NEW CENTURY WORLD·WIDE

ITALIAN DICTIONARY

THE *NEW CENTURY* DICTIONARIES

VELAZQUEZ SPANISH/ENGLISH DICTIONARY

VEST-POCKET DICTIONARIES

French

German

Italian

Spanish

INSTANT CONVERSATION GUIDES

French

German

Spanish

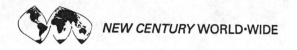
NEW CENTURY WORLD·WIDE

ITALIAN
DICTIONARY

ITALIAN-ENGLISH / ENGLISH-ITALIAN
(American English)

compiled by
VITTORE E. BOCCHETTA, Ph.D.
Formerly Professor of Humanities, Verona, Italy

NEW CENTURY PUBLISHERS, INC.

Printing Code
16 17 18 19 20 21

Library of Congress Catalog Card Number: 81-85508

ISBN 0-8329-9696-3

Editors: R. J. Nelson, Ph.D.
Jean Rich, M.S.

Cover Design: Jean M. Krause

Printed in the United States of America

A DICTIONARY OF FIRSTS

Recent years have brought a tremendous upsurge of interest in everything Italian, including the country, its people, its music and art, its literature—and its LANGUAGE. A growing number of Americans proudly claim Italian as their favorite foreign tongue. And with good reason! For it is, without question, one of the most beautiful and expressive languages in the world.

However, the means of acquiring a good speaking acquaintance with this language have not kept pace with the increasing demand. Outside the universities there have been few opportunitities for oral instruction, and until now there has never been available in this country an Italian-English, English-Italian dictionary thoroughly designed to teach American students how the language is pronounced. The WORLD-WIDE ITALIAN DICTIONARY is the *first* to meet this need. Each of the Italian main entries and solid subentries is phonetically transcribed, and a clear and concise set of rules is provided for pronouncing any word in the language just from seeing it spelled.

But pronounciation is only one of the *firsts* which users of this work will enjoy.

Included in both languages are many scientific and general words of recent origin that have never before appeared in any Italian-English dictionary. The knowledge of Italian here conveyed is completely up to date.

When entry words have two or more distinct meanings, subject labels (in parentheses) guide the user to the particular translation that fits the meaning. This feature guarantees the appropriate word for every occasion, thereby avoiding the embarrassment that comes from using the wrong word to translate a given meaning.

All entries of Italian irregular verbs are identified by means of asterisks. These asterisks signify that complete conjugations for such verbs are supplied in alphabetical order in the Italian grammar section on pages 27 to 37.

Hundreds of the more common personal names in both languages are conveniently assembled and translated in separate lists on pages 270 to 277 and 513 to 519.

Translations and pronunciations are provided at the end of the book for hundreds of conversational questions and expressions in both English and Italian. This section will prove useful to travelers and students alike.

5

For motorists and others who may be interested, six pages of traffic information are included, much of it in the form of pictures for quick recognition.

In addition to these *firsts*, this dictionary has all the usual features common to other good foreign language dictionaries, such as gender indication for all noun entries on the Italian side of the work. On the English side, all noun equivalents in Italian are also indicated as to gender, with the exception of masculine nouns ending in **-o** and feminine nouns ending in **-a**, **-sione**, **-tione**, and **-zione**.

The vocabulary includes just about every word in both languages that American users will have need of.

Especially helpful are the translations of abundant idioms, each entered under its appropriate key word.

The last three pages contain the sort of special statistical information that travelers sooner or later feel an interest in but seldom find conveniently at hand when wanted.

The compiler and publisher of this dictionary have spared no pains or expense in their effort to make it the best of its kind. It is hoped, therefore, that purchasers will begin their use of it by thoroughly acquainting themselves with its many features. Only by so doing will they get from it all the benefits that it is capable of providing.

THE PUBLISHER

CONTENTS

7

PRONUNCIATION KEY

Symbols	English Sounds
	Vowels
â	*a*rm, f*a*ther
ā	b*a*by, g*a*te
e	b*e*t, m*e*n
ē	b*e*, h*e*
ō	g*o*, sp*o*ke
ô	g*o*ne, n*o*rth
ū	bl*u*e, t*oo*
	Consonants
b	*b*aby, tu*b*
ch	*ch*ild, cat*ch*
d	*d*ad, su*dd*en
f	*f*at, a*f*ter
g	*g*ate, ba*g*
j	*j*et, a*j*ar
k	*k*itten, ta*k*e
l	*l*ate, *l*i*l*y
m	*m*et, da*m*p
n	*n*ot, se*n*d
p	*p*at, sto*p*
r	ve*r*y (with a trill)
s	*s*at, la*s*t
sh	*sh*op, di*sh*
t	*t*ell, *t*as*t*e
v	*v*ery, gi*v*e
w	*w*e, q*u*ack
y	*y*es, *y*ou
z	*z*ero, ro*s*e

9

GUIDE TO ITALIAN PRONUNCIATION

Beginning students of Italian will find the pronunciations in this dictionary very helpful in learning to speak the language. Not only are all the main entries accurately pronounced throughout, but complete Italian pronunciations are provided for all the various inflected endings of regular verbs and for hundreds of conversational phrases. With such help readily available at the flip of a page, acquiring a good speaking accquaintance with this new language is almost as simple as learning to pronounce the unfamiliar words we sometimes encounter in our native language.

But it won't always be convenient to consult a WORLD-WIDE ITALIAN DICTIONARY every time one wants the pronunciation of an Italian word. Sooner or later the serious student will need a sufficient mastery of the language to enable him to pronounce any word from seeing it spelled. Fortunately, such a mastery is not hard to acquire.

Italian is one of the easiest new languages for Americans to learn to speak. It has only 21 letters, one of which is always silent. It has only 26 sounds, all but one of which are completely familiar to English-speaking students. But like American English, the language is pronounced somewhat differently in different parts of the country. In most parts of Italy it is correct to give the letters *e* and *o* only one sound apiece, regardless of stress or position. But in Central Italy (which includes Florence and Rome) each of these letters has two different sounds, depending, first, on whether it is stressed or unstressed and, second, on where it occurs in the word. Because of these regional variations, it is impossible to provide pronunciations or rules that are wholly accurate for such widely scattered places as Milan, Venice, Florence, Rome, Naples and Palermo.

Nevertheless, American visitors to Italy will have little difficulty with regional differences once they become sufficiently familiar with the pronunciations and guide rules provided in this dictionary.

The first rule of good Italian pronunciation is to utter every syllable of every word clearly and distinctly. More use is made of the lips, tongue, and lower jaw than is customary in English speech. Vowel sounds, even when they are unstressed, are always pure and full-rounded—never slurred. Consonants (except *h*) are always plainly audible—never dropped (as the *t* in lis*t*en and the *b* in clim*b*).

Stress and Accent

There are no rules that will enable anyone unfamiliar with the language to tell where the stress falls in Italian words. It usually falls on the next-to-last syllable. *Examples*: **anno** (ân'nō), **madre** (mâ'drā), **economia** (ā·kō·nō·mē'â), **esitare** (ā·zē·tâ'rā). But in many words the stress falls on other syllables. *Examples*: **edile** (e'dē·lā), **piccolo** (pēk'-kō·lō), **perchè** (pār·kā').

In the inflection of verbs the stress often changes position from form to form. *Examples*: **esitare** (ā·zē·tâ'rā), **esito** (e'zē·tō), **esitano** (e'zē·tâ·nō), **esiterò** (ā·zē·tâ·rō').

When the stress falls on the last vowel of a word, the vowel is written or printed with an accent mark, thus: **ò**. This accent is part of the spelling and must always appear in writing and printing. *Examples*: **più** (pyū) **perchè** (pār·kā'), **civiltà** (chē·vēl·tâ').

Some one-syllable words are written with accent marks to distinguish them from words similar in spelling and sound but different in meaning. *Examples*: **di** (meaning *of*) and **dì** (meaning *day*), **se** (meaning *if*) and **sè** (meaning *oneself*).

The Italian Alphabet and Its Sounds

Asterisks (*) refer to the explanatory notes on the following pages.

Italian Letter	English Sound	Phonetic Symbol	Italian Word	Phonetic Respelling
a	father	â	capra	kâ′prâ
b	baby	b	basta	bâ′stâ
c*	car	k	cava	kâ′vâ
	child	ch	cine	chē′nā
d	dim	d	donna	dōn′nâ
e*	they	ā	mente	mān′tā
	bet	e	fegato	fe′gâ·tō
f	fat	f	fede	fā′dā
g*	gate	g	gamba	gâm′bâ
	gentle	j	gente	jän′tā
h*	(silent)	(none)	hanno	ân′nō
i*	police	ē	di	dē
	yes	y	dieci	dyā′chē
l	lap	l	lana	lâ′nâ
m	met	m	meno	mā′nō
n	not	n	nano	nâ′nō
o*	spoken	ō	piccolo	pēk′kō·lō
	gone	ô	gomito	gô′mē·tō
p	pat	p	pasta	pâ′stâ
q	quack	k	quando	kwân′dō
r*	(see below)	r	caro	kâ′rō
s*	sat	s	sala	sâ′lâ
	rose	z	rosa	rō′zâ
t	taste	t	tardi	târ′dē
u*	too	ū	uno	ū′nō
	quit	w	uomo	wō′mō
v	valve	v	vivo	vē′vō
z, zz*	lets	ts	razza	râ′tsâ
	adz	dz	mezzo	mā′dzō

Combined Letters

ch	chorus	k	chiaro	kyâ′rō
ci*	chart	ch	ciao	châ′ō
	cheese	chē	ciclo	chē′klō
gh	ghost	g	ghiro	gē′rō
gi*	digest	j	giorno	jōr′nō
	gee	jē	giglio	jē′lyō
gli*	million	ly	foglia	fô′lyâ
	will ye	lyē	egli	ā′lyē
gn	onion	ny	bagno	bâ′nyō
qu	quack	kw	questo	kwā′stō
sc*	shine	sh	scena	shā′nâ
	scar	sk	scusa	skū′zâ
sch	scheme	sk	schema	skā′mâ
sci*	shop	sh	scialle	shâl′lā
	she	shē	sci	shē

Guide to Italian Pronunciation

Explanation of the Sounds

c has the sound of *k* when it is followed by the letters a, o, u, h, l, or r. *Examples*: **caro** (kâ′rō), **corpo** (kōr′pō), **cuore** (kwō′rā), **che** (kā), **classe** (klâs′sā), **credo** (krā′dō).

has the sound of *ch* when it is followed by e or i. *Examples*: **cena** (chā′nâ), **cine** (chē′nā), **cielo** (chā′lō), **ciao** (châ′ō). (See the two sounds of **ci** below.)

e has the sound of *e* in b*e*t when it occurs with stress:

    1) in the third-from-last (or fourth-from-last) syllable of a word. *Examples*: **iberico** (ē·be′rē·kō), **medico** (me′dē·kō).

    2) in the next-to-last syllable when the last syllable is spelled with two vowels. *Examples*: **sedia** (se′dyâ), **secchio** (sek′kyō).

has the sound of *ey* in *they* (*a* in b*a*by) in all other situations, both stressed and unstressed. *Examples*: **cine** (chē′nā), **quel** (kwāl), **temere** (tā·mā′rā), **genovese** (jā·nō·vā′zā), **gentilmente** (jān·tēl·mān′tā).

g has the sound of *g* in *g*ate when followed by a, o, u, h, l, or r. *Examples*: **gamba** (gâm′bâ), **gola** (gō′lâ), **gusto** (gū′stō), **ghiro** (gē′rō), **globo** (glō′bō), **grande** (grân′dā). *Exception*: **gl** has the sound of *ly* in certain words. See below.

has the sound of *g* in *g*entle (*j* in *j*et) when followed by e or i. *Examples*: **gente** (jān′tā), **gigante** (jē·gân′tā), **giallo** (jâl′lō). See the two sounds of **gi** below.

i has the sound of *i* in police (*e* in b*e*) when it is the only vowel in a syllable or follows another vowel in the same syllable. *Examples*: **di** (dē), **Dio** (dē′ō), **idea** (ē·dā′â), **difficile** (dēf·fē′chē·lā), **eroico** (ā·rô′ē·kō), **eroicamente** (ā·rōē·kâ·mān′tā).

has the sound of *y* in *y*et when it is unstressed and is followed by another vowel. *Examples*: **dieci** (dyā′chē), **più** (pyū), **bestia** (be′styâ). *Exception*: **i** is silent before a, e, o, and u when it follows c or g: **ciao** (châ′ō), **giocare** (jō·kâ′rā).

o has the sound of *o* in g*o*ne when it occurs with stress:

    1) in the third-from-last (or fourth-from-last) syllable of a word. *Examples*: **povero** (pô′vā·rō), **geografo** (jā·ô′grâ·fō).

    2) in the next-to-last syllable when the last syllable is spelled with two vowels. *Examples*: **goccia** (gô′châ), **gloria** (glô′ryâ).

has the sound of *o* in *go* in all other situations, both stressed and unstressed. *Examples*: **piccolo** (pēk′kō·lō), **nove** (nō′vâ), **orbo** (ōr′bō), **opporre** (ōp·pōr′rā).

r is unlike any sound natural to English. It is produced by rapidly vibrating the tip of the tongue against the base of the upper front teeth. *Examples*: **caro** (kâ′rō), **rosa** (rō′zâ), **tardi** (târ′dē).

s has the sound *s* in ro*s*e (*z* in *z*ero):

    1) between vowels. *Examples*: **rosa** (rō·zâ), **contesa** (kōn·tā′zâ).

    2) before b, d, g, l, m, n, r, or v. *Examples*: **sguardo** (zgwâr′dō), **slavo** (zlâ′vō), **mutismo** (mū·tē′zmō), **svolta** (zvōl′tâ).

has the sound *s* in *s*at in all other situations; *Examples*: **sano** (sâ′nō), **scala** (skâ′lâ), **scansia** (skân·sē′â), **stesso** (stās′sō), **gres** (grās).

u has the sound of *oo* in *too* when it is the only vowel sound in a syllable or follows another vowel in the same syllable. *Examples*: **uno** (ū'nō), **tutto** (tūt'tō), **più** (pyū), **rauco** (râ'ū·kō), **raucedine** (râū·che'dē·nä).

has the sound of *w* in *way* when followed by a vowel in the same syllable. *Examples*: **nuovo** (nwō'vō), **guerra** (gwär'râ), **quel** (kwäl), **cuore** (kwō'rä).

z, zz usually has the sound of *dz* in *adz*:

1) at the start of words. *Examples*: **zampa** (dzâm'pâ), **zio** (dzē'ō), **zuppa** (dzūp'pâ).

2) in all verbs ending in **-izzare**, including all their inflected forms: **-izzante**, **-izzato**, etc. *Examples*: **scandalizzare** (skân·dâ·lē·dzâ'rä), **fertilizzante** (fär·tē·lē·dzân'tä).

usually has the sound of *ts* in *lets* when it occurs elsewhere. *Examples*: **azionare** (â·tsyō·nâ'rä), **ambizioso** (âm·bē·tsyō'zō), **altezza** (âl·tä'tsâ), **alleanza** (âl·lä·ân'-tsâ).

Exceptions: there are too many exceptions, however, to account for them all. Certain words may be pronounced either *dz* or *ts* within the same region.

ci has the sound of *ch* in *ch*art when it is followed by a, e, o, or u. *Examples*: **ciao** (châ'ō), **provincia** (prō·vēn'châ), **ciò** (chō), **ciuco** (chū'kō), **sufficiente** (sūf·fē·chän'tä).

has the sound of *chee* in *chee*se when it is not followed in the same syllable by another vowel. *Examples*: **ci** (chē), **dieci** (dyä'chē), **ciclo** (chē'klō).

gi has the sound of *g* in *g*entle (*j* in *j*ug) when it is followed in the same syllable by a, o, or u. *Examples*: **già** (jâ), **grigio** (grē'jō), **giubba** (jūb'bâ).

has the same sound of *gee* (*jee* in *jee*p) when it is not followed in the same syllable by another vowel. *Examples*: **dogi** (dō'jē), **geologia** (jä·ō·lō·jē'â).

gl has the sound of *gl* in *gl*ad when followed by a, e, o, or u. *Examples*: **glaciale** (glâ·châ'lä), **gleba** (glä'bâ), **globo** (glō'bō).

gli has the sound of *lli* in mi*lli*on when it is followed in the same syllable by another vowel (a, e, o, u). *Examples*: **foglia** (fô'lyâ), **biglietto** (bē·lyät'tō), **figlio** (fē'lyō).

has the sound of *l ye* in wi*ll ye* when it occurs at the end of a word. *Examples*: **gli** (lyē), **egli** (ā'lyē).

has the sound of *glee* when it is followed in the same word by a consonant. *Examples*: **glicogeno** (glē·kô'jä·nō), **negligenza** (nä·glē·jän'tsâ).

sc has the sound of *sh* in *sh*ine before e or i. *Examples*: **scena** (shä'nâ), **scimmia** (shēm'myâ).

has the sound of *sc* in *sc*ar in all other cases. *Examples*: **scusa** (skū'zâ), **schema** (skā'mâ), **scritto** (skrēt'tō).

sci has the sound of *sh* in *sh*op when it is followed by another vowel. *Examples*: **scialle** (shâl'lä), **scienza** (shän'tsâ), **sciocco** (shōk'kō), **sciupare** (shū·pâ'rä).

has the sound of *she* when it is not followed in the same syllable by another vowel. *Examples*: **sci** (shē), **scibile** (shē'bē·lä), **trascinare** (trâ·shē·nâ'rä).

Guide to Italian Pronunciation

Diphthongs

When two vowels occur together in words, they are usually pronounced as one syllable. Such one-syllable combinations are known as *diphthongs*. Some well-known English examples are *oi* in *boil* and *ou* in *house*. Diphthongs are frequent occurrences in Italian, and it is therefore important to know how to pronounce them.

The five vowels occur in just about every possible combination. But the more common diphthongs combine a *strong* vowel with a *weak* one. Strong vowels (**a, e,** and **o**) are so-called because they usually *sound* stronger (louder) than weak vowels (**i** and **u**) when combined. *Examples:* **mai** (mâ′ē), **causa** (kâ′ū·zâ), **poi** (pō′ē), **Europa** (āū·rō′pâ), **piace** (pyâ′chā), **dieci** (dyā′chē), **Pasqua** (pâ′skwâ), **uomo** (wō′mō).

When the two weak vowels (**i, u**) combine to form a diphthong, it is usually the **u** that is stressed. *Examples:* **piuma** (pyū′mâ), **più** (pyū). Where the **i** is stressed, **u** has the sound of w. *Examples:* **guida** (gwē′dâ), **qui** (kwē).

The combination of two strong vowels (**a, e, o**) results, not in a diphthong, but in two syllables. *Examples:* **paese** (pâ·ā′zā), **poeta** (pō·ā′tâ), **ciao** (châ′ō), **boa** (bō′â), **eroe** (ā·rō′ā), **poeticamente** (pō·ā·tē·kâ·mān′tā).

Two syllables also result when **i** and **u** carry the stress in combination with **a, e,** or **o**. *Examples:* **zio** (dzē′ō), **siano** (sē′â·nō), **Aida** (â·ē′dâ) **eroina** (ā·rō·ē′nâ), **due** (dū′ā), **tuo** (tū′ō).

Syllable Division

Both in speaking and writing, Italian words divide into syllables according to the following simple rules:

1) a single consonant always belongs with the vowel which follows it. *Examples:* **rosa** (rō′zâ), **capitolo** (kâ·pē′tō·lō).

2) When **l, m, n,** and **r** are followed by other consonants, these four letters belong with the preceding vowels. *Examples:* **alto** (âl′tō), **lento** (lān′tō), **corpo** (kōr′pō).

3) All double consonants are separated. *Examples:* **accollare** (âk·kōl·lâ′rā), **passato** (pâs·sâ′tō), **correre** (kôr′râ·râ).

4) When **s** is followed by a consonant (or consonants) other than s, it is never separated from what follows. *Examples:* **basta** (bâ′stâ), **questo** (kwā′stō), **destro** (dā′strō), **lasciare** (lâ·shâ′râ).

5) Any consonant followed by **l** or **r** belongs in the syllable that follows it. *Examples:* **ciclo** (chē′klō), **madre** (mâ′drâ).

14

A BRIEF GUIDE TO ITALIAN GRAMMAR

GENDER OF NOUNS AND ADJECTIVES

1 The Noun

Nouns in Italian are either masculine or feminine, the gender having been determined by custom and usage. Those ending in **-o** are usually masculine, and those ending in **-a, -sione, -tione,** and **-zione** are usually feminine.

Examples:
il libro the book
la coperta the cover
la tensione the tension
la questione the question
la rivoluzione the revolution

Nouns referring to people usually have a masculine and a feminine form, often contrary to English. Masculine nouns ending in **-o** customarily change the **-o** to **-a** for the feminine form. Those ending in **-e** usually change the **-e** to **-a**; others have no special feminine form, the difference being shown by the feminine article. Some change **-ore** to **-oressa** or **-rice.** Those masculine nouns ending in **-a** usually have no special form for the feminine, the difference being shown by the gender of the article; a few change the **-a** to **-essa.**

Examples:

ladro male thief	**ladra** woman thief
signore gentleman	**signora** lady
il cantante the male singer	**la cantante** the female singer
professore male professor	**professoressa** lady professor
pittore male painter	**pittrice** woman painter
il socialista the man socialist	**la socialista** the woman socialist
poeta male poet	**poetessa** woman poet

As in English, some nouns are completely different in the feminine form.

Examples:

uomo man	**donna** woman
marito husband	**moglie** wife
genero son-in-law	**nuora** daughter-in-law
fratello brother	**sorella** sister

15

2 The Adjective

Contrary to English usage, in Italian the adjective always takes the gender of the noun it modifies. Masculine adjectives that end in -o change the -o to -a for the feminine form; masculine adjectives that end in -e are unchanged in the feminine.

Examples:

lo studente serio	la studentessa seria
l'uomo gentile	la donna gentile

NUMBER OF NOUNS AND ADJECTIVES

1 The Noun

Masculine singular forms ending in -o and -a change the -o or -a to -i to form the plural.

Examples:

ragazzo boy	**ragazzi** boys
soldato soldier	**soldati** soldiers
artista male artist	**artisti** male artists

Feminine singular forms ending in -a change the -a to -e to form the plural.

Examples:

donna woman	**donne** women
ragazza girl	**ragazze** girls
artista woman artist	**artiste** woman artists

Masculine and feminine singular forms ending in -e change the -e to -i to form the plural.

Examples:

il cantante the male singer	**i cantanti** the male singers
la cantante the woman singer	**le cantanti** the woman singers
l'origine the origin	**le origini** the origins
il pittore the male painter	**i pittori** the male painters
la pittrice the woman painter	**le pittrici** the woman painters

Masculine and feminine singular forms of one syllable, those in which the last vowel is accented, and those ending in -i, do not change in the plural.

Examples:

il re the king	**i re** the kings
la virtù the virtue	**le virtù** the virtues
la civiltà the civilization	**le civiltà** the civilizations
l'analisi the analysis	**le analisi** the analyses

Feminine singular forms that end in -cia and -gia preceded by a consonant, and in which the i is not stressed, change -cia and -gia to -ce and -ge respectively. Otherwise, the general rule of change from -a to -e applies.

Examples:

guancia cheek	**guance** cheeks
mancia tip	**mance** tips
farmacia drug store	**farmacie** drug stores
valigia suitcase	**valigie** suitcases
camicia shirt	**camicie** shirts

Masculine and feminine singular forms ending in **-co, -go, -ca,** and **-ga** generally change to **-chi, -ghi, -che,** and **-ghe,** inserting the **h** to maintain the hard sound of **c** and **g**. There are some common words which are exceptions, however.

Examples:

tacco heel	**tacchi** heels
lago lake	**laghi** lakes
monaca nun	**monache** nuns
spiga ear of corn	**spighe** ears of corn
amico friend	**amici** friends
greco Greek	**greci** Greeks

As in English, in Italian some plural forms are entirely different.

Examples:

bue ox	**buoi** oxen
uomo man	**uomini** men
dio god	**dei** gods

Some masculine singular forms become feminine in the plural by changing **-o** to **-a**. Such nouns often have a regular plural which has a figurative meaning.

Examples:

l'uovo the egg	**le uova** the eggs
il dito the finger	**le dita** the fingers
il braccio the arm	**le braccia** the arms (human)
	i bracci the arms (of the sea)

2 The Adjective

Masculine singular forms ending in **-o** change **-o** to **-i** to form the plural.

Examples:

il libro giallo the yellow book	**i libri gialli** the yellow books
il cappello rosso the red hat	**i cappelli rossi** the red hats

Feminine singular forms ending in **-a** change **-a** to **-e** to form the plural.

Example:

la camicia rossa the red shirt	**le camicie rosse** the red shirts

Masculine and feminine singular forms ending in **-e** change the **-e** to **-i** to form the plural.

Examples:

una signora gentile a kind woman   **delle signore gentili** some kind women
un signore gentile a kind man   **dei signori gentili** some kind men

The use of **h** to retain the hard sound of **c** and **g** is the same as for the plural of nouns.

Example:

un libro bianco a white book   **dei libri bianchi** some white books

ARTICLES

1 The Definite Article "the"

	Singular			Plural	
Masculine:	il	lo	l'	i	gli
Feminine:	la	l'		le	

The eight forms of the definite article are used as follows:

MASCULINE SINGULAR

- **il** before nouns beginning with any consonant *except* **s** followed by another consonant, or **z**

    Examples: **il maestro**   **il padre**   **il salone**

- **lo** before nouns beginning with **s** followed by another consonant, or **z**

    Examples: **lo sbaglio**   **lo zucchero**   **lo zio**

- **l'** before nouns beginning with any vowel

    Examples: **l'amico**   **l'uovo**   **l'occhio**

FEMININE SINGULAR

- **la** before nouns beginning with any consonant

    Examples: **la parola**   **la donna**   **la spazzola**

- **l'** before nouns beginning with any vowel

    Examples: **l'amica**   **l'ostrica**   **l'uva**

MASCULINE PLURAL

- **i** before nouns beginning with any consonant *except* **s** followed by another consonant, or **z**

    Examples: **i maestri**   **i padri**   **i saloni**

- **gli** before nouns beginning with any vowel, **s** followed by another consonant, or **z**

    Examples: **gli amici**   **gli sbagli**   **gli zii**

- **le** before all nouns

    Examples: **le parole**   **le donne**   **le amiche**

2 The Indefinite Article "a" or "an"

Masculine:	**un**	**uno**
Feminine:	**una**	**un'**

The four forms of the indefinite article are used as follows:

MASCULINE

- **un** before nouns beginning with any vowel or consonant except **s** followed by another consonant, or **z**

    Examples: **un uomo**   **un cavallo**   **un tavolo**

- **uno** before nouns beginning with **s** followed by another consonant, or **z**

    Examples: **uno sbaglio**   **uno sfogo**   **uno zio**

FEMININE

- **una** before nouns beginning with any consonant

    Examples: **una donna**   **una stanza**   **una tazza**

- **un'** before nouns beginning with any vowel

    Examples: **un'amica**   **un'estasi**   **un'unità**

3 The Combined Preposition

	a	da	di	in	su	con
il	al	dal	del	nel	sul	col
lo	allo	dallo	dello	nello	sullo	
l'	all'	dall'	dell'	nell'	sull'	
la	alla	dalla	della	nella	sulla	
i	ai	dai	dei	nei	sui	coi
gli	agli	dagli	degli	negli	sugli	
le	alle	dalle	delle	nelle	sulle	

The various forms of the definite article combine with the prepositions **a, da, di, in, su,** and **con** as shown above. Those forms not given for **con** exist, but are considered obsolete.

Examples:

del padre of the father	**dei padri** of the fathers
dalla madre from the mother	**dalle madri** from the mothers
nello sguardo in the glance	**negli sguardi** in the glances
sul libro in the book	**sui libri** in the books
nel paese in the village	**nei paesi** in the villages
col ragazzo with the boy	**coi ragazzi** with the boys

In Italian, the combined prepositions formed with **di** are often used to indicate the partitive quality of the following noun. In English translation, this same idea is usually rendered by the words *some* or *any*.

Examples:

dei libri some books	**dell'antipasto** some hors d'oeuvres
del denaro some money	**degli sbagli** some mistakes
dello zucchero some sugar	**della frutta** some fruit

PRONOUNS

1 The Subject Pronouns

	Singular		Plural
I	**io**	we	**noi**
you *(familiar)*	**tu**	you *(familiar)*	**voi**
he	**lui, egli**	they *(m)*	**loro, essi**
she	**lei, ella**	they *(f)*	**loro, esse**
you *(formal)*	**Lei**	you *(formal)*	**Loro**

The subject pronouns are used much less than in English, since the verb ending is usually enough to clarify the subject. They are used when stress on the subject is indicated. The forms **egli, ella, essi,** and **esse** are literary. In conversation the alternatives are always used.

Examples:

Io dico che non è vero!	I say it isn't so!
Ci sono andato io, non lui	I'm the one who's been there, not he.
Noi americani viaggiamo assai.	We Americans travel quite a bit.
Lei è molto gentile.	You're very kind.

2 The Object Pronouns

	Singular					Plural		
	direct	*indirect*	*preposition*			*direct*	*indirect*	*preposition*
me	mi	mi (me)	me		us	ci	ci (ce)	noi
you *(fam)*	ti	ti (te)	te		you *(fam)*	vi	vi (ve)	voi
him, it *(m)*	lo	gli (glie)	lui		them *(m)*	li	loro	loro
her, it *(f)*	la	le (glie)	lei		them *(f)*	le	loro	loro
you *(for m)*	La	Le (Glie)	Lei		you *(for m)*	Li	Loro	Loro
you *(for f)*	La	Le (Glie)	Lei		you *(for f)*	Le	Loro	Loro

The pronouns precede all indicative and subjunctive forms of the verb and all formal commands (those using **Lei** or **Loro**). They follow and are attached to the present participle, the infinitive, and all familiar commands. (However, the pronouns may also *precede* negative familiar commands, at the speaker's option.) The forms **loro** and **Loro** are exceptions to the foregoing: they always follow *all* forms of the verb and are never attached to them. The indirect object pronouns precede the direct when used in combination. When pronouns are attached, the final **e** of the infinitive is dropped.

Examples:

Mi scrive ogni settimana.	He writes me every week.
Ti dico la verità.	I'm telling you *(fam)* the truth.
Non posso dirti il perchè.	I can't tell you the reason.
Mi dica subito.	Tell me at once. *(for)*
Dimmi pure.	Go right ahead and tell me. *(fam)*
Ci ha visto ieri sera.	He saw us yesterday evening.
È stato fatto per noi.	It was done for us.
Sono andato da lei.	I went over to her place.
Non la vedo più.	I don't see her any longer.
Non La vedo quasi mai.	I almost never see you *(for)*.
Manderò loro il libro stasera.	I'll send them the book tonight.
Scriverò Loro una lettera subito.	I'll write you *(for)* at once.
Non farlo adesso.	Don't do it now. *(fam)*
Non la scrivere adesso.	Don't write it now. *(fam)*
Faccia pure.	Go right ahead and do it. *(for)*
Non lo faccia oggi.	Don't do it today.
Non posso descriverlo.	I can't describe it.

The indirect forms **mi**, **ti**, **ci**, and **vi** change to **me**, **te**, **ce**, and **ve**, respectively, when used in combination with other pronouns. The indirect forms **gli** and **le** change to **glie** when combined with other pronouns and are fused with them. The indirect form **Le** changes to **Glie** when combined with other pronouns and also fuses with them.

Examples:

Adesso Glielo faccio io.	I'll do it for you this time. (*for*)
Non posso dirtelo.	I can't tell it to you. (*fam*)
Me lo racconti dopo.	Tell me about it later. (*for*)
Te l'ho detto tante volte.	I've told you about it so many times.
Ce lo dirai tu.	You'll tell us about it.
Non posso spiegarglielo.	I can't explain it to him.

The prepositional forms of the pronoun are often used as substitutes for the direct and indirect forms, whenever the speaker wishes to stress or emphasize the pronoun. In such cases, the prepositional forms normally follow the verb.

Examples:

Ho visto lui, non lei.	I saw *him*, not *her*.
Riguarda noi, non te.	It's *our* concern, not *yours*.
Scrive a noi, non a te.	He's writing *us*, not *you*.

ADVERBS

Most adverbs are derived from the corresponding adjective by adding the suffix **-mente** to the feminine form of the adjective.

Examples:

Adjective	*Adverb*
rapido quick	**rapidamente** quickly
garbato polite	**garbatamente** politely

In the case of invariable adjectives ending in **e**, the **e** is dropped before adding **-mente** in adjectives ending in **-le** or **-re** preceded by a vowel. Otherwise, **-mente** is added *without* dropping the final **e**.

Examples:

Adjective	*Adverb*
generale general	**generalmente** generally
cortese courteous	**cortesemente** courteously

NEGATION

Italian does not make use of any auxiliary verb, such as the English *do*, to form negative statements. The adverb **non** is regularly placed before the conjugated verb to convey the negative idea. The double negative is common when the negative adjective or pronoun follows the verb. If they precede, the adverb **non** is no longer used.

Examples:

Mi dispiace, ma non so dirtelo.	I'm sorry, but I can't tell you.
Non è partito ancora.	He hasn't left yet.
Nessuno lo sa.	No one knows.
Non ha scritto a nessuno.	He has written no one.
Non vedo nessuno.	I don't see anyone.

QUESTIONS

As in the case of negative statements, there is no Italian form which corresponds to the English auxiliary *do*. Questions are regularly formed by the inversion of subject and verb, as in English questions formed with the verb *to be*.

Examples:

È italiano Lei?	Are you Italian?
Gliel'ha detto lui?	Did he tell him?
È tornata la sua sorella?	Has his sister returned?

CONJUGATION OF VERBS

1 Regular Verbs

All regular verbs entered in the dictionary conform to one of the following basic patterns.

In the regular conjugations below, the verb forms are given in the following order: first, second, and third person singular; followed by first, second, and third person plural. Italian speakers should note that in the following conjugations the designation "present participle" corresponds to the usage assigned the **gerundio** in Italian.

–ARE VERBS *Example:* **amare** (â·mâ′rā) to love

PRESENT PARTICIPLE **amando** (â·mân′dō)
PAST PARTICIPLE **amato** (â·mâ′tō)
PRESENT **amo** (â′mō), **ami** (â′mē), **ama** (â′mâ), **amiamo** (â·myâ′mō), **amate** (â·mâ′tā), **amano** (â′mâ·nō)
FUTURE **amerò** (â·mā·rō′), **amerai** (â·mā·râ′ē), **amerà** (â·mā·râ′), **ameremo** (â·mā·rā′mō), **amerete** (â·mā·rā′tā), **ameranno** (â·mā·rân′nō)
CONDITIONAL **amerei** (â·mā·râ′ē), **ameresti** (â·mā·rā′stē), **amerebbe** (â·mā·rāb′bā), **ameremmo** (â·mā·rām′mō), **amereste** (â·mā·rā′stā), **amerebbero** (â·mā·reb′bā·rō)
PRESENT SUBJUNCTIVE **ami** (â′mē), **ami** (â′mē), **ami** (â′mē), **amiamo** (â·myâ′mō), **amiate** (â·myâ′tā), **amino** (â′mē·nō)
IMPERFECT **amavo** (â·mâ′vō), **amavi** (â·mâ′vē), **amava** (â·mâ′vâ), **amavamo** (â·mâ·vâ′mō), **amavate** (â·mâ·vâ′tā), **amavano** (â·mâ′vâ·nō)
PAST DEFINITE **amai** (â·mâ′ē), **amasti** (â·mâ′stē), **amò** (â·mō′), **amammo** (â·mâm′mō), **amaste** (â·mâ′stā), **amarono** (â·mâ′rō·nō)
PAST SUBJUNCTIVE **amassi** (â·mâs′sē), **amassi** (â·mâs′sē), **amasse** (â·mâs′sā), **amassimo** (â·mâs′sē·mō), **amaste** (â·mâ′stā), **amassero** (â·mâs′sā·rō)

–ERE VERBS *Example:* **credere** (kre′dā·rā) to believe

PRESENT PARTICIPLE **credendo** (krā·dān′dō)
PAST PARTICIPLE **creduto** (krā·dū′tō)
PRESENT **credo** (krā′dō), **credi** (krā′dē), **crede** (krā′dā), **crediamo** (krā·dyâ′mō), **credete** (krā·dā′tā), **credono** (kre′dō·nō)
FUTURE **crederò** (krā·dā·rō′), **crederai** (krā·dā·râ′ē), **crederà** (krā·dā·râ′), **crederemo** (krā·dā·rā′mō), **crederete** (krā·dā·rā′tā), **crederanno** (krā·dā·rân′nō)
CONDITIONAL **crederei** (krā·dā·râ′ē), **crederesti** (krā·dā·rā′stē), **crederebbe** (krā·dā·rāb′bā), **crederemmo** (krā·dā·rām′mō), **credereste** (krā·dā·rā′stā), **crederebbero** (krā·dā·reb′bā·rō)
PRESENT SUBJUNCTIVE **creda** (krā′dâ), **creda** (krā′dâ), **creda** (krā′dâ), **crediamo** (krā·dyâ′mō), **crediate** (krā·dyâ′tā), **credano** (kre′dâ·nō)
IMPEFECT **credevo** (krā·dā′vō), **credevi** (krā·dā′vē), **credeva** (krā·dā′vâ), **credevamo** (krā·dā·vâ′mō), **credevate** (krā·dā·vâ′tā), **credevano** (krā·de′vâ·nō)
PAST DEFINITE **credei** (krā·dā′ē), **credesti** (krā·dā′stē), **credè** (krā·dā′), **credemmo** (krā·dām′mō), **credeste** (krā·dā′stā), **crederono** (krā·de′rō·nō)
PAST SUBJUNCTIVE **credessi** (krā·dās′sē), **credessi** (krā·dās′sē), **credesse** (krā·dās′sā), **credessimo** (krā·des′sē·mō), **credeste** (krā·dā′stā), **credessero** (krā·des′sā·rō)

Conjugation of Verbs

–IRE VERBS (ISC) *Example:* **capire** (kâ·pē′rā) to understand

PRESENT PARTICIPLE **capendo** (kâ·pān′dō)
PAST PARTICIPLE **capito** (kâ·pē′tō)
PRESENT **capisco** (kâ·pē′skō), **capisci** (kâ·pē′shē), **capisce** (kâ·pē′shā), **capiamo** (kâ·pyâ′mō), **capite** (kâ·pē′tā), **capiscono** (kâ·pē′skō·nō)
FUTURE **capirò** (kâ·pē·rō′), **capirai** (kâ·pē·râ′ē), **capirà** (kâ.pē·râ′), **capiremo** (kâ·pē·rā′mō), **capirete** (kâ·pē·rā′tā), **capiranno** (kâ·pē·rân′nō)
CONDITIONAL **capirei** (kâ·pē·rā′ē), **capiresti** (kâ·pē·rā′stē), **capirebbe** (kâ·pē·rāb′bā), **capiremmo** (kâ·pē·rām′mō), **capireste** (kâ·pē·rā′stā), **capirebbero** (kâ·pē·reb′bā·rō)
PRESENT SUBJUNCTIVE **capisca** ((kâ·pē′skâ), **capisca** (kâ·pē′skâ), **capisca** (kâ·pē′skâ), **capiamo** (kâ·pyâ′mō), **capiate** (kâ·pyâ′tā), **capiscano** (kâ·pē′skâ·nō)
IMPERFECT **capivo** (kâ·pē′vō), **capivi** (kâ·pē′vē), **capiva** (kâ·pē′vâ), **capivamo** (kâ·pē·rā′mō), **capirete** (kâ·pē·rā′tā), **capiranno** (kâ·pē·rân′nō)
PAST DEFINITE **capii** (kâ·pē′ē), **capisti** (kâ·pē′stē), **capì** (kâ·pē′), **capimmo** (kâ·pēm′mō) **capiste** (kâ·pē′stā), **capirono** (kâ·pē′rō·nō)
PAST SUBJUNCTIVE **capissi** (kâ·pēs′sē), **capissi** (kâ·pēs′sē), **capisse** (kâ·pēs′sā), **capissimo** (kâ·pēs′sē·mō), **capiste** (kâ·pē′stā), **capissero** (kâ·pēs′sā·rō)

–IRE VERBS *Example:* **dormire** (dōr·mē′rā) to sleep

PRESENT PARTICIPLE **dormendo** (dōr·mān′dō)
PAST PARTICIPLE **dormito** (dōr·mē′tō)
PRESENT **dormo** (dōr′mō), **dormi** (dōr′mē), **dorme** (dōr′mā), **dormiamo** (dōr·myâ′mō), **dormite** (dōr·mē′tā), **dormono** (dôr′mō·nō)
FUTURE **dormirò** (dōr·mē·rō′), **dormirai** (dōr·mē·râ′ē), **dormirà** (dōr·mē·râ′), **dormiremo** (dōr·mē·rā′mō), **dormirete** (dōr·mē.rā′tā), **dormiranno** (dōr·mē·rân′nō)
CONDITIONAL **dormirei** (dōr·mē·rā′ē), **dormiresti** (dōr·mē·rā′stē), **dormirebbe** (dōr·mē·rāb′bā), **dormiremmo** (dōr·mē·rām′mō), **dormireste** (dōr·mē·rā′stā), **dormirebbero** (dōr·mē·reb′bā·rō)
PRESENT SUBJUNCTIVE **dorma** (dōr′mâ), **dorma** (dōr′mâ), **dorma** (dōr′mâ), **dormiamo** (dōr·myâ′mō), **dormiate** (dōr·myâ′tā), **dormano** (dôr′mâ·nō)
IMPERFECT **dormivo** (dōr·mē′vō), **dormivi** (dōr·mē′vē), **dormiva** (dōr·mē′vâ), **dormivamo** (dōr·mē·vâ′mō), **dormivate** (dōr·mē·vâ′tā), **dormivano** (dōr·mē′vâ·nō)
PAST DEFINITE **dormii** (dōr·mē′ē), **dormisti** (dōr·mē′stē), **dormì** (dōr·mē′), **dormimmo** (dōr·mēm′mō), **dormiste** (dōr·mē′stā), **dormirono** (dōr·mē′rō·nō)
PAST SUBJUNCTIVE **dormissi** (dōr·mēs′sē), **dormissi** (dōr·mēs′sē), **dormisse** (dōr·mēs′sā), **dormissimo** (dōr·mēs′sē·mō), **dormiste** (dōr·mē′stā), **dormissero** (dōr·mēs′sā·rō)

VERB USAGE

The present tense in Italian is sometimes used in cases where the future is called for in English, when the future is immediate.

Examples:

Vado subito.	I'll go at once.
Partiamo stasera.	We'll leave this evening.

24

The imperfect tense is used in Italian instead of the past definite or the compound past when repeated or habitual action is implied in the past. The modal *used to* is often used in English to convey the same idea. The imperfect is also used when indefinite time is implied in the past.

Examples:

Andavo alla spiaggia ogni fine di settimana.	I used to go to the beach every weekend.
Andavamo in città ogni domenica.	We went to town every Sunday.
Eravamo lì nel pomeriggio.	We were there in the afternoon.

The compound past **(passato prossimo)** or present perfect, is used for a single action in the past, or when definite time limits are indicated.

Examples:

Sono andati a Fiesole ieri sera.	They went to Fiesole last night.
Siamo rimasti a Volterra per tre giorni.	We stayed in Volterra for three days.

The past definite is also used for a single action in the past, or when definite time limits are indicated. It is a more formal tense and is found in writing more often than conversation. It is also used in combination with the compound past to clarify the time element of actions in the past.

Examples:

Dante scrisse la Divina Commedia, capolavoro del medioevo italiano.	Dante wrote *The Divine Comedy,* a masterpiece of the Italian Middle Ages.
Le ho dato il libro che comprai l'altro ieri.	I gave her the book that I bought the day before yesterday.

2 Auxiliary Verbs avere and essere

As in English, the verb **avere** *(to have)* is used to form the compound tenses, *but not exclusively.* Many verbs of motion, all reflexive and reciprocal verb forms, verbs that imply change in condition, and verbs in the passive voice are conjugated with the verb **essere** *(to be).* The Italian equivalent of our present perfect, using the auxiliary in the present tense with the past participle, is often used with the idea of the simple past in English. The past participle always agrees with the subject when the verb **essere** is used; it never does when **avere** is used.

Examples:

L'ho fatto io ieri l'altro.	I did it the day before yesterday.
Mia sorella non è ancora partita.	My sister hasn't left yet.
La lettera è stata scritta da me.	The letter was written by me.

Conjugation of Verbs

È stato visto dappertutto.	He has been seen everywhere.
Si è fatta male.	She hurt herself.
Si sono parlati per mezz'ora.	They talked to one another for a half-hour.
Ci siamo visti in città.	We saw each other in town.
Non ho mai sentito una cosa simile.	I've never heard anything like that before.

In the conjugations below, the verb forms are given in the following order: first, second, and third person singular; followed by first, second, and third person plural.

avere (â·vā′rā) to have
PRESENT PARTICIPLE **avendo** (â·vān′dō)
PAST PARTICIPLE **avuto** (â·vū′tō)
PRESENT **ho** (ō), **hai** (â′ē), **ha** (â), **abbiamo** (âb·byâ′mō), **avete** (â·vā′tā), **hanno** (ân′nō)
FUTURE **avrò** (â·vrō′), **avrai** (â·vrâ′ē), **avrà** (â·vrâ′), **avremo** (â·vrā′mō), **avrete** (â·vrā′tā), **avranno** (â·vrân′nō)
CONDITIONAL **avrei** (â·vrā′ē), **avresti** (â·vrā′stē), **avrebbe** (â·vrāb′bā), **avremmo** (â·vrām′mō), **avreste** (â·vrā′stā), **avrebbero** (â·vreb′bā·rō)
PRESENT SUBJUNCTIVE **abbia** (âb′byâ), **abbia** (âb′byâ), **abbia** (âb′byâ), **abbiamo** (âb·byâ′mō), **abbiate** (âb·byâ′tā), **abbiano** (âb′byâ·nō)
IMPERFECT **avevo** (â·vā′vō), **avevi** (â·vā′vē), **aveva** (â·vā′vâ), **avevamo** (â·vā·vâ′mō), **avevate** (â·vā·vâ′tā), **avevano** (â·ve′vâ·nō)
PAST DEFINITE **ebbi** (āb′bē), **avesti** (â·vā′stē), **ebbe** (āb′bā), **avemmo** (â·vām′mō), **aveste** (â·vā′stā), **ebbero** (eb′bā·rō)
PAST SUBJUNCTIVE **avessi** (â·vās′sē), **avessi** (â·vās′sē), **avesse** (â·vās′sā), **avessimo** (â·ves′sē·mō), **aveste** (â·vā′stā), **avessero** (â·ves′sā·rō)

essere (es′sā·rā) to be
PRESENT PARTICIPLE **essendo** (ās·sān′dō)
PAST PARTICIPLE **stato** (stâ′tō)
PRESENT **sono** (sō′nō), **sei** (sā′ē), **è** (ā), **siamo** (syâ′mō), **siete** (syā′tā), **sono** (sō′nō)
FUTURE **sarò** (sâ·rō′), **sarai** (sâ·râ′ē), **sarà** (sâ·râ′), **saremo** (sâ·rā′mō), **sarete** (sâ·rā′tā), **saranno** (sâ·rân′nō)
CONDITIONAL **sarei** (sâ·rā′ē), **saresti** (sâ·rā′stē), **sarebbe** (sâ·rāb′bā), **saremmo** (sâ·rām′mō), **sareste** (sâ·rā′stā), **sarebbero** (sâ·reb′bā·rō)
PRESENT SUBJUNCTIVE **sia** (sē′â), **sia** (sē′â), **sia** (sē′â), **siamo** (syâ′mō), **siate** (syâ′tā), **siano** (sē′â·nō)
IMPERFECT **ero** (ā′rō), **eri** (ā′rē), **era** (ā′râ), **eravamo** (ā·râ·vâ′mō), **eravate** (ā·râ·vâ′tā), **erano** (e′râ·nō)
PAST DEFINITE **fui** (fū′ē), **fosti** (fō′stē), **fu** (fū), **fummo** (fūm′mō), **foste** (fō′stā), **furono** (fū′rō·nō)
PAST SUBJUNCTIVE **fossi** (fōs′sē), **fossi** (fōs′sē), **fosse** (fōs′sā), **fossimo** (fôs′sē·mō), **foste** (fō′stā), **fossero** (fôs′sā·rō)

3 Irregular Verbs

The following list contains all the irregular verbs entered in this dictionary. For those verbs whose conjugation is identical to a root verb, the user is referred to that verb (for example, **rimettere** see **mettere**).

In the conjugations offered below, only those tenses containing one or more irregular forms are given. Other tenses are formed on the model of the regular verbs given previously.

The present subjunctive is not given when the regular subjunctive endings are used with the stem of the first person singular of the present indicative (for example, **dica**, **dica**, **dica**, **diciamo**, **diciate**, **dicano** from **dico**).

It will be noted that many of the verbs given below show an irregularity only in the past participle and in the past definite. As stated previously, the past participle always agrees with the subject when the verb **essere** is used, and never does so with forms of the verb **avere**. However, when the verb **avere** is employed, the past participle *always* agrees with third-person direct object pronouns, singular or plural. The past participle may or may not agree in gender and number with first- and second-person direct object pronouns, noun objects, or preceding relative pronouns, at the speaker's option.

Space does not permit including the pronunciation of inflected forms of irregular verbs. But comparison with the pronunciations already given for the inflected forms of regular verbs plus the rules of pronunciation set forth on pages 10-14, should enable the reader to supply his own pronunciation for the words listed here.

The verb forms are given in the following order: first, second, and third person singular; followed by first, second, and third person plural.

accadere to happen, see **cadere**
accendere to ignite
  PAST PARTICIPLE **acceso**
  PAST DEFINITE **accesi, accendesti, accese, accendemmo, accendeste, accesero**
accludere to enclose
  PAST PARTICIPLE **accluso**
  PAST DEFINITE **acclusi, accludesti, accluse, accludemmo, accludeste, acclusero**
accogliere to receive, see **cogliere**
accorgersi to perceive
  PAST PARTICIPLE **accorto**
  PAST DEFINITE **accorsi, accorgesti, accorse, accorgemmo, accorgeste, accorsero**
accorrere to run up, see **correre**
addurre to allege
  PRESENT PARTICIPLE **adducendo**
  PAST PARTICIPLE **addotto**
  PRESENT **adduco, adduci, adduce, adduciamo, adducete, adducono**
  IMPERFECT **adducevo, adducevi, adduceva, adducevamo, adducevate, adducevano**
  PAST DEFINITE **addussi, adducesti, addusse, adducemmo, adduceste, addussero**

  PAST SUBJUNCTIVE **adducessi, adducessi, adducese, adducessimo, adduceste, adducessero**
adempiere to fulfill, see **compiere**
affliggere to afflict
  PAST PARTICIPLE **afflitto**
  PAST DEFINITE **afflissi, affliggesti, afflisse, affliggemmo, affliggeste, afflissero**
aggiungere to add, see **giungere**
ammettere to admit, see **mettere**
andare to go
  PRESENT **vado, vai, va, andiamo, andate, vanno**
  FUTURE **andrò, andrai, andrà, andremo, andrete, andranno**
  CONDITIONAL **andrei, andresti, andrebbe, andremmo, andreste, andrebbero**
  PRESENT SUBJUNCTIVE **vada, vada, vada, andiamo, andiate, vadano**
apparire to appear
  PAST PARTICIPLE **apparso**
  PRESENT **appaio, appari, appare, appariamo, apparite, appaiono**
  PAST DEFINITE **apparsi, apparisti, apparse, apparimmo, appariste, apparsero**
appartenere to belong, see **tenere**
appendere to hang up, see **pendere**
apprendere to learn, see **prendere**

Conjugation of Verbs

aprire to open
PAST PARTICIPLE **aperto**
PAST DEFINITE **apersi, apristi, aperse, aprimmo, apriste, apersero**

ardere to burn
PAST PARTICIPLE **arso**
PAST DEFINITE **arsi, ardesti, arse, ardemmo, ardeste, arsero**

arrendersi to surrender, see **rendere**
ascendere to ascend, see **scendere**
ascrivere to ascribe, see **scrivere**
assistere to attend
PAST PARTICIPLE **assistito**

assolvere to absolve, see **solvere**
assumere to assume
PAST PARTICIPLE **assunto**
PAST DEFINITE **assunsi, assumesti, assunse, assumemmo, assumeste, assunsero**

astrarre to abstract, see **trarre**
attendere to wait for, see **tendere**
attenere to maintain, see **tenere**
attingere to reach, see **tingere**
attrarre to attract, see **trarre**
avvenire to happen, see **venire**
avvincere to bind, see **vincere**
avvolgere to roll up, see **volgere**

benedire to bless, see **dire**
benvolere to like, see **volere**
bere to drink
PRESENT PARTICIPLE **bevendo**
PAST PARTICIPLE **bevuto**
PRESENT **bevo, bevi, beve, beviamo, bevete, bevono**
FUTURE **berrò, berrai, berrà, berremo, berrete, berranno**
CONDITIONAL **berrei, berresti, berrebbe, berremmo, berreste, berrebero**
IMPERFECT **bevevo, bevevi, beveva, bevevamo, bevevate, bevevano**
PAST DEFINITE **bevvi, bevesti, bevve, bevemmo, beveste, bevvero**
PAST SUBJUNCTIVE **bevessi, bevessi, bevesse, bevessimo, beveste, bevessero**

cadere to fall
FUTURE **cadrò, cadrai, cadrà, cadremo, cadrete, cadranno**
CONDITIONAL **cadrei, cadresti, cadrebbe, cadremmo, cadreste, cadrebbero**
PAST DEFINITE **caddi, cadesti, cadde, cademmo, cadeste, caddero**

capovolgere to upset, see **volgere**
chiedere to request
PAST PARTICIPLE **chiesto**
PAST DEFINITE **chiesi, chiedesti, chiese, chiedemmo, chiedeste, chiesero**

chiudere to close
PAST PARTICIPLE **chiuso**
PAST DEFINITE **chiusi, chiudesti, chiuse, chiudemmo, chiudeste, chiusero**

cingere to encircle
PAST PARTICIPLE **cinto**
PAST DEFINITE **cinsi, cingesti, cinse, cingemmo, cingeste, cinsero**

circoncidere to circumcise, see **decidere**
circonvenire to circumvent, see **venire**
cogliere to gather
PAST PARTICIPLE **colto**
PRESENT **colgo, cogli, coglie, cogliamo, cogliete, colgono**
PAST DEFINITE **colsi, cogliesti, colse, cogliemmo, coglieste, colsero**

coinvolgere to involve, see **volgere**
commuovere to move, see **muovere**
comparire to appear, see **apparire**
compiangere to regret, see **piangere**
compiere or **compire** to accomplish
PRESENT PARTICIPLE **compiendo**
PAST PARTICIPLE **compiuto** or **compito**
PRESENT **compio, compi, compie, compiamo, compite, compiono**
FUTURE **compirò, compirai, compirà, compiremo, compirete, compiranno**
CONDITIONAL **compirei, compiresti, compirebbe, compiremmo, compireste, compirebbero**
PRESENT SUBJUNCTIVE **compia, compia, compia, compiamo, compiate, compiano**
IMPERFECT **compivo, compivi, compiva, compivamo, compivate, compivano**
PAST DEFINITE **compii, compisti, compì, compimmo, compiste, compirono**
PAST SUBJUNCTIVE **compissi, compissi, compisse, compissimo, compiste, compissero**

comporre to compose, see **porre**
comprendere to understand, see **prendere**
comprimere to squeeze
PAST PARTICIPLE **compresso**
PAST DEFINITE **compressi, comprimesti, compresse, comprimemmo, comprimeste, compressero**

compromettere to risk, see **mettere**
concludere to conclude, see **accludere**
concorrere to compete, see **correre**
condividere to share in, see **dividere**
condolersi to sympathize, see **dolere**
condurre to conduct, see **addurre**
confarsi to suit, see **fare**
confondere to confuse, see **fondere**

28

congiungere to connect, see **giungere**
connettere to connect
  PAST PARTICIPLE **connesso**
  PAST DEFINITE **connessi, connettesti, connesse, connettemmo, connetteste, connessero**
conoscere to know
  PAST DEFINITE **conobbi, conoscesti, conobbe, conoscemmo, conosceste, conobbero**
consistere to consist
  PAST PARTICIPLE **consistito**
contendere to contest, see **tendere**
contenere to contain, see **tenere**
contorcere to contort, see **torcere**
contraddire to contradict, see **dire**
contraffare to counterfeit, see **fare**
contrarre to contract, see **trarre**
convergere to converge
  PAST PARTICIPLE **converso**
  PAST DEFINITE **conversi, convergesti, converse, convergemmo, convergeste, conversero**
convincere to convince, see **vincere**
convivere to cohabit, see **vivere**
coprire to cover
  PAST PARTICIPLE **coperto**
correre to run
  PAST PARTICIPLE **corso**
  PAST DEFINITE **corsi, corresti, corse, corremmo, correste, corsero**
corrispondere to correspond, see **rispondere**
corrodere to corrode, see **rodere**
corrompere to corrupt, see **rompere**
cospargere to sprinkle, see **spargere**
crescere to grow
  PAST DEFINITE **crebbi, crescesti, crebbe, crescemmo, cresceste, crebbero**
crocifiggere to crucify, see **figgere**
cuocere to cook
  PRESENT PARTICIPLE **cocendo**
  PAST PARTICIPLE **cotto**
  PRESENT **cuocio, cuoci, cuoce, cociamo, cocete, cuociono**
  FUTURE **cocerò, cocerai, cocerà, coceremo, cocerete, coceranno**
  CONDITIONAL **cocerei, coceresti, cocerebbe, coceremmo, cocereste, cocerebbero**
  PRESENT SUBJUNCTIVE **cuocia, cuocia, cuocia, cociamo, cociate, cuociano**
  IMPERFECT **cocevo, cocevi, coceva, cocevamo, cocevate, cocevano**
  PAST DEFINITE **cossi, cocesti, cosse, cocemmo, coceste, cossero**
  PAST SUBJUNCTIVE **cocessi, cocessi, cocesse, cocessimo, coceste, cocessero**

dare to give
  PRESENT **do, dai, dà, diamo, date, danno**
  FUTURE **darò, darai, darà, daremo, darete, daranno**
  CONDITIONAL **darei, daresti, darebbe, daremmo, dareste, darebbero**
  PRESENT SUBJUNCTIVE **dia, dia, dia, diamo, diate, diano**
  PAST DEFINITE **diedi, desti, diede, demmo, deste, diedero**
  PAST SUBJUNCTIVE **dessi, dessi, desse, dessimo, deste, dessero**
decadere to decay, see **cadere**
decidere to decide
  PAST PARTICIPLE **deciso**
  PAST DEFINITE **decisi, decidesti, decise, decidemmo, decideste, decisero**
decomporre to decompose, see **porre**
decorrere to elapse, see **correre**
decrescere to decrease, see **crescere**
dedurre to deduce, see **addurre**
deflettere to deflect
  PAST PARTICIPLE **deflesso**
  PAST DEFINITE **deflessi, deflettesti, deflesse, deflettemmo, defletteste, deflessero**
deludere to delude
  PAST PARTICIPLE **deluso**
  PAST DEFINITE **delusi, deludesti, deluse, deludemmo, deludeste, delusero**
deporre to deposit, see **porre**
descrivere to describe, see **scrivere**
desistere to desist, see **esistere**
desumere to infer, see **assumere**
detenere to detain, see **tenere**
detrarre to detract, see **trarre**
devolvere to devolve, see **volvere**
difendere to defend
  PAST PARTICIPLE **difeso**
  PAST DEFINITE **difesi, difendesti, difese, difendemmo, difendeste, difesero**
dimettere to dismiss, see **mettere**
dipendere to depend, see **pendere**
dipingere to paint
  PAST PARTICIPLE **dipinto**
  PAST DEFINITE **dipinsi, dipingesti, dipinse, dipingemmo, dipingeste, dipinsero**
dire to say
  PRESENT PARTICIPLE **dicendo**
  PAST PARTICIPLE **detto**
  PRESENT **dico, dici, dice, diciamo, dite, dicono**
  IMPERFECT **dicevo, dicevi, diceva, dicevamo, dicevate, dicevano**

Conjugation of Verbs

PAST DEFINITE dissi, dicesti, disse, dicemmo, diceste, dissero
PAST SUBJUNCTIVE dicessi, dicessi, dicesse, dicessimo, diceste, dicessero
dirigere to direct
PAST PARTICIPLE diretto
PAST DEFINITE diressi, dirigesti, diresse, dirigemmo, dirigeste, diressero
dischiudere to disclose, see chiudere
disciogliere to untie, see sciogliere
disconoscere to ignore, see conoscere
discorrere to discourse, see correre
discutere to discuss
PAST PARTICIPLE discusso
PAST DEFINITE discussi, discutesti, discusse, discutemmo, discuteste, discussero
disdire to deny, see dire
disfare to undo, see fare
disgiungere to detach, see giungere
disperdere to disperse, see perdere
dispiacere to displease, see piacere
disporre to dispose, see porre
dissolvere to dissolve, see solvere
dissuadere to dissuade
PAST PARTICIPLE dissuaso
PAST DEFINITE dissuasi, dissuadesti, dissuase, dissuademmo, dissuadeste, dissuasero
distendere to stretch, see tendere
distinguere to distinguish
PAST PARTICIPLE distinto
PAST DEFINITE distinsi, distinguesti, distinse, distinguemmo, distingueste, distinsero
distogliere to divert, see togliere
distrarre to distract, see trarre
distruggere to destroy
PAST PARTICIPLE distrutto
PAST DEFINITE distrussi, distruggesti, distrusse, distruggemmo, distruggeste, distrussero
divellere to uproot
PAST PARTICIPLE divelso
PAST DEFINITE divelsi, divellesti, divelse, divellemmo, divelleste, divelsero
divenire to become, see venire
dividere to divide
PAST PARTICIPLE diviso
PAST DEFINITE divisi, dividesti, divise, dividemmo, divideste, divisero
dolere to pain
PRESENT dolgo, duoli, duole, dogliamo, dolete, dolgono
FUTURE dorrò, dorrai, dorrà, dorremo, dorrete, dorranno

CONDITIONAL dorrei, dorresti, dorrebbe, dorremmo, dorreste, dorrebbero
PRESENT SUBJUNCTIVE dolga, dolga, dolga, dogliamo, dogliate, dolgano
PAST DEFINITE dolsi, dolesti, dolse, dolemmo, doleste, dolsero
dovere to owe
PRESENT devo, devi, deve, dobbiamo, dovete, devono
FUTURE dovrò, dovrai, dovrà, dovremo, dovrete, dovranno
CONDITIONAL dovrei, dovresti, dovrebbe, dovremmo, dovreste, dovrebbero
PRESENT SUBJUNCTIVE deva, deva, deva, dobbiamo, dobbiate, devano

eccellere to excel
PAST PARTICIPLE eccelso
PAST DEFINITE eccelsi, eccellesti, eccelse, eccellemmo, eccelleste, eccelsero
eleggere to elect
PAST PARTICIPLE eletto
PAST DEFINITE elessi, eleggesti, elesse, eleggemmo, eleggeste, elessero
elidere to elide
PAST PARTICIPLE eliso
PAST DEFINITE elisi, elidesti, elise, elidemmo, elideste, elisero
eludere to elude, see deludere
emergere to emerge
PAST PARTICIPLE emerso
PAST DEFINITE emersi, emergesti, emerse, emergemmo, emergeste, emersero
emettere to emit, see mettere
empire to fill
PRESENT PARTICIPLE empiendo
PRESENT empio, empi, empie, empiamo, empite, empiono
PRESENT SUBJUNCTIVE empia, empia, empia, empiamo, empiate, empiano
erigere to erect
PAST PARTICIPLE eretto
PAST DEFINITE eressi, erigesti, eresse, erigemmo, erigeste, eressero
erompere to erupt, see rompere
escludere to exclude, see accludere
esigere to exact
PAST PARTICIPLE esatto
esistere to exist, see assistere
espandere to expand, see spandere
espellere to expel
PAST PARTICIPLE espulso
PAST DEFINITE espulsi, espellesti, espulse, espellemmo, espelleste, espulsero
esplodere to explode

PAST PARTICIPLE **esploso**
PAST DEFINITE **esplosi, esplodesti, esplose, esplodemmo, esplodeste, esplosero**
esporre to expose, see **porre**
esprimere to express, see **comprimere**
estendere to extend, see **tendere**
estinguere to extinguish, see **distinguere**
estollere to extol
PAST PARTICIPLE **estolto**
PAST DEFINITE **estolsi, estollesti, estolse, estollemmo, estolleste, estolsero**
estorcere to extort, see **torcere**
estrarre to extract, see **trarre**
estromettere to oust, see **mettere**
evadere to escape
PAST PARTICIPLE **evaso**
PAST DEFINITE **evasi, evadesti, evase, evademmo, evadeste, evasero**

fare to make
PRESENT PARTICIPLE **facendo**
PAST PARTICIPLE **fatto**
PRESENT **faccio, fai, fa, facciamo, fate, fanno**
FUTURE **farò, farai, farà, faremo, farete, faranno**
CONDITIONAL **farei, faresti, farebbe, faremmo, fareste, farebbero**
PRESENT SUBJUNCTIVE **faccia, faccia, faccia, facciamo, facciate, facciano**
IMPERFECT **facevo, facevi, faceva, facevamo, facevate, facevano**
PAST DEFINITE **feci, facesti, fece, facemmo, faceste, fecero**
PAST SUBJUNCTIVE **facessi, facessi, facesse, facessimo, faceste, facessero**
fendere to split
PAST PARTICIPLE **fesso**
figgere to fix
PAST PARTICIPLE **fitto**
PAST DEFINITE **fissi, figgesti, fisse, figgemmo, figgeste, fissero**
fingere to feign
PAST PARTICIPLE **finto**
PAST DEFINITE **finsi, fingesti, finse, fingemmo, fingeste, finsero**
flettere to flex
PAST PARTICIPLE **flesso**
PAST DEFINITE **flessi, flettesti, flesse, flettemmo, fletteste, flessero**
fondere to cast
PAST PARTICIPLE **fuso**
PAST DEFINITE **fusi, fondesti, fuse, fondemmo, fondeste, fusero**

fraintendere to misunderstand, see **tendere**
frangere to break
PAST PARTICIPLE **franto**
PAST DEFINITE **fransi, frangesti, franse, frangemmo, frangeste, fransero**
frapporre to insert, see **porre**
friggere to fry
PAST PARTICIPLE **fritto**
PAST DEFINITE **frissi, friggesti, frisse, friggemmo, friggeste, frissero**

genuflettersi to genuflect, see **flettere**
giacere to lie
PRESENT **giaccio, giaci, giace, giacciamo, giacete, giacciono**
PRESENT SUBJUNCTIVE **giaccia, giaccia, giaccia, giacciamo, giacciate, giacciano**
PAST DEFINITE **giacqui, giacesti, giacque, giacemmo, giaceste, giacquero**
giungere to arrive
PAST PARTICIPLE **giunto**
PAST DEFINITE **giunsi, giungesti, giunse, giungemmo, giungeste, giunsero**

illudere to deceive, see **deludere**
immergere to immerse, see **emergere**
immettere to infuse, see **mettere**
imporre to impose, see **porre**
imprimere to print, see **comprimere**
includere to include, see **accludere**
incorrere to incur, see **correre**
indire to notify, see **dire**
indisporre to upset, see **porre**
indulgere to gratify
PAST PARTICIPLE **indulto**
PAST DEFINITE **indulsi, indulgesti, indulse, indulgemmo, indulgeste, indulsero**
indurre to induce, see **addurre**
infliggere to inflict
PAST PARTICIPLE **inflitto**
PAST DEFINITE **inflissi, infliggesti, inflisse, infliggemmo, infliggeste, inflissero**
infondere to infuse, see **fondere**
inframmettere to interpose, see **mettere**
infrangere to violate, see **frangere**
ingiungere to enjoin, see **giungere**
insistere to insist
PAST PARTICIPLE **insistito**
intendere to intend, see **tendere**
intercorrere to elapse, see **correre**
interdire to forbid, see **dire**
interporre to interpose, see **porre**
interrompere to interrupt, see **rompere**

Conjugation of Verbs

intervenire to intervene, see **venire**
intingere to dip, see **tingere**
intraprendere to undertake, see **prendere**
intrattenere to entertain, see **tenere**
introdurre to insert, see **addurre**
intrommettersi to interfere, see **mettere**
invadere to invade, see **evadere**
involgere to involve, see **volgere**
irrompere to break out, see **rompere**
iscrivere to enroll, see **scrivere**

ledere to injure
  PAST PARTICIPLE **leso**
  PAST DEFINITE **lesi, ledesti, lese, ledemmo, ledeste, lesero**
leggere to read
  PAST PARTICIPLE **letto**
  PAST DEFINITE **lessi, leggesti, lesse, leggemmo, leggeste, lessero**

malintendere to misunderstand, see **tendere**
mantenere to maintain, see **tenere**
mettere to put
  PAST PARTICIPLE **messo**
  PAST DEFINITE **misi, mettesti, mise, mettemmo, metteste, misero**
mordere to bite
  PAST PARTICIPLE **morso**
  PAST DEFINITE **morsi, mordesti, morse, mordemmo, mordeste, morsero**
morire to die
  PAST PARTICIPLE **morto**
  PRESENT **muoio, muori, muore, moriamo, morite, muoiono**
  FUTURE **morrò, morrai, morrà, morremo, morrete, morranno**
  CONDITIONAL **morrei, morresti, morrebbe, morremmo, morreste, morrebbero**
  PRESENT SUBJUNCTIVE **muoia, muoia, muoia, moriamo, moriate, muoiano**
mungere to milk
  PAST PARTICIPLE **munto**
  PAST DEFINITE **munsi, mungesti, munse, mungemmo, mungeste, munsero**
muovere to move
  PAST PARTICIPLE **mosso**
  PAST DEFINITE **mossi, movesti, mosse, movemmo, moveste, mossero**

nascere to be born
  PAST PARTICIPLE **nato**
  PAST DEFINITE **nacqui, nascesti, nacque, nascemmo, nasceste, nacquero**
nascondere to hide
  PAST PARTICIPLE **nascosto**
  PAST DEFINITE **nascosi, nascondesti, nascose, nascondemmo, nascondeste, nascosero**
nuocere to harm
  PAST PARTICIPLE **nociuto**
  PRESENT **nuoccio, nuoci, nuoce, nociamo, nocete, nuocciono**
  PRESENT SUBJUNCTIVE **noccia, noccia, noccia, nociamo, nociate, nocciano**
  PAST DEFINITE **nocqui, nocesti, nocque, nocemmo, noceste, nocquero**

occorrere to be necessary, see **correre**
offendere to offend
  PAST PARTICIPLE **offeso**
  PAST DEFINITE **offesi, offendesti, offese, offendemmo, offendeste, offesero**
offrire to offer
  PAST PARTICIPLE **offerto**
omettere to omit, see **mettere**
opporre to oppose, see **porre**
opprimere to oppress, see **comprimere**
ottenere to obtain, see **tenere**

parere to appear
  PAST PARTICIPLE **parso**
  PRESENT **paio, pari, pare, pariamo, parete, paiono**
  FUTURE **parrò, parrai, parrà, parremo, parrete, parranno**
  CONDITIONAL **parrei, parresti, parrebbe, parremmo, parreste, parrebbero**
  PRESENT SUBJUNCTIVE **paia, paia, paia, pariamo, pariate, paiano**
  PAST DEFINITE **parvi, paresti, parve, paremmo, pareste, parvero**
pendere to hang
  PAST PARTICIPLE **peso**
  PAST DEFINITE **pesi, pendesti, pese, pendemmo, pendeste, pesero**
percorrere to travel across, see **correre**
percuotere to strike
  PRESENT PARTICIPLE **percotendo**
  PAST PARTICIPLE **percosso**
  PRESENT **percuoto, percuoti, percuote, percotiamo, percotete, percuotono**
  FUTURE **percoterò, percoterai, percoterà, percoteremo, percoterete, percoteranno**
  CONDITIONAL **percoterei, percoteresti, percoterebbe, percoteremmo, percote-**

reste, percoterebbero
PRESENT SUBJUNCTIVE percuota, percuota, percuota, percotiamo, percotiate, percuotano
IMPERFECT percotevo, percotevi, percoteva, percotevamo, percotevate, percotevano
PAST DEFINITE percossi, percotesti, percosse, percotemmo, percoteste, percossero
PAST SUBJUNCTIVE percotessi, percotessi, percotesse, percotessimo, percoteste, percotessero
perdere to lose
PAST PARTICIPLE perso
PAST DEFINITE persi, perdesti, perse, perdemmo, perdeste, persero
permanere to stay
PAST PARTICIPLE permaso
PRESENT permango, permani, permane, permaniamo, permanete, permangono
FUTURE permarrò, permarrai, permarrà, permarremo, permarrete, permarranno
CONDITIONAL permarrei, permarresti, permarrebbe, permarremmo, permarreste, permarrebbero
PRESENT SUBJUNCTIVE permanga, permanga, permanga, permaniamo, permaniate, permangano
PAST DEFINITE permasi, permanesti, permase, permanemmo, permaneste, permasero
permettere to permit, see mettere
persistere to persist
PAST PARTICIPLE persistito
persuadere to persuade
PAST PARTICIPLE persuaso
PAST DEFINITE persuasi, persuadesti, persuase, persuademmo, persuadeste, persuasero
pervenire to achieve, see venire
piacere to please
PRESENT piaccio, piaci, piace, piacciamo, piacete, piacciono
PRESENT SUBJUNCTIVE piaccia, piaccia, piaccia, piacciamo, piacciate, piacciano
PAST DEFINITE piacqui, piacesti, piacque, piacemmo, piaceste, piacquero
piangere to cry
PAST PARTICIPLE pianto
PAST DEFINITE piansi, piangesti, pianse, piangemmo, piangeste, piansero
piovere to rain
PAST DEFINITE piovvi, piovesti, piovve, piovemmo, pioveste, piovvero
porgere to hand over

PAST PARTICIPLE porto
PAST DEFINITE porsi, porgesti, porse, porgemmo, porgeste, porsero
porre to place
PRESENT PARTICIPLE ponendo
PAST PARTICIPLE posto
PRESENT pongo, poni, pone, poniamo, ponete, pongono
FUTURE porrò, porrai, porrà, porremo, porrete, porranno
CONDITIONAL porrei, porresti, porrebbe, porremmo, porreste, porrebbero
PRESENT SUBJUNCTIVE ponga, ponga, ponga, poniamo, poniate, pongano
IMPERFECT ponevo, ponevi, poneva, ponevamo, ponevate, ponevano
PAST DEFINITE posi, ponesti, pose, ponemmo, poneste, posero
PAST SUBJUNCTIVE ponessi, ponessi, ponesse, ponessimo, poneste, ponessero
posporre to postpone, see porre
possedere to own, see sedere
potere to be able
PRESENT posso, puoi, può, possiamo, potete, possono
FUTURE potrò, potrai, potrà, potremo, potrete, potranno
CONDITIONAL potrei, potresti, potrebbe, potremmo, potreste, potrebbero
predire to foretell, see dire
predisporre to predispose, see porre
prefiggere to prefix, see figgere
premettere to premise, see mettere
prendere to take
PAST PARTICIPLE preso
PAST DEFINITE presi, prendesti, prese, prendemmo, prendeste, presero
prescindere to disregard
PAST PARTICIPLE prescisso
PAST DEFINITE prescissi, prescindesti, prescisse, prescindemmo, prescindeste, prescissero
prescrivere to prescribe, see scrivere
presiedere to preside, see sedere
presumere to presume
PAST PARTICIPLE presunto
PAST DEFINITE presunsi, presumesti, presunse, presummemo, presumeste, presunsero
presupporre to imply, see porre
pretendere to claim, see tendere
prevalere to prevail, see valere
prevedere to foresee, see vedere
prevenire to warn, see venire
produrre to produce, see addurre
profondere to squander, see fondere

Conjugation of Verbs

promettere to promise, see **mettere**
promuovere to promote, see **muovere**
propendere to incline, see **pendere**
proporre to propose, see **porre**
prorompere to break out, see **rompere**
prosciogliere to free, see **sciogliere**
proscrivere to banish, see **scrivere**
proteggere to protect
   PAST PARTICIPLE **protetto**
   PAST DEFINITE **protessi, proteggesti, protesse, proteggemmo, proteggeste, protessero**
protrarre to prolong, see **trarre**
povenire to originate, see **venire**
provvedere to provide, see **vedere**
pungere to sting
   PAST PARTICIPLE **punto**
   PAST DEFINITE **punsi, pungesti, punse, pungemmo, pungeste, punsero**
putrefare to rot, see **fare**

racchiudere to lock in, see **chiudere**
raccogliere to collect, see **cogliere**
radere to shave
   PAST PARTICIPLE **raso**
   PAST DEFINITE **rasi, radesti, rase, rademmo, radeste, rasero**
raggiungere to reach, see **giungere**
rarefare to rarefy, see **fare**
ravvedersi to repent, see **vedere**
recidere to cut off
   PAST PARTICIPLE **reciso**
   PAST DEFINITE **recisi, recidesti, recise, recidemmo, recideste, recisero**
redigere to edit
   PAST PARTICIPLE **redatto**
   PAST DEFINITE **redassi, redigesti, redasse, redigemmo, redigeste, redassero**
redimere to redeem
   PAST PARTICIPLE **redento**
   PAST DEFINITE **redensi, redimesti, redense, redimemmo, redimeste, redensero**
reggere to uphold
   PAST PARTICIPLE **retto**
   PAST DEFINITE **ressi, reggesti, resse, reggemmo, reggeste, ressero**
rendere to render
   PAST PARTICIPLE **reso**
   PAST DEFINITE **resi, rendesti, rese, rendemmo, rendeste, resero**
reprimere to repress, see **comprimere**
resistere to resist
   PAST PARTICIPLE **resistito**
respingere to repel, see **spingere**
restringere to restrict, see **stringere**
richiedere to request, see **chiedere**

riconoscere to recognize, see **conoscere**
ricorrere to appeal, see **correre**
ridere to laugh
   PAST PARTICIPLE **riso**
   PAST DEFINITE **risi, ridesti, rise, ridemmo, rideste, risero**
ridurre to reduce, see **addurre**
riempire to fill, see **empire**
rifare to redo, see **fare**
riflettere to reflect, see **flettere**
rimanere to remain
   PAST PARTICIPLE **rimasto**
   PRESENT **rimango, rimani, rimane, rimaniamo, rimanete, rimangono**
   FUTURE **rimarrò, rimarrai, rimarrà, rimarremo, rimarrete, rimarranno**
   CONDITIONAL **rimarrei, rimarresti, rimarrebbe, rimarremmo, rimarreste, rimarrebbero**
   PRESENT SUBJUNCTIVE **rimanga, rimanga, rimanga, rimaniamo, rimaniate, rimangano**
   PAST DEFINITE **rimasi, rimanesti, rimase, rimanemmo, rimaneste, rimasero**
rimettere to replace, see **mettere**
rimpiangere to regret, see **piangere**
rinchiudere to enclose, see **chiudere**
rincrescere to cause regret, see **crescere**
rinvenire to find, see **venire**
riporre to put back, see **porre**
riprodurre to reproduce, see **addurre**
riscuotere to cash, see **scuotere**
risiedere to reside, see **sedere**
risolvere to resolve, see **solvere**
rispondere to answer
   PAST PARTICIPLE **risposto**
   PAST DEFINITE **risposi, rispondesti, rispose, rispondemmo, rispondeste, risposero**
ritenere to hold, see **tenere**
ritorcere to twist, see **torcere**
riuscire to succeed, see **uscire**
rivedere to revise, see **vedere**
rivolgersi to apply, see **volgere**
rodere to gnaw
   PAST PARTICIPLE **roso**
   PAST DEFINITE **rosi, rodesti, rose, rodemmo, rodeste, rosero**
rompere to break
   PAST PARTICIPLE **rotto**
   PAST DEFINITE **ruppi, rompesti, ruppe, rompemmo, rompeste, ruppero**

salire to go up
   PRESENT **salgo, sali, sale, saliamo, salite, salgono**

PRESENT SUBJUNCTIVE **salga, salga, salga, saliamo, saliate, salgano**
sapere to know
PRESENT **so, sai, sa, sappiamo, sapete, sanno**
FUTURE **saprò saprai, saprà, sapremo, saprete, sapranno**
CONDITIONAL **saprei, sapresti, saprebbe, sapremmo, sapreste, saprebbero**
PRESENT SUBJUNCTIVE **sappia, sappia, sappia, sappiamo, sappiate, sappiano**
PAST DEFINITE **seppi, sapesti, seppe, sapemmo, sapeste, seppero**
scadere to fall due, see **cadere**
scegliere to choose
PAST PARTICIPLE **scelto**
PRESENT **scelgo, scegli, sceglie, scegliamo, scegliete, scelgono**
PRESENT SUBJUNCTIVE **scelga, scelga, scelga, scegliamo, scegliate, scelgano**
scendere to go down
PAST PARTICIPLE **sceso**
PAST DEFINITE **scesi, scendesti, scese, scendemmo, scendeste, scesero**
scindere to split
PAST PARTICIPLE **scisso**
PAST DEFINITE **scissi, scindesti, scisse, scindemmo, scindeste, scissero**
sciogliere to untie
PAST PARTICIPLE **sciolto**
PRESENT **sciolgo, sciogli, sciolgie, sciogliamo, sciogliete, sciolgono**
PRESENT SUBJUNCTIVE **sciolga, sciolga, sciolga, sciogliamo, sciogliate, sciolgano**
PAST DEFINITE **sciolsi, sciogliesti, sciolse, sciogliemmo, scioglieste, sciolsero**
scommettere to bet, see **mettere**
scomparire to disappear, see **apparire**
scomporre to upset, see **porre**
sconfiggere to defeat, see **figgere**
scoprire to uncover, see **coprire**
scorgere to perceive, see **accorgersi**
scorrere to scan, see **correre**
scrivere to write
PAST PARTICIPLE **scritto**
PAST DEFINITE **scrissi, scrivesti, scrisse, scrivemmo, scriveste, scrissero**
scuotere to shake
PAST PARTICIPLE **scosso**
PAST DEFINITE **scossi, scotesti, scosse, scotemmo, scoteste, scossero**
sedere to sit
PRESENT **siedo, siedi, siede, sediamo, sedete, siedono**
PRESENT SUBJUNCTIVE **sieda, sieda, sieda, sediamo, sediate, siedano**
sedurre to seduce, see **addurre**

smettere to stop, see **mettere**
soccorrere to help, see **correre**
soddisfare to satisfy, see **fare**
soffriggere to brown, see **friggere**
soffrire to suffer, see **offrire**
soggiungere to reply, see **giungere**
solere to be used to
PAST PARTICIPLE **solito**
PRESENT **soglio, suoli, suole, sogliamo, solete, sogliono**
PRESENT SUBJUNCTIVE **soglia, soglia, soglia, sogliamo, sogliate, sogliano**
solvere to solve
PAST PARTICIPLE **solto**
sommergere to submerge, see **immergere**
sopprimere to suppress, see **comprimere**
sopraffare to overpower, see **fare**
sopraggiungere to overtake, see **giungere**
sopravvivere to survive, see **vivere**
sorgere to rise
PAST PARTICIPLE **sorto**
PAST DEFINITE **sorsi, sorgesti, sorse, sorgemmo, sorgeste, sorsero**
sorprendere to surprise, see **prendere**
sorreggere to support, see **reggere**
sorridere to smile, see **ridere**
sospendere to suspend, see **pendere**
sostenere to uphold, see **tenere**
sottomettere to subjugate, see **mettere**
sottoporre to submit, see **porre**
sottoscrivere to subscribe, see **scrivere**
sottrarre to subtract, see **trarre**
spargere to scatter
PAST PARTICIPLE **sparso**
PAST DEFINITE **sparsi, spargesti, sparse, spargemmo, spargeste, sparsero**
spegnere to extinguish
PAST PARTICIPLE **spento**
PRESENT **spengo, spegni, spegne, spegniamo, spegnete, spengono**
PRESENT SUBJUNCTIVE **spenga, spenga, spenga, spegniamo, spegniate, spengano**
PAST DEFINITE **spensi, spegnesti, spense, spegnemmo, spegneste, spensero**
spendere to spend
PAST PARTICIPLE **speso**
PAST DEFINITE **spesi, spendesti, spese, spendemmo, spendeste, spesero**
spingere to push
PAST PARTICIPLE **spinto**
PAST DEFINITE **spinsi, spingesti, spinse, spingemmo, spingeste, spinsero**
stare to be
PRESENT **sto, stai, sta, stiamo, state, stanno**
FUTURE **starò, starai, starà, staremo, starete, staranno**

Conjugation of Verbs

CONDITIONAL **starei, staresti, starebbe, staremmo, stareste, starebbero**
PRESENT SUBJUNCTIVE **stia, stia, stia, stiamo, stiate, stiano**
PAST DEFINITE **stetti, stesti, stette, stemmo, steste, stettero**
PAST SUBJUNCTIVE **stessi, stessi, stesse, stessimo, steste, stessero**
stendere to stretch, see **tendere**
storcere to twist, see **torcere**
strafare to overdo, see **fare**
stringere to squeeze
PAST PARTICIPLE **stretto**
PAST DEFINITE **strinsi, stringesti, strinse, stringemmo, stringeste, strinsero**
succedere to happen
PAST PARTICIPLE **successo**
PAST DEFINITE **successi, succedesti, successe, succedemmo, succedeste, successero**
supporre to suppose, see **porre**
svolgere to unroll, see **volgere**

tacere to keep quiet
PRESENT **taccio, taci, tace, tacciamo, tacete, tacciono**
PRESENT SUBJUNCTIVE **taccia, taccia, taccia, tacciamo, tacciate, tacciano**
PAST DEFINITE **tacqui, tacesti, tacque, tacemmo, taceste, tacquero**
tendere to tend
PAST PARTICIPLE **teso**
PAST DEFINITE **tesi, tendesti, tese, tendemmo, tendeste, tesero**
tenere to hold
PRESENT **tengo, tieni, tiene, teniamo, tenete, tengono**
FUTURE **terrò, terrai, terrà, terremo, terrete, terranno**
CONDITIONAL **terrei, terresti, terrebbe, terremmo, terreste, terrebbero**
PRESENT SUBJUNCTIVE **tenga, tenga, tenga, teniamo, teniate, tengano**
PAST DEFINITE **tenni, tenesti, tenne, tenemmo, teneste, tennero**
tergere to wipe
PAST PARTICIPLE **terso**
PAST DEFINITE **tersi, tergesti, terse, tergemmo, tergeste, tersero**
tingere to dye
PAST PARTICIPLE **tinto**
PAST DEFINITE **tinsi, tingesti, tinse, tingemmo, tingeste, tinsero**
togliere to take away

PAST PARTICIPLE **tolto**
PRESENT **tolgo, togli, toglie, togliamo, togliete, tolgono**
PRESENT SUBJUNCTIVE **tolga, tolga, tolga, togliamo, togliate, tolgano**
PAST DEFINITE **tolsi, togliesti, tolse, togliemmo, toglieste, tolsero**
torcere to twist
PAST PARTICIPLE **torto**
PAST DEFINITE **torsi, torcesti, torse, torcemmo, torceste, torsero**
tradurre to translate, see **addurre**
transigere to compromise, see **esigere**
trarre to take in
PRESENT PARTICIPLE **traendo**
PAST PARTICIPLE **tratto**
PRESENT **traggo, trai, trae, traiamo, traete, traggono**
FUTURE **trarrò, trarrai, trarrà, trarremo, trarrete, trarranno**
CONDITIONAL **trarrei, trarresti, trarrebbe, trarremmo, trarreste, trarrebbero**
PRESENT SUBJUNCTIVE **tragga, tragga, tragga, traiamo, traiate, traggano**
IMPERFECT **traevo, traevi, traeva, traevamo, traevate, traevano**
PAST DEFINITE **trassi, traesti, trasse, traemmo, traeste, trassero**
PAST SUBJUNCTIVE **traessi, traessi, traesse, traessimo, traeste, traessero**
trascendere to transcend, see **scendere**
trascorrere to elapse, see **correre**
trasmettere to transmit, see **mettere**
trattenere to withhold, see **tenere**
travolgere to overcome, see **volgere**

uccidere to kill
PAST PARTICIPLE **ucciso**
PAST DEFINITE **uccisi, uccidesti, uccise, uccidemmo, uccideste, uccisero**
udire to hear
PRESENT **odo, odi, ode, udiamo, udite, odono**
PRESENT SUBJUNCTIVE **oda, oda, oda, udiamo, udiate, odano**
ungere to grease
PAST PARTICIPLE **unto**
PAST DEFINITE **unsi, ungesti, unse, ungemmo, ungeste, unsero**
uscire to exit
PRESENT **esco, esci, esce, usciamo, uscite, escono**
PRESENT SUBJUNCTIVE **esca, esca, esca, usciamo, usciate, escano**

valere to be worth
PAST PARTICIPLE **valso**
PRESENT **valgo, vali, vale, valiamo, valete, valgono**
FUTURE **varrò, varrai, varrà, varremo, varrete, varranno**
CONDITIONAL **varrei, varresti, varrebbe, varremmo, varreste, varrebbero**
PRESENT SUBJUNCTIVE **valga, valga, valga, valiamo, valiate, valgano**
PAST DEFINITE **valsi, valesti, valse, valemmo, valeste, valsero**

vedere to see
PAST PARTICIPLE **visto**
FUTURE **vedrò, vedrai, vedrà, vedremo, vedrete, vedranno**
CONDITIONAL **vedrei, vedresti, vedrebbe, vedremmo, vedreste, vedrebbero**
PAST DEFINITE **vidi, vedesti, vide, vedemmo, vedeste, videro**

venire to come
PRESENT PARTICIPLE **venuto**
PRESENT **vengo, vieni, viene, veniamo, venite, vengono**
FUTURE **verrò, verrai, verrà, verremo, verrete, verranno**
CONDITIONAL **verrei, verresti, verrebbe, verremmo, verreste, verrebbero**
PRESENT SUBJUNCTIVE **venga, venga, venga, veniamo, veniate, vengano**

PAST DEFINITE **venni, venisti, venne, venimmo, veniste, vennero**

vincere to win
PAST PARTICIPLE **vinto**
PAST DEFINITE **vinsi, vincesti, vinse, vincemmo, vinceste, vinsero**

vivere to live
PAST PARTICIPLE **vissuto**
FUTURE **vivrò, vivrai, vivrà, vivremo, vivrete, vivranno**
CONDITIONAL **vivrei, vivresti, vivrebbe, vivremmo, vivreste, vivrebbero**
PAST DEFINITE **vissi, vivesti, visse, vivemmo, viveste, vissero**

volere to want
PRESENT **voglio, vuoi, vuole, vogliamo, volete, vogliono**
FUTURE **vorrò, vorrai, vorrà, vorremo, vorrete, vorranno**
CONDITIONAL **vorrei, vorresti, vorrebbe, vorremmo, vorreste, vorrebbero**
PRESENT SUBJUNCTIVE **voglia, voglia, voglia, vogliamo, vogliate, vogliano**
PAST DEFINITE **volli, volesti, volle, volemmo, voleste, vollero**

volgere to turn
PAST PARTICIPLE **volto**
PAST DEFINITE **volsi, volgesti, volse, volgemmo, volgeste, volsero**

ABBREVIATIONS

a	adjective	*interj*	interjection
adv	adverb	*lit*	literature
aesp	aerospace	*m*	masculine
agr	agriculture	*math*	mathematics
anat	anatomy	*mech*	mechanics
arch	architecture	*med*	medicine
art	article	*mil*	military
ast	astronomy	*min*	mineralogy
auto	automobile	*mus*	music
avi	aviation	*n*	noun
biol	biology	*naut*	nautical
bot	botany	*phot*	photography
chem	chemistry	*phys*	physics
coll	colloquial	*pl*	plural
com	commerce	*pol*	politics
comp	compound	*prep*	preposition
conj	conjunction	*print*	printing
dent	dentistry	*pron*	pronoun
eccl	ecclesiastic	*rad*	radio
elec	electricity	*rail*	railway
f	feminine	*sl*	slang
fam	familiar	*theat*	theatre
fig	figuratively	*TV*	television
for	formal	*vi*	verb intransitive
		vr	verb reflexive
geog	geography	*vt*	verb transitive
geol	geology	*vt&i*	verb transitive and intransitive
gram	grammar	*zool*	zoology

* An asterisk following an Italian entry indicates that it is one of the irregular verbs for which conjugation is supplied in the grammar section, pages 27 to 37.

Italian-English

A

a (â) *prep* to, at, in, until
abate (â·bâ′tā) *m* abbot
abbacchiamento (âb·bâk·kyâ·mān′tō) *m* dejection, depression
abbacchiare (âb·bâk·kyâ′rā) *vt* to deject, depress
abbacchiarsi (âb·bâk·kyâr′sē) *vr* to lose one's courage; to become dejected
abbacchiato (âb·bâk·kyâ′tō) *a* dejected, dispirited, depressed
abbacchio (âb·bâk′kyō) *m* lamb
abbacinamento (âb·bâ·chē·nâ·mān′tō) *m* dazzling; bewilderment
abbacinare (âb·bâ·chē·nâ′rā) *vt* to dazzle, blind
abbaco (âb′bâ·kō) *m* abacus
abbadessa (âb·bâ·dās′sâ) *f* abbess
abbadia (âb·bâ·dē′â) *f* abbey
abbagliamento (âb·bâ·lyâ·mān′tō) *m* mistake, confusion
abbagliante (âb·bâ·lyân′tā) *a* dazzling; — *m* (*auto*) high-beam headlight
abbagliare (âb·bâ·lyâ′rā) *vt* to dazzle; to confuse, bewilder
abbaglio (âb·bâ′lyō) *m* dazzling, bewilderment; mistake
abbaiamento (âb·bâ·yâ·mān′tō) *m* barking
abbaiare (âb·bâ·yâ′rā) *vi* to bark
abbaiatore (âb·bâ·yâ·tō′rā) *m* muckraker
abbaino (âb·bâ·ē′nō) *m* dormer; attic window
abbandonamento (âb·bân·dō·nâ·mān′tō) *m* abandonment; surrender
abbandonare (âb·bân·dō·nâ′rā) *vt* to

abandon; to fail
abbandonarsi (âb·bân·dō·nâr′sē) *vr* to indulge oneself; to lose one's spirits
abbandonatamente (âb·bân·dō·nâ·tâ·mān′tā) *adv* carelessly; passionately
abbandonato (âb·bân·dō·nâ′tō) *a* abandoned, deserted
abbandono (âb·bân·dō′nō) *m* abandonment; recklessness
abbarbagliamento (âb·bâr·bâ·lyâ·mān′tō) *m* dazzling; dizziness
abbarbagliare (âb·bâr·bâ·lyâ′rā) *vt* to dazzle; to deceive, bewilder
abbarbicare (âb·bâr·bē·kâ′rā) *vi* to take root; to become established
abbarbicato (âb·bâr·bē·kâ′tō) *a* rooted; settled
abbarcare (âb·bâr·kâ′rā) *vt* to heap, pile up
abbassamento (âb·bâs·sâ·mān′tō) *m* abatement; reduction
abbassare (âb·bâs·sâ′rā) *vt* to lower; to cut off, reduce
abbassarsi (âb·bâs·sâr′sē) *vr* to stoop, bow down; to humble oneself; to debase oneself
abbasso (âb·bâs′sō) *adv* down; low; —! *interj* down with!
abbastanza (âb·bâ·stân′tsâ) *adv* enough; quite
abbattere (âb·bât′tā·rā) *vt* to knock down; to shoot down; to fell; to deject
abbattersi (âb·bât′tār·sē) *vr* to be dejected; to lose one's spirits; to be demolished
abbattimento (âb·bât·tē·mān′tō) *m* dem-

---

k kid, **l** let, **m** met, **n** not, **p** pat, **r** very, **s** sat, **sh** shop, **t** tell, **v** vat, **w** we, **y** yes, **z** zero

olition; cutting down; dejection

abbattuto (âb·bât·tū′tō) *a* demolished; dejected

abbazia (âb·bâ·tsē′â) *f* abbey

abbecedario (âb·bā·chā·dâ′ryō) *m* primer, first reader

abbellimento (âb·bāl·lē·mān′tō) *m* embellishment, beautifying

abbellire (âb·bāl·lē′rā) *vt* to embellish, beautify

abbeverare (âb·bā·vā·râ′rā) *vt* to water (*livestock*)

abbigliamento (âb·bē·lyâ·mān′tō) *m* wearing apparel; **industria dell'—** clothing industry

abbigliare (âb·bē·lyâ′rā) *vt* to dress; to adorn; to clothe

abbigliarsi (âb·bē·lyâr′sē) *vr* to get dressed; to attire oneself

abbinare (âb·bē·nâ′rā) *vt* to couple, join

abbindolare (âb·bēn·dō·lâ′rā) *vt* to cheat, deceive, defraud

abboccamento (âb·bōk·kâ·mān′tō) *m* interview

abboccare (âb·bōk·kâ′rā) *vt* to bite (*fish*); **— all'amo** to take the bait

abboccarsi (âb·bōk·kâr′sē) *vr* to confer with; to converse in private

abboccato (âb·bōk·kâ′tō) *a* sweetish; palatable

abbonamento (âb·bō·nâ·mān′tō) *m* subscription

abbonare (âb·bō·nâ′rā) *vt* to give a discount to

abbonarsi (âb·bō·nâr′sē) *vr* to subscribe; to take a subscription

abbondanza (âb·bōn·dân′tsâ) *f* abundance, wealth

abbondare (âb·bōn·dâ′rā) *vi* to abound; to teem

abbondevole (âb·bōn·de′vō·lā) *a* abundant, plentiful

abbondevolezza (âb·bōn·dā·vō·lā′tsâ) *f* abundance, plenty

abbondevolmente (âb·bōn·dā·vōl·mān′tā) *adv* abundantly; in large numbers

abbottonare (âb·bōt·tō·nâ′rā) *vt* to button

abbottonato (âb·bōt·tō·nâ′tō) *a* buttoned

abbozzare (âb·bō·tsâ′rā) *vt* to delineate; to sketch; to outline, rough in

abbracciare (âb·brâ·châ′rā) *vt* to hug, embrace

abbraccio (âb·brâ′chō) *m* embrace, hug

abbreviare (âb·brā·vyâ′rā) *vt* to abbreviate; to curtail

abbreviatura (âb·brā·vyâ·tū′râ) *f* abbreviation, shortening

abbronzare (âb·brōn·dzâ′rā) *vt* to bronze; to tan

abbronzato (âb·brōn·dzâ′tō) *a* suntanned

abbronzatura (âb·brōn·dzâ·tū′râ) *f* sunburn; bronzing; tanning

abbrunare (âb·brū·nâ′rā), **abbrunire** (âb·brū·nē′rā) *vt* to brown; to tan

abbrunarsi (âb·brū·nâr′sē), **abbrunirsi** (âb·brū·nēr′sē) *vr* to become sunburned; to wear mourning

abbrunato (âb·brū·nâ′tō), **abbrunito** (âb·brū·nē′tō) *a* browned; dark; tanned

abbrustolire (âb·brū·stō·lē′rā) *vt* to roast; to broil; to toast

abbrutimento (âb·brū·tē·mān′tō) *m* brutishness

abbrutire (âb·brū·tē′rā) *vt* to brutalize

abbrutirsi (âb·brū·tēr′sē) *vr* to become brutal

abbrutito (âb·brū·tē′tō) *a* brutalized.

abbuono (âb·bwō′nō) *m* allowance

abdicare (âb·dē·kâ′rā) *vi* to abdicate

abdicato (âb·dē·kâ′tō) *a* abdicated

abdicazione (âb·dē·kâ·tsyō′nā) *f* abdication

aberrazione (â·bār·râ·tsyō′nā) *f* aberration

abete (â·bā′tā) *m* fir tree

abietto (âb·byāt′tō) *a* despicable, low, mean

abigeato (â·bē·jā·â′tō) *m* rustling, cattle theft

abile (â′bē·lā) *a* able, skillful

abilità (â·bē·lē·tâ′) *f* ability, aptitude

abilitazione (â·bē·lē·tâ·tsyō′nā) *f* certificate of competence

abilmente (â·bēl·mān′tā) *adv* ably

abisso (â·bēs′sō) *m* abyss, chasm

abitabile (â·bē·tâ′bē·lā) *a* habitable

abitacolo (â·bē·tâ′kō·lō) *m* (*avi*) cockpit

abitante (â·bē·tân′tā) *m* inhabitant

abitare (â·bē·tâ′rā) *vt&i* to live in, inhabit

abitazione (â·bē·tâ·tsyō′nā) *f* residence, home

abito (â′bē·tō) *m* suit (*clothing*)

abituale (â·bē·twâ′lā) *a* habitual, accustomed

abitualmente (â·bē·twâl·mān′tā) *adv* usually, customarily

abituare (â·bē·twâ′ra) *vt* to accustom

abituarsi (â·bē·twâr′sē) *vr* to accustom oneself; to grow used to

abituato (â·bē·twâ′tō) *a* used to, in the habit of

abitudine (â·bē·tū′dē·nā) *f* custom; usage

abluzione (â·blū·tsyō′nā) *f* ablution

â ârm, ā bāby, e bet, ē bē, ō gō, ô gône, ū blūe, b bad, ch child, d dad, f fat, g gay, j jet

abolire (â·bō·lē′rā) *vt* to abolish; to do away with

abolizione (ā·bō·lē·tsyō′nā) *f* abolition

abominabile (â·bō·mē·nâ′bē·lā) *a* abominable, loathsome

abominare (â·bō·mē·nâ′rā) *vt* to abominate, loathe

abominazione (â·bō·mē·nâ·tsyō′nā) *f* abomination

abominevole (â·bō·mē·ne′vō·lā) *a* abominable

aborrire (â·bōr·rē′rā) *vt* to abhor; to detest

abortire (â·bōr·tē′rā) *vi* to miscarry; to come to nothing, fall short

aborto (â·bōr′tō) *m* miscarriage; abortion; falling short

abrasione (â·brâ·zyō′nā) *f* abrasion

abrogare (â·brō·gâ′rā) *vt* to abrogate

abside (âb′zē·dā) *f* apse

abusare (â·bū·zâ′rā) *vi* to take advantage of; to abuse; to impose on

abusato (â·bū·zâ′tō) *a* abused; misused

abusivamente (â·bū·zē·vâ·mān′tā) *adv* unjustly

abusivo (â·bū·zē′vō) *a* abusive; unjust

abuso (â·bū′zō) *m* abuse; imposition

accademia (âk·kâ·de′myâ) *f* academy

accademico (âk·kâ·de′mē·kō) *a* academic; scholastic

accademista (âk·kâ·dā·mē′stâ) *m&f* academy member

accadere * (âk·kâ·dā′rā) *vi* to happen

accalappiare (âk·kâ·lâp·pyâ′rā) *vt* to inveigle, entrap; to hoodwink

accalappiacani (âk·kâ·lâp·pyâ·kâ′nē) *m* dogcatcher

accalorarsi (âk·kâ·lō·râr′sē) *vr* to become excited; to be aroused

accampamento (âk·kâm·pâ·mān′tō) *m* encampment, camp

accampare (âk·kâm·pâ′rā) *vi* to encamp; to state, contend

accanire (âk·kâ·nē′rā) *vt* to irritate; to vex

accanirsi (âk·kâ·nēr′sē) *vr* to be persistent

accanito (âk·kâ·nē′to) *a* furious; obstinate

accanto (âk·kân′tō) *adv&prep* near, by, beside

accapparrare (âk·kâp·pâr·râ′rā) *vt (com)* to corner; to hoard

accappatoio (âk·kâp·pâ·tô′yō) *m* bathrobe

accapigliarsi (âk·kâ·pē·lyâr′sē) *vr* to come to blows; to scuffle, grapple

accapponare (âk·kâp·pō·nâ′rā) *vt* to castrate; **— la pelle** *(fig)* to cause goose pimples

accarezzare (âk·kâ·râ·tsâ′rā) *vt* to caress, pet

accasciamento (âk·kâ·shâ·mān′tō) *m* depression; fatigue

accasciare (âk·kâ·shâ′rā) *vt* to depress

accasciarsi (âk·kâ·shâr′sē) *vr* to become depressed

accattone (âk·kât·tō′nā) *m* mendicant, beggar

accecare (â·chā·kâ′rā) *vt* to blind; to bewilder

accedere (â·che′dā·rā) *vi* to approach; to consent to, accept

accelerare (â·chā·lā·râ′rā) *vt* to speed up, accelerate

accelerato (â·chā·lā·râ′tō) *a* accelerated; **— m** local train; **—re** (â·chā·lā·râ·tō′rā) *m (auto)* accelerator pedal

accelerazione (â·chā·lā·râ·tsyō′nā) *f* acceleration; *(auto)* pickup

accendere * (â·chen′dā·rā) *vt* to light; to illuminate; to motivate, stir

accendersi * (â·chen′dār·sē) *vr* to catch fire; to burn

accendisigari (â·chân·dē·sē′gâ·rē) *m* cigarette lighter

accennare (â·chân·nâ′rā) *vt&i* to hint; to point out; to treat, deal with

accensione (â·chân·syō′nā) *f (auto)* ignition

accento (â·chân′tō) *m* accent

accerchiare (â·châr·kyâ′rā) *vt* to surround; to ring

accertare (â·châr·tâ′rā) *vt* to make sure of; to verify

acceso (â·châ′zō) *a* lighted, lit, on

accessibile (â·châs·sē′bē·lā) *a* approachable

accesso (â·châs′sō) *m* access; spasm, fit

accessorio (â·châs·sô′ryō) *a* accessory; **— m** fixture; equipment

accetta (â·chāt′tâ) *f* hatchet

accettabile (â·chât·tâ′bē·lā) *a* acceptable, agreeable

accettare (â·chât·tâ′rā) *vt* to accept

accettazione (â·chât·tâ·tsyō′nā) *f* acceptance, agreement

accettevole (â·chât·te′vō·lā) *a* pleasant; acceptable

accettevolmente (â·chât·tā·vōl·mān′tā) *adv* acceptably

accezione (â·châ·tsyō′nā) *f* accepted meaning of a word; accepted expression

acchiappare (âk·kyâp·pâ′rā) *vt* to catch; to snare

acchito (âk·kē′tō) *m* lead, leading off

acciacchi (â·châk′kē) *mpl* infirmities;

---

k kid, **l** let, **m** met, **n** not, **p** pat, **r** very, **s** sat, **sh** shop, **t** tell, **v** vat, **w** we, **y** yes, **z** zero

weaknesses
acciaio (â·châ′yō) *m* steel
accidentale (â·chē·dän·tâ′lā) *a* accidental; casual, happenstance
accidentalmente (â·chē·dän·tâl·mān′tā) *adv* accidentally
accidentato (â·chē·dän·tâ′tō) *a* uneven
accidente (â·chē·dän′tā) *m* apoplectic stroke; accident
accidia (â·chē′dyâ) *f* indolence; laziness
accigliarsi (â·chē·lyâr′sē) *vr* to knit one's brows; to scowl
accigliato (â·chē·lyâ′tō) *a* frowning; unhappy
accingersi (â·chēn′jär·sē) *vr* to get ready
accinto (â·chēn′tō) *a* ready, prepared
acciottolato (â·chôt·tō·lâ′tō) *m* cobblestone pavement
acciuffare (â·chūf·fâ′rā) *vt* to catch; to grasp, grab
acciuga (ā·chū′gâ) *f* anchovy
acclamare (âk·klâ·mâ′rā) *vt* to acclaim
acclamazione (âk·klâ·mâ·tsyō′nā) *f* acclamation
acclimatazione (âk·klē·mâ·tâ·tsyō′nā) *f* acclimatation
acclimatarsi (âk·klē·mâ·târ′sē) *vr* to grow acclimated; to get used to
accludere * (âk·klū′dā·rā) *vt* to enclose, attach
accluso (âk·klū′zō) *a* enclosed, attached
accogliere * (âk·kó′lyā·rā) *vt* to welcome; to receive
accoglienza (âk·kō·lyän′tsâ) *f* welcome; reception
accoglimento (âk·kō·lyē·mān′tō) *m* reception; assemblage
accollare (âk·kōl·lâ′rā) *vt* to shoulder; to join
accollarsi (âk·kōl·lâr′sē) *vr* to take charge of; to assume
accollato (âk·kōl·lâ′tō) *a* high-necked
accoltellare (âk·kōl·tāl·lâ′rā) *vt* to stab with a knife
accomandare (âk·kō·mân·dâ′rā) *vt* to give into custody; to commend, hand over
accomandatario (âk·kō·mân·dâ·tâ′ryō) *m (com)* general partner
accomandita (âk·kō·mân·dē′tâ) *f* limited partnership
accomiatarsi (âk·kō·myâ·târ′sē) *vr* to take one's leave; to say good-bye; to part
accomodamento (âk·kō·mō·dâ·mān′tō) *m* adjustment, settlement; repair
accomodare (âk·kō·mō·dâ′rā) *vt* to adjust; to repair

accomodarsi (âk·kō·mō·dâr′sē) *vr* to sit down, be seated
accomodato (âk·kō·mō·dâ′tō) *a* adjusted; repaired
accomodatura (âk·kō·mō·dâ·tū′râ) *f* adjusting; fixing, repairing
accompagnare (âk·kōm·pâ·nyâ′rā) *vt* to accompany, go with
accompagnatore (âk·kōm·pâ·nyâ·tō·rā) *m* escort; *(mus)* accompanist
acconciare (âk·kōn·châ′rā) *vt* to ready; to adapt
acconciatura (âk·kōn·châ·tū′râ) *f* hairdo
acconsentimento (âk·kōn·sän·tē·mān′tō) *m* consent, agreement
acconsentire (âk·kōn·sän·tē′rā) *vi* to consent, agree
accontentare (âk·kōn·tän·tâ′rā) *vt* to please; to make happy
aconto (âk·kōn′tō) *m (com)* account; deposit
accoppare (âk·kōp·pâ′rā) *vt* to kill; to beat to death
accoppiamento (âk·kōp·pyâ·mān′tō) *m* coupling
accoppiare (âk·kōp·pyâ′rā) *vt* to match; to unite
accorciare (âk·kōr·châ′rā) *vt* to make shorter, abbreviate
accordare (âk·kōr·dâ′rā) *vt* to grant; *(mus)* to tune; to permit
accordo (âk·kōr′dō) *m* agreement, consensus; d′—! agreed!
accorgersi * (âk·kôr′jär·sē) *vr* to notice, observe
accorgimento (âk·kōr·jē·mān′tō) *m* shrewdness; circumspection; prudence
accorrere * (âk·kôr′rā·rā) *vi* to run; to rush up
accortamente (âk·kōr·tâ·mān′tā) *adv* shrewdly, cunningly
accorto (âk·kōr′tō) *a* shrewd, circumspect
accostamento (âk·kōs·tâ·mān′tō) *m* approach, access
accostare (âk·kō·stâ′rā) *vt* to approach, draw near
accreditare (âk·krā·dē·tâ′rā) *vt (com)* to extend credit to, credit
accreditarsi (âk·krā·dē·târ′sē) *vr* to gain esteem, be credited
accreditato (âk·krā·dē·tâ′tō) *a* accredited; authorized; estimable, worthy
accrescere * (âk·krē′shā·rā) *vt* to increase
accudire (âk·kū·dē′rā) *vi* to care for
accumulare (âk·kū·mū·lâ′rā) *vt* to accumulate
accumulatore (âk·kū·mū·lâ·tō′rā) *m (elec)* battery

â ârm, ā bāby, e bet, ē bē, ō gō, ô gône, ū blūe, b bad, ch child, d dad, f fat, g gay, j jet

accumulazione (âk·kū·mū·lâ·tsyō′nä) *f* accumulation

accuratamente (âk·kū·râ·tâ·män′tä) *adv* accurately, exactly

accurato (âk·kū·râ′tō) *a* accurate, precise

accuratezza (âk·kū·râ·tä′tsä) *f* accuracy

accusa (âk·kū′zä) *f* accusation; **atto d'**— indictment; **capo d'**— count of an indictment **–re** (âk·kū·zâ′rä) *vt* to accuse, indict; **–to** (âk·kū·zâ′tō) *a* accused; **–to** *m* defendant

acerbo (â·chär′bō) *a* not ripe; sour

acerrimo (â·cher′rē·mō) *a* very fierce

acetico (â·che′tē·kō) *a* acetic

aceto (â·chä′tō) *m* vinegar; **–liera** (â·chä·tō·lyä′râ) *f* set of cruets for oil and vinegar

acidità (â·chē·dē·tâ′) *f* acidity

acido (â′chē·dō) *a&m* acid

acino (â′chē·nō) *m* grape; grapeseed

acqua (âk′kwâ) *f* water; **— ossigenata** hydrogen peroxide; **— potabile** drinking water; **— di Colonia** cologne, toilet water; **–forte** (âk·kwâ·fōr′tä) *f* etching; **–io** (âk·kwâ′yō) *m* sink; **–plano** (âk·kwâ·plâ′nō) *m* aquaplane; **–rio** (âk·kwâ′ryō) *m* aquarium; **–vite** (âk·kwâ·vē′tä) *f* brandy; **–zzone** (âk·kwâ·tsō′nä) *m* shower of rain

acquattarsi (âk·kwât·târ′sē) *vr* to crouch; to hide

acquerello (âk·kwä·räl′lō) *m* water color

acquirente (âk·kwē·rän′tä) *m&f* purchaser, customer

acquisire (âk·kwē·zē′rä) *vt* to acquire

acquistare (âk·kwē·stâ′rä) *vt* to buy

acquitrino (âk·kwē·trē′nō) *m* swamp, marsh

acre (â′krä) *a* acrid, sharp

acrobata (â·krô′bâ·tâ) *m&f* acrobat

acromatico (â·krō·mâ′tē·kō) *a* achromatic

acuire (â·kwē′rä) *vt* to whet, sharpen

aculeo (â·kū′lä·o) *m* sting; goad, spur; stimulus

acume (â·kū′mä) *m* sharpness, insight; subtlety

acustica (â·kū′stē·kâ) *f* acoustics

acutezza (â·kū·tä′tsâ) *f* acuteness

acuto (â·kū′tō) *a* sharp

adagiare (â·dâ·jâ′rä) *vt* to lay; to put

adagio (â·dâ′jō) *adv* slowly; easily

adattabile (â·dât·tâ′bē·lä) *a* applicable

adattabilità (â·dât·tâ·bē·lē·tâ′) *f* suitability, aptitude

adattamento (â·dât·tâ·män′tō) *m* adaptation; adjustment

adattare (â·dât·tâ′rä) *vt* to adapt

adatto (â·dât′tō) *a* fitting, suitable, fit

addebitare (âd·dä·bē·tâ′rä) *vt* to debit

addebito (âd·de′bē·tō) *m* debit

addentare (âd·dän·tâ′rä) *vt* to bite

addestrare (âd·dä·strâ′rä) *vt* to drill; to instruct; to prepare

addetto (âd·dä′tō) *m* attendant; — **d'ambasciata** attaché

addio (âd·dē′ō) *interj&m* good-bye

addirittura (âd·dē·rēt·tū′râ) *adv* absolutely, altogether

additamento (âd·dē·tâ·män′tō) *m* indication, designation

additare (âd·dē·tâ′rä) *vt* to indicate, show

addizionale (âd·dē·tsyō·nâ′lä) *a* additional

addizionare (âd·dē·tsyō·nâ′rä) *vt* to add

addizionatrice (âd·dē·tsyō·nâ·trē′chä) *f* adding machine

addizione (âd·dē·tsyō′nä) *f (math)* addition

addolcimento (âd·dōl·chē·män′tō) *m* softening; mitigation

addolcire (âd·dōl·chē′rä) *vt* to sweeten; to soften

addolcitore (âd·dōl·chē·tō′rä) *m* softener; sweetener; water softener

addolorare (âd·dō·lō·râ′rä) *vt* to afflict, grieve; to sadden

addolorarsi (âd·dō·lō·râr′sē) *vr* to grieve; to be saddened

addolorato (âd·dō·lō·râ′tō) *a* saddened

addome (âd·dō′mä) *m* abdomen, belly

addormentare (âd·dōr·män·tâ′rä) *vt* to put to sleep

addormentarsi (âd·dōr·män·târ′sē) *vr* to fall asleep

addosso (âd·dōs′sō) *prep&adv* on; on one's back

addurre * (âd·dūr′rä) *vt* to adduce

adeguatamente (â·dä·gwâ·tâ·män′tä) *adv* equally; adequately

adeguato (â·dä·gwâ′tō) *a* adequate

adempiere * (â·dem′pyä·rä) *vt* to accomplish; to perform

adempimento (â·däm·pē·män′tō) *m* execution, accomplishment; performance

aderente (â·dä·rän′tä) *m* follower; — *a* tight-fitting

aderire (â·dä·rē′rä) *vi* to join; to consent; to adhere

adesione (â·dä·zyō′nä) *f* adherence

adesivo (â·dä·zē′vō) *a* adhesive

adesso (â·däs′sō) *adv* now, at the present time

adiacente (â·dyâ·chän′tä) *a* adjacent, contiguous

---

adiacenza (â·dyâ·chän'tsâ) *f* contiguity

adipe (â'dē·pā) *m* grease, fat

adiposo (â·dē·pō'zō) *a* adipose, fatty

adirare (â·dē·râ'rä) *vt* to anger

adirarsi (â·dē·râr'sē) *vr* to get angry

adirato (â·dē·râ'tō) *a* angry

adocchiare (â·dōk·kyâ'rä) *vt* to behold; to eye, ogle

adocchiato (â·dōk·kyâ'tō) *a* beheld; eyed

adolescente (â·dō·lä·shän'tä) *mf&a* adolescent; — *m&f* teenager

adolescenza (â·dō·lä·shän'tsâ) *f* adolescence

adombramento (â·dōm·brâ·män'tō) *m* offense; shade; resentment

adombrare (â·dōm·brâ'rä) *vt* to shade

adombrarsi (â·dōm·brâr'sē) *vr* to get hurt; to become suspicious

adoperabile (â·dō·pä·râ'bē·lä) *a* employable; usable

adoperare (â·dō·pä·râ'rä) *vt* to use

adorabile (â·dō·râ'bē·lä) *a* adorable

adorare (â·dō·râ'rä) *vt* to adore, worship

adoratore (â·dō·râ·tō'rä) *m* adorer, worshiper

adornare (â·dōr·nâ'rä) *vt* to adorn

adorno (â·dōr'nō) *a* adorned; — *m* ornament

adottare (â·dōt·tâ'rä) *vt* to adopt; to make use of

adottato (â·dōt·tâ'tō) *a* adopted; used

adottivo (â·dōt·tē'vō) *a* adoptive; adopted

adozione (â·dō·tsyō'nä) *f* adoption

adulare (â·dū·lâ'rä) *vt* to flatter

adulatore (â·dū·lâ·tō'rä) *m* flatterer

adulazione (â·dū·lâ·tsyō'nä) *f* flattery

adulterare (â·dūl·tä·râ'rä) *vt* to adulterate; to represent falsely

adulterio (â·dūl·te'ryō) *m* adultery

adultero (â·dūl'tä·rō) *m* adulterer; — *a* adulterous

adulto (â·dūl'tō) *a&m* adult

adunare (â·dū·nâ'rä) *vt* to convene, gather

adunata (â·dū·nâ'tâ) *f* rally, meeting, gathering

aereo (â·e'rä·ō) *a* air; — *m* airplane; **in** — by plane

aerodinamico (â·ä·rō·dē·nâ'mē·kō) *a* streamlined

aerodromo (â·ä·rô'drō·mō) *m* airport

aerofaro (â·ä·rō·fâ'rō) *m* aerial beacon

aerogramma (â·ä·rō·grâm'mâ) *m* air letter

aerolito (â·ä·rô'·lē·tō) *m* (*ast*) aerolite

aerometro (â·ä·rô'mä·trō) *m* aerometer

aeronauta (â·ä·rō·nâ'ū·tâ) *m&f* aeronaut, airman

aeronautica (â·ä·rō·nâ'ū·tē·kâ) *f* aero-

nautics; — **militare** air force

aeroplano (â·ä·rō·plâ'nō) *m* airplane

aeroporto (â·ä·rō·pōr'tō) *m* airport

aerosilurante (â·ä·rō·sē·lū·rân'tä) *m* torpedo plane

aerospazio (â·ä·rō·spâ'tsyō) *m* aerospace

aerostatica (â·ä·rō·stâ'tē·kâ) *f* aerostatics

aerostazione (â·ä·rō·stâ·tsyō'nä) *f* air terminal

aerostiere (â·ä·rō·styä'rä) *m* balloonist

aerotermo (â·ä·rō·tär'mō) *m* unit heater

aerotrasportato (â·ä·rō·trâ·spōr·tâ'tō) *a* transported by airplane, airborne

afa (â'fâ) *f* closeness, sultry weather

afelio (â·fe'lyō) *m* (*ast*) aphelion

affabile (âf·fâ'bē·lä) *a* affable, civil, pleasant

affabilità (âf·fâ·bē·lē·tâ') *f* affability, pleasantness

affabilmente (âf·fâ·bēl·män'tä) *adv* affably, pleasantly

affaccendato (âf·fâ·chän·dâ'tō) *a* busy, occupied

affacciarsi (âf·fâ·châr'sē) *vr* to show oneself, appear; to lean out

affamare (âf·fâ·mâ'rä) *vt* to famish

affamato (âf·fâ·mâ'tō) *a* starved, famished

affannare (âf·fân·nâ'rä) *vt* to bother, worry

affannarsi (âf·fân·nâr'sē) *vr* to bustle, be anxious; to go to a lot of trouble

affannato (âf·fân·nâ'tō) *a* anxious, upset

affanno (âf·fân'nō) *m* affliction; trouble

affannosamente (âf·fân·nō·zâ·män'tä) *adv* asthmatically; anxiously

affare (âf·fâ'rä) *m* affair; business; transaction

affarista (âf·fâ·rē'stâ) *m* (*com*) speculator; go-getter

affascinante (âf·fâ·shē·nân'tä) *a* fascinating, charming

affaticare (âf·fâ·tē·kâ'rä) *vt* to fatigue

affatto (âf·fât'tō) *adv* completely; **non** — not at all

affermare (âf·fär·mâ'rä) *vt* to affirm; to certify

affermarsi (âf·fär·mâr'sē) *vr* to succeed; to make a good showing

afferrare (âf·fär·râ'rä) *vt* to grab; to conceive of, comprehend

affettare (âf·fät·tâ'rä) *vt* to slice; to affect, make a show of

affettato (âf·fät·tâ'tō) *a* sliced; affected

affetto (âf·fät'tō) *m* affection

affettivo (âf·fät·tē'vō) *a* emotional

affettuoso (âf·fät·twō'zō) *a* affectionate

affettuosamente (âf·fät·twō·zâ·män'tä)

â ârm, ā bāby, e bet, ē bē, ō gō, ô gône, ū blūe, b bad, ch child, d dad, f fat, g gay, j jet

adv affectionately

affettuosità (âf·fāt·twō·zē·tâ') *f* fondness

affezionare (âf·fā·tsyō·nâ'rā) *vt* to make fond; to endear oneself to

affezionarsi (âf·fā·tsyō·nâr'sē) *vr* to grow fond of, become attached to

affezionato (âf·fā·tsyō·nâ'tō) *a* fond; affectionate; attached

affidare (âf·fē·dâ'rā) *vt* to commit, trust; to give to one's keeping

affidarsi (âr·fē·dâr'sē) *vr* to have confidence; to depend on

affilare (âf·fē·lâ'rā) *vt* to sharpen

affinchè (âf·fēn·kâ') *conj* so that; in order that; in order to

affine (âj·fē'nā) *a* related

affinità (âf·fē·nē·tâ') *f* affinity

affissione (âf·fēs·syō'nā) *f* posting; **proibita l'**— post no bills

affisso (âf·fēs'sō) *m* poster; **vietati gli affissi** post no bills

affittare (âf·fēt·tâ'rā) *vt* to rent

affitto (âf·fēt'tō) *m* rent

affliggere * âf·flēj'jā·rā) *vt* to afflict; to upset, bother

afflitto (âf·flēt'tō) *a* afflicted; sad

afflizione (âf·flē·tsyō'nā) *f* affliction; grief

affogare (âf·fō·gâ'rā) *vt&i* to drown; to overwhelm

affogato (âf·fō·gâ'tō) *a* drowned; (*egg*) poached

affondamento (âf·fōn·dâ·mān'tō) *m* sinking; submerging

affondare (âf·fōn·dâ'rā) *vt* to sink

affrancatura (âf·frân·kâ·tū'râ) *f* postage

affresco (âf·frā'skō) *m* fresco

affrettare (âf·frāt·tâ'rā) *vt* to hurry, speed up

affrettato (âf·frāt·tâ'tō) *a* hasty; in a hurry

affrontare (âf·frōn·tâ'rā) *vt* to defy; to face; to insult

affronto (âf·frōn'tō) *m* affront, insult

affumicare (âf·fū·mē·kâ'rā) *vt* to cure, smoke

affumicato (âf·fū·mē·kâ'tō) *a* smoked, cured

affusolato (âf·fū·zō·lâ'tō) *a* slender; tapering

afoso (â·fō'zō) *a* sultry; excessively hot

Africa (â'frē·kâ) *f* Africa

africano (â·frē·kâ'nō) *a* African

agenda (â·jān'dâ) *f* notebook

agente (â·jān'tā) *m* agent; — **di cambio** stockbroker; — **di polizia** policeman; — **investigativo** detective; — **delle tasse** tax collector

agenzia (â·jān·tsē'â) *f* agency; — **di collocamento** employment agency; — **di trasporti** freight company; — **di viaggi** travel agency

agevolazione (â·jā·vō·lâ·tsyō'nā) *f* facility; ease; (*com*) easy terms

aggeggio (âj·je'jō) *m* gadget

aggettivo (âj·jāt·tē'vō) *m* adjective

aggiornamento (âj·jōr·nâ·mān'tō) *m* updating

aggiornare (aj·jōr·nâ'rā) *vt* to adjourn; to update; — *vi* to dawn

aggiornato (âj·jōr·nâ'tō) *a* up-to-date

aggiramento (âj·jē·râ·mān'tō) *m* circumvention; fraud

aggirare (âj·jē·râ'rā) *vt* to surround; to turn around; to take in, defraud

aggirarsi (âj·jē·râr'sē) *vr* to ramble; to roam; to tramp

aggiratore (âj·jē·râ·tō'rā) *m* rambler; deceiver, swindler

aggiungere * (âj·jūn'jā·rā) *vt* to add; to rejoin

aggiunta (âj·jūn'tâ) *f* addition

aggiunto (âj·jūn'tō) *a* added

aggiustaggio (âj·jū·stâj'jō) *m* (*mech*) adjustment, alignment

aggiustare (âj·jū·stâ'rā) *vt* to fix; to adjust

aggiustatore (âj·jū·stâ·tō'rā) *m* (*mech*) fitter

aggrappare (âg·grâp·pâ'rā) *vt* to grapple; to grab hold of

aggrapparsi (âg·grâp·pâr'sē) *vr* to cling to tightly

aggravamento (âg·grâ·vâ·mān'tō) *m* surcharge; aggravation

aggravante (âg·grâ·vân'tā) *a* aggravating

aggravare (âg·grâ·vâ'rā) *vt* to make worse, worsen

aggravarsi (âg·grâ·vâr'sē) *vr* to get worse, worsen

aggravio (âg·grâ'vyō) *m* injury; burden, charge

aggredire (âg·grā·dē'rā) *vt* to attack

aggregare (âg·grā·gâ'rā) *vt* to aggregate, mass together

aggregarsi (âg·grā·gâr'sē) *vr* to join, become a member

aggregato (âg·grā·gâ'tō) *a* aggregated; — *m* aggregation, assembly

aggressione (âg·grās·syō'nā) *f* aggression

aggressivo (âg·grās·sē'vō) *a* aggressive

aggressore (âg·grās·sō'rā) *m* aggressor

aggrottare (âg·grōt·tâ'rā) *vt* to pucker; (*agr*) to embank; — **le ciglia** to frown

agguantare (âg·gwân·tâ'rā) *vt* to catch hold of, clasp

---

k kid, **l** let, **m** met, **n** not, **p** pat, **r** very, **s** sat, **sh** shop, **t** tell, **v** vat, **w** we, **y** yes, **z** zero

agiatamente (â·jâ·tâ·mān'tā) adv comfortably, easily

agiatezza (â·jâ·tā'tsâ) f welfare, wellbeing

agiato (â·jâ'tō) a well off; wealthy

agilità (â·jē·lē·tâ') f agility; quickness

agire (â·jē'rā) vi to act; to behave

agitare (â·jē·tâ'rā) vt to shake; to upset

agitarsi (â·jē·târ'sē) vr to get excited

agitatore (â·jē·tâ·tō'rā) m agitator; ringleader

agitazione (â·jē·tâ·tsyō'nā) f agitation, excitement

agli (â'lyē) prep to the

aglio (â'lyō) m garlic

agnello (â·nyāl'lō) m lamb

ago (â'gō) m needle

agonia (â·gō·nē'â) f agony

agosto (â·gō'stō) m August

agricolo (â·grē'kō·lō) a agricultural

agricoltore (â·grē·kōl·tō'rā) m farmer

agricultura (â·grē·kūl·tū'râ) f farming

agrifoglio (â·grē·fō'lyō) m holly

agrimensore (â·grē·mān·sō'rā) m surveyor

agrumeto (â·grū·mā'tō) m citrus grove

agrumi (â·grū'mē) mpl citrus fruit

ai (â'ē) prep to the

aia (â'yâ) f threshing area; governess, tutor

aiuola (â·ywō'lâ) f flower bed

aiutante (â·yū·tân'tā) m helper, aid

aiutare (â·yū·tâ'rā) vt to help, be of assistance to

aiuto (â·yū'tō) m help

al (âl), allo (âl'lō), alla (âl'lâ), all' (âll) prep to the, on the; with; in the manner of

ala (â'lâ) f wing; –to (â·lâ'tō) a winged

alare (â·lâ'rā) m andiron

alba (âl'bâ) f dawn

Albania (âl·bâ·nē'â) f Albania

albanese (âl·bâ·nä'zā) a&m Albanian

albatro (âl'bâ·trō) m (bot) arbutus; (zool) albatross

albeggiare (âl·bāj·jâ'rā) vi to break (day); to dawn

albergatore (âl·bār·gâ·tō'rā) m hotel manager; hotelman

albergo (âl·bār'gō) m hotel; — diurno public bathing and washing facilities

albero (âl'bā·rō) m tree

albicocca (âl·bē·kōk'kâ) f apricot

albume (âl·bū'mā) m albumen

alcali (âl'kâ·lē) m alkali; –no (âl·kâ·lē'nō) a alkaline

alcole (âl·kō'lā), alcool (āl'kō·ōl) m alcohol

alcuno (âl·kū'nō) a&pron some, any, none, no

alesatore (â·lā·zâ·tō'rā) m ream, bore

alettone (â·lāt·tō'nā) m (avi) aileron

alga (âl'gâ) f seaweed

algebra (âl'jā·brâ) f algebra

algebrico (âl·je'brē·kō) a algebraic

aliante (â·lyân'tā) m (avi) glider

alice (â·lē'chā) f anchovy

alienare (â·lyā·nâ'rā) vi to alienate; to make over

alienato (â·lyā·nâ'tō) a alienated; — mentale lunatic, madman

alimentare (â·lē·mān·tâ'rā) a alimentary; paste alimentari spaghetti; generi alimentari groceries

alimentarista (â·lē·mān·tâ·rē'stâ) m grocer

alimentazione (â·lē·mān·tâ·tsyō'nā) f feeding; (mech) stoking

alimento (â·lē·mān'tō) m nourishment

aliscafo (â·lē·skâ'fō) m hydrofoil speedboat

alito (â'lē·tō) m breath; breeze

allacciamento (â·lâ·châ·mān'tō) m lacing; (elec) connection, link

allacciare (âl·lâ·châ'rā) vt to lace

allargare (âl·lâr·gâ'rā) vt to broaden; to extend

allarme (âl·lâr'mā) m alarm

allattare (âl·lât·tâ'rā) vt to nurse, breastfeed

alleanza (âl·lā·ân'tsâ) f alliance

alleato (âl·lā·â'tō) a allied

allegato (âl·lā·gâ'tō) a enclosed; — m enclosure, attachment

alleggerire (âl·lāj·jā·rē'rā) vt to lighten; to make easier

alleggerirsi (âl·lāj·jā·rēr'sē) vr to relieve oneself; (fig) to undress

alleggerito (âl·lāj·jā·rē'tō) a lightened, alleviated

allegoria (âl·lā·gō·rē'â) f allegory

allegria (âl·lā·grē'â) f gaiety, happiness

allegro (âl·lā'grō) a cheerful, gay

allenamento (âl·lā·nâ·mān'tō) m training, workout, exercise

allenatore (âl·lā·nâ·tō'rā) m trainer, coach

allevare (âl·lā·vâ'rā) vt to breed; to raise, educate

alleviare (âl·lā·vyâ'rā) vt to alleviate

allibratore (âl·lē·brâ·tō'rā) m bookie, bookmaker

allievo (âl·lyā'vō) m pupil

allineare (âl·lē·nā·â'rā) vt to form into ranks; to line up

allinearsi (âl·lē·nā·âr'sē) vr to align oneself; to get in line

allodola (âl·lô'dō·là) *f* skylark

allogeno (âl·lô'jä·nō) *m* alien

alloggiare (âl·lôj·jâ'rā) *vt* to house, lodge; — *vi* to stay, be accommodated

alloggio (âl·lôj'jō) *m* lodging

allontanamento (âl·lōn·tâ·nâ·mān'tō) *m* distance; remoteness

allontanare (âl·lōn·tâ·nâ'rā) *vt* to keep away; to take away

allora (âl·lō'râ) *adv* then

alloro (âl·lô'rō) *m* laurel; **foglie d'**— bay leaves

allume (âl·lū'mā) *m* alum

alluminio (âl·lū·mē'nyō) *m* aluminum

allungamento (âl·lūn·gâ·mān'tō) *m* lengthening, prolonging

allungare (âl·lūn·gâ'rā) *vt* to lengthen; to prolong

allusione (âl·lū·zyō'nā) *f* allusion

alluvionato (âl·lū·vyō·nâ'tō) *m* flood victim; — *a* flooded

alluvione (âl·lū·vyō'nā) *f* flood

almanacco (âl·mâ·nâk'kō) *m* almanac

almeno (âl·mā'nō) *adv* at least

alone (â·lō'nā) *m* halo

Alpi (âl'pē) *fpl*

alpinista (âl·pē·nē'stâ) *m&f* mountain climber

alquanto (âl·kwân'tō) *adv* somewhat; a bit

alt! (âlt) *interj* stop!

altalena (âl·tâ·lā'nâ) *f* swing

altamente (âl·tâ·mān'tā) *adv* highly; nobly

altare (âl·tâ'rā) *m* altar

alterare (âl·tâ·râ'rā) *vt* to alter; to distort

alterazione (âl·tâ·râ·tsyō'nā) *f* alteration; distortion

alternare (âl·tār·nâ'rā) *vt* to alternate

alternarsi (âl·tār·nâr'sē) *vr* to follow each other; to take turns

alternativa (âl·tār·nâ·tē'vâ) *f* alternative

alternato (âl·tār·nâ'tō) *a* alternating; **corrente alternata** alternating current

alternatore (âl·tār·nâ·tō'rā) *m (elec)* alternator

altezza (âl·tā'tsâ) *f* height; loftiness

altigiano (âl·tē·jâ'nō) *m* mountaineer

altimetro (âl·tē'mâ·trō) *m* altimeter

altipiano (âl·tē·pyâ'nō) *m* plateau

alto (âl'tō) *a* high; tall; loud; **–forno** (âl·tō·fōr'nō) *m* blast furnace; **–locato** (âl·tō·lô·kâ'tō) *a* prominent; **–mare** (âl·tō·mâ'rā) *m* high sea; **–parlante** (âl·tō·pâr·lân'tā) *m* loudspeaker

altrimenti (âl·trē·mān'tē) *adv* otherwise, if not

altro (âl'trō) *a* other; **un** — another

altrove (âl·trō'vā) *adv* elsewhere, somewhere else

altrui (âl·trū'ē) *pron* another's, others', of others

alunno (â·lūn'nō) *m* pupil, scholar

alveare (âl·vâ·â'rā) *m* beehive

alzare (âl·tsâ'rā) *vt* to lift, raise

alzarsi (âl·tsâr'sē) *vr* to get up, arise

amabile (â·mâ'bē·lā) *a* amiable, friendly

amabilità (â·mâ·bē·lē·tâ') *f* amiability, friendliness

amabilmente (â·mâ·bēl·mān'tā) *adv* kindly, friendly

amante (â·mân'tā) *a* fond; — *f&m* mistress; lover

amare (â·mâ'rā) *vt* to love

amaretto (â·mâ·rāt'tō) *m* macaroon

amareggiare (â·mâ·rāj·jâ'rā) *vt* to embitter

amarezza (â·mâ·rā'tsâ) *f* bitterness; resentfulness

amaro (â·mâ'rō) *a* bitter; — *m* bitters

ambasciata (âm·bâ·shâ'tâ) *f* embassy

ambasciatore (âm·bâ·shâ·tō'rā) *m* ambassador

ambedue (âm·bā·dū'ā) *a&pron* both

ambiente (âm·byān'tā) *m* atmosphere, environment

ambiguamente (âm·bē·gwâ·mān'tā) *adv* ambiguously, vaguely

ambiguità (âm·bē·gwē·tâ') *f* ambiguity, vagueness

ambiguo (âm·bē'gwō) *a* ambiguous, vague

ambizione (âm·bē·tsyō'nā) *f* ambition, heart's desire

ambizioso (âm·bē·tsyō'zō) *a* ambitious; covetous

ambo (âm'bō) *a&pron* both

ambra (âm'brâ) *f* amber

ambulanza (âm·bū·lân'tsâ) *f* ambulance

ambulatorio (âm·bū·lâ·tō'ryō) *m* dispensary

ameno (â·mā'nō) *a* cheerful, gay

America (â·me'rē·kâ) *f* America

americanata (â·mâ·rē·kâ·nâ'tâ) *f* something spectacular; eccentric and exaggerated action

americano (â·mâ·rē·kâ'nō) *m* American

amianto (â·myân'tō) *m* asbestos

amica (â·mē'kâ) *f* girl friend; sweetheart

amichevole (â·mē·ke'vō·lā) *a* friendly

amicizia (â·mē·chē'tsyâ) *f* friendship; **fare** — to become friendly, establish a friendship

amico (â·mē'kō) *m* friend

amido (â'mē·dō) *m* starch

---

k kid, **l** let, **m** met, **n** not, **p** pat, **r** very, **s** sat, **sh** shop, **t** tell, **v** vat, **w** we, **y** yes, **z** zero

ammaccare (âm·mâk·kâ′rā) *vt* to bruise
ammaccato (âm·mâk·kâ′tō) *a* battered; bruised
ammaccatura (âm·mâk·kâ·tū′râ) *f* bruise; knob; lump; hammer mark; contusion
ammainare (âm·mâē·nâ′rā) *vt* to lower; to haul down (*sails*)
ammalarsi (âm·mâ·lâr′sē) *vt* to become ill, get sick
ammalato (âm·mâ·lâ′tō) *a* ill, sick; — *m* patient
ammannire (âm·mân·nē′rā) *vt* to prime, prepare
ammanco (âm·mân′kō) *m* deficit, shortage
ammansare (âm·mân·sâ′rā), **ammansire** (âm·mân·sē′rā) *vt* to tame; to calm; to pacify
ammassare (âm·mâs·sâ′rā) *vt* to amass; to heap; to gather
ammasso (âm·mâs′sō) *m* heap; mass
ammattire (âm·mât·tē′rā) *vi* to go mad, lose one's mind
ammattito (âm·mât·tē′tō) *a* mad, insane
ammazzare (âm·mâ·tsâ′rā) *vt* to kill, do away with
ammenda (âm·mān′dâ) *f* fine
ammettere * (âm·met′tā·rā) *vt* to admit
amministrare (âm·mē·nē·strâ′rā) *vt* to administer
amministrativamente (âm·mē·nē·strâ·tē·vâ·mān′tâ) *adv* administratively
amministrativo (âm·mē·nē·strâ·tē′vō) *a* administrative
amministrato (âm·mē·nē·strâ′tō) *a* administered
amministratore (âm·mē·nē·strâ·tō′rā) *m* administrator, manager
amministrazione (âm·mē·nē·strâ·tsyō′nä) *f* administration; business office
ammirabile (âm·mē·râ′bē·lä) *a* admirable
ammiraglio (âm·mē·râ′lyō) *m* admiral
ammirare (âm·mē·râ′rā) *vt* to admire; to think highly of
ammirativo (âm·mē·râ·tē′vō) *a* admirable
ammiratore (âm·mē·râ·tō′rā) *m* admirer
ammirazione (âm·mē·râ·tsyō′nä) *f* admiration
ammissibile (âm·mēs·sē′bē·lä) *a* admissible
ammissibilità (âm·mēs·sē·bē·lē·tâ′) *f* admissibility
ammissione (âm·mēs·syō′nä) *f* admission
ammobiliato (âm·mō·bē·lyâ′tō) *a* furnished

ammogliare (âm·mō·lyâ′rā) *vt* to give in marriage; to marry
ammogliarsi (âm·mō·lyâr′sē) *vr* to get married; to marry
ammogliato (âm·mō·lyâ′tō) *a* married; — *m* married man
ammoniaca (âm·mō·nē′â·kâ) *f* ammonia
ammonire (âm·mō·nē′rā) *vt* to warn
ammonito (âm·mō·nē′tō) *a* admonished; under surveillance
ammonizione (âm·mō·nē·tsyō′nä) *f* admonition
ammontare (âm·mōn·tâ′rā) *vi* to amount; to cost; — *m* amount
ammorbidire (âm·mōr·bē·dē′rā) *vt* to make soft; to make supple
ammortamento (âm·mōr·tâ·mân′tō) *m* amortization
ammortizzare (âm·mōr·tē·dzâ′rā) *vt* to amortize; to break, deflect; to deaden, cushion
ammortizzatore (âm·mōr·tē·dzâ·tō′rā) *m* (*auto*) shock absorber
ammucchiare (âm·mūk·kyâ′rā) *vt* to pile up, amass, collect
ammuffire (âm·mūf·fē′rā) *vi* to get musty
ammuffito (âm·mūf·fē′tō) *a* moldy
ammutinarsi (âm·mū·tē·nâr′sē) *vr* to mutiny; to rebel
amnistia (âm·nē·stē′â) *f* amnesty
amo (â′mō) *m* fishhook
amore (â·mō′rā) *m* love; **–ggiare** (â·mō·räj·jâ′rā) *vt&i* to make love; to flirt **–vole** (â·mō·re′vō·lä) *a* loving; lovely; affectionate; **–volmente** (â·mō·rā·vōl·mān′tä) *adv* kindly; lovably
amorosamente (â·mō·rō·zâ·mān′tä) *adv* with love, lovingly
amoroso (â·mō·rō′zō) *a* amorous; fond; — *m* lover, suitor
amper (âm·pär′) *m* (*elec*) ampere; **–aggio** (âm·pä·räj′jō) *m* amperage; **–ometro** (âm·pä·rō′mä·trō) *m* ammeter
ampiezza (âm·pyâ′tsâ) *f* largeness; amplitude
ampio (âm′pyō) *a* abundant; ample
amplesso (âm·plās′sō) *m* hug, embrace
ampliare (âm·plyâ′rā) *vt* to amplify, extend
amplificare (âm·plē·fē·kâ′rā) *vt* to amplify; to enrich
amplificatore (âm·plē·fē·kâ·tō′rā) *m* amplifier
amplificazione (âm·plē·fē·kâ·tsyō′nä) *f* amplification
amputare (âm·pū·tâ′rā) *vt* to amputate
anabbagliante (â·nâb·bâ·lyân′tä) *a* anti-

â ârm, ā bāby, e bet, ē bē, ō gō, ô gône, ū blūe, b bad, ch child, d dad, f fat, g gay, j jet

glare

anagrafe (â·nâ′grâ·fä) *f* vital statistics; **ufficio d'** — bureau of records

analfabeta (â·nâl·fâ·bä′tâ) *a* illiterate

analisi (â·nâ′lē·zē) *f* analysis

analitico (â·nâ·lē′tē·kō) *a* analytical, analytic

analizzare (â·nâ·lē·dzâ′rä) *vt* to analyse; to break down, decompose

analizzatore (â·nâ·lē·dzâ·tō′rä) *m* analyst; *(TV)* scanning disk

ananasso (â·nâ·nâs′sō) *m* pineapple

anarchia (â·nâr·kē′â) *f* anarchy

anarchico (â·nâr′kē·kō) *m* anarchist

anatomia (â·nâ·tō·mē′â) *f* anatomy

anatra (â′nâ·trä) *f* duck

anca (ân′kâ) *f* hip

anche (ân′kä) *adv* too, as well, also

ancora (ân′kō·râ) *f* anchor; **–ggio** (ân·kō·râj′jō) *m* anchorage, anchoring; **–re** (ân·kō·râ′rä) *vt* to anchor, cast anchor; **–rsi** (ân·kō·râr′sē) *vr* to anchor; lay anchor

ancora (ân·kō′râ) *adv* still, yet, as yet

andare * ân·dâ′râ) *vi* to go; — **a piedi** to walk; — **in macchina** to drive; to ride

andata (ân·dâ′tâ) *f* going; **biglietto di** — **semplice** one-way ticket; **biglietto di** — **e ritorno** round-trip ticket

aneddoto (â·ned′dō·tō) *m* anecdote

anello (ân·nâl′lō) *m* ring

anemografo (â·nâ·mô′grâ·fō) *m* anemograph

anemometro (â·nâ·mô′mâ·trō) *m* anemometer

anemoscopio (â·nâ·mō·skô′pyō) *m* anemoscope

aneroide (â·nâ·rô′ē·dä) *m* aneroid

anestesia (â·nâ·stâ·zē′â) *f* anesthesia

anestesista (â·nâ·stâ·zē′stâ) *m* anesthetist

anestetico (â·nâ·ste′tē·kō) *a&m* anesthetic

anestizzante (â·nâ·stē·dzân′tâ) *m* anesthetic

anestizzare (â·nâ·stē·dzâ′rä) *vt* to anesthetize

anestizzato (â·nâ·stē·dzâ′tō) *a* anesthetized

aneto (â·nâ′tō) *m* (*bot*) dill

anfibio (ân·fē′byō) *a* amphibious; — *m* amphibian; — (*mil*) duck, amphibious truck

anfiteatro (ân·fē·tâ·â′trō) *m* amphitheater

anfora (ân′fō·râ) *f* amphora

angelo (ân′jä·lō) *m* angel

angheria (ân·gä·rē′â) *f* vexation; an-

noyance

angolo (ân′gō·lō) *m* corner

angoscia (ân·gô′shâ) *f* anguish, torment

anguilla (ân·gwēl′lâ) *f* eel

anguria (ân·gū′ryâ) *f* watermelon

anima (â′nē·mâ) *f* soul; **–le** (â·nē·mâ′lä) *m* animal, beast; **–le** *a* bestial, beastly; stupid

animare (â·nē·mâ′rä) *vt* to animate; to encourage

animarsi (â·nē·mâr′sē) *vi* to take courage

animazione (â·nē·mâ·tsyō′nä) *f* animation

animella (â·nē·mäl′lâ) *f* sweetbread

animosità (â·nē·mō·zē·tâ′) *f* animosity

animoso (â·nē·mō′zō) *a* bold; malevolent, evil

anione (â·nyō′nä) *m* (*phys*) anion

annacquare (ân·nâk·kwâ′rä) *vt* to water; to add water to, dilute

annaffiare (ân·nâf·fyâ′rä) *vt* to water, sprinkle

annegare (ân·nâ·gâ′rä) *vt* to drown

annerire (ân·nâ·rē′rä) *vt&i* to blacken; to get black

annessione (ân·nâs·syō′nä) *f* annexation

annientare (ân·nyân·tâ′rä) *vt* to annihilate; to wipe out

anniversario (ân·nē·vâr·sâ′ryō) *m* anniversary

anno (ân′nō) *m* year; — **bisestile** leap year

annodare (ân·nō·dâ′rä) *vt* to tie; to knot

annoiare (ân·nō·yâ′rä) *vt* to bore; to tire out

annoiarsi (ân·nō·yâr′sē) *vi* to get bored; to be worn-out

annoiato (ân·nō·yâ′tō) *a* bored; weary

annotare (ân·nō·tâ′rä) *vt* to annotate; to footnote

annotazione (ân·nō·tâ·tsyō′nä) *f* annotation; note

annuale (ân·nwâ′lä), **annuo** (ân′nwō) *a* yearly, annual

annuario (ân·nwâ′ryō) *m* yearbook; directory

annullamento (ân·nūl·lâ·mân′tō) *m* annulment

annullare (ân·nūl·lâ′rä) *vt* to annul

annunziare (ân·nūn·tsyâ′rä) *vt* to announce; to publicize

annunziatore (ân·nūn·tsyâ·tō′rä) *m* announcer

annunzio (ân·nūn′tsyō) *m* announcement; — **pubblicitario** advertisement

ano (â′nō) *m* anus

anodico (â·nô′dē·kō) *a* anodic

anodino (â·nô′dē·nō) *a* anodyne

anodo (â'nō·dō) *m* (*elec*) anode
anonimo (â·nô'nē·mō) *a* anonymous
anormale (â·nōr·mâ'lā) *a* abnormal
anormalità (â·nōr·mâ·lē·tâ') *f* abnormality
ansia (ân'syâ), **ansietà** (ân·syā·tâ') *f* anxiety
ansiosamente (ân·syō·zâ·mān'tā) *adv* anxiously
ansioso (ân·syō'zō) *a* anxious
antartico (ân·târ'tē·kō) *m&a* antarctic
antenato (ân·tā·nâ'tō) *m* ancestor; predecessor
antenna (ân·tān'nâ) *f* antenna
antecessore (ân·tā·chās·sō'rā) *m* predecessor
anteprima (ân·tā·prē'mâ) *f* preview
anteriore (ân·tā·ryō'rā) *a* previous; front
anteriorità (ân·tā·ryō·rē·tâ') *f* priority
anteriormente (ân·tā·ryōr·mān'tā) *adv* previously, before
antiacido (ân·tyâ'chē·dō) *m&a* antacid
anticamente (ân·tē·kâ·mān'tā) *adv* formerly; in days of yore
anticamera (ân·tē·kâ'mā·râ) *f* waiting room
antichità (ân·tē·kē·tâ') *f* antiquity
anticipare (ân·tē·chē·pâ'rā) *vt* to advance; to anticipate
anticipatamente (ân·tē·chē·pâ·tâ·mān'tā) *adv* in advance
anticipato (ân·tē·chē·pâ'tō) *a* in advance; **pagamento** — advance payment
anticipo (ân·tē'chē·pō) *m* advance
anticlericale (ân·tē·klā·rē·kâ'lā) *a* anticlerical
antico (ân·tē'kō) *a* ancient
anticongelante (ân·tē·kōn·jā·lân·tā) *m* (*auto*) antifreeze
antidetonante (ân·tē·dā·tō·nân'tā) *a* antiknock
antidoto (ân·tē'dō·tō) *m* antidote
antifrizione (ân·tē·frē·tsyō'nā) *f* antifriction
antiincendio (ân·tē·ēn·chen'dyō) *a* fireproofing
antimagnetico (ân·tē·mâ·nye'tē·kō) *a* antimagnetic
antimeridiano (ân·tē·mā·rē·dyâ'nō) *a* forenoon, morning
antimonio (ân·tē·mô'nyō) *m* (*chem*) antimony
antipasto (ân·tē·pâ'stō) *m* hors d'oeuvres, appetizers
antipatia (ân·tē·pâ·tē'â) *f* dislike
antipatico (ân·tē·pâ'tē·kō) *a* disagreeable
antiquariato (ân·tē·kwâ·ryâ'tō) *m* rare

book business; antiquarianism
antiquario (ân·tē·kwâ'ryō) *m* antique dealer
antiquato (ân·tē·kwâ'tō) antiquated
antisemita (ân·tē·sâ·mē'tâ) *a* anti-semitic
antisettico (ân·tē·set'tē·kō) *a* antiseptic
antologia (ân·tō·lō·jē'â) *f* anthology
antracene (ân·trâ·chā'nā) *m* (*chem*) anthracene
antracite (ân·trâ·chē'tā) *m* anthracite
anzi (ân'tsē) *adv* rather, instead
anzianità (ân·tsyâ·nē·tâ') *f* seniority
anziano (ân·tsyâ'nō) *a* elder; elderly
anzichè (ân·tsē·kâ') *conj* rather than, in place of
anzitutto (ân·tsē·tūt'tō) *adv* above all
ape (â'pā) *f* bee
aperitivo (â·pā·rē·tē'vō) *m* aperitif
apertamente (â·pâr·tâ·mān'tā) *adv* openly, publicly
aperto (â·pâr'tō) *a* open
apertura (â·pâr·tū'râ) *f* opening, aperture, hole
apoplessia (â·pō·plās·sē'â) *f* stroke
apostolo (â·pō'stō·lō) *m* apostle
appaiare (âp·pâ·yâ'rā) *vt* to match, find a mate for
appaltatore (âp·pâl·tâ·tō'rā) *m* contractor
appalto (âp·pâl'tō) *m* contract; bid
appannato (âp·pân·nâ'tō) *a* dim; dull
apparecchiare (âp·pâ·rāk·kyâ'rā) *vt* to prepare; — **la tavola** to set the table
apparecchiatura (âp·pâ·rāk·kyâ·tū'râ) *f* equipment
apparecchio (âp·pâ·rek'kyō) *m* apparatus; telephone; radio; plane
apparente (âp·pâ·rēn'tā) *a* apparent; —**mente** (âp·pâ·rān·tā·mān'tā) *adv* apparently, seemingly
apparenza (âp·pâ·rān'tsâ) *f* appearance
apparire * (âp·pâ·rē'rā) *vi* to appear
apparizione (âp·pâ·rē·tsyō'nā) *f* apparition, vision
appartamento (âp·pâr·tâ·mān'tō) *m* apartment
appartenere * (âp·pâr·tā·nā'rā) *vi* to belong; to be in one's field
appassire (âp·pâs·sē'rā) *vt&i* to dry; to wither
appassito (âp·pâs·sē'tō) *a* faded
appellarsi (âp·pāl·lâr'sē) *vi* to appeal
appello (âp·pāl'lō) *m* appeal; roll call; **corte d'** — court of appeals, appellate court
appena (âp·pā'nâ) *adv* hardly; as soon as; just as
appendere * (âp·pen'dâ·rā) *vt* to hang

appendice (âp·pän·dē'chä) *f* appendix; **romanzo d'—** serial novel

appendicite (âp·pän·dē·chē'tä) *f* appendicitis

appetito (âp·pā·tē'tō) *m* appetite; **buon —!** enjoy your dinner!

appetitoso (âp·pā·tē·tō'zō) *a* appetizing, delicious

appiccicare (âp·pē·chē·kâ'rä) *vt* to stick; to glue together

applaudire (âp·plâû·dē'rä) *vt* to applaud

applauso (âp·plâ'ü·zō) *m* applause

applicare (âp·plē·kâ'rä) *vt* to apply; to place

applicazione (âp·plē·kâ·tsyō'nä) *f* application; appliance

appoggiare (âp·pōj·jâ'rä) *vt* to support

appoggiarsi (âp·pōj·jâr'sē) *vr* to lean against

appoggio (âp·pôj'jō) *m* support, backing

apporto (äp·pôr'tō) *m* contribution

appositamente (âp·pō·zē·tâ·mān'tä) *adv* on purpose

apprendere * (âp·pren'dä·rä) *vt* to learn

apprendista (âp·prän·dē'stä) *m* apprentice

appresso (âp·präs'sō) *adv* later; next; nearby

apprezzare (âp·prä·tsâ'rä) *vt* to appreciate; to value

approdare (âp·prō·dâ'rä) *vi* to land

approdo (âp·prō'dō) *m* landing

approffittare (âp·prōf·fēt·tâ'rä) *vi* to make the most of, profit by

approffittarsi (âp·prōf·fēt·târ'sē) *vr* to draw profit from, avail oneself of, take advantage of

appropriare (âp·prō·pryâ'rä) *vt* to adjust; to suit; to appropriate

appropriarsi (âp·prō·pryâr'sē) *vi* to steal, make off with

appropriato (âp·prō·pryâ'tō) *a* proper, fitting

appropriazione (âp·prō·pryâ·tsyō'nä) *f* appropriation; **— indebita** embezzlement

approssimativo (âp·prōs·sē·mâ·tē'vō) *a* approximate

approssimato (âp·prōs·sē·mâ'tō) *a* approached

approssimazione (âp·prōs·sē·mâ·tsyō'nä) *f* approximation

approvabile (âp·prô·vâ'bē·lä) *a* commendable

approvare (âp·prō·vâ'rä) *vt* to approve, commend

approvazione (âp·prō·vâ·tsyō'nä) *f* approval; commendation

appuntamento (âp·pün·tâ·mān'tō) *m* appointment, date

appuntare (âp·pün·tâ'rä) *vt* to sharpen; to pin on; to note

appunto (âp·pün'tō) *m* remark; note; **per l'— ** *adv* exactly, precisely

aprile (â·prē'lä) *m* April; **pesce d'—** April fool

apripista (â·prē·pē'stä) *m* bulldozer

aprire * (â·prē'rä) *vt* to open; to split

aprirsi * (â·prēr'sē) *vi* to burst; to split open

apriscatole (â·prē·skâ'tō·lä) *m* can opener

aquila (â'kwē·lâ) *f* eagle

aquilino (â·kwē·lē'nō) *a* hooked, aquiline

aquilone (â·kwē·lō'nä) *m* kite

arabo (â'râ·bō) *m* Arab; **—** *a* Arabian

arachide (â·râ'kē·dä) *f* peanut

aragosta (â·râ·gō'stä) *f* lobster

araldica (â·râl'dē·kâ) *f* heraldry

aranceto (â·rân·châ'tō) *m* orange grove

arancia (â·rân'châ) *f* orange; **—ta** (â·rân·châ'tä) *f* orangeade

aratro (â'râ·trō) *m* plow

arazzo (â·râ'tsō) *m* tapestry

arbitro (âr'bē·trō) *m* judge; referee

arcangelo (âr·kân'jä·lō) *m* archangel

architetto (âr·kē·tät'tō) *m* architect

architettura (âr·kē·tât·tü'râ) *f* architecture

archiviare (âr·kē·vyâ'rä) *vt* to file; to put on file

archivio (âr·kē'vyō) *m* file; archives

arcivescovo (âr·chē·ve'skō·vō) *m* archbishop

arco (âr'kō) *m* arch; **strumenti ad —** string instruments; **tiro con l'—** archery; **—baleno** (âr·kō·bâ·lä'nō) *m* rainbow

ardente (âr·dän'tä) *a* burning; passionate

ardere * (âr'dä·rä) *vt&i* to burn

ardesia (âr·de'zyâ) *f* slate

ardito (âr·dē'tō) *a* bold, intrepid

area (â'râ·â) *f* area, zone

arena (â·râ'nä) *f* arena; sand

arenoso (â·râ·nō'zō) *a* sandy

argano (âr'gâ·nō) *m* winch; capstan

argentato (âr·jän·tâ'tō) *a* silver-plated

argenteria (âr·jän·tä·rē'â) *f* silverware

argento (âr·jän'tō) *m* silver

argilla (âr·jēl'lâ) *f* clay

argine (âr'jē·nä) *m* embankment; barricade

argo (âr'gō) *m* argon

argomento (âr·gō·mān'tō) *m* argument subject; reason; indication

argutamente (âr·gü·tâ·mān'tä) *adv*

---

shrewdly, artfully; wittily
arguto (âr·gū'tō) *a* witty, sharp
arguzia (âr·gū'tsyâ) *f* wit, humor; guile
aria (â'ryâ) *f* air; appearance
arido (â'rē·dō) *a* arid; dull, insipid
ariete (â·ryā'tā) *m* (*zool*) ram; (*mil*) battering ram
aringa (â·rēn'gâ) *f* herring
arioso (â·ryō'zō) *a* airy, light
aristocratico (â·rē·stō·krâ'tē·kō) *a* aristocratic; patrician; noble
aristocrazia (â·rē·stō·krâ·tsē'â) *f* aristocracy, nobility
aritmetica (â·rēt·me'tē·kâ) *f* arithmetic
arlecchino (âr·lāk·kē'nō) *m* buffoon, jester
arma (âr'mâ) *f* armament, arm
armadietto (âr·mâ·dyāt'tō) *m* small cabinet; — **per medicinali** medicine chest
armadio (âr·mâ'dyō) *m* wardrobe; — **a muro** closet
armamentario (âr·mâ·mān·tâ'ryō) *m* outfit; — **chirurgico** surgical instruments
armamento (âr·mâ·mān'tō) *m* (*mil*) armament; ship's rigging; (*mech*) assembly
armare (âr·mâ'rā) *vt* to arm; to put together, assemble
armata (âr·mâ'tâ) *f* fleet; **corpo d'—** army corps
armato (âr·mâ'tō) *a* armed; **–re** (âr·mâ·tō'rā) *m* shipowner
armatura (âr·mâ·tū'râ) *f* armor; (*elec*) armature; framework
arme (âr'mā) *f* weapon; **–ria** (âr·mā·rē'â) *f* armory
armistizio (âr·mē·stē'tsyō) *m* armistice
armonia (âr·mō·nē'â) *f* harmony
armonica (âr·mō'nē·kâ) *f* harmonica
armonioso (âr·mō·nyō'zō) *a* harmonious, melodious
armonizzare (âr·mō·nē·dzâ'râ) *vt&i* to harmonize
arnese (âr·nā'zā) *m* tool; **cattivo —** rogue
arnione (âr·nyō'nā) *m* kidney
aroma (â·rō'mâ) *m* flavor, aroma; **–tico** (â·rō·mâ'tē·kō) *a* flavorful, aromatic
arpa (âr'pâ) *f* harp
arpia (âr·pē'â) *f* (*fig*) shrew, scold
arrabbiarsi (âr·râb·byâr'sē) *vr* to get angry
arrampicarsi (âr·râm·pē·kâr'sē) *vr* to climb
arrecare (âr·rā·kâ'râ) *vt* to cause, bring about, give
arredamento (âr·rā·dâ·mān'tō) *m* furnishings
arredare (âr·rā·dâ'rā) *vt* to furnish

arredatore (âr·rā·dâ·tō'rā) *m* interior decorator
arredo (âr·rā'dō) *m* outfit; (*eccl*) vestments
arrembare (âr·rām·bâ'râ) *vt* to board, get aboard (*forcibly*)
arrendevole (âr·rān·de'vō·lā) *a* limber, flexible; (*fig*) tractable; **–zza** (âr·rān·dā·vō·lā'tsâ) *f* litheness; willing obedience; pliancy
arrendersi * (âr·ren'dār·sē) *vr* to give oneself up, surrender, yield
arrestare (âr·rā·stâ'râ) *vt* to arrest
arresto (âr·rā'stō) *m* arrest; failure; — **alla dogana** customs stop
arretrare (âr·rā·trâ'râ) *vt&i* to withdraw; — *vi* to fall back
arretrato (âr·rā·trâ'tō) *m* arrears; — *a* backward; delinquent; **numero —** back issue
arricchimento (âr·rēk·kē·mān'tō) *m* enrichment; embellishment
arricchire (âr·rēk·kē'râ) *vt* to enrich; (*fig*) to enhance, point up
arricchirsi (âr·rēk·kēr'sē) *vr* to get rich, become rich
arricchito (âr·rēk·kē'tō) *a* enriched; — *m* parvenu; — **di guerra** war profiteer
arricciare (âr·rē·châ'râ) *vt* to curl; — **il naso** to turn up one's nose
arringa (âr·rēn'gâ) *f* harangue; (*law*) plea
arrischiare (âr·rē·skyâ'râ) *vt* to risk
arrischiato (âr·rē·skyâ'tō) *a* risky
arrivare (âr·rē·vâ'râ) *vt* to arrive; to succeed in
arrivato (âr·rē·vâ'tō) *a* arrived; successful; — *m* success
arrivederci (âr·rē·vā·dâr'chē) *inter* goodbye, so long, see you later
arrivista (âr·rē·vē'stâ) *m* (*coll*) social climber
arrivo (âr·rē'vō) *m* arrival
arrogante (âr·rō·gân'tā) *a* overbearing; supercilious; **–mente** (âr·rō·gân·tā·mān'tā) *adv* domineeringly, haughtily
arroganza (âr·rō·gân'tsâ) *f* arrogance; insolence
arrossire (âr·rōs·sē'râ) *vi* to blush
arrostire (âr·rō·stē'râ) *vt* to roast
arrostito (âr·rō·stē'tō) *a* roasted
arrosto (âr·rō'stō) *m* roast
arrotare (âr·rō·tâ'râ) *vt* to sharpen, hone; to smooth out
arrotino (âr·rō·tē'nō) *m* knife sharpener
arrotolare (âr·rō·tō·lâ'râ) *vt* to roll
arrotondare (âr·rō·tōn·dâ'râ) *vt* to make round; to round off (*a figure*)

arroventare (âr·rō·vän·tâ′rä) *vt* to make red-hot
arroventato (âr·rō·vän·tâ′tō) *a* red-hot
arruffare (âr·rüf·fâ′rä) *vt* to ruffle; to tangle; to make disorderly
arrugginirsi (âr·rüj·jē·nēr′sē) *vr* to rust
arrugginito (âr·rüj·jē·nē′tō) *a* rusty
arruvidire (âr·rü·vē·dē′rä) *vt* to roughen, make rough
arsella (âr·säl′lä) *f* mussel
arsenico (âr·se′nē·kō) *m* arsenic
arso (âr′sō) *a* burnt, burned
arte (âr′tä) *f* art; — **sacra** religious art; –**fatto** (âr·tä·fât′tō) *a* adulterated; –**fice** (âr·te′fē·chä) *m* skilful craftsman; (*fig*) author, perpetrator
arteria (âr·te′ryâ) *f* artery
artico (âr′tē·kō) *a&m* arctic
articolazione (âr·tē·kō·lâ·tsyō′nä) *f* articulation; joint
articolo (âr·tē′kō·lō) *m* article
artificiale (âr·tē·fē·châ′lä) *a* artificial
artificialmente (âr·tē·fē·châl·män′tä) *adv* artificially
artificio (âr·tē·fē′chō) *m* ingenuity; device; trick, wile; **fuochi d'**— fireworks; –**so** (âr·tē·fē·chō′zō) *a* sly, cunning, tricky
artigianato (âr·tē·jâ·nâ′tō) *m* arts and crafts
artigiano (âr·tē·jâ′nō) *m* craftsman
artiglieria (âr·tē·lyä·rē′â) *f* artillery
artiglio (âr·tē′lyō) *m* claw
artista (âr·tē′stä) *m&f* artist; — **di canto** singer; — **drammatico** actor
artistico (âr·tē′stē·kō) *a* artistic; tasteful
arto (âr′tō) *m* limb
artrite (âr·trē′tä) *f* arthritis
arzillo âr·dzēl′lō) *a* sprightly, active
asbesto (â·zbä′stō) *m* asbestos
ascella (â·shäl′lä) *f* armpit
ascendente (â·shän·dän′tä) *a* ascending, upward; — *m* (*astr*) ascendant; forebear; power, influence
ascendere * (â·schen′dä·rä) *vt&i* to go up, climb; to rise
Ascensione (â·shän·syō′nä) *f* Ascension
ascensionista (â·shän·syō·nē′stä) *m* mountain climber
ascensore (â·shän·sō′rä) *m* elevator
ascensorista (â·shän·sō·rē′stä) *m* elevator operator
ascesa (â·shä′zä) *f* ascent; climb
ascesso (â·shäs′sō) *m* abscess
ascia (â′shä) *f* ax
asciugacapelli (â·shū·gâ·kâ·päl′lē) *m* hair dryer

asciugamano (â·shū·gâ·mâ′nō) *m* hand towel
asciugante (â·shū·gân′tä) *a* drying, absorbent; **carta** — blotting paper
asciugare (â·shū·gâ′rä) *vt* to wipe, dry off; to absorb
asciugato (â·shū·gâ′tō) *a* dried; wiped up
asciugatoio (â·shū·gâ·tô′yō) *m* towel
asciutto (â·shūt′tō) *a* dry; hard, merciless
ascoltare (â·skōl·tâ′rä) *vt* to listen to; to pay attention
ascoltatore (â·skōl·tâ·tō′rä) *m* listener
ascolto (â·skōl′tō) *m* listening; attention; **prestare** — to listen, pay attention
ascrivere * (â·skrē′vä·rä) *vt* to attribute; to impute; to assign
asettico (â·set′tē·kō) *a* aseptic, antiseptic
asfalto (â·sfäl′tō) *m* asphalt
asfissia (â·sfēs′syä) *f* asphyxia; –**re** (â·sfēs·syâ′rä) *vt* to asphyxiate
Asia (â′zyä) *f* Asia
asiatico (â·zyâ′tē·kō) *m&a* Asiatic
asilo (â·zē′lō) *m* asylum; — **infantile** kindergarten; — **notturno** welfare center
asimmetria (â·sēm·mâ·trē′â) *f* asymmetry
asimmetrico (â·sēm·me′trē·kō) *a* asymmetrical
asino (â′zē·nō) *m* donkey, ass
asma (â′zmâ) *f* asthma
asola (â′zō·lä) *f* buttonhole
asparago (â·spâ′râ·gō) *m* asparagus
aspettare (â·spät·tâ′rä) *vt* to wait for, await
aspettarsi (â·spät·târ′sē) *vr* to expect; to count on
aspettativa (ä·spät·tâ·tē′vâ) *f* expectancy, anticipation; leave of absence
aspetto (â·spät′tō) *m* appearance; **sala d'**— waiting room
aspirante (â·spē·rân′tä) *m* applicant
aspirapolvere (â·spē·râ·pōl′vä·rä) *m* vacuum cleaner
aspirare (â·spē·râ′rä) *vt* to aspire to; to inhale
aspirativo (â·spē·râ·tē′vō) *a* aspirate, to be aspirated
aspirato (â·spē·râ′tō) *a* sought after; aspired to; (*gram*) aspirated; –**re** (â·spē·râ·tō′rä) *m* vacuum cleaner
aspirazione (â·spē·râ·tsyō′nä) *f* desire, aim; inhalation
aspirina (â·spē·rē′nâ) *f* aspirin
aspo (â′spō) *m* reel
asportare (â·spōr·tâ′rä) *vt* to take out, remove
asprezza (â·sprä′tsä) *f* curtness, asperity; acidity, tart taste

aspro (â'sprō) *a* sour; harsh

assaggiare (âs·sâj·jâ'rā) *vt* to taste

assai (âs·sâ'ē) *adv* enough; much

assale (âs·sâ'lā) *m* axle (*auto*)

assalire (âs·sâ·lē'rā) *vt* to attack

assalitore (âs·sâ·lē·tō'rā) *m* aggressor; attacker

assaltare (âs·sâl·tâ'rā) *vt* to assault, assail

assalto (âs·sâl'tō) *m* assault, aggression

assassinare (âs·sâs·sē·nâ'rā) *vt* to murder; to assassinate

assassinio (âs·sâs·sē'nyō) *m* murder

assassino (âs·sâs·sē'nō) *m* murderer

asse (âs'sā) *m* axis; axle; wooden board

assediare (âs·sā·dyâ'rā) *vt* to lay siege to

assediato (âs·sā·dyâ'tō) *a* beset, attacked

assediante (âs·sā·dyân'tā) *m* besieger; — *a* besieging

assedio (âs·se'dyō) *m* siege

assegnamento (âs·sā·nyâ·mān'tō) *m* reliance; assignment

assegnare (âs·sā·nyâ'rā) *vt* to grant, award; to designate

assegno (âs·sā'nyō) *m* check; — **per viaggiatori** traveler's check

assemblea (âs·sâm·blā'â) *f* assembly, gathering

assembramento (âs·sâm·brâ·mān'tō) *m* concourse, assemblage, crowd

assennatezza (âs·sân·nâ·tâ'tsâ) *f* sagacity; common sense, prudence

assennato (âs·sân·nâ'tō) *a* judicious; wise

assentarsi (âs·sān·târ'sē) *vr* to absent oneself; not to be present

assente (âs·sān'tā) *a* absent; missing

assenza (âs·sān'tsâ) *f* absence

asserire (âs·sā·rē'rā) *vt* to assert; to claim

asserzione (âs·sār·tsyō'nā) *f* declaration, affirmation

assestamento (âs·sā·stâ·mān'tō) *m* settlement, adjustment

assestare (âs·sā·stâ'rā) *vt* to put in order, arrange; to balance; — **un colpo** to deliver a blow

assetato (âs·sā·tâ'tō) *a* thirsty

assiale (âs·syâ'lā) *a* axial

assicurare (âs·sē·kū·râ'rā) *vt* to insure; to make certain of

assicurarsi (âs·sē·kū·râr'sē) *vr* to make sure, be certain

assicurata (âs·sē·kū·râ'tâ) *f* insured letter

assicurazione (âs·sē·kū·râ·tsyō'nā) *f* insurance; — **sulla vita** life insurance; — **per la responsabilità civile** liability insurance

assiduamente (âs·sē·dwâ·mān'tā) *adv* perseveringly

assiduo (âs·sē'dwō) *a* diligent

assieme (âs·syä'mā) *adv* together

assillare (âs·sēl·lâ'rā) *vt* to incite, goad; to urge, spur on; — *vi* to be riled up; to be upset

assillo (âs·sēl'lō) *m* urge, impulse; tormenting thought; bête noire, bugbear

assimilare (âs·sē·mē·lâ'rā) *vt* to assimilate, digest; (*fig*) to take in, grasp

assimilarsi (âs·sē·mē·lâr'sē) *vr* to be assimilated; to become like

assimilazione (âs·sē·mē·lâ·tsyō'nā) *f* assimilation

assistente (âs·sē·stān·tā) *m* assistant; — **sociale** social worker

assistenza (âs·sē·stān'tsâ) *f* assistance; — **sociale** social work

assistenziale (âs·sē·stān·tsyâ'lā) *a* charitable; **opere assistenziali** social welfare

assistenziario (âs·sē·stān·tsyâ'ryō) *m* welfare department

assistere * (âs·sē'stâ·rā) *vt* to assist; — *vi* to be present

assistiti (âs·sē·stē'tē) *mpl* welfare cases, relief recipients

asso (âs'sō) *m* ace

associare (âs·sō·châ'rā) *vt* to associate

associarsi (âs·sō·châr'sē) *vi* to associate; to be associated; to join

associazione (âs·sō·châ·tsyō'nā) *f* association; — **a delinquere** crime syndicate

assodare (âs·sō·dâ'rā) *vt* to make solid; to make sure of

assolto (âs·sōl'tō) *a* acquitted

assolutamente (âs·sō·lū·tâ·mān'tā) *adv* absolutely

assoluto (âs·sō·lū'tō) *a&m* absolute; positive

assoluzione (âs·sō·lū·tsyō'nā) *f* absolution; acquittal

assolvere * (âs·sōl'vâ·rā) *vt* to absolve; to perform (*task*)

assomigliare (âs·sō·mē·lyâ'rā) *vi* to resemble

assonante (âs·sō·nân'tā) *a* assonant

assonanza (âs·sō·nân'tsâ) *f* assonance

assorbente (âs·sōr·bân'tā) *a* absorbent

assorbire (âs·sōr·bē'rā) *vt* to absorb; to engulf

assordire (âs·sōr·dē'rā) *vt* to deafen; to stun; — *vi* to become deaf

assortimento (âs·sōr·tē·mān'tō) *adv* assortment, line; variety

assortire (âs·sōr·tē'rā) *vt* to sort; to furnish, provide

â ârm, ā bāby, e bet, ē bē, ō gō, ô gône, ū blūe, b bad, ch child, d dad, f fat, g gay, j jet

assortito (âs·sōr·tē'tō) *a* assorted; various

assumere * (âs·sū'mä·rä) *vt* to assume; to employ; to fulfill

Assunzione (âs·sūn·tsyō'nä) *f* Assumption

assurdità (âs·sūr·dē·tâ') *f* absurdity; nonsense

assurdo (âs·sūr'dō) *a* absurd, ridiculous

asta (â'stä) *f* pole; **vendita all'**— auction sale

astemio (â·ste'myō) *m* teetotaler; — *a* abstemious

astenersi (â·stä·när'sē) *vr* to abstain

astensione (â·stän·syō'nä) *f* abstention

asterisco (â·stä·rē'skō) *m* asterisk

astio (â'styō) *m* grudge

astracan (â·strä'kân) *m* astrakhan; **pelliccia d'**— astrakhan fur

astrale (â·strä'lä) *a* astral

astrarre * (â·strâr'rä) *vt&i* to abstract; to set apart, highlight

astrarsi * (â·strâr'sē) *vr* to wander off

astrattismo (â·strät·tē'zmō) *m* abstract art

astro (â'strō) *m* star; **–fisica** (â·strō·fē'zē·kâ) *f* astrophysics; **–fotometrico** (â·strō·fō·tō·me'trē·kō) *a* astrophotometric; **–logia** (â·strō·lō·jē'â) *f* astrology; **–logo** (â·strō'lō·gō) *m* astrologer; **–metria** (â·strō·mä·trē'â) *f* astrometry; **–nauta** (â·strō·nâ'ū·tâ) *m* astronaut; **–nautica** (â·strō·nâ'ū·tē·kâ) *f* space travel, astronautics; **–nave** (â·strō·nâ'vä) *f* spaceship; **–nomia** (â·strō·nō·mē'â) *f* astronomy; **–nomico** (â·strō·nô'mē·kō) *a* astronomical; **–nomo** (â·strô'nō·mō) *m* astronomer

astuccio (â·stū'chō) *m* case, box

astuto (â·stū'tō) *a* shrewd, clever

astuzia (â·stū'tsyâ) *f* craftiness, asstuteness; ruse

ateismo (â·tä·ē'zmō) *m* atheism

ateo (â'tä·ō) *a* atheist

atlante (â·tlân'tä) *m* atlas

atlantico (â·tlân'tē·kō) *a* Atlantic

atleta (â·tlä'tâ) *m* athlete

atletica (â·tle'tē·kâ) *f* athletics, sports

atmosfera (â·tmō·sfä'râ) *f* atmosphere

atomico (â·tô'mē·kō) *a* atomic; **energia atomica** atomic energy

atomizzare (â·tō·mē·dzä'rä) *vt* to annihilate; to destroy

atomo (â'tō·mō) *m* atom; **scissione dell'**— atomic fission

atrio (â'tryō) *m* hall

atroce (â·trō'chä) *a* frightful, atrocious

atrocità (â·trō·chē·tâ') *f* atrocity

atrofia (â·trō·fē'â) *f* atrophy

attaccamento (ât·tâk·kâ·mân'tō) *m* devotion, love

attaccapanni (ât·tâk·kâ·pân'nē) *m* coat hanger

attaccare (ât·tâk·kâ'râ) *vt* to attack; to attach; to sew; to stick

attacco (ât·tâk'kō) *m* attack

attecchire (ât·täk·kē'râ) *vt* to stick, take hold

atteggiamento (ât·tâj·jâ·mân'tō) *m* attitude

atteggiare (ât·tâj·jâ'râ) *vt* to adapt, make conform; to cause to comply

atteggiarsi (ât·tâj·jâr'sē) *vr* to take an attitude, take a position

attempato (ât·tâm·pâ'tō) *a* grown old, elderly

attendarsi (ât·tân·dâr'sē) *vr* to camp out, pitch camp

attendente (ât·tân·dân'tä) *m* orderly

attendere * (ât·ten'dä·râ) *vt* to wait for, anticipate

attendibile (ât·tân·dē'bē·lä) *a* reliable

attendibilità (ât·tân·dē·bē·lē·tâ') *f* trustworthiness; assurance

attenere * (ât·tä·nâ'râ) *vi* to belong to

attenersi * (ât·tä·nâr'sē) *vr* to conform to; to stick to; — **alle istruzioni** to follow instructions

attentamente (ât·tân·tâ·mân'tä) *adv* carefully

attentare (ât·tân·tâ'râ) *vi* to attempt

attentato (ât·tân·tâ'tō) *m* attempt

attento (ât·tân'tō) *a* careful; **attenti a** beware of; watch out for; **attenti ai treni** railroad crossing

attenuare (ât·tä·nwâ'râ) *vt* to lessen; to diminish

attenzione (ât·tân·tsyō'nä) *f* attention; **—! lavori in corso!** caution! road under repair!; — **agli animali** beware of animals; **fare** — to be careful

atterraggio (ât·târ·râj'jō) *m* (*avi*) landing; — **di fortuna** emergency landing; — **cieco** blind landing; — **strumentale** instrument landing; **carrello di** — landing gear

atterrare (ât·târ·râ'râ) *vi* to land; — *vt* to fell; to knock to the ground

atterrire (ât·târ·rē'râ) *vt* to frighten

attesa (ât·tä'zä) *f* waiting

attestare (ât·tä·stâ'râ) *vt* to testify to; to declare

attestato (ât·tä·stâ'tō) *m* testimonial

attiguo (ât·tē'gwō) *a* adjoining, next

attillato (ât·tēl·lâ'tō) *a* close-fitting; dressed up; coquettish

attimo (ât'tē·mō) *m* instant

---

k kıd, **l** let, **m** met, **n** not, **p** pat, **r** very, **s** sat, **sh** shop, **t** tell, **v** vat, **w** we, **y** yes, **z** zero

attingere * (ât·tēn'jä·rā) *vt* to draw, come by, obtain; to arrive at
attinico (ât·tē'nē·kō) *a* actinic
attirare (ât·tē'râ'rā) *vt* to attract, call; to appeal to
attitudine (ât·tē·tū'dē·nä) *f* aptitude, talent, natural ability
attivamente (ât·tē·vä·mān'tä) *adv* actively
attività (ât·tē·vē·tâ') *f* activity
attivo (ât·tē'vō) *a* active; animated
attizzare (ât·tē·tsâ'rā) *vt* to stir, poke (*fire*); to instigate; to egg on
attizzatoio (ât·tē·tsâ·tô'yō) *m* poker
atto (ât'tō) *m* act; action; deed; — **di nascita** birth certificate; — **di morte** death certificate
attonito *a* (ât·tô'nē·tō) *a* astonished
attorcigliare (ât·tōr·chē·lyâ'rā) *vt* to wind around, twist about
attorcigliarsi (ât·tōr·chē·lyâr'sē) *vr* to twist around, twine about
attore (ât·tō'rā) *m* actor; plaintiff (*law*)
attorno (ât·tōr'nō) *adv* around, all about
attraccare (ât·trâk·kâ'rā) *vt* to dock at, come alongside
attraente (ât·trâ·ān'tä) *a* attractive, charming
attrarre * (ât·trâr'rā) *vt* to attract; to appeal to
attrattiva (ât·trât·tē'vâ) *f* charm, appeal
attrattivo (ât·trât·tē'vō) *a* attractive, appealing
attraversamento (ât·trâ·vär·sâ·mān'tō) *m* crossing; — **pedonale** crosswalk
attraversare (ât·trâ·vär·sâ'rā) *vt* to cross, go across
attraverso (ât·trâ·vär'sō) *adv* across, to the other side of
attrazione (ât·trâ·tsyō'nä) *f* attraction; appeal
attrezzare (ât·trā·tsâ'rā) *vt* to equip, provide
attrezzatura (ât·trā·tsâ·tū'râ) *f* equipment
attrezzi (ât·trā'tsē) *mpl* tools; **borsa degli** — tool kit
attribuire (ât·trē·bwē'rā) *vt* to attribute, lay; to regard, consider
attributo (ât·trē·bū'tō) *m* attribute
attrice (ât·trē'chä) *f* actrice
attrito (ât·trē'tō) *m* attrition
attuale (ât·twâ'lä) *a* actual; contemporary
attualità (ât·twâ·lē·tâ') *f* current events
attualmente (ât·twâl·mān'tä) *adv* now, at the present time
attuare (ât·twâ'rā) *vt* to actuate; to accomplish, execute; to implement

attutire (ât·tū·tē'rā) *vt* to deaden, muffle; to alleviate
attutirsi (ât·tū·tēr'sē) *vr* to be muffled; to be alleviated
audace (âū·dâ'chä) *a* bold, daring
audacia (âū·dâ'châ) *f* daring, boldness, audacity
audiofrequenza (âū·dyō·frä·kwän'tsâ) *f* (*rad*) audiofrequency
auditorio (âū·dē·tô'ryō) *m* auditorium; television studio
audizione (âū·dē·tsyō'nä) *f* hearing, audition
augurare (âū·gū·râ'rā) *vt* to wish; to hope for
augurio (âū·gū'ryō) *m* wish; omen
aula (â'ū·lâ) *f* hall; schoolroom
aumentare (âū·mān·tâ'rā) *vt* to increase; to broaden
aumento (âū·mān'tō) *m* raise, increase; broadening
aureo (â'ū·rä·ō) *a* golden
aureomicina (âū·rä·ō·mē·chē'nâ) *f* aureomycin
auricolare (âū·rē·kō·lâ'rā) *a* auricular
aurora (âū·rō'râ) *f* daybreak, dawn
ausiliario (âū·zē·lyâ'ryō) *m* auxiliary
ausilio (âū·zē'lyō) *m* assistance, aid
auspici (âū·spē'chē) *mpl* auspices
auspicio (âū·spē'chō) *m* omen
austerità (âū·stä·rē·tâ') *f* austerity
austero (âū·stä'rō) *a* sober, austere; plain
austriaco (âū·strē'â·kō) *a&m* Austrian
autarchia (âū·târ·kē'â) *f* self-sufficiency
autenticare (âū·tän·tē·kâ'rā) *vt* to notarize; to authenticate
autentico (âū·ten'tē·kō) *a* authentic, real
autista (âū·tē'stâ) *m* driver
auto (â'ū·tō) *m* car; **–accensione** (âū·tō·â·chän·syō'nä) *f* autoignition; **–adescante** (âū·tō·â·dä·skân'tä) *a* (*mech*) self-starting; **–biografia** (âū·tō·byō·grâ·fē'â) *f* autobiography; **–blinda** (âū·tō·blēn'dâ) *f* armored car; **–bus** (âū·tō·būs') *m* bus; **–campeggio** (âū·tō·kâm·pej'jō) *m* camping in a trailer; **–carro** (âū·tō·kâr'rō) *m* truck; **–cisterna** (âū·tō·chē·stär'nâ) *f* tank truck; **–clave** (âū·tō·klâ'vä) *f* autoclave (*med*) sterilizer; **–corriera** (âū·tō·kōr·ryâ'râ) *f* intercity bus; **–crazia** (âū·tō·krâ·tsē'â) *f* autocracy; **–decisione** (âū·tō·dä·chē·zyō'nä) *f* self-determination; **–dromo** (âū·tō·drō'mō) *m* motordrome; **–fficina** (âū·tō·fē·chē'nâ) *f* auto repair shop; **–genesi** (âū·tō·je'nä·zē) *f* abiogenesis; spontaneous generation; **–geno** (âū·tō'jä·nō) autogenic;

â ârm, **ā** bāby, **e** bet, **ē** bē, **ō** gō, **ô** gône, **ū** blūe, **b** bad, **ch** child, **d** dad, **f** fat, **g** gay, **j** jet

autogenetic; **–giro** (aū·tō·jē′rō) *m* gyroplane; autogyro; **–grafo** (aū·tô′grä·fō) *m* autograph; **–lesione** (aū·tō·lā·zyō′nä) *f* self-inflicted wound; **–lettiga** (aū·tō·lät·tē′gä) *f* ambulance; **–linea** (aū·tō·lē′nä·ä) *f* bus line; **–ma** (aū·tō′mä) *m* robot, automation; **–matico** (aū·tō·mä′tē·kō) *a* automatic; **–mazione** (aū·tō·mä·tsyō′nä) *f* automation; **–mezzo** (aū·tō·mä′dzō) *m* motor vehicle; **–mobile** (aū·tō·mô′bē·lä) *m* automobile; **–mobilismo** (aū·tō·mō·bē·lē′zmō) *m* motoring; **–mobilista** (aū·tō·mō·bē·lē′stä) *m* driver; **–motrice** (aū·tō·mō·trē′chä) *f* self-propelled railroad car; **–nomia** (aū·tō·nō·mē′ä) *f* self-government; *(avi)* cruising range; **–parcheggio** (aū·tō·pâr·kej′jō) *m* parking lot; **–pompa** (aū·tō·pōm′pä) *f* fire engine; **–psia** (aū·tō·psē′ä) *f* autopsy; **–pubblica** (aū·tō·pūb′blē·kä) *f* taxi, taxicab; **–pullman** (aū·tō·pūl′män) *m* luxury bus; **–raduno** (aū·tō·rä·dū′nō) *m* automobile meet; **–re** (aū·tō′rä) *m* author; **–rimessa** (aū·tō·rē·mäs′sä) *f* garage; **–rità** (aū·tō·rē·tâ′) *f* authority; **–rizzare** (aū·tō·rē·dzä′rä) *vt* to authorize; **–rizzazione** (aū·tō·rē·dzä·tsyō′nä) *f* authorization; **–scafo** (aū·tō·skä′fō) *m* motor boat; **–scatto** (aū·tō·skät′tō) *m* *(phot)* automatic release; **–stello** (aū·tō·stäl′lō) *m* motel; **–stop** (aū·tō·stōp′) *m* hitchhiking; **–stoppista** (aū·tō·stōp·pē′stä) *m&f* hitchhiker; **–strada** (aū·tō·strä′dä) *f* superhighway, expressway, turnpike; **–suggestione** (aū·tō·sūj·jä·styō′nä) *f* autosuggestion; **–tipia** (aū·tō·tē·pē′ä) *f* autotype, facsimile; **–trasporto** (aū·tō·trä·spōr′tō) *m* trucking; **–treno** (aū·tō·trä′nō) *m* trailer truck; **–veicolo** (aū·tō·vä·ē′kō·lō) *m* motor vehicle; **–vettura** (aū·tō·vät·tū′rä) *f* passenger car

autunno (aū·tūn′nō) *m* fall, autumn
avallare (ä·väl·lä′rä) *vt* to guarantee
avambraccio (ä·väm·brä′chō) *m* forearm
Avana (ä·vä′nä) *f* Havana; **a–** *m* Havana cigar
avanguardia (ä·vän·gwär′dyä) *f* vanguard
avanguardista (ä·vän·gwär·dē′stä) *m* scout
avanscoperta (ä·vän·skō·pär′tä) *f (mil)* scouting
avanti (ä·vän′tē) *adv* ahead; come in!; **–eri** (ä·vän·tyä′rē) *adv* day before yesterday
avanzamento (ä·vän·tsä·män′tō) *m* progression; promotion

avanzare (ä·vän·tsä′rä) *vt* to advance; — *vi* to be left over
avanzata (ä·vän·tsä′tä) *f* advance
avanzato (ä·vän·tsä′tō) *a* advanced; **cibo** — leftover food; **notte avanzata** late at night; **età avanzata** great age, old age
avanzo (ä·vän′tsō) *m* leftover
avaro (ä·vä′rō) *a* stingy; — *m* miser
avena (ä·vä′nä) *f* oats
avere * (ä·vä′rä) *vt* to have
avi (ä′vē) *mpl* ancestors
aviatore (ä·vyä·tō′rä) *m* aviator
aviatrice (ä·vyä·trē′chä) *f* aviatrix
aviazione (ä·vyä·tsyō′nä) *f* aviation
avidità (ä·vē·dē·tâ′) *f* great eagerness; greed
avido (ä′vē·dō) *a* avid, anxious
aviere (ä·vyä′rä) *m* aviator
aviogetto (ä·vyō·jät′tō) *m* jet plane
aviolinea (ä·vyō·lē′nä·ä) *f* air line
avioraduno (ä·vyō·rä·dū′nō) *m* air meet
aviorimessa (ä·vyō·rē·mäs′sä) *f* hangar
avitaminosi (ä·vē·tä·mē·nō′zē) *f* avitaminosis
avo (ä′vō) *m* grandfather
avorio (ä·vô′ryō) *m* ivory
avvallamento (äv·väl·lä·män′tō) *m* valley; hollow
avvallare (äv·väl·lä′rä) *vt* to hollow out; to level *(land)*
avvallarsi (äv·väl·lär′sē) *vr* to sink; *(fig)* to give up, admit defeat
avvalorare (äv·vä·lō·rä′rä) *vt* to increase the value of; to strengthen
avvalorarsi (äv·vä·lō·rär′sē) *vr* to increase in value; to make oneself valuable; to become stronger
avvantaggiamento (äv·vän·täj·jä·män′tō) *m* advantage, benefit; improvement
avvantaggiare (äv·vän·täj·jä′rä) *vt* to improve; to benefit
avvantaggiarsi (äv·vän·täj·jär′sē) *vr* to get profit from; to take advantage of
avvedutezza (äv·vä·dū·tä′tsä) *f* prudence; keenness; astuteness
avveduto (äv·vä·dū′tō) *a* wary; prudent; shrewd
avvelenare (äv·vä·lä·nä′rä) *vt* to poison
avvelenatore (äv·vä·lä·nä·tō′rä) *m* poisoner
avvenenza (äv·vä·nän′tsä) *f* charm; prettiness
avvenimento (äv·vä·nē·män′tō) *m* event, happening
avvenire * (äv·vä·nē′rä) *vi* to happen; — *m* future
avventare (äv·vän·tä′rä) *vt* to hazard; to rush at; to fling

---

k kid, **l** let, **m** met, **n** not, **p** pat, **r** very, **s** sat, **sh** shop, **t** tell, **v** vat, **w** we, **y** yes, **z** zero

avventarsi (âv·vän·târ'sē) *vr* to pounce; to rush upon

avventato (âv·vän·tâ'tō) *a* rash, heedless

avventore (âv·vän·tō'rā) *m* customer

avventura (âv·vän·tū'râ) *f* adventure; **–re** (âv·vän·tū·râ'rā) *vt* to venture; **–rsi** (âv·vän·tū·râr'sē) *vr* to venture, dare; **–to** (âv·vän·tū·râ'tō) *a* fortunate, lucky

avventuriere (âv·vän·tū·ryā'rā) *m* adventurer

avverbio (âv·ver'byō) *m* adverb

avversario (âv·vär·sâ'ryō) *m* adversary; enemy

avversione (âv·vär·syō'nä) *f* dislike

avversità (âv·vär·sē·tâ') *f* adversity

avvertenza (âv·vär·tän'tsä) *f* notice, warning; foreword, preface

avvertimento (âv·vär·tē·mān'tō) *m* warning

avvertire (âv·vär·tē'rā) *vt* to notify; to warn; to sense, notice

avvezzare (âv·vä·tsâ'rā) *vt* to accustom

avviamento (âv·vyä·mān'tō) *m* introduction to a subject; *(auto)* starter; **scuola d'— commerciale** business school, commercial college

avviare (âv·vyâ'rā) *vt* to start, activate

avviarsi (âv·vyâr'sē) *vr* to set out; to advance, proceed

avvicendamento (âv·vē·chän·dâ·mān'tō) *m* rotation; alternation

avvicinamento (âv·vē·chē·nâ·mān'tō) *m* approach, drawing near

avvicinare (âv·vē·chē·nâ'rā) *vt* to bring closer

avvicinarsi (âv·vē·chē·nâr'sē) *vr* to get closer, draw nearer

avvilimento (âv·vē·lē·mān'tō) *m* dejection; debasement

avvilire (âv·vē·lē'rā) *vt* to mortify; to deject; to debase

avvilirsi (âv·vē·lēr'sē) *vr* to lose heart; to debase oneself

avviluppare (âv·vē·lūp·pâ'rā) *vt* to enfold; to wrap

avvilupparsi (âv·vē·lūp·pâr'sē) *vr* to wrap up, bundle up; to become involved

avvinazzato (âv·vē·nâ·tsâ'tō) *a* tipsy

avvincere * (âv·vēn'chā·rā) *vt* to truss up; to bind; to fascinate

avvincersi * (âv·vēn'chār·sē) *vr* to hug each other; to become obligated, obligate oneself

avvinto (âv·vēn'tō) *a* tied, bound; *(fig)* fascinated

avvisare (âv·vē·zâ'rā) *vt* to inform, advise

avviso (âv·vē'zō) *m* notice, advice

avvitamento (âv·vē·tâ·mān'tō) *m* *(avi)* spin; screwing

avvitare (âv·vē·tâ'rā) *vt* to screw

avvivare (âv·vē·vâ'rā) *vt* to animate; to make vivacious

avvizzire (âv·vē·tsē'rā) *vi* to wither

avvocato (âv·vō·kâ'tō) *m* lawyer

avvocatura (âv·vō·kâ·tū'râ) *f* practice of law

avvolgere * (âv·vôl'jā·rā) *vt* to wrap up; to envolve, mix up

avvolgimento (âv·vōl·jē·mān'tō) *m* winding; hoodwinking

avvoltoio (âv·vōl·tō'yō) *m* vulture

azienda (â·tsyän'dâ) *f* business, firm; **— di soggiorno** municipal tourist bureau; **-le** (â·tsyän·dâ'lā) *a* pertaining to business, business

azionare (â·tsyō·nâ'rā) *vt* to operate; to activate

azione (â·tsyō'nä) *f* action; share

azionista (â·tsyō·nē'stä) *m* stockholder

azoto (â·dzō'tō) *m* nitrogen

azzannare (â·dzân·nâ'rā) *vt* to gore, tusk

azzardare (â·dzär·dâ'rā) *vt* to risk

azzardo (â·dzär'dō) *m* risk; **giuoco d'—** gambling

azzeccare (â·dzäk·kâ'rā) *vt* to guess

azzimo (â'dzē·mō) *a* unleavened

azzuffarsi (â·dzūf·fâr'sē) *vr* to come to blows, fight

azzurro (â·dzūr'rō) *a* blue; **–gnolo** (â·dzūr·rô'nyō·lō) *a* bluish

B

babbeo (bâb·bā'ō) *m* idiot, simpleton

babbo (bâb·bō) *m* dad

babordo (bâ·bôr'dō) *m* *(naut)* port

bacato (bâ·kâ'tō) *a* rotten; worm-eaten

bacca (bâk'kâ) *f* berry

baccalà (bâk·kâ·lâ') *m* codfish, cod

baccano (bâk·kâ'nō) *m* noise, racket

baccello (bâ·chäl'lō) *m* *(bot)* pod

bacchetta (bâk·kät'tâ) *f* *(mus)* baton

baciare (bâ·châ'rā) *vt* to kiss

bacile (bâ·chē'lä) *m* basin

bacinella (bâ·chē·nāl'lâ) *f* shallow bowl; *(phot)* tray

bacio (bâ'chō) *m* kiss

baco (bâ'kō) *m* caterpillar; **— da seta** silkworm

â ârm, ā bāby, e bet, ē bē, ō gō, ô gône, ū blūe, b bad, ch child, d dad, f fat, g gay, j jet

badare (bâ·dâ′rä) *vi* to mind; to be careful

badessa (bâ·dās′sâ) *f* abbess

badia (bâ·dē′â) *f* abbey

badile (bâ·dē′lä) *m* shovel

baffi (bâf′fē) *mpl* mustache

bagagliaio (bâ·gâ·lyâ′yō) *m* baggage car

bagaglio (bâ·gâ′lyô) *m* baggage; **deposito bagagli** checkroom; **ufficio bagagli** baggage room

bagarino (bâ·gâ·rē′nō) *m* scalper on the stock market; ticket scalper

bagattella (bâ·gât·tāl′lâ) *f* bagatelle, trifle

baggianata (bâj·jâ·nâ′tâ) *f* foolishness, nonsense

bagliore (bâ·lyō′rä) *m* gleam, dazzle; beam, ray

bagnante (bâ·nyân′tä) *m&f* bather

bagnare (bâ·nyâ′rä) *vt* to wet; to dampen

bagnarola (bâ·nyâ·rō′lâ) *f* bathtub

bagnarsi (bâ·nyâr′sē) *vr* to get wet; to bathe; **vietato —** no swimming

bagnasciuga (bâ·nyâ·shū′gâ) *f* shoreline

bagnino (bâ·nyē′nō) *m* lifeguard

bagno (bâ′nyō) *m* bath; **costume da —** bathing suit; **stanza da —** bathroom; **vasca da —** bathtub; **–maria** (bâ·nyō·mâ·rē′â) *m* bain-marie

baia (bâ′yâ) *f* bay, harbor

baio (bâ′yō) *m* bay (*horse*)

baionetta (bâ·yō·nāt′tâ) *f* bayonet

baita (bâ′ē·tâ) *f* mountain hut

balaustra (bâ·lâ·ū′strâ), **balaustrata** (bâ·lâū·strâ′tâ) *f* railing

balbettare (bâl·bāt·tâ′rä) *vt* to stammer; to speak haltingly

balbuziente (bâl·bū·tsyän′tä) *m* stammerer

balcone (bâl·kō′nä) *m* balcony

baldacchino (bâl·dâk·kē′nō) *m* canopy

baldoria (bâl·dô′ryâ) *f* revelry, wassail

balena (bâ·lā′nâ) *f* whale

balenare (bâ·lā·nâ′rä) *vi* to flash; to lightning; (*fig*) to cross the mind

balenio (bâ·lā·nē′ō) *m* flashing, dazzling

baleno (bâ·lā′nō) *m* lightning flash; **in un —** in a flash, instantly

balestra (bâ·lā′strâ) *f* leaf spring

balestre (bâ·lā′strä) *fpl* auto springs

balia (bâ·lyâ) *f* wet nurse

balistico (bâ·lē′stē·kō) *a* ballistic

balla (bâl′lâ) *f* bale

ballare (bâl·lâ′rä) *vt&i* to dance

ballatoio (bâl·lâ·tô′yō) *m* balcony, gallery

ballerina (bâl·lā·rē′nâ) *f* dancer

balletto (bâl·lāt′tō) *m* ballet

ballo (bâl′lō) *m* ball, dance

balneare (bâl·nā·â′râ) *a* bathing; **stazione —** bathing resort

balocco (bâ·lōk′kō) *m* toy

balordo (bâ·lōr′dō) *a* silly; mentally slow

balordaggine (bâ·lōr·dâj′jē·nä) *f* silliness; foolish conduct; mental deficiency

balsamo (bâl′sâ·mō) *m* balsam

balsamico (bâl·sâ′mē·kō) *a* balmy; like balsam

baluardo (bâ·lwâr′dō) *m* bulwark

balza (bâl′tsâ) *f* cliff; wide ruffle

balzano (bâl·tsâ′nō) *a* strange, unpredictable; white-footed (*horse*)

balzare (bâl·tsâ′rä) *vi* to jump, leap; **— dal letto** to jump out of bed; **— in piedi** to jump to one's feet

bambagia (bâm·bâ′jâ) *f* cotton batting

bambinaia (bâm·bē·nâ′yâ) *f* nursemaid; **— a ore** baby-sitter

bambinesco (bâm·bē·nā′skō) *a* childish

bambino (bâm·bē′nō) *m* baby; child

bambola (bâm′bō·lâ) *f* doll

banca (bân′kâ) *f* bank; **–rella** (bân·kâ·rāl′lâ) *f* street stall; pushcart; **–rio** (bân·kâ′ryō) *a* banking; **–rotta** (bân·kâ·rōt′tâ) *f* bankruptcy

banchetto (bân·kāt′tō) *m* banquet

banchiere (bân·kyä′rä) *m* banker

banchina (bân·kē′nâ) *f* pier; platform

banco (bân′kō) *m* counter; bench; bank; **–nota** (ban·kō·nō′tâ) *f* banknote, bill

banda (bân′dâ) *f* band; gang

bandiera (bân·dyä′râ) *f* flag

bandito (bân·dē′tō) *m* bandit

banditore (bân·dē·tō′rä) *m* auctioneer

bando (bân′dō) *m* exile; banishment; (*pol*) proclamation

bandoliera (bân·dō·lyä′râ) *f* (*mil*) shoulder belt

bandolo (bân′dō·lō) *m* last of a skein; **— di un problema** clue for solving a problem

bar (bâr) *m* bar; café

bara (bâ′râ) *f* casket; bier

baracca (bâ·râk′kâ) *f* hut; barrack; **piantare — e burattini** to give it up as a bad job, give it up as a lost cause

barare (bâ·râ′rä) *vi* to cheat in a game

baratro (bâ′râ·trō) *m* crevice; abyss; gulf

barattare (bâ·rât·tâ′rä) *vt* (*com*) to trade on; to exchange, barter

baratto (bâ·rât′tō) *m* board of trade; bartering

barattolo (bâ·rât′tō·lō) *m* can; jar; tin

barba (bâr′bâ) *f* beard; **che —!** what a nuisance! **fare la —** to shave

barbabietola (bâr·bâ·bye′tō·lâ) *f* beet

barbagianni (bâr·bâ·jân′nē) *m* owl; (*fig*)

---

k kid, l let, m met, n not, p pat, r very, s sat, sh shop, t tell, v vat, w we, y yes, z zero

simpleton
barbaro (bâr'bâ·rō) *a* barbarous
barberia (bâr·bā·rē'â) *f* barbershop
barbetta (bâr·bāt'tâ) *f* goatee
barbiere (bâr·byā'rā) *m* barber
barbiturico (bâr·bē·tū'rē·kō) *m* barbiturate
barbone (bâr·bō'nā) *m* (*coll*) hobo; long-bearded man
barboso (bâr·bō'zō) *a* boring
barbuto (bâr·bū'tō) *a* bearded
barca (bâr'kā) *f* boat; **–iuolo** (bâr·kâ·ywō'lō) *m* boatman
barcollare (bâr·kōl·lâ'rā) *vi* to reel, stagger
barella (bâ·rāl'lâ) *f* stretcher; **–re** (bâ·rāl·lâ'rā) *vt* to transport by stretcher; **—** *vi* to stagger
baricentro (bâ·rē·chān'trō) *m* center of gravity
barile (bâ·rē'lā) *m* barrel, cask
baritono (bâ·rē'tō·nō) *m* baritone
baro (bâ'rō) *m* cardsharp; cheat
baroccio (bâ·rô'chō) *m* handcart
barometro (bâ·rô'mā·trō) *m* barometer
barone (bâ·rō'nā) *m* baron
baronessa (bâ·rō·nās'sâ) *f* baroness
barra (bâr'râ) *f* bar; (*naut*) tiller
barricata (bâr·rē·kâ'tâ) *f* barricade
barriera (bâr·ryā'râ) *f* barrier; **—** **doganale** customs station
baruffa (bâ·rūf'fâ) *f* fight, brawl
barzelletta (bâr·dzāl·lāt'tâ) *f* joke; witty story
basalto (bâ·zâl'tō) *m* (*min*) basalt
basare (bâ·zâ'rā) *vt* to base
base (bâ'zā) *f* base; basis
basetta (bâ·zāt'tâ) *f* sideburn
basilica (bâ·zē'lē·kâ) *f* basilica
basilico (bâ·zē'lē·kō) *m* (*bot*) basil
bassifondi (bâs·sē·fōn'dē) *mpl* scum of society, underworld
basso (bâs'sō) *m* bass; **—** *a* low; mean
bassorilievo (bâs·sō·rē·lyā'vō) *m* bas-relief
bassotto (bâs·sōt'tō) *m* basset (*dog*)
basta! (bâ'stâ) *interj* that's enough!; **–re** (bâ·stâ'rā) *vt* to suffice, be sufficient
bastardo (bâ·stâr'dō) *m&a* hybrid; bastard
bastimento (bâ·stē·mān'tō) *m* ship, boat
bastione (bâ·styō'nā) *m* rampart; fortification
basto (bâ'stō) *m* packsaddle
bastonare (bâ·stō·nâ'rā) *vt* to beat, club
bastone (bâ·stō'nā) *m* club; cane
bastoni (bâ·stō'nē) *mpl* clubs (*cards*)
batosta (bâ·tō'stâ) *f* blow, calamity

battaglia (bât·tâ'lyâ) *f* battle
battaglione (bât·tâ·lyō'nā) *m* battalion
battelliere (bât·tāl·lyā'rā) *m* boatman
battello (bât·tāl'lō) *m* boat, small craft
battere (bât'tā·rā) *vt&i* to strike; to hit; to beat; to defeat; **— alla porta** to knock at the door; **— bandiera** (*fig*) to fly a flag; **—d'occhi** to blink one's eyes; **— di piedi** to stamp one's feet; **— il nemico** to defeat the enemy; **— il tacco** (*fig*) to abscond; to take to one's heels; **— le mani** to applaud, clap
batteria (bât·tā·rē'â) *f* battery; (*mus*) percussion instruments; **— da cucina** cooking utensils
batteriologia (bât·tā·ryō·lō·jē'â) *f* bacteriology
batteriologo (bât·tā·ryô'lō·gō) *f* bacteriologist
batterista (bât·tā·rē'stâ) *m* drummer
battersi (bât'tār·sē) *vr* to hit oneself; to beat each other up; to fight, battle; **battersela** to flee, take flight
battesimo (bât·te'zē·mō) *m* baptism; **nome di —** Christian name
battezzare (bât·tā·dzâ'rā) *vt* to christen; to baptize
batticuore (bât·tē·kwō'rā) *m* heartbeat
battistero (bât·tē·stā'rō) *m* baptistry
battistrada (bât·tē·strâ'dâ) *m* scout; tread (*tire*)
battuta (bât·tū'tâ) *f* beat; stroke; cue; (*mus*) bar
batuffolo (bâ·tūf'fō·lō) *m* wad
baule (bâ·ū'lā) *m* trunk
bauxite (bâūk·sē'tā) *f* (*min*) bauxite
bava (bâ'vâ) *f* foam (*mouth*); slobber; silk floss; **–glino** (bâ·vâ·lyē'nō) *m* bib
bavaglio (bâ·vâ'lyō) *m* gag
bavero (bâ'vā·rō) *m* coat collar
bazza (bâ'dzâ) *f* prominent chin; (*fig*) good fortune; windfall; trick (*cards*)
bazzicare (bâ·tsē·kâ'rā) *vt* to frequent
bazzotto (bâ·dzōt'tō) *a* soft-boiled
beatificare (bā·â·tē·fē·kâ'rā) *vt* (*eccl*) to beatify
beatificazione (bā·â·tē·fē·kâ·tsyō'nā) *f* beatification
beatitudine (bā·â·tē·tū'dē·nā) *f* exalted happiness, beautitude; bliss; **Sua B–** His Holiness
beato (bā·â'tō) *a* blessed; lucky
beccaccia (bāk·kâ'châ) *f* woodcock
beccaio (bāk·kâ'yō) *m* butcher
beccamorto (bāk·kâ·mōr'tō) *m* gravedigger; (*fig*) unpleasantness
beccare (bāk·kâ'rā) *vt* to peck
beccarsi (bāk·kâr'sē) *vi* to peck each

â arm, ā bāby, e bet, ē bē, ō gō, ô gône, ū blūe, b bad, ch child, d dad, f fat, g gay, j jet other; (*fig*) to get; — **un raffreddore** to catch a cold

beccheggio (bāk·kej'jō) *m* pitching (*ship*)

becchino (bāk·kē'nō) *m* gravedigger

becco (bāk'kō) *m* beak; burner; he-goat; cuckold

befana (bā·fâ'nâ) *f* Epiphany; Italian counterpart of Santa Claus

beffa (bāf'fâ) *f* mockery, derision; **–rdo** (bāf·fâr'dō) *m* derider; **–rdo** *a* mocking; **–re** (bāf·fâ'rā) *vt* to mock, poke fun at; **–rsi** (bāf·fâr'sē) *vr* to hold up to ridicule, make fun of

belare (bā·lâ'rā) *vi* to bleat

belga (bāl'gâ) *m&a* Belgian

belladonna (bāl·lâ·dōn'nâ) *f* (*bot*) belladonna

belletto (bāl·lāt'tō) *m* makeup; cosmetic

bellezza (bāl·lā'tsâ) *f* beauty; **concorso di** — beauty contest; **istituto di** —, **salone di** — beauty parlor, beauty shop

bellico (bel'lē·kō) *a* having to do with war; **materiale** — military supplies; **–so** (bāl·lē·kō'zō) *a* pugnacious; bellicose; quarrelsome

belligerante (bāl·lē·jā·rân'tā) *m&a* belligerent

bellimbusto (bāl·lēm·bū'stō) *m* fop, dandy

bellino (bāl·lē'nō) *a* cute; pretty; darling

bello (bāl'lō) *a* beautiful; handsome; lovely; fine; wonderful

beltà (bāl·tâ') *f* beauty; loveliness; handsomeness

belva (bāl'vâ) *f* wild beast; (*fig*) savage person

belvedere (bāl·vā·dā'rā) *m* observation car; belvedere

benaccetto (bān·nâ·chāt'tō) *a* welcome; well-received

benallevato (bā·nâl·lā·vâ'tō) *a* well-bred

benalzato! (bā·nâl·tsâ'tō) *a* (*coll*) good morning!

benamato (bā·nâ·mâ'tō) *a* beloved

benarrivato (bā·nâr·rē·vâ'tō) *a* welcome, pleasant

benaugurato (bā·nâû·gū·râ'tō) *a* auspicious; well-received

benavventurato (bā·nâv·vān·tū·râ'tō) *a* lucky, fortunate

bencreato (bān·krā·â'tō) *a* well-bred; well-born

benda (bān'dâ) *f* bandage; **–re** (bān·dâ'rā) *vt* to bandage; to swathe

bene (bā'nā) *adv* well; O.K. (*coll*); — *m* good; love; **beni immobili** real estate

benedettino (bā·nā·dāt·tē'nō) *m&a* Benedictine

benedetto (bā·nā·dāt'tō) *a* blessed, holy

benedire * (bā·nā·dē'rā) *vt* to bless

benedizione (bā·nā·dē·tsyō'nâ) *f* benediction

beneducato (bā·nā·dū·kâ'tō) *a* well brought up, well-mannered

benefattore (bā·nā·fât·tō'rā) *m* benefactor

beneficare (bā·nā·fē·kâ'rā) *vt* to benefit

beneficato (bā·nā·fē·kâ'tō) *a* benefited

beneficenza (bā·nā·fē·chān'tsâ) *f* charity

beneficiario (bā·nā·fē·châ'ryō) *m* beneficiary; — *a* beneficial

beneficiata (bā·nā·fē·châ'tâ) *f* benefit performance

beneficio (bā·nā·fē'chō) *m* benefit

benefico (bā·ne'fē·kō) *a* altruistic, beneficent

benemerenza (bā·nā·mā·rān'tsâ) *f* merit, worth; good turn, favor

benemerito (bā·nā·me'rē·tō) *a* deserving

beneplacito (bā·nā·plâ'chē·tō) *m* approbation; consent

benessere (bā·nes'sā·rā) *m* well-being

benestante (bā·nā·stân'tâ) *a* well-to-do

benevolo (bā·ne'vō·lō) *a* kind, gentle, benevolent

benfatto (bān·fât'tō) *a* handsome, well built (*person*)

beniamino (bān·yâ·mē'nō) *m* favorite

benigno (bā·nē'nyō) *a* benign

benino (bā·nē'nō) *adv* pretty well

beninteso (bā·nēn·tâ'zō) *adv* of course, certainly; — *conj* provided; with the understanding that

benissimo (bā·nēs'sē·mō), **benone** (bā·nō'nâ) *adv&a* very well; swell

benpensante (bān·pān·sân'tâ) *a* sensible; judicious; — *m* a judicious, moderate person

benservito (bān·sār·vē'tō) *m* reference; **dare il** — (*fig*) to discharge, fire

bensì (bān·sē') *adv* indeed, of course

bentornato (bān·tōr·nâ'tō) *m* welcome; —! *interj* welcome back!

benvenuto (bān·vā·nū'tō) *m&a* welcome

benvisto (bān·vē'stō) *a* liked; welcome

benvolere * (bān·vō·lā'rā) *vt* to like very much; — *m* attachment, affection, love

benzina (bān·dzē'nâ) *f* gasoline; — **per l'accenditore** lighter fuel

bere * (bā'rā) *vt* to drink; to absorb

berlina (bār·lē'nâ) *f* (*auto*) sedan

berlinetta (bār·lē·nāt'tâ) *f* (*auto*) two-door sedan

bernoccolo (bār·nôk'kō·lō) *m* bump; knock; swelling

berretto (bār·rāt'tō) *m* cap

bersaglio (bār·sâ'lyō) *m* target

bertuccia (bār·tū'châ) *f* monkey; ape

bestemmia (bā·stem′myâ) f blasphemy, swear word; **–re** (bā·stäm·myâ′rā) vt to curse
bestia (be′styâ) f animal; — a stupid; **–le** (bā·styâ′lā) a brutal, beastly; **–lità** (bā·styâ·lē·tâ′) f bestiality; absurdity; **–me** (bā·styâ′mā) m cattle
betatrone (bā·tâ·trō′nā) m betatron
betoniera (bā·tō·nyā′râ) f concrete mixer
bettola (bet′tō·lâ) f saloon; tavern
bevanda (bā·vän′dâ) f beverage
biacca (byâk′kâ) f white lead
biada (byâ′dâ) f fodder
biancastro (byân·kâ′strō) a whitish
biancheria (byân·kā·rē′â) f linen; — **intima** lingerie
bianco (byân′kō) a white; **–segno** (byân·kō·sā′nyō) m blank check; **–spino** (byân·kō·spē′nō) m hawthorn
biasimare (byâ·zē·mâ′rā) vt to reprove; to criticize; to blame
biasimo (byâ′zē·mō) m blame
biasimevole (byâ·zē·me′vō·lā) a blameworthy, reproachable
Bibbia (Bēb′byâ) f Bible
biberone (bē·bâ·rō′nā) m nursing bottle
bibita (bē′bē·tâ) f drink; — **gasata** soft drink
bibliografia (bē·blyō·grâ·fē′â) f bibliography
biblioteca (bē·blyō·tā′kâ) f library; — **di prestito** lending library; — **pubblica** public library; **–rio** (bē·blyō·tā·kâ′ryō) m librarian
bicarbonato (bē·kâr·bō·nâ′tō) m bicarbonate
bicchiere (bēk·kyâ′rā) m drinking glass, tumbler
bicicletta (bē·chē·klät′tâ) f bicycle
bicimotore (bē·chē·mō·tō′rā) m motorbike
bidello (bē·dâl′lō) m janitor, custodian
bidone (bē·dō′nā) m drum; large can; (fig) swindle
bieco (byâ′kō) a angry (look); sinister; evil; squinting
biella (byâl′lâ) f connecting rod
biennale (byân·nâ′lā) a biennial
bietola (bye′tō·lâ) f beet
bifolco (bē·fōl′kō) m peasant; farm laborer
biforcazione (bē·fōr·kâ·tsyō′nâ) f junction, fork
biga (bē′gâ) f chariot
bigamia (bē·gâ·mē′â) f bigamy
bigamo (bē′gâ·mō) a bigamous; — m bigamist

bigio (bē′jō) a gray; dull
bigiotteria (bē·jōt·tā·rē′â) f costume jewelry
bigliettaio (bē·lyät·tâ′yō) m ticket seller; conductor
biglietteria (bē·lyät·tā·rē′â) f ticket office
biglietto (bē·lyät′tō) m ticket; — **da visita** calling card
bigodino (bē·gō·dē′nō) m hair curler
bilancia (bē·lân′châ) f scales; **–re** (bē·lân·châ′rā) vt to counterbalance; **–re** vi to balance; **–rsi** (bē·lân·châr′sē) vi to be in balance; to weigh one alternative against another; to evaluate one's possibilities
bilanciere (bē·lân·chä′rā) m pendulum; scale; beam (scale); balance wheel (watch)
bilancio (bē·lân′chō) m budget; balance sheet
bile (bē′lā) f bile
bilia (bē′lyâ) f billiard ball; table pocket; **–rdo** (bē·lyâr′dō) m billiards
bilico (bē′lē·kō) m balance
bilingue (bē·lēn′gwä) a bilingual
bilione (bē·lyō′nä) m billion
bimbo (bēm′bō) m baby; child
bimetallico (bē·mā·tâl′lē·kō) a bimetallic
bimotore (bē·mō·tō′rā) m twin-engine plane
binario (bē·nâ′ryō) m track, rails
binoccolo (bē·nôk′kō·lō) m binoculars
biochimica (byō·kē′mē·kâ) f biochemistry
biografia (byō·grâ·fē′â) f biography
biologia (byō·lō·jē′â) f biology
biologo (byō′lō·gō) m biologist
biondo (byōn′dō) a blond, fair
biossido (byôs′sē·dō) m dioxide
bipede (bē′pā·dā) m&a biped
biplano (bē·plâ′nō) m biplane
bipolare (bē·pō·lâ′rā) a bipolar
biposto (bē·pō′stō) a two-seat
birbante (bēr·bân′tä) m rascal
biricchino (bē·rēk·kē′nō) m prankster, mischief (person)
birillo (bē·rēl′lō) m bowling pin
birmano (bēr·mâ′nō) m&a Burmese
biro (bē′rō) m ballpoint pen
birra (bēr′râ) f beer
birreria (bēr·râ·rē′â) f beer garden; bar, saloon
bisavolo (bē·zâ′vō·lō) great-grandfather
bisbigliare (bē·zbē·lyâ′rā) vt to whisper
biscazziere (bē·skâ·tsyä′rā) m gambling house operator
biscia (bē′shâ) f water snake, garter snake

â ȧrm, ā bāby, e bet, ē bē, ō gō, ô gône, ū blūe, b bad, ch child, d dad, f fat, g gay, j jet

biscotto (bē·skŏt′tō) *m* cracker; cookie

bisestile (bē·zā·stē′lä) *a* bissextile; **anno — leap year**

bisettrice (bē·zāt·trē′chä) *f* bisector

bisognare (bē·zō·nyâ′rä) *vi* to be needed, be wanting

bisogno (bē·zō′nyō) *m* need, necessity; **–so** (bē·zō·nyō′zō) *a* needy; destitute

bisso (bēs′sō) *m* fine linen

bistecca (bē·stāk′kâ) *f* beefsteak; **— ai ferri** broiled steak

bisticciarsi (bē·stē·châr′sē) *vi* to quarrel, wrangle, argue

bistrattare (bē·strât·tä′rä) *vt* to abuse; to mistreat

bisturì (bē·stū·rē′) *m* surgeon's knife, scalpel

bitume (bē·tū′mä) *m* bitumen

bituminoso (bē·tū·mē·nō′zō) *a* bituminous

bivalente (bē·vâ·lān′tä) *a* bivalent

bivalenza (bē·vâ·län′tsâ) *f* bivalence

bivio (bē′vyō) *m* junction, fork

bizza (bē′dzâ) *f* brief anger; whim; **fare le bizze** to be in a foul mood; **–rria** (bē·dzâr·rē′â) *f* oddness; whimsy; **–rro** (bē·dzâr′rō) *a* bizarre, fantastic; **cavallo –rro** spirited horse

blandire (blân·dē′rä) *vt* to blandish; to fondle

blando (blân′dō) *a* soft; weak

blasone (blä·zō′nä) *m* escutcheon

blatta (blât′tâ) *f* cockroach

bleso (blā′zō) *m* lisper; **—** *a* lisping

blinda (blēn′dâ) *f* armor; **–to** (blēn·dä′tō) *a* armored; **carro –to** armored car

bloccare (blōk·kä′rä) *vt* to block; **— i freni** to jam the brakes

blocco (blōk′kō) *m* block; blockade

blu (blū′) *a* blue

bluffare (blūf·fä′rä) *vt* to bluff, deceive

blusa (blū′zâ) *f* blouse

boa (bō′â) *f* buoy; (*zool*) boa

bobina (bō·bē′nâ) *f* coil; spool

bocca (bōk′kâ) *f* mouth; **in — al lupo!** good luck to you!; **–le** (bōk·kä′lä) *m* pitcher; **–porto** (bōk·kâ·pōr′tō) *m* (*naut*) hatch

bocce (bō′chä) *fpl* game of bowling

boccetta (bō·chāt′tâ) *f* small bottle, flask

bocchino (bōk·kē′nō) *m* cigarette holder

boccia (bō′châ) *f* carafe; flower bud; bowling ball

bocciare (bō·châ′rä) *vt* to flunk

bocciodromo (bō·chō·drō′mō) *m* bowling alley

bocciuolo (bō·chwō′lō) *m* bud

boccone (bōk·kō′nä) *m* bite, mouthful

bocconi (bōk·kō′nē) *adv* flat on one's face; **cadere —** to fall flat on one's face

boia (bō′yâ) *m* executioner

boicottare (bōē·kōt·tä′rä) *vt* to boycott

bolla (bōl′lâ) *f* bubble; blister

bollare (bōl·lä′rä) *vt* to stamp

bollente (bōl·lān′tä) *a* boiling

bolletta (bōl·lāt′tâ) *f* bill; **— del gas** gas bill; **essere in —** to be flat broke (*coll*)

bollettino (bōl·lāt·tē′nō) *m* bulletin; **— meteorologico** weather bulletin

bollire (bōl·lē′rä) *vt* to boil

bollito (bōl·lē′tō) *a* boiled; **—** *m* boiled beef; **–re** (bōl·lē·tō′rä) *m* kettle; boiler

bollitura (bōl·lē·tū′râ) *f* boiling

bollo (bōl′lō) *m* stamp; **carta da — official paper; marca da — revenue stamp**

bomba (bōm′bâ) *f* bomb; **— atomica** atomic bomb; **— all'idrogeno** H-bomb; **–rdamento** (bōm·bâr·dä·mān′tō) *m* bombing; (*phys*) bombardment; **–rdare** (bōm·bâr·dä′rä) *vt* to bomb, shell; to bombard; **–rdiere** (bōm·bâr·dyä′rä) *m* bombardier; bomber (*plane*)

bombetta (bōm·bāt′tâ) *f* derby, bowler (*hat*)

bombola (bôm′bō·lâ) *f* cylinder; glass tank

bonario (bō·nâ′ryō) *a* gentle, meek, kind, good-natured

bonifica (bō·nē′fē·kâ) *f* land reclamation

bonsenso (bōn·sän′sō) *m* common sense

bontà (bōn·tâ′) *f* goodness

borace (bō·râ′chä) *m* borax

borbottare (bōr·bōt·tä′rä) *vt* to mutter

bordata (bōr·dä′tâ) *f* (*naut*) broadside; tack

bordeggiare (bōr·dāj·jä′rä) *vi* to veer; (*naut*) to tack

bordello (bōr·dāl′lō) *m* brothel; racket

borderò (bōr·dä·rō′) *m* list; note

bordo (bōr′dō) *m* edge; board; **a — on board**

borghese (bōr·gä′zä) *a* middle-class, bourgeois; **abito — civilian clothes**

borgo (bōr′gō) *m* suburb; village; **–mastro** (bōr·gō·mä′strō) *m* mayor

boria (bō′ryâ) *f* arrogance, vainglory

borico (bō′rē·kō) *a* boric

borraccia (bōr·râ′châ) *f* canteen, bottle, water bottle

borsa (bōr′sâ) *f* handbag; briefcase; scholarship, fellowship; stock exchange; **— di gomma per acqua calda** hot-water bottle; **— di ghiaccio** ice bag; **–iolo** (bōr·sâ·yō′lō) *m* pickpocket; **–nerista** (bōr·sâ·nä·rē′stâ) *m* black marketeer

borsellino (bōr·säl·lē′nō) *m* purse

borsetta (bōr·sät′tâ) *f* handbag
borsista (bōr·sē′stâ) *m* stockbroker
boscaglia (bō·skå′lyâ) *f* wood, forest
boscaiolo (bō·skå·yō′lō) *m* woodsman
boschetto (bō·skät′tō) *m* grove, thicket
bosco (bō′skō) *m* woods; –so (bō·skō′zō) *a* woody
bossolo (bôs′sō·lō) *m* cartridge case (*gun*)
botanico (bō·tâ′nē·kō) *a* botanical
botta (bōt′tâ) *f* blow; misfortune
botte (bôt′tâ) *f* cask
bottega (bōt·tä′gâ) *f* store, shop
botteghino (bōt·tä·gē′nō) *m* box office
bottiglia (bōt·tē′lyâ) *f* bottle
bottiglieria (bōt·tē·lyä·rē′â) *f* store where bottled wine is sold; wineshop
bottino (bōt·tē′nō) *m* loot
bottone (bōt·tō′nâ) *m* button
bove (bō′vâ) *m* ox
bovini (bō·vē′nē) *mpl* cattle
bovino (bō·vē′nō) *a* bovine
bozza (bō′tsâ) *f* printer's proof, galley; sketch
bozzetto (bō·tsät′tō) *m* draft; sketch
braccialetto (brâ·châ·lät′tō) *m* bracelet
bracciante (brâ·chân′tä) *m* laborer
braccio (brâ′chō) *m* arm
bracciuolo (brâ·chwō′lō) *m* arm (*chair*)
bracco (bräk′kō) *m* setter (*dog*)
brace (brâ′châ) *f* embers
braciere (brâ·chyä′rä) *m* brazier
braciuola (brâ·chwō′lâ) *f* chop, cutlet
brado (brâ′dō) *a* untamed (*animal*)
brama (brâ′mâ) *f* desire; greed; –re (brâ·mâ′rä) *vt* to covet; to wish for
bramoso (brâ·mō′zō) *a* yearning, greedy, desirous
branca (brân′kâ) *f* branch, speciality; claw
branco (brân′kō) *m* flock; crowd; herd
brancolare (brân·kō·lâ′rä) *vi* to grope one's way
branda (brân′dâ) *f* cot
brandire (brân·dē′rä) *vt* to brandish
brando (brân′dô) *m* sword
brano (brâ′nō) *m* passage, selection (*literature*)
bravamente (brâ·vâ·män′tä) *adv* bravely, courageously
bravare (brâ·vâ′rä) *vt&i* to menace; to brag
bravata (brâ·vâ′tâ) *f* bravado
bravo (brâ′vō) *a* skillful; —! *interj* well done! fine!
bravura (brâ·vū′râ) *f* ability, skill; courage
breccia (bre′châ) *f* gap; breach; breccia
brefotrofio (brä·fō·trō′fyō) *m* foundling home

bretelle (brä·täl′lä) *fpl* suspenders
breve (brä′vä) *a* brief; **in —** in brief; **–mente** (brä·vä·män′tä) *adv* briefly
brevettare (brä·vät·tâ′rä) *vt* to patent
brevetto (brä·vät′tō) *m* patent
brezza (brä′tsâ) *f* breeze
bricco (brēk′kō) *m* kettle; pot; **— del caffè** coffee pot; **— del tè** teapot
briccone (brēk·kō′nä) *m* scoundrel
briciola (brē′chō·lâ) *f* crumb
bridgista (brēd′jē′stâ) *m* bridge player
briga (brē′gâ) *f* care, worry; exertion
brigadiere (brē·gâ·dyä′rä) *m* brigadier; police sergeant
brigante (brē·gân′tä) *m* highwayman; brigand
brigantino (brē·gân·tē′nō) *m* (*naut*) brigantine
brigantaggio (brē·gân·tâj′jō) *m* robbery, banditry
brigare (brē·gâ′rä) *vt&i* to intrigue; to strive; to solicit, petition
brigata (brē·gâ′tâ) *f* (*coll*) gang, crew; (*mil*) brigade
briglia (brē′lyâ) *f* bridle
brillamento (brēl·lâ·män′tō) *m* brilliance
brillante (brēl·lân′tä) *a* brilliant; — *m* diamond
brillantina (brēl·lân·tē′nâ) *f* brilliantine
brillare (brēl·lâ′rä) *vi* to shine; to glisten
brillo (brēl′lō) *a* tipsy
brina (brē′nâ) *f* frost
brindare (brēn·dâ′rä) *vi* to drink a toast
brindisi (brēn′dē·zē) *m* toast
brio (brē′ō) *m* vivacity; cheerfulness; spirit; **–sità** (bryō·zē·tâ′) *f* vivacity; **–so** (bryō′zō) *a* lively; cheerful
britannico (brē·tân′nē·kō) *a* British
brivido (brē′vē·dō) *m* chill; thrill
brizzolato (brē·tsō·lâ′tō) *a* grey-haired, grizzled
brocca (brōk′kâ) *f* pitcher
broccolo (brôk′kō·lō) *m* broccoli
brodo (brō′dō) *m* broth
brogliaccio (brō·lyâ′chō) *m* scratch pad
bromatologia (brō·mâ·tō·lō·jē′â) *f* dietetics
bromuro (brō·mū′rō) *m* bromide
bronchi (brōn′kē) *mpl* bronchi (*anat*); **–te** (brōn·kē′tä) *f* bronchitis
broncio (brōn′chō) *m* pouting
brontolare (brōn·tō·lâ′rä) *vi* to grumble; to complain
bronzina (brōn·dzē′nâ) *f* (*mech*) bushing
bronzo (brōn′dzō) *m* bronze
brossura (brōs·sū′râ) *f* paperback book
brucare (brū·kâ′rä) *vt* to browse
bruciare (brū·châ′rä) *vt* to burn

---

bruciato (brü·châ′tō) *a* burnt, burned
bruciatura (brü·châ·tü′râ) *f* scorch, burn; burning
bruciore (brü·chō′rā) *m* burning, smarting; — **di stomaco** heartburn
bruco (brü′kō) *m* caterpillar
brullo (brül′lō) *a* bare, naked; forsaken, abandoned
bruma (brü′mâ) *f* fog
bruna (brü′nâ), **brunetta** (brü·nāt′tâ) *f* brunette
brunire (brü·nē′rā) *vt* to brown; to burnish
brunito (brü·nē′tō) *a* browned; burnished
brunitura (brü·nē·tü′râ) *f* browning; burnishing
bruno (brü′nō) *a* brown; dark
brusco (brü′skō) *a* rude, brusque, sharp; (*fig*) unexpected, sudden; sour, sharp (*taste*); **una brusca decisione** a quick decision; **con le brusche** brusquely
bruscolo (brü′skō·lō) *m* cinder
brutale (brü·tâ′lâ) *a* brutal
brutalità (brü·tâ·lē·tâ′) *f* brutality
bruto (brü′tō) *m&a* brute
bruttezza (brü·tâ′tsâ) *f* ugliness; unpleasantness
brutto (brüt′tō) *a* ugly; unvarnished, plain
buca (bü′kâ) *f* hole, perforation; — **delle lettere** mail drop; **–re** (bü·kâ′rā) *vt* to puncture; to make a hole in
bucatini (bü·kâ·tē′nē) *mpl* medium-size macaroni
bucato (bü·kâ′tō) *m* laundry, wash
buccia (bü′châ) *f* skin, rind
buccina (bü·chē′nâ) *f* bugle
buco (bü′kō) *m* hole
budello (bü·dāl′lō) *m* intestine
budino (bü·dē′nō) *m* pudding
bue (bü′ā) *m* ox; **carne di** — beef
bufalo (bü′fâ·lō) *m* buffalo
bufera (bü·fâ′râ) *f* storm; tempest; hurricane
buffo (büf′fō) *a* comic, funny, droll; —, **–ne** (büf·fō′nâ) *m* buffoon, jester, clown
bugia (bü·jē′â) *f* falsehood; **–rdo** (bü·jâr′dō) *m* liar; **–rdo** *a* false
bugigattolo (bü·jē·gât′tō·lō) *m* cubbyhole
bugno (bü′nyō) *m* beehive
buio (bü′yō) *m* darkness; — *a* dark

bullo (bül′lō) *m* (*coll*) hoodlum
bullone (bül·lō′nâ) *m* bolt
buono (bwō′nō) *a* good; — *m* bond; **Buon Capo d'Anno** Happy New Year; **Buon Natale** Merry Christmas; **Buona Pasqua** Happy Easter; **Buona sera** Good evening; **Buona notte** Good night; **Buon viaggio** Have a pleasant journey
buonaccordo (bwō·nâk·kōr′dō) *m* harmony; (*mus*) harpsichord
buonanima (bwō·nâ′nē·mâ) *a* dearly departed
buonanno! (bwō·nân′nō) *m* Happy New Year!
buonappetito! (bwō·nâp·pā·tē′tō) *m* enjoy your meal!
buonavoglia (bwō·nâ·vô′lyâ) *f* willingness, good will; **di** — willingly
buondì (bwōn·dē′), **buongiorno** (bwōn·jōr′nō) *m* good day, good morning
buongustaio (bwōn·gü·stâ′yō) *m* gourmet, gastronome, epicure
buongusto (bwōn·gü′stō) *m* good taste, discernment
buonsenso (bwōn·sân′sō) *m* common sense, sense
buontempo (bwōn·tâm′pō) *m* good weather
burattino (bü·rât·tē′nō) *m* puppet
burbero (bür′bâ·rō) *a* rough, surly
burla (bür′lâ) *f* practical joke; **–re** (bür·lâ′rā) *vt&i* to poke fun at, to jest; to fool; **–rsi** (bür·lâr′sē) *vr* to ridicule, laugh at
burocrazia (bü·rō·krâ·tsē′â) *f* bureaucracy
burrasca (bür·râ′skâ) *f* storm
burrato (bür·râ′tō) *a* buttered
burro (bür′rō) *m* butter
burrone (bür·rō′nâ) *m* ravine
busecca (bü·zāk′kâ) *f* tripe
bussare (büs·sâ′rā) *vi* to knock
bussola (büs′sō·lâ) *f* compass; inner door
busta (bü′stâ) *f* envelope
bustina (bü·stē′nâ) *f* little envelope; (*mil*) overseas cap
busto (bü′stō) *m* bust; corset
buttare (büt·tâ′rā) *vt* to throw
buttero (büt′tâ·rō) *m* pockmark; cowboy

C

cabala (kâ′bâ·lâ) *f* cabala, occultism; cabal
cabalista (kâ·bâ·lē′stâ) *m* cabalist
cabalistico (kâ·bâ·lē′stē·kō) *a* cabalistic
cabina (kā·bē′nâ) *f* cabin; cockpit;

— **rimorchio** house trailer; — **telefonica** telephone booth
cablografare (kâ·blō·grâ·fâ′rā) *vi* to cable, send a cablegram
cablogramma (kâ·blō·grâm′mâ) *m* cable-

gram
cabotaggio (kâ·bōt·tâj'jō) *m* (*naut*) coastal trade; limited trade
cacao (kâ·kâ'ō) *m* cocoa
caccia (kâ'châ) *f* hunting; — *m* fighter plane; **–gione** (kâ·châ·jō'nā) *f* game, venison; **–re** (kâ·châ'rā) *vt* to chase; to pursue; to banish; **–tore** (kâ·châ·tō'rā) *m* hunter; **–torpediniera** (kâ·châ·tōr·pā·dē·nyā'râ) *f* (*naut*) destroyer; **–vite** (kâ·châ·vē'tā) *m* screwdriver
cacio (kâ'chō) *m* cheese
cacofonia (kâ·kō·fō·nē'â) *f* cacophony
cacografia (kâ·kō·grâ·fē'â) *f* cacography, poor handwriting
cacto (kâk'tō) *m* cactus
cadauno (kâ·dâ·ū'nō) *pron* each one, every
cadavere (kâ·dâ'vā·rā) *m* corpse, body, cadaver
cadenza (kâ·dān'tsâ) *f* cadence, rhythm; **–to** (kâ·dān·tsâ'tō) *a* rhythmical
cadere * (kâ·dā'rā) *vi* to fall
cadetto (kâ·dāt'tō) *m* cadet
caduco (kâ·dū'kō) *a* perishable; transitory
caffè (kâf·fā') *m* coffee; café; coffee-house; — **concerto** café chantant; — **in polvere**, — **solubile** instant coffee
caffeina (kâf·fā·ē'nâ) *f* caffeine
caffelatte (kâf·fā·lât'tā) *m* coffee with milk
cafettiera (kâf·fā·tyā'râ) *f* coffeepot; jalopy
cafone (kâ·fō'nâ) *m* yokel
cagionare (kâ·jō·nâ'rā) *vt* to cause, be the reason for
cagione (kâ·jō'nâ) *f* cause
cagionevole (kâ·jō·nē'vō·lā) *a* sickly, infirm; weak
cagna (kâ'nyâ) *f* bitch; **–ra** (kâ·nyâ'râ) *f* barking; commotion, racket
cagnolino (kâ·nyō·lē'nō) *m* puppy
cala (kâ'lâ) *f* (*naut*) bay; creek
calabrese (kâ·lâ·brâ'zâ) *mf&a* Calabrian
calafatare (kâ·lâ·fâ·tâ'râ) *vt* (*naut*) to caulk
calamaio (kâ·lâ·mâ'yō) *m* inkwell
calamaro (kâ·lâ·mâ'rō) *m* squid
calamita (kâ·lâ·mē'tâ) *f* magnet
calamità (kâ·lâ·mē·tâ') *f* calamity, disaster
calamitoso (kâ·lâ·mē·tō'zō) *a* calamitous, disastrous
calapranzi (kâ·lâ·prân'dzē) *m* dumbwaiter
calare (kâ·lâ'rā) *vt* to lower; — *vi* to pounce upon
calca (kâl'kâ) *f* crowd

calcare (kâl·kâ'rā) *vt* to tread; to press; (*fig*) to lay stress upon
calcare (kâl·kâ'rā) *a* calcarious; — *m* limestone
calcagno (kâl·kâ'nyō) *m* heel
calce (kâl'chā) *f* lime, quicklime; **–struzzo** (kâl·chā·strū'tsō) *m* concrete
calciatore (kâl·châ·tō'rā) *m* soccer player
calcina (kâl·chē'nâ) *f* mortar, lime; **–ccio** (kâl·chē·nâ'chō) *m* fragment of mortar, piece of concrete
calcinare (kâl·chē·nâ'rā) *vt* to render (*fat*); to put lime on
calcio (kâl'chō) *m* kick; soccer; calcium
calcistico (kâl·chē'stē·kō) *a* soccer
calco (kâl'kō) *m* plaster cast
calcolare (kâl·kō·lâ'rā) *vt* to figure, compute
calcolatore (kâl·kō·lâ·tō'rā) *m* computer
calcolatrice (kâl·kō·lâ·trē'chā) *f* calculating machine
calcolo (kâl'kō·lō) *m* calculation; calculus; (*med*) stone
caldaia (kâl·dâ'yâ) *f* boiler
caldarrosta (kâl·dâr·rō'stâ) *f* roast chestnut
calderaio (kâl·dā·râ'yō) *m* coppersmith
caldo (kâl'dō) *m* heat; — *a* warm; hot; sentir — to be warm, feel hot
calendario (kâ·lān·dâ'ryō) *m* calendar
calesse (kâ·lās'sâ) *m* buggy, carriage
calibro (kâ'lē·brō) *m* gauge
calice (kâ'lē·châ) *f* chalice
caligine (kâ·lē'jē·nā) *f* fog; smog; mist; (*fig*) ignorance
callifugo (kâl·lē·fū'gō) *m* corn pad
calligrafia (kâl·lē·grâ·fē'â) *f* penmanship
callo (kâl'lō) *m* corn (*foot*)
calma (kâl'mâ) *f* calm; —! Don't get excited!; **–nte** (kâl·mân'tâ) *m* sedative; **–re** (kâl·mâ'rā) *vt* to calm down
calmiere (kâl·myâ'rā) *m* official price list, schedule of controlled prices
calmo (kâl'mō) *a* calm
calo (kâ'lō) *m* descent; diminishing; reduction
calore (kâ·lō'rā) *m* heat
caloria (kâ·lō·rē'â) *f* calorie
calorifero (kâ·lō·rē'fâ·rō) *m* heater
caloroso (kâ·lō·rō'zō) *a* warm
caloscia (kâ·lō'shâ) *f* overshoe, rubber
calotta (kâ·lōt'tâ) *f* scull cap; (*anat*) skull
calpestare (kâl·pā·stâ'rā) *vt* to trample, step on
calunnia (kâ·lūn'nyâ) *f* calumny; **–re** (kâ·lūn·nyâ'rā) *vt* to defame; **–tore**

â ârm, ā bāby, e bet, ē bē, ō gō, ô gône, ū blūe, b bad, ch child, d dad, f fat, g gay, j jet

(kâ·lūn·nyâ·tō′rā) *m* defamer
Calvario (kâl·vä′ryō) *m* Calvary
Calvinismo (kâl·vē·nē′zmō) *m* Calvinism
calvinista (kâl·vē·nē′stä) *m* Calvinist
calvizie (kâl·vē′tsyā) *f* baldness
calvo (kâl′vō) *a* bald
calza (kâl′tsâ) *f* sock; stocking
calzare (kâl·tsâ′rā) *vt* to wear; — *vi* to fit
calzatoio (kâl·tsâ·tô′yō) *m* shoehorn
calzatura (kâl·tsâ·tū′râ) *f* footwear
calzaturificio (kâl·tsâ·tū·rē·fē′chō) *m* shoe factory
calzino (kâl·tsē′nō) *m* anklet, sock
calzolaio (kâl·tsō·lâ′yō) *m* cobbler, shoe-maker; shoe dealer
calzoni (kâl·tsō′nē) *mpl* trousers
camaleonte (kâ·mâ·lā·ōn′tā) *m* (*zool*) chameleon
camarilla (kâ·mâ·rēl′lâ) *f* gang, clique
cambiabile (kâm·byâ′bē·lā) *a* changeable, fickle
cambiale (kâm·byâ′lā) *f* promissory note
cambiamento (kâm·byâ·män′tō) *m* change; mutation
cambiare (kâm·byâ′rā) *vt* to change
cambiato (kâm·byâ′tō) *a* changed
cambiavalute (kâm·byâ·vâ·lū′tä) *m* foreign money changer
cambio (kâm′byō) *m* change; — **di velocità** gearshift; **corso del** — exchange rate; **leva di** — gear shift
cambusa (kâm·bū′zä) *f* (*naut*) galley; storage room
camera (kâ′mä·râ) *f* bedroom; — **ardente** mortuary chapel; — **d'aria** inner tube; — **di commercio** chamber of commerce
camerata (kâ·mä·râ′tä) *m* comrade
cameriera (kâ·mä·ryā′râ) *f* waitress; maid
cameriere (kâ·mä·ryā′rä) *m* waiter; steward
camerino (kâ·mä·rē′nō) *m* dressing room; small room
camice (kâ′mē·chä) *m* smock
camiceria (kâ·mē·chä·rē′â) *f* shirt shop
camicetta (kâ·mē·chät′tä) *f* blouse
camicia (kâ·mē′châ) *f* shirt; — **da notte** nightgown; **–io** (kâ·mē·châ′yō) *m* shirtmaker
camiciotto (kâ·mē·chōt′tō) *m* overalls; coverall
camiciuola (kâ·mē·chwō′lâ) *f* bodice; vest
caminetto (kâ·mē·nät′tō) *m* fireplace, hearth
camino (kâ·mē′nō) *m* fireplace, chimney
camionale (kâ·myō·nä′lä) *f* highway
camioncino (kâ·myōn·chē′nō) *m* pick-up truck

camione (kâ·myō′nä) *m* motor truck; **–tta** (kâ·myō·nät′tä) *f* jeep
camionista (kâ·myō·nē′stä) *m* truck driver
cammello (kâm·mäl′lō) *m* camel
cammeo (kâm·mä′ō) *m* cameo
camminare (kâm·mē·nâ′rä) *vi* to walk; to stroll
camminata (kâm·mē·nâ′tä) *f* walk
cammino (kâm·mē′nō) *m* walk; way
camomilla (kâ·mō·mēl′lä) *f* camomile
camorra (kâ·mōr′râ) *f* secret criminal gang; racket, extortion
camorrista (kâ·mōr·rē′stä) *m* racketeer, gangster
camoscio (kâ·mô′shō) *m* chamois
campagna (kâm·pâ′nyâ) *f* country, rural areas; campaign
campagnuolo (kâm·pâ·nywō′lō) *m* peasant; — *a* rustic
campale (kâm·pâ′lä) *a* hard (*fig*); **battaglia** — pitched battle; **giornata** — hard day
campana (kâm·pâ′nâ) *f* bell; **–io** (kâm·pâ·nâ′yō), **–ro** (kâm·pâ·nâ′rō) *m* bellman
campanello (kâm·pâ·näl′lō) *m* small bell; doorbell
campanile (kâm·pâ·nē′lä) *m* belfry
campanilismo (kâm·pâ·nē·lē′zmō) *m* sectionalism
campanilista (kâm·pâ·nē·lē′stä) *m* sectionalist
campare (kâm·pâ′rä) *vi* to manage to get along, stick it out; **si campa** we get by
campata (kâm·pâ′tä) *f* (*arch*) bay; bridge span
campeggiare (kâm·pāj·jâ′rä) *vi* to camp
campeggio (kâm·pej′jō) *m* camping
campestre (kâm·pä′strä) *a* rural, country
Campidoglio (kâm·pē·dô′lyō) *m* Capitol
campionario (kâm·pyō·nâ′ryō) *m* sample case
campionato (kâm·pyō·nâ′tō) *m* championship
campione (kâm·pyō·nä) *m* champion; sample
campo (kâm′pō) *m* field; — **di tennis** tennis court; — **sportivo** stadium; **–santo** (kâm·pō·sân′tō) *m* cemetery
camuffare (kâ·mūf·fâ′rä) *vt* to camouflage
camuso (kâ·mū′zō) *a* flat; **dal naso** — snub-nosed
canadese (kâ·nâ·dä′zä) *m&a* Canadian
canaglia (kâ·nâ′lyâ) *f* rabble, mob
canale (kâ·nä′lä) *m* canal; channel
canapa (kâ′nâ·pâ) *f* hemp
canapè (kâ·nâ·pä′) *m* sofa

---

k kid, **l** let, **m** met, **n** not, **p** pat, **r** very, **s** sat, **sh** shop, **t** tell, **v** vat, **w** we, **y** yes, **z** zero

canapo (kâ·nâ·pō) *m* cable, rope; towline
canarino (kâ·nâ·rē′nō) *m* canary
canavaccio (kâ·nâ·vâ′chō) *m* canvass; (*lit*) plot
cancellare (kân·chāl·lâ′rā) *vt* to cancel; to erase
cancellata (kân·chāl·lâ′tâ) *f* fence, railing
cancellatura (kân·chāl·lâ·tū′râ) *f* erasure, taking out
cancellazione (kân·chāl·lâ·tsyō′nâ) *f* cancelling, annulment
cancelleria (kân·chāl·lā·rē′â) *f* chancellery; chancery; **oggetti di —** stationery
cancelliere (kân·chāl·lyā′rā) *m* chancellor; court clerk
cancello (kân·chāl′lō) *m* gate
canceroso (kân·chā·rō′zō) *a* cancerous
cancrena (kân·krā′nâ) *f* gangrene
cancro (kân′krō) *m* cancer
candeggina (kân·dāj·jē′nâ) *f* bleach
candela (kân·dā′lâ) *f* candle; spark plug; **–bro** (kân·dā·lâ′brō) *m* candelabrum
candeliere (kân·dā·lyā′rā) *m* candlestick
candelora (kân·dā·lō′râ) *f* Candlemas
candente (kân·dān′tâ) *a* glowing, incandescent
candidato (kân·dē·dâ′tō) *m* candidate
candidatura (kân·dē·dâ·tū′râ) *f* candidacy
candidezza (kân·dē·dā′tsâ) *f*, **candore** (kân·dō′râ) *m* dazzling whiteness; (*fig*) candor, innocence
candido (kân′dē·dō) *a* white; (*fig*) candid; artless
candito (kân·dē′tō) *a* candied
cane (kâ′nâ) *m* dog; **— da caccia** hunting dog; **— da fermo** setter; **— da guardia** watch dog; **— da presa** retriever; **— da punta** pointer; **— poliziotto** police dog; **— randagio** stray dog
canestra (kâ·nâ′strâ) *f*, **canestro** (kâ·nâ′strō) *m* basket; **palla —** basketball
canfora (kân′fō·râ) *f* camphor
canicola (kâ·nē′kō·lâ) *f* dog days; (*ast*) Dog Star; **–re** (kâ·nē·kō·lâ′râ) *a* sultry (*weather*)
canile (kâ·nē′lâ) *m* doghouse
canino (kâ·nē′nō) *m* puppy, whelp; **— a** canine; **dente —** eyetooth; **tosse canina** whooping cough
canizie (kâ·nē′tsyâ) *f* hoariness, gray hairs
canna (kân′nâ) *f* cane; reed; organ pipe; gun barrel
cannella (kân·nāl′lâ) *f* cinnamon
cannello (kân·nāl′lō) *m* tube; welding torch; blowpipe; **— della pipa** pipe stem; **–ni** (kân·nāl·lō′nē) *mpl* large macaroni

cannibale (kân·nē′bâ·lā) *m* cannibal
cannocchiale (kân·nōk·kyâ′lā) *m* binoculars
cannolo (kân·nō′lō) *m* cylindrical pastry filled with sweet cream
cannonata (kân·nō·nâ′tâ) *f* cannon shot; (*sl*) smash hit
cannone (kân·nō′nā) *m* cannon; clever person; big shot; **–ggiamento** (kân·nō·nāj·jâ·mān′tō) *m* gun shot; bombardment; **–ggiare** (kân·nō·nāj·jâ′rā) *vt* to bombard (*cannon*); to cannonade
cannoniera (kân·nō·nyā′râ) *f* gunboat
cannoniere (kân·nō·nyā′rā) *m* gunner
cannuccia (kân·nū′châ) *f* pipe stem; **— da bere** drink
canoa (kâ·nō′â) *f* canoe
canone (kâ′nō·nā) *m* canon; rent; **— della radio** annual fee paid by owners of radio sets
canonica (kâ·nô′nē·kâ) *f* rectory
canonico (kâ·nô′nē·kō) *m* canon; **— a** canonical; **diritto —** canon law
canonizzare (kâ·nō·nē·dzâ′rā) *vt* to canonize
canoro (kâ·nō′rō) *a* melodious; musical
canottaggio (kâ·nōt·tâj′jō) *m* rowing
canottiera (kâ·nōt·tyā′râ) *f* T-shirt; straw hat
canottiere (kâ·nōt·tyā′rā) *m* rower, oarsman
canotto (kâ·nōt′tō) *m* canoe; shell
cantante (kân·tân′tâ) *m&f* singer
cantare (kân·tâ′rā) *vt&i* to sing
cantero (kân′tā·rō) *m* chamber pot
cantico (kân′tē·kō) *m* canticle
cantiere (kân·tyā′rā) *m* shipyard; construction yard
cantilena (kân·tē·lā′nâ) *f* singsong
cantina (kân·tē′nâ) *f* cellar
cantiniere (kân·tē·nyā′râ) *m* butler; wine steward
canto (kân′tō) *m* song; singing; corner; canto
cantonata (kân·tō·nâ′tâ) *f* corner; angle; (*fig*) stupid mistake
cantone (kân·tō′nâ) *m* corner; Swiss canton; (*arch*) corner stone
cantuccio (kân·tū′chō) *m* nook
canuto (kâ·nū′tō) *a* hoary
canzonare (kân·tsō·nâ′rā) *vt* to jeer, to poke fun at
canzone (kân·tsō′nā) *f* song; **–tta** (kân·tsō·nât′tâ) *f* chanson, ballad; **–ttista** (kân·tsō·nât·tē′stâ) *m&f* balladeer, singer of chansons
canzoniere (kân·tsō·nyā′rā) *m* songbook

â ârm, **ā** bāby, **e** bet, **ē** bē, **ō** gō, **ô** gône, **ū** blūe, **b** bad, **ch** child, **d** dad, **f** fat, **g** gay, **j** jet

caos (kâ′ōs) *m* chaos
capace (kâ·pâ′chä) *a* ample; able
capacità (kâ·pâ·chē·tâ′) *f* capacity
capanna (kâ·pân′nâ) *f* cottage
capannone (kâ·pân·nō′nä) *m* shed
caparbio (kâ·pâr′byō) *a* stubborn
caparra (kâ·pâr′râ) *f* earnest money
capeggiare (kâ·pāj·jâ′rä) *vt* to head, lead
capellini (kâ·pāl·lē′nē) *mpl* very thin spaghetti
capello (kâ·pāl′lō) *m* hair
capelluto (kâ·pāl·lū′tō) *a* hairy; **cuoio — ** scalp
capestro (kâ·pā′strō) *m* halter; gallows
capezzale (kâ·pā·tsâ′lä) *m* bolster; **al — di** at the bedside of
capezzolo (kâ·pe′tsō·lō) *m* teat, nipple
capillare (kâ·pēl·lâ′rä) *a* capillary; **vasi capillari** capillaries
capire (kâ·pē′rä) *vt* to understand, comprehend
capitale (kâ·pē·tâ′lä) *a&m* capital
capitalista (kâ·pē·tâ·lē′stâ) *m* capitalist
capitalizzare (kâ·pē·tâ·lē·dzâ′rä) *vt* to capitalize on
capitano (kâ·pē·tâ′nō) *m* captain
capitare (kâ·pē·tâ′rä) *vi* to arrive; to reach; to happen unexpectedly; to be by chance
capitello (kâ·pē·tāl′lō) *m* (*arch*) capital
capitolare (kâ·pē·tō·lâ′rä) *vi* to surrender, capitulate
capitolazione (kâ·pē·tō·lâ·tsyō′nä) *f* surrender, capitulation
capitolo (kâ·pē′tō·lō) *m* chapter
capitombolo (kâ·pē·tôm′bō·lō) *m* tumble, cropper
capo (kâ′pō) *m* head; **—banda** (kâ·pō·bân′dâ) *m* ringleader; (*mus*) bandmaster; **—caccia** (kâ·pō·kâ′châ) *m* master of the hounds (*hunt*); **—cchia** (kâ·pōk′-kyâ) *f* head (*nail, pin*); **—ccia** (kâ·pô′-châ) *m* family head; foreman; boss; **—chino** (kâ·pō·kē′nō) *adv* with bowed head; **—chino** *a* nodding; **—comico** (kâ·pō·kô′mē·kō) *m* leading comedian; actor-manager; **—cronista** (kâ·pō·krō·nē′stâ) *m* city editor; **—cuoco** (kâ·pō·kwō′kō) *m* chef; **—danno** (kâ·pō·dân′nō) *m* New Year's Day; **—fabbrica** (kâ·pō·fâb′brē·kâ) *m* foreman; **—fila** (kâ·pō·fē′lâ) *m* first in line; **—fitto** (kâ·pō·fēt′tō) *adv* headlong; **—giro** (kâ·pō·jē′rō) *m* dizziness; **—lavoro** (kâ·pō·lâ·vō′rō) *m* masterpiece; **—linea** (kâ·pō·lē′nä·â) *m* transportation terminal; **—lino** (kâ·pō·lē′nō) *m* little head; **—lino** to peep out; **—lista** (kâ·pō·lē′stâ)

m head of list; **—luogo** (kâ·pō·lwō′gō) *m* chief city; **—mastro** (kâ·pō·mâ′strō) *m* contractor; foreman (*building*); **—posto** (kâ·pō·pō′stō) *m* corporal of the guard; **—rale** (kâ·pō·râ′lä) *m* corporal; **—rione** (kâ·pō·ryō′nä) *m* chief; ward alderman; **—sala** (kâ·pō·sâ′lâ) *m* maître d'hôtel; master of ceremonies; **—saldo** (kâ·pō·sâl′dō) *m* stronghold; main point; key position; **—scuola** (kâ·pō·skwō′lâ) *m* founder of a literary movement; **—sezione** (kâ·pō·sä·tsyō′nä) *m* section head, department manager; **—squadra** (kâ·pō·skwâ′drâ) *m* group leader; foreman; **—stazione** (kâ·pō·stâ·tsyō′nä) *m* station master; **—stipite** (kâ·pō·stē′pē·tä) *m* family founder; (*arch*) column shaft; **—tare** (kâ·pō·tâ′rä) *vi* to capsize; **—treno** (kâ·pō·trä′nō) *m* train conductor; **—verso** (kâ·pō·vär′sō) *m* paragraph; **—volgere** * (kâ·pō·vôl′jä·rä) *vt* to turn over; **—volto** (kâ·pō·vōl′tō) *a* upside down; capsized
cappa (kâp′pâ) *f* topcoat; cape; k (*alphabet*)
cappare (kâp·pâ′rä) *vt* to pick out, select
cappella (kâp·pāl′lâ) *f* chapel; **—no** (kâp·pāl·lâ′nō) *m* chaplain
cappellaio (kâp·pāl·lâ′yō) *m* hatter
cappelleria (kâp·pāl·lâ·rē′â) *f* hat store
cappelliera (kâp·pāl·lyä′râ) *f* hat box
cappello (kâp·pāl′lō) *m* hat
capperi (kâp′pâ·rē) *mpl* (*bot*) capers
cappone (kâp·pō′nä) *m* capon
cappotta (kâp·pōt′tâ) *f* convertible car top
cappotto (kâp·pōt′tō) *m* overcoat; slam (*bridge game*)
cappuccino (kâp·pū·chē′nō) *m* Capuchin; demitasse with whipped cream
cappuccio (kâp·pū′chō) *m* hood
capra (kâ′prâ) *f* nanny goat; **—io** (kâ·prâ′-yō) *m* goatherd
capretto (kâ·prät′tō) *m* kid
capriata (kâ·pryâ′tâ) *f* truss; scaffolding
capriccio (kâ·prē′chō) *m* whim
capriola (kâ·pryō′lâ) *f* somersault
capro (kâ′prō) *m* billy goat; **— espiatorio** (*fig*) scapegoat
capsula (kâ′psū·lâ) *f* capsule
carabina (kâ·râ·bē′nâ) *f* carbine
carabiniere (kâ·râ·bē·nyä′rä) *m* national policeman in Italy
caracollare (kâ·râ·cōl·lâ′rä) *vt&i* to wheel about, prance on horseback; to caracole
caraffa (kâ·râf′fâ) *f* carafe, decanter
caramella (kâ·râ·mäl′lâ) *f* caramel candy;

monocle; **–io** (kâ·râ·mäl·lâ'yō) *m* confectioner

carato (kâ·râ'tō) *m* carat

carattere (kâ·rât'tā·rā) *m* character; type

caratterista (kâ·rât·tā·rē'stâ) *m* character actor

caratteristica (kâ·rât·tā·rē'stē·kâ) *f* peculiarity; trait

caratteristico (kâ·rât·tā·rē'stē·kō) *a* characteristic

caratterizzare (kâ·rât·tā·rē·dzâ'rā) *vt* to characterize

carbonaia (kâr·bō·nâ'yâ) *f* coal pit; (*naut*) bunker; coaler (*ship*)

carbonaio (kâr·bō·nâ'yō) *m* coal dealer; charcoal burner; coalman

carbonaro (kâr·bō·nâ'rō) *m* (*pol*) Carbonaro

carbonchio (kâr·bôn'kyō) *m* (*med*) carbuncle

carbone (kâr·bō'nā) *m* charcoal; coal; carbon

carboniera (kâr·bō·nyâ'râ) *f* (*naut*) collier, coal barge

carbonizzare (kâr·bō·nē·dzâ'rā) *vt* to char, carbonize

carborundum (kâr·bō·rūn'dūm) *m* carborundum

carburante (kâr·bū·rân'tā) *m* fuel

carburatore (kâr·bū·râ·tō'rā) *m* carburetor

carburo (kâr·bū'rō) *m* carbide

carcassa (kâr·kâs'sâ) *f* carcass; (*naut*) derelict

carcere (kâr'chā·rā) *m* jail

carceriere (kâr·chā·ryā'rā) *m* jailer

carciofo (kâr·chō'fō) *m* artichoke

carda (kâr'dâ) *f* carding machine; **–re** (kâr·dâ'rā) *vt* to comb out, card (*fibers*)

cardanico (kâr·dâ'nē·kō) *a* universal; **giunto** — (*mech*) universal joint

cardellino (kâr·dāl·lē'nō) *m* goldfinch

cardinale (kâr·dē·nâ'lā) *m&a* cardinal

cardine (kâr'dē·nā) *m* hinge

cardiologo (kâr·dyō'lō·gō) *m* cardiologist, heart specialist

cardo (kâr'dō) *m* thistle

carena (kâ·rā'nâ) *f* (*naut*) keel; **–re** (kâ·rā·nâ'rā) *vt* (*naut*) to careen; (*avi*) to fair

carestia (kâ·rā·stē'â) *f* famine

carezza (kâ·rā'tsâ) *f* caress; **–re** (kâ·rā·tsâ'rā) *vt* to caress; to coax, wheedle

carezzevole (kâ·rā·tse'vō·lā) *a* caressing; cajoling

cariato (kâ·ryâ'tō) *a* carious, decayed

carica (kâ'rē·kâ) *f* office; charge; **–re**

(kâ·rē·kâ'rā) *vt* to load; to wind a clock; to charge with; **–to** (kâ·rē·kâ'tō) *a* enriched; loaded

caricatura (kâ·rē·kâ·tū'râ) *f* caricature

carico (kâ'rē·kō) *m* load, burden

carie (kâ'ryâ) *f* decay; cavity (*tooth*)

carità (kâ·rē·tâ') *f* charity; mercy; **per —!** for goodness' sake!

caritatevole (kâ·rē·tâ·te'vō·lā), **caritativo** ((kâ·rē·tâ·tē'vō) *a* charitable

carlinga (kâr·lēn'gâ) *f* cockpit; fuselage

carminio (kâr·mē'nyō) *m* carmine; (*coll*) lipstick

carnagione (kâr·nâ·jō'nā) *f* complexion

carnale (kâr·nâ'lā) *a* carnal, sensual; corporeal

carne (kâr'nā) *f* meat; flesh; **–fice** (kâr·ne'fē·châ) *m* hangman; **–vale** (kâr·nā·vâ'lā) *m* carnival; pre-Lenten period

carnivoro (kâr·nē'vō·rō) *a* carnivorous

caro (kâ'rō) *a* dear; expensive

carogna (kâ·rō'nyâ) *f* carrion; (*fig*) cad

carosello (kâ·rō·zäl'lō) *m* merry-go-round

carota (kâ·rō'tâ) *f* carrot

carovana (kâ·rō·vâ'nâ) *f* convoy; caravan

carpentiere (kâr·pän·tyā'rā) *m* carpenter

carreggiata (kâr·rāj·jâ'tâ) *f* roadbed; lane

carrettiere (kâr·rāt·tyâ'rā) *m* carter

carriaggio (kâr·ryâj'jō) *m* cartage

carriera (kâr·ryâ'râ) *f* career

carrista (kâr·rē'stâ) *m* driver of military tank

carro (kâr'rō) *m* car, wagon, truck; **— armato** tank; **— funebre** hearse; **–zza** (kâr·rō'tsâ) *f* carriage, coach; **–zzabile** (kâr·rō·tsâ'bē·lā) *a* passable (*road*); **–zzella** (kân·rō·tsâl'lâ) *f* baby carriage; **–zzeria** (kâr·rō·tsâ·rē'â) *f* (*auto*) body; **–zziere** (kâr·rō·tsyâ'râ) *m* (*auto*) body maker; **–zzino** (kâr·rō·tsē'nō) *m* sulky

carrucola (kâr·rū'kō·lâ) *f* pulley

carta (kâr'tâ) *f* paper; card; map; **— carbone, — copiativa** carbon paper; **— da bollo** official paper; **— da parati** wall paper; **— da scrivere** writing paper **— di tornasole** litmus paper; **— d'identità** identity card; **— eliografica** heliographic paper; **— geografica** map; **— gommata** gummed paper; **— igienica** toilet paper; **— incatramata** tarred paper; **— intestata** letterhead; **— milimetrata** squared paper; **— moschicida** fly paper; **— oleata** oilpaper; **— ondulata** corrugated paper; **— pergamena** parchment paper; **— smerigliata** sandpaper; **— sugante** blotting paper; **— velina** tissue paper; **— vetrata** sandpaper; glass paper; **aver —**

bianca to have carte blanche; **–ceo** (kâr·tâ·chä′ō) *a* paper, papery; **–pecora** (kâr·tâ·pe′kō·râ) *f* vellum, parchment; **–pesta** (kâr·tâ·pā′stâ) *f* papiermâché; **carte da giuoco** playing cards

carteggio (kâr·tej′jō) *m* documents; correspondence

cartella (kâr·tāl′lâ) *f* folder; schoolbag; portfolio

cartelliera (kâr·tāl·lyä′râ) *f* filing cabinet

cartello (kâr·tāl′lō) *m* sign; placard; **–ne** (kâr·tāl·lō′nä) *m* poster

cartiera (kâr·tyä′râ) *f* paper mill

çartilagine (kâr·tē·lâ′jē·nä) *f* cartilage

cartoccio (kâr·tō′chō) paper bag; paper cornucopia

cartolaio (kâr·tō·lâ′yō) *m* stationer

cartoleria (kâr·tō·lâ·rē′â) *f* stationery store

cartolina (kâr·tō·lē′nâ) *f* postcard; — **illustrata** picture postcard; — **postale** postal card, postcard

cartoncino (kâr·tōn·chē′nō) *m* thin cardboard

cartone (kâr·tō′nä) *m* cardboard; — **animato** animated cartoon

cartuccia (kâr·tū′châ) *f* cartridge

casa (kâ′zâ) *f* house; home; firm; — **colonica** farmhouse; — **communale** town hall; — **di ricovero** poorhouse; — **di salute** sanitarium; private hospital; — **di tolleranza** brothel; — **editrice** publishing company; — **signorile** mansion; **partita in** — (*sport*) home game

casacca (kâ·zâk′kâ) *f* jacket

casaccio (kâ·zâ′chō) *m* nasty business; **a** — carelessly; at random

casale (kâ·zâ′lâ) *m* hamlet

casalingo (kâ·zâ·lēn′gō) *a* homemade; homey, cozy; **oggetti casalinghi** household appliances

casamento (kâ·zâ·mān′tō) *m* apartment house

casato (kâ·zâ′tō) *m* birth; lineage; family name

cascame (kâ·skâ′mä) *m* waste

cascare (kâ·skâ′râ) *vi* to fall, tumble

cascata (kâ·skâ′tâ) *f* waterfall

cascina (kâ·shē′nâ) *f* dairy farm

casco (kâ′skō) *m* helmet

caseificio (kâ·zāē·fē′chō) *m* cheese factory

caseina (kâ·zâ·ē′nâ) *f* casein

casella (kâ·zāl′lâ) *f* pigeonhole, compartment; — **postale** post-office box

caserma (kâ·zär′mâ) *f* barracks; — **dei pompieri** firehouse

casetta (kâ·zät′tâ) *f* cottage

casimiro (kâ·zē·mē′rō) *m* cashmere

casino (kâ·zē′nō) *m* casino; clubhouse; (*coll*) brothel

caso (kâ′zō) *m* case; chance; — **a parte** particular case; **far** — **a** to pay attention to; **in** — **che** in case; **in** — **contrario** otherwise, on the contrary; **in tal** — under such circumstances; **puta** — **che** supposing that; **a** — **by** chance; **mero** — mere chance; **non fa il** — it doesn't matter

casolare (kâ·zō·lâ′râ) *m* hovel

caspita! (kâ′spē·tâ) *interj* heavens!

cassa (kâs′sâ) *f* box; crate; cash; cashier's counter; — **cranica** cranium; — **da morto** casket; — **dell'orologio** watch case; — **di risparmio** savings bank; — **toracica** chest; **avanzo di** — cash on hand; **gran** — (*mus*) bass drum; **–forte** (kâs·sâ·fōr′tâ) *f* safe; **–panca** (kâs·sâ·pân′kâ) wooden bench, seat

cassata (kâs·sâ′tâ) *f* cream cake tart; — **siciliana** ice cream; sherbert

casseruola (kâs·sä·rūō′lâ) *f* saucepan

cassetta (kâs·sät′tâ) *f* box; — **di sicurezza** safe-deposit box; — **postale** mailbox

cassetto (kâs·sät′tō) *m* drawer; **–ne** (kâs·sät·tō′nä) *m* chest of drawers

cassiere (kâs·syä′râ) *m* cashier; teller

casta (kâ′stâ) *f* caste

castagna (kâ·stâ′nyâ) *f* chestnut

castagno (kâ·stâ′nyō) *m* chestnut tree; chestnut color

castello (kâ·stāl′lō) *m* castle

castigare (kâ·stē·gâ′râ) *vt* to punish

castigo (kâ·stē′gō) *m* punishment

castità (kâ·stē·tâ′) *f* chastity

casto (kâ′stō) *a* chaste

castoro (kâ·stō′rō) *m* beaver

castrare (kâ·strâ′râ) *vt* to emasculate, castrate

castrato (kâ·strâ′tō) *a* castrated; — *m* mutton; wether; eunuch

castroneria (kâ·strō·nä·rē′â) *f* absurdity; gross error

casuale (kâ·zwâ′lâ) *a* by chance; casual

casualità (kâ·zwâ·lē·tâ′) *f* happenstance, chance; fortuitousness

catacomba (kâ·tâ·kōm′bâ) *f* catacomb

catafalco (kâ·tâ·fâl′kō) *f* catafalque; scaffold

catalessi (kâ·tâ·lās′sē) *f* trance, catalepsy

catalogo (kâ·tâ′lō·gō) *m* catalog

catapecchia (kâ·tâ·pek′kyâ) *f* slum dwelling

cataplasma (kâ·tâ·plâ′zmâ) *m* poultice

catarifrangente (kâ·tâ·rē·frân·jän′tâ) *m*

reflector

catarro (kâ·târ'rō) *m* catarrh

catasta (kâ·tâ'stâ) *f* heap, mound

catasto (kâ·tâ'stō) *m* real estate register

catastrofe {kâ·tâ'strō·fā) *f* catastrophe

catechismo (kâ·tâ·kĕ'zmō) *m* catechism

categoria (kâ·tā·gō·rē'â) *f* category

catena (kâ·tā'nâ) *f* chain; **–ccio** (kâ·tā·nā'chō) *m* bolt

cateratta (kâ·tā·rât'tâ) *f* cataract

catinella (kâ·tē·nāl'lâ) *f* washbowl

catino (kâ·tē'nō) *m* basin

catrame (kâ·trâ'mâ) *m* tar

cattedra (kât'tā·drâ) *f* chair, professorship

cattedrale (kât·tā·drâ'lā) *f* cathedral

cattivo (kât·tē'vō) *a* bad; poor, badly done

cattolicismo (kât·tō·lē·chē'zmō), **cattolicesimo** (kât·tō·lē·che'zē·mō) *m* Catholicism

cattolico (kât·tô'lē·kō) *m&a* Catholic

cattura (kât·tū'râ) *f* capture; **mandato di** — warrant for arrest; **–re** (kât·tū·râ'rā) *vt* to seize, capture; **–to** (kât·tū·râ'tō) *a* seized, captured

cauccìù (kâū·chū') *m* rubber

causa (kâ'ū·zâ) *f* cause; lawsuit; **a** — **di** because of; **far** — to sue, bring action; **–re** (kâū·zâ'rā) *vt* to cause; to effect, produce

caustico (kâ'ū·stē·kō) *a* caustic; trenchant

cautela (kâū·tā'lâ) *f* caution

cauterio (kâū·te'ryō) *m* (*med*) cauterizing

cauto (kâ'ū·tō) *a* careful; cautious

cauzione (kâū·tsyō'nâ) *f* guarantee; bail

cava (kâ'vâ) *f* quarry

cavalcare (kâ·vâl·kâ'rā) *vi* to ride horseback; — *vt* to straddle

cavalcavia (kâ·vâl·kâ·vē'â) *m* overpass

cavaliere (kâ·vâ·lyâ'rā) *m* horseman; gentleman; knight; partner, escort

cavalla (kâ·vâl'lâ) *f* mare

cavalleresco (kâ·vâl·lā·rā'skō) *a* chivalrous

cavalleria (kâ·vâl·lā·rē'â) *f* cavalry; chivalry

cavalletta (kâ·vâl·lāt'tâ) *f* grasshopper

cavalletto (kâ·vâl·lāt'tō) *m* easel

cavallo (kâ·vâl'lō) *m* horse; (*chess*) knight

cavallone (kâ·vâl·lō'nâ) *m* large wave, comber

cavare (kâ·vâ'rā) *vt* to take out; to get, obtain

cavatappi (kâ·vâ·tâp'pē), **cavaturaccioli** (kâ·vâ·tū·râ'chō·lē) *m* corkscrew

cavatina (kâ·vâ·tē'nâ) *f* (*mus*) cavatina;

sustained air, lilting melody

caverna (kâ·vâr'nâ) *f* grotto; cave

cavernoso (kâ·vâr·nō'zō) *a* deep; deep-set (*eyes*)

cavezza (kâ·vā'tsâ) *f* halter (*horse*)

cavia (kâ'vyâ) *f* guinea pig

caviale (kâ·vyâ'lā) *m* caviar

caviglia (kâ·vē'lyâ) *f* ankle

cavillare (kâ·vēl·lâ'rā) *vi* to cavil, find fault

cavillo (kâ·vēl'lō) *m* cavil, unnecessary faultfinding; **–so** (kâ·vēl·lō'zō) *a* captious, faultfinding

cavità (kâ·vē·tâ') *f* hole; cavity

cavo (kâ'vō) *m* cable; — *a* hollow

cavolfiore (kâ·vōl·fyō'rā) *m* cauliflower

cavolo (kâ'vō·lō) *m* cabbage

cazzotto (kâ·tsōt'tō) *m* punch, blow

cazzuola (kâ·tswō'lâ) *f* trowel

ce (chā) *pron* to us, us; — *adv* here, there

cece (châ'chā) *m* chick-pea

cecità (chā·chē·tâ') *f* blindness; (*fig*) heedlessness, foolishness

ceco (chā'kō) *m&a* Czech

cedere (che'dā·rā) *vt&i* to yield, give in; to fall down, collapse

cedevole (chā·de'vō·lā) *a* yielding; (*fig*) docil

cedimento (chā·dē·mân'tō) *m* yielding, ceding; settling, subsidence

cedola (che'dō·lâ) *f* coupon

cedro (chā'drō) *m* cedar; citron

ceduo (che'dwō) *a* ready for clearing; **bosco** — cordwood

ceffo (châf'fō) *m* muzzle; snout; **brutto** — rascally face; **–ne** (châf·fō'nâ) *m* slap, smack

celare (chā·lâ'rā) *vt* to hide; to cover up, dissemble

celata (chā·lâ'tâ) *f* ambush; visor (*helmet*)

celebrare (chā·lā·brâ'rā) *vt* to celebrate; to extole

celebrazione (chā·lā·brâ·tsyō'nâ) *f* celebration

celebre (che'lā·brā) *a* famous; illustrious

celebrità (chā·lā·brē·tâ') *m* celebrity

celere (che'lā·rā) *a* quick; — *f* police riot squad

celerimetro (chā·lā·rē'mâ·trō) *m* speedometer

celeste (chā·lā'stâ) *a* celestial; blue

celia (che'lyâ) *f* joke, lark

celibe (che'lē·bā) *a* single; — *m* bachelor

cella (châl'lâ) *f* cell; cellar; cave

cellofane (châl·lō·fâ'nâ) *f* cellophane

cellula (chel'lū·lâ) *f* cell; **–re** (châl·lū·lâ'rā) *a* cellular; **–re** *m* jail; patrol wagon

---

â ârm, **ā** bāby, **e** bet, **ē** bē, **ō** gō, **ô** gône, **ū** blūe, **b** bad, **ch** child, **d** dad, **f** fat, **g** gay, **j** jet

cell 73 cesu

celluloide (chăl·lū·lô′ē·dā) *f* celluloid

cembalo (chem′bâ·lō) *m* harpsichord; tambourine

cemento (chā·mān′tō) *m* cement, concrete; — **armato** reinforced concrete

cena (chā′nâ) *f* supper; –**re** (chā·nâ′rā) *vi* to have supper

cenciaiuolo (chān·châ·ywō′lō) *m* rag picker

cencio (chen′chō) *m* rag; –**so** (chān·chō′zō) *a* ragged

cenere (che′nā·rā) *f* ash

cenno (chān′nō) *m* hint; indication

censimento (chān·sē·mān′tō) *m* census

censo (chān′sō) *m* census; –**re** (chān·sō′rā) *m* critic, censor

censura (chān·sū′râ) *f* censorship; –**re** (chān·sū·râ′rā) *vt* to censure; to blame; to criticize

centauro (chān·tâ′ū·rō) *m* centaur

centellinare (chān·tāl·lē·nâ′rā) *vt* to sip on, drink in sips

centenario (chān·tā·nâ′ryō) *m&a* centennial

centesimo (chān·te′zē·mō) *m* centime; hundredth part

centigrado (chān·tē′grâ·dō) *m* centigrade

centimetro (chān·tē′mā·trō) *m* centimeter

centina (chen′tē·nâ) *f* truing; (*arch*) fantail; (*avi*) rib

centinaio (chān·tē·nâ′yō) *m* hundred; **a centinaia** by hundreds

cento (chān′tō) *a* hundred; –**mila** (chān·tō·mē′lâ) *a* hundred thousand

centrale (chān·trâ′lā) *a* central; — *f* central office; — **elettrica** power plant

centralinista (chān·trâ·lē·nē′stâ) *m&f* switchboard operator

centralino (chān·trâ·lē′nō) *m* telephone switchboard

centrare (chān·trâ′rā) *vt* to center; to hit dead center

centrifugo (chān·trē′fū·gō) *a* centrifugal

centripeto (chān·trē′pā·tō) *a* centripetal

centro (chān′trō) *m* center; centerpiece; downtown

centuplicare (chān·tū·plē·kâ′rā) to multiply by one hundred

centuria (chān·tū′ryâ) *f* century

ceppo (chāp′pō) *m* log

cera (chā′râ) *f* wax; mien; –**lacca** (chā·râ·lâk′kâ) *f* sealing wax

ceramica (chā·râ′mē·kâ) *f* ceramics; pottery

cerata (chā·râ′tâ) *f* oilskin, oilcloth

cerbiatto (chār·byât′tō) *m* young deer, fawn

cerbottana (chār·bōt·tâ′nâ) peashooter; blowpipe

cerca (chār′kâ) *f* search; –**re** (chār·kâ′rā) *vt&i* to seek; to try, make an attempt

cerchio (cher′kyō) *m* circle; loop; –**ne** (chār·kyō′nā) *m* rim (*wheel*)

cereale (chā·rā·â′lā) *m* cereal

cerebrale (chā·rā·brâ′lā) *a* cerebral; — *m* intellectual

cereo (che′rā·ô) *a* waxy; wan, pale

cerfoglio (chār·fô′lyō) *m* chervil

cerimonia (chā·rē·mô′nyâ) *f* ceremony; –**le** (chā·rē·mō·nyâ′lā) *m* protocol

cerimoniere (chā·rē·mō·nyâ′rā) *m* master of ceremonies

cerimonioso (chā·rē·mō·nyō′zō) *a* formal; ceremonious

cerino (chā·rē′nō) *m* wax match

cerniera (chār·nyâ′râ) *f* hinge; — **lampo** zipper

cero (chā′rō) *m* taper, candle

cerotto (chā·rōt′tō) *m* plaster

certamente (chār·tâ·mān′tā) *adv* surely, of course

certezza (chār·tā′tsâ) *f* certainty

certificato (chār·tē·fē·kâ′tō) *m* certificate; — **medico** health certificate

certo (chār′tō) *a* certain, sure; — *adv* certainly

certosa (chār·tō′zâ) *f* charterhouse

certosino (chār·tō·zē′nō) *m* Carthusian monk

ceruleo (chā·rū′lâ·ō) *a* cerulean

cerume (chā·rū′mā) *m* cerumen, wax in the ear

cerusico (chā·rū′zē·kō) *m* surgeon

cervello (chār·vāl′lō) *m* brain

cervo (chār′vō) *m* deer; — **volante** kite

cerziorare (chār·tsyō·râ′rā) *vt* to assure; to ascertain

cesellare (chā·zāl·lâ′rā) *vt* to chisel; to engrave

cesellatore (chā·zāl·lâ·tō′rā) *m* carver; engraver

cesello (chā·zāl′lō) *m* chisel

cesoia (chā·zô′yâ) *f* scissors

cespite (che′spē·tā) *m* source of one's income

cespuglio (chā·spū′lyō) *m* thicket; shrubbery

cessare (chās·sâ′rā) *vt* to cease, stop

cesso (chās′sō) *m* toilet

cesta (chā′stâ) *f* basket

cestinare (chā·stē·nâ′rā) *vt* to reject; to discard

cestino (chā·stē′nō) *m* small basket; — **da viaggio** lunch basket

cesura (chā·zū′râ) *f* caesura

k kid, **l** let, **m** met, **n** not, **p** pat, **r** very, **s** sat, **sh** shop, **t** tell, **v** vat, **w** we, **y** yes, **z** zero

ceto (chä'tō) *m* class; order; rank
cetra (chä'trä) *f* cithern; harp; lyre
cetriuolo (chä·trywō'lō) *m* cucumber; (*fig*) fool
che (kā) *conj* than, that; — *pron* what, which, who
chè (kā) *conj* because
chellerina (kāl·lä·rē'nä) *f* waitress
cheppia (kep'pyä) *f* shad
cherubino (kā·rū·bē'nō) *m* cherub
chi (kē) *pron* who, that, whom
chiacchiera (kyäk'kyä·rä) *f* gossip; **–re** (kyä·kyä·rä'rä) *vi* to chat; **–ta** (kyä·kyä·rä'tä) *f* tittle-tattle, prattle
chiacchierone (kyä·kyä·rō'nä) *m* prattler; gossip; windbag
chiamare (kyä·mä'rä) *vt* to call; to call upon
chiamata (kyä·mä'tä) *f* call
chiara (kyä'rä) *f* egg white
chiaramente (kyä·rä·män'tä) *adv* clearly, obviously
chiarezza (kyä·rä'tsä) *f* plainness; clearness
chiarificazione (kyä·rē·fē·kä·tsyō'nä) *f* clarification
chiarimento (kyä·rē·män'tō) *m* explanation
chiarire (kyä·rē'rä) *vt* to clear up; to clarify
chiaro (kyä'rō) *a* clear; light; **–re** (kyä·rō'rä) *m* glimmer; **–scuro** (kyä·rō·skū'rō) *m* interplay of light and shadow; chiaroscuro; **–veggente** (kyä·rō·väj·jän'tä) *a* clearsighted; **–veggente** *m&f* clairvoyant
chiasso (kyâs'sō) *m* noise; **–so** (kyâs·sō'zō) *a* noisy; loud
chiatta (kyät'tä) *f* barge
chiave (kyä'vä) *f* key; — **inglese** monkey wrench
chiazza (kyâ'tsä) *f* stain, spot; scar; mottling; **–to** (kyâ·tsä'tō) *a* mottled, speckled, spotted
chiavica (kyâ'vē·kä) *f* sewer
chiavistello (kyâ·vē·stäl'lō) *m* door bolt
chicca (kēk'kä) *f* candy
chicchera (kēk'kä·rä) *f* cup
chicchessia (kēk·käs·sē'ä) *pron* anybody, whoever
chicco (kēk'kō) *m* bean; grain
chiedere * (kye'dä·rä) *vt* to ask; to implore
chiesa (kyä'zä) *f* church
chiesto (kyä'stō) *a* asked, requested, sought
chifel (kē'fäl) *m* crescent-shaped roll
chiglia (kē'lyä) *f* keel

chilo (kē'lō) *m* kilogram; **–ciclo** (kē·lō·chē'klō) *m* kilocycle; **–gramma** (kē·lō·grâm'mä) *m* kilogram; **–metro** (kē·lō'·mä·trō) *m* kilometer; **–watt** (kē·lō·vât') *m* kilowatt
chimera (kē·mä'rä) *f* chimera
chimica (kē'mē·kä) *f* chemistry
chimico (kē'mē·kō) *m* chemist; — *a* chemical
chimo (kē'mō) *m* chyme
chimono (kē·mō'nō) *m* kimono
china (kē'nä) *f* slope; **–re** (kē·nä'rä) *vt* to bow; to bend; **–rsi** (kē·nâr'sē) *vi* to bow down; to bend oneself; to stoop; (*fig*) to submit oneself
chincaglie (kēn·kä'lyä) *fpl* trinkets
chineseria (kē·nä·zä·rē'ä) *f* chinoiserie; red tape
chinino (kē·nē'nō) *m* quinine
chino (kē'nō) *a* inclined, bent
chioccia (kyō'chä) *f* brooding hen; **–re** (kyō·chä'rä) *vi* to cluck, to cackle
chiocciola (kyō'chō·lä) *f* snail
chiodo (kyō'dō) *m* nail; — **di garofano** clove
chioma (kyō'mä) *f* hair, head of hair; (*animal*) mane
chiosa (kyō'zä) *f* annotation; comment
chiosco (kyō'skō) *m* newsstand; stand
chiostro (kyō'strō) *m* cloister
chiotto (kyōt'tō) *a* still, silent
chiromante (kē·rō·mân'tä) *m&f* palmist
chiromanzia (kē·rō·mân·tsē'ä) *f* chiromancy, palmistry
chirurgia (kē·rūr·jē'ä) *f* surgery
chirurgico (kē·rūr'jē·kō) *a* surgical
chirurgo (kē·rūr'gō) *m* surgeon
chissà (kēs·sâ') *interj* heaven only knows, who knows
chitarra (kē·târ'rä) *f* guitar
chiudere * (kyū'dä·rä) *vt* to close; — **a chiave** to lòck
chiunque (kyūn'kwä) *pron* anybody, whoever
chiusa (kyū'zä) *f* lock (*canal*); dam
chiuso (kyū'zō) *a* closed, shut
chiusura (kyū·zū'rä) *f* closing; — **lampo** zipper
ci (chē) *pron* us, to us; — *adv* here, there
ciabatta (chä·bät'tä) *f* old shoe; slipper; **–re** (chä·bät·tä'rä) *vi* to move with a shuffle
ciabattino (chä·bät·tē'nō) *m* cobbler
ciabattone (châ·bät·tō'nä) *m* fumbler
cialda (châl'dä) *f* waffle
cialtrone (châl·trō'nä) *m* scoundrel
ciambella (châm·bäl'lä) *f* ring-shaped cake; doughnut

â ârm, **ā** bāby, **e** bet, **ē** bē, **ō** gō, **ô** gône, **ū** blūe, **b** bad, **ch** child, **d** dad, **f** fat, **g** gay, **j** jet

ciamberlano (châm·bär·lâ′nō) *m* chamberlain

cianfrusaglia (chân·frū·zâ′lyâ) *f* trifle

cianidrico (châ·nē′drē·kō) *a* hydrocyanic, prussic

cianina (châ·nē′nâ) *f* cyanin

cianogeno (châ·nō′jä·nō) *m* cyanogen

cianotico (châ·nō′tē·kō) *a* cyanic; blue in color

cianotipia (châ·nō·tē·pē′â) *f* blueprint

cianuro (châ·nū′rō) *m* cyanide

ciao (châ′ō) *interj* hello, good-bye

ciaramella (châ·râ·mäl′lâ) *f* bagpipe

ciarlare (châr·lâ′rā) *vi* to chatter

ciarlatano (châr·lâ·tâ′nō) *m* charlatan

ciascuno (châ·skū′nō) *a* each, every; — *pron* each one, every one

cibare (chē·bâ′rā) *vt* to nourish; to feed

cibaria (chē·bâ′ryâ) *f* foodstuff

cibo (chē′bō) *m* food

cicala (chē·kâ′lâ) *f* cicada

cicalino (chē·kâ·lē′nō) *m* electric buzzer

cicatrice (chē·kâ·trē′chā) *f* scar

cicca (chēk′kâ) *f* butt; stump

ciccia (chē′châ) *f* flesh, meat; *(coll)* fat

ciccioli (chē′chō·lē) *mpl* fatty scraps of meat

ciccione (chē·chō′nā) *m* fleshy individual; fat person

cicerone (chē·chā·rō′nā) *m* cicerone, guide

cicisbeo (chē·chē·zbā′ō) *m* gallant; gigolo; ladies' man

ciclamino (chē·klâ·mē′nō) *m* cyclamen

ciclismo (chē·klē′zmō) *m* cycling

ciclista (chē·klē′stâ) *m&f* cyclist

ciclo (chē′klō) *m* cycle

ciclomotore (chē·klō·mō·tō′rā) *m* motorbike

ciclone (chē·klō′nā) *m* tornado, cyclone

ciclope (chē·klō′pā) *m* cyclops

ciclopico (chē·klō′pē·kō) *a* enormous, cyclopean

ciclopista (chē·klō·pē′stâ) *f* bicycle path

ciclostile (chē·klō·stē′lā) *m* mimeograph

ciclotrone (chē·klō·trō′nā) *m (phys)* cyclotron

cicogna (chē·kō′nyâ) *f* stork

cicoria (chē·kô′ryâ) *f* chicory

ciecamente (chā·kâ·mān′tâ) *adv* blindly; *(fig)* inconsiderately

cieco (chā′kō) *a* blind

cielo (châ′lō) *m* sky, heaven

cifra (chē′frâ) *f* figure, amount; **–rio** (chē·frâ′ryō) *m* code

ciglio (chē′lyō) *m* eyelash; edge

cigno (chē′nyō) *m* swan

cignone (chē·nyō′nā) *m* chignon

cigolare (chē·gō·lâ′rā) *vi* to squeak

cilecca (chē·lāk′kâ) *f* misfiring; jamming; **far — to** misfire

cilicio (chē·lē′chō) *m* sackcloth

ciliegia (chē·lye′jâ) *f* cherry

cilindrata (chē·lēn·drâ′tâ) *f (auto)* displacement of a cylinder

cilindro (chē·lēn′drō) *m* cylinder

cima (chē′mâ) *f* peak; summit

cimare (chē·mâ′rā) *vt* to shear *(fabric);* to lop off, trim

cimasa (chē·mâ′zâ) *f (arch)* cyma, curved molding

cimelio (chē·me′lyō) *m* ancient remains

cimentare (chē·mān·tâ′rā) *vt* to attempt, try; to risk

cimentarsi (chē·mān·târ′sē) *vi* to incur a risk; to test one's ability

cimice (chē′mē·châ) *f* bedbug

cimiero (chē·myâ′rō) *m* crest *(helmet)*

ciminiera (chē·mē·nyā′râ) *f* smokestack

cimitero (chē·mē·tâ′rō) *m* cemetery

cimosa (chē·mō′zâ) *f* selvage *(fabric)*

cimurro (chē·mūr′rō) *m* glanders *(horse);* distemper *(dog)*

Cina (chē′nâ) *f* China

cinabro (chē·nâ′brō) *m* cinnabar

cincin (chēn·chēn′) *interj* Here's to you!; To your health!

cine (chē′nā) *m* movie, movies, movie theater; **–asta** (chē·nâ·â′stâ) *m* film star; movie fan; **–città** (chē·nâ·chēt·tâ′) *f* movie studio; **–ma** (chē′nâ·mâ) *m* movie, movies; **–mateatro** (chē·nâ·mâ·tâ·â′trō) *m* movie theater; **–matografaio** (chē·nâ·mâ·tō·grâ·fâ′yō) *m* motion picture man; **–matografare** (chē·nâ·mâ·tō·grâ·fâ′râ) *vt* to film; **–matografia** (chē·nâ·mâ·tō·grâ·fē′â) *f* filmmaking; **–matografo** (chē·nâ·mâ·tô′grâ·fō) *m* motion picture theater; **–presa** (chē·nâ·prâ′zâ) *f* movie shot; **–scopio** (chē·nâ·skô′pyō) *m* TV picture tube, kinescope; **–scrittore** (chē·nâ·skrēt·tō′rā) *m* motion picture writer; **–teca** (chē·nâ·tâ′kâ) *f* film library

cinese (chē·nâ′zā) *a&m* Chinese

cinetica (chē·ne′tē·kâ) *f* kinetics

cingere * (chēn′jä·râ) *vt* to gird; to encompass

cinghia (chēn′gyâ) *f* belt

cinghiale (chēn·gyâ′lâ) *m* wild boar

cinguettare (chēn·gwât·tâ′rā) *vi* to chirp; to chatter; to twitter

cinguettio (chēn·gwât·tē′ō) *m* chirping

cinico (chē′nē·kō) *a* cynical

ciniglia (chē·nē′lyâ) *f* chenille

cinodromo (che·nō′drō·mō) *m* dog track

k kid, **l** let, **m** met, **n** not, **p** pat, **r** very, **s** sat, **sh** shop, **t** tell, **v** vat, **w** we, **y** yes, **z** zero

cinofilo (chē·nô′fē·lō) *m* dog lover

cinquanta (chēn·kwän′tâ) *a* fifty

cinquantenario (chēn·kwän·tā·nâ′ryō) *m* fiftieth anniversary

cinquantesimo (chēn·kwän·te′zē·mō) *a* fiftieth

cinquantina (chēn·kwän·tē′nâ) *f* about fifty

cinque (chēn′kwā) *a* five

cinquecento (chēn·kwä·chān′tō) *a* five hundred; **il C–** the sixteenth century

cinquennio (chēn·kwen′nyō) *m* five-year period

cinta (chēn′tâ) *f* fence, enclosure

cintura (chēn·tū′râ) *f* belt; girdle

cinturino (chēn·tū·rē′nō) *m* belt; **— per orologio** wristwatch band

ciò (chō′) *pron* this, that, it

ciocca (chōk′kâ) *f* cluster; lock

cioccolata (chōk·kō·lâ′tâ) *f* chocolate

cioccolatino (chōk·kō·lâ·tē′nō) *m* chocolate candy

ciocia (chō′châ) *f* sandal worn in the area of Rome; **–ro** (chō·châ′rō) *m* Roman peasant

cioè (chō·ā′) *conj* that is, namely

ciondolare (chōn·dō·lâ′rā) *vt* to dangle, swing

ciondolo (chôn′dō·lō) *m* locket

ciotola (chô′tō·lâ) *f* cup, bowl

ciottolo (chôt′tō·lō) *m* cobblestone; pebble

cipiglio (chē·pē′lyō) *m* scowl, frown

cipolla (chē·pōl′lâ) *f* onion

cipresso (chē·prās′sō) *m* cypress

cipria (chē′pryâ) *f* face powder

circa (chēr′kâ) *adv* about; almost; circa

circo (chēr′kō) *m* circus

circolare (chēr·kō·la′rā) *a&f* circular; **—** *f* circular letter; **—** *vi* to circulate, move around

circolazione (chēr·kō·lâ·tsyō′nâ) *f* circulation; traffic; **— vietata** do not enter; **documento di —** registration card

circolo (chēr′kō·lō) *m* circle; club

circoncidere * (chēr·kōn·chē′dä·rā) *vt* to circumcise

circoncisione (chēr·kōn·chē·zyō′nā) *f* circumcision

circondare (chēr·kōn·dâ′rā) *vt* to surround

circondario (chēr·kōn·dâ′ryō) *m* provincial district

circonferenza (chēr·kōn·fā·rān′tsâ) *f* circumference

circonflesso (chēr·kōn·flās′sō) *a* circumflex

circonlocuzione (chēr·kōn·lō·cū·tsyō′nä)

f circumlocution; evasion

circonvallazione (chēr·kōn·vâl·lâ·tsyō′ nä) *f* belt highway; belt bus line; bypass

circonvenire * (chēr·kōn·vä·nē′rä) *vt* to circumvent; to baffle

circoscritto (chēr·kō·skrēt′tō) *a* circumscribed, limited

circostanza (chēr·kō·stân′tsâ) *f* circumstance

circuire (chēr·kwē′rā) *vt* to surround, enclose; *(fig)* to entrap; to go around, bypass

circuitare (chēr·kwē·tâ′rā) *vi (avi)* to circle before landing

circuito (chēr·kwē′tō) *m* circuit; **corto —** short circuit

cirro (chēr′rō) *m* lock *(hair)*; *(bot)* cirrus, tendril; cirrus cloud; *(med)* scirrhus

cispa (chē′spâ) *f* bleariness; discharge of rheum from the eye

cisposo (chē·spō′zō) *a* bleary-eyed

cisterna (chē·stār′nâ) *f* cistern, tank; **acqua di —** rain water; **nave —** tanker *(naut)*

cistifellea (chē·stē·fel′lā·â) *f* gall bladder

citare (chē·tâ′rā) *vt* to cite, mention; to sue

citazione (chē·tâ·tsyō′nā) *f* subpoena; summons; quotation, citation

citofono (chē·tô′fō·nō) *m* intercom

citrato (chē·trâ′tō) *m* citrate; **— di magnesio** magnesium; **— di magnesia** effervescent antacid

citroniera (chē·trō·nyä′râ) *f* hothouse

citrullo (chē·trūl′lō) *m* nincompoop

città (chēt·tâ′) *f* city; **— giardino** garden city

cittadina (chēt·tâ·dē′nâ) *f* town; **–nza** (chēt·tâ·dē·nân′tsâ) *f* citizenship

cittadino (chēt·tâ·dē′nō) *m* citizen; **—** *a* civic

ciuco (chū′kō) *m* jackass

ciuffo (chūf′fō) *m* lock, tuft

ciurma (chūr′mâ) *f* ship's crew; mob; hands; **–glia** (chūr·mâ′lyâ) *f* rabble, mob; **–re** (chūr·mâ′rā) *vt* to swindle, trick, cheat; to charm

civetta (chē·vāt′tâ) *f* screechowl; *(fig)* flirt, coquette; **–re** (chē·vāt·tâ′rā) *vi* to flirt

civetteria (chē·vāt·tā·rē′â) *f* coquetry

civettuolo (chē·vāt·twô′lō) *a* saucy, coquettish

civile (chē·vē′lā) *a&m* civilian; **—** *a* civilized; civil

civilista (chē·vē·lē′stâ) *m* civil lawyer

civilizzare (chē·vē·lē·dzâ′rā) *vt* to civilize

civilizzato (chē·vē·lē·dzâ′tō) *a* civilized;

–re (chē·vē·lē·dzâ·tō′rā) *a* civilizing
civilmente (chē·vēl·mân′tā) *adv* politely, civilly
civiltà (chē·vēl·tâ′) *f* civilization; politeness
civismo (chē·vē′zmō) *m* civic pride, civic duty
clackson (klâk′sōn) *m* (*auto*) horn
clamoroso (klâ·mō·rō′zō) *a* sensational
clandestino (klân·dā·stē′nō) *a* underhand, clandestine
clarinetto (klâ·rē·nāt′tō) *m* clarinet
classe (klâs′sā) *f* class
classicista (klâs·sē·chē′stâ) *m* classical scholar
classico (klâs′sē·kō) *a* classic; classical
classifica (klâs·sē′fē·kâ) *f* rating, grading; **–re** (klâs·sē·fē·kâ′rā) *vt* to classify; **–tore** (klâs·sē·fē·kâ·tō′rā) *m* folder; **–zione** (klâs·sē·fē·kâ·tsyō′nā) *f* classification
classismo (klâs·sē′zmō) *m* class consciousness
clausola (klâ′ū·zō·lâ) *f* clause
claustrale (klâū·strâ′lā) *a* cloistered, solitary
claustro (klâ′ū·strō) *m* cloister
clausura (klâū·zū′râ) *f* seclusion, cloistering
clava (klâ′vâ) *f* club
clavicembalo (klâ·vē·chem′bâ·lō) *m* harpsichord
clavicola (klâ·vē′kō·lâ) *f* collarbone
clemente (klā·mân′tā) *a* mild, merciful, clement
clemenza (klā·mân′tsâ) *f* clemency
cleptomania (klāp·tō·mâ·nē′â) *f* kleptomania
clericale (klā·rē·kâ′lā) *a* clerical, pertaining to the clergy
clero (klā′rō) *m* clergy
clessidra (klās·sē′drâ) *f* water clock, clepsydra
cliente (kyān′tā) *m&f* customer, client; **–la** (klyān·tā′lâ) *f* patronage; clients, customers
clima (klē′mâ) *m* climate; **–tico** (klē·mâ′tē·kō) *a* climatic; **stazione climatica** health resort, spa
clinica (klē′nē·kâ) *f* clinic, hospital
clinico (klē′nē·kō) *a* clinical
clistere (klē·stā′râ) *m* enema
cloaca (klō·â′kâ) *f* drain; sewer
clorato (klō·râ′tō) *m* chlorate
cloro (klō′rō) *m* chlorine; **–filla** (klō·rō·fēl′lâ) *f* chlorophyl; **–formio** (klō·rō·fôr′myŏ) *m* chloroform
cloruro (klō·rū′rō) *m* chloride

coabitare (kō·â·bē·tâ′rā) *vi* to cohabit
coadiuvare (kō·â·dyū·vâ′rā) *vt* to aid, assist, help; **—** *vi* to cooperate, to collaborate
coagulare (kō·â·gū·lâ′rā) *vt* to coagulate
coagulo (kō·â′gū·lō) *m* coagulum, clot (*blood*); curd (*milk*)
coalizione (kō·â·lē·tsyō′nā) *f* coalition
coalizzarsi (kō·â·lē·dzâr′sē) *vi* to form a coalition
coartare (kō·âr·tâ′rā) *vt* to force, coerce
coassiale (kō·âs·syâ′lā) *a* coaxial
cobalto (kō·bâl′tō) *m* cobalt
cocainomane (kō·kâē·nô′mâ·nā) *m* cocaine addict
coccarda (kōk·kâr′dâ) *f* cockade, rosette
cocchiere (kōk·kyā′râ) *m* coachman
cocchio (kōk′kyō) *m* carriage, coach; chariot
cocciniglia (kō·chē·nē′lyâ) *f* cochineal, red dye
coccio (kô′chō) *m* pottery fragment
cocciuto (kō·chū′tō) *a* stubborn
cocco (kōk′kō) *m* coconut; (*fig*) darling
coccodrillo (kōk·kō·drēl′lō) *m* crocodile
cocomero (kō·kô′mā·rō) *m* watermelon
coda (kō′dâ) *f* tail; **far —** to stand in line
codardia (kō·dâr·dē′â) *f* cowardice
codardo (kō·dâr′dō) *a* cowardly; **— *m*** coward
codesto (kō·dā′stō) *a&pron* that
codice (kô′dē·châ) *m* code; **— della strada** traffic regulations; **— penale** criminal law code
coefficiente (kō·âf·fē·chân′tā) *m* coefficient
coerente (kō·ā·rân′tā) *a* consistent
coesione (kō·ā·zyō′nā) *f* cohesion
coesistenza (kō·ā·zē·stân′tsâ) *f* coexistence
coesore (kō·ā·zō′rā) *m* (*elec*) coherer
coetaneo (kō·ā·tâ′nā·ō) *a* coetaneous, contemporary, coeval
cofano (kô′fâ·nō) *m* (*auto*) hood; coffer
coffa (kōf′fâ) *f* (*naut*) crow's nest, top, foretop
cogliere * (kô′lyā·rā) *vt* to pick; to take hold of
cognata (kō·nyâ′tâ) *f* sister-in-law
cognato (kō·nyâ′tō) *m* brother-in-law
cognizione (kō·nyē·tsyō′nā) *f* knowledge; recognition
cognome (kō·nyō′mā) *m* family name, last name
coibente (kōē·bân′tā) *m* (*phys*) non-conducting, insulating material
coincidenza (kōēn·chē·dân′tsâ) *f* coincidence; connection, transfer

---

k kid, **l** let, **m** met, **n** not, **p** pat, **r** very, **s** sat, **sh** shop, **t** tell, **v** vat, **w** we, **y** yes, **z** zero

coincidere (kōēn·chē'dā·rā) *vi* to coincide

coinvolgere * (kōēn·vôl'jā·rā) *vt* to involve; to implicate

coito (kô'ē·tō) *m* coition

col (kōl) *prep* with the

colà (kō·lâ') *adv* there

colabrodo (kō·lâ·brō'dō) *m* strainer

colare (kō·lâ'rā) *vt* to strain

colata (kō·lâ'tâ) *f* metal casting

colazione (kō·lâ·tsyō'nā) *f* lunch; breakfast; **prima — ** breakfast

colei (kō·lā'ē) *pron* she

colera (kō·lā'râ) *f* cholera

colesterina (kō·lā·stā·rē'nâ) *f* cholesterol

colibrì (kō·lē·brē') *m* hummingbird

colica (kô'lē·kâ) *f* colic

colla (kōl'lâ) *f* glue

collaborare (kōl·lâ·bō·râ'rā) *vi* to contribute; to collaborate

collaborazione (kōl·lâ·bō·râ·tsyō'nā) *f* collaboration

collaborazionista (kōl·lâ·bō·râ·tsyō·nē'stâ) *m* collaborationist

collana (kōl·lâ'nâ) *f* necklace; collection; series of related books

collare (kōl·lâ'rā) *m* collar

collasso (kōl·lâs'sō) *m* collapse; **— cardiaco** heart attack

collaterale (kōl·lâ·tā·râ'lā) *a&m* collateral

collaudare (kōl·lâū·dâ'rā) *vt* to test

collaudo (kōl·lâ'ū·dō) *m* testing

colle (kôl'lā) *m* hill

collega (kōl·lā'gâ) *m* colleague; **—mento** (kōl·lā·gâ·mān'tō) *m* liaison; relationship

collegiale (kōl·lā·jâ'lā) *m* student at a boarding school

collegio (kōl·le'jō) *m* academy; boarding school

collera (kôl'lā·râ) *f* rage; anger

colletta (kōl·lāt'tâ) *f* collection

collettivismo (kōl·lāt·tē·vē'zmō) *m* collectivism

collettività (kōl·lāt·tē·vē·tâ') *f* community

collettivo (kōl·lāt·tē'vō) *a* collective

colletto (kōl·lāt'tō) *m* collar; **— floscio** soft collar

collettore (kōl·lāt·tō'rā) *m* (*mech*) exhaust manifold; (*elect*) commutator; main sewer; **— a** collecting

collezione (kōl·lā·tsyō'nā) *f* collection

collezionista (kōl·lā·tsyō·nē'stâ) *m* collector

collimare (kōl·lē·mâ'rā) *vi* to agree, be in accord, jibe; to coincide

collina (kōl·lē'nâ) *f* hill

collisione (kōl·lē·zyō'nā) *f* collision

collo (kōl'lō) *m* neck; parcel

collocamento (kōl·lō·kâ·mān'tō) *m* employment; situation

collocare (kōl·lō·kâ'rā) *vt* to place; to situate

collocarsi (kōl·lō·kâr'sē) *vr* to place oneself, range, take a position

collocazione (kōl·lō·kâ·tsyō'nā) *f* placement, placing

collodio (kōl·lô'dyō) *m* (*chem*) collodion

colloidale (kōl·lōē·dâ'lā) *a* (*chem*) colloidal

colloquio (kōl·lô'kwēō) *m* interview, talk

collusione (kōl·lū·zyō'nā) *f* collusion

colluttazione (kōl·lūt·tâ·tsyō'nā) *f* brawl, fight

colmare (kōl·mâ'rā) *vt* to fill

colmo (kōl'mō) *a* full; **— ** *m* height, upper reaches

colombaia (kō·lōm·bâ'yâ) *f* dove cote

Colombia (kō·lōm'byâ) *f* Colombia; **–no** (kō·lōm'byâ'nō) *m&a* Colombian

colombo (kō·lōm'bō) *m* pigeon

colonia (kō·lô'nyâ) *f* colony; **— estiva** summer camp; **–li** (kō·lō·nyâ'lē) *mpl* spices

colonizzare (kō·lō·nē·dzâ'rā) *vt* to colonize

colonna (kō·lōn'nâ) *f* column; **–to** (kō·lōn·nâ'tō) *m* colonnade

colonnello (kō·lōn·nāl'lō) *m* colonel

colono (kō·lō'nō) *m* tenant farmer; sharecropper

colorante (kō·lō·rân'tā) *a* coloring

colore (kō·lō'rā) *m* color; paint

colorire (kō·lō·rē'râ) *vt* to color, paint

colorito (kō·lō·rē'tō) *m* complexion, coloring

colossale (kō·lōs·sâ'lā) *a* colossal

Colosseo (kō·lōs·sā'ō) *m* Colosseum

colosso (kō·lōs'sō) *m* giant, colossus

colpa (kōl'pâ) *f* fault

colpevole (kōl·pe'vō·lā) *a* guilty

colpire (kōl·pē'râ) *vt* to hit

colpo (kōl'pō) *m* blow

coltellata (kōl·tāl·lâ'tâ) *f* knife wound

coltelleria (kōl·tāl·lā·rē'â) *f* cutlery

coltello (kōl·tāl'lō) *m* knife

coltivare (kōl·tē·vâ'rā) *vt* to cultivate

coltivatore (kōl·tē·vâ·tō'rā) *m* cultivator; farmer; grower

coltivazione (kōl·tē·vâ·tsyō'nā) *f* cultivation

colto (kōl'tō) *a* educated, cultivated

coltre (kōl'trā) *f* blanket

coltrone (kōl·trō'nâ) *m* quilt

coltura (kōl·tū'râ), **cultura** (kūl·tū'râ) *f*

culture

colubro (kō·lū′brō) *m* snake, serpent

colui (kō·lū′ē) *pron* he, the one who, he who

comandamento (kō·mân·dâ·mān′tō) *m* commandment

comandante (kō·mân·dân′tā) *m* commander; captain of a ship

comandare (kō·mân·dâ′rā) *vt* to command

comando (kō·mân′dō) *m* command

comare (kō·mâ′rā) *f* crony; housewife; godmother

combaciare (kōm·bâ·châ′rā) *vi* to tally, jibe, agree

combattente (kōm·bât·tān′tā) *m* combatant; **ex —** veteran

combattere (kōm·bât′tā·rā) *vt&i* to fight; to struggle against

combattimento (kōm·bât·tē·mān′tō) *m* fight, struggle

combinare (kōm·bē·nâ′rā) *vt* to arrange; to bring together

combinazione (kōm·bē·nâ·tsyō′nā) *m* combination; coincidence; **per —** by chance

combriccola (kōm·brēk′kō·lâ) *f* clique, ring, gang

combustibile (kōm·bū·stē′bē·lā) *m* fuel

come (kō′mā) *prep&conj* as, like; **— adv** how; **— mai?** how in the world?

cometa (kō·mā′tâ) *f* comet

comico (kō′mē·kō) *a* funny; **— m** comedian

comignolo (kō·mē′nyō·lō) *m* chimney top; gable

cominciare (kō·mēn·châ′rā) *vt&i* to begin

comitato (kō·mē·tâ′tō) *m* committee

comitiva (kō·mē·tē′vâ) *f* party; **viaggio in —** conducted tour

comizio (kō·mē′tsyō) *m* meeting, rally

comma (kōm′mâ) *m* paragraph; *(gram)* clause between commas; comma

commedia (kōm·me′dyâ) *f* comedy

commediografo (kōm·mā·dyō′grâ·fō) *m* playwright

commemorare (kōm·mā·mō·râ′rā) *vt* to commemorate, celebrate

commenda (kōm·mān′dâ) *f* allowance; order of knighthood; **–tore** (kōm·mān·dâ·tō′rā) *m* commander; knight commander

commensale (kōm·mān·sâ′lā) *m* table companion

commentare (kōm·mān·tâ′rā) *vt* to comment on; to footnote

commentatore (kōm·mān·tâ·tō′rā) *m* commentator

commento (kōm·mān′tō) *m* comment;

annotation

commerciale (kōm·mār·châ′lā) *a* commercial

commercialista (kōm·mār·châ·lē′stâ) *m* business lawyer

commerciante (kōm·mār·chân′tā) *m* merchant, businessman

commerciare (kōm·mār·châ′rā) *vi* to be in business; **— vt** to deal in

commercio (kōm·mer′chō) *m* commerce; **— librario** book business

commessa (kōm·mās′sâ) *f* order; salesgirl

commesso (kōm·mās′sō) *m* clerk; **— viaggiatore** traveling salesman

commestibile (kōm·mā·stē′bē·lā) *m* foodstuff

commettere (kōm·met′tā·rā) *vt* to perpetrate; to commit

commiato (kōm·myâ′tō) *m* leave; departure

commilitone (kōm·mē·lē·tō′nā) *m* fellow soldier; companion; comrade

commissariato (kōm·mēs·sâ·ryâ′tō) *m* commissariat; **— di polizia** police station

commissario (kōm·mēs·sâ′ryō) *m* commissioner; **— di bordo** purser; **— di pubblica sicurezza** local chief of police

commissionare (kōm·mēs·syō·nâ′rā) *vt* to order, place an order for

commissionario (kōm·mēs·syō·nâ′ryō) *m* sales agent; commission salesman

commissione (kōm·mēs·syō′nā) *f* commission; committee; order

commisto (kōm·mē′stō) *a* mixed

commosso (kōm·mōs′sō) *a* moved; saddened

commovente (kōm·mō·vān′tā) *a* moving, touching; saddening

commozione (kōm·mō·tsyō′nā) *f* emotion; commotion

commuovere * (kōm·mwō′vā·rā) *vt* to move; to cause to feel sympathy for

commutare (kōm·mū·tâ′rā) *vt* to commute, set aside

commutatore (kōm·mū·tâ·tō′rā) *m* (*elec*) switch

comò (kō·mō′) *m* chest of drawers

comodino (kō·mō·dē′nō) *m* bedside table

comodità (kō·mō·dē·tâ′) *f* comfort; convenience

comodo (kō′mō·dō) *a* comfortable; convenient

compagnia (kōm·pâ·nyē′â) *f* company

compagno (kōm·pâ′nyō) *m* companion

companatico (kōm·pâ·nâ′tē·kō) *m* food eaten with bread

comparare (kōm·pâ·râ′rā) *vt* to compare

---

k kid, **l** let, **m** met, **n** not, **p** pat, **r** very, **s** sat, **sh** shop, **t** tell, **v** vat, **w** we, **y** yes, **z** zero

comparativo (kōm·på·rå·tē'vō) *a&m*
comparative
comparazione (kōm·på·rå·tsyō'nā) *f*
comparison, likening
compare (kōm·på'rā) *m* godfather; buddy
(*coll*)
comparire * (kōm·på·rē'rā) *vi* to appear;
to make one's appearance
comparsa (kôm·pär'så) *f* (*theat*) extra
compartimento (kōm·pär·tē·mān'tō) *m*
compartment
compartire (kōm·pär·tē'rā) *vt* to share,
divide, partition
compassione (kōm·pâs·syō'nā) *f* sympathy; **–vole** (kōm·pâs·syō·ne'vō·lä) *a*
pitiful, piteous, woeful; sympathizing,
pitying
compasso (kōm·pâs'sō) *m* compass
compatibile (kōm·på·tē'bē·lä) *a* consistent; compatible
compatibilità (kōm·på·tē·bē·lē·tâ') *f*
consistency; compatibility
compatire (kōm·på·tē'rā) *vt* to pity
compatto (kōm·pât'tō) *a* compact
compendiare (kōm·pän·dyâ'rā) *vt* to resume, summarize, make a compendium
of
compendio (kōm·pen'dyō) *m* summary
compenetrare (kōm·pä·nä·trâ'rā) *vt* to
penetrate, pervade
compenetrarsi (kōm·pä·nä·trâr'sē) *vr* to
become diffused; to penetrate thoroughly
compensare (kōm·pän·sâ'rā) *vt* to reward
compensato (kōm·pän·sâ'tō) *a* compen-
sated; — *m* plywood
compenso (kōm·pän'sō) *m* reward
competente (kōm·pä·tän'tā) *a* qualified,
competent; — *m* expert
competenza (kōm·pä·tän'tsâ) *f* competence
competizione (kōm·pä·tē·tsyō'nā) *f* contest, competition
compiacente (kōm·pyâ·chän'tā) *a* indulgent, complaisant, obliging
compiangere * (kōm·pyân'jä·rā) *vt* to
pity
compilare (kōm·pē·lâ'rā) *vt* to compile
compire * (kōm·pē'rā), **compiere** (kōm'-
pyä·rā) *vt* to complete, do, carry out
compito (kôm'pē·tō) *m* school work; duty;
task
compiuto (kōm·pyū'tō) *a* completed, finished, accomplished
compleanno (kōm·plä·ân'nō) *m* birthday
complessivamente (kōm·pläs·sē·vâ·mān'-
tä) *adv* inclusively, on the whole, totally
complessivo (kōm·pläs·sē'vō) *a* inclusive,

encompassing; complete
complesso (kōm·pläs'sō) *a&m* complex;
— *m* organization, outfit
completare (kōm·plā·tâ'rā) *vt* to complete, fulfill
completo (kōm·plā'tō) *a* complete; full;
— *m* man's suit of clothing
complicare (kōm·plē·kâ'rā) *vt* to complicate; to confuse
complicato (kōm·plē·kâ'tō) *a* complicated
complicazione (kōm·plē·kâ·tsyō'nā) *f*
complication
complice (kôm'plē·chā) *m&f* accomplice
complimentare (kōm·plē·mān·tâ'rā) *vt*
to compliment, congratulate
complimenti (kōm·plē·mān'tē) *mpl* regards; congratulations; **fare i —** to compliment; to be ceremonious; to congratulate
complimento (kōm·plē·mān'tō) *m* compliment
complottare (kōm·plōt·tâ'rā) *vt&i* to plot
componente (kōm·pō·nän'tä) *m* component part
componimento (kōm·pō·nē·mān'tō) *m*
composition; structure
comporre * (kōm·pōr'rā) *vt* to compose;
to construct; to write up
comportamento (kōm·pōr·tâ·mān'tō) *m*
behavior
comportarsi (kōm·pōr·târ'sē) *vr* to behave
compositoio (kōm·pō·zē·tô'yō) *m* (*print*)
composing stick
compositore (kōm·pō·zē·tō'rā) *m* composer; typesetter
composizione (kōm·pō·zē·tsyō'nā) *f* composition; typesetting
composta (kōm·pō'stâ) *f* compote
compostezza (kōm·pō·stä'tsâ) *f* composure, self-possession, self-assurance
compostiera (kōm·pō·styä'râ) *f* compote
(*dish*)
composto (kōm·pō'stō) *a* composed; compound; — *m* compound
compra (kōm'prâ) *f* purchase; — **vendita**
terreni real estate agency; **–re** (kōm·
prâ'rā) *vt* to purchase, buy; **–tore** (kōm·
prâ·tō'rā) *m* buyer
comprendere * (kōm·pren'dä·rā) *vt* to
understand; to contain, include
comprensorio (kōm·prän·sô'ryō) *m* reclamation area
compreso (kōm·prä'zō) *a* included, including; understood
compressa (kōm·präs'sâ) *f* tablet; pad
compressione (kōm·präs·syō'nā) *f* compression
compressore (kōm·präs·sō'rā) *m* com-

pressor; — **stradale** steam roller
comprimere * (kōm·prē'mā·rā) *vt* to press, squeeze; to compress; to repress (*feeling*)
compromesso (kōm·prō·mäs'sō) *a* involved; compromised; — *m* compromise
compromettere * (kōm·prō·met'tā·rā) *vt* to compromise; to involve
comproprietario (kōm·prō·pryā·tâ'ryō) *m* co-owner, joint owner
comprovare (kōm·prō·vä'rā) *vt* to evidence, prove
compulsare (kōm·pūl·sä'rā) *vt* to consult, have reference to
compunto (kōm·pūn'tō) *a* contrite; ashamed; afflicted; demure
computare (kōm·pū·tä'rā) *vt* to compute
computista (kōm·pū·tē'stä) *m* accountant
computisteria (kōm·pū·tē·stä·rē'â) *f* bookkeeping
computo (kôm'pū·tō) *m* computation, calculation
comunale (kō·mū·nâ'lä) *a* municipal; **palazzo** — city hall
comune (kō·mū'nä) *a* common; — *m* municipality; **-lla** (kō·mū·näl'lâ) *f* gang, clique; **-mente** (kō·mū·nä·mān'tā) *adv* usually, commonly
comunicare (kō·mū·nē·kâ'rā) *vt* to communicate with; — *vi* to be connected
comunicato (kō·mū·nē·kâ'tō) *m* communiqué
communicazione (kō·mū·nē·kâ·tsyō'nä) *f* communication; telephone connection
comunione (kō·mū·nyō'nä) *f* Communion; communion
comunismo (kō·mū·nē'zmō) *m* Communism
comunista (kō·mū·nē'stâ) *m&a* Communist
comunità (kō·mū·nē·tâ') *f* community
comunque (kō·mūn'kwä) *adv* however
con (kōn) *prep* with
conato (kō·nâ'tō) *m* impulse; effort; attempt
conca (kōn'kâ) *f* vase; basin; tub; (*geog*) valley; lock (*canal*)
concatenare (kōn·kâ·tā·nâ'rā) *vt* to join; to link, unite
concatenazione (kōn·kâ·tā·nâ·tsyō'nä) *f* linking, connection, union
concavo (kōn'kâ·vō) *a* concave
concedere (kōn·che'dā·rā) *vt* to grant
concentramento (kōn·chān·trâ·män'tō) *m* concentration
concentrare (kōn·chān·trâ'rā) *vt* to concentrate
concentrato (kōn·chān·trâ'tō) *m* concen-

trate; — *a* concentrated
concentrazione (kōn·chān·trâ·tsyō'nä) *f* concentration
concentrico (kōn·chen'trē·kō) *a* concentric
concepire (kōn·chä·pē'rā) *vt* to conceive; to originate
conceria (kōn·chä·rē'â) *f* tannery
concertista (kōn·chär·tē'stâ) *m&f* concert artist
concerto (kōn·chär'tō) *m* concert; agreement, accord
concessionario (kōn·chäs·syō·nâ'ryō) *m* sole agent; distributor; dealer
concessione (kōn·chäs·syō'nä) *f* concession; dealership
concetto (kōn·chät'tō) *m* concept, idea
concezione (kōn·chä·tsyō'nä) *f* conception
conchiglia (kōn·kē'lyâ) *f* shell
concia (kôn'châ) *f* tanning; tannery; **-re** (kōn·châ'rā) *vt* to tan; to fix
conciliare (kōn·chē·lyä'rā) *vt* to reconcile, conciliate
conciliarsi (kōn·chē·lyâr'sē) *vr* to agree with; to gain one's esteem, win one over
conciliazione (kōn·chē·lyä·tsyō'nä) *f* conciliation, reconciliation
concilio (kōn·chē'lyō) *m* council
concimare (kōn·chē·mâ'rā) *vt* to fertilize; to manure
concime (kōn·chē'mä) *m* manure
conciso (kōn·chē'zō) *a* concise
concistoro (kōn·chē·stō'rō) *m* concistory
concitato (kōn·chē·tâ'tō) *a* excited, aroused
concittadino (kōn·chēt·tâ·dē'nō) *m* fellow citizen, countryman
concludere * (kōn·klū'dā·rā) *vt&i* to conclude; to come to a decision
conclusione (kōn·klū·zyō'nä) *f* conclusion
concordanza (kōn·kōr·dân'tsâ) *f* accord, agreement; concordance
concordare (kōn·kōr·dâ'rā) *vt* to cause to agree; to bring into harmony
concordato (kōn·kōr·dâ'tō) *a* arranged, agreed upon; — *m* agreement; concordate
concordia (kōn·kôr'dyâ) *f* harmony, peace; mutual consent, concord
concorrente (kōn·kōr·rän'tä) *m* competitor
concorrenza (kōn·kōr·rän'tsâ) *f* competition
concorrere * (kōn·kôr'rā·rā) *vi* to compete
concorso (kōn·kōr'sō) *m* attendance; contest

---

k kid, **l** let, **m** met, **n** not, **p** pat, **r** very, **s** sat, **sh** shop, **t** tell, **v** vat, **w** we, **y** yes, **z** zero

concreto (kōn·krā'tō) *a* concrete, actual

concubina (kōn·kū·bē'nä) *f* concubine; **—to** (kōn·kū·bē·nä'tō) *m* concubinage

concupiscente (kōn·kū·pē·shän'tä) *a* concupiscent

concupiscenza (kōn·kū·pē·shän'tsâ) *f* lust, concupiscence

concussione (kōn·kūs·syō'nä) *f* extortion; concussion

condanna (kōn·dân'nä) *f* condemnation; sentence; **—re** (kōn·dân·nä'rä) *vt* to sentence; **—to** (kōn·dân·nä'tō) *m* convict

condensare (kōn·dän·sâ'rä) *vt* to condense; to abridge

condensatore (kōn·dän·sâ·tō'rä) *m* condenser

condimento (kōn·dē·män'tō) *m* seasoning

condire (kōn·dē'rä) *vt* to season

condividere * (kōn·dē·vē'dä·rä) *vt* to share

condizionale (kōn·dē·tsyō·nä'lä) *a* conditional; **condanna — suspended** sentence; **—** *m* (*gram*) conditional mood

condizionare (kōn·dē·tsyō·nä'rä) *vt* to condition; to prepare, ready

condizionato (kōn·dē·tsyō·nä'tō) *a* conditioned; **aria condizionata** air conditioning; **—re** (kōn·dē·tsyō·nä·tō'rä) *m* air conditioner

condizione (kōn·dē·tsyō'nä) *f* condition, term

condoglianza (kōn·dō·lyân'tsâ) *f* sympathy, condolence

condolersi * (kōn·dō·lär'sē) *vr* to sympathize with, condole with

condonare (kōn·dō·nä'rä) *vt* to pardon, forgive, condone

condonato (kōn·dō·nä'tō) *a* pardoned, condoned

condono (kōn·dō'nō) *m* pardon, forgiveness

condotta (kōn·dōt'tâ) *f* behavior; management

condottiero (kōn·dōt·tyä'rō) *m* leader, condottiere, mercenary soldier

condotto (kōn·dōt'tō) *m* pipeline; **— a** led

conducente (kōn·dū·chän'tä) *a* leading; **—** *m* conductor; driver

conducibilità (kōn·dū·chē·bē·lē·tâ') *f* (*phys*) conductivity

condurre * (kōn·dūr'rä) *vt* to take, escort

conduttività (kōn·dūt·tē·vē·tâ') *f* (*phys*) conductivity

conduttore (kōn·dūt·tō'rä) *m* driver; train conductor; operator

confabulare (kōn·fâ·bū·lâ'rä) *vi* to talk, chat

confacente (kōn·fâ·chän'tä) *a* proper, suitable; agreeable to; becoming

confarsi * (kōn·fâr'sē) *vr* to fit; to agree; to suit; to content oneself

confederare (kōn·fä·dä·râ'rä) *vt* to confederate

confederato (kōn·fä·dä·râ'tō) *a* confederated; **—** *m* confederate

confederazione (kōn·fä·dä·râ·tsyō'nä) *f* confederacy, confederation

conferenza (kōn·fä·rän'tsâ) *f* lecture; **— al vertice** summit conference; **— stampa** press conference

conferenziere (kōn·fä·rän·tsyä'rä) *m* lecturer

conferire (kōn·fâ·rē'rä) *vt&i* to confer

conferma (kōn·fär'mâ) *f* confirmation; **—re** (kōn·fär·mâ'rä) *vt* to confirm

confessare (kōn·fäs·sâ'rä) *vt* to confess

confessionale (kōn·fäs·syō·nä'lä) *m&a* confessional

confessione (kōn·fäs·syō'nä) *f* confession

confessore (kōn·fäs·sō'rä) *m* confessor

confettiera (kōn·fät·tyä'râ) *f* candy box

confettiere (kōn·fät·tyä'rä) *m* confectioner

confetto (kōn·fät'tō) *m* piece of candy

confettura (kōn·fät·tū'râ) *f* marmalade

confezionare (kōn·fâ·tsyō·nä'rä) *vt* to manufacture; to draw up; to outline

confezione (kōn·fâ·tsyō'nä) *f* ready-to-wear manufacture

conficcare (kōn·fēk·kâ'rä) *vt* to nail in, drive in; to embed

conficcarsi (kōn·fēk·kâr'sē) *vr* to be embedded, be thrust in

confidare (kōn·fē·dâ'rä) *vt&i* to trust; to confide in; to be on familiar terms with

confidenza (kōn·fē·dän'tsâ) *f* familiarity; confidence

confidenziale (kōn·fē·dän·tsyâ'lä) *a* confidential

configurare (kōn·fē·gū·râ'rä) *vt* to shape, outline; (*fig*) to idealize

configurazione (kōn·fē·gū·râ·tsyō'nä) *f* configuration, contour

confinare (kōn·fē·nä'rä) *vt* to intern; **— vi** to border

confine (kōn·fē'nä) *m* border

confino (kōn·fē'nō) *m* internment

confiscare (kōn·fē·skâ'rä) *vt* to confiscate

conflitto (kōn·flēt'tō) *m* conflict

confluente (kōn·flūän'tä) *m* confluent, tributary

confondere * (kōn·fôn'dä·rä) *vt* to confuse; to mistake

â ârm, ā bāby, e bet, ē bē, ō gō, ô gône, ū blūe, b bad, ch child, d dad, f fat, g gay, j jet

conformare (kōn·fōr·mä'rä) *vt* to conform
conformarsi (kōn·fōr·mär'sē) *vr* to content oneself; to adapt oneself, accustom oneself
conforme (kōn·fōr'mä) *adv* in conformity; — *a* conforming
conformista (kōn·fōr·mē'stä) *m* conformist
conformità (kōn·fōr·mē·tâ) *f* conformity
confortabile (kōn·fōr·tâ'bē·lä) *a* consolable
confortare (kōn·fōr·tâ'rä) *vt* to comfort, solace
confortevole (kōn·fōr·te'vō·lä) *a* comfortable
conforto (kōn·fōr'tō) *m* comfort
confraternità (kōn·frâ·tär·nē·tâ') *f* brotherhood; fraternity
confrontare (kōn·frōn·tâ'rä) *vt* to compare; to relate
confronto (kōn·frōn'tō) *m* comparison; (*law*) confrontation
confusione (kōn·fū·zyō'nä) *f* confusion
confuso (kōn·fū'zō) *a* confused
confutare (kōn·fū·tâ'rä) *vt* to refute; to deny
confutazione (kōn·fū·tâ·tsyō'nä) *f* refutation, confutation
congedare (kōn·jä·dâ'rä) *vt* to dismiss
congedo (kōn·jä'dō) *m* discharge; leave
congegno (kōn·jä'nyō) *m* device
congelare (kōn·jä·lâ'rä) *vt* to freeze
congelato (kōn·jä·lâ'tō) *a* frozen
congenito (kōn·je'nē·tō) *a* congenital
congestione (kōn·jä·styō'nä) *f* congestion; traffic jam
congettura (kōn·jät·tū'râ) *f* supposition
congiungere * (kōn·jūn'jä·rä) *vt* to join, unite
congiuntivo (kōn·jūn·tē'vō) *m* subjunctive
congiunto (kōn·jūn'tō) *m* relative
congiuntura (kōn·jūn·tū'râ) *f* trade outlook, market conditions; emergency
congiunzione (kōn·jūn·tsyō'nä) *f* conjunction
congiura (kōn·jū'râ) *f* plot; **-re** (kōn·jū·râ'rä) *vt&i* to plot; to conjure; **-to** (kōn·jū·râ'tō) *a* plotted; conjured
conglomerato (kōn·glō·mä·râ'tō) *m* concrete; conglomerate
congratulare (kōn·grâ·tū·lâ'rä) *vt* to congratulate
congratulazione (kōn·grâ·tū·lâ·tsyō'nä) *f* congratulation
congrega (kôn'grä·gâ) *f* congregation; **-re** (kōn·grä·gâ'rä) *vt* to congregate;

-zione (kōn·grä·gâ·tsyō'nä) *f* congregation
congressista (kōn·gräs·sē'stâ) *m* member of a convention; congressman
congresso (kōn·gräs'sō) *m* congress; convention, meeting
congruente (kōn·grūän'tä) *a* congruent
congruenza (kōn·grūän'tsâ) *f* congruence; consistency
congruo (kôn'grūō) *a* congruous
conguaglio (kōn·gwä'lyō) *m* balance
coniare (kō·nyä'rä) *vt* to coin
conico (kô'nē·kō) *a* conic
coniglio (kō·nē'lyō) *m* rabbit
conio (kô'nyō) *m* coinage
coniugare (kō·nyū·gâ'rä) *vt* to conjugate
coniugazione (kō·nyū·gâ·tsyō'nä) *f* conjugation
coniuge (kô'nyū·jä) *m* spouse
coniugi (kô'nyū·jē) *mpl* husband and wife, couple
connaturale (kōn·nâ·tū·râ'lä) *a* connatural, inborn
connazionale (kōn·nä·tsyō·nâ'lä) *m* compatriot
connessione (kōn·näs·syō'nä) *f* connection
connettere * (kōn·net'tä·rä) *vt* to connect
connivenza (kōn·nē·vän'tsâ) *f* connivance
connubio (kōn·nū'byō) *m* marriage, match; blend, union
cono (kō'nō) *m* cone; — **gelato** ice cream cone
conoscente (kō·nō·shän'tä) *m&f* acquaintance
conoscenza (kō·nō·shän'tsâ) *f* knowledge; acquaintance
conoscere * (kō·nô'shä·rä) *vt* to know; to be aware of
conoscitore (kō·nō·shē·tō'rä) *m* connoisseur
conosciuto (kō·nō·shū'tō) *a* known
conquista (kōn·kwē'stä) *f* conquest; **-re** (kōn·kwē·stâ'rä) *vt* to conquer; **-tore** (kōn·kwē·stâ·tō'rä) *m* conqueror; (*coll*) ladies' man
consacrare (kōn·sâ·krâ'rä) *vt* to consecrate
consacrazione (kōn·sâ·krâ·tysō'nä) *f* consecration
consanguineo (kōn·sân·gwē'nä·ō) *a* akin; consanguineous
consanguinità (kōn·sân·gwē·nē·tâ') *f* consanguinity
consapevole (kōn·sâ·pe'vō·lä) *a* aware, knowing; informed
conscio (kôn'shō) *a* conscious

---

k kid, **l** let, **m** met, **n** not, **p** pat, **r** very, **s** sat, **sh** shop, **t** tell, **v** vat, **w** we, **y** yes, **z** zero

consecutivo (kōn·sā·kū·tē′vō) *a* successive, consecutive; following

consegna (kōn·sā′nyâ) *f* assignment; delivery; **–re** (kōn·sā·nyâ′rā) *vt* to deliver; **–tario** (kōn·sā·nyâ·tâ′ryō) *m* consignee

conseguente (kōn·sā·gwān′tā) *a* ensuing, resulting, consequent; **–mente** (kōn·sā·gwān·tā·mān′tā) *adv* consequently, as a result

conseguenza (kōn·sā·gwān′tsâ) *f* consequence

conseguire (kōn·sā·gwē′rā) *vt* to attain

consenso (kōn·sān′sō) *m* consent

consentimento (kōn·sān·tē·mān′tō) *m* consent

consentire (kōn·sān·tē′rā) *vi* to consent

conserva (kōn·sār′vâ) *f* preserve; **— di pomodoro** tomato paste; **in —** canned; **conserve alimentari** canned foods; **–re** *vt* (kōn·sār·vâ′rā) to conserve; **–tivo** (kōn·sār·vâ·tē′vō) *a* conservative; **–tore** (kōn·sār·vâ·tō′rā) *a* conservative; *(coll)* traditionalist; **–torio** (kōn·sār·vâ·tô′ryō) *m* conservatory of music; finishing school; **–zione** (kōn·sār·vâ·tsyō′nā) *f* preservation, conservation

consesso (kōn·sās′sō) *m* meeting, assembly

considerare (kōn·sē·dā·râ′rā) *vt* to consider

considerazione (kōn·sē·dā·râ·tsyō′nā) *f* consideration

considerevole (kōn·sē·dā·re′vō·lā) *a* considerable

consigliare (kōn·sē·lyâ′rā) *vt* to advise

consigliere (kōn·sē·lyā′rā) *m* adviser; **— delegato** member of board of directors

consiglio (kōn·sē′lyō) *m* advice; council

consistente (kōn·sē·stān′tā) *a* solid, strong; consisting of

consistenza (kōn·sē·stān′tsâ) *f* solidity, firmness; consistency

consistere * (kōn·sē′stā·rā) *vi* to consist, be composed

consociazione (kōn·sō·châ·tsyō′nā) *f* association

consocio (kōn·sô′chō) *m* partner

consolare (kōn·sō·lâ′rā) *vt* to console; **— a** consular

consolato (kōn·sō·lâ′tō) *m* consulate; **— a** consoled

consolazione (kōn·sō·lâ·tsyō′nā) *f* consolation

console (kôn′sō·lā) *m* consul

consolidare (kōn·sō·lē·dâ′rā) *vt* to strengthen; to consolidate

consolidarsi (kōn·sō·lē·dâr′sē) *vr* to become firm; to strengthen oneself; to be consolidated; to take root

consolidato (kōn·sō·lē·dâ′tō) *m* funded debt

consonante (kōn·sō·nân′tā) *f* consonant

consorte (kōn·sōr′tā) *m&f* spouse

consorzio (kōn·sôr′tsyō) *m* combine, syndicate; **— agrario** farmers' cooperative

consueto (kōn·swā′tō) *a* customary, habitual, usual; **— m** custom, habit, wont

consuetudine (kōn·swā·tū′dē·nā) *f* custom

consulente (kōn·sū·lān′tā) *a&m* consultant

consultare (kōn·sūl·tâ′rā) *vt* to consult

consultivo (kōn·sūl·tē′vō) *a* advisory

consulto (kōn·sūl′tō) *m* consultation; **–re** (kōn·sūl·tō′rā) *m* adviser, counsellor

consumare (kōn·sū·mâ′rā) *vt* to consume; to use up

consumato (kōn·sū·mâ′tō) *m* consommé; **— a** used up; accomplished, finished

consumazione (kōn·sū·mâ·tsyō′nā) *f* consummation; drinks; meal

consumo (kōn·sū′mō) *m* consumption

consunto (kōn·sūn′tō) *a* consumptive

consunzione (kōn·sūn·tsyō′nā) *f* consumption

contabile (kōn·tâ′bē·lā) *m* accountant; bookkeeper

contabilità (kōn·tâ·bē·lē·tâ′) *f* auditing; bookkeeping

contachilometro (kōn·tâ·kē·lô′mâ·trō) *m* speedometer

contadino (kōn·tâ·dē′nō) *m* peasant; farm hand

contagio (kōn·tâ′jō) *m* contagion; **–so** (kōn·tâ·jô′zō) *a* contagious

contagiri (kōn·tâ·jē′rē) *m (mech)* revolutions indicator, speedometer

contagocce (kōn·tâ·gô′chā) *f* medicine dropper

contaminare (kōn·tâ·mē·nâ′rā) *vt* to infect

contaminazione (kōn·tâ·mē·nâ·tsyō′nā) *f* contamination

contante (kōn·tân′tā) *a&m* cash

contare (kōn·tâ′rā) *vt* to count; to expect; to depend on

contatore (kōn·tâ·tō′rā) *m* meter

contatto (kōn·tât′tō) *m* contact

conte (kōn′tā) *m* count; **–a** (kōn·tā′â) *f* county; earldom; **–ssa** (kōn·tās′sâ) *f* countess

conteggiare (kōn·tāj·jâ′rā) *vt* to figure

conteggio (kōn·tej′jō) *m* count; **— alla rovescia** *(aesp)* countdown

contegno (kōn·tā′nyō) *m* behavior, deportment; aloofness

contemplare (kōn·tām·plâ′rā) *vt* to contemplate; to view

contemplativo (kōn·tām·plâ·tē′vō) *a* contemplative

contemplazione (kōn·tām·plâ·tsyō′nä) *f* contemplation

contemporaneo (kōn·tām·pō·râ′nä·ō) *a* contemporary

contendere * (kōn·ten′dā·rä) *vi* to contend

contenente (kōn·tä·nän′tä) *a* containing

contenere * (kōn·tä·nä′rä) *vt* to contain; to encompass

contentare (kōn·tän·tâ′rä) *vt* to please; to satisfy

contentezza (kōn·tän·tä′tsä) *f* joy

contento (kōn·tän′tō) *a* glad; satisfied

contenuto (kōn·tä·nū′tō) *m* contents

contenzione (kōn·tän·tsyō′nä) *f* debate; contention

contenzioso (kōn·tän·tsyō′zō) *a* contentious, quarrelsome

contesa (kōn·tä′zä) *f* contest; contention

conteso (kōn·tä′zō) *a* opposed; contested

contestare (kōn·tä·stâ′rä) *vt* to object; to contest

contestazione (kōn·tä·stâ·tsyō′nä) *f* objection; dispute; opposition; contention

contesto (kōn·tä′stō) *m* context; compound; structure; texture; — *a* formed; interwoven

contiguo (kōn·tē′gwō) *a* adjoining

continente (kōn·tē·nän′tä) *m* continent; — *a* temperate, continent

continenza (kōn·tē·nän′tsä) *f* continence

contingentare (kōn·tēn·jän·tâ′rä) *vt* to ration

contingente (kōn·tēn·jän′tä) *a&m* contingent

contingenza (kōn·tēn·jän′tsâ) *f* contingence

continuamente (kōn·tē·nwâ·män′tä) *adv* always, continually

continuamento (kōn·tē·nwâ·män′tō) *m* continuation; prolongation

continuare (kōn·tē·nwâ′rä) *vt&i* to continue; to prolong

continuato (kōn·tē·nwâ′tō) *a* continued

continuazione (kōn·tē·nwâ·tsyō′nä) *f* continuation

continuità (kōn·tē·nwē·tâ′) *f* continuity

continuo (kōn·tē′nwō) *a* continuous

conto (kōn′tō) *m* count; account; bill

contorcere * (kōn·tôr′chä·rä) *vt* to twist

contorno (kōn·tōr′nō) *m* side dish; contour; outline

contorsione (kōn·tōr·syō′nä) *f* contortion

contorto (kōn·tōr′tō) *a* twisted, contorted

contrabbandiere (kōn·trâb·bân·dyä′rä) *m* smuggler

contrabbando (kōn·trâb·bân′dō) *m* smuggling

contrabbasso (kōn·trâb·bâs′sō) *m* contrabass

contraccambiare (kōn·trâk·kâm·byâ′rä) *vt* to reciprocate; to exchange; to return

contraccolpo (kōn·trâk·kōl′pō) *m* counterblow; repercussion; retaliation

contrada (kōn·trâ′dâ) *f* district, region; country road

contradetto (kōn·trâd·dät′tō) *a* contradicted

contraddire * (kōn·trâd·dē′rä) *vt* to contradict, gainsay

contraddizione (kōn·trâd·dē·tsyō′nä) *f* contradiction

contraente (kōn·trâ·än′tä) *a* contracting; — *m* contractor

contraereo (kōn·trâ·e′rä·ō) *a* antiaircraft

contraffare * (kōn·trâf·fâ′rä) *vt* to counterfeit; to impersonate

contraffatto (kōn·trâf·fât′tō) *a* false; —re (kōn·trâf·fât·tō′rä) *m* counterfeiter

contraffazione (kōn·trâf·fâ·tsyō′nä) *f* forgery

contrafforte (kōn·trâf·fōr′tä) *m (arch)* buttress, pier

contralto (kōn·trâl′tō) *m* contralto

contrammiraglio (kōn·trâm·mē·râ′lyō) *m* rear admiral

contrappeso (kōn·trâp·pä′zō) *m* counterpoise, counterweight

contrappunto (kōn·trâp·pūn′tō) *m* counterpoint

contrariamente (kōn·trâ·ryâ·män′tä) *adv* contrarily

contrariare (kōn·trâ·ryâ′rä) *vt* to contradict; to oppose, counteract

contrarietà (kōn·trâ·ryä·tâ′) *f* adversity

contrario (kōn·trâ′ryō) *a* contrary

contrarre * (kōn·trâr′rä) *vt* to contract

contrassegno (kōn·trâs·sä′nyō) *m* sign, token

contrastante (kōn·trâ·stân′tä) *a* contrasting; — *m&f* contestant

contrastare (kōn·trâ·stâ′rä) *vt* to contrast

contrasto (kōn·trâ′stō) *m* contrast

contrattare (kōn·trât·tâ′rä) *vt&i* to bargain; to contract; to deal

contrattempo (kōn·trât·tâm′pō) *m* mishap; misfortune

contratto (kōn·trât′tō) *m* contract; — *a* contracted

contravvenzione (kōn·trâv·vän·tsyō′nä) *f* violation

contrazione (kōn·trâ·tsyō′nä) *f* contrac-

tion
contribuente (kōn·trē·bwän'tä) *m* tax-
payer
contribuire (kōn·trē·bwē'rā) *vt* to contribute
contributo (kōn·trē·bū'tō) *m* contribution
contrito (kōn·trē'tō) *a* contrite
contrizione (kōn·trē·tsyō'nä) *f* contrition
contro (kōn'trō) *prep* against
controcurva (kōn·trō·kūr'vä) *f* S-curve
controfigura (kōn·trō·fē·gū'râ) *f* stand-in;
substitute
controllare (kōn·trōl·lâ'rä) *vt* to verify,
check
controllo (kōn·trōl'lō) *m* control, check;
—re (kōn·trōl·lō'rä) *m* train conductor;
auditor; ticket collector
contromarca (kōn·trō·mâr'kâ) *f* check,
ticket stub
contromarcia (cōn·trō·mâr'châ) *f* reverse
(auto)
controproducente (kōn·trō·prō·dū·chän'-
tä) *a* self-defeating
controrivoluzione (kōn·trō·rē·vō·lū·
tsyō'nä) *f* counterrevolution
controversia (kōn·trō·ver'syâ) *f* controversy
contumacia (kōn·tū·mâ'châ) *f* default
contumelia (kōn·tū·me'lyâ) *f* contumely,
outrage, insult
conturbante (kōn·tūr·bân'tä) *a* glamorous; disturbing
conturbare (kōn·tūr·bâ'rä) *vt* to disturb;
to upset
contusione (kōn·tū·zyō'nä) *f* bruise
contuttochè (kōn·tūt·tō·kä') *conj* although, though, despite the fact that
contuttociò (kōn·tūt·tō·chō') *adv* however, nevertheless
convalescente (kōn·vâ·lā·shän'tä) *m&f*
convalescent
convalescenza (kōn·vâ·lā·shän'tsä) *f* recovery, convalescence
convalescenziario (kōn·vâ·lā·shän·tsyâ'-
ryō) *m* convalescent home, sanitarium
convalidare (kōn·vâ·lē·dâ'rä) *vt* to validate; to prove
convegno (kōn·vā'nyō) *m* meeting, convention
convenevoli (kōn·vā·ne'vō·lē) *mpl* ameni-
ties, pleasantries
conveniente (kōn·vā·nyän'tä) *a* convenient; appropriate; profitable
convenienza (kōn·vā·nyän'tsä) *f* convenience
convenire * (kōn·vā·nē'rä) *vi* to agree; to
be proper
convento (kōn·vän'tō) *m* monastery; con-

vent
convenuto (kōn·vā·nū'tō) *m* defendant
convenzione (kōn·vän·tsyō'nä) *f* convention
convergere * (kōn·ver'jä·rä) *vi* to converge
conversare (kōn·vär·sâ'rä) *vi* to converse
conversazione (kōn·vär·sâ·tsyō'nä) *f* conversation
conversione (kōn·vär·syō'nä) *f* conversion
converso (kōn·vär'sō) *m* lay brother
convertire (kōn·vär·tē'rä) *vt* to convert
convertito (kōn·vär·tē'tō) *m* convert
convesso (kōn·väs'sō) *a* convex
convincente (kōn·vēn·chän'tä) *a* convincing
convincere * (kōn·vēn'chä·rä) *vt* to convince; to satisfy
convinzione (kōn·vēn·tsyō'nä) *f* conviction
convitare (kōn·vē·tâ'rä) *vt* to invite
convitato (kōn·vē·tâ'tō) *m* guest; — *a*
invited
convito (kōn·vē'tō) *m* feast; banquet
convitto (kōn·vēt'tō) *m* academy, boarding school, private school; —re (kōn·vēt·
tō'rä) *m* student at a boarding school
convivente (kōn·vē·vän'tä) *m* cohabitant
convivenza (kōn·vē·vän'tsä) *f* cohabita-
tion
convivere * (kōn·vē'vä·rä) *vi* to cohabit
convocare (kōn·vō·kâ'rä) *vt* to convoke;
to bring into play
convogliare (kōn·vō·lyâ'rä) *vt* to convey;
to convoy
convoglio (kōn·vô'lyō) *m* convoy
convulsione (kōn·vul·syō'nä) *f* convulsion
cooperare (kō·ō·pä·râ'rä) *vi* to cooperate
cooperativa (kō·ō·pä·râ·tē'vâ) *f* cooperative
coordinare (kō·ōr·dē·nâ'rä) *vt* to co-
ordinate
copale (kō·pâ'lä) *f* patent leather; lacquer
coperchio (kō·per'kyō) *m* top, lid
coperta (kō·pär'tâ) *f* blanket; *(naut)* deck;
sopra — on deck
copertina (kō·pär·tē'nâ) *f* book jacket,
dust jacket
coperto (kō·pär'tō) *m* cover; cover charge;
—ne (kō·pär·tō'nä) *m* tire; tarpaulin
copertura (kō·pär·tū'râ) *f* coverage
copia (kô'pyä) *f* copy; print; —lettere
(kō·pyä·let'tä·rä) *f* automatic typewrit-
ing unit; —re (kō·pyâ'rä) *vt* to copy; —tivo
(kō·pyä·tē'vō) *a* copying; —tore (kō·
pyâ·tō'rä) *m* imitator
copione (kō·pyō'nä) *m* script

copiosità (kō·pyō·zē·tâ′) f plentifulness, abundance, copiousness
copioso (kō·pyō′zō) a plentiful, abundant, copious
copista (kō·pē′stâ) m copyist
copisteria (kō·pē·stä·rē′â) f letter service
coppa (kōp′pâ) f cup; bowl
coppia (kôp′pyâ) f couple, pair
copribusto (kō·prē·bü′stō) m bodice
copricapo (kō·prē·kâ′pō) m headgear
coprifuoco (kō·prē·fwō′kō) m curfew
copriletto (kō·prē·lät′tō) m bedspread
coprire * (kō·prē′râ) vt to cover
copula (kô′pü·lâ) f conjunction; copulation; (gram) copula, conjunction; –re (kō·pü·lâ′râ) vt to copulate
coraggio (kō·râj′jō) m courage; –so (kō·râj·jō′zō) a brave
corale (kō·râ′lä) a choral
corallo (kō·râl′lō) m coral
coramella (kō·râ·mäl′lâ) f razor strop
coratella (kō·râ·täl′lâ) f pluck
corazza (kō·râ′tsâ) f armor; –ta (kō·râ·tsâ′tâ) f battleship
corazziere (kō·râ·tsyâ′râ) m (mil) cuirassier
corbellare (kōr·bāl·lâ′râ) vt to make fun of; to tease
corbelleria (kōr·bāl·lä·rē′â) f nonsense
corbello (kōr·bāl′lō) m basket
corbezzoli! (kōr·be′tsō·lē) interj gosh!
corda (kōr′dâ) f rope; string
cordiale (kōr·dyâ′lä) a&m cordial
cordialità (kōr·dyä·lē·tâ′) f cordiality; regards
cordicella (kōr·dē·chäl′lâ) f string, lace
cordigliera (kōr·dē·lyâ′râ) f (geog) cordillera
cordoglio (kōr·dô′lyō) m sorrow
cordoncino (kōr·dōn·chē′nō) m string, lace
cordone (kōr·dō′nä) m cordon
coreografia (kō·râ·ō·grâ·fē′â) f choreography
coreografo (kō·râ·ô′grâ·fō) m choreographer
coriaceo (kō·ryâ′chä·ō) a leathery; (fig) tough
coriandoli (kō·ryân′dō·lē) mpl confetti
coricare (kō·rē·kâ′râ) vt to put to bed
coricarsi (kō·rē·kâr′sē) vr to go to bed
corifeo (kō·rē·fâ′ō) m coryphaeus
corindone (kō·rēn·dō′nä) m (min) corundum
corinzio (kō·rēn′tsyō) a Corinthian
corista (kō·rē′stâ) m chorister; diapason
corna (kōr′nâ) fpl horns
cornacchia (kōr·nâk′kyâ) f crow

cornamusa (kōr·nâ·mü′zâ) f bagpipe
cornata (kōr·nâ′tâ) f butt, ram
cornea (kôr′nä·â) f (anat) cornea
corneo (kôr′nä·ō) a horny, corneous
cornetta (kōr·nät′tâ) f (mus) cornet
cornice (kōr·nē′châ) f frame
cornicione (kōr·nē·chō′nä) m eaves, cornice; entablature
corniolo (kōr·nyō′lō) m (bot) dogwood
corno (kōr′nō) m horn
cornucopia (kōr·nü·kô′pyâ) f horn of plenty, cornucopia
cornuto (kōr·nü′tō) a horned; — m cuckold
coro (kō′rō) m choir, chorus
corollario (kō·rōl·lâ′ryō) m corollary
corona (kō·rō′nâ) f crown
coronario (kō·rō·nâ′ryō) a coronary
corpacciuto (kōr·pâ·chü′tō) a stout, fleshy
corpo (kōr′pō) m body; undershirt; –rale (kōr·pō·râ′lä) a bodily, corporeal; –ralmente (kōr·pō·râl·mân′tä) adv bodily, corporally; –ratura (kōr·pō·râ·tü′râ) f physique, build; –razione (kōr·pō·râ·tsyō′nä) f guild; corporation
corpulento (kōr·pü·län′tō) a stout, corpulent
corpuscolo (kōr·pü′skō·lō) m corpuscle
corredare (kōr·rä·dâ′râ) vt to equip, provide, furnish
corredo (kōr·rä′dō) m trousseau; outfit
correggia (kōr·rej′jâ) f girdle; leather belt
correggere (kōr·rej′jä·râ) vt to correct
correlativo (kōr·rä·lâ·tē′vō) a correlative
corrente (kōr·rän′tâ) f stream; current; — a running; — alternata alternating current; — continua direct current; al — up-to-date
correo (kōr·rä′ō) m accomplice
correre * (kôr′rä·râ) vi to run
corretto (kōr·rät′tō) a correct; –re (kōr·rät·tō′râ) m corrector; (print) proofreader
correzionale (kōr·rä·tsyō·nâ′lä) m reformatory
correzione (kōr·rä·tsyō′nä) f correction
corridoio (kōr·rē·dô′yō) m corridor
corridore (kōr·rē·dō′râ) m runner
corriera (kōr·ryâ′râ) f intercity bus
corriere (kōr·ryâ′râ) m messenger, courier; mail
corrispettivo (kōr·rē·spät·tē′vō) m recompense; — a corresponding
corrispondente (kōr·rē·spōn·dän′tä) m correspondent
corrispondenza (kōr·rē·spōn·dän′tsâ) f correspondence

k kid, **l** let, **m** met, **n** not, **p** pat, **r** very, **s** sat, **sh** shop, **t** tell, **v** vat, **w** we, **y** yes, **z** zero

corrispondere * (kŏr·rē·spôn'dā·rā) *vi* to correspond

corrodere * (kŏr·rô'dā·rā) *vt* to corrode; to waste

corrompere * (kôr·rôm'pā·rā) *vt* to bribe, corrupt

corrosione (kŏr·rō·zyō'nā) *f* corrosion

corrosivo (kŏr·rō·zē'vō) *a* corrosive

corroso (kŏr·rō'zō) *a* corroded

corrotto (kŏr·rōt'tō) *a* corrupted

corrugare (kŏr·rū·gâ'rā) *vt* to corrugate

corruzione (kŏr·rū·tsyō'nā) *f* corruption

corsa (kŏr'sâ) *f* race; fare; stroke

corsaro (kŏr·sâ'rō) *m* pirate, corsair

corseggiare (kŏr·sāj·jâ'rā) *vi* to pirate

corsetto (kŏr·sāt'tō) *m* corset

corsia (kŏr·sē'â) *f* lane; ward

corsivo (kŏr·sē'vō) *m* italics

corso (kŏr'sō) *m* course; main street; Corsican

corte (kŏr'tā) *f* court; courtship; courtyard; **–ggiare** (kŏr·tāj·jâ'rā) *vt* to court; **–ggiatore** (kŏr·tāj·jâ·tō'rā) *m* suitor; wooer

corteo (kŏr·tā'ō) *m* parade, procession

cortese (kŏr·tā'zā) *a* polite, courteous; **–mente** (kŏr·tā·zā·mān'tā) *adv* courteously, politely, kindly

cortesia (kŏr·tā·zē'â) *f* politeness, courtesy

cortigiana (kŏr·tē·jâ'nâ) *f* courtesan

cortigiano (kŏr·tē·jâ'nō) *m* courtier; *(fig)* flatterer

cortile (kŏr·tē'lā) *m* courtyard

cortina (kŏr·tē'nâ) *f* curtain; **— di acciaio** iron curtain; **— di fumo** smoke screen; **–ggio** (kŏr·tē·nâj'jō) *m* curtains, drapes; *(mil)* barrage

corto (kŏr'tō) *a* short; **— circuito** short circuit; **— di vista** shortsighted; **–metraggio** (kŏr·tō·mā·trâj'jō) *m* short subject *(movies)*

corvetta (kŏr·vāt'tâ) *f* (*naut*) corvette

corvino (kŏr·vē'nō) *a* crowlike; raven, jet black, corvine

corvo (kŏr'vō) *m* crow

cosa (kō'zâ) *f* thing; matter; **che —?** what?

coscia (kô'shâ) *f* thigh

coscienza (kō·shân'tsâ) *f* conscience; consciousness

coscio (kô'shō), **cosciotto** (kô·shŏt'tō) *m* leg; **— d'agnello** leg of lamb

coscritto (kō·skrēt'tō) *m* draftee

coscrizione (kō·skrē·tsyō'nā) *f* (*mil*) draft

così (kō·zē') *adv* thus, so, in this way

cosmetico (kō·zme'tē·kō) *m&a* cosmetic

cosmico (kô'zmē·kō) *a* cosmic

cosmo (kô'zmō) *m* cosmos; **–grafia** (kō·zmō·grâ·fē'â) *f* cosmography; **–logia** (kō·zmō·lō·jē'â) *f* cosmology; **–polita** (kō·zmō·pō·lē'tâ) *a&m* cosmopolitan

cospargere * (kō·spâr'jā·rā) *vt* to sprinkle, to bedew; to strew

cospetto (kō·spāt'tō) *m* view; presence; sight

cospicuo (kō·spē'kwō) *a* conspicuous; in evidence

cospirare (kō·spē·râ'rā) *vi* to plot, conspire

cospiratore (kō·spē·râ·tō'rā) *m* conspirator

cospirazione (kō·spē·râ·tsyō'nā) *f* plot, conspiracy

costa (kō'stâ) *f* coast; rib; slope; side

costà (kō·stâ') *adv* over there, there

costanza (kō·stân'tsâ) *f* constancy; faithfulness

costare (kō·stâ'rā) *vi* to cost

costata (kō·stâ'tâ) *f* chop (*meat*)

costatare (kō·stâ·tâ'rā) *vt* to ascertain

costei (kō·stâ'ē) *pron* she, that girl, that woman

costellazione (kō·stāl·lâ·tsyō'nā) *f* constellation

costernare (kō·stār·nâ'rā) *vt* to consternate; to upset

costernarsi (kō·stār·nâr'sē) *vi* to be dismayed

costernazione (kō·stār·nâ·tsyō'nā) *f* dismay

costiero (kō·styā'rō) *a* coastal

costipazione (kō·stē·pâ·tsyō'nā) *f* constipation; cold

costituire (kō·stē·twē'rā) *vt* to constitute; to set up

costituirsi (kō·stē·twēr'sē) *vr* to give oneself up, surrender; to be composed of

costituzione (kō·stē·tū·tsyō'nā) *f* constitution

costo (kō'stō) *m* cost

costola (kô'stō·lâ) *f* rib

costoletta (kō·stō·lāt'tâ) *f* cutlet, chop

costoro (kō·stō'rō) *pron* these; those

costoso (kō·stō'zō) *a* costly, expensive

costringere * (kō·strēn'jā·rā) *vt* to compel, make

costruire (kō·strūē'rā) *vt* to construct

costruttore ((kō·strūt·tō'rā) *m* builder

costruzione (kō·strū·tsyō'nā) *f* construction

costui (kō·stū'ē) *pron* he, that fellow, that man

costumatezza (kō·stū·mâ·tā'tsâ) *f* politeness

costumato (kō·stū·mâ'tō) *a* well-bred

costume (kō·stū'mā) *m* custom; costume;

habit
costumista (kō·stū·mē'stâ) _m_ (_theat_) costumer
costura (kō·stū'râ) _f_ seam
cotale (kō·tâ'lä) _pron_ such a one, such
cotanto (kō·tân'tō) _a_ as much; — _adv_ so much
cote (kō'tä) _f_ hone
cotechino (kō·tä·kē'nō) _m_ pork sausage
cotenna (kō·tän'nä) _f_ rind; pigskin
cotesto (kō·tä'stō), **codesto** (kō·dä'stō) _a_ that; — _pron_ that one by you
cotogna (kō·tō'nyä) _f_ quince; **–ta** (kō·tō·nyâ'tä) _f_ quince jam
cotone (kō·tō'nä) _m_ cotton; — **idrofilo** absorbent cotton
cotoniere (kō·tō·nyä'rä) _m_ cotton merchant
cotonificio (kō·tō·nē·fē'chō) _m_ cotton mill
cotonina (kō·tō·nē'nä) _f_ calico
cottimo (kôt'tē·mō) _m_ piecework
cotto (kôt'tō) _a_ cooked; **ben** — well done; **poco** — rare
cottura (kôt·tū'râ) _f_ cooking
cova (kō'vä) _f_ brooding, brood; **–re** (kō·vâ'rä) _vt_ to hatch, brood; **–ta** (kō·vâ'tä) _f_ covey, brood; hatch
covo (kō'vō) _m_ hole, den; lair
covone (kō·vō'nä) _m_ sheaf
cozza (kō'tsä) _f_ mussel
cozzare (kō·tsä'rä) _vt&i_ to bump, bump into
cozzo (kō'tsō) _m_ shock; collision; butt; clash; (_fig_) conflict, contrast
crac (krâk) _m_ (_com_) crash, failure
crampo (krâm'pō) _m_ cramp
cranio (krâ'nyō) _m_ skull
crapula (krâ'pū·lä) _f_ intemperance in food and drink
crapulone (krâ·pū·lō'nä) _m_ reveller; guzzler; debauchee
crasso (krâs'sō) _a_ coarse, crass, gross; **ignoranza crassa** gross ignorance
cratere (krä·tä'rä) _m_ crater
crauti (krâ'ū·tē) _mpl_ sauerkraut
cravatta (krâ·vât'tä) _f_ necktie
creanza (krä·ân'tsä) _f_ education; breeding; politeness
creare (krä·â'rä) _vt_ to create; to bring up
creatore (krä·â·tō'rä) _m_ creator
creatura (krä·â·tū'râ) _f_ creature
creazione (krä·â·tsyō'nä) _f_ creation
credente (krä·dän'tä) _m&f_ believer
credenza (krä·dän'tsä) _f_ belief; cupboard; credit
credere (kre'dä·rä) _vi&t_ to believe; to think

credibile (krä·dē'bē·lä) _a_ credible
credibilità (krä·dē·bē·lē·tâ') _f_ credibility
credito (kre'dē·tō) _m_ credit; **–re** (krä·dē·tō'rä) _m_ creditor
credo (krä'dō) _m_ creed, belief
credulo (kre'dū·lō) _a_ gullible
crema (krä'mâ) _f_ cream; — **da scarpe** shoe polish; — **per la pelle** cold cream
cremagliera (krä·mâ·lyä'râ) _f_ rack; **ferrovia a** — cog railway
crematoio (krä·mâ·tô'yō) _m_ crematory
cremazione (krä·mâ·tsyō'nä) _f_ cremation
cremisi (kre'mē·zē) _m_ crimson
Cremlino (kräm·lē'nō) _m_ Kremlin
cremore (krä·mō'rä) _m_ essence; — **tartaro** cream of tartar
crepa (krä'pä) _f_ crack
crepare (krä·pâ'rä) _vi_ to crack open, split open; to burst; (_coll_) to feel stuffed; (_sl_) to kick the bucket
crepitare (krä·pē·tâ'rä) _vi_ to crackle
crepuscolo (krä·pü'skō·lō) _m_ twilight
crescere * (kre'shä·rä) _vt_ to grow
crescione (krä·shō'nä) _m_ watercress
cresima (kre'zē·mâ) _f_ (_eccl_) confirmation; **–re** (krä·zē·mâ'rä) _vt_ to confirm
crespo (krä'spō) _m_ crepe; — _a_ curly, crisp, woolly
cresta (krä'stä) _f_ crest; comb of a cock
creta (krä'tä) _f_ clay; **–ceo** (krä·tâ'chä·ō) _a_ chalky, claylike
cretino (krä·tē'nō) _m_ moron, idiot
cricco (krēk'kō) _m_ jack
criminale (krē·mē·nâ'lä) _m_ criminal
criminalista (krē·mē·nâ·lē'stä) _m_ criminal lawyer; criminologist
criminalità (krē·mē·nâ·lē·tâ') _f_ criminality
crimine (krē'mē·nä) _m_ crime
crine (krē'nä) _m_ horsehair
criniera (krē·nyä'rä) _f_ mane
cripta (krēp'tä) _f_ crypt
crisi (krē'zē) _f_ crisis
cristalleria (krē·stâl·lä·rē'â) _f_ crystalware
cristallizzare (krē·stâl·lē·dzä'rä) _vt_ to crystallize
cristallizzato (krē·stâl·lē·dzä'tō) _a_ crystallized
cristallizzazione (krē·stâl·lē·dzâ·tsyō'nä) _f_ crystallization
cristallo (krē·stâl'lō) _m_ crystal, glass
cristianesimo (krē·styâ·ne'zē·mō) _m_ Christianity
cristiano (krē·styâ'nō) _m_ Christian
Cristo (krē'stō) _m_ Christ
criterio (krē·te'ryō) _m_ criterion
critica (krē'tē·kä) _f_ criticism; **–re** (krä·tē·kâ'rä) _vt_ to criticize, find fault with

---

k kid, **l** let, **m** met, **n** not, **p** pat, **r** very, **s** sat, **sh** shop, **t** tell, **v** vat, **w** we, **y** yes, **z** zero

critico (krē'tē·kō) *a* critical; — *m* critic

crivellare (krē·vāl·lā'rā) *vt* to riddle; to sift

crivello (krē·vāl'lō) *m* riddle; sieve

croccante (krōk·kán'tä) *a* crisp

crocchetta (krōk·kāt'tä) *f* croquette

croce (krō'chä) *f* cross; **—rossina** (krō·chä·rōs·sē'nä) *f* Red Cross nurse; **—via** (krō·chä·vē'ä) *f* intersection

crociata (krō·chä'tä) *f* crusade

crociera (krō·chä'rä) *f* cruise

crocifiggere * (krō·chē·fēj'jä·rä) *vt* to crucify

crocifissione (krō·chē·fēs·syō'nä) *f* crucifixion

crocifisso (krō·chē·fēs'sō) *m* crucifix

crogiuolo (krō·jwō'lō) *m* melting pot

crollare (krōl·lä'rä) *vi* to fall in, collapse; — *vt* to shrug, shake

crollo (krōl'lō) *m* crash, collapse

cromatico (krō·mä'tē·kō) *a* chromatic

cromo (krō'mō) *m* chromium

cromotelevisore (krō·mō·tä·lä·vē·zō'rä) *m* color television set

cronaca (krō'nä·kä) *f* news; chronicle

cronico (krô'nē·kō) *a* chronic

cronista (krō·nē'stä) *m* reporter

cronologico (krō·nō·lô'jē·kō) *a* chronological

cronometrista (krō·nō·mä·trē'stä) *m* timekeeper

cronometro (krō·nô'mä·trō) *m* stop watch

crosta (krō'stä) *f* crust; **—ceo** (krō·stä'·chä·ō) *m* shellfish; **—ta** (krō·stä'tä) *f* pie

crostino (krō·stē'nō) *m* toast; canapé

crucciare (krū·chä'rä) *vt* to irritate; to worry

crucciarsi (krū·chär'sē) *vr* to get irritated; to get vexed

cruccio (krū'chō) *m* grief; anger, vexation; worry

cruciale (krū·chä'lä) *a* crucial; critical; decisive

cruciare (krū·chä'rä) *vt* to torment, grieve

cruciverba (krū·chē·vär'bä) *m* crossword puzzle

crudele (krū·dä'lä) *a* cruel

crudeltà (krū·däl·tâ') *f* cruelty

crudezza (krū·dä'tsä) *f* rawness; crudeness; coarseness; (*fig*) rudeness

crudo (krū'dō) *a* raw; cruel

cruento (krūän'tō) *a* bloody; dreadful

crumiro (krū·mē'rō) *m* scab; strikebreaker

cruna (krū'nä) *f* eye of a needle

crusca (krū'skä) *f* bran

cruscotto (krū·skōt'tō) *m* dashboard

cubico (kū'bē·kō) *a* cubic

cubismo (kū·bē'zmō) *m* cubism

cubito (kū'bē·tō) *m* elbow; cubit (*measure*)

cubo (kū'bō) *m* cube

cuccagna (kūk·kâ'nyä) *f* land of plenty; **albero di —** greased pole

cuccetta (kū·chät'tä) *f* berth

cucchiaiata (kūk·kyâ·yä'tä) *f* spoonful

cucchiaino (kūk·kyä·ē'nō) *m* teaspoon

cucchiaio (kūk·kyä'yō) *m* spoon; **— da tavola** tablespoon

cuccia (kū'chä) *f* doghouse; dog bed

cucciolo (kū·chō'lō) *m* puppy

cucco (kūk'kō) *m* pet, favorite; **vecchio —** stupid old man

cuccù (kū·kū'), **cuculo** (kū'kū·lō) *m* cuckoo

cuccuma (kūk'kū·mä) *f* kettle

cucina (kū·chē'nä) *f* kitchen; range; cuisine; **libro di —** cookbook; **—re** (kū·chē·nä'rä) *vt&i* to cook

cuciniere (kū·chē·nyä'rä) *m* cook

cucinino (kū·chē·nē'nō) *m* kitchenette

cucire (kū·chē'rä) *vt* to sew; **macchina da cucire** sewing machine

cucitura (kū·chē·tū'rä) *f* sewing

cuffia (kūf'fyä) *f* baby cap; hood; bathing cap; headphone

cugina (kū·jē'nä) *f*, **cugino** (kū·jē'nō) *m* cousin

cui (kū'ē) *pron* whom, to whom

culatta (kū·lät'tä) *f* breech (*gun barrel*); rump, seat

culla (kūl'lä) *f* cradle; **—re** (kūl·lä'rä) *vt* to rock, lull

culo (kū'lō) *m* bottom (*bottle*); arse; rump

culto (kūl'tō) *m* worship

cultura (kūl·tū'rä) *f* culture

cumulativo (kū·mū·lä·tē'vō) *a* cumulative

cumulo (kū'mū·lō) *m* heap

cuna (kū'nä) *f* cradle

cuneo (kū'nä·ō) *m* wedge

cunetta (kū·nät'tä) *f* ditch

cuoca (kwō'kä) *f* woman cook

cuocere * (kwô'chä·rä) *vt* to cook

cuoco (kwō'kō) *m* cook; **capo —** chef

cuoio (kwō'yō) *m* leather

cuore (kwō'rä) *m* heart

cupidigia (kū·pē·dē'jä) *f* greed

cupido (kū'pē·dō) *a* greedy, covetous, eager

cupo (kū'pō) *a* dark; deep

cupola (kū'pō·lä) *f* cupola, dome

cupone (kū·pō'nä) *m* coupon

cura (kū'rä) *f* care, treatment; **—re** (kū·râ'rä) *vt* to treat; to edit; **—to** (kū·râ'·tō) *m* curate; pastor; **—to** *a* cured; **—to·re** (kū·râ·tō'rä) *m* (*law*) receiver

â ârm, ā bāby, e bet, ē bē, ō gō, ô gône, ū blūe, b bad, ch child, d dad, f fat, g gay, j jet

curia (kū′ryâ) *f* (*eccl*) curia; — **vescovile** bishop's court

curiosare (kū·ryō·zâ′rā) *vi* to pry, look around

curiosità (kū·ryō·zē·tâ′) *f* curiosity; place of interest, tourist attraction

curioso (kū·ryō′zō) *a* curious

curva (kūr′vâ) *f* curve; — **e controcurva** double curve; — **stretta** sharp turn; **–re** (kūr·vâ′rā) *vt* to curve; to bend; **–rsi** (kūr·vâr′sē) *vr* to stoop, bow down **–tura** (kūr·vâ·tū′râ) *f* bending, curvature

curvo (kūr′vō) *a* curved, stooped

cuscinetto (kū·shē·nāt′tō) *m* pincushion; **stato** — buffer state; — **a sfere** ball bearing

cuscino (kū·shē′nō) *m* pillow

cuspide (kū′spē·dā) *f* point; peak

custode (kū·stō′dā) *m&f* caretaker

custodia (kū·stō′dyâ) *f* care; custody; keeping

custodire (kū·stō·dē′rā) *vt* to keep; to take care of, look after

cutaneo (kū·tâ′nā·ō) *a* cutaneous, of the skin

cute (kū′tā) *f* skin (*human*)

cuticola (kū·tē′kō·lâ) *f* cuticle

D

da (dâ) *prep* from, by, at; as

dabbenaggine (dâb·bā·nâj′jē·nā) *f* simplicity; simplemindedness

dabbene (dâb·bā′nā) *a* naive, simple

daccapo (dâk·kâ′pō) *adv* once more, over again

dacchè (dâk·kā′) *conj* since

dadi (dâ′dē) *mpl* dice

dado (dâ′dō) *m* die; cube; nut

daga (dâ′gâ) *f* dagger

dagherrotipo (dâ·gār·rô′tē·pō) *m* daguerrotype

dagli (dâ′lyē), **dai** (dâ′ē), **dalla** (dâl′lâ), **dalle** (dâl′lā), **dallo** (dâl′lō) *prep* from the; by the; at the

daino (dâ·ē′nō) *m* deer, buck; **pelle di** — buckskin

dalia (dâ′lyâ) *f* dahlia

daltonico (dâl·tô′nē·kō) *a* color-blind

daltonismo (dâl·tō·nē′zmō) *m* color blindness, daltonism

dama (dâ′mâ) *f* lady; checkers; — **di compagnia** lady-in-waiting

damascare (dâ·mâ·skâ′rā) *vt* to damask

damascato (dâ·mâ·skâ′tō) *a* damasked

damascatura (dâ·mâ·skâ·tū′râ) *f* damasking

damaschinare (dâ·mâ·skē·nâ′rā) *vt* to damascene

damasco (dâ·mâ′skō) *m* damask

damerino (dâ·mā·rē′nō) *m* fop, dandy

damigella (dâ·mē·jāl′lâ) *f* young maiden; — **d'onore** bridesmaid

damigiana (dâ·mē·jâ′nâ) *f* demijohn

damma (dâm′mâ) *f* doe, deer

danaro (dâ·nâ′rō) *m* money; **–so** (dâ·nâ·rō′zō) *a* moneyed, rich, well-to-do

danese (dâ·nā′zâ) *a* Danish

Danimarca (dâ·nē·mâr′kâ) *f* Denmark

dannabile (dân·nâ′bē·lâ) *a* blameworthy;

damnable

dannare (dân·nâ′rā) *vt* to condemn, damn; to harrass; to lay the blame on

dannato (dân·nâ′tō) *a* damned; blamed

dannazione (dân·nâ·tsyō′nā) *f* damnation

danneggiare (dân·nāj·jâ′rā) *vt* to damage

danneggiato (dân·nāj·jâ′tō) *a* damaged; — *m* victim

danno (dân′nō) *m* damage; **–so** (dân·nō′zō) *a* harmful

dante (dân′tā) *m* buck; **pelle di** — buckskin

dantesco (dân·tā′skō) *a* Dantesque, in the style of Dante

danza (dân′tsâ) *f* dance; **–nte** (dân·tsân′tā) *a* dancing

dappertutto (dâp·pār·tūt′tō) *adv* everywhere

dappocaggine (dâp·pō·kâj′jē·nā) *f* worthlessness; ineptness

dappoco (dâp·pō′kō) *a* worthless; inept

dappresso (dâp·prās′sō) *adv* close by, near, near at hand

dapprima (dâp·prē′mâ) *adv* first, at first

dardeggiare (dâr·dāj·jâ′rā) *vt* to dart; to shoot out

dardo (dâr′dō) *m* arrow; dart

dare * (dâ′rā) *vt* to give; — *vi* to look on; — *m* (*com*) debit; — **e avere** debits and credits; **passare al** — to transfer to the debit side of the ledger

darsena (dâr′sā·nâ) *f* (*naut*) basin, wet dock

darsi * (dâr′sē) *vr* to be a devotee of; to surrender; to addict oneself; — **agli affari** to go into business; — **all'alcool** to become an alcoholic; — **alla fuga** to flee; **darsela a gambe** to take to one's heels; — **al mare** to sail; — **d'attorno**, — **da fare** to work painstakingly; — **la**

briga di to go to the trouble of; — **il caso** to happen; — **pace** to become resigned; — **per vinto** to give in; **può** — maybe, perhaps

data (dâ'tâ) *f* date; **-re** (dâ·tâ'rā) *vt* to date

datario (dâ·tâ'ryō) *m* (*eccl*) datary

dati (dâ'tē) *mpl* data, facts

dativo (dâ·tē'vō) *m* (*gram*) dative

dato (dâ'tō) *m* element; factor; indication; hint; — *a* established; given; indicated; devoted to; addicted; — **che** since, seeing that, in view of the fact that

datore (dâ·tō'rā) *m* giver; — **di lavoro** boss; patron

dattero (dât'tâ·rō) *m* date; date palm

dattilografare (dât·tē·lō·grâ·fâ'rā) *vt* to type, typewrite

dattilografia (dât·tē·lō·grâ·fē'â) *f* typing

dattilografo (dât·tē·lô'grâ·fō) *m*, **dattilografa** (dât·tē·lô'grâ·fâ) *f* typist

dattiloscopia (dât·tē·lō·skō·pē'â) *f* verification of finger prints

dattiloscritto (dât·tē·lō·skrēt'tō) *a* typed, typewritten

dattorno (dât·tōr'nō) *adv* around; **levarsi** — to get rid of; **qui** — around here, in this area

davanti (dâ·vân'tē) *adv* in front, before

davanzale (dâ·vân·tsâ'lā) *m* window sill

davvero (dâv·vā'rō) *adv* really, indeed, in all earnestness

daziario (dâ·tsyâ'ryō) *a* concerning customs, customs; **cinta daziaria** series of toll gates; customs; **tariffa daziaria** customs duty

daziere (dâ·tsyā'rā) *m* customs official

dazio (dâ'tsyō) *m* duty, excise, tax

dea (dā'â) *f* goddess

deambulare (dā·âm·bū·lâ'rā) *vi* to walk about, stroll around

debellamento (dā·bāl·lâ·mān'tō) *m* defeat, overthrow

debellare (dā·bāl·lâ'rā) *vt* to defeat; to subdue; to conquer

debellatore (dā·bāl·lâ·tō'rā) *m* conqueror

debilitante (dā·bē·lē·tân'tē) *a* weakening, debilitating

debilitare (dā·bē·lē·tâ'rā) *vt* to weaken

debilitazione (dā·bē·lē·tâ·tsyō'nā) *f* weakening, debilitation

debitamente (dā·bē·tâ·mān'tā) *adv* properly, correctly

debito (de'bē·tō) *m* debt; — **ipotecario** mortgage; **essere pieno di debiti** to be up to one's neck in debts; **farsi — di** to make a special point of; **mettere a —**, **scrivere a —** to debit; **uscire di —** to

pay one's debts; — *a* proper, due; **a tempo** — in good time; — **modo** proper way; **-re** (dā·bē·tō'rā) *m* debtor

debole (de'bō'lā) *a* weak; **-zza** (dā·bō'lā'tsâ) *f* weakness

debosciato (dā·bō·shâ'tō) *a* debauched

debraiare (dā·brâ·yâ'rā) *vt* (*auto*) to declutch, release the clutch of

debuttante (dā·būt·tân'tā) *m&f* (*theat*) actor or actress making his first stage appearance

debuttare (dā·būt·tâ'rā) *vi* to make one's debut

debutto (dā·būt'tō) *m* debut

decade (de'kâ·dā) *f* decade; group of ten

decadente (dā·kâ·dān'tā) *a* decadent, declining

decadenza (dā·kâ·dān'tsâ) *f* decline, decadence

decadere * (dā·kâ·dā'rā) *vi* to decay; — **da una carica** to end a term in office; to lose one's office

decaduto (dā·kâ·dū'tō) *a* deposed; declining; impoverished

decaedro (dā·kâ·â'drō) *m* (*geom*) decahedron

decagono (dā·kâ'gō·nō) *m* (*geom*) decagon

decagrammo (dā·kâ·grâm'mō) *m* decagram

decalcare (dā·kâl·kâ'rā) *vt* to trace, make a tracing of

decalco (dā·kâl'kō) *m* tracing; **-mania** (dā·kâl·kō·mâ·nē'â) *f* decalcomania, transfer

decalitro (dā·kâ'lē·trō) *m* ten liters

decalogo (dā·kâ'lō·gō) *m* decalogue

decampare (dā·kâm·pâ'rā) *vi* to decamp

decano (dā·kâ'nō) *m* dean

decantare (dā·kân·tâ'rā) *vt* to extol; to decant (*alcohol*)

decantazione (dā·kân·tâ·tsyō'nā) *f* decanting; water purification

decapitare (dā·kâ·pē·tâ'rā) *vt* to behead

decapitazione (dā·kâ·pē·tâ·tsyō'nā) *f* beheading, decapitation

decappotabile (dā·kâp·pōt·tâ'bē·lā) *a* convertible

decarburare (dā·kâr·bū·râ'rā) *vt* to decarbonize

decatlon (dā·kât·lōn') *m* decathlon

decedere (dā·che'dâ·rā) *vi* to die, pass on

deceduto (dā·chā·dū'tō) *a* dead, passed on

decennale (dā·chān·nâ'lā) *m* decennium

decenne (dā·chān'nā) *a* decennial, ten years old

decennio (dā·chen'nyō) *m* decade

decente (dā·chān'tā) *a* proper, decent

â ârm, **ā** bāby, **e** bet, **ē** bē, **ō** gō, **ô** gône, **ū** blūe, **b** bad, **ch** child, **d** dad, **f** fat, **g** gay, **j** jet

decentrare (dā·chän·trâ′rā) *vt* to decentralize

decenza (dā·chän′tsâ) *f* decency

decesso (dā·chās′sō) *m* death, demise

decidere * (dā·chē′dā·rā) *vt* to decide

decidersi * (dā·chē′dâr·sē) *vr* to arrive at a decision, make up one's mind

deciduo (dā·chē′dwō) *a* deciduous

decifrabile (dā·chē·frâ′bē·lā) *a* decipherable

decifrare (dā·chē·frâ′rā) *vt* to decode

decifrazione (dā·chē·frâ·tsyō′nä) *f* deciphering; decoding; explanation

decima (de′chē·mâ) *f* tithe; **–le** (dā·chē·mâ′lā) *a* decimal; **–re** (dā·chē·mâ′rā) *vt* to decimate, ravage

decimazione (dā·chē·mâ·tsyō′nä) *f* decimation

decimetro (dā·chē′mâ·trō) *m* decimeter

decimo (de′chē·mō) *m* tithe, tenth part; **— a** tenth; **–primo** (dā·chē·mō·prē′mō) *a* eleventh; **–secondo** (dā·chē·mō·sā·kōn′dō) *a* twelfth; **–terzo** (dā·chē·mō·tär′tsō) *a* thirteenth

decina (dā·chē′nâ) *f* about ten

decisamente (dā·chē·zâ·män′tā) *adv* positively, definitely, decidedly

decisione (dā·chē·zyō′nä) *f* decision

decisivamente (dā·chē·zē·vâ·män′tā) *adv* conclusively, finally, decisively

decisivo (dā·chē·zē′vō) *a* conclusive, final, decisive

deciso (dā·chē′zō) *a* decided, resolved, settled

declamare (dā·klâ·mâ′rā) *vt&i* to declaim, orate

declamazione (dā·klâ·mâ·tsyō′nä) *f* declaiming, harangue

declassare (dā·klâs·sâ′rā) *vt* to downgrade

declinare (dā·klē·nâ′rā) *vt&i* to decline

declinazione (dā·klē·nâ·tsyō′nä) *f* declination

declive (dā·klē′vä) *a* sloping, declining

declivio (dā·klē′vyō) *m* declivity, slope, hillside

decollaggio (dā·kōl·lâj′jō), **decollo** (dā·kōl′lō) *m* (*avi*) take-off

decollare (dā·kōl·lâ′rā) *vi* (*avi*) to take off

decolorante (dā·kō·lō·rân′tā) *m* decolorizer; bleach

decolorare (dā·kō·lō·râ′rā) *vt* to bleach; to decolorize

decolorazione (dā·kō·lō·râ·tsyō′nä) *f* bleaching

decomporre * (dā·kōm·pōr′rā) *vt* to take apart; (*math*) to factor; to decay

decomporsi * (dā·kōm·pōr′sē) *vr* to putrefy, become decomposed

decomposizione (dā·kōm·pō·zē·tsyō′nä) *f* putrefaction, decomposition

decomposto (dā·kōm·pō′stō) *a* decomposed, rotten

decompressione (dā·kōm·präs·syō′nä) *f* decompression

decorare (dā·kō·râ′rā) *vt* to decorate

decorativo (dā·kō·râ·tē′vō) *a* decorative

decorato (dā·kō·râ′tō) *a* decorated; **— m** medal winner; **–re** (dā·kō·râ·tō′rā) *m* decorator

decorazione (dā·kō·râ·tsyō′nä) *f* decoration

decoro (dā·kō′rō) *m* decorum; decency; **–samente** (dā·kō·rō·zâ·mān′tä) *adv* decently; decorously; **–so** (dā·kō·rō′zō) *a* proper; decorous

decorrenza (dā·kōr·rān′tsä) *f* beginning; coming into force; end of a period

decorrere * (dā·kôr′rā·rā) *vi* to go by, elapse; to accrue; **a — da** from, starting with

decorso (dā·kōr′sō) *m* development, course; lapse, period **— d'una malattia** the course of an illness; **— a** elapsed, gone by

decotto (dā·kōt′tō) *m* extract; decoction

decrepito (dā·krē′pē·tō) *a* ailing, decrepit

decrescente (dā·krā·shän′tä) *a* decreasing

decrescere * (dā·kre′shā·rā) *vi* to lessen; to decrease, diminish

decretare (dā·krā·tâ′rā) *vt* to decree; to stipulate

decreto (dā·krā′tō) *m* decree

decuplicare (dā·kū·plē·kâ′rā) *vt* to multiply by ten

decuplicazione (dā·kū·plē·kâ·tsyō′nä) *f* tenfold increase

decuplo (de′kū·plō) *a* ten times larger, multiplied by ten

decurtare (dā·kūr·tâ′rā) *vt* to cut down, curtail

dedalo (de′dâ·lō) *m* labyrinth, maze

dedica (de′dē·kâ) *f* dedication; **–re** (dā·dē·kâ′rā) *vt* to dedicate; **–rsi** (dā·dē·kâr′sē) *vr* to devote oneself, dedicate oneself; **–toria** (dā·dē·kâ·tô′ryâ) *f* dedication; **–torio** (dā·dē·kâ·tô′ryō) *a* dedicatory; **–zione** (dā·dē·kâ·tsyō′nä) *f* dedication, devotion

dedito (de′dē·tō) *a* dedicated; devoted; addicted

dedizione (dā·dē·tsyō′nä) *f* abnegation; submission

dedotto (dā·dōt′tō) *a* deducted; deduced, derived

dedurre * (dā·dūr′rā) *vt* to deduct, deduce, reason

---

k kid, **l** let, **m** met, **n** not, **p** pat, **r** very, **s** sat, **sh** shop, **t** tell, **v** vat, **w** we, **y** yes, **z** zero

deduttivo (dā·dŭt·tē′vō) *a* deductive

deduzione (dā·dū·tsyō′nä) *f* deduction, reasoning

defalcamento (dā·fâl·kâ·mān′tō) *m* defection; default; curtailment

defalcare (dā·fâl·kâ′rä) *vt* to deduct; to curtail

defalcazione (dā·fâl·kâ·tsyō′nä) *f* defalcation; abatement

defecare (dā·fä·kâ′rä) *vt&i* to defecate; to empty *(bowels); (chem)* to purify *(a liquid)*

defecazione (dā·fä·kâ·tsyō′nä) *f* bowel movement, defecation; excrement

defenestrare (dā·fä·nä·strâ′rä) *vt* to oust, turn out

deferente (dā·fä·rän′tä) *a* deferential

deferenza (dā·fä·rän′tsâ) *f* respect, deference; consideration; compliance

deferimento (dā·fä·rē·mān′tō) *m* deferment; regard, deference

deferire (dā·fä·rē′rä) *vt&i* to defer; — all'autorità to denounce; to submit for legal action

defezionare (dā·fä·tsyō·nâ′rä) *vi* to defect; — *vt* to betray

defezione (dā·fä·tsyō′nä) *f* defection; betrayal

deficiente (dā·fē·chän′tä) *a* feeble-minded

deficienza (dā·fē·chän′tsâ) *f* lack, insufficience, deficiency

deficit (de′fē·chĕt) *m* deficit

definibile (dā·fē·nē′bē·lä) *a* definable

definire (dā·fē·nē′rä) *vt* to define; to limit

definitivamente (dā·fē·nē·tē·vâ·mān′tä) *adv* definitely, absolutely; once and for all

definitivo (dā·fē·nē·tē′vō) *a* conclusive, definitive

definizione (dā·fē·nē·tsyō′nä) *f* definition; limitation

deflazione (dā·flâ·tsyō′nä) *f* deflation

deflettere * (dā·flet′tä·rä) *vi* to deflect

deflettore (dā·flet·tō′rä) *m (avi)* deflector

deflorare (dā·flō·râ′rä) *vt* to rape, ravish; to deflower

deflorazione (dā·flō·râ·tsyō′nä) *f* rape, violation

deformare (dā·fōr·mâ′rä) *vt* to deform

deformazione (dā·fōr·mâ·tsyō′nä) *f* deformation

deforme (dā·fōr′mä) *a* deformed; ugly

deformità (dā·fōr·mē·tâ′) *f* deformity

defraudare (dā·frâû·dâ′rä) *vt* to defraud; to deceive

defraudazione (dā·frâû·dâ·tsyō′nä) *f* deceit, defrauding

defunto (dā·fūn′tō) *a* dead; late

degenerare (dā·jä·nä·râ′rä) *vi* to degenerate

degenerato (dā·jä·nä·râ′tō) *a&m* degenerate

degente (dā·jän′tä) *a* sick in bed; — *m* bed patient

degenza (dā·jän′tsâ) *f* period of illness; hospital stay; **certificato di —** medical certificate of illness

deglutire (dā·glū·tē′rä) *vt* to swallow

deglutizione (dā·glū·tē·tsyō′nä) *f* swallowing

degnamente (dā·nyâ·mān′tä) *adv* properly, worthily; adequately

degnare (dā·nyâ′rä) *vt* to grant

degnarsi (dā·nyâr·sē) *vr* to deign, see fit

degnazione (dā·nyâ·tsyō′nä) *f* compliance; condescension; graciousness, affability

degno (dā′nyō) *a* worthy; adequate

degradare (dā·grâ·dâ′rä) *vt* to degrade

degradazione (dā·grâ·dâ·tsyō′nä) *f* debasement, degradation

degrassaggio (dā·grâs·sâj′jō) *m* greasing

degustare (dā·gū·stâ′rä) *vt* to taste; to make a sampling of

degustazione (dā·gū·stâ·tsyō′nä) *f* tasting

deificare (dāē·fē·kâ′rä) *vt* to idolize, deify

deificazione (dāē·fē·kâ·tsyō′nä) *f* deification

delatore (dā·lâ·tō′rä) *m* informer

delazione (dā·lâ·tsyō′nä) *f* secret accusal; informing

delebile (dā·le′bē·lä) *a* removable, delible

delega (de′lâ·gâ) *f* power of attorney; **–re** (dā·lâ·gâ′rä) *vt* to delegate; **–to** (dā·lâ·gâ′tō) *m* delegate; director; **–zione** (dā·lâ·gâ·tsyō′nä) *f* commission; delegation

delibera (dā·lē′bâ·râ) *f* deliberation; auction sale; **–re** (dā·lē·bâ·râ′rä) *vt&i* to deliberate; **–tamente** (dā·lē·bâ·râ·tâ·mān′tä) *adv* on purpose, deliberately; **–to** (dā·lē·bâ·râ′tō) *a* resolved; **–to** *m* resolution

delicatamente (dā·lē·kâ·tâ·mān′tä) *adv* sensitively, delicately

delicatezza (dā·lē·kâ·tâ′tsâ) *f* delicacy; tact

delicato (dā·lē·kâ′tō) *a* delicate; tactful

delinquente (dā·lēn·kwän′tä) *a&m* criminal

delinquenza (dā·lēn·kwän′tsâ) *f* crime

delinquere (dā·lēn′kwä·rä) *vi (law)* to commit a crime; **associazione a —** crime syndicate

delirare (dā·lē·râ′rä) *vi* to be delirious

delirio (dā·lē′ryō) *m* delirium

delitto (dā·lēt′tō) *m* crime

â ârm, ā bāby, e bet, ē bē, ō gō, ô gône, ū blūe, b bad, ch child, d dad, f fat, g gay, j jet

delizia (dā·lē′tsyâ) *f* great joy, delight; tastiness

delizioso (dā·lē·tsyō′zō) *a* delightful; delicious; exquisite

delucidazione (dā·lū·chē·dâ·tsyō′nä) *f* explanation, elucidation

deludere * (dā·lū′dā·rä) *vt* to disappoint; to avoid

delusione (dā·lū·zyō′nä) *f* disappointment

deluso (dā·lū′zō) *a* tricked; disappointed

demagogia (dā·mâ·gō·jē′â) *f* demagoguery

demagogico (dā·mâ·gô′jē·kō) *a* demagogic

demagogo (dā·mâ·gō′gō) *m* demagogue

demaniale (dā·mâ·nyä′lä) *a* owned by the government

demanio (dā·mâ′nyō) *m* public property; government property

demarcazione (dā·mâr·kâ·tsyō′nä) *f* demarcation

demente (dā·mān′tä) *a* demented

demenza (dā·mān′tsä) *f* madness, insanity

demilitarizzare (dā·mē·lē·tâ·rē·dzâ′rä) *vt* to demilitarize

democratico (dā·mō·krâ′tē·kō) *a* democratic

democrazia (dā·mō·krâ·tsē′â) *f* democracy

democristiano (dā·mō·krē·styâ′nō) *a&m* Christian Democrat

demodossologia (dā·mō·dōs·sō·lō·jē′â) *f* study of public opinion

demografico (dā·mō·grâ′fē·kō) *a* demographic

demolire (dā·mō·lē′rä) *vt* to wreck, knock down

demolizione (dā·mō·lē·tsyō′nä) *f* demolition

demone (de′mō·nä), **demonio** (dā·mô′nyō) *m* demon

demonietto (dā·mō·nyät′tō) *m* little devil, imp

demoralizzare (dā·mō·râ·lē·dzâ′rä) *vt* to demoralize; to cause to lose heart

demoralizzazione (dā·mō·râ·lē·dzâ·tsyō′nä) *f* demoralization, losing heart

denaro (dā·nâ′rō) *m* money; — **contante** cash; **denari** diamonds (*cards*)

denaturante (dā·nâ·tū·rân′tä) *m* denaturant

denaturare (dā·nâ·tū·râ′rä) *vt* to denature

denaturato (dā·nâ·tū·râ′tō) *a* denatured; **alcool** — denatured alcohol

denicotinizzare (dē·nē·kō·tē·nē·dzâ′rä) *vt* to denicotinize

denigrare (dā·nē·grâ′rä) *vt* to defame, cast aspersions on

denigratore (dā·nē·grâ′tō′rä) *m* slanderer

denigrazione (dā·nē·grâ·tsyō′nä) *f* detraction; defamation, slander

denominare (dā·nō·mē·nâ′rä) *vt* to name

denominativo (dā·nō·mē·nâ·tē′vō) *a* denominative

denominatore (dā·nō·mē·nâ·tō′rä) *m* (*math*) denominator

denominazione (dā·nō·mē·nâ·tsyō′nä) *f* title, denomination

denotare (dā·nō·tâ′rä) *vt* to signify, mean

densità (dān·sē·tâ′) *f* density

denso (dān′sō) *a* dense

dentale (dān·tâ′lä), **dentario** (dān·tâ′ryō) *a* dental

dentaruolo (dān·tâ·rūō′lō) *m* pacifier

dentata (dān·tâ′tâ) *f* bite; bite mark

dentato (dān·tâ′tō) *a* notched; toothed; cogged; (*bot*) dentate

dentatura (dān·tâ·tū′râ) *f* set of teeth, denture

dente (dān′tä) *m* tooth; — **canino** eye tooth; — **d'elefante** tusk; — **del giudizio** wisdom tooth; — **per** — tit for tat; **otturare un** — to fill a tooth; **denti d'ingranaggio** cogs (*gear*); **dai denti lunghi** (*fig*) greedy; **mal di denti** toothache; **mettere i denti** to cut one's teeth; **mostrare i denti** (*fig*) to show one's teeth (*fig*); **non è pane per i tuoi denti** (*fig*) it's not your cup of tea; it's out of your field

dentellare (dān·tāl·lâ′rä) *vt* to indent, tooth; to make notches in

dentellatura (dān·tāl·lâ·tū′râ) *f* notching; toothing

dentello (dān·tāl′lō) *m* (*mech*) notch, tooth; (*arch*) dentil

dentiera (dān·tyâ′râ) *f* denture, plate

dentifricio (dān·tē·frē′chō) *m* dentrifice

dentista (dān·tē′stä) *m* dentist

dentro (dān′trō) *adv* inside, within

denudare (dā·nū·dâ′rä) *vt* to lay bare, denude

denudarsi (dā·nū·dâr′sē) *vr* to strip oneself; to undress

denuncia (dā·nūn′châ), **denunzia** (dā·nūn′tsyâ) *f* report; complaint, censuring

denunciare (dā·nūn·châ′rä), **denunziare** (dā·nūn·tsyâ′rä) *vt* to denounce; to report

denutrito (dā·ñū·trē′tō) *a* undernourished

denutrizione (dā·nū·trē·tsyō′nä) *f* undernourishment, inadequate diet

deodorante (dā·ō·dō·rân′tä) *a&m* deodorant; antiperspirant

---

k kid, **l** let, **m** met, **n** not, **p** pat, **r** very, **s** sat, **sh** shop, **t** tell, **v** vat, **w** we, **y** yes, **z** zero

deossidante (dā·ōs·sē·dân'tä) *a (chem)* deoxidizer
deossidazione (dā·os·sē·dâ·tsyō'nä) *f* deoxygenation
deperibile (dā·pā·rē'bē·lä) *a* perishable
deperimento (dā·pā·rē·mān'tō) *m* decay; wasting away; decline; — **nervoso** nervous exhaustion
depilare (dā·pē·lâ'rä) *vt* to depilate
depilatorio (dā·pē·lâ'tō'ryō) *m* depilatory
depilazione (dā·pē·lâ·tsyō'nä) *f* hair removal
deplorare (dā·plō·râ'rä) *vt* to deplore
deplorevole (dā·plō·re'vō·lä) *a* deplorable
depolarizzare (dā·pō·lâ·rē·dzä'rä) *vt (elec)* to depolarize
deponente (dā·pō·nān'tä) *m (law)* witness; — *a&m* deponent
deporre * (dā·pōr'rä) *vt* to lay down; — *vi* to testify, give testimony
deportare (dā·pōr·tâ'rä) *vt* to deport
deportazione (dā·pōr·tâ·tsyō'nä) *f* deportation
depositante (dā·pō·zē·tân'tä) *m* depositor
depositario (dā·pō·zē·tâ'ryō) *m* depository
deposito (dā·pô'zē·tō) *m* deposit; — **bagagli** baggage room; — **di colli a mano** checkroom
deposizione (dā·pō·zē·tsyō'nä) *f* deposition; declaration
depravare (dā·prâ·vâ'rä) *vt* to corrupt, deprave
depravato (dā·prâ·vâ'tō) *a* depraved
depravazione (dā·prâ·vâ·tsyō'nä) *f* corruption, depravation
deprecare (dā·prâ·kâ'rä) *vt* to deprecate; to disapprove of
depressione (dā·prās·syō'nä) *f* depression
depresso (dā·prās'sō) *a* dejected, saddened
deprezzamento (dā·prā·tsâ·mān'tō) *m* depreciation, drop in value
deprezzare (dā·prā·tsâ'rä) *vt* to disparage
deprimente (dā·prē·mān'tä) *a* depressing
depurare (dā·pū·râ'rä) *vt* to purify
depuratore (dā·pū·râ·tō'rä) *m* cleaner; — **d'acqua** water softener; — **d'aria** air cleaner; air filter
deputato (dā·pū·tâ'tō) *m* deputy; delegate
deputazione (dā·pū·tâ·tsyō'nä) *f* committee; delegation, authorized commission
deragliamento (dā·râ·lyâ·mān'tō) *m* derailment
deragliare (dā·râ·lyâ'rä) *vi* to derail
derapare (dā·râ·pâ'rä) *vi* to skid, career
derapata (dā·râ·pâ'tä) *f (avi)* skidding
derelitto (dā·rā·lēt'tō) *m* derelict, waif; **ospizio dei derelitti** home for lost chil-

dren; — *a* abandoned, forsaken *(children)*
deretano (dā·rā·tâ'nō) *m* buttocks, derriere
deridere (dā·rē'dä·rä) *vt* to deride
derisione (dā·rē·zyō'nä) *f* ridicule
deriva (dā·rē'vâ) *f* drift; **–re** (dā·rē·vâ'rä) *vi* to derive; **–zione** (dā·rē·vâ·tsyō'nä) *f* derivation; telephone extension
derma (dār'mâ) *f (anat)* skin; dermis; **–tite** (dār·mâ·tē'tä) *f (med)* dermatitis; **–tologia** (dār·mâ·tō·lō·jē'â) *f (med)* dermatology
dermoide (dār·mô'ē·dä) *f* imitation leather, leatherette
deroga (de'rō·gâ) *f* noncompliance; **–re** (dā·rō·gâ'rä) *vi* to fail to comply; to depart from; **–toria** (dā·rō·gâ·tō'ryâ) *f (law)* conditional clause
derrata (dār·râ'tâ) *f* foodstuff
derubare (dā·rū·bâ'rä) *vt* to rob
desco (dā'skō) *m* table; table ready for dinner
descrittivamente (dā·skrēt·tē·vâ·mān'tä) *adv* descriptively
descrittivo (dā·skrēt·tē'vō) *a* descriptive
descrivere * (dā·skrē'vä·rä) *vt* to describe
descrizione (dā·skrē·tsyō'nä) *f* description
desensibilizzatore (dā·sān·sē·bē·lē·dzä·tō'rä) *m (phot)* desensitizer
deserto (dā·zār'tō) *m* desert; — *a* abandoned, deserted
desiderabile (dā·zē·dâ·râ'bē·lä) *a* desirable
desiderare (dā·zē·dâ·râ'rä) *vt* to wish
desiderio (dā·zē·de'ryō) *m* desire, wish
desideroso (dā·zē·dâ·rō'zō) *a* anxious
designare (dā·zē·nyâ'rä) *vt* to designate
designazione (dā·zē·nyâ·tsyō'nä) *f* nomination, designation
desinare (dā·zē·nâ'rä) *m* dinner, supper; — *vi* to dine; **dopo** — after dinner
desinenza (dā·zē·nân'tsä) *f* ending, suffix
desistere * (dā·zē'stä·rä) *vi* to desist; to refrain
desolante (dā·zō·lân'tä) *a* grievous, trying *(fig)*; distressing; discouraging
desolatamente (dā·zō·lâ·tâ·mān'tä) *adv* desolately
desolato (dā·zō·lâ'tō) *a* dejected, desolate; **–re** (dā·zō·lâ·tō'rä) *m* destroyer, desolator
desolazione (dā·zō·lâ·tsyō'nä) *f* grief, anguish, distress; desolation; ruin
despota (de'spō·tâ) *m* despot
desquamazione (dā·skwâ·mâ·tsyō'nä) *f* scaling *(fish)*
destare (dā·stâ'rä) *vt* to awaken; to arouse,

â ârm, ā bāby, e bet, ē bē, ō gō, ô gône, ū blūe, b bad, ch child, d dad, f fat, g gay, j jet

stir up

destarsi (dā·stâr′sē) *vr* to wake up, arise

destinare (dā·stē·nâ′rā) *vt* to destine, decree; to appoint; to address, send

destinatario (dā·stē·nâ·tâ′ryō) *m* addressee

destinato (dā·stē·nâ′tō) *a* intended; ordained, destined; — **a perire** doomed to perish; — **a New York** appointed to New York

destinazione (dā·stē·nâ·tsyō′nā) *f* destination

destino (dā·stē′nō) *m* fate; destination

destituire (dā·stē·twē′rā) *vt* to remove, turn out of office

destituzione (dā·stē·tū·tsyō′nā) *f* removal

desto (dā′stō) *a* wide awake *(fig)*; fast, sharp, lively

destra (dā′strâ) *f* right hand; **a** — to the right

destramente (dā·strâ·mān′tā) *adv* cleverly, dexterously

destreggiare (dā·strāj·jâ′rā) *vi*, **destreggiarsi** (dā·strāj·jâr′sē) *vr* to devise, contrive, manage smartly; to strive; to manipulate

destrezza (dā·strā′tsâ) *f* dexterity

destriero (dā·stryā′rō) *m* steed, war-horse

destro (dā′strō) *a* clever; — *m* chance; righthand side; **–rso** (dā·strōr′sō) *a* righthanded; clockwise

destrosio (dā·strô′zyō) *m* dextrose

desumere * (dā·zū′mā·rā) *vt* to deduce

desumibile (dā·zū·mē′bē·lā) *a* deducible; inferential

desunto (dā·zūn′tō) *a* deduced, inferred; derived

detenere * (dā·tā·nā′rā) *vt* to keep; to hold under arrest; to detain; to retain; — **un incarico** to hold a job, occupy a post

detentore (dā·tān·tō′rā) *m* holder; possessor

detenuto (dā·tā·nū′tō) *a* detained; — *m* prisoner, convict

detenzione (dā·tān·tsyō′nā) *f* detention

detergente (dā·tār·jān′tā) *a&m* detergent

detergere (dā·ter′jā·rā) *vt* to clean

deteriorabile (dā·tā·ryō·râ′bē·lā) *a* susceptible to deterioration

deterioramento (dā·tā·ryō·râ·mān′tō) *m* deterioration

deteriorare (dā·tā·ryō·râ′rā) *vt&i* to deteriorate, spoil

deteriorato (dā·tā·ryō·râ′tō) *a* deteriorated; damaged, wasted, spoiled

determinante (dā·tār·mē·nân′tā) *a* determining; **causa** — determining factor

determinare (dā·tār·mē·nâ′rā) *vt* to estab-

lish; to cause; to resolve, decide

determinarsi (dā·tār·mē·nâr′sē) *vr* to resolve, make up one's mind

determinatamente (dā·tār·mē·nâ·tâ·mān′tā) *adv* determinedly

determinatezza (dā·tār′mē·nâ·tā′tsâ) *f* resoluteness, firmness *(spirit)*; determination

determinativo (dā·tār·mē·nâ·tē′vō) *a* determining, decisive; clinching *(coll)*

determinato (dā·tār·mē·nâ′tō) *a* determined, fixed

determinismo (dā·tār·mē·nē′zmō) *m* determinism

detersivo (dā·tār·sē′vō) *m* detergent

detestabile (dā·tā·stâ′bē·lā) *a* hateful, detestable

detestare (dā·tā·stâ′rā) *vt* to detest, hate

detettore (dā·tāt·tō′rā) *m* detector

detonazione (dā·tō·nâ·tsyō′nā) *f* detonation

detrarre * (dā·trâr′rā) *vt* to deduct; to detract from

detrattore (dā·trât·tō′rā) *m* detractor

detrimento (dā·trē·mân′tō) *m* detriment, harm

detrito (dā·trē′tō) *m* debris; rubbish

detronizzare (dā·trō·nē·dzâ′rā) *vt* to dethrone

detta (dāt′tâ) *f* opinion; word; **a — di tutti** according to general opinion; **a — tua** according to you; **–fono** (dāt·tâ′fô·nō) *m* dictaphone; **–re** (dāt·tâ′rā) *vt* to dictate; **–to** (dāt·tâ′tō) *m* dictation; **–tura** (dāt·tâ·tū′râ) *f* dictation *(act)*; **scrivere sotto –tura** to write from dictation

dettagliante (dāt·tâ·lyân′tâ) *m* retailer

dettagliare (dāt·tâ·lyâ′rā) *vt* to retail; to detail, relate in detail

dettagliatamente (dāt·tâ·lyâ·tâ·mān′tā) *adv* detailedly, in detail

dettaglio (dāt·tâ′lyō) *m* specific, detail; retail sale

detto (dāt′tō) *m* expression; saying, proverb, maxim; motto; witticism; **secondo il** — as the saying goes; **detti memorabili** memorable words, **i detti di Cristo** Christ's words; — *a* said, called, named; — **fatto** no sooner said than done; **Alessandro** — **il Grande** Alexander the Great; **è presto** — it is easy to say

deturpare (dā·tūr·pâ′rā) *vt* to disfigure; to spoil; to deface

deturpazione (dā·tūr·pâ·tsyō′nā) *f* disfigurement

devastare (dā·vâ·stâ′rā) *vt* to devastate, ruin

devastazione (dā·vâ·stâ·tsyō′nā) *f* ruin,

waste, havoc, devastation

deviare (dā·vyâ'rā) *vi* to deviate; to detour, switch

deviatore (dā·vyâ·tō'rā) *m* switchman

deviazione (dā·vyâ·tsyō'nā) *f* detour

deviazionista (dā·vyâ·tsyō·nē'stä) *m* deviationist; deviate

devitalizzare (dā·vē·tâ·lē·dzâ'rā) *vt* to devitalize

devoluto (dā·vō·lū'tō) *a* transmitted, delivered over, transferred

devoluzione (dā·vō·lū·tsyō'nā) *f* transmission, transfer, devolution

devolvere * (dā·vōl'vā·rā) *vt* to transfer, devolve; to appropriate

devolversi * (dā·vōl'vär·sē) *vr* to be transferred, devolve; to be assigned; to turn

devotissimo (dā·vō·tēs'sē·mō) *a* very devoted; highly devout; very sincerely

devoto (dā·vō'tō) *a* devout, pious; devoted, attached; destined; — *m* devout person

devozione (dā·vō·tsyō'nā) *f* devotion; **fare le proprie devozioni** to do one's devotions

di (dē) *prep* of, about, from, any, by, at, some, with

dì (dē) *m* day; **a — 10 di dicembre** on the 10th of December; **al — d'oggi** nowadays; **buon — ** good day; **mezzodì** midday; **sul fare del — ** at dawn

diabete (dyâ·bā'tā) *m* diabetes

diabolicamente (dyâ·bō·lē·kâ·mān'tā) *adv* devilishly, diabolically

diabolico (dyâ·bô'lē·kō) *a* devilish, diabolic

diacono (dyâ'kō·nō) *m (eccl)* deacon

diadema (dyâ·dā'mâ) *m* tiara

diafano (dyâ'fâ·nō) *a* transparent

diaframma (dyâ·frâm'mâ) *m* diaphragm

diagnosi (dyâ'nyō·zē) *f* diagnosis

diagnosticare (dyâ·nyō·stē·kâ'rā) *vt* to diagnose

diagnostico (dyâ·nyō'stē·kō) *a* diagnostic; — *m* diagnostician

diagonale (dyâ·gō·nâ'lā) *a* diagonal

diagramma (dyâ·grâm'mâ) *m* diagram

dialettale (dyâ·lät·tâ'lā) *a* dialectical

dialettica (dyâ·let'tē·kâ) *f* dialectics

dialetto (dyâ·lāt'tō) *m* dialect

dialogo (dyâ'lō·gō) *m* dialogue

diamante (dyâ·mân'tā) *m* diamond

diamantifero (dyâ·mân·tē'fâ·rō) *a* diamond-bearing

diamantino (dyâ·mân·tē'nō) *a* adamant, rigid

diametro (dyâ'mā·trō) *m* diameter

diamine! (dyâ'mē·nā) *interj* good heavens!

diana (dyâ'nâ) *f* morning star; *(mil)* **suonar la — ** to sound reveille

diapason (dyâ'pâ·zōn) *m* tuning fork

diapositiva (dyâ·pō·zē·tē'vâ) *f* slide; color transparency

diaria (dyâ'ryâ) *f* travelling allowance

diario (dyâ'ryō) *m* diary; — *a* daily

diarrea (dyâr·rā'â) *f* diarrhea

diavoleria (dyâ·vō·lā·rē'â) *f* mischief, deviltry

diavoletto (dyâ·vō·lāt'tō) *m* little devil, imp, mischief

diavolo (dyâ'vō·lō) *m* devil; —! *interj* heck! what the heck!

dibattere (dē·bât'tā·rā) *vt* to discuss, debate

dibattersi (dē·bât'tār·sē) *vr* to struggle; to contest; to flounder

dibattimento (dē·bât·tē·mān'tō) *m* debate

dibattuto (dē·bât·tū'tō) *a* discussed, debated; controversial; contested; **questione dibattuta** controversial issue

dicastero (dē·kâ·stā'rō) *m* government department; department of a Cabinet member

dicembre (dē·chām'brā) *m* December

diceria (dē·chā·rē'â) *f* rumor, gossip

dichiarare (dē·kyâ·râ'rā) *vt* to declare

dichiarazione (dē·kyâ·râ·tsyō'nā) *f* declaration; — **giurata** affidavit

diciannove (dē·chân·nō'vā) *a* nineteen; **–simo** (dē·chân·nō·ve'zē·mō) *a* nineteenth

diciassette (dē·châs·sāt'tā) *a* seventeen; **–simo** (dē·châs·sät·te'zē·mō) *a* seventeenth

diciottesimo (dē·chōt·te'zē·mô) *a* eighteenth

diciotto (dē·chōt'tō) *a* eighteen

dicitore (dē·chē·tō'rā) *m* speaker, lecturer

dicitura (dē·chē·tū'râ) *f* phrasing, wording; style; delivery; pronunciation; **con la seguente — ** worded as follows; **una bella — ** a good delivery *(speech)*

dicotiledone (dē·kō·tē·le'dō·nā) *m (bot)* dicotyledon

didascalia (dē·dâ·skâ·lē'â) *f* caption; stage directions

didattico (dē·dât'tē·kô) *a* educational

dieci (dyâ'chē) *a* ten; **–mila** (dyâ·chē·mē'lä) *a* ten thousand; **–millesimo** (dyâ·chē·mēl·le'zē·mō) *a* ten thousandth; **–na** (dyâ·chē'nâ) *f* about ten; half a score

diesis (dyâ'zēs) *m (mus)* sharp

dieta (dyâ'tâ) *f* diet

dietetica (dyâ·te'tē·kâ) *f* dietetics

dietetico (dyâ·te'tē·kō) *a* dietetic

dietro (dyā'trō) *prep&adv* behind, after; — accettazione *(com)* on agreement, upon acceptance; — **front!** *(mil)* about face!; — **le quinte** *(fig)* behind the scene; — **le spalle** behind one's back; — **ricevuta** against receipt; — **richiesta** upon request; — **sborso di** on payment of; **andar** — to follow behind; **per di** — from behind; **tener** — to follow; **to agree**

difatti (dē·fât'tē) *adv* really, in fact

difendere * (dē·fen'dā'rā) *vt* to defend; to uphold

difensore (dē·fān·sō'rā) *m* defender

difesa (dē·fā'zä) *f* defense; — **legittima** self defense; **prendere la — di** to take the side of; to go to the defense of; **senza** — defenseless

difeso (dē·fā'zō) *a* sheltered; protected, defended

difetto (dē·fāt'tō) *m* fault, flaw; **–so** (dē·fāt·tō'zō) *a* faulty; fallible

diffamare (dēf·fâ·mâ'rā) *vt* to defame

diffamazione (dēf·fâ·mâ·tsyō'nä) *f* defamation

differente (dēf·fä·rän'tä) *a* different

differenziale (dēf·fä·rän·tsyâ'lä) *a&m* differential

differire (dēf·fä·rē'rä) *vi* to delay, put off

difficile (dēf·fē'chē·lä) *a* difficult

difficilmente (dēf·fē·chēl·män'tä) *adv* with difficulty; barely; hardly possible

difficoltà (dēf·fē·kōl·tä') *f* difficulty

diffida (dēf·fē'dä) *f* warning; notice; **–re** (dēf·fē·dâ'rä) *vt* to enjoin, warn; **–re** *vi* to distrust

diffidente (dēf·fē·dän'tä) *a* distrustful

diffidenza (dēf·fē·dän'tsâ) *f* suspicion, diffidence

diffondere (dēf·fôn'dā·rä) *vt* to spread

diffusamente (dēf·fū·zâ·män'tä) *adv* abundantly

diffusione (dēf·fū·zyō'nä) *f* diffusion

diffuso (dēf·fū'zō) *a* widespread, rife

difterite (dēf·tä·rē'tä) *f* diphtheria

diga (dē'gâ) *f* dam

digeribile (dē·jä·rē'bē·lä) *a* digestible

digerire (dē·jä·rē'rä) *vt* to digest

digerito (dē·jä·rē'tō) *a* digested

digestione (dē·jä·styō'nä) *f* digestion

digestivo (dē·jä·stē'vō) *a* digestive

digesto (dē·jä'stō) *m (law)* digest

digiunare (dē·jū·nâ'rä) *vi* to fast

digiuno (dē·jū'nō) *m* fast

dignità (dē·nyē·tâ') *f* dignity

dignitario (dē·nyē·tâ'ryō) *m* dignitary

dignitosamente (dē·nyē·tō·zâ·män'tä) *adv* with dignity, properly.

dignitoso (dē·nyē·tō'zō) *a* dignified

digressione (dē·grâs·syō'nä) *f* digression

digrignare (dē·grē·nyâ'rä) *vi* to grind one's teeth, gnash one's teeth

dilagare (dē·lâ·gâ'rä) *vi* to overflow, run over

dilaniare (dē·lâ·nyâ'rä) *vt* to lacerate, tear

dilapidare (dē·lâ·pē·dâ'rä) *vt* to squander, spend foolishly

dilapidato (dē·lâ·pē·dâ'tō) *a* squandered, spent recklessly

dilatare (dē·lâ·tâ'rä) *vt* to dilate

dilatazione (dē·lâ·tâ·tsyō'nä) *f* expansion; dilation

dilazionare (dē·lâ·tsyō·nâ'rä) *vt* to delay

dilazione (dē·lâ·tsyō'nä) *f* respite, delay

dileguare (dē·lä·gwâ'rä) *vt* to disperse, scatter; to route, set to route

dilemma (dē·lām'mâ) *m* dilemma

dilettante (dē·lät·tân'tä) *m&a* amateur

dilettevole (dē·lät·te'vō·lä) *a* delightful, charming

diletto (dē·lât'tō) *m* delight; — *a* beloved

diligente (dē·lē·jän'tä) *a* diligent

diligenza (dē·lē·jän'tsâ) *f* diligence

diluire (dē·lwē'rä) *vt* to dilute

diluvio (dē·lū'vyō) *m* deluge

dimagrare (dē·mâ·grâ'rä), **dimagrire** (dē·mâ·grē'rä) *vi* to reduce, lose weight

dimensione (dē·mān·syō'nä) *f* dimension

dimenticanza (dē·mān·tē·kân'tsâ) *f* oversight; absentmindedness

dimenticare (dē·mān·tē·kâ'rä) *vt* to forget

dimesso (dē·mâs'sō) *a* humble; dismissed

dimettere * (dē·met'tä·rä) *vt* to dismiss; to stop, give up

dimettersi * (dē·met'tär·sē) *vr* to resign

diminuire (dē·mē·nwē'rä) *vt&i* to decrease, abate, lessen

diminutivo (dē·mē·nū·tē'vō) *a&m* diminutive

diminuzione (dē·mē·nū·tysō'nä) *f* decrease

dimissionare (dē·mēs·syō·nâ'rä) *vt* to discharge, dismiss; — *vi* to resign

dimissionario (dē·mēs·syō·nâ'ryō) *a* resigning

dimissione (dē·mēs·syō'nä) *f* resignation

dimora (dē·mō'râ) *f* residence; **–re** (dē·mō·râ'rä) *vt* to stay, dwell, live; to delay

dimostrare (dē·mō·strâ'rä) *vt* to demonstrate; to evidence, show

dimostrazione (dē·mō·strâ·tsyō'nä) *f* evidence, demonstration

dinamica (dē·nâ'mē·kâ) *f* dynamics

dinamico (dē·nâ'mē·kō) *a* dynamic

dinamite (dē·nâ·mē'tä) *f* dynamite

---

k kid, **l** let, **m** met, **n** not, **p** pat, **r** very, **s** sat, **sh** shop, **t** tell, **v** vat, **w** we, **y** yes, **z** zero

dinamo (dē'nà·mō) *f* generator; dynamo
dinanzi (dē·nân'tsē) *prep&adv* before
dinastia (dē·nà·stē'à) *f* dynasty
dindo (dēn'dō), **dindio** (dēn'dyō) *m* turkey
dinoccolato (dē·nōk·kō·là'tō) *a* awkward; slouchy; sloppy
dinosauro (dē·nō·sâ'ū·rō) *m* dinosaur
dintorni (dēn·tōr'nē) *mpl* environs
Dio (dē'ō) *m* God, Almighty, Lord
dio (dē'ō) *m* deity, god
diocesi (dyō'chā·zē) *f* diocese
diodo (dyō'dō) *m* diode
dipanare (dē·pà·nâ'rà) *vt* to unravel; to clear up, solve
dipartimento (dē·pâr·tē·mān'tō) *m* department
dipendente (dē·pān·dān'tà) *a&m* dependent
dipendenza (dē·pān·dān'tsà) *f* dependence
dipendere * (dē·pen'dà·rà) *vi* to depend
dipingere * (dē·pēn'jà·rà) *vt* to paint; to describe, depict
dipinto (dē·pēn'tō) *a* painted; — *m* painting, picture
diploma (dē·plō'mà) *m* diploma; **–re** (dē·plō·mâ'rà) *vt* to confer a diploma; **–rsi** (dē·plō·mâr'sē) *vr* to obtain a diploma, be graduated; **–tica** (dē·plō·mâ'tē·kâ) *f* art of diplomacy; **–ticamente** (dē·plō·mâ·tē·kâ·mān'tà) *adv* diplomatically; **–tico** (dē·plō·mâ'tē·kō) *a* diplomatic; **–tico** *m* diplomat; **–to** (dē·plō·mâ'tō) *m* graduate; **–zia** (dē·plō·mâ·tsē'à) *f* diplomacy
diporto (dē·pōr'tō) *m* pleasure
diramare (dē·râ·mâ'rà) *vt* to send out, circulate
diramarsi (dē·râ·mâr'sē) *vr* to ramify, branch out
diramazione (dē·râ·mâ·tsyō'nà) *f* ramification, branching out
dire * (dē'rà) *vt* to say; to tell; — **pane al pane** (*fig*) to call a spade a spade (*fig*); **a — il vero** to tell the truth; **aver a che — con qualcuno** to quarrel with somebody; **che cosa vuol —?** what does it mean?; **come si suol —** as the saying goes; **lasciar —** to let people talk; **mandare a —** to send word; **per così —** as it were, so to speak; **si dice** it is said; **vale a —** that is to say; **voler —** to mean to say; **al — di tutti** according to public opinion; **l'arte del —** public speaking; **oltre ogni —** beyond description
direttamente (dē·rāt·tâ·mān'tà) *adv* directly
direttissimo (dē·rāt·tēs'sē·mō) *m* through train; — *a* very direct

direttiva (dē·rāt·tē'và) *f* directive; policy; direction
diretto (dē·rāt'tō) *a* direct; — *m* fast train
direttore (dē·rāt·tō'rà) *m*, **direttrice** (dē·rāt·trē'chā) *f* director, manager
direzione (dē·rā·tsyō'nà) *f* direction, management; board of directors
dirigente (dē·rē·jān'tà) *a&m* executive
dirigere * (dē·rē'jà·rà) *vt* to manage, run; (*mus*) to conduct
dirigersi * (dē·rē'jàr·sē) *vr* to apply
dirigibile (dē·rē·jē'bē·là) *m* dirigible
dirigismo (dē·rē·jē'zmō) *m* planned economy
dirimpetto (dē·rēm·pāt'tō) *adv&prep* opposite
diritto (dē·rēt'tō) *m* right; law; — *a* straight; — **canonico** canon law; — **d'autore** copyright; **a buon —** with good reason, justifiedly; **maggior —** all the more reason; **sempre —** straight ahead; **a — o a rovescio** by fair means or foul
diroccato (dē·rōk·kâ'tō) *a* in ruins
dirottamente (dē·rōt·tâ·mān'tà) *adv* excessively, extremely, torrentially; **piangere —** to shed floods of tears
dirottare (dē·rōt·tâ'rà) *vt* to detour
dirotto (dē·rōt'tō) *a* pouring; torrential; **pioggia dirotta** downpour; **a —** freely, without restraint; **piove a —** it's raining cats and dogs
dirozzare (dē·rō·dzâ'rà) *vt* to educate; to polish; to refine
dirupo (dē·rū'pō) *m* precipice; ravine
disabbigliare (dē·zâb·bē·lyâ'rà) *vt* to undress
disabitato (dē·zâ·bē·tâ'tō) *a* deserted
disaccordo (dē·zâk·kōr'dō) *m* disaccord, disagreement
disadatto (dē·zâ·dât'tō) *a* maladjusted; not suitable
disadorno (dē·zâ·dōr'nō) *a* bare, plain, unadorned; **stile —** terse style
disagevole (dē·zâ·je'vō·là) *a* uneasy; hard, difficult; uncomfortable, rough
disagio (dē·zâ'jō) *m* discomfort; anxiety, disquiet
disanimare (dē·zâ·nē·mâ'rà) *vt* to dispirit, discourage
disanimato (dē·zâ·nē·mâ'tō) *a* dispirited, discouraged
disapprovare (dē·zâp·prō·vâ'rà) *vt* to disapprove of
disappunto (dē·zâp·pūn'tō) *m* disappointment
disarcionare (dē·zâr·chō·nâ'rà) *vt* to unsaddle; to unhorse
disarmamento (dē·zâr·mâ·mān'tō) **di-**

sarmo (dē·zâr′mō) *m* disarmament
disarmare (dē·zâr·mâ′rā) *vt* to dismantle; to disarm; *(naut)* to unrig; *(fig)* to subdue, quiet
disarmonico (dē·zâr·mô′nē·kō) *a* discordant
disarticolare (dē·zâr·tē·kō·lâ′rā) *vt* to disjoint, throw out of joint
disarticolarsi (dē·zâr·tē·kō·lâr′sē) *vr* to get dislocated, be thrown out of joint
disastrato (dē·zâ·strâ′tō) *m* victim
disastro (dē·zâ′strō) *m* disaster
disastroso (dē·zâ·strō′zō) *a* catastrophic
disattento (dē·zât·tān′tō) *a* careless
disattenzione (dē·zât·tān·tsyō′nä) *f* carelessness, negligence, lack of attention
disavanzo (dē·zâ·vân′tsō) *m* deficit
disavventura (dē·zâv·vän·tū′râ) *f* bad luck, mishap, misfortune
disavvezzare (dē·zâv·vā·tsâ′rā) *vt* to dissuade; to help break the habit of; to disaccustom, wean away from
disavvezzato (dē·zâv·vā·tsâ′tō) *a* unaccustomed, not used
disboscamento (dē·zbō·skâ·män′tō) *m* deforestation
disboscare (dē·zbō·skâ′rā) *vt* to deforest
disbrigare (dē·zbrē·gâ′rā) *vt* to disentangle, disengage; to expedite, dispatch
disbrigarsi (dē·zbrē·gâr′sē) *vr* to hurry; to get rid of; to acquit oneself
disbrigo (dē·zbrē′gō) *m* dispatch; carrying through, completion
discapito (dē·skâ′pē·tō) *m* loss, damage; spoilage
discendente (dē·shän·dän′tä) *m* descendant; — *a* descending
discendenza (dē·shän·dän′tsä) *f* extraction, lineage; origin, descent
discepolo (dē·she′pō·lō) *m* disciple
discernare (dē·shâr′nä·râ) *vt* to discern
discernimento (dē·shâr·nē·män′tō) *m* discernment; **aver** — to have good sense, have good judgment
discesa (dē·shä′zä) *f* descent; — **dei prezzi** decline in prices; — **in picchiata** *(avi)* nose dive; — **rapida** steep grade; **la** — **dei barbari** the barbarian invasion of Italy; **forte** — steep descent; **in** — downhill, going down
dischiudere * (dē·skyū′dä·rā) *vt* to disclose, reveal
dischiuso (dē·skyū′zō) *a* disclosed; open, above board
discinto (dē·shēn′tō) *a* undressed; messy; unprepared
disciogliere * (dē·shô′lyä·rā) *vt* to loosen; to untie, unbind; to release; to melt

disciolto (dē·shōl′tō) *a* loose; dissolved; melted
disciplina (dē·shē·plē′nä) *f* discipline; **–re** (dē·shē·plē·nâ′rā) *vt* to discipline; **–tamente** (dē·shē·plē·nâ·tâ·män′tä) *adv* with discipline; **–to** (dē·shē·plē·nâ′tō) *a* disciplined, well-trained
disco (dē′skō) *m* record; *(sports)* disc, quoit; *(rail)* signal; — **combinatore** telephone dial; — **sul ghiaccio** ice hockey; — **volante** flying saucer; **–teca** (dē·skō·tä′kâ) *f* record library
discolorare (dē·skō·lō·râ′rä) *vt* to discolor
discolpare (dē·skōl·pâ′rä) *vt* to justify, vindicate
discolparsi (dē·skōl·pâr′sē) *vr* to vindicate oneself, clear oneself
disconoscere * (dē·skō·nō′shä·rä) *vt* to disavow; to show ingratitude for
discordanza (dē·skōr·dân′tsä) *f* disagreement, discordance; *(mus)* discord
discorde (dē·skōr′dä) *a* discordant, not agreed; dissonant
discordia (dē·skōr′dyä) *f* dissension
discorrere * (dē·skōr′rä·rä) *vi* to talk
discorsa (dē·skōr′sä) *f* tiresome talk
discorso (dē·skōr′sō) *m* talk, speech
discosto (dē·skō′stō) *adv&a* distant, far away; detached
discreditare (dē·skrâ·dē·tâ′rä) *vt* to discredit
discredito (dē·skre′dē·tō) *m* discredit
discrepanza (dē·skrä·pân′tsä) *f* discrepancy, variance
discretamente (dē·skrä·tâ·män′tä) *adv* discreetly, fairly, tolerably
discretezza (dē·skrä·tä′tsä) *f* moderation, discretion; prudence
discreto (dē·skrä′tō) *a* fair; discreet
discrezione (dē·skrä·tsyō′nä) *f* discretion
discriminare (dē·skrē·mē·nâ′rä) *vt* to discriminate between, choose among
discriminazione (dē·skrē·mē·nâ·tsyō′nä) *f* discrimination, taste
discussione (dē·skūs·syō′nä) *f* argument; debate; discussion
discutere * (dē·skū′tä·rä) *vt* to discuss; to argue
discutibile (dē·skū·tē′bē·lä) *a* debatable
disdegnare (dē·zdā·nyâ′rä) *vt* to disdain
disdegno (dē·zdā′nyō) *m* disdain
disdetta (dē·zdāt′tō) *f* mishap, bad luck
disdire * (dē·zdē′rä) *vt* to cancel; to deny; — **la camera** to check out of a hotel
disdoro (dē·zdō′rō) *m* dishonor
disegnare (dē·zā·nyâ′rä) *vt* to draw
disegnatore (dē·zā·nyâ·tō′rä) *m* draftsman, designer

---

k kid, **l** let, **m** met, **n** not, **p** pat, **r** very, **s** sat, **sh** shop, **t** tell, **v** vat, **w** we, **y** yes, **z** zero

disegno (dē·zā′nyō) *m* drawing, design; — **di legge** parliamentary bill; **punta da —** thumbtack

diseredare (dē·zā·rā·dâ′rā) *vt* to disinherit

disertare (dē·zār·tâ′ra) *vt* to desert

diserzione (dē·zār·tsyō′nä) *f* desertion

disfare * (dē·sfä′rā) *vt* to undo, untie; to disassemble

disfarsi * (dē·sfâr′sē) *vr* to dispose of; to be dissolved; — **di qualcuno** to get rid of someone, shake someone

disfatta (dē·sfât′tä) *f* defeat

disfattista (dē·sfât·tē′stä) *m* defeatist

disfida (dē·sfē′dâ) *f* defiance; challenge

disfunzione (dē·sfūn·tsyō′nä) *f (med)* disorder, malfunction; derangement

disgelo (dē·zjä′lō) *m* thawing

disgiungere * (dē·zjūn′jä·rä) *vt* to detach, disjoin

disgiuntivo (dē·zjūn·tē′vō) *a (gram)* disjunctive

disgrazia (dē·zgrâ′tsyä) *f* accident; misfortune; **cadere in —** to fall into disfavor; **per —** unfortunately; **–tamente** (dē·zgrâ·tsyâ·tâ·mān′tä) *adv* unfortunately, unhappily; **–to** (dē·zgrâ·tsyâ′tō) *a* unfortunate; **–to m** wretch

disguido (dē·zgwē′dō) *m* error in mail delivery, misrouting

disgustare (dē·zgū·stâ′rā) *vt* to disgust

disgustarsi (dē·zgū·stâr′sē) *vr* to feel disgust; to fall out, quarrel

disgusto (dē·zgū′stō) *m* disgust; disliking

disillusione (dē·zēl·lū·zyō′nä) *f* rude awakening; disappointment

disimpegnare (dē·zēm·pä·nyâ′rä) *vt* to free, disentangle; to carry out, discharge

disincagliare (dē·zēn·kâ·lyâ′rä) *vt (naut)* to refloat

disincantato (dē·zēn·kân·tâ′tō) *a* disenchanted; disappointed

disinfestante (dē·zēn·fä·stân′tä) *m* exterminator

disinfestare (dē·zēn·fä·stâ′rä) *vt* to exterminate; to fumigate

disinfettante (dē·zēn·fät·tân′tä) *a&m* disinfectant

disinfettare (dē·zēn·fät·tâ′rä) *vt* to disinfect

disinfezione (dē·zēn·fä·tsyō′nä) *f* disinfection

disingannare (dē·zēn·gân·nâ′rä) *vt* to disillusion, disenchant; to give the true picture

disinganno (dē·zēn·gân′nō) *m* disenchantment, rude awakening

disinnestare (dē·zēn·nä·stâ′rä) *vt* to disconnect, separate

disintegrare (dē·zēn·tä·grâ′rä) *vt* to split

disintegrazione (dē·zēn·tä·grâ·tsyō′nä) *f* fission, splitting

disinteressato (dē·zēn·tä·rās·sâ′tō) *a* impartial

disinvolto (dē·zēn·vōl′tō) *a* nonchalant

disinvoltura (dē·zēn·vōl·tū′râ) *f* nonchalance; ease of manner

dislivello (dē·zlē·vâl′lō) *m* unevenness; gradient; drop

dislocamento (dē·zlō·kâ·mān′tō) *m* displacement

disobbediente (dē·zōb·bä·dyän′tä) *a* disobedient

disobbedire (dē·zōb·bä·dē′rä) *vt* to disobey

disobbligante (dē·zōb·blē·gân′tä) *a* rude

disobbligarsi (dē·zōb·blē·gâr′sē) *vi* to return a favor

disoccupare (dē·zōk·kū·pâ′rä) *vt* to terminate one's employment; to idle, put out of work

disoccuparsi (dē·zōk·kū·pâr′sē) *vr* to give up one's job; to curtail one's commitments

disoccupato (dē·zōk·kū·pâ′tō) *a* unemployed

disoccupazione (dē·zōk·kū·pâ·tsyō′nä) *f* unemployment

disonestà (dē·zō·nä·stâ′) *f* dishonesty

disonesto (dē·zō·nä′stō) *a* dishonest

disonorante (dē·zō·nō·rân′tä) *a* dishonoring

disonorare (dē·zō·nō·râ′rä) *vt* to dishonor

disonorato (dē·zō·nō·râ′tō) *a* without honor

disonore (dē·zō·nō′rä) *m* disgrace, shame; **–vole** (dē·zō·nō·re′vō·lä) *a* dishonorable

disopra (dē·sō′prâ) *adv* above, upstairs; **— m** top, upperside; **al —** above, up above; **al — di ogni sospetto** above suspicion; **il piano —** upstairs, the floor above

disordinare (dē·zōr·dē·nâ′rä) *vt* to disarrange, disorder; **— vi** to exceed

disordinatamente (dē·zōr·dē·nâ·tâ·mān′tä) *adv* disorderly; inordinately

disordinato (dē·zōr·dē·nâ′tō) *a* untidy, messy

disordine (dē·zôr′dē·nä) *m* disorder

disorganizzato (dē·zōr·gâ·nē·dzâ′tō) *a* disorganized

disorganizzazione (dē·zōr·gâ·nē·dzâ·tsyō′nä) *f* disorganization

disorientamento (dē·zō·ryän·tâ·mān′tō)

m bewilderment

disorientare (dē·zō·ryän·tâ'rä) *vt* to bewilder, disorient

disorientarsi (dē·zō·ryän·târ'sē) *vr* to lose one's way

disorientato (dē·zō·ryän·tä'tō) *a* bewildered; **essere — to** have lost one's bearings

disossato (dē·zōs·sâ'tō) *a* boned, without bones

disotto (dē·sōt'tō) *adv* below, downstairs; **— m** bottom, under side; **al — di** below, beneath; **— a** lower; **il piano —** downstairs, the lower floor; **la parte —** the lower part

dispaccio (dē·spä'chō) *m* dispatch; **— telegrafico** telegraph message

disparatamente (dē·spä·râ·tâ·män'tä) *adv* disparately; unevenly

dispari (dē'spä·rē) *a* odd, uneven

disparte (dē·spär·tä) *adv* aside, apart; **in — to** one side; separately

dispensa (dē·spän·sâ) *f* pantry; section; dispensation; **–re** (dē·spän·sâ'rä) *vt* to dispense; **–rio** (dē·spän·sâ'ryō) *m* dispensary; **–to** (dē·spän·sâ'tō) *a* dispensed; distributed; exonerated; **–to dal servizio** exempted from service; **–to dalla posta** distributed by mail

dispepsia (dē·spä·psē'â) *f* dyspepsia

disperare (dē·spä·râ'rä) *vi* to despair; **far — to** drive to despair; to be the death of *(fig)*

disperarsi (dē·spä·râr'sē) *vr* to give up hope

disperatamente (dē·spä·râ·tâ·män'tä) *adv* desperately

disperato (dē·spä·râ'tō) *a* hopeless; useless; **— m** penniless man

disperazione (dē·spä·râ·tsyō'nä) *f* despair; uselessness

disperdere * (dē·sper'dä·rä) *vt* to disperse

dispersione (dē·spär·syō'nä) *f* dispersal

disperso (dē·spär'sō) *a* missing

dispetto (dē·spät'tō) *m* spite; **a — di** despite, in spite of; **far — to** annoy, vex; to spite; **–samente** (dē·spät·tō·zä·män'tä) *adv* maliciously; **–so** (dē·spät·tō'zō) *a* malicious, spiteful

dispiacente (dē·spyâ·chän'tä) *a* unpleasant; sorry

dispiacere (dē·spyâ·chä'rä) *m* sorrow; regret; **— * *vi* to be displeasing, displease; to inconvenience; **mi dispiace** I am sorry; **se non ti dispiace** if you please

dispiaceri (dē·spyâ·chä'rē) *mpl* troubles *(fig)*; **aver — to** be in trouble

disponibile (dē·spō·nē'bē·lä) *a* available

disponibilità (dē·spō·nē·bē·lē·tâ') *f* availability

disporre * (dē·spōr'rä) *vt* to arrange; to dispose of; to order; **— di mezzi** to have means at one's disposal; **— le cose in modo da** to arrange matters so that; **poter — di** to be able to dispose of; **l'uomo propone e Dio dispone** man proposes, God disposes

disporsi * (dē·spōr'sē) *vr* to place oneself; to be prepared; to be ready for; **— a uscire** to be ready to leave

dispositivo (dē·spō·zē·tē'vō) *m* device; **— di segnalazione** indicator

disposizione (dē·spō·zē·tsyō'nä) *f* disposal; arrangement; order; **a — available;** on hand; at one's service; **d'accordo alla — in** accordance with the rules; **— per la musica** talent for music

disposto (dē·spō'stō) *a* inclined; prepared

dispotico (dē·spō'tē·kō) *a* despotic

dispotismo (dē·spō·tē'zmō) *m* despotism

dispregiativo (dē·sprä·jâ·tē'vō) *a* disparaging; *(gram)* pejorative

disprezzabile (dē·sprä·tsâ'bē·lä) *a* despicable

disprezzare (dē·sprä·tsâ'rä) *vt* to despise

disprezzo (dē·sprä'tsō) *m* contempt

disputa (dē'spū·tâ) *f* dispute, quarrel; **–re** (dē·spū·tâ'rä) *vt&i* to contend; to argue

disquisizione (dē·skwē·zē·tsyō'nä) *f* dissertation

dissanguare (dēs·sân·gwâ'rä) *vt* to bleed; to draw blood from

dissapore (dēs·sâ·pō'rä) *m* disappointment; disagreement, difference

dissecare (dēs·sä·kâ'rä) *vt* to dissect

disseminare (dēs·sä·mē·nâ'rä) *vt* to spread, disseminate

disseminato (dēs·sä·mē·nâ'tō) *a* strewn; covered; disseminated; **— di fiori** covered with flowers; **— di pietre** strewn with stones

dissenso (dēs·sän'sō) *m* dissent, dissension

dissenteria (dēs·sän·tä·rē'â) *f* dysentery

dissentire (dēs·sän·tē'rä) *vi* to disagree, be in disagreement

disseppellire (dēs·säp·päl·lē'rä) *vt* to exhume, disinter; *(fig)* to revive

dissertazione (dēs·sär·tâ·tsyō'nä) *f* dissertation

disservizio (dēs·sär·vē'tsyō) *m* poor service

dissesto (dēs·sä'stō) *m* failure; trouble

dissetare (dēs·sä·tâ'rä) *vt* to quench one's thirst

dissezione (dēs·sä·tsyō'nä) *f* dissection

dissidente (dēs·sē·dän'tä) *m* dissenter

---

k kid, **l** let, **m** met, **n** not, **p** pat, **r** very, **s** sat, **sh** shop, **t** tell, **v** vat, **w** we, **y** yes, **z** zero

dissidio (dēs·sē′dyō) *m* disagreement

dissimile (dēs·sē′mē·lā) *a* dissimilar

dissimulare (des·sē·mū·lâ′rā) *vt* to dissimulate, hide, feign

dissimularsi (dēs·sē·mū·lâr′sē) *vr* to disguise oneself; to be hidden

dissimulatamente (dēs·sē·mū·lâ·tâ·mān′tā) *adv* deceptively; deceitfully

dissimulazione (dēs·sē·mū·lâ·tsyō′nā) *f* dissimulation; deceit, trickery

dissipare (dēs·sē·pâ′rā) *vt* to dispel; to waste; to squander; — **gli averi** to squander one's patrimony; — **i sospetti** to remove one's suspicions; to cast off one's doubts

dissiparsi (dēs·sē·pâr′sē) *vr* to vanish, disappear

dissociazione (dēs·sō·châ·tsyō′nā) *f* disassociation

dissodare (dēs·sō·dâ′rā) *vt* to clear *(land)*; to break up *(soil)*

dissoluto (dēs·sō·lū′tō) *a* dissolute

dissoluzione (dēs·sō·lū·tsyō′nā) *f* dissolution

dissolvere * (dēs·sôl′vā·rā) *vt* to dissolve; to dispel

dissonanza (dēs·sō·nân′tsâ) *f* dissonance

dissotterrare (dēs·sōt·tār·râ′rā) *vt* to disinter

dissuadere * (dēs·swâ·dā′rā) *vt* to dissuade

dissuasione (dēs·swâ·zyō′nā) *f* dissuasion

distaccamento (dē·stâk·kâ·mān′tō) *m* detachment

distaccare (dē·stâk·kâ′rā) *vt* to detach

distacco (dē·stâk′kō) *m* aloofness; distance; separation; parting; difference; — **doloroso** painful parting; — **notevole** considerable distance; **il — fra i due** the difference between the two

distante (dē·stân′tā) *a* distant, far

distanza (dē·stân′tsâ) *f* distance

distanziare (dē·stân·tsyâ′rā) *vt* to leave behind; to keep at a distance

distare (dē·stâ′rā) *vi* to be distant

distendere * (dē·sten′dā·rā) *vt* to stretch out, extend

distensione (dē·stān·syō′nā) *f* relaxation

distesa (dē·stā′zâ) *f* expanse; —**mente** (dē·stā·zâ·mān′tā) *adv* at length, extensively

disteso (dē·stā′zō) *a* stretched out; **lungo** — at full length; **per** — in detail

distillare (dē·stēl·lâ′rā) *vt* to distill

distillarsi (dē·stēl·lâr′sē) *vr* to be distilled, be extracted; — **il cervello** to rack one's brain

distilleria (dē·stēl·lā·rē′â) *f* distillery

distinguere * (dē·stēn′gwā·rā) *vt* to distinguish

distinguersi * (dē·stēn′gwâr·sē) *vr* to stand out, be preeminent

distinta (dē·stēn′tâ) *f* list; itemized invoice; price list; —**mente** (dē·stēn·tâ·mān′tā) *adv* distinctly

distintivo (dē·stēn·tē′vō) *m* badge; — *a* distinctive

distinto (dē·stēn′tō) *a* distinct; distinguished; **modo** — different way; refined manners; **famiglia distinta** eminent family; **nascita distinta** aristocratic birth; **pronuncia distinta** clear pronunciation

distinzione (dē·stēn·tsyō′nā) *f* distinction; **senza** — indiscriminately

distogliere * (dē·stô′lyā·rā) *vt* to distract, divert, deter; to dissuade; to draw away

distorsione (dē·stōr·syō′nā) *f* sprain

distrarre * (dē·strâr′rā) *vt* to distract; to entertain, amuse, divert; — **fondi** to misappropriate funds

distrarsi * (dē·strâr′sē) *vr* to become distracted, divert one's attention; to relax

distrattamente (dē·strât·tâ·mān′tā) *adv* absentmindedly, inattentively, heedlessly

distratto (dē·strât′tō) *a* absent-minded, inattentive

distrazione (dē·strâ·tsyō′nā) *f* distraction; relaxation; misappropriation; amusement

distretto (dē·strāt′tō) *m* district

distrettuale (dē·strāt·twâ′lā) *a* of a district; **giudice** — district judge

distribuire (dē·strē·bwē′rā) *vt* to distribute

distributore (dē·strē·bū·tō′rā) *m* distributor

distribuzione (dē·strē·bū·tsyō′nā) *f* distribution

districare (dē·strē·kâ′rā) to disentangle; to extricate

districato (dē·strē·kâ′tō) *a* disentangled; extricated

distrofia (dē·strō·fē′â) *f* dystrophy

distruggere * (dē·strūj′jā·rā) *vt* to destroy

distrutto (dē·strūt′tō) *a* destroyed; —**re** (dē·strūt·tō′rā) *m* destroyer

distruzione (dē·strū·tsyō′nā) *f* destruction

disturbare (dē·stūr·bâ′rā) *vt* to disturb

disturbarsi (dē·stūr·bâr′sē) *vr* to bother, take the trouble

disturbo (dē·stūr′bō) *m* trouble

disubbidiente (dē·zūb·bē·dyān′tā) *a* disobedient

disubbidienza (dē·zūb·bē·dyān′tsâ) *f* disobedience

disubbidire (dē·zūb·bē·dē′rā) *vt&i* to disobey, disregard; to be heedless of

disuguaglianza (dē·zū·gwâ·lyân'tsâ) *f* unevenness; inequality; difference, disparity

disuguagliare (dē·zū·gwâ·lyâ'rä) *vt* to make unequal

disuguale (dē·zū·gwâ'lä) *a* unequal; uneven

disunione (dē·zū·nyō'nä) *f* disunity, discord

disunire (dē·zū·nē'rä) *vt* to disunite

disunirsi (dē·zū·nēr'sē) *vr* to become disunified, split up

disunito (dē·zū·nē'tō) *a* disunited

disusato (dē·zū·zâ'tō) *a* obsolete

disuso (dē·zū'zō) *m* disuse, obsolescence

disutile (dē·zū'tē·lä) *a* harmful; useless

disviare (dē·zvyâ'rä) *vt* to mislead, lead astray

disviarsi (dē·zvyâr'sē) *vr* to go astray, lose one's bearings

disvio (dē·zvē'ō) *m* straying; misrouting

dita (dē'tâ) *fpl* fingers; **mordersi le —** to regret something bitterly

ditale (dē·tâ'lä) *m* thimble

ditali (dē·tâ'lē) *mpl* elbow macaroni

dito (dē'tō) *m* finger; toe; **— alluce** big toe; **— annulare** ring finger; **— indice** forefinger, index finger; **— medio** middle finger; **— mignolo** little finger **— pollice** thumb; **a un — della tragedia** on the brink of tragedy; **il — di Dio** *(fig)* the hand of God; **legarsela al —** to bear a grudge; to make a point of remembering; **mostrare a —** to point at; **un — di vino** a drop of wine

ditta (dēt'tâ) *f* firm, concern

dittatore (dēt·tâ·tō'rä) *m* dictator

dittatoriale (dēt·tâ·tō·ryâ'lä) *a* dictatorial

dittatura (dēt·tâ·tū'râ) *f* dictatorship

dittongo (dēt·tōn'gō) *m* diphthong

diuretico (dyū·re'tē·kō) *a&m* diuretic

diurnista (dyūr·nē'stâ) *m* temporary employee; worker paid by the day; dayworker

diurno (dyūr'nō) *a* daily; **albergo —** public baths; **lavoro —** work paid by the day; daywork; **scuola diurna** day school

diuturno (dyū·tūr'nō) *a* continual; eternal

diva (dē'vâ) *f (theat)* star

divagare (dē·vâ·gâ'rä) *vi* to roam, ramble

divagazione (dē·vâ·gâ·tsyō'nä) *f* deviation; diversion

divano (dē·vâ'nō) *m* sofa, couch

divario (dē·vâ'ryō) *m* difference, discrepancy

divampare (dē·vâm·pâ'rä) *vi* to burst into flames; *(fig)* to break out; to flare up

divaricare (dē·vâ·rē·kâ'rä) *vt* to spread

apart; to stretch out, extend

divellere * (dē·vel'lä·rä) *vt* to uproot

divenire * (dē·vâ·nē'rä), **diventare** (dē·vân·tâ'rä) *vi* to become, get; **— amici** to become friends; **— pallido** to turn pale; **— ricco** to grow wealthy; **— vecchio** to grow old; **far — matto** to drive mad

diverbio (dē·ver'byō) *m* argument, quarrel

divergenza (dē·vär·jän'tsâ) *f* disagreement, difference of opinion

diversamente (dē·vär·sâ·mân'tä) *adv* in a different way, differently

diversità (dē·vär·sē·tâ') *f* variety, unlikeness; diversity

diversivo (dē·vär·sē'vō) *m* pastime

diverso (dē·vär'sō) *a* different; diverse

divertente (dē·vär·tän'tä) *a* amusing

divertimento (dē·vär·tē·mân'tō) *m* fun, recreation; **buon —!** have fun!

divertire (dē·vär·tē'rä) *vt* to amuse; to give pleasure to

divertirsi (dē·vär·tēr'sē) *vr* to have a good time, enjoy oneself

divetta (dē·vät'tâ) *f (theat)* starlet

dividendo (dē·vē·dän'dō) *m* dividend

dividere * (dē·vē'dä·rä) *vt* to divide; to share; to take part in

divieto (dē·vyä'tō) *m* prohibition; **— di fumare** no smoking; **— di parcheggio, — di posteggio** no parking; **— di passaggio** do not enter; **— di segnalazione acustica** horn blowing forbidden; **— di sorpasso** no passing; **— di sosta** no parking; **— di svolta a destra** no right turn; **— di svolta a sinistra** no left turn; **— di svolta a destra o a sinistra** no turns; **— di transito** no thoroughfare

divinamente (dē·vē·nâ·mân'tä) *adv* exquisitely, divinely, beautifully

divinatorio (dē·vē·nâ·tô'ryō) *a* forecasting, predicting; divining

divinazione (dē·vē·nâ·tsyō'nä) *f* divining

divinità (dē·vē·nē·tâ') *f* divinity

divinizzare (dē·vē·nē·dzâ'rä) *vt* to deify

divino (dē·vē'nō) *a* divine

divisa (dē·vē'zâ) *f* uniform; currency, bills

divisare (dē·vē·zâ'rä) *vt* to plan, design, devise

divisibile (dē·vē·zē'bē·lä) *a* divisible

divisione (dē·vē·zyō'nä) *f* division

divismo (dē·vē'zmō) *m* filmdom, movie world; worship of movie stars

divisore (dē·vē·zō'rä) *m* divisor

divisorio (dē·vē·zô'ryō) *a* dividing; **muro —** partition

divo (dē·vō) *m (theat)* star

divorare (dē·vō·râ'rä) *vt* to devour

divorato (dē·vō·râ'tō) *a* devoured; wasted; **— dalla febbre** wasted by fever; **–re** (dē·vō·râ·tō'rā) *m* big eater; **–re di ricchezze** squanderer, wastrel

divorziare (dē·vōr·tsyâ'rā) *vi* to get a divorce

divorzio (dē·vôr'tsyō) *m* divorce; **chiedere il —** to ask for a divorce

divulgare (dē·vūl·gâ'rā) *vt* to divulge, disclose

divulgazione (dē·vūl·gâ·tsyō'nā) *f* divulgation, spreading; **opera di —** popular literary work

dizionario (dē·tsyō·nâ'ryō) *m* dictionary

dizione (dē·tsyō'nā) *f* diction

do (dō) *m* (*mus*) do

doccia (dō'chä) *f* shower, shower bath

docente (dō·chān'tä) *m* teacher; **libero —** guest professor

docenza (dō·chān'tsâ) *f* teaching profession

docile (dô'chē·lä) *a* docile, tame

docilità (dō·chē·lē·tâ') *f* tameness, docility

docilmente (dō·chēl·män'tä) *adv* submissively, mildly

documentare (dō·kū·män·tâ'rā) *vt* to document, prove

documentario (dō·kū·män·tâ'ryō) *m* documentary film

documenti (dō·kū·män'tē) *mpl* papers

documento (dō·kū·män'tō) *m* document

dodicenne (dō·dē·chān'nā) *a* twelve years old

dodicesimo (dō·dē·che'zē·mō) *a* twelfth

dodici (dô'dē·chē) *a* twelve

doga (dō'gâ) *f* stave; **–re** (dō·gâ'rā) *vt* to put the staves on (*barrel*)

dogale (dō·gâ'lä) *a* of the doge

dogana (dō·gâ'nä) *f* duty, customs; **–le** (dō·gâ·nâ'lä) *a* customs, concerning customs

doganiere (dō·gâ·nyä'rā) *m* customs official

dogaressa (dō·gâ·räs'sâ) doge's wife

dogato (dō·gâ'tō) *m* office of the doge

doge (dō'jä) *m* doge

doglia (dō'lyä) *f* labor pains; birth pains

dogma (dōg'mâ) *m* dogma; **–tico** (dōg·mâ'·tē·kō) *a* dogmatic; **–tizzare** (dōg·mâ·tē·dzâ'rā) *vt* to dogmatize

dolce (dōl'chä) *a* sweet; soft; mild; (*mus*) dolce; (*gram*) soft; **— m** candy; **— ricordo** pleasant memory; **acqua —** fresh water; soft water; **carattere —** mild temper; **carbone —** charcoal; **clima —** mild climate; **–mente** (dōl·chä·män'tä) *adv* softly; **–ria** (dōl·chä·rē'â) *f* candy

store; **–zza** (dōl·chä'tsâ) *f* sweetness; **–zza mia!** sweetheart!

dolciastro (dōl·châ'strō) *a* sweetish

dolciumi (dōl·chū'mē) *mpl* candies

dolente (dō·lān'tä) *a* sorry

dolere * (dō·lā'rā) *vi* to hurt, ache; to cause sorrow; to make grieve

dolicocefalo (dō·lē·kō·che'fâ·lō) dolichocephalous

dollaro (dôl'lâ·rō) *m* dollar

dolo (dō'lō) *m* fraud; **–so** (dō·lō'zō) *a* deceitful, fraudulent; **incendio –so** arson

dolore (dō·lō'rā) *m* sorrow; pain; **— di denti** toothache; **— di stomaco** stomachache; **— di testa** headache

dolorosamente (dō·lō·rō·zâ·män'tä) *adv* painfully; unfortunately

doloroso (dō·lō·rō'zō) *a* sad; painful; unfortunate

domanda (dō·mân'dâ) *f* question; application; request; **–re** (dō·mân·dâ'rā) *vt* to ask; to inquire about; **-rsi** (dō·mân·dâr'sē) *vr* to wonder, question

domani (dō·mâ'nē) *m&adv* tomorrow; **dopo–** (dō·pō·dō·mâ'nē),**— l'altro** day after tomorrow; **— otto** week from tomorrow; **pensare a —** to think of the future; **un — non lontano** the near future

domare (dō·mâ'rā) *vt* to tame; **— una sommossa** to suppress a rebellion; **— un cavallo** to break a horse; **— un incendio** to get a fire under control

domato (dō·mâ'tō) *a* subdued; quenched; broken; tamed; **–re** (dō·mâ·tō'rā) *m* tamer, trainer

domattina (dō·mât·tē'nä) *adv* tomorrow morning

domenica (dō·me'nē·kâ) *f* Sunday; **–le** (dō·mä·nē·kâ'lä) *a* Sunday, concerning Sunday

domenicano (dō·mä·nē·kâ'nō) *a&m* Dominican

domestica (dō·me'stē·kâ) *f* housemaid; **–re** (dō·mä·stē·kâ'rā) *vt* to tame

domestichezza (dō·mä·stē·kä'tsâ) *f* familiarity

domestico (dō·me'stē·kō) *m* servant; **— a** domestic

domicilio (dō·mē·chē'lyō) *m* home address; residence

dominante (dō·mē·nân'tä) *a* prevailing; outstanding; dominant

dominare (dō·mē·nâ'rā) *vt&i* to dominate

dominatore (dō·mē·nâ·tō'rā) *m* ruler; **— a** ruling, dominant

dominazione (dō·mē·nâ·tsyō'nä) *f* domination

â ârm, **ā** bāby, **e** bet, **ē** bē, **ō** gō, **ô** gône, **ū** blūe, **b** bad, **ch** child, **d** dad, **f** fat, **g** gay, **j** jet

dominio (dō·mē'nyō) *m* control, power

domino (dô'mē·nō) *m* domino

donare (dō·nâ'rā) *vt* to donate

donatore (dō·nâ·tō'rā) *m* donor; — **di sangue** blood donor

donazione (dō·nâ·tsyō'nā) *f* donation

donde (dōn'dā) *adv* from where; as a result, consequently

dondolare (dōn·dō·lâ'rā) *vt* to rock, sway

dondolo (dôn'dō·lō) *m* swing; swaying; **sedia a —** rocking chair

donna (dōn'nâ) *f* woman; queen (*cards*); **— di servizio** housemaid; **–ccia** (dōn·nâ'châ) *f* woman of easy virtue; illtempered woman; **–iuolo** (dōn·nâ·ywō'lō) *m* ladies' man

dono (dō'nō) *m* gift

donzella (dōn·dzāl'lâ) *f* maid, maiden

dopo (dō'pō) *prep* after; *adv* later; **–guerra** (dō·pō·gwâr'râ) *m* postwar period; **–pranzo** (dō·pō·prân'dzō) *m* afternoon; **— si vedrà** we'll see later on; **il giorno —** the next day; **poco —** shortly afterwards

doppiaggio (dōp·pyâj'jō) *m* film dubbing

doppiamente (dōp·pyâ·mān'tā) *adv* doubly

doppiare (dōp·pyâ'rā) *vt* (*naut*) to double, sail around; to dub (*movies*)

doppietta dōp·pyāt'tâ) *f* double-barreled shotgun

doppio (dōp'pyō) *a* double; two-faced; **–ne** (dōp·pyō'nā) *m* copy, duplicate

dorare (dō·râ'rā) *vt* to gild

dorato (dō·râ'tō) *a* gilded, gilt

dorico (dô'rē·kō) *a* Doric; Dorian

dormiglione (dōr·mē·lyō'nā) *m* sleepyhead; lazybones

dormire (dōr·mē'rā) *vi* to sleep; **chi dorme non piglia pesci** (*fig*) the early bird catches the worm

dormitina (dōr·mē·tē'nâ) *f* nap, short sleep

dormitorio (dōr·mē·tō'ryō) *m* dormitory

dormiveglia (dōr·mē·ve'lyâ) *m* doze; fitful sleep

dorsale (dōr·sâ'lā) *a* dorsal

dorso (dōr'sō) *m* back

dosaggio (dō·zâj'jō) *m* dosage

dosare (dō·zâ'rā) *vt* to dose

dose (dō'zā) *f* dose

dosso (dōs'sō) *m* back; **togliersi di —** to get rid of; to take off

dotare (dō·tâ'rā) *vt* to endow; to furnish, provide

dotazione (dō·tâ·tsyō'nā) *f* endowment; donation

dote (dō'tā) *f* dowry; talent; quality

dotto (dōt'tō) *a* learned; **–re** (dōt·tō'rā) *m* doctor; scholar; **–ressa** (dōt·tō·rās'sâ) *f* woman doctor

dottrina (dōt·trē'nâ) *f* doctrine; **— cristiana** catechism

dove (dō'vā) *adv* where; **il — the place; per ogni —** everywhere

dovere (dō·vā'rā) *m* duty; **avere il — di** to have the duty of, be obliged; **farsi un — di** to make a point of, consider it one's duty to; **prima il —, dopo il** piacere work before pleasure; **stare a —** to behave properly; **— * vt&i** to owe; to have to; to be obliged to; to feel it one's duty to; to be due

doveroso (dō·vâ·rō'zō) *a* right; dutiful; legitimate

dovunque (dō·vūn'kwā) *adv* wherever

dovuto (dō·vū'tō) *a* right, just, proper; due; rightful; **a tempo —** in due time; **in modo —** in the proper way; **in dovuta considerazione** in just consideration

dozzina (dō·dzē'nâ) *f* dozen; board; **–le** (dō·dzē·nâ'lā) *a* common, cheap; **–nte** (dō·dzē·nân'tā) *m* boarder, lodger

draga (drâ'gâ) *f* dredge; **–ggio** (drâ·gâj'jō) *m* dredging; **–mine** (drâ·gâ·mē'nâ) *m* minesweeper; **–re** (drâ·gâ'rā) *vt* to dredge

drago (drâ'gō) *m* dragon

dramma (drâm'mâ) *m* drama; **–tica** (drâm·mâ'tē·kâ) *f* dramatic art, dramatics; **–tico** (drâm·mâ'tē·kō) *a* dramatic; **–tizzare** (drâm·mâ·tē·dzâ'rā) *vt* to dramatize; **–turgo** (drâm·mâ·tūr'gō) *m* playwright

drappeggio (drâp·pej'jō) *m* drapery

drappello (drâp·pāl'lō) *m* platoon

drappo (drâp'pō) *m* cloth; drapery; **— funebre** pall

drastico (drâ'stē·kō) *a* drastic

drenaggio (drā·nâj'jō) *m* drainage

drenare (drā·nâ'rā) *vt* to drain

dribblare (drēb·blâ'rā) *vt* to dribble (*sport*)

dritto (drēt'tō) *a* straight; honest

drizzare (drē·tsâ'rā) *vt* to straighten

droga (drō'gâ) *f* drug; spice; **–re** (drō·gâ'rā) *vt* to drug, dope; to spice

drogheria (drō·gâ·rē'â) *f* grocery store

droghiere (drō·gyâ'rā) *m* grocer

dromedario (drō·mâ·dâ'ryō) *m* dromedary

dualismo (dwâ·lē'zmō) *m* dualism; duality

dualista (dwâ·lē'stâ) *m&f* dualist

dualità (dwâ·lē·tâ') *f* duality; dualism

dubbio (dūb'byō) *m* doubt; **—, –so** (dūb·byō'zō) *a* doubtful, dubious

---

k kid, **l** let, **m** met, **n** not, **p** pat, **r** very, **s** sat, **sh** shop, **t** tell, **v** vat, **w** we, **y** yes, **z** zero

dubitabile (dū·bē·tâ′bē·lā) *a* questionable, open to doubt
dubitare (dū·bē·tâ′rā) *vi* to doubt
duca (dū′kâ) *m* duke; **–le** (dū·kâ′lā) *a* ducal
duce (dū′chā) *m* captain; leader, chief
duchessa (dū·kās′sâ) *f* duchess
due (dū′ā) *a* two; — **volte** twice; **tutt'e** — both; **uno dei** — one or the other, one of the two
duecento (dwā·chān′tō) *a* two hundred; **il D–** the thirteenth century
duellante (dwāl·lān′tā) *m* duelist
duellare (dwāl·lâ′rā) *vi* to duel, fight a duel
duemila (dwā·mē′lâ) *a* two thousand
duetto (dwāt′tō) *m* duet
duna (dū′nâ) *f* dune
dunque (dūn′kwā) *adv* so, therefore
duodeno (dwō·dā′nō) *m* duodenum
duo (dū′ō) *m* (*mus*) duo, duet; **–decimo** (dwō·de′chē·mō) *a* twelfth
duolo (dwō′lō) *m* suffering, grief
duomo (dwō′mō) *m* cathedral
duplex (dū′plāks) *m* telephone party line
duplicare (dū·plē·kâ′rā) *vt* to duplicate

duplicato (dū·plē·kâ′tō) *m* duplicate
duplice (dū′plē·chā) *a* double, twofold; **in — copia** in duplicate
duplicità (dū·plē·chē·tâ′) *f* duplicity, falseness
durabile (dū·râ′bē·lā) *a* durable
duramente (dū·râ·mān′tā) *adv* hard; harshly; bitterly; sharply; roughly; cruelly
durante (dū·rân′tā) *prep* during; — *a* lasting
durare (dū·râ′rā) *vt* to endure; — *vi* to last
durata (dū·râ′tâ) *f* duration
duraturo (dū·râ·tū′rō), **durevole** (dū·re′vō·lā) *a* durable, lasting
durevolezza (dū·rā·vō·lā′tsâ) *f* durability
durevolmente (dū·rā·vōl·mān′tā) *adv* lastingly, durably
durezza (dū·rā′tsâ) *f* hardness, harshness
duro (dū′rō) *a* hard, tough; stale; **–ne** (dū·rō′nā) *a* stupid; **–ne** *m* callous
duttile (dūt′tē·lā) *a* ductile, plastic; yielding
duttilità (dūt·tē·lē·tâ′) *f* plasticity; pliability

E

e (ā) *conj* and; well then? and so?
ebanista (ā·bâ·nē′stâ) *m* cabinet maker
ebano (e′bâ·nō) *m* ebony
ebbene (āb·bā′nā) *adv* well then
ebbrezza (āb·brā′tsâ) *f* intoxication; (*fig*) rapture
ebbro (āb′brō) *a* drunk; — **d'amore** mad with love; — **di gioia** exultant with joy
ebdomadario (āb·dō·mâ·dâ′ryō) *a&m* weekly
ebete (e′bā·tā) *a* stupid, obtuse
ebetismo (ā·bā·tē′zmō) *m* stupidity, dullness
ebollizione (ā·bōl·lē·tsyō′nā) *f* boiling; (*fig*) enthusiasm, excitement
ebraico (ā·brâ′ē·kō) *a&m* Hebrew
ebreo (ā·brā′ō) *a* Jewish; — *m* Jew
ecatombe (ā·kâ·tōm′bā) *f* massacre, slaughter
eccedenza (ā·chā·dān′tsâ) *f* excess; surplus
eccedere (ā·che′dā·rā) *vt&i* to exceed; to exaggerate, carry too far
eccellente (ā·chāl·lān′tā) *a* excellent; **–mente** (ā·chāl·lān·tā·mān′tā) *adv* very well, excellently
eccellenza (ā·chāl·lān′tsâ) *f* excellence; **Vostra Eccellenza** Your Excellency

eccellere * (ā·chel′lā·rā) *vt* to excel; to outshine
eccentricamente (ā·chān·trē·kâ·mān′tā) *adv* eccentrically
eccentricità (ā·chān·trē·chē·tâ′) *f* eccentricity
eccentrico (ā·chen′trē·kō) *a&m* eccentric
eccepibile (ā·chā·pē′bē·lā) *a* questionable, objectionable
eccepire (ā·chā·pē′rā) *vt* to take exception to, object to
eccessivamente (ā·chās·sē·vâ·mān′tā) *adv* excessively, overly
eccessività (ā·chās·sē·vē·tâ′) *f* excessiveness; overstatement
eccessivo (ā·chās·sē′vō) *a* excessive, overdone
eccesso (ā·chās′sō) *m* excess
eccetera (ā·che′tā·râ) *m* and so forth
eccetto (ā·chāt′tō) *prep* except; but; **tutti — uno** all but one
eccettuare (ā·chāt·twâ′rā) *vt* to except
eccettuato (ā·chāt·twâ′tō) *a* excepted; omitted, left out
eccezionale (ā·chā·tsyō·nâ′lā) *a* exceptional
eccezione (ā·chā·tsyō′nā) *f* exception
eccidio (ā·chē′dyō) *m* massacre

â ârm, ā bāby, e bet, ē bē, ō gō, ô gône, ū blūe, b bad, ch child, d dad, f fat, g gay, j jet

eccitabile (ā·chē·tâ′bē·lā) *a* excitable, emotional

eccitamento (ā·chē·tâ·mān′tō) *m* excitement; fervor

eccitante (ā·chē·tân′tā) *m* stimulant; — *a* stimulating, moving

eccitare (ā·chē·tâ′rā) *vt* to excite, stir; to arouse, move

eccitativo (ā·chē·tâ·tē′vō) *a* moving, rousing

eccitato (ā·chē·tâ′tō) *a* excited; –re (ā·chē·tâ·tō′rā) *m* arouser; –re *a* exciting

eccitazione (ā·chē·tâ·tsyō′nā) *f* excitement, arousing, stimulation

ecclesiastico (āk·klā·zyâ′stē·kō) *a* ecclesiastical; — *m* clergyman

ecco (āk′kō) *adv* here; —! *interj* look!; –mi qua! Here I am!; — fatto that's done; — tutto that's all

eccome (āk·kō′mā) *adv* and how, how in the world

echeggiante (ā·kāj·jân′tā) *a* resounding, reverberating

echeggiare (ā·kāj·jâ′rā) *vi* to echo; to reverberate

eclettico (ā·klet′tē·kō) *a&m* eclectic

eclissare (ā·klēs·sâ′rā) *vt* to eclipse

eclissarsi (ā·klēs·sâr′sē) *vr* to abscond, disappear

eclissi (ā·klēs′sē) *m* eclipse

eclittica (ā·klēt′tē·kâ) *f* ecliptic

eco (ā′kō) *m* echo; — della stampa service providing newspaper clippings; fare — alle parole di to mouth the words of; farsi — della diceria to repeat a rumor

economato (ā·kō·nō·mâ′tō) *m* stewardship; administration

economia (ā·kō·nō·mē′â) *f* economy; — planificata controlled economy; — politica political economy; political economics

economicamente (ā·kō·nō·mē·kâ·mān′tā) *adv* economically

economico (ā·kō·nō′mē·kō) *a* economical; cheap

economista (ā·kō·nō·mē′stâ) *m* economist

economizzare (ā·kō·nō·mē·dzâ′rā) *vt* to economize; to husband

economizzatore (ā·kō·nō·mē·dzâ·tō′rā) *m* economizer; saver

economo (ā·kō′nō·mō) *m* administrator; steward; — *a* saving, thrifty

ecumenico (ā·kū·me′nē·kō) *a* ecumenical

eczema (āk·dzā′mâ) *m* eczema

ed (ād) *conj* and

edema (ā·dā′mâ) *m (med)* edema

edera (e′dā·râ) *f* ivy

edicola (ā·dē′kō·lâ) *f* newsstand

edicolista (ā·dē·kō·lē′stâ) *m* newsstand operator

edificare (ā·dē·fē·kâ′rā) *vt* to build; to edify, educate

edificante (ā·dē·fē·kân′tā) *a* educative, edifying

edificio (ā·dē·fē′chō) *m* building

edile (e′dē·lā) *a* building; — *m* building contractor

edilizia (ā·dē·lē′tsyâ) *f* construction; building industry

edilizio (ā·dē·lē′tsyō) *a* building

edito (e′dē·tō) *a* published; edited

editore (ā·dē·tō′rā) *m* publisher; editor; — *a* publishing; casa editrice publishing house

editoriale (ā·dē·tō·ryâ′lā) *m* editorial

editto (ā·dēt′tō) *m* edict

edizione (ā·dē·tsyō′nā) *f* edition; — esaurita edition out of print

edonista (ā·dō·nē′stâ) *mf&a* hedonist

edotto (ā·dōt′tō) *a* notified, informed

educare (ā·dū·kâ′rā) *vt* to educate, teach

educatamente (ā·dū·kâ·tâ·mān′tā) *adv* politely, in a well-bred manner

educativo (ā·dū·kâ·tē′vō) *a* educational

educato (ā·dū·kâ′tō) *a* well-mannered, polite

educatore (ā·dū·kâ·tō′rā) *m* educator

educazione (ā·dū·kâ·tsyō′nā) *f* good manners; education; senza — rowdy, ill-mannered

effeminatamente (āf·fā·mē·nâ·tâ·mān′tā) *adv* effeminately

effeminatezza (āf·fā·mē·nâ·tā′tsâ) *f* effeminacy

efferatamente (āf·fā·râ·tâ·mān′tā) *adv* brutally

efferatezza (āf·fā·râ·tā′tsâ) *f* ferociousness; barbarism

efferato (āf·fā·râ′tō) *a* savage, ferocious

effervescente (āf·fār·vā·shān′tā) *a* effervescent

effervescenza (āf·fār·vā′shān′tsâ) *f* effervescence; (*fig*) agitation, excitement

effetti (āf·fāt′tē) *mpl* possessions; effects; bills

effettista (āf·fāt·tē′stâ) *m* sensationalist

effettivamente (āf·fāt·tē·vâ·mān′tā) *adv* really, as a matter of fact

effettivo (āf·fāt·tē′vō) *a* actual, true; present, current

effetto (āf·fāt′tō) *m* effect; (*mech*) action; (*com*) bill; a quest' — to this purpose; far l' — di to seem; to give the appearance of; in — really, truly; in fact

effettuabile (āf·fāt·twâ′bē·lā) *a* feasible

effettuare (āf·fāt·twâ'rā) *vt* to fulfill, complete

effettuazione (āf·fāt·twâ·tsyō'nā) *f* completion, fulfillment, carrying out

efficace (āf·fē·kâ'chā) *a* effective; **–mente** (āf·fē·kâ·chā·mān'tā) *adv* efficiently, effectively

efficacia (āf·fē·kâ'châ) *f* efficacy, effect

efficiente (āf·fē·chyän'tā) *a* efficient; **–mente** (āf·fē·chyän·tā·mān'tā) *adv* efficiently, effectively

efficienza (āf·fē·chyän'tsâ) *f* efficiency **essere in —** to be in good working order

effige (āf·fē'jā) *f* effigy

effimero (āf·fē'mä·rō) *a* short-lived

efflusso (āf·flüs'sō) *m* outflow

effrazione (āf·frâ·tsyō'nā) *f* housebreaking

effusione (āf·fū·zyō'nā) *f* effusion; (*fig*) warmheartedness

effuso (āf·fū'zō) *a* given out; diffused; distributed

egemonia (ā·jā·mō·nē'â) *f* hegemony

egida (e'jē·dâ) *f* auspices, sponsorship

Egitto (ā·jēt'tō) *m* Egypt

egiziano (ā·jē·tsyâ'nō) *a&m* Egyptian

egli (ā'lyē) *pron* he

egloga (e'glō·gâ) *f* eglogue

egoismo (ā·gō·ē'zmō) *m* egoism

egoista (ā·gō·ē'stâ) *m* egoist

egoisticamente (ā·gōē·stē·kâ·mān'tā) *adv* selfishly

egoistico (ā·gō·ē'stē·kō) *a* selfish

egotismo (ā·gō·tē'zmō) *m* egotism

egotista (ā·gō·tē'stâ) *m* egotist

egregiamente (ā·grā·jâ·mān'tā) *adv* excellently

egregio (ā·gre'jō) *a* distinguished

egresso (ā·gräs'sō) *m* way out, exit

egretta (ā·grāt'tâ) *f* egret

eguaglianza (ā·gwâ·lyân'tsâ) *f* equality

eguagliare (ā·gwâ·lyâ'rā) *vt* to equalize; to make even

eguale (ā·gwâ'lā) *a* equal; **rendere —** to level; to smooth out

eiaculare (ā·yâ·kū·lâ'rā) *vt* to ejaculate

eiaculazione (ā·yâ·kū·lâ·tsyō'nā) *f* ejaculation

eiettore (ā·yāt·tō'rā) *m* (*mech*) release, ejector

eiezione (ā·yā·tsyō'nā) *f* ejection, release

elaborare (ā·lâ·bō·râ'rā) *vt* to work out in detail; to elaborate

elaborato (ā·lâ·bō·râ'tō) *a* carefully done; detailed

elaborazione (ā·lâ·bō·râ·tsyō'nā) *f* elaboration; refinement

elargire (ā·lâr·jē'rā) *vt* to lavish, expend profusely

elargizione (ā·lâr·jē·tsyō'nā) *f* lavish donation; munificence

elasticamente (ā·lâ·stē·kâ·mān'tā) *adv* resiliently, bouyantly

elasticità (ā·lâ·stē·chē·tâ') *f* elasticity; bouyancy

elastico (ā·lâ'stē·kō) *m* rubber band; spring; **— a** elastic; bouyant, adaptable

elefante (ā·lā·fân'tā) *m* elephant; **–essa** (ā·lā·fân·tās'sâ) *f* female elephant

elegante (ā·lā·gân'tā) *a* smart, elegant; **–mente** (ā·lā·gân·tā·mān'tā) *adv* smartly, elegantly

elegantone (ā·lā·gân·tō'nā) *a* overly elegant; chic

eleganza (ā·lā·gân'tsâ) *f* elegance

eleggere * (ā·lej'jā·rā) *vt* to elect; to select

eleggibile (ā·lāj·jē'bē·lā) *a* eligible

eleggibilità (ā·lāj·jē·bē·lē·tâ') *f* qualification, eligibility

elegia (ā·lā·jē'â) *f* elegy

elementale (ā·lā·mān·tâ'lā) *a* elemental

elementare (ā·lā·mān·tâ'rā) *a* elementary

elemento (ā·lā·mān'tō) *m* element; component

elemosina (ā·lā·mô'zē·nâ) *f* charity; **–re** (ā·lā·mō·zē·nâ'rā) *vt&i* to solicit alms, beg; to entreat

elencare (ā·lān·kâ'rā) *vt* to list

elenco (ā·lān'kō) *m* list; **— telefonico** telephone book

elettivo (ā·lāt·tē'vō) *a* elective

eletto (ā·lāt'tō) *a* elected; chosen

elettorale (ā·lāt·tō·râ'lā) *a* electoral; **scheda —** ballot; **urna —** ballot box

elettorato (ā·lāt·tō·râ'tō) *m* right to vote, suffrage

elettore (ā·lāt·tō'rā) *m* voter

elettricamente (ā·lāt·trē·kâ·mān'tā) *adv* electrically, with electricity

elettricista (ā·lāt·trē·chē'stâ) *m* electrician

elettricità (ā·lāt·trē·chē·tâ') *f* electricity

elettrico (ā·let'trē·kō) *a* electrical, electric

elettrificare (ā·lāt·trē·fē·kâ'rā) *vt* to electrify; to charge with a current

elettrificazione (ā·lāt·trē·fē·kâ·tsyō'nā) *f* electrification

elettrizzare (ā·lāt·trē·dzâ'rā) *vt* to thrill, to excite, electrify

elettro (ā·lāt'trō) *m* yellow amber; **–biologia** (ā·lāt·trō·byō·lō·jē'â) *f* electrobiology; **–calamita** (ā·lāt·trō·kâ·lâ·mē'tâ) *f* electromagnet; **–cardiogramma** (ā·lāt·trō·kâr·dyō·grâm'mâ) *m* electrocardiogram; **–cuzione** (ā·lāt·trō·kū·tsyō'nā) *f* electrocution; **–dinamica** (ā·lāt·trō·

dē·nâ′mē·kâ) *f* electrodynamics; **–do** (ā·lāt·trō′dō) *m* electrode; **–domestico** (ā·lāt·trō·dō·me′stē·kō) *m* electrical appliance; **–dotto** (ā·lāt·trō·dōt′tō) *m* power line; **–lisi** (ā·lāt·trô′lē·zē) *f* electrolysis; **–lito** (ā·lāt·trō·lē′tō) *m* electrolyte; **–metallurgia** (ā·lāt·trō·mā·tâl·lūr·jē′á) *f* electrometallurgy; **–metro** (ā·lāt·trô′mā·trō) *m* electrometer; **–motore** (ā·lāt·trō·mō·tō′rā) *m&a* electromotor; **–motrice** (ā·lāt·trō·mō·trē′chā) *f* electrified railroad car; **–ne** (ā·lāt·trō′nā) *m* electron; **–nica** (ā·lāt·trô′nē·kâ) *f* electronics; **–nico** (ā·lāt·trô′nē·kō) *a* electronic; **–scopio** (ā·lāt·trō·skô′pyō) *m* electroscope; **–squasso** (ā·lāt·trō·skwâs′sō) *m* electric shock; jolt of electricity; **–statica** (ā·lāt·trō·stâ′tē·kâ) *f* electrostatics; **–statico** (ā·lāt·trō·stâ′tē·kō) *a* electrostatic; **–tecnica** (ā·lāt·trō·tek′nē·kâ) *f* electrical engineering; **–tecnico** (ā·lāt·trō·tek′nē·kō) *a* electric; **–terapia** (ā·lāt·trō·tā·râ·pē′â) *f* electrotherapy; **–termica** (ā·lāt·trō·ter′mē·kâ) *f* electrothermics; **–termico** (ā·lāt·trō·ter′mē·kō) *a* electrothermic; **–tipia** (ā·lāt·trō·tē·pē′â) *f* electrotype; **–treno** (ā·lāt·trō·trā′nō) *m* electrified train

elevare (ā·lā·vâ′rā) *vt* to raise; to hoist
elevarsi (ā·lā·vâr′sē) *vr* to raise oneself; to stand out, tower above
elevatamente (ā·lā·vâ·tâ·mān′tā) *adv* highly, loftily
elevatezza (ā·lā·vâ·tā′tsā) *f* loftiness, highness; nobility
elevato (ā·lā·vâ′tō) *a* high, raised
elevatore (ā·lā·vâ·tō′rā) *m* elevator
elevazione (ā·lā·vâ·tsyō′nā) *f* elevation
elezione (ā·lā·tsyō′nā) *f* election; appointment; choice; option
elfo (āl′fō) *m* elf
elica (e′lē·kâ) *f* propeller; (*naut*) screw
elicottero (ā·lē·kôt′tâ·rō) *m* helicopter
elidere * (ā·lē′dā·rā) *vt* to cancel out; to elide; to suppress
eliminare (ā·lē·mē·nâ′rā) *vt* to eliminate; to delete; to exclude; to obviate
eliminarsi (ā·lē·mē·nâr′sē) *vr* to be eliminated; to be obviated
eliminatoria (ā·lē·mē·nâ·tô′ryâ) *f* (*sport*) heat
eliminatorio (ā·lē·mē·nâ·tô′ryō) *a* eliminating; deleting
eliminazione (ā·lē·mē·nâ·tsyō′nā) *f* elimination, removal; exclusion; suppression
ella (āl′lâ) *pron* she
ellisse (āl·lēs′sā) *f* ellipse

ellissoide (āl·lēs·sô′ē·dā) *m&a* ellipsoid
ellissi (āl·lēs′sē) *f* ellipsis
ellittico (āl·lēt′tē·kō) *a* elliptical
ellenico (āl·le′nē·kō) *m&a* Hellenic
elmetto (āl·māt′tō) (*mil*) helmet
elmo (āl′mō) *m* helmet
elocuzione (ā·lō·kū·tsyō′nā) *f* elocution; oratorical style
elogiare (ā·lō·jâ′rā) *vt* to praise, commend
elogiabile (ā·lō·jâ′bē·lā) *a* commendable, praiseworthy
elogiatore (ā·lō·jâ·tō′rā) *m* eulogist
elogio (ā·lô′jō) *m* praise
eloquente (ā·lō·kwän′tā) *a* eloquent; golden-tongued; **–mente** (ā·lō·kwān·tā·mān′tā) *adv* forcefully, eloquently
eloquenza (ā·lō·kwän′tsâ) *f* eloquence
elsa (āl′sâ) *f* hilt
elucubrare (ā·lū·kū·brâ′rā) *vt* to muse, mull over
elucubrazione (ā·lū·kū·brâ·tsyō′nā) *f* musing, thoughtful consideration
eludere * (ā·lū′dā·rā) *vt* to elude, evade; to avoid
elusione (ā·lū·zyō′nā) *f* evasion, avoidance
elusivo (ā·lū·zē′vō) elusive, evasive
emaciato (ā·mâ·châ′tō) *a* emaciated
emanare (ā·mâ·nâ′rā) *vt&i* to emanate from, spring from, originate; to publicize
emanazione (ā·mâ·nâ·tsyō′nā) *f* issue, issuing; promulgation
emancipare (ā·mân·chē·pâ′rā) *vt* to free, liberate
emancipazione (ā·mân·chē·pâ·tsyō′nā) *f* liberation, emancipation
emarginare (ā·mâr·jē·nâ′rā) *vt* to note on the margin; to make marginal notes on
emarginato (ā·mâr·jē·nâ′tō) *a* annotated; foot-noted
emblema (ām·blā′mâ) *m* emblem, sign
embolia (ām·bō·lē′â) *f* embolism
embolo (em′bō·lō) *m* embolus, blood clot
embrice (em′brē·châ) *m* roofing tile
embriologia (ām·bryō·lō·jē′â) *f* embryology
embriologo (ām·bryô′lō·gō) *m* embryologist
embrionale (ām·bryō·nâ′lā) *a* embryonic, inchoate
embrione (ām·bryō′nā) *m* embryo
emendamento (ā·mān·dâ·mān′tō) *m* amendment
emendare (ā·mān·dâ′rā) *vt* to amend
emendarsi (ā·mān·dâr′sē) *vr* to correct oneself, reform

k kid, l let, m met, n not, p pat, r very, s sat, sh shop, t tell, v vat, w we, y yes, z zero

emergenza (ā·mär·jän'tsâ) *f* emergency

emergere * (ā·mēr'jä·rā) *vi* to distinguish oneself; to out, become public

emerso (ā·mär'sō) *a* emerged

emerito (ā·me'rē·tō) *a* emeritus; eminent

emeroteca (ā·mā·rō·tā'kâ) *f* periodical room

emesso (ā·mās'sō) *a* emitted, issued

emettere * (ā·met'tä·rā) *vt* to emit; — un grido to cry out

emicrania (ā·mē·krâ'nyâ) *f* migraine headache

emigrante (ā·mē·grân'tä) *a&m* emigrant

emigrare (ā·mē·grâ'rā) *vi* to emigrate

emigrato (ā·mē·grâ'tō) *m* emigrant

emigrazione (ā·mē·grâ·tsyō'nä) *f* emigration

eminente (ā·mē·nän'tä) *a* eminent, wellknown; —mente (ā·mē·nän·tä·män'tä) *adv* eminently; highly, greatly

eminenza (ā·mē·nän'tsâ) *f* eminence

emisfero (ā·mē·sfä'rō) *m* hemisphere

emissario (ā·mēs·sä'ryō) *m* emissary

emissione (ā·mēs·syō'nä) *f* emission; broadcast

emittente (ā·mēt·tän'tä) *m* broadcaster; broadcasting station; — *a* broadcasting; issuing

emofilia (ā·mō·fē·lē'â) *f* hemophilia

emoglobina (ā·mō·glō·bē'nâ) *f* hemoglobin

emolliente (ā·mōl·lyän'tä) *a&m* emollient

emolumento (ā·mō·lū·män'tō) *m* fee; wages

emorragia (ā·mōr·râ·jē'â) *f* hemorrhage

emorroidi (ā·mōr·rô'ē·dē) *fpl* hemorrhoids

emostatico (ā·mō·stâ'tē·kō) *m&a* hemostatic

emoteca (ā·mō·tā'kâ) *f* blood bank

emotivo (ā·mō·tē'vō) *a* excitable

emozionale (ā·mō·tsyō·nâ'lä) *a* emotional, excitable

emozionante (ā·mō·tsyō·nän'tä) *adv* touching, thrilling

emozione (ā·mō·tsyō'nä) *f* emotion; suspense

empietà (äm·pyä·tâ') *f* impiety

empio (em'pyō) *a* impious; cruel

empire * (äm·pē'rā) *vt* to fill; to fill in, close up

empiricamente (äm·pē·rē·kâ·män'tä) *adv* empirically, experimentally

empirico (äm·pē'rē·kō) *a* empirical

emporio (äm·pô'ryō) *m* bazaar; market place; department store

emù (ā·mū') *m* (*zool*) emu

emulare (ā·mū·lâ'rā) *vt* to emulate; to rival

emulazione (ā·mū·lâ·tsyō'nä) *f* emulation

emulsione (ā·mūl·syō'nä) *f* emulsion

encefalite (ān·chä·fâ·lē'tä) *f* encephalitis

enciclica (ān·chē'klē·kâ) *f* encyclical

enciclopedia (ān·chē·klō·pä·dē'â) *f* encyclopedia

enciclopedico (ān·chē·klō·pe'dē·kō) *a* encyclopedic

encomiabile (ān·kō·myâ'bē·lä) *a* laudable, worthy of commendation

encomiare (ān·kō·myâ'rā) *vt* to commend, praise

encomio (ān·kô'myō) *m* praise

endemico (ān·de'mē·kō) *a* endemic

endivia (ān·dē'vyâ) *f* endive

endocardo (ān·dō·kâr'dō) *m* endocardium

endocrino (ān·dô'krē·nō) *a* endocrine; —logia (ān·dō·krē·nō·lō·jē'â) *f* endocrinology

endogeno (ān·dô'jä·nō) *a* endogenous

endogetto (ān·dō·jät'tō) *m* rocket

endovenoso (ān·dō·vä·nō'zō) *a* intravenous

energetico (ā·nār·je'tē·kō) *m* tonic

energia (ā·nār·jē'â) *f* power; energy; determination

energicamente (ā·nār·jē·kâ·män'tä) *adv* energetically, forcefully

energico (ā·ner'jē·kō) *a* vigorous, resolute

energumeno (ā·nār·gū'mä·nō) *m* demoniac

enfasi (en'fâ·zē) *f* stress, emphasis

enfaticamente (ān·fâ·tē·kâ·män'tä) *adv* emphatically

enigma (ā·nēg'mâ) *f* puzzle, riddle

enigmista (ā·nēg·mē'stâ) *m* puzzler

enigmistico (ā·nēg·mē'stē·kō) *a* puzzling

enimmistica (ān·nēm·mē'stē·kâ) *a* brainteaser

enologo (ā·nô'lō·gō) *m* wine-making expert; expert in wines

enorme (ā·nôr'mä) *a* enormous

enormità (ā·nôr·mē·tâ') *f* hugeness; enormity

ente (än'tä) *m* being; agency; institution; — morale (*law*) body corporate; (*com*) corporation

enteroclisma (ān·tä·rō·klē'zmâ) *m* enema

entità (ān·tē·tâ') *f* entity; significance, import

entomologia (ān·tō·mō·lō·jē'â) *f* entomology

entrambi (ān·trâm'bē) *pron* both

entrante (ān·trân'tä) *a* next, coming

entrare (ān·trâ'rā) *vi* to enter; — in particolari to go into details; — in

possesso di to take possession of
entrata (ān·trä′tä) *f* entrance; *(com)* income, asset; — **libera** free admission; — **in vigore** *(law)* enforcement; — **pubblica** government revenue
entro (ān′trō) *prep* within
entusiasmare (ān·tū·zyâ·zmâ′rä) *vt* to enthuse; to awaken the interest of
entusiasmarsi (ān·tū·zyâ·zmâr′sē) *vr* to become enthusiastic; to be inspired
entusiasmo (ān·tū·zyâ′zmō) *m* enthusiasm
entusiasta (ān·tū·zyâ′stä) *a* enthusiastic
enumerare (ā·nū·mä·râ′rä) *vt* to enumerate
enunciare (ā·n̄ūn·châ′rä) *vt* to enunciate
enunciato (ā·nūn·châ′tō) *a* enunciated
enunciazione (ā·nūn·châ·tsyō′nä) *f* enunciation
epa (ā′pä) *f* belly
epatite (ā·pâ·tē′tä) *f* hepatitis
epicentro (ā·pē·chän′trō) *m* focal point; epicenter
epiciclo (ā·pē·chē′klō) *m* epicycle
epico (e′pē·kō) *a* epic
epicureo (ā·pē·kū·rä′ō) *a&m* epicurean
epidemia (ā·pē·dä·mē′â) *f* epidemic
epidermide (ā·pē·der′mē·dä) *f* epidermis
Epifania (ā·pē·fâ·nē′â) *f* Epiphany
epiglottide (ā·pē·glôt′tē·dä) *f* epiglottis
epigrafe (ā·pē′grâ·fä) *f* dedication, preface
epigramma (ā·pē·grâm′mâ) *m* epigram
epilessia (ā·pē·läs·sē′â) *f* epilepsy
epilettico (ā·pē·let′tē·kō) *a* epileptic
epilogo (ā·pē′lō·gō) *m* epilogue
episcopale (ā·pē·skō·pâ′lä) *a* episcopal
episodio (ā·pē·zô′dyō) *m* episode
epistolario (ā·pē·stō·lâ′ryō) *m* exchange of letters; correspondence
epitaffio (ā·pē·tâf′fyō) *m* epitaph
epitelio (ā·pē·te′lyō) *m* epithelium
epiteto (ā·pē′tä·tō) *m* epithet
epoca (e′pō·kâ) *f* epoch, age
epopea (ā·pō·pä′â) *f* epic poem, saga
eppure (āp·pū′rä) *conj* yet, nonetheless, nevertheless
epurare (ā·pū·râ′rä) *vt* to purge
epurazione (ā·pū·râ·tsyō′nä) *f* purge, purification
equamente (ā·kwâ·män′tä) *adv* fairly, justly
equanime (ā·kwâ′nē·mä) *a* just, fair; calm, composed
equanimità (ā·kwâ·nē·mē·tâ′) *f* justness; composure
equatore (ā·kwâ·tō′rä) *m* equator
equatoriale (ā·kwâ·tō·ryâ′lä) *a* equatorial
equazione (ā·kwâ·tsyō′nä) *f* equation

equestre (ā·kwä′strä) *a* equestrian
equidistante (ā·kwē·dē·stân′tä) *a* equidistant
equilibrato (ā·kwē·lē·brâ′tō) *a* sensible, stable
equilibrio (ā·kwē·lē′bryō) *m* balance; stability
equilibrismo (ā·kwē·lē·brē′zmō) *m* acrobatics
equilibrista (ā·kwē·lē·brē′stâ) *m* tightrope walker
equinozio (ā·kwē·nô′tsyō) *m* equinox
equipaggiare (ā·kwē·pâj·jâ′rä) *vt* to equip
equipaggio (ā·kwē·pâj′jō) *m* crew
equità (ā·kwē·tâ′) *f* equity; fairness
equitazione (ā·kwē·tâ·tsyō′nä) *f* horsemanship
equivalente (ā·kwē·vâ·lān′tä) *a&m* equivalent
equivoco (ā·kwē′vō·kō) *m* misunderstanding; — *a* equivocal, unclear
equo (e′kwō) *a* fair; equitable
era (ā′râ) *f* era
erario (ā·râ′ryō) *m* treasury
erba (âr′bâ) *f* grass; herb; **in** — immature; inexperienced; latent
erbaccia (âr·bâ′châ) *f* weed
erbaggio (âr·bâj′jō) *m* vegetable
erbivendolo (âr·bē·ven′dō·lō) *m* vegetable dealer
erbivoro (âr·bē′vō·rō) *a* herbivorous
erede (ā·rā′dä) *m* heir
ereditiera (ā·râ·dē·tyâ′râ) *f* heiress
eredità (ā·râ·dē·tâ′) *f* inheritance; **lasciare in** — to bequeath, leave in one's will
ereditario (ā·râ·dē·tâ′ryō) *a* hereditary
ereditato (ā·râ·dē·tâ′tō) *a* inherited
eremita (ā·râ·mē′tä) *m* hermit
eremo (ā·râ′mō) *m* hermitage
eresia (ā·râ·zē′â) *f* heresy
eretico (ā·re′tē·kō) *a&m* heretic
eretto (ā·rät′tō) *a* erect
erezione (ā·râ·tsyō′nä) *f* erection
ergastolano (âr·gâ·stō·lâ′nō) *m* prisoner convicted for life
ergastolo (âr·gâ′stō·lō) *m* penitentiary; life sentence; life imprisonment
erica (e′rē·kâ) *f* heather
erigere * (ā·rē′jâ·rä) *vt* to erect; to build; to found; to institute
ermellino (âr·mäl·lē′nō) *m* ermine
ermetico (âr·me′tē·kō) *a* hermetic
ernia (er′nyâ) *f* rupture, hernia
eroe (ā·rō′â) *m* hero
eroina (ā·rō·ē′nâ) *f* heroine; *(med)* heroin
eroicamente (ā·rōē·kâ·män′tä) *adv* hero-

ically

eroico (ā·rô′ē·kō) *a* heroic

eroismo (ā·rō·ē′zmō) *m* heroism

erogare (ā·rō·gâ′rā) *vt* to give, distribute, deal out

erogatore (ā·rō·gâ·tō′rā) *m* distributor; — *a* distributing

erogazione (ā·rō·gâ·tsyō′nā) *f* distribution; donation

erompere * (ā·rôm′pā·rā) *vi* to break out

erosione (ā·rō·zyō′nā) *f* erosion

erotico (ā·rô′tē·kō) *a* erotic

erpete (er′pā·tā) *m (med)* shingles

erpice (er′pē·chā) *m* harrow, cultivator

errare (ār·râ′rā) *vi* to err; to make a mistake; to wander

errabondo (ār·râ·bōn′dō) *a* rambling, wandering

errante (ār·rân′tā) *a* errant; wandering; roaming; **cavaliere** — knight errant

errata corrige (ār·râ′tâ kôr′rē·jā) *(print)* errata

errato (ār·râ′tō) *a* wrong, mistaken

erroneo (ār·rô′nā·ō) *a* wrong, mistaken

errore (ār·rō′rā) *m* mistake

erta (ār′tā) *f* ascent; slope

erto (ār′tō) *a* steep

erudire (ā·rū·dē′rā) *vt* to educate, teach

erudirsi (ā·rū·dēr′sē) *vr* to educate oneself

erudito (ā·rū·dē′tō) *a* learned; — *m* scholar

erudizione (ā·rū·dē·tsyō′nā) *f* erudition

eruttare (ā·rūt·tâ′rā) *vi* to belch

eruttazione (ā·rūt·tâ·tsyō′nā) *f* belching

eruzione (ā·rū·tsyō′nā) *f* eruption; *(med)* inflammation, rash

esacerbare (ā·zâ·chār·bâ′rā) *vt* to aggravate; to exasperate

esacerbarsi (ā·zâ·chār·bâr′sē) *vr* to be exasperated; to be at one's wit's end

esaedro (ā·zâ·â′drō) *m* hexahedron

esagono (ā·zâ′gō·nō) *m* hexagon

esagonale (ā·zâ·gō·nâ′lā) *a* hexagonal

esagerare (ā·zâ·jā·râ′rā) *vt* to exaggerate; — *vi* to go too far

esageratamente (ā·zâ·jā·râ·tâ·mān′tâ) *adv* exaggeratedly

esagerato (ā·zâ·jā·râ′tō) *a* exaggerated

esagerazione (ā·zâ·jā·râ·tsyō′nā) *f* exaggeration

esalare (ā·zâ·lâ′rā) *vt&i* to exhale

esalante (ā·zâ·lân′tā) *a* exhaling

esaltare (ā·zâl·tâ′rā) *vt* to extol, praise highly

esaltarsi (ā·zâl·târ′sē) *vr* to sing one's own praises; to become overly enthusiastic

esaltato (ā·zâl·tâ′tō) *a* fanatical; — *m* fanatic

esaltazione (ā·zâl·tâ·tsyō′nā) *f* exaltation; excess enthusiasm

esame (ā·zâ′mā) *f* examination

esaminando (ā·zâ·mē·nân′dō) *m* candidate for an academic degree

esaminare (ā·zâ·mē·nâ′rā) *vt* to examine; to put to the test

esangue (ā·zân′gwā) *a* bloodless

esanime (ā·zâ′nē·mā) *a* lifeless

esasperare (ā·zâ·spâ·râ′rā) *vt* to exasperate

esasperarsi (ā·zâ·spâ·râr′sē) *vr* to become irritated

esasperato (ā·zâ·spâ·râ′tō) *a* exasperated, irritated

esasperazione (ā·zâ·spâ·râ·tsyō′nā) *f* exasperation, irritation

esattezza (ā·zât·tā′tsâ) *f* exactness, precision, care

esatto (ā·zât′tō) *a* exact, correct

esattore (ā·zât·tō′rā) *m* revenue agent, tax collector

esattoria (ā·zât·tō·rē′â) *f* internal revenue office

esaudimento (ā·zâū·dē·mān′tō) *m* agreement; granting

esaudire (ā·zâū·dē′rā) *vt* to grant; to agree to

esaudito (ā·zâū·dē′tō) *a* granted; complied with

esauriente (ā·zâū·ryān′tā) *a* exhaustive, complete

esaurimento (ā·zâū·rē·mān′tō) *m* exhaustion; breakdown

esaurire (ā·zâū·rē′rā) *vt* to exhaust; *(com)* to sell out

esaurirsi (ā·zâū·rēr′sē) *vr* to overwork oneself; to become exhausted

esaurito (ā·zâū·rē′tō) *a* sold out; out of print

esausto (ā·zâ′ū·stō) *a* exhausted

esautorare (a·zâū·tō·râ′rā) *vt* to discredit, cast aspersions on

esazione (ā·zâ·tsyō′nā) *f* tax collection

esca (ā′skā) *f* bait; *(fig)* temptation

escandescenza (ā·skân·dā·shân′tsâ) *f* fit of anger, outburst of rage

escavatore (ā·skâ·vâ·tō′rā) *m* excavator

escavazione (ā·skâ·vâ·tsyō′nā) *f* excavation

esclamare (ā·sklâ·mâ′rā) *vi* to exclaim

esclamativo (ā·sklâ·mâ·tē′vō) *a* exclamatory

esclamazione (ā·sklâ·mâ·tsyō′nā) *f* exclamation

escludere * (ā·sklū′dā·rā) *vt* to exclude; to

rule out
esclusione (ā·sklū·zyō'nā) *f* exclusion
esclusiva (ā·sklū·zē'và) *f* exclusive right; sole dealership
esclusivo (ā·sklū·zē'vō) *a* exclusive
escluso (ā·sklū'zō) *a* excluded; expected
escomiare (ā·skō·myâ'rā) *vt* to dismiss
escremento (ā·skrā·mān'tō) *m* excrement
escrescenza (ā·skrā·shān'tsā) *f* outgrowth
escursione (ā·skūr·syō'nā) *f* excursion
escursionista (ā·skūr·syō·nē'stâ) *m&f* member of a tour
escussione (ā·skūs·syō'nā) *f* examination of witnesses
esecrare (ā·zā·krâ'rā) *vt* to detest, have a loathing for
esecutivo (ā·zā·kū·tē'vō) *a* executive; — *m* executive board, board of directors
esecutore (ā·zā·kū·tō'rā) *m (law)* executor; executioner; performer; *(pol)* enactor
esecuzione (ā·zā·kū·tsyō'nā) *f* execution; performance; *(pol)* enactment
esedra (ā·zā'drā) *f* exedra
eseguire (ā·zā·gwē'rā) *vt* to execute; to perform; to accomplish; to fulfill; — **un progetto** to carry out a plan; — **un pagamento** to make a payment
esempio (ā·zem'pyō) *m* example; sample, demonstration; instance
esemplare (ā·zām·plâ'rā) *m* copy, pattern; — *a* exemplary
esentare (ā·zān·tâ'rā) *vt* to exempt
esente (ā·zān'tā) *a* exempt, free
esenzione (ā·zān·tsyō'nā) *f* exemption
esequie (ā·ze'kwēā) *fpl* funeral services
esercente (ā·zār·chān'tā) *a* practicing; — *m* dealer; shopkeeper, merchant; tradesman
esercire (ā·zār·chē'rā) *vt* to operate, carry on *(business)*
esercitare (ā·zār·chē·tâ'rā) *vt* to exercize; to exert; to practice, make use of
esercitarsi (ā·zār·chē·târ'sē) *vr* to practice; *(sport)* to train, work out
esercitato (ā·zār·chē·tâ'tō) *a* trained; experienced
esercitazione (ā·zār·chē·tâ·tsyō'nā) *f* exercise
esercito (ā·zer'chē·tō) *m* army
esercito (ā·zār·chē'tō) *a* operated, managed; carried on
esercizio (ā·zār·chē'tsyō) *m* drill; exercize; business
esibire (ā·zē·bē'rā) *vt* to show, display; to sport, make a show of
esibirsi (ā·zē·bēr'sē) *vr* to show oneself; to volunteer; *(theat)* to play a part

esibitore (ā·zē·bē·tō'rā) *m,* **esibitrice** (ā·zē·bē·trē'chā) *f* exhibitor
esibizione (ā·zē·bē·tsyō'nā) *f* exhibit, display
esibizionismo (ā·zē·bē·tsyō·nē'zmō) *m* exhibitionism; show, pomp
esibizionista (ā·zē·bē·tsyō·nē'stâ) *m* show-off *(coll)*
esigente (ā·zē·jān'tā) *a* demanding
esigenza (ā·zē·jān'tsâ) *f* exigency; requirement
esigere * (ā·zē'jā·rā) *vt* to collect; to demand, exact, require
esigibile (ā·zē·jē'bē·lā) *a* collectible
esiguo (ā·zē'gwō) *a* meager
esile (e'zē·lā) *a* slender, slight
esilità (ā·zē·lē·tâ') *f* slenderness, slightness
esiliare (ā·zē·lyâ'rā) *vt* to exile
esiliarsi (ā·zē·lyâr'sē) *vr* to seclude oneself
esiliato (ā·zē·lyâ'tō) *a* exiled; — *m* exile *(person)*
esilio (ā·zē'lyō) *m* exile
esimere (ā·zē'mā·rā) *vt* to exempt, release; to dispense with, do away with
esimersi (ā·zē'mār·sē) *vr* to evade; to avoid; to shirk, to get out of doing; to be able to help, refrain from
esistente (ā·zē·stān'tā) *a* existent; existing, living; extant
esistenza (ā·zē·stān'tsâ) *f* existence
esistere * (ā·zē'stā·rā) *vi* to exist, live
esitabile ā·zē·tâ'bē·lā) *a* a marketable
esitante (ā·zē·tân'tā) *a* hesitant, hesitating
esitare (ā·zē·tâ'rā) *vt* to hesitate
esitazione (ā·zē·tâ·tsyō'nā) *f* hesitation
esito (e'zē·tō) *m* success; outcome, upshot; *(com)* sale
esiziale (ā·zē·tsyâ'lā) *a* fatal, deadly
esodo (e'zō·dō) *m* exodus; flight
esofago (ā·zō'fâ·gō) *m* esophagus
esoftalmico (ā·zōf·tâl'mē·kō) *a (med)* exophthalmic
esonerare (ā·zō·nā·râ'rā) *vt* to exonerate, clear
esonero (ā·zô'nā·rō) *m* exoneration; exemption
esorbitante (ā·zōr·bē·tân'tā) *a* exorbitant
esorbitare (ā·zōr·bē·tâ'rā) *vi* to exceed
esorcismo (ā·zōr·chē'zmō) *m* exorcism
esorcizzare (ā·zōr·chē·dzâ'rā) *vt* to exorcise
esordire (ā·zōr·dē'rā) *vi* to start, begin
esordio (ā·zôr'dyō) *m* debut; beginning
esoso (ā·zō'zō) *a* hateful; stingy; greedy
esotico (ā·zô'tē·kō) *a* exotic
espandere * (ā·spân'dā·rā) *vt* to spread; to

---

k kid, **l** let, **m** met, **n** not, **p** pat, **r** very, **s** sat, **sh** shop, **t** tell, **v** vat, **w** we, **y** yes, **z** zero

expand, enlarge

espansione (ā·spân·syō'nā) *f* expansion

espansionismo (ā·spân·syō·nē'zmō) *m* *(pol)* expansionism

espansività (ā·spân·sē·vē·tâ') *f* expansiveness

espansivo (ā·spân·sē'vō) *a* demonstrative; expansive

espatriare (ā·spâ·tryâ'rā) *vt* to exile, banish

espatrio (ā·spâ'tryō) *m* expatriation

espediente (ā·spā·dyân'tā) *m* expedient

espellere * (ā·spel'lā·rā) *vt* to expel; to shoot out, eject

esperienza (ā·spā·ryân'tsä) *f* experiment; experience

esperimentare (ā·spā·rē·mān·tâ'rā) *vt* to experience, undergo; to test, put to the test

esperimentato (ā·spā·rē·mān·tâ'tō) *a* experienced, skillful; proven, tested

esperimentatore (ā·spā·rē·mān·tâ·tō'rā) *m* tester, experimenter

esperimento (ā·spā·rē·mān'tō) *m* experiment

espertamente (ā·spär·tâ·mān'tä) *adv* skillfully

esperto (ā·spär'tō) *a* skilled; — *m* expert

espettorare (ā·spät·tō·râ'rā) *vt* to expectorate

espiare (ā·spyâ'rā) *vt* to expiate

espiatorio (ā·spyâ·tô'ryō) *a* expiatory, serving as an atonement; **capro —** whipping boy, scapegoat

espiazione (ā·sypâ·tsyō'nā) *f* expiation

espirare (ā·spē·râ'rā) *vt* to expire

espirazione (ā·spē·râ·tsyō'nā) *f* expiration

espletare (ā·splâ·tâ'rā) *vt* to complete, fulfill; to execute, perform

esplicare (ā·splē·kâ'rā) *vt* to explain in detail; to detail

esplicito (ā·splē'chē·tō) *a* explicit

esplodere * (ā·splō'dā·rā) *vt&i* to explode

esplorare (ā·splō·râ'rā) *vt* to explore

esploratore (ā·splō·râ·tō'rā) *m* explorer; **giovane —** boy scout

esplorazione (ā·splō·râ·tsyō'nā) *f* exploration; *(mil)* reconnaissance

esplosione (ā·splō·zyō'nā) *f* explosion

esplosivo (ā·splō·zē'vō) *a&m* explosive

esploso (ā·splō'zō) exploded

esponente (ā·spō·nān'tä) *a&m* exponent

esporre * (ā·spōr'rā) *vt* to display, exhibit, show; to open, expose

esportare (ā·spōr·tâ'rā) *vt* to export

esportatore (ā·spōr·tâ·tō'rā) *m*, **esportatrice** (ā·spōr·tâ·trē'chä) *f* exporter

esportazione (ā·spōr·tâ·tsyō'nā) *f* export, exporting

esposimetro (ā·spō·zē'mā·trō) *m* exposure meter

espositore (ā·spō·zē·tō'rā) *m*, **espositrice** (ā·spō·zē·trē'chä) *f* exhibitor

esposizione (ā·spō·zē·tsyō'nā) *f* exposition, exhibit; show, demonstration

esposto (ā·spō'stō) *a* displayed; — *m* report

espressamente (ā·sprās·sâ·mān'tä) *adv* purposely; on purpose

espressione (ā·sprās·syō'nā) *f* expression

espressività (ā·sprās·sē·vē·tâ') *f* expressiveness

espressivo (ā·sprās·sē'vō) *a* clear, meaningful

espresso (ā·sprās'sō) *m* special delivery

esprimere * (ā·sprē'mā·rā) *vt* to express

esprimersi * (ā·sprē'mär·sē) *vr* to express oneself

espropriare (ā·sprō·pryâ'rā) *vt* to take over, expropriate; to evict

espropriazione (ā·sprō·pryâ·tsyō'nā) *f* expropriation; eviction

espugnare (ā·spū·nyâ'rā) *vt* to conquer; to storm, overrun

espulsione (ā·spūl·syō'nā) *f* expulsion

espulso (ā·spūl'sō) *a* expelled; **–re** (ā·spūl·sō'rā) *m* *(mech)* ejector, release

essa (ās'sâ) *pron* she

esse (ās'sā) *pron fpl* they

essenza (ās·sān'tsä) *f* essence

essenziale (ās·sān·tsyâ'lä) *a* essential

essenzialmente (ās·sān·tsyâl·mān'tä) *adv* essentially

essere * (es'sā·rā) *vi* to be, exist; to become; to happen; to stand; — **di** to belong to; — **in grado di** to be able to

essicare (ās·sē·kâ'rā) *vt* to dry up

essicarsi (ās·sē·kâr'sē) *vr* to become dry, dry up

essicativo (ās·sē·kâ·tē'vō) *a* drying, dehydrating

essicazione (ās·sē·kâ·tsyō'nā) *f* drying, dehydrating

esso (ās'sō) *pron* he

essi (ās'sē) *pron mpl* they

essudare (ās·sū·dâ'rā) *vt&i* to exude

essudazione (ās·sū·dâ·tsyō'nā) *f* exudation

est (āst) *m* east; East; Orient; **dell'—** eastern; Oriental

estasi (e'stâ·zē) *f* ecstasy; great enthusiam

estasiare (ā·stâ·zyâ'rā) *vt* to enrapture; to enthuse

estasiarsi (ā·stâ·zyâr'sē) *vr* to become enthusiastic; to gush

---

â ârm, **ā** bāby, **e** bet, **ē** bē, **ō** gō, **ô** gône, **ū** blūe, **b** bad, **ch** child, **d** dad, **f** fat, **g** gay, **j** jet

estasiato (ā·stä·zyâ'tō) *a* enraptured; highly enthused

estatico (ā·stä'tē·kō) *a* ecstatic

estate (ā·stä'tä) *f* summer

estendere * (ā·sten'dä·rä) *vt* to extend; to reach out

estendersi * (ā·sten'där·sē) *vr* to expand; to stretch oneself

estensamente (ā·stän·sâ·män'tä) *adv* extensively; fully

estensione (ā·stän·syō'nä) *f* extension

estensivo (ā·stän·sē'vō) *a* extensive

estenuante (ā·stä·nwân'tä) *a* oppressive, exhausting

esteriore (ā·stä·ryō'rä) *a* external; — *m* exterior; outer surface

esteriorità (ā·stä·ryō·rē·tâ') *f* external appearances

esternamente (ā·stär·nâ·män'tä) *adv* externally, outwardly

esterno (ā·stär'nō) *a* external; — *m* outside; alunno — day pupil

estero (e'stä·rō) *a* foreign; all'— abroad, overseas

esterrefatto (ā·stär·rä·fât'tō) *a* frightened, horrified

esteso (ā·stä'zō) *a* extensive; far-reaching

esteta (ā·stä'tä) *m* aesthete

estetica (ā·ste'tē·kä) *f* aesthetics

estetista (ā·stä·tē'stä) *m* beautician

estimare (ā·stē·mä'rä) *vt* to estimate

estimativo (ā·stē·mä·tē'vō) *a* estimated; approximate

estimatore (ā·stē·mä·tō'rä) *m* appraiser, estimator

estimazione (ā·stē·mä·tsyō'nä) *f* estimation; appraisal

estimo (e'stē·mō) *m* survey; appraisal

estinguere * (ā·stēn·gwä·rä) *vt* to extinguish; — il conto to pay the bill

estinguersi * (ā·stēn'gwär·sē) *vr* to be extinguished, die out

estinto (ā·stēn'tō) *a* extinct; dead; —re (ā·stēn·tō'rä) *m* fire extinguisher

estinzione (ā·stēn·tsyō'nä) *f* extinction

estivo (ā·stē'vō) *a* summer; scuola estiva summer school

estollere * (ā·stôl'lä·rä) *vt* to extol, praise

estorcere * (ā·stôr'chä·rä) *vt* to extort

estorsione (ā·stôr·syō'nä) *f* extortion

estradare (ā·strä·dä'rä) *vt* to extradite

estradizione (ā·strä·dē·tsyō'nä) *f* extradition

estraneo (ā·strä'nä·ō) *m* stranger; alien; — *a* extraneous

estrarre * (ā·strär'rä) *vt* to extract; to pull out, draw out

estratto (ā·strät'tō) *m* extract; — *a* drawn

out, extracted; —re (ā·strât·tō'rä) *m* extractor

estrazione (ā·strâ·tsyō'nä) *f* extraction

estremista (ā·strä·mē'stä) *m* extremist

estremità (ā·strä·mē·tâ') *f* extremity; da una — all'altra from one end to the other

estremo (ā·strä'mō) *a&m* extreme

estro (ä'strō) *m* imagination, fancy; inspiration; —so (ā·strō'zō) *a* whimsical

estromettere * (ā·strō·met'tä·rä) *vt* to oust

estuario (ā·stwâ'ryō) *m* estuary, mouth

esuberante (ā·zū·bä·rân'tä) *a* exuberant; —mente (ā·zū·bä·rân·tä·män'tä) *adv* exuberantly

esuberanza (ā·zū·bä·rân'tsä) *f* exuberance; plenty

esulare (ā·zū·lâ'rä) *vi* to go into exile

esule (e'zū·lä) *m* refugee, exile

esultante (ā·zūl·tân'tä) *a* exultant, jubilant

esultanza (ā·zūl·tân'tsä) *f* exultation

esultare (ā·zūl·tâ'rä) *vi* to exult

esumare (ā·zū·mä'rä) *vt* to exhume

età (ā·tâ') *f* age

etano (ā·tä'nō) *m* ethane

etere (e'tä·rä) *m* ether

etereo (ā·te'rä·ō) *a* ethereal

eternamente (ā·tär·nâ·män'tä) *adv* eternally

eternare (ā·tär·nâ'rä) *vt* to perpetuate

eternit (e'tär·nēt) *m* building material of asbestos and cement

eternità (ā·tär·nē·tâ') *f* eternity

eterno (ā·tär'nō) *a* eternal; in — forever

eterodina (ā·tä·rō·dē'nä) *f* heterodyne

eterodosso (ā·tä·rō·dōs'sō) *a* unorthodox

eterogeneo (ā·tä·rō·je'nä·ō) *a* heterogeneous

etica (e'tē·kâ) *f* ethics

eticamente (ā·tē·kâ·män'tä) *adv* ethically

etichetta (ā·tē·kät'tâ) *f* label; etiquette; senza — unceremoniously

etico (e'tē·kō) *a* ethical; *(med)* consumptive

etile (ā·tē'lä) *m (chem)* ethyl; —ne (ā·tē·lä'nä) *m* ethylene

etimologia (ā·tē·mō·lō·je'â) *f* etymology

etimologico (ā·tē·mō·lō'je·kō) *a* etymological

Etiopia (ā·tyô'pyä) *f* Ethiopia

etnico (et'nē·kō) *a* ethnic

etnologia (āt·nō·lō·je'â) *f* ethnology

etnologo (āt·nô'lō·gō) *m* ethnologist

etrusco (ā·trü'skō) *a&m* Etruscan

ettagono (āt·tâ'gō·nō) *m* heptagon

ettaro (et'tâ·rō) *m* hectare

ettogrammo (āt·tō·grâm'mō) *m* hecto-

---

k kid, **l** let, **m** met, **n** not, **p** pat, **r** very, **s** sat, **sh** shop, **t** tell, **v** vat, **w** we, **y** yes, **z** zero

gram, 100 grams
ettolitro (ăt·tō′lē·trō) *m* hectoliter
ettowatt (ăt·tō′vât) *m* 100 watts
eucaristia (āū·kâ·rē·stē′â) *f* Eucharist
eucaristico (āū·kâ·rē′stē·kō) *a* Eucharistic
eufemismo (āū·fā·mē′zmō) *m* euphemism
eufonia (āū·fō·nē′â) *f* euphony
eugenetica (āū·jā·ne′tē·kâ) *f* eugenics
eunuco (āū·nū′kō) *m* eunuch
Europa (āū·rō′pâ) *f* Europe
europeo (āū·rō·pā′ō) *a&m* European
eutanasia (āū·tâ·nâ′zyâ) *f* euthanasia
evacuare (ā·vâ·kwâ′rā) *vt* to evacuate
evadere * (ā·vâ′dā·rā) *vt&i* to escape; to flee; to settle *(obligation)*; to fill *(an order)*
evanescente (ā·vâ·nā·shān′tā) *a* evanescent, ephemeral
evangelista (ā·vân·jā·lē′stâ) *m* evangelist
evangelizzare (ā·vân·jā·lē·dzâ′rā) *vt&i* to evangelize
evaporare (ā·vâ·pō·râ′rā) *vt&i* to evaporate
evaporazione (ā·vâ·pō·râ·tsyō′nā) *f* evaporation
evasione (ā·vâ·zyō′nā) *f* evasion
evasivamente (ā·vâ·zē·vâ·mān′tā) *adv* evasively
evaso (ā·vâ′zō) *m* fugitive
evenienza (ā·vā·nyān′tsâ) *f* occurrence; emergency; eventuality; **per ogni —** just in case
evento (ā·vān′tō) *m* event

eventuale (ā·vān·twâ′lā) *a* possible; eventual
eventualmente (ā·vān·twâl·mān′tā) *adv* later on; possibly
eventualità (ā·vān·twâ·lē·tâ′) *f* possibility; need, necessity
evidente (ā·vē·dān′tā) *a* evident, obvious
evidentemente (ā·vē·dān·tā·mān′tā) *adv* clearly, obviously
evidenza (ā·vē·dān′tsâ) *f* evidence; **arrendersi all' — dei fatti** to be convinced of the truth of the evidence
evirare (ā·vē·râ′rā) *vt* to emasculate; to weaken
evirato (ā·vē·râ′tō) *a* emasculated
evitare (ā·vē·tâ′rā) *vt* to avoid; to get around, get out of
evitabile (ā·vē·tâ′bē·lā) *a* preventable, avoidable
evo (ā′vō) *m* age; **— medio** Middle Ages; **— moderno** present day, present
evocare (ā·vō·kâ′rā) *vt* to call upon, evoke; to bring to mind
evocazione (ā·vō·kâ·tsyō′nā) *f* evoking; remembrance
evolutista (ā·vō·lū·tē′stâ) *m* evolutionist
evolutivo (ā·vō·lū·tē′vō) *a* evolutive, evolutionary
evolto (ā·vōl′tō) *a* evolved; civilized
evoluzione (ā·vō·lū·tsyō′nā) *f* evolution
evolvere (ā·vōl′vā·rā) *vt* to evolve, develop
evolversi (ā·vōl′vār·sē) *vr* to develop
ex (ăks) *prefix* late, past, former

F

fa (fâ) *adv* ago; **tempo —** some time ago; **— m** *(mus)* F, fa; **— diesis** F sharp
fabbisogno (fâb·bē·zō′nyō) *m* needs, necessary items
fabbrica (fâb′brē·kâ) *f* factory; building; **marca di —** trademark
fabbricare (fâb·brē·kâ′rā) *vt* to manufacture, fabricate; to construct
fabbricato (fâb·brē·kâ′tō) *m* building; *a* built, made manufactured
fabbricatore (fâb·brē·kâ·tō′rā) *m* manufacturer, builder
fabbricazione (fâb·brē·kâ·tsyō′nā) *f* manufacture
faccenda (fâ·chān′dâ) *f* business, affair; chore, task
faccendiere (fâ·chān·dyā′rā) *m* meddler
faccetta (fâ·chāt′tâ) *f* facet
facchinata (fâk·kē·nâ′tâ) *f* toil, drudgery; foul language

facchino (fâk·kē′nō) *m* porter
faccia (fâ′châ) *f* face; front; **cambiar —** to change completely; **— tosta** effrontery; nerve *(sl)* **—le** (fâ·châ′lā) *a* facial; **—ta** (fâ·châ′tâ) *f* façade
face (fâ′châ) *f* flame, torch
faceto (fâ·châ′tō) *a* witty, humorous
facezia (fâ·che′tsyâ) *f* joke; note of humor
fachiro (fâ·kē′rō) *m* fakir
facile (fâ′chē·lā) *a* easy; inclined
facilità (fâ·chē·lē·tâ′) *f* ease, facility
facilitare (fâ·chē·lē·tâ′rā) *vt* to facilitate, make easy
facilitazione (fâ·chē·lē·tâ·tsyō′nā) *f (com)* easy credit terms; making easy
facilmente (fâ·chēl·mān′tā) *adv* easily; more than likely
facilone (fâ·chē·lō′nā) *m* easy-going person; person easy to get along with
facinoroso (fâ·chē·nō·rō′zō) *a* wicked;

lawless
facoltà (fâ·kŏl·tâ′) _f_ faculty; power; means
facoltativo (fâ·kŏl·tâ·tē′vō) _a_ optional
facoltoso (fâ·kŏl·tō′zō) _a_ well-to-do, with means
facondia (fâ·kôn′dyâ) _f_ eloquence
facondo (fâ·kŏn′dō) _a_ talkative; eloquent
fagiano (fâ·jâ′nō) _m_ pheasant
fagiolini (fâ·jō·lē′nē) _mpl_ string beans
fagiuolo (fâ·jwō′lō) _m_ bean; **andare a —** _(coll)_ to be fine with, please
fagotto (fâ·gŏt′tō) _m_ bundle; _(mus)_ bassoon
faina (fâ·ē′nâ) _f (zool)_ marten
falange (fâ·lân′jä) _f_ phalanx
falce (fâl′chä) _f_ scythe; **–tto** (fâl·chät′tō) _m_ sickle
falciare (fâl·châ′rä) _vt_ to mow
falciatore (fâl·châ·tō′rä) _m_ harvester
falciatrice (fâl·châ·trē′chä) _f_ mechanical harvester
falco (fâl′kō) _m_ hawk; **–ne** (fâl·kō′nä) _m_ falcon
falda (fâl′dâ) _f_ brim _(hat)_; flap; bottom _(coat)_; **— di monte** foot of a mountain; **— di neve** snowflake
falegname (fâ·lä·nyâ′mä) _m_ carpenter; **–ria** (fâ·lä·nyâ·mâ·rē′â) _f_ carpentry
falena (fâ·lä′nâ) _f_ moth
falla (fâl′lâ) _f_ leak; weaving fault
fallace (fâl·lâ′chä) _a_ fallacious
fallacia (fâl·lâ′châ) _f_ fallacy
fallibile (fâl·lē′bē·lä) _a_ fallible
fallibilità (fâl·lē·bē·lē·tâ′) _f_ fallibility
fallimentare (fâl·lē·män·tâ′râ) _a_ ruinous; causing bankruptcy; **procedura —** bankruptcy proceedings
fallimento (fâl·lē·män′tō) _m_ failure; _(com)_ bankruptcy
fallire (fâl·lē′râ) _vi_ to fail; _(com)_ to go bankrupt
fallito (fâl·lē′tō) _a_ failed; bankrupt
fallo (fâl′lō) _m_ fault, error
falò (fâ·lō′) _m_ bonfire
falsamente (fâl·sâ·män′tä) _adv_ falsely
falsare (fâl·sâ′râ) _vt_ to forge; to distort, falsify
falsariga (fâl·sâ·rē′gâ) _f_ example, sample
falsario (fâl·sâ′ryō) _m_ counterfeiter
falsificare (fâl·sē·fē·kâ′râ) _vt_ to falsify; to counterfeit
falsificatore (fâl·sē·fē·kâ·tō′râ) _m_ forger
falsificazione (fâl·sē·fē·kâ·tsyō′nä) _f_ forgery; counterfeiting
falsità (fâl·sē·tâ′) _f_ falsehood
falso (fâl′sō) _a_ false; forged
fama (fâ′mâ) _f_ fame

fame (fâ′mä) _f_ hunger; **aver — to be hungry; –lico** (fâ′me′lē·kō) _a_ starving; famished
famigerato (fâ·mē·jä·râ′tō) _a_ notorious; of ill repute, with a bad reputation
famiglia (fâ·mē′lyâ) _f_ family
familiare (fâ·mē·lyâ′râ) _a_ familiar; colloquial; **— m** relative; servant
familiarità (fâ·mē·lyâ·rē·tâ′) _f_ familiarity
familiarizzarsi (fâ·mē·lyâ·rē·dzâr′sē) _vr_ to become familiar
famosamente (fâ·mō·zâ·män′tâ) _adv_ famously
famoso (fâ·mō′zō) _a_ famous; notorious
fanale (fâ·nâ′lē) _m_ lamp; _(auto)_ headlight
fanaticamente (fâ·nâ·tē·kâ·män′tä) _adv_ fanatically
fanatico (fâ·nâ′tē·kō) _a_ fanatical; **— m** fanatic
fanatismo (fâ·nâ·tē′zmō) _m_ bigotry
fanciulla (fân·chūl′lâ) _f_ girl
fanciullaggine (fân·chūl·lâj′jē·nä) _f_ puerility, childishness
fanciullescamente (fân·chūl·lä·skâ·män′tä) _adv_ childishly
fanciullezza (fân·chūl·lä′tsâ) _f_ childhood
fanciullo (fân·chūl′lō) _m_ boy
fandonia (fân·dō′nyâ) _f_ humbug, tall tale
fanfara (fân·fâ′râ) _f_ brass band
fanfaronata (fân·fâ·rō·nâ′tâ) _f_ bravado, blustering manner
fanfarone (fân·fâ·rō′nâ) _m_ braggart
fanghiglia (fân·gē′lyâ) _f_ slush, mire
fango (fân′gō) _m_ mud; **–so** (fân·gō′zō) _a_ muddy
fannullone (fân·nūl·lō′nâ) _m_ loafer, idler
fantascienza (fân·tâ·shyän′tsâ) _f_ science fiction
fantasia (fân·tâ·zē′â) _f_ fancy; fiction
fantasioso (fân·tâ·zyō′zō) _a_ fanciful, whimsical
fantasma (fân·tâ′zmâ) _m_ phantom
fantasticamente (fân·tâ·stē·kâ·män′tä) _adv_ fantastically
fantasticare (fân·tâ·stē·kâ′râ) _vi_ to daydream; to engage in flights of fancy
fantasticheria (fân·tâ·stē·kä·rē′â) _f_ reverie, daydreaming
fante (fân′tä) _m_ infantryman; jack _(cards)_; **–ria** (fân·tä·rē′â) _f_ infantry
fantino (fân·tē′nō) _m_ jockey
fantoccio (fân·tō′chō) _m_ puppet; figurehead
fantomatico (fân·tō·mâ′tē·kō) _a_ ghostly
farabutto (fâ·râ·būt′tō) _m_ crook; _(coll)_ rogue, cad
farad (fâ′râd) _m_ farad

k kid, **l** let, **m** met, **n** not, **p** pat, **r** very, **s** sat, **sh** shop, **t** tell, **v** vat, **w** we, **y** yes, **z** zero

faraglione (fâ·râ·lyō'nä) *m* crag, pinnacle
farcire (fâr·chē'rä) *vt* to stuff
farcito (fâr·chē'tō) *a* stuffed
fardello (fâr·dāl'lō) *m* bundle; burden;
  far — to leave, make one's departure
fare * (fâ'rä) *vt* to make; to do; — **caldo**
  to be warm; — **coraggio** to encourage;
  — **fiasco** to fail; — **finta** to feign; —
  freddo to be cold; — **fronte a** to face;
  — **il maestro** to teach; — **le carte** to
  deal the cards; — **male** to injure; —
  onore to honor; — **paura** to scare; —
  sapere to inform; — **silenzio** to be silent;
  — **tardi** to be late; — **una domanda** to
  question; — **una parte** to play a part; —
  uno scherzo to play a trick; — **vedere** to
  show; — **visita** to visit; **fa lo stesso** it
  makes no difference
faretra (fâ·rä'trä) *f* quiver
farfalla (fâr·fâl'lä) *f* butterfly; (*mech*)
  throttle
farina (fâ·rē'nä) *f* flour; **–ceo** *a* (fâ·rē·
  nâ'chā·ō) farinaceous
farinoso (fâ·rē·nō'zō) *a* floury
faringe (fâ·rēn'jä) *f* pharynx
fariseo (fâ·rē·zä'ō) *a* hypocrite
farmaceutica (fâr·mâ·che'ū·tē·kâ) *f*
  pharmaceutics
farmaceutico (fâr·mâ·che'ū·tē·kō) *a*
  pharmaceutical
farmacia (fâr·mâ·chē'â)*f* drugstore
farmacista (fâr·mâ·chē'stä) *m* druggist
farmaco (fâr'mâ·kō) *m* medicine
faro (fâ'rō) *m* headlight; lighthouse; — **di**
  atterraggio (*avi*) landing light
farragine (fâr·râ'jē·nä) *f* hodgepodge,
  potpourri
farsa (fâr'sâ) *f* farce
farsi * (fâr'sē) *vr* to become; to be done;
  — **capire** to make oneself understood;
  — **la barba** to shave; — **male** to hurt
  oneself
fascia (fâ'shâ) *f* strip; bandage; **–re** (fâ·
  shâ'rä) *vt* to bandage
fasciatura (fâ·shâ·tū'râ) *f* bandaging
fascicolo (fâ·shē'kō·lō) *m* pamphlet
fascino (fâ'shē·nō) *m* charm, glamour
fascio (fâ'shō) *m* bundle
fascismo (fâ·shē'zmō) *m* Fascism
fascista (fâ·shē'stä) *m&a* Fascist
fase (fâ'zä) *f* phase; period; era
fastidio (fâ·stē'dyō) *m* trouble; **–samente**
  (fâ·stē·dyō·zâ·mān'tä) *adv* with difficulty; **–so** (fâ·stē·dyō'zō) *a* annoying;
  tiresome
fasto (fâ'stō) *m* display, pomp; **–samente**
  (fâ·stō·zâ·mān'tä) *adv* pompously; **–so**
  (fâ·stō'zō) *a* pompous

fata (fâ'tâ) *f* fairy
fatale (fâ·tä'lä) *a* fatal; inevitable
fatalista (fâ·tâ·lē'stä) *m* fatalist
fatalità (fâ·tâ·lē·tâ') *f* destiny, fate
fatica (fâ·tē'kâ) *f* effort, toil; fatigue; **–re**
  (fâ·tē·kâ'rä) *vi* to work hard
faticosamente (fâ·tē·kō·zâ·mān'tä) *adv*
  laboriously, with great effort
faticoso (fâ·tē·kō'zō) *a* fatiguing
fato (fâ'tō) *m* fortune; destiny
fatta (fât'tâ) *f* sort; action; **–ccio** (fât·tâ'-
  chō) *m* crime, evildoing
fattezze (fât·tā'tsä) *fpl* features (*face*);
  outline
fattibile (fât·tē'bē·lä) *a* feasible
fatto (fât'tō) *m* fact; deed; — *a* done;
  made; **badare al — suo** to mind one's
  own business; **cogliere sul —** to catch
  in the act; **giorno —** broad daylight; **in**
  — **di** regarding, as concerns
fattore (fât·tō'rä) *m* factor; farmer; maker
fattoria (fât·tō·rē'â) *f* farm
fattorino (fât·tō·rē'nō) *m* messenger; bus
  conductor; mailman
fattura (fât·tū'râ) *f* (*com*) invoice; **–re**
  (fât·tū·râ'rä) *vt* to invoice
fatuamente (fâ·twâ·mān'tä) *adv* foolishly
fatuità (fâ·twē·tâ') *f* foolishness
fatuo (fâ'twō) *a* silly, foolish
fausto (fâ'ū·stō) *a* lucky; happy
fautore (fâū·tō'râ) *m* patron, supporter
fava (fâ'vâ) *f* broad bean
favilla (fâ·vēl'lä) *f* spark
favo (fâ'vō) *m* (*med*) carbuncle; honey-
  comb
favola (fâ'vō·lâ) *f* fable
favolosamente (fâ·vō·lō·zâ·mān'tä) *adv*
  fabulously; incredibly
favore (fâ·vō'rä) *m* favor; **fare un —** to
  do a favor; **giorni di —** (*com*) days of
  grace; **–ggiare** (fâ·vō·rāj·jâ'rä) *vt* to
  support, favor; **–ggiamento** (fâ·vō·râj·
  jâ·mān'tō) *m* support, backing; **–vole**
  (fâ·vō·re'vō·lä) *a* favorable; **tempo**
  –vole opportune time
favorire (fâ·vō·rē'râ) *vt* to aid; to oblige
favoritismo (fâ·vō·rē·tē'zmō) *m* partiality
favorito (fâ·vō·rē'tō) *a* favorite; favored
fazione (fâ·tsyō'nä) *f* faction; political
  party
faziosamente (fâ·tsyō·zâ·mān'tä) *adv*
  contentiously; in an argumentive way
fazioso (fâ·tsyō'zō) *a* dissentive; argumentive
fazzoletto (fâ·tsō·lät'tō) *m* handkerchief
febbraio (fāb·brâ'yō) *m* February
febbre (fāb'brä) *f* fever; **aver —** to run
  a fever; — **da cavallo** high fever

â ârm, **ā** bāby, **e** bet, **ē** bē, **ō** gō, **ô** gône, **ū** blūe, **b** bad, **ch** child, **d** dad, **f** fat, **g** gay, **j** jet

febbrile (fāb·brē'lā) *a* feverish; agitated
fecale (fā·kâ'lā) *a* fecal
feccia (fā'châ) *f* scum
fecola (fe'kō·lâ) *f* starch
fecondare (fā·kōn'dâ·rā) *vt* to pollinate; to fertilize
fecondativo (fā·kōn·dâ·tē'vō) *a* creative
fecondo (fā·kōn'dō) *a* fertile
fede (fā'dā) *f* faith; wedding ring; certificate; — **di nascita** birth certificate; **degno di** — trustworthy; **far** — to bear witness; **prestar** — to give credence to; **romper** — to break one's word
fedele (fā·dā'lā) *a* faithful
fedelmente (fā·dāl·mān'tā) *adv* loyally; exactly
fedeltà (fā·dāl·tâ') *f* faithfulness; exactness
federa (fe'dā·râ) *f* pillowcase
federale (fā·dā·râ'lā) *a* federal
federare (fā·dā·râ'rā) *vt* to federate
federazione (fā·dā·râ·tsyō'nā) *f* federation
fedina (fā·dē'nâ) *f* police record
fegataccio (fā·gâ·tâ'chō) *m* madcap, daredevil
fegato (fe'gâ·tō) *m* liver; (*sl*) courage; **aver** — to be brave; **-so** (fā·gâ·tō'zō) (*med*) bilious; cross, testy
felce (fāl'chā) *f* fern
felice (fā·lē'chā) *a* happy; **-mente** (fā·lē·châ·mān'tā) *adv* happily; safely
felicità (fā·lē·chē·tâ') *f* happiness
felicitare (fā·lē·chē·tâ'rā) *vt* to congratulate; to bless; to make happy
felicitazione (fā·lē·chē·tâ·tsyō'nā) *f* congratulation
felino (fā·lē'nō) *a* feline
fellone (fāl·lō'nā) *a* ruthless
fellonia (fāl·lō·nē'â) *f* felony; treason
felpato (fāl·pâ'tō) *a* soft, carpet-like
feltro (fāl'trō) *m* felt
femmina (fem'mē·nâ) *f* woman; female
femminile (fām·mē·nē'lā) *a* feminine
femore (fe'mō·râ) *m* thighbone
fendere * (fen'dā·rā) *vt* to split, cleave
fenditura (fān·dē·tū'râ) *f* cleft, split, opening
fenico (fe'nē·kō) *a* carbolic
fenolo (fā·nō'lō) *m* phenol
fermentare (fār·mān·tâ'rā) *vt* to ferment; to foment
fermentazione (fār·mān·tâ·tsyō'nā) *f* fermentation; fomenting
fermento (fār·mān'tō) *m* ferment; agitation, foment
feroce (fā·rō'chā) *a* ferocious; wild; **-mente** (fā·rō·chā·mān'tā) *adv* sav-

agely, fiercely
ferragosto (fār·râ·gō'stō) *m* Assumption Day
ferramenta (fār·râ·mān'tâ) *fpl* hardware
ferravecchio (fār·râ·vek'kyō) *m* scrap iron dealer
ferreo (fer'rā·ō) *a* iron; strong
ferri (fār'rē) *mpl* tools; **cuocere ai** — to grill (*food*)
ferriera (fâr·ryā'râ) *f* steel mill, iron works
ferro (fār'rō) *m* iron; (*fig*) sword; — **da calze** knitting needle; — **da stiro** flat-iron; **-via** (fār·rō·vē'â) *f* railroad; **-viario** (fār·rō·vyâ'ryō) *a* railroad; **-viere** (fār·rō·vyâ'rā) *m* railroad man
fertile (fer'tē·lā) *a* fertile
fertilità (fār·tē·lē·tâ') *f* fertility
fertilizzante (fār·tē·lē·dzân'tā) *m* fertilizer
fertilizzare (fār·tē·lē·dzâ'rā) *vt* to fertilize
fertilizzazione (fār·tē·lē·dzâ·tsyō'nā) *f* fertilization
fertilmente (fār·tēl·mān'tā) *adv* fruitfully
fervente (fār·vān'tā) *a* fervent; **-mente** (fār·vān·tā·mān'tā) *adv* fervently
fervore (fār·vō'râ) *m* zeal, fervor
fesso (fās'sō) *a* cleft, cracked open
fessura (fās·sū'râ) *f* crack, crevice
festa (fā'stâ) *f* feast; party; holiday; **far** — a to welcome; to fete
festeggiamento (fā·stāj·jâ·mān'tō) *m* rejoicing
festeggiare (fā·stāj·jâ'rā) *vt* to celebrate; to rejoice over
festino (fā·stē'nō) *m* banquet
festività (fā·stē·vē·tâ') *f* festivity; celebration
festivo (fā·stē'vō) *a* festive; **giorno** — holiday
fetale (fā·tâ'lā) *a* fetal
feto (fā'tō) *m* fetus
fetente (fā·tān'tā) *a* stinking
fetido fe'tē·dō) *a* malodorous
fetore (fā·tō'râ) *m* stench
fetta (fāt'tâ) *f* slice; rasher
fettuccia (fāt·tū'châ) *f* ribbon
fettuccine (fāt·tū·chē'nā) *fpl* noodles
feudale (fāū·dâ'lā) *a* feudal
feudalismo (fāū·dâ·lē'zmō) *m* feudalism
fiaba (fyâ'bâ) *f* fable
fiacca (fyâk'kâ) *f* laziness; weakness; **batter** — (*coll*) to be sluggish; **-re** (fyâk·kâ'rā) *vt* to tire; to break down
fiacchere (fyâk'kā·rā) *m* carriage
fiacco (fyâk'kō) *a* weary; sluggish; lazy
fiaccola (fyâk'kō·lâ) *f* torch; **-ta** (fyâk·kō·lâ'tâ) *f* torchlight parade

---

fiacre (fyâ'krā) *m* hansom, carriage

fiala (fyâ'lâ) *f* vial

fiamma (fyâm'mâ) *f* flame; **–nte** (fyâm·mân'tā) *a* flaming; **nuovo –nte** brand-new

fiammifero (fyâm·mē'fā·rō) *m* match (*light*)

fiammingo (fyâm·mēn'gō) *m&a* Flemish

fiancheggiare (fyân·kāj·jâ'rā) *vt* to border on; *(fig)* to help, support; *(mil)* to flank

fianco (fyân'kō) *m* hip; flank; side; **di —** sideways; on one side; **— destro!** right turn!; **— sinistro!** left turn!

fiaschetteria (fyâ·skät·tā·rē'â) *f* wine shop

fiasco (fyâ'skō) *m* flask; fiasco

fiatare (fyâ·tâ'rā) *vi* to breathe; *(fig)* to tell in secret

fiato (fyâ'tō) *m* breath

fibbia (fēb'byâ) *f* buckle

fibra (fē'brâ) *f* fiber; *(fig)* character, moral fiber

fibroso (fē·brō'zō) *a* fibrous

ficcanaso (fēk·kâ·nâ'zō) *m* busybody; intruder

fico (fē'kō) *m* fig; **non valere un —** to be absolutely worthless

fidanzamento (fē·dân·tsâ·mān'tō) *m* engagement

fidanzarsi (fē·dân·tsâr'sē) *vr* to get engaged

fidanzata (fē·dân·tsâ'tâ) *f* fiancée

fidanzato (fē·dân·tsâ'tō) *m* fiancé; **— a** engaged

fidare (fē·dâ'rā) *vt* to trust, have confidence in

fidarsi (fē·dâr'sē) *vr* to rely upon; to confide in; to dare

fidatamente (fē·dâ·tâ·mān'tā) *adv* trustingly

fidato (fē·dâ'tō) *a* faithful; devoted

fido (fē'dō) *m* faithful; devoted; **— m** (*com*) credit

fiducia (fē·dū'châ) *f* trust, confidence

fiduciario (fē·dū·châ'ryō) *m* trustee

fiduciosamente (fē·dū·chō·zâ·mān'tā) *adv* confidently, trustfully

fiducioso (fē·dū·chō'zō) *a* confident; hopeful

fiele (fyä'lā) *m* gall; *(fig)* grudge

fienile (fyâ·nē'lâ) *m* hayloft

fieno (fyä'nō) *m* hay; **febbre del —** hay fever

fiera (fyä'râ) *f* fair; **— di beneficenza** charity bazaar

fiera (fyä'râ) *f* wild animal

fieramente (fyä·râ·mān'tā) *adv* fiercely

fierezza (fyä·rā'tsâ) *f* fierceness; pride

fiero (fyä'rō) *a* proud; violent

fievole (fye'vō·lā) *a* feeble, weak

fievolmente (fyä·vōl·mān'tā) *adv* feebly, weakly

fifa (fē'fâ) *f* cowardice; fear

fifone (fē·fō'nä) *m* coward; softie (*coll*)

figgere * (fēj'jä·rā) *vt* to drive in, stick in

figlia (fē'lyâ) *f* daughter

figliastra (fē·lyâ'strâ) *f* step-daughter

figliastro (fē·lyâ'strō) *m* step-son

figlio (fē'lyō) *m* son; **–ccia** (fē·lyô'châ) *f* goddaughter; foster daughter; **–ccio** (fē·lyô'chō) *m* godson; godchild; foster son

figliuola (fē·lywō'lâ) *f* daughter

figliuoli (fē·lywō'lē) *mpl* children

figliuolo (fē·lywō'lō) *m* son

figura (fē·gū'râ) *f* figure; picture; appearance; face card; **far la — di** to seem to be; **–bile** (fē·gū·râ'bē·lā) *a* imaginable

figurare (fē·gū·râ'rā) *vt* (*math*) to figure; **— vi** to appear; to look well

figurarsi (fē·gū·râr'sē) *vr* to imagine, suppose

figurina (fē·gū·rē'nâ) *f* figurine

figurinista (fē·gū·rē·nē'stâ) *m* fashion designer

figurino (fē·gū·rē'nō) *m* fashion plate; pattern

figuro (fē·gū'rō) *m* rascal

fila (fē'lâ) *f* row; line; suite; **di —** one after the other

filaccia (fē·lâ'châ) *f* raveling

filamento (fē·lâ·mân'tō) *m* filament

filantropia (fē·lân·trō·pē'â) *f* philanthropy

filantropo (fē·lân'trō·pō) *m* philanthropist

filare (fē·lâ'rā) *vt&i* to spin; to run; to woo; **— diritto** to go straight ahead; to behave properly; **far — qualcuno** *(fig)* to make someone toe the mark

filarmonico (fē·lâr·mô'nē·kō) *a* philharmonic

filastrocca (fē·lâ·strōk'kâ) *f* hodgepodge, rigmarole

filatelista (fē·lâ·tā·lē'stâ) *m&f* stamp collector, philatelist

filato (fē·lâ'tō) *a* spun; **— m** yarn

filatura (fē·lâ·tü'râ) *f* spinning

filetto (fē·lāt'tō) *m* thread (*screw*); fillet

fili (fē'lē) *mpl* electric wiring; **— ad alta tensione** high-tension wires

filiale (fē·lyâ'lā) *a* filial; **— f** (*com*) branch, regional office

filibustiere (fē·lē·bū·styä'rā) *m* filibuster, freebooter

film (fēlm) *m* movie film

filo (fē'lō) *m* thread; wire; clue; cutting

edge; — **d'erba** blade of grass; — **di voce** thin voice; **per — e per segno** exactly; in detail; **-bus** *m* trolley bus; **-ne** *m* vein; long loaf of bread; **-via** *f* trolley line

filodrammatico (fē·lō·dräm·mâ'tē·kō) *m* (*theat*) amateur performer

filologo (fē·lô'lō·gō) *m* philologist

filosofia (fē·lō·zō·fē'â) *f* philosophy

filosofico (fē·lō·zô'fē·kō) *a* philosophic

filosofo (fē·lô'zō·fō) *m* philosopher

filtrare (fēl·trâ'rä) *vt&i* to filter

filtro (fēl'trō) *m* filter

finale (fē·nä'lä) *a* final; *m* — finale; finish

finalista (fē·nä·lē'stä) *m* finalist

finalità (fē·nä·lē·tâ') *f* end; purpose

finalmente (fē·nâl·män'tä) *adv* at last; in the long run

finanche (fē·nân'kä) *adv* even; too

finanza (fē·nân'tsä) *f* finance; **guardia di — revenue** official

finanziamento (fē·nân·tsyä·män'tō) *m* financing, financial backing

finanziare (fē·nân·tsyä'rä) *vt* to finance

finanziario (fē·nân·tsyä'ryō) *a* financial

finanziatore (fē·nân·tsyâ·tō'rä) *m* backer; angel (*sl*)

finanziere (fē·nân·tsyä'rä) *m* financier

finca (fēn'kä) *f* (*print*) column

finchè (fēn·kä') *conj* while; until

fine (fē'nä) *m* end, reason; — *f* close; limit; result; — **a thin**; refined; **-zza** (fē·nä'tsä) *f* finesse; refinement

finestra (fē·nä'strä) *f* window

fingere * (fēn'jä·rä) *vt* to pretend, feign; to counterfeit

fingersi * (fēn'jär·sē) *vr* to pretend to be; to act

finimento (fē·nē·män'tō) *m* accomplishment; completion; ornament; harness (*horse*)

finire (fē·nē'rä) *vt* to finish, end; — **male** to come to grief, come to a bad end

finito (fē·nē'tō) *a* finished; perfect; accomplished; finite

Finlandia (fēn·lân'dyâ) *f* Finland

finlandese (fēn·lân·dä'zä) *a* Finnish

fino (fē'nō) *a* shrewd; thin, fine; **udito —** keen ear; — *prep* until; — **a** up to; — **là** up to that point; — **a che** until

finocchio (fē·nôk'kyō) *m* fennel

finora (fē·nō'râ) *adv* up to now, previously

finta (fēn'tä) *f* pretense; **far – di** to feign, pretend

finto (fēn'tō) *a* false, artificial

finzione (fēn·tsyō'nä) *f* pretense; humbug

fioccare (fyōk·kâ'rä) *vi* to fall in flakes, snow

fiocco (fyōk'kō) *m* tassel; flake

fionda (fyōn'dâ) *f* sling

fiore (fyō'rä) *m* flower; club (*card*) — **di** cream of, best of

fiorentino (fyō·rän·tē'nō) *a&m* Florentine

fioretto (fyō·rät'tō) *m* foil (*fencing*)

fiorancio (fyō·rân'chō) *m* marigold

fioraio (fyō·râ·yō) *m* florist

fiorire (fyō·rē'rä) *vi* to bloom, flower; (*fig*) to prosper, thrive

fiorista (fyō·rē'stä) *m* florist, nurseryman

fiorito (fyō·rē'tō) *a* blooming, flowering

fiotto (fyōt'tō) *m* gush; stream; (*naut*) wave

Firenze (fē·rän'tsä) *f* Florence

firma (fēr'mâ) *f* signature; **-re** (fēr·mâ'rä) *vt* to sign; **-tario** (fēr·mâ·tâ'ryō) *m* signer

firmamento (fēr·mâ·män'tō) *m* firmament

fisarmonica (fē·zâr·mô'nē·kâ) *f* accordion

fisarmonicista (fē·zâr·mō·nē·chē'stä) *m* accordion player

fischiare (fē·skyâ'rä) *vt&i* to whistle; to hiss

fischio (fē'skyō) *m* whistle; hiss

fiscale (fē·skä'lä) *a* fiscal; **avvocato —** public prosecutor

fisco (fē'skō) *m* treasury

fisica (fē'zē·kâ) *f* physics

fisico (fē'zē·kō) *a* physical, bodily; — *m* physique; physicist

fisiologia (fē·zyō·lō·jē'â) *f* physiology

fisionomia (fē·zyō·nō·mē'â) *f* physiognomy

fisima (fē'zē·mâ) *f* whim

fissare (fēs·sâ'rä) *vt* to fasten, fix; to stare at; to decide, determine; — **un posto** to reserve a seat

fissarsi (fēs·sâr'sē) *vr* to establish oneself; to settle down

fissazione (fēs·sâ·tsyō'nä) *f* fixation; obsession

fissile (fēs'sē·lä) *a* fissionable

fissione (fēs·syō'nä) *f* fission

fisso (fēs'sō) *a* fixed; — *adv* steadily

fistola (fē'stō·lä) *f* (*med*) fistula

fitta (fēt'tä) *f* pang, sharp pain

fittabile (fēt·tâ'bē·lä) *m* lessee, tenant farmer

fittamente (fēt·tâ·män'tä) *adv* thickly, densely; frequently

fittizio (fēt·tē'tsyō) *a* fictitious

fitto (fēt'tō) *m* rent; income; lease

fitto (fēt'tō) *a* dense, thick; **notte fitta** pitch dark; **a capo fitto** headlong

fiumana (fyū·mâ'nâ) *f* stream; **una — di**

---

k kid, **l** let, **m** met, **n** not, **p** pat, **r** very, **s** sat, **sh** shop, **t** tell, **v** vat, **w** we, **y** yes, **z** zero

gente (fig) a crowd of people

fiume (fyū'mā) m river; **un — di parole** (fig) a flood of words

fiutare (fyū·tâ'rā) vt to smell; to scent; (fig) to foresee

fiuto (fyū'tō) m scent; (fig) talent, flair; acute perception

flaccido (flâ'chē·dō) a spineless; flabby, soft

flacone (flâ·kō'nā) m flacon, vial

flagellare (flâ·jäl·lâ'rā) vt to whip, scourge

flagellazione (flâ·jäl·lâ·tsyō'nā) f whipping

flagello (flâ·jäl'lō) m scourge; utter ruin

flagrante (flâ·grân'tā) a evident; **in —** in the act

flagranza (flâ·grân'tsâ) f flagrancy; **colto in —** surprised red-handed

flanella (flâ·näl'lâ) f flannel

flangia (flân'jâ) f flange

flautista (flâū·tē'stâ) m flutist

flauto (flâ'ū·tō) m flute

flebile (fle'bē·lâ) a mournful, wailing

flebilmente (flâ·bēl·män'tā) adv mournfully, plaintively; weakly

flebite (flâ·bē'tā) f (med) phlebitis

flemma (flâm'mâ) f calmness; **–ticamente** (flâm·mâ·tē·kâ·män'tā) adv calmly, coolly

flemmone (flâm·mō'nā) m (med) phlegm

flessibile (flâs·sē'bē·lâ) a flexible

flessibilità (flâs·sē·bē·lē·tâ') f flexibility

flessibilmente (flâs·sē·bēl·män'tā) adv flexibility

flessione (flâs·syō'nā) f bend; (gram) inflection

flessuoso (flâs·swō'zō) a sinuous; bending

flettere * (flet'tā·rā) vt to flex; to bend

flirtare (flēr·tâ'rā) vi to flirt

florido (flō'rē·dō) a florid

florilegio (flô·rē·le'jō) m anthology, collection

floscio (flô'shō) a limp, flabby

flotta (flōt'tâ) f (naut) fleet; **–nte** (flōt·tân'tā) a floating

flottiglia (flōt·tē'lyâ) f flotilla

fluente (flūān'tā) a flowing; fluent

fluidamente (flūē·dâ·män'tā) adv fluently; smoothly

fluidezza (flūē·dâ'tsâ) f fluency

fluido (flū'ē·dō) m&a fluid

fluorescente (flūō·rā·shân'tā) a flourescent

fluorescenza (flūō·rā·shân'tsâ) f fluorescence

fluoridrico (flūō·rē'drē·kō) a hydrofluoric

fluoro (flūō'rō) m fluorine

fluoruro (flūō·rū'rō) m fluorine

flusso (flūs'sō) m flux

flutto (flūt'tō) m (naut) wave

fluttuante (flūt·twân'tā) a floating; fluctuating

fluttuare (flūt·twâ'rā) vi to fluctuate; to swing

fluttuazione (flūt·twâ·tsyō'nā) f fluctuation

fobia (fō·bē'â) f phobia; aversion

foca (fō'kâ) f seal

focaccia (fō·kâ'châ) f cake; **rendere pan per —** (fig) to give blow for blow

foce (fō'chā) f river mouth

fochista (fō·kē'stâ) m fireman

focolare (fō·kō·lâ'rā) m fireplace; home

focoso (fō·kō'zō) a fiery, impetuous

fodera (fô'dā·râ) f lining; **–re** (fō·dā·râ'rā) vt to line

foga (fō'gâ) f élan, ardor

foggia (fôj'jâ) f shape; manner; **a — di** like; **alla — di** after the fashion of; **–re** (fôj·jâ'rā) vt to shape

foglia (fô'lyâ) f leaf; **mangiare la —** to take a hint; to catch on; **–me** (fō·lyâ'mā) m foliage

foglietto (fō·lyāt'tō) m small leaf of paper; **— volante** handbill

foglio (fô'lyō) m sheet; (print) folio, page number; **–lina** (fō·lyō·lē'nâ) f leaflet

fogna (fō'nyâ) f sewer; **–tura** (fō·nyâ·tū'râ) f drainage system, sewers

folata (fō·lâ'tâ) f gust, puff (wind); sudden flight of birds

folgorante (fōl·gō·rân'tā) a shining; flashing; burning

folgorare (fōl·gō·râ'rā) vt&i to flash; to strike (lightning); to burn

folgorato (fōl·gō·râ'tō) a struck by lightning; electrocuted

folgore (fôl'gō·rā) f thunderbolt

folla (fōl'lâ) f mob, crowd

folle (fōl'lâ) a insane, mad; (mech) unfastened; **in —** (mech) in neutral; **–mente** (fōl·lâ·män'tā) adv madly, foolishly

follia (fōl·lē'â) f folly; insanity

folto (fōl'tō) a thick, dense

fomentare (fō·män·tâ'rā) vt to foment; to incite

fomentatore (fō·män·tâ·tō'rā) m agitator, inciter

fomento (fō·män'tō) m agitation, forment

fonda (fōn'dâ) f holster; **alla —** at anchor; **–ccio** (fōn·dâ'chō) m remnant; sediment; **–co** (fôn'dâ·kō) m warehouse; **–le** (fōn·dâ'lā) m (theat) backdrop; seabed; **–mentale** (fōn·dâ·män·tâ'lâ) a fundamental; **–mentalmente** (fōn·dâ·män·

tâl·mān'tâ) *adv* fundamentally; **–mento** (fōn·dâ·mān'tō) *m* principle, basis; **–re** (fōn·dâ'rā) *vt* to found; to base; **–tezza** (fōn·dâ·tā'tsâ) *f* base, basis; **–tore** (fōn·dâ·tō'rā) *m* founder; **–zione** (fōn·dâ·tsyō'nā) *f* foundation

fondente (fōn·dān'tâ) *a* melting; fusing; — *m* fondant

fondere * (fōn'dā·rā) *vt&i* to melt; to fuse

fonderia (fōn·dâ·rē'â) *f* foundry

fondersi (fōn'dār·sē) *vr* to melt; to dissolve

fondina (fōn·dē'nâ) *f* holster; *(coll)* soup plate

fonditore (fōn·dē·tō'rā) *m* smelter

fonditura (fōn·dē·tū'râ) *f* smelting

fondo (fōn'dō) *m* fund; bottom; property, land; **— di magazzino** stock on hand; **—dei pantaloni** seat of the pants; **articolo di —** *(press)* editorial; feature article; **dar —** *(naut)* to anchor; **gara di —** endurance test; **in — alla strada** at the end of the street; **— a** deep

fonetica (fō·ne'tē·kâ) *f* phonetics

fonetico (fō·ne'tē·kō) *a* phonetic

fonico (fô'nē·kō) *a* phonic

fonogeno (fō·nô'jâ·nō) *m* *(rad)* pickup

fonografico (fō·nō·grâ'fē·kō) *a* phonographic; **disco —** phonograph record

fonografo (fō·nô'grâ·fō) *m* phonograph

fontana (fōn·tâ'nâ) *f* fountain

fonte (fōn'tâ) *f* spring *(water)*; font; origin

foraggio (fō·râj'jō) *m* fodder

forare (fō·râ'rā) *vt* to pierce; to drill *(hole)*; to punch *(ticket)*

foratrice (fō·râ·trē'châ) *f* *(mech)* drill

foratura (fō·râ·tū'râ) *f* puncture; flat tire

forbici (fôr'bē·chē) *fpl* scissors

forbire (fōr·bē'rā) *vt* to furbish, polish

forbito (fōr·bē'tō) *a* elegant; polished

forca (fōr'kâ) *f* gallows; pitchfork; **far la — a** to be untrue to; to treat someone shabbily; to do someone dirt *(sl)*; **–iuolo** (fōr·kâ·ywō'lō) *m* *(pol)* reactionary

forcella (fōr·châl'lâ) *f* hairpin; tree fork; bicycle fork

forchetta (fōr·kāt'tâ) *f* fork *(table)*

forchettone (fōr·kāt·tō'nâ) *m* carving fork

forcina (fōr·chē'nâ) *f* hairpin

forcipe (fôr'chē·pā) *m* forceps

forense (fō·rān'sā) *a* forensic

foresta (fō·re'stâ) *f* forest; **una — di capelli** *(fig)* a mop of hair

forestale (fō·rā·stâ'lâ) *a* forest; **guardia —** forest ranger

forestiero (fō·rā·styā'rō) *m* foreigner;

stranger; — *a* foreign

forfora (fôr'fō·râ) *f* dandruff

forgia (fôr'jâ) *f* forge; **–re** (fōr·jâ'rā) *vt* to forge, shape

forma (fōr'mâ) *f* form; way; **–le** (fōr·mâ'lā) *a* formal; usual; **–lità** (fōr·mâ·lē·tâ') *f* formality; **–lizzare** (fōr·mâ·lē·dzâ'rā) *vt* to shock, astonish; **–lizzarsi** (fōr·mâ·lē·dzâr'sē) *vr* to be astonished, be shocked; to be offended; **–lmente** (fōr·mâl·mān'tâ) *adv* with formality; **–re** (fōr·mâ'rā) *vt* to form; **–rsi** (fōr·mâr'sē) *vr* to mature, develop; **–tivo** (fōr·mâ·tē'vō) *a* formative; **–to** (fōr·mâ'tō) *m* format; size; **–to** *a* formed; shaped; molded; **–tore** (fōr·mâ·tō'rā) *m*, **–trice** (fōr·mâ·trē'châ) *f* modeler; creator; educator; **–zione** (fōr·mâ·tsyō'nā) *f* formation; forming

formaggio (fōr·mâj'jō) *m* cheese

formaldeide (fōr·mâl·de'ē·dā) *f* formaldehyde

formica (fōr·mē'kâ) *f* ant; **–io** (fōr·mē·kâ'yō) *m* ant hill; *(fig)* swarm

formico (fōr'mē·kō) *a* *(chem)* formic; **acido —** formic acid; **–lante** (fōr·mē·kō·lân'tâ) *a* swarming; **–lare** (fōr·mē·kō·lâ'rā) *vi* to swarm; **–lio** (fōr·mē·kō·lē'ō) *n* tingling sensation, prickling

formidabile (fōr·mē·dâ'bē·lâ) *a* formidable

formidabilmente (fōr·mē·dâ·bēl·mān'tâ) *adv* dreadfully; formidably

formoso (fōr·mō'zō) *a* shapely; buxom

formula (fôr'mū·lâ) *f* formula; **–re** (fōr·mū·lâ'rā) *vt* to formulate; to express, couch

fornace (fōr·nâ'châ) *f* furnace; oast

fornaio (fōr·nâ'yō) *m* baker

fornello (fōr·nāl'lō) *m* kitchen range, stove

fornire (fōr·nē'rā) *vt* to supply

fornitore (fōr·nē·tō'rā) *m* caterer; supplier

fornitura (fōr·nē·tū'râ) *f* supplies; equipment

forno (fōr'nō) *m* bakery; oven; *(theat)* empty house; **al —** baked; **alto —** blast furnace; **— crematorio** crematory

foro (fō'rō) *m* hole; forum; *(law)* bar

forse (fōr'sā) *adv* perhaps; — *m* doubt

forsennato (fōr·sān·nâ'tō) *a* crazy; — *m* madman

forte (fōr'tâ) *a* strong; loud; — *adv* strongly; loudly; — **guadagno** large profit; — **pioggia** heavy rain; **dar man — to** uphold; **–zza** (fōr·tâ'tsâ) *f* fortress

fortificare (fōr·tē·fē·kâ'rā) *vt* to fortify

---

k kid, **l** let, **m** met, **n** not, **p** pat, **r** very, **s** sat, **sh** shop, **t** tell, **v** vat, **w** we, **y** yes, **z** zero

fortificarsi (fōr·tē·fē·kâr'sē) *vr* to be fortified; to become strengthened

fortuitamente (fōr·twē·tâ·mān'tā) *adv* by chance

fortuito (fōr·tū'ē·tō) *a* casual; accidental; **caso** — coincidence

fortuna (fōr·tū'nâ) *f* luck; fortune; success; **atterraggio di** — (avi) forced landing; **–le** (fōr·tū·nâ'lā) *m* storm; tempest; **–tamente** (fōr·tū·nâ·tâ·mān'-tā) *adv* fortunately; luckily; **–to** (fōr·tū·nâ'tō) *a* lucky; fortunate; successful; happy

fortunosamente (fōr·tū·nō·zâ·mān'tā) *adv* tempestuously

fortunoso (fōr·tū·nō'zō) *a* stormy; risky, dangerous

foruncolo (fō·rūn'kō·lō) *m (med)* boil

forviare (fōr·vyâ'rā) *vt* to lead astray

forza (fōr'tsâ) *f* force, power; strength; — **motrice** driving power; **a viva** — with might and main; **a — di** by dint of; **farsi** — to gather courage; **–re** (fōr·tsâ'rā) *vt* to compel, force; **–re una serratura** to pick a lock; **–re un blocco** to run a blockade; **–tamente** (fōr·tsâ·tâ·mān'tā) *adv* necessarily; **–to** (fōr·tsâ'tō) *a* forced; **–to** *m* convict; **lavoro –to** forced labor

forziere (fōr·tsyâ'rā) *m* strongbox

forzosamente (fōr·tsō·zâ·mān'tā) *adv* forcibly

forzoso (fōr·tsō'zō) *a* forced

foscamente (fō·skâ·mān'tā) *adv* darkly; gloomily; obscurely

foschia (fō·skē'â) *f* mist; fog

fosco (fō'skō) *a* dark; gloomy, dull

fosfato (fō·sfâ'tō) *m* phosphate

fosforescente (fō·sfō·rā·shān'tā) *a* phosphorescent

fosforo (fō'sfō·rō) *m* phosphorus

fossa (fōs'sâ) *f* ditch; grave; moat; **–to** (fōs·sâ'tō) *m* ditch

fossetta (fōs·sāt'tâ) *f* dimple

fossile (fôs'sē·lā) *m&a* fossil

fossilizzare (fōs·sē·lē·dzâ'rā) *vt* to fossilize

fotocalcografia (fō·tō·kâl·kō·grâ·fē'â) *f* photogravure

fotocellula (fō·tō·chel'lū·lâ) *f* photoelectric cell

fotochimica (fō·tō·kē'mē·kâ) *f* photochemistry

fotocollografia (fō·tō·kōl·lō·grâ·fē'â) *f* colortype

fotoelettrico (fō·tō·ā·let'trē·kō) *a* photoelectric

fotogenico (fō·tō·je'nē·kō) *a* photogenic

fotografare (fō·tō·grâ·fâ'rā) *vt* to photograph

fotografia (fō·tō·grâ·fē'â) *f* photograph; — **istantanea** *f* snapshot

fotografico (fō·tō·grâ'fē·kō) *a* photographic

fotografo (fō·tô'grâ·fō) *m* photographer

fotoincisione (fō·tō·ēn·chē·zyō'nā) *f* photoengraving

fotometro (fō·tô'mā·trō) *m* light meter

fotone (fō·tō'nā) *m* photon

fotoritocco (fō·tō·rē·tōk'kō) *m* (*photo*) retouching

fotosfera (fō·tō·sfâ'râ) *f* photosphere

fototerapia (fō·tō·tā·râ·pē'â) *f* phototherapy

fra (frâ) *prep* among; between; within, in (*time*); — **di noi** between us; — **me e** me to myself; — **poco** soon

frac (frâk) *m* frock coat; (*sl*) tails

fracassare (frâ·kâs·sâ'rā) *vt* to smash, break up

fracassarsi (frâ·kâs·sâr'sē) *vr* to smash, shatter; to crash

fracasso (frâ·kâs'sō) *m* racket, uproar

fradicio (frâ'dē·chō) *a* rotten; soaked; **ubriaco** — dead drunk

fradiciume (frâ·dē·chū'mā) *m* rottenness

fragile (frâ'jē·lā) *a* frail, fragile; brittle

fragilità (frâ·jē·lē·tâ') *f* brittleness; weakness

fragola (frâ'gō·lâ) *f* strawberry

fragore (frâ·gō'râ) *m* loud noise; rumble; clang

fragorosamente (frâ·gō·rō·zâ·mān'tā) *adv* noisily, loudly

fragoroso (frâ·gō·rō'zō) *a* noisy, loud

fragrante (frâ·grân'tā) *a* fragrant

fragranza (frâ·grân'tsâ) *f* fragrance

fraintendere * (frâēn·ten'dā·rā) *vt* to misunderstand; to understand in part

frainteso (frâēn·tā'zō) *a* misunderstood

frammentario (frâm·mān·tâ'ryō) *a* fragmentary; — *m* fragment

frana (frâ'nâ) *f* landslide

francamente (frân·kâ·mān'tā) *adv* frankly, openly

francatura (frân·kâ·tū'râ) *f* postage

francese (frân·chā'zā) *a* French; — *m* Frenchman

franchezza (frân·kā'tsâ) *f* frankness

franchigia (frân·kē'jâ) *f* franchise; — **postale** free postage

franco (frân'kō) *a* frank, candid; — **a bordo** (*com*) F.O.B. free on board; — **di porto** (*com*) postpaid; **essere** — **con** to be frank with; **farla franca** to go scot-free; **–bollo** (frân·kō·bōl'lō) *m* postage stamp; **–tiratore** (frân·kō·tē·râ·tō'rä) *m* sniper; guerilla

frangente (frân·jän'tä) *m* bad situation, tight spot; *(naut)* breaker; reef

frangere * (frân'jä·rä) *vt* to crush; to dash to pieces

frangia (frân'jâ) *f* fringe

frantumare (frân·tū·mâ'rä) *vt* to shatter; to sliver

frantumi (frân·tū'mē) *mpl* splinters; small pieces; slivers; **andare in —** to break into small pieces

frapporre * (frâp·pōr'rä) *vt* to interpose

frapporsi * (frâp·pōr'sē) *vr* to interfere; to step between

frapposizione (frâ·pō·zē·tsyō'nä) *f* interference

frasca (frä'skä) *f (bot)* branch; frivolous person; frivolity; **saltar di palo in —** *(coll)* to ramble, speak disjointedly

frase (frä'zä) *f* sentence; phrase; **–ggiare** (frâ·zäj·jâ'rä) *vt&i* to phrase; **–ologia** (frâ·zä·ō·lō·jē'â) *f* phraseology

frassino (frâs'sē·nō) *m* ash *(tree)*

frastagliamento (frâ·stä·lyâ·män'tō) *m* indentation; notching

frastagliare (frâ·stä·lyâ'rä) *vt* to notch; to indent

frastagliato (frâ·stä·lyâ'tō) *a* jagged; indented

frastornare (frâ·stōr·nâ'rä) *vt* to disturb, upset

frastuono (frâ·stwō'nō) *m* uproar; din

frate (frä'tä) *m* friar; **–llanza** (frâ·täl·lân'tsâ) *f* brotherhood; **–ellastro** (frâ·täl·lâ'strō) *m* half-brother; **–llo** (frâ·täl'lō) *m* brother; **–rnamente** (frâ·tär·nâ·män'tä) *adv* fraternally; **–rnità** (frâ·tär·nē·tâ') *f* fraternity, brotherhood; **–rnizzare** (frâ·tär·nē·dzâ'rä) *vi* to fraternize; **–rno** (frâ·tär'nō) *a* fraternal

fratricida (frâ·trē·chē'dâ) *m* fratricide *(person)*

fratta (frât'tä) *f* hedge, bush

frattaglie (frât·tâ'lyä) *fpl* giblets

frattanto (frât·tân'tō) *adv* meanwhile

frattempo (frât·täm'pō) *m* meantime; interval

frattura (frât·tū'râ) *f* fracture; **–re** (frât·tū·râ'rä) *vt* to break, fracture

fraudolentemente (frâū·dō·lân·tä·män'tä) *adv* deceitfully; fraudulently

fraudolento (frâū·dō·lân'tō) *a* deceitful; fraudulent

frazionamento (frâ·tsyō·nâ·män'tō) *m* division; separation

frazionare (frâ·tsyō·nâ'rä) *vt* to divide, separate; *(chem)* to fractionate

frazionario (frâ·tsyō·nâ'ryō) *a* fragmentary

frazione (frâ·tsyō'nä) *f* fraction; *(fig)* whistle-stop, one-horse town

freccia (fre'châ) *f* arrow; indicating needle; **–ta** (frâ·châ'tâ) *(fig)* bitter word; gibe, taunt

freddamente (frâd·dâ·män'tä) *adv* coolly, coldly

freddezza (frâd·dä'tsâ) *f* coolness; coldness

freddo (frâd'dō) *a&m* cold; **aver —** *(person)* to be cold; **far —** *(weather)* to be cold; **sentir —** to feel cold; **–loso** (frâd·dō·lō'zō) *a* cold-blooded, susceptible to the cold

freddura (frâd·dū'râ) *f* pun; witticism

fregare (frâ·gâ'rä) *vt* to rub; *(coll)* to swindle

fregarsene (frâ·gâr'sä·nä) *vr (coll)* not to give a hang

fregatura (frâ·gâ·tū'râ) *f* rubbing; *(coll)* swindle, deceit

fregiare (frâ·jâ'rä) *vt* to decorate

fregiarsi (frâ·jâr'sē) *vr* to deck oneself out

fregio (fre'jō) *m* adornment

frego (frä'gō) *m* cancellation; striking out

fremente (frâ·män'tä) *a* quivering; shuddering

fremere (fre'mä·rä) *vi* to fume, fret; to tremble

fremito (fre'mē·tō) *m* thrill; quiver

frenare (frâ·nâ'rä) *vt* to check, restrain; *(mech)* to brake

frenarsi (frâ·nâr'sē) *vr* to restrain oneself; to keep one's temper

frenatore (frâ·nâ·tō'râ) *m* brakeman

frenesia (frâ·nä·zē'â) *f* frenzy, flurry

freneticamente (frâ·nä·tē·kâ·män'tä) *adv* frantically

frenetico (frâ·ne'tē·kō) *a* frantic; **applauso —** loud cheers

freno (frä'nō) *m* brake; restraint; **senza —** unrestrained

frenologia (frâ·nō·lō·jē'â) *f* phrenology

frequentare (frâ·kwän·tâ'rä) *vt* to frequent; to attend

frequente (frâ·kwän'tä) *a* frequent; **–mente** *adv* frequently

frequenza (frâ·kwän'tsâ) *f* frequency; attendance; **modulazione di —** frequency modulation

fresa (frä'zâ) *f (mech)* cutter; milling machine

frescamente (frâ·skâ·män'tä) *adv* freshly; coolly; recently

freschezza (frâ·skä'tsâ) *f* freshness; coolness *(weather)*

---

k kid, l let, m met, n not, p pat, r very, s sat, sh shop, t tell, v vat, w we, y yes, z zero

fresco (frā'skō) *a* fresh, new; — *m* cool weather; **al** — outdoors
fretta (frāt'tâ) *f* hurry, haste; **in** — **e furia** hurriedly
frettolosamente (frāt·tō·lō·zâ·mān'tā) *adv* swiftly
friabile (fryâ'bē·lā) *a* brittle; friable
friabilità (fryâ·bē·lē·tâ') *f* brittleness; friability
friggere * (frēj'jā·rā) *vt* to fry
frigorifero (frē·gō·rē'fā·rō) *m* refrigerator
frittata (frēt·tâ'tâ) *f* omelet; **fare una** — *(fig)* to mess things up, botch a job
frittella (frēt·tāl'lâ) *f* fritter
fritto (frēt'tō) *a* fried; **essere** — *(fig)* to be done for; to be worn out; — **e rifritto** *(fig)* trite
frivolamente (frē·vō·lâ·mān'tā) *adv* frivolously
frivoleggiare (frē·vō·lāj·jâ'rā) *vi* to trifle; to fritter away one's time
frivolezza (frē·vō·lā'tsâ) *f* frivolity
frivolo (frē'vō·lō) *a* frivolous
frizione (frē·tsyō'nā) *f* massage; *(auto)* clutch; friction
frizzante (frē·tsân'tā) *a* racy; piquant
frizzo (frē'tsō) *m* witticism; witty remark
frodare (frō·dâ'rā) *vt* to defraud; to hoax
frodatore (frō·dâ·tō'rā) *m* defrauder
frodo (frō'dō) *m* smuggling; **cacciatore di** — poacher
frollare (frōl·lâ'rā) *vt&i* to tenderize *(meat)*; to make soft, fluff up
frollo (frōl'lō) *a* fluffy, soft
frondoso (frōn·dō'zō) *a* leafy
frontale (frōn·tâ'lā) *a* frontal
fronte (frōn'tā) *f* forehead; **–ggiare** (frōn·tāj·jâ'rā) *vt* to confront; **–spizio** (frōn·tā·spē'tsyō) *m* title page; — **a** — face to face; **far** — **al pericolo** to face danger; **far** — **alle spese** to meet expenses; **mettere di** — **a** to confront with; **di** — **a** in front of, facing
frontiera (frōn·tyā'râ) *f* border, frontier
fronzolo (frōn'dzō·lō) *m* ribbon; *(fig)* trifle
frotta (frōt'tâ) *f* crowd, flock
frottola (frôt'tō·lâ) *f* fib; nonsense
frugare (frū·gâ'rā) *vt* to search through carefully, comb through
fruire (frūē'rā) *vt* to enjoy the use of
frullare (frūl·lâ'rā) *vt* to beat up, whisk; — *vi* to flutter; — **per il capo** *(fig)* to get into one's head
frumento (frū·mān'tō) *m* wheat; **–ne** (frū·mān·tō'nā) *m* maize
frusciare (frū·shâ'rā) *vi* to rustle
fruscio (frū·shē'ō) *m* rustle

frusta (frū'stâ) *f* whip
frustare (frū·stâ'rā) *vt* to scourge
frustata (frū·stâ'tâ) *f* lash; whipping
frustino (frū·stē'nō) *m* horsewhip
frutta (frūt'tâ) *f* fruit
fucina (fū·chē'nâ) *f* forge
fuco (fū'kō) *m (zool)* drone
fuga (fū'gâ) *f* fleeing, flight; *(mus)* fugue; **–ce** (fū·gâ'chā) *a* transient, fleeting; **–cemente** (fū·gâ·chā·mān'tā) *adv* fleetingly; **–re** (fū·gâ'rā) *vt* to frighten away, put to flight
fuggiasco (fūj·jâ'skō) *m* fugitive
fuggibile (fūj·jē'bē·lā) *a* avoidable
fuggifuggi (fūj·jē·fūj'jē) *m (coll)* panic, stampede
fuggire (fūj·jē'rā) *vi* to flee, escape; — *vt* to avoid; to shrink from
fuggitivo (fūj·jē·tē'vō) *m&a* fugitive
fulcro (fūl'krō) *m* fulcrum
fulgido (fūl'jē·dō) *a* bright, shining
fuliggine (fū·lēj'jē·nā) *f* soot
fulminare (fūl·mē·nâ'rā) *vt* to strike down
fulmine (fūl'mē·nā) *m* lightning; thunderbolt; **–ità** (fūl·mē·nāē·tâ') *f* extreme rapidity; **–o** (fūl·mē'nā·ō) *a* extremely fast
fulvo (fūl'vō) *a* tawny, tan
fumaiolo (fū·mâ·yō'lō) *m* funnel; smokestack
fumare (fū·mâ'rā) *vt&i* to smoke; **vietato** — no smoking
fumata (fū·mâ'tâ) *f* smoke
fumetto (fū·māt'tō) *m* comic strip
fumigare (fū·mē·gâ'rā) *vi* to fumigate
fumigazione (fū·mē·gâ·tsyō'nā) *f* fumigation
fumista (fū·mē'stâ) *m* heating technician
fumo (fū'mō) *m* smoke; *(fig)* humbug; **mandare in** — *(fig)* to reduce to nothing; **vendere** — *(fig)* to humbug; **–so** (fū·mō'zō) *a* smoky
fumogeno (fū·mō'jā·nō) *a* producing smoke; **cortina fumogena** smokescreen
fune (fū'nā) *f* cable; rope
funebre (fū'nā·brā) *a* funerial, mournful
funebri (fū'nā·brē) *fpl* funeral; **impresario di pompe** — funeral director, undertaker
funestare (fū·nā·stâ'rā) *vt* to ruin, wreck; to cast a pall over, sadden
fungo (fūn'gō) *m* fungus; mushroom
funicolare (fū·nē·kō·lâ'rā) *f* cable railway
funzionale (fūn·tsyō·nâ'lā) *a* functional
funzionare (fūn·tsyō·nâ'rā) *vi* to function
funzionario (fūn·tsyō·nâ'ryō) *m* official
funzione (fūn·tsyō'nā) *f* function
fuoco (fwō'kō) *m* fire; **fuochi d'artificio**

â ârm, **ā** bāby, **e** bet, **ē** bē, **ō** gō, **ô** gône, **ū** blūe, **b** bad, **ch** child, **d** dad, **f** fat, **g** gay, **j** jet

fireworks; **a —** *(phot)* in focus
fuorchè (fwōr·kä') *prep* except, with the exception of; **—** *conj* unless
fuori (fwō'rē) *prep* outside of; **—** *adv* outside, out; **— casa** not at home; **— di sè** beside oneself; **— di tempo** badly timed; **— d'uso** obsolete; **— giuoco** *(sport)* offside; **— servizio** off duty; **— strada** astray; mistaken; **lasciar —** to omit; **tutti fuori tu** all except you; **— legge** outlaw; **— serie** *a* custom-built
fuoruscito (fwō·rū·shē'tō) *m* exile
fuorviare (fwōr·vyâ'rā) *vt* to mislead, lose
fuorviarsi (fwōr·vyâr'sē) *vr* to become lost
furberia (fūr·bā·rē'â) *f* cunning, artfulness; craftiness
furbesco (fūr·bā'skō) *a* artful, crafty
furbo (fūr'bō) *a* crafty, sly; clever
furente (fū·rān'tā) *a* furious; **— d'ira** infuriated
furetto (fū·rāt'tō) *m (zool)* ferret
furfante (fūr·fân'tā) *m* rogue; villain
furgone (fūr·gō'nä) *m* van; wagon
furia (fū'ryâ) *f* rage, fury; **aver —** to be in a great hurry; **a — di** by force of
furiosamente (fū·ryō·zâ·mān'tä) *adv*

furiously; violently
furioso (fū·ryō'zō) *a* furious
furore (fū·rō'râ) *m* fury, wrath; *(fig)* enthusiasm; **–ggiare** (fū·rō·rāj·jâ'rā) *vi* to be highly successful; to be the rage
furtivamente (fūr·tē·vâ·mān'tä) *adv* furtively, on the sly
furtivo (fūr·tē'vō) *a* furtive, sly
furto (fūr'tō) *m* theft; **— con scasso** burglary
fusibile (fū·zē'bē·lä) *m* fuse
fusione (fū·zyo'nä) *f* fusion; *(com)* merger
fuso (fū'zō) *m* spindle; **–liera** (fū·zō·lyä'râ) *f (avi)* fuselage; **— orario** time zone; **diritto come un —** straight as a ramrod; **fare le fusa** to purr
fuso (fū'zō) *a* fused; melted
fustigare (fū·stē·gâ'rā) *vt* to flog
fustigazione (fū·stē·gâ·tsyō'nä) *f* flogging
fusto (fū'stō) *m (bot, anat)* trunk; mannequin; cask
futile (fū'tē·lä) *a* futile, useless; frivolous
futilità (fū·tē·lē·tâ') *f* futility, uselessness
futurista (fū·tū·rē'stä) *m* futurist
futuro (fū·tū'rō) *a&m* future

G

gabbanella (gâb·bâ·nāl'lâ) *f* smock
gabbare (gâb·bâ'rā) *vt* to mock; to trick
gabbarsi (gâb·bâr'sē) *vr* to make sport of
gabella (gâ·bāl'lâ) *f* duty, excise tax; **–re** (gâ·bāl·lâ'rā) *vt* to charge; to tax; to pretend to be, pass oneself off as
gabbia (gâb'byâ) *f* cage; crate; **mettere in —** *(fig)* to put into prison
gabbiano (gâb·byâ'nō) *m* seagull
gabinetto (gâ·bē·nāt'tō) *m (pol)* cabinet; office; washroom; **— di decenza** toilet; **— di lettura** reading room
gaffa (gâf'fâ) *f (coll)* blunder
gagà (gâ·gâ') *m (sl)* dandy, dude
gaggia (gâj·jē'â) *f* acacia
gagliardetto (gâ·lyâr·dāt'tō) *m* pennant
gagliardo (gâ·lyâr'dō) *a* vigorous; stouthearted
gaglioffo (gâ·lyōf'fō) *m* loafer, lout
gaiamente (gâ·yâ·mān'tä) *adv* gaily, brightly
gaiezza (gâ·yā'tsâ) *f* gaiety; vividness
gaio (gâ'yō) *a* merry, gay; bright
gala (gâ'lâ) *f* festivity; **pranzo di —** formal dinner
galante (gâ·lân'tä) *a* polite; courteous; **— *m*** gallant; **donna —** call girl;

avventura — love affair; **–ria** (gâ·lân·tā·rē'â) *f* politeness; courtesy
galantuomo (gâ·lân·twō'mō) *m* honest man; gentleman
galateo (gâ·lâ·tā'ō) *m* etiquette
galeotto (gâ·lā·ōt'tō) *m* convict; rascal; galley slave
galera (gâ·lā'râ) *f* jail; *(naut)* galley; **vita da —** wretched life
galla (gâl'lâ) *f* blister; **a —** afloat
galleggiante (gâl·lāj·jân'tä) *a* floating **— *m (naut)* float
galleria (gâl·lā·rē'â) *f* gallery; tunnel
galletto (gâl·lāt'tō) *m* spring chicken
gallina (gâl·lē'nâ) *f* hen, chicken; **–ccio** (gâl·lē·nâ'chō) *m* turkey
gallo (gâl'lō) *m* rooster
gallone (gâl·lō'nä) *m* stripe, chevron; braid; gallon
galoppare (gâ·lōp·pâ'rā) *vi* to gallop
galoppatoio (gâ·lōp·pâ·tô'yō) *m* bridle path
galoppino (gâ·lōp·pē'nō) *m* errand boy; *(pol)* solicitor
galoppo (gâ·lōp'pō) *m* gallop
galvani (gâl·vâ'nē) *mpl (print)* electrotype
galvanizzare (gâl·vâ·nē·dzâ'rā) *vt* to gal-

vanize
galvanoplastica (gâl·vâ·nō·plâ′stē·kâ) *f* electroplating
gamba (gâm′bâ) *f* leg; **andare a gambe levate** fall headlong; **darsela a gambe** to take to one's heels; **essere in —** to be smart; **fare il passo secondo la —** *(fig)* to cut the coat according to the cloth; **–le** (gâm·bâ′lâ) *m* legging
gamberetto (gâm·bâ·rât′tō) *m* shrimp
gambero (gâm′bâ·rō) *m* crayfish
gambo (gâm′bō) *m* stem
gamella (gâ·mâl′lâ) *f* mess kit
gamma (gâm′mâ) *f* range, gamut; *(mus)* scale
ganascia (gâ·nâ′shâ) *f (anat)* jaw
gancio (gân′chō) *m* hook; clasp
ganghero (gân′gâ·rō) *m* hinge; **uscir dai gangheri** to fly off the handle
ganglio (gân′glyō) *m* ganglion
gara (gâ′râ) *f* contest, match; competition; **andare a —** to compete
garagista (gâ·râ·jē′stâ) *m* garageman, automobile mechanic
garante (gâ·rân′tâ) *m* guarantor
garantire (gâ·rân·tē′râ) *vt* to guarantee, vouch for
garanzia (gâ·rân·tsē′â) *f* guaranty, security
garbare (gâr·bâ′râ) *vi* to please
garbatamente (gâr·bâ·tâ·mân′tâ) *adv* politely
garbatezza (gâr·bâ·tâ′tsâ) *f* kindness; courtesy
garbato (gâr·bâ′tō) *a* polite
garbo (gâr′bō) *m* politeness; **con —** graciously; **mal —** rudeness; **senza —** clumsy, awkward
garbuglio (gâr·bū′lyō) *m* confusion; mess
gareggiare (gâ·râj·jâ′râ) *vi* to compete
gargarismo (gâr·gâ·rē′zmō) *m* gargle, gargling
garguglia (gâr·gū′lyâ) *f* gargoyle
garofano (gâ·rô′fâ·nō) *m* carnation
garrese (gâr·râ′zâ) *m* withers *(horse)*
garretto (gâr·rât′tō) *m* fetlock *(horse)*; *(anat)* ankle
garrulo (gâr′rū·lō) *a* garrulous
garza (gâr′dzâ) *f* gauze
gas (gâs) *m* gas; **–odotto** (gâ·zō·dōt′tō) *m* gasline; **–olio** (gâ·zô′lyō) *m* fuel oil; **–sare** (gâs·sâ′râ) *vt* to charge *(liquid)*; **–sato** (gâs·sâ′tō) *a* charged; **–ista** (gâ·zē′stâ) *m* gasman; **–osa** (gâ·zō′zâ) *f* soft drink; **–oso** (gâ·zō′zō) *a* gaseous, fizzy
gastrico (gâ′strē·kō) *a* gastric
gastrite (gâ·strē′tâ) *f (med)* gastritis

gatta (gât′tâ) *f* female cat; **— ci cova** *(coll)* there is something brewing; **avere una — da pelare** *(fig)* to be in trouble; **–buia** (gât·tâ·bū′yâ) *f* jail; **–morta** (gât·tâ·môr′tâ) *f* hypocrite
gattino (gât·tē′nō) *m* kitten
gatto (gât′tō) *m* tomcat; **essere in quattro gatti** to be few in number
gattò (gât·tō′) *m* French pastry
gaudente (gâū·dān′tâ) *a* epicurean; cheerful; **— m** bon vivant
gaudio (gâ′ū·dyō) *m* joy; **mal comune mezzo —** trouble shared is trouble halved
gavazzare (gâ·vâ·tsâ′râ) *vi* to wassail, revel
gavitello (gâ·vē·tâl′lō) *m* buoy
gazzarra (gâ·dzâr′râ) *f* racket, uproar
gazzella (gâ·dzâl′lâ) *f* gazelle
gazzettino (gâ·dzât·tē′nō) *m* bulletin; *(fig)* gossip
gelare (jâ·lâ′râ) *vt&i* to freeze
gelarsi (jâ·lâr′sē) *vr* to be frozen, freeze
gelateria (jâ·lâ·tâ·rē′â) *f* ice cream shop
gelatiere (jâ·lâ·tyâ′râ) *m* ice cream seller
gelatina (jâ·lâ·tē′nâ) *f* gelatin
gelatinoso (jâ·lâ·tē·nō′zō) *a* gelatinous
gelato (jâ·lâ′tō) *m* ice cream; **— a** frozen
gelidamente (jâ·lē·dâ·mân′tâ) *adv* icily
gelido (je′lē·dō) *a* icy; freezing
gelo (jâ′lō) *m* frost; *(fig)* chilly manner; **–ne** (jâ·lô′nâ) *m* chilblain
gelosamente (jâ·lō·zâ·mân′tâ) *adv* jealously
gelosia (jâ·lō·zē′â) *f* jealousy; jalousie, venetian blind
geloso (jâ·lō′zō) *a* jealous, showing envy
gelsomino (jâl·sō·mē′nō) *m* jasmine
gemello (jâ·mâl′lō) *a&m* twin; **bottoni gemelli** cuff links
gemere (je′mâ·râ) *vi* to groan, moan
gemito (je′mē·tō) *m* lament, groan
geminare (jâ·mē·nâ′râ) *vt* to pair, couple
geminazione (jâ·mē·nâ·tsyō′nâ) *f* gemination, pairing
gemma (jâm′mâ) *f* gem; bud; **–zione** (jâm·mâ·tsyō′nâ) *f (bot)* budding
gemmato (jâm·mâ′tō) *a* studded with gems
gendarme (jân·dâr′mâ) *m* policeman; **–ria** (jân·dâr·mâ·rē′â) *f* police force
genealogia (jâ·nâ·â·lō·jē′â) *f* genealogy
genealogico (jâ·nâ·â·lô′je·kō) *a* genealogical; **albero —** family tree
generale (jâ·nâ·râ′lâ) *a&m* general; **tenersi sulle generali** to be vague
generalità (jâ·nâ·râ·lē·tâ′) *f* generality; **— fpl** personal data
generalizzare (jâ·nâ·râ·lē·dzâ′râ) *vt&i* to

generalize

generalmente (jā·nā·rál·mãn'tā) *adv* generally, as a rule

generare (jā·nā·rá'rā) *vt* to generate, bring forth

generatore (jā·nā·rá·tō'rā) *m* generator

generazione (jā·nā·rá·tsyō'nā) *f* generation

genere (je'nā·rā) *m* kind; genus; *(gram)* gender; **generi di prima necessità** primary needs of life; **generi alimentari** groceries; **il — tragico** *(lit)* tragedy, tragic genre

generico (jā·ne'rē·kō) *a* generic; indefinite

genero (je'nā·rō) *m* son-in-law

generosamente (jā·nā·rō·zä·mãn'tā) *adv* generously

generosità (jā·nā·rō·zē·tâ') *f* generosity

generoso (jā·nā·rō'zō) *a* generous

genesi (je'nā·zē) *f* genesis; origin

genetica (jā·ne'tē·kä) *f* genetics

gengiva (jän·jē'vä) *f (dent)* gum

gengivite (jän·jē·vē'tä) *f* gingivitis

geniale (jā·nyä'lā) *a* genial, pleasant; talented

genialità (jā·nyä·lē·tâ') *f* geniality; ingeniousness

genialmente (jā·nyâl·mãn'tā) *adv* genially; ingeniously

genio (je'nyō) *m* genius, talent; *(mil)* engineer; **— civile** public works administration; **andare a —** to be to one's liking

genitale (jā·nē·tâ'lā) *a&m* genital

genitivo (jā·nē·tē'vō) *m* genitive

genitore (jā·nē·tō'rā) *m*, **genitrice** (jā·nē·trē'chä) *f* parent

genitura (jā·nē·tū'rä) *f* procreation

gennaio (jā·nā·nâ'yō) *m* January

Genova (je'nō·vä) *f* Genoa

genovese (jā·nō·vā'zā) *a&m* Genovese

gentaglia (jān·tâ'lyä) *f* mob, rabble

gente (jān'tā) *f* people; **— di mare** seamen; **diritto delle genti** international law

gentildonna (jän·tēl·dōn'nä) *f* lady

gentile (jän·tē'lā) *a* polite; kind; **–zza** (jän·tē·lä'tsä) *f* kindness

gentilizio (jän·tē·lē'tsyō) *a* noble; **stemma gentilizia** coat of arms

gentilmente (jän·tēl·mãn'tā) *adv* kindly; courteously

gentiluomo (jän·tē·lwō'mō) *m* gentleman

genuflessione (jā·nū·flās·syō'nä) *f* genuflection

genuflesso (jā·nū·flãs'sō) *a* knelt in prayer

genuflettersi * (jā·nū·flet'tār·sē) *vr* to

genuflect

genuinità (jā·nwē·nē·tâ') *f* genuineness

genuino (jā·nwē'nō) *a* genuine

geofisica (jā·ō·fē'zē·kä) *f* geophysics

geografia (jā·ō·grä·fē'ä) *f* geography

geografico (jā·ō·grä'fē·kō) *a* geographical

geografo (jā·ô'grä·fō) *m* geographer

geologia (jā·ō·lō·jē'ä) *f* geology

geologico (jā·ō·lô'jē·kō) *a* geological

geologo (jā·ô'lō·gō) *m* geologist

geometria (jā·ō·mä·trē'ä) *f* geometry

geometrico (jā·ō·me'trē·kō) *a* geometrical

geranio (jā·rä'nyō) *m* geranium

gerarca (jā·rär'kä) *m* leader, head

gerarchia (jā·rär·kē'ä) *f* hierarchy

gerente (jā·rän'tā) *m* director, manager

gerenza (jā·rän'tsä) *f* board of directors, management

gergo (jär'gō) *m* slang

Germania (jär·mâ'nyä) *f* Germany

germano (jär·mâ'nō) *a* germane; **— m** full brother; mallard duck; **cugino —** first cousin

germe (jär'mā) *m* germ, sprout, shoot; *(fig)* root, cause

germinare (jär·mē·nâ'rā) *vt&i* to germinate

germinazione (jär·mē·nâ·tsyō'nä) *f* germination

germogliare (jär·mō·lyä'rā) *vt&i* to sprout, shoot up

germoglio (jär·mô'lyō) *m* shoot, bud

geroglifico (jā·rō·glē'fē·kō) *m&a* hieroglyphic

gerontocomio (jā·rōn·tō·kô'myō) *m* old people's home

gerontoiatria (jā·rōn·tō·yä·trē'â) *f* geriatrics

gerundio (jā·rūn'dyō) *m* gerund

Gerusalemme (jā·rū·zä·lãm'mä) *f* Jerusalem

gessaio (jās·sâ'yō) *m* plasterer; maker of plaster statues

gessare (jās·sâ'rā) *vt* to plaster

gessatura (jās·sâ·tū'râ) *f* plastering

gesso (jās·sō) *m* chalk; plaster of Paris; **–so** (jās·sō'zō) *a* chalk-like, chalky

gesta (jä'stä) *fpl* achievements; feats of derring-do

gestante (jā·stân'tā) *f* pregnant woman

gestazione (jā·stä·tsyō'nä) *f* pregnancy; question

gesticolare (jā·stē·kō·lâ'rā) *vi* to gesticulate

gesticolazione (jā·stē·kō·lâ·tsyō'nä) *f* gesticulation, gesturing

gestione (jā·styō'nä) *f* administering, managing

---

k kid, **l** let, **m** met, **n** not, **p** pat, **r** very, **s** sat, **sh** shop, **t** tell, **v** vat, **w** we, **y** yes, **z** zero

gestire (jä·stē'rä) *vt (com)* to operate; to gesture

gesto (jä'stō) *m* gesture; **-re** (jä·stō'rä) *m* manager; operator

Gesù (jä·zü') *m* Jesus

gesuita (jä·zwē'tä) *m* Jesuit

gettare (jät·tâ'rä) *vt* to throw, cast; — *vi (bot)* to bud, shoot up; — **a terra** to knock down; — **l'ancora** *(naut)* to cast anchor; — **le fondamenta** to lay the foundation; — **la moneta** to toss a coin; — **via il denaro** to waste one's money, throw away one's money

gettarsi (jät·târ'sē) *vr* to cast oneself, dash oneself; to spring forward

gettata (jät·tâ'tä) *f* rough cast

gettatore (jät·tâ·tō'rä) *m* caster, molder

gettito (jet'tē·tō) *m* yield, output

getto (jät'tō) *m* throw; jet, spout; **a — continuo** uninterruptedly; **opera di —** inspired work; **-ne** (jät·tō'nä) *m* token

gheriglio (gä·rē'lyō) *m* center, kernel

gherminella (gär·mē·nāl'lä) *f* trickery; mischief

ghermire (gär·mē'rä) *vt* to snatch, grab; to hold tightly

gherone (gä·rō'nä) *m* gore *(clothing)*

ghetta (gät'tä) *f* spat *(clothing)*

ghiacciaia (gyä·chä'yä) *f* refrigerator; ice box

ghiacciaio (gyä·chä'yō) *m* glacier

ghiacciare (gyä·chä'rä) *vt* to ice over; to freeze

ghiacciarsi (gyä·chär'sē) *vr* to freeze, become frozen

ghiacciata (gyä·chä'tä) *f* cool drink

ghiacciato (gyä·chä'tō) *a* iced, ice-cold; frozen

ghiaccio (gyä'chō) *m* ice; **rompere il —** to break the ice *(fig)*

ghiacciuolo (gyä·chwō'lō) *m* icicle

ghiaia (gyä'yä) *f* gravel

ghianda (gyän'dä) *f* acorn; **-ia** (gyän·dâ'-yä) *f* jay

ghiera (gyä'rä) *f* ferrule

ghigliottina (gē·lyōt·tē'nä) *f* guillotine **-re** (gē·lyōt·tē·nâ'rä) *vt* to guillotine

ghignare (gē·nyä'rä) *vi* to sneer, leer

ghigno (gē'nyō) *m* smirk, sneer

ghiotta (gyōt'tä) *f* drip pan

ghiotto (gyōt'tō) *a* gluttonous; tasty; **-ne** (gyōt·tō'nä) *m* glutton; gourmand; **-neria** (gyōt·tō·nä·rē'ä) *f* delicacy; gluttony

ghiribizzo (gē·rē·bē'tsō) *m* whim

ghirigoro (gē·rē·gō'rō) *m* doodle

ghirlanda (gēr·lân'dä) *f* wreath, garland

ghiro (gē'rō) *m* dormouse; **dormire come**

un — to sleep like a top

ghisa (gē'zä) *f* cast iron

già (jä) *adv* formerly, already; **G–!** *adv* Right! Of course!

giacchè (jäk·kä') *conj* now that; since, in view of the fact that

giacchetta (jäk·kät'tä) *f* jacket, coat

giacente (jä·chän'tä) *a* lying down; in abeyance

giacere * (jä'chä·rä) *vi* to lie, lie at rest

giacimento (jä·chē·män'tō) *m (min)* deposit, layer

giacinto (jä·chēn'tō) *m* hyacinth

giaculatoria (jä·kü·lä·tō'ryä) *f* short prayer

giada (jä'dä) *m (min)* jade

giaggiolo (jäj·jō'lō) *m (bot)* iris

giaguaro (jä·gwä'rō) *m* jaguar

giallastro (jäl·lä'strō) *a* yellowish

giallo (jäl'lō) *a* yellow; — **d'uovo** yolk; **romanzo —** mystery novel; **-gnolo** (jäl·lō'nyō·lō) *a* yellowish

Giamaica (jä·mâ'ē·kä) Jamaica

giammai (jäm·mâ'ē) *adv* never

gianduiotto (jän·dü·yōt'tō) *m* chocolate candy

giannizzero (jan·nē'tsä·rō) *m (fig)* underling, hireling

Giappone (jäp·pō'nä) *m* Japan; **-se** (jä·pō·nä'zä) *m&a* Japanese

giara (jä'rä) *f* jug

giardinaggio (jär·dē·nâj'jō) *m* gardening

giardinetta (jär·dē·nät'tä) *f* station wagon

giardiniera (jär·dē·nyä'rä) *f* vegetable soup; jardiniere; woman gardener; **maestra —** kindergarten teacher

giardiniere (jär·dē·nyä'rä) *m* gardener

giardino (jär·dē'nō) *m* garden; — **d'infanzia** kindergarten; — **publico** public park; — **zoologico** zoo

giarrettiera (jär·rät·tyä'rä) *f* garter

giavazzo (jä·vâ'tsō) *m (min)* jet

gigante (jē·gän'tä) *a&m* giant; **far passi da —** *(fig)* to make great progress; **-ggiare** (jē·gän·tâj·jä'rä) *vi* to tower; **-sco** (jē·gän·tä'skō) *a* gigantic

gigione (jē·jō'nä) *m (sl)* ham actor

giglio (jē'lyō) *m* lily

gilè (jē·lä') *m* vest

ginecologia (jē·nä·kō·lō·jē'â) *f* gynecology

ginecologo (jē·nä·kô'lō·gō) *m* gynecologist

ginepraio (jē·nä·prä'yō) *m* confused situation; **cacciarsi in un —** to be in a mess

ginepro (jē·nä'prō) *m* juniper

Ginevra (jē·nä'vrä) *f* Geneva

gingillare (jēn·jēl·lä'rä) *vi* to dawdle

gingillarsi (jēn·jēl·lâr'sē) *vr* to toy with,

trifle

gingillo (jēn·jēl′lō) *m* knicknack, trinket; **— fantasia** costume jewelry

ginnasiale (jēn·nâ·zyâ′lā) *a* high-school; **licenza —** high-school diploma

ginnasio (jēn·nâ′zyō) *m* high school

ginnasta (jēn·nâ′stâ) *m* gymnast, athlete

ginnastica (jēn·nâ′stē·kâ) *f* gymnastics

ginnastico (jēn·nâ′stē·kō) *a* athletic, gymnastic

ginocchio (jē·nôk′kyō) *m* knee; **–ni** (jē·nōk·kyō′nē) *adv* kneeling, knelt

giocare (jō·kâ′rā) *vt&i* to play; to bet; to make a fool of; to deceive; **— d'azzardo** to gamble

giocatore (jō·kâ·tō′rā) *m* player; **— di borsa** stockbroker

giocattolo (jō·kât′tō·lō) *m* toy

giochetto (jō·kāt′tō) *m* trick

giocoforza (jō·kō·fōr′tsâ) *f* necessity, essential

giocoliere (jō·kō·lyā′rā) *m* juggler

giocondità (jō·kōn·dē·tâ′) *f* gaiety

giocondo (jō·kōn′dō) *a* gay

giocosamente (jō·kō·zâ·mān′tā) *adv* jokingly

giocoso (jō·kō′zō) *a* facetious, humorous

giogaia (jō·gâ′yâ) *f* mountain range

giogo (jō′gō) *m* yoke

gioia (jō′yâ) *f* joy, delight; jewel; **fuoco di —** bonfire

gioielleria (jō·yāl·lā·rē′â) *f* jewelry store; jewelry

gioielliere (jō·yāl·lyā′rā) *m* jeweler

gioiello (jō·yāl′lō) *m* gem

gioiosamente (jō·yō·zâ·mān′tā) *adv* joyfully

gioioso (jō·yō′zō) *a* joyful

gioire (jō·ē′rā) *vi* to rejoice

giornalaio (jōr·nâ·lâ′yō) *m* newsboy; newspaper dealer

giornale (jōr·nâ′lā) *m* newspaper; **— di bordo** logbook; **— settimanale** weekly; **— radio** newscast

giornaliero (jōr·nâ·lyā′rō) *a* daily; **— m** day laborer

giornalismo (jōr·nâ·lē′zmō) *m* journalism

giornalista (jōr·nâ·lē′stâ) *m* newspaperman, journalist

giornalmente (jōr·nâl·mān′tā) *adv* daily, every day

giornata (jōr·nâ′tâ) *f* day; **vivere alla —** to live from hand to mouth; **–ccia** (jōr·nâ·tâ′châ) bad day

giorno (jōr′nō) *m* day;**— feriale** weekday; **— festivo** holiday; **di —** in the daytime; **allo spuntar del —** at daybreak; **al cader del —** at sunset; **ai nostri giorni** in our

time; **al — d'oggi** nowadays; **metter a —** to bring up-to-date; **essere a —** to be conversant with

giostra (jō′strâ) *f* merry-go-round; tournament; **–re** (jō·strâ′rā) *vi* to joust

giovamento (jō·vâ·mān′tō) *m* aid; advantage

giovane (jō′vâ·nā), **giovine** (jō′vē·nā) *a* young; **— m** youth; **–tto** (jō·vâ·nāt′tō) boy; **–tta** (jō·vâ·nāt′tâ) *f* girl

giovanile (jō·vâ·nē′lā) *a* juvenile; youthful

giovanotto (jō·vâ·nōt′tō) *m* young man

giovare (jō·vâ′rā) *vi* to be of help; to avail

giovarsi (jō·vâr′sē) *vr* to profit by; to avail oneself of; **— a vicenda** to aid each other

giovenca (jō·vān′kâ) *f* heifer

gioventù (jō·vān·tū′) *f* youth

giovevole (jō·ve′vō·lā) *a* advantageous; profitable

giovevolmente (jō·vâ·vōl·mān′tā) *adv* profitably

giovinastro (jō·vē·nâ′strō) *m* scamp

giovinezza (jō·vē·nâ′tsâ) *f* youth

giraffa (jē·râf′fâ) *f* giraffe

girare (jē·râ′rā) *vt* to turn, spin, revolve; *(movies)* to film; *(com)* to endorse; **— un pericolo** to avoid a danger; **— l'occhio intorno** to glance around; **— al largo** to keep aloof

giracapo (jē·râ·kâ′pō) *m* vertigo

giradischi (jē·râ·dē′skē) *m* record player

giramento (jē·râ·mān′tō) *m* turning; **aver — di testa** to be dizzy

giramondo (jē·râ·mōn′dō) *m* adventurer; world traveler

girandola (jē·rân′dō·lâ) *f* pinwheel

girante (jē·rân′tā) *m (com)* endorser; **—** *a* revolving, turning

girarrosto (jē·râr·rō′stō) *m* rotisserie

girarsi (jē·râr′sē) *vr* to turn about; **— sui tacchi** to turn on one's heels

girasole (jē·râ·sō′lā) *m* sunflower

girata (jē·râ′tâ) *f* turn; *(com)* endorsement; **–rio** (jē·râ·tâ′ryō) *m* endorsee

giratorio (jē·râ·tō′ryō) *a* revolving, spinning

giravolta (jē·râ·vōl′tâ) *f* twirl, pirouette; *(fig)* about-face

giretto (jē·rāt′tō) *m* short walk

girevole (jē·re′vō·lā) *a* whirling, revolving

girino (jē·rē′nō) *m* tadpole

giro (jē′rō) *m* turn; walk; **fare un —** to take a walk; **prendere in —** to make fun of; **a — di posta** by return mail;

---

k kid, **l** let, **m** met, **n** not, **p** pat, **r** very, **s** sat, **sh** shop, **t** tell, **v** vat, **w** we, **y** yes, **z** zero

mettere in — notizie to spread rumors; mettersi in — to form a circle; — d'affari *(com)* turnover; cambiali in — *(com)* outstanding bills; –pilota (jē·rō·pē·lō'tâ) *m* automatic pilot; –scopio (jē·rō·skô'pyō) *m* gyroscope; –stato (jē·rō·stâ'tō) *m* gyrostat; –vagare (jē·rō·vâ·gâ'rā) *vi* to loaf, idle; –vago (jē·rô'vâ·gō) *m* peddler; vagrant; –vago *a* roaming

gita (jē'tâ) *f* trip, outing; — in comitiva conducted tour

gitana (jē·tâ'nâ) *f* gypsy

giù (jū) *adv* downstairs; down, below; essere — di morale *(coll)* to have the blues, be discouraged; su per — approximately; non mi va — *(fig)* I can't believe it

giubba (jūb'bâ) *f* jacket

giubilante (jū·bē·lân'tâ) *a* exultant, jubilant

giubilare (jū·bē·lâ'rā) *vi* to exult, be overjoyed

giubileo (jū·bē·lā'ō) *m* jubilee, celebration

giubilo (jū'bē·lō) *m* jubilation

giudaismo (jū·dâ·ē'zmō) *m* Judaism

giudeo (jū·dā'ō) *m* Jew; — *a* Jewish

giudicare (jū·dē·kâ'rā) *vt&i* to judge, pass judgment; to believe

giudicato (jū·dē·kâ'tō) *a* judged; — *m* sentence *(law)*

giudice (jū'dē·chā) *m* judge; — istruttore coroner; — di pace, — conciliatore justice of the peace

giudiziale (jū·dē·tsyâ'lâ) *a* judicial

giudizialmente (jū·dē·tsyâl·mân'tâ) *adv* judicially

giudiziario (jū·dē·tsyâ'ryō) *a* judicial, court

giudizio (jū·dē'tsyō) *m* wisdom, judgment; formare un — to form an opinion; dente del — wisdom tooth; a mio — in my opinion; aver — to be wise; senza — careless, rash; metter — to become wise; to grow up emotionally; citare in — to sue; comparire in — to appear in court

giudiziosamente (jū·dē·tsyō·zâ·mân'tâ) *adv* judiciously, wisely

giugno (jū'nyō) *m* June

giugulare (jū·gū·lâ'rā) *a (anat)* jugular; — *vt* to strangle

giulebbe (jū·lāb'bā) *m* julep

giulivo (jū·lē'vō) *a* happy, joyful

giullare (jūl·lâ'rā) *m* clown, jester

giumenta (jū·mān'tâ) *f* mare

giunchiglia (jūn·kē'lyâ) *f* jonquil

giunco (jūn'kō) *m (bot)* rush

giungere * (jūn'jā·rā) *vt&i* to arrive, reach; to connect

giungla (jūn'glâ) *f* jungle

giunta (jūn'tâ) *f* board, commission; per — besides

giunto (jūn'tō) *a* arrived; joined; — *m (mech)* joint; — cardanico universal joint

giuntura (jūn·tū'râ) *f* articulation; joint

giuoco (jwō'kō) *m* game; *(mech)* play; — d'azzardo gambling; — di prestigio; sleight of hand; — di parole pun; farsi — di to make a fool of

giuramento (jū·râ·man'tō) *m* oath *(law)*

giurare (jū·râ'rā) *vt* to swear *(oath)*

giurato (jū·râ'tō) *a* sworn; — *m* juror

giuria (jū·rē'â) *f* jury

giureconsulto (jū·rā·kōn·sūl'tō) *m* law expert, jurist

giuridicamente (jū·rē·dē·kâ·mân'tâ) *adv* legally, juridically

giurisdizione (jū·rē·dzē·tsyō'nâ) *f* jurisdiction

giurisprudenza (jū·rē·sprū·dân'tsâ) *f* law, jurisprudence

giurista (jū·rē'stâ) *m* jurist

giusta (jū'stâ) *prep* in accordance with

giustamente (jū·stâ·mân'tâ) *adv* correctly; justly; precisely

giustificabile (jū·stē·fē·kâ'bē·lâ) *a* justifiable

giustificare (jū·stē·fē·kâ'rā) *vt* to justify

giustificarsi (jū·stē·fē·kâr'sē) *vr* to justify one's actions; to explain oneself

giustificativo (jū·stē·fē·kâ·tē'vō) *m* statement; documento — voucher

giustificazione (jū·stē·fē·kâ·tsyō'nâ) *f* explanation; justification

giustizia (jū·stē'tsyâ) *f* justice; con — equitably; farsi — da sè to take the law into one's own hands; render — to be fair, to do justice to; –re (jū·stē·tsyâ'rā) *vt* to execute; –to (jū·stē·tsyâ'tō) *a* put to death

giustiziere (jū·stē·tsyā'rā) *m* executioner

giusto (jū'stō) *a* just; correct; — *adv* right; exactly; — mezzo golden mean

glabro (glâ'brō) *a* hairless

glaciale (glâ·châ'lâ) *a* icy, ice; glacial

gladiatore (glâ·dyâ·tō'râ) *m* gladiator

gladiolo (glâ·dyō'lō) *m* gladiola

glandola (glân'dō·lâ) *f* gland

glandolare (glân·dō·lâ'rā) *a* glandular

glaucoma (glâū·glâ·kō'mâ) *f* glaucoma

gleba (glā'bâ) *f* earth; servo della — serf; proletarian

gli (lyē) *art mpl* the; — *pron* to him, to it

glicerina (glē·châ·rē'nâ) *f* glycerine

glicerofosfato (glē·chā·rō·fō·sfâ′tō) *m* glycerophosphate
glicogeno (glē·kô′jä·nō) *m* glycogen
globale (glō·bâ′lä) *a* global; overall; lump *(payment)*
globalmente (glō·bâl·män′tä) *adv* in the aggregate
globo (glō′bō) *m* globe
globulo (glô′bū·lō) *m* globule; corpuscle
gloria (glô′ryä) *f* glory; *(eccl)* aureole
gloriarsi (glō·ryâr′sē) *vr* to pride oneself on
glorificare (glō·rē·fē·kâ′rä) *vt* to glorify; to worship
glorificazione (glō·rē·fē·kâ·tsyō′nä) *f* glorification, worship
gloriosamente (glō·ryō·zâ·män′tä) *adv* magnificently; gloriously
glossare (glōs·sâ′rä) *vt* to gloss
glossario (glōs·sâ′ryō) *m* glossary
glottide (glōt′tē·dä) *f* glottis
glutine (glū′tē·nä) *m* gluten
glutinoso (glū·tē·nō′zō) *a* glutinous
gnocco (nyōk′kō) *m* dumpling
gnomo (nyō′mō) *m* goblin, gnome
gnorri (nyōr′rē) *m* ignorance; **fare lo —** to turn a deaf ear; to pretend ignorance
gobba (gōb′bä) *f* hump
gobbo (gōb′bō) *m* hunchback
goccia (gô′chä) *f* drop; **assomigliarsi come due gocce d'acqua** to be like two peas in a pod
gocciolare (gō·chō·lâ′rä) *vi* to drip
gocciolio (gō·chō·lē′ō) *m* trickle; dripping
godere * (gō·dā′rä) *vt&i* to enjoy; to rejoice; **godersi la vita** to enjoy life; **godersela** to enjoy oneself; **— credito** to have a good credit rating
godimento (gō·dē·män′tō) *m* enjoyment; possession
goffaggine (gōf·fâj′jē·nä) *f* awkwardness; gaucheness
goffo (gōf′fō) *a* clumsy; gauche
gogna (gō′nyä) *f* pillory; **mettere alla —** to expose to public ridicule
gol (gōl) *m* goal *(sport)*
gola (gō′lä) *f* throat; gorge; gullet; groove; **far —** to tempt; to make one's mouth water; **aver l'acqua alla —** to be in dire straits
goletta (gō·lāt′tä) *f* schooner
golfo (gōl′fō) *m* gulf; pullover, sweater
Golgota (gôl′gō·tä) *m* Golgotha
goliardo (gō·lyär′dō) *m* university student
golosamente (gō·lō·zâ·män′tä) *adv* greedily, gluttonously
golosità (gō·lō·zē·tâ′) *f* gluttony

goloso (gō·lō′zō) *a* gluttonous; **— n** glutton
gomena (gô′mä·nâ) *f* hawser, cable
gomitata (gō·mē·tâ′tä) *f* nudge, shove with one's elbow
gomito (gō′mē·tō) *m* elbow; **alzare il —** *(fig)* to drink heavily; **alzare troppo il — to** drink too much
gomma (gōm′mâ) *f* rubber; eraser; inner-tube; tire; **— lacca** shellac; **— liquida** mucilage; **— piuma** foam rubber; **–to** (gōm·mâ′tō) *a* gummed
gommoso (gōm·mō′zō) *a* gummy, sticky
gommosità (gōm·mō·zē·tâ′) *f* stickiness, gumminess
gondola (gôn′dō·lâ) *f* gondola
gondoliere (gōn·dō·lyä′rä) *m* gondolier
gonfiamento (gōn·fyâ·män′tō) *m* swelling; *(fig)* exaggeration
gonfiare (gōn·fyâ′rä) *vt* to inflate, swell; to exaggerate
gonfiarsi (gōn·fyâr′sē) *vr* to swell up, swell
gonfiatura (gōn·fyâ·tū′râ) *f* puffiness; *(fig)* overstatement
gonfio (gôn′fyō) *a* swollen
gonfiore (gōn·fyō′rä) *m* swelling
gongolante (gōn·gō·lân′tä) *a* elated
gongolare (gōn·gō·lâ′rä) *vi* to rejoice
goniometria (gō·nyō·mä·trē′â) *f* goniometry
goniometro (gō·nyô′mä·trō) *m* protractor
gonna (gōn′nâ) *f* skirt
gonnella (gōn·nāl′lâ) *f* petticoat, slip; skirt
gonorrea (gō·nōr·rä′â) *f* gonorrhea
gonzo (gōn′dzō) *m* fool
gora (gō′râ) *f* pond; canal, ditch
gorgheggiare (gōr·gāj·jâ′rä) *vi* to warble
gorgo (gōr′gō) *m* whirlpool
gorgogliare (gōr·gō·lyâ′rä) *vi* to gurgle
gorgoglio (gōr·gō·lyē′ō) *m* gurgle
gorilla (gō·rēl′lâ) *m* gorilla
gota (gō′tâ) *f* cheek
gotico (gô′tē·kō) *a* Gothic
gotta (gōt′tâ) *f* gout
governante (gō·vär·nân′tä) *m* ruler; **— f** governess; housekeeper
governare (gō·vär·nâ′rä) *vt* to rule, govern
governarsi (gō·vär·nâr′sē) *vr* to control oneself; to govern oneself
governativo (gō·vär·nâ·tē′vō) *a* governmental; **impiegato —** government employee
governatore (gō·vär·nâ·tō′râ) *m* governor
governo (gō·vär′nō) *m* government, administration; control, steering
gozzo (gō′dzō) *m* crop *(bird)*; goiter
gozzoviglia (gō·dzō·vē′lyä) *f* excessive

drinking, debauchery

gozzovigliare (gō·dzō·vē·lyâ'rā) *vi* to debauch; to revel; to eat and drink excessively

gracidare (grâ·chē·dâ'rā) *vi* to croak; to cluck

gracile (grâ'chē·lā) *a* delicate; slender

gracilità (grâ·chē·lē·tâ') *f* slimness; feebleness

gracilmente (grâ·chēl·mān'tā) *adv* gracefully

gradatamente (grâ·dâ·tâ·mān'tā) *adv* gradually

gradevole (grâ·de'vō·lā) *a* pleasant, nice

gradevolezza (grâ·dā·vō·lâ'tsâ) *f* agreeableness

gradevolmente (grâ·dā·vōl·mān'tā) *adv* pleasantly, agreeably

gradimento (grâ·dē·mān'tō) *m* approval, liking

gradinata (grâ·dē·nâ'tâ) *f* stairway; tier *(seats)*

gradino (grâ·dē'nō) *m* step *(stair)*

gradire (grâ·dē'rā) *vt* to accept; to like; to appreciate

gradito (grâ·dē'tō) *a* pleasant; welcome

grado (grâ'dō) *m* liking; grade, degree, rank; **mettere in — di** to enable to; **essere in — di** to be able to; **di buon — willingly; di proprio —** of one's own accord

graduale (grâ·dwâ'lā) *a* gradual

gradualmente (grâ·dwâl·mān'tā) *adv* gradually

graduare (grâ·dwâ'rā) *vt* to graduate, adjust

graduato (grâ·dwâ'tō) *a* graduated; graduate; **— m** non-commissioned officer

graduatoria (grâ·dwâ·tô'ryâ) *f* classification

graduazione (grâ·dwâ·tsyō'nā) *f* graduation

graffiare (grâf·fyâ'rā) *vt* to scratch

graffiatura (grâf·fyâ·tū'râ) *f* scratch

graffio (grâf'fyō) *m* scratch

grafia (grâ·fē'â) *f* spelling; handwriting

graficamente (grâ·fē·kâ·mān'tā) *adv* graphically

grafico (grâ'fē·kō) *a* graphic; **— m** graph; blue print

grafite (grâ·fē'tā) *f* graphite

grafologia (grâ·fō·lō·jē'â) *f* graphology

grafologo (grâ·fô'lō·gō) *m* graphologist

gramaglie (grâ·mâ·lyā) *fpl* mourning

grammatica (grâm·mâ'tē·kâ) *f* grammar

grammaticale (grâm·mâ·tē·kâ'lā) *a* grammatical

grammaticalmente (grâm·mâ·tē·kâl·

mān'tā) *adv* grammatically

grammatico (grâm·mâ'tē·kō) *m* grammarian

grammo (grâm'mō) *m* gram

grammofono (grâm·mō'fō·nō) *m* phonograph

gramo (grâ'mō) *a* miserable, wretched

grana (grâ'nâ) *f* grain; *(sl)* trouble, difficulty; **formaggio —** Parmesan cheese

granaglie (grâ·nâ'lyā) *fpl* cereals

granaio (grâ·nâ'yō) *m* barn; granary

granata (grâ·nâ'tâ) *f* grenade; broom

granatina (grâ·nâ·tē'nâ) *f* grenadine

granato (grâ·nâ'tō) *m* pomegranate; garnet

grancassa (grân·kâs'sâ) *f* bass drum; **suonare la —** to broadcast loudly

granchio (grân'kyō) *m* crab; **prendere un — to** make a gross error

grandangolare (grân·dân·gō·lâ'rā) *a (phot)* wide-angle

grande (grân'dā) *a* great; big, large; tall; **— m** great man; **in —** wholesale; **— conoscenza di** vast knowledge of; **fare il —** to put on airs; **fare le cose in —** to do things on a large scale; **farsi — to** grow up

grandeggiare (grân·dāj·jâ'rā) *vi* to tower over; to act in a haughty manner

grandemente (grân·dā·mān'tā) *adv* greatly; very much

grandezza (grân·dā'tsâ) *f* greatness; grandeur; largeness

grandinare (grân·dē·nâ'rā) *vi* to hail *(weather)*

grandinata (grân·dē·nâ'tâ) *f* hailstorm

grandiosamente (grân·dyō·zâ·mān'tā) *adv* majestically; pompously

grandiosità (grân·dyō·zē·tâ') *f* grandeur

grandioso (grân·dyō'zō) *a* majestic; pompous

granduca (grân·dū'kâ) *m* grand duke

granduchessa (grân·dū·kās'sâ) *f* grand duchess

granello (grâ·nāl'lō) *m* grain; speck

granfia (grân'fyâ) *f* claw

granita (grâ·nē'tâ) *f* sherbet

granitico (grâ·nē'tē·kō) *a* granite; *(fig)* adamant, unyielding

granito (grâ·nē'tō) *m* granite

grano (grâ'nō) *m* grain *(cereal)*; wheat **— d'uva** grape; **— di rosario** rosary bead; **— di caffè** coffee bean

granulare (grâ·nū·lâ'rā) *a* granular; **— vt** to granulate

granulato (grâ·nū·lâ'tō) *a* granulated

granulo (grâ'nū·lō) *m* granule

granuloso (grâ·nū·lō'zō) *a* granular

â ârm, **ā** bāby, **e** bet, **ē** bē, **ō** gō, **ô** gône, **ū** blūe, **b** bad, **ch** child, **d** dad, **f** fat, **g** gay, **j** jet

grappa (gräp'på) f clamp; brandy
grappolo (gräp'pō·lō) m cluster
grascia (grä'shä) f lard
grassamente (gräs·sä·män'tä) adv plentifully; (fig) lasciviously
grassatore (gräs·sä·tō'rä) m bandit, highwayman
grassazione (gräs·sä·tsyō'nä) m holdup
grassetto (gräs·sät'tō) m bold-faced type
grassezza (gräs·sä'tsä) f fatness; (fig) licentiousness
grasso (gräs'sō) a fat, stout; productive; gross; greasy; — m fat, grease; **martedì** — Shrove Tuesday, Mardi Gras; **grasse risate** peals of laughter
grassoccio (gräs·sō'chō) a chubby, plump
grassume (gräs·sū'mä) m fatness; grease; smut
grata (grä'tä) f grate
gratamente (grä·tä·män'tä) adv gratefully
gratella (grä·täl'lä) f grill
graticcio (grä·tē'chō) m basketry; trellis work
gratificare (grä·tē·fē·kä'rä) vt to reward; to gratify; to tip
gratificazione (grä·tē·fē·kä·tsyō'nä) f bonus, tip; reward, satisfaction
gratis (grä'tēs) adv gratis, free
grato (grä'tō) a grateful; pleasing
grattacapo (grät·tä·kä'pō) m worry, trouble
grattacielo (grät·tä·chä'lō) m skyscraper
grattamento (grät·tä·män'tō) m rubbing; scraping, scratching
grattare (grät·tä'rä) vt&i to scratch; to grate; (sl) to steal
grattato (grät·tä'tō) a grated
grattugia (grät·tū'jä) f grater; –re (grät·tū·jä'rä) vt to grate
gratuitamente (grä·twē·tä·män'tä) adv gratis, gratuitously
gratuito (grä·twē'tō) a free, gratis; unmotivated; — **patrocinio** free legal aid
gravabile (grä·vä'bē·lä) a dutiable; liable
gravame (grä·vä'mä) m taxation; lien; mortgage; burden
gravato (grä·vä'tō) a burdened; loaded; — **d'assegno** C.O.D., cash on delivery; — **di lavoro** overworked
grave (grä'vä) a serious, grave; dangerous; — **negligenza** gross negligence; **essere** — to be seriously ill; — **d'anni** aged
gravemente (grä·vä·män'tä) adv gravely; dangerously; solemnly
gravezza (grä·vä'tsä) f seriousness, gravity
gravida (grä'vē·dä) a pregnant
gravidanza (grä·vē·dän'tsä) f pregnancy

gravido (grä'vē·dō) a full; heavy; **panino** — sandwich
gravina (grä·vē'nä) f pickax
gravità (grä·vē·tä') f seriousness; importance; gravity; weight
gravitare (grä·vē·tä'rä) vi to gravitate
gravitazionale (grä·vē·tä·tsyō·nä'lä) gravitational
gravitazione (grä·vē·tä·tsyō'nä) f gravitation
gravosità (grä·vō·zē·tä') f heftiness, weight; bother
gravoso (grä·vō'zō) a burdensome
grazia (grä'tsyä) f grace; pardon; attractiveness; **far la** — to pardon; to grant a favor; to answer a prayer; **anno di** — A.D., year of Our Lord; **colpo di** — death blow; **in** — **di** on behalf of; **senza** — awkward; **troppa** — excess of a good thing
graziare (grä·tsyä'rä) vt to pardon, reprieve
grazie! (grä'tsyä) interj thank you!, thanks!
grazioso (grä·tsyō'zō) a pretty, charming
graziosamente (grä·tsyō·zä·män'tä) adv gracefully
grecale (grä·kä'lä) m northeast wind
Grecia (grä'chä) f Greece
greco (grä'kō) a&m Greek
gregario (grä·gä'ryō) m follower; — a sociable
gregge (gräj'jä) m herd
grembiale (gräm·byä'lä) m apron
grembo (gräm'bō) m bosom; lap (anat)
gremire (grä·mē'rä) vt to fill; to crowd
gremito (grä·mē'tō) a full, packed; overcrowded
greppia (grep'pyä) f crib, manger; livelihood
greppo (gräp'pō) m cliff
gres (gräs) m sandstone
grettamente (grät·tä·män'tä) adv avariciously; meanly
grettezza (grät·tä'tsä) f pettiness; avarice
gretto (grät'tō) a miserly
greve (grä'vä) a oppressive, irksome
grezzo (grä'dzō) a raw; coarse
gridare (grē·dä'rä) vi to cry, scream
grido (grē'dō) m cry, shout; **di** — famous, well-known
grifagno (grē·fä'nyō) a rapacious
griffa (grēf'fä) f jaw (mech)
grifo (grē'fō) m snout
grigiastro (grē·jä'strō) a grayish
grigio (grē'jō) a gray
griglia (grē'lyä) f grill; grate; grid (rad)
grilletto (grēl·lät'tō) m trigger
grillo (grēl'lō) m (zool) cricket; (coll)

whim, caprice

grinfia (grēn'fyâ) *f* claw

grinta (grēn'tâ) *f* stern look; sulky expression

grinza (grēn'dzâ) *f* wrinkle; **non fare una** — to be perfect, be without a flaw

grippaggio (grēp·pâj'jō) *m* jamming *(mech)*

grippare (grēp·pâ'rā) *vi* to jam *(mech)*

grippe (grēp'pā) *m* influenza

grissino (grēs·sē'nō) *m* bread stick

gronda (grōn'dâ) *f* eaves; **–ia** (grōn·dâ'yâ) *f* gutter; **–re** (grōn·dâ'rā) *vi* to drip; to pour out; **–nte** (grōn·dân'tā) *a* streaming; dripping

groppa (grōp'pâ) *f* back, croup *(horse)*; **avere molti anni sulla** — *(fig)* to be very old; **in** — on one's back

groppone (grōp·pō'nā) *m* back; **piegare il** — to yield; to be submissive

grossa (grōs'sâ) *f* gross

grossezza (grōs·sā'tsâ) *f* bigness; thickness; uncouthness

grossista (grōs·sē'stâ) *m* wholesaler

grosso (grōs'sō) *a* big; thick; large; **pezzo** — big shot; **sbagliarsi di** — to be completely wrong; **farle grosse** to act ridiculously; **in modo** — roughly speaking; **fare la voce grossa** to threaten; **mare** — rough sea

grossolanità (grōs·sō·lâ·nē·tâ') *f* vulgarity; lack of refinement; uncouthness

grossolano (grōs·sō·lâ'nō) *a* coarse; common, vulgar

grotta (grōt'tâ) *f* grotto, cavern

grottesco (grōt·tā'skō) *a* grotesque

groviglio (grō·vē'lyō) *m* knot; snare; entanglement; *(fig)* mess

gru (grū) *f* crane

gruccia (grū'châ) *f* crutch; *(coll)* coat hanger

grufolare (grū·fō·lâ'rā) *vi* to root; to rummage

grugnire (grū·nyē'rā) *vi* to grunt

grugnito (grū·nyē'tō) *m* grunt

grugno (grū'nyō) *m* snout, muzzle; **fare il** — *(coll)* to sulk; **un brutto** — *(coll)* a homely face

grullagine (grūl·lâ'jē·nā) *f* foolishness

grullo (grūl'lō) *m* simpleton; — *a* foolish

grumo (grū'mō) *m* clot; **–so** (grū·mō'zō) *a* clotted

grumolo (grū'mō·lō) *m* core

gruppo (grūp'pō) *m* group; flock

gruviera (grū·vyâ'râ) *f* Gruyère

gruzzolo (grū'tsō·lō) *m* savings, nest egg

guadagnare (gwâ·dâ·nyâ'rā) *vt* to earn, gain; to win; — **un porto** to reach a

port; **—il tempo perduto** to make up time

guadagnarsi (gwâ·dâ·nyâr'sē) *vr* to earn for oneself; — **un raffreddore** to catch cold

guadagno (gwâ·dâ'nyō) *m* earnings, profit

guadare (gwâ·dâ'rā) *vt* to ford

guado (gwâ'dō) *m* ford

guaina (gwâ·ē·nâ) *f* scabbard, sheath

guaio (gwâ'yō) *m* misfortune; trouble; breakdown *(mech)*

guaire (gwâ·ē'rā) *vi* to yelp, whine

gualcire (gwâl·chē'rā) *vt* to crumple, rumple

gualcito (gwâl·chē'tō) *a* crumpled

guancia (gwân'châ) *f* cheek; **–le** (gwân·châ'lā) *m* pillow

guantaio (gwân·tâ'yō) *m* glovemaker

guanteria (gwân·tā·rē'â) *f* glove shop

guanto (gwân'tō) *m* glove; **trattare coi guanti** to handle with care

guantone (gwân·tō'nâ) *m* boxing glove

guardaboschi (gwâr·dâ·bō'skē) *m* forester

guardacaccia (gwâr·dâ·kâ'châ) *m* gamekeeper

guardacosta (gwâr·dâ·kō'stâ) *m* coastguard

guardamano (gwâr·dâ·mâ'nō) *m* handrail

guardaportone (gwâr·dâ·pōr·tō'nâ) *m* doorman

guardare (gwâr·dâ'rā) *vt* to look at; to consider; to guard; — **il letto** *(fig)* to stay in bed; — **per il sottile** to be very squeamish

guardaroba (gwâr·dâ·rō'bâ) *f* cloakroom; wardrobe

guardarsi (gwâr·dâr'sē) *vr* to be careful of; to abstain from; to look at one another

guardata (gwâr·dâ'tâ) *f* look; **–ccia** (gwâr·dâ·tâ'châ) *f* scowling look

guardia (gwâr'dyâ) *f* guard; watchman; policeman; — **del corpo** bodyguard; — **forestale** forest ranger; — **doganale** customs agent

guardiamarina (gwâr·dyâ·mâ·rē'nâ) *m* ensign

guardiano (gwâr·dyâ'nō) *m* watchman

guardingo (gwâr·dēn'gō) *a* cautious

guaribile (gwâ·rē·bē·lâ) *a* curable

guarigione (gwâ·rē·jō'nâ) *f* recovery, cure

guarire (gwâ·rē'rā) *vi* to recover one's health; — *vt* to cure, heal

guaritore (gwâ·rē·tō'rā) *m* healer

guarnigione (gwâr·nē·jō'nâ) *f* garrison

guarnire (gwâr·nē'rā) *vt* to garnish, trim; to fortify *(mil)*

guarnizione (gwâr·nē·tsyō'nâ) *f* trimming; garnish; gasket, packing *(mech)*

â ârm, ā bāby, e bet, ē bē, ō gō, ô gône, ū blūe, b bad, ch child, d dad, f fat, g gay, j jet

guasconata (gwâ·skō·nâ'tâ) *f* bragging
guastafeste (gwâ·stâ·fā'stä) *m* killjoy, wet blanket
guastamestieri (gwâ·stâ·mā·styā'rē) *m* strikebreaker; bungler
guastare (gwâ·stâ'rā) *vt* to spoil, ruin
guastarsi (gwâ·stâr'sē) *vr* to go bad, spoil
guastatore (gwâ·stâ·tō'rā) *m* destroyer, despoiler
guasto (gwâ'stō) *a* out of order; spoiled; — *m* damage; — **al motore** breakdown, engine trouble
guatare (gwâ·tâ'rā) *vt* to look askance at; to ogle
guazza (gwâ'tsâ) *f* dew
guazzabuglio (gwâ·tsâ·bū'lyō) *m* hodgepodge; potpourri
guazzo (gwâ'tsō) *m* slush
guercio (gwer'chō) *a* squint-eyed; one-eyed
guerra (gwār'râ) *f* war; **ministero della —** war department
guerrafondaio (gwār·râ·fōn·dâ'yō) *m* warmonger
guerreggiare (gwār·rāj·jâ'rā) *vt&i* to fight; to wage war; to wage war
guerresco (gwār·rā'skō) *a* martial
guerriglia (gwār·rē'lyâ) *f* guerrilla war
gufo (gū'fō) *m* screech owl
guglia (gū'lyâ) *f* spire

Guiana (gū·yâ'nâ) *f* Guiana
guida (gwē'dâ) *f* guide; guidance; leadership; drive *(auto)*; — **telefonica** telephone book; **–re** (gwē·dâ'rā) *vt* to guide, conduct, lead; to drive; **–tore** (gwē·dâ·tō'rā) *m* driver, motorist
guiderdone (gwē·dâr·dō'nä) *m* reward
guidoslitta (gwē·dō·zlēt'tâ) *f* bobsled
guinzaglio (gwēn·tsâ'lyō) *m* leash
guisa (gwē'zâ) *f* way; manner; **a — di** as, like; **in tal —** in such a manner; **in ogni —** in every way; **di — che** so that
guizzare (gwē·tsâ'rā) *vi* to dart; to flash *(light)*
guscio (gū'shō) *m* pod; shell; **restar nel proprio —** to be unsociable, be withdrawn
gustare (gū·stâ'rā) *vt* to taste; — *vi* to like, enjoy
gustevole (gū·ste'vō·lä) *a* tasty
gusto (gū'stō) *m* taste, flavor; gusto
gustosamente (gū·stō·zâ·män'tä) *adv* tastefully; agreeably
gustoso (gū·stō'zō) *a* tasty; savory; amusing
gutturale (gūt·tū·râ'lä) *a* guttural
gutturalmente (gūt·tū·râl·män'tä) *adv* gutturally

I

i (ē) *art mpl* the
iarda (yâr'dâ) *f* yard *(measure)*
iato (yâ'tō) *m* hiatus; gap
iattanza (yât·tân'tsâ) *f* bragging
iattura (yât·tū'râ) *f* misfortune
iberico (ē·be'rē·kō) *a&m* Iberian
ibernazione (ē·bār·nâ·tsyō'nä) *f* hibernation
ibridazione (ē·brē·dâ·tsyō'nä) *f* hybridization
ibrido (ē'brē·dō) *m&a* hybrid
icona (ē·kō'nâ) *f* icon
iconoclastico (ē·kō·nō·klâ'stē·kō) *a* iconoclastic
Iddio (ēd·dē'ō) *m* God, Lord
idea (ē·dā'â) *f* idea, opinion; **–le** (ē·dâ·â'lä) *n&a* ideal; **–lismo** (ē·dâ·â·lē'zmō) *m* idealism; **–lista** (ē·dâ·â·lē'stä) *m* idealist; **–lizzare** (ē·dâ·â·lē·dzâ'rā) *vt* to idealize; **–lizzazione** (ē·dâ·â·lē·dzâ·tsyō'nä) *f* idealization; **–lmente** (ē·dâ·âl·män'tä) *adv* ideally; **–re** (ē·dâ·â'râ) *vt* to conceive, plan; **–tore** (ē·dâ·â·tō'rā) *m* inventor, creator; **–zione** (ē·dâ·â·tsyō'nä) *f* ideation

idem (ē'dām) *adv* idem
identicamente (ē·dân·tē·kâ·män'tä) *adv* exactly, identically
identico (ē·den'tē·kō) *a* identical
identificare (ē·dân·tē·fē·kâ'rā) *vt* to identify
identificarsi (ē·dân·tē·fē·kâr'sē) *vr* to identify onself; to feel drawn toward
identificazione (ē·dân·tē·fē·kâ·tsyō'nä) *f* identification
identità (ē·dân·tē·tâ') *f* identity; **carta d' —** identification card
ideologia (ē·dâ·ō·lō·jē'â) *f* ideology
ideologico (ē·dâ·ō·lô'jē·kō) *a* ideological
idillio (ē·dēl'lyō) *m* romance, idyl
idioma (ē·dyō'mâ) *m* vernacular; language
idiomatico (ē·dyō·mâ'tē·kō) *a* idiomatic; **espressione idiomatica** idiom
idiosincrasia (ē·dyō·sēn·krâ·zē'â) *f* allergy; repugnance; aversion; peculiarity
idiota (ē·dyō'tâ) *a* idiotic — *m* idiot
idiotismo (ē·dyō·tē'zmō) *m* idiocy; idiom; expression
idolatrare (ē·dō·lâ·trâ'rā) *vt* to idolize
idolo (ē'dō·lō) *m* idol

k kid, **l** let, **m** met, **n** not, **p** pat, **r** very, **s** sat, **sh** shop, **t** tell, **v** vat, **w** we, **y** yes, **z** zero

idoneamente (ē·dō·nā·â·mān'tā) *adv* conveniently

idoneità (ē·dō·nāē·tâ') *f* fitness, aptness

idoneo (ē·dô'nā·ō) *a* qualified; fit

idrante (ē·drân'tā) *m* hydrant

idrato (ē·drâ'tō) *m* hydrate; — **di carbone** carbohydrate

idraulica (ē·drâ'ū·lē·kâ) *f* hydraulics

idraulico (ē·drâ'ū·lē·kō) *a* hydraulic; — *m* plumber

idrocarburo (ē·drō·kâr·bū'rō) *m* hydrocarbon

idrodinamica (ē·drō·dē·nâ'mē·kâ) *f* hydrodynamics

idroelettrico (ē·drō·ā·let'trē·kō) *a* hydroelectric

idrofilo (ē·drô'fē·lō) *a* absorbent; **cotone** — absorbent cotton

idrofobia (ē·drō·fō·bē'â) *f* hydrophobia

idrofobo (ē·drô'fō·bō) *a* hydrophobic

idrografia (ē·drō·grâ·fē'â) *f* hydrography

idrografo (ē·drô'grâ·fō) *m* hydrographer

idrogeno (ē·drô'jā·nō) *m* hydrogen

idrolisi (ē·drō·lē'zē) *f* hydrolysis

idrometria (ē·drō·mā·trē'â) *f* hydrometry

idrometro (ē·drô'mā·trō) *m* water gauge

idropico (ē·drô'pē·kō) *a* dropsical

idropisia (ē·drō·pē·zē'â) *f* dropsy

idroplano (ē·drō·plâ'nō) *m* hydroplane

idroponica (ē·drō·pô'nē·kâ) *f* hydroponics

idroscalo (ē·drō·skâ'lō) *m* seaplane station

idroscì (ē·drō·shē') *m* water ski

idrosilurante (ē·drō·sē·lū·rân'tā) *m* torpedoplane

idrostatica (ē·drō·stâ'tē·kâ) *f* hydrostatics

idrovia (ē·drō·vē'â) *f* waterway

iena (yā'nâ) *f* hyena

ieri (yā'rē) *adv* yesterday; — **l'altro** the day before yesterday; — **sera** yesterday evening

iettatura (yā·tâ·tū'râ) *f* evil eye; **portare** — to bring misfortune; **avere la** — to be unlucky

igiene (ē·jā'nā) *f* hygienics, hygiene

igienico (ē·je'nē·kō) *a* hygenic; **carta igienica** toilet paper, bathroom tissue

ignaro (ē·nyâ'rō) *a* unaware, lacking information

ignavia (ē·nyâ'vyâ) *f* indolence

ignifugo (ē·nyē'fū·gō) *a* fire-resistant

ignizione (ē·nyē·tsyō'nā) *f* ignition

ignobile (ē·nyō'bē·lā) *a* base, ignoble

ignobilmente (ē·nyō·bēl·mān'tā) *adv* ignobly

ignominia (ē·nyō·mē'nyâ) *f* disgrace

ignominiosamente (ē·nyō·mē·nyō·zâ·mān'tā) *adv* shamefully, dishonorably

ignominioso (ē·nyō·mē·nyō'zō) *a* shameful; dishonorable

ignorante (ē·nyō·rân'tā) *a* ignorant; — *m* ignoramus

ignoranza (ē·nyō·rân'tsâ) *f* ignorance

ignorare (ē·nyō·râ'rā) *vt* to be ignorant, be unaware; to lack information; to ignore

ignorato (ē·nyō·râ'tō) *a* disregarded; unknown

ignoto (ē·nyō'tō) *a* unknown

ignudo (ē·nyū'dō) *a* stripped, nude

il (ēl) *art m* the

ilare (ē·lâ'râ) *a* cheerful

ilarità (ē·lâ·rē·tâ') *f* hilarity; merriment; **scoppio d'** — burst of laughter; **destare** — to provoke laughter

illanguidimento (ēl·lân·gwē·dē·mān'tō) *m* listlessness; languishing

illanguidire (ēl·lân·gwē·dē'râ) *vt&i* to weaken; to become languid

illazione (ēl·lâ·tsyō'nâ) *f* inference, deduction

illecitamente (ēl·lā·chē·tâ·mān'tā) *adv* illicitly

illecito (ēl·le'chē·tō) *a* illicit

illegale (ēl·lā·gâ'lā) *a* illegal

illegalità (ēl·lā·gâ·lē·tâ') *f* illegality

illegalmente (ēl·lā·gâl·mān'tā) *adv* illegally

illeggibile (ēl·lāj·jē'bē·lā) *a* illegible

illegittimo (ēl·lā·jēt'tē·mō) *a* illegitimate

illeso (ēl·lā'zō) *a* unharmed

illetterato (ēl·lāt·tā·râ'tō) *a* illiterate

illibato (ēl·lē·bâ'tō) *a* pure, innocent

illimitatamente (ēl·lē·mē·tâ·tâ·mān'tā) *adv* without bounds, unlimitedly

illimitato (ēl·lē·mē·tâ'tō) *a* unlimited

illividire (ēl·lē·vē·dē'râ) *vt* to make livid; — *vi* to become livid

illividito (ēl·lē·vē·dē'tō) *a* livid

illogico (ēl·lô'jē·kō) *a* illogical

illudere * (ēl·lū'dā·râ) *vt* to deceive

illuminante (ēl·lū·mē·nân'tā) *a* lighting up; illuminating

illuminare (ēl·lū·mē·nâ'râ) *vt* to light up; to enlighten

illuminarsi (ēl·lū·mē·nâr'sē) *vr* to grow bright

illuminato (ēl·lū·mē·nâ'tō) *a* lighted; enlightened

illuminazione (ēl·lū·mē·nâ·tsyō'nâ) *f* lighting; illumination; enlightenment

illusione (ēl·lū·zyō'nâ) *f* illusion; **farsi illusioni** to build dream castles; **vivere di illusioni** to live in a dream world

---

â ârm, **ā** bāby, **e** bet, **ē** bē, **ō** gō, **ô** gône, **ū** blūe, **b** bad, **ch** child, **d** dad, **f** fat, **g** gay, **j** jet

illusionista (ēl·lū·zyō·nē′stâ) *m* magician

illuso (ēl·lū′zō) *a* deluded — *m* daydreamer

illusorio (ēl·lū·zō′ryō) *a* fallacious; unreal

illustrare (ēl·lū·strâ′rā) *vt* to illustrate; to make famous; to explain

illustrativo (ēl·lū·strâ·tē′vō) *a* illustrative

illustratore (ēl·lū·strâ·tō′rā) *m* illustrator

illustrazione (ēl·lū·strâ·tsyō′nā) *f* illustration; explanation; glory

illustre (ēl·lū′·strā) *a* illustrious

imbaldanzire (ēm·bâl·dân·tsē′rā) *vt* to make bold; — *vi* to become bold

imballaggio (ēm·bâl·lâj′jō) *m* packing

imballare (ēm·bâl·lâ′rā) *vt* to pack; *(mech)* to race

imballatore (ēm·bâl·lâ·tō′rā) *m* packer

imballatrice (ēm·bâl·lâ·trē′chā) *f* packing machine; baling machine

imballo (ēm·bâl′lō) *m* packing; *(mech)* racing

imbalsamare (ēm·bâl·sâ·mâ′rā) *vt* to embalm; to stuff

imbambolato (ēm·bâm·bō·lâ′tō) *a* listless; sleepy

imbandierare (ēm·bân·dyā·râ′rā) *vt* to decorate with flags

imbandierato (ēm·bân·dyā·râ′tō) *a* decorated with flags

imbandigione (ēm·bân·dē·jō′nā) *f* banquet preparations

imbandire (ēm·bân·dē′rā) *vt* to set *(table)*; to ready, prepare; to serve; — **un pranzo** to serve a feast

imbarazzante (ēm·bâ·râ·tsân′tā) *a* embarrassing; puzzling; obstructing

imbarazzare (ēm·bâ·râ·tsâ′rā) *vt* to embarrass; to perplex; to obstruct

imbarazzarsi (ēm·bâ·râ·tsâr′sē) *vr* to become confused, grow embarrassed; *(coll)* to interfere with

imbarazzato (ēm·bâ·râ·tsâ′tō) *a* embarrassed; bewildered

imbarazzo (ēm·bâ·râ′tsō) *m* embarrassment; constipation; financial difficulties; **essere d'** — to be in the way; **trovarsi in imbarazzi** to find oneself in a difficult situation; **levarsi d'** — to get out of trouble; — **di stomaco** indigestion

imbarcadero (ēm·bâr·kâ·dā′rō) *m* pier

imbarcare (ēm·bâr·kâ′rā) *vt* to take on board; to ship

imbarcarsi (ēm·bâr·kâr′sē) *vr* to go aboard, board; to sail; — **in un'impresa difficile** to embark on a difficult task

imbarcatoio (ēm·bâr·kâ·tô′yō) *m* wharf

imbarcazione (ēm·bâr·kâ·tsyō′nā) *f* boat, ship

imbarco (ēm·bâr′kō) *m* loading pier; embarkation; shipping

imbardare (ēm·bâr·dâ′rā) *vi* to yaw *(avi)*

imbarilare (ēm·bâ·rē·lâ′rā) *vt* to put into barrels

imbastardire (ēm·bâ·stâr·dē′rā) *vt* to corrupt; to debase

imbastardirsi (ēm·bâ·stâr·dēr′sē) *vr* to degenerate

imbastardito (ēm·bâ·stâr·dē′tō) *a* degenerate; corrupted

imbastire (ēm·bâ·stē′rā) *vt* to baste; — **un discorso** to prepare a speech

imbattersi (ēm·bât′tār·sē) *vr* to run across

imbattibile (ēm·bât·tē′bē·lā) *a* unbeatable

imbattuto (ēm·bât·tū′tō) *a* unsurpassed; unbeaten

imbavagliare (ēm·bâ·vâ·lyâ′rā) *vt* to gag

imbeccare (ēm·bāk·kâ′rā) *vt* *(fig)* to coach, prompt

imbeccata (ēm·bāk·kâ′tâ) *f* cue, prompting

imbecillaggine (ēm·bā·chēl·lâj′jē·nā) *f* imbecility, foolishness

imbecille (ēm·bā·chēl′lā) *m* imbecile, simpleton

imbelle (ēm·bāl′lā) *a* cowardly, fainthearted; unwarlike

imbellettarsi (ēm·bāl·lāt·târ′sē) *vr* to put on make-up

imbellire (ēm·bāl·lē′rā) *vt* to beautify; to ornament; — *vi* to become more handsome; to grow more beautiful

imberbe (ēm·bār′bā) *a* beardless; young

imbestialire (ēm·bā·styâ·lē′rā) *vt* to brutalize

imbestialirsi (ēm·bā·styâ·lēr′sē) *vr* to become brutal; to get furious

imbevere (ēm·be′vâ·rā) *vt* to drench; to absorb

imbeversi (ēm·be′vār·sē) *vr* to become soaked; — **di** to be imbued with, to absorb, to assimilate

imbevuto (ēm·bā·vū′tō) *a* drenched; imbued

imbiancamento (ēm·byân·kâ·mān′tō) *m* whitewashing; bleaching; turning white *(hair)*

imbiancare (ēm·byân·kâ′rā) *vt* to whitewash; to whiten

imbiancato (ēm·byân·kâ′tō) *a* whitened

imbiancatura (ēm·byân·kâ·tū′râ) *f* whitewash; bleach

imbianchino (ēm·byân·kē′nō) *m* house painter

imbizzarrirsi (ēm·bē·dzâr·rēr′sē) *vr* to

become enraged; to frisk *(animals)*

imboccare (ēm·bōk·kâ′rā) *vt* to feed; to enter; — *vi* to fit in *(mech)*

imbocco (ēm·bōk′kō) *m* aperture; entrance; mouth

imboscare (ēm·bō·skâ′rā) *vt* to ambush; to conceal

imboscarsi (ēm·bō·skâr′sē) *vr* to lie in ambush; *(fig)* to shirk

imboscata (ēm·bō·skâ′tâ) *f* ambush

imboscato (ēm·bō·skâ′tō) *m* slacker

imbottigliamento (ēm·bōt·tē·lyâ·mān′tō) *m* bottling; *(fig)* blockade

imbottita (ēm·bōt·tē′tâ) *f* quilt

imbottito (ēm·bōt·tē′tō) *a* padded, stuffed

imbottitura (ēm·bōt·tē·tū′râ) *f* quilting; padding

imbracciatura (ēm·brâ·châ·tū′râ) *f* rifle sling

imbrattare (ēm·brât·tâ′rā) *vt* to soil, stain

imbrattatele (ēm·brât·tâ·tā′lā) *m* dauber; bad painter

imbrigliare (ēm·brē·lyâ′rā) *vt* to bridle; to check

imbroccare (ēm·brōk·kâ′rā) *vt* to hit; to guess right

imbrogliare (ēm·brō·lyâ′rā) *vt* to cheat; to confuse

imbrogliarsi (ēm·brō·lyâr′sē) *vr* to become confused; to meddle with

imbroglio (ēm·brō′lyō) *m* fraud; mess

imbroglione (ēm·brō·lyō′nâ) *m* crook; swindler

imbronciarsi (ēm·brōn·châr′sē) *vr* to pout; to grow dark *(sky)*

imbrunire (ēm·brū·nē′râ) *vi* to get dark; to turn brown

imbruttire (ēm·brūt·tē′rā) *vt* to disfigure; to make homely

imbucare (ēm·bū·kâ′rā) *vt* to mail; to put in the mailbox

imburrare (ēm·būr·râ′rā) *vt* to butter

imburrato (ēm·būr·râ′tō) *a* buttered

imbuto (ēm·bū′tō) *m* funnel

imene (ē·mâ′nā) *m* hymen

imitare (ē·mē·tâ′rā) *vt* to imitate

imitato (ē·mē·tâ′tō) *a* imitated

imitatore (ē·mē·tâ·tō′râ) *m* imitator, mimic

imitazione (ē·mē·tâ·tsyō′nâ) *f* imitation

immacolato (ēm·mâ·kō·lâ′tō) *a* immaculate; **l'Immacolata** the Virgin Mary

immagazzinaggio (ēm·mâ·gâ·dzē·nâj′jō) *m* storage, storing

immagazzinare (ēm·mâ·gâ·dzē·nâ′rā) *vt* to store; to lay by

immaginabile (ēm·mâ·jē·nâ′bē·lâ) *a* imaginable

immaginare (ēm·mâ·jē·nâ′rā) *vt* to imagine

immaginario (ēm·mâ·jē·nâ′ryō) *a* imaginary

immaginativa (ēm·mâ·jē·nâ·tē′vâ) *f* imagination

immaginativo (ēm·mâ·jē·nâ·tē′vō) *a* imaginative

immaginazione (ēm·mâ·jē·nâ·tsyō′nâ) *f* imagination

immagine (ēm·mâ′jē·nā) *f* image

immancabile (ēm·mân·kâ′bē·lâ) *a* sure; unfailing

immancabilmente (ēm·mân·kâ·bēl·mān′-tā) *adv* without fail; certainly

immane (ēm·mâ′nā) *a* enormous

immanente (ēm·mâ·nān′tā) *a* inherent

immantinente (ēm·mân·tē·nān′tā) *adv* immediately, at once

immateriale (ēm·mâ·tā·ryâ′lā) *a* immaterial

immatricolarsi (ēm·mâ·trē·kō·lâr′sē) *vr* to register, matriculate *(school)*

immaturità (ēm·mâ·tū·rē·tâ′) *f* immaturity

immaturo (ēm·mâ·tū′rō) *a* immature, not ripe

immediatamente (ēm·mā·dyâ·tâ·mān′tā) *adv* immediately

immediato (ēm·mā·dyâ′tō) *a* immediate

immemorabile (ēm·mā·mō·râ′bē·lâ) *a* immemorial

immemore (ēm·me′mō·râ) *a* forgetful

immensamente (ēm·mān·sâ·mān′tā) *adv* immensely

immensità (ēm·mān·sē·tâ′) *f* immensity

immenso (ēm·mān′sō) *a* immense

immergere * (ēm·mer′jā·rā) *vt* to dip, immerse

immergersi * (ēm·mer′jâr·sē) *vr* to plunge, dive into

immeritato (ēm·mâ·rē·tâ′tō) *a* undeserved

immeritevole (ēm·mâ·rē·te′vō·lā) *a* unworthy

immeritevolmente (ēm·mâ·rē·tā·vōl·mān′lā) *adv* undeservingly

immersione (ēm·mâr·syō′nâ) *f* immersion
linea d' — waterline

immerso (ēm·mâr′sō) *a* immersed

immettere * (ēm·met′tā·rā) *vt* to bring in; *(fig)* to infuse, inspire

immettersi * (ēm·met′târ·sē) *vr* to enter into; to penetrate

immigrante (ēm·mē·grân′tā) *a&m* immigrant

immigrare (ēm·mē·grâ′rā) *vi* to immigrate

immigrato (ēm·mē·grä′tō) *a* immigrant

immigrazione (ēm·mē·grä·tsyō′nä) *f* immigration

imminente (ēm·mē·nän′tā) *a* impending

imminenza (ēm·mē·nän′tsä) *f* imminence

immischiare (ēm·mē·skyâ′rä) *vt* to entangle; to implicate

immischiarsi (ēm·mē·skyâr′sē) *vr* to interfere, meddle

immiserire (ēm·mē·zä·rē′rä) *vt* to impoverish

immiserirsi (ēm·mē·zä·rēr′sē) to become destitute

immissario (ēm·mēs·sâ′ryō) *a* tributary *(river)*

immobile (ēm·mô′bē·lä) *a* motionless; immovable; — *m* property

immobili (ēm·mô′bē·lē) *mpl* property, real estate

immobiliare (ēm·mō·bē·lyâ′rä) *a* pertaining to real estate; **credito** — real estate mortgage

immobilità (ēm·mō·bē·lē·tâ′) *f* immobility; stability

immobilizzare (ēm·mō·bē·lē·dzä′rä) *vt* to immobilize; to freeze *(capital)*

immolare (ēm·mō·lâ′rä) *vt* to sacrifice, offer up

immolarsi (ēm·mō·lâr′sē) *vr* to sacrifice oneself

immolazione (ēm·mō·lâ·tsyō′nä) *f* sacrifice, immolation

immondizia (ēm·mōn·dē′tsyâ) *f* filth; garbage

immondo (ēm·mōn′dō) *a* filthy, impure

immorale (ēm·mō·râ′lä) *a* immoral

immoralità (ēm·mō·râ·lē·tâ′) *f* immorality

immoralmente (ēm·mō·râl·män′tä) *adv* immorally

immortalare (ēm·mōr·tâ·lâ′rä) *vt* to immortalize

immortale (ēm·mōr·tâ′lä) *a* immortal, everlasting

immortalità (ēm·mōr·tâ·lē·tâ′) *f* immortality

immoto (ēm·mō′tō) *a* motionless

immune (ēm·mü′nä) *a* immune; exempt; unhurt

immunità (ēm·mü·nē·tâ′) *f* immunity

immunizzare (ēm·mü·nē·dzâ′rä) *vt* to immunize

immunizzazione (ēm·mü·nē·dzâ·tsyō′nä) *f* immunization

immutabile (ēm·mü·tâ′bē·lä) *a* immutable

immutabilità (ēm·mü·tâ·bē·lē·tâ′) *f* constancy

immutato (ēm·mü·tâ′tō) *a* unchanged, unvaried

imo (ē′mō) *a* lowest; — *m* bottom

impaccare (ēm·pâk·kâ′rä) *vt* to pack, make a package of

impacchettare (ēm·pâk·kät·tâ′rä) *vt* to put in a package; to pack

impacciare (ēm·pâ·châ′rä) *vt* to trouble; to impede, hinder

impacciato (ēm·pâ·châ′tō) *a* embarrassed, ill at ease

impaccio (ēm·pâ′chō) *m* embarrassment; trouble; hindrance; **levarsi d'**— to get out of a difficult situation

impacco (ēm·pâk′kō) *m (med)* compress

impadronirsi (ēm·pâ·drō·nēr′sē) *vr* to get possession, seize; to become master

impagabile (ēm·pâ·gâ′bē·lä) *a* irreplaceable; priceless

impaginare (ēm·pâ·jē·nâ′rä) *vt* to make into pages, paginate

impaginazione (ēm·pâ·jē·nâ·tsyō′nä) *f* numbering of pages, pagination

impagliare (ēm·pâ·lyâ′rä) *vt* to stuff; to cover with straw

impalare (ēm·pâ·lâ′rä) *vt* to impale

impalato (ēm·pâ·lâ′tō) *a* stiff; impaled

impalcatura (ēm·pâl·kâ·tü′râ) *f* scaffolding

impallidire (ēm·pâl·lē·dē′rä) *vi* to turn pale

impalpabile (ēm·pâl·pâ′bē·lä) *a* intangible; inappreciable

impanare (ēm·pâ·nâ′rä) *vt* to bread; to thread *(mech)*

impantanarsi (ēm·pân·tâ·nâr′sē) *vr* to bog down; to get stuck in the mud; to wallow; *(fig)* to get mixed up in

impaperarsi (ēm·pâ·pâ·râr′sē) *vr* to fluff a line *(theat)*; to mispronounce; to stammer

impappinarsi (ēm·pâp·pē·nâr′sē) *vr* to get flustered

imparagonabile (ēm·pâ·râ·gō·nâ′bē·lä) *a* incomparable, peerless

imparare (ēm·pâ·râ′rä) *vt* to learn; — **a memoria** to memorize

impareggiabile (ēm·pâ·râj·jâ′bē·lä) *a* incomparable

imparentarsi (ēm·pâ·rän·târ′sē) *vr* to marry into

imparentato (ēm·pâ·rän·tâ′tō) *a* related

impari (ēm·pâ′rē) *a* odd, uneven; inadequate

impartire (ēm·pâr·tē′rä) *vt* to give, bestow

imparziale (ēm·pâr·tsyâ′lä) *a* impartial

imparzialità (ēm·pâr·tsyâ·lē·tâ′) *f* im-

partiality
imparzialmente (ēm·pâr·tsyâl·mān'tā) *adv* impartially
impassibile (ēm·pâs·sē'bē·lā) *a* impassive; unfeeling, insensible
impassibilità (ēm·pâs·sē·bē·lē·tâ') *f* aloofness, impassiveness
impassibilmente (ēm·pâs·sē·bēl·mān'tā) *adv* impassively, aloofly
impastare (ēm·pâ·stâ'rā) *vt* to knead; to paste
impasticciare (ēm·pâ·stē·châ'rā) *vt* to make a mess of; to soil
impasto (ēm·pâ'stō) *m* mixture
impattare (ēm·pât·tâ'rā) *vi* to be quits; to tie the score
impavidamente (ēm·pâ·vē·dâ·mān'tā) *adv* undauntedly
impavido (ēm·pâ'vē·dō) *a* brave, fearless
impaurire (ēm·pâū·rē'rā) *vt* to frighten
impaurirsi (ēm·pâū·rēr'sē) *vr* to become frightened; to be intimidated
impazientare (ēm·pâ·tsyān·tâ'rā) *vt* to bore; to annoy; to irritate
impazientarsi (ēm·pâ·tsyān·târ'sē) *vr* to get impatient
impazientemente (ēm·pâ·tsyān·tā·mān'-tā) *adv* impatiently
impazienza (ēm·pâ·tsyān'tsâ) *f* impatience
impazzata (ēm·pâ·tsâ'tâ) *f* folly, madness; **all'**— rashly; madly
impazzito (ēm·pâ·tsē'tō) *a* demented
impazzire (ēm·pâ·tsē'rā) *vi* to go mad
impeccabile (ēm·pāk·kâ'bē·lā) *a* impeccable
impeccabilità (ēm·pāk·kâ·bē·lē·tâ') *f* impeccability, flawlessness
impeccabilmente (ēm·pāk·kâ·bēl·mān'tā) *adv* impeccably, faultlessly
impedenza (ēm·pā·dān'tsâ) *f (elec)* impedance
impedimento (ēm·pā·dē·mān'tō) *m* impediment; obstacle, hindrance
impedire (ēm·pā·dē'rā) *vt* to prevent; to impede; — **la circolazione** to block traffic
impegnare (ēm·pā·nyâ'rā) *vt* to pawn; to hire; to pledge
impegnarsi (ēm·pā·nyâr'sē) *vr* to involve oneself; to give one's services
impegnativo (ēm·pā·nyâ·tē'vō) *a* binding, obliging
impegnato (ēm·pā·nyâ'tō) *a* involved; occupied; pawned
impegno (ēm·pā'nyō) *m* pledge; obligation
impegolarsi (ēm·pā·gō·lâr'sē) *vr* to become involved, get mixed up

impellente (ēm·pāl·lān'tā) *a* urgent
impellicciato (ēm·pāl·lē·châ'tō) *a* dressed in furs; furred; veneered *(furniture)*
impenetrabile (ēm·pā·nā·trâ'bē·lā) *a* impenetrable; — **all'aria** airtight
impenetrabilmente (ēm·pā·nā·trâ·bēl·mān'tā) *adv* impenetrably
impenitente (ēm·pā·nē·tān'tā) *a* unrepenting
impennarsi (ēm·pān·nâr'sē) *vr (fig)* to get angry; to rise up on its hind legs
impennato (ēm·pān·nâ'tō) *a* rearing, prancing *(horse)*
impensabile (ēm·pān·sâ'bē·lā) *a* unthinkable
impensato (ēm·pān·sâ'tō) *a* unexpected
impensierire (ēm·pān·syā·rē'rā) *vt* to cause alarm; to worry
impensierirsi (ēm·pān·syā·rēr'sē) *vr* to grow anxious, become uneasy
imperante (ēm·pā·rân'tā) *a* reigning, prevailing
imperativo (ēm·pā·râ·tē'vō) *a* imperative; — *m* imperative *(gram)*
imperatore (ēm·pā·râ·tō'rā) *m* emperor
impercettibile (ēm·pār·chāt·tē'bē·lā) *a* unnoticeable
imperdonabile (ēm·pār·dō·nâ'bē·lā) *a* unpardonable
imperfetto (ēm·pār·fāt'tō) *a* defective; — *m* imperfect *(gram)*
imperfezione (ēm·pār·fā·tsyō'nā) *f* imperfection
imperiale (ēm·pā·ryâ'lā) *a* imperial
imperialismo (ēm·pā·ryâ·lē'zmō) *m* imperialism
imperialista (ēm·pā·ryâ·lē'stâ) *m* imperialist
imperiosamente (ēm·pā·ryō·zâ·mān'tā) *adv* dictatorially
imperioso (ēm·pā·ryō'zō) *a* peremptory; arrogant
imperituro (ēm·pā·rē·tū'rō) *a* undying
imperizia (ēm·pā·rē'tsyâ) *f* awkwardness; lack of skill
impermalirsi (ēm·pār·mâ·lēr'sē) *vr* to resent; to take offense
impermeabile (ēm·pār·mā·â'bē·lā) *a* waterproof; — *m* raincoat
imperniare (ēm·pār·nyâ'rā) *vt* to pivot; to base; to found
impero (ēm·pā'rō) *m* empire
imperseveranza (ēm·pār·sā·vā·rân'tsâ) *f* inconstancy
impersonare (ēm·pār·sō·nâ'rā) *vt* to impersonate
imperterrito (ēm·pār·ter'rē·tō) *a* fearless, intrepid

â ârm, ā bāby, e bet, ē bē, ō gō, ô gône, ū blūe, b bad, ch child, d dad, f fat, g gay, j jet

impertinente (ēm·pär·tē·nän'tā) *a* impertinent, saucy, fresh

impertinenza (ēm·pär·tē·nän'tsâ) *f* impudence, impertinence

imperturbabile (ēm·pär·tūr·bâ'bē·lä) *a* imperturbable, calm, serene

imperturbabilità (ēm·pär·tūr·bâ·bē·lē·tâ') *f* calmness, serenity

imperturbabilmente (ēm·pär·tūr·bâ·bēl·män'tā) *adv* imperturbably, calmly

imperversare (ēm·pär·vär·sâ'rä) *vi* to storm, rage *(weather)*; to become furious, rampage

impervio (ēm·per'vyō) *a* impervious

impetigine (ēm·pä·tē'jē·nä) *f (med)* impetigo

impeto (ēm'pä·tō) *m* impetus; **di primo —** impulsively; at first; **fare — su** to attack; **pieno d'—** vigorous

impettito (ēm·pät·tē'tō) *a* stiff; erect; **camminare —** to strut

impetuosamente (ēm·pä·twō·zâ·män'tā) *adv* impulsively; violently

impetuosità (ēm·pä·twō·zē·tâ') *f* impetuousness; fervor

impetuoso (ēm·pä·twō'zō) *a* impetuous

impiantare (ēm·pyân·tâ'rä) *vt* to plant; to set up; to establish

impiantito (ēm·pyân·tē'tō) *m* flooring

impianto (ēm·pyân'tō) *m* installation, establishment; plant *(com)*; **spese d'—** initial expenses

impiastro (ēm·pyâ'strō) *m* poultice; *(fig)* bore

impiccagione (ēm·pēk·kâ·jō'nä) *f* hanging *(person)*

impiccare (ēm·pēk·kâ'rä) *vt* to hang *(person)*

impiccato (ēm·pēk·kâ'tō) *a&m* hanged

impicciarsi (ēm·pē·chär'sē) *vr* to meddle, become involved

impiccio (ēm·pē'chō) *m* trouble; obstacle

impiccolire (ēm·pēk·kō·lē'rä) *vt* to diminish, reduce

impiccolirsi (ēm·pēk·kō·lēr'sē) *vr* to diminish, grow smaller

impiegare (ēm·pyä·gâ'rä) *vt* to employ; to use; *(com)* to invest

impiegarsi (ēm·pyä·gâr'sē) *vr* to be hired; to find a job

impiegato (ēm·pyä·gâ'tō) *m* employee; clerk; **—** *a* employed

impiego (ēm·pyä'gō) *m* employment, job; use; investment

impigliarsi (ēm·pē·lyâr'sē) *vr* to get entangled; to be caught in

impinguare (ēm·pēn·gwâ'rä) *vt* to fatten

impiombare (ēm·pyōm·bâ'rä) *vt* to cover

with lead; to fill *(tooth)*

impiparsi (ēm·pē·pär'sē) *vr* not to give a hang; to be totally unconcerned

implacabile (ēm·plâ·kâ'bē·lä) *a* unrelenting; implacable

implacabilità (ēm·plâ·kâ·bē·lē·tâ') *f* implacability

implacabilmente (ēm·plâ·kâ·bēl·män'tä) *adv* unrelentingly, implacably

implicare (ēm·plē·kâ'rä) *vt* to involve; to imply

implicitamente (ēm·plē·chē·tâ·män'tä) *adv* implicity

implicito (ēm·plē'chē·tō) *a* implicit

implorare (ēm·plō·râ'rä) *vt* to implore

implorazione (ēm·plō·râ·tsyō'nä) *f* imploring, entreaty

implume (ēm·plū'mä) *a* without feathers

impolverare (ēm·pōl·vä·râ'rä) *vt* to cover with dust, make dusty

impolverarsi (ēm·pōl·vä·râr'sē) *vr* to get dusty

imponente (ēm·pō·nän'tä) *a* imposing

imponenza (ēm·pō·nän'tsâ) *f* impressiveness, grandeur

imponibile (ēm·pō·nē'bē·lä) *a* taxable

impopolare (ēm·pō·pō·lâ'rä) *a* unpopular

impopolarità (ēm·pō·pō·lâ·rē·tâ') *f* unpopularity

imporre * (ēm·pōr'rä) *vt* to impose; to inflict

imporsi * (ēm·pōr'sē) *vr* to impose upon; to intrude oneself

importante (ēm·pōr·tân'tä) *a* important

importanza (ēm·pōr·tân'tsâ) *f* importance; **darsi —** to give oneself airs; to throw one's weight around

importare (ēm·pōr·tâ'rä) *vt* to import; **—** *vi* to matter, be of concern

importatore (ēm·pōr·tâ·tō'rä) *m* importer

importazione (ēm·pōr·tâ·tsyō'nä) *f* importation, import

importo (ēm·pōr'tō) *m* cost, amount

importunare (ēm·pōr·tū·nâ'rä) *vt* to importune; to bother

importuno (ēm·pōr·tū·nō) *a* inopportune; annoying; troublesome

imposizione (ēm·pō·zē·tsyō'nä) *f* imposition

impossessarsi (ēm·pōs·sās·sâr'sē) *vr* to get possession of

impossibile (ēm·pōs·sē'bē·lä) *a* impossible

impossibilità (ēm·pōs·sē·bē·lē·tâ') *f* impossibility

imposta (ēm·pō'stâ) *f* tax; shutter

impostazione (ēm·pō·stâ·tsyō'nä) *f* statement; mailing; setting up, positioning

---

k kid, **l** let, **m** met, **n** not, **p** pat, **r** very, **s** sat, **sh** shop, **t** tell, **v** vat, **w** we, **y** yes, **z** zero

impostare (ēm·pō·stä'rā) *vt* to mail; to place

impostore (ēm·pō·stō'rā) *m* impostor

impostura (ēm·pō·stū'râ) *f* imposture; deception; swindle

impotente (ēm·pō·tän'tā) *a* impotent; powerless

impotenza (ēm·pō·tän'tsä) *f* impotence

impoverire (ēm·pō·vä·rē'rā) *vt* to impoverish

impraticabile (ēm·prâ·tē·kâ'bē·lä) *a* impassable; not feasible; impracticable; impractical

imprecare (ēm·prā·kâ'rā) *vi* to curse

imprecazione (ēm·prā·kâ·tsyō'nä) *f* curse, imprecation

imprecisabile (ēm·prā·chē·zâ'bē·lä) *a* undeterminable

imprecisione (ēm·prā·chē·zyō'nä) *f* inaccuracy; lack of precision

impreciso (ēm·prā·chē'zō) *a* vague

impregnare (ēm·prā·nyâ'rā) *vt* to impregnate

imprendere (ēm·pren'dä·rā) *vt* to undertake; to start

imprendibile (ēm·prän·dē'bē·lä) *a* untakeable; unassailable; impregnable

imprenditore (ēm·prän·dē·tō'rā) *m* contractor

impreparato (ēm·prā·pâ·râ'tō) *a* unprepared

impreparazione (ēm·prā·pâ·râ·tsyō'nä) *f* lack of preparation

impresa (ēm·prā'zä) *f* undertaking; exploit; *(com)* firm; *(theat)* management

impresario (ēm·prā·zâ'ryō) *m* contractor; *(theat)* impresario; — **di pompe funebri** mortician

imprescindibile (ēm·prā·shēn·dē'bē·lä) *a* unavoidable; indispensable

impressionabile (ēm·präs·syō·nâ'bē·lä) *a* sensitive, impressionable

impressionare (ēm·präs·syō·nâ'rā) *vt* to stir; to impress

impressionarsi (ēm·präs·syō·nâr'sē) *vr* to be deeply stirred

impressione (ēm·präs·syō'nä) *f* impression

impressionismo (ēm·präs·syō·nē'zmō) *m* impressionism

impressionista (ēm·präs·syō·nē'stä) *m* impressionist

impresso (ēm·präs'sō) *a* pressed; imprinted, engraved

impressore (ēm·präs·sō'rā) *m* pressman *(print)*

imprevedibile (ēm·prā·vä·dē'bē·lä) *a* unforeseeable

imprevidente (ēm·prā·vē·dän'tä) *a* improvident

imprevisto (ēm·prā·vē'stō) *a* unforeseen

imprigionamento (ēm·prē·jō·nâ·män'tō) *m* confinement, imprisonment

imprigionare (ēm·prē·jō·nâ'rā) *vt* to imprison

imprimere * (ēm·prē'mä·rā) *vt* to impress; to print; to engrave

improbabile (ēm·prō·bâ'bē·lä) *a* improbable

improbabilità (ēm·prō·bâ·bē·lē·tâ') *f* improbability

improbabilmente (ēm·prō·bâ·bēl·män'tä) *adv* improbably

improbo (ēm'prō·bō) *a* dishonest; wicked; *(fig)* hard, difficult

impronta (ēm·prōn'tâ) *f* print; mark; — **digitale** fingerprint

improperio (ēm·prō·pe'ryō) *m* abuse, insult, impropriety

impropriamente (ēm·prō·pryâ·män'tä) *adv* improperly

improprietà (ēm·prō·pryä·tâ') *f* impropriety

improprio (ēm·prô'pryō) *a* improper, unbecoming

improrogabile (ēm·prō·rō·gâ'bē·lä) *a* not postponable, not deferrable

improrogabilmente (ēm·prō·rō·gâ·bēl·män'tä) *adv* without delay, without postponement

improvvido (ēm·prôv'vē·dō) *a* improvident

improvvisamente (ēm·prōv·vē·zâ·män'tä) *adv* suddenly; unexpectedly

improvvisare (ēm·prōv·vē·zâ'rā) *vi* to improvise; to extemporize; to ad-lib

improvvisazione (ēm·prōv·vē·zâ·tsyō'nä) *f* extemporization, improvisation

improvviso (ēm·prōv·vē'zō) *a* unforeseen; sudden; **all'** — suddenly

imprudente (ēm·prū·dän'tä) *a* imprudent

imprudentemente (ēm·prū·dän·tä·män'tä) *adv* rashly

imprudenza (ēm·prū·dän'tsä) *f* imprudence

impudente (ēm·pū·dän'tä) *a* impudent

impudenza (ēm·pū·dän'tsä) *f* impudence, brazenness

impudicamente (ēm·pū·dē·kâ·män'tä) *adv* immodestly, shamelessly

impudicizia (ēm·pū·dē·chē'tsyâ) *f* shamelessness, immodesty

impugnabile (ēm·pū·nyâ'bē·lä) *a* questionable; impugnable

impugnare (ēm·pū·nyâ'rā) *vt* to contest; to grip

impugnatura (ēm·pū·nyâ·tū'râ) *f* grip

(hand); hilt

impulsivo (ēm·pūl·sē'vō) *a* impulsive

impulso (ēm·pūl'sō) *m* impulse; **dare — a** to set in motion, put into operation

impunemente (ēm·pū·nā·mān'tā) *adv* with impunity

impunità (ēm·pū·nē·tâ') *f* impunity

impuntarsi (ēm·pūn·târ'sē) *vr* to be stubborn

impuntigliarsi (ēm·pūn·tē·lyâr'sē) *vr* to be obstinate; to get it into one's head

impuramente (ēm·pū·râ·mān'tā) *adv* impurely

impurità (ēm·pū·rē·tâ') *f* impurity

impuro (ēm·pū'rō) *a* impure

imputare (ēm·pū·tâ'rā) *vt* to blame, accuse; *(law)* to indict

imputato (ēm·pū·tâ'tō) *m (law)* defendant; **— a** accused

imputazione (ēm·pū·tâ·tsyō'nā) *f* accusation

imputridire (ēm·pū·trē·dē'rā) *vi* to rot

in (ēn) *prep* in; at; by; to; into

inabile (ē·nâ'bē·lā) *a* unable; unfit

inabilità (ē·nâ·bē·lē·tâ') *f* inability

inabissare (ē·nâ·bēs·sâ'rā) *vt* to engulf; to sink

inabissarsi (ē·nâ·bēs·sâr'sē) *vr* to be submerged, sink

inaccessibile (ē·nâ·chās·sē'bē·lā) *a* inaccessible

inaccettabile (ēn·nâ·chāt·tâ'bē·lā) *a* unacceptable

inacidire (ē·nâ·chē·dē'rā) *vt&i* to sour

inadattabile (ē·nâ·dât·tâ'bē·lā) *a* unadaptable

inadeguato (ē·nâ·dā·gwâ'tō) *a* inadequate

inadempiuto (ē·nâ·dām·pyū'tō) *a* uncompleted; unfulfilled

inadoprabile (ē·nâ·dō·prâ'bē·lā) *a* unusable

inalare (ē·nâ·lâ'rā) *vt* to inhale

inalatore (ē·nâ·lâ·tō'rā) *m* inhaler *(med)*

inalazione (ē·nâ·lâ·tsyō'nā) *f* inhalation

inalberare (ē·nâl·bâ·râ'rā) *vt* to hoist

inalienabile (ē·nâ·lyā·nâ'bē·lā) *a* inalienable

inalienare (ē·nâ·lyā·nâ'rā) *vt* to estrange, alienate

inalterabile (ē·nâl·tā·râ'bē·lā) *a* unalterable

inalterato (ē·nâl·tā·râ'tō) *a* unaltered, unchanged

inamidare (ē·nâ·mē·dâ'rā) *vt* to starch

inammissibile (ē·nâm·mēs·sē'bē·lā) *a* inadmissible

inamovibile (ē·nâ·mō·vē'bē·lā) *a* irremovable

inane (ē·nâ'nā) *a* vapid; inane

inanimato (ē·nâ·nē·mâ'tō) *a* inanimate

inanizione (ē·nâ·nē·tsyō'nā) *f* exhaustion; emptiness, vapidness

inappetenza (ē·nâp·pā·tān'tsâ) *f* lack of appetite

inapplicabile (ē·nâp·plē·kâ'bē·lā) *a* inapplicable

inapprezzabile (ē·nâp·prā·tsâ'bē·lā) *a* imperceptible; invaluable

inaridire (ē·nâ·rē·dē'rā) *vt* to dry up

inaridirsi (ē·nâ·rē·dēr'sē) *vr* to become sere, grow arid

inarrivabile (ē·nâr·rē·vâ'bē·lā) *a* unsurpassable; unattainable

inarticolato (ē·nâr·tē·kō·lâ'tō) *a* inarticulate

inaspettatamente (ē·nâ·spāt·tâ·tâ·mān'-tā) *adv* unexpectedly

inaspettato (ē·nâ·spāt·tâ'tō) *a* unexpected

inasprimento (ē·nâ·sprē·mān'tō) *m* aggravation; embitterment; harshness

inasprire (ē·nâ·sprē'rā) *vt* to embitter

inasprirsi (ē·nâ·sprēr'sē) *vr* to become exasperated; to grow embittered

inattivo (ē·nât·tē'vō) *a* inactive

inaudito (ē·nâū·dē'tō) *a* unprecedented; unheard-of

inaugurale (ē·nâū·gū·râ'lā) *a* inaugural

inaugurare (ē·nâū·gū·râ'rā) *vt* to inaugurate

inaugurazione (ē·nâū·gū·râ·tsyō'nā) *f* inauguration

incagliare (ēn·kâ·lyâ'rā) *vi* to be stranded; to be brought to a halt; **— vt** to jam; to obstruct, bring to a halt

incagliarsi (ēn·kâ·lyâr'sē) *vr* to be hindered; to run aground

incaglio (ēn·kâ'lyō) *m* deterrent; *(fig)* deadlock

incalcolabile (ēn·kâl·kō·lâ'bē·lā) *a* incalculable, uncountable

incallire (ēn·kâl·lē'rā) *vi* to become callous; to get hard

incalzante (ēn·kâl·tsân'tā) *a* in pursuit, chasing

incalzare (ēn·kâl·tsâ'rā) *vt* to press, harass; to pursue

incamerare (ēn·kâ·mā·râ'rā) *vt* to appropriate; to annex

incamminare (ēn·kâm·mē·nâ'rā) *vt* to set in motion; to give a start to

incamminarsi (ēn·kâm·mē·nâr'sē) *vr* to start out; to set out for

incanalare (ēn·kâ·nâ·lâ'rā) *vt* to channel

incancellabile (ēn·kân·chāl·lâ'bē·lā) *a* unforgettable; indelible, irradicable

incandescente (ēn·kân·dā·shān'tā) *a* in-

---

k kid, **l** let, **m** met, **n** not, **p** pat, **r** very, **s** sat, **sh** shop, **t** tell, **v** vat, **w** we, **y** yes, **z** zero

candescent

incantare (ēn·kân·tâ'rā) *vt* to charm

incantatore (ēn·kân·tâ·tō'rā) *m* enchanter, charmer

incantesimo (ēn·kân·te'zē·mō) *m* charm; enchantment; magic, sorcery

incantevole (ēn·kân·te'vō·lā) *a* enchanting

incanto (ēn·kân'tō) *m* magic; charm; auction sale

incapace (ēn·kâ·pâ'chā) *a* incapable

incapacità (ēn·kâ·pâ·chē·tâ') *f* incapacity, inability

incappare (ēn·kâp·pâ'rā) *vi* to run into, come upon

incappucciare (ēn·kâp·pū·châ'rā) *vt* to hood; to bundle up

incarcerare (ēn·kâr·chā·râ'rā) *vt* to imprison

incarcerazione (ēn·kâr·chā·râ·tsyō'nā) *f* incarceration, imprisonment

incaricare (ēn·kâ·rē·kâ'rā) *vt* to entrust

incaricarsi (ēn·kâ·rē·kâr'sē) *vr* to take upon oneself

incaricato (ēn·kâ·rē·kâ'tō) *a* entrusted, charged; — *m* agent; — **d'affari** chargé d'affaires

incarico (ēn·kâ'rē·kō) *m* appointment; duty; task

incartare (ēn·kâr·tâ'rā) *vt* to wrap in paper

incassare (ēn·kâs·sâ'rā) *vt* to cash; to collect; to case

incasso (ēn·kâs'sō) *m* collection, take

incastonare (ēn·kâ·stō·nâ'rā) *vt* to set *(gems)*

incastrare (ēn·kâ·strâ'rā) *vt* to insert, fit in

incastrarsi (ēn·kâ·strâr'sē) *vr* to be embedded; to fit in

incastro (ēn·kâ'strō) *m* recess *(arch)*; groove, joint; — **a coda di rondine** dovetailing

incatenare (ēn·kâ·tā·nâ'rā) *vt* to chain; *(fig)* to fascinate

incatramare (ēn·kâ·trâ·mâ'rā) *vt* to tar

incautamente (ēn·kâū·tâ·mān'tā) ' *adv* rashly, carelessly

incauto (ēn·kâ'ū·tō) *a* incautious, rash

incavato (ēn·kâ·vâ'tō) *a* hollow

incavo (ēn·kâ'vō) *m* hole; hollow

incendiare (ēn·chān·dyâ'rā) *vt* to put fire to

incendiario (ēn·chān·dyâ'ryō) *m* arsonist

incendiarsi (ēn·chān·dyâr'sē) *vr* to catch fire

incendio (ēn·chen'dyō) *m* fire; — **doloso** arson

incenerire (ēn·chā·nā·rē'rā) *vt* to incinerate

incensamento (ēn·chān·sâ·mân'tō) *m (fig)* flattery; incensing

incensare (ēn·chān·sâ'rā) *vt* to incense; *(fig)* to flatter

incenso (ēn·chān'sō) *m* incense; *(fig)* flattery

incensurabile (ēn·chān·sū·râ'bē·lā) *a* above criticism

incensurato (ēn·chān·sū·râ'tō) *a* uncensured

incentivo (ēn·chān·tē'vō) *m* incentive

incepparsi (ēn·chāp·pâr'sē) *vr* to jam, become obstructed

incerare (ēn·chā·râ'rā) *vt* to wax *(surface)*

incerata (ēn·chā·râ'tâ) *f* oilskin

incertezza (ēn·chār·tā'tsâ) *f* uncertainty; indecision; **tenere nell'**—; to keep in suspense; — **del tempo** unsettled weather

incerto (ēn·chār'tō) *a* dubious, uncertain; irresolute; **luce incerta** dim light; — *m* uncertainty; gratuity, perquisite

incerti (ēn·chār'tē) *mpl* perquisites

incessante (ēn·chās·sân'tā) *a* incessant; **—mente** (ēn·chās·sân·tā·mân'tā) *adv* incessantly

incetta (ēn·chāt'tâ) *f* cornering *(goods)*; buying up

incettare (ēn·chāt·tâ'rā) *vt* to buy up; to corner *(goods)*

inchiesta (ēn·kyā'stâ) *f* investigation; inquiry; inquest

inchinare (ēn·kē·nâ'rā) *vt* to bend; — *vi* to bow

inchinarsi (ēn·kē·nâr'sē) *vr* to lower oneself; to bow to

inchino (ēn·kē'nō) *m* bow

inchiodare (ēn·kyō·dâ'rā) *vt* to rivet; to nail; — **al letto** *(fig)* to confine to bed

inchiostro (ēn·kyō'strō) *m* ink

inciampare (ēn·châm·pâ'rā) *vi* to stumble, trip

inciampo (ēn·châm'pō) *m* obstacle, hindrance; *(fig)* difficulty

incidentalmente (ēn·chē·dân·tâl·mān'tā) *adv* accidentally; incidentally

incidente (ēn·chē·dân'tā) *m* accident; incident; — **automobilistico** automobile accident

incidere * (ēn·chē'dā·rā) *vt* to engrave; to record; to cut into; — **una canzone** to record a song; — **all'acquaforte** to etch

incinta (ēn·chēn'tâ) *a* pregnant

incipriare (ēn·chē·pryâ'rā) *vt* to powder

incipriarsi (ēn·chē·pryâr'sē) *vr* to powder oneself; to put on powder

---

â ârm, **ā** bāby, **e** bet, **ē** bē, **ō** gō, **ô** gône, **ū** blūe, **b** bad, **ch** child, **d** dad, **f** fat, **g** gay, **j** jet

incisione (ēn·chē·zyō′nā) *f* engraving; etching; incision

incisivo (ēn·chē·zē′vō) *a* incisive; — *m* incisor

incisore (ēn·chē·zō′rā) *m* engraver

incitamento (ēn·chē·tâ·mān′tō) *m* incitement

incitare (ēn·chē·tâ′rā) *vt* to incite

incivile (ēn·chē·vē′lā) *a* uncivilized; ill-mannered, discourteous

incivilirsi (ēn·chē·vē·lēr′sē) *vr* to become civilized

inclemente (ēn·klā·mān′tā) *a* inclement

inclinare (ēn·klē·nâ′rā) *vt&i* to bend; to incline; to be inclined

inclinarsi (ēn·klē·nâr′sē) *vr* to incline toward; to lean

inclinazione (ēn·klē·nâ·tsyō′nā) *f* inclination

incline (ēn·klē′nā) *a* apt to; inclined

includere * (ēn·klū′dā·rā) *vt* to include

inclusione (ēn·klū·zyō′nā) *f* inclusion

incluso (ēn·klū′zō) *a* included

incoerente (ēn·kō·ā·rān′tā) *a* incoherent; inconsistent

incognita (ēn·kô′nyē·tâ) *f* unknown quantity

incognito (ēn·kô′nyē·tō) *a* unknown; **in** — incognito

incollare (ēn·kōl·lâ′rā) *vt* to glue, paste

incollerito (ēn·kōl·lā·rē′tō) *a* angry

incollerirsi (ēn·kōl·lā·rēr′sē) *vr* to get angry

incolore (ēn·kō·lō′rā) *a* colorless

incolpabilità (ēn·kōl·pâ·bē·lē·tâ′) *f* innocence

incolpare (ēn·kōl·pâ′rā) *vt* to blame

incolto (ēn·kōl′tō) *a* uncouth; uncultivated

incolume (ēn·kô′lū·mā) *a* uninjured, safe and sound

incolumità (ēn·kō·lū·mē·tâ′) *f* safety

incombenza (ēn·kōm·bān′tsâ) *f* task; errand

incombere (ēn·kôm′bā·rā) *vi* to be incumbent; to impend

incombustibile (ēn·kōm·bū·stē′bē·lā) *a* fireproof; incombustible

incominciare (ēn·kō·mēn·châ′rā) *vt&i* to begin, start

incommestibile (ēn·kōm·mā·stē′bē·lā) *a* inedible

incomodare (ēn·kō·mō·dâ′rā) *vt* to disturb

incomodarsi (ēn·kō·mō·dâr′sē) *vr* to take the trouble, trouble oneself

incomodità (ēn·kō·mō·dē·tâ′) *f* annoyance; trouble; discomfort

incomodo (ēn·kô′mō·dō) *m* trouble; — *a* bothersome; uncomfortable

incomparabile (ēn·kōm·pâ·râ′bē·lā) *a* incomparable

incompatibile (ēn·kōm·pâ·tē′bē·lā) *a* inconsistent; incompatible

incompatibilità (ēn·kōm·pâ·tē·bē·lē·tâ′) *f* inconsistency; incompatibility

incompetente (ēn·kōm·pā·tān′tā) *a* incompetent

incompleto (ēn·kōm·plā′tō) *a* incomplete

incomprensibile (ēn·kōm·prān·sē′bē·lā) *a* incomprehensible

incomprensione (ēn·kōm·prān·syō′nā) *f* incomprehension, misunderstanding

incompreso (ēn·kōm·prā′zō) *a* unappreciated; misunderstood

inconcepibile (ēn·kōn·chā·pē′bē·lā) *a* inconceivable

incondizionatamente (ēn·kōn·dē·tsyō·nâ·tâ·mān′tā) *f* unreservedly, unconditionally

incondizionato (ēn·kōn·dē·tsyō·nâ′tō) *a* unconditional

inconfessabile (ēn·kōn·fās·sâ′bē·lā) *a* unmentionable

inconfondibile (ēn·kōn·fōn·dē′bē·lā) *a* unmistakable

inconfutabile (ēn·kōn·fū·tâ′bē·lā) *a* irrefutable

incongruente (ēn·kōn·grūān′tā) *a* incongruous

incongruenza (ēn·kōn·grūān′tsâ) *f* incongruity

inconsapevole (ēn·kōn·sâ·pe′vō·lā) *a* unaware; unconscious; unknowing

inconsapevolmente (ēn·kōn·sâ·pā·vōl·mān′tā) unwittingly, unknowingly

inconsiderato (ēn·kōn·sē·dā·râ′tō) *a* inconsiderate; rash

inconsistente (ēn·kōn·sē·stān′tā) *a* unfounded; inconsistent

inconsolabile (ēn·kōn·sō·lâ′bē·lā) *a* inconsolable

inconsueto (ēn·kōn·swā′tō) *a* unusual

incontaminato (ēn·kōn·tâ·mē·nâ′tō) *a* stainless; uncontaminated

incontentabile (ēn·kōn·tān·tâ′bē·lā) *a* exacting; impossible to please; never satisfied

incontrare (ēn·kōn·trâ′rā) *vt* to meet; — **favore** to be successful

incontrarsi (ēn·kōn·trâr′sē) *vr* to meet, get together

incontro (ēn·kōn′trō) *m* meeting; match *(sport)*; — *prep* towards, to; **andare** — **a qualcuno** to go to meet someone; **andare** — **a spese** to incure expenses;

andare — al pericolo to face danger
inconveniente (ēn·kŏn·vā·nyän'tā) *m* inconvenience; **—** *a* inconvenient; unbecoming
incoraggiamento (ēn·kŏ·râj·jâ·män'tō) *m* encouragement; **per —** by way of encouragement
incoraggiante (ēn·kŏ·râj·jân'tā) *a* encouraging
incoraggiare (ēn·kŏ·râj·jâ'rā) *vt* to encourage
incoraggiarsi (ēn·kŏ·râj·jâr'sē) *vr* to take heart, muster one's courage
incoronare (ēn·kŏ·rō·nâ'rā) *vt* to crown
incoronazione (ēn·kŏ·rō·nâ·tsyō'nä) *f* coronation
incorporare (ēn·kŏr·pō·râ'rā) *vt* to annex; to incorporate
incorporarsi (ēn·kŏr·pō·râr'sē) *vr* to be incorporated
incorreggibile (ēn·kŏr·râj·jē'bē·lä) *a* incorregible
incorrere * (ēn·kôr'rā·rā) *vi* to incur
incorrettamente (ēn·kŏr·rāt·tâ·män'tā) *adv* incorrectly
incorrettezza (ēn·kŏr·rāt·tā'tsä) *f* incorrectness
incorruttibile (ēn·kŏr·rūt·tē'bē·lä) *a* incorruptible
incosciente (ēn·kŏ·shän'tā) *a* unconscious; irresponsible
incoscienza (ēn·kŏ·shän'tsä) *f* unconsciousness; lack of responsibility
incostante (ēn·kŏ·stän'tā) *a* changeable; fickle, inconstant
incostituzionale (ēn·kŏ·stē·tū·tsyō·nâ'lä) *a* unconstitutional
incredibile (ēn·krä·dē'bē·lä) *a* incredible
incrementare (en·krä·män·tâ'rā) *vt* to increase
incremento (ēn·krä·män'tō) *m* increase, increment; **dare — a** to favour; to foster
increscioso (ēn·krä·shō'zō) *a* unpleasant, regrettable
incriminare (ēn·krē·mē·nâ'rā) *vt* to impeach; to incriminate
incriminazione (ēn·krē·mē·nâ·tsyō'nä) *f* impeachement; accusation
incrinatura (ēn·krē·nâ·tū'râ) *f* flaw; crack
incrociare (ēn·krō·châ'rā) *vt* to cross; **— le braccia** to fold one's arms
incrociato (ēn·krō·châ'tō) *a* crossed; **parole incrociate** crossword puzzle
incrociatore (ēn·krō·châ·tō'rā) *m* (*naut*) cruiser
incrocio (ēn·krô'chō) *m* crossing; junction

incrostare (ēn·krō·stâ'rā) *vt* to encrust
incrostarsi (ēn·krō·stâr'sē) *vr* to become encrusted
incubatrice (ēn·kū·bâ·trē'chä) *f* incubator
incubazione (ēn·kū·bâ·tsyō'nä) *f* incubation
incubo (ēn'kū·bō) *m* nightmare
incudine (ēn·kū'dē·nä) *f* anvil
inculcare (ēn·kūl·kâ'rā) *vt* to impress; to inculcate
incurabile (ēn·kū·râ'bē·lä) *a* incurable
incurante (ēn·kū·rân'tā) *a* negligent, heedless, careless
incuranza (ēn·kū·rân'tsâ) *f* inaccuracy; carelessness
incuriosire (ēn·kū·ryō·zē'rā) *vt* to make curious
incuriosirsi (ēn·kū·ryō·zēr'sē) *vr* to become curious
incursionare (ēn·kūr·syō·nâ'rā) *vt* to raid; to make inroads upon
incursione (ēn·kūr·syō'nä) *f* inroad; raid
incutere * (ēn·kū'tā·rā) *vt* to command; to inspire
indaffarato (ēn·dâf·fâ·râ'tō) *a* very busy
indagare (ēn·dâ·gâ'rā) *vt* to investigate
indagine (ēn·dâ'jē·nä) *f* investigation; poll; research
indebitamente (ēn·dâ·bē·tâ·män'tā) *adv* unduly; improperly
indebitarsi (ēn·dâ·bē·târ'sē) *vr* to get into debt
indebito (ēn·de'bē·tō) *a* undue; unbecoming; **appropriazione indebita** embezzlement
indebolimento (ēn·dâ·bō·lē·män'tō) *m* weakening
indebolire (ēn·dâ·bō·lē'rā) *vt&i* to weaken
indebolirsi (ēn·dâ·bō·lēr'sē) *vr* to become weak
indecente (ēn·dâ·chân'tā) *a* indecent
indecenza (ēn·dâ·chân'tsâ) *f* indecency; **e un'—** it's a shame
indecisione (ēn·nâ·chē·zyō'nä) *f* indecision; hesitation
indeciso (ēn·dâ·chē'zō) *a* not decided; irresolute
indecoroso (ēn·dâ·kō·rō'zō) *a* indecorous
indefesso (ēn·dâ·fâs'sō) *a* tireless
indefinibile (ēn·dâ·fē·nē'bē·lä) *a* hard to define; indescribable
indefinito (ēn·dâ·fē·nē'tō) *a* indefinite
indegnamente (ēn·dâ·nyâ·män'tā) *adv* unworthily
indegnità (ēn·dâ·nyē·tâ') *f* indignity; unworthiness
indegno (ēn·dā'nyō) *a* unworthy

indelebile (ēn·dā·le′bē·lā) *a* indelible

indelicatezza (ēn·dā·lē·kâ·tā′tsâ) *f* indelicacy

indelicato (ēn·dā·lē·kâ′tō) *a* indelicate

indemagliabile (ēn·dā·mâ·lyâ′bē·lā) *a* runproof

indemoniato (ēn·dā·mō·nyâ′tō) *a* possessed, demonic

indennità (ēn·dān·nē·tâ′) *f* indemnity

indennizzare (ēn·dān·nē·dzâ′rā) *vt* to compensate for; to indemnify

indennizzo (ēn·dān·nē′dzō) *m* compensation; indemnity

indescrivibile (ēn·dā·skrē·vē′bē·lā) *a* indescribable

indeterminato (ēn·dā·tār·mē·nâ′tō) *a* indeterminate, indefinite

indetto (ēn·dāt′tō) *a* established; fixed; announced

India (ēn′dyâ) *f* India

indiano (ēn·dyâ′nō) *a* Indian; **in fila indiana** in single file; **far l'—** to feign ignorance

indiavolato (ēn·dyâ·vō·lâ′tō) *a* difficult; furious; devilish

indicante (ēn·dē·kân′tā) *a* indicative of, indicating

indicare (ēn·dē·kâ′rā) *vt* to indicate; to point at; to mean

indicativo (ēn·dē·kâ·tē′vō) *a* indicative

indicato (ēn·dē·kâ′tō) *a* suitable, right

indicatore (ēn·dē·kâ·tō′rā) *m* indicator; sign; directory

indicazione (ēn·dē·kâ·tsyō′nā) *f* indication; information

indice (ēn′dē·chā) *m* index; sign *(fig)*

indicibile (ēn·dē·chē′bē·lā) *a* hard to express; unutterable

indietreggiare (ēn·dyā·trāj·jâ′rā) *vi* to draw back; to fall back; to back up

indietro (ēn·dyā′trō) *adv* behind, back; **voltarsi —** to turn round; **all'—** backwards; **essere —** to run slow *(watch)*

indifferente (ēn·dēf·fā·rān′tā) *a* indifferent

indifferenza (ēn·dēf·fā·rān′tsâ) *f* indifference; coldness

indigeno (ēn·dē′jā·nō) *a&m* native

indigente (ēn·dē·jân′tā) *a* indigent, destitute

indigeribile (ēn·dē·jā·rē′bē·lā) *a* indigestible

indigestione (ēn·dē·jā·styō′nā) *f* indigestion; **fare —** to eat too much

indigesto (ēn·dē·jā′stō) *a* indigestible; unpleasant, tiresome

indignare (ēn·dē·nyâ′rā) *vt* to make indignant; to anger

indignarsi (ēn·dē·nyâr′sē) *vr* to become indignant; to get angry

indignazione (ēn·dē·nyâ·tsyō′nā) *f* indignation

indimenticabile (ēn·dē·mān·tē·kâ′bē·lā) *adv* unforgettable

indipendente (ēn·dē·pān·dān′tā) *a* independent

indipendentemente (ēn·dē·pān·dān·tā·mān′tā) *adv* independently

indipendenza (ēn·dē·pān·dān′tsâ) *f* independence

indire * (ēn·dē′rā) *vt* to order; to notify; **— una riunione** to call a meeting

indirettamente (ēn·dē·rāt·tâ·mān′tā) *adv* indirectly

indiretto (ēn·dē·rāt′tō) *a* indirect

indirizzare (ēn·dē·rē·tsâ′rā) *vt* to direct; to address *(mail)*

indirizzario (ēn·dē·rē·tsâ′ryō) *m* mailing list

indirizzarsi (ēn·dē·rē·tsâr′sē) *vr* to apply oneself to; to go toward

indirizzo (ēn·dē·rē′tsō) *m* address *(mail)*; course, direction

indisciplina (ēn·dē·shē·plē′nâ) *f* unruliness, lack of discipline

indisciplinato (ēn·dē·shē·plē·nâ′tō) *a* unruly, lacking in discipline

indiscretamente (ēn·dē·skrā·tâ·mān′tā) *adv* indiscreetly

indiscreto (ēn·dē·skrā′tō) *a* indiscreet

indiscrezione (ēn·dē·skrā·tsyō′nā) *f* indiscretion

indiscusso (ēn·dē·skūs′sō) *a* undisputed; undiscussed

indispensabile (ēn·dē·span·sâ′bē·lā) *a* indispensable; necessary; **— m** necessity

indispensabilmente (ēn·dē·span·sâ·bēl·mān′tā) *adv* indispensably, necessarily

indispettire (ēn·dē·spāt·tē′rā) *vt* to irritate; to annoy

indispettirsi (ēn·dē·spāt·tēr′sē) *vr* to get irritated, become vexed

indisporre * (ēn·dē·spōr′rā) *vt* to disincline; to upset

indisposizione (ēn·dē·spō·zē·tsyō′nā) *f* indisposition

indisposto (ēn·dē·spō′stō) *a* indisposed

indissolubile (ēn·dēs·sō·lū′bē·lā) *a* indissoluble; permanent

indistintamente (ēn·dē·stēn·tâ·mān′tā) *adv* dimly; indistinctly

indistinto (ēn·dē·stēn′tō) *a* vague, indistinct

indistruttibile (ēn·dē·strūt·tē′bē·lā) *a* indestructible

---

k kid, **l** let, **m** met, **n** not, **p** pat, **r** very, **s** sat, **sh** shop, **t** tell, **v** vat, **w** we, **y** yes, **z** zero

indivia (ēn·dē′vyâ) *f* endive, chicory

individuale (ēn·dē·vē·dwâ′lā) *a* individual

individualista (ēn·dē·vē·dwâ·lē′stâ) *m* individualist

individualità (ēn·dē·vē·dwâ·lē·tâ′) *f* individuality

individualizzare (ēn·dē·vē·dwâ·lē·dzâ′rā) *vt* to specify

individuare (ēn·dē·vē·dwâ′rā) *vt* to identify; to specify; to single out

individuo (ēn·dē·vē′dwō) *m* individual; person, fellow

indivisibile (ēn·dē·vē·zē′bē·lā) *a* indivisible

indiviso (ēn·dē·vē′zō) *a* undivided, whole

indiziare (ēn·dē·tsyâ′rā) *vt* to suspect

indiziario (ēn·dē·tsyâ′ryō) *a* circumstantial

indizio (ēn·dē′tsyō) *m* circumstance; clue; indication

Indocina (ēn·dō·chē′nâ) *f* Indochina

indoeuropeo (ēn·dō·āū·rō·pā′ō) *a* Indo-European

indole (ēn′dō·lā) *f* disposition, character; **uomo di buona —** good-natured man

indolente (ēn·dō·lān′tā) *a* indolent, lazy

indolenza (ēn·dō·lān′tsâ) *f* laziness, indolence

indolenzito (ēn·dō·lān·tsē′tō) *a* numb

indomabile (ēn·dō·mâ′bē·lā) *a* indomitable; untamable; unconquerable

indomani (ēn·dō·mâ′nē) *m* next day

indorare (ēn·dō·râ′rā) *vt* to gild

indorato (ēn·dō·râ′tō) *a* gilded; browned

indossare (ēn·dōs·sâ′rā) *vt* to wear; to put on, don

indossatrice (ēn·dōs·sâ·trē′châ) *f* model, mannequin

indosso (ēn·dōs′sō) *adv* on (*oneself*)

indotto (ēn·dōt′tō) *a* induced; **corrente indotta** induced current; **—** *m* (*elec*) armature, rotor; induction coil

indovinare (ēn·dō·vē·nâ′rā) *vt&i* to guess; to foresee; to hit the mark

indovinato (ēn·dō·vē·nâ′tō) *a* guessed; well done; fine

indovinello (ēn·dō·vē·nāl′lō) *m* riddle, puzzle

indovino (ēn·dō·vē′nō) *m* fortuneteller

indubbiamente (ēn·dūb·byâ·mān′tā) *adv* certainly, undoubtedly

indubbio (ēn·dūb′byō) *a* undoubted, sure; undisputed

indubitabile (ēn·dū·bē·tâ′bē·lā) *a* indubitable, doubtless

indugiare (ēn·dū·jâ′rā) *vi* to delay; to

hesitate

indugio (ēn·dū′jō) *m* delay; **rompere gl'indugi** to come to a decision

indulgente (ēn·dūl·jān′tā) *a* indulgent

indulgenza (ēn·dūl·jān′tsâ) *f* indulgence

indulgere * (ēn·dūl′jā·rā) *vi* to indulge in; to be indulgent; **—** *vt* to allow; to grant; to gratify

indumento (ēn·dū·mān′tō) *m* garment

indurire (ēn·dū·rē′rā) *vt&i* to harden; to inure

indurirsi (ēn·dū·rēr′sē) *vr* to become inured; to become hardened

indurre * (ēn·dūr′rā) *vt* to induce

indursi * (ēn·dūr′sē) *vt* to make up one's mind; to decide; to bring upon oneself

industria (ēn·dū′stryâ) *f* industry

industriale (ēn·dū·stryâ′lā) *m* industrialist; **—** *a* industrial; **stabilimento —** factory

industrializzare (ēn·dū·stryâ·lē·dzâ′rā) *vt* to industrialize

industrialmente (ēn·dū·stryâl·mān′tā) *adv* industrially

industriarsi (ēn·dū·stryâr′sē) *vr* to strive; to do one's utmost

industriosamente (ēn·dū·stryō·zâ·mān′tā) *adv* industriously

induttanza (ēn·dūt·tân′tsâ) *f* (*elec*) inductance

induttivo (ēn·dūt·tē′vō) *a* inductive

induttore (ēn·dūt·tō′rā) *m* (*elec*) inductor

induzione (ēn·dū·tsyō′nā) *f* induction

inebriare (ē·nā·bryâ′rā) *vt* to intoxicate, make drunk

inebriarsi (ē·nā·bryâr′sē) *vr* to go into raptures; to get drunk

inedia (ē·ne′dyâ) *f* starvation

inedito (ē·ne′dē·tō) *a* unpublished

ineducato (ē·nā·dū·kâ′tō) *a* ill-bred, rude

ineffabile (ē·nāf·fâ′bē·lā) *a* ineffable

inefficace (ē·nāf·fē·kâ′châ) *a* ineffectual, inefficacious

ineguaglianza (ē·nā·gwâ·lyân′tsâ) *f* inequality

ineguale (ē·nā·gwâ′lā) *a* uneven, unequal

ineluttabile (ē·nā·lūt·tâ′bē·lā) *a* inevitable

inerente (ē·nā·rān′tā) *a* inherent; concerning, with relation to; incidental

inerme (ē·nār′mā) *a* unarmed

inerpicarsi (ē·nār·pē·kâr′sē) *vr* to clamber

inerte (ē·nār′tā) *a* inert; inactive

inerzia (ē·ner′tsyâ) *f* inertia; inertness

inesatto (ē·nā·zât′tō) *a* inaccurate; inexact

inesauribile (ē·nā·zâū·rē′bē·lā) *a* inexhaustible

inesistente (ē·nā·zē·stän'tā) *a* nonexistent

inesorabile (ē·nā·zō·râ'bē·lā) *a* inexorable, relentless

inesorabilmente (ē·nā·zō·râ·bēl·män'tā) *adv* inexorably

inesperto (ē·nā·spär'tō) *a* inexperienced, lacking in experience

inesplicabile (ē·nā·splē·kâ'bē·lā) *a* inexplicable

inesplorato (ē·nā·splō·râ'tō) *a* unexplored

inesploso (ē·nā·splō'zō) *a* unexploded

inestimabile (ē·nā·stē·mâ'bē·lā) *adv* invaluable, inestimable

inettitudine (ē·nāt·tē·tū'dē·nā) *f* ineptitude, incapacity, unfitness

inetto (ē·nāt'tō) *a* inept, unfit

inevaso (ē·nā·vâ'zō) *a* outstanding, pending

inevitabile (ē·nā·vē·tâ'bē·lā) *a* inevitable

inevitabilmente (ē·nā·vē·tâ·bēl·män'tā) *adv* inevitably, unavoidably

inezia (ē·ne'tsyâ) *f* trifle

infallibile (ēn·fâl·lē'bē·lā) *a* infallible

infame (ēn·fâ'mā) *a* infamous, outrageous

infamia (ēn·fâ'myâ) *f* infamy, ignominy

infangare (ēn·fân·gâ'rā) *vt* to spatter with mud; to defame

infangarsi (ēn·fân·gâr'sē) *vr* to get muddy

infantile (ēn·fân·tē'lā) *a* infantile; **asilo —** kindergarten; **capriccio —** childish whim

infanzia (ēn·fân'tsyâ) *f* childhood; infancy

infarcire (ēn·fâr·chē'rā) *vt* to stuff; (*fig*) to cram

infarinare (ēn·fâ·rē·nâ'rā) *vt* to flour

infarinarsi (ēn·fâ·rē·nâr'sē) *vr* (*coll*) to powder oneself; (*fig*) to get a smattering of, dabble in

infarinatura (ēn·fâ·rē·nâ·tū'râ) *f* (*fig*) smattering; dabbling

infastidire (ēn·fâ·stē·dē'rā) *vt* to annoy, bother

infastidirsi (ēn·fâ·stē·dēr'sē) *vr* to be annoyed; to get bored

infaticabile (ēn·fâ·tē·kâ'bē·lā) *a* tireless

infatti (ēn·fât'tē) *adv* indeed, in fact

infatuazione (ēn·fâ·twâ·tsyō'nā) *f* infatuation

infausto (ēn·fâ'ū·stō) *a* unlucky; inauspicious

infedele (ēn·fā·dā'lā) *a* unfaithful; infidel

infedeltà (ēn·fā·dāl·tâ') *f* unfaithfulness; infidelity

infelice (ēn·fā·lē'chā) *a* unhappy

infelicità (ēn·fā·lē·chē·tâ') *f* unhappiness

inferiore (ēn·fā·ryō'rā) *a* inferior; lower

inferiorità (ēn·fā·ryō·rē·tâ') *f* inferiority

inferire (ēn·fâ·rē'rā) *vt&i* to infer, deduce; **—** *vt* to inflict

infermeria (ēn·fār·mâ·rē'â) *f* infirmary

infermiera (ēn·fār·myā'râ) *f* nurse

infermiere (ēn·fār·myā'rā) *m* male nurse

infermità (ēn·fār·mē·tâ') *f* infirmity

infermo (ēn·fār'mō) *a* ill, sick

infernale (ēn·fār·nâ'lā) *a* hellish

inferno (ēn·fār'nō) *m* hell

inferriata (ēn·fār·ryâ'tâ) *f* metal grating

infervorato (ēn·fār·vō·râ'tō) *a* fervent

infestare (ēn·fā·stâ'rā) *vt* to infest

infesto (ēn·fā'stō) *a* harmful

infettare (ēn·fât·tâ'rā) *vt* to infect

infettarsi (ēn·fât·târ'sē) *vr* to be infected

infettivo (ēn·fât·tē'vō) *a* infectious

infetto (ēn·fât'tō) *a* infected

infezione (ēn·fā·tsyō'nā) *f* infection

infiammabile (ēn·fyâm·mâ'bē·lā) *a* combustible, inflammable

infiammarsi (ēn·fyâm·mâr'sē) *vr* (*med*) to become inflamed; (*fig*) to become excited

infiammazione (ēn·fyâm·mâ·tsyō'nā) *f* inflammation

infido (ēn'fē·dō) *a* untrustworthy

infierire (ēn·fyâ·rē'rā) *vi* to rage; to be merciless

infilare (ēn·fē·lâ'rā) *vt* to thread; to slip into, put on; to string

infiltrarsi (ēn·fēl·trâr'sē) *vr* to penetrate, infiltrate

infiltrazione (ēn·fēl·trâ·tsyō'nā) *f* infiltration, penetration

infimo (ēn'fē·mō) *a* lowest

infine (ēn·fē'nā) *adv* after all; at last

infingardo (ēn·fēn·gâr'dō) *a* lazy

infinità (ēn·fē·nē·tâ') *f* infinity; **un'— di gente** a crowd of people

infinitamente (ēn·fē·nē·tâ·män'tā) *adv* infinitely

infinito (ēn·fē·nē'tō) *a&m* infinite; (*gram*) infinitive

infinocchiare (ēn·fē·nōk·kyâ'rā) *vt* to hoodwink; to fool

infischiarsi (ēn·fē·skyâr'sē) *vr* not to care a bit; to treat lightly

inflazione (ēn·flâ·tsyō'nā) *f* inflation

inflessibile (ēn·flās·sē'bē·lā) *a* inflexible, rigid

inflessibilmente (ēn·flās·sē·bēl·män'tā) *adv* inflexibly, rigidly

infliggere * (ēn·flēj'jâ·rā) *vt* to inflict

influente (ēn·flūän'tā) *a* prominent, influential

influenza (ēn·flūän'tsâ) *f* influence; (*med*) influenza

influenzare (ēn·flūän·tsâ'rā) *vt* to influence; to bias

influire (ēn·flūē′rā) *vi* to affect; to exert influence on

influsso (ēn·flūs′sō) *m* influence; influx

infocato (ēn·fō·kâ′tō) *a* inflamed; angry; red-hot

infondatezza (ēn·fōn·dâ·tā′tsâ) *f* lack of support

infondato (ēn·fōn·dâ′tō) *a* groundless

infondere * (ēn·fôn′dā·rā) *vt* to infuse; — **coraggio a** to give courage to

informare (ēn·fōr·mâ′rā) *vt* to inform; to acquaint

informarsi (ēn·fōr·mâr′sē) *vr* to inquire; to obtain information

informatore (ēn·fōr·mâ·tō′rā) *m* informant; informer

informazione (ēn·fōr·mâ·tsyō′nā) *f* information; inquiry; investigation; **servizio** — **intelligence agency**

informe (ēn·fōr′mā) *a* shapeless

informicolamento (ēn·fōr·mē·kō·lâ·mān′tō) *m* tingling sensation

infornare (ēn·fōr·nâ′rā) *vt* to place in the oven

infornata (ēn·fōr·nâ′tâ) *f* ovenful; batch

infortunio (ēn·fōr·tū′nyō) *m* accident

infossare (ēn·fōs·sâ′rā) *vt* to bury; to dig

infossato (ēn·fōs·sâ′tō) *a* fallen in, sunken; **occhi infossati** hollow eyes

infradiciare (ēn·frâ·dē·châ′rā) *vt* to soak; to drench

infradiciarsi (ēn·frâ·dē·châr′sē) *vr* to get soaked; to be drenched

inframmettere * (ēn·frâm·met′tā·rā) *vt* to interpose

inframmettersi * (ēn·frâm·met′tār·sē) *vr* to intervene; to interfere; to meddle

infrangere * (ēn·frân′jā·rā) *vt* to shatter, break; to violate

infrangersi * (ēn·frân′jār·sē) *vr* to break up; to be smashed; to shatter

infrangibile (ēn·frân·jē′bē·lā) *a* unbreakable; **vetro** — safety glass

infrazione (ēn·frâ·tsyō′nā) *f* infraction

infreddatura (ēn·frād·dâ·tū′râ) *f* cold (*med*)

infruttifero (ēn·frūt·tē′fâ·rō) *a* unprofitable, unfruitful; **capitale** — capital not bearing interest

infuori (ēn·fwō′rē) *adv* out; outwards; **all'** — **di** except

infuriarsi (ēn·fū·ryâr′sē) *vr* to lose one's temper

ingaggiare (ēn·gâj·jâ′rā) *vt* to enlist, hire; (*mech*) to start

ingannare (ēn·gân·nâ′rā) *vt* to deceive; — **il tempo** to while away the time

ingannarsi (ēn·gân·nâr′sē) *vr* to deceive oneself; to be mistaken

inganno (ēn·gân′nō) *m* deception, trick; fraud; stratagem

ingegnarsi (ēn·jā·nyâr′sē) *vr* to strive, try; to do everything possible

ingegnere (ēn·jā·nyā′rā) *m* engineer; — **elettrotecnico** electrical engineer

ingegneria (ēn·jā·nyā·rē′â) *f* engineering

ingegnosamente (ēn·jā·nyō·zâ·mān′tā) *adv* ingeniously

ingegnoso (ēn·jā·nyō′zō) *a* clever, witty

ingelosire (ēn·jā·lō·zē′rā) *vt* to make jealous, make envious

ingelosirsi (ēn·jā·lō·zēr′sē) *vr* to become jealous

ingenio (ēn·je′nyō) *m* brains, talent; wits

ingente (ēn·jān′tā) *a* huge

ingenuamente (ēn·jā·nwâ·mān′tā) *adv* innocently, ingenuously

ingenuità (ēn·jā·nwē·tâ′) *f* ingenuousness

ingenuo (ēn·je′nwō) *a* naive

ingerenza (ēn·jā·rān′tsâ) *f* interference

ingerire (ēn·jā·rē′rā) *vt* to swallow

ingerirsi (ēn·jā·rēr′sē) *vr* to meddle

inghiottire (ēn·gyōt·tē′rā) *vt* to swallow; to engulf (*fig*)

ingiallire (ēn·jâl·lē′rā) *vt&i* to yellow, turn yellow

inginocchiarsi (ēn·jē·nōk·kyâr′sē) *vr* to kneel down, fall to one's knees

inginocchiatoio (ēn·jē·nōk·kyâ·tō′yō) *m* prie-dieu

ingiungere * (ēn·jūn′jā·rā) *vt* to command; to enjoin

ingiunzione (ēn·jūn·tsyō′nā) *f* injunction

ingiuria (ēn·jū′ryâ) *f* insult; abuse

ingiuriare (ēn·jū·ryâ′rā) *vt* to abuse; to insult

ingiuriosamente (ēn·jū·ryō·zâ·mān′tā) *adv* offensively; insultingly

ingiurioso (ēn·jū·ryō′zō) *a* outrageous; insulting; offending

ingiustamente (ēn·jū·stâ·mān′tā) *adv* unfairly, unjustly

ingiustificabile (ēn·jū·stē·fē·kâ′bē·lā) *a* unjustifiable

ingiustizia (ēn·jū·stē′tsyâ) *f* injustice

ingiusto (ēn·jū′stō) *a* unjust, unfair

inglese (ēn·glā′zā) *a&m* English

ingoiare (ēn·gō·yâ′rā) *vt* to swallow; to down

ingombrante (ēn·gōm·brân′tā) *a* bulky, encumbering

ingombrare (ēn·gōm·brâ′rā) *vt* to clutter; to encumber; (*rail*) to block (*tracks*)

ingombrarsi (ēn·gōm·brâr′sē) *vr* to become obstructed; to block up

---

â **ârm**, ā **bāby**, e **bet**, ē **bē**, ō **gō**, ô **gône**, ū **blūe**, b **bad**, ch **child**, d **dad**, f **fat**, g **gay**, j **jet**

ingombro (ēn·gōm′brō) *m* obstruction; impediment; — *a* encumbered; **essere d'— a qualcuno** to be in someone's way

ingordigia (ēn·gōr·dē′jâ) *f* greed, greediness; avarice

ingordo (ēn·gōr′dō) *a* gluttonous

ingorgare (ēn·gōr·gâ′rā) *vt* to bar the way; to obstruct; to choke up

ingorgo (ēn·gōr′gō) *m* obstruction; traffic jam; (*med*) engorgement

ingranaggio (ēn·grâ·nâj′jō) *m* gearing, gears; works; **ingranaggi d'orologio** cogwheels of a clock

ingranare (ēn·grâ·nâ′rā) *vt* (*auto*) to throw into gear; to engage; (*mech*) to mesh

ingrandimento (ēn·grân·dē·mān′tō) *m* enlargement; amplification; **lente d'—** magnifying glass

ingrandire (ēn·grân·dē′rā) *vt* to enlarge; to increase

ingrandirsi (ēn·grân·dēr′sē) *vr* to increase; to grow larger

ingrassaggio (ēn·grâs·sâj′jō) *m* greasing, lubrication

ingrassare (ēn·grâs·sâ′rā) *vt* to fatten; to grease; — *vi* to get fat

ingrassarsi (ēn·grâs·sâr′sē) *vr* (*fig*) to take pleasure in; to get fat; to become larger; to increase

ingrassatore (ēn·grâs·sâ·tō′rā) *m* greaser; grease gun

ingratitudine (ēn·grâ·tē·tū′dē·nā) *f* ingratitude

ingrato (ēn·grâ′tō) *a* ungrateful; hard, unpleasant; sterile, unproductive (*soil*)

ingresso (ēn·grās′sō) *m* entrance; — **libero** free admission; **vietato l'—** no admittance

ingrossamento (ēn·grōs·sâ·mān′tō) *m* swelling; increase; thickening

ingrossare (ēn·grōs·sâ′rā) *vt* to increase, swell; to make bigger

ingrossarsi (ēn·grōs·sâr′sē) *vr* to increase; to become bigger; to swell; to grow rough (*sea*)

ingrosso (ēn·grōs·sō) **all'—** wholesale; approximately

inguaiare (ēn·gwâ·yâ′rā) *vt* to get into trouble; to cause trouble

inguaiarsi (ēn·gwâ·yâr′sē) *vr* to get oneself into trouble

inguantarsi (ēn·gwân·târ′sē) *vr* to put on one's gloves

inguaribile (ēn·gwâ·rē′bē·lā) *a* incurable

inguine (ēn′gwē·nā) *m* (*anat*) groin

inibire (ē·nē·bē′rā) *vt* to inhibit

inibizione (ē·nē·bē·tsyō′nā) *f* inhibition

iniettare (ē·nyāt·tâ′rā) *vt* to inject

iniettore (ē·nyāt·tō′rā) *m* injector; jet

iniezione (ē·nyâ·tsyō′nā) *f* injection

inimicizia (ē·nē·mē·chē′tsyâ) *f* enmity

ininterrottamente (ē·nēn·tār·rōt·tâ·mān′tā) *adv* uninterruptedly

ininterrotto (ē·nēn·tār·rōt′tō) *a* uninterrupted

iniquità (ē·nē·kwē·tâ′) *f* iniquity; injustice

iniziale (ē·nē·tsyâ′lā) *a&f* initial

iniziare (ē·nē·tsyâ′rā) *vt* to start; to initiate; to commence

iniziarsi (ē·nē·tsyâr′sē) *vr* to begin, commence

iniziativa (ē·nē·tsyâ·tē′vâ) *f* initiative

inizio (ē·nē′tsyō) *m* beginning

innamorare (ēn·nâ·mō·râ′rā) *vt* to captivate, charm; to make fall in love

innamorarsi (ēn·nâ·mō·râr′sē) *vr* to become enamored; to fall in love

innamorato (ēn·nâ·mō·râ′tō) *a* in love; — *m* sweetheart, lover

innanzi (ēn·nân′tsē) *prep* before; — **tutto** above all, first

innato (ēn·nâ′tō) *a* innate

innegabile (ēn·nā·gâ′bē·lā) *a* undeniable

innestare (ēn·nā·stâ′rā) *vt* to graft; (*mech*) to throw into gear; to inoculate

innesto (ēn·nā′stō) *m* inoculation; graft; — **del vaccino** vaccination

inno (ēn′nō) *m* hymn; anthem

innocente (ēn·nō·chân′tā) *a* innocent; guiltless; simple

innocentemente (ēn·nō·chân·tā·mān′tā) *adv* innocently

innocenza (ēn·nō·chân′tsâ) *f* innocence; simplicity

innocuo (ēn·nô′kwō) *a* harmless

innovazione (ēn·nō·vâ·tsyō′nā) *f* innovation, change

inoculare (ē·nō·kū·lâ′rā) *vt* to inoculate

inoculazione (ē·nō·kū·lâ·tsyō′nā) *f* inoculation

inodoro (ē·nō·dō′rō) *a* odorless

inoffensivo (ē·nôf·fân·sē′vō) *a* harmless, inoffensive

inoltrare (ē·nōl·trâ′rā) *vt* to forward

inoltrarsi (ē·nōl·trâr′sē) *vr* to penetrate; to advance

inoltrato (ē·nōl·trâ′tō) *a* advanced; forwarded; **in inverno** late in winter

inoltre (ē·nōl′trā) *adv* besides; furthermore

inoltro (ē·nōl′trō) *m* forwarding

inondare (ē·nōn·dâ′rā) *vt* to flood

inondazione (ē·nōn·dâ·tsyō′nā) *f* flooding; inundation

---

k kid, **l** let, **m** met, **n** not, **p** pat, **r** very, **s** sat, **sh** shop, **t** tell, **v** vat, **w** we, **y** yes, **z** zero

inoperoso (ē·nō·pā·rō′zō) *a* idle, indolent; inactive

inopportuno (ē·nōp·pōr·tū′nō) *a* awkward, inopportune; badly timed

inorganico (ē·nōr·gâ′nē·kō) *a* inorganic

inorgoglirsi (ē·nōr·gō·lyēr′sē) *vr* to swell with pride

inorridire (ē·nōr·rē·dē′rā) *vt* to instill horror in; to frighten; to terrify; — *vi* to be terrified; to become horror-struck; to be filled with fear

inospitabile (ē·nō·spē·tâ′bē·lā) *a* inhospitable, forbidding

inosservato (ē·nōs·sār·vâ′tō) *a* unobserved

inossidabile (ē·nōs·sē·dâ′bē·lā) *a* stainless (*metal*)

inquietante (ēn·kwēā·tân′tā) *a* alarming

inquietare (ēn·kwēā·tâ′rā) *vt* to make nervous; to worry; to upset

inquietarsi (ēn·kwēā·târ′sē) *vr* to become alarmed; to grow uneasy

inquieto (ēn·kwēā′tō) *a* restless; upset; apprehensive

inquietudine (ēn·kwēā·tū′dē·nā) *f* apprehension, nervousness

inquilino (ēn·kwē·lē′nō) *m* tenant

inquisizione (ēn·kwē·zē·tsyō′nā) *f* inquisition

insabbiare (ēn·sâb·byâ′rā) *vt* to sand, fill with sand; (*fig*) to pigeonhole

insabbiarsi (ēn·sâb·byâr′sē) *vr* to get stuck in the sand; (*coll*) to be hindered, be delayed; to be handicapped

insaccare (ēn·sâk·kâ′rā) *vt* to put in a sack; to bag

insaccato (ēn·sâk·kâ′tō) *a* in a sack; bagged; **carne insaccata** sausage

insalata (ēn·sâ·lâ′tâ) *f* salad

insalatiera (ēn·sâ·lâ·tyâ′râ) *f* salad bowl

insalubre (ēn·sâ·lū′brā) *a* insalubrious, unhealthful

insanabile (ēn·sâ·nâ′bē·lā) *a* incurable

insanguinare (ēn·sân·gwē·nâ′rā) *vt* to stain with blood

insaponare (ēn·sâ·pō·nâ′rā) *vt* to lather; to soap

insaponarsi (ēn·sâ·pō·nâr′sē) *vr* to lather oneself; to soap oneself

insaponata (ēn·sâ·pō·nâ′tâ) *f* lathering; soaping

insapore (ēn·sâ·pō′rā) *a* tasteless, insipid

insaputa (ēn·sâ·pū′tâ) **all′— di** unknown to, without one's knowledge

insaziabile (ēn·sâ·tsyâ′bē·lā) *a* unappeasable, insatiable, implacable

inscenare (ēn·shā·nâ′rā) *vt* to promote; to stage

insegna (ēn·sā′nyâ) *f* flag; sign, indication

insegnamento (ēn·sā·nyâ·mân′tō) *m* teaching; tuition; education

insegnante (ēn·sā·nyân′tā) *m&f* teacher

insegnare (ēn·sā·nyâ′rā) *vt* to teach

inseguimento (ēn·sā·gwē·mân′tō) *m* chase, pursuit

inseguire (ēn·sā·gwē′rā) *vt* to pursue, chase

insellare (ēn·sāl·lâ′rā) *vt* to saddle

insenatura (ēn·sā·nâ·tū′râ) *f* harbor, inlet

insensibile (ēn·sān·sē′bē·lā) *a* insensible; hardhearted, insensitive

insensibilità (ēn·sān·sē·bē·lē·tâ′) *f* indifference, insensitivity; insensibility

inseparabile (ēn·sā·pâ·râ′bē·lā) *a* inseparable; inextricable

inseparabilmente (ēn·sā·pâ·râ·bēl·mân′-tā) *adv* inseparably; inextricably

inserire (ēn·sā·rē′rā) *vt* to insert

inserirsi (ēn·sā·rēr′sē) *vr* to be contained in, form part of

inservibile (ēn·sār·vē′bē·lā) *a* useless

inserviente (ēn·sār·vyân′tā) *m* attendant

inserzione (ēn·sār·tsyō′nā) *f* advertisement; insertion

inserzionista (ēn·sār·tsyō·nē′stâ) *m* advertiser

insetticida (ēn·sāt·tē·chē′dâ) *m* insecticide

insetto (ēn·sāt′tō) *m* insect

insidia (ēn·sē′dyâ) *f* trap, snare; peril; —**re** (ēn·sē·dyâ′rā) *vt* to tempt; to trap

insidiosamente (ēn·sē·dyō·zâ·mân′tā) *adv* insidiously

insidioso (ēn·sē·dyō′zō) *a* insidious

insieme (ēn·syā′mā) *adv* together; — *m* ensemble, whole; **mettere una fortuna** — to amass a fortune; **mettere** — (*mech*) to assemble

insigne (ēn·sē′nyâ) *a* famous, notable; notorious

insignificante (ēn·sē·nyē·fē·kân′tā) *a* insignificant, inconsequential; lacking in meaning

insindacabile (en·sēn·dâ·kâ′bē·lā) *a* unobjectionable; irreproachable; undisputable

insinuante (ēn·sē·nwân′tā) *a* insinuating, winning

insinuare (ēn·sē·nwâ′rā) *vt* to insinuate, suggest; to introduce, instill

insinuarsi (ēn·sē·nwâr′sē) *vr* to creep into, enter stealthily

insipido (ēn·sē′pē·dō) *a* tasteless; uninteresting

insistente (ēn·sē·stān′tā) *a* insistent

insistere * (ēn·sē′stâ·rā) *vi* to insist

â ârm, ā bāby, e bet, ē bē, ō gō, ô gône, ū blūe, b bad, ch child, d dad, f fat, g gay, j jet

insoddisfatto (ēn·sŏd·dē·sfât'tō) *a* dissatisfied; displeased

insofferenza (ēn·sŏf·fā·rän'tsâ) *f* impatience; intolerance

insolazione (ēn·sō·lâ·tsyō'nä) *f* sunstroke

insolente (ēn·sō·län'tä) *a* insolent, impudent

insolenza (ēn·sō·län'tsâ) *f* sauciness; insolence, impudence

insolitamente (ēn·sō·lē·tâ·män'tä) *adv* seldom, infrequently

insolito (ēn·sô'lē·tō) *a* unusual, rare

insolubile (ēn·sō·lū'bē·lä) *a* insolvable; insoluble

insolvente (ēn·sōl·vän'tä) *a* insolvent

insolvibile (ēn·sōl·vē'bē·lä) *a* insolvent; insoluble; uncollectible

insomma (ēn·sōm'mâ) *adv* in conclusion; briefly; after all

insonne (ēn·sŏn'nä) *a* sleepless

insonnia (ēn·sŏn'nyâ) *f* insomnia

insopportabile (ēn·sōp·pōr·tâ'bē·lä) *adv* unbearable

insormontabile (ēn·sōr·mōn·tâ'bē·lä) *adv* insurmountable, insuperable

insospettabile (ēn·sō·spät·tâ'bē·lä) *a* above suspicion; not suspect

insostenibile (ēn·sō·stä·nē'bē·lä) *a* indefensible, untenable; insufferable

instabile (ēn·stâ'bē·lä) *a* unsure, unsteady, insecure

installare (ēn·stâl·lâ'rä) *vt* to install; to set up

installarsi (ēn·stâl·lâr'sē) *vr* to get settled

installazione (ēn·stâl·lâ·tsyō'nä) *f* installation

instancabile (ēn·stän·kâ'bē·lä) *a* indefatigable, unwearying

instancabilmente (ēn·stän·kâ·bēl·män'tä) *adv* untiringly

instaurare (ēn·stâū·râ'rä) *vt* to establish; to institute

instaurazione (ēn·stâū·râ·tsyō'nä) *f* establishing, installation

insù (ēn·sū') *adv* upward, up; **naso all'—** pug nose

insubordinazione (ēn·sū·bōr·dē·nâ·tsyō'nä) *f* insubordination

insuccesso (ēn·sū·chäs'sō) *m* failure

insudiciare (ēn·sū·dē·châ'rä) *vt* to tarnish; to soil

insudiciarsi (ēn·sū·dē·châr'sē) *vr* to get dirty; to become tarnished

insufficiente (ēn·sūf·fē·chän'tä) *a* insufficient

insufficienza (ēn·sūf·fē·chän'tsâ) *f* insufficiency; **— di prove** lack of sufficient evidence

insulina (ēn·sū·lē'nâ) *f* insulin

insulso (ēn·sūl'sō) *a* vapid, stupid, empty

insultare (ēn·sūl·tâ'rä) *vt* to insult; to vilify

insulto (ēn·sūl'tō) *m* insult; (*med*) attack, stroke

insuperabile (ēn·sū·pä·râ'bē·lä) *a* unsurmountable

insuperbirsi (ēn·sū·pär·bēr'sē) *vr* to fill with pride; to become arrogant

insurrezionale (ēn·sūr·rä·tsyō·nâ'lä) *a* insurgent, insurrectionary

insurrezione (ēn·sūr·rä·tsyō'nä) *f* uprising, insurrection

intaccare (ēn·tâk·kâ'rä) *vt* to notch; to indent; to damage; to eat away

intagliare (ēn·tâ·lyâ'rä) *vt* to carve; to sculpt

intagliato (ēn·tâ·lyâ'tō) *a* carved

intagliatore (ēn·tâ·lyâ·tō'rä) *m* engraver; sculptor

intaglio (ēn·tâ'lyō) *m* carving; intaglio

intangibile (ēn·tân·jē'bē·lä) *a* intangible; impalpable

intanto (ēn·tân'tō) *adv* meanwhile; **— che** until; while

intarsiare (ēn·târ·syâ'rä) *vt* to veneer; to inlay

intarsio (ēn·târ'syō) *m* veneering; inlaid work

intasato (ēn·tâ·zâ'tō) *a* stopped up; clogged

intatto (ēn·tât'tō) *a* intact

integrale (ēn·tā·grâ'lä) *a* whole; integral; **pane —** wholewheat bread

integrare (ēn·tā·grâ'rä) *vt* to integrate

integrazione (ēn·tā·grâ·tsyō'nä) *f* integration

integrità (ēn·tā·grē·tâ') *f* integrity

intelaiare (ēn·tā·lâ·yâ'rä) *vt* to frame

intelaiatura (ēn·tā·lâ·yâ·tū'râ) *f* frame; chassis (*auto*)

intelletto (ēn·tāl·lāt'tō) *m* intellect; judgment

intellettuale (ēn·tāl·lät·twâ'lä) *a&m* intellectual

intelligente (ēn·tāl·lē·jän'tä) *a* intelligent; skillful

intelligentemente (ēn·tāl·lē·jän·tä·män'tä) *adv* skillfully; intelligently

intelligenza (ēn·tāl·lē·jän'tsâ) *f* intelligence

intemerato (ēn·tā·mā·râ'tō) *a* spotless, pure, honorable

intemperante (ēn·tām·pä·rân'tä) *a* intemperate; immoderate

intemperanza (ēn·tām·pä·rân'tsâ) *f* intemperance; immoderation

---

intemperie (ēn·tām·pe′ryä) *fpl* bad weather, unpleasant weather

intempestivamente (ēn·tām·pä·stē·vä·män′tä) *adv* out of turn; at the wrong time

intempestivo (ēn·tām·pä·stē′vō) *a* badly timed, inopportune

intendente (ēn·tän·dän′tä) *m* superintendent, head

intendenza (ēn·tän·dän′tsä) *f* superintendency; — **di finanza** excise office

intendere * (ēn·ten′dä·rä) *vt* to understand; to plan, intend; **darla ad —** to lead one to believe

intendersi * (ēn·ten′där·sē) *vr* to be well versed in, know a great deal about; to come to terms; **intendersela** to be in agreement; to get along well with one another

intendimento (ēn·tän·dē·män′tō) *m* understanding; aim, purpose

intenditore (ēn·tän·dē·tō′rä) *m* connoisseur

intenerire (ēn·tä·nä·rē′rä) *vt* to move, stir (*emotions*); to soften

intenerirsi (ēn·tä·nä·rēr′sē) *vr* to be moved to pity, feel compassion; to become tender

intensamente (ēn·tän·sä·män′tä) *adv* deeply, intensely

intensificare (ēn·tän·sē·fē·kä′rä) *vt* to intensify; to heighten; to redouble

intensità (ēn·tän·sē·tä′) *f* intensity

intensivo (ēn·tän·sē′vō) *a* intensive

intenso (ēn·tän′sō) *a* intense

intentare (ēn·tän·tä′rä) *vt* (*law*) to bring (*action*), file (*suit*)

intento (ēn·tän′tō) *m* aim; — *a* intent, concentrated

intenzionale (ēn·tän·tsyō·nä′lä) *a* deliberate

intenzionalmente (ēn·tän·tsyō·näl·män′tä) *adv* intentionally

intenzionato (ēn·tän·tsyō·nä′tō) *a* inclined, predisposed

intenzione (ēn·tän·tsyō′nä) *f* intention; **aver l' — di fare** to mean to do; **aver buone intenzioni** to mean well

interamente (ēn·tä·rä·män′tä) *adv* entirely

interasse (ēn·tä·räs′sä) *m* (*auto*) wheelbase

intercalare (ēn·tär·kä·lä′rä) *vt* to insert

intercedere (ēn·tär·che′dä·rä) *vi* to intercede; to intervene

intercessione (ēn·tär·chäs·syō′nä) *f* intercession

intercettare (ēn·tär·chät·tä′rä) *vt* to intercept; to tap (*telephone*)

intercezione (ēn·tär·chä·tsyō′nä) *f* interception; intervention

intercomunicante (ēn·tär·kō·mū·nē·kän′tä) *a* connecting, linking

intercorrere * (ēn·tär·kôr′rä·rä) *vi* to elapse; to come between

intercostale (ēn·tär·kō·stä′lä) *a* (*anat*) intercostal

intercutaneo (ēn·tär·kū·tâ′nä·ō) *a* subcutaneous

interdetto (ēn·tär·dät′tō) *a* forbidden, prohibited

interdire * (ēn·tär·dē′rä) *vt* to forbid; to disqualify

interdizione (ēn·tär·dē·tsyō′nä) *f* loss of civil rights; restraint; interdiction

interessamento (ēn·tä·räs·sä·män′tō) *m* interest, care

interessante (ēn·tä·räs·sän′tä) *a* interesting

interessare (ēn·tä·räs·sä′rä) *vt&i* to interest; to concern; to be important; — **qualcuno in un affare** to form a business partnership with someone

interessarsi (ēn·tä·räs·sär′sē) *vr* to take an interest in; to attend to

interessato (ēn·tä·räs·sä′tō) *a* interested; partial; having an interest

interesse (ēn·tä·räs′sä) *m* interest

interessenza (ēn·tä·räs·sän′tsä) *f* (*com*) percentage, commission

interferenza (ēn·tär·fä·rän′tsä) *f* interference; meddling

interferire (ēn·tär·fä·rē′rä) *vi* to interfere

interiezione (ēn·tä·ryä·tsyō′nä) *f* interjection

interim (ēn′tä·rēm) *m* interim; meanwhile

interinale (ēn·tä·rē·nä′lä) *a* provisional, temporary

interiora (ēn·tä·ryō′rä) *fpl* intestines

interiore (ēn·tä·ryō′rä) *a&m* interior

interlocutore (ēn·tär·lō·kū·tō′rä) *m* questioner; speaker

interloquire (ēn·tär·lō·kwē′rä) *vi* to break in (*conversation*); to intrude, interfere

interludio (ēn·tär·lū′dyō) *m* interlude

intermediario (ēn·tär·mä·dyâ′ryō) *m* intermediary, middleman

intermezzo (ēn·tär·mä′dzō) *m* intermezzo, intermission; interval

interminabile (ēn·tär·mē·nâ′bē·lä) *a* endless

intermittente (ēn·tär·mēt·tän′tä) *a* intermittent, recurrent

internamente (ēn·tär·nä·män′tä) *adv* internally, within

internare (ēn·tär·nä′rä) *vt* to confine,

intern

internazionale (ēn·tär·nâ·tsyō·nâ'lā) *a* international

internazionalista (ēn·tär·nâ·tsyō·nâ·lē'-stä) *m* internationalist

interno (ēn·tär'nō) *a* internal; **commercio** — domestic trade; — *m* interior; **Ministro dell'**— Secretary of the Interior

intero (ēn·tā'rō) *m* total, whole; — *a* complete, entire

interporre * (ēn·tär·pōr'rā) *vt* to interpose; to interject

interporsi * (ēn·tär·pōr'sē) *vr* to intercede; to mediate

interposizione (ēn·tär·pō·zē·tsyō'nä) *f* intervention

interpretare (ēn·tär·prā·tâ'rā) *vt* to interpret; to construe

interpretazione (ēn·tär·prā·tâ·tsyō'nä) *f* version, account; interpretation; — **erronea** misinterpretation

interprete (ēn·ter'prā·tā) *m&f* interpreter; actor, actress

interrogante (ēn·tär·rō·gân'tā) *a* questioning

interrogare (ēn·tär·rō·gâ'rā) *vt* to question; query; to consult

interrogativo (ēn·tär·rō·gâ·tē'vō) *a* interrogative; **punto** — question mark

interrogatorio (ēn·tär·rō·gâ·tô'ryō) *m* questioning; cross-examination

interrompere * (ēn·tär·rôm'pā·rā) *vt* to interrupt; *(elec)* to disconnect, turn off

interrompersi * (ēn·tär·rôm'pär·sē) *vr* to stop; to interrupt oneself

interrotto (ēn·tär·rōt'tō) *a* interrupted; discontinued

interruttore (ēn·tär·rūt·tō'rā) *m* interrupter; switch *(elec)*

interruzione (ēn·tär·rū·tsyō'nä) *f* interruption; **senza** — uninterruptedly, continuously

interurbano (ēn·tä·rūr·bâ'nō) *a* long-distance

intervallo (ēn·tär·vâl'lō) *m* break; interval

intervenire * (ēn·tär·vä·nē'rā) *vi* to intervene; to take part in, participate in

intervento (ēn·tär·vän'tō) *m* intervention; attendance

intervista (ēn·tär·vē'stä) *f* interview; **–re** (ēn·tär·vē·stä'rā) *vt* to interview

intesa (ēn·tā'zä) *f* understanding, agreement

inteso (ēn·tā'zō) *a* heard; understood; **non darsi per** — not to give a rap; to turn a deaf ear

intestato (ēn·tä·stâ'tō) *a* headed; *(com)*

registered; *(law)* intestate; **carta intestata** letterhead

intestazione (ēn·tä·stâ·tsyō'nä) *f* headline, heading

intestino (ēn·tä·stē'nō) *m* intestine; — *a* domestic; internal

intimamente (ēn·tē·mâ·mān'tä) *adv* intimately, closely

intimare (ēn·tē·mâ'rā) *vt* to summon; to intimate

intimazione (ēn·tē·mâ·tsyō'nä) *f* injunction, order

intimidazione (ēn·tē·mē·dâ·tsyō'nä) *f* intimidation; threat

intimità (ēn·tē·mē·tâ') *f* intimacy; confidence

intimo (ēn'tē·mō) *a* intimate; private

intingere * (ēn·tēn'jä·rā) *vt&i* to dip

intingolo (ēn·tēn'gō·lō) *m* gravy, sauce

intirizzire (ēn·tē·rē·tsē'rā) *vt* to freeze, benumb

intitolare (ēn·tē·tō·lâ'rā) *vt* to dedicate; to name

intitolato (ēn·tē·tō·lâ'tō) *a* entitled, named

intollerabile (ēn·tōl·lä·râ'bē·lä) *a* unbearable; insufferable

intollerante (ēn·tōl·lä·rân'tä) *a* intolerant

intolleranza (ēn·tōl·lä·rân'tsä) *f* intolerance

intonaco (ēn·tô'nâ·kō) *m* plaster

intonazione (ēn·tō·nâ·tsyō'nä) *f* intonation

intontire (ēn·tōn·tē'rā) *vt* to daze, stun

intontirsi (ēn·tōn·tēr'sē) *vr* to be dazed; to be stunned

intontito (ēn·tōn·tē'tō) *a* stunned; dazed

intoppo (ēn·tōp'pō) *m* obstacle; *(fig)* difficulty

intorbidire (ēn·tōr·bē·dē'rā) *vt* to muddy; to confuse

intorbidirsi (ēn·tōr·bē·dēr'sē) *vr* to grow muddy; to become confused

intorno (ēn·tōr'nō) *adv* around

intossicare (ēn·tōs·sē·kâ'rā) *vt* to poison

intossicazione (ēn·tōs·sē·kâ·tsyō'nä) *f* poisoning; — **da cibi** ptomaine poisoning

intraducibile (ēn·trâ·dū·chē'bē·lä) *a* untranslatable

intralciare (ēn·trâl·châ'rā) *vt* to obstruct

intralcio (ēn·trâl'chō) *m* obstacle, obstruction

intrallazzo (ēn·trâl·lâ'tsō) *m* *(sl)* racket, black market

intransigente (ēn·trân·sē·jän'tä) *a* uncompromising, hard

intransigenza (ēn·trân·sē·jän'tsä) *f* sever-

---

k kid, **l** let, **m** met, **n** not, **p** pat, **r** very, **s** sat, **sh** shop, **t** tell, **v** vat, **w** we, **y** yes, **z** zero

ity, intransigence

intransitivo (ēn·trân·sē·tē′vō) *a* (*gram*) intransitive

intraprendente (ēn·trâ·prän·dän′tā) *a* resourceful; enterprising, industrious

intraprendenza (ēn·trâ·prän·dän′tsä) *f* initiative, enterprise, industry

intraprendere * (ēn·trâ·pren′dā·rā) *vt* to undertake; to take on

intrattabile (ēn·trät·tâ′bē·lā) *a* hard; intractable, unruly

intrattenere * (ēn·trät·tā·nā′rā) *vt* to entertain

intrattenersi * (ēn·trät·tā·när′sē) *vr* to dwell on; to linger; to pause

intrattenimento (ēn·trät·tā·nē·män′tō) *m* entertainment

intrattenitrice (ēn·trät·tā·nē·trē′chä) *f* B-girl

intravenoso (ēn·trâ·vä·nō′zō) *a* intravenous

intreccio (ēn·tre′chō) *m* story, plot

intrepido (ēn·tre′pē·dō) *a* brave, intrepid

intrigante (ēn·trē·gän′tä) *a* scheming, tricky

intrigare (ēn·trē·gâ′rā) *vt* to plot; to scheme

intrigarsi (ēn·trē·gâr′sē) *vr* to meddle

intrigo (ēn·trē′gō) *m* plot, intrigue, scheme

intrinseco (ēn·trēn′sä·kō) *a* intrinsic

intriso (ēn·trē′zō) *a* sodden, soaked; — *m* mixture

introdotto (ēn·trō·dōt′tō) *a* shown in, admitted (*entry*); introduced

introdurre * (ēn·trō·dūr′rā) *vt* to insert; to show in; to introduce

introduzione (ēn·trō·dü·tsyō′nä) *f* introduction

introitare (ēn·trōē·tâ′rā) *vt* to collect; to cash

introito (ēn·trô′ē·tō) *m* receipts; income; (*eccl*) introit

intromettersi * (ēn·trō·met′tär·sē) *vt* to interfere with, meddle in; to arbitrate

introspezione (ēn·trō·spä·tsyō′nä) *f* introspection, self-examination

intruso (ēn·trü′zō) *m* intruder

intuire (ēn·twē′rā) *vi* to guess; to sense; to intuit

intuito (ēn·tü′ē·tō) *m* intuition; insight

intuizione (ēn·twē·tsyō′nä) *f* intuition; intuitiveness

inumano (ē·nü·mâ′nō) *a* inhuman; brutal

inumidire (ē·nü·mē·dē′rā) *vt* to moisten, dampen

inumidirsi (ē·nü·mē·dēr′sē) *vr* to become moist, dampen

inusitato (ē·nü·zē·tâ′tō) *a* unusual, strange; obsolete

inutile (ē·nü′tē·lä) *a* useless

inutilità (ē·nü·tē·lē·tâ′) *f* uselessness; futility

inutilmente (ē·nü·tēl·män′tä) *adv* uselessly; in vain

invadente (ēn·vâ·dän′tä) *a* aggressive, pushy; invading

invadenza (ēn·vâ·dän′tsä) *f* aggressiveness, pushiness; interference

invadere * (ēn·vâ′dā·rā) *vt* to invade

invalidità (ēn·vâ·lē·dē·tâ′) *f* invalidity

invalido (ēn·vâ′lē·dō) *a&m* invalid; — **di guerra** disabled war veteran

invano (ēn·vâ′nō) *adv* in vain, vainly, to no avail

invariabile (ēn·vâ·ryâ′bē·lä) *a* invariable; unvarying

invasione (ēn·vâ·zyō′nä) *f* invasion; incursion

invasore (ēn·vâ·zō′rä) *m* invader

invecchiare (ēn·vāk·kyâ′rä) *vt* to age, make old; — *vi* to become old, age

invece (ēn·vā′chä) *adv* on the contrary; rather, instead

inventare (ēn·vän·tâ′rä) *vt* to invent, create; to discover

inventario (ēn·vän·tâ′ryō) *f* inventory

inventiva (ēn·vän·tē′vâ) *f* inventiveness

inventivo (ēn·vän·tē′vō) *a* inventive, creative

inventore (ēn·vän·tō′rä) *m* inventor

invenzione (ēn·vän·tsyō′nä) *f* invention; **brevetto d'**— patent

invernale (ēn·vär·nâ′lä) *a* winter

inverno (ēn·vär′nō) *m* winter

invero (ēn·vā′rō) *adv* really, indeed

inverosimile (ēn·vä·rō·sē′mē·lä) *a* unlikely; hard to believe; implausible

inversamente (ēn·vär·sâ·män′tä) *adv* inversely

inversione (ēn·vär·syō′nä) *f* reverse; reversal; inversion

inverso (ēn·vär′sō) *a* inverted, inverse; **senso** — opposite direction; — *adv* toward; **all'**— backwards; **all'inversa** badly, wrong

invertibile (ēn·vär·tē′bē·lä) *a* reversible

invertire (ēn·vär·tē′rä) *vt* to reverse; to invert

investigare (ēn·vä·stē·gâ′rä) *vt* to investigate; to research

investigatore (ēn·vä·stē·gâ·tō′rä) *m* investigator; — **privato** private investigator, detective

investigazione (ēn·vä·stē·gâ·tsyō′nä) *f* research; investigation; scrutiny

---

â ârm, ā bāby, e bet, ē bē, ō gō, ô gône, ū blūe, b bad, ch child, d dad, f fat, g gay, j jet

investimento (ēn·vä·stē·män'tō) *m (com)* investment; collision, smashup

investire (ēn·vä·stē'rä) *vt* to invest; to run over; to smash into; to assail

investirsi (ēn·vä·stēr'sē) *vr* to collide with, crash into; *(naut)* to run aground; to take a deep interest; to go into thoroughly

invetriata (ēn·vä·tryâ'tâ) *f* skylight; glass door

invettiva (ēn·vät·tē'vâ) *f* invective, vituperation

invidia (ēn·vē'dyâ) *n* jealousy, envy; **–bile** (ēn·vē·dyâ'bē·lä) *a* enviable

invincibile (ēn·vēn·chē'bē·lä) *a* invincible

invio (ēn·vē'ō) *m* shipment; remittance

invitante (ēn·vē·tân'tä) *a* inviting

invitare (ēn·vē·tâ'rä) *vt* to invite

invitato (ēn·vē·tâ'tō) *a* invited; — *m* guest

invito (ēn·vē'tō) *m* invitation

invocare (ēn·vō·kâ'rä) *vt* to invoke; to call upon

invocazione (ēn·vō·kâ·tsyō'nä) *f* appeal; invocation

involgere * (ēn·vôl'jä·rä) *vt* to involve; to envelop

involontariamente (ēn·vō·lōn·tâ·ryâ·män'tä) *adv* involuntarily; unintentionally

involtini (ēn·vōl·tē'nē) *mpl* meat rolls

involto (ēn·vōl'tō) *m* package; — *a* wrapped

involucro (ēn·vô'lū·krō) *m* wrapper; cover; envelope

inzuccherare (ēn·dzūk·kä·râ'rä) *vt* to sweeten, put sugar in; *(fig)* to wheedle

inzuppare (en·dzūp·pâ'rä) *vt* to soak; to dunk

inzupparsi (ēn·dzūp·pâr'sē) *vr* to get drenched, get soaked to the skin

io (ē'ō) *pron* I; — **stesso** I myself

iodio (yô'dyō) *m* iodine

iosa (yō'sâ) *adv* **a** — in great quantity, in abundance

iperbole (ē·per'bō·lä) *f* hyperbole; *(geom)* hyperbola

iperbolico (ē·pär·bô'lē·kō) *a* hyperbolic, given to hyperbole

ipersonico (ē·pär·sô'nē·kō) *a* hypersonic

ipnosi (ēp·nō'zē) *f* hypnosis; trance

ipnotismo (ēp·nō·tē'zmō) *m* hypnotism

ipnotizzare (ēp·nō·tē·dzä'rä) *vt* to hypnotize

ipocrisia (ē·pō·krē·zē'â) *f* hypocrisy

ipocrita (ē·pô'krē·tâ) *m* hypocrite

ipoteca (ē·pō·tā'kâ) *f* mortgage

ipotenusa (ē·pō·tä·nū'zâ) *f* hypotenuse

ipotesi (ē·pô'tä·zē) *f* hypothesis; assumption

ippica (ēp'pē·kâ) *f* horse racing

ippico (ēp'pē·kō) *a* relating to horses

ippodromo (ēp·pô'drō·mō) *m* racetrack

ippopotamo (ēp·pō·pô'tâ·mō) *m* hippopotamus

ira (ē'râ) *f* anger, wrath

iracheno (ē·râ·kä'nō) *a&m* Iraqi

Irak, Iraq (ē'râk) *m* Iraq

iranico (ē·râ'nē·kō) *a&m* Iranian

irascibile (ē·râ·shē'bē·lä) *a* irascible, short-tempered

irato (ē·râ'tō) *a* angry, wrathful

iride (ē'rē·dä) *f* iris; rainbow

Irlanda (ēr·lân'dâ) *f* Ireland

irlandese (ēr·lân·dä'zä) *a&m* Irish; — *m* Irishman

ironia (ē·rō·nē'â) *f* irony

ironico (ē·rô'nē·kō) *a* ironic; sarcastic

irradiare (ēr·râ·dyâ'rä) *vt* to radiate; to irradiate

irradiarsi (ēr·râ·dyâr'sē) *vr* to shine, radiate

irradiazione (ēr·râ·dyâ·tsyō'nä) *f* irradiation, shining

irragionevole (ēr·râ·jō·ne'vō·lä) *a* unreasonable; unfair

irreale (ēr·rä·â'lä) *a* unreal

irrealtà (ēr·rä·âl·tâ') *f* unreality

irregolare (ēr·rä·gō·lâ'rä) *a* irregular; uneven

irregolarità (ēr·rä·gō·lâ·rē·tâ') *f* irregularity; nonconformity; disorder

irremovibile (ēr·rä·mō·vē'bē·lä) *a* irremovable; steadfast, firm

irreparabile (ēr·râ·pâ·râ'bē·lä) *a* irreparable; beyond repair

irreperibile (ēr·rä·pä·rē'bē·lä) *a* elusive; impossible to find

irreprensibile (ēr·rä·prän·sē'bē·lä) *a* irreproachable; blameless, faultless

irrequieto (ēr·rä·kwēâ'tō) *a* restless; uneasy

irresistibile (ēr·rä·zē·stē'bē·lä) *a* irresistible

irresponsabile (ēr·rä·spōn·sâ'bē·lä) *a* heedless; irresponsible

irrevocabile (ēr·rä·vō·kâ'bē·lä) *a* irrevocable; unchangeable

irriconoscibile (ēr·rē·kō·nō·shē'bē·lä) *a* unrecognizable

irrigare (ēr·rē·gâ'rä) *vt* to irrigate

irrigazione (ēr·rē·gâ·tsyō'nä) *f* irrigation, watering

irrigidire (ēr·rē·jē·dē'rä) *vt&i* to stiffen; to tighten

irrigidirsi (ēr·rē·jē·dēr'sē) *vr* to become

rigid; to harden; to become obdurate; to be unyielding in one's attitude

irrisorio (ĕr·rē·zō'ryō) *a* trifling, paltry; ridiculous

irritabile (ĕr·rē·tâ'bē·lā) *a* irritable

irritabilità (ĕr·rē·tâ·bē·lē·tâ') *f* irritability

irritante (ĕr·rē·tân'tā) *a* irritating, chafing

irritare (ĕr·rē·tâ'rā) *vt* to irritate, aggravate, chafe; to rub the wrong way

irritarsi (ĕr·rē·târ'sē) *vr* to get angry, become irritated; to fret

irritazione (ĕr·rē·tâ·tsyō'nā) *f* irritation; exasperation

irrompere * (ĕr·rôm'pā·rā) *vi* to overflow; to break out

irruente (ĕr·rūân'tā) *a* rash, impetuous

irruzione (ĕr·rū·tsyō'nā) *f* irruption; incursion; overflowing

iscrivere * (ē·skrē'vä·rā) *vt* to enroll; to register

iscriversi * (ē·skrē'vär·sē) *vr* to enroll; to join; to register

iscrizione (ē·skrē·tsyō'nā) *f* registration; enlistment; membership; **domanda d'—** application; **modulo d'—** entry blank; **tassa d'—** entry fee, registration fee

Islanda (ē·zlân'dä) *f* Iceland

isola (ē'zō·lä) *f* island

isolamento (ē·zō·lâ·mān'tō) *m* isolation; *(elec)* insulation

isolano (ē·zō·lâ'nō) *m* islander; **—** *a* island

isolante (ē·zō·lân'tā) *m* insulator; **—** *a* insulating

isolare (ē·zō·lâ'rā) *vt* to seclude; to isolate; to keep apart; *(elec)* to insulate

isolarsi (ē·zō·lâr'sē) *vr* to live in seclusion; to isolate oneself

isolatamente (ē·zō·lâ·tâ·mān'tā) *adv* isolatedly; separately

isolato (ē·zō·lâ'tō) *a* isolated; insulating; **—** *m* city block

isolatore (ē·zō·lâ·tō'rā) *m (elec)* insulator

isolazionismo (ē·zō·lâ·tsyō·nē'zmō) *m* isolationism

isolazionista (ē·zō·lâ·tsyō·nē'stâ) *m* isolationist

isoscele (ē·sô'shā·lā) *a (geom)* isosceles

isotopo (ē·zō'tō·pō) *m* isotope

ispanico (ē·spâ'nē·kō) *a* Hispanic

ispettore (ē·spät·tō'rā) *m* inspector; examiner

ispezionare (ē·spā·tsyō·nâ'rā) *vt* to inspect; to examine

ispezione (ē·spā·tsyō'nā) *f* inspection; examination

ispirare (ē·spē·râ'rā) *vt* to inspire; to enthuse

ispirarsi (ē·spē·râr'sē) *vr* to become inspired; to draw inspiration

ispirazione (ē·spē·râ·tsyō'nā) *f* inspiration; enthusiasm

Israele (ē·zrâ·ä'lā) *m* Israel

israelita (ē·zrâ·ā·lē'tâ) *a* Jewish; **—** *m&f* Jew

istantanea (ē·stân·tâ'nā·â) *f* snapshot

istantaneamente (ē·stân·tâ·nā·â·mān'tā) *adv* at once, immediately; momentarily

istantaneo (ē·stân·tâ'nā·ō) *a* instantaneous; momentary

istante (ē·stân'tā) *m* instant; **—** *a* urgent, pressing; **sull'—** immediately; on the spot

istanza (ē·stân'tsâ) *f* petition; plea

isterismo (ē·stā·rē'zmō) *m* hysteria

istigazione (ē·stē·gâ·tsyō'nā) *f* instigation; incitement

istintivamente (ē·stēn·tē·vâ·mān'tā) *adv* instinctively

istinto (ē·stēn'tō) *m* instinct

istituire (ē·stē·twē'rā) *vt* to establish; to institute

istituto (ē·stē·tū'tō) *m* institute, institution

istmo (ēst'mō) *m* isthmus

istrice (ē'strē·chä) *m* porcupine

istruire (ē·strūē'rā) *vt* to teach, educate, instruct

istruirsi (ē·strūēr'sē) *vr* to learn; to become proficient

istruito (ē·strūē'tō) *a* educated

istruttivo (ē·strūt·tē'vō) *a* educational; instructive

istruttore (ē·strūt·tō'rā) *m* instructor

istruttoria (ē·strūt·tô'ryâ) *f* inquest

istruzione (ē·strū·tsyō'nā) *f* instruction; education

istupidirsi (ē·stū·pē·dēr'sē) *vr* to grow stupid; to become stupified

Italia (ē·tâ'lyä) *f* Italy; **— meridionale** Southern Italy; **— settentrionale** Northern Italy

italianista (ē·tâ·lyä·nē'stâ) *m* Italian scholar, Italianist

italianità (ē·tâ·lyä·nē·tâ') *f* Italian characteristics, Italian feeling

italianizzare (ē·tâ·lyä·nē·dzâ'rā) *vt* to italianize

italiano (ē·tâ·lyä'nō) *m&a* Italian

itinerario (ē·tē·nä·râ'ryō) *m* itinerary

itterizia (ēt·tä·rē'tsyä) *f (med)* jaundice

ittiologia (ēt·tyō·lō·jē'ä) *f* ichthyology

Iugoslavia (yū·gō·slâ'vyä) *f* Yugoslavia

iugoslavo (yū·gō·slâ'vō) *m&a* Yugoslav

iuta (yū'tâ) *f* jute

ivi (ē'vē) *adv* there

â ârm, ā bāby, e bet, ē bē, ō gō, ô gône, ū blūe, b bad, ch child, d dad, f fat, g gay, j jet

L

la (lâ) *art f* the; — *pron* her; it; you
là (lâ) *adv* there; **al di** — beyond; on the other side
labaro (lâ′bâ·rō) *m* flag; standard
labbra (lâb′brâ) *fpl* lips
labbro (lâb′brō) *m* lip; rim
labile (lâ′bē·lā) *a* shaky; feeble; fleeting, ephemeral
labirinto (lâ·bē·rēn′tō) *m* labyrinth
laboratorio (lâ·bō·râ·tô′ryō) *m* laboratory; workshop
laborioso (lâ·bō·ryō′zō) *a* industrious; difficult; painstaking
laburismo (lâ·bū·rē′zmō) *m* labor movement; labor party
laburista (lâ·bū·rē′stâ) *a (pol)* labor; — *m* laborite
lacca (lâk′kâ) *f* lacquer; hair spray
lacchè (lâk·kā′) *m* lackey; flunky
laccio (lâ′chō) *m* string; noose; snare; — **da scarpe** shoelace
lacerante (lâ·chā·rân′tā) *a* rending, piercing
lacerare (lâ·chā·râ′rā) *vt* to tear; to rip
lacerazione (lâ·chā·râ·tsyō′nâ) *f* laceration; rip; tear
laconico (lâ·kô′nē·kō) *a* succinct, concise
lacrima (lâ′krē·mâ), **lagrima** (lâ′grē·mâ) *f* tear
lacrimare (lâ·krē·mâ′rā) *vi* to weep; to water *(eyes); (fig)* to trickle
lacrimogeno (lâ·krē·mô′jā·nō) *a* tear-producing; **gas** — teargas
lacuna (lâ·kū′nâ) *f* blank, gap
ladro (lâ′drō) *m* thief
ladrone (lâ·drō′nâ) *m* highwayman
ladruncolo (lâ·drūn′kō·lō) *m* petty thief
laggiù (lâj·jū′) *adv* down there
lagnanza (lâ·nyân′tsâ) *f* complaint; criticism
lagnarsi (lâ·nyâr′sē) *vr* to complain
laico (lâ′ē·kō) *m* layman; — *a* laic, lay
lama (lâ′mâ) *f* blade, cutting edge; — *m* lama; *(zool)* llama
lambiccare (lâm·bēk·kâ′rā) *vt* to distill; **lambiccarsi il cervello** to rack one's brains
lambire (lâm·bē′rā) *vt* to touch lightly; to skim over; to lap
lamentare (lâ·mân·tâ′rā) *vt* to regret; to complain about
lamentarsi (lâ·mân·târ′sē) *vr* to complain, grumble
lamentela (lâ·mân·tā′lâ) *f* complaint
lamento (lâ·mân′tō) *m* moan; complaining; **-so** (lâ·mân·tō′zō) *a* sorrowful

lamiera (lâ·myâ′râ) *f* sheet *(metal);* — **di ferro** sheet iron
laminatoio (lâ·mē·nâ·tô′yō) *m* rolling mill
lampada (lâm′pâ·dâ) *f* lamp
lampadario (lâm·pâ·dâ′ryō) *m* chandelier
lampadina (lâm·pâ·dē′nâ) *f* light bulb; — **tascabile** flashlight
lampante (lâm·pân′tā) *a* clear; obvious; flashing
lampeggiare (lâm·pāj·jâ·rā) *vi* to lightning; to flash
lampeggiatore (lâm·pāj·jâ·tō′râ) *m (auto)* directional light
lampeggio (lâm·pej′jō) *m* flashing; lightning
lampione (lâm·pyō′nâ) *m* lamppost; street light
lampo (lâm′pō) *m* lightning flash; **chiusura** — zipper; **guerra** — blitzkrieg
lampone (lâm·pō′nâ) *m* raspberry
lana (lâ′nâ) *f* wool; — **di acciaio** steel wool; **buona** — rascal
lancetta (lân·chāt′tâ) *f* watch hand; clock hand
lancia (lân′châ) *f* spear; launch
lanciafiamme (lân·châ·fyâm′mā) *m* flamethrower
lanciarazzo (lân·châ·râ′tsō) *m* bazooka
lanciare (lân·châ′rā) *vt* to hurl, throw; to launch
lanciarsi (lân·châr′sē) *vr* to hurl oneself, fling oneself; to leap
lanciatore (lân·châ·tō′râ) *m* baseball pitcher
lancinante (lân·chē·nân′tā) *a* excruciating; **dolore** — piercing pain
lancio (lân′chō) *m* throw; leap; — **del disco** discus throw; — **del peso** shotput; — **del martello** hammer throw; **pista di** — *(avi)* runway
languido (lân′gwē·dō) *a* languorous; logy
languire (lân·gwē′rā) *vi* to languish
languore (lân·gwō′rā) *m* languor; sluggishness
laniero (lâ·nyā′rō) *a* woolen
lanificio (lâ·nē·fē′chō) *m* woolen mill
lanterna (lân·târ′nâ) *f* lantern
lanugine (lâ·nū′jē·nâ) *f* down; soft hair; fuzz
lapide (lâ′pē·dā) *f* stone slab; tombstone
lapis (lâ′pēs) *m* pencil; — **per le labbra** lipstick; — **per le ciglia** eyebrow pencil
lardo (lâr′dō) *m* lard; bacon
larghezza (lâr·gā′tsâ) *f* breadth, width
largo (lâr′gō) *a* broad, wide; — *m* width;

farsi — to push one's way through; **prendere il** — *(fig)* to sneak away; **di manica larga** placid, easygoing

laringite (lâ·rēn·jē'tā) *f* laryngitis

larvato (lâr·vâ'tō) *a* disguised, concealed

lasagna (lâ·zâ'nyâ) *f* large noodle

lasagnone (lâ·zâ·nyō'nā) *m (fig)* foolish fellow, dolt

lasciapassare (lâ·shâ·pâs·sâ'rā) *m* permit, authorization

lasciare (lâ·shâ'rā) *vt* to leave; to let; to stop; — **cadere** to drop

lasciarsi (lâ·shâr'sē) *vr* to allow oneself; to part

lascito (lâ'shē·tō) *m* legacy

lascivo (lâ·shē'vō) *a* lascivious

lassativo (lâs·sâ·tē'vō) *a&m* laxative

lassù (lâs·sū') *adv* up there

lastra (lâ'strâ) *f* plate, slab

lastrico (lâ'strē·kō) *m* flagstone; pavement

lastrone (lâ·strō'nā) *m* large slab

latente (lâ·tān'tā) *a* latent; quiescent

laterale (lâ·tā·râ'lā) *a* lateral

laterizi (lâ·tā·rē'tsē) *mpl* bricks

latifondista (lâ·tē·fōn·dē'stâ) *m* owner of a landed estate; big landowner

latifondo (lâ·tē·fōn'dō) *m* large landed estate

latino (lâ·tē'nō) *m&a* Latin

latitante (lâ·tē·tân'tā) *a&m* fugitive

latitudine (lâ·tē·tū'dē·nā) *f* latitude

lato (lâ'tō) *m* side; — *a* broad

latore (lâ·tō'râ) *m* bearer

latrare (lâ·trâ'râ) *vi* to howl; to bark

latrina (lâ·trē'nâ) *f* latrine, toilet

latta (lât'tâ) *f* tin; tinplate; tin can

lattaio (lât·tâ'yō) *m* milkman

lattante (lât·tân'tā) *a* unweaned; — *m* suckling

latte (lât'tā) *m* milk; — **condensato** condensed milk; — **scremato** skimmed milk; **fratello di** — foster brother

latteria (lât·tā·rē'â) *f* dairy; dairy farm

latticini (lât·tē·chē'nē) *mpl* dairy products

lattico (lât'tē·kō) *a* lactic; **acido** — lactic acid

lattoniere (lât·tō·nyā'râ) *m* tinman, tinsmith

lattuga (lât·tū'gâ) *f* lettuce

laurea (lâ'ū·râ·â) *f* academic degree

laurearsi (lâu·râ·âr'sē) *vr* to take one's degree; to be graduated

lauro (lâ'ū·rō) *m* laurel; **foglie di** — bay leaves

lauto (lâ'ū·tō) *a* sumptuous; magnificent

lava (lâ'vâ) *f* lava

lavabiancheria (lâ·vâ·byân·kā·rē'â) *f* washing machine

lavabile (lâ·vâ'bē·lā) *a* washable

lavabo (lâ·vâ'bō) *m.* washbowl, washbasin

lavaggio (lâ·vâj'jō) *m* washing; — **del cervello** brainwashing

lavagna (lâ·vâ'nyâ) *f* blackboard

lavamano (lâ·vâ·mâ'nō) *m* washstand

lavanda (lâ·vân'dâ) *f (bot)* lavender

lavandaia (lâ·vân·dâ'yâ) *f* washwoman, laundress

lavandaio (lâ·vân·dâ'yō) *m* laundryman

lavanderia (lâ·vân·dā·rē'â) *f* laundry

lavandino (lâ·vân·dē'nō) *m* sink; washstand

lavapiatti (lâ·vâ·pyât'tē) *m* dishwasher

lavare (lâ·vâ'rā) *vt* to wash; — **a secco** to dry-clean

lavarsi (lâ·vâr'sē) *vr* to wash oneself; to wash up; — **le mani** *(fig)* to wash one's hands

lavata (lâ·vâ'tâ) *f* wash; — **di capo** scolding; severe reproof

lavativo (lâ·vâ·tē'vō) *m* enema; *(fig)* bore

lavina (lâ·vē'nâ) *f* landslide

lavorante (lâ·vō·rân'tâ) *m* worker

lavorare (lâ·vō·râ'rā) *vt&i* to work; — **la terra** to work the soil

lavorativo (lâ·vō·râ·tē'vō) *a* working; **giorno** — workday

lavorato (lâ·vō·râ'tō) *a* worked; processed; wrought

lavoratore (lâ·vō·râ·tō'râ) *m* workman; — *a* working

lavoratrice (lâ·vō·râ·trē'châ) *f* workwoman

lavorazione (lâ·vō·râ·tsyō'nā) *f* workmanship; processing; working

lavoro (lâ·vō'rō) *m* work; **lavori stradali** road under construction; **camera del** — trade union

lazzaretto (lâ·dzâ·rāt'tō) *m* isolation hospital, lazaretto

lazzarone (lâ·dzâ·rō'nâ) *m* beggar; bum; *(sl)* rascal

le (lā) *art fpl* the; — *pron* them; to her; to it

leale (lā·â'lā) *a* sincere, true; loyal

lealtà (lā·âl·tâ') *f* loyalty; fairness

lebbra (lāb'brâ) *f* leprosy

lebbroso (lāb·brō'zō) *a* leprous; — *m* leper

leccapiedi (lāk·kâ·pyā'dē) *m* toady, flatterer

leccare (lāk·kâ'rā) *vt* to lick; *(fig)* to flatter

leccornia (lāk·kôr'nyâ) *f (food)* delicacy

lecito (le'chē·tō) *a* permissible; legal

ledere * (le'dā·rā) *vt* to injure, hurt

â ârm, ā bāby, e bet, ē bē, ō gō, ô gône, ū blūe, b bad, ch child, d dad, f fat, g gay, j jet

lega (lā′gâ) *f* league; union; alloy

legaccio (lā·gâ′chō) *m* string; shoelace; garter

legale (lā·gâ′lā) *a* statutory; legal; **per via —** through legal means; **—** *m* lawyer

legalizzare (lā·gâ·lē·dzâ′rā) *vt* to legalize; to notarize

legame (lā·gâ′mā) *m* tie; bond

legare (lā·gâ′rā) *vt* to tie; to bind; to bequeath

legarsi (lā·gâr′sē) *vr* to bind oneself; **legarsela al dito** *(fig)* to hold a grudge

legato (lā·gâ′tō) *a* tied; bound; **—** *m* envoy; ambassador; *(law)* legacy

legatore (lā·gâ·tō′rā) *m* bookbinder

legatura (lā·gâ·tū′râ) *f* binding; *(mus)* slur

legazione (lā·gâ·tsyō′nā) *f* legation

legge (lāj′jā) *f* law; **di —** of necessity; **proposta di —** *(pol)* bill

leggenda (lāj·jān′dâ) *f* legend; caption

leggere * (lej′jā·rā) *vt* to read

leggerezza (lāj·jā·rā′tsâ) *f* levity; lightness; thoughtlessness

leggermente (lāj·jār·mān′tā) *adv* lightly; easily

leggero (lāj·jā′rō) *a* light *(weight)*; nimble; inconsiderate; easy

leggiadro (lāj·jâ′drō) *a* lovely; graceful

leggibile (lāj·jē′bē·lā) *a* legible

leggio (lāj·jē′ō) *m (eccl)* lectern; reading desk

leghista (lā·gē′stâ) *m* club member; union member

legislativo (lā·jē·zlâ·tē′vō) *a* legislative, lawmaking

legislatore (lā·jē·zlâ·tō′rā) *m* legislator, lawmaker

legislatura (lā·jē·zlâ·tū′râ) *f* legislature

legislazione (lā·jē·zlâ·tsyō′nā) *f* legislation, lawmaking

legittima (lā·jēt′tē·mâ) *f (law)* legitim

legittimo (lā·jēt′tē·mō) *a* lawful, legal; legitimate

legna (lā′nyâ) *f* firewood; brushwood

legnaiolo (lā·nyâ·yō′lō) *m* woodcutter

legname (lā·nyâ′mā) *m* lumber; **deposito —** lumberyard

legnata (lā·nyâ′tā) *f* beating, thrashing

legno (lā′nyō) *m* wood; timber; **testa di —** *(fig)* blockhead, dunce; **— compensato** plywood

legume (lā·gū′mā) *m* legume; vegetable

lei (lā′ē) *pron* you *(for)*; she; her

lembo (lām′bō) *m* flap; edge; **all'estremo — della terra** to the ends of the earth

lemme lemme (lām′mā lām′mā) *adv* slowly

lendine (len′dē·nā) *m* nit

lenire (lā·nē′rā) *vt* to soothe, calm; to allay

lenone (lā·nō′nā) *m* procurer, pimp; white slaver

lentamente (lān·tâ·mān′tā) *adv* slowly; gradually

lente (lān′tā) *f* lens; **— d'ingrandimento** magnifying glass

lentezza (lān·tâ′tsâ) *f* slothfulness; slowness

lenti (lān′tē) *fpl* eyeglasses

lenticchia (lān·tēk′kyâ) *f* lentil

lentiggine (lān·tēj′jē·nā) *f* freckle

lento (lān′tō) *a* slow; loose, slack; **—** *adv* slowly

lenza (lān′tsâ) *f* fishing line, line for angling

lenzuola (lān·tswō′lâ) *fpl* bedsheets

lenzuolo (lān·tswō′lō) *m* bedsheet

leone (lā·ō′nā) *m* lion

leonessa (lā·ō·nās′sâ) *f* lioness

leopardo (lā·ō·pâr′dō) *m* leopard

lepre (lā′prā) *f* hare

lesina (le′zē·nâ) *f* awl; parsimony

lesinare (lā·zē·nâ′rā) *vi* to be stingy; to be very sparing

lesione (lā·zyō′nā) *f* lesion; wound

leso (lā′zō) *a* hurt; damaged

lessare (lās·sâ′rā) *vt* to boil

lesso (lās′sō) *m* boiled beef

lestofante (lā·stō·fân′tā) *m* swindler; shyster

letamaio (lā·tâ·mâ′yō) *m* manure pile

letame (lā·tâ′mā) *m* manure

letizia (lā·tē′tsyâ) *f* joy, gaiety

lettera (let′tâ·rā) *f* letter; **alla —** literally

letteralmente (lāt·tā·râl·mān′tā) *adv* literally

letterario (lāt·tā·râ′ryō) *a* literary; **proprietà letteraria** copyright

letterato (lāt·tā·râ′tō) *m* man of letters, man of learning; **—** *a* learned

letteratura (lāt·tā·râ·tū′râ) *f* literature

lettiga (lāt·tē′gâ) *f (med)* stretcher

lettino (lāt·tē′nō) *m* small bed; cot

letto (lāt′tō) *m* bed; **— da campeggio** camp bed; **— a sacco** sleeping bag; **figli del primo —** children of the first marriage

lettura (lāt·tū′râ) *f* reading

leva (lā′vâ) *f* lever; *(mil)* draft

levante (lā·vân′tā) *m* Levant; East

levare (lā·vâ′rā) *vt* to remove, take out; to lift; **— il campo** to break camp; **— il bollore** to bring to a boil; **— il tacco** to decamp; **— l'ancora** to weigh anchor; **— la seduta** to adjourn the meeting

levarsi (lā·vâr′sē) *vr* to get off; to get up; to rise; **— il pane dalla bocca** *(fig)* to make great sacrifices; — **del sole** sunrise

levata (lā·vâ'tâ) *f* rising; removal; — **delle lettere** mail collection

levatrice (lā·vâ·trē'chā) *f* midwife

levigato (lā·vē·gâ'tō) *a* smooth, smoothed

levriere (lā·vryā'rā) *m* greyhound

lezione (lā·tsyō'nā) *f* lesson; class

li (lē) *pron* them

lì (lē) *adv* there

Libano (lē'bâ·nō) *m* Lebanon

libbra (lēb'brâ) *f* pound *(weight)*

libellula (lē·bel'lū·lâ) *f* dragonfly

liberale (lē·bā·râ'lā) *a* generous, free; liberal

liberamente (lē·bā·râ·mān'tā) *adv* freely; openly

liberare (lē·bā·râ'rā) *vt* to free, set free

liberarsi (lē·bā·râr'sē) *vr* to rid oneself; to free oneself

liberato (lē·bā·râ'tō) *a* liberated, freed, set free

liberatore (lē·bā·râ·tō'rā) *m* liberator

liberazione (lē·bā·râ·tsyō'nā) *f* liberation, setting free, freeing

liberismo (lē·bā·rē'zmō) *m* free trade

liberista (lē·bā·rē'stâ) *m* free trader

libero (lē'bā·rō) *a* free; vacant; unhampered; **a piede** — out on bail; **all'aria libera** outdoors; — **arbitrio** free will; **verso** — free verse

libertà (lē·bār·tâ') *f* freedom, liberty; lack of restraint

libertario (lē·bār·tâ'ryō) *m&a* libertarian

libertinaggio (lē·bār·tē·nâj'jō) *m* libertinism, licentiousness

libertino (lē·bār·tē'nō) *m* libertine, rake

libidine (lē·bē'dē·nā) *f* lust

libraio (lē·brâ'yō) *m* bookdealer

libreria (lē·brā·rē'stâ) *f* bookstore; bookcase

librettista (lē·brāt·tē'stâ) *m* librettist

libretto (lē·brāt'tō) *m* booklet; libretto

libro (lē'brō) *m* book; — **di bordo** *(naut)* log; — **mastro** *(com)* ledger

licenza (lē·chān'tsâ) *f* license; leave; authorization

licenziare (lē·chān·tsyâ'rā) *vt* to dismiss, fire; to authorize

licenziarsi (lē·chān·tsyâr'sē) *vr* to resign; to take one's degree

licenzioso (lē·chān·tsyō'zō) *a* licentious, debauched

liceo (lē·chā'ō) *m* high school; — **scientifico** technical school

licitazione (lē·chē·tâ·tsyō'nā) *f* bid; auction sale

lido (lē'dō) *m* beach, shore

lietamente (lyā·tâ·mān'tā) *adv* happily, gleefully

lieto (lyā'tō) *a* glad, happy

lieve (lyā'vā) *a* light *(weight)*; simple, easy

lievemente (lyā·vā·mān'tā) *adv* lightly; softly

lievito (lye'vē·tō) *m* yeast

ligure (lē·gū'rā) *m&a* Ligurian

lilla (lēl'lâ) *f* lilac; — *m* lilac color

lima (lē'mâ) *f* file

limare (lē·mâ'rā) *vt* to file

limatura (lē·mâ·tū'râ) *f* filings

limetta (lē·māt'tâ) *f* lime *(fruit)*

limitare (lē·mē·tâ'rā) *vt* to limit, check

limitarsi (lē·mē·târ'sē) *vr* to confine oneself, limit oneself

limitatamente (lē·mē·tâ·tâ·mān'tā) *adv* in a limited way, limitedly

limitazione (lē·mē·tâ·tsyō'nā) *f* limitation, check

limite (lē'mē·tā) *m* limit; — **massimo di velocità** speed limit

limonata (lē·mō·nâ'tâ) *f* lemonade

limone (lē·mō'nā) *m* lemon

limoso (lē·mō'zō) *a* slimy, muddy, miry

limpido (lēm'pē·dō) *a* clear, limpid

lince (lēn'chā) *f* lynx

linciaggio (lēn·châj'jō) *m* lynching

linciare (lēn·châ'rā) *vt* to lynch

lindo (lēn'dō) *a* neat; orderly

linea (lē'nā·â) *f* line; figure; — **tranviaria** streetcar line; — **automobilistica** bus line

lineetta (lē·nā·āt'tâ) *f* dash; hyphen

lingotto (lēn·gōt'tō) *m* ingot

lingua (lēn'gwâ) *f* language; tongue; **conoscere una** — **correntemente** to speak a language fluently; **in** — **povera** in plain words

linguista (lēn·gwē'stâ) *m* linguist

linguistica (lēn·gwē'stē·kâ) *f* linguistics

lino (lē'nō) *m* linen; flax

linoleum (lē·nô'lāūm) *m* linoleum

linosa (lē·nō'zâ) *f* linseed

linotipia (lē·nō·tē·pē'â) *f* linotype composition

linotipista (lē·nō·tē·pē'stâ) *m&f* linotype operator

liocorno (lyō·kōr'nō) *m* unicorn

Lipsia (lē'psyâ) *f* Leipzig

liquefare (lē·kwâ·fâ'rā) *vt&i* to melt

liquefazione (lē·kwâ·fâ·tsyō'nā) *f* melting

liquidare (lē·kwē·dâ'rā) *vt* to liquidate

liquidazione (lē·kwē·dâ·tsyō'nā) *f* liquidation; clearance sale

liquido (lē'kwē·dō) *a&m* liquid; **denaro** — cash

liquirizia (lē·kwē·rē'tsyâ) *f* licorice

â ârm, **ā** bāby, **e** bet, **ē** bē, **ō** gō, **ô** gône, **ū** blūe, **b** bad, **ch** child, **d** dad, **f** fat, **g** gay, **j** jet

liquore (lē·kwō'rā) *m* liquor; liqueur
liquoroso (lē·kwō·rō'zō) *a* highly alcoholic
lira (lē'râ) *f* lira; lyre
lirico (lē'rē·kō) *a* lyrical
Lisbona (lē·zbō'nâ) *f* Lisbon
lisca (lē'skâ) *f* fishbone
lisciare (lē·shâ'rā) *vt* to smooth; to flatter
lisciarsi (lē·shâr'sē) *vr* to dress carefully; to groom oneself; to preen
liscio (lē'shō) *a* smooth; straight *(drink)*
liscivia (lē·shē'vyâ) *f* lye
lista (lē'stâ) *f* list; bill of fare; — **dei vini** wine list
listino (lē·stē'nō) *m* bulletin; price list
litania (lē·tâ·nē'â) *f* litany; *(fig)* long list
lite (lē'tā) *f* argument, row; lawsuit
litigare (lē·tē·gâ'rā) *vt* to argue, dispute, contend; — *vi* to quarrel
litigio (lē·tē'jō) *m* lawsuit; quarrel, dispute
litografia (lē·tō·grâ·fē'â) *f* lithography
litorale (lē·tō·râ'lâ) *a* coastal; — *m* coastline
litro (lē'trō) *m* liter; **un quarto di** — a half-pint
Lituania (lē·twâ'nyâ) *f* Lithuania
lituano (lē·twâ'nō) *a&m* Lithuanian
liturgia (lē·tūr·jē'â) *f* liturgy
liutaio (lyū·tâ'yō) *m* stringed-instrument maker
liuto (lyū'tō) *m* lute
livellare (lē·vâl·lâ'rā) *vt* to level; to make uniform
livellazione (lē·vâl·lâ·tsyō'nâ) *f* levelling; standardization
livello (lē·vâl'lō) *m* level; **passaggio a** — railroad crossing; **sul** — **del mare** above sea level; — **delle acque** water level; waterline
livido (lē'vē·dō) *a* livid; pale; *(fig)* jealous; — *m* contusion, bruise
lo (lō) *art m* the; — *pron* it, him
lobbia (lōb'byâ) *f* fedora
lobo (lō'bō) *m (anat)* lobe
locale (lō·kâ'lâ) *a* local; — *m* room; place; — **di lusso** high-class establishment
località (lō·kâ·lē·tâ') *f* position; town
localizzare (lō·kâ·lē·dzâ'rā) *vt* to localize; to find, locate
locanda (lō·kân'dâ) *f* inn
locandiere (lō·kân·dyā'rā), *m* **locandiera** (lō·kân·dyâ'râ) *f* innkeeper
locandina (lō·kân·dē'nâ) *f (theat)* handbill
locare (lō·kâ'rā) *vt* to rent; **locasi** for rent
locatario (lō·kâ·tâ'ryō) *m* tenant
locativo (lō·kâ·tē'vō) *a (gram)* locative

locatore (lō·kâ·tō'rā) *m* lessor
locazione (lō·kâ·tsyō'nâ) *f* rent; lease
locomotiva (lō·kō·mō·tē'vâ) *f* engine, locomotive
locomozione (lō·kō·mō·tsyō'nâ) *m* locomotion
locusta (lō·kū'stâ) *f* locust
lodare (lō·dâ'rā) *vt* to praise; to extol
lodarsi (lō·dâr'sē) *vr* to praise oneself; to swell with pride
lode (lō'dâ) *f* praise
lodevole (lō·de'vō·lâ) *a* laudable
logaritmo (lō·gâ·rēt'mō) *m* logarithm
loggia (lôj'jâ) *f (theat)* box, loge; balcony
loggione (lōj·jō'nâ) *m (theat)* gallery
logorare (lō·gō·râ'rā) *vt* to wear out
logorarsi (lō·gō·râr'sē) *vr* to wear oneself out; to become worn out
logorio (lō·gō·rē'ō) *m* waste; wear
logoro (lô'gō·rō) *a* worn-out
lombaggine (lōm·bâj·jē·nâ) *f* lumbago
Lombardia (lōm·bâr·dē'â) *f* Lombardy
lombata (lōm·bâ'tâ) *f* loin *(meat)*
lombo (lōm'bō) *m* sirloin; loin
Londra (lōn'drâ) *f* London
lontananza (lōn·tâ·nân'tsâ) *f* time away, absence; distance
lontano (lōn·tâ'nō) *a* distant; absent; — *adv* far, a long way
lontra (lōn'trâ) *f* otter
loquace (lō·kwâ'châ) *a* talkative
lordare (lōr·dâ'rā) *vt* to dirty; to foul
lordo (lōr'dō) *a* dirty, filthy; *(com)* gross
loro (lō'rō) *pron* they, them, to them; you, to you; yours; theirs; — *a* your; their
losco (lō'skō) *a* one-eyed; shady, sinister
lotta (lōt'tâ) *f* struggle; wrestling; — **libera** catch-as-catch-can wrestling; **partita di** — wrestling match
lottare (lōt·tâ'râ) *vi* to struggle; to wrestle
lottatore (lōt·tâ·tō'rā) *m* fighter; wrestler; struggler
lotteria (lōt·tā·rē'â) *f* lottery
lottizzare (lōt·tē·dzâ'rā) *vt* to parcel out; to allot
lotto (lōt'tō) *m* lottery; parcel, plot *(land)*
lozione (lō·tsyō'nâ) *f* lotion; — **per la barba** shaving lotion; — **per gli occhi** eyewash
lubrificante (lū·brē·fē·kân'tā) *a* lubricating; — *m* lubricant
lubrificare (lū·brē·fē·kâ'rā) *vt* to lubricate
lubrificazione (lū·brē·fē·kâ·tsyō'nâ) *f* lubrication
lucchetto (lūk·kât'tō) *m* padlock
luccicare (lū·chē·kâ'rā) *vi* to gleam; to

---

k kid, **l** let, **m** met, **n** not, **p** pat, **r** very, **s** sat, **sh** shop, **t** tell, **v** vat, **w** we, **y** yes, **z** zero

shimmer
luccichio (lū·chē·kē′ō) *m* glimmer
luccio (lū′chō) *m* pike *(fish)*
lucciola (lū′chō·lå) *f* firefly
luce (lū′chā) *f* light; — **di arresto** stop-light; — **di posizione** parking light; **filtro** — light filter
lucente (lū·chān′tā) *a* luminous, shining; sparkling; gleaming
lucernario (lū·chär·nâ′ryō) *m* skylight
lucertola (lū·cher′tō·lå) *f* lizard
lucidare (lū·chē·då′rā) *vt* to polish, shine; to trace *(drawing)*
lucidatrice (lū·chē·då·trē′chā) *f* floor polisher
lucidità (lū·chē·dē·tâ′) *f* lucidity; — **di mente** clearness of mind
lucido (lū′chē·dō) *a* shining; lucid; — *m* polish; — **per le scarpe** shoe polish
lucignolo (lū·chē′nyō·lō) *m* wick
lucro (lū′krō) *m* profit
luglio (lū′lyō) *m* July
lui (lū′ē) *pron* he; him
lumaca (lū·mâ′kå) *f* snail; **a passo di** — at a snail's pace
lume (lū′mā) *m* light; lamp *(fig)* under-standing; **a** — **di naso** at first glance; roughly speaking
luminoso (lū·mē·nō′zō) *a* shining, bright
luna (lū′nå) *f* moon; — **di miele** honey-moon; **al chiaro di** — by moonlight; **avere la** — to be in an ugly mood
lunario (lū·nâ′ryō) *m* almanac; **sbarcare il** — *(fig)* to make both ends meet
lunatico (lū·nâ′tē·kō) *a* moody, capri-cious; lunatical
lunedì (lū·nā·dē′) *m* Monday
lungamente (lūn·gâ·mān′tā) *adv* length-ily, at length

lunghezza (lūn·gā′tså) *f* length
lungimirante (lūn·jē·mē·rân′tā) *a* far-sighted
lungo (lūn′gō) *a* long; thin; — *prep* beside, along; **a** — **andare** in the long run; — **disteso** headlong; **tirare in** — to put off, delay
lungomare (lūn·gō·mâ′rā) *m* boardwalk; street by the sea
luogo (lwō′gō) *m* place; spot; **aver** — to take place; to happen; **in** — **di** instead of
lupo (lū′pō) *m* wolf; **In bocca al** —! Good luck to you! — **di mare** veteran seaman
lurido (lū′rē·dō) *a* filthy, lewd, lurid
lusinga (lū·zēn′gå) *f* flattery
lusingare (lū·zēn·gâ′rā) *vt* to cajole; to flatter
lusingarsi (lū·zēn·gâr′sē) *vr* to trust, hope; to feel confident; to flatter
lusinghiero (lū·zēn·gyā′rō) *a* flattering; promising
lussazione (lūs·så·tsyō′nā) *f (med)* dis-location
lusso (lūs′sō) *m* luxury
lussuoso (lūs·swō′zō) *a* deluxe, magnifi-cent
lussureggiante (lūs·sū·rāj·jân′tā) *a* luxuri-ant; overabundant
lustrare (lū·strâ′rā) *vt* to shine; to clean; to polish
lustrascarpe (lū·strâ·scâr′pā) *m* boot-black, shoeblack; shoeshine boy
lustro (lū′strō) *m* luster; — *a* bright, shin-ing; polished
lutto (lūt′tō) *m* mourning; — **pesante** deep sorrow
luttuoso (lūt·twō′zō) *a* sorrowful, mourn-ful; saddening

M

ma (mâ) *conj* but
macabro (mâ·kâ′brō) *a* macabre; eerie
maccheroni (mâk·kā·rō′nē) *mpl* macaroni
macchia (mâk′kyå) *f* stain; blemish; thicket
macchiare (mâk·kyâ′rā) *vt* to dirty; to stain
macchiarsi (mâk·kyâr′sē) *vr* to ruin one's reputation; to get dirty
macchietta (mâk·kyāt′tå) *f* eccentric; odd character
macchiettista (mâk·kyāt·tē′stå) *m* mimic
macchina (mâk′kē·nå) *f* machine; auto-mobile; engine; — **fotografica** camera; — **da cucire** sewing machine; — **da scrivere** typewriter

macchinalmente (mâk·kē·nâl·mān′tā) *adv* mechanically; automatically
macchinario (mâk·kē·nâ′ryō) *m* ma-chinery; works, working parts
macchinazione (mâk·kē·nâ·tsyō′nā) *f* in-trigue; conspiracy
macchinetta (mâk·kē·nāt′tâ) *f* little ma-chine; — **per i capelli** hair clippers; — **del caffè** coffeepot
macchinista (mâk·kē·nē′stâ) *m* machinist; engineer; stoker; stagehand
macchinosamente (mâk·kē·nō·zâ·mān′-tā) *adv* heavily; complicatedly
macedonia (mâ·châ·dō′nyå) *m* fruit salad
macellaio (mâ·châl·lâ′yō) *m* butcher

â ârm, **ā** bāby, **e** bet, **ē** bē, **ō** gō, **ô** gône, **ū** blūe, **b** bad, **ch** child, **d** dad, **f** fat, **g** gay, **j** jet

macellare (mâ·chäl·lâ'rä) *vt* to butcher
macellazione (mâ·chäl·lâ·tsyō'nä) *f* slaughtering, butchering
macelleria (mâ·chäl·lä·rē'â) *f* butcher shop
macello (mâ·chäl'lō) *m* slaughterhouse; *(fig)* slaughter, massacre
macerare (mâ·chä·râ'rä) *vt* to steep, macerate
maceria (mâ·che'ryâ) *f* ruins, debris
macero (mâ'chä·rō) *a* macerated
macigno (mâ·chē'nyō) *m* boulder, large rock
macilento (mâ·chē·län'tō) *a* cadaverous, emaciated
macina (mâ'chē·nâ) *f* millstone
macinacaffè (mâ·chē·nâ·kâf·fä') *m* coffee mill
macinapepe (mâ·chē·nâ·pä'pä) *m* pepper mill
macinare (mâ·chē·nâ'rä) *vt* to grind; to pulverize
macinato (mâ·chē·nâ'tō) *a* ground; milled; — *m* flour; ground grain
macinino (mâ·chē·nē'nō) *m* small mill; *(coll)* old car; *(sl)* jalopy
macrocosmo (mâ·krō·kō'zmō) *m* macrocosm
madornale (mâ·dōr·nâ'lä) *a* huge, behemoth
madre (mâ'drä) *f* mother
madreperla (mâ·drä·pär'lâ) *f* mother-of-pearl, nacre
madrigna (mâ·drē'nyâ) *f* stepmother
madrina (mâ·drē'nâ) *f* godmother; foster mother
maestà (mâ·ä·stâ') *f* majesty, stateliness
maestosamente (mâ·ä·stō·zâ·män'tä) *adv* majestically; regally
maestra (mâ·ä'strä) *f* teacher
maestranza (mâ·ä·strân'tsâ) *f* workmen
maestria (mâ·ä·strē'â) *f* proficiency; dexterity
maestro (mâ·ä'strō) *m* teacher; master; — *a* main; masterful; **strada maestra** highway; main road; **vento** — northwest wind
magari (mâ·gâ'rē) *adv* perhaps, maybe; — ! *interj* God grant!, if only!
magazzinaggio (mâ·gâ·dzē·nâj'jō) *m* storage
magazziniere (mâ·gâ·dzē·nyä'rä) *m* warehouseman
magazzino (mâ·gâ·dzē'nō) *m* warehouse; depot; store
maggio (mâj'jō) *m* May
maggiorana (mâj·jō·râ'nâ) *f* marjoram
maggioranza (mâj·jō·rân'tsâ) *f* majority

maggiorare (mâj·jō·râ'rä) *vt* to raise; to increase
maggiorato (mâj·jō·râ'tō) *a* raised; increased
maggiorazione (mâj·jō·râ·tsyō'nä) *f* increase
maggiordomo (mâj·jōr·dō'mō) *m* majordomo
maggiore (mâj·jō'rä) *a* greater; elder; larger; — *m (mil)* major
maggiorenne (mâj·jō·rän'nä) *a* of age
maggiormente (mâj·jōr·män'tä) *adv* greatly; all the more
magia (mâ·jē'â) *f* magic; witchcraft
magistrale (mâ·jē·strâ'lä) *a* dextrous; skillful; masterful; **istituto** — teachers college; **scuola** — normal school; **con tono** — in a commanding voice
magistralmente (mâ·jē·strâl·män'tä) *adv* adroitly; masterfully
magistrato (mâ·jē·strâ'tō) *m* judge
magistratura (mâ·jē·strâ·tū'râ) *f* judiciary, bench
maglia (mâ'lyâ) *f* mesh; undershirt; **lavorare a** — to knit
maglieria (mâ·lyä·rē'â) *f* knitted goods; hosiery
maglietta (mâ·lyät'tâ) *f* undershirt
maglione (mâ·lyō'nä) *m* sweater
magnanimità (mâ·nyâ·nē·mē·tâ') *f* magnanimity; largess
magnanimo (mâ·nyâ'nē·mō) *a* generous, liberal
magnano (mâ·nyâ'nō) *m* locksmith
magnate (mâ·nyâ'tä) *m* patron; magnate
magnesia (mâ·nye'zyâ) *f* magnesia
magnesio (mâ·nye'zyō) *m* magnesium
magnete (mâ·nyâ'tä) *m* magneto; magnet
magnetico (mâ·nye'tē·kō) *a* magnetic
magnetofono (mâ·nyä·tō·fō'nō) *m* tape recorder
magnificamente (mâ·nyē·fē·kâ·män'tä) *adv* magnificently, splendidly
magnificenza (mâ·nyē·fē·chän'tsâ) *f* pomp; magnificence
magnifico (mâ·nyē'fē·kō) *a* magnificent
mago (mâ'gō) *m* magician
magrezza (mâ·grä'tsâ) *f* skinniness; scantiness
magro (mâ'grō) *a* lean, thin; — *m* lean meat; abstinence
mai (mâ'ē) *adv* ever, never; **non si sa** — one never can tell; **caso** — if, just in case; **come** —? how in the world?, how ever?; — **più** never again
maiale (mâ·yâ'lä) *m* swine; **carne di** — pork; **grasso di** — lard
maialetto (mâ·yâ·lät'tō) *m* suckling pig

---

k kid, **l** let, **m** met, **n** not, **p** pat, **r** very, **s** sat, **sh** shop, **t** tell, **v** vat, **w** we, **y** yes, **z** zero

maiolica (mâ·yô'lē·kâ) f majolica

maionesa (mâ·yō·nā'zâ) f mayonnaise

maiuscola (mâ·yū'skō·lâ) f capital letter

maiuscolo (mâ·yū'skō·lō) a capital; large, gross

mal (mâl) m pain; sickness; — di mare seasickness; — d'aereo airsickness; — di denti toothache; — di pancia stomachache; — di testa headache

malafede (mâ·lâ·fā'dā) f bad faith

malaffare (mâ·lâf·fâ'rā) m dissolute living; donna di — woman of easy virtue

malagiato (mâ·lâ·jâ'tō) a ill at ease; badly off

malagrazia (mâ·lâ·grâ'tsyâ) f rudeness; disfavor

malalingua (mâ·lâ·lēn'gwâ) f gossip; slanderer

malamente (mâ·lâ·mān'tā) adv badly

malandato (mâ·lân·dâ'tō) a in poor condition; worn-out

malandrino (mâ·lân·drē'nō) m ruffian, tough; gangster

malanimo (mâ·lâ'nē·mō) m spitefulness; ill will, malice

malanno (mâ·lân'nō) m calamity; sickness

malapena (mâ·lâ·pā'nâ) adv hardly; scarcely; just

malaria (mâ·lâ'ryâ) f (med) malaria

malato (mâ·lâ'tō) a sick; — m patient

malattia (mâ·lât·tē'â) f disease, illness

malaugurio (mâ·lâū·gū'ryō) m bad omen, bad sign

malavita (mâ·lâ·vē'tā) f underworld

malcaduco (mâl·kâ·dū'kō) m (med) epilepsy

malcapitato (mâl·kâ·pē·tâ'tō) a unlucky, unfortunate

malcauto (mâl·kâ'ū·tō) a unwary, rash; heedless

malcerto (mâl·chār'tō) a uncertain, dubious

malconcio (mâl·kôn'chō) a bruised, beaten; ill-used, mistreated

malcontento (mâl·kōn·tān'tō) a discontented; dissatisfied; — m dissatisfaction; malcontent

malcostume (mâl·kō·stū'mâ) m dissipation; bad habit; immorality

maldestro (mâl·dā'strō) a awkward, clumsy; unexperienced, unskillful

maldicente (mâl·dē·chān'tā) a slanderous; gossipy; — n slanderer; gossip (person)

maldicenza (mâl·dē·chān'tsâ) f slander; gossip (act)

male (mâ'lā) m evil; disease; pain; misfortune; — adv badly; far — to hurt;

to harm; farsi — to hurt oneself; to injure oneself; niente di — everything's all right

maledetto (mâ·lā·dāt'tō) a damned, cursed

maledire (mâ·lā·dē'rā) vt to curse

maledizione (mâ·lā·dē·tsyō'nā) f curse, malediction; (fig) bad luck

maleducato (mâ·lā·dū·kâ'tō) a ill-bred; unmannerly

maleficio (mâ·lā·fē'chō) m sorcery; spell, enchantment

malefico (mâ·le'fē·kō) a evil; harmful; ruinous

maleodorante (mâ·lā·ō·dō·rân'tā) a smelly, malodorous

maleolente (mâ·lā·ō·lān'tā) a evil-smelling; foul-smelling

malerba (mâ·lār'bâ) f weed

malessere (mâ·les'sā·rā) m uneasiness; indisposition; discomfort

malfatto (mâl·fât'tō) m misdeed; evil act; — a misshapen; poorly made

malfattore (mâl·fât·tō'rā) m criminal

malgarbo (mâl·gâr'bō) m lack of grace; rudeness; awkwardness

malgrado (mâl·grâ'dō) prep despite, notwithstanding; a mio — against my will; — ciò however, nevertheless

malgusto (mâl·gū'stō) m poor taste

malia (mâ·lē'â) f fascination, charm

maliarda (mâ·lyâr'dâ) f enchantress

maligno (mâ·lē'nyō) a malignant; wicked; evil-minded

malinconia (mâ·lēn·kō·nē'â) f melancholy; unhappiness; depression

malinconico (mâ·lēn·kô'nē·kō) a melancholy

malincuore (mâ·lēn·kwō'rā) adv unwillingly

malintendere * (mâ·lēn·ten'dā'rā) vt to misunderstand

malinteso (mâ·lēn·tā'zō) m misunderstanding

malizia (mâ·lē'tsyâ) f malice; cunning

maliziosamente (mâ·lē·tsyō·zâ·mân'tā) adv maliciously, evilly

malizioso (mâ·lē·tsyō'zō) a malicious; roguish; tricky

malleabile (mâl·lā·â'bē·lā) a pliable, yielding

malleolo (mâl·le'ō·lō) m anklebone

malmenare (mâl·mā·nâ'rā) vt to manhandle; to mishandle; to mistreat

malo (mâ'lō) a bad; evil; mala voglia ill will; mala riuscita failure

malocchio (mâ·lôk'kyō) m evil eye

malore (mâ·lō'rā) m indisposition, sickness; sudden collapse

malsano (mâl·sä'nō) *a* unhealthy

maltempo (mâl·tām'pō) *m* bad weather

maltrattare (mâl·trât·tä'rā) *vt* to mistreat, treat badly

malumore (mâ·lū·mō'rā) *m* bad humor; bad mood

malvagio (mâl·vä'jō) *a* wicked

malvagità (mâl·vä·jē·tâ') *f* evil, wickedness

malversazione (mâl·vär·sä·tsyō'nā) *f* embezzlement, defalcation

malvisto (mâl·vē'stō) *a* unpopular; disliked; not well-thought-of

malvivente (mâl·vē·vän'tā) *m* gangster; scoundrel

malvolentieri (mâl·vō·lān·tyä'rē) *adv* unwillingly; against one's will

malvolere (mâl·vō·lā'rä) *m* malevolence

mamma (mâm'mâ) *f* mother

mammalucco (mâm·mâ·lūk'kō) *m* (*sl*) nitwit, dope

mammella (mâm·māl'lâ) *f* breast; udder; teat

mammifero (mâm·mē'fä·rō) *m* mammal

mammola (mâm'mō·lâ) *f* (*bot*) violet

manata (mâ·nä'tâ) *f* handful; slap

mancante (mân·kân'tā) *a* missing; short

mancanza (mân·kân'tsä) *f* want; lack; fault; **in — di** in the absence of; **in — di meglio** for want of something better; **sentire la — di** to miss

mancare (mân·kâ'rä) *vi* to be lacking; to be at fault; to be missing; — *vt* to miss; to fall short of; — **alla parola** to break one's word; **Non ci mancherebbe altro!** That's the last straw!

mancia (mân'châ) *f* tip

manciata (mân·châ'tâ) *f* handful

mancino (mân·chē'nō) *a* left-handed; **colpo —** shady deal; dishonest action

Manciuria (mân·chū'ryâ) *f* Manchuria

manco (mân'kō) *adv* not even; — *a* left

mandamento (mân·dâ·mān'tō) *m* local jurisdiction

mandare (mân·dâ'rä) *vt* to send; — **via** to dismiss; — **a gambe all'aria** to knock head over heels; (*fig*) to upset; to put an end to; — **a picco** (*naut*) to sink; — **ad effetto** to carry out; accomplish; — **per le lunghe** to delay, put off; — **giù** to swallow; (*fig*) to stomach, brook

mandarino (mân·dâ·rē'nō) *m* (*bot*) tangerine

mandatario (mân·dâ·tâ'ryō) (*pol*) mandatary; (*law*) abettor, accomplice; (*com*) agent

mandato (mân·dâ'tō) *m* mandate; warrant

mandibola (mân·dē'bō·lâ) *m* (*anat*) jaw

mandolinista (mân·dō·lē·nē'stâ) *m* mandolin player

mandolino (mân·dō·lē'nō) *m* mandolin

mandorla (mân'dōr·lâ) *f* almond

mandorlato (mân·dōr·lâ'tō) *m* almond cake

mandorlo (mân'dōr·lō) *m* almond tree

mandria (mân'dryâ) *f* large group, drove; herd; flock

maneggiare (mâ·nāj·jâ'rä) *vt* to handle; to manipulate

maneggiarsi (mâ·nāj·jâr'sē) *vr* to manage; to get along

manesco (mâ·nä'skō) *a* quarrelsome

manette (mâ·nät'tā) *fpl* handcuffs

manganello (mân·gâ·nāl'lō) *m* billy, club

mangiare (mân·jâ'rä) *vt* to eat; to corrode; (*fig*) to squander; to take (*chess*)

mangiatoia (mân·jâ·tô'yâ) *f* manger; crib

mangiatore (mân·jâ·tō'rä) *m* big eater

mangime (mân·jē'mä) *m* chicken feed; fodder

mania (mâ·nē'â) *f* mania; pet project, special interest

maniaco (mâ·nē'â·kō) *a* fanatic; — *m* maniac

manica (mâ'nē·kâ) *f* sleeve; gang; **un altro paio di maniche** a horse of a different color; **di — larga** lenient, indulgent; **la M—** the English channel

manicaretto (mâ·nē·kâ·rät'tō) *m* tidbit, delicacy

manichino (mâ·nē·kē'nō) *m* mannequin, dummy

manico (mâ'nē·kō) *m* handle

manicomio (mâ·nē·kô'myō) *m* mental hospital, mental institution

manicotto (mâ·nē·kōt'tō) *m* muff; large stuffed macaroni

maniera (mâ·nyä'râ) *f* manner, way; **in nessuna —** by no means; **in ogni —** anyhow; **bella —** fine manner; **in una — o nell'altra** one way or another; **di — che** so that; **in che — ?** by what means?, how?

manifattura (mâ·nē·fât·tū'râ) *f* manufacture; production

manifatturare (mâ·nē·fât·tū·râ'rä) *vt* to manufacture; to produce

manifatturiero (mâ·nē·fât·tū·ryä'rō) *a* manufacturing

manifestare (mâ·nē·fä·stä'rä) *vt* to manifest; to evince, evidence

manifestarsi (mâ·nē·fä·stâr'sē) *vr* to declare oneself; to show oneself

manifestazione (mâ·nē·fä·stä·tsyō'nā) *f*

display; manifestation; show

manifestino (mâ·nē·fä·stē'nō) *m* handbill

manifesto (mâ·nē·fä'stō) *m* poster; waybill; manifest; — *a* obvious; evident

maniglia (mâ·nē'lyâ) *f* handle, knob

manipolare (mâ·nē·pō·lâ'rä) *vt* to manipulate

maniscalco (mâ·nē·skâl'kō) *m* blacksmith

mannaia (mân·nâ'yâ) *f* axe

mano (mâ'nō) *f* hand; coat of paint; **venire alle mani** to come to blows; **chiedere la** — to ask in marriage; **a** — **a** — little by little; **alla** — easy to get along with, tractable; **far man bassa** to rob; **–dopera** (mâ·nō·dô'pä·râ) *f* labor, work with the hands; **–pola** (mâ·nô'pō·lâ) *f* handgrip, handle; handlebar

manovella (mâ·nō·väl'lâ) *f* handle; crank

manovrare (mâ·nō·vrâ'rä) *vt* to operate; to maneuver; to switch

manovratore (mâ·nō·vrâ·tō'rä) *m* motorman; driver

manrovescio (mân·rō·ve'shō) *m* backhanded blow; backhand

mansione (mân·syō'nä) *f* task; duty

mansueto (mân·swä'tō) *a* tame; meek

mantello (mân·tâl'lō) *m* cloak; wrap; coat (*animal*)

mantenere * (mân·tä·nâ'rä) *vt* to keep; — **la destra** to keep to the right

mantenersi * (mân·tä·nâr'sē) *vr* to maintain oneself; to keep

mantenimento (mân·tä·nē·mân'tō) *m* support; maintenance

mantice (mân'tē·chä) *m* bellows

manuale (mâ·nwâ'lä) *m* handbook; — *a* manual, done by hand

manubrio (mâ·nū'bryō) *m* handlebar; dumbbell

manutenzione (mâ·nū·tän·tsyō'nä) *f* upkeep; servicing

manzo (mân'dzō) *m* beef

mappamondo (mâp·pâ·mōn'dō) *m* globe; map of the world

marachella (mâ·râ·kâl'lâ) *f* trick; fraud

maramaldo (mâ·râ·mâl'dō) *m* coward

marasma (mâ·râ'zmâ) *m* (*fig*) chaos

marca (mâr'kâ) *f* brand; make; trademark; mark

marcare (mâr·kâ'rä) *vt* to mark

marchesa (mâr·kā'zâ) *f* marquise

marchese (mâr·kā'zä) *m* marquis

marchiano (mâr·kyâ'nō) *a* gross, enormous

marchio (mâr'kyō) *m* brand; stamp

marcia (mâr'châ) *f* gear, speed; march; pus

marciapiede (mâr·châ·pyä'dä) *m* sidewalk; platform (*railroad station*)

marciare (mâr·châ'rä) *vi* to march; to function, work

marciatram (mâr·châ·trâm') *f* streetcar platform

marcio (mâr'chō) *a* rotten; — *m* rot

marcire (mâr·chē'rä) *vt* to rot

marciume (mâr·chū'mä) *m* rottenness

marconigramma (mâr·kō·nē·grâm'mâ) *m* radiogram

marconista (mâr·kō·nē'stâ) *m* wireless operator

mare (mâ'rä) *m* sea; (*fig*) huge amount

marea (mâ·rä'â) *f* tide

maremoto (mâ·rä·mō'tō) *m* tidal wave

maresciallo (mâ·rä·shâl'lō) *m* marshal; warrant officer

margarina (mâr·gâ·rē'nâ) *f* margarine

margherita (mâr·gä·rē'tâ) *f* (*bot*) daisy

margine (mâr'jē·nä) *m* edge; margin

marina (mâ·rē'nâ) *f* shore; navy; seascape; — **mercantile** merchant marine

marinaio (mâ·rē·nâ'yō) *m* sailor; marine

marinare (mâ·rē·nâ'rä) *vt* to marinate; to pickle; — **la scuola** to play hooky

marionetta (mâ·ryō·nät'tâ) *f* marionette

maritare (mâ·rē·tâ'rä) *vt* to marry, join in marriage

maritarsi (mâ·rē·târ'sē) *vr* to get married

marito (mâ·rē'tō) *m* husband

marittimo (mâ·rēt'tē·mō) *m* seaman; — *a* maritime

mariuolo (mâ·rywō'lō) *m* swindler, thief

marmaglia (mâr·mâ'lyâ) *f* rabble; mob

marmellata (mâr·mâl·lâ'tâ) *f* jam, preserve

marmitta (mâr·mēt'tâ) *f* large pot, kettle

marmo (mâr'mō) *m* marble

marmocchio (mâr·môk'kyō) *m* brat, spoiled child

marmotta (mâr·mōt'tâ) *f* (*zool*) marmot

maroso (mâ·rō'zō) *m* billow, wave, breaker

marrone (mâr·rō'nä) *m* chestnut; — *a* chestnut (*color*)

marsina (mâr·sē'nâ) *f* dress coat; tails (*coll*)

marsupiale (mâr·sū·pyâ'lä) *m&a* marsupial

martedì (mâr·tä·dē') *m* Tuesday

martellare (mâr·tâl·lâ'rä) *vt* to hammer; — *vi* to pulse, throb

martellista (mâr·tâl·lē'stâ) *m* (*sport*) hammer thrower

martello (mâr·tâl'lō) *m* hammer

martire (mâr'tē·rä) *m* martyr

martirio (mâr·tē'ryō) *m* martyrdom

â ârm, **ā** bäby, **e** bet, **ē** bē, **ō** gō, **ô** gône, **ū** blūe, **b** bad, **ch** child, **d** dad, **f** fat, **g** gay, **j** jet

martirizzare (mâr·tē·rē·dzä′rä) *vt* to martyr

martirizzarsi (mâr·tē·rē·dzâr′sē) *vr* to martyr oneself

martora (mâr′tō·râ) *f* (*zool*) marten

marzapane (mâr·dzä·pâ′nä) *f* marzipan

marziale (mâr·tsyâ′lä) *a* martial; war

marziano (mâr·tsyâ′nō) *a&m* Martian

marzo (mâr′tsō) *m* March

mascalzone (mâ·skâl·tsō′nä) *m* cad, scoundrel

mascella (mâ·shāl′lä) *f* jaw

maschera (mâ′skä·râ) *f* mask; (*theat*) usher; (*fencing*) face guard

mascherare (mâ·skä·râ′rä) *vt* to mask; to hide, conceal

mascherarsi (mâ·skä·râr′sē) *vr* to masquerade; to wear a mask

maschietta (mâ·skyät′tâ) *f* tomboy; **capelli alla — ** bobbed hair

maschile (mâ·skē′lä) *m* masculine; male

maschio (mâ′skyō) *a&m* male; **— a** manly

masnada (mâ·znâ′dâ) *f* gang of toughs

massa (mâs′sâ) *f* mass

massacrare (mâs·sâ·krâ′rä) *vt* to massacre

massacro (mâs·sâ′krō) *m* massacre

massaggiare (mâs·sâj·jâ′rä) *vt* to massage

massaggiatore (mâs·sâj·jâ·tō′rä) *m* masseur

massaggiatrice (mâs·sâj·jâ·trē′chä) *f* masseuse

massaggio (mâs·sâj′jō) *m* massage

massaia (mâs·sâ′yâ) *f* housewife

masseria (mâs·sä·rē′â) *f* farm; herd

masserizie (mâs·sä·rē′tsyä) *fpl* utensils; household goods

massicciata (mâs·sē·châ′tâ) *f* roadbed

massiccio (mâs·sē′chō) *a* huge, bulky

massima (mâs′sē·mâ) *f* rule; maxim

massimamente (mâs·sē·mâ·mân′tä) *adv* most of all; especially

massimo (mâs′sē·mō) *a* greatest; best; utmost; **— m** maximum

masso (mâs′sō) *m* large rock; boulder

massone (mâs·sō′nä) *m* Freemason

massoneria (mâs·sō·nä·rē′â) *f* Freemasonry

mastello (mâ·stāl′lō) *m* tub

masticare (mâ·stē·kâ′rä) *vt* to chew; (*fig*) to meditate; to grumble about

masticazione (mâ·stē·kâ·tsyō′nä) *f* chewing, mastication

mastice (mâ′stē·chä) *m* rubber cement

mastino (mâ·stē′nō) *m* mastiff

mastodonte (mâ·stō·dōn′tä) *m* mastodon

mastro (mâ′strō) *m* master; (*com*) ledger

matassa (mâ·tâs′sâ) *f* skein

matematica (mâ·tä·mâ′tē·kâ) *f* mathematics

matematico (mâ·tä·mâ′tē·kō) *a* mathematical; **— m** mathematician

materasso (mâ·tä·râs′sō) *m* mattress

materia (mâ·te′ryâ) *f* matter, substance; (*med*) pus

materiale (mâ·tä·ryâ′lä) *a&m* material

materialista (mâ·tä·ryâ·lē′stä) *m* materialist

materializzare (mâ·tä·ryâ·lē·dzâ′rä) *vt* to materialize

materialmente (mâ·tä·ryâl·mān′tä) *adv* materially

maternità (mâ·tär·nē·tâ′) *f* maternity

materno (mâ·tär′nō) *a* maternal

matita (mâ·tē′tâ) *f* pencil

matricola (mâ·trē′kō·lâ) *f* freshman; register; registration

matricolazione (mâ·trē·kō·lâ·tsyō′nä) *f* matriculation

matrigna (mâ·trē′nyâ) *f* stepmother

matrimoniale (mâ·trē·mō·nyâ′lä) *a* wedding, matrimonial; **anello — ** wedding ring; **letto — ** double bed

matrimonio (mâ·trē·mô′nyō) *m* marriage

mattacchione (mât·tâk·kyō′nä) *m* wit, joker

mattarello (mât·tâ·râl′lō) *m* rolling pin

mattatoio (mât·tâ·tô′yō) *m* slaughterhouse, abattoir

mattina (mât·tē′nâ) *f* morning

mattinata (mât·tē·nâ′tâ) *f* morning hours; matinee; whole morning long

mattino (mât·tē′nō) *m* early morning

matto (mât′tō) *a* crazy; insane; **— m** maniac; **scacco — ** (*chess*) checkmate

mattonato (mât·tō·nâ′tō) *m* tile floor

mattone (mât·tō′nä) *m* brick; dull book; boring article; tiresome person

mattonella (mât·tō·nāl′lâ) *f* floor tile

mattutino (mât·tū·tē′nō) *a* early; morning; **— m** (*eccl*) Matins

maturare (mâ·tū·râ′rä) *vt&i* to ripen; to fall due, come due

maturazione (mât·tū·râ·tsyō′nä) *f* ripening; (*com*) maturity

maturità (mâ·tū·rē·tâ′) *f* maturity; **esame di — ** final exam before graduation

maturo (mâ·tū′rō) *a* mature, ripe

mausoleo (mâû·zō·lâ′ō) *m* mausoleum

mazza (mâ′tsâ) *f* club; cane; (*sport*) bat

mazzo (mâ′tsō) *m* bunch; deck (*cards*); classification

me (mä) *pron* me

meccanica (māk·kâ′nē·kâ) *f* mechanics

meccanico (māk·kâ′nē·kō) *a* mechanical; **— m** mechanic

meccanismo (māk·kâ·nē'zmō) *m* mechanism; working parts, works

meccanizzare (māk·kâ·nē·dzâ'rā) *vt* to mechanize; to automate

meccanizzazione (māk·kâ·nē·dzâ·tsyō'nā) *f* mechanization; automation

mecenate (mā·chā·nä'tā) *m* patron

meco (mā'kō) *pron* with me

medaglia (mā·dâ'lyâ) *f* medal

medaglione (mā·dâ·lyō'nā) *m* medallion

medesimo (mā·de'zē·mō) *a* same

media (me'dyâ) *f* average; **in —** on the average

mediano (mā·dyâ'nō) *m* football halfback; **— a** mean

mediante (mā·dyân'tā) *prep* by means of, with, by

mediatore (mā·dyâ·tō'rā) *m (com)* stockbroker; mediator

medicamento (mā·dē·kâ·män'tō) *m* medicine; medication

medicare (mā·dē·kâ'rā) *vt* to medicate; to dress; to treat

medicarsi (mā·dē·kâr'sē) *vr* to treat oneself, doctor oneself; to take medication

medicastro (mā·dē·kâ'strō) *m* quack, charlatan

medicazione (mā·dē·kâ·tsyō'nā) *f (med)* dressing; medication; treatment

medicina (mā·dē·chē'nâ) *f* medication, medicine; remedy

medicinali (mā·dē·chē·nâ'lē) *mpl* drugs

medico (me'dē·kō) *m* doctor; physician; **— chirurgo** physician and surgeon; **— condotto** town doctor

medio (me'dyō) *a* average; middle; **—** *m* average, mean

mediocre (mā·dyō'krā) *a* mediocre, ordinary

mediocrità (mā·dyō·krē·tâ') *f* mediocrity; lack of distinction

medioevale (mā·dyō·ā·vâ'lā) *a* Medieval

medioevo (mā·dyō·ā'vō) *m* Middle Ages

meditare (mā·dē·tâ'rā) *vt&i* to meditate; to mull over; to deliberate

meditazione (mā·dē·tâ·tsyō'nā) *f* meditation; deliberation

Mediterraneo (mā·dē·tär·râ'nä·ō) *m&a* Mediterranean

megafono (mā·gâ'fō·nō) *m* megaphone

megalomane (mā·gâ·lô'mâ·nä) *m&a* megalomaniac

megaton (me'gâ·tōn) *m* megaton

meglio (me'lyō) *a&adv* better; **il —** the best

mela (mā'lâ) *f* apple

melacotogna (mā·lâ·kō·tō'nyâ) *f* quince

melagrana (mā·lâ·grä'nâ) *f* pomegranate

melanzana (mā·lân·dzâ'nâ) *f* eggplant

melassa (mā·lâs'sâ) *f* molasses

melenso (mā·lān'sō) *a* retarded; silly

mellifluo (māl·lē'flūō) *a (speech)* honeyed, flattering

melma (māl'mâ) *f* mire

melo (mā'lō) *m* apple tree

melodia (mā·lō·dē'â) *f* melody

melodioso (mā·lō·dyō'zō) *a* melodious

melodramma (mā·lō·drâm'mâ) *m* melodrama

melograno (mā·lō·grâ'nō) *m* pomegranate tree

melone (mā·lō'nâ) *m* melon, cantaloupe; **— d'inverno** honeydew melon

membra (mâm'brâ) *fpl (anat)* limbs

membrana (mâm·brâ'nâ) *f* membrane

membro (mâm'brō) *m* member; *(anat)* limb

memorabile (mā·mō·râ'bē·lā) *a* notable; memorable

memoria (mā·mô'ryâ) *f* memory; memento; remembrance; **imparare a —** to memorize

memoriale (mā·mō·ryâ'lā) *m* memorial

memorie (mā·mô'ryâ) *fpl* memoirs

mena (mā'nâ) *f* intrigue; plot

menare (mā·nâ'rā) *vt* to lead, guide; to wag *(tail)*; **— le mani** to come to blows; **— per le lunghe** to postpone, put off; **— il can per l'aia** *(coll)* to beat around the bush; **— vanto** to brag, boast

mendicante (mān·dē·kân'tā) *m* beggar; **— a** begging; beggarly

mendicare (mān·dē·kâ'rā) *vt&i* to beg; to entreat

mendicità (mān·dē·chē·tâ') *f* begging; mendicancy; **ricovero di —** poorhouse; poor farm

meneghino (mā·nā·gē'nō) *a&m* Milanese

menestrello (mā·nā·strāl'lō) *m* minstrel

meningite (mā·nēn·jē'tā) *f* meningitis

meno (mā'nō) *m prep* less; **—** *adv* save, excepting; less; **il —** the least; **a — che** except that; only; **a — che non** unless; **fare a —** to do without; **— male** so much the better; it's a good thing

menomamente (mā·nō·mâ·mân'tā) *adv* not in the least, by no means, not at all

menomare (mā·nō·mâ'rā) *vt* to belittle; to prejudice, have an adverse affect on; to decrease

menomazione (mā·nō·mâ·tsyō'nā) *f* impairment; decrease

mensa (mān'sâ) *f* table; *(mil)* mess

mensile (mān·sē'lā) *a* monthly; **—** *m* salary

mensilità (mān·sē·lē·tâ') *f* monthly in-

stallment
mensilmente (mān·sēl·mān′tā) *adv* monthly, every month
mensola (men′sō·lâ) *f* console table; bracket
menta (mān′tâ) *f* mint
mentale (mān·tâ′lā) *a* mental, cerebral
mentalità (mān·tâ·lē·tâ′) *f* mentality, mind
mentalmente (mān·tâl·mān′tā) *adv* mentally
mente (mān′tā) *m* mind
mentire (mān·tē′rā) *vi* to lie; — *vt* to misrepresent, falsify
mentitore (mān·tē·tō·rā) *m* liar; falsifier
mento (mān′tō) *m* chin
mentolo (mān·tō′lō) *m* menthol
mentre (mān′trā) *conj* while
menzionare (mān·tsyō·nâ′rā) *vt* to mention; to cite
menzione (mān·tsyō′nā) *f* mention; citing
menzogna (mān·dzō′nyâ) *f* lie; misrepresentation
menzognero (mān·dzō·nyā′rō) *m* liar; — *a* lying, false
meramente (mā·râ·mān′tā) *adv* simply, merely
meraviglia (mā·râ·vē′lyâ) *f* wonder; astonishment
meravigliare (mā·râ·vē·lyâ′rā) *vt* to astonish
meravigliarsi (mā·râ·vē·lyâr′sē) *vr* to wonder; to be surprised
meravigliosamente (mā·râ·vē·lyō·zâ·mān′tā) *adv* wonderfully, splendidly
meraviglioso (mā·râ·vē·lyō′zō) *a* wonderful, splendid
mercante (mār·kân′tā) *m* merchant; dealer; **fare orecchie da —** (*fig*) to turn a deaf ear; to ignore someone completely
mercanteggiare (mār·kân·tāj·jâ′rā) *vt* to haggle over, bargain over
mercantile (mār·kân·tē′lā) *a* mercantile; commercial
mercanzia (mār·kân·tsē′â) *f* merchandise
mercatino (mār·kâ·tē′nō) *m* market vendor; marketeer
mercato (mār·kâ′tō) *m* market; — **nero** black market; **a buon —** cheap
merce (mār′chā) *f* merchandise
mercede (mār·chā′dā) *f* pay; wages; reward
mercenario (mār·chā·nâ′ryō) *m&a* mercenary
merceria (mār·chā·rē′â) *f* notions store
mercoledì (mār·kō·lā·dē′) *m* Wednesday
mercurio (mār·kū′ryō) *m* mercury, quick-

silver
merda (mār′dâ) *f* filth; feces; dung
merenda (mā·rān′dâ) *f* afternoon snack; **— all'aperto** picnic
meridiana (mā·rē·dyâ′nâ) *f* sundial; meridian line
meridiano (mā·rē·dyâ′nō) *m&a* meridian
meridionale (mā·rē·dyō·nâ′lā) *a* southern; — *m* Southerner
meridione (mā·rē·dyō′nā) *m* south; **il M–** Southern Italy
meringa (mā·rēn′gâ) *f* meringue
meritare (mā·rē·tâ′rā) *vt* to deserve, be worthy of
meritarsi (mā·rē·târ′sē) *vr* to merit, deserve; to have a right to
meritatamente (mā·rē·tâ·tâ·mān′tā) *adv* deservedly; with just cause
meritevole (mā·rē·te′vō·lā) *a* worthy
merito (me′rē·tō) *m* merit; reward; value; **in — a** with reference to; **entrare in — a** to go fully into the matter of
merletto (mār·lāt′tō) *m* lace
merlo (mār′lō) *m* blackbird
merluzzo (mār·lū′tsō) *m* codfish; **olio di fegato di —** cod-liver oil
mero (mā′rō) *a* mere; absolute
meschino (mā·skē′nō) *a* unfortunate, destitute; stingy
mescita (me′shē·tâ) *f* bar; wine shop
mescolanza (mā·skō·lân′tsâ) *f* hodgepodge; mixture
mescolare (mā·skō·lâ′râ) *vt* to mix
mescolarsi (mā·skō·lâr′sē) *vr* to meddle; to get involved; to participate
mese (mā′zā) *m* month
messa (mās′sâ) *f* Mass; placement; positioning; **— cantata** High Mass; **— in piega** finger wave; **— in scena** staging, mise-en-scène; **— a fuoco** (*photo*) focus; **— in vigore** putting into effect, enforcement
messaggero (mās·sâj·jā′rō) *m* messenger
messaggio (mās·sâj′jō) *m* message
messicano (mās·sē·kâ′nō) *a&m* Mexican
Messico (mes′sē·kō) *m* Mexico
messo (mās′sō) *m* messenger; — *a* placed, laid
mesticheria (mā·stē·kā·rē′â) *f* paint store
mestiere (mā·styâ′rā) *m* trade; profession; business
mestizia (mā·stē′tsyâ) *f* sadness, sorrow
mesto (mā′stō) *a* unhappy, sad; melancholy
mestola (me′stō·lâ) *f* ladle
mestruo (me′strūō) *m* menses
meta (mā′tâ) *f* goal, ambition; target (*fig*)
metà (mā·tâ′) *f* half

---

k kid, **l** let, **m** met, **n** not, **p** pat, **r** very, **s** sat, **sh** shop, **t** tell, **v** vat, **w** we, **y** yes, **z** zero

metafora (mā·tâ'fō·râ) *f* metaphor
metaforicamente (mā·tâ·fō·rē·kâ·mān'-tā) *adv* metaphorically
metallico (mā·tâl'lē·kō) *a* metallic
metallurgico (mā·tâl·lūr'jē·kō) *m* metallurgical worker; — *a* metallurgical
metano (mā·tâ'nō) *m* natural gas; methane
metanodotto (mā·tâ·nō·dōt'tō) *m* gas pipeline
meteorologia (mā·tā·ō·rō·lō·jē'a) *f* meteorology
meteorologico (mā·tā·ō·rō·lô'jē·kō) *a* meteorological; **bollettino** — weather report
meticcio (mā·tē'chō) *m&a* half-breed; mongrel
meticoloso (mā·tē·kō·lō'zō) *a* overly exact; finicky; meticulous
metodico (mā·tô'dē·kō) *a* methodical
metodo (me'tō·dō) *m* method
metraggio (mā·trâj'jō) *m* measurement in meters; yardage
metrico (me'trē·kō) *a* metric; **sistema** — **decimale** metric system
metro (mā'trō) *m* meter; yardstick
metropoli (mā·trô'pō·lē) *f* metropolis
metropolitana (mā·trō·pō·lē·tâ'nâ) *f* subway (*train*)
metropolitano (mā·trō·pō·lē·tâ'nō) *a* metropolitan; — *m* policeman
mettere * (met'tā·râ) *vt* to put, set, place; — **al corrente** to inform, acquaint; to bring up to date; — **in atto** to accomplish, bring about; — **in dubbio** to put in doubt; — **in marcia** to start; to put into operation; — **in opera** to bring into play, make use of; — **in salvo** to rescue; — **i punti sugli i** (*fig*) to dot one's i's
mettersi * (met'tär·sē) *vr* to put on; to dress in; to place oneself; — **in cammino** to start off, set out; — **in mezzo** to interfere; — **d'accordo** to come to an agreement
mezzadro (mā·dzâ'drō) *m* sharecropper
mezzaluna (mā·dzâ·lū'nâ) *f* halfmoon
mezzanino (mā·dzâ·nē'nō) *m* mezzanine
mezzano (mā·dzâ'nō) *m* pander, pimp; — *a* middle
mezzanotte (mā·dzâ·nōt'tâ) *f* midnight
mezzo (mā'dzō) *adj&adv* half; — *m* half; means; **per** — **di** by means of; **togliersi di** — to get out of the way
mezzogiorno (mā·dzō·jōr'nō) *m* south; noon
mezzotermine (mā·dzō·ter'mē·nā) *m* compromise; modus vivendi
mi (mē) *pron* me; to me

miagolare (myâ·gō·lâ'râ) *vi* to mew
mica (mē'kâ) *adv* not in the least; not at all; — *f* crumb; mica
miccia (mē'châ) *f* fuse (*explosive*)
micidiale (mē·chē·dyâ'lâ) *a* fatal; deadly
micio (mē'chō) *m* tomcat
microbo (mē'krō·bō) *m* microbe
microcamera (mē·krō·kâ'mâ·râ) *f* pocket camera
microcosmo (mē·krō·kō'zmō) *m* microcosm
microfilm (mē·krō·fēlm') *m* microfilm
microfono (mē·krô'fō·nō) *m* microphone
microfotografia (mē·krō·fō·tō·grâ·fē'â) *f* microphotograph, microprint
microlettore (mē·krō·lāt·tō'râ) *m* microfilm viewer
micromotore (mē·krō·mō·tō'râ) *m* bicycle motor
microscopio (mē·krō·skô'pyō) *m* microscope
microsolco (mē·krō·sōl'kō) *a* microgroove; **disco** — long-playing record
midolla (mē·dōl'lâ) *f* crumb
midollo (mē·dōl'lō) *m* (*anat*) marrow; — **spinale** spinal cord
miei (myā'ē) *pron* mine; — *a* my
miele (myā'lâ) *m* honey
mietere (mye'tâ·râ) *vt* to harvest; to mow
mietitore (myâ·tē·tō'râ) *m* reaper, harvester
mietitrice (myâ·tē·trē'châ) *f* harvester; (*mech*) reaper, reaping machine
migliaio (mē·lyâ'yō) *m* thousand
miglio (mē'lyō) *m* mile; millet
miglioramento (mē·lyō·râ·mān'tō) *m* improvement; bettering
migliorare (mē·lyō·râ'râ) *vt&i* to improve; to better
migliorarsi (mē·lyō·râr'sē) *vr* to improve oneself; to grow better
migliore (mē·lyō'râ) *a* better; superior; **il** — the best
miglioria (mē·lyō·rē'â) *f* improvement
mignolo (mē'nyō·lō) *m* little finger; little toe
Milano (mē·lâ'nō) *f* Milan
miliardo (mē·lyâr'dō) *m* billion
milionario (mē·lyō·nâ'ryō) *m* millionaire
milione (mē·lyō'nâ) *m* million
militante (mē·lē·tân'tâ) *a* aggressive, militant
militare (mē·lē·tâ'râ) *a* military; — *m* serviceman; — *vi* to militate
militarismo (mē·lē·tâ·rē'zmō) *m* militarism
militarmente (mē·lē·târ·mān'tâ) *adv* by armed force; militarily

---

â ârm, **ā** bāby, **e** bet, **ē** bē, **ō** gō, **ô** gône, **ū** blūe, **b** bad, **ch** child, **d** dad, **f** fat, **g** gay, **j** jet

milite (mē'lē·tā) *m* soldier; — **ignoto** unknown soldier; — **della polizia stradale** highway patrolman

millantatore (mēl·lân·tâ·tō'rā) *m* braggart

mille (mēl'lā) *a* thousand

millenario (mēl·lā·nâ'ryō) *a* millenial

millennio (mēl·len'nyō) *m* millennium

millesimo (mēl·le'zē·mō) *a* thousandth

millimetro (mēl·lē'mā·trō) *m* millimeter

milza (mēl'tsâ) *f* spleen

mimica (mē'mē·kâ) *f* mimicry

mimetizzare (mē·mā·tē·dzâ'rā) *vt* to camouflage

mimo (mē'mō) *m* mimic; pantomime dancer

mina (mē'nâ) *f* mine

minaccia (mē·nâ'châ) *f* threat

minacciare (mē·nâ·châ'rā) *vt* to threaten

minaccioso (mē·nâ·chō'zō) *a* menacing

minare (mē·nâ'rā) *vt* to mine; to weaken, undermine

minareto (mē·nâ·rā'tō) *m* minaret

minatore (mē·nâ·tō'rā) *m* miner

minerale (mē·nâ·râ'lā) *m&a* mineral

mineralogia (mē·nâ·râ·lō·jē'â) *f* mineralogy

minerario (mē·nâ·râ'ryō) *a* mining

minestra (mē·nâ'strâ) *f* soup

minestrone (mē·nâ·strō'nâ) *m* vegetable soup; (*fig*) potpourri, hodgepodge

mingherlino (mēn·gâr·lē'nō) *a* thin; lithe, svelte

miniatura (mē·nyâ·tū'râ) *f* miniature

miniera (mē·nyâ'râ) *f* mine; — **di ferro** iron mine

minimamente (mē·nē·mâ·mân'tā) *adv* by no means; not in the least

minimizzare (mē·nē·mē·dzâ'rā) *vt* to minimize; to belittle

minimo (mē'nē·mō) *m* minimum; — *a* least, lowest, smallest; cheapest; slightest

minio (mē'nyō) *m* red lead

ministero (mē·nē·stā'rō) *m* ministry, department; **M— degli Esteri** State Department; **pubblico —** public prosecutor, prosecuting attorney, district attorney

ministro (mē·nē'strō) *m* minister; secretary, cabinet member

minoranza (mē·nō·rân'tsâ) *f* minority

minorativo (mē·nō·râ·tē'vō) *a* lessening, diminishing

minorato (mē·nō·râ'tō) *a* disabled, handicapped

minorazione (mē·nō·râ·tsyō'nā) *f* diminishing, reduction; handicap

minore (mē·nō'rā) *a* less; minor; younger

minorenne (mē·nō·rân'nā) *m&a* minor

minuscola (mē·nū'skō·lâ) *f* small letter, lowercase letter

minuscolo (mē·nū'skō·lō) *a* tiny, minute

minuta (mē·nū'tâ) *f* rough copy; draft

minutante (mē·nū·tân'tā) *m* retailer

minuteria (mē·nū·tā·rē'â) *f* nicknack

minuto (mē·nū'tō) *m* minute; — *a* small; **al —** at retail

minuziosamente (mē·nū·tsyō·zâ·mân'tā) *adv* minutely, in detail

minuzioso (mē·nū·tsyō'zō) *a* detailed; accurate; complete

mio (mē'ō) *pron* mine; — *a* my

miope (mē'ō·pā) *a* shortsighted; nearsighted

mira (mē'râ) *f* aim; sight; target

mirabilmente (mē·râ·bēl·mân'tā) *adv* wonderfully; admirably

miracolo (mē·râ'kō·lō) *m* miracle

miracolosamente (mē·râ·kō·lō·zâ·mân'tā) *adv* miraculously; astoundingly

miracoloso (mē·râ·kō·lō'zō) *a* miraculous; astounding

miraggio (mē·râj'jō) *m* mirage, vision

mirare (mē·râ'rā) *vt* to look at; — *vi* to aim

mirarsi (mē·râr'sē) *vr* to gaze at oneself; — **intorno** to look around; to be on the qui vive

miriade (mē·rē'â·dā) *f* great number

mirino (mē·rē'nō) *m* gunsight; (*photo*) viewfinder

mirra (mēr'râ) *f* myrrh

mirto (mēr'tō) *m* myrtle

misantropo (mē·zân'trō·pō) *m* misanthrope; — *a* misanthropic

miscela (mē·shā'lâ) *f* blending; mixture

mischia (mē'skyâ) *f* fight, fray

mischiare (mē·skyâ'rā) *vt* to jumble; to mix up

mischiarsi (mē·skyâr'sē) *vr* to interfere; to meddle

miscredente (mē·skrā·dân'tā) *a* unbelieving; — *m* unbeliever

miscuglio (mē·skū'lyō) *m* blending, mix

miserabile (mē·zā·râ'bē·lā) *a* contemptible; miserable; vile

miserabilmente (mē·zā·râ·bēl·mân'tā) *adv* badly; wretchedly

miseria (mē·ze'ryâ) *f* want; poverty; (*fig*) bagatelle, trifle

misericordia (mē·zā·rē·kôr'dyâ) *f* pity; mercy

misfatto (mē·sfât'tō) *m* wrongdoing, offense

missile (mēs·sē'lā) *m* missile; — **balistico** ballistic missile; — **guidato** guided missile

missionario (mē·syō·nâ'ryō) *m* missionary

missione (mēs·syō'nä) *f* mission

misterioso (mē·stä·ryō'zō) *a* mysterious, arcane

mistero (mē·stä'rō) *m* mystery

misticismo (mē·stē·chē'zmō) *m* mysticism

mistificare (mē·stē·fē·kâ'rä) *vt* to adulterate; to deceive, hoodwink

mistificazione (mē·stē·fē·kâ·tsyō'nä) *f* hoax, deceit, trick

misto (mē'stō) *a* mixed; **scuola mista** co-educational school

misura (mē·zū'râ) *f* measure; criterion, yardstick

misurare (mē·zū·râ'rä) *vt* to measure; to evaluate

misurarsi (mē·zū·râr'sē) *vr* to evaluate oneself; to vie, compete; to try on (*clothing*)

misurato (mē·zū·râ'tō) *a* measured; cautious

mite (mē'tä) *a* temperate; mellow, gentle

mitigare (mē·tē·gâ'rä) *vt* to mitigate; to ease

mitigarsi (mē·tē·gâr'sē) *vr* to abate, subside

mito (mē'tō) *m* myth

mitra (mē'trâ) *f* miter; submachine gun

mitragliatrice (mē·trâ·lyâ·trē'chä) *f* machine gun

mittente (mēt·tän'tä) *m* sender; — *a* sending

mobile (mô'bē·lä) *m* piece of furniture; — *f* riot squad; — *a* mobile; shifting; undependable, flighty; **sabbie mobili** quicksand

mobilia (mō·bē'lyâ) *f* furniture

mobiliare (mō·bē·lyâ'rä) *a* personal; movable; **proprietà —** personal property

mobiliere (mō·bē·lyä'rä) *m* furniture manufacturer; furniture dealer

mobilità (mō·bē·lē·tâ') *f* mobility; flightiness; fickleness

mobilitare (mō·bē·lē·tâ'rä) *vt* to marshal; to mobilize

mobilitazione (mō·bē·lē·tâ·tsyō'nä) *f* mobilization; marshaling

mocassino (mō·kâs·sē'nō) *m* mocassin

moccioso (mō·chō'zō) *m* brat; nasty individual

moda (mō'dä) *f* fashion; **di —** fashionable, **fuori di —** out of style; **ultima —** latest style

modalità (mō·dâ·lē·tâ') *f* form, characteristic

modello (mō·dāl'lō) *m* sample; pattern;

model

moderare (mō·dä·râ'rä) *vt* to moderate; to relax, cool

moderarsi (mō·dä·râr'sē) *vr* to hold oneself back; to control oneself, keep oneself under control

moderato (mō·dä·râ'tō) *a* moderate; temperate

moderazione (mō·dä·râ·tsyō'nä) *f* moderation

modernamente (mō·där·nâ·män'tä) *adv* modernly; in the latest style; fashionably

modernizzare (mō·där·nē·dzâ'rä) *vt* to modernize; to update

moderno (mō·dâr'nō) *a* modern; current

modestamente (mō·dä·stâ·män'tä) *adv* modestly; unassumingly

modestia (mō·de'styâ) *f* modesty; reserve; unassumingness

modesto (mō·dä'stō) *a* modest; reserved

modifica (mō·dē'fē·kâ) *f* alteration; —**re** (mō·dē·fē·kâ'rä) *vt* to change, alter, modify

modificazione (mō·dē·fē·kâ·tsyō'nä) *f* revision; change; modification

modista (mō·dē'stâ) *f* milliner

modisteria (mō·dē·stä·rē'â) *f* millinery shop; millinery

modo (mō'dō) *m* way; manner; habit; **in ogni —** anyhow; in any event; **oltre —** extremely; excessively; **fare a — suo** to get one's own way; to do as one pleases; **in — da** so as to; **in nessun —** by no means; **per — di dire** as it were, so to speak

modulazione (mō·dū·lâ·tsyō'nä) *f* modulation; intonation

modulo (mô'dū·lō) *m* blank, form

moffetta (mōf·fät'tâ) *f* skunk

mogano (mô'gâ·nō) *m* mahogany

moglie (mô'lyä) *f* wife

mola (mō'lâ) *f* grindstone

molare (mō·lâ'rä) *vt* to grind; — *a&m* molar

mole (mō'lä) *f* bulk, mass; greater part

molecola (mō·le'kō·lâ) *f* molecule

molestare (mō·lä·stâ'rä) *vt* to bother; to annoy; to trouble

molestia (mō·le'styâ) *f* nuisance; trouble; bother; annoyance

molla (mōl'lâ) *f* spring

mollare (mōl·lâ'rä) *vt* to loosen; — *vi* to yield

molle (mōl'lä) *a* soft; tender; effeminate, weak

molle (mōl'lä) *fpl* tongs

mollette (mōl·lät'tä) *fpl* small tongs;

paper clips; — **per la biancheria** clothespins

mollettiere (mŏl·lāt·tyā'rā) *fpl* leggings

mollezza (mŏl·lā'tsâ) *f* effeminacy; softness; weakness

mollica (mŏl·lē'kâ) *f* bread crumb

mollusco (mŏl·lŭ'skō) *m* shellfish, mollusk

molo (mō'lō) *m* pier

molteplice (mŏl·te'plē·chā) *a* multiple, manifold

moltiplicare (mŏl·tē·plē·kâ'rā) *vt* to multiply

moltiplicatore (mŏl·tē·plē·kâ·tō'rā) *m* multiplier

moltiplicazione (mŏl·tē·plē·kâ·tsyō'nā) *f* multiplication

moltissimo (mŏl·tēs'sē·mō) *a&adv* very much, a great deal

moltitudine (mŏl·tē·tū'dē·nā) *f* throng, multitude

molto (mŏl'tō) *a* much; — *adv* very

momentaneamente (mō·mān·tâ·nā·â·mān'tā) *adv* temporarily; for the moment; at any moment

momentaneo (mō·mān·tâ'nā·ō) *a* ephemeral; transitory

momento (mō·mān'tō) *m* moment

monaca (mô'nâ·kâ) *f* nun

monaco (mô'nâ·kō) *m* friar; monk

Monaco (mô'nā·kō) *m* Monaco; — **di Baviera** Munich

monarca (mō·nâr'kâ) *m* monarch

monarchia (mō·nâr·kē'â) *f* monarchy

monarchico (mō·nâr'kē·kō) *a* monarchical; — *m (pol)* monarchist

monastero (mō·nâ'stā'rō) *m* monastery; cloister; convent

moncherino (mōn·kā·rē'nō) *m* stump

mondanità (mōn·dâ·nē·tâ') *f* mundanity, worldliness

mondano (mōn·dâ'nō) *a* worldly; **vita mondana** society life; high society

mondezzaio (mōn·dā·tsâ'yō) *m* garbage dump

mondiale (mōn·dyâ'lā) *a* world-wide; world

mondo (mōn'dō) *m* world; **un — di gente** a very large crowd; **da che — è —** since the dawn of time; **andare all'altro —** to die, pass on; **caschi il —!** come what may!; **venire al —** to be born; — *a* pure, spotless

monello (mō·nāl'lō) *m* urchin; street arab

moneta (mō·nā'tâ) *f* money; coin

mongolo (môn'gō·lō) *m&a* Mongolian, Mongol

monile (mō·nē'lā) *m* necklace

monocolo (mō·nô'kō·lō) *m* monocle

monofase (mō·nō·fâ'zā) *a (elec)* single-phase

monolito (mō·nō·lē'tō) *m* monolith

monologo (mō·nô'lō·gō) *m* monologue

monopattino (mō·nō·pât·tē'nō) *m* scooter

monopolizzare (mō·nō·pō·lē·dzâ'rā) *vt* to monopolize; to corner

monopolio (mō·nō·pô'lyō) *m* monopoly

monotonia (mō·nō·tō·nē'â) *f* tedium, monotony

monotono (mō·nô'tō·nō) *a* tiresome; monotonous

montacarico (mōn·tâ·kâ'rē·kō) *m* freight elevator

montaggio (mōn·tâj'jō) *m* montage; *(mech)* assemblage; editing *(movies)*

montagna (mōn·tâ'nyâ) *f* mountain

montagnoso (mōn·tâ·nyō'zō) *a* mountainous

montanaro (mōn·tâ·nâ'rō) *m* mountaineer; — *a* mountain

montante (mōn·tân'tā) *m* uppercut *(boxing)*; — *f* amount; *(avi)* strut

montare (mōn·tâ'rā) *vt* to climb up; *(mech)* to assemble; to praise, boost; — *vi* to ascend, go up

montarsi (mōn·târ'sē) *vr* to make a scene; to get upset

montatura (mōn·tâ·tū'râ) *f* ballyhoo; publicity buildup; publicity stunt

montavivande (mōn·tâ·vē·vân'dā) *m* dumbwaiter

monte (mōn'tā) *m* mountain; lots, large quantity; — **di pietà** pawnshop; **andare a —** to amount to nothing; to fall through; **mandare a —** to ruin, upset, foil

montone (mōn·tō'nā) *m* mutton; ram

montuoso (mōn·twō'zō) *a* mountainous

monumento (mō·nū·mān'tō) *m* monument

mora (mō'râ) *f* blackberry; delay

morale (mō·râ'lā) *a* moral; — *f* morals; — *m* morale, spirits

moralità (mō·râ·lē·tâ') *f* moral character; morality

moratoria (mō·râ·tô'ryâ) *f* moratorium; suspension

morbidezza (mōr·bē·dā'tsâ) *f* softness; weakness

morbido (môr'bē·dō) *a* soft; weak; effete

morbillo (mōr·bēl'lō) *m* measles

mordace (mōr·dâ'chā) *a* biting, sarcastic, trenchant

mordere * (môr'dā·rā) *vt* to bite; to eat away

---

k kid, **l** let, **m** met, **n** not, **p** pat, **r** very, **s** sat, **sh** shop, **t** tell, **v** vat, **w** we, **y** yes, **z** zero

more   180   mugg

morente (mō·rän'tä) *a* fading away; dying
moretta (mō·rät'tä) *f* brunette
morfina (mōr·fē'nä) *f* morphine
moribondo (mō·rē·bōn'dō) *a* dying
morigerato (mō·rē·jä·rä'tō) *a* wellbred; mannerly
morire * (mō·rē'rä) *vi* to die; to fade away; to pass away
mormorare (mōr·mō·rä'rä) *vi&t* to murmur; to grumble; to rustle
mormorio (mōr·mō·rē'ō) *m* murmur; rustling
moro (mō'rō) *m* Negro; Moor; blackberry bush
moroso (mō·rō'zō) *a* in arrears, late
morsa (mōr'sä) *f* vise
morsetto (mōr·sät'tō) *m* clamp
morso (mōr'sō) *m* bite; sting; morsel
mortaio (mōr·tä'yō) *m* mortar
mortale (mōr·tä'lä) *a&m* mortal
morte (mōr'tä) *f* death
mortella (mōr·täl'lä) *f* myrtle; — **di palude** cranberry
mortificare (mōr·tē·fē·kä'rä) *vt* to mortify; to humble, shame
mortificarsi (mōr·tē·fē·kär'sē) *vr* to humiliate oneself; to be ashamed
mortificazione (mōr·tē·fē·kä·tsyō'nä) *f* mortification; shame
morto ((mōr'tō) *a* dead; **capitale** — (*com*) dormant capital; **binario** — (*rail*) siding; **giorno dei morti** All Souls' Day
mosaico (mō·zä'ē·kō) *m* mosaic
mosca (mō'skä) *f* fly; — **bianca** (*fig*) oddity, rarity; exception
Mosca (mō'skä) *f* Moscow
moscerino (mō·shä·rē'nō) *m* gnat
moschea (mō·skä'ä) *f* mosque
moschetto (mō·skät'tō) *m* rifle, musket
moscone (mō·skō'nä) *m* bluebottle fly; (*fig*) hanger-on
moscovita (mō·skō·vē'tä) *m&a* Muscovite
mossa (mōs'sä) *f* move, movement; gesture; impetus; — **di corpo** bowel movement
mossiere (mōs·syä'rä) *m* starter (*race*)
mosso (mōs'sō) *a* moved; removed; **mare** — rough sea
mostarda (mō·stär'dä) *f* mustard
mosto (mō'stō) *m* must; –**so** (mō·stō'zo) *a* rich in must
mostra (mō'strä) *f* show, exhibit; **far** — **di** to pretend; to feign; to make a great show of; **far** — **di sè** to make oneself conspicuous
mostrare (mō·strä'rä) *vt* to show; to evidence
mostrarsi (mō·strär'sē) *vr* to appear,

seem; to turn out, prove
mostro (mō'strō) *m* monster
mostruoso (mō·strūō'zō) *a* monstrous
mota (mō'tä) *f* slime, mire; mud
motivare (mō·tē·vä'rä) *vt* to motivate; to account for; to justify
motivazione (mō·tē·vä·tsyō'nä) *f* motivation; motive
motivo (mō·tē'vō) *m* motive; motif; reason, cause; (*mus*) theme
moto (mō'tō) *m* motion: uprising; –**aratura** (mō·tō·ä·rä·tū'rä) *f* mechanized farming; –**cicletta** (mō·tō·chē·klät'tä) *f* motorcycle; –**ciclista** (mō·tō·chē·klē'stä) *m* motorcyclist; –**dromo** (mō·tō·drō'mō) *m* motordrome; –**furgoncino** (mō·tō·fūr·gōn·chē'nō) *m* motorcycle truck; –**leggiera** (mō·tō·läj·jä'rä) *f* motorbike; motor scooter; –**nave** (mō·tō·nä'vä) *f* motor ship; –**peschereccio** (mō·tō·pä·skä·rä'chō) *m* motorized fishing boat; –**re** (mō·tō'rä) *m* motor; –**re** *a* driving, propelling; forcing; **forza motrice** driving force; –**retta** (mō·tō·rät'tä) *f* motor scooter; –**rino** (mō·tō·rē'nō) *m* small motor; (*auto*) self-starter; –**rista** (mō·tō·rē'stä) *m* motorman; driver; mechanic; machinist; –**rizzare** (mō·tō·rē·dzä'rä) *vt* to motorize; –**scafo** (mō·tō·skä'fō) *m* motorboat; –**vedetta** (mō·tō·vä·dät'tä) *f* police motorboat; –**veicolo** (mō·tō·vä·ē'kō·lō) *m* motor vehicle; –**zattera** (mō·tō·tsät'tä·rä) *f* (*mil*) landing craft
motto (mōt'tō) *m* motto; — **di spirito** witticism
movente (mō·vän'tä) *m* motive, reason; — *a* moving
movimento (mō·vē·män'tō) *m* movement; hustle; gesture; — **ferroviario** railway traffic; — **d'affari** (*com*) turnover
mozione (mō·tsyō'nä) *f* (*pol*) motion, resolution
mozzafiato (mō·tsä·fyä'tō) *a* breathtaking; thrilling
mozzare (mō·tsä'rä) *vt* to cut, sever
mozzicone (mō·tsē·kō'nä) *m* cigar stub; stump
mozzo (mō'tsō) *m* (*naut*) cabin boy; hub (*wheel*); — *a* severed
mucca (mūk'kä) *f* cow
mucchio (mūk'kyō) *m* pile; (*coll*) lot, great deal
mucosa (mū·kō'zä) *f* mucous membrane
muffa (mūf'fä) *f* mould
muffola (mūf'fō·lä) *f* kiln
mugghiare (mūg·gyä'rä), **muggire** (mūj·jē'rä) *vi* to bellow; to low; to roar; to howl

â ârm, ā bāby, e bet, ē bē, ō gō, ô gône, ū blūe, b bad, ch child, d dad, f fat, g gay, j jet

mughetto (mū·gāt'tō) *m* lily of the valley
mugnaio (mū·nyâ'yō) *m* miller
mugolare (mū·gō·lâ'rā) *vi* to whine
mulatto (mū·lât'tō) *m* mulatto
mulinello (mū·lē·nāl'lō) *m* whirlwind; whirlpool; windlass; whirl
mulino (mū·lē'nō) *m* mill
mulo (mū'lō) *m* mule
multa (mūl'tâ) *f* fine; **—re** (mūl·tâ'rā) *vt* to fine; to penalize
mummia (mūm'myâ) *f* mummy
mungere * (mūn'jā·rā) *vt* to milk; (*fig*) to sweat, fleece
municipale (mū·nē·chē·pâ'lā) *a* municipal
municipalità (mū·nē·chē·pâ·lē·tâ') *f* municipal authority
municipio (mū·nē·chē'pyō) *m* city hall; town hall
munificenza (mū·nē·fē·chān'tsâ) *f* liberality, largess
munifico (mū·nē'fē·kō) *a* generous; munificent
munire (mū·nē'rā) *vt* to fortify; to provide
munirsi (mū·nēr'sē) *vr* to prepare oneself; to get ready
munizione (mū·nē·tsyō'nā) *f* ammunition
muovere * (mwô'vā·rā) *vt* to cause; to move; to stir up; **— una domanda** to ask a question
muoversi * (mwô'vār·sē) *vr* to move; to stir; to shake
mura (mū'râ) *fpl* city walls
muraglione (mū·râ·lyō'nā) *m* bulwark; high wall
murare (mū·râ'rā) *vt* to wall; to close up
muratore (mū·râ·tō'rā) *m* bricklayer; mason
muratura (mū·râ·tū'râ) *f* masonry

muro (mū'rō) *m* wall; impediment
muschio (mū'skyō) *m* moss
muscolo (mū'skō·lō) *m* muscle
muscoloso (mū·skō·lō'zō) *a* muscular; sinewy
museo (mū·zā'ō) *m* museum
museruola (mū·zā·rūō'lâ) *f* muzzle; nose (*animal*)
musica (mū'zē·kâ) *f* music
musicale (mū·zē·kâ'lā) *a* musical
musicante (mū·zē·kân'tā) *m* professional musician
musicista (mū·zē·chē'stâ) *m* musician
muso (mū'zō) *m* muzzle; nose (*animal*)
mussolina (mūs·sō·lē'nâ) *f* muslin
musulmano (mū·zūl·mâ'nō) *m&a* Muslim, Moslem
mutabile (mū·tâ'bē·lā) *a* capricious, changeable; mutable
mutamento (mū·tâ·mān'tō) *m* variation; change; mutation
mutande (mū·tân'dā) *fpl* underpants, drawers
mutandine (mū·tân·dē'nā) *fpl* panties; shorts; briefs; **— da bagno** swimming trunks
mutare (mū·tâ'rā) *vt* to change; to mutate
mutevole (mū·te'vō·lā) *a* changeable
mutilato (mū·tē·lâ'tō) *a* maimed; **— m** cripple; **— della guerra** disabled war veteran
mutismo (mū·tē'zmō) *m* muteness; uncommunicativeness
muto (mū'tō) *a* mute; **cinema —** silent film
mutria (mū'tryâ) *f* haughtiness; nerve, cheek, gall
mutuamente (mū·twâ·mān'tā) *adv* mutually
mutuo (mū'twō) *a* mutual; **— m** loan

N

nacchere (nâk'kā·rā) *fpl* castanets
nafta (nâf'tâ) *f* naphtha; fuel oil
naftalina (nâf·tâ·lē'nâ) *f* napthaline
naia (nâ'yâ) *f* cobra
nailon (nâ'ē·lōn) *m* nylon
nano (nâ'nō) *a&m* dwarf
napoletano (nâ·pō·lā·tâ'nō) *a&m* Neapolitan
Napoli (nâ'pō·lē) *f* Naples
narcotico (nâr·kô'tē·kō) *a&m* narcotic
narcotizzare (nâr·kō·tē·dzā'rā) *vt* to anesthetize; to drug
narice (nâ·rē'chā) *f* nostril
narrare (nâr·râ'rā) *vt* to relate, tell

narratore (nâr·râ·tō'rā) *m* storyteller; narrator
narrazione (nâr·râ·tsyō'nā) *f* telling, narration; narrative, account
nasale (nâ·zâ'lā) *a* nasal
nascere * (nâ'shā·rā) *vt* to be born; to spring up; to originate
nascita (nâ'shē·tâ) *f* birth; provenance
nascondere * (nâ·skôn'dā·rā) *vt* to hide; to cover, disguise
nascondersi * (nâ·skôn'dār·sē) *vr* to keep out of sight, conceal oneself
nascondiglio (nâ·skōn·dē'lyō) *m* cache; hiding place

---

k kid, **l** let, **m** met, **n** not, **p** pat, **r** very, **s** sat, **sh** shop, **t** tell, **v** vat, **w** we, **y** yes, **z** zero

nascostamente (nâ·skō·stâ·mān′tä) *adv*
stealthily; secretly; underhandedly

nascosto (nâ·skō′stō) *a* hidden; underhanded, sly

nasello (nâ·zāl′lō) *m* door latch

naso (nâ′zō) *m* nose; — **a** — face to face;
restare con un palmo di — (*fig*) to be
disappointed; to be taken aback

nastro (nâ′strō) *m* tape; ribbon; — **isolante** friction tape; — **trasportatore**
conveyor belt; **sega a** — band saw

Natale (nâ·tâ′lä) *m* Christmas, Yule;
vigilia di — Christmas Eve; **Buon** — !
Merry Christmas!

natale (nâ·tâ′lä) *a* native; — *m* birth;
ancestry

natalità (nâ·tâ·lē·tâ′) *f* birthrate

natalizio (nâ·tâ·lē′tsyô) *m* birthday; — *a*
natal

natante (nâ·tân′tä) *a* afloat, floating; — *m*
watercraft

natica (nâ′tē·kâ) *f* buttock

nativo (nâ·tē′vō) *a&m* native

nato (nâ′tō) *a* born; sprung up, originated

natura (nâ·tū′râ) *f* nature; type; — **morta**
(*art*) still life

naturale (nâ·tū·râ′lä) *a* natural; **di grandezza** — life-size

naturalezza (nâ·tū·râ·lä′tsâ) *f* artlessness;
naturalness; **con** — naively; simply

naturalismo (nâ·tū·râ·lē′zmō) *m* natural-
ism

naturalista (nâ·tū·râ·lē′stä) *m* naturalist

naturalizzare (nâ·tū·râ·lē·dzâ′rä) *vt* to
naturalize; to grant citizenship to

naturalizzarsi (nâ·tū·râ·lē·dzâr′sē) *vr* to
become naturalized; to become a citizen

naturalizzazione (nâ·tū·râ·lē·dzâ·tsyō′-
nä) *f* naturalization

naturalmente (nâ·tū·râl·mān′tä) *adv* of
course

naturismo (nâ·tū·rē′zmō) *m* nudism

naufragare (nâû·frâ·gâ′rä) *vi* to be ship-
wrecked; to fail, be spoiled; **far** — to
shipwreck, cast away; to ruin, spoil,
upset

naufragio (nâû·frâ′jō) *m* shipwreck; (*fig*)
failure; ruining, upsetting

naufrago (nâ′ū·frâ·gō) *m* cast away, ship-
wrecked; ruined, upset; — *m* shipwreck
victim, castaway; — **della vita** (*fig*)
pariah, outcast

nausea (nâ′ū·zä·â) *f* nausea; **far** — **a** to
repulse, disgust

nauseante (nâû·zä·ân′tä) *a* disgusting,
loathsome

nautica (nâ′ū·tē·kâ) *f* science of navigation, navigation

nautico (nâ′ū·tē·kō) *a* nautical

navale (nâ·vâ′lä) *a* naval

navata (nâ·vâ′tâ) *f* (*arch*) nave, aisle

nave (nâ′vä) *f* boat; ship

navetta (nâ·vät′tâ) *f* shuttle; **fare la** — to
ply back and forth

navicella (nâ·vē·chāl′lâ) *f* (*avi*) nacelle;
small vessel

navigabile (nâ·vē·gâ′bē·lä) *a* navigable

navigante (nâ·vē·gân′tä) *m* sailor; — *a*
sailing

navigare (nâ·vē·gâ′rä) *vt* to sail; to navigate

navigato (nâ·vē·gâ′tō) *a* (*fig*) sly, experienced, knowing

navigazione (nâ·vē·gâ·tsyō′nä) *f* navigation

nazionale (nâ·tsyō·nâ′lä) *a&m* national

nazionalismo (nâ·tsyō·nâ·lē′zmō) *m* na-
tionalism

nazionalista (nâ·tsyō·nâ·lē′stä) *m* nation-
alist

nazionalità (nâ·tsyō·nâ·lē·tâ′) *f* nationality

nazionalizzare (nâ·tsyō·nâ·lē·dzâ′rä) *vt*
to nationalize

nazione (nâ·tsyō′nä) *f* nation

ne (nä) *pron* some, any; of him, of it, of
her; from there

nè (nä) *conj* neither, nor; — **. . .** —
neither . . . nor

neanche (nä·ân′kä) *adv* not even, even;
— *conj* neither; — **per sogno** by no
means; I shouldn't dream of it

nebbia (neb′byâ) *f* fog

nebbioso (näb·byō′zō) *a* hazy, foggy

nebulizzare (nä·bū·lē·dzâ′rä) *vt* to ne-
bulize, atomize

nebulizzatore (nä·bū·lē·dzâ·tō′rä) *m*
aerosol bomb; atomizer

nebulosa (nä·bū·lō′zâ) *f* (*astr*) nebula

nebuloso (nä·bū·lō′zō) *a* cloudy; nebulous, indistinct

necessariamente (nä·chäs·sâ·ryâ·mān′tä)
adv by necessity, necessarily

necessario (nä·chäs·sâ′ryō) *a* necessary

necessità (nä·chäs·sē·tâ′) *f* poverty; necessity

necessitare (nä·chäs·sē·tâ′rä) *vt* to compel; to need, be in need of; to necessitate; — *vi* to be needed, be necessary

necrologia (nä·krō·lō·jē′â) *f* obit, death
notice; eulogy

necrologio (nä·krō·lô′jō) *m* obituary

necrosi (nä·krō′zē) *f* gangrene, necrosis

nefando (nä·fân′dō) *a* wicked, infamous

nefasto (nä·fâ′stō) *a* ill-fated, ill-starred;
unfavorable

â ârm, ā bāby, e bet, ē bē, ō gō, ô gône, ū blūe, b bad, ch child, d dad, f fat, g gay, j jet

nefrite (nā·frē'tā) *f* nephritis
negare (nā·gâ'rā) *vt* to deny; to gainsay; to negate
negativa (nā·gâ·tē'vâ) *f* negative; denial
negativamente (nā·gâ·tē·vâ·mān'tā) *adv* negatively
negazione (nā·gâ·tsyō'nā) *f* denial; negation; contradiction
negli (nā'lyē) *prep* in the
negligente (nā·glē·jān'tā) *a* lax, heedless, negligent
negligentemente (nā·glē·jān·tā·mān'tā) *adv* negligently, heedlessly
negligenza (nā·glē·jān'tsâ) *f* laxity, negligence
negoziante (nā·gō·tsyân'tā) *m* storekeeper; merchant; dealer
negoziare (nā·gō·tsyâ'rā) *vt&i* (*com*) to do business; to negotiate
negoziato (nā·gō·tsyâ'tō) *m* negotiation; deal
negozio (nā·gô'tsyō) *m* store, shop
negra (nā'grâ) *f* Negro woman
negriero (nā·gryā'rō) *m* slave dealer; — *a* slave
negro (nā'grō) *m* Negro
negromante (nā·grō·mân'tā) *m* sorcerer
nei (nā'ē), **nel** (nāl), **nella** (nāl'lâ), **nelle** (nāl'lā), **negli** (nā'lyē) *prep* in the
nemico (nā·mē'kō) *m* enemy; — *a* enemy; hostile
nemmeno (nām·mā'nō) *adv* not even, even; — *conj* neither
neo (nā'ō) *m* mole (*growth*); (*fig*) imperfection, flaw
neon (nā'ōn) *m* neon; **luci al** — neon lights
neonato (nā·ō·nâ'tō) *a* newborn
nepotismo (nā·pō·tē'zmō) *m* partiality; nepotism
neppure (nāp·pū'rā) *adv* not even, even; — *conj* neither
nerastro (nā·râ'strō) *a* somewhat black, blackish
nerbata (nār·bâ'tâ) *f* flogging, whipping
nerbo (nār'bō) *m* thong; sinew; whip; **il** — **del partito** the backbone of the party
nerboruto (nār·bō·rū'tō) *a* sinewy, muscular
neretto (nā·rāt'tō) *m* (*print*) boldface type
nero (nā'rō) *a* black
nervo (nār'vō) *m* nerve; (*arch*) rib
nervosismo (nār·vō·zē'zmō) *m* nervousness; nervous condition
nervoso (nār·vō'zō) *a* nervous
nespola (ne'spō·lâ) *f* medlar; (*coll*) blow; beating
nessuno (nās·sū'nō) *a* any, no; — *pron* nobody, none, no one, anyone

nettare (nāt·tâ'rā) *vt* to clean
nettare (net'tâ·rā) *m* nectar
nettezza (nāt·tā'tsâ) *f* tidiness; cleanness
netto (nāt'tō) *a* clean; distinct; (*com*) net; — **di spese** free of charge
neurologia (nāū·rō·lō·jē'â) *f* neurology
neurologo (nāū·rô'lō·gō) *m* neurologist
neutrale (nāū·trâ'lā) *a* neutral; imparital; undecided
neutralità (nāū·trâ·lē·tâ') *f* neutrality
neutralizzare (nāū·trâ·lē·dzâ'rā) *vt* to neutralize
neutralizzazione (nāū·trâ·lē·dzâ·tsyō'nā) *f* neutralization
neutralmente (nāū·trâl·mān'tā) *adv* neutrally
neutro (ne'ū·trō) *a* neutral; — *m* neuter
neutrone (nāū·trō'nā) *m* neutron
neve (nā'vā) *f* snow
nevicare (nā·vē·kâ'rā) *vi* to snow
nevicata (nā·vē·kâ'tā) *f* snowfall
nevischio (nā·vē'skyō) *m* fine snow; sleet
nevoso (nā·vō'zō) *a* snow-capped; snowy
nevralgia (nā·vrâl·jē'â) *f* neuralgia
nevrastenico (nā·vrâ·ste'nē·kō) *a&m* neurasthenic
nevrotico (nā·vrô'tē·kō) *a&m* neurotic
nevvero (nāv·vā'rō) *interj* isn't that right?; don't you think?; aren't they?; isn't it?
nicchia (nēk'kyâ) *f* niche; cranny, nook
nichel (nē'kāl) *m* nickel
nichelare (nē·kā·lâ'rā) *vt* to nickel; to nickel-plate
nichelato (nē·kā·lâ'tō) *a* nickel-plated
nicotina (nē·kō·tē'nâ) *f* nicotine
nidiata (nē·dyâ'tâ) *f* brood, nest
nidificare (nē·dē·fē·kâ'rā) *vi* to build one's nest
nido (nē'dō) *m* nest
niente (nyân'tā) *m* nothing, nothingness; — *adv* not at all; — *a* no; **far finta di** — to close one's eyes to a situation; to feign indifference; — **affatto** not at all; — **altro?** anything else?; — **di nuovo?** is there any news?; **non fa** — it doesn't matter; don't worry about it; — **meno della verità** nothing less than the truth
nientemeno (nyân·tā·mā'nō) *adv* nevertheless; —! *interj* well really!; you don't say!
nimbo (nēm'bō) *m* halo; rain cloud
ninfa (nēn'fâ) *f* nymph; (*zool*) chrysalis
ninnananna (nēn·nâ·nân'nâ) *f* cradlesong, lullaby
ninnolo (nēn'nō·lō) *m* trinket
nipote (nē·pō'tā) *m&f* nephew; niece; grandson; granddaughter
nipponico (nēp·pô'nē·kō) *a* Japanese

---

k kid, **l** let, **m** met, **n** not, **p** pat, **r** very, **s** sat, **sh** shop, **t** tell, **v** vat, **w** we, **y** yes, **z** zero

nitidamente (nē·tē·dâ·mān'tā) *adv* limpidly; obviously
nitidezza (nē·tē·dā'tsâ) *f* brightness; clearness; brilliance
nitido (nē'tē·dō) *a* clear, distinct; brilliant, bright
nitrico (nē'trē·kō) *a* nitric
nitrito (nē·trē'tō) *m* winny, neigh
nitrocellulosa (nē·trō·chāl·lū·lō'zā) *f* guncotton
nitrogeno (nē·trô'jā·nō) *m* nitrogen
Nizza (nē'tsâ) *f* Nice
no (nō) *adv* no
nobile (nô'bē·lā) *a* noble; — *m* noble, nobleman
nobiltà (nō·bēl·tâ') *f* nobility
nocca (nŏk'kâ) *f* knuckle
nocciola (nō·chō'lâ) *f* hazelnut
nocciolo (nô'chō·lō) *m* stone, pit (*fruit*); kernel
noce (nō'chā) *f* walnut; nut; — **moscata** nutmeg; — **del piede** anklebone
nocivo (nō·chē'vō) *a* harmful; injurious
nocumento (nō·kū·mān'tō) *m* detriment; damage
nodo (nō'dō) *m* knot; (*anat*) joint; (*rail*) junction
nodoso (nō·dō'zō) *a* knotty
noi (nō'ē) *pron* we, us
noia (nô'yâ) *f* boredom
noioso (nō·yō'zō) *a* boring, dull
noleggiare (nō·lāj·jâ'rā) *vt* to hire; to rent
noleggiatore (nō·lāj·jâ·tō'rā) *m* (*com*) freighter
nolo (nō'lō) *m* hire; rental; — **di biciclette** bicycles for rent; bicycle rental
nomade (nô'mâ·dā) *m&a* nomad
nome (nō'mā) *m* name; — **di battesimo** first name; — **di famiglia** family name, surname
nomenclatura (nō·mān·klâ·tū'râ) *f* nomenclature
nomignolo (nō·mē'nyō·lō) *m* nickname
nomina (nô'mē·nâ) *f* nomination; reputation, name
nominare (nō·mē·nâ'rā) *vt* to name; to appoint; to mention; to cite
nominarsi (nō·mē·nâr'sē) *vr* to be nominated; to be called
nominativo (nō·mē·nâ·tē'vō) *a* nominative; — *m* name; (*gram*) nominative
nominato (nō·mē·nâ'tō) *a* cited, mentioned; appointed
non (nōn) *adv* not; — **fumatore** nonsmoker
nonagesimo (nō·nâ·je'zē·mō) *a* ninetieth
noncurante (nōn·kū·rân'tā) *a* heedless;

slipshod, careless
noncuranza (nōn·kū·rân'tsâ) *f* indifference; carelessness
nondimeno (nōn·dē·mā'nō) *adv* nevertheless; however; despite that
nonna (nōn'nâ) *f* grandmother
nonno (nōn'nō) *m* grandfather
nonnulla (nōn·nūl'lâ) *f* trifle, nothing, bagatelle
nono (nō'nō) *a* ninth
nonostante (nō·nō·stân'tā) *prep* in spite of, despite, notwithstanding
nord (nōrd) *m* north
nordico (nôr'dē·kō) *a* northern, north; Nordic
norma (nōr'mâ) *f* rule; guidance; **–le** (nōr·mâ'lā) *a* normal; **–lista** (nōr·mâ·lē'stâ) *m&f* normal-school student; **–lità** (nōr·mâ·lē'tâ') *f* normality; **–lizzare** (nōr·mâ·lē·dzâ'rā) *vt* to normalize; to stabilize
normalmente (nōr·mâl·mān'tā) *adv* normally; customarily
norvegese (nōr·vâ·jā'zā) *a&m* Norwegian
Norvegia (nōr·ve'jâ) *f* Norway
nosocomio (nō·zō·kô'myō) *m* hospital
nostalgia (nō·stâl·jē'â) *f* nostalgia
nostrano (nō·strâ'nō) *a* domestic, local
nostro (nō'strō) *a* our; — *pron* ours
nostromo (nō·strō'mō) *m* (*naut*) boatswain
nota (nō'tâ) *f* note; bill
notaio (nō·tâ'yō) *m* notary
notare (nō·tâ'rā) *vt* to note; to notice; **far** — to comment on; to point out; **farsi** — to attract attention to oneself
notarile (nō·tâ·rē'lā) *a* notarial
notevole (nō·te'vō·lā) *a* notable, remarkable; conspicuous
notevolmente (nō·tâ·vōl·mān'tā) *adv* noticeably; remarkably; conspicuously
notifica (nō·tē'fē·kâ) *f* notification; **–re** (nō·tē·fē·kâ'rā) *vt* to notify, advise; to let know
notizia (nō·tē'tsyâ) *f* news; notice; **–rio** (nō·tē·tsyâ'ryō) *m* news bulletin
noto (nō'tō) *a* known; famous
notoriamente (nō·tō·ryâ·mān'tā) *adv* notoriously; in public
notorietà (nō·tō·ryā·tâ') *f* fame; notoriety
notorio (nō·tô'ryō) *a* notorious; legal; famous, well-known
nottambulo (nŏt·tâm'bū·lō) *m* night owl; nighthawk
nottata (nŏt·tâ'tâ) *f* nighttime; entire night
notte (nŏt'tā) *f* night; **buona —!** good night!; **questa —** tonight; **si fa —** it's getting dark out; **di — tempo** at night,

nights
notturno (nŏt·tūr'nō) *a* nightly; nocturnal;
— *m* (*mus*) nocturne
novanta (nō·vän'tâ) *a* ninety
novantesimo (nō·vân·te'zē·mō) *a* ninetieth
nove (nō'vä) *a* nine
novecento (nō·vä·chän'tō) *a* nine hundred; **il N**– the twentieth century
novella (nō·väl'lâ) *f* short story; novelette
novellino (nō·väl·lē'nō) *m* greenhorn;
novice; — *a* inexperienced; beginning
novellista (nō·väl·lē'stâ) *m* short-story
writer; writer of fiction
novello (nō·väl'lō) *a* novel, new
novembre (nō·väm'brä) *m* November
novità (nō·vē·tâ') *f* novelty; latest news
novizio (nō·vē'tsyō) *a* new, beginning;
— *m* novice
nozione (nō·tsyō'nä) *f* knowledge; idea,
conception
nozze (nō'tsä) *fpl* wedding
nube (nū'bä) *f* cloud
nubifragio (nū·bē·frâ'jō) *m* cloudburst,
sudden rainstorm
nubile (nū'bē·lä) *f* single woman; — *a*
unmarried
nuca (nū'kâ) *f* (*anat*) nape
nucleare (nū·klä·â'rä) *a* nuclear; **fisica**
— nuclear physics
nucleo (nū'klä·ō) *m* nucleus; gist
nucleone (nū·klä·ō'nä) *m* nucleon
nudamente (nū·dâ·män'tä) *adv* plainly;
bluntly; barefacedly
nudista (nū·dē'stä) *m&f* nudist
nudità (nū·dē·tâ') *f* nudity
nudo (nū'dō) *a* nude; bare
nulla (nūl'lâ) *m* nothing, nothingness; —
adv not at all; **non fa** — it doesn't matter, that's quite alright
nullaosta (nūl·lâ·ō'stä) *m* visa, permit
nullatenente (nūl·lâ·tä·nän'tä) *a&m* proletarian, have-not
nullità (nūl·lē·tâ') *f* nonentity, cipher;
nothingness

nullo (nūl'lō) *a* null, void, nil
nume (nū'mä) *m* deity
numerare (nū·mä·râ'rä) *vt* to number
numerato (nū·mä·râ'tō) *a* numbered
numerazione (nū·mä·râ·tsyō'nä) *f* numbering
numero (nū'mä·rō) *m* number; issue, (*periodical*); (*theat*) act
numerosamente (nū·mä·rō·zâ·män'tä)
adv numerously
numeroso (nū·mä·rō'zō) *a* numerous;
many
numismatica (nū·mē·zmâ'tē·kâ) *f* numismatics
nunzio (nūn'tsyō) *m* nuncio
nuocere * (nwô'chä·rä) *vt* to harm; to
damage
nuora (nwō'râ) *f* daughter-in-law
nuotare (nwō·tâ'rä) *vi* to swim; (*fig*) to
roll, wallow
nuotatore (nwō·tâ·tō'rä) *m* swimmer
nuoto (nwō'tō) *m* swimming; — **a rana**
breaststroke; — **sul dorso** backstroke;
— **a stile libero** freestyle swimming
nuova (nwō'vä) *f* news
nuovo (nwō'vō) *a* new; different; another
nutriente (nū·tryän'tä) *a* nourishing, substantial
nutrice (nū·trē'chä) *f* foster mother; wet
nurse
nutrimento (nū·trē·män'tō) *m* nourishment
nutrire (nū·trē'rä) *vt* to nourish; —
speranze to entertain hopes; — **affetto
per** to love; to be fond of
nutrirsi (nū·trēr'sē) *vr* to thrive on; to
feed on
nutrito (nū·trē'tō) *a* well-fed
nutrizione (nū·trē·tsyō'nä) *f* nourishment
nuvola (nū'vō·lâ) *f* cloud; **cader dalle
nuvole** (*fig*) to be amazed; to be astonished
nuvoloso (nū·vō·lō'zō) *a* cloudy, overcast
nuziale (nū·tsyâ'lä) *a* bridal, nuptial;
veste — bridal gown

O

o (ō) *conj* either, or; —...— either ... or
oasi (ô'â·zē) *f* oasis
obbediente (ōb·bä·dyän'tä) *a* tractable,
obedient
obbedienza (ōb·bä·dyän'tsâ) *f* acquiescence; obedience; submission
obbedire (ōb·bä·dē'rä) *vt&i* to comply
with; to obey
obbligare (ōb·blē·gâ'rä) *vt* to oblige; to

compel; to make, force
obbligarsi (ōb·blē·gâr'sē) *vr* to undertake;
to oblige oneself
obbligatoriamente (ōb·blē·gâ·tō·ryâ·
män'tä) *adv* under obligation
obbligatorio (ōb·blē·gâ·tō'ryō) *a* required; mandatory
obbligazione (ōb·blē·gâ·tsyō'nä) *f* bond;
duty, obligation

obbligazionista (ōb·blē·gâ·tsyō·nē'stâ) *m* bondholder

obbligo (ôb'blē·gō) *m* obligation

obbrobrio (ôb·brō'bryō) *m* opprobrium, disgrace, shame

obbrobrioso (ōb·brō·bryō'zō) *a* disgraceful, opprobrious

obelisco (ō·bā·lē'skō) *m* obelisk

oberato (ō·bā·râ'tō) *a* laden, weighed down

obeso (ō·bā'zō) *a* obese, excessively fat, corpulent

obice (ô'bē·chā) *m* howitzer

obiettare (ō·byāt·tâ'rā) *vt* to object to; to argue against

obiettivamente (ō·byāt·tē·vâ·mān'tā) *adv* objectively; impartially

obiettività (ō·byāt·tē·vē·tâ') *f* fairness; objectivity

obiettivo (ō·byāt·tē'vō) *a&m* objective; (*phot*) lens; — *a* objective, impersonal

obiettore (ō·byāt·tō'rā) *m* objector; — **di coscienza** conscientious objector

obiezione (ō·byā·tsyō'nā) *f* objection

obitorio (ō·bē·tô'ryō) *m* morgue

oblatore (ō·blâ·tō'rā) *m* donor

oblazione (ō·blâ·tsyō'nā) *f* gift, donation

oblio (ō·blē'ō) *m* oblivion

obliquo (ō·blē'kwō) *a* indirect; oblique; (*fig*) sly

oblò (ō·blō') *m* porthole

obolo (ô'bō·lō) *m* tiny coin; insignificant sum

oca (ō'kâ) *f* goose; stupid girl; **collo d'** — (*mech*) crankshaft

ocarina (ō·kâ·rē'nâ) *f* (*mus*) ocarina

occasionale (ōk·kâ·zyō·nâ'lā) *a* casual

occasionalmente (ōk·kâ·zyō·nâl·mān'tā) *adv* occasionally, now and then; by chance

occasionare (ōk·kâ·zyō·nâ'rā) *vt* to cause, engender; to bring on

occasione (ōk·kâ·zyō'nā) *f* chance; opportunity; bargain

occhiaia (ōk·kyâ'yâ) *f* eye socket

occhialaio (ōk·kyâ·lâ'yō) *m* optician

occhiali (ōk·kyâ'lē) *mpl* eyeglasses; — **da automobile** goggles; — **da sole** sunglasses

occhialoni (ōk·kyâ·lō'nē) *mpl* goggles

occhiata (ōk·kyâ'tâ) *f* look, glance

occhiello (ōk·kyāl'lō) *m* buttonhole; flyleaf; half title

occhio (ōk'kyō) *m* eye; **a quattr'occhi** tête-à-tête, privately; **dare nell'** — to attract attention; **a** — **e croce** roughly speaking; **costare un** — to be extremely costly

occhiolino (ōk·kyō·lē'nō) *m* wink; **fare l'** — to wink

occidentale (ō·chē·dān·tâ'lā) *a* western; Occidental

occidente (ō·chē·dān'tā) *m* west; Occident, West

occorrente (ōk·kōr·rān'tā) *a* necessary; — *m* necessity, requisite

occorrenza (ōk·kōr·rān'tsâ) *f* circumstance; necessity; **all'** — in case of emergency; **if necessary**

occorrere * (ōk·kôr'rā·rā) *vi* to happen; to be necessary; to be fitting

occultare (ōk·kūl·tâ'rā) *vt* to keep secret; to secrete, hide

occulto (ōk·kūl'tō) *a* mysterious; esoteric; hidden; occult

occupare (ōk·kū·pâ'rā) *vt* to take possession of; to occupy

occuparsi (ōk·kū·pâr'sē) *vr* to engage in; to interest oneself in

occupato (ōk·kū·pâ'tō) *a* taken; busy; occupied

occupazione (ōk·kū·pâ·tsyō'nā) *f* work, job; occupation

oceano (ō·che'â·nō) *m* ocean

oculare (ō·kū·lâ'rā) *a* ocular; **testimonio** — eyewitness

oculato (ō·kū·lâ'tō) *a* cautious, wary

oculista (ō·kū·lē'stâ) *m* oculist

od (ōd) *conj* or

odiare (ō·dyâ'rā) *vt* to hate

odiernamente (ō·dyār·nâ·mān'tā) *adv* nowadays, currently, presently

odierno (ō·dyār'nō) *a* of today, current, present

odio (ō'dyō) *m* hatred

odiosamente (ō·dyō·zâ·mān'tā) *adv* hatefully; disgustingly

odioso (ō·dyō'zō) *a* odious; hateful

Odissea (ō·dēs·sā'â) *f* Odyssey; (*fig*) ups and downs of life

odontoiatria (ō·dōn·tō·yâ·trē'â) *f* dentistry, odontology

odorare (ō·dō·râ'rā) *vt&i* to smell

odorato (ō·dō·râ'tō) *m* sense of smell

odore (ō·dō'rā) *m* scent, smell

odoroso (ō·dō·rō'zō) *a* sweet-scented, fragrant

offendere * (ōf·fen'dā·rā) *vt* to offend

offendersi * (ōf·fen'dār·sē) *vr* to feel hurt, take offense; to be irritated; to be piqued

offensiva (ōf·fān·sē'vâ) *f* offensive; onslaught

offensivo (ōf·fān·sē'vō) *a* insulting

offensore (ōf·fān·sō'rā) *m* offender

offerente (ōf·fā·rān'tā) *m* bidder

offerta (ōf·fār'tâ) *f* offer; bid

offesa (ōf·fā'zâ) *f* insult; offense

officina (ōf·fē·chē'nâ) *f* shop; plant; **capo** — foreman

officioso (ōf·fē·chō'zō) *a* polite; obliging; unofficial; semiofficial

offrire * (ōf·frē'rā) *vt* to afford, present; to offer

offrirsi * (ōf·frēr'sē) *vr* to present oneself; volunteer

offuscare (ōf·fū·skâ'rā) *vt* to darken; to obscure, eclipse

offuscarsi (ōf·fū·skâr'sē) *vr* to darken; to get dim; to decline

oggetto (ōj·jāt'tō) *m* object; purpose

oggi (ōj'jē) *m&adv* today

oggidì (ōj·jē·dē') *adv* nowadays, at present

ogni (ō'nyē) *a* each, every; — **tanto** now and then, from time to time; **in** — **luogo** everywhere; **in** — **modo** in any case; anyhow

Ognissanti (ō·nyēs·sân'tē) *m* All Saints' Day

ognuno (ō·nyū'nō) *pron* each one; everyone

Olanda (ō·lân'dâ) *f* Holland

olandese (ō·lân·dā'zā) *a* Dutch

oleandro (ō·lā·ân'drō) *m* oleander

oleificio (ō·lāē·fē'chō) *m* oil mill

oleodotto (ō·lā·ō·dōt'tō) *m* oil pipeline

oleografia (ō·lā·ō·grâ·fē'â) *f* oleograph

oleoso (ō·lā·ō'zō) *a* oily

olezzante (ō·lā·tsân'tā) *a* fragrant, sweet-scented

olezzare (ō·lā·tsâ'rā) *vi* to smell sweet

olfatto (ōl·fât'tō) *m* sense of smell

oliare (ō·lyâ'rā) *vt* to lubricate, oil

oliatore (ō·lyâ·tō'rā) *m* oilcan; oiler

oliera (ō·lyā'râ) *f* set of cruets for oil and vinegar

oligarchia (ō·lē·gâr·kē'â) *f* oligarchy

olimpiadi (ō·lēm·pē'â·dē) *fpl* Olympic games

olimpico (ō·lēm'pē·kō) *a* Olympic; Olympian; **giuochi olimpici** Olympic games

olimpionico (ō·lēm·pyō'nē·kō) *m* Olympic champion

olio (ō'lyō) *m* oil; — **d'oliva** olive oil; — **di fegato di merluzzo** codliver oil; — **di ricino** castor oil; — **lubrificante** lubricating oil

oliva (ō·lē'vâ) *f* olive

olivastro (ō·lē·vâ'strō) *a* olive (*color*)

oliveto (ō·lē·vā'tō) *m* olive grove

olivo (ō·lē'vō) *m* olive tree

olmo (ōl'mō) *m* elm

oltraggiare (ōl·trâj·jâ'rā) *vt* to ravage; to insult; to outrage

oltraggio (ōl·trâj'jō) *m* insult; outrage; — **al pudore** obscenity; — **alla giustizia** contempt of court

oltraggioso (ōl·trâj·jō'zō) *a* insulting; outrageous

oltranza (ōl·trân'tsâ) *f* extreme, uttermost, utmost; excess; **ad** — out and out; to the bitter end; **guerra ad** — war to the death

oltranzista (ōl·trân·tsē'stâ) *m* diehard; extremist; radical

oltre (ōl'trā) *prep* past, beyond; — *adv* further, farther; ahead; on; — **un mese** over a month; — **a ciò** besides, moreover; in addition to that; —**chè** (ōl·trā·kā') *conj* aside from the fact that; –**mare** (ōl·trā·mâ'rā) *m* ultramarine, deep blue; –**mare** *adv* overseas; –**modo** (ōl·trā·mō'dō) *adv* exceedingly; –**passare** (ōl·trā·pâs·sâ'rā) *vt* to exceed; to overtake; –**passare i limiti** to go too far; to go overboard (*fig*); –**tomba** (ōl·trā·tōm'bâ) *f* afterlife, next world

omaccione (ō·mâ·chō'nâ) *m* big fellow

omaggi (ō·mâj'jē) *mpl* respects

omaggiare (ō·mâj·jâ'rā) *vt* to present; to pay one's respects to

omaggio (ō·mâj'jō) *m* compliment; gift; homage; — **di** compliments of

ombelico (ō·mā·bē·lē'kō) *m* navel

ombra (ōm'brâ) *f* shadow; resentment, umbrage; shade

ombreggiare (ōm·brāj·jâ'rā) *vt* to shade; to cast a shadow on

ombreggiatura (ōm·brāj·jâ·tū'râ) *f* shading, shade

ombrellino (ōm·brāl·lē'nō) *m* parasol

ombrello (ōm·brāl'lō) *m* umbrella

ombrellone (ōm·brāl·lō'nā) *m* beach umbrella

ombroso (ōm·brō'zō) *a* shady; easily offended; skittish

omeopatia (ō·mā·ō·pâ·tē'â) *f* homeopathy

omero (ô'mā·rō) *m* shoulder; humerus

omertà (ō·mār·tâ') *f* code of silence among criminals

omesso (ō·mās'sō) *a* omitted

omettere * (ō·met'tā·râ) *vt* to omit; to disregard

ometto (ō·māt'tō) *m* little man; (*coll*) coat hanger

omicida (ō·mē·chē'dâ) *m* murderer

omicidio (ō·mē·chē'dyō) *m* homicide; — **premeditato** premeditated murder; — **colposo** manslaughter; **tentato** — attempted murder omino (ō·mē'nō) *m* little fellow

omissione (ō·mēs·syō'nā) *f* omission; mistake; disregard

omnibus (ôm'nē·būs) *m* local train; bus

omogeneità (ō·mō·jā·nāē·tâ') *f* uniformity; homogeneity

omogeneo (ō·mō·je'nā·ō) *a* homogeneous; correspondent

omogenizzato (ō·mō·jā·nē·dzâ'tō) *a* homogenized

omologare (ō·mō·lō·gâ'rā) *vt* to probate; to ratify

omologia (ō·mō·lō·jē'â) *f* homology

omonimo (ō·mô'nē·mō) *a* having the same name; — *m* namesake

omosessuale (ō·mō·sās·swâ'lā) *m&a* homosexual

oncia (ôn'châ) *f* ounce

onda (ōn'dä) *f* wave; andare in — (*rad*) to go on the air

ondata (ōn·dâ'tä) *f* breaker, surf; wave; outbreak; — di freddo cold wave

onde (ōn'dä) *adv* from where; through where; consequently; — *pron* whose; of which; with which; by which; of whom; with whom; — *conj* so that, in order that

ondeggiare (ōn·dāj·jâ'rā) *vt* to wave; to waver

ondina (ōn·dē'nâ) *f* siren, water nymph, undine

ondulare (ōn·dū·lâ'rā) *vt&i* to undulate, wave; — i capelli to wave one's hair

ondulato (ōn·dū·lâ'tō) *a* wavy; cartone — corrugated board

ondulazione (ōn·dū·lâ·tsyō'nä) *f* waving; — permanente permanent wave

onere (ô'nā·rä) *m* burden

oneroso (ō·nā·rō'zō) *a* burdensome

onestà (ō·nā·stâ') *f* integrity; honesty

onesto (ō·nā'stō) *a* fair; true; honest; straightforward, upstanding

onnipotente (ōn·nē·pō·tān'tä) *a* almighty, omnipotent

onnivoro (ōn·nē'vō·rō) *a* omnivorous

onomastico (ō·nō·mâ'stē·kō) *m* name day

onorabilità (ō·nō·râ·bē·lē·tâ') *f* honor; good name

onoranza (ō·nō·rân'tsâ) *f* tribute, honor; esteem, regard

onorare (ō·nō·râ'rā) *vt* to honor; to regard, esteem

onorario (ō·nō·râ'ryō) *a* honorary; — *m* fee

onorarsi (ō·nō·râr'sē) *vr* to take pride; to have the honor

onore (ō·nō'rä) *m* honor; acclaim; serata d' — benefit performance; fare — ai

propri impegni to keep one's commitments

onorevole (ō·nō·re'vō·lä) *a* honorable; esteemed

onorevolmente (ō·nō·rä·vōl·mān'tä) *adv* honorably; with distinction

onorificenza (ō·nō·rē·fē·chān'tsâ) *f* decoration

onta (ōn'tâ) *f* disgrace; dishonor

ontano (ōn·tâ'nō) *m* alder

ontologia (ōn·tō·lō·jē'â) *f* ontology

ONU (ō'nū) *f* United Nations

opaco (ō·pâ'kō) *a* opaque; lackluster

opera (ô'pä·râ) *f* work; opera

operaio (ō·pä·râ'yō) *m* workman

operare (ō·pä·râ'rā) *vt* to work, operate; to cause; — *vi* to function, perform

operatore (ō·pä·râ·tō'rä) *m* operator; cameraman

operatorio (ō·pä·râ·tô'ryō) *a* (*med*) operable

operazione (ō·pä·râ·tsyō'nä) *f* transaction; operation

operetta (ō·pä·rät'tâ) *f* musical comedy

operosità (ō·pä·rō·zē·tâ') *f* industry, diligence

operoso (ō·pä·rō'zō) *a* industrious, diligent

opificio (ō·pē·fē'chō) *m* plant, factory

opinare (ō·pē·nâ'rā) *vi* to suppose; to opine; to consider

opinione (ō·pē·nyō'nä) *f* opinion, idea

oppio (ôp'pyō) *m* opium

opponente (ōp·pō·nän'tä) *m* opponent; — *a* adverse; opposing

opporre * (ōp·pōr'rä) *vt* to oppose

opporsi * (ōp·pōr'sē) *vr* to withstand; to be opposed

opportunamente (ōp·pōr·tū·nâ·mān'tä) *adv* opportunely; at the right time

opportunista (ōp·pōr·tū·nē'stâ) *m* opportunist

opportunità (ōp·pōr·tū·nē·tâ') *f* opportunity; timeliness

opportuno (ōp·pōr·tū'nō) *a* opportune; considerare — to think advisable; a tempo — at the right time

oppositore (ōp·pō·zē·tō'rā) *m* antagonist; opponent

opposizione (ōp·pō·zē·tsyō'nä) *f* opposition

opposto (ōp·pō'stō) *a&m* opposed; opposite; contrary

oppressione (ōp·präs·syō'nä) *f* oppression

oppressore (ōp·präs·sō'rä) *m* oppressor

opprimente (ōp·prē·mān'tä) *a* oppressing, oppressive

opprimere * (ōp·prē'mä·rä) *vt* to oppress;

to lord it over; to bully

oppugnare (ōp·pū·nyâ′râ) *vt* to confute; to refute

oppure (ōp·pū′rā) *conj* or else, or

optare (ōp·tâ′râ) *vi* to choose, make a choice, opt

optometria (ōp·tō·mā·trē′â) *f* optometry

opulento (ō·pū·lān′tō) *a* well-to-do, affluent

opulenza (ō·pū·lān′tsâ) *f* affluence

opuscolo (ō·pū′skō·lō) *m* pamphlet, leaflet

ora (ō′râ) *f* time; hour; — **di punta** rush hour; — *adv* now; **che** — **è?** What time is it?; **di buon′**— early in the morning; — **legale** daylight saving time

orafo (ō′râ·fō) *m* goldsmith

orale (ō·râ′lâ) *a* oral

oralmente (ō·râl·mān′tā) *adv* verbally, orally

orare (ō·râ′râ) *vi* to pray

orario (ō·râ′ryō) *m* timetable; — *a* hourly; — **di visita** visiting hours; **segnale** — (*rad*) time signal

oratore (ō·râ·tō′râ) *m* public speaker, orator

oratoria (ō·râ·tô′ryâ) *f* public speaking, oratory

oratorio (ō·râ·tô′ryō) *m* private chapel; (*mus*) oratorio; — *a* oratorical

orazione (ō·râ·tsyō′nā) *f* prayer; public discourse, oration

orbene (ōr·bā′nā) *adv* well; so; well now

orbita (ôr′bē·tâ) *f* orbit

orbo (ōr′bō) *a* blind; (*fig*) lacking

orchestra (ōr·kā′strâ) *f* orchestra

orchestrale (ōr·kā·strâ′lā) *m* orchestra member; — *a* orchestral

orchestrare (ōr·kā·strâ′râ) *vt* to score, orchestrate

orchestrazione (ōr·kā·strâ·tsyō′nā) *f* orchestration

orchidea (ōr·kē·dā′â) *f* orchid

orco (ōr′kō) *m* ogre

orda (ōr′dâ) *f* horde, swarm, throng

ordigno (ōr·dē′nyō) *m* device; implement; tool, instrument

ordinale (ōr·dē·nâ′lā) *a* ordinal (*number*)

ordinamento (ōr·dē·nâ·mân′tō) *m* arrangement, placement; ordinance

ordinanza (ōr·dē·nân′tsâ) *f* order; writ; (*mil*) ordinance

ordinare (ōr·dē·nâ′râ) *vt* to order; (*eccl*) to ordain; to set up, place

ordinariamente (ōr·dē·nâ·ryâ·mān′tā) *adv* usually, commonly; routinely

ordinario (ōr·dē·nâ′ryō) *a* ordinary; common; coarse; regular; — *m* professor

ordinarsi (ōr·dē·nâr′sē) *vr* to get organized; to put one's house in order (*fig*)

ordinatamente (ōr·dē·nâ·tâ·mân′tā) *adv* orderly; methodically; neatly

ordinato (ōr·dē·nâ′tō) *a* put in order, tidied; orderly; ordered; methodical

ordinazione (ōr·dē·nâ·tsyō′nā) *f* order; ordination; (*med*) prescription

ordine (ôr′dē·nā) *m* order, decree

ordire (ōr·dē′râ) *vt* to scheme, plot

ordito (ōr·dē′tō) *m* warp (*weaving*); scheming; network

orecchino (ō·râk·kē′nō) *m* earring

orecchio (ō·rek′kyō) *m* ear

orecchioni (ō·râk·kyō′nē) *mpl* mumps

orefice (ō·re′fē·châ) *m* goldsmith; jeweler

oreficeria (ō·râ·fē·châ·rē′â) *f* jewelry store; jewelry

orfanello (ōr·fâ·nāl′lō) *f* orphan boy

orfano (ôr′fâ·nō) *m&a* orphan

orfanotrofio (ōr·fâ·nō·trô′fyō) *m* orphanage

organetto (ōr·gâ·nāt′tō) *m* accordion; — **di Barberia** hurdy-gurdy

organico (ōr·gâ′nē·kō) *a* organic; — *m* staff, personnel

organismo (ōr·gâ·nē′zmō) *m* organism

organista (ōr·gâ·nē′stâ) *m&f* organist

organizzare (ōr·gâ·nē·dzâ′râ) *vt* to set up, organize; to constitute

organizzatore (ōr·gâ·nē·dzâ·tō′râ) *m* organizer

organizzazione (ōr·gâ·nē·dzâ·tsyō′nā) *f* organization, setup; makeup

organo (ôr′gâ·nō) *m* organ

orgia (ôr′jâ) *f* orgy

orgoglio (ōr·gō′lyō) *m* pride; boastfulness

orgogliosamente (ōr·gō·lyō·zâ·mān′tā) *adv* haughtily; with pride

orgoglioso (ōr·gō·lyō′zō) *a* proud; swelled with pride

orientale (ō·ryān·tâ′lā) *a* eastern; Oriental; — *m* Oriental

orientamento (ō·ryān·tâ·mān′tō) *m* bearings; orientation

orientare (ō·ryān·tâ′râ) *vt* to orient

orientarsi (ō·ryān·târ′sē) *vr* to get one's bearings; to adapt oneself, get used to

orientazione (ō·ryān·tâ·tsyō′nā) *f* orientation; bearings; position

oriente (ō·ryān′tā) *m* East, Orient; east

origano (ō·rē′gâ·nō) *m* oregano, marjoram

originale (ō·rē·jē·nâ′lā) *a* original; strange, unusual; — *m&f* eccentric person; — *m* original

originalità (ō·rē·jē·nâ·lē·tâ′) *f* originality; strangeness

originalmente (ō·rē·jē·nâl·mān′tā) *adv*
originally; strangely
originare (ō·rē·jē·nâ′rā) *vt&i* to originate; to spring from
originariamente (ō·rē·jē·nâ·ryâ·mān′tā)
adv originally; at first
originario (ō·rē·jē·nâ′ryō) *a* of a specified origin; — **iltaiano** of Italian extraction
origine (ō·rē′jē·nā) *f* source; font; origin
orina (ō·rē′nâ) *f* urine
orinare (ō·rē·nâ′rā) *vi* to urinate
orinatoio (ō·rē·nâ·tô′yō) *m* urinal
oriundo (ō·ryūn′dō) *a* of a specified descent; from a specified country; —
svedese of Swedish descent
orizzontale (ō·rē·dzōn·tâ′lā) *a* horizontal
orizzontalmente (ō·rē·dzōn·tâl·mān′tā)
adv horizontally
orizzontarsi (ō·rē·dzōn·târ′sē) *vr* to get
one's bearings; to grow used to
orizzonte (ō·rē·dzōn′tā) *m* horizon
orlare (ōr·lâ′rā) *vt* to hem
orlatura (ōr·lâ·tū′râ) *f* hem; hemming
orlo (ōr′lō) *m* edge; brim; hem; verge
orma (ōr′mâ) *f* footstep; track
ormai (ōr·mâ′ē) *adv* by now; from now on
orme (ōr′mā) *fpl* trail; spoor
ormeggiare (ōr·māj·jâ′rā) *vt* to tie up,
dock, moor
ormeggiarsi (ōr·māj·jâr′sē) *vr* to lie at
anchor
ormeggio (ōr·mej′jō) *m* mooring, docking
ormone (ōr·mō′nâ) *m* hormone
ornamentale (ōr·nâ·mān·tâ′lā) *a* decorative
ornamento (ōr·nâ·mān′tō) *m* ornament;
adornment
ornare (ōr·nâ′rā) *vt* to ornament; to adorn
ornato (ōr·nâ′tō) *m* design; ornamental
motif; — *a* adorned; ornamented
ornitologo (ōr·nē·tô′lō·gō) *m* ornithologist
ornitorinco (ōr·nē·tō·rēn′kō) *m* duckbill,
platypus
oro (ō′rō) *m* gold; riches
orologeria (ō·rō·lō·jā·rē′â) *f* watchmaker's shop
orologiaio (ō·rō·lō·jâ′yō) *m* watchmaker
orologio (ō·rō·lō′jō) *m* clock; watch; —
da polso wristwatch
oroscopo (ō·rô′skō·pō) *m* horoscope
orpello (ōr·pāl′lō) *m* tinsel; gold foil
orrendamente (ōr·rān·dâ·mān′tā) *adv*
dreadfully, frightfully
orrendo (ōr·rān′dō) *a* horrible, horrifying
orribile (ōr·rē′bē·lā) *a* horrible, terrible
orribilmente (ōr·rē·bēl·mān′tā) *adv* horri-

bly, frightfully
orrido (ôr′rē·dō) *a* horrid, horrible; —
m cliff, precipice
orripilante (ōr·rē·pē·lân′tā) *a* thrilling;
hair-raising
orrore (ōr·rō′râ) *m* fright, horror
orsa (ōr′sâ) *f* female bear
orsacchiotto (ōr·sâ·kyōt′tō) *m* bear cub
orso (ōr′sō) *m* bear
orsù (ōr·sū′) *interj* come on now, well then
ortaggi (ōr·tâj′jē) *mpl* vegetables
ortica (ōr·tē′kâ) *f* nettle; (*fig*) prod, goad
orticaria (ōr·tē·kâ′ryâ) *f* (*med*) nettle rash
orticolo (ōr·tē′kō·lō) *a* horticultural
orticoltore (ōr·tē·kūl·tō′râ) *m* truck
farmer
orticoltura (ōr·tē·kūl·tū′râ) *f* truck farming
orto (ōr′tō) *m* orchard; truck farm; —
botanico botanical garden
ortofrutticoli (ōr·tō·frūt·tē′kō·lē) *mpl*
farm produce
ortografia (ōr·tō·grâ·fē′â) *f* spelling
ortolano (ōr·tō·lâ′nō) *m* truck farmer;
vegetable dealer
ortopedico (ōr·tō·pe′dē·kō) *a* orthopedic;
— *m* orthopedist
orzaiolo (ōr·dzâ·yō′lō) *m* (*med*) sty
orzare (ōr·dzâ′rā) *vi* (*naut*) to luff
orzo (ōr′dzō) *m* barley
osare (ō·zâ′rā) *vt&i* to dare
oscenità (ō·shā·nē·tâ′) *f* obscenity, lewdness
osceno (ō·shā′nō) *a* obscene, lewd
oscillare (ō·shēl·lâ′rā) *vi* to sway, swing;
to delay, hesitate
oscillazione (ō·shēl·lâ·tsyō′nā) *f* oscillation, swaying; hesitation
oscuramente (ō·skū·râ·mān′tā) *adv* dimly, obscurely
oscuramento (ō·skū·râ·mān′tō) *m* blackout; darkening
oscurare (ō·skū·râ′rā) *vt* to darken
oscurarsi (ō·skū·râr′sē) *vr* to become dim;
to get dark
oscurità (ō·skū·rē·tâ′) *f* obscurity; dark;
darkness
oscuro (ō·skū′rō) *a* obscure; unknown;
dim, dark; uncertain
ospedale (ō·spâ·dâ′lā) *m* hospital
ospitale (ō·spē·tâ′lā) *a* hospitable
ospitalità (ō·spē·tâ·lē·tâ′) *f* hospitality
ospitalmente (ō·spē·tâl·mān′tā) *adv* hos-
pitably
ospitare (ō·spē·tâ′rā) *vt* to entertain; to
accommodate; to fete
ospite (ô′spē·tā) *m* host; guest; boarder;
— *f* hostess

â ârm, **ā** bāby, **e** bet, **ē** bē, **ō** gō, **ô** gône, **ū** blūe, **b** bad, **ch** child, **d** dad, **f** fat, **g** gay, **j** jet

ospizio (ō·spē′tsyō) *m* poorhouse; orphanage; old people's home

ossa (ōs′sâ) *fpl* bones

ossario (ōs·sä′ryō) *m* charnel

ossatura (ōs·sä·tü′râ) *f* skeleton; framework, structure; build, physique

osseo (ôs′sä·ō) *a* bony

ossequi (ōs·se′kwē) *mpl* respects, greetings, best regards

ossequio (ōs·se′kwēō) *m* respect, homage

ossequiosamente (ōs·sä·kwēō·zä·män′tä) *adv* respectfully

ossequioso (ōs·sä·kwēō′zō) *a* deferential, respectful

osservanza (ōs·sär·vän′tsâ) *f* observance; **con —** respectfully yours

osservare (ōs·sär·vâ′rä) *vt* to observe; to follow, comply with

osservatorio (ōs·sär·vâ·tô′ryō) *m* observatory

osservazione (ōs·sär·vâ·tsyō′nä) *f* observation; remark

ossessionare (ōs·sās·syō·nâ′rä) *vt* to obsess, preoccupy

ossessionato (ōs·sās·syō·nâ′tō) *a* possessed, obsessed

ossessione (ōs·sās·syō′nä) *f* obsession; fear

ossia (ōs·sē′â) *conj* or, in other words, that is to say

ossidare (ōs·sē·dâ′rä) *vt* to oxidize

ossido (ôs′sē·dō) *m* oxide

ossigenare (ōs·sē·jä·nâ′rä) *vt* to oxygenate; to bleach *(hair)*

ossigeno (ōs·sē′jä·nō) *m* oxygen

osso (ōs′sō) *m* bone; **— buco** bone marrow

ostacolare (ō·stâ·kō·lâ′rä) *vt* to impede; to hinder

ostacolista (ō·stâ·kō·lē′stâ) *m (sport)* hurdler

ostacolo (ō·stâ′kō·lō) *m* obstacle; handicap; bar; *(sport)* hurdle

ostaggio (ō·stâj′jō) *m* hostage

ostante (ō·stân′tä) *a* hindering; impeding; **ciò non —** nevertheless, however

oste (ō′stä) *m* host; innkeeper

ostello (ō·stäl′lō) *m* hostel; **— della gioventù** youth hostel

ostensibilmente (ō·stän·sē·bēl·män′tä) *adv* ostensibly, visibly

ostensivamente (ō·stän·sē·vâ·män′tä) *adv* visibly, apparently

ostensorio (ō·stän·sô′ryō) *m (eccl)* monstrance

ostentare (ō·stän·tâ′rä) *vt* to show off; to brag about

ostentazione (ō·stän·tâ·tsyō′nä) *f* display; affectation; brag, bragging

osteria (ō·stä·rē′â) *f* tavern

ostessa (ō·stās′sâ) *f* hostess; airline stewardess; landlady

ostetrica (ō·ste′trē·kâ) *f* midwife

ostetricia (ō·stä·trē′châ) *f* obstetrics

ostetrico (ō·ste′trē·kō) *m* obstetrician

ostia (ô′styâ) *f* wafer; *(eccl)* Host

ostico (ô′stē·kō) *a* unpleasant; hard

ostile (ō·stē′lä) *a* hostile

ostilità (ō·stē·lē·tâ′) *f* hostility, enmity

ostilmente (ō·stēl·män′tä) *adv* inimically

ostinarsi (ō·stē·nâr′sē) *vr* to stick to; to persist in; to be obstinate

ostinato (ō·stē·nâ′tō) *a* obstinate

ostinazione (ō·stē·nâ·tsyō′nä) *f* obstinacy

ostracismo (ō·strâ·chē′zmō) *m* ostracism; avoidance

ostracizzare (ō·strâ·chē·dzâ′rä) *vt* to ostracize; to avoid

ostrica (ô′strē·kâ) *f* oyster

ostruire (ō·strüē′rä) *vt* to obstruct; to impede

ostruzionismo (ō·strü·tsyō·nē′zmō) *m* obstructionism

otite (ō·tē′tä) *f* otitis

otre (ō′trä) *m* wineskin

ottaedro (ōt·tâ·ä′drō) *m* octahedron

ottagono (ōt·tâ′gō·nō) *m* octagon

ottano (ōt·tâ′nō) *m* octane

ottanta (ōt·tân′tâ) *a* eighty

ottantesimo (ōt·tân·te′zē·mō) *a* eightieth

ottantina (ōt·tân·tē′nâ) *f* about eighty

ottava (ōt·tâ′vâ) *f* octave

ottavino (ōt·tâ·vē′nō) *m* piccolo

ottavo (ōt·tâ′vō) *a* eighth; **— n** *(mus)* octave; *(print)* octavo

ottemperare (ōt·täm·pä·râ′rä) *vi* to comply

ottemperanza (ōt·täm·pä·rân′tsâ) *f* compliance, obedience

ottenere * (ōt·tä·nä′rä) *vt* to obtain; to get

ottica (ôt′tē·kâ) *f* optics

ottico (ôt′tē·kō) *m* optician; **— a** optical

ottimamente (ōt·tē·mâ·män′tä) *adv* very well; fine; excellently

ottimismo (ōt·tē·mē′zmō) *m* optimism

ottimista (ōt·tē·mē′stâ) *m&f* optimist

ottimo (ôt′tē·mō) *a* excellent; fine

otto (ōt′tō) *m* eight; **oggi a —** a week from today

ottobre (ōt·tō′brä) *m* October

ottocento (ōt·tō·chân′tō) *a* eight hundred; **l'O-** the nineteenth century

ottomana (ōt·tō·mâ′nâ) *f* sofa, ottoman

ottone (ōt·tō′nä) *m* brass

ottuagenario (ōt·twâ·jä·nâ′ryō) *a&m* octogenarian

otturare (ōt·tü·râ′rä) *vt* to fill in; to plug up

---

k kid, **l** let, **m** met, **n** not, **p** pat, **r** very, **s** sat, **sh** shop, **t** tell, **v** vat, **w** we, **y** yes, **z** zero

otturatore (ōt·tū·râ·tō'rā) *m* *(photo)* shutter

otturazione (ōt·tū·râ·tsyō'nā) *f* filling; obstruction

ottuso (ōt·tū'zō) *a* obtuse, dull

ovaia (ō·vâ'yâ) *f* ovary

ovale (ō·vä'lā) *a* oval

ovatrice (ō·vâ·trē'chā) *f* incubator

ovatta (ō·vât'tâ) *f* wadding

ovazione (ō·vä·tsyō'nā) *f* ovation

ove (ō'vā) *conj* whereas; — *adv* where, wherein

ovest (ō'vāst) *m* west

ovile (ō·vē'lā) *m* sheepfold

ovini (ō·vē'nē) *mpl* sheep

ovino (ō·vē'nō) *a* sheep, ovine

ovunque (ō·vūn'kwā) *adv* everywhere

ovvero (ōv·vā'rō) *conj* or; or otherwise

ovviare (ō·vyâ'rā) *vt* to avoid; to obviate

ovvio (ōv'vyō) *a* clear, obvious

oziare (ō·tsyâ'rā) *vi* to laze; to idle

ozio (ō'tsyō) *m* idleness

oziosamente (ō·tsyō·zâ·mān'tā) *adv* idly; lazily

ozioso (ō·tsyō'zō) *a* lazy; idle

ozono (ō·dzō'nō) *m* ozone

P

pacatamente (pâ·kâ·tâ·mān'tā) *adv* calmly, peacefully

pacatezza (pâ·kâ·tā'tsâ) *f* calmness; quiet

pacato (pâ·kâ'tō) *a* calm, quiet

pacchetto (pâk·kät'tō) *m* package, parcel

pacchia (pâk'kyâ) *f* good things of life; cakes and ale *(fig)*

pacchianata (pâk·kyâ·nâ'tâ) *f* vulgarity

pacchiano pâk·kyâ'nō) *a* common, cheap

pacco (pâk'kō) *m* package, parcel; — **postale** parcel post

paccotiglia (pâk·kō·tē'lyâ) *f* inferior merchandise, rubbish

pace (pâ'chā) *f* peace; **lasciare in** — to leave alone

pachiderma (pâ·kē·där'mâ) *m* pachyderm

paciere (pâ·chä'rā) *m* peacemaker

pacificamente (pâ·chē·fē·kâ·mān'tā) *adv* peacefully

pacificare (pâ·chē·fē·kâ'rā) *vt* to pacify; to assuage, quiet

pacificarsi (pâ·chē·fē·kâr'sē) *vr* to be reconciled; to settle one's differences

pacifico (pâ·chē'fē·kō) *a* peaceful; pacific; quiet; **Oceano P–** Pacific Ocean

pacifismo (pâ·chē·fē'zmō) *m* pacifism

pacioccone (pâ·chōk·kō'nā) *m*, **pacioccona** (pâ·chōk·kō'nâ) *f* fat, easygoing person

padella (pâ·dāl'lâ) *f* frying pan; bedpan

padiglione (pâ·dē·lyō'nā) *m* pavilion; exhibition hall

Padova (pâ'dō·vâ) *f* Padua

padovano (pâ·dō·vâ'nō) *m&f* Paduan

padre (pâ'drä) *m* father

padrigno (pâ·drē'nyō) *m* stepfather

padrino (pâ·drē'nō) *m* godfather, foster father

padrona (pâ·drō'nâ) *f* lady, mistress *(household)*; landlady; proprietress

padronanza (pâ·drō·nân'tsâ) *f* mastery; composure; — **di una lingua** command of a language

padrone (pâ·drō'nā) *m* master; employer; landlord; proprietor; owner

padroneggiare (pâ·drō·nāj·jâ'rā) *vt* to control; to domineer

padroneggiarsi (pâ·drō·nāj·jâr'sē) *vr* to exhibit self-control

paesaggio (pâ·ä·zâj'jō) *m* scenery; landscape

paesano (pâ·ä·zâ'nō) *m* fellow townsman; peasant

paese (pâ·ä'zā) *m* country; town; village

paesista (pâ·ä·zē'stâ) *m* landscape painter

paffuto (pâf·fū'tō) *a* chubby, plump

paga (pâ'gâ) *f* wage, pay

pagaia (pâ·gâ'yâ) *f* paddle *(canoe)*

pagamento (pâ·gâ·mân'tō) *m* payment; — **alla consegna** COD, collect on delivery

paganesimo (pâ·gâ·ne'zē·mō) *m* paganism

pagano (pâ·gâ'nō) *a&m* heathen

pagare (pâ·gâ'rā) *vt* to pay, pay for

pagella (pâ·jäl'lâ) *f* report card

paggio (pâj'jō) *m* valet, page

pagina (pâ'jē·nâ) *f* page *(book)*

paglia (pâ'lyâ) *f* straw

pagliaccio (pâ·lyâ'chō) *m* clown; jester

pagliaio (pâ·lyâ'yō) *m* haystack

paglierino (pâ·lyâ·rē'nō) *a* yellowish

paglietta (pâ·lyät'tâ) *f* straw hat

pagnotta (pâ·nyōt'tâ) *f* loaf of bread; *(fig)* daily bread, daily wages

pago (pâ'gō) *a* satisfied

paio (pâ'yō) *m* couple; pair; two; **un altro** — **di maniche** *(fig)* a horse of a different color; a different matter

pala (pâ'lâ) *f* shovel; blade *(propeller)*

palanca (pâ·lân'kâ) *f* stake; *(coll)* money

palata (pâ·lâ'tâ) *f* shovelful

â ârm, ā bāby, e bet, ē bē, ō gō, ô gône, ū blūe, b bad, ch child, d dad, f fat, g gay, j jet

palato (pâ·lâ′tō) *m* palate

palazzo (pâ·lâ′tsō) *m* palace; large apartment building; **— di giustizia** court house

palco (pâl′kō) *m* (*theat*) box

palcoscenico (pâl·kō·she′nē·kō) *m* stage

paleolitico (pâ·lā·ō·lē′tē·kō) *a* paleolithic

paleontologia (pâ·lā·ōn·tō·lō·jē′â) *f* paleontology

palesare (pâ·lā·zâ′rā) *vt* to disclose, reveal

palesarsi (pâ·lā·zâr′sē) *vr* to prove oneself to be; to turn out to be

palese (pâ·lā′zā) *a* obvious, apparent

palesemente (pâ·lā·zā·mān′tā) *adv* obviously, apparently

Palestina (pâ·lā·stē′nâ) *f* Palestine

palestra (pâ·lā′strâ) *f* gymnasium

paletta (pâ·lāt′tâ) *f* palette; blade (*fan*); small shovel

paletto (pâ·lāt′tō) *m* bolt, bar; small post

palio (pâ′lyō) *m* prize, race; **mettere in —** to raffle off

palizzata (pâ·lē·tsâ′tâ) *f* palisade

palla (pâl′lâ) *f* ball; **— salutare** medicine ball; **— soffice a basi** softball; **cogliere la — al balzo** (*fig*) to take advantage of an opportunity; **–base** (pâl·lâ·bâ′zā) *f* baseball; **–canestro** (pâl·lâ·kâ·nā′strō) *m* basketball; **–corda** (pâl·lâ·kōr′dâ) *f* tennis; **–maglio** (pâl·lâ·mâ′lyō) *f* croquet; **–nuoto** (pâl·lâ·nwō′tō) *f* water polo; **–tavola** (pâl·lâ·tâ′vō·lâ) *f* table tennis; **–volo** (pâl·lâ·vō′lō) *f* volley ball

palliare (pâl·lyâ′rā) *vt* to veil; to disguise

palliativo (pâl·lyâ·tē′vō) *a* palliative

pallidamente (pâl·lē·dâ·mān′tā) *adv* faintly; wanly

pallidezza (pâl·lē·dā′tsâ) *f* wanness; paleness

pallido (pâl′lē·dō) *a* pale

pallina (pâl·lē′nâ) *f* marble (*toy*); small ball

pallini (pâl·lē′nē) *mpl* buckshot

pallonaio (pâl·lō·nâ′yō) *m* balloon man

palloncino (pâl·lōn·chē′nō) *m* toy balloon; Chinese lantern

pallone (pâl·lō′nâ) *m* balloon; football; **— americano** bubble gum; **— gonfiato** (*fig*) pretentious nobody, windbag (*coll*)

pallore (pâl·lō′rā) *m* paleness

pallottola (pâl·lôt′tō·lâ) *f* bullet

pallottolaia (pâl·lōt·tō·lâ′yâ) *f* bowling alley; bowling green

pallottoliere (pâl·lōt·tō·lyā′rā) *m* abacus

pallovale (pâl·lō·vâ′lâ) *f* rugby

palma (pâl′mâ) *f* palm

palmare (pâl·mâ′rā) *a* evident, obvious

palmeto (pâl·mā′tō) *m* palm grove

palmipede (pâl·mē′pā·dā) *m* webfooted

palmo (pâl′mō) *m* span; palm (*hand*)

palo (pâ′lō) *m* pole; stick; post

palombaro (pâ·lōm·bâ′rō) *m* deep-sea diver

palombo (pâ·lōm′bō) *m* dove

palpare (pâl·pâ′rā) *vt* to feel, touch; to palpate

palpebra (pâl′pā·brâ) *f* eyelid

palpitante (pâl·pē·tân′tā) *a* throbbing; exciting

palpitare (pâl·pē·tâ′rā) *vi* to palpitate, throb

palpitazione (pâl·pē·tâ·tsyō′nā) *f* palpitation

palpito (pâl′pē·tō) *m* throb

paltò (pâl·tō′) *m* overcoat

palude (pâ·lū′dā) *f* swamp

panama (pâ′nâ·mâ) *m* Panama hat

panare (pâ·nâ′rā) *vt* to bread; to crumb

panca (pân′kâ) *f* bench

pancetta (pân·chāt′tâ) *f* bacon; protruding stomach, potbelly

panchina (pân·kē′nâ) *f* (*rail*) platform; garden seat

pancia (pân′châ) *f* belly

panciera (pân·chā′râ) *f* abdominal belt; girdle

panciotto (pân·chōt′tō) *m* vest

pandemonio (pân·dā·mô′nyō) *m* pandemonium; din

pandorato (pân·dō·râ′tō) *m* French toast

pane (pâ′nā) *m* bread

panetteria (pâ·nāt·tā·rē′â) *f* bakery

panettiere (pâ·nāt·tyā′rā) *m* baker

panettone (pâ·nāt·tō′nā) *m* raisin bread

panfilo (pân′fē·lō) *m* yacht

pania (pâ′nyâ) *f* birdlime

panico (pâ′nē·kō) *m* panic

paniere (pâ·nyâ′râ) *m* basket

panificare (pâ·nē·fē·kâ′rā) *vt* to make into bread

panificazione (pâ·nē·fē·kâ·tsyō′nā) *f* baking of bread

panificio (pâ·nē·fē′chō) *m* wholesale bakery

panino (pâ·nē′nō) *m* roll; **— imbottito** sandwich

panna (pân′nâ) *f* cream; (*auto*) engine trouble; flat tire; **— montata** whipped cream

pannello (pân·nāl′lō) *m* panel

panno (pân′nō) *m* cloth

pannocchia (pân·nôk′kyâ) *f* (*bot*) spike; corncob

pannolino (pân·nō·lē′nō) *m* diaper; sanitary napkin

panorama (pâ·nō·râ′mâ) *m* view, pano-

rama
pantaloni (pân·tâ·lō′nē) *mpl* pants, trousers
pantano (pân·tâ′nō) *m* quagmire, swamp
pantera (pân·tā′râ) *f* panther
pantofola (pân·tō′fō·lâ) *f* slipper
pantostato (pân·tō·stā′tō) *m* toast
panzana (pân·dzâ′nâ) *f* tall tale, yarn
Papa (pâ′pâ) *m* (*eccl*) Pope
papà (pâ·pâ′) *m* father, papa
papale (pâ·pâ′lâ) *a* papal
papalina (pâ·pâ·lē′nâ) *f* skullcap
papato (pâ·pâ′tō) *m* papacy
papavero (pâ·pâ′vā·rō) *m* poppy; (*fig*) important person
papera (pâ′pā·râ) *f* goose; (*theat*) muffing a line
papero (pâ′pā·rō) *m* gander
pappa (pâp′pâ) *f* pap
pappagallo (pâp·pâ·gâl′lō) *m* parrot
pappagorgia (pâp·pâ·gôr′jâ) *f* double chin
para (pâ′râ) *f* latex; crepe rubber
parabola (pâ·râ′bō·lâ) *f* parable; (*math*) parabola
parabrezza (pâ;râ·brā′tsâ) *m* windshield
paracadute (pâ·râ·kâ·dū′tâ) *m* parachute
paracadutista (pâ·râ·kâ·dū·tē′stâ) *m* paratrooper
paracalli (pâ·râ·kâl′lē) *m* corn pad
paracarro (pâ·râ·kâr′rō) *m* highway guard post; guard rail
paracolpi (pâ·râ·kōl′pē) *m* (*auto*) fender
paracqua (pâ·râk′kwâ) *m* umbrella
paradisiaco (pâ·râ·dē·zē′â·kō) *a* heavenly
paradiso (pâ·râ·dē′zō) *m* heaven, empyrean, paradise
paradosso (pâ·râ·dōs′sō) *m* paradox
parafango (pâ·râ·fân′gō) *m* (*auto*) fender
parafare (pâ·râ·fâ′râ) *vt* to initial
paraffina (pâ·râf·fē′nâ) *f* paraffin
parafrasare (pâ·râ·frâ·zâ′râ) *vt* to paraphrase; to restate
parafulmine (pâ·râ·fūl′mē·nâ) *m* lightning rod
parafuoco (pâ·râ·fwō′kō) *m* fire screen
paraggi (pâ·râj′jē) *mpl* surroundings; environs
paragonabile (pâ·râ·gō·nâ′bē·lâ) *a* comparable
paragonare (pâ·râ·gō·nâ′râ) *vt* to compare
paragone (pâ·râ·gō′nâ) *m* comparison; **pietra di —** standard, guage
paragrafo (pâ·râ′grâ·fō) *m* paragraph
paralisi (pâ·râ′lē·zē) *f* paralytic stroke; paraiysis

paralizzare (pâ·râ·lē·dzâ′râ) *vt* to paralyze
paralizzarsi (pâ·râ·lē·dzâr′sē) *vr* to become paralyzed
parallela (pâ·râl·lā′lâ) *f* parallel
parallelo (pâ·râl·lā′lō) *a* parallel
paralume (pā·râ·lū′mâ) *m* lamp shade
paranco (pâ·rân′kō) *m* (*mech*) tackle
paraocchi (pâ·râ·ōk′kē) *mpl* goggles
parapetto (pâ·râ·pāt′tō) *m* rampart; parapet
parapiglia (pâ·râ·pē′lyâ) *m* hurry-scurry, turmoil
parapioggia (pâ·râ·pyôj′jâ) *m* umbrella
parare (pâ·râ′râ) *vt* to parry; to adorn
pararsi (pâ·râr′sē) *vr* to take shelter; to dress up
parasole (pâ·râ·sō′lâ) *m* parasol
parassita (pâ·râs·sē′tâ) *m* parasite
parastatale (pâ·râ·stâ·tâ′lâ) *a* government-recognized
parata (pâ·râ′tâ) *f* parry; parade
parato (pâ·râ′tō) *m* tapestry; **carta da parati** wallpaper
paraurti (pâ·râ·ūr′tē) *m* (*auto*) bumper
parcamente (pâr·kâ·mān′tâ) *adv* frugally; parsimoniously
parcella (pâr·châl′lâ) *f* bill; lawyer's fee
parcheggiare (pâr·kâj·jâ′râ) *vt* to park
parcheggio (pâr·kej′jō) *m* parking lot; parking; **— avanti** parking ahead
parchimetro (pâr·kē′mâ·trō) *m* parking meter
parco (pâr′kō) *m* park
parco (pâr′kō) *a* frugal
parecchio (pâ·rek′kyō) *a* enough; some; **— adv** much
pareggiare (pâ·râj·jâ′râ) *vt* (*com*) to balance; to equalize
pareggiarsi (pâ·râj·jâr′sē) *vi* to be an equal match; to match oneself
pareggio (pâ·rej′jō) *m* balance; tie, even score
parente (pâ·rân′tâ) *m&f* relative
parentela (pâ·rân·tâ′lâ) *f* relationship, relation
parentesi (pâ·ren′tâ·zē) *f* parenthesis; **fra —** in brackets; (*fig*) by the way
parere (pâ·râ′râ) *m* opinion; **— * ** *vi* to appear, seem
parete (pâ·râ′tâ) *f* wall (*interior*)
pari (pâ′rē) *a* even, equal
Parigi (pâ·rē′jē) *f* Paris
parigino (pâ·rē·jē′nō) *m&a* Parisian
pariglia (pâ·rē′lyâ) *f* pair; **rendere la —** (*coll*) to retaliate in kind; to give blow for blow
parità (pâ·rē·tâ′) *f* parity

â ârm, ā bāby, e bet, ē bē, ō gō, ô gône, ū blūe, b bad, ch child, d dad, f fat, g gay, j jet

parlamentare (pär·lä·mān·tä′rā) *a* parliamentary; — *m* member of a parliament; — *vi* to confer

parlamento (pär·lä·män′tō) *a* parley; parliament

parlantina (pär·län·tē′nä) *f* glibness; talkativeness

parlare (pär·lä′rā) *vt* to talk, speak

parlata (pär·lä′tä) *f* accent; way of speaking, speech

parlato (pär·lä′tō) *a* spoken; **cinema —** sound movie

parmigiano (pär·mē·jä′nō) *a&m* Parmesan

parodia (pä·rō·dē′ä) *f* parody

parola (pä·rō′lä) *f* word; parole

parolaccia (pä·rō·lä′chä) *f* indecent expression; abusive word

paroliere (pä·rō·lyä′rā) *m* lyricist

parolina (pä·rō·lē′nä) *f* term of endearment; affectionate word

parossismo (pä·rōs·sē′zmō) *m* paroxysm

parrocchia (pär·rōk′kyä) *f* parish

parrocchiale (pär·rōk·kyä′lä) *a* parochial

parrocchiano (pär·rōk·kyä′nō) *m* parishioner

parroco (pär′rō·kō) *m* pastor; priest

parrucca (pär·rūk′kä) *f* wig

parrucchiere (pär·rūk·kyä′rä) *m* barber; hairdresser

parsimonia (pär·sē·mō′nyä) *f* parsimony; thriftiness

parte (pär′tä) *f* part; share; role

partecipare (pär·tä·chē·pä′rā) *vt* to announce; — *vi* to participate

partecipazione (pär·tä·chē·pä·tysō′nä) *f* participation; announcement

partecipe (pär·te′chē·pä) *a* sharing; participating

parteggiare (pär·täj·jä′rä) *vi* to take sides, side; to be partial

partenza (pär·tän′tsä) *f* leave-taking, departure

participio (pär·tē·chē′pyō) *m* participle

particola (pär·tē′kō·lä) *f* (*eccl*) Host; particle

particolare (pär·tē·kō·lä′rä) *a* particular; — *m* detail

particolarità (pär·tē·kō·lä·rē·tä′) *f* peculiarity; characteristic

particolarmente (pär·tē·kō·lär·män′tä) *adv* particularly, specially

partigiano (pär·tē·jä′nō) *m&a* partisan

partita (pär·tē′tä) *f* game, match; (*com*) lot; — **doppia** (*com*) double entry

partito (pär·tē′tō) *m* political party; match (*in marriage*)

partitura (pär·tē·tū′rä) *f* (*mus*) score

partizione (pär·tē·tsyō′nä) *f* division

parto (pär′tō) *m* childbirth; (*fig*) fruit, result

partoriente (pär·tō·ryän′tä) *a* in childbirth

partorire (pär·tō·rē′rä) *vt* to give birth to, be delivered of; — *vi* to give birth

parvenza (pär·vän′tsä) *f* appearance, sham

parziale (pär·tsyä′lä) *a* partial

parzialità (pär·tsyä·lē·tä′) *f* bias

parzialmente (pär·tsyäl·män′tä) *adv* in part; in a biased manner

pascolare (pä·skō·lä′rä) *vt&i* to browse; to graze; to pasture

pascolo (pä′skō·lō) *m* pasture

Pasqua (pä′skwä) *f* Easter

passabile (päs·sä′bē·lä) *a* bearable; passable

passaggio (päs·säj′jō) *m* passage; (*auto*) lift; ride; — **a livello** railroad crossing; — **a livello con barriera** guarded crossing; — **a strisce** marked crosswalk

passamaneria (päs·sä·mä·nä·rē′ä) *f* dry goods store; ribbon manufacture

passamano (päs·sä·mä′nō) *m* ribbon; braid; passing from hand to hand

passamontagna (päs·sä·mōn·tä′nyä) *m* winter cap

passante (päs·sän′tä) *m* pedestrian; passerby

passaporto (päs·sä·pōr′tō) *m* passport

passare (päs·sä′rä) *vt&i* to pass; to surpass; to spend (*time*); **passarla liscia** to go scot-free; to escape uninjured; — **la vita** to spend one's life; — **oltre** to progress, go ahead; to go beyond

passatempo (päs·sä·täm′pō) *m* pastime

passato (päs·sä′tō) *a&m* past

passeggero (päs·säj·jä′rō) *m* passenger; — *a* temporary, transitory

passeggiare (päs·säj·jä′rä) *vi* to take a walk; to go for a drive

passeggiata (päs·säj·jä′tä) *f* walk; drive

passeggio (päs·sej′jō) *m* walkway; promenade, walk

passerella (päs·sä·räl′lä) *f* gangway

passero (päs′sä·rō) *m* sparrow

passibile (päs·sē′bē·lä) *a* liable

passionale (päs·syō·nä′lä) *a* vehement; ardent

passione (päs·syō′nä) *f* passion; love

passivamente (päs·sē·vä·män′tä) *adv* passively

passività (päs·sē·vē·tä′) *fpl* (*com*) liabilities; — *f* passiveness

passivo (päs·sē′vō) *a* passive; — *m* liability

passo (päs′sō) *m* pace, step; passage (*book*); (*geog*) straits; **al —** slow;

slowly; — **carrabile** driveway
pasta (pâ′stâ) *f* spaghetti; paste, dough; pastry; — **dentifricia** toothpaste; — **frolla** puff pastry; **–io** (pâ·stâ′yō) *m* spaghetti maker; spaghetti dealer
pastello (pâ·stäl′lō) *m* pastel; pastel drawing
pastetta (pâ·stät′tâ) *f* batter (*food*)
pasticca (pâ·stēk′kâ) *f* (*med*) tablet; — **per la tosse** cough drop
pasticcere (pâ·stē·chä′rā) *m* pastry cook
pasticceria (pâ·stē·chä·rē′â) *f* pastry shop
pasticcino (pâ·stē·chē′nō) *m* cake; cookie
pasticcio (pâ·stē′chō) *m* pie; (*fig*) jumble; trouble; bungling
pasticcione (pâ·stē·chō′nā) *m* bungler
pastificio (pâ·stē·fē′chō) *m* spaghetti factory
pastiglia (pâ·stē′lyâ) *f* (*med*) tablet
pastinaca (pâ·stē·nâ′kâ) *f* parsnip
pasto (pâ′stō) *m* meal; **vino da** — table wine
pastoia (pâ·stô′yä) *f* hobble, fetter
pastore (pâ·stō′rä) *m* shepherd; pastor
pastorizia (pâ·stō·rē′tsyâ) *f* stock raising
pastorizzato (pâ·stō·rē·dzä′tō) *a* pasteurized
pastoso (pâ·stō′zō) *a* pasty; mellow
pastrano (pâ·strâ′nō) *m* heavy overcoat, greatcoat
patata (pâ·tâ′tâ) *f* potato
patatine (pâ·tâ·tē′nâ) *fpl* little potatoes; — **fritte** potato chips
patema (pâ·tä′mâ) *m* anxiety; anguish
patentare (pâ·tän·tâ′rä) *vt* to grant a license to; to award a degree to
patente (pâ·tän′tä) *a* patent, clear; — *f* license; patent; — **di guida** driver's license
paternale (pâ·tär·nâ′lä) *f* rebuke, reprimand; — *a* paternal
paternità (pâ·tär·nē·tâ′) *f* paternity
paterno (pâ·tär′nō) *a* paternal, fatherly
paternostro (pâ·tär·nō′strō) *m* the Lord's Prayer
patetico (pâ·te′tē·kō) *a* pathetic; sentimental
patibolare (pâ·tē·bō·lâ′rä) *a* criminal, guilty; **faccia** — hangdog appearance
patibolo (pâ·tē′bō·lō) *m* gallows
patimento (pâ·tē·mān′tō) *m* sorrow, anguish; pain
patina (pâ′tē·nâ) *f* patina; (*med*) furring; **–re** (pâ·tē·nâ′rä) *vt* to varnish; to daub
patire (pâ·tē′râ) *vt&i* to suffer; to tolerate; to undergo; — **la fame** to be starving
patito (pâ·tē′tō) *a* emaciated; lean
patologia (pâ·tō·lō·jē′â) *f* pathology

patologo (pâ·tô′lō·gō) *m* pathologist
patria (pâ′tryâ) *f* one's own country; one's native land
patricidio (pâ·trē·chē′dyō) *m* patricide
patrigno (pâ·trē′nyō) *m* stepfather
patrimonio (pâ·trē·mô′nyō) *m* estate; fortune; inheritance
patriotta (pâ·tryōt′tâ) *m&f* patriot
patriottico (pâ·tryôt′tē·kō) *a* patriotic
patrizio (pâ·trē′tsyō) *a* aristocratic; patrician
patrocinare (pâ·trō·chē·nâ′rā) *vt* to sponsor; to defend; to protect
patrocinatore (pâ·trō·chē·nâ·tō′rā) *m* protector; (*law*) counsel for the defense; (*com*) sponsor
patrocinio (pâ·trō·chē′nyō) *m* legal assistance; patronage; sponsorship; protection
patronato (pâ·trō·nâ′tō) *m* charitable organization; patronage; — **scolastico** agency to assist school children
patrono (pâ·trō′nō) *m* patron; protector; **santo** — patron saint
patteggiare (pât·täj·jâ′rā) *vt&i* to bargain; to reach an agreement
pattinaggio (pât·tē·nâj′jō) *m* skating; — **artistico** figure skating
pattinare (pât·tē·nâ′rä) *vi* to skate
pattinatore (pât·tē·nâ·tō′rä) *m*, **pattinatrice** (pât·tē·nâ·trē′chä) *f* skater
pattino (pât′tē·nō) *m* skate; (*avi*) skid; **sled runner**; — **a rotelle** roller skate; — **da ghiaccio** ice skate
patto (pât′tō) *m* agreement, pact; **a** — **che** providing, on condition that; **a nessun** — by no means; under no circumstances
pattuglia (pât·tū′lyâ) *f* patrol
pattuire (pât·twē′rä) *vt&i* to bargain; to agree on
pattuito (pât·twē′tō) *a* agreed upon
pattume (pât·tū′mä) *m* garbage, rubbish
pattumiera (pât·tū·myä′rä) *f* garbage can
pauperismo (pâū·pä·rē′zmō) *m* pauperism; extreme poverty
paura (pâ·ū′râ) *f* fear; **aver** — to be afraid; **far** — to fill with dread, frighten
paurosamente (pâū·rō·zâ·mân′tâ) *adv* fearfully, filled with dread
pauroso (pâū·rō′zō) *a* frightened; timid
pausa (pâ′ū·zâ) *f* pause; interval
pavese (pâ·vä′zä) *m* banner, standard
pavimentazione (pâ·vē·mān·tâ·tsyō′nâ) *f* pavement; flooring
pavimento (pâ·vē·mân′tō) *m* floor; pavement
pavone (pâ·vō′nä) *m* peacock
pavoneggiarsi (pâ·vō·nâj·jâr′sē) *vr* to

strut; to prance

pazientare (pâ·tsyän·tâ′rä) *vi* to be patient; to be long-suffering

paziente (pâ·tsyän′tä) *am&f* patient; **–mente** (pâ·tsyän·tä·män′tä) *adv* patiently

pazienza (pâ·tsyän′tsä) *f* patience; longsuffering

pazzamente (pâ·tsä·män′tä) *adv* rashly; madly

pazzesco (pâ·tsä′skō) *a* crazy, reckless, foolish

pazzia (pâ·tsē′â) *f* madness; rashness

pazzo (pâ′tsō) *a* insane, demented

pecca (pāk′kâ) *f* flaw; **–minoso** (pâk·kâ·mē·nō′zō) *a* sinful; **–re** (pāk·kâ′rä) *vi* to sin; to fall short, be inadequate; **–tore** (pāk·kâ·tō′rä) *m* sinner, transgressor

peccato (pāk·kâ′tō) *m* sin; shame, pity, bad luck; **che —!** what a shame!

pece (pā′chä) *f* pitch; **— liquida** tar

pecora (pe′kō·râ) *f* sheep; (*fig*) servile individual; **–io** (pā·kō·râ′yō) *m* shepherd

peculato (pā·kū·lä′tō) *m* embezzlement

peculio (pā·kū′lyō) *m* nest egg, savings

pedaggio (pā·dâj′jō) *m* toll, fee

pedalare (pā·dâ·lâ′rä) *vt&i* to pedal

pedale (pā·dâ′lä) *m* pedal

pedana (pā·dâ′nä) *f* platform; mat (*sport*)

pedante (pā·dân′tä) *a* pedantic; **— m** pedant

pedata (pā·dâ′tâ) *f* kick; footprint

pedestre (pā·dâ′strä) *a* pedestrian, unimaginative, commonplace

pediatra (pā·dyâ′trâ) *m* pediatrician

pediatria (pā·dyâ·trē′â) *f* pediatrics

pedicure (pā·dē·kū′rä) *m&f* chiropodist

pediluvio (pā·dē·lū′vyō) *m* footbath

pedina (pā·dē′nä) *f* (*chess*) man, pawn

pedinare (pā·dē·nâ′rä) *vt* to shadow, tail

pedone (pā·dō′nä) *m* pedestrian; (*chess*) pawn, man

peggio (pej′jō) *adv* worse; **il —** the worst

peggioramento (pâj·jō·râ·män′tō) *m* aggravation; worsening

peggiorare (pâj·jō·râ′rä) *vi* to get worse; to worsen

peggiore (pâj·jō′rä) *a* worse; **il —** the worst

pegno (pā′nyō) *m* forfeit; pledge; **in — d'amore** as a token of love

pelame (pā·lâ′mä) *m* plumage; coat of hair (*animal*)

pelare (pā·lâ′rä) *vt* to peel, skin; to fleece, swindle

pelarsi (pā·lâr′sē) *vr* to lose its leaves (*tree*); to grow bald

pellaio (pāl·lâ′yō) *m* leather dealer; tan-

ner

pellame (pāl·lâ′mä) *m* pelts

pelle (pāl′lä) *f* skin; rind; hide; **lasciarci la — (fig)** to die

pellegrinaggio (pāl·lä·grē·nâj′jō) *m* pilgrimage

pellegrino (pāl·lä·grē′nō) *m* pilgrim; **— a** wandering

pelletterie (pāl·lät·tä·rē′ä) *fpl* leather goods

pellicceria (pāl·lē·châ·rē′â) *f* fur store

pelliccia (pāl·lē′châ) *f* fur; fur coat

pellicciaio (pāl·lē·châ′yō) *m* furrier

pellicola (pāl·lē′kō·lä) *f* film

pellirossa (pāl·lē·rōs′sâ) *m* North American Indian, redskin

pelo (pā′lō) *m* fur (*animal*); hair; **contro — against the grain; aver il — sul cuore** to be unscrupulous; **montare a —** to ride bareback; **non aver peli sulla lingua** to be frank; **–so** (pā·lō′zō) *a* hairy; **carità pelosa** selfish kindness

peltro (pāl′trō) *m* pewter

peluria (pā·lū′ryâ) *f* fuzz, down

pena (pā′nâ) *f* punishment; trouble; **— capitale** capital punishment; **a mala —** hardly; **non vale la —** it isn't worthwhile; **fare —** to move to pity; to be a shame; **–le** (pā·nâ′lä) *a* penal; **–lista** (pā·nâ·lē′stä) *m* criminal lawyer

pendente (pān·dān′tä) *a* leaning; in abeyance; **— m** pendant

pendere * (pen′dä·rä) *vi* to hang; to be unsettled

pendio (pān·dē′ō) *m* grade, slope

pendola (pen′dō·lâ) *f* pendulum clock

pendolo (pen′dō·lō) *m* pendulum

pene (pā′nä) *m* penis

penetrante (pā·nä·trân′tä) *a* penetrating; pervading

penetrare (pā·nä·trâ′rä) *vi* to penetrate, enter

penetrazione (pā·nä·trâ·tsyō′nä) *f* keenness; penetration

penna (pān′nâ) *f* pen; feather; **— a sfera** ballpoint pen; **— stilografica** fountain pen

pennacchio (pān·nâk′kyō) *m* plume, panache

pennellare (pān·nāl·lâ′rä) *vt&i* to paint

pennello (pān·nāl′lō) *m* brush; **— da barba** shaving brush

pennino (pān·nē′nō) *m* nib; pen point

pennone (pān·nō′nä) *m* pennant

pennuto (pān·nū′tō) *a* feathered

penombra (pā·nōm′brâ) *f* dim light

penosamente (pā·nō·zâ·män′tä) *adv* distressingly; painfully

penoso (pā·nō'zō) *a* painful
pensare (pān·sâ'rā) *vt&i* to think; to intend
pensata (pān·sâ'tâ) *f* thought
pensatore (pān·sâ·tō'rā) *m* thinker; **libero —** free thinker
pensiero (pān·syā'rō) *m* thought; **–so** (pān·syā·rō'zō) a thoughtful; serious
pensile (pān·se'lā) *a* hanging; **giardino —** roof garden
pensilina (pān·se·le'nâ) *f* marquee; shelter
pensionante (pān·syō·nân'tā) *m* boarder
pensione (pān·syō'nā) *f* pension; boarding house; **mezza —** room with breakfast and one other meal; **in —** retired
pensosamente (pān·sō·zâ·mān'tā) *adv* pensively
pentagono (pān·tâ'gō·nō) *m* pentagon
Pentecoste (pān·tā·kō'stā) *f* Pentecost; Whitsunday
pentimento (pān·te·mān'tō) *m* repentance
pentirsi (pān·ter'se) *vr* to change one's mind; to have a change of heart; to repent, regret
pentola (pen'tō·lâ) *f* pot; **— a pressione** pressure cooker
penultimo (pā·nūl'te·mō) *m&a* next to last
penuria (pā·nū'ryâ) *f* need, penury
penzolare (pān·tsō·lâ'rā) *vi* to hang down; to swing
penzoloni (pān·tsō·lō'ne) *adv* swinging, dangling
pepaiola (pā·pâ·yō'lâ) *f* pepper shaker, pepper mill
pepato (pā·pâ'tō) *a* peppery: *(fig)* expensive; **pan —** gingerbread
pepe (pā'pā) *m* pepper
peperita (pā·pâ·re'tâ) *f* peppermint
peperone (pā·pâ·rō'nā) *m* (*bot*) pepper; chili
pepita (pā·pe'tâ) *f* nugget
per (pār) *prep* for; through; in order to; on account of; by means of; **— favore** if you please; **— lo meno** at least; **— piacere** please; **— quanto** however; **— così dire** in a manner of speaking, so to speak; **— l'appunto** exactly; **— ora** for now
pera (pā'râ) *f* pear
perbene (pār·bā'nā) *a* nice; refined; respectable; **persona —** decent person, well-bred person; **— adv** nicely, carefully
percalle (pār·kâl'lā) *m* percale
percentuale (pār·chān·twâ'lā) *f* percentage

percepibile (pār·chā·pe'be·lā) *a* perceptible
percepire (pār·chā·pe'rā) *vt* to conceive; to gain, secure; to collect; to descry, make out
percettività (pār·chāt·te·vē·tâ') *f* perceptiveness
percettore (pār·chāt·tō'rā) *m* collector
percezione (pār·chā·tsyō'nā) *f* perception; collecting
perchè (pār·kā') *conj* why; because
perciò (pār·chō') *conj* therefore
percorrere * (pār·kôr'rā·rā) *vt* to run over, travel across
percorso (pār·kôr'sō) *m* route; trip, run; **— filoviario** trolleybus route; **durante il —** on the way
percossa (pār·kōs'sâ) *f* blow, shock
percuotere * (pār·kwô'tā·rā) *vt* to strike; to shock; to hit
percussore (pār·kūs·sō'rā) *m* firing pin
perdere * (per'dā·rā) *vt* to lose; to waste; to miss; **— il treno** to miss the train
perdersi * (per'dār·se) *vr* to be spoiled; to vanish; to get lost, be lost; to miscarry
perdita (per'dē·tâ) *f* loss
perdizione (pār·dē·tsyō'nā) *f* perdition; ruin
perdonare (pār·dō·nâ'rā) *vt* to forgive
perdono (pār·dō'nō) *m* forgiveness; pardon
perdutamente (pār·dū·tâ·mān'tā) *adv* desperately; head over heels, deeply
perduto (pār·dū'tō) *a* lost
perenne (pā·rān'nā) *a* perennial; eternal
perennemente (pā·rān·nā·mān'tā) *adv* eternally
perennità (pā·rān·ne·tâ') *f* eternity
perentoriamente (pā·rān·tō·ryâ·mān'tā) *adv* peremptorily, imperiously
perentorio (pā·rān·tō'ryō) *a* without delay; decisive
perequazione (pā·rā·kwâ·tsyō'nā) *f* equalization; standardization
perfettamente (pār·fāt·tâ·mān'tā) *a* perfectly, flawlessly
perfetto (pār·fāt'tō) *a* perfect, flawless
perfezionamento (pār·fā·tsyō·nâ·mān'tō) *m* improvement; perfection; **corso di —** postgraduate course
perfezionare (pār·fā·tsyō·nâ'rā) *vt* to perfect; to complete
perfezionarsi (pār·fā·tsyō·nâr'se) *vr* to improve oneself; to achieve perfection; to learn perfectly
perfezione (par·fā·tsyō'nā) *f* perfection
perfidia (pār·fē'dyâ) *f* perfidy

â ârm, **ā** bāby, **e** bet, **ē** bē, **ō** gō, **ô** gône, **ū** blūe, **b** bad, **ch** child, **d** dad, **f** fat, **g** gay, **j** jet

perfido (per'fē·dō) *a* perfidious

perfino (pär·fē'nō) *adv* even, the very

perforare (pär·fō·râ'rä) *vt* to perforate, pierce

perforatrice (pär·fō'râ·trē'chä) *f* (*mech*) drill

perforazione (pär·fō·râ·tsyō'nä) *f* perforation

pergamena (pär·gâ·mä'nâ) *f* parchment

pergolato (pär·gō·lâ'tō) *m* arbor; pergola

pericolante (pä·rē·kō·lân'tä) *a* shaky, unsound, rickety

pericolo (pä·rē'kō·lō) *m* danger

pericolosamente (pä·rē·kō·lō·zâ·män'tä) *adv* dangerously

pericoloso (pä·rē·kō·lō'zō) *a* dangerous

periferia (pä·rē·fä·rē'â) *f* periphery; suburbs

perimetro (pä·rē'mä·trō) *m* perimeter

periodicamente (pä·ryō·dē·kâ·män'tä) *adv* periodically

periodico (pä·ryō'dē·kō) *a&m* periodical

periodo (pä·rē'ō·dō) *m* period

peripezia (pä·rē·pä·tsē'â) *f* ups and downs, vicissitudes

perire (pä·rē'rä) *vi* to perish

periscopio (pä·rē·skō'pyō) *m* periscope

perito (pä·rē'tō) *a* perished; expert; — *m* expert

perizia (pä·rē'tsyâ) *f* survey, examination; skill; **–re** (pä·rē·tsyâ'rä) *vt* to estimate

perla (pär'lâ) *f* pearl

perlustrare (pär·lū·strä'rä) *vt* (*mil*) to scout

permaloso (pär·mâ·lō'zō) *a* hypersensitive; ill-tempered

permanente (pär·mâ·nän'tä) *a* permanent; — *f* permanent wave; — *m* railroad pass

permanentemente (pär·mâ·nän·tä·män'tä) *adv* permanently

permanenza (pär·mâ·nän'tsâ) *f* stay

permanere * (pär·mâ·nä'rä) *vi* to remain; to stay

permeabile (pär·mä·â'bē·lä) *a* penetrable; permeable

permesso (pär·mäs'sō) *m* permit; excuse me, pardon me; — *a* permitted, allowed; È — ? May I?

permettere * (pär·met'tä·rä) *vt* to tolerate; to authorize, permit

permettersi (pär·met'tär·sē) *vr* to allow oneself to; to take the liberty of

permuta (pär·mū'tâ) *f* trade-in; exchange; **–re** (pär·mū·tâ'rä) *vt* to turn in; to trade in; to trade, swap

pernice (pär·nē'chä) *f* partridge

perniciosamente (pär·nē·chō·zâ·män'tä) *adv* perniciously

pernicioso (pär·nē·chō'zō) *a* extremely harmful; fatal

perno (pär'nō) *m* turning point; pivot

pernottare (pär·nōt·tâ'rä) *vi* to spend the night

pero (pä'rō) *m* pear tree

però (pä·rō') *conj* but, however; consequently

perorare (pä·rō·râ'rä) *vt&i* to defend; to plead (*a case*)

perpendicolare (pär·pän·dē·kō·lâ'rä) *a&f* perpendicular

perpetuamente (pär·pä·twâ·män'tä) *adv* perpetually

perpetuare (pär·pä·twâ'rä) *vt* to perpetuate

perpetuarsi (pär·pä·twâr'sē) *vr* to be perpetuated

perpetuo (pär·pe'twō) *a* perpetual

perplessità (pär·pläs·sē·tâ') *f* perplexity

perplesso (pär·pläs'sō) *a* perplexed

perquisire (pär·kwē·zē'rä) *vt* to search, make an official search of

perquisizione (pär·kwē·zē·tsyō'nä) *f* investigation; police search

persecuzione (pär·sä·kū·tsyō'nä) *f* persecution

perseguitare (pär·sä·gwē·tâ'rä) *vt* to persecute

perseverante (pär·sä·vä·rân'tä) *a* unrelenting

perseveranza (pär·sä·vä·rân'tsâ) *f* perseverance

perseverare (pär·sä·vä·râ'rä) *vi* to persist, persevere

persiana (pär·syâ'nâ) *f* shutter — **avvolgibile** venetian blind

persico (per'sē·kō) *a&m* Persian; **pesce** — perch (*fish*)

persistenza (pär·sē·stän'tsä) *f* perserverance; pertinacity; stick-to-itiveness

persistere * (pär·sē'stä·rä) *vi* to persist

perso (pär'sō) *a* lost

persona (pär·sō'nâ) *f* person; **–ggio** (pär·sō·nâj'jō) *m* person of note; (*theat*) character; **–le** (pär·sō·nâ'lä) *m* personnel; staff; **–le** *f* one-man show; **–le** *a* personal

personalità (pär·sō·nâ·lē·tâ') *f* personality

personalmente (pär·sō·nâl·män'tä) *adv* in person

personificare (pär·sō·nē·fē·kâ'rä) *vt* to embody; to symbolize; to impersonate

personificazione (pär·sō·nē·fē·kâ·tsyō'nä) *f* embodiment, personification; symbol perspicace (pär·spē·kâ'chä) *a* penetrating, shrewd

perspicacia (pär·spē·kâ'châ) *f* shrewdness, penetration

persuadere * (pär·swâ·dä'rä) *vt* to persuade; to win over

persuadersi * (pär·swâ·dār'sē) *vr* to be convinced; to be persuaded; to be won over

persuasione (pär·swâ·zyō'nä) *f* persuasion

persuasivo (pär·swâ·zē'vō) *a* persuasive

pertanto (pär·tân'tō) *adv* therefore, as a result, for that reason

pertica (per'tē·kâ) *f* pole

pertinacia (pär·tē·nâ'châ) *f* pertinacity

pertinenza (pär·tē·nän'tsä) *f* competence

pertosse (pär·tōs'sä) *f* whooping cough

perturbare (pär·tūr·bâ'rä) *vt* to disturb, upset

perturbazione (pär·tūr·bâ·tsyō'nä) *f* upsetting, disturbance

Perù (pā·rū') *m* Peru; **valere un —** *(coll)* to be extremely valuable

peruviano (pā·rū·vyâ'nō) *a* Peruvian

pervenire * (pär·vā·nē'rä) *vi* to reach, arrive; to achieve

perversione (pär·vär·syō'nä) *f* perversion

perversità (pär·vär·sē·tâ') *f* depravity; perversity

perverso (pär·vär'sō) *a* perverse; wicked

pervertire (pär·vär·tē'rä) *vt* to pervert

pervertirsi (pär·vär·tēr'sē) *vr* to degenerate: to become perverted

pesa (pā'zâ) *f* scale; **–ggio** (pā·zâj'jō) *m* weighing; **–nte** (pā·zän'tä) *a* heavy; boring; hard (*work*); **–ntemente** (pā·zân·tä·mān'tä) *adv* heavily; **–ntezza** (pā·zân·tā'tsä) *f* heaviness; **–ntezza allo stomaco** indigestion; **–re** (pā·zâ'rä) *(fig)* to consider; to influence; to weigh; **–rsi** (pā·zâr'sē) *vr* to weigh oneself

pesca (pā'skâ) *f* peach; fishing; bazaar; raffle; **–ggio** (pā·skâj'jō) *m* (*naut*) draft; **–re** (pā·skâ'rä) *vt&i* to fish; **–re nel torbido** *(fig)* to fish in troubled waters; **–tore** (pā·skâ·tō'rä) *m* fisherman

pesce (pā'shä) *m* fish; **— d'aprile** April Fool joke; **–cane** (pā·shä·kâ'nä) *m* shark; *(coll)* profiteer; **–spada** (pā·shä·spâ'dâ) *m* swordfish

peschereccio (pā·skä·re'chō) *a* concerning fishing, fishing; **—** *m* fishing boat

pescheria (pā·skä·rē'â) *f* fish market

pescivendolo (pā·shē·ven'dō·lō) *m* fish dealer

pesco (pā'skō) *m* peach tree

pesista (pā·zē'stâ) *m* (*sport*) weightlifter

peso (pā'zō) *m* weight; **— gallo** bantam-weight; **— leggero** lightweight; **— lordo** gross weight; **— massimo** heavyweight; **— medio** middleweight; **— mosca** flyweight; **— piuma** featherweight

pessimamente (pās·sē·mâ·män'tä) *adv* very badly

pessimismo (pās·sē·mē'zmō) *m* pessimism

pessimista (pās·sē·mē'stâ) *m* pessimist

pessimo (pes'sē·mō) *a* worst; very bad

pestaggio (pā·stâj'jō) *m* beating, drubbing

pestare (pā·stâ'rä) *vt* to pound; to trample

peste (pā'stä) *f* plague

pestello (pā·stäl'lō) *m* pestle

pestifero (pā·stē'fa·rō) *a* pernicious; pestilential; deadly

pestilenza (pā·stē·län'tsä) *f* plague, pestilence; *(fig)* stench

pesto (pā'stō) *a* pounded; **occhio —** black eye; **buio —** black, extremely dark; **carta pesta** papier mâché

petalo (pe'tâ·lō) *m* petal

petardo (pā·târ'dō) *m* firecracker

petente (pā·tän'tä) *n* petitioner

petizione (pā·tē·tsyō'nä) *f* petition

petonciano (pā·tōn·châ'nō) *m* eggplant

petroliera (pā·trō·lyâ'râ) *f* tanker

petrolio (pā·trō'lyō) *m* oil; kerosene; petroleum

pettegolezzo (pāt·tā·gō·lä'tsō) *m* gossip, idle chatter

pettegolo (pāt·te'gō·lō) *a* gossipy; **—** *m* gossip

pettinare (pāt·tē·nâ'rä) *vt* to comb

pettinarsi (pāt·tē·nâr'sē) *vr* to comb one'ↄ hair

pettinatore (pāt·tē·nâ·tō'rä) *m*, **pettinatrice** (pāt·tē·nâ·trē'chä) *f* hairdresser

pettinatura (pāt·tē·nâ·tū'râ) *f* hairdo

pettine (pet'tē·nä) *m* comb; **tutti i nodi vengono al —** *(coll)* murder will out; it will all come out in the wash

pettiniera (pāt·tē·nyâ'râ) *f* dressing table; comb case

pettirosso (pāt·tē·rōs'sō) *m* robin

petto (pāt'tō) *m* breast; chest; **a due petti** double-breasted; **— a —** vis-à-vis; **prendere di —** to face squarely; **prendersela a —** to throw oneself into something heart and soul; to be deeply hurt

petulante (pā·tū·lân'tä) *a* saucy; nervy *(sl)*; peevish

pezza (pā'tsâ) *f* patch; bolt of cloth

pezzente (pā·tsän'tä) *m* miser; beggar

pezzettino (pā·tsät·tē'nō) *m* little bit

pezzo (pā'tsō) *m* piece; story; **— di ricambio** spare part; **— grosso** important person; big shot *(sl)*; **un — d'uomo** a well-built man

---

piacente (pyâ·chän'tä) *a* attractive, pleasing

piacere (pyâ·chä'rä) *m* favor; pleasure; — * *vi* to please; to like; **Molto** — ! **P- di conoscerla!** I am glad to know you!, Very happy to meet you!; **per** — please

piacevole (pyâ·che'vō·lä) *a* pleasant, pleasing, gracious

piacevolmente (pyâ·chä·vōl·män'tä) *adv* graciously, pleasantly

piacimento (pyâ·chē·män'tō) *m* liking, pleasure

piaga (pyä'gä) *f* sore; *(fig)* catastrophe; **mettere il dito sulla** — *(fig)* to hit the nail on the head; to find the rub; **-re** (pyâ·gâ'rä) *vt* to cause a sore, form a sore; to wound; **-rsi** (pyâ·gâr'sē) *vr* to ulcerate

piagnucolare (pyâ·nyū·kō·lâ'rä) *vi* to whine

pialla (pyâl'lä) *f* plane *(tool)*; **-re** (pyâl·lâ'rä) *vt* to plane

piallatrice (pyâl·lâ·trē'chä) *f* planer *(machine)*

pianamente (pyâ·nâ·män'tä) *adv* in a smooth way; clearly; softly; simply

pianale (pyâ·nâ'lä) *m (rail)* flatcar

pianella (pyâ·näl'lä) *f* slipper, mule; tile

pianerottolo (pyâ·nä·rôt'tō·lō) *m* landing *(stairway)*

pianeta (pyâ·nä'tä) *m* planet; — *f (eccl)* chasuble

piangere * (pyân'jä·rä) *vi&t* to cry; to mourn; to weep

pianificare (pyâ·nē·fē·kâ'rä) *vt* to plan; to outline

pianificato (pyâ·nē·fē·kâ'tō) *a* planned, outlined

pianificazione (pyâ·nē·fē·kâ·tsyō'nä) *f* planning; outline

pianino (pyâ·nē'nō) *m* barrel organ, hurdy-gurdy; — *adv* slowly; gently

pianista (pyâ·nē'stä) *m* pianist

piano (pyâ'nō) *m* plan, project; story, floor; *(mus)* piano; — **regolatore** city planning; — *a* flat; level; plain, clear; — *adv* slowly; softly; quietly; **primo** — *(photo)* close-up

pianoforte (pyâ·nō·fôr'tä) *m* piano; — **a coda** grand piano; — **verticale** upright piano

pianta (pyân'tä) *f* plant; map; sole of foot; **-gione** (pyân·tâ·jō'nä) *f* planting; plantation; **-re** (pyân·tâ'rä) *vt* to plant; to jilt; to cast aside; **-re in asso** to leave in the lurch; **-re chiodi** *(fig)* to incur debts; **-rsi** (pyân·târ'sē) *vr* to take a stance; to settle, establish oneself;

Piantala! *(coll)* Stop it!; **-tore** (pyân·tâ· tō'rä) *m* planter

pianto (pyân'tō) *m* crying, weeping; — *a* rued; mourned

piantonare (pyân·tō·nâ'rä) *vt* to watch over; to guard

piantone (pyân·tō'nä) *m (mil)* sentinel, orderly; *(bot)* shoot

pianura (pyâ·nū'râ) *f* plain

piastra (pyâ'strä) *f* sheet, plate

piastrella (pyâ·sträl'lä) *f* tile

piattaforma (pyât·tâ·fôr'mä) *f* platform

piattino (pyât·tē'nō) *m* saucer

piatto (pyât'tō) *m* dish; plate; *(mus)* cymbal; — *a* flat; dull

piattola (pyât'tō·lä) *f* crab louse; thumbtack; *(fig)* bore, nuisance

piazza (pyâ'tsä) *f* square; market place; **letto a due piazze** double bed; **prezzo di** — market price; **far** — **pulita** to make a clean sweep; — **d'armi** *(mil)* drill field; **-le** (pyâ·tsâ'lä) *m* large open square; **-re** (pyâ·tsâ'rä) *vt* to sell; *(sport)* to place; **-rsi** (pyâ·tsâr'sē) *vr (sport)* to place

piazzista (pyâ·tsē'stä) *m* traveling salesman; agent; dealer

picca (pēk'kä) *f* ruffled pride; lance; pick; *(cards)* spade; **per** — *(fig)* out of spite; **-rsi** (pēk·kâr'sē) *vr* to be offended; **-nte** (pēk·kân'tä) *a* sharp; racy

picchè (pēk·kä') *m* piqué

picchetto (pēk·kät'tō) *m* picket

picchiare (pēk·kyâ'rä) *vt* to hit, beat

picchiarsi (pēk·kyâr'sē) *vr* to beat one another; to scuffle, fight

picchiata (pēk·kyâ'tä) *f* beating; *(avi)* dive

picchio (pēk'kyō) *m* knock; woodpecker

piccineria (pē·chē·nä·rē'â) *f* pettiness, narrowness

piccino (pē·chē'nō) *m* child; — *a* small; petty, narrow; cheap; narrow-minded; unimportant

piccionaia (pē·chō·nâ'yâ) *f* dovecote; *(theat)* upper gallery

piccione (pē·chō'nä) *m* dove; pigeon

picciuolo (pē·chwō'lō) *m* stem

picco (pēk'kō) *m* peak; **andare a** — to go to the bottom, sink

piccolezza (pēk·kō·lä'tsä) *f* trifle; smallness; unimportance

piccolo (pēk'kō·lō) *a* small, little; — *m* little fellow

piccone (pēk·kō'nä) *m* pick

piccoso (pēk·kō'zō) *a* touchy, hypersensitive

piccozza (pēk·kō'tsä) *f* pickax

pidocchio (pē·dôk'kyō) *m* louse; *(coll)*

---

k kid, **l** let, **m** met, **n** not, **p** pat, **r** very, **s** sat, **sh** shop, **t** tell, **v** vat, **w** we, **y** yes, **z** zero

stingy person, miser; **–so** (pē·dōk·kyō'-zō) *a* lousy; *(coll)* stingy, miserly

piede (pyā'dā) *m* foot; **stare in piedi** to stand; **a piedi** on foot

piedistallo (pyā·dē·stäl'lō) *m* pedestal

piega (pyā'gä) *f* fold; crease; pleat; **–mento** (pyā·gä·mān'tō) *m* bending; pleating, creasing; *(mil)* retreat; **–re** (pyā·gâ'rā) *vt* to fold; to bend; to yield; **–rsi** (pyā·gâr'sē) *vr* to submit; to bend

pieghevole (pyā·ge'vō·lā) *a* folding, pliable; — *m* folder

pieghevolmente (pyā·gä·vōl·män'tā) *adv* flexibly

Piemonte (pyā·mōn'tā) *m* Piedmont

piemontese (pyā·mōn·tā'zä) *a&m* Piedmontese

piena (pyā'nâ) *f* flood; mob

pienamente (pyā·nâ·män'tā) *adv* absolutely; entirely; quite

pienezza (pyā·nä'tsä) *f* fullness; plenty

pieno (pyā'nō) *a* full; — *m* fullness; climax; **fare il —** to fill the gas tank; **in piena notte** in the dead of night; **in — giorno** in broad daylight; **–ne** (pyā·nō'nä) *m* huge crowd; *(theat)* full house

pietà (pyā·tâ') *f* piety; pity; mercy; *(art)* Pietà; **Monte di P–** pawnshop

pietanza (pyā·tân'tsä) *f* dish, course

pietosamente (pyā·tō·zä·män'tä) *adv* mercifully; charitably; pitifully

pietoso (pyā·tō'zō) *a* pitiful; pitiable; merciful

pietra (pyā'trâ) *f* stone; **metterci una — sopra** *(fig)* to let bygones be bygones

pietrificare (pyā·trē·fē·kâ'rā) *vt* to petrify, turn to stone

pietrisco (pyā·trē'skō) *m* gravel

pievano (pyā·vâ'nō) *m* rural parish priest

pieve (pyā'vä) *f* rural parish

piffero (pēf'fä·rō) *m (mus)* fife

pigiama (pē·jä'mä) *m* pajamas

pigiare (pē·jä'rā) *vt* to crush; to press

pigiarsi (pē·jâr'sē) *vr* to crowd together; to mill around

pigione (pē·jō'nä) *f* rent

pigliare (pē·lyâ'rä) *vt* to take; **— a sinistra** to turn to the left; **— fuoco** to catch fire

pigliarsi (pē·lyâr'sē) *vr* to catch, take; **— a pugni** to come to blows; **— la sbornia** to get drunk; **— un raffreddore** to catch cold

pigmeo (pēg·mā'ō) *m* pygmy

pigna (pē'nyâ) *f* pine cone

pignatta (pē·nyät'tâ) *f* pot *(cooking)*

pignolo (pē·nyō'lō) *a* faultfinding; fussy; pedantic

pignolo (pē·nyō'lō) *m* pine nut

pignoramento (pē·nyō·râ·män'tō) *m* distraint; attachment, legal seizure

pignorare (pē·nyō·râ'rä) *vt* to distrain; to attach; to seize legally

pigolare (pē·gō·lâ'rä) *vi* to chirp

pigolio (pē·gō·lē'ō) *m* chirping; chirp

pigramente (pē·grâ·män'tä) *adv* lazily

pigrizia (pē·grē'tsyâ) *f* laziness

pigro (pē'grō) *a* lazy

pila (pē'lâ) *f* pile; battery; baptismal font

pilastro (pē·lä'strō) *m* pillar

pillacchera (pēl·läk'kä·râ) *f* mud splash

pillola (pēl'lō·lä) *f* pill

pillotare (pēl·lōt·tâ'rä) *vt* to baste *(meat)*; *(fig)* to lambaste

pilota (pē·lō'tâ) *m* pilot; **–ggio** (pē·lō·täj'jō) *m* piloting; **corso di –ggio** aviation course; **–re** (pē·lō·tâ'rä) *vt* to drive; to fly

pinacoteca (pē·nâ·kō·tā'kâ) *f* art gallery; art museum

pineta (pē·nā'tâ) *f* pine wood

pingue (pēn'gwä) *a* lucrative; fat; rich

pinguino (pēn·gwē'nō) *m* penguin

pinna (pēn'nâ) *f* fin

pino (pē'nō) *m* pine tree

pinze (pēn'tsä) *fpl* pliers; pincers; **–tte** (pēn·tsät'tä) *fpl* tweezers

pio (pē'ō) *a* pious, charitable

pioggia (pyōj'jä) *f* rain

piombare (pyōm·bâ'rä) *vt* to seal; to fall upon; *(dent)* to fill

piombino (pyōm·bē'nō) *m* plumb, plumb line

piombo (pyōm'bō) *m* plummet; lead; **procedere con i piedi di —** *(fig)* to proceed with great caution

pioniere (pyō·nyä'rä) *m* pioneer

pioppo (pyōp'pō) *m* poplar

piorrea (pyōr·rä'â) *f* pyorrhea

piovere * (pyō'vä·rä) *vi* to rain

piovigginare (pyō·vēj·jē·nâ'rä) *vi* to drizzle

piovigginoso (pyō·vēj·jē·nō'zō) *a* drizzling

piovoso (pyō·vō'zō) *a* rainy

pipa (pē'pâ) *f* pipe

pipistrello (pē·pē·sträl'lō) *m (zool)* bat

pira (pē'râ) *f* pyre

piramide (pē·râ'mē·dä) *f* pyramid

pirata (pē·râ'tä) *m* pirate

piroga (pē·rō'gä) *f* canoe

pirometro (pē·rō'mä·trō) *m* pyrometer

piroscafo (pē·rō'skâ·fō) *m* steamship

pirotecnica (pē·rō·tek'nē·kâ) *f* fireworks

pisciare (pē·shâ'rä) *vi* to urinate

piscina (pē·shē'nâ) *f* swimming pool

â ârm, **ā** bāby, **e** bet, **ē** bē, **ō** gō, **ô** gône, **ū** blūe, **b** bad, **ch** child, **d** dad, **f** fat, **g** gay, **j** jet

piscio (pē'shō) *m* urine
pisello (pē·zăl'lō) *m* pea
pisolino (pē·zō·lē'nō) *m* doze, nap; catnap; **fare un —** to catnap
pista (pē'stâ) *f* track; racetrack; **— di decollaggio** runway; **— d'atterraggio** landing strip; **— d'involo** runway; **— da ballo** dance floor; **seguire la — di** to track; to shadow
pistacchio (pē·stâk'kyō) *m* pistachio
pistola (pē·stō'lâ) *f* pistol; gun
pistone (pē·stō'nā) *m* piston
pitone (pē·tō'nā) *m* python
pitonessa (pē·tō·nās'sâ) *f* prophetess
pittima (pēt'tē·mâ) *f* hairsplitter, pedant
pittore (pēt·tō'rā) *m*, **pittrice** (pēt·trē'chā) *f* painter
pittoresco (pēt·tō·rā'skō) *a* picturesque
pittura (pēt·tū'râ) *f* painting; paint; **—re** (pēt·tū·râ'rā) *vt* to paint
più (pyū) *adv* more; **— prep** plus; **— presto** sooner; more quickly; **— volte** several times; **sempre —** more and more; **mai —** never again; **in —** in addition; **tutt'al —** at most; **per lo —** generally, for the most part; **per di —** besides, moreover; **a — non posso** as much as I could
piuma (pyū'mâ) *f* feather
piumino (pyū·mē'nō) *m* powder puff; feather duster
piuolo (pywō'lō) *m* peg
piuttosto (pyūt·tō'stō) *adv* rather, instead
pizza (pē'tsâ) *f* pizza, Neapolitan open meat and cheese pie
pizzardone (pē·tsâr·dō'nā) *m (⬤⬤)* policeman; cop *(sl)*
pizzicagnolo (pē·tsē·kâ'nyō·lō) *m* grocer
pizzicare (pē·tsē·kâ'rā) *vt* to nip; to pinch; *(mus)* to pluck
pizzicheria (pē·tsē·kā·rē'â) *f* delicatessen; grocery
pizzico (pē'tsē·kō) *m* smarting, tingling; tiny bit, pinch; **—tto** (pē·tsē·kōt'tō) *m* pinch
pizzo (pē'tsō) *m* lace
placare (plâ·kâ'rā) *vt* to appease, placate
placarsi (plâ·kâr'sē) *vr* to subside; to be placated
placca (plâk'kâ) *f* metal badge; **—re** (plâk·kâ'rā) *vt* to plate; **—to** (plâk·kâ'tō) *a* plated; **—tura** (plâk·kâ·tū'râ) *f* plating
placidamente (plâ·chē·dâ·mān'tâ) *adv* tranquilly, placidly
placido (plâ'chē·dō) *a* placid
plafone (plâ·fō'nā) *m* ceiling
plaga (plâ'gâ) *f* country, locality
plagiario (plâ·jâ'ryō) *m* plagiarist

plagio (plâ'jō) *m* plagiarism
planare (plâ·nâ'rā) *vi* to glide, volplane
plancia (plân'châ) *f (naut)* bridge
plantigrado (plân·tē'grâ·dō) *a&m* plantigrade
plasma (plâ'zmâ) *f* plasma; **—re** (plâ·zmâ'rā) *vt* to mould, shape
plastico (plâ'stē·kō) *a* plastic
platano (plâ'tâ·nō) *m (bot)* sycamore
platea (plâ·tā'â) *f (theat)* orchestra pit
platino (plâ'tē·nō) *m* platinum
plausibile (plâū·zē'bē·lâ) *a* reasonable; likely; plausible
plebe (plā'bā) *f* populace; mob; **—o** (plā·bā'ō) *a* plebeian
plebiscitario (plā·bē·shē·tâ'ryō) *a* unanimous
plebiscito (plā·bē·shē'tō) *m* plebiscite
plenario (plā·nâ'ryō) *a* plenary
plenilunio (plā·nē·lū'nyō) *m* moonlight; full moon
plenipotenziario (plā·nē·pō·tān·tsyâ'ryō) *a* plenipotentiary
pletora (ple'tō·râ) *f* excess, plethora
plettro (plât'trō) *m* plectrum
pleurite (plāū·rē'tâ) *f* pleurisy
plico (plē'kō) *m* envelope
plotone (plō·tō'nā) *m* platoon; **— d'esecuzione** firing squad
plumbeo (plūm'bā·ō) *a* leaden; dull
plurale (plū·râ'lâ) *m&a* plural
plutocrate (plū·tō·krâ'tâ) *m* plutocrat
plutocrazia (plū·tō·krâ·tsē'â) *f* plutocracy
plutonio (plū·tō'nyō) *m (min)* plutonium
pluviale (plū·vyâ'lâ) *a* rain
pluviometro (plū·vyō'mâ·trō) *m* rain guage
pneumatico (pnāū·mâ'tē·kō) *a* pneumatic, air; **—** *m* inner tube; tire
po' (pō) *a&adv* little
poco (pō'kō) *a&adv* little; **fra —** soon, in a short while; **a — a —** gradually, little by little
podagra (pō·dâ'grâ) *f* gout
podere (pō·dā'rā) *m* farm
poderosamente (pō·dā·rō·zâ·mān'tâ) *adv* powerfully
poderoso (pō·dā·rō'zō) *a* ponderous; powerful
podestà (pō·dā·stâ') *m* mayor; **—** *f* authority, power
podio (pō'dyō) *m* podium; dais
podista (pō·dē'stâ) *m* foot racer
poema (pō·ā'mâ) *m* long poem; epopee
poesia (pō·â·zē'â) *f* poetry; short poem
poeta (pō·ā'tâ) *m*, **poetessa** (pō·â·tās'sâ) *f* poet

---

k kid, **l** let, **m** met, **n** not, **p** pat, **r** very, **s** sat, **sh** shop, **t** tell, **v** vat, **w** we, **y** yes, **z** zero

poggiacapo (pōj·jà·kâ′pō) *m* headrest
poggiapiedi (pōj·jà·pyà′dē) *m* footstool
poggiare (pōj·jà′rä) *vt&i* to rest; to place; to lean on; — **a sinistra** to keep to the left
poggiarsi (pōj·jâr′sē) *vr* to lean on
poggiolo (pōj·jō′lō) *m* balcony
poi (pō′ē) *adv* then; later; afterwards
poichè (pōē·kä′) *conj* after; when; since; as; for
polacco (pō·lâk′kō) *a&m* Polish; — *m* Pole
polemica (pō·le′mē·kâ) *f* controversy; polemic
polemico (pō·le′mē·kō) *a* controversial; polemical
polemizzare (pō·lä·mē·dzâ′rä) *vi* to argue
polenta (pō·län′tâ) *f* cornmeal mush
policlinico (pō·lē·klē′nē·kō) *m* general hospital; medical center
poligamia (pō·lē·gà·mē′â) *f* poligamy
poliglotta ((pō·lē·glōt′tâ) *a&m* polyglot
poligono (pō·lē′gō·nō) *m* target range
poliomielite (pō·lyō·myä·lē′tä) *f* infantile paralysis, poliomyelitis
polipo (pō′lē·pō) *m* polyp
politeama (pō·lē·tä·â′mä) *m* theater
politecnico (pō·lē·tek′nē·kō) *m* engineering school; polytechnical institute
politica (pō·lē′tē·kâ) *f* policy, regulation; politics; **-nte** (pō·lē·tē·kân′tä) *m* political dabbler, small-time politician
politico (pō·lē′tē·kō) *a* political; — *m* statesman; politician; **-ne** (pō·lē·tē·kō′nä) *m* schemer; cunning person
polizia (pō·lē·tsē′â) *f* police; **agente di —** police officer; — **stradale** highway patrol; traffic police; — **dei costumi** vice squad
poliziesco (pō·lē·tsyä′skō) *a* police; **romanzo —** detective story
poliziotto (pō·lē·tsyōt′tō) *m* policeman; — **in borghese** plainclothesman
polizza (pō′lē·dzä) *f* insurance policy; pawn ticket; certificate; — **di carico** bill of lading
pollaio (pōl·lâ′yō) *m* hencoop
pollame (pōl·lâ′mä) *m* poultry
pollastra (pōl·lâ′strä) *f*, **pollastro** (pōl·lâ′strō) *m* spring chicken
polleria (pōl·lä·rē′â) *f* poultry store
pollice (pōl′lē·chä) *m* thumb; big toe; inch
polline (pōl′lē·nä) *m* pollen
pollivendolo (pōl·lē·ven′dō·lō) *m* poultry dealer
pollo (pōl′lō) *m* chicken
polmone (pōl·mō′nä) *m* lung; — **d'acciaio** iron lung

polmonite (pōl·mō·nē′tä) *f* pneumonia
polo (pō′lō) *m* (*geog, phys*) pole; polo
Polonia (pō·lō′nyâ) *f* Poland
polonio (pō·lō′nyō) *m* (*min*) polonium
polpa (pōl′pâ) *f* pulp; flesh (*animal*); **-ccio** (pōl·pà′chō) *m* (*anat*) calf; **-strello** (pōl·pâ·strâl′lō) *m* tip of the finger
polpetta (pōl·pät′tâ) *f* meat ball; croquette
polpettone (pōl·pät·tō′nä) *m* hash; hodgepodge; meat loaf
polpo (pōl′pō) *m* octopus
polsino (pōl·sē′nō) *m* cuff
polso (pōl′sō) *m* wrist; pulse; (*fig*) energy, strength
poltiglia (pōl·tē′lyâ) *f* mash; slush, mud
poltrona (pōl·trō′nä) *f* easy chair; (*theat*) orchestra seat
poltronaggine (pōl·trō·nâj′jē·nä) *f* laziness; lassitude
poltrone (pōl·trō′nä) *a* lazy; — *m* loafer; **-ria** (pōl·trō·nä·rē′â) *f* laziness
polvere (pōl′vâ·rä) *f* powder; dust
polveriera (pōl·vâ·ryä′rä) *f* powder magazine
polverizzare (pōl·vâ·rē·dzâ′rä) *vt* to pulverize
polverizzatore (pōl·vâ·rē·dzâ·tō′rä) *m* atomizer
polverone (pōl·vâ·rō′nä) *m* dust cloud
polveroso (pōl·vâ·rō′zō) *a* dusty
pomata (pō·mâ′tâ) *f* pomade
pomello (pō·mäl′lō) *m* cheekbone
pomeridiano (pō·mä·rē·dyâ′nō) *a* P.M.; afternoon
pomeriggio (pō·mä·rēj′jō) *m* afternoon
pomice (pō′mē·chä) *f* pumice
pomiciare (pō·mē·chä′rä) *vt* to polish with pumice; to flatter; to softsoap (*coll*)
pomodoro (pō·mō·dō′rō) *m* tomato
pompa (pōm′pâ) *f* pomp; parade; pump; — **da incendio** fire engine; **-re** (pōm·pâ′rä) *vt* to pump; (*fig*) to praise; **pompe funebri** funeral; **impresario di pompe funebri** funeral director, undertaker
pompelmo (pōm·pâl′mō) *m* grapefruit
pompiere (pōm·pyä′rä) *m* fireman
pomposamente (pōm·pō·zâ·män′tä) *adv* pompously, ostentatiously
pomposo (pōm·pō′zō) *a* pompous, swelled
ponderare (pōn·dä·râ′rä) *vt&i* to ponder; to ruminate (*fig*)
ponderato (pōn·dä·râ′tō) *a* considered; pondered
ponderoso (pōn·dä·rō′zō) *a* ponderous; weighty
ponente (pō·nän′tä) *m* West; west; west wind

â ârm, ā bāby, e bet, ē bē, ō gō, ô gône, ū blūe, b bad, ch child, d dad, f fat, g gay, j jet

ponte (pōn′tā) *m* bridge; (*naut*) deck; — **levatoio** drawbridge; — **stretto** narrow bridge; — **passeggiata** promenade deck; — **aereo** airlift

pontefice (pōn·te′fē·chä) *m* pontiff; Pope

pontificio (pōn·tē·fē′chō) *a* papal, pontifical

pontile (pōn·tē′lä) *m* pier, dock

pontone (pōn·tō′nä) *m* pontoon

popolano (pō·pō·lä′nō) *m* commoner; — *a* of the masses, popular

popolare (pō·pō·lä′rä) *a* popular; low-priced; — *vt* to people

popolarità (pō·pō·lä·rē·tä′) *f* popularity, celebrity

popolarizzare (pō·pō·lä·rē·dzä′rä) *vt* to popularize

popolarsi (pō·pō·lär′sē) *vr* to crowd, get crowded; to become populated

popolazione (pō·pō·lä·tsyō′nä) *f* population

popolo (pô′pō·lō) *m* people

popone (pō·pō′nä) *m* cantaloupe; melon

poppa (pōp′pä) *f* (*anat*) breast; (*naut*) stern; **–re** (pōp·pä′rä) *vt&i* to nurse; **–toio** (pōp·pä·tō′yō) *m* rubber nipple; nursing bottle

porcellana (pōr·chäl·lä′nä) *f* porcelain; china

porcellino (pōr·chäl·lē′nō) *m* suckling pig

porcheria (pōr·kä·rē′ä) *f* dirt, trash; monkey business (*sl*)

porchetta (pōr·kät′tä) *f* roast duckling, pig

porcile (pōr·chē′lä) *m* pigsty, pigpen

porcino (pōr·chē′nō) *a* porcine

porco (pōr′kō) *m* pig, hog; pork

porgere * (pôr′jä·rä) *vt* to hand over; to offer; to give

porgersi * (pôr′jär·sē) *vr* to come forward, volunteer one's services

poro (pō′rō) *m* pore; **–oso** (pō·rō′zō) *a* porous

porre * (pōr′rä) *vt* to place, put

porro (pōr′rō) *m* leek; (*med*) wart

porta (pōr′tä) *f* door; gate

portaaerei (pōr·tä·ä·e′rāē) *f* aircraft carrier

portabagagli (pōr·tä·bä·gä′lyē) *m* redcap, porter; (*auto*) trunk; (*rail*) rack

portabastoni (pōr·tä·bä·stō′nē) *m* golf caddie

portacarte (pōr·tä·kär′tä) *m* file folder

portacenere (pōr·tä·che′nä·rä) *m* ashtray

portacipria (pōr·tä·chē′pryä) *m* compact

portafiori (pōr·tä·fyō′rē) *m* flower stand

portafogli (pōr·tä·fō′lyē) *m* wallet

portafoglio (pōr·tä·fō′lyō) *m* portfolio

portafortuna (pōr·tä·fōr·tū′nä) *m* charm; amulet

portagioielli (pōr·tä·jō·yäl′lē) *m* jewelry case

portalampada (pōr·tä·läm′pä·dä) *f* lamp socket

portale (pōr·tä′lä) *m* door; portal

portalettere (pōr·tä·let′tä·rä) *m* mailman

portamento (pōr·tä·män′tō) *m* behavior, bearing

portamonete (pōr·tä·mō·nä′tä) *m* purse

portantina (pōr·tän·tē′nä) *f* sedan chair

portaordine (pōr·tä·ôr′dē·nä) *m* messenger

portapenne (pōr·tä·pän′nä) *m* penholder

portare (pōr·tä′rä) *vt* to take, bring, carry; to wear

portaritratti (pōr·tä·rē·trät′tē) *m* picture frame

portarsi (pōr·tär′sē) *vr* to behave, demean oneself

portasapone (pōr·tä·sä·pō′nä) *m* soap dish

portasigarette (pōr·tä·sē·gä·rät′tä) *m* cigarette case

portasigari (pōr·tä·sē′gä·rē) *m* cigar case

portata (pōr·tä′tä) *f* course (*meal*); reach; range; **a — di mano** within reach

portatile (pōr·tä′tē·lä) *a* portable

portatore (pōr·tä·tō′rä) *m* bearer

portauovo (pōr·tä·wō′vō) *m* eggcup

portavoce (pōr·tä·vō′chä) *m* speaking tube; megaphone; spokesman

portellino (pōr·täl·lē′nō) *m* porthole

portento (pōr·tän′tō) *m* miracle; marvel; **–samente** (pōr·tän·tō·zä·män′tä) *adv* marvelously, prodigiously; **–so** (pōr·tän·tō′zō) *a* wonderful, portentous

portico (pōr′tē·kō) *m* porch; portico

portiera (pōr·tyä′rä) *f* door curtain, portiere; door (*auto*)

portiere (pōr·tyä′rä) *m* doorman; (*sport*) goalkeeper

portinaia (pōr·tē·nä′yä) *f* woman doorkeeper

portinaio (pōr·tē·nä′yō) *m* janitor; doorman

portineria (pōr·tē·nä·rē′ä) *f* doorman's quarters

porto (pōr′tō) *m* port; postage; shipping charge; — **assegnato** COD; **franco di —** postpaid; — **d'armi** gun license

Portogallo (pōr·tō·gäl′lō) *m* Portugal

portoghese (pōr·tō·gä′zä) *a&m* Portuguese

portone (pōr·tō′nä) *m* gate; main door

portuale (pōr·twä′lä) *m* dockhand; — *a* port

---

k kid, **l** let, **m** met, **n** not, **p** pat, **r** very, **s** sat, **sh** shop, **t** tell, **v** vat, **w** we, **y** yes, **z** zero

porzione (pōr·tsyō′nä) *f* share; portion; serving

posa (pō′zä) *f* pose; pause; (*photo*) exposure; **senza** — continuously; **–mine** (pō·zä·mē′nä) *m* minelayer; **–piano** (pō·zä·pyâ′nō) *m* slowpoke; "handle with care" (*label*); **–re** (pō·zä′rä) *vt* to lay; to rest; to pose; **–rsi** (pō·zär′sē) *vr* to come to rest; to place oneself; to alight; **–ta** (pō·zâ′tä) *f* cover (*knife, fork, spoon*); **–mente** (pō·zä·tä·mān′tä) *adv* calmly, sedately; **–tezza** (pō·zä·tä′tsâ) *f* gravity, composure, sedateness; **–to** (pō·zä′tō) *a* laid; staid, quiet

posbellico (pō·zbel′lē·kō) *a* postwar

poscia (pō′shä) *adv* afterwards, subsequently

poscritto (pō·skrēt′tō) *m* postscript, PS

posdatato (pō·zdâ·tâ′tō) *a* postdated

positiva (pō·zē·tē′vâ) *f* (*photo*) positive

positivamente (pō·zē·tē·vâ·mān′tä) *adv* positively

positivo (pō·zē·tē′vō) *a* positive; matter-of-fact, factual

posizione (pō·zē·tsyō′nä) *f* position; status

posporre * (pō·spōr′rä) *vt* to postpone, delay

possedere * (pōs·sä·dä′rä) *vt* to have; to own

possedimento (pōs·sä·dē·mān′tō) *m* property, holdings; possession; colony

possesso (pōs·sās′sō) *m* possession; **–re** (pōs·sās·sō′rä) *m* owner

possibile (pōs·sē′bē·lä) *a* possible; workable

possibilità (pōs·sē·bē·lē·tâ′) *f* possibility, occasion

possibilmente (pōs·sē·bēl·mān′tä) *adv* possibly, perhaps

possidente (pōs·sē·dän′tä) *m* property owner; possessor

posta (pō′stä) *f* mail; post office; stake; — **aerea** air mail; **fermo in** — general delivery; **a** — purposely; **stare alla** — to watch; **–le** (pō·stâ′lä) *a* postal; **casella –le** post-office box; **cassetta –le** mailbox; **cassa –le** postal savings; **vaglia –le** money order

posteggiare (pō·stäj·jâ′rä) *vt* to park

posteggio (pō·stej′jō) *m* parking; parking lot; place to park; — **per auto pubbliche** taxi stand

postelegrafico (pō·stä·lä·grâ′fē·kō) *m* postal telegraph office employee

postergare (pō·stär·gâ′rä) *vt* to procrastinate; to postpone, delay

posteri (pō′stä·rē) *mpl* posterity

posteriore (pō·stä·ryō′rä) *a* rear; posterior; later

posteriormente (pō·stä·ryōr·mān′tä) *adv* later, subsequently; posteriorly

posticcio (pō·stē′chō) *a* fake, false; artificial

posticipare (pō·stē·chē·pâ′rä) *vt* to postpone

posticipatamente (pō·stē·chē·pâ·tâ·mān′tä) *adv* afterward, after the event; too late

posticipazione (pō·stē·chē·pâ·tsyō′nä) *f* postponement

postilla (pō·stēl′lâ) *f* footnote

postino (pō·stē′nō) *m* mailman

posto (pō′stō) *m* place; seat; site; job; — *a* placed; — **che** supposing that

postribolo (pō·strē′bō·lō) *m* brothel

postulante (pō·stū·lân′tä) *m* applicant; candidate

postulare (pō·stū·lâ′rä) *vt* to make application for; to request

postumo (pō′stū·mō) *a* posthumous; — *m* aftermath

potabile (pō·tâ′bē·lä) *a* drinkable

potare (pō·tâ′rä) *vt* to prune; to lop off

potassa (pō·tâs′sâ) *f* potash

potassio (pō·tâs′syō) *m* potassium

potentato (pō·tän·tâ′tō) *m* potentate

potente (pō·tän′tä) *a* powerful; **–mente** (pō·tän·tä·mān′tä) *adv* vigorously

potenza (pō·tän′tsâ) *f* power, dominion

potenzialmente (pō·tän·tsyâl·mān′tä) *adv* potentially

potere (pō·tä′rä) *m* power; — * *vi* to be able; **può essere** it may be, perhaps; **non può essere** it can't be true; **non ne posso più** I can't take it any longer

potestà (pō·tä·stâ′) *f* power; authority; **la P– divina** the Almighty

poveraccio (pō·vä·râ′chō) *m* poor wretch, poor fellow

poveramente (pō·vä·râ·mān′tä) *adv* miserably; poorly

povero (pō′vä·rō) *a* poor; unlucky

povertà (pō·vär·tâ′) *f* poverty, lack

pozione (pō·tsyō′nä) *f* potion

pozzanghera (pō·tsän′gä·râ) *f* puddle

pozzo (pō′tsō) *m* well; **un — di sapienza** (*fig*) a fountain of knowledge

Praga (prâ′gä) *f* Prague

prammatica (prâm·mâ′tē·kâ) *f* custom, way; **di** — required

pranzare (prân·dzâ′rä) *vi* to dine

pranzo (prân′dzō) *m* dinner

prassi (prâs′sē) *f* procedure; practice, praxis

prateria (prâ·tä·rē′â) *f* prairie

pratica (prâ'tē·kâ) *f* practice; experience; file, papers; **–mente** (prâ·tē·kâ·mān'tä) *adv* practically; **–re** (prâ·tē·kâ'rä) *vt&i* to practice; to associate with

praticità (prâ·tē·chē·tâ') *f* usefulness; practicability

pratico (prâ'tē·kō) *a* experienced; practical; — *m* expert

prato (prâ'tō) *m* meadow

preaccennato (prā·â·chān·nâ'tō) *a* aforementioned

preambolo (prā·âm'bō·lō) *m* preamble

preavvisare (prā·âv·vē·zâ'rä) *vt* to preinform, advise in advance

preavviso (prā·âv·vē'zō) *m* notice; warning

prebellico (prā·bel'lē·kō) *a* prewar

precario (prā·kâ'ryō) *a* precarious, risky

precauzione (prā·kâū·tsyō'nä) *f* precaution

precedente (prā·chā·dān'tä) *a* previous; — *m* precedent; **–mente** (prā·chā·dān·tâ·mān'tä) *adv* previously

precedenti (prā·chā·dān'tē) *mpl* background

precedenza (prā·chā·dān'tsâ) *f* precedence; **diritto di** — right of way

precedere (prā·che'dā·rä) *vi* to precede; to outstrip

precetto (prā·chāt'tō) *m* maxim; rule; — **pasquale** (*eccl*) Easter duty; **–re** (prā·chât·tō'rä) *m* tutor

precipitare (prā·chē·pē·tâ'rä) *vt&i* to fall, crash; to precipitate; to collapse

precipitarsi (prā·chē·pē·târ'sē) *vr* to dash; to hurl oneself

precipitatamente (prā·chē·pē·tâ·tâ·mān'tä) *adv* rashly, headlong

precipitazione (prā·chē·pē·tâ·tsyō'nä) *f* rashness; precipitation

precipitosamente (prā·chē·pē·tō·zâ·mān'tä) *adv* precipitously; hastily

precipizio (prā·chē·pē'tsyō) *m* cliff, precipice

precipuo (prā·chē'pwō) *a* chief, main, head

precisamente (prā·chē·zâ·mān'tä) *adv* exactly, just

precisare (prā·chē·zâ'rä) *vt* to specify; to make clear; to point up, underline

precisione (prā·chē·zyō'nä) *f* accuracy, precision

preciso (prā·chē'zō) *a* exact; precise; accurate

preclaro (prā·klâ'rō) *a* prominent, famous

precoce (prā·kō'chā) *a* precocious; **–mente** (prā·kō·chā·mān'tä) *adv* precociously; prematurely

precursore (prā·kūr·sō'rä) *m* forerunner

preda (prā'dâ) *f* prey; **–re** (prā·dâ'rä) *vt* to prey upon; to rob

predecessore (prā·dā·chās·sō'rä) *m* forerunner

predellino (prā·dāl·lē'nō) *m* step; (*auto*) running board; baby's high chair

predestinare (prā·dā·stē·nâ'rä) *m* forerunner, predecessor

predestinazione (prā·dā·stē·nâ·tsyō'nä) *f* predestination

predetto (prā·dāt'tō) *a* aforementioned

predica (pre'dē·kâ) *f* sermon; **–re** (prā·dē·kâ'rä) *vt* to preach; to lecture; to reprove; **–tore** (prā·dē·kâ·tō'rä) *m* preacher

prediletto (prā·dē·lāt'tō) *a&m* favorite, pet

predire * (prā·dē'rä) *vt* to foretell

predisporre * (prā·dē·spōr'rä) *vt* to predispose; to arrange in advance

predisposizione (prā·dē·spō·zē·tsyō'nä) *f* prearrangement; tendency

predisposto (prā·dē·spō'stō) *a* favorable; predisposed

predominare (prā·dō·mē·nâ'rä) *vt&i* to dominate; to hold sway

predominio (prā·dō·mē'nyō) *m* supremacy, predominance

predone (prā·dō'nä) *m* robber

prefazione (prā·fâ·tsyō'nä) *f* preface

prefabbricato (prā·fâb·brē·kâ'tō) *a* prefabricated

preferenza (prā·fā·rān'tsâ) *f* partiality, preference

preferenziale (prā·fā·rān·tsyâ'lä) *a* preferential; **azioni preferenziali** (*com*) preferred stock

preferibile (prā·fā·rē'bē·lä) *a* preferable

preferibilmente (prā·fâ·rē·bēl·mān'tä) *adv* preferably, rather

preferire (prā·fâ·rē'rä) *vt* to prefer

preferito (prā·fâ·rē'tō) *a* preferred; favorite

prefetto (prā·fāt'tō) *m* prefect, provincial governor

prefettura (prā·fât·tū'râ) *f* prefecture, office of provincial governor

prefiggere * (prā·fēj'jâ·rä) *vi* to predetermine; to arrange in advance; (*gram*) to prefix

prefiggersi * (prā·fēj'jâr·sē) *vr* to aim, intend; to make up one's mind to

prefisso (prā·fēs'sō) *m* prefix; — *a* intended, arranged beforehand

pregare (prā·gâ'rä) *vt* to beg; to pray; to supplicate

pregevole (prā·je'vō·lä) *a* valuable

---

k kid, **l** let, **m** met, **n** not, **p** pat, **r** very, **s** sat, **sh** shop, **t** tell, **v** vat, **w** we, **y** yes, **z** zero

preghiera (prā·gyä′rä) *f* request; supplication; prayer

pregiare (prā·jâ′rä) *vt* to esteem; to prize; to appreciate

pregiarsi (prā·jâr′sē) *vr* to have the honor to; to be pleased to

pregiato (prā·jâ′tō) *a* valued, esteemed

pregio (pre′jō) *m* merit; value

pregiudicare (prā·jū·dē·kâ′rä) *vt* to prejudge; to prejudice

pregiudicarsi (prā·jū·dē·kâr′sē) *vr* to ruin one's chances; to damage one's reputation

pregiudicato (prā·jū·dē·kâ′tō) *m* ex-convict

pregiudizio (prā·jū·dē′tsyō) *m* prejudice

prego! (prā′gō) *interj* Please! You're welcome! Don't mention it! Not at all!

pregustare (prā·gū·stä′rä) *vt* to look forward to, anticipate; to foretaste

preistorico (prāē·stô′rē·kō) *a* prehistoric

prelevamento (prā·lā·vä·män′tō) *m* (*com*) draft; withdrawal

prelevare (prā·lā·vä′rä) *vt* to pick up; to withdraw

prelibato (prā·lē·bâ′tō) *a* delicious; superb

preliminare (prā·lē·mē·nä′rä) *a&m* preliminary

prematuro (prā·mâ·tū′rō) *a* premature

premeditare (prā·mä·dē·tä′rä) *vt* to premeditate; to plan in advance

premeditato (prā·mä·dē·tâ′tō) *a* intentional; premeditated

premeditazione (prā·mä·dē·tâ·tsyō′nä) *f* premeditation; advance planning

premere (pre′mä·rä) *vt* to press, squeeze; (*fig*) to urge; — *vi* to be urgent; to be of great importance

premessa (prā·mäs′sä) *f* premise

premettere * (prā·met′tä·rä) *vt* to lay down in advance; to give preference to; to premise; to prefix

premiare (prā·myä′rä) *vt* to reward

premiato (prā·myâ′tō) *m* prize winner; — *a* rewarded

premiazione (prā·myâ·tsyō′nä) *f* prize distribution, awarding of prizes

preminenza (prā·mē·nän′tsä) *f* preeminence

premio (pre′myō) *m* reward; prize; (*com*) premium

premunire (prā·mū·nē′rä) *vt* to forewarn; to arm in advance; to caution

premunirsi (prā·mū·nēr′sē) *vr* to guard against; to protect oneself against

premura (prā·mū′rä) *f* care; haste; concern

premuroso (prā·mū·rō′zō) *a* eager to help; obliging

prendere * (pren′dä·rä) *vt* to take; to catch, seize; to turn; — **a sinistra** to make a left turn; — **una malattia** to catch a disease; — **quota** (*avi*) to gain altitude; (*fig*) to catch on, gain in favor; — **terra** (*naut&avi*) to land; — **il mare** to put out to sea; — **a noleggio** to hire; — **di mira** to stare at

prendersi * (pren′där·sē) *vr* to become entangled; to be taken; — **a pugni** to come to blows; — **la libertà di** to take the liberty of; — **prendersela** to take it wrong; to have one's feelings hurt

prendisole (prān·dē·sō′lä) *m* sunsuit

prenotare (prā·nō·tä′rä) *vt* to reserve; to engage; to subscribe to; to book

prenotarsi (prā·nō·târ′sē) *vr* to take out a subscription; to make a reservation

prenotazione (prā·nō·tä·tsyō′nä) *f* reservation; subscription

preoccupare (prā·ōk·kū·pâ′rä) *vt* to worry, bother; to annoy

preoccuparsi (prā·ōk·kū·pâr′sē) *vr* to worry; to be preoccupied

preoccupato (prā·ōk·kū·pâ′tō) *a* upset, worried, bothered

preoccupazione (prā·ōk·kū·pâ·tsyō′nä) *f* worry, bother; annoyance

preparare (prā·pâ·râ′rä) *vt* to prepare, ready

prepararsi (prā·pâ·râr′sē) *vr* to ready oneself; to prepare oneself

preparato (prā·pâ·râ′tō) *a* prepared; — *m* (*med*) preparation

preponderante (prā·pōn·dä·rân′tä) *a* predominant

preposizione (prā·pō·zē·tsyō′nä) *f* preposition

prepotente (prā·pō·tän′tä) *a* tyrannical; arrogant; overbearing; — *m* bully; tyrant

prepotenza (prā·pō·tän′tsä) *f* domineering manner; abuse of power; arrogance

prerogativa (prā·rō·gâ·tē′vä) *f* privilege; prerogative

presa (prā′zä) *f* seizure; grasp; influence; (*elec*) outlet; plug; (*photo*) shot; **macchina da —** movie camera

presagio (prā·zä′jō) *m* foreboding, omen

presagire (prā·zä·jē′rä) *vt&i* to forebode; to be a forewarning

presbite (pre′zbē·tä) *a* farsighted

prescindere * (prā·shēn′dä·rä) *vt* to disregard; to depart from

prescrivere * (prā·skrē′vä·rä) *vt* to prescribe

â ârm, **ā** bāby, **e** bet, **ē** bē, **ō** gō, **ô** gône, **ū** blūe, **b** bad, **ch** child, **d** dad, **f** fat, **g** gay, **j** jet

prescrizione (prā·skrē·tsyō'nä) *f* prescription

presentare (prā·zān·tâ'rā) *vt* to present; to introduce

presentarsi (prā·zān·târ'sē) *vr* to appear, come into view; to introduce oneself, present oneself

presentatore (prā·zān·tâ·tō'rā) *m* master of ceremonies

presentazione (prā·zān·tâ·tsyō'nä) *f* presentation

presente (prā·zān'tä) *a&m* present

presentimento (prā·zān·tē·mān'tō) *m* foreboding, feeling

presenza (prā·zān'tsä) *f* presence

presenziare (prā·zān·tsyâ'rā) *vt&i* to attend; to witness; to take part; to intervene

presepio (prā·ze'pyō) *m* crib, manger, crèche

preservare (prā·zār·vâ'rā) *vt* to maintain, keep; to save

preservativo (prā·zār·vâ·tē'vō) *a* preservative; — *m* prophylactic

preservazione (prā·zār·vâ·tsyō'nä) *f* preservation

preside (pre'zē·dä) *m* presiding officer; principal of a secondary school; dean; **–nte** (prā·zē·dān'tä) *m*, **–ntessa** (prā·zē·dān·tās'sâ) *f* president; **–nza** (prā·zē·dān'tsâ) *f* president's office; presidency; **–nziale** (prā·zē·dān·tsyâ'lä) *a* presidential

presidiare (prā·zē·dyâ'rā) *vt* to garrison; (*mil*) to defend

presidio (prā·zē'dyō) *m* garrison

presiedere * (prā·sye'dä·rā) *vi* to preside

preso (prā'zō) *a* captured; taken

pressa (prās'sâ) *f* press; crowd

pressante (prās·sân'tä) *a* momentous, great concern

pressappoco (prās·sâp·pō'kō) *adv* approximately; almost

pressi (prās'sē) *mpl* neighborhood, environment

pressione (prās·syō'nä) *f* pressure

presso (prās'sō) *adv* near; — *prep* in care of; — **a poco** just about; **–chè** (prās·sō·kâ') *adv* nearly, almost

prestabilire (prā·stâ·bē·lē'rā) *vt* to pre-establish; to fix in advance

prestanome (prā·stâ·nō'mä) *m* (*coll*) figurehead; dupe, cat's-paw

prestare (prā·stâ'rā) *vt* to impute; to lend; — **fede** to trust; — **ascolto** to listen, pay attention; — **giuramento** to take an oath; — **obbedienza** to obey; — **attenzione** to pay attention, be attentive

prestarsi (prā·stâr'sē) *vr* to volunteer one's services; to adapt oneself; to lend itself

prestazione (prā·stâ·tsyō'nä) *f* service, favor

prestigiatore (prā·stē·jâ·tō'rā) *m* juggler

prestigio (prā·stē'jō) *m* prestige; **giuoco di** — sleight of hand, legerdemain

prestissimo (prā·stēs'sē·mō) *a* very early; very quickly

prestito (pre'stē·tō) *m* loan; **dare in** — to lend

presto (prā'stō) *adv* soon; quickly; early; **si fa — a dire** it's very easy to say

presumere * (prā·zū'mā·rā) *vi* to presume; to boast

presunto (prā·zūn'tō) *a* alleged; presumed

presuntuoso (prā·zūn·twō'zō) *a* conceited

presunzione (prā·zūn·tsyō'nä) *f* conceit

presupporre * (prā·sūp·pōr'rā) *vt* to imply; to presuppose

prete (prā'tä) *m* priest

pretendente (prā·tān·dān'tä) *m* suitor; pretender

pretendere * (prā·ten'dä·rā) *vt&i* to claim, pretend; to charge; to demand

preterintenzionale (prā·tā·rēn·tān·tsyō·nâ'lä) *a* involuntary, unintentional

pretesa (prā·tā'zä) *f* pretense; claim; pretension; demand

pretesto (prā·tā'stō) *m* pretext

pretore (prā·tō'rā) *m* municipal judge

prettamente (prāt·tâ·mān'tä) *adv* merely; clearly

pretto (prāt'tō) *a* pure; mere

pretura (prā·tū'rä) *f* district court

prevalente (prā·vâ·lān'tä) *a* prevalent; prevailing

prevalenza (prā·vâ·lān'tsä) *f* prevalence

prevalere * (prā·vâ·lā'rā) *vi* to prevail

prevalersi * (prā·vâ·lār'sē) *vr* to avail oneself of; to make use of

prevaricazione (prā·vâ·rē·kâ·tsyō'nä) *f* graft; collusion; malfeasance

prevedere * (prā·vā·dā'rā) *vt* to forecast; to anticipate; to foresee

prevedibile (prā·vā·dē'bē·lä) *a* foreseeable

preveggenza (prā·vāj·jān'tsä) *f* foresight

prevenire * (prā·vā·nē'rā) *vt* to warn; to precede; to prevent

preventivare (prā·vān·tē·vâ'rā) *vt* to estimate

preventivato (prā·vān·tē·vâ'tō) *a* estimated

preventivo (prā·vān·tē'vō) *m* estimated budget; — *a* preventive

prevenuto (prā·vā·nū'tō) *a* forewarned; disposed; — *m* defendant

k kid, **l** let, **m** met, **n** not, **p** pat, **r** very, **s** sat, **sh** shop, **t** tell, **v** vat, **w** we, **y** yes, **z** zero

prevenzione (prā·văn·tsyō′nä) *f* prevention; bias; precaution
previamente (prā·vyâ·män′tä) *adv* formerly
previdente (prā·vē·dän′tä) *a* provident
previdenza (prā·vē·dän′tsâ) *f* providence; prudence; — **sociale** social security
previsione (prā·vē·zyō′nä) *f* forecast
prezioso (prā·tsyō′zō) *a* precious
prezzemolo (prā·tse′mō·lō) *m* parsley
prezzo (prā′tsō) *m* price; — **fisso** set price; **pranzo a** — **fisso** table d'hôte
prezzolato (prā·tsō·lâ′tō) *a* bribed; hired
prigione (prē·jō′nä) *f* prison
prigionia (prē·jō·nē′â) *f* imprisonment
prigioniero (prē·jō·nyä′rō) *m* prisoner
prima (prē′mâ) *adv* before; at first; — *f* première; **quanto** —, — **possibile** as soon as possible; —**rio** (prē·mâ′ryō) *a* primary; —**rio** *m* hospital head of staff; —**tista** (prē·mâ·tē′stâ) *m* record holder; —**to** (prē·mâ′tō) *m* supremacy; (*sport*) record
primavera (prē·mâ·vā′râ) *f* spring
primeggiare (prē·māj·jâ′rä) *vi* to excel; to stand out
primitivo (prē·mē·tē′vō) *a&m* primitive
primizia (prē·mē′tsyâ) *f* early fruit
primo (prē′mō) *a&m* first; —**genito** (prē·mō·ge′nē·tō) *a* firstborn
primula (prē′mū·lâ) *f* primrose
principale (prēn·chē·pâ′lä) *a* principal; primary; — *m* boss; employer
principalmente (prēn·chē·pâl·män′tä) *adv* primarily; essentially; mainly
principe (prēn′chē·pä) *m* prince; —**sco** (prēn·chē·pä′skō) *a* princely; —**ssa** (prēn·chē·pās′sâ) *f* princess
principiante (prēn·chē·pyân′tä) *m&f* beginner; — *a* beginning, elementary
principiare (prēn·chē·pyâ′rä) *vt&i* to begin, start out
principio (prēn·chē′pyō) *m* beginning, start; precept
priore (pryō′rä) *m* prior
priorità (pryō·rē·tâ′) *f* priority
prisma (prē′zmâ) *m* prism
privare (prē·vâ′rä) *vt* to deprive
privarsi (prē·vâr′sē) *vr* to do without, get along without; to abstain from
privatamente (prē·vâ·tâ·män′tä) *adv* privately, in private
privatista (prē·vâ·tē′stâ) *m* student in a private school
privativa (prē·vâ·tē′vâ) *f* exclusive right; monopoly; patent; — **dei tabacchi** tobacco shop
privato (prē·vâ′tō) *a&m* private

privazione (prē·vâ·tsyō′nä) *f* suffering; privation
privilegio (prē·vē·le′jō) *m* privilége
privo (prē′vō) *a* deprived, wanting
pro (prō) *m* advantage, profit
probabile (prō·bâ′bē·lä) *a* probable; believable
probabilità (prō·bâ·bē·lē·tâ′) *f* probability
probabilmente (prō·bâ·bēl·män′tä) *adv* probably
problema (prō·blā′mâ) *m* problem; difficulty; —**tico** (prō·blā·mâ′tē·kō) *a* questionable; difficult
probo (prō′bō) *a* honest, upright
proboscide (prō·bō′shē·dä) *f* proboscis; trunk (*elephant*)
procaccia (prō·kâ′châ) *m* rural mailman; —**re** (prō·kâ·châ·râ) *vt* to obtain; to procure; —**rsi** (prō·kâ·châr′sē) *vr* to secure; to earn for oneself
procace (prō·kâ′chä) *a* forward; coquettish; shapely, provocative
procedente (prō·chā·dän′tä) *a* proceeding
procedere (prō·che′dā·rä) *vi* to proceed; (*law*) to prosecute; — *m* conduct
procedimenti (prō·chā·dē·män′tē) *mpl* transactions, proceedings
procedimento (pro·chā·dē·män′tō) *m* method; procedure
procedura (prō·chā·dū′râ) *f* procedure
processare (prō·chās·sâ′râ) *vt* to try, prosecute
processione (prō·chās·syō′nä) *f* procession
processo (prō·chās′sō) *m* trial; lawsuit; process; — **verbale** official record, minutes of a meeting
processuale (prō·chās·swâ′lä) *a* (*law*) trial
procinto (prō·chēn′tō) *m* preparations; **essere in** — **di** to be about to
proclama (prō·klâ′mâ) *m* proclamation; —**re** (prō·klâ·mâ′rä) *vt* to proclaim
proclamazione (prō·klâ·mâ·tsyō′nä) *f* proclamation
proclive (prō·klē′vä) *a* disposed, inclined, amenable
procrastinare (prō·krâ·stē·nâ′rä) *vi* to procrastinate; to temporize
procreare (prō·krā·â′rä) *vt* to procreate; to give birth to
procura (prō·kū′râ) *f* power of attorney; proxy
procurare (prō·kū·râ′rä) *vt* to secure; to try; to supply
procurarsi (prō·kū·râr′sē) *vr* to secure; to obtain for oneself

---

â ârm, ā bāby, e bet, ē bē, ō gō, ô gône, ū blūe, b bad, ch child, d dad, f fat, g gay, j jet

procuratore (prō·kū·râ·tō′rā) *m* prosecutor; administrator; attorney

proda (prō′dâ) *f* bank, shore; (*naut*) prow

prode (prō′dā) *a* brave; — *m* hero; **–zza** (prō·dā′tsâ) *f* valor, bravery

prodigare (prō·dē·gâ′rā) *vt* to lavish, give in profusion

prodigarsi (prō·dē·gâr′sē) *vr* to devote oneself; to spare no pains, do one's best

prodigio (prō·dē′jō) *m* marvel; prodigy **–samente** (prō·dē·jō·zâ·mān′tā) *adv* prodigiously

prodigo (prō′dē·gō) *m* spendthrift; — *a* prodigal; lavish

proditorio (prō·dē·tô′ryō) *a* sneaky, treacherous

prodotto (prō·dōt′tō) *m* product; child (*fig*) — *a* produced

prodromo (prō′drō·mō) *m* symptom, sign

produrre * (prō·dūr′rā) *vt* to produce

prodursi * (prō·dūr′sē) *vr* to happen, take place

produttivo (prō·dūt·tē′vō) *a* fruitful, productive

produttore (prō·dūt·tō′rā) *m* producer

produzione (prō·dū·tsyō′nā) *f* production

profanare (prō·fâ·nâ′rā) *vt* to desecrate, profane

profanazione (prō·fâ·nâ·tsyō′nā) *f* desecration, profaning

profano (prō·fâ′nō) *m* layman; outsider; — *a* worldly, secular, profane; unskilled

proferire (prō·fâ·rē′rā) *vt* to utter

proferirsi (prō·fâ·rēr′sē) *vr* to offer one's assistance, volunteer one's aid

professare (prō·fās·sâ′rā) *vt&i* to profess

professarsi (prō·fās·sâr′sē) *vr* to profess oneself to be; to declare oneself

professione (prō·fās·syō′nā) *f* profession

professionista (prō·fās·syō·nē′stâ) *m&f* professional

professore (prō·fās·sō′rā) *m*, **professoressa** (prō·fās·sō·rās′sâ) *f* professor

profeta (prō·fā′tâ) *m* prophet

profetico (prō·fe′tē·kō) *a* prophetic

profetizzare (prō·fâ·tē·dzâ′rā) *vt* to foretell; to prophesy

profezia (prō·fâ·tsē′â) *f* prophecy

proficuo (prō·fē′kwō) *a* profitable, fruitful

profilare (prō·fē·lâ′rā) *vt* to outline

profilarsi (prō·fē·lâr′sē) *vr* to be evident, stand out

profilassi (prō·fē·lâs′sē) *f* prevention; (*med*) prophylaxis

profilo (prō·fē′lō) *m* profile; side view

profittare (prō·fēt·tâ′rā) *vi* to profit; to derive benefit

profitto (prō·fēt′tō) *m* advantage, profit

profondamente (prō·fōn·dâ·mān′tā) *adv* deeply

profondere * (prō·fōn′dâ·rā) *vt* to squander, throw away

profondersi * (prō·fōn′dār·sē) *vr* to be lavish; to show munificence

profondità (prō·fōn·dē·tâ′) *f* depth

profondo (prō·fōn′dō) *a* profound, deep

profugo (prô′fū·gō) *m* refugee

profumare (prō·fū·mâ′rā) *vt* to scent, perfume

profumarsi (prō·fū·mâr′sē) *vr* to wear perfume; to put on perfume

profumatamente (prō·fū·mâ·tâ·mān′tā) *adv* dearly; munificently

profumeria (prō·fū·mâ·rē′â) *f* perfume shop, perfumery

profumo (prō·fū′mō) *m* scent, perfume

profusione (prō·fū·zyō′nā) *f* profusion; great number

progenitore (prō·jâ·nē·tō′rā) *m*, **progenitrice** (prō·jâ·nē·trē′châ) *f* ancestor

progettare (prō·jât·tâ′rā) *vt* to plan; to design

progettista (prō·jât·tē′stâ) *m* designer; planner

progetto (prō·jât′tō) *m* plan; design

programma (prō·grâm′mâ) *m* program; — **di viaggio** itinerary; **–re** (prō·grâm·mâ′rā) *vt* to schedule; **–zione** (prō·grâm·mâ·tsyō′nā) *f* theater bill; programming

progredire (prō·grâ·dē′rā) *vi* to make progress; to advance

progresso (prō·grās′sō) *m* progress

proibire (prōē·bē′rā) *vt* to forbid

proibito (prōē·bē′tō) *a* forbidden; è — **fumare** no smoking

proibizione (prōē·bē·tsyō′nā) *f* prohibition

proiettare (prō·yât·tâ′rā) *vt* to project; to show (*movie*)

proiettile (prō·yet′tē·lā) *m* bullet; missile

proiettore (prō·yât·tō′rā) *m* projector; searchlight

proiezione (prō·yâ·tsyō′nā) *f* projection; showing (*movie*)

prole (prō′lā) *f* offspring; issue

proletario (prō·lā·tâ′ryō) *a&m* proletarian

prolificare (prō·lē·fē·kâ′rā) *vi* to spread, multiply

prolifico (prō·lē′fē·kō) *a* fruitful; inventive, creative

prolisso (prō·lēs′sō) *a* verbose; longwinded; pedantic

prologo (prô′lō·gō) *m* introduction; pro-

logue
prolungamento (prō·lŭn·gâ·mān'tō) *m*
lengthening, prolongation
prolungare (prō·lŭn·gâ'rā) *vt* to extend;
to stretch out .
prolungarsi (prō·lŭn·gâr'sē) *vr* to continue, extend
promemoria (prō·mā·mô'ryâ) *m* memorandum, note
promessa (prō·mās'sâ) *f* promise
promesso (prō·mās'sō) *a* promised; be-
trothed, engaged
promettente (prō·māt·tān'tā) *a* hopeful,
promising
promettere * (prō·met'tā·rā) *vt* to promise
promiscuo (prō·mē'skwō) *a* mixed; promiscuous; **scuola promiscua** coeducational school; **matrimonio** — mixed
marriage
promontorio (prō·mōn·tô'ryō) *m* promontory
promosso (prō·mōs'sō) *a* passed (*student*);
promoted
promozione (prō·mō·tsyō'nā) *f* promotion; advancement
promulgare (pro·mŭl·gâ'rā) *vt* to issue;
to proclaim, promulgate
promuovere * (prō·mwô'vā·rā) *vt* to promote; to pass (*students*)
pronipote (prō·nē·pō'tā) *m&f* grand-
nephew, grandniece
pronipoti (prō·nē·pō'tē) *mpl* descendants
pronome (prō·nō'mā) *m* pronoun
pronostico (prō·nô'stē·kō) *m* omen, forecast; prediction
prontamente (prōn·tâ·mān'tā) *adv* readily; quickly
prontezza (prōn·tā'tsâ) *f* promptness
pronto (prōn'tō) *a* ready; hello (*telephone*); — **soccorso** first aid
pronunzia (prō·nŭn'tsyâ) *f* pronunciation;
—**re** (prō·nŭn·tsyâ'rā) *vt* to pronounce;
to utter; —**rsi** (prō·nŭn·tsyâr'sē) *vr* to
declare oneself, avow oneself
propaganda (prō·pâ·gân'dâ) *f* propaganda; advertisement; advertising; **a titolo
di** — for advertising purposes
propagandista (prō·pâ·gân·dē'stâ) *m*
propagandist; canvasser
propagare (prō·pâ·gâ'rā) *vt* to spread;
to distribute
propagarsi (prō·pâ·gâr'sē) *vr* to extend;
to propagate; to spread
propalare (prō·pâ·lâ'rā) *vt* to divulge
propendere * (prō·pen'dā·rā) *vi* to lean;
to incline
propensione (prō·pān·syō'nā) *f* propensity, inclination; native ability

propenso (prō·pān'sō) *a* inclined, amenable
propinquo (prō·pēn'kwō) *a* related; similar; near
propiziamente (prō·pē·tsyâ·mān'tā) *adv*
propitiously
propizio (prō·pē'tsyō) *a* favorable
proponimento (prō·pō·nē·mān'tō) *m* intent, resolution
proporre * (prō·pōr'rā) *vt* to propose; to
suggest
proporsi * (prō·pōr'sē) *vr* to volunteer
oneself; to resolve, mean
proporzionato (prō·pōr·tsyō·nâ'tō) *a* pro-
portionate
proporzione (prō·pōr·tsyō'nā) *f* proportion
proposito (prō·pô'zē·tō) *m* determination; purpose; reason; **a** — by the way
proposizione (prō·pō·zē·tsyō'nā) *f* proposition, proposal
proposta ((prō·pō'stâ) *f* proposal
propriamente (prō·pyrâ·mān'tā) *adv* ap-
propriately, properly
proprietà (prō·pryā·tâ') *f* property; decorum
proprietario (prō·pryā·tâ'ryō) *m* proprietor
proprio (prō'pryō) *a* one's own; proper;
exact; — *adv* just; really; **lavorare in** —
to be in business for oneself
propugnare (prō·pū·nyâ'rā) *vt* to advocate, be in favor of; to rally around
propulsione (prō·pŭl·syō'nā) *f* propulsion; — **a reazione** jet propulsion
propulsore (prō·pŭl·sō'rā) *m* propeller
prora (prō'râ) *f* (*naut*) bow
proroga (prō'rō·gâ) *f* deferment; postponement; —**re** (prō·rō·gâ'rā) *vt* to put
off; to defer; (*com*) to extend
prorompere * (prō·rôm'pā·rā) *vi* to break
out; — **in pianto** to burst into tears
prosa (prō'zâ) *f* prose; **teatro di** — legitimate theater; —**ico** (prō·zâ'ē·kō) *a*
prosaic; hackneyed, trite
prosciogliere * (prō·shô'lyâ·rā) *vt* to free,
liberate; to absolve
prosciugamento (prō·shū·gâ·mān'tō) *m*
draining
prosciugare (prō·shū·gâ'rā) *vt* to drain;
to dry
prosciutto (prō·shūt'tō) *m* ham
proscrivere * (prō·skrē'vā·rā) *vt* to banish, outlaw
proscrizione (prō·skrē·tsyō'nā) *f* banishment, proscription
proseguimento (prō·sā·gwē·mān'tō) *m*
resuming; continuation

â ârm, ā bāby, e bet, ē bē, ō gō, ô gône, ū blūe, b bad, ch child, d dad, f fat, g gay, j jet

proseguire (prō·sā·gwē′rā) *vt&i* to continue; to resume, make a fresh start; — **diritto** to keep going straight ahead

prosopopea (prō·zō·pō·pā′ä) *f* pose, self-importance, affectation

prosperare (prō·spā·rä′rā) *vi* to thrive; to do well

prosperità (prō·spä·rē·tä′) *f* prosperity

prosperosamente (prō·spä·rō·zä·mān′tä) *adv* prosperously

prosperoso (prō·spä·rō′zō) *a* prosperous; thriving; plump

prospettare (prō·spät·tä′rā) *vt* to describe; to outline, lay out

prospettiva (prō·spät·tē′vä) *f* project; prospective; prospect

prospetto (prō·spät′tō) *m* prospect; plan; prospectus

prospiciente (prō·spē·chän′tä) *a* facing; looking over, opening on

prossimamente (prōs·sē·mä·mān′tä) *adv* in the near future, soon, shortly

prossimità (prōs·sē·mē·tä′) *f* proximity

prossimo (prōs′sē·mō) *a* next; — *m* fellowman; neighbor

prostituta (prō·stē·tū′tä) *f* prostitute

prostrazione (prō·strä·tsyō′nä) *f* prostration; depression (*mental*)

protagonista (prō·tä·gō·nē′stä) *m&f* protagonist

proteggere * (prō·tej′jä·rā) *vt* to protect

protervo (prō·tär′vō) *a* stubborn

protesta (prō·tä′stä) *f* protest; protestation; –**nte** (prō·tä·stän′tä) *m&a* Protestant; –**re** (prō·tä·stä′rā) *vt&i* to protest

protetto (prō·tät′tō) *m* favorite; protégé; –**rato** (prō·tät·tō·rä′tō) *m* protectorate; –**re** (prō·tät·tō′rā) *m* protector

protezione (prō·tä·tsyō′nä) *f* protection; aegis

protocollare (prō·tō·kōl·lä′rā) *vt* to file; to enter on the record

protocollo (prō·tō·kōl′lō) *m* protocol; file, record

prototipo (prō·tō·tē′pō) *m* prototype

protozoo (prō·tō·dzō′ō) *m* protozoan

protrarre * (prō·trär′rā) *vt* to drag out, prolong

protuberanza (prō·tū·bä·rän′tsä) *f* protuberance

prova (prō′vä) *f* test; proof; (*theat*) rehearsal; (*law*) evidence, testimony; –**re** (prō·vä′rā) *vt&i* to prove; to try; to experience; –**rsi** (prō·vär′sē) *vr* to make an attempt

proveniente (prō·vä·nyän′tä) *a* arising, originating

provenienza (prō·vä·nyän′tsä) *f* origin,

font

provenire * (prō·vä·nē′rā) *vi* to originate, come from

provento (prō·vän′tō) *m* profit, income

proverbiale (prō·vär·byä′lä) *a* notorious; proverbial; **essere** — to be a byword

proverbio (prō·ver′byō) *m* proverb

provetta (prō·vät′tä) *f* test tube

provetto (prō·vät′tō) *a* skillful, able

provincia (prō·vēn′chä) *f* province; –**le** (prō·vēn·chä′lä) *a* provincial; insular (*fig*)

provino (prō·vē′nō) *m* test tube; screen test

provocante (prō·vō·kän′tä) *a* provoking; seductive

provocare (prō·vō·kä′rā) *vt* to provoke, create

provocativo (prō·vō·kä·tē′vō) *a* provocative

provocatore (prō·vo·kä·tō′rā) *m* instigator; — *a* provocative

provocazione (prō·vō·kä·tsyō′nä) *f* provocation

provolone (prō·vō·lō′nä) *m* hard cheese made from goat's milk

provvedere * (prōv·vä·dä′rā) *vt&i* to provide; to supply

provvedersi * (prōv·vä·där′sē) *vr* to furnish oneself with; to lay in

provvedimento (prōv·vä·dē·mān′tō) *m* measure, precaution; (*pol*) ordinance

provveditore (prōv·vä·dē·tō′rā) *m* (*com*) supplier; superintendent; — **agli studi** superintendent of schools

provvidenza (prōv·vē·dän′tsä) *f* providence

provvidenziale (prōv·vē·dän·tsyä′lä) *a* providential

provvido (prōv′vē·dō) *a* provident

provvigione (prōv·vē·jō′nä) *f* provision; (*com*) commission

provvisoriamente (prōv·vē·zō·ryä·män′tä) *adv* temporarily

provvisorio (prōv·vē·zō′ryō) *a* provisional, temporary

provvista (prōv·vē′stä) *f* stock, supplies, provisions

prozia (prō·dzē′ä) *f* great-aunt

prozio (prō·dzē′ō) *m* great-uncle

prua (prū′ä) *f* (*naut*) bow, prow

prudente (prū·dän′tä) *a* prudent; –**mente** (prū·dän·tä·män′tä) *adv* prudently

prudenza (prū·dän′tsä) *f* prudence; husbandry

prudenziale (prū·dän·tsyä′lä) *a* precautionary; prudent

prudere (prū′dä·rā) *vi* to itch

---

prugna (prū'nyâ) *f* plum; — **secca** prune
pruno (prū'nō) *m* bramble
prurito (prū·rē'tō) *m* itching, itch
Prussia (prūs'syâ) *f* Prussia
pseudonimo (psāū·dô'nē·mō) *m* pseudonym; pen name
psicanalisi (psē·kâ·nâ'lē·zē) *f* psychoanalysis
psichiatra (psē·kyâ'trâ) *m* psychiatrist
psichiatria (psē·kyâ·trē'â) *f* psychiatry
psichico (psē'kē·kō) *a* psychic
psicologo (psē·kô'lō·gō) *m* psychologist
psicopatico (psē·kō·pâ'tē·kō) *m* psychopath; — *a* psychopathic
psicosi (psē·kō'zē) *f* psychosis
pubblicamente (pūb·blē·kâ·mān'tā) *adv* publicly, in public
pubblicare (pūb·blē·kâ'rā) *vt* to publish; to publicize, make public
pubblicazione (pūb·blē·kâ·tsyō'nā) *f* publication
pubblicista (pūb·blē·chē'stâ) *m* press agent
pubblicità (pūb·blē·chē·tâ') *f* advertising; publicity
pubblicitario (pūb·blē·chē·tâ'ryō) *a* advertising
pubblico (pūb'blē·kō) *m&a* public; audience
pubertà (pū·bâr·tâ') *f* puberty
pudicizia (pū·dē·chē'tsyâ) *f* chastity; bashfulness; modesty
pudico (pū'dē·kō) *a* modest; decent
pudore (pū·dō'rā) *m* modesty; decency
puerile (pwā·rē'lā) *a* childish
puerilità (pwā·rē·lē·tâ') *f* childishness
puerizia (pwā·rē'·tsyâ) *f* childhood
pugilato (pū·jē·lâ'tō) *m* boxing, prizefighting
pugilista (pū·jē·lē'stâ) *m* prizefighter, boxer
pugilistica (pū·jē·lē'stē·kâ) *f* boxing
pugilistico (pū·jē·lē'stē·kō) *a* boxing
pugnalare (pū·nyâ·lâ'rā) *vt* to stab
pugnalata (pū·nyâ·lâ'tâ) *f* stab
pugnale (pū·nyâ'lā) *m* dagger
pugno (pū'nyō) *m* fist; handful
pulce (pūl'chā) *f* flea; **mettere una — nell'orecchio** to put a bee in one's bonnet
pulcino (pūl·chē'nō) *m* chick
puledra (pū·lā'drâ) *f* filly
puledro (pū·lā'drō) *m* colt
puleggia (pū·lej'jâ) *f* pulley
pulire (pū·lē'rā) *vt* to clean; to polish
pulirsi (pū·lēr'sē) *vr* to clean up; to tidy up; — **il naso** to blow one's nose; — **la bocca** to wipe one's lips

pulito (pū·lē'tō) *a* clean; polished
pulitura (pū·lē·tū'râ) *f* cleaning; — **a secco** dry cleaning
pulizia (pū·lē·tsē'â) *f* cleanliness; cleaning
pullulare (pūl·lū·lâ'rā) *vi* to swarm, teem
pulpito (pūl'pē·tō) *m* pulpit; **Senti da che — viene la predica!** *(coll)* Just look who's talking! You're a fine one!
pulsante (pūl·sân'tā) *m* push button
pulsare (pūl·sâ'rā) *vi* to throb, pulsate
pulsazione (pūl·sâ·tsyō'nā) *f* pulsation; vibration
pungente (pūn·jān'tā) *a* piercing, sharp, caustic
pungere * (pūn'jā·rā) *vt* to sting; to irritate; to hurt the feelings of; to arouse, provoke, spur on
pungersi * (pūn'jär·sē) *vr* to prick oneself; to take offense
pungiglione (pūn·jē·lyō'nā) *m* insect sting; stimulus, goad
pungolo (pūn'gō·lō) *m* goad
punire (pū·nē'·rā) *vt* to punish
punitivo (pū·nē·tē'vō) *a* punitive
punizione (pū·nē·tsyō'nā) *f* punishment
punta (pūn'tâ) *f* tip; point; **ora di —** rush hour; **fare la — alla matita** to sharpen one's pencil; **-re** (pūn·tâ'rā) *vt* to aim, point; to stake, wager; — *vi* to bet; **-ta** (pūn·tâ'tâ) *f* installment; issue *(magazine)*
punteggiare (pūn·tāj·jâ'rā) *vt&i* to punctuate; to dot
punteggiatura (pūn·tāj·jâ·tū'râ) *f* dotting; punctuation
punteggio (pūn·tej'jō) *m (sport)* score
puntellare (pūn·tāl·lâ'rā) *vt* to prop, support; to shore up
puntello (pūn·tāl'lō) *m* stay, prop
punteruolo (pūn·tā·rūō'lō) *m* awl, punch
puntiglio (pūn·tē'lyō) *m* false pride; point of honor; spite; **-so** (pūn·tē·lyō'zō) *a* stubborn; punctilious
puntina (pūn·tē'nâ) *f* thumbtack
puntino (pūn·tē'nō) *m* dot; **a — *(coll)* just right, perfectly; **cuocere a — to cook just right
punto (pūn'tō) *m* point; period; dot; mark *(school)*; — *a* pricked; — *adv* by no means; — **e virgola** semicolon; **due punti** colon; — **esclamativo** exclamation point; — **interrogativo** question mark; **giungere a buon —** to arrive at the right moment
puntuale (pūn·twâ'lā) *a* punctual; careful
puntualità (pūn·twâ·lē·tâ') *f* punctuality
puntualmente (pūn·twâl·mān'tā) *adv*

---

punctually; precisely, carefully
puntuazione (pŭn·twä·tsyō'nä) *f* punctuation
puntura (pŭn·tū'râ) *f* sting; *(med)* injection; — **di zanzara** mosquito bite
punzecchiare (pŭn·dzäk·kyâ'rä) *vt* to tease; to prick; to spur
punzone (pŭn·tsō'nä) *m* punch
pupa (pū'pâ) *f (coll)* baby, little girl; doll; **-zzo** (pū·pâ'tsō) *m* puppet, marionette
pupilla (pū·pēl'lä) *f* pupil of the eye
pupillo (pū·pēl'lō) *m* ward, charge
pupo (pū'pō) *m (coll)* baby, little boy
puramente (pū·râ·mān'tä) *adv* merely, simply
purchè (pūr·kā') *conj* provided
pure (pū'rä) *adv* also, too; yet, still, even; by all means
purè (pū·rä') *m* thick soup; — **di patate** mashed potatoes
purezza (pū·rä'tsä) *f* purity
purga (pūr'gä) *f* purging, purge; **-nte** (pūr·gän'tä) *m* laxative, purge, physic; **-re** (pūr·gâ'rä) *vt* to purify; to purge; to expurgate
purgatorio (pūr·gâ·tô'ryō) *m* Purgatory
purificare (pū·rē·fē·kâ'rä) *vt* to purify
puritano (pū·rē·tâ'nō) *m&a* puritan

puro (pū'rō) *a* pure; genuine; mere, plain; **-sangue** (pū·rō·sân'gwä) *m* thoroughbred
purtroppo (pūr·trōp'pō) *adv* unfortunately
purulento (pū·rū·lān'tō) *a* purulent
pus (pūs) *m* pus
pusillanime (pū·zēl·lâ'nē·mä) *a* pusillanimous, cowardly
pustola (pū'stō·lä) *f (med)* boil, pustule
putativo (pū·tâ·tē'vō) *a* reputed; supposed, putative
putiferio (pū·tē·fe'ryō) *m* racket, uproar, row
putredine (pū·tre'dē·nä) *f* rottenness
putrefare * (pū·trä·fâ'rä) *vi* to rot
putrefarsi * (pū·trä·fär'sē) *vr* to putrify; to decompose
putrefazione (pū·trä·fâ·tsyō'nä) *f* putrefaction
putrido (pū'trē·dō) *a* rotten, putrid
puttana (pūt·tâ'nä) *f* whore, prostitute
puzza (pū'tsâ) *f* stench, foul odor; **-re** (pū·tsâ'rä) *vi* to stink, have an unpleasant smell
puzzo (pū'tsō) *m* stench, stink
puzzola (pū'tsō·lä) *f* polecat, skunk
puzzolente (pū·tsō·län'tä) *a* stinking, foulsmelling

Q

qua (kwâ') *adv* here; — **e là** here and there
quaderno (kwâ·där'nō) *m* notebook
quadrangolo (kwâ·drân'gō·lō) *m* quadrangle
quadrante (kwâ·drân'tä) *m* quadrant; face *(clock)*; dial *(watch)*
quadrare (kwâ·drâ'rä) *vt&i* to fit; to make square; to please, be to one's liking; to adjust; *(com)* to balance
quadrato (kwâ·drâ'tō) *a* squared; — *m* square; ring *(sport)*
quadrettato (kwâ·drät·tâ'tō) *a* checkered
quadretto (kwâ·drät'tō) *m* small square; check
quadri (kwâ'drē) *mpl (cards)* diamonds
quadrifoglio (kwâ·drē·fô'lyō) *m* four-leaf clover
quadriglia (kwâ·drē'lyâ) *f* quadrille
quadrilatero (kwâ·drē·lâ'tä·rō) *a&m* quadrilateral
quadrimotore (kwâ·drē·mō·tō'rä) *m* four-engine plane
quadro (kwâ'drō) *m* painting; picture; — *a* square; — **commutatore** *(elec)* switchboard
quadrupede (kwâ·drū'pä·dä) *m&a* quadruped

quadruplicare (kwâ·drū·plē·kâ'rä) *vt* to quadruple
quadruplo (kwâ'drū·plō) *m* quadruple
quaggiù (kwâj·jū') *adv* down here; on earth
quaglia (kwâ'lyä) *f (zool)* quail
quagliare (kwâ·lyâ'rä) *vt&i* to curdle; to coagulate
qualche (kwâl'kä) *a* some, any
qualcosa (kwâl·kō'zä) *pron* something, anything
qualcuno (kwâl·kū'nō) *pron* someone, anyone
quale (kwâ'lä) *a&pron* what, which
qualifica (kwâ·lē'fē·kâ) *f* qualification; requisite; **-re** (kwâ·lē·fē·kâ'rä) *vt* to qualify
qualità (kwâ·lē·tâ') *f* quality; type
qualora (kwâ·lō'râ) *adv* just in case; whenever; if and when
qualsiasi (kwâl·sē'â·sē) *a&pron* whatever, any
qualunque (kwâ·lūn'kwä) *a* any, whatever
qualvolta (kwâl·vōl'tä) *adv* whenever; in the event that; **ogni** — whenever

---

quando (kwân'dō) *adv* when; whenever

quanti (kwân'tē) *a&pron* how many

quantico (kwân'tē·kō), **quantistico** (kwân·tē'stē·kō) *a (math)* quantic

quantità (kwân·tē·tâ') *f* quantity

quantitativo (kwân·tē·tâ·tē'vō) *m* quantity, sum, amount

quanto (kwân'tō) *a&pron* as much, how much; — **a** as to, as concerns

quantunque (kwân·tūn'kwā) *conj* although, even though

quaranta (kwâ·rân'tâ) *a* forty; —**mila** (kwâ·rân·tâ·mē'lâ) *a* forty thousand

quarantenne (kwâ·rân·tān'nā) *a* forty years old

quarantesimo (kwâ·rân·te'zē·mō) *a* fortieth

quaresima (kwâ·re'zē·mâ) *f* Lent; —**le** (kwâ·rā·zē·mâ'lā) *a* Lenten

quartetto (kwâr·tāt'tō) *m* quartet

quartiere (kwâr·tyā'rā) *m* area, district; quarter; apartment

quarto (kwâr·tō) *a* fourth; — *m* quarter

quarzo (kwâr'tsō) *m* quartz

quasi (kwâ'sē) *adv* almost

quassù (kwâs·sū') *adv* up here; here above

quatto (kwât'tō) *a* squat; crouched, huddled; cowed

quattordicenne (kwât·tōr·dē·chān'nā) *a* fourteen years old

quattordicesimo (kwât·tōr·dē·che'zē·mō) *a* fourteenth

quattordici (kwât·tôr'dē·chē) *a* fourteen

quattrino (kwât·trē'nō) *m* cent; money

quattro (kwât'trō) *a* four; **fare — passi** to go for a walk; **dirgliene — to** give someone a piece of one's mind; to tell someone off; **in — e quattr'otto** in a hurry, quickly; **farsi in — to** do one's best; **a quattr'occhi** privately, secretly

quattrocento (kwât·trō·chān'tō) *a* four hundred; **il Q—** the fifteenth century

quegli (kwā'lyē) *a* those; — *pron* he

quei (kwā'ē) *a* those

quel (kwāl) *a&pron* that

quelli (kwāl'lē) *pron* those

quello (kwāl'lō) *a&pron* that

quercia (kwer'châ) *f* oak

querela (kwâ·rā'lâ) *f* legal action; complaint; —**re** (kwâ·rā·lâ'rā) *vt* to sue

quesito (kwâ·zē'tō) *m* question, query

questi (kwā'stē) *a&pron* these

questionamento (kwā·styō·nâ·mān'tō) *m* quarrel, altercation

questionare (kwā·styô·nâ'rā) *vi* to argue; to altercate

questionario (kwā·styō·nâ'ryō) *m* questionaire

questione (kwā·styō'nā) *f* argument; problem, matter

questo (kwā'stō) *a&pron* this, the latter

questore (kwā·stō'râ) *m* provincial chief of police

questua (kwe'stwâ) *f* collection for charity

questura (kwā·stū'râ) *f* police headquarters

questurino (kwā·stū·rē'nō) *m* policeman

qui (kwē) *adv* here

quiescenza (kwēā·shān'tsâ) *f* retirement; quiescence

quietanza (kwēā·tân'tsâ) *f* receipt; —**re** (kwēā·tân·tsâ'rā) *vt* to receipt

quietare (kwēā·tâ'rā) *vt* to calm, quiet down; to silence

quietarsi (kwēā·târ'sē) *vr* to become quiet; to grow silent

quiete (kwēā'tā) *f* peace and quiet; silence

quieto (kwēā'tō) *a* quiet; peaceful; shy, retiring

quindi (kwēn'dē) *adv* therefore; afterwards; as a result

quindicenne (kwēn·dē·chān'nā) *a* fifteen years old

quindicesimo (kwēn·dē·che'zē·mō) *a* fifteenth

quindici (kwēn'dē·chē) *a* fifteen; —**mila** (kwēn·dē·che·mē'lâ) *a* fifteen thousand; —**na** (kwēn·dē·che'nâ) *f* about fifteen; two weeks

quinquagenario (kwēn·kwâ·jā·nâ'ryō) *a* fifty years old

quintale (kwēn·tâ'lā) *m* quintal

quintessenza (kwēn·tās·sān'tsâ) *f* quintessence

quintetto (kwēn·tāt'tō) *m* quintet

quinto (kwēn'tō) *a* fifth

quintuplicare (kwēn·tū·plē·kâ'rā) *vt* to quintuple

quisquilia (kwē·skwē'lyâ) *f* trifle; bagatelle

quota (kwō'tâ) *f* share; quota; installment; *(avi)* height; —**re** (kwō·tâ'râ) *vt* to quote; to assess; —**zione** (kwō·tâ·tsyō'nâ) *f* quotation; **prendere —** *(avi)* to gain altitude, climb; **volare a bassa — to** fly at a low altitude

quotidianamente (kwō·tē·dyâ·nâ·mān'tâ) *adv* every day, daily

quotidiano (kwō·tē·dyâ'nō) *a* daily; — *m* daily newspaper

quotizzare (kwō·tē·dzâ'rā) *vt* to assess, evaluate

quotizzazione (kwō·tē·dzâ·tsyō'nā) *f* assessment, evaluation

quoto (kwō'tō), **quoziente** (kwō·tsyān'tā) *m* quotient

â ârm, ā bāby, e bet, ē bē, ō gō, ô gône, ū blūe, b bad, ch child, d dad, f fat, g gay, j jét

R

rabarbaro (râ·bâr′bâ·rō) *m* rhubarb
rabberciare (râb·bār·châ′rā) *vt* to patch
rabbia (râb′byâ) *f* anger, rage; hydrophobia
rabbino (râb·bē′nō) *m* rabbi
rabbiosamente (râb·byō·zâ·mān′tā) *adv* furiously; rabidly
rabbioso (râb·byō′zō) *a* furious, angry; rabid
rabbrividire (râb·brē·vē·dē′rā) *vi* to shiver, shake
rabbuffare (râb·būf·fâ′rā) *vt* to scold; to ruffle, upset
rabbuffarsi (râb·būf·fâr′sē) *vr* to become disturbed; to get upset
rabbuffo (râb·būf′fō) *m* reprimand, scolding
rabdomante (râb·dō·mân′tā) *m* water witch, dowser
raccappezzarsi (râk·kâp·pā·tsâr′sē) *vr* to figure out, understand
raccapricciante (râk·kâ·prē·chân′tā) *a* frightful, horrifying
raccapriccio (râk·kâ·prē′chō) *m* horror
raccattare (râk·kât·tâ′rā) *vt* to pick up, gather
racchetta (râk·kāt′tâ) *f* tennis racket; snowshoe
racchiudere * (râk·kyū′dā·rā) *vt* to contain; to lock in
raccogliere * (râk·kô′lyā·rā) *vt* to gather, collect; to marshal; to accept
raccogliersi * (râk·kô′lyār·sē) *fr* to reflect, ponder; to assemble, gather together; to concentrate one's mind
raccoglimento (râk·kō·lyē·mân′tō) *m* self-absorption; gathering; mental concentration
raccolta (râk·kōl′tâ) *f* collection; harvest
raccoltamente (râk·kōl·tâ·mān′tā) *adv* pensively, musingly
raccolto (râk·kōl′tō) *m* harvest, crop; — *a* gathered; quiet
raccomandare (râk·kō·mân·dâ′rā) *vt* to recommend; to register
raccomandarsi (râk·kō·mân·dâr′sē) *vr* to urge, entreat; to remind
raccomandata (râk·kō·mân·dâ′tâ) *f* registered letter
raccomandazione (râk·kō·mân·dâ·tsyō′nā) *f* recommendation; registry *(letter)*
raccomodare (râk·kō·mō·dâ′rā) *vt* to repair; to set right
raccontare (râk·kōn·tâ′rā) *vt* to relate, tell

racconto (râk·kōn′tō) *m* story; account
raccordo (râk·kōr′dō) *m* junction; connection
rachitico (râ·kē′tē·kō) *a* rickety
racimolare (râ·chē·mō·lâ′rā) *vt* to scrape together; to gather at random
rada (râ′dâ) *f (naut)* roadstead
radar (râ′dâr) *m* radar; –ista (râ·dâ·rē′-stâ) *m* radarman
raddolcire (râd·dōl·chē′rā) *vt* to sweeten; to make mild
raddolcirsi (râd·dōl·chēr′sē) *vr* to become mild; to get sweet; *(fig)* to be soothed
raddoppiare (râd·dōp·pyâ′rā) *vt* to double
raddoppio (râd·dōp′pyō) *m* doubling
raddrizzare (râd·drē·tsâ′rā) *vt* to make straight
raddrizzarsi (râd·drē·tsâr′sē) *vr* to right; to straighten up
raddrizzatore (râd·drē·dzâ·tō′rā) *m (elec)* rectifier, converter
radere * (râ′dā·rā) *vt* to shave; to raze
radersi * (râ′dār·sē) *vr* to shave, shave oneself
radiare (râ·dyâ′rā) *vt* to expel; to cross out, delete; — *vi* to beam; to radiate
radiatore (râ·dyâ·tō′rā) *m* radiator
radicalmente (râ·dē·kâl·mān′tā) *adv* radically; completely
radicarsi (râ·dē·kâr′sē) *vr* to take root; to take hold
radicchio (râ·dēk′kyō) *m* wild chicory
radice (râ·dē′châ) *f* root
radio (râ′dyō) *f* radio; — *m (min)* radium; — stazione radio station; –amatore (râ·dyō·â·mâ·tō′rā) *m* ham *(sl)*; –attività (râ·dyō·ât·tē·vē·tâ′) *f* radioactivity; –auditore (râ·dyō·âū·dē·tō′rā) *m* radio listener; –comandato (râ·dyō·kō·mân·dâ′tō) *a* radiocontrolled; –comando (râ·dyō·kō·mân′dō) *m* remote control; radio control; –commentatore (râ·dyō·kōm·mân·tâ·tō′rā) *m* radio commentator; –cronista (râ·dyō·krō·nē′stâ) *m* newscaster; –diffusione (râ·dyō·dēf·fū·zyō′nâ) *f* broadcasting; –faro (râ·dyō·fâ′rō) *m* radio beacon; –fonico (râ·dyō·fô′nē·kō) *a* radio; trasmissione radiofonica broadcast; –frequenza (râ·dyō·frā·kwān′tsâ) *f* radio frequency; –goniometro (râ·dyō·gō·nyô′mâ·trō) *m* direction finder; –grafia (râ·dyō·grâ·fē′â) *f* X ray; –gramma (râ·dyō·grâm′mâ) *m* radiogram; –localizzatore (râ·dyō·lō·kâ·lē·dzâ·tō′rā) *m* radar; –logia

(râ·dyō·lō·jē′â) *f* radiology; **–logo** (râ·dyô′lō·gō) *m* radiologist; **–scopia** (râ·dyō·skō·pē′â) *f* radioscopy; **–so** (râ·dyō′zō) *a* bright, radiant; **–telefono** (râ·dyō·tā·le′fō·nō) *m* radiotelephone; **–telegrafia** (râ·dyō·tā·lā·grâ·fē′â) *f* radiotelegraphy; **– telegrafista** (râ·dyō·tā·lā·grâ·fē′stâ) *m* wireless operator; **–telegramma** (râ·dyō·tā·lā·grâm′mâ) *m* radiotelegram; **–terapia** (râ·dyō·tā·râ·pē′â) *f* radiotherapy; **–trasmissione** (râ·dyō·trâ·zmēs·syō′nä) *f* broadcast; **-trasmittente** (râ·dyō·trâ·zmēt·tän′tâ) *a* broadcasting

rado (râ′dō) *a* thin; rare; **di** — seldom

radunare (râ·dū·nâ′rā) *vt* to collect, gather

radunarsi (râ·dū·nâr′sē) *vr* to assemble, meet

raduno (râ·dū′nō) *m* rally; meeting, assembly

radura (râ·dū′râ) *f* clearing, glade

rafano (râ′fâ·nō) *m* horseradish

raffermo (râf·fâr′mō) *a* stale

raffica (râf′fē·kâ) *f* gust; shower

raffigurare (râf·fē·gū·râ′rā) *vt* to symbolize; to recognize; to represent

raffigurarsi (râf·fē·gū·râr′sē) *vr* to imagine

raffigurazione (râf·fē·gū·râ·tsyō′nä) *f* recognition; representation

raffinamento (râf·fē·nâ·mān′tō) *m* thinning, refining

raffinare (râf·fē·nâ′rā) *vt* to refine

raffinarsi (râf·fē·nâr′sē) *vr* to become refined

raffinatezza (râf·fē·nâ·tā′tsâ) *f* refinement

raffinato (râf·fē·nâ′tō) *a* refined; cultured; *(fig)* sly, clever

raffineria (râf·fē·nā·rē′â) *f* refinery

rafforzare (râf·fōr·tsâ′râ) *vt* to reinforce

rafforzarsi (râf·fōr·tsâr′sē) *vr* to be strengthened, become stronger

raffreddamento (râf·frād·dâ·mān′tō) *m* cooling; **— ad acqua** *(mech)* water cooling

raffreddare (râf·frād·dâ′rā) *vt* to cool

raffreddarsi (râf·frād·dâr′sē) *vr* to get cold; to catch a cold

raffreddato (râf·frād·dâ′tō) *a* cooled; **essere** — to have a cold

raffreddore (râf·frād·dō′râ) *m* cold

raffronto (râf·frōn′tō) *m* comparison

raganella (râ·gâ·nāl′lâ) *f* rattle

ragazza (râ·gâ′tsâ) *f* girl; **nome di** — maiden name

ragazzata (râ·gâ·tsâ′tâ) *f* boyish prank

ragazzo (râ·gâ′tsō) *m* boy

raggiante (râj·jân′tā) *a* beaming, radiant

raggio (râj′jō) *m* ray; spoke; *(geom)* radius

raggirare (râj·jē·râ′rā) *vt* to swindle

raggirarsi (râj·jē·râr′sē) *vr* to turn about; to ramble

raggiro (râj·jē′rō) *m* trick; subterfuge

raggiungere * (râj·jūn′jä·rä) *vt* to reach

raggiungersi * (râj·jūn′jär·sē) *vr* to meet again; to rejoin

raggomitolare (râg·gō·mē·tō·lâ′rä) *vt* to coil; to roll up

raggomitolarsi (râg·gō·mē·tō·lâr′sē) *vr* to coil up; to roll oneself up

raggranellare (râg·grâ·nāl·lâ′rä) *vt* to scrape together

raggrinzire (râg·grēn·dzē′rä) *vt&i* to become wrinkled; to wrinkle

raggrinzirsi (râg·grēn·dzēr′sē) *vr* to become wrinkled

raggrinzito (râg·grēn·dzē′tō) *a* wrinkled

raggruppare (râg·grūp·pâ′rä) *vt* to collect; to group; to regroup

raggrupparsi (râg·grūp·pâr′sē) *vr* to cluster; to form a group

raggruzzolare (râg·grū·tsō·lâ′rä) *vt* to put together, save up

ragguaglio (râg·gwâ′lyō) *m* report; comparison

ragguardevole (râg·gwâr·de′vō·lä) *a* prominent

ragionamento (râ·jō·nâ·mān′tō) *m* argument

ragionare (râ·jō·nâ′rä) *vt* to reason; to talk

ragione (râ·jō′nä) *f* reason; motive; **— sociale** trade name; **aver —** to be right; **rendersi —** to understand; to account for; **dar —** di to explain about; **in — di 10 km all'ora** at the rate of 10 kilometers an hour; **–ria** (râ·jō·nä·rē′â) *f* accounting, bookkeeping; **–vole** (râ·jō·ne′vō·lä) *a* reasonable; **–volmente** (râ·jō·nä·vōl·mân′tä) *adv* reasonably

ragioniere (râ·jō·nyä′rä) *m* accountant

ragliare (râ·lyâ′rä) *vi* to bray

ragnatela (râ·nyâ·tā′lâ) *f* spider web

ragno (râ′nyō) *m* spider

rallegramenti (râl·lā·grâ·mān′tē) *mpl* congratulations

rallegramento (râl·lā·grâ·mān′tō) *m* rejoicing

rallegrare (râl·lā·grâ′rä) *vt* to cheer, make glad

rallegrarsi (râl·lā·grâr′sē) *vr* to be glad; **— con** to congratulate; to be glad for

rallentamento (râl·lān·tâ·mān′tō) *m* relaxing; slowing

rallentare (râl·lān·tâ′rä) *vt* to slow down

rallentarsi (râl·län·târ'sē) *vr* to slow down; to become slack; *(mech)* to get loose

ramaiolo (râ·mä·yō'lō) *m* ladle

ramanzina (râ·män·dzē'nä) *f* scolding

rame (râ'mä) *m* copper

ramificare (râ·mē·fē·kâ'rā) *vi* to branch; to ramify

ramificazione (râ·mē·fē·kâ·tsyō'nä) *f* branching; ramification

rammaricare (râm·mâ·rē·kâ'rā) *vt* to vex; to sadden; to mortify

rammaricarsi (râm·mâ·rē·kâr'sē) *vr* to complain; to regret; to grieve

rammarico (râm·mâ'rē·kō) *m* regret

rammendare (râm·män·dâ'rā) *vt* to mend; to repair; to darn

rammendo (râm·män'dō) *m* darning, mending

rammentare (râm·män·tâ'rā) *vt* to remind; to recall

rammentarsi (râm·män·târ'sē) *vr* to remember, recollect

rammollire (râm·mōl·lē'rā) *vt* to soften; to pacify

rammollirsi (râm·mōl·lēr'sē) *vr* to become effeminate; to grow senile; to become soft

rammollito (râm·mōl·lē'tō) *a* soft; senile; effeminate

ramo (râ'mō) *m* branch; line

ramolaccio (râ·mō·lä'chō) *m* radish

ramoscello (râ·mō·shäl'lō) *m* twig

rampa (râm'pä) *f* rail; ramp

rampicante (râm·pē·kân'tä) *a* climbing; — *m (bot)* creeper

rampino (râm·pē'nō) *m* hook

rampogna (râm·pō'nyä) *f* rebuke

rampollo (râm·pōl'lō) *m* scion, offspring; *(coll)* child

rampone (râm·pō'nä) *m* harpoon

rana (râ'nä) *f* frog

rancidezza (rän·chē·dä'tsä) *f* rancidity

rancido (rän'chē·dō) *a* rancid; rank

rancore (rän·kō'rä) *m* grudge; malice

randagio (rän·dâ'jō) *a* stray

randello (rän·däl'lō) *m* club, cudgel

rango (rän'gō) *m* rank, station

rannicchiarsi (rän·nēk·kyâr'sē) *vr* to crouch

rannuvolarsi (rän·nū·vō·lâr'sē) *vr* to cloud over; to darken

rantolare (rän·tō·lâ'rā) *vi* to have a rattle in one's throat

rantolo (rän'tō·lō) *m* death rattle; rattle

rapa (râ'pä) *f* turnip; **testa di** — ignoramus

rapace (râ·pâ'chä) *a* greedy; plundering;

— *m* bird of prey

rapare (râ·pâ'rā) *vt* to shave; to crop

rapida (râ'pē·dä) *f* rapids

rapidamente (râ·pē·dâ·män'tä) *adv* rapidly

rapidità (râ·pē·dē·tâ') *f* rapidity

rapido (râ'pē·dō) *a* quick; — *m* express train

rapimento (râ·pē·män'tō) *m* abduction

rapina (râ·pē'nä) *f* robbery; holdup; **–tore** (râ·pē·nâ·tō'rä) *m* holdup man

rapire (râ·pē'rä) *vt* to kidnap; to ravish

rapitore (râ·pē·tō'rä) *m* kidnapper; rapist

rappacificare (râp·pâ·chē·fē·kâ'rā) *vt* to reconcile; to pacify

rappacificarsi (râp·pâ·chē·fē·kâr'sē) *vr* to become reconciled

rappacificazione (râp·pâ·chē·fē·kâ·tsyō'nä) *f* reconciliation

rappezzare (râp·pä·tsâ'rā) *vt* to patch up

rappezzo (râp·pä'tsō) *m* patch

rapportare (râp·pōr·tâ'rā) *vt* to relate, report

rapporto (râp·pōr'tō) *m* reference; relationship; intercourse; statement; ratio; report; **rapporti sessuali** sexual relations; **in — a** in relation to; **in — di due a quattro** in the ratio of two to four; **sotto tutti i rapporti** in every respect

rappresaglia (râp·prä·zâ'lyä) *f* retaliation

rappresentante (râp·prä·zän·tân'tä) *m* representative; agent

rappresentanza (râp·prä·zän·tân'tsä) *f* agency; representation

rappresentare (râp·prä·zän·tâ'rā) *vt* to represent; to act as agent for; *(theat)* to perform

rappresentazione (râp·prä·zän·tâ·tsyō'nä) *f* representation; *(theat)* performance

raramente (râ·râ·män'tä) *adv* infrequently; rarely

rarefare * (râ·râ·fâ'rā) *vt* to rarefy

rarefazione (râ·râ·fâ·tsyō'nä) *f* rarefaction

raro (râ'rō) *a* unusual, strange; rare; hard to come by

rasare (râ·zâ'rā) *vt* to shave

raschiare (râ·skyâ'rä) *vt* to scrape

rasentare (râ·zän·tâ'rā) *vt* to brush; to touch lightly, shave

rasente (râ·zän'tä) *prep* very near, close to

raso (râ'zō) *m* satin

raso (râ'zō) *a* shaved; cut close; **–io** (râ·zô'yō) *m* razor

raspa (râ'spä) *f* rasp; **–re** (râ·spâ'rā) *vt* to scrape, rasp; to paw

rassegna (râs·sä'nyä) *f* review; **–re** (râs-

sā·nyâ′rā) *vt* to resign; **–rsi** (râs·sā·nyâr′sē) *vr* to resign oneself; **–zione** (râs·sā·nyâ·tsyō′nā) *f* resignation

rasserenare (râs·sā·rā·nâ′rā) *vt* to calm, clear up

rasserenarsi (râs·sā·rā·nâr′sē) *vr* to calm down; *(weather)* to clear up; *(sky)* to brighten

rassettare (râs·sāt·tâ′rā) *vt* to tidy up; to repair

rassicurare (râs·sē·kū·râ′rā) *vt* to reassure

rassicurarsi (râs·sē·kū·râr′sē) *vr* to make sure; to reassure oneself

rassomiglianza (râs·sō·mē·lyân′tsâ) *f* resemblance

rassomigliare (râs·sō·mē·lyâ′rā) *vi* to resemble, look like

rastrellamento (râ·strāl·lâ·mān′tō) *m* raking; *(mil)* mop up

rastrellare (râ·strāl·lâ′rā) *vt* to rake; *(mil)* to mop up

rastrello (râ·strāl′lō) *m* rake *(tool)*

rata (râ′tâ) *f* installment

rateale (râ·tā·â′lā) *a* by installments; **pagamento —** partial payment

ratealmente (râ·tā·âl·mān′tā) *adv* in installments

ratifica (râ·tē′fē·kâ) *f* ratification; **–re** (râ·tē·fē·kâ′rā) *vt* to ratify

ratto (rât′tō) *m* abduction; rape; rat

rattoppare (rât·tōp·pâ′rā) *vt* to patch

rattoppo (rât·tōp′pō) *m* patch

rattrappirsi (rât·trâp·pēr′sē) *vr* to become contracted

rattristare (rât·trē·stâ′rā) *vt* to grieve, sadden

rattristarsi (rât·trē·stâr′sē) *vr* to be sorry; to become sad

raucedine (râū·che′dē·nā) *f* hoarseness

rauco (râ′ū·kō) *a* hoarse

ravanello (râ·vâ·nāl′lō) *m* radish

ravvedersi * (rāv·vā·dār′sē) *vr* to repent

ravvedimento (râv·vā·dē·mān′tō) *m* reformation; repentance

ravviare (râv·vyâ′rā) *vt* to fix up

ravviarsi (râv·vyâr′sē) *vr* to primp; to tidy up; **i capelli** to comb one's hair

ravvisare (râv·vē·zâ′rā) *vt* to recognize

ravvivare (râv·vē·vâ′rā) *vt* to revive

ravvolgimento (râv·vōl·jē·mān′tō) *m* winding; rolling up

raziocinio (râ·tsyō·chē′nyō) *m* reason; sense; reasoning

razionale (râ·tsyō·nâ′lā) *a* rational

razionare (râ·tsyō·nâ′rā) *vt* to ration

razione (râ·tsyō′nā) *f* ration

razza (rât′tsâ) *f* race; kind; **di — pura** thoroughbred

razzia (râ·tsē′â) *f* raid

razzismo (râ·tsē′zmō) *m* racialism; racism

razzo (râ′tsō) *m* rocket; **motore a —** jet engine; **— interplanetario** spaceship

re (rā) *m* king; *(mus)* re

reagire (rā·â·jē′rā) *vi* to react

reale (rā·â′lā) *a* royal; real

realizzare (rā·â·lē·dzâ′rā) *vt* to realize; *(com)* to make a profit of; to achieve, attain; to collect

realizzarsi (rā·â·lē·dzâr′sē) *vr* to come true; to happen

realizzazione (rā·â·lē·dzâ·tsyō′nā) *f* achievement; execution; collection

realmente (rā·âl·mân′tā) *adv* really

reato (rā·â′tō) *m* crime; **corpo del —** evidence

reattore (rā·ât·tō′rā) *m* reactor; inductor; *(avi)* jet plane

reazionario (rā·â·tsyō·nâ′ryō) *a* reactionary

reazione (rā·â·tsyō′nā) *f* reaction; **— a catena** chain reaction; **propulsione a — jet** propulsion

recapitare (rā·kâ·pē·tâ′rā) *vt* to deliver

recapito (rā·kâ′pē·tō) *m* delivery address

recare (rā·kâ′rā) *vt* to bring; to take

recarsi (rā·kâr′sē) *vr* to go to; to have recourse to

recensione (rā·chān·syō′nā) *f* book review

recensionista (rā·chān·syō·nē′stâ) *f* book reviewer

recensire (rā·chān·sē′rā) *vt* to review

recente (rā·chān′tā) *a* recent; **–mente** (rā·chān·tā·mān′tā) *adv* recently

recessione (rā·chās·syō′nā) *f* recession

recidere * (rā·chē′dā·rā) *vt* to cut off

recidivo (rā·chē·dē′vō) *m* repeater; habitual offender

recinto (rā·chēn′tō) *m* enclosure

recipiente (rā·chē·pyān′tā) *m* container

reciprocamente (rā·chē·prō·kâ·mân′tā) *adv* reciprocally

reciproco (rā·chē′prō·kō) *a* mutual

reciso (rā·chē′zō) *a* cut off; curt

recita (re′chē·tâ) *f* performance, recital

recitare (rā·chē·tâ′rā) *vt* to recite; *(theat)* to perform, act; **— a soggetto** *(theat)* to improvise

reclamare (rā·klâ·mâ′rā) *vt* to claim, demand; **— vi** to complain; to file a complaint

reclame (rā·klâ′mā) *f* advertisement

reclamo (rā·klâ′mō) *m* claim, complaint

recluso (rā·klū′zō) *m* convict, recluse; **–rio** (rā·klū·zō′ryō) *m* penitentiary

---

â ârm, **ā** bāby, **e** bet, **ē** bē, **ō** gō, **ô** gône, **ū** blūe, **b** bad, **ch** child, **d** dad, **f** fat, **g** gay, **j** jet

recluta (re'klū·tâ) *f* recruit; selectee; **–mento** (rā·klū·tâ·mān'tō) *m* recruiting
recondito (rā·kôn'dē·tō) *a* hidden
redarguire (rā·dâr·gwē'rā) *vt* to scold; to censure
redattore (rā·dât·tō'rā) *m* editor
redazione (rā·dâ·tsyō'nä) *f* editorial staff; editing
redditizio (rād·dē·tē'tsyō) *a* profitable
reddito (red'dē·tō) *m* income
redentore (rā·dān·tō'rā) *m* redeemer; **il R–** the Saviour
redenzione (rā·dān·tsyō'nä) *f* redemption
redigere * (rā·dē'jā·rā) *vt* to draw up, draft; to edit
redimere * (rā·dē'mā·rā) *vt* to redeem
redimersi * (rā·dē'mār·sē) *vr* to redeem oneself
redine (re'dē·nä) *f* rein; bridle
redivivo (rā·dē·vē'vō) *a* come back to life; another of the same type, second
reduce (re'dū·chä) *m* veteran; **– a** returning
refe (rā'fä) *m* thread
referenza (rā·fā·rān'tsä) *f* reference
refettorio (rā·fāt·tô'ryō) *m* refectory; *(mil)* mess hall
refezione (rā·fā·tsyō'nä) *f* light meal, snack
refrattario (rā·frât·tâ'ryō) *a* intractable; unruly
refrigerare (rā·frē·jā·râ'rā) *vt* to refrigerate; to refresh, restore
refrigerio (rā·frē·je'ryō) *m* relief; refreshment
refurtiva (rā·fūr·tē'vâ) *f* stolen property, stolen goods
regalare (rā·gâ·lâ'rā) *vt* to present; to make a gift of
regalo (rā·gâ'lō) *m* gift, present
reggente (rāj·jān'tä) *m&f* regent
reggere * (rej'jā·rā) *vt&i* to uphold; to support; to rule
reggersi * (rej'jār·sē) *vr* to stand, endure; to control oneself
reggia (rej'jâ) *f* palace, royal residence
reggicalze (rāj·jē·kâl'tsä) *m* garter belt
reggimento (rāj·jē·mān'tō) *m* regiment
reggipetto (rāj·jē·pāt'tō), **reggiseno** (rāj·jē·sä'nō) *m* brassiere
regia (rā·jē'â) *f* directing *(movie, play)*; *(theat)* producing; **– dei tabacchi** tobacco monopoly
regime (rā·jē'mä) *m* regime; diet
regina (rā·jē'nâ) queen
regio (re'jō) *a* royal, regal
regione (rā·jō'nä) *f* district; region

regista (rā·jē'stä) *m* director *(movie, play)*; *(theat)* producer
registrare (rā·jē·strā'rā) *vt* to register; to record
registratore (rā·jē·strâ·tō'rā) *m* recorder; register; **– di cassa** cash register; **– a nastro** tape recorder
registrazione (rā·jē·strâ·tsyō'nä) *f* registration; recording
registro (rā·jē'strō) *m* register; record
regnare (rā·nyâ'rā) *vi* to reign, rule
regno (rā'nyō) *m* kingdom; rule
regola (re'gō·lâ) *f* rule; **–mento** (rā·gō·lâ·mān'tō) *m* regulation; **–re** (rā·gō·lâ'rā) *a* regular; **–re** *vt* to adjust; **–rizzare** (rā·gō·lâ·rē·dzâ'rā) *vt* to remedy; to straighten; to make regular; **–rmente** (rā·gō·lâr·mān'tä) *adv* regularly; **–rsi** (rā·gō·lâr'sē) *vr* to act, behave; **–tezza** (rā·go·lâ·tä'tsâ) *f* order; moderation; **–tore** (rā·gō·lâ·tō'rā) *m* regulator; **–tore** *a* regulating
regolo (re'gō·lō) *m* ruler; **– calcolatore** slide rule
regresso (rā·grās'sō) *m* regression
reincarnazione (rāēn·kâr·nâ·tsyō'nä) *f* reincarnation
reintegrare (rāēn·tā·grâ'rā) *vt* to reinstate
reintegrazione (rāēn·tā·grâ·tsyō'nä) *f* reinstatement
relativamente (rā·lâ·tē·vâ·mān'tä) *adv* relatively
relativo (rā·lâ·tē'vō) *a* relative; related
relatore (rā·lâ·tō'rā) *m* reporter
relazione (rā·lâ·tsyō'nä) *f* relation, connection; account, report
relegare (rā·lā·gâ'rā) *vt* to relegate; to confine, enclose
religione (rā·lē·jō'nä) *f* religion
religiosamente (rā·lē·jō·zâ·mān'tä) *adv* religiously
religioso (rā·lē·jō'zō) *a* religious
reliquia (rā·lē'kwêâ) *f* relic
relitto (rā·lēt'tō) *m* wreck, remains
remare (rā·mâ'rā) *vi* to row
rematore (rā·mâ·tō'rā) *m* oarsman
reminiscenza (rā·mē·nē·shān'tsä) *f* reminiscence, memory
remissivo (rā·mēs·sē'vō) *a* obedient; humble; docile
remo (rā'mō) *m* oar
remoto (rā·mō'tō) *a* secluded; remote; **passato –** *(gram)* past definite
rendere * (ren'dā·rā) *vt* to render; to yield; to make; to return
rendersi * (ren'dār·sē) *vr* to become; **– necessario** to become necessary; **– conto di** to realize; to take note of,

notice
rendiconto (rän·dē·kōn'tō) *m* report; statement
rendita (ren'dē·tâ) *f* income, return
rene (rā'nä) *m* kidney
renitente (rā·nē·tän'tā) *a* unwilling; opposed; **—alla leva** (*mil*) draft dodger
renna (rän'nâ) *f* reindeer
reo (rā'ō) *m&a* accused; convict; **—** *a* guilty
reostato (rā·ō'stâ·tō) *m* (*elec*) rheostat
reparto (rā·pâr'tō) *m* department; (*mil*) detachment
repentaglio (rā·pän·tâ'lyō) *m* danger, risk
repente (rā·pän'tä) *a* sudden
repentino (rā·pän·tē'nō) *a* unexpected, sudden
reperibile (rā·pā·rē'bē·lä) *a* to be found; available
reperto (rā·pär'tō) *m* (*law*) findings, evidence; (*med*) report
repertorio (rā·pär·tô'ryō) *m* repertory
replica (re'plē·kâ) *f* reply; retort; repetition
repressione (rā·prās·syō'nä) *f* repression
reprimere * (rā·prē'mä·rä) *vt* to repress, stifle; to hold back
reprimersi * (rā·prē'mär·sē) to restrain oneself, control oneself
reprobo (re'prō·bō) *a* depraved
repubblica (rā·pūb'blē·kâ) *f* republic
repulsione (rā·pūl·syō'nä) *f* repulsion
repulsivo (rā·pūl·sē'vō) *a* repellent; repulsive
reputare (rā·pū·tâ'rä) *vt* to deem, think
reputarsi (rā·pū·târ'sē) *vr* to regard oneself, think oneself
reputazione (rā·pū·tâ·tsyō'nä) *f* reputation
requie (re'kwēä) *f* rest; peace; requiem; **senza —** unceasingly
requisire (rā·kwē·zē'rä) *vt* to requisition, request
requisito (rā·kwē·zē'tō) *m* requirement
requisizione (rā·kwē·zē·tsyō'nä) *f* requisition
resa (rā'zä) *f* surrender; return; yield
residente (rā·zē·dän'tä) *a&m* resident
residenza (rā·zē·dän'tsâ) *f* residence
residuo (rā·zē'dwō) *m* remainder; residue
resina (re'zē·nä) *f* rosin; resin
resipola (rā·zē'pō·lä) *f* erysipelas
resistente (rā·sē·stän'tä) *a* strong; fast (*color*); resistant
resistenza (rā·zē·stän'tsâ) *f* resistance
resistere * (rā·zē'stä·rä) *vi* to resist, oppose; to endure, withstand
resoconto (rā·zō·kōn'tō) *m* account, report

respingere * (rā·spēn'jä·rä) *vt* to reject; to repel; **— al mittente** to return to the sender
respinto (rā·spēn'tō) *a* rejected; refused; returned to the sender
respirare (rā·spē·râ'rä) *vi* to breathe
respirazione (rā·spē·râ·tsyō'nä) *f* respiration
respiro (rā·spē'rō) *m* breath; respite; delay; **esalare l'ultimo —** to breath one's last; to die
responsabile (rā·spōn·sâ'bē·lä) *a* answerable; liable; responsible
responsabilità (rā·spōn·sâ·bē·lē·tâ') *f* responsibility; **— civile** personal liability
ressa (räs'sâ) *f* crowd, mob
restare (rā·stâ'rä) *vi* to stay, remain
restaurare (rā·stâū·râ'rä) *vt* to restore
restaurazione (rā·stâū·râ·tsyō'nä) *f* restoration
restauro (rā·stâ'ū·rō) *m* repair; restoration
restio (rā·stē'ō) *a* reluctant; obstinate
restituire (rā·stē·twē'rä) *vt* to return, bring back
restituzione (rā·stē·tū·tsyō'nä) *f* restitution
resto (rā'stō) *m* remainder; change
restringere * (rā·strēn'jä·rä) *vt* to tighten; to restrict; to cut down
restringersi * (rā·strēn'jär·sē) *vr* to shrink, contract; to restrain oneself, limit oneself
restrizione (rā·strē·tsyō'nä) *f* restriction; **— mentale** mental reservation; **senza —** unreservedly
resurrezione (rā·zūr·râ·tsyō'nä) *f* resurrection
resuscitare (rā·zū·shē·tâ'rä) *vt&i* to resuscitate; to revive
retata (rā·tâ'tâ) *f* haul; netful; police raid
rete (rā'tä) *f* net; network; (*soccer*) goal; **— metallica** wire mesh; **— ferroviaria** railway system
reticella (rā·tē·chäl'lâ) *f* hairnet; baggage rack
reticente (rā·tē·chän'tä) *a* reticent; reluctant
reticolato (rā·tē·kō·lâ'tō) *m* barbed wire
retina (re'tē·nä) *f* (*anat*) retina
retribuire (rā·trē·bwē'rä) *vt* to reward
retribuzione (rā·trē·bū·tsyō'nä) *f* compensation
retrobottega (rā·trō·bōt·tä'gâ) *f* back room of a store
retrocarica (rā·trō·kâ'rē·kâ) *f* (*mil*) breechloading; **a —** breechloading;

â ärm, **ā** bāby, **e** bet, **ē** bē, **ō** gō, **ô** gône, **ū** blūe, **b** bad, **ch** child, **d** dad, **f** fat, **g** gay, **j** jet

fucile a — breechloader

retrocedere (rā·trō·che′dā·rā) *vi* to go back, recede; — *vt* to demote

retrocessione (rā·trō·chās·syō′nā) *f* demotion; recession

retrogrado (rā·trō′grä·dō) *m* reactionary; — *a* backward, retrograde

retroguardia (rā·trō·gwâr′dyä) *f* (*mil*) rearguard

retromarcia (rā·trō·mâr′chä) *f* (*auto*) reverse gear; backing up

retroscena (rā·trō·shā′nä) *f* (*theat*) backstage

retta (rät′tâ) *f* charges; fee; **dar** — to pay attention

rettangolo (rät·tân′gō·lō) *m* rectangle

rettificare (rät·tē·fē·kâ′rā) *vt* to rectify, set right

rettificazione (rät·tē·fē·kâ·tsyô′nä) *f* rectification

rettile (ret′tē·lä) *m* reptile

rettilineo (rät·tē·lē′nä·ō) *a* rectilinear; — *m* straight line

rettitudine (rät·tē·tū′dē·nä) *f* honesty

retto (rät′tō) *a* straight; honest

rettore (rät·tō′rä) *m* director; rector; — **magnifico** university president

reuma (re′ū·mä) *m* rheumatism

reverendo (rā·vä·rän′dō) *a* reverend; — *m* ecclesiastic

revisionare (rā·vē·zyō·nâ′rä) *vt* to revise; (*mech*) to overhaul; (*com*) to audit

revisione (rā·vē·zyō′nä) *f* audit; (*mech*) overhauling

revisore (rā·vē·zō′rä) *m* reviser; auditor; — **di bozze** proofreader

revoca (re′vō·kä) *f* revocation; –**re** (rā·vō·kâ′rä) *vt* to revoke

revolver (rā·vōl′vâr) *m* revolver, pistol; –**ata** (rā·vōl·vä·râ′tâ) *f* pistol shot

riabilitare (ryä·bē·lē·tâ′rä) *vt* to rehabilitate; to reform

riabilitazione (ryä·bē·lē·tâ·tsyō′nä) *f* rehabilitation; reformation

rialzare (ryâl·tsâ′rä) *vt* to raise

rialzarsi (ryâl·tsâr′sē) *vr* to get up again; to rise

rianimare (ryä·nē·mâ′rä) *vt* to cheer up; to reanimate

rianimarsi (ryä·nē·mâr′sē) *vr* to take heart; to cheer up

riassunto (ryäs·sūn′tō) *m* recapitulation; summary

riattaccare (ryät·tâk·kâ′rä) *vt* to start again; to reattach; — **il ricevitore** to hang up the receiver

riattivare (ryät·tē·vâ′rä) *vt* to reactivate

ribalta (rē·bâl′tâ) *f* (*theat*) stage apron;

luci della — footlights

ribassare (rē·bâs·sâ′rä) *vt* to reduce; to lower; to cut (*prices*); to curtail

ribasso (rē·bâs′sō) *m* reduction, cut; curtailment

ribattere (rē·bât′tā·rä) *vt* to repel; to hit again; — *vi* to retort

ribellarsi (rē·bäl·lâr′sē) *vr* to rebel; to rise in revolt

ribelle (rē·bâl′lä) *m&a* rebel

ribellione (rē·bäl·lyō′nä) *f* rebellion

ribrezzo (rē·brä′tsō) *m* nausea; disgust

ricaduta (rē·kâ·dū′tâ) *f* relapse

ricalcare (rē·kâl·kâ′rä) *vt* to trample; to retrace; to trace (*drawing*)

ricamare (rē·kâ·mâ′rä) *vt* to embroider

ricambiare (rē·kâm·byâ′rä) *vt* to reciprocate

ricambio (rē·kâm′byō) *m* exchange, interchange; metabolism; **pezzo di** — spare part

ricamo (rē·kâ′mō) *m* embroidery

ricapitolazione (rē·kâ·pē·tō·lâ·tsyō′nä) *f* recapitulation

ricattatore (rē·kât·tâ·tō′rä) *m* blackmailer

ricatto (rē·kât′tō) *m* blackmail

ricavare (rē·kâ·vâ′rä) *vt* to derive; to get out, obtain

ricavato (rē·kâ·vâ′tō) *m* proceeds

riccamente (rēk·kâ·män′tä) *adv* richly

ricchezza (rēk·kä′tsä) *f* wealth

riccio (rē′chō) *m* curl of hair; — *a* curly

ricco (rēk′kō) *a* rich

ricerca (rē·châr′kä) *f* search; –**re** *vt* (rē·châr·kâ′rä) *vt* to search; to research; –**tezza** (rē·châr·kâ·tä′tsä) *f* affectation; –**to** (rē·châr·kâ′tō) *a* wanted; popular; affected

ricetta (rē·chät′tâ) *f* prescription, recipe

ricettatore (rē·chät·tâ·tō′rä) *m* fence, receiver of stolen goods

ricevente (rē·chä·vän′tä) *m* receiver, recipient

ricevere (rē·che′vä·rä) *vt&i* to receive

ricevimento (rē·châ·vē·män′tō) *m* reception, receipt

ricevitore (rē·châ·vē·tō′rä) *m* receiver

ricevuta (rē·châ·vū′tâ) *f* receipt

richiamare (rē·kyâ·mâ′rä) *vt* to call back; to rebuke; to recall

richiamarsi (rē·kyâ·mâr′sē) *vr* to have recourse to, resort to

richiamo (rē·kyâ′mō) *m* reproof; recall

richiedente (rē·kyä·dän′tä) *m* applicant

richiedere * (rē·kye′dä·rä) *vt* to request; to require; to apply for; to send for

richiesta (rē·kyä′stä) *f* demand

k kid, **l** let, **m** met, **n** not, **p** pat, **r** very, **s** sat, **sh** shop, **t** tell, **v** vat, **w** we, **y** yet, **z** zero

ricino (rē'chē·nō) *m* castor-oil plant; **olio di —** castor oil
ricognizione (rē·kō·nyē·tsyō'nä) *f* military reconnaissance
ricolmo (rē·kōl'mō) *a* brimful, chock-full
ricompensa (rē·kōm·pän'sâ) *f* reward
riconoscenza (rē·kō·nō·shän'tsâ) *f* gratitude
riconoscere * (rē·kō·nô'shä·rä) *vt* to recognize
riconoscimento (rē·kō·nō·shē·män'tō) *m* identification; recognition
ricordare (rē·kōr·dâ'rä) *vt&i* to remember, recall
ricordarsi (rē·kōr·dâr'sē) *vr* to remember, recall
ricordo (rē·kōr'dō) *m* souvenir; memory; recollection
ricorrere * (rē·kôr'rä·rä) *vi* to appeal; to recur; to take recourse
ricorso (rē·kōr'sō) *m* appeal
ricostituente (rē·kō·stē·twän'tä) *m* tonic; restorative
ricoverare (rē·kō·vä·râ'rä) *vt* to shelter, give refuge to
ricoverarsi (rē·kō·vä·râr'sē) *vr* to take refuge, seek shelter
ricovero (rē·kô'vä·rō) *m* refuge; shelter
ricreazione (rē·krä·â·tsyō'nä) *f* rest; recreation
ricuperare (rē·kŭ·pä·râ'rä) *vt* to regain; to salvage
ricupero (rē·kŭ'pä·rō) *m* salvage; recovery
ricusare (rē·kŭ·zâ'rä) *vt* to reject, refuse; to spurn
ridda (rēd'dâ) *f* confusion
ridere * (rē'dä·rä) *vi* to laugh
ridersi * (rē'där·sē) *vr* to make fun of
ridicolo (rē·dē'kō·lō) *a* ridiculous; funny
ridotto (rē·dōt'tō) *m* (*theat*) lobby, foyer; **— a** reduced
ridurre * (rē·dūr'rä) *vt* to reduce
ridursi * (rē·dūr'sē) *vr* to be reduced; to sink, be degraded
riduzione (rē·dū·tsyō'nä) *f* reduction; adaptation; (*mus*) arrangement
riecheggiare (ryä·kāj·jâ'rä) *vi* to resound
riempire * (ryäm·pē'rä) *vt* to fill
rievocare (ryä·vō·kâ'rä) *vt* to recall; to bring to mind
rifare * (rē·fâ'rä) *vt* to do again; redo
rifarsi * (rē·fâr'sē) *vr* to get even; to begin; to recoup; to become once more
riferire (rē·fä·rē'rä) *vt* to refer; to report
riferirsi (rē·fä·rēr'sē) *vr* to refer to; to concern, deal with
riffa (rēf'fâ) *f* raffle; lottery

rifiutare (rē·fyū·tâ'rä) *vt&i* to refuse; to deny
rifiutarsi (rē·fyū·târ'sē) *vr* to decline; to refuse
rifiuto (rē·fyū'tō) *m* refusal; rubbish; garbage; (*cards*) revoking
riflessione (rē·flās·syō'nä) *f* reflection
riflessivo (rē·flās·sē'vō) *a* thoughtful; meditative; (*gram*) reflexive
riflettere * (rē·flet'tä·rä) *vt* to reflect
riflettore (rē·flät·tō'rä) *m* searchlight; reflector
riflusso (rē·flūs'sō) *m* reflux, ebb
riforma (rē·fōr'mä) *f* reform; reformation
riformatorio (rē·fōr·mâ·tō'ryō) *m* reformatory
rifornimento (rē·fōr·nē·män'tō) *m* supply
rifornire (rē·fōr·nē'rä) *vt* to supply
rifornirsi (rē·fōr·nēr'sē) *vr* to supply oneself with, lay in a supply
rifrazione (rē·frâ·tsyō'nä) *f* refraction
rifugiarsi (rē·fū·jâr'sē) *vr* to take shelter
rifugio (rē·fū'jō) *m* shelter
riga (rē'gâ) *f* line; ruler (*measure*); (*mus*) staff
rigattiere (rē·gât·tyä'rä) *m* junkman
rigenerazione (rē·jä·nä·râ·tsyō'nä) *f* regeneration
rigidamente (rē·jē·dâ·män'tä) *adv* severely; rigidly
rigido (rē'jē·dō) *a* stiff; severe
rigore (rē·gō'rä) *m* severity; rigor
rigoroso (rē·gō·rō'zō) *a* strict; severe
riguardo (rē·gwâr'dō) *m* respect; consideration; viewpoint
rigurgitare (rē·gūr·jē·tâ'rä) *vi* to overflow; to regurgitate
rilasciare (rē·lâ·shâ'rä) *vt* to release
rilascio (rē·lâ'shō) *m* release
rilassamento (rē·lâs·sâ·män'tō) *m* slackening, relaxation
rilassarsi (rē·lâs·sâr'sē) *vr* to slacken
rilassato (rē·lâs·sâ'tō) *a* slack; loose
rilegare (rē·lä·gâ'rä) *vt* to retie; to bind (*book*); to refasten
rilevare (rē·lä·vâ'rä) *vt* to point out; to relieve
rilievo (rē·lyä'vō) *m* relief
riluttanza (rē·lūt·tân'tsâ) *f* reluctance
rima (rē'mä) *f* rhyme
rimandare (rē·mân·dâ'rä) *vt* to send back; to put off; to postpone
rimanenza (rē·mâ·nän'tsâ) *f* remainder
rimanere * (rē·mâ·nä'rä) *vi* to remain
rimarchevole (rē·mâr·ke'vō·lä) *a* remarkable, extraordinary
rimarginare (rē·mâr·jē·nâ'rä) *vt* to heal
rimarginarsi (rē·mâr·jē·nâr'sē) *vr* to heal

â ârm, **ā** bāby, **e** bet, **ē** bē, **ō** gō, **ô** gône, **ū** blūe, **b** bad, **ch** child, **d** dad, **f** fat, **g** gay, **j** jet

up
rimasuglio (rē·mâ·zū'lyō) *m* leavings; residue
rimbalzare (rēm·bâl·tsâ'rā) *vi* to bounce
rimbambito (rēm·bâm·bē'tō) *a* senile; silly
rimboccare (rēm·bōk·kâ'rā) *vt* to tuck up
rimbombo (rēm·bōm'bō) *m* roar, boom
rimborsare (rēm·bōr·sâ'rā) *vt* to refund
rimborso (rēm·bōr'sō) *m* refund
rimediare (rē·mā·dyâ'rā) *vt* to remedy
rimedio (rē·me'dyō) *m* remedy
rimenata (rē·mā·nâ'tâ) *f* upbraiding, talking-to
rimessa (rē·mās'sâ) *f* remittance; hangar; garage
rimettere * (rē·met'tä·rā) *vt* to put back, replace; to postpone; to remit
rimettersi * (rē·met'tär·sē) *vr* to get better; to resume; to put on again; (*weather*) to improve
rimodernare (rē·mō·där·nâ'rā) *vt* to modernize
rimorchiare (rē·mōr·kyâ'rā) *vt* to tow; to tug
rimorchiatore (rē·mōr·kyâ·tō'rā) *m* tugboat
rimorchio (rē·môr'kyō) *m* (*auto*) trailer
rimorso (rē·mōr'sō) *m* remorse
rimostranza (rē·mō·strân'tsâ) *f* remonstrance
rimpatriare (rēm·pâ·tryâ'rā) *vt* to repatriate
rimpiangere * (rēm·pyân'jä·rā) *vt* to regret; to feel sorry about
rimpianto (rēm·pyân'tō) *m* regret; — *a* regretted
rimproverare (rēm·prō·vā·râ'rā) *vt* to reproach
rimproverarsi (rēm·prō·vā·râr'sē) *vr* to regret; to blame oneself
rimprovero (rēm·prô'vä·rō) *m* scolding
rimunerare (rē·mū·nā·râ'rā) *vt* to reward
rimunerazione (rē·mū·nā·râ·tsyō'nâ) *f* repayment; reward
rinascimento (rē·nâ·shē·mān'tō) *m* Renaissance; rebirth
rincalzo (rēn·kâl'tsō) *m* support; reinforcement
rincaro (rēn·kâ'rō) *m* rising costs; increasing prices
rinchiudere * (rēn·kyū'dä·rā) *vt* to shut in; to enclose
rinchiudersi * (rēn·kyū'där·sē) *vr* to shut oneself up
rincrescere * (rēn·kre'shä·rā) *vi* to cause regret; to cause sorrow; **mi rincresce** I am sorry

rinforzare (rēn·fōr·tsâ'rā) *vt* to reinforce; to support, prop
rinforzarsi (rēn·fōr·tsâr'sē) *vr* to grow stronger
rinforzo (rēn·fōr'tsō) *m* reinforcement
rinfrescarsi (rēn·frā·skâr'sē) *vr* to cool off; to refresh oneself
rinfresco (rēn·frā'skō) *m* refreshment
rinfusa (rēn·fū'zâ) *f* **alla —** pell-mell, confusedly; (*com*) in bulk
ringhiare (rēn·gyâ'rā) *vi* to growl, snarl
ringhiera (rēn·gyä'râ) *f* banister, balcony
ringraziamento (rēn·grâ·tsyâ·mân'tō) *m* thanks
ringraziare (rēn·grâ·tsyâ'rā) *vt* to thank
rinnegare (rēn·nā·gâ'rā) *vt* to disown; to repudiate
rinnegato (rēn·nā·gâ'tō) *m* renegade
rinnovare (rēn·nō·vâ'rā) *vt* to renew
rinnovo (rēn·nō'vō) *m* renewal
rinoceronte (rē·nō·chā·rōn'tâ) *m* rhinoceros
rinomato (rē·nō·mâ'tō) *a* renowned, known
rintocco (rēn·tōk'kō) *m* toll, knell
rintracciare (rēn·trâ·châ'rā) *vt* to trace
rinunzia (rē·nūn'tsyâ) *f* renunciation; **–re** (rē·nūn·tsyâ'rā) *vt&i* to renounce
rinvenire * (rēn·vā·nē'rā) *vt* to find; to rediscover; — *vi* to recover one's senses
rinvio (rēn·vē'ō) *m* adjournment; postponement
rionale (ryō·nâ'lā) *a* neighborhood
rione (ryō'nā) *m* district, section, neighborhood
riparare (rē·pâ·râ'rā) *vt* to repair
ripararsi (rē·pâ·râr'sē) *vr* to take shelter
riparazione (rē·pâ·râ·tsyō'nā) *f* repair; amends
ripartizione (rē·pâr·tē·tsyō'nā) *f* allotment; distribution
ripasso (rē·pâs'sō) *m* review; repetition
ripercussione (rē·pär·kūs·syō'nā) *f* repercussion
ripetere (rē·pe'tā·rā) *vt* to repeat; to rehearse
ripetitore (rē·pā·tē·tō'rā) *m* coach; — **televisivo** television relay
ripetizione (rē·pā·tē·tsyō'nā) *f* repetition; **fucile a —** repeater rifle
ripetutamente (rē·pā·tū·tâ·mān'tā) *adv* repeatedly
ripiano (rē·pyâ'nō) *m* shelf; ledge
ripido (rē'pē·dō) *a* steep
ripiego (rē·pyä'gō) *m* expedient
ripieno (rē·pyä'nō) *a* stuffed, crammed
riporre * (rē·pōr'rā) *vt* to put back, replace

---

k kid, l let, m met, n not, p pat, r very, s sat, sh shop, t tell, v vat, w we, y yet, z zero

riportare (rē·pōr·tâ'rä) *vt* to bring back; to receive; to carry over

riposarsi (rē·pō·zâr'sē) *vr* to rest

riposo (rē·pō'zō) *m* rest

ripostiglio (rē·pō·stē'lyō) *m* closet; locker

ripresa (rē·prä'zä) *f* capture; resumption; retrieving; (*sport*) round

riprodurre * (rē·prō·dūr'rä) *vt* to reproduce

riprodursi * (rē·prō·dūr'sē) *vr* to recur; to reproduce, be reproduced

riproduzione (rē·prō·dū·tsyō'nä) *f* reproduction

ripugnante (rē·pū·nyân'tä) *a* repulsive, loathsome

ripugnare (rē·pū·nyâ'rä) *vi* to disgust; to be repugnant to

risacca (rē·zäk'kä) *f* surf

risalto (rē·zâl'tō) *m* prominence; evidence

risaputo (rē·sä·pū'tō) *a* well-known, widely known

risarcimento (rē·zâr·chē·män'tō) *m* reparation; indemnification

risarcire (rē·zâr·chē'rä) *vt* to indemnify

risata (rē·zä'tä) *f* laugh, peal of laughter

riscaldamento (rē·skäl·dä·män'tō) *m* heating, warming

riscaldare (rē·skäl·dâ'rä) *vt* to heat; to excite

riscaldarsi (rē·skäl·dâr'sē) *vr* to warm up; to become excited

riscaldo (rē·skäl'dō) *m* inflammation

riscattare (rē·skät·tâ'rä) *vt* to redeem

riscattarsi (rē·skät·târ'sē) *vr* to get revenge, get even

rischiarare (rē·skyâ·râ'rä) *vt* to light up; to make clear

rischiare (rē·skyä'rä) *vt* to risk

rischio (rē'skyō) *m* risk

risciacquare (rē·shâk'kwâ·rä) *vt* to rinse, wash out

riscontro (rē·skōn'trō) *m* reply; verification

riscossa (rē·skōs'sä) *f* revenge; rebellion; rescue

riscossione (rē·skōs'syō'nä) *f* collection

riscuotere * (rē·skwô'tä·rä) *vt* to cash; to collect

risentimento (rē·zän·tē·män'tō) *m* resentment

risentito (rē·zän·tē'tō) *a* resentful

riserva (rē·zär'vä) *f* reserve; **–re** (rē·zär·vâ'rä) *vt* to reserve; to set aside; **–to** (rē·zär·vâ'tō) *a* reserved; confidential

risiedere * (rē·zye'dä·rä) *vi* to reside

risipola (rē·zē'pō·lä) *f* erysipelas

risma (rē'zmä) *f* ream (*paper*); kind

riso (rē'zō) *m* laugh; rice

risolto (rē·zōl'tō) *a* settled, resolved

risoluto (rē·zō·lū'tō) *a* resolute

risoluzione (rē·zō·lū·tsyō'nä) *f* resolution; solution

risolvere * (rē·zōl'vä·rä) *vt&i* to resolve; to solve

risolversi * (rē·zōl'vär·sē) *vr* to end in, come to; to decide

risonanza (rē·sō·nân'tsä) *f* resonance

risorgimento (rē·sōr·jē·män'tō) *m* revival, renaissance

risorsa (rē·zōr'sä) *f* resource

risparmiare (rē·spâr·myâ'rä) *vt* to save

risparmio (rē·spâr'myō) *m* saving

rispecchiare (rē·späk·kyâ'rä) *vt* to reflect, mirror

rispettabile (rē·spät·tâ'bē·lä) *a* respectable, proper; considerable

rispettare (rē·spät·tâ'rä) *vt* to respect

rispettivamente (rē·spät·tē·vâ·män'tä) *adv* respectively

rispettivo (rē·spät·tē'vō) *a* one's own; particular, respective

rispetto (rē·spät'tō) *m* respect; **–so** (rē·spät·tō'zō) *a* respectful

rispondere * (rē·spôn'dä·rä) *vt&i* to answer, reply

risposta (rē·spō'stä) *f* answer

rissa (rēs'sä) *f* brawl

ristampa (rē·stâm'pâ) *f* reprint

ristorante (rē·stō·rân'tä) *m* restaurant; **vettura —** dining car

ristrettezza (rē·strät·tä'tsä) *f* restriction; narrowness; **— economica** financial difficulties

risultare (rē·zūl·tâ'rä) *vi* to result, end

risultato (rē·zūl·tä'tō) *m* result

risveglio (rē·zve'lyō) *m* revival; awakening

risvolta (rē·zvôl'tä) *f* lapel, cuff

ritaglio (rē·tä'lyō) *m* clipping; **— di tempo** free moment

ritardare (rē·târ·dâ'rä) *vt&i* to delay

ritardo (rē·târ'dō) *m* delay; postponement

ritegno (rē·tä'nyō) *m* restraint

ritenere * (rē·tä·nä'rä) *vt* to hold

ritenersi * (rē·tä·när'sē) *vr* to think oneself; to refrain from

ritirare (rē·tē·râ'rä) *vt* to withdraw, take back

ritirarsi (rē·tē·râr'sē) *vr* to shrink (*materials*); to retreat; to retire

ritirata (rē·tē·râ'tä) *f* water closet; bathroom, lavatory; retreat

ritiro (rē·tē'rō) *m* retirement; withdrawal

ritmo (rēt'mō) *m* cadence, rhythm

rito (rē'tō) *m* rite

ritoccare (rē·tōk·kâ'rä) *vt* to retouch

ritocco (rē·tōk′kō) *m* retouching; finishing touch

ritorcere * (rē·tôr′chä·rä) *vt* to twist; to retort

ritorcersi * (rē·tôr′chär·sē) *vr* to get twisted

ritornare (rē·tōr·nâ′rä) *vt&i* to return, go back

ritornello (rē·tōr·näl′lō) *m* refrain; (*coll*) boring repetition, same old thing

ritorno (rē·tōr′nō) *m* return; **di andata e —** round-trip

ritrattare (rē·trât·tâ′rä) *vt* to retract; to paint a portrait of

ritrattazione (rē·trât·tâ·tsyō′nä) *f* withdrawal, retraction

ritratto (rē·trât′tō) *m* portrait

ritrovare (rē·trō·vâ′rä) *vt* to meet again, meet; to find again

ritrovarsi (rē·trō·vâr′sē) *vr* to meet, meet again; to rendezvous

ritrovato (rē·trō·vâ′tō) *m* finding; expedient

ritrovo (rē·trō′vō) *m* meeting place; **— notturno** night club

ritto (rēt′tō) *a* upright; straight; erect; **—** *adv* straight ahead; directly

rituale (rē·twâ′lä) *a* customary; ritual

riunione (ryū·nyō′nä) *f* reunion; meeting

riunire (ryū·nē′rä) *vt* to assemble; to draw together

riunirsi (ryū·nēr′sē) *vr* to get together; to reunite

riuscire * (ryū·shē′rä) *vt* to succeed in; to go out again; **— negli esami** to pass one's exams; **non —** to fail

riuscita (ryū·shē′tâ) *f* outcome; success; **cattiva —** failure

riva (rē′vä) *f* shore, bank

rivale (rē·vâ′lä) *a&m* rival

rivedere * (rē·vä·dä′rä) *vt* to see again; to revise, go over; **arrivederla** good-bye, I'll be seeing you

rivelare (rē·vä·lâ′rä) *vt* to reveal, uncover

rivelarsi (rē·vä·lâr′sē) *vr* to show oneself to be, prove oneself

rivelatore (rē·vä·lâ·tō′rä) *m* revealer; (*rad*) detector

rivelazione (rē·vä·lâ·tsyō′nä) *f* revelation, uncovering

rivendicazione (rē·vän·dē·kâ·tsyō′nä) *f* vindication, vengeance

rivendita (rē·ven′dē·tâ) *f* shop; retail selling; **— di sale e tabacchi** tobacco shop, tobacconist

rivenditore (rē·vän·dē·tō′rä) *m* retailer, retail merchant

riverenza (rē·vä·rän′tsâ) *f* reverence; bow

rivestimento (rē·vä·stē·män′tō) *m* lining, covering, coating

riviera (rē·vyä′rä) *f* shore, seashore

rivincita (rē·vēn′chē·tâ) *f* revenge; (*sport*) return match

rivista (rē·vē′stä) *f* review, parade; magazine; musical comedy

rivolgersi * (rē·vôl′jär·sē) *vr* to apply to; to have recourse to, turn to

rivolta (rē·vōl′tä) *f* revolt

rivoltella (re·vōl·tāl′lâ) *f* revolver

rivoluzione (rē·vō·lū·tsyō′nä) *f* revolution

roba (rō′bâ) *f* things; stuff; belongings, possessions

robivecchio (rō·bē·vek′kyō) *m* junkman

robusto (rō·bū′stō) *m* robust; sturdy, sinewy

rocca (rōk′kâ) *f* rock; fortress

rocchetto (rōk·kät′tō) *m* spool; reel

roccia (rô′chä) *f* cliff; rock; precipice

rodere * (rô′dä·rä) *vt* to gnaw; to corrode away

rodersi * (rô′där·sē) *vr* to be worried; to be upset; **— le unghie** to bite one's nails

roditore (rō·dē·tō′rä) *m* rodent

rogna (rō′nyâ) *f* (*med*) mange; scab

rognone (rō·nyō′nä) *m* kidney

Roma (rō′mâ) *f* Rome

romano (rō·mâ′nō) *a&m* Roman

romantico (rō·mân′tē·kō) *a* romantic

romanziere (rō·mân·dzyä′rä) *m* novelist

romanzo (rō·mân′dzō) *m* novel; **— a** Romance

rombo (rōm′bō) *m* roar, thunder; (*math*) rhombus; turbot (*fish*)

rompere * (rôm′pä·rä) *vt* to break; to shatter

rompersi * (rôm′pär·sē) *vr* to get shattered; to break

rompighiaccio (rōm·pē·gyâ′chō) *m* (*naut*) icebreaker

rompiscatole (rōm·pē·skâ′tō·lä) *m* pest, bore, nuisance

ronda (rōn′dâ) *f* rounds, patrol, watch

rondella (rōn·dâl′lâ) *f* (*mech*) washer

rondine (rôn′dē·nä) *f* swallow (*bird*)

rondone (rōn·dō′nä) *m* swift (*bird*)

ronzare (rōn·dzâ′rä) *vi* to whir; to buzz; to flirt

ronzino (rōn·dzē′nō) *m* nag, jade (*horse*)

ronzio (rōn·dzē′ō) *m* buzzing, whirring

rosa (rō′zâ) *f* rose; **— dei venti** rose compass; **all'acqua di —** (*fig*) quasi; so-called

rosario (rō·zâ′ryō) *m* rosary

rosicante (rō·zē·kân′tä) *a&m* rodent

rosicchiare (rō·zēk·kyâ′rä) *vt* to nibble at,

nibble; to eat away gradually
rosmarino (rō·zmâ·rē'nō) *m* rosemary
rosolare (rō·zō·lâ'rā) *vt* to brown
rosolia (rō·zō·lē'á) *f* German measles
rosolio (rō·zō'lyō) *m* cordial, liqueur
rospo (rō'spō) *m* (*zool*) toad; **ingoiare un** — (*fig*) to swallow a bitter pill
rossetto (rōs·sāt'tō) *m* rouge; — **per le labbra** lipstick
rosso (rōs'sō) *a* red; —**re** (rōs·sō'rā) *m* blush; (*fig*) shame
rosticceria (rō·stē·chā·rē'á) *f* rotisserie
rotaia (rō·tâ'yâ) *f* rail
rotante (rō·tân'tā) *a* rotating
rotativa (rō·tâ·tē'vâ) *f* rotary press
rotella (rō·tāl'lâ) *f* caster; (*anat*) knee cap; **pattini a rotelle** roller skates
rotocalco (rō·tō·kâl'kō) *m* rotogravure
rotolare (rō·tō·lâ'rā) *vt&i* to roll up, roll
rotolarsi (rō·tō·lâr'sē) *vr* to wallow; to roll around
rotondamente (rō·tōn·dâ·mān'tā) *adv* roundly; (*coll*) frankly
rotondo (rō·tōn'dō) *a* round
rotta (rōt'tâ) *f* route; **a — di collo** (*fig*) headlong; from bad to worse
rottame (rōt·tâ'mā) *m* wreckage
rottami (rōt·tâ'mē) *mpl* ruins; rubbish
rotto (rōt'tō) *a* broken
rottura (rōt·tū'râ) *f* break; breach
rovente (rō·vān'tā) *a* red-hot
rovesciare (rō·vä·shâ'rā) *vt* to ruin, overturn, upset
rovesciarsi (rō·vä·shâr'sē) *vr* to capsize; to be upset
rovescio (rō·ve'shō) *m* reverse; **a —** inside out; upside down
rovina (rō·vē'nâ) *f* ruin; —**re** (rō·vē·nâ'rā) *vt* to ruin; —**rsi** (rō·vē·nâr'sē) to ruin oneself, become ruined; —**to** (rō·vē·nâ'tō) *a* ruined
rovistare (rō·vē·stâ'rā) *vt&i* to rummage through, sift through
rozzamente (rō·dzâ·mān'tā) *adv* awkwardly; roughly
rozzo (rō'dzō) *a* course, rough, awkward

rubare (rū·bâ'rā) *vt* to steal
rubinetto (rū·bē·nät'tō) *m* faucet, tap
rubino (rū·bē'nō) *m* ruby
rubrica (rū'brē·kâ) *f* newspaper column; address book; directory
rudemente (rū·dā·mān'tā) *adv* coarsely, rudely
rudere (rū'dā·rā) *m* ruin
rudimentale (rū·dē·mân·tâ'lā) *a* rudimentary
rudimento (rū·dē·mân'tō) *m* rudiment
ruffiano (rūf·fyâ'nō) *m* pander; go-between
ruga (rū'gâ) *f* wrinkle
ruggine (rūj'jē·nâ) *f* rust; grudge, bad blood
ruggire (rūj·jē'rā) *vi* to roar
ruggito (rūj·jē'tō) *m* roar
rullio (rūl·lē'ō) *m* rolling, roll
rullo (rūl'lō) *m* roller; cylinder
Rumania (rū·mâ·nē'á) *f* Romania
rumeno (rū·mā'nō) *a&m* Romanian
ruminante (rū·mē·nân'tā) *a&m* ruminant
rumore (rū·mō'rā) *m* noise; loudness
rumorosamente (rū·mō·rō·zâ·mān'tā) *adv* noisily, loudly
rumoroso (rū·mō·rō'zō) *a* noisy, loud
ruolo (rūō'lō) *m* list; (*theat*) role
ruota (rūō'tâ) *f* wheel
rupe (rū'pā) *f* cliff, precipice
rurale (rū·râ'lā) *a* rural
ruscello (rū·shäl'lō) *m* brook, rivulet
russare (rūs·sâ'rā) *vi* to snore
Russia (rūs'syâ) *f* Russia
russo (rūs'sō) *a&m* Russian
rustico (rū'stē·kō) *a* rustic, country
ruttare (rūt·tâ'rā) *vi* to belch
rutto (rūt'tō) *m* belch
ruvidamente (rū·vē·dâ·mān'tā) *adv* coarsely
ruvidezza (rū·vē·dā'tsâ) *f* roughness
ruvido (rū'vē·dō) *a* coarse; rough
ruzzolare (rū·tsō·lâ'rā) *vt* to knock down, topple; — *vi* to tumble down, topple over
ruzzolone (rū·tsō·lō'nâ) *m* fall, tumble

S

sabato (sâ'bâ·tō) *m* Saturday
sabbia (sâb'byâ) *f* sand
sabbioso (sâb·byō'zō) *a* sandy
sabotaggio (sâ·bō·tâj'jō) *m* sabotage
sabotare (sâ·bō·tâ'rā) *vt* to sabotage
saccarina (sâk·kâ·rē'nâ) *f* saccharine
saccente (sâ·chān'tā) *m* smart aleck; dilettante; — *a* knowing, apparently wise

saccheggiare (sâk·kāj·jâ'rā) *vt* to plunder, sack
saccheggio (sâk·kej'jō) *m* pillage, sacking
sacco (sâk'kō) *m* bag; — **a pelo** sleeping bag; — **da montagna** knapsack
saccoccia (sâk·kô'châ) *f* pocket
sacerdote (sâ·châr·dō'tā) *m* priest; —**ssa** (sâ·châr·dō·tās'sâ) *f* priestess

â ârm, ā bāby, e bet, ē bē, ō gō, ô gône, ū blūe, b bad, ch child, d dad, f fat, g gay, j jet

sacerdozio (sä·chär·dô′tzyō) *m* priest-hood

sacramento (sä·krä·mān′tō) *m* sacrament

sacrario (sä·krä′ryō) *m* sanctuary

sacrificare (sä·krē·fē·kä′rā) *vt* to sacrifice

sacrificarsi (sä·krē·fē·kär′sē) *vr* to sacrifice oneself; to make great sacrifices

sacrificio (sä·krē·fē′chō) *m* sacrifice

sacrilegio (sä·krē·le′jō) *m* sacrilege

sacro (sä′krō) *a* holy; sacred

sadismo (sä·dē′zmō) *m* sadism

saetta (sä·ät′tä) *f* arrow; lightning flash

sagace (sä·gä′chä) *a* sagacious, wise

saggezza (säj·jä′tsä) *f* prudence, wisdom

saggiare (säj·jä′rā) *vt* to taste

saggio (säj′jō) *m* wise man, savant; essay; sample; — *a* wise

sagoma (sä′gō·mä) *f* outline; shape; mold; –**re** (sä·gō·mä′rā) *vt* to form, mold

sagra (sä′grä) *f* festival; –**to** (sä·grä′tō) *m* church square

sagrestano (sä·grä·stä′nō) *m* sexton

sagrestia (sä·grä·stē′ä) *f* sacristy

saio (sä′yō) *m* (*eccl*) frock, habit

sala (sä′lä) *f* room; — **d'aspetto** waiting room; — **da ballo** dance hall; — **da pranzo** dining room

salace (sä·lä′chä) *a* salacious, racy

salame (sä·lä′mä) *m* salami

salamoia (sä·lä·mô′yä) *f* pickle, brine

salare (sä·lä′rä) *vt* to salt, put salt on

salario (sä·lä′ryō) *m* salary, wages

salatino (sä·lä·tē′nō) *m* salted cracker

salato (sä·lä′tō) *a* salted; (*fig*) very expensive, dear

saldamente (säl·dä·mān′tä) *adv* solidly, firmly

saldare (säl·dä′rä) *vt* to weld; to solder; (*com*) to balance, settle; — **un conto** to pay a bill

saldatura (säl·dä·tū′rä) *f* welding, soldering; — **ossidrica** oxyhydrogen welding

saldo (säl′dō) *m* (*com*) balance; — *a* steadfast, dependable

sale (sä′lä) *m* salt; (*fig*) wit

salgemma (säl·jäm′mä) *m* rock salt

salice (sä′lē·chä) *m* willow

salina (sä·lē′nä) *f* saltworks; salt marsh

salire * (sä·lē′rä) *vt&i* to go up, climb, rise

saliscendi (sä·lē·shän′dē) *m* latch; going up and down, up-and-down movement

salita (sä·lē′tä) *f* rise, climb

saliva (sä·lē′vä) *f* saliva

salma (säl′mä) *f* body, corpse

salmo (säl′mō) *m* psalm

salmone (säl·mō′nä) *m* salmon

salnitro (säl·nē′trō) *m* niter, saltpeter

salone (sä·lō′nä) *m* salon, hall

salotto (sä·lōt′tō) *m* living room

salsa (säl′sä) *f* sauce; –**manteria** (säl·sä·mân·tä·rē′ä) *f* delicatessen

salsedine (säl·se′dē·nä) *f* saltiness

salsiccia (säl·sē′chä) *f* sausage

salso (säl′sō) *a* salty, briny

saltare (säl·tä′rä) *vt&i* to jump; to skip

saltellare (säl·täl·lä′rä) *vi* to skip, hop, jump about

saltimbanco (säl·tēm·bân′kō) *m* mountebank; acrobat

salto (säl′tō) *m* jump, bound; precipice

saltuariamente (säl·twä·ryä·mān′tä) *adv* fitfully; desultorily

salubre (sä′lū·brä) *a* wholesome, healthful

salumeria (sä·lū·mä·rē′ä) *f* delicatessen

salumi (sä·lū′mē) *mpl* salted products

salutare (sä·lū·tä′rä) *vt* to greet; to salute; — *a* healthy

salute (sä·lū′tä) *f* health; salvation; well-being; **S—!** *interj* To your health!; **casa di** — nursing home

saluto (sä·lū′tō) *m* greeting; **saluti cordiali** cordially yours

salvacondotto (säl·vä·kōn·dōt′tō) *m* safe-conduct

salvadanaio (säl·vä·dä·nä′yō) *m* piggy bank

salvagente (säl·vä·jän′tä) *m* life belt

salvaguardia (säl·vä·gwär′dyä) *f* safeguard

salvare (säl·vä′rä) *vt* to save, rescue

salvarsi (säl·vär′sē) *vr* to take shelter; to save oneself

salvataggio (säl·vä·täj′jō) *m* rescue; **barca da** — lifeboat

salvezza (säl·vä′tsä) *f* safety; salvation

salvia (säl′vyä) *f* (*bot*) sage

salvietta (säl·vyät′tä) *f* napkin

salvo (säl′vō) *a* safe; — *adv&prep* except; — **in** safekeeping

sanatoria (sä·nä·tô′ryä) *f* indemnity; sanction

sanatorio (sä·nä·tô′ryō) *m* sanatorium

sancire (sän·chē′rä) *vt* to decree; to authorize, sanction

sandalino (sän·dä·lē′nō) *m* light kayak

sandalo (sän′dä·lō) *m* sandal

sanforizzare (sän·fō·rē·dzä′rä) *vt* to sanforize

sangue (sän′gwä) *m* blood; **al** — rare

sanguinare (sän·gwē·nä′rä) *vi* to bleed

sanguinario (sän·gwē·nä′ryō) *a* sanguinary

sanguinoso (sän·gwē·nō′zō) *a* bloody

sanguisuga (sän·gwē·sū′gä) *f* (*fig*) bloodsucker; (*zool*) leech

---

k kid, **l** let, **m** met, **n** not, **p** pat, **r** very, **s** sat, **sh** shop, **t** tell, **v** vat, **w** we, **y** yet, **z** zero

sanitario (sâ·nē·tâ′ryō) *a* sanitary; **ufficio**
— health officer
sano (sâ′nō) *a* sane; wholesome; — **e salvo**
safe and sound
santamente (sân·tâ·mān′tä) *adv* piously
santificare (sân·tē·fē·kâ′rä) *vt* to sanctify;
to canonize
santità (sân·tē·tâ′) *f* holiness
santo (sân′tō) *a* holy; — *m* saint; **-la** (sân′-tō·lä) *f* godmother; **-lo** (sân′tō·lō) *m* godfather
santuario (sân·twâ′ryō) *m* shrine
sanzione (sân·tsyō′nä) *f* sanction
sapere * (sâ·pā′rä) *vt&i* to know; to taste of; to smell of; — *m* erudition, learning
sapido (sâ′pē·dō) *a* tasty, delectable, delicious
sapiente (sâ·pyän′tä) *a* learned; — *m&f* scholar; **-mente** (sâ·pyēn·tâ·mān′tä) *adv* wisely, learnedly
sapientone (sâ·pyän·tō′nä) *m* wiseacre, smart aleck; dabbler, dilettante
sapienza (sâ·pyän′tsä) *f* wisdom
saponata (sâ·pō·nâ′tâ) *f* lather; soapy water
sapone (sâ·pō′nä) *m* soap; — **da bucato** laundry soap; — **da barba** shaving stick; shaving cream; **-tta** (sâ·pō·nät′tâ) *f* cake of soap
saponiera (sâ·pō·nyä′râ) *f* soap dish
sapore (sâ·pō′rä) *m* taste, savor
saporito (sâ·pō·rē′tō) *a* tasty, delectable
sarcasmo (sâr·kâ′zmō) *m* sarcasm
sarcastico (sâr·kâ′stē·kō) *a* sarcastic
sarda (sâr·dâ), **sardella** (sâr·dāl′lâ), **sardina** (sâr·dē′nâ) *f* sardine
Sardegna (sâr·dā′nyâ) *f* Sardinia
sardo (sâr′dō) *a&m* Sardinian
sardonico (sâr·dô′nē·kō) *a* scornful, sardonic
sarta (sâr′tâ) *f* dressmaker, seamstress
sarto (sâr′tō) *m* tailor; **-ria** (sâr·tō·rē′â) *f* tailor shop
sasso (sâs′sō) *m* stone
sassofonista (sâs·sō·fō·nē′stâ) *m* saxophone player
sassofono (sâs·sô′fō·nō) *m* saxophone
satellite (sâ·tel′lē·tä) *m* satellite
satira (sâ′tē·râ) *f* satire
satiro (sâ′tē·rō) *m* satyr
saturazione (sâ·tū·râ·tsyō′nä) *f* saturation
saturnismo (sâ·tūr·nē′zmō) *m* lead poisoning
saturo (sâ′tū·rō) *a* saturated
savio (sâ′vyō) *a* wise; well-behaved
saziare (sâ·tsyâ′rä) *vt* to sate; to satisfy completely
saziarsi (sâ·tsyâr′sē) *vr* to tire of; to be

come sated
sazietà (sâ·tsyā·tâ′) *f* surfeit, satiety
sazio (sâ′tsyō) *a* full, satiated
sbadataggine (zbâ·dâ·tâj′jē·nä) *f* carelessness
sbadatamente (zbâ·dâ·tâ·mān′tä) *adv* carelessly
sbadato (zbâ·dâ′tō) *a* careless
sbadigliare (zbâ·dē·lyâ′rä) *vi* to yawn
sbadiglio (zbâ·dē′lyō) *m* yawn
sbagliare (zbâ·lyâ′rä) *vi* to make a mistake, commit an error; — *vt* to miss; to misjudge
sbagliato (zbâ·lyâ′tō) *a* wrong, mistaken
sbaglio (zbâ′lyō) *m* mistake; error
sballare (zbâl·lâ′rä) *vt* to unpack; **sballarle grosse** *(fig)* to talk big; to tell tall tales
sballato (zbâl·lâ′tō) *a* false; *(fig)* unbalanced; foolish
sbalordimento (zbâ·lōr·dē·mān′tō) *m* amazement, astonishment
sbalordire (zbâ·lōr·dē′rä) *vt* to astound
sbalordirsi (zbâ·lōr·dēr′sē) *vr* to be astounded, be amazed
sbalorditivo (zbâ·lōr·dē·tē′vō) *a* amazing, astounding
sbalzare (zbâl·tsâ′rä) *vt* to overthrow; to discharge, to dismiss
sbalzo (zbâl′tsō) *m* leap; jump; **a** — **in bas-relief**
sbandamento (zbân·dâ·mān′tō) *m* dispersing; disbanding; *(auto)* skidding; *(naut)* listing
sbandare (zbân·dâ′rä) *vi* to swerve; to go out of control; — *vt* to break up, scatter
sbandarsi (zbân·dâr′sē) *vr* to disband; *(auto)* to skid; *(naut)* to heel, tip
sbaragliare (zbâ·râ·lyâ′rä) *vt* to rout, scatter, set to flight
sbaraglio (zbâ·râ′lyō) *m* hubbub; rout; dispersion; *(fig)* jeopardy; **gettarsi allo** — to jeopardize oneself, put oneself in a dangerous position
sbarazzare (zbâ·râ·tsâ′rä) *vt* to rid; to clear; to disencumber, extricate
sbarazzarsi (zbâ·râ·tsâr′sē) *vr* to dispose of; to get rid of
sbarazzino (zbâ·râ·tsē′nō) *m* urchin, scamp, mischief
sbarbare (zbâr·bâ′rä) *vt* to shave
sbarbarsi (zbâr·bâr′sē) *vr* to shave
sbarbatello (zbâr·bâ·tāl′lō) *m* stripling, young lad
sbarcare (zbâr·kâ′rä) *vt&i* to land; — **il lunario** to make both ends meet
sbarco (zbâr′kō) *m* landing; disembarkation

â ârm, ā bāby, e bet, ē bē, ō gō, ô gône, ū blūe, b bad, ch child, d dad, f fat, g gay, j jet

sbarra (zbâr′râ) *f* lever; crowbar; *(print)* dash; *(naut)* tiller; **–mento** (zbâr·râ·mān′tō) *m* barrier; barrage; **–re** (zbâr·râ′rā) *vt* to bar

sbattere (zbât′tā·rā) *vt* to slam, bang; to stamp; to beat *(eggs)*; **— gli occhi** to blink one's eyes

sbellicarsi (zbäl·lē·kâr′sē) *vr* **— dalle risa** to split one's sides with laughter

sberleffo (zbär·lāf′fō) *m* grimace; scar

sbiadire (zbyâ·dē′rā) *vi* to fade, fade out

sbieco (sbyā′kō) *a* oblique; awry; **di —** askance; askew

sbigottito (zbē·gōt·tē′tō) *a* dismayed

sbilanciare (zbē·lân·châ′rā) *vt&i* to unbalance; *(fig)* to derange

sbilanciarsi (zbē·lân·châr′sē) *vr* to lose one's balance; *(fig)* to live beyond one's income

sbirciare (zbēr·châ′rā) *vt&i* to eye, ogle, glance at, peer at

sbirro (zbēr′rō) *m (coll)* cop

sbizzarrirsi (zbē·dzâr·rēr′sē) *vr* to follow one's whims

sboccare (zbōk·kâ′rā) *vi* to flow into

sboccato (zbōk·kâ′tō) *a* foulmouthed

sbocciare (zbō·châ′rā) *vi* to bloom

sbocco (zbōk′kō) *m* outlet

sbollire (zbōl·lē′rā) *vi* to stop boiling; *(fig)* to calm down

sbornia (zbôr′nyâ) *f* intoxication

sborsare (zbōr·sâ′rā) *vt* to pay out, lay out

sbottonare (zbōt·tō·nâ′rā) *vt* to unbutton

sbottonarsi (zbōt·tō·nâr′sē) *vi* to open up; *(fig)* to speak freely

sbraitare (zbrâē·tâ′rā) *vi* to shout; to shriek

sbranare (zbrâ·nâ′rā) *vt* to rip to shreds

sbrigare (zbrē·gâ′rā) *vt* to finish off; to hurry up

sbrigarsi (zbrē·gâr′sē) *vr* to rush, hurry up

sbrigativamente (zbrē·gâ·tē·vâ·mān′tā) *adv* promptly, rapidly

sbrigliato (zbrē·lyâ′tō) *a* unbridled, untrammeled

sbrinatore (zbrē·nâ·tō′rā) *m* defroster

sbrogliare (zbrō·lyâ′rā) *vt* to unravel; to untangle; to clear away

sbrogliarsi (zbrō·lyâr′sē) *vr* to rid oneself of; to untangle oneself

sbronzo (zbrōn′dzō) *a (sl)* drunk

sbucare (zbū·kâ′rā) *vi* to come out

sbucciare (zbū·châ′rā) *vt* to peel

sbuffare (zbūf·fâ′rā) *vi* to pant; to puff

scabbia (skâb′byâ) *f* scabies; mange

scabroso (skâ·brō′zō) *a* rugged; hard; complicated

scacchi (skâk′kē) *mpl* chess; **a —** check-ered

scacchiera (skâk·kyā′râ) *f* chessboard

scacciare (skâ·châ′rā) *vt* to drive out, eject; to disperse, scatter

scacco (skâk′kō) *m* square; chessboard; **subire uno — to** suffer a defeat; **— matto** checkmate

scadente (skâ·dān′tā) *a* of poor quality, inferior

scadenza (skâ·dān′tsâ) *f* expiration

scadere * (skâ·dā′rā) *vi* to fall due

scaduto (skâ·dū′tō) *a* expired, run out

scafandro (skâ·fân′drō) *m* deep-sea diving

scaffale (skâf·fâ′lâ) *m* shelf

scafo (skâ′fō) *m* hull of a ship

scaglia (skâ′lyâ) *f* scale *(fish)*; flake; shell *(tortoise)*; spangle; chip

scagliare (skâ·lyâ′rā) *vt* to hurl

scagliarsi (skâ·lyâr′sē) *vr* to hurl oneself at, rush at

scagliola (skâ·lyō′lâ) *f* plaster of Paris

scala (skâ′lâ) *f* stairs, ladder; **–re** (skâ·lâ′rā) *vt* to scale down, reduce; to climb, ascend; **–re** *a* graduated

scalcinato (skâl·chē·nâ′tō) *a (fig)* seedy, shabby; run-down

scaldabagno (skâl·dâ·bâ′nyō) *m* water heater

scaldare (skâl·dâ′rā) *vt* to warm up, heat

scaldarsi (skâl·dâr′sē) *vr* to warm up; to get roiled up

scalea (skâ·lā′â) *f* stairway

scalfittura (skâl·fēt·tū′râ) *f* scratch, scrape

scalinata (skâl·lē·nâ′tâ) *f* stairway

scalino (skâ·lē′nō) *m* step

scalmanato (skâl·mâ·nâ′tō) *a* excited, upset

scalo (skâ′lō) *m* port of call; **— merci** freight yard; **senza —** nonstop

scalogna (skâ·lō′nyâ) *f* jinx, whammy

scalpello (skâl·pāl′lō) *m* chisel; *(med)* scalpel

scaltrezza (skâl·trâ′tsâ) *f* sharpness, artfulness

scaltro (skâl′trō) *a* shrewd

scalzo (skâl′tsō) *a* barefooted

scambiare (skâm·byâ′rā) *vt* to take for, exchange

scambio (skâm′byō) *m* exchange; *(com)* trade

scampagnàta (skâm·pâ·nyâ′tâ) *f* picnic

scampare (skâm·pâ′rā) *vt&i* to avoid; to escape; to get out of

scampo (skâm′pō) *m* escape; prawn

scampolo (skâm′pō·lō) *m* remnant; mill end

scanalatura (skâ·nâ·lâ·tū′râ) *f* rabbet *(carpentry)*; channeling

k kid, **l** let, **m** met, **n** not, **p** pat, **r** very, **s** sat, **sh** shop, **t** tell, **v** vat, **w** we, **y** yet, **z** zero

scandaglio (skăn·dä′lyō) *m (naut)* sounding; sounding line

scandalistico (skăn·dä·lē′stē·kō) *a* sensational

scandalizzare (skăn·dä·lē·dzä′rā) *vt* to scandalize

scandalizzarsi (skăn·dä·lē·dzär′sē) *vr* to be scandalized

scandalo (skăn′dä·lō) *m* scandal; **pietra dello —** stumbling block; **–so** (skăn·dä·lō′zō) *a* shocking; libelous

Scandinavia (skăn·dē·nä′vyä) *f* Scandinavia

scandinavo (skăn·dē′nä·vō) *a* Scandinavian

scannare (skăn·nä′rā) *vt* to butcher

scansafatiche (skăn·sä·fä·tē′kä) *m* loafer, ne'er-do-well

scansare (skăn·sä′rā) *vt* to dodge; to shun; to avoid

scansarsi (skăn·sär′sē) *vr* to dodge; to step aside, get out of the way

scansia (skăn·sē′ä) *f* shelf; bookcase

scanso (skăn′sō) *m* avoidance; **a — di malintesi** in order to avoid misunderstandings

scantinato (skăn·tē·nä′tō) *m* basement

scanzonato (skăn·tsō·nä′tō) *a* free and easy, devil-may-care; frisky

scapaccione (skä·pä·chō′nä) *m* cuff, slap

scapestrato (skä·pä·strä′tō) *m* rake; **— a** dissolute

scapigliato (skä·pē·lyä′tō) *a* disheveled

scapito (skä′pē·tō) *m* detriment

scapola (skä′pō·lä) *f* shoulder blade; scapula

scapolo (skä′pō·lō) *m* bachelor

scappamento (skăp·pä·män′tō) *m* gas escape; *(mech)* exhaust

scappare (skăp·pä′rā) *vi* to flee; to escape; **lasciarsi — l'occasione** to miss one's chance; **lasciarsi — la parola** to let a word slip, forget oneself

scappata (skăp·pä′tä) *f* escapade; excursion

scappatoia (skăp·pä·tô′yä) *f* means of escaping; loophole

scarabocchiare (skä·rä·bōk·kyä′rä) *vt&i* to scrawl

scarabocchio (skä·rä·bôk′kyō) *m* blot; scribble, scrawl

scarafaggio (skä·rä·fäj′jō) *m* bug; cockroach

scaramuccia (skä·rä·mū′chä) *f* skirmish

scaraventare (skä·rä·vän·tä′rä) *vt* to hurl, throw

scaraventarsi (skä·rä·vän·tär′sē) *vr* to throw oneself

scarcerare (skär·chä·rä′rä) *vt* to release from prison

scaricare (skä·rē·kä′rä) *vt* to unload; to discharge

scaricarsi (skä·rē·kär′sē) *vr* to run down *(timepiece)*; to relieve oneself; to empty into

scaricatore (skä·rē·kä·tō′rä) *m* stevedore

scarico (skä′rē·kō) *m* discharge; **— a** discharged; not loaded; **tubo di —** exhaust pipe, **a — di coscienza** in order to relieve one's mind, to ease one's conscience

scarlattina (skär·lät·tē′nä) *f* scarlet fever

scarno (skär′nō) *a* emaciated

scarola (skä·rō′lä) *f* escarole

scarpa (skär′pä) *f* shoe

scarseggiare (skär·säj·jä′rä) *vi* to be scarce; to be short in supply

scarsità (skär·sē·tä′) *f* scarcity, dearth

scarso (skär′sō) *a* scarce, short

scarto (skär′tō) *m* rejected goods; dodge, side movement

scassinare (skäs·sē·nä′rä) *vt* to break into

scassinatore (skäs·sē·nä·tō′rä) *m* burglar

scasso (skäs′sō) *m* housebreaking; burglary

scatenare (skä·tä·nä′rä) *vt* to unchain; *(fig)* to cause

scatenarsi (skä·tä·när′sē) *vr* to break loose; *(fig)* to fly into a rage

scatola (skä′tō·lä) *f* box; **in —** canned; **–me** (skä·tō·lä′mä) *m* canned goods

scattare (skät·tä′rä) *vi* to spring up; *(photo)* to click *(shutter)*

scatto (skät′tō) *m* outburst; click; spring lock

scaturire (skä·tū·rē′rä) *vi* to spring, gush up

scavare (skä·vä′rä) *vt* to dig up, uncover

scavatrice (skä·vä·trē′chä) *f* excavating machine

scavo (skä′vō) *m* excavation

scegliere * (shē′lyä·rä) *vt* to choose

scelleratezza (shāl·lä·rä·tä′tsä) *f* wickedness, evil

scellerato (shāl·lä·rä′tō) *a* wicked; **— m** miscreant

scelta (shāl′tä) *f* choice, selection

scelto (shāl′tō) *a* chosen; choice, select

scemenza (shā·män′tsä) *f* foolishness

scemo (shā′mō) *a* foolish; stupid; **— m** fool

scempiaggine (shām·pyäj′jē·nä) *f* foolishness

scempio (shem′pyō) *m* devastation; confusion; massacre, slaughter

scena (shā′nä) *f* scene; stage; **–rio** (shä·

nâ'ryō) *m* scenario; *(theat)* set; **–rista**
(shā·nâ·rē'stâ) *m* scriptwriter; **–ta** (shā·
nâ'tâ) *f* row, scene
scendere * (shen'dā·rā) *vi* to get down, go
down, come down
sceneggiatore (shā·nāj·jâ·tō'rā) *m* scenar-
ist, movie writer; TV writer
scenografia (shā·nō·grâ·fē'â) *f* scene
painting; scenography
scenografo (shā·nō'grâ·fō) *m* scene painter
scervellarsi (shār·vāl·lâr'sē) *vr* to cudgel
one's brains, ponder deeply
scettro (shāt'trō) *m* scepter
scheda (skā'dâ) *f* index card; ballot; **–re**
(skā·dâ'rā) *vt* to classify; **–rio** (skā·dâ'-
ryō) *m* card file
schedina (skā·dē'nâ) *f* index card; **— del
totocalcio** football pool ticket
scheggia (skej'jâ) *f* chip; splinter
scheletro (ske'lā·trō) *m* skeleton
schema (skā'mâ) *m* outline, sketch; plan,
blueprint
schematicamente (skā·mâ·tē·kâ·mān'tâ)
adv schematically
scherma (skār'mâ) *f* fencing
schermitore (skār·mē·tō'rā) *m* fencer
schermo (skār'mō) *m* screen *(TV, movies)*;
defense, protection
schernire (skār·nē'rā) *vt* to mock, make
fun of
scherno (skār'nō) *m* ridicule; contempt;
sneering
scherzare (skār·tsā'rā) *vi* to joke; to trifle
scherzo (skār'tsō) *m* joke; trick *(mischief)*;
–so (skār·tsō'zō) *a* playful; **–samente**
(skār·tsō·zâ·mān'tâ) *adv* jokingly, play-
fully
schiaccianoci (skyâ·châ·nō'chē) *m* nut-
cracker
schiacciante (skyâ·chân'tâ) *a* overwhelming, decisive
schiacciare (skyâ·châ'rā) *vt* to crush; to
put down, quell
schiacciarsi (skyâ·châr'sē) *vr* to be
crushed; to be squashed; to be sup-
pressed
schiaffo (skyâf'fō) *m* slap
schiamazzare (skyâ·mâ·tsâ'rā) *vi* to howl,
clamor; to squawk
schiamazzo (skyâ·mâ'tsō) *m* howling;
shouting; clamor
schianto (skyân'tō) *m* clap, crash; noise;
(fig) pang; **di —** suddenly
schiarire (skyâ·rē'rā) *vt* to clear up; **— vi**
to fade
schiarirsi (skyâ·rēr'sē) *vr* to grow light;
to become clear, lighten
schiavista (skyâ·vē'stâ) *m* slave trader;

stato — slave state
schiavitù (skyâ·vē·tū') *f* slavery
schiavo (skyâ'vō) *m&a* slave
schiena (skyā'nâ) *f* *(anat)* back; **–le**
(skyā·nâ'lā) *m* back *(chair)*
schiera (skyā'râ) *f* band, group; *(mil)* rank;
–rsi (skyā·râr'sē) *vr* *(mil)* to draw up
schiettamente (skyāt·tâ·mān'tâ) *adv*
straightforwardly, frankly
schiettezza (skyāt·tā'tsâ) *f* openness;
frankness
schietto (skyāt'tō) *a* sincere, frank
schifare (skē·fâ'rā) *vt* to loathe
schifiltoso (skē·fēl·tō'zō) *a* fastidious
schifo (skē'fō) *m* disgust; **fare — a** to
make sick, be repugnant to; **–so** (skē·
fō'zō) *a* disgusting
schioppo (skyōp'pō) *m* shotgun
schiuma (skyū'mâ) *f* froth, foam
schizzare (skē·tsâ'rā) *vt&i* to splash; to
sketch
schizzinoso (skē·tsē·nō'zō) *a* snooty
(coll); fastidious; hypercritical
schizzo (skē'tsō) *m* sketch; splash; squirt
sci (shē) *m* ski; **— nautico** water ski; **fare
il — nautico** to water-ski
scia (shē'â) *f* wake; track
sciabola (shâ'bō·lâ) *f* saber
sciacquare (shâk·kwâ'rā) *vt* to rinse
sciacquarsi (shâk·kwâr'sē) *vr* to rinse out
one's mouth
sciagura (shâ·gū'râ) *f* misfortune; accident; adversity; **–to** (shâ·gū·râ'tō) *m*
wretch; **–to** *a* unhappy; unfortunate
scialacquare (shâ·lâk·kwâ'rā) *vt* to
squander
scialbo (shâl'bō) *a* pallid, drab; vague
scialle (shâl'lā) *m* shawl
scialuppa (shâ·lūp'pâ) *f* launch
sciamare (shâ·mâ'rā) *vi* to swarm; to
crowd together
sciame (shâ'mā) *m* swarm
sciampagna (shâm·pâ'nyâ) *f* champagne
sciampagnino (shâm·pâ·nyē'nō) *m* soft
drink
sciampagnone (shâm·pâ·nyō'nā) *m* playboy
sciancato (shân·kâ'tō) *m* cripple; **— a**
lame, crippled
sciare (shâ'rā) *vi* to ski
sciarada (shâ·râ'dâ) *f* charade
sciarpa (shâr'pâ) *f* scarf, muffler; sash
sciatore (shâ·tō'rā) *m* skier
sciatto (shât'tō) *a* slovenly, untidy, unkempt
scibile (shē'bē·lā) *m* knowledge, information
scientificamente (shān·tē·fē·kâ·mān'tâ)

adv scientifically
scientifico (shän·tē'fē·kō) *a* scientific
scienza (shän'tsâ) *f* science
scienziato (shän·tsyâ'tō) *m* scientist
scilinguagnolo (shē·lēn·gwâ'nyō·lō) *m (anat)* tongue ligament; *(coll)* **aver lo — sciolto** to have a gift for gab; to be a great talker
scimmia (shēm'myâ) *f* monkey, ape
scimmiottare (shēm·myōt·tâ'rā) *vt&i* to imitate; to mimic; to parody
scimunito (shē·mū·nē'tō) *a* foolish, moronic; — *m* moron, fool
scindere * (shēn'dä·rā) *vt* to split
scintilla (shēn·tēl'lâ) *f* sparkle; **—nte** (shēn·tēl·lân'tä) *a* sparkling; **—re** (shēn·tēl·lâ'rā) *vi* to sparkle
scioccamente (shōk·kâ·mān'tä) *adv* foolishly, nonsensically
sciocchezza (shōk·kā'tsâ) *f* nonsense; trifle
sciocco (shōk'kō) *a* foolish, silly; nonsensical
sciogliere * (shô'lyä·rā) *vt* to unite; to solve; to free; **— la lingua** to become talkative; **— un voto** to fulfill a vow; **— un dubbio** to settle a doubt; **— un contratto** to annul a contract
sciogliersi * (shô'lyär·sē) *vr* to dissolve, melt; to get loose
scioglilingua (shō·lyē·lēn'gwâ) *m* tongue-twister
sciolto (shōl'tō) *a* loose; unrestrained; free
scioperante (shō·pä·rân'tä) *m* striker *(labor)*; **—** *a* striking
scioperare (shō·pä·rä'rā) *vi* to go on strike
scioperato (shō·pä·rä'tō) *a&m* ne'er-do-well
sciopero (shô'pä·rō) *m* strike
sciovia (shō·vē'â) *f* ski lift
sciovinismo (shō·vē·nē'zmō) *m* chauvinism
scipito (shē·pē'tō) *a* dull; tasteless
scirocco (shē·rōk'kō) *m* hot, dry wind; sirocco
sciroppo (shē·rōp'pō) *m* syrup
scissione (shēs·syō'nâ) *f* fission; split
sciupare (shū·pâ'rā) *vt* to spoil; to waste
sciuparsi (shū·pâr'sē) *vr* to spoil, get spoiled
sciupone (shū·pō'nä) *m* squanderer, spendthrift, wastrel
scivolare (shē·vō·lâ'rā) *vi* to slide; to slip
scivolone (shē·vō·lō'nä) *m* slip *(footing)*
scocciante (skō·chân'tä) *a* tiresome, annoying
scocciare (skō·châ'rā) *vt (coll)* to bother, annoy; to shell *(nut)*; to break *(egg)*
scocciarsi (skō·châr'sē) *vr* to become

bored; to be annoyed
scodella (skō·dāl'lâ) *f* soup plate; bowl; **—re** (skō·dāl·lâ'rā) *vt* to dish up, serve
scodinzolare (skō·dēn·tsō·lâ'rā) *vi* to wag its tail
scogliera (skō·lyä'râ) *f* cliff
scoglio (skō'lyō) *m* rock; *(fig)* problem
scoiattolo (skō·yât'tō·lō) *m* squirrel
scolare (skō·lâ'rā) *vt&i* to drain
scolaresca (skō·lâ·rä'skâ) *f* school children
scolastico (skō·lâ'stē·kō) *a* scholastic; **anno —** school year
scolaro (skō·lâ'rō) *m* pupil
scollacciato (skōl·lâ·châ'tō) *a* low-necked, décolleté; suggestive, risqué
scollatura (skōl·lâ·tū'râ) *f* ungluing; decolletage
scolo (skō'lō) *m* drainpipe; drain; drainage; *(sl)* gonorrhea
scolorina (skō·lō·rē'nâ) *f* ink eradicator
scolorire (skō·lō·rē'rā) *vi* to fade
scolorirsi (skō·lō·rēr'sē) *vr* to get pale; to lose one's color
scolorito (skō·lō·rē'tō) *a* discolored
scolpire (skōl·pē'rā) *vt* to sculpture, sculpt
scombro (skōm'brō) *m* mackerel
scombussolare (skōm·būs·sō·lâ'rā) *vt* to upset; to confuse, disorganize
scommessa (skōm·mäs'sâ) *f* wager, bet
scommettere * (skōm·met'tä·rā) *vt* to bet
scomodare (skō·mō·dâ'rā) *vt* to disturb; to put out
scomodarsi (skō·mō·dâr'sē) *vr* to disturb oneself; to put oneself out
scomodo (skō'mō·dō) *a* uncomfortable, inconvenient; — *m* discomfort
scomparire * (skōm·pâ·rē'rā) *vi* to disappear
scomparsa (skōm·pâr'sâ) *f* disappearance
scompartimento (skōm·pâr·tē·mân'tō) *m* compartment; section
scompigliare (skōm·pē·lyâ'rā) *vt* to disarrange, upset; to disorganize
scompiglio (skōm·pē'lyō) *m* to-do *(coll)*; bustle; disorder
scomporre * (skōm·pōr'rā) *vt* to take apart; *(fig)* to ruffle, upset; *(math)* to resolve
scomporsi * (skōm·pōr'sē) *vr* to get mad, lose one's temper; to become decomposed, decompose
scomunica (skō·mū'nē·kâ) *f* excommunication
sconcertare (skōn·châr·tâ'rā) *vt* to baffle, disconcert, upset
sconcertante (skōn·châr·tân'tä) *a* baffling, upsetting

sconcezza (skōn·chā′tsâ) *f* immodesty; obscenity

sconcio (skôn′chō) *a* indecent; — *m* shame; indecency

sconclusionato (skōn·klū·zyō·nâ′tō) *a* disjointed; rambling; meaningless

sconfiggere * (skōn·fēj′jä·rä) *vt* to defeat

sconfinato (skōn·fē·nâ′tō) *a* limitless, boundless

sconfitta (skōn·fēt′tâ) *f* defeat

sconforto (skōn·fōr′tō) *m* discomfort, distress; depression

scongiurare (skōn·jū·râ′rä) *vt* to implore; to plead

scongiuro (skōn·jū′rō) *m* plea; exorcism

sconnesso (skōn·nās′sō) *a* disconnected

sconosciuto (skō·nō·shū′tō) *a* unknown; — *m* stranger

sconquassare (skōn·kwâs·sâ′rä) *vt* to wreck; to smash

sconquasso (skōn·kwâs′sō) *m* ruin; smash

sconsigliare (skōn·sē·lyä′rä) *vt* to discourage; to convince against

sconsolato (skōn·sō·lâ′tō) *a* disconsolate, grieving

scontare (skōn·tâ′rä) *vt* to pay for, do penance for; *(com)* to discount

scontento (skōn·tän′tō) *a* dissatisfied; — *m* discontent

sconto (skōn′tō) *m* discount; allowance

scontrino (skōn·trē′nō) *m* check, ticket

scontro (skōn′trō) *m* crash, collision; *(sport)* bout, match

scontroso (skōn·trō′zō) *a* touchy, hypersensitive

sconvolgere (skōn·vôl′jä·rä) *vt* to throw into disorder; to upset, turn over

sconvolto (skōn·vōl′tō) *a* troubled, upset

scopa (skō′pâ) *f* broom; **–re** (skō·pâ′rä) *vt&i* to sweep

scoperta (skō·pär′tâ) *f* discovery

scoperto (skō·pär′tō) *a* uncovered; bare

scopo (skō′pō) *m* purpose, aim, objective

scoppiare (skōp·pyä′rä) *vi* to burst; to break out; — **dall'invidia** to turn green with envy; — **in pianto** to burst into tears

scoppio (skôp′pyō) *m* explosion; **motore a** — internal combustion engine

scoprire * (skō·prē′rä) *vt* to discover; to uncover

scoprirsi * (skō·prēr′sē) *vr* to make one's purpose known; *(coll)* to tip one's hat

scoraggiamento (skō·râj·jâ·mān′tō) *m* discouragement, dejection

scoraggiare (skō·râj·jä′rä) *vt* to discourage, deject

scoraggiarsi (skō·râj·jâr′sē) *vr* to lose

heart, become downhearted

scorciatoia (skōr·châ·tô′yâ) *f* shortcut

scordare (skōr·dâ′rä) *vt* to put out of tune; to forget

scordarsi (skōr·dâr′sē) *vr* to forget; to get out of tune

scorgere * (skôr′jä·rä) *vt* to perceive, observe, see

scoria (skô′ryâ) *f* scum; dross

scorno (skōr′nō) *m* disgrace, shame

scorpacciata (skōr·pâ·châ′tâ) *f* bellyful

scorrere * (skôr′rä·rä) *vt* to scan; — *vi* to pass, go by *(time)*; to flow by, run by

scorrettamente (skōr·rät·tâ·mān′tä) *adv* unsuitably, incorrectly

scorrettezza (skōr·rät·tä′tsâ) *f* misbehavior; faultiness

scorretto (skōr·rät′tō) *a* incorrect, faulty

scorrevole (skōr·re′vō·lä) *a* sliding; fluent

scorrimento (skōr·rē·män′tō) *m* sliding; **porta a** — sliding door

scorso (skōr′sō) *a* last; past

scorsoio (skōr·sô′yō) *a* slipping, running; **nodo** — slipknot

scorta (skōr′tâ) *f* escort; stock, reserve supply

scortese (skōr·tä′zā) *a* rude, ill-mannered

scorticare (skōr·tē·kâ′rä) *vt* to skin; *(fig)* to fleece

scorza (skōr′tsâ) *f* bark; *(fig)* outer surface

scosceso (skō·shä′zō) *a* sheer, steep

scossa (skōs′sâ) *f* shake; shock; **a scosse** in an irregular way, by fits and starts

scostare (skō·stâ′rä) *vt* to remove, take away

scostarsi (skō·stâr′sē) *vr* to step aside; to move away

scostumato (skō·stū·mâ′tō) *a* dissolute; ill-mannered

scotennare (skō·tān·nâ′rä) *vt* to scalp; to skin

scottare (skōt·tâ′rä) *vt&i* to burn; to sting; to scald; to be very hot

scottarsi (skōt·târ′sē) *vr* to get burned; to scald oneself

scottatura (skōt·tâ·tū′râ) *f* burn

Scozia (skô′tsyâ) *f* Scotland

scozzese (skō·tsä′zä) *a* Scotch; — *m* Scot

screditato (skrä·dē·tâ′tō) *a* discredited, disreputed

scremato (skrä·mâ′tō) *a* skimmed

screpolato (skrä·pō·lâ′tō) *a* chapped; cracked, split

screzio (skre′tsyō) *m* spat, difference

scribacchiare (skrē·bâk·kyâ′rä) *vt* to scribble

scricchiolare (skrēk·kyō·lâ′rä) *vi* to creak; to rasp

k kid, **l** let, **m** met, **n** not, **p** pat, **r** very, **s** sat, **sh** shop, **t** tell, **v** vat, **w** we, **y** yet, **z** zero

scricchiolio (skrēk·kyō·lē'ō) *m* rasping; creaking

scrigno (skrē'nyō) *m* jewel case; cashbox

scriteriato (skrē·tā·ryâ'tō) *a* foolish, rash, unwise

scritta (skrēt'tâ) *f* sign; caption; inscription

scritto (skrēt'tō) *a* written; — *m* writing; **–io** (skrēt·tô'yō) *m* desk; **–re** (skrēt·tō'-rā) *m*, **scrittrice** (skrēt·trē'chā) *f* writer

scrittura (skrēt·tū'rā) *f* handwriting; *(law)* deed; *(theat)* booking; *(com)* entry; **la Sacra** — the Holy Scriptures; **avere bella** — to have a good handwriting; **–re** (skrēt·tū·râ'rā) *vt (theat)* to book, engage

scrivania (skrē·vâ·nē'â) *f* writing desk

scrivano (skrē·vâ'nō) *m* clerk; transcriber

scrivere * (skrē'vā·rā) *vt&i* to write, write up

scroccare (skrōk·kâ'rā) *vt* to live at another's expense; to sponge *(coll)*

scroccone (skrōk·kō'nā) *m* parasite; sponger *(coll)*

scrofa (skrō'fâ) *f* sow

scroscio (skrô'shō) *m* burst; shower *(rain)*; **piovere a** — to rain cats and dogs *(coll)*

scrupolo (skrū'pō·lō) *m* scruple; **–samente** (skrū·pō·lō·zâ·mān'tā) *adv* scrupulously

scrutatore (skrū·tâ·tō'rā) *m* investigator

scrutinio (skrū·tē'nyō) *m* grade average *(school)*; scrutiny, careful examination

scucire (skū·chē'rā) *vt* to rip, unstitch

scucito (skū·chē'tō) *a* ripped, unsewed

scucitura (skū·chē·tū'râ) *f* ripped seam

scuderia (skū·dā·rē'â) *f* stable

scudiscio (skū·dē'shō) *m* whip, lash

scudo (skū'dō) *m* shield; escutcheon; *(fig)* protection, aegis

sculacciare (skū·lâ·châ'rā) *vt* to spank

sculacciatura (skū·lâ·châ·tū'râ) *f* spanking

sculaccione (skū·lâ·chō'nā) *m* spanking

scultore (skūl·tō'rā) *m* sculptor

scultura (skūl·tū'râ) *f* sculpture

scuola (skwō'lâ) *f* school; — **professionale** vocational school

scuotere * (skwô'tā·rā) *vt* to shake

scuotersi * (skwô'tār·sē) *vr* to bestir oneself; to rouse oneself

scure (skū'rā) *f* hatchet, ax

scuro (skū'rō) *a* dark; swarthy; — *m* obscurity; shading *(art)*

scusa (skū'zâ) *f* excuse; apology; justification; — **magra** poor excuse; **–re** (skū·zâ'rā) *vt* to excuse; to justify

scusarsi (skū·zâr'sē) *vr* to justify one-

self; to excuse oneself

sdebitarsi (zdā·bē·târ'sē) *vr* to meet one's obligations; to return a favor

sdegno (zdā'nyō) *m* indignation; **–samente** (zdā·nyō·zâ·mān'tâ) *adv* scornfully; haughtily; **–so** (zdā·nyō'zō) *a* haughty, disdainful

sdentato (zdān·tâ'tō) *a* toothless

sdoganare (zdō·gâ·nâ'rā) *vt* to clear through customs

sdolcinato (zdōl·chē·nâ'tō) *a* affected, cloying

sdraiarsi (zdrâ·yâr'sē) *vi* to stretch out; to lie extended

sdraio (zdrâ'yō) *a* reclining, stretched out; **sedia a** — deck chair

sdrucciolare (zdrū·chō·lâ'rā) *vi* to slip

sdrucciolevole (zdrū·chō·le'vō·lā) *a* slippery, slick

sdrucito (zdrū·chē'tō) *a* ripped, torn

se (sā) *conj* if; — **mai** if at all

sè (sā) *pron* herself, himself; itself; oneself; themselves

sebbene (sāb·bā'nā) *conj* although, despite the fact that

seccante (sāk·kân'tā) *a* boresome, tiring

seccare (sāk·kâ'rā) *vt&i* to bother, annoy; to dry; to sere

seccarsi (sāk·kâr'sē) *vr* to wither; *(coll)* to be bored

seccatore (sāk·kâ·tō'rā) *m* pest, bore

seccatura (sāk·kâ·tū'râ) *f* nuisance

secchia (sek'kyâ) *f*, **secchio** (sek'kyō) *m* pail

secco (sāk'kō) *a* dry; sharp; cold

secessione (sā·chās·syō'nā) *f* secession

secolare (sā·kō·lâ'rā) *m* layman; — *a* worldly, secular

secolo (se'kō·lō) *m* century

secondo (sā·kōn'dō) *m&a* second; — *prep* according to

secrezione (sā·krā·tsyō'nā) *f* secretion

sedano (se'dâ·nō) *m* celery

sedare (sā·dâ'rā) *vt* to quell; to appease

sedativo (sā·dâ·tē'vō) *m&a* sedative

sede (sā'dā) *f* see *(eecl)*; main office, home office

sedentario (sā·dān·tâ'ryō) *a* sedentary

sedere * (sā·dā'rā) *vi* to sit; — *m* rump

sedersi * (sā·dār'sē) *vr* to seat oneself

sedia (se'dyâ) *f* chair; — **a rotelle** wheel chair; — **a sdraio** deck chair, chaise longue

sedicenne (sā·dē·chân'nā) *a* sixteen years old

sedicente (sā·dē·chân'tā) *a* self-styled

sedicesimo (sā·dē·che'zē·mō) *a* sixteenth

sedici (se'dē·chē) *a* sixteen

â ârm, ā bāby, e bet, ē bē, ō gō, ô gône, ū blūe, b bad, ch child, d dad, f fat, g gay, j jet

sedile (sā·dē'lā) *m* seat
sedizione (sā·dē·tsyō'nä) *f* mutiny; sedition
seducente (sā·dū·chän'tä) *a* seductive; glamorous, attractive
sedurre * (sā·dūr'rä) *vt* to seduce; to entrance
seduta (sā·dū'tâ) *f* meeting
seduzione (sā·dū·tsyō'nä) *f* seduction; attraction, glamour
sega (sā'gâ) *f* saw; **–re** (sā·gâ'rä) to saw; **–tura** (sā·gâ·tū'râ) *f* sawdust
segale (sā·gâ'lä) *f* rye
segaligno (sā·gâ·lē'nyō) *a* slim, wiry
segnalare (sā·nyâ·lâ'rä) *vt* to indicate, point out
segnalarsi (sā·nyâ·lâr'sē) *vr* to distinguish oneself; to become well known
segnalazione (sā·nyâ·lâ·tsyō'nä) *f* signal; indication
segnale (sā·nyâ'lä) *m* signal; **— acustico** auto horn
segnalibro (sā·nyâ·lē'brō) *m* bookmark
segnare (sā·nyâ'rä) *vt* to mark; to note, point to
segno (sā'nyō) *m* sign; token; **cogliere il — to** to hit the mark; **in — d'affetto** as a token of affection; **per filo e per — with** all the details, completely
segregare (sā·grā·gâ'rä) *vt* to segregate; to keep isolated
segregarsi (sā·grā·gâr'sē) *vr* to isolate oneself; to live in seclusion
segregazione (sā·grā·gâ·tsyō'nä) *f* segregation; solitary confinement *(prison)*
segretaria (sā·grā·tâ'ryâ) *f*, **segretario** (sā·grā·tâ'ryō) *m* secretary
segreteria (sā·grā·tā·rē'â) *f* secretariat; central office
segretezza (sā·grā·tâ'tsâ) *f* secrecy, privacy
segreto (sā·grā'tō) *m* privacy, secret; **—** *a* private, secret
seguace (sā·gwâ'chä) *m* follower
seguente (sā·gwän'tä) *a* following, coming
segugio (sā·gū'jō) *m* bloodhound
seguire (sā·gwē'rä) *vt* to follow; to continue; **far — to** forward *(mail)*
seguito (se'gwē·tō) *m* continuation; following; party; retinue
sei (sā'ē) *a* six
seicento (sāē·chän'tō) *a* six hundred; **il S–** the seventeenth century
seimila (sāē·mē'lâ) *a* six thousand
selettore (sā·lät·tō'rä) *m* selector
selezionare (sā·lā·tsyō·nâ'rä) *vt* to select; to make a selection of

selezione (sā·lā·tsyō'nä) *f* selection; digest
sella (sāl'lâ) *f* saddle
selvaggina (sāl·vâj·jē'nâ) *f* game
selvaggio (sāl·vâj'jō) *a&m* savage
selvatico (sāl·vâ'tē·kō) *a* wild
selz (sālts) *f* soda water; seltzer
semaforo (sā·mâ'fō·rō) *m* traffic light
sembrare (sām·brâ'râ) *vt&i* to seem; to appear to be
seme (sā'mä) *m* seed; cause, origin
semestre (sā·mā'strä) *m* six months; semester
semina (se'mē·nâ) *f* seed; sowing; **–re** (sā·mē·nâ'râ) *vt* to sow; **–tore** (sā·mē·nâ·tō'râ) *m* sower; **–trice** (sā·mē·nâ·trē'chä) *f* mechanical seeder
semita (sā·mē'tâ) *m* Semite
semola (se'mō·lâ) *f* fine flour; bran; freckle; **pan di —** white bread
semolino (sā·mō·lē'nō) *m* semolina
semovente (sā·mō·vän'tä) *a* self-propelled
semplice (sem'plē·chä) *a* simple; plain; easy; **–mente** (sām·plē·chä·män'tä) *adv* plainly, obviously; easily
semplicione (sām·plē·chō'nä), **sempliciotto** (sām·plē·chōt'tō) *m* simpleton
semplicità (sām·plē·chē·tâ') *f* simplicity; ease
sempre (sām'prä) *adv* ever; always; **–chè** (sām·prâ·kä') *conj* with the condition that; **–verde** (sām·prâ·vâr'dä) *m&a* evergreen
senape (se'nâ·pä) *f* mustard
senato (sā·nâ'tō) *m* senate; **–re** (sā·nâ·tō'râ) *m* senator
senilità (sā·nē·lē·tâ') *f* senility
senno (sän'nō) *m* wisdom; common sense
seno (sā'nō) *m* breast; bay; *(math)* sine
senonchè (sā·nōn·kä') *adv* otherwise, if not; **—** *conj* except for the fact that; unless
sensale (sān·sâ'lä) *m* middleman; broker; agent
sensato (sān·sâ'tō) *a* sensible, reasonable; wise; rational
sensazionale (sān·sâ·tsyō·nâ'lä) *a* sensational; moving, stirring
sensazione (sān·sâ·tsyō'nä) *f* sensation
sensibile (sān·sē'bē·lä) *a* sensitive
sensibilità (sān·sē·bē·lē·tâ') *f* sensitivity; susceptibility
senso (sān'sō) *m* sense; meaning; direction; way; **— unico** one way; **— vietato** do not enter *(street)*; **buon —** common sense; **in — contrario** in the opposite way; to the contrary
sensuale (sān·swâ'lä) *a* sensual
sentenza (sān·tān'tsâ) *f* sentence; verdict

k kid, **l** let, **m** met, **n** not, **p** pat, **r** very, **s** sat, **sh** shop, **t** tell, **v** vat, **w** we, **y** yet, **z** zero

sentiero (sān·tyā′rō) *m* path, trail

sentimentale (sān·tē·män·tâ′lā) *a* sentimental; romantic

sentimento (sān·tē·män′tō) *m* feeling; viewpoint

sentinella (sān·tē·näl′lâ) *f* sentinel

sentire (sān·tē′rā) *vt* to hear; to feel

sentirsi (sān·tēr′sē) *vr* to feel

sentitamente (sān·tē·tâ·män′tā) *adv* sincerely, cordially, deeply

sentore (sān·tō′rā) *m* feeling, premonition, forewarning

senza (sān′tsâ) *prep* without

senzatetto (sān·tsâ·tāt′tō) *m* homeless person

separare (sā·pâ·râ′rā) *vt* to separate

separarsi (sā·pâ·râr′sē) *vr* to part, diverge

separazione (sā·pâ·râ·tsyō′nä) *f* separation

sepolcro (sā·pōl′krō) *m* tomb; burial vault

sepolto (sā·pōl′tō) *a* buried

sepoltura (sā·pōl·tū′râ) *f* burial

seppellire (sāp·pāl·lē′rā) *vt* to bury

sequenza (sā·kwän′tsâ) *f* sequence

sequestrare (sā·kwä·strä′rā) *vt* to attach, seize; to seclude, keep hidden

sequestro (sā·kwä′strō) *m* attachment, confiscating; **— guidiziale** distraint; **— di stipendio** attachment of salary

sera (sā′râ) *f* evening; **verso —** at dusk; **di —** at night; **—le** (sā·râ′lä) *a* evening; **—ta** (sā·râ′tâ) *f* evening; *(theat)* evening performance

serbare (sār·bâ′rā) *vt* to keep, reserve

serbarsi (sār·bâr′sē) *vr* to keep for oneself; to take care of

serbatoio (sār·bâ·tō′yō) *m* tank; cistern, storage tank

serenata (sā·rā·nâ′tâ) *f* serenade

serenità (sā·rā·nē·tâ′) *f* calm; serenity

sereno (sā·rā′nō) *a* serene; clear, cloudless; **— m** cloudless sky

sergente (sār·jän′tä) *m* sargeant

seriamente (sā·ryâ·män′tä) *adv* solemnly; seriously

serie (se′ryā) *f* series; **fuori —** custombuilt; **produzione in —** mass production

serietà (sā·ryä·tâ′) *f* seriousness

serio (se′ryō) *a* serious; responsible; **sul —** seriously, earnestly

sermone (sār·mō′nä) *m* sermon

sermoneggiare (sār·mō·näj·jâ′rā) *vi* to harangue, lecture

serpe (sār′pä) *m* snake; **—ggiare** (sār·pāj·jâ′rä) *vi* to wander, meander; **—ntino** (sār·pān·tē′nō) *a* snaky; **—ntino** *m* coil

serpente (sār·pän′tä) *m* snake, serpent

serra (sār′râ) *f* hothouse; **—glio** (sār·râ′lyō) *m* menagerie; **—nda** (sār·rân′dâ) *f* rolling shutter; **—re** (sār·râ′rā) *vt* to lock; to close; to squeeze; to close up *(ranks)*; **—ta** (sār·râ′tâ) *f* lockout; **—tura** (sār·râ·tū′râ) *f* lock; **—tura di sicurezza** safety lock

serva (sār′vâ) *f* maid

servilismo (sār·vē·lē′zmō) *m* fawning; servility

servire (sār·vē′rā) *vt&i* to serve

servirsi (sār·vēr′sē) *vr* to make use of; to help oneself *(food)*

servitore (sār·vē·tō′rä) *m* servant

servitù (sār·vē·tū′) *f* servitude; 'bondage; servants

servizievole (sār·vē·tsye′vō·lä) *a* convenient; serviceable; helpful

servizio (sār·vē′tsyō) *m* service; **mezzo —** part-time service; **donna di —** maid

servo (sār′vō) *m* servant; **— a** servile; **—freno** (sār·vō·frä′nō) *m* hydraulic brake booster; **—sterzo** (sār·vō·stär′tsō) *m* hydraulic steering

sessagenario (sās·sâ·jä·nâ′ryō) *a&m* sexagenarian

sessagesima (sās·sâ·je′zē·mâ) *f* *(eccl)* Sexagesima

sessanta (sās·sân′tâ) *a* sixty

sessantesimo (sās·sân·te′zē·mō) *a* sixtieth

sessione (sās·syō′nä) *f* meeting; session

sesso (sās′sō) *m* sex

sessuale (sās·swâ′lä) *a* sexual

sestetto (sā·stāt′tō) *m* sextet

sesto (sā′stō) *a* sixth

seta (sā′tâ) *f* silk

setaccio (sā·tâ′chō) *m* sieve; crib

sete (sā′tä) *f* thirst; **aver —** to be thirsty

setificio (sā·tē·fē′chō) *m* silk mill

setola (se′tō·lâ) *f* bristle

setta (sāt′tâ) *f* sect

settanta (sāt·tân′tâ) *a* seventy

settantesimo (sāt·tân·te′zē·mō) *a* seventieth

sette (sāt′tä) *a* seven

settecento (sāt·tä·chän′tō) *a* seven hundred; **il S—** the eighteenth century

settemila (sāt·tā·mē′lâ) *a* seven thousand

settembre (sāt·täm′brä) *m* September

settennale (sāt·tän·nâ′lä) *a* septennial

settentrionale (sāt·tän·tryō·nâ′lä) *a* northern

settentrione (sāt·tän·tryō′nä) *m* north

settenne (sāt·tän′nä) *a* seven years old

settimana (sāt·tē·mâ′nä) *f* week; **—le** (sāt·tē·mâ·nâ′lä) *a&m* weekly

settimo (set′tē·mō) *a* seventh

settore (sāt·tō′rā) *m* department, field,

area
settuagenario (sāt·twâ·jā·nâ′ryō) *a&m* septuagenarian
severamente (sā·vā·râ·mān′tā) *adv* severely; with austerity
severità (sā·vā·rē·tâ′) *f* strictness, severity
severo (sā·vā′rō) *a* strict; severe
seviziare (sā·vē·tsyâ′rā) *vt* to torture; to mistreat, treat badly
sezione (sā·tsyō′nā) *f* section
sfaccendato (sfâ·chān·dâ′tō) *m* loafer, ne′er-do-well; — *a* lazy, idle
sfacciataggine (sfâ·châ·tâj′jē·nā) *f* impudence
sfacciatamente (sfâ·châ·tâ·mān′tā) *adv* impudently
sfacciato (sfâ·châ′tō) *a* brazen; impudent
sfacelo (sfâ·châ′lō) *m* collapse, ruin
sfamare (sfâ·mâ′rā) *vt* to feed; to satisfy one's hunger
sfarzo (sfâr′tsō) *m* pomp
sfasciarsi (sfâ·shâr′sē) *vr* to be smashed up; to collapse; to come apart
sfavillante (sfâ·vēl·lân′tā) *a* scintillating, sparkling
sfavorevole (sfâ·vō·re′vō·lā) *a* unfavorable
sfavorevolmente (sfâ·vō·rā·vōl·mān′tā) *adv* unfavorably
sfegatato (sfā·gâ·tâ′tō) *a* passionate; — *m* hothead
sfera (sfā′râ) *f* sphere; **penna** — ballpoint pen
sferrare (sfār·râ′rā) *vt* to release; — **uno schiaffo** to slap violently; — **un attacco** (*mil*) to launch an attack
sfiatato (sfyâ·tâ′tō) *a* breathless
sfibrante (sfē·brân′tā) *a* weakening, enervating
sfida (sfē′dâ) *f* defiance; challenge; **-re** (sfē·dâ′rā) *vt* to challenge
sfiducia (sfē·dū′châ) *f* distrust
sfigurato (sfē·gū·râ′tō) *a* disfigured
sfilata (sfē·lâ′tâ) *f* parade; fashion show; procession
sfinge (sfēn′jā) *f* sphinx
sfinimento (sfē·nē·mān′tō) *m* breakdown; faint; exhaustion
sfinirsi (sfē·nēr′sē) *vr* to become run-down
sfinito (sfē·nē′tō) *a* exhausted, run-down
sfiorare (sfyō·râ′rā) *vt* to brush, graze; to go over quickly, scan hurriedly
sfiorire (sfyō·rē′rā) *vt* to wither
sfociare (sfō·châ′rā) *vi* to flow into
sfoderare (sfō·dā·râ′rā) *vt* to unsheath; (*fig*) to vaunt, make a great display of
sfogare (sfō·gâ′rā) *vt* to vent, unleash
sfogarsi (sfō·gâr′sē) *vr* to give vent to

one's emotions, vent one's wrath
sfoggio (sfôj′jō) *m* ostentation, parade
sfogliatella (sfō·lyâ·tāl′lâ) *f* puff pastry
sfogo (sfō′gō) *m* vent; relief; (*med*) rash; **dar** — **a** to give free rein to
sfollagente (sfōl·lâ·jän′tā) *m* billy, night stick
sfollare (sfōl·lâ′rā) *vt* to evacuate; — *vi* to disperse
sfollato (sfōl·lâ′tō) *m* evacuee
sfondare (sfōn·dâ′rā) *vt* to succeed in; to achieve; to break through, break open; to make it (*coll*)
sfondo (sfōn′dō) *m* background
sformato (sfōr·mâ′tō) *a* deformed
sfornare (sfōr·nâ′rā) *vt* to take out of the oven
sfornito (sfōr·nē′tō) *a* devoid; lacking; destitute
sfortuna (sfōr·tū′nâ) *f* bad luck; **–tamente** (sfōr·tū·nâ·tâ·mān′tā) *adv* unluckily; **–to** (sfōr·tū·nâ′tō) *a* unlucky
sforzare (sfōr·tsâ′rā) *vt* to force, make one's best
sforzarsi (sfōr·tsâr′sē) *vr* to strive; to do one's best
sforzo (sfōr′tsō) *m* effort, attempt
sfracellare (sfrâ·châl·lâ′rā) *vt* to smash, crash
sfracellarsi (sfrâ·châl·lâr′sē) *vr* to be smashed, dash to pieces
sfrattare (sfrât·tâ′rā) *vt* to evict; to expel, oust
sfratto (sfrât′tō) *m* eviction
sfregio (sfre′jō) *m* scar; gash; (*fig*) insult
sfrenato (sfrā·nâ′tō) *a* dissolute; unrestrained, untrammeled
sfrontato (sfrōn·tâ′tō) *a* brazen
sfruttamento (sfrūt·tâ·mān′tō) *m* exploitation; depletion
sfruttare (sfrūt·tâ′rā) *vt* to deplete; to exploit
sfruttatore (sfrūt·tâ·tō′rā) *m* exploiter; — **di donne** pimp, pander
sfuggire (sfūj·jē′rā) *vi* to escape; — *vt* to avoid, evade
sfuggita (sfūj·jē′tâ) *f* **di** — in passing; incidentally, by the way
sfumare (sfū·mâ′rā) *vi* to vanish, disappear; — *vt* (*art*) to shade; (*mus*) to diminish
sfumatura (sfū·mâ·tū′râ) *f* nuance, shade
sfuriata (sfū·ryâ′tâ) *f* tirade, fit of rage
sfuso (sfū′zō) *a* (*com*) in bulk
sgabello (zgâ·bāl′lō) *m* stool
sgambettare (zgâm·bāt·tâ′rā) *vi* to trip along; to toddle
sgambetto (zgâm·bāt′tō) *m* caper, gambol; **fare lo** — **a** (*fig*) to oust

sganciare (zgân·châ′rā) *vt* to unfasten; to unhook; (*avi*) to drop (*bombs*)

sgangheratamente (zgân·gā·râ·tâ·mān′tā) *adv* grossly, immoderately; **ridere —** to guffaw

sgangherato (zgân·gā·râ′tō) *a* rickety; rude, gross

sgarbato (zgâr·bâ′tō) *a* rude

sgarbo (zgâr′bō) *m* discourtesy, impoliteness

sgelare (zjā·lâ′rā) *vi* to melt, thaw

sgelo (zjā′lō) *m* thaw

sgobbare (zgōb·bâ′rā) *vt* to work doggedly

sgobbone (zgōb·bō′nā) *m* (*coll*) hard worker; grind (*coll*)

sgocciolare (zgō·chō·lâ′rā) *vi* to drip

sgomberare (zgōm·bā·râ′rā), **sgombrare** (zgōm·brâ′rā) *vt* to clear out; to leave, depart from

sgombero (zgôm′bā·rō), **sgombro** (zgōm′-brō) *m* clearance, removal; **— a** clear, free; empty

sgomentare (zgō·mān·tâ′rā) *vt* to upset; to dismay; to frighten

sgomentarsi (zgō·mān·târ′sē) *vr* to lose heart; to become frightened

sgomento (zgō·mān′tō) *m* panic; fear

sgonfiare (zgōn·fyâ′rā) *vt* to deflate

sgonfiarsi (zgōn·fyâr′sē) *vr* to deflate, be deflated; (*med*) to go down (*swelling*)

sgorbio (zgôr′byō) *m* blot; daub; scrawl; stain

sgozzare (zgō·dzâ′rā) *vt* to slaughter; to slit the throat of

sgradevole (zgrâ·de′vō·lā) *a* disagreeable, displeasing

sgradevolmente (zgrâ·dā·vōl·mān′tā) *adv* unpleasantly

sgradito (zgrâ·dē′tō) *a* unwelcome, badly received, unpleasant

sgrammaticato (zgrâm·mâ·tē·kâ′tō) *a* ungrammatical

sgranare (zgrâ·nâ′rā) *vt* to shell, husk; **— gli occhi** (*fig*) to open one's eyes wide

sgranchire (zgrân·kē′rā) *vt* to stretch out, extend

sgranchirsi (zgrân·kēr′sē) *vr* to stretch oneself; **— le gambe** to stretch one's legs; (*fig*) to go for a short walk

sgravare (zgrâ·vâ′rā) *vt* to ease; to unload

sgravarsi (zgrâ·vâr′sē) *vr* to relieve oneself; (*med*) to be delivered; to litter (*animals*); **— la coscienza** (*fig*) to assuage one's conscience

sgraziato (zgrâ·tsyâ′tō) *a* awkward

sgridare (zgrē·dâ′rā) *vt* to reprimand, scold

sgridata (zgrē·dâ′tâ) *f* scolding

sguaiatamente (zgwâ·yâ·tâ·mān′tā) *adv* uncouthly, coarsely

sguaiato (zgwâ·yâ′tō) *a* vulgar, low

sguainare (zgwâē·nâ′rā) *vt* to uncover, unsheathe

sgualcito (zgwâl·chē′tō) *a* crumpled, rumpled

sgualdrina (zgwâl·drē′nâ) *f* prostitute

sguardo (zgwâr′dō) *m* glance, look

sguattero (zgwât′tā·rō) *m* dishwasher

sgusciare (zgū·shâ′rā) *vt* to shell; to remove the husk from; **—** *vi* to slip away unnoticed, make off unobserved

sì (sē) *adv* yes

si (sē) *pron* one, oneself; himself, herself; we, ourselves; each other, themselves

sia (sē′â) *conj* either; or; whether

sicario (sē·kâ′ryō) *m* hired assassin, mercenary

sicchè (sēk·kā′) *conj* so that, in order that

siccità (sē·chē·tâ′) *f* drought

siccome (sēk·kō′mā) *conj* since, in view of the fact that

Sicilia (sē·chē′lyā) *f* Sicily

siciliano (sē·chē·lyā′nō) *a&m* Sicilian

sicuramente (sē·kū·râ·mān′tā) *adv* safely, surely

sicurezza (sē·kū·rā′tsā) *f* assurance; safety; security; **consiglio di —** security council; **pubblica —** police; **uscita di —** emergency door

sicuro (sē·kū′rō) *a* safe; reliable, sure; **— m** safety; **andare sul —** to play safe; **— adv** surely; **di —** certainly, surely

siderurgico (sē·dā·rūr′jē·kō) *a* iron and steel; **stabilimento —** steel mill

siepe (syā′pā) *f* hedge

siero (syā′rō) *m* serum

sifilide (sē·fē′lē·dā) *f* (*med*) syphilis

sifilitico (sē·fē·lē′tē·kō) *a* (*med*) syphilitic

sigaraio (sē·gâ·râ′yō) *m* cigar maker; cigar dealer

sigaretta (sē·gâ·rât′tâ) *f* cigarette; **sigarette sciolte** cigarettes sold individually

sigaretto (sē·gâ·rât′tō) *m* cigarillo, small cigar

sigaro (sē′gâ·rō) *m* cigar

sigillare (sē·jēl·lâ′rā) *vt* to seal

sigillo (sē·jēl′lō) *m* seal

sigla (sē′glâ) *f* monogram; initials; **–re** (sē·glâ′rā) *vt* to initial

significare (sē·nyē·fē·kâ′rā) *vt* to mean

significativamente (sē·nyē·fē·kâ·tē·vâ·mān′tā) *adv* meaningfully; significantly

significativo (sē·nyē·fē·kâ·tē′vō) *a* significant, meaningful

significato (sē·nyē·fē·kâ′tō) *m* meaning, importance

signora (sē·nyō′rä) *f* lady; mistress, Mrs.; madam

signore (sē·nyō′rā) *m* gentleman; lord; Mister, Mr.

signorile (sē·nyō·rē′lā) *a* refined, dignified

signorina (sē·nyō·rē′nâ) *f* young lady; Miss

silenziatore (sē·lān·tsyâ·tō′rā) *m* muffler

silenzio (sē·len′tsyō) *m* silence; **–samente** (sē·lān·tsyō·zâ·mān′tä) *adv* noiselessly; silently; **–so** (sē·lān·tsyō′zō) *a* silent

silice (sē′lē·chä) *f* flint, silica

silicio (sē′lē·chō) *m* silicon

sillaba (sēl′lâ·bâ) *f* syllable; **–re** (sēl·lâ·bâ′rā) *vt* to spell out; to syllable; to syllabify; **–rio** (sēl·lâ·bâ′ryō) *m* primer; speller

silo (sē′lō) *m* silo

silografia (sē·lō·grâ·fē′â) *f* wood engraving

siluetta (sē·lūät′tâ) *f* silhouette

silurante (sē·lū·rân′tä) *f* torpedo boat, destroyer; **aereo —** (*avi*) torpedo-carrying airplane

silurare (sē·lū·râ′rā) *vt* to torpedo; (*fig*) to dismiss, fire

siluro (sē·lū′rō) *m* torpedo

silvestre (sēl·vä′strä) *a* wild; sylvan; rustic

simbolizzare (sēm·bō·lē·dzâ′rā) *vt&i* to represent; to symbolize

simbolo (sēm′bō·lō) *m* symbol

simile (sē′mē·lä) *a* alike, similar; like

simpatia (sēm·pâ·tē′â) *f* sympathy; liking

simpatico (sēm·pâ′tē·kō) *a* nice; likable

simpatizzante (sēm·pâ·tē·dzân′tä) *a* friendly; pleasant; **—** *m* advocate

simpatizzare (sēm·pâ·tē·dzâ′rā) *vt&i* to be favorable to; to hit it off with, get along well with

simulare (sē·mū·lâ′rā) *vt&i* to simulate, pretend

simulatore (sē·mū·lâ·tō′rā) *m*, **simulatrice** (sē·mū·lâ·trē′chä) *f* pretender; liar

simulazione (sē·mū·lâ·tsyō′nä) *f* pretense; lying

simultaneamente (sē·mūl·tâ·nä·â·mān′tä) *adv* simultaneously

simultaneo (sē·mūl·tâ′nä·ō) *a* simultaneous

sinagoga (sē·nâ·gō′gâ) *f* synagogue

sinceramente (sēn·chä·râ·mān′tä) *adv* really; sincerely; with conviction; truthfully speaking

sincerarsi (sēn·chä·râr′sē) *vr* to be convinced; to make sure; to be certain

sincerità (sēn·chä·rē·tâ′) *f* honesty; sincerity; conviction

sincero (sēn·chä′rō) *a* sincere, frank; honest

sincronizzare (sēn·krō·nē·dzâ′rā) *vt&i* to synchronize

sindacabile (sēn·dâ·kâ′bē·lä) *a* blameworthy, faulty; controllable; subject to verification

sindacale (sēn·dâ·kâ′lä) *a* pertaining to a trade union, trade-union; syndical

sindacalista (sēn·dâ·kâ·lē′stâ) *m* trade unionist

sindacare (sēn·dâ·kâ′rā) *vt* to verify; to control; to find fault with, blame

sindacato (sēn·dâ·kâ′tō) *m* trade union; syndicate

sindaco (sēn′dâ·kō) *m* mayor; auditor

sinfonia (sēn·fō·nē′â) *f* symphony

singhiozzare (sēn·gyō·tsâ′rā) *vi* to sob

singhiozzo (sēn·gyō′tsō) *m* sob; hiccup

singolare (sēn·gō·lâ′rä) *a* peculiar; odd; strange; (*gram*) singular

sinistra (sē·nē′strâ) *f* left; left hand; **–to** (sē·nē·strâ′tō) *m* accident victim

sinistro (sē·nē′strō) *a* left; sinister, eerie; **—** *m* accident

sino (sē′nō) *prep* as far as; till; up to; until; **–ra** (sē·nō′râ) *adv* hitherto, as yet, till now

sintetico (sēn·te′tē·kō) *a* synthetic

sintomo (sēn′tō·mō) *m* symptom

sintonizzare (sēn·tō·nē·dzâ′rā) *vt* (*rad*) to tune in

sipario (sē·pâ′ryō) *m* (*theat*) curtain

sirena (sē·rā′nâ) *f* siren

siringa (sē·rēn′gâ) *f* syringe

sistema (sē·stä′mâ) *m* method; system; procedure; **–re** (sē·stä·mâ′rā) *vt* to arrange, organize, set up; **–rsi** (sē·stä·mâr′sē) *vr* to settle, get settled; **–zione** (sē·stä·mâ·tsyō′nä) *f* settlement; arranging; organization

situazione (sē·twâ·tsyō′nä) *f* situation

slacciare (zlâ·châ′rā) *vt* to untie; to undo

slacciarsi (zlâ·châr′sē) *vr* to undo one's buttons; to come undone, become unfastened

slanciare (zlân·châ′rā) *vt* to throw, hurl; to give rise to; to spur on, incite

slanciarsi (zlân·châr′sē) *vr* to throw oneself, rush; to become slender

slanciato (zlân·châ′tō) *a* slim, slender; thrown; incited, spurred on

slancio (zlân′chō) *m* dash; impulse; goad, motivation; **prendere lo —** to start off, rush off; to begin hurriedly; **— di generosità** impulse of generosity; **pieno di —** full of energy, full of vigor

slavo (zlä′vō) *a* Slavonic, Slavic; — *m* Slav

sleale (zlä·â′lä) *a* disloyal

slegare (zlä·gâ′rä) *vt* to untie

slegarsi (zlä·gâr′sē) *vr* to get loose; to become undone

slegato (zlä·gâ′tō) *a* untied; loose

slitta (zlēt′tä) *f* sled; toboggan; **–re** (zlēt· tä′rä) *vi* to skid; to slide

slogare (zlō·gâ′rä) *vt* to sprain; to dislocate

slogarsi (zlō·gâr′sē) *vr* to be dislocated; to be sprained; — **una caviglia** to dislocate one's ankle

slogatura (zlō·gâ·tū′râ) *f* dislocation; sprain

sloggiare (zlōj·jâ′rä) *vt* to evict; to oust; to dislodge

smacchiare (zmâk·kyâ′rä) *vt* to clean; to take out the stains on

smacco (zmâk′kō) *m* disgrace; affront

smagliatura (zmâ·lyâ·tū′râ) *f* ravel; run in one's stocking

smaltare (zmâl·tâ′rä) *vt* to glaze; to enamel

smaltire (zmâl·tē′rä) *vt* to free oneself of, get rid of; to digest; (*com*) to sell out; — **la sbornia** to sleep off a drunk

smalto (zmâl′tō) *m* enamel; — **per le unghie** nail polish

smania (zmâ′nyâ) *f* frenzy, mania; urge; delirium

smarrimento (zmâr·rē·mân′tō) *m* miscarriage of justice; loss, losing; perturbation

smarrire (zmâr·rē′rä) *vt* to lose; to bewilder

smarrirsi (zmâr·rēr′sē) *vr* to become lost

smarrito (zmâr·rē′tō) *a* lost

smemorato (zmā·mō·râ′tō) *a* forgetful; absent-minded

smentire (zmän·tē′rä) *vt* to deny; to give the lie to; to discredit

smentita (zmän·tē′tä) *f* disapproval; denial; refutation

smeraldo (zmä·râl′dō) *m* emerald

smerigliato (zmâ·rē·lyâ′tō) *a* emery; **vetro** — ground glass

smeriglio (zmâ·rē′lyō) *m* emery

smettere * (zmet′tä·rä) *vt&i* to stop, put a stop to

smidollato (zmē·dōl·lâ′tō) *a* pithless, feeble, spineless

smilzo (zmēl′tsō) *a* slender, thin

smistamento (zmē·stâ·mân′tō) *m* assortment, distribution; (*rail*) switching

smisurato (zmē·zū·râ′tō) *a* limitless, immeasurable

smobiliato (zmō·bē·lyâ′tō) *a* unfurnished

smobilitazione ' (zmō·bē·lē·tâ·tsyō′nä) *f* demobilization

smodatamente (zmō·dâ·tâ·mân′tä) *adv* excessively, immoderately

smoderato (zmō·dä·râ′tō) *a* intemperate, immoderate; overdone

smoking (zmō′kēn) *m* tuxedo

smontare (zmōn·tâ′rä) *vt* to dismantle, take apart; — *vi* to get off

smorfia (zmōr′fyâ) *f* grimace

smorzare (zmōr·tsâ′rä) *vt* to quench; to put out (*light*); to deaden (*sound*); to tone down

smorzarsi (zmōr·tsâr′sē) *vr* to die away, fade away; to go off, go out (*light*)

smunto (zmūn′tō) *a* wan, gaunt, pale

snaturato (znâ·tū·râ′tō) *a* pitiless, unfeeling; unnatural, twisted

snello (znāl′lō) *a* slender; quick, spry

snervante (znâr·vân′tä) *a* very tiring, enervating

snobismo (znō·bē′zmō) *m* snobbery

snodato (znō·dâ′tō) *a* articulate, expressive; plastic, adaptable

snudare (znū·dâ′rä) *vt* to bare; to uncover, expose

soave (sō·â′vä) *a* soft; sweet; **–mente** (sō· â·vä·mân′tä) *adv* gently, softly

sobborgo (sōb·bōr′gō) *m* suburb

sobillare (sō·bēl·lâ′rä) *vt* to stir up; to foment

sobillatore (sō·bēl·lâ·tō′rä) *m* instigator

sobrietà (sō·bryä·tâ′) *f* moderation, soberness

socchiuso (sōk·kyū′zō) *a* ajar

soccorrere * (sōk·kōr′rä·rä) *vt* to help; — *vi* to take place

soccorso (sōk·kōr′sō) *m* help; **pronto** — first aid

sociale (sō·châ′lä) *a* social

socialismo (sō·châ·lē′zmō) *m* socialism

socialista (sō·châ·lē′stä) *m&a* socialist

soddisfacente (sōd·dē·sfâ·chān′tä) *a* sufficient, satisfactory

soddisfare * (sōd·dē·sfâ′rä) *vt* to satisfy, content '

soddisfarsi * (sōd·dē·sfâr′sē) *vr* to be satisfied, be contented

soddisfatto (sōd·dē·sfât′tō) *a* satisfied, contented

soddisfazione (sōd·dē·sfâ·tsyō′nä) *f* satisfaction, contentment

sodo (sō′dō) *a* solid, hard; stable; **uovo** — hard-boiled egg

sofferenza (sōf·fä·rân′tsä) *f* pain, suffering

soffiare (sōf·fyâ′rä) *vt&i* to puff; to blow

soffice (sôf′fē·chā) *a* soft
soffietto (sôf·fyät′tō) *m* bellows; *(fig)* publicity, advertisement
soffio (sôf′fyō) *m* puff; breath of air
soffitta (sôf·fēt′tâ) *f* attic
soffitto (sôf·fēt′tō) *m* ceiling
soffocare (sôf·fō·kâ′rā) *vt&i* to choke
soffriggere * (sôf·frēj′jā·rā) *vt* to fry lightly, brown
soffrire * (sôf·frē′rā) *vi&t* to suffer; to undergo; to endure, bear
sofisticato (sō·fē·stē·kâ′tō) *a* adulterated; sophisticated
sofisticheria (sō·fē·stē·kā·rē′â) *f* cavil, quibbling
soggetto (sōj·jät′tō) *m* theme, subject; — *a* under the control of, subject to
soggezione (sōj·jä·tsyō′nä) *f* awe; discomfort
soggiorno (sōj·jōr′nō) *m* residence, stay; sala di — living room
soggiungere * (sōj·jūn′jā·rā) *vt&i* to reply; to add, attach
soglia (sô′lyâ) *f* threshold
sogliola (sô′lyō·lâ) *f* sole *(fish)*
sognare (sō·nyâ′rā) *vt&i* to dream
sognatore (sō·nyâ·tō′rā) *m* daydreamer; dreamer
sogno (sō′nyō) *m* dream
solaio (sō·lâ′yō) *m* loft
solamente (sō·lâ·mān′tâ) *adv* only
solcare (sōl·kâ′rā) *vt* to furrow, plow
solco (sōl′kō) *m* furrow
soldato (sōl·dâ′tō) *m* soldier
soldo (sōl′dō) *m* penny; wages; **non aver un** — to be penniless
sole (sō′lā) *m* sun
soleggiato (sō·lāj·jâ′tō) *a* bright, sunny
solenne (sō·lān′nä) *a* downright; serious, solemn
solere * (sō·lā′rā) *vi* to be in the habit of, have the custom of, be used to
solerte (sō·lār′tâ) *a* industrious
solerzia (sō·ler′tsyâ) *f* diligence, zeal
soletta (sō·lāt′tâ) *f* insole
solfatara (sōl·fâ·tâ′râ) *f* sulphur mine
solforico (sōl·fô′rē·kō) *a* sulphuric; **acido** — sulphuric acid
solforoso (sōl·fō·rō′zō) *a* sulphurous
solfuro (sōl·fū′rō) *m* sulphide
solidarietà (sō·lē·dâ·ryä·tâ′) *f* solidarity
solidezza (sō·lē·dā′tsâ) *f* soundness, firmness
solidità (sō·lē·dē·tâ′) *f* solidity, firmness
solido (sô′lē·dō) *a&m* solid; reliable, firm
solitario (sō·lē·tâ′ryō) *a* lonely; — *m* hermit; solitaire *(gem, cards)*
solito (sô′lē·tō) *a* usual; customary; **al** —

as usual; **il** — **ritornello** the same old thing; **essere** — **di** to be accustomed to; **di** — usually, customarily
solitudine (sō·lē·tū′dē·nä) *f* loneliness
sollecitare (sōl·lā·chē·tâ′rā) *vt* to urge, request; to plead with
sollecitazione (sōl·lā·chē·tâ·tsyō′nä) *f* plea; urging, request
sollecito (sōl·le′chē·tō) *a* prompt
sollecitudine (sōl·lā·chē·tū′dē·nä) *f* promptness; concern
solleone (sōl·lā·ō′nä) *m* sultry weather
solleticare (sōl·lā·tē·kâ′rā) *vt* to tickle; to excite; — **la fantasia** to stir one's imagination; — **l'appetito** to whet one's appetite
solletico (sōl·le′tē·kō) *m* tickling; **fare il** — to tickle
sollevare (sōl·lā·vâ′rā) *vt* to lift; to relieve
sollevarsi (sōl·lā·vâr′sē) *vr* to revolt; to rise; *(avi)* to take off
sollevazione (sōl·lā·vâ·tsyō′nä) *f* uprising, revolt
solo (sō′lō) *m* *(mus)* solo; — *a* alone; lonely; **a** — solo; **una sola persona** one person only; **da** — by oneself; **da** — **a** — privately, in private; — *adv* only; **non** — not only
solstizio (sōl·stē′tsyō) *m* solstice
solubile (sō·lū′bē·lä) *a* soluble
soluzione (sō·lū·tsyō′nä) *f* solution *(liquid)*
solvente (sōl·vän′tâ) *a&m* solvent
solvere * (sôl′vä·rā) *vt* to solve; to dissolve
solvibile (sōl·vē′bē·lä) *a* sound, able to pay, solvent
soma (sō′mâ) *f* load, weight; —**ro** (sō·mâ′rō) *m* donkey, jackass
somatico (sō·mâ′tē·kō) *a* physical, somatic
somigliante (sō·mē·lyân′tâ) *a* resembling; alike
somiglianza (sō·mē·lyân′tsâ) *f* resemblance
somigliare (sō·mē·lyâ′rā) *vi* to resemble; — **come due gocce d'acqua** to be like two peas in a pod
somma (sōm′mâ) *f* sum, amount; *(math)* adding; —**re** (sōm·mâ′rā) *vt&i* to add; to amount to, come to; —**rio** (sōm·mâ′ryō) *m* summary
sommergere * (sōm·mer′jä·rā) *vt* to sink; to flood; to submerge; to inundate; *(fig)* to overcome, upset
sommergersi * (sōm·mer′jär·sē) *vr* to be swamped, be inundated; to dive; to sink
sommergibile (sōm·mār·jē′bē·lä) *m* sub-

marine

sommerso (sŏm·mär'sō) *a* submerged, inundated, sunken

sommessamente (sŏm·mäs·sâ·män'tä) *adv* submissively; in a low voice; in a subdued tone

somministrare (sŏm·mē·nē·strâ'rä) *vt* to supply; to administer; — **una medicina** to give a medicine

sommissione (sŏm·mēs·syō'nä) *f* submission

sommo (sŏm'mō) *a* highest; — *m* top

sommossa (sŏm·mōs'sä) *f* uprising

sommozzatore (sŏm·mō·tsâ·tō'rä) *m* frogman

sonaglio (sō·nâ'lyō) *m* rattle; harness bell; **serpente a sonagli** rattlesnake

sonda (sŏn'dä) *f (med)* probe; sounding line; —**ggio** (sŏn·dâj'jō) *m* sounding; poll, concensus

sonico (sō'nē·kō) *a* sonic; **barriera sonica** sound barrier

sonnambulo (sŏn·nâm'bū·lō) *m* sleepwalker

sonnellino (sŏn·nāl·lē'nō) *m* nap

sonnifero (sŏn·nē'fä·rō) *m* narcotic; sleeping pill; — *a* sleep-inducing

sonno (sŏn'nō) *m* sleep; **aver** — to be sleepy; —**lenza** (sŏn·nō·lān'tsâ) *f* drowsiness

sonoro (sō·nō'rō) *a* resonant, resounding; **onde sonore** sound waves

sontuosamente (sŏn·twō·zâ·män'tä) *adv* sumptuously, splendidly

sontuoso (sŏn·twō'zō) *a* splendid, sumptuous

sopore (sō·pō'rä) *m* sleepiness, torpor

soppiatto (sŏp·pyät'tō) *m* **di** — stealthily, on the sly

sopportabile ((sŏp·pōr·tâ'bē·lä) *a* tolerable, bearable

sopportare (sŏp·pōr·tâ'rä) *vt&i* to bear, stand, abide

sopportazione (sŏp·pōr·tâ·tsyō'nä) *f* fortitude, restraint, tolerance

soppressione (sŏp·prās·syō'nä) *f* abolition; suppression

sopprimere * (sŏp·prē'mä·rä) to suppress; to abolish

sopra (sō'prâ) *prep* over, above; — *adv* upstairs; up above; —**bito** (sō·prâ'bē·tō) *m* overcoat; —**ccennato** (sō·prâ·chān·nâ'tō) *a* aforesaid, previously mentioned; —**cciglio** (sō·prâ·chē'lyō) *m* eyebrow; —**ccoperta** (sō·prâk·kō·pär'tä) *f* bedspread; book jacket; —**ddetto** (sō·prâd·dät'tō) *a* above mentioned; —**ffare** * (sō·prâf·fâ'rä) *vt* to overpower; —**ffa-**

zione (sō·prâf·fâ·tsyō'nä) *f* overwhelming, oppression; —**ggiungere** * (sō·prâj·jūn'jä·rä) *vt&i* to occur; to overtake; —**luogo** (sō·prâ·lwō'gō) *m* on-the-spot investigation; —**mmobile** (sō·prâm·mō'bē·lä) *m* knick-knack; —**nnome** (sō·prân·nō'mä) *m* nickname; surname; —**nnumero** (sō·prân·nū'mä·rō) *m* surplus; **in** —**nnumero** in excess; —**no** (sō·prâ'nō) *m&a* soprano; —**scarpe** (sō·prâ·skâr'pä) *fpl* overshoes; —**ssalto** (sō·prâs·sâl'tō) *m* jolt, start; **di** — **ssalto** with a start; suddenly; —**ssedere** (sō·prâs·sā·dā'rä) *vi* to preside; to defer, wait; —**ttassa** (sō·prât·tâs'sä) *f* surtax; —**ttutto** (sō·prât·tūt'tō) *adv* above all; —**vvalutare** (sō·prâv·vâ·lū·tâ'rä) *vt* to overestimate; —**vvento** (sō·prâv·vān'tō) *m* advantage, whip hand; —**vvivere** * (sō·prâv·vē'vä·rä) *vi* to survive; —**vvivere a** to outlive

sopruso (sō·prū'zō) *m* abuse, imposition; assault

soqquadro (sōk·kwâ'drō) *m* ado, confusion

sorbetto (sōr·bāt'tō) *m* sherbet; ice cream

sorbire (sōr·bē'rä) *vt* to sip; to drink slowly

sorbirsi (sōr·bēr'sē) *vr* to swallow; to submit to; — **una predica** *(fig)* to have to endure a scolding

sorcio (sōr'chō) *m* mouse

sordità (sōr·dē·tâ') *f* deafness

sordo (sōr'dō) *a&m* deaf; —**muto** (sōr·dō·mū'tō) *a&m* deaf-mute

sorella (sō·rāl'lä) *f* sister; —**stra** (sō·râl·lâ'strâ) *f* stepsister; halfsister

sorgente (sōr·jän'tä) *f* spring; source; — *a* rising, ascendant

sorgere * (sōr'jä·rä) *vi* to rise; to ascend; to be due to, be the result of

sormontare (sōr·mōn·tâ'rä) *vt* to overcome, surmount

sornione (sōr·nyō'nä) *a* wily, sly

sorpassare (sōr·pâs·sâ'rä) *vt* to pass; to exceed

sorpassarsi (sōr·pâs·sâr'sē) *vr* to outdo oneself

sorpassato (sōr·pâs·sâ'tō) *a* obsolete, passé

sorpasso (sōr·pâs'sō) *m* passing *(auto)*; **divieto di** — no passing

sorprendente (sōr·prân·dän'tä) *a* astounding, amazing

sorprendere * (sōr·pren'dä·rä) *vt* to surprise; to take by surprise; — **la buona fede di** to deceive

sorpresa (sōr·prā'zâ) *f* surprise

â ârm, **ā** bāby, **e** bet, **ē** bē, **ō** gō, **ô** gône, **ū** blūe, **b** bad, **ch** child, **d** dad, **f** fat, **g** gay, **j** jet

sorreggere * (sōr·rej′jä·rā) *vt* to bolster, hold up, support

sorridere * (sōr·rē′dä·rā) *vi* to smile

sorriso (sōr·rē′zō) *m* smile

sorso (sōr′sō) *m* sip

sorta (sōr′tä) *f* type, sort

sorte (sōr′tä) *f* luck; lot; fate; doom; **–ggiare** (sōr·täj·jâ′rā) *vt* to draw by lot

sortilegio (sōr·tē·le′jō) *m* necromancy, witchcraft

sorvegliante (sōr·vä·lyân′tä) *m* watchman

sorveglianza (sōr·vä·lyân′tsâ) *f* surveillance, watch

sorvegliare (sōr·vä·lyâ′rā) *vt* to watch over, keep watch over

sosia (sō′zyâ) *m* double, counterpart

sospendere * (sō·spen′dä·rā) *vt* to suspend; to hold in abeyance

sospensione (sō·spän·syō′nä) *f* discontinuing, suspension

sospettare (sō·spät·tâ′rā) *vt* to suspect; to suppose

sospetto (sō·spät′tō) *m* suspicion; supposition; **–samente** (sō·spät·tō·zâ·män′tä) *adv* suspiciously; **–so** (sō·spät·tō′zō) *a* suspicious; cautious, fearful

sospirare (sō·spē·râ′rā) *vt&i* to sigh; to yearn for

sospiro (sō·spē′rō) *m* sigh

sossopra (sōs·sō′prâ) *adv* upside down; topsy-turvy

sosta (sō′stä) *f* stop; — **vietata** no parking; — **regolamentata** limited parking; **senza** — persistently, unremittingly

sostanza (sō·stân′tsâ) *f* substance

sostanzioso (sō·stân·tsyō′zō) *a* nutritive; substantial

sostare (sō·stâ′rā) *vi* to stop; to pause; to park

sostegno (sō·stä′nyō) *m* support

sostenere * (sō·stä·nâ′rā) *vt* to support; to uphold; to hold; to back up

sostenitore (sō·stä·nē·tō′rā) *m* supporter

sostentamento (sō·stän·tâ·män′tō) *m* maintenance, support

sostituire (sō·stē·twē′rā) *vt* to substitute; to act in the stead of

sostituto (sō·stē·tū′tō) *a* substitute

sostituzione (sō·stē·tū·tsyō′nä) *f* substitution

sottaceti (sōt·tâ·chä′tē) *mpl* pickles

sottana (sōt·tâ′nâ) *f* petticoat; skirt; cassock

sotterfugio (sōt·tär·fū′jō) *m* subterfuge

sotterraneo (sōt·tär·râ′nä·ō) *a* underground; — *m* basement

sotterrare (sōt·tär·râ′rā) *vt* to bury

sottigliezza (sōt·tē·lyâ′tsâ) *f* subtlety; *(fig)*

insight; tenuousness

sottile (sōt·tē′lä) *a* thin; subtle, crafty

sottinteso (sōt·tēn·tä′zō) *a* understood, implied; — *m* implication

sotto (sōt′tō) *prep* under, below, — *adv* down, down below; **–bicchiere** (sōt·tō·bēk·kyä′rā) *m* coaster; **–coperta** (sōt·tō·kō·pär′tâ) *adv* below deck; **–coperta** *f* (naut) lower decks; **–fascia** (sōt·tō·fâ′shâ) *m* printed matter; **–gola** (sōt·tō·gō′lâ) *f* chin strap; **–lineare** (sōt·tō·lē·nä·â′rä) *vt* to underline; to stress, point up; **–mano** (sōt·tō·mâ′nō) *adv* at hand; on hand; **di –mano** stealthily, underhandedly; **–marino** (sōt·tō·mâ·rē′nō) *m* submarine; **–messo** (sōt·tō·mäs′sō) *a* docile, submissive; **–mettere** * (sōt·tō·met′tä·rā) *vt* to conquer, subjugate; to submit; **–mettersi** * (sōt·tō·met′tär·sē) *vr* to cede, surrender; **–missione** (sōt·tō·mēs·syō′nä) *f* self-abasement; subdual; submission; **–passaggio** (sōt·tō·pâs·sâj′jō) *m* underpass; **–porre** * (sōt·tō·pōr′rä) *vt* to submit; **–porsi** * (sōt·tō·pōr′sē) *vr* to submit to; to undergo; **–scrivere** * (sōt·tō·skrē′vä·rä) *vt&i* to sign; to subscribe to; **–scriversi** * (sōt·tō·skrē′vär·sē) *vr* to subscribe to; to approve; **–segretario** (sōt·tō·sâ·grä·tâ′ryō) *m* undersecretary; **–sopra** (sōt·tō·sō′prâ) *adv* in confusion; upside down; **–suolo** (sōt·tō·swō′lō) *m* subsoil; **–valutare** (sōt·tō·vâ·lū·tâ′rä) *vt* to underestimate; **–veste** (sōt·tō·vä′stä) *f* underwear; man's vest; **–voce** (sōt·tō·vō′chä) *adv* softly; in a low voice

sottrarre * (sōt·trâr′rā) *vt* to deduct, subtract

sottrarsi * (sōt·trâr′sē) *vr* to escape, elude, avoid

sottrazione (sōt·trâ·tsyō′nä) *f* subtraction, deduction

sottufficiale (sōt·tūf·fē·châ′lä) *m* noncommissioned officer

sovente (sō·vän′tä) *adv* often, with frequency

sovrano (sō·vrâ′nō) *a&m* sovereign

sovrumano (sō·vrū·mâ′nō) *a* superhuman

sovvenzionare (sōv·vän·tsyō·nâ′rä) *vt* to subsidize, provide financial backing for

sovvenzione (sōv·vän·tsyō′nä) *f* subsidy; scholarship

sovversivo (sōv·vär·sē′vō) *a* subversive

sozzo (sō′tsō) *a* filthy

spaccalegna (spâk·kâ·lä′nyâ) *m* wood cutter

spaccare (spâk·kâ′rā) *vt* to split

spaccarsi (spåk·kâr'sē) *vr* to cleave, split, crack open

spaccato (spåk·kâ'tō) *m* cross section

spacciare (spå·châ'rā) *vt* to spread, circulate; to sell; to palm off

spacciarsi (spå·châr'sē) *vr* to masquerade as; to pass for

spacciatore (spå·châ·tō'rā) *m* peddler

spaccone (spåk·kō'nā) *m* braggart

spada (spå'då) *f* sword

spaesato (spå·ā·zâ'tō) *a* out of one's natural environment; ill at ease

Spagna (spå'nyå) *f* Spain

spagnolo (spå·nyō'lō) *a* Spanish; — *m* Spaniard

spago (spå'gō) *m* twine, string

spaiato (spå·yâ'tō) *a* unmatched, mateless, odd

spalancare (spå·lân·kâ'rā) *vt* to open wide, throw open

spalare (spå·lâ'rā) *vt* to shovel

spalla (spål'lå) *f* shoulder

spalleggiare (spål·lāj·jâ'rā) *vt* to back; to endorse

spalliera (spål·lyä'râ) *f* chair back

spallina (spål·lē'nâ) *f* epaulet

spalmare (spål·mâ'rā) *vt* to spread with; to cover with

sparadrappo (spå·râ·drâp'pō) *m* adhesive plaster; adhesive tape

sparare (spå·râ'rā) *vt&i* to shoot

sparatoia (spå·râ·tō'yâ) *f* shooting

sparecchiare (spå·rāk·kyâ'rā) *vt* to remove, clear away; to clear *(table)*

spargere * (spår'jä·rā) *vt* to scatter; to shed, drop

spargimento (spår·jē·mân'tō) *m* spilling; scattering; — **di sangue** bloodshed

sparire (spå·rē'rā) *vi* to disappear

sparlare (spår·lâ'rā) *vi* to slander

sparo (spå'rō) *m* shot

spartito (spår·tē'tō) *m (mus)* score

spartitraffico (spår·tē·trâf'fē·kō) *m* safety island

spartizione (spår·tē·tsyō'nā) *f* distribution, apportionment

spasimante (spå·zē·mân'tā) *a* lovelorn; — *m* lover, swain

spasimo (spå'zē·mō) *m* pang; *(med)* spasm

spasmodico (spå·zmô'dē·kō) *a* spasmodic; *(med)* spastic

spassionatamente (spâs·syō·nâ·tâ·mân'tā) *adv* fairly; without emotion

spasso (spâs'sō) *m* relaxation; **andare a** — to take a walk; **–so** (spâs·sō'zō) *a* funny, amusing

spauracchio (spåü·râk'kyō) *m* bugbear; scarecrow

spavalderia (spå·vâl·dā·rē'â) *f* haughtiness

spaventapasseri (spå·vân·tâ·pâs'sā·rē) *m* scarecrow

spaventare (spå·vân·tâ'rā) *vt* to frighten

spaventarsi (spå·vân·târ'sē) *vr* to be frightened, be aghast, be terrified

spaventevole (spå·vân·te'vō·lā) *a* dreadful, horrifying

spaventosamente (spå·vân·tō·zâ·mân'tā) *adv* awfully; frightfully

spavento (spå·vân'tō) *m* scare; fright; **–so** (spå·vân·tō'zō) *a* awful

spaziale (spå·tsyâ'lā) *a* spatial

spazientirsi (spå·tsyân·tēr'sē) *vr* to lose one's patience

spazio (spå'tsyō) *m* room, space; **–so** (spå·tsyō'zō) *a* roomy

spazzacamino (spå·tsâ·kâ·mē'nō) *m* chimney sweep

spazzamine (spå·tsâ·mē'nā) *m (naut)* mine sweeper

spazzaneve (spå·tsâ·nâ'vā) *m* snowplow

spazzare (spå·tsâ'rā) *vt* to sweep

spazzatura (spå·tsâ·tū'râ) *f* sweepings

spazzino (spå·tsē'nō) *m* street cleaner

spazzola (spå'tsō·lâ) *f* brush; **–re** (spå·tsō·lâ'rā) *vt* to brush

spazzolino (spå·tsō·lē'nō) *m* small brush; — **da denti** toothbrush

specchiarsi (spāk·kyâr'sē) *vr* to look at one's reflection; to be mirrored, be reflected

specchiera (spāk·kyä'râ) *f* dressing table; mirror

specchio (spek'kyō) *m* mirror; — **retrovisivo** *(auto)* rearview mirror

speciale (spå·châ'lā) *a* special; unusual

specialista (spå·châ·lē'stâ) *m* specialist

specialità (spå·châ·lē·tâ') *f* specialty

specie (spe'chā) *f* kind, species; — *adv* especially, above all

specificare (spå·chē·fē·kâ'rā) *vt* to specify, detail

specifico (spå·chē'fē·kō) *a* specific, detailed; — *m* specific, particular

speculazione (spå·kū·lâ·tsyō'nā) *f* speculation

spedire (spå·dē'rā) *vt* to ship; to mail; to send

spedizione (spå·dē·tsyō'nā) *f* shipment; expedition; — **di bagaglio** forwarding of luggage

spedizioniere (spå·dē·tsyō·nyä'rā) *m* forwarding agent

spegnere * (spe'nyä·rā) *vt* to put out; to quench; to extinguish; — **la radio** to turn off the radio

---

â ârm, **ā** bāby, **e** bet, **ē** bē, **ō** gō, **ô** gône, **ū** blūe, **b** bad, **ch** child, **d** dad, **f** fat, **g** gay, **j** jet

spegnersi * (spe'nyār·sē) *vr* to disappear; to die out

spelonca (spā·lōn'kâ) *f* den, cavern

spendere * (spen'dā·rā) *vt&i* to spend; to make use of

spensierato (spān·syā·râ'tō) *a* carefree, troublefree

speranza (spā·rân'tsâ) *f* hope

sperare (spā·râ'rā) *vt&i* to hope; to intend, plan

sperduto (spār·dū'tō) *a* lost, led astray

spergiuro (spār·jū'rō) *m* perjurer; perjury

sperimentare (spā·rē·mān·tâ'rā) *vt* to experiment with, try out, put to the test

sperma (spār'mâ) *m* sperm

sperone (spā·rō'nā) *m (naut)* ram; *(arch)* abutment

spesa (spā'zâ) *f* expense; **fare le spese to** shop

spesso (spās'sō) *adv* often; — *a* frequent; thick, heavy; **–re** (spās·sō'rā) *m* thickness

spettacolare (spāt·tâ·kō·lâ'rā) *a* spectacular

spettacolo (spāt·tâ'kō·lō) *m* show; — **continuo** continuous performance; **–so** (spāt·tâ·kō·lō'zō) *a* striking, unusual

spettanza (spāt·tân'tsâ) *f* concern; due, right

spettare (spāt·tâ'rā) *vi* to be one's turn; to belong to; to be one's business; to be one's duty

spettatore (spāt·tâ·tō'rā) *m* spectator

spettinare (spāt·tē·nâ'rā) *vt* to tousle one's hair; to ruin one's hairdo

spezie (spe'tsyā) *fpl* spices

spezzare (spā·tsâ'rā) *vt* to break

spezzarsi (spā·tsâr'sē) *vr* to be broken; to break, shatter

spezzatino (spā·tsâ·tē'nō) *m* stew

spia (spē'â) *f* spy

spiacevole (spyâ·che'vō·lā) *a* unpleasant

spiaggia (spyâj'jâ) *f* beach, strand

spiare (spyâ'rā) *vt* to spy on

spiccare (spēk·kâ'rā) *vt* to detach; — *vi* to stand out

spiccarsi (spēk·kâr'sē) *vr* to be outstanding; to become detached; to isolate oneself

spicchio (spēk'kyō) *m* garlic clove; segment of fruit, slice of fruit

spicciarsi (spē·châr'sē) *vr* to hurry up, rush

spicciativo (spē·châ·tē'vō) *a* efficient; prompt, quick

spiccioli (spē'chō·lē) *mpl* small change

spiedo (spyā'dō) *m* spit *(cooking)*

spiegamento (spyā·gâ·mān'tō) *m* spread-

ing out; *(mil)* deployment

spiegare (spyā·gâ'rā) *vt* to explain

spiegarsi (spyā·gâr'sē) *vr* to explain oneself, make oneself understood; **Mi spiego?** Do I make myself clear?

spiegazione (spyā·gâ·tsyō'nā) *f* explanation

spietato (spyā·tâ'tō) *a* relentless; without pity

spiga (spē'gâ) *f (bot)* ear

spilla (spēl'lâ) *f* brooch; tie-pin

spillo (spēl'lō) *m* pin; — **di sicurezza** safety pin

spilorcio (spē·lôr'chō) *a* stingy; — *m* miser

spilungone (spē·lūn·gō'nā) *m* lanky fellow; *(fig)* lamppost; — *a* tall and thin

spina (spē'nâ) *f* thorn; spine; fish bone; *(elec)* plug

spinacio (spē·nâ'chō) *m* spinach

spingere * (spēn'jā·rā) *vt* to push; — **all'eccesso** to go too far, carry things to extremes

spinoso (spē·nō'zō) *a* thorny; ticklish, delicate

spinta (spēn'tâ) *f* shove; push; *(fig)* impetus

spinterogeno (spēn·tā·rō'jā·nō) *m (auto)* distributor

spinto (spēn'tō) *a* daring, suggestive; immoderate; **–ne** (spēn·tō'nā) *m* violent shove

spionaggio (spyō·nâj'jō) *m* espionage

spioncino (spyōn·chē'nō) *m* peephole

spiraglio (spē·râ'lyō) *m* fissure; vent; hole; *(fig)* gleam, glimmering, ray of hope

spirale (spē·râ'lā) *f&a* spiral; **a —** in spiral fashion

spirare (spē·râ'rā) *vt&i* to expire, die; to fall due; to infuse, inspire

spiritismo (spē·rē·tē'zmō) *m* spirit rapping; spiritualism

spirito (spē'rē·tō) *m* wit; spirit; ghost; alcohol; — **denaturato** denatured alcohol; **prontezza di —** ready wit; **povero di —** narrow-minded; **S– Santo** Holy Ghost; **–so** (spē·rē·tō'zō) *a* witty, humorous

spirituale (spē·rē·twâ'lā) *a* spiritual

splendere (splen'dā·rā) *vi* to shine; to gleam, glisten

splendidamente (splān·dē·dâ·mān'tā) *adv* magnificently, stupendously

splendido (splen'dē·dō) *a* glorious; sumptuous, magnificent

splendore (splān·dō'rā) *m* magnificence; radiance; splendor

spoglia (spō'lyâ) *f* skin, hide; loot; — **mortale** mortal remains; **–re** (spō·lyâ'-

rā) *vt* to strip; *(fig)* to examine minutely; **–rello** (spō·lyä·rāl'lō) *m* strip tease; **–rsi** (spō·lyâr'sē) *vr* to undress; **–toio** (spō·lyâ·tô'yō) *m* dressing room; locker room

spola (spō'lä) *f* shuttle; **fare la —** *(fig)* to ply, go back and forth

spolverare (spōl·vä·râ'rā) *vt* to dust off

sponda (spōn'dä) *f* shore

spontaneo (spōn·tä'nä·ō) *a* spontaneous

sporadicamente (spō·râ·dē·kâ·män'tä) *adv* sporadically

sporcaccione (spōr·kâ·chō'nä) *m* filthy person, swine

sporcare (spōr·kâ'rä) *vt* to dirty, soil

sporco (spōr'kō) *a* unclean, filthy, dirty

sport (spōrt) *m* sport

sporta (spōr'tä) *f* shopping bag

sportello (spōr·tāl'lō) *m* ticket window

sportivo (spōr·tē'vō) *a* sporting; **—** *m* sportsman

sposa (spō'zä) *f* wife, bride; **–lizio** (spō·zâ·lē'tsyō) *m* wedding; **–re** (spō·zâ'rä) *vt* to marry; **–rsi** (spō·zâr'sē) *vr* to get married; **–to** (spō·zâ'tō) *a* married

sposo (spō'zō) *m* husband, bridegroom

sposi (spō'zē) *mpl* bride and groom, wedding couple

spostare (spō·stâ'rä) *vt* to move; to change

spostarsi (spō·stâr'sē) *vr* to change one's place; to move to another seat

spostato (spō·stâ'tō) *m* misfit; **—** *a* maladjusted

sprazzo (sprâ'tsō) *m* flash, gleam; **— d'intelligenza** glimmer of understanding

sprecare (sprä·kâ'rä) *vt* to waste

spreco (sprä'kō) *m* waste; **–ne** (sprä·kō'nä) *m* waster, spendthrift

spregio (spre'jō) *m* despising; disrespect; scorn

spregiudicato (sprä·jū·dē·kâ'tō) *a* impartial; broadminded; unprejudiced

spremere (spre'mä·rä) *vt* to squeeze; to wring out

spremilimoni (sprä·mē·lē·mō'nē) *m* lemon squeezer

spremuta (sprä·mū'tä) *f* fruit juice; **— di arancia** orange juice

sprezzante (sprä·tsän'tä) *a* contemptuous, despising

sproloquio (sprō·lô'kwyō) *m* long-winded talk, very wordy speech

spronare (sprō·nâ'rä) *vt* to stimulate, rouse; to spur on; *(naut)* to ram

sproporzionato (sprō·pōr·tsyō·nâ'tō) *a* out of proportion

sproposito (sprō·pô'zē·tō) *m* nonsense; error; faux pas; **fare uno —** to make a

blunder; **parlare a —** to get off the subject; **costare uno —** to cost a fortune

spropriazione (sprō·pryâ·tsyō'nä) *f* expropriation

sprovvisto (sprōv·vē'stō) *a* deficient in; unprovided for; **alla sprovvista** unexpectedly, by surprise

spruzzare (sprū·tsâ'rä) *vt* to spatter; to sprinkle

spruzzatore (sprū·tsâ·tō'rä) *m* sprayer

spudoratezza (spū·dō·râ·tä'tsä) *f* brazenness; lack of decorum

spudorato (spū·dō·râ'tō) *a* shameless; insolent

spugna (spū'nyâ) *f* sponge

spulciare (spūl·châ'rä) *vt* to deflea; *(fig)* to scrutinize, inspect minutely

spuma (spū'mâ) *f* froth, foam; **–nte** (spū·mân'tä) *a* sparkling, foaming; **–nte** *m* champagne, sparkling wine

spuntare (spūn·tâ'rä) *vt* to blunt; to break the point of; *(com)* to check off; to unfasten; **—** *vi* to show up; to rise; to peep out; to cut *(teeth)*; **spuntarcela** to win out, overcome all difficulties; **lo — del giorno** daybreak, dawn

spuntarsi (spūn·târ'sē) *vr* to become blunt; to lose its point *(pencil)*

spuntino (spūn·tē'nō) *m* snack

sputacchiera (spū·tâk·kyä'râ) *f* cuspidor

sputare (spū·tâ'rä) *vt&i* to spit, expectorate

sputo (spū'tō) *m* saliva, spit

squadra (skwâ'drä) *f* team; square; *(avi)* squadron; **— mobile** riot squad

squagliare (skwâ·lyâ'rä) *vt* to melt

squagliarsi (skwâ·lyâr'sē) *vr* to take French leave; to vanish, disappear

squalificare (skwâ·lē·fē·kâ'rä) *vt* to disqualify

squallido (skwâl'lē·dō) *a* bleak, miserable

squallore (skwâl·lō'rä) *m* dismalness, gloominess; squalor, misery

squalo (skwâ'lō) *m* shark

squama (skwâ'mâ) *f* scale *(fish, reptile)*; flake of paint

squarciare (skwâr·châ'rä) *vt* to tear apart, rip apart

squarciarsi (skwâr·châr'sē) *vr* to rip in two, tear apart, be torn up

squarcio (skwâr'chō) *m;* tear, rip; gash, cut

squattrinato (skwât·trē·nâ'tō) *a* penniless, broke

squilibrato (skwē·lē·brâ'to) *a* deranged; mentally unbalanced; **—** *m* madcap; hare-brained individual

squillo (skwēl'lō) *m* ring; blare, blast; peal

â ârm, ā bāby, e bet, ē bē, ō gō, ô gône, ū blūe, b bad, ch child, d dad, f fat, g gay, j jet

of bells
squisitezza (skwē·zē·tā′tsâ) *f* exquisiteness; deliciousness
squisito (skwē·zē′tō) *a* delicious; exquisite
squoiare (skwō·yâ′rā) *vt* to skin
sradicare (zrâ·dē·kâ′rā) *vt* to abolish; to pull out by the roots; to eradicate
sregolatezza (zrâ·gō·lâ·tā′tsâ) *f* debauchery, dissipation; confusion
stabile (stâ′bē·lā) *m* building; piece of real estate; — *a* stable, constant
stabilimento (stā·bē·lē·mān′tō) *m* establishment
stabilire (stâ·bē·lē′rā) *vt* to establish, found; to lay down
stabilirsi (stâ·bē·lēr′sē) *vr* to settle, take up residence
stabilità (stâ·bē·lē·tâ′) *f* steadiness
staccare (stâk·kâ′rā) *vt* to detach, separate
staccarsi (stâk·kâr′sē) *vr (avi)* to take off; to come loose; to stand out, be outstanding
staccio (stâ′chō) *m* sieve
stadio (stâ′dyō) *m* stadium; phase, level
staffa (stâf′fâ) *f* stirrup; **perdere le staffe** *(fig)* to lose one's temper
staffetta (stâf·fāt′tâ) *f* courier; messenger; **corsa a —** relay race
staffilata (stâf·fē·lâ′tâ) *f* whipping; lash; *(fig)* taunt
staffile (stâf·fē′lā) *m* whip
stagione (stâ·jō′nā) *f* season
stagno (stâ′nyō) *m* tin; — *a* watertight; **–la** (stâ·nyō′lâ) *f* tinfoil
stagno (stâ′nyō) *m* pond
stalla (stâl′lâ) *f* stable, stall
stallone (stâl·lō′nâ) *m* stallion
stamani (stâ·mâ′nē) *adv* this morning
stamattina (stâ·mât·tē′nâ) *adv* this morning
stampa (stâm′pâ) *f* press; printing; **–re** (stâm·pâ′rā) *vt* to print
stampe (stâm′pā) *fpl* printed matter
stampella (stâm·pāl′lâ) *f* crutch; coat hanger
stamperia (stâm·pâ·rē′â) *f* printing office
stampiglia (stâm·pē′lyâ) *f (mech)* stamp
stampino (stâm·pē′nō) *m* stencil
stampo (stâm′pō) *m* sort; stamp, mould
stancare (stân·kâ′rā) *vt* to tire
stancarsi (stân·kâr′sē) *vr* to grow tired
stanchezza (stân·kâ′tsâ) *f* fatigue; exhaustion
stanco (stân′kō) *a* tired, worn-out
stanga (stân′gâ) *f* bar; shaft
stanotte (stâ·nōt′tâ) *adv* last night; tonight
stantio (stân·tē′ō) *a* insipid, stale, inane

stantuffo (stân·tūf′fō) *m* plunger; piston
stanza (stân′tsâ) *f* room
stanziamento (stân·tsyâ·mān′tō) *m* appropriation, grant
stanziare (stân·tsyâ′rā) *vt* to appropriate, allocate
stare * (stâ′rā) *vi* to be; to stand; to remain; — **in piedi** to stand; — **fermo** to stand still; — **per** to be about to
starnutire (stâr·nū·tē′rā) *vi* to sneeze
starnuto (stâr·nū′tō) *m* sneeze
stasera (stâ·sâ′râ) *f* tonight
statale (stâ·tâ′lā) *a* governmental
statistica (stâ·tē′s′tē·kâ) *f* statistics
stato (stâ′tō) *m* condition, state
statua (stâ′twâ) *f* statue
statunitense (stâ·tū·nē·tân′sā) *a* American, of the United States.
statura (stâ·tū′râ) *f* stature
statuto (stâ·tū′tō) *m* constitution; by-law; *(law)* statute
stavolta (stâ·vōl′tâ) *adv* this time, on this occasion
stazionare (stâ·tsyō·nâ′rā) *vi* to park; to stay, remain
stazione (stâ·tsyō′nā) *f* station; — **climatica** health resort; — **di villeggiatura** summer resort
stazza (stâ′tsâ) *f (naut)* displacement
stecca (stāk′kâ) *f* stick; spoke; billiard cue; plectrum; carton of cigarettes; *(mus)* false note; umbrella rib
stecchino (stāk·kē′nō) *m* toothpick
stecconata (stāk·kō·nâ′tâ) *f* fence
stella (stāl·lâ) *f* star; *(fig)* destiny; asterisk; — **filante** shooting star; streamer
stelo (stā′lō) *m (bot)* stem
stemma (stām′mâ) *m* coat of arms
stemperare (stām·pâ·râ′rā) *vt* to dilute; to melt
stendere * (sten′dā·rā) *vt* to stretch; to spread; to compose, draft *(document)*
stendersi * (sten′dār·sē) *vr* to relax; to reach; to stretch out
stenodattilografo (stā·nō·dât·tē·lō′grâ·fō) *m* stenographer
stento (stān′tō) *m* struggle; suffering; lack; **a —** with difficulty; hardly
steppa (stāp′pâ) *f* steppe, prairie
sterco (stār′kō) *m* dung
sterile (ste′rē·lā) *a* sterile; of no avail, useless
sterilità (stâ·rē·lē·tâ′) *f* sterility
sterilizzare (stâ·rē·lē·dzâ′rā) *vt* to sterilize
sterminare (stâr·mē·nâ′rā) *vt* to exterminate
sterminato (stār·mē·nâ′tō) *a* immense; limitless

k kid, **l** let, **m** met, **n** not, **p** pat, **r** very, **s** sat, **sh** shop, **t** tell, **v** vat, **w** we, **y** yet, **z** zero

sterminio (stär·mē′nyō) *m* enormity; extermination

sterpo (stär′pō) *m* underbrush; brambles

sterratore (stär·rä·tō′rä) *m* ditchdigger

sterzare (stär·tsä′rä) *vt&i* to swerve; to steer

sterzo (stär′tsō) *m (auto)* steering mechanism

stesso (stās′sō) *a* same, very same; **fa lo — it's immaterial,** it makes no difference

stia (stē′â) *f* hencoop

stilare (stē·lâ′rä) *vt* to draw up *(document)*

stile (stē′lä) *m* style; stylus

stilografica (stē·lō·grä′fē·kâ) *f* fountain pen

stima (stē′mâ) *f* esteem; opinion; *(com)* estimate; **-re** (stē·mä′rä) *vt* to esteem; to consider, deem; *(com)* to estimate; **-rsi** (stē·mâr′sē) to consider oneself, deem oneself

stimolare (stē·mō·lâ′rä) *vt* to stimulate; to urge

stimolo (stē′mō·lō) *m* stimulus; urging

stinco (stēn′kō) *m* shin

stipendio (stē·pen′dyō) *m* salary

stipite (stē′pē·tä) *m* jamb; stalk, stem; lineage

stipo (stē′pō) *m* cabinet

stipulare (stē·pū·lâ′rä) *vt* to stipulate

stipulazione (stē·pū·lâ·tsyō′nä) *f* stipulation

stirare (stē·râ′rä) *vt* to iron; to stretch

stirarsi (stē·râr′sē) *vr* to stretch out; to stretch one's limbs

stiratrice (stē·râ·trē′chä) *f* laundress

stireria (stē·rä·rē′â) *f* laundry

stiro (stē′rō) *m* ironing; **ferro da —** flatiron

stirpe (stēr′pä) *f* lineage, origin

stitichezza (stē·tē·kä′tsä) *f* constipation

stitico (stē′tē·kō) *a* constipated; *(fig)* stingy

stiva (stē′vâ) *f (naut)* hold

stivale (stē·vä′lä) *m* boot

stizza (stē′tsä) *f* anger, ire

stizzire (stē·tsē′rä) *vt* to vex, irritate

stizzirsi (stē·tsēr′sē) *vr* to become angry

stoffa (stōf′fâ) *f* cloth; material

stoino (stō·ē′nō) *m* door mat

stolto (stōl′tō) *a* foolish

stomachevole (stō·mâ·ke′vō·lä) *a* disgusting

stomaco (stô′mâ·kō) *m* stomach; **dolor di — stomach** ache

stomatico (stō·mâ′tē·kō) *m* tonic

stonare (stō·nä′rä) *vi* to sing off key; to be out of tune; to be out of place; to jar;

(fig) to be at loggerheads

stonatura (stō·nâ·tū′rä) *f* blunder; dissonant note; dissonance; *(fig)* disagreement

stoppa (stōp′pâ) *f* oakum

stoppino (stōp·pē′nō) *m* wick

storcere * (stôr′chä·rä) *vt* to twist; to sprain

stordimento (stōr·dē·mân′tō) *m* daze, bewilderment; dulling of one's senses

stordire (stōr·dē′rä) *vt* to deafen; to bewilder, confuse; to dull *(senses)*

stordirsi (stōr·dēr′sē) *vr* to have one's senses dulled; to become dazed

stordito (stōr·dē′tō) *a* dizzy; dulled; confused, bewildered

storia (stô′ryâ) *f* story; history

storicamente (stō·rē·kâ·mān′tä) *adv* historically

storico (stô′rē·kō) *a* historical; **— m** historian

storione (stō·ryō′nä) *m* sturgeon

stormo (stôr′mō) *m* swarm, flock; *(avi)* flight, wing; **suonare a —** to sound the alarm, sound the alert

storpio (stôr′pyō) *m* cripple; **— a** maimed

storta (stôr′tä) *f (med)* sprain; *(chem)* retort

storto (stôr′tō) *a* twisted; distorted; **avere gli occhi storti** to be squint-eyed

stoviglie (stō·vē′lyä) *fpl* pottery; china, dishes

strabene (strâ·bä′nä) *adv* extremely well

strabico (strâ′bē·kō) *a* squint-eyed, squinting

strabiliante (strâ·bē·lyân′tä) *a* surprising, astonishing

stracciare (strâ·châ′rä) *vt* to tear, rip; to lacerate

stracciato (strâ·châ′tō) *a* in rags; torn to shreds

straccio (strâ′chō) *m* rag; **-ne** (strâ·chō′nä) *m* ragamuffin

stracco (strâk′kō) *a* very tired, worn-out

strada (strâ′dä) *f* street; road; **— interrotta** road closed; **— in costruzione** road repairs; **— secondaria** by-pass; **— maestra** highway

stradale (strâ·dâ′lä) *m* avenue; **— a** street, road; **polizia —** traffic patrol; **carta —** road map

strafalcione (strâ·fâl·chō′nä) *m* blunder

strafare * (strâ·fâ′rä) *vi* to work too hard; to overdo

strage (strâ′jä) *f* massacre, butchering; *(fig)* plenty

stramazzare (strâ·mâ·tsä′rä) *vi* to fall in, collapse; **— vt** to knock over, knock down

strame (strä'mä) *m* fodder, litter

strampalato (strâm·pâ·lâ'tō) *a* absurd; odd; bizarre

stranezza (strâ·nä'tsâ) *f* whimsy; singularity; oddity

strangolare (strän·gō·lâ'rä) *vt* to choke

straniero (strä·nyä'rō) *a* foreign; — *m* foreigner; stranger

strano (strä'nō) *a* stranger, peculiar

straordinario (strâ·ōr·dē·nâ'ryō) *a* extraordinary; — *m* overtime

strapazzare (strâ·pâ·tsâ'rä) *vt* to scold; to mistreat; to scramble *(eggs)*

strapazzarsi (strâ·pâ·tsâr'sē) *vr* to overdo oneself; to act carelessly about one's health

strapazzo (strâ·pâ'tsō) *m* excess; strain; **vestito da** — working cloths; **pittore da** — inferior painter

strapiombo (strâ·pyōm'bō) *m* **a** — jutting out; sheer

strappare (strâp·pâ'rä) *vt* to tear apart; to pull; to snatch; — **il cuore a qualcuno** *(fig)* to break someone's heart

strapparsi (strâp·pâr'sē) *vr* to tear oneself away; — **i capelli** to tear one's hair

strappo (strâp'pō) *m* tear, rent; jerk, start; — **muscolare** muscle strain

strapuntino (strâ·pūn'tē·nō) *m* *(auto)* bucket seat

straripare (strâ·rē·pâ'rä) *vi* to overflow; to flood its banks *(river)*

strascico (strâ'shē·kō) *m* train *(dress)*; results, aftermath

stratagemma (strâ·tâ·jäm'mâ) *m* stratagem, policy, device

stratega (strâ·tä'gâ) *m* strategist

strato (strâ'tō) *m* layer, coat; **-sfera** (strâ·tō·sfä'rä) *f* stratosphere

stravagante (strâ·vâ·gân'tä) *a* eccentric, odd

stravolto (strâ·vōl'tō) *a* agitated, upset

strazio (strâ'tsyō) *m* anguish, torture

strega (strä'gâ) *f* witch

stregone (strä·gō'nä) *m* wizard, warlock

strenna (strän'nâ) *f* gift; tip, gratuity

strenuamente (strä·nwâ·män'tä) *adv* strenuously, vigorously

strenuo (stre'nwō) *active, vigorous

strepito (stre'pē·tō) *m* noise; **-so** (strâ·pē·tō'zō) *a* resounding; sensational; noisy

stretta (strät'tâ) *f* grip, grasp, squeeze; — **al cuore** tug at the heart; — **di mano** handshake; — **di spalle** shrug of one's shoulders

strettezza (strät·tä'tsâ) *f* difficulty; strict-

ness; narrowness; — **economica** economic difficulties, money worries

stretto (strät'tō) *a* narrow; — *m* *(geog)* straits

strillare (strēl·lâ'rä) *vi* to scream

strillo (strēl'lō) *m* scream, shriek; **-ne** (strēl·lō'nä) *m* newsboy

stringa (strēn'gâ) *f* shoelace

stringere * (strēn'jä·rä) *vt&i* to squeeze; to press; to make tighter; — **la mano** to shake hands

stringersi * (strēn'jär·sē) *vr* to narrow; to come close; to draw near; — **nelle spalle** to shrug one's shoulders

striscia (strē'shâ) *f* strip; **-re** (strē·shâ'rä) *vt* to creep; to graze, touch lightly

stritolare (strē·tō·lâ'rä) *vt* to smash; to crush

strizzalimoni (strē·tsâ·lē·mō'nē) *m* lemon squeezer

strizzare (strē·tsâ'rä) *vt* to wring; to squeeze

strofinaccio (strō·fē·nâ'chō) *m* rag; duster

strozzare (strō·tsâ'rä) *vt* to strangle

strozzino (strō·tsē'nō) *m* loan shark *(coll)*

strumento (strū·män'tō) *m* instrument

strutto (strūt'tō) *m* lard

struzzo (strū'tsō) *m* ostrich

studente (stū·dän'tä) *m*, **studentessa** (stū·dän·täs'sâ) *f* student

studiare (stū·dyâ'rä) *vt* to study

studio (stū'dyō) *m* study; studio

stufa (stū'fâ) *f* stove

stufato (stū·fâ'tō) *m* stew

stufo (stū'fō) *a* fed up, tired, bored

stuoia (stwō'yâ) *f* doormat; matting

stuolo (stwō'lō) *m* crowd, group

stupefacente (stū·pâ·fâ·chän'tä) *a* astounding; awe-inspiring; bewildering; — *m* narcotic

stupendo (stū·pän'dō) *a* stupendous, magnificent, wonderful

stupidaggine (stū·pē·dâj'jē·nä) *f* absurdness; foolishness

stupido (stū'pē·dō) *a* dull, stupid, foolish, mentally slow

stupire (stū·pē'rä) *vt* to amaze, astound

stupirsi (stū·pēr'sē) *vr* to be astonished; to wonder at

stupore (stū·pō'rä) *m* stupefaction; wonderment; *(med)* stupor

stupro (stū'prō) *m* rape

sturare (stū·râ'rä) *vt* to uncork

stuzzicadenti (stū·tsē·kâ·dän'tē) *m* toothpick

stuzzicante (stū·tsē·kân'tä) *a* provocative, stimulating; vexing

stuzzicare (stū·tsē·kâ'rä) *vt* to whet; to

stimulate; to tease, needle

stuzzicarsi (stŭ·tsē·kâr'sē) *vr* to pick one's teeth

su (sū) *adv&prep* on; over; above; about

subacqueo (sū·bâk'kwä·ō) *a* underwater; **pescatore** — skin diver

subaffittare (sū·bâf·fēt·tâ'rā) *vt* to sublet

subbuglio (sūb·bū'lyō) *m* uproar, bustle, hubbub

subcoscienza (sūb·kō·shän'tsâ) *f* subconscious

subdolo (sūb'dō·lō) *a* shifty, insidious, crafty

subire (sū'·bē'rā) *vt* to suffer, undergo

subito (sū'bē·tō) *adv* at once; — *a* sudden; rapid

sublimato (sū·blē·mâ'tō) *m* sublimate; — **corrosivo** mercuric chloride

sublimazione (sū·blē·mâ·tsyō'nä) *f* sublimation

subodorare (sū·bō·dō·râ'rā) *vt* to suspect; to get an inkling of; to know intuitively

succedere * (sū·che'dä·rā) *vi* to happen; to follow

successivamente (sū·chäs·sē·vâ·mān'tā) *adv* consecutively; in succession; thereafter, afterward

successivo (sū·chäs·sē'vō) *a* following, next

successo (sū·chäs'sō) *m* success; — *a* succeeded; followed

succhiare (sūk·kyâ'rā) *vt* to suck

succhiello (sūk·kyäl'lō) *m* gimlet

succo (sūk'kō) *m* juice; —**so** (sūk·kō'zō) *a* juicy; *(fig)* meaty, substantial

succursale (sūk·kūr·sâ'lä) *f* branch office; agency

sud (sūd) *m* south; —**africano** (sū·dâ·frē·kâ'nō) *a&m* South African; —**americano** (sū·dâ·mä·rē·kâ'nō) *m&a* South American

sudare (sū·dâ'rā) *vi* to perspire; — *vt* to ooze

sudario (sū·dâ'ryō) *m* shroud

suddetto (sūd·dät'tō) *a* aforementioned

suddito (sūd'dē·tō) *m* citizen, subject

sudicio (sū'dē·chō) *a* filthy, dirty; lewd, smutty

sudiciume (sū·dē·chū'mä) *m* smut; dirt

sudore (sū·dō'rā) *m* perspiration, sweat

sufficiente (sūf·fē·chän'tä) *a* sufficient; —**mente** (sūf·fē·chän·tä·mān'tä) *adv* sufficiently, adequately

sufficienza (sūf·fē·chän'tsâ) *f* sufficiency; abundance

suffragare (sūf·frâ·gâ'rā) *vt* to support, aid, back

suggellare (sūj·jäl·lâ'rā) *vt* to seal

suggerimento (sūj·jä·rē·mān'tō) *m* proposal, advice; suggestion

suggerire (sūj·jä·rē'rā) *vt* to prompt; to suggest

suggeritore (sūj·jä·rē·tō'rā) *m* prompter

suggestione (sūj·jä·styō'nä) *f* suggestion

suggestivo (sūj·jä·stē'vō) *a* interesting; enchanting

sughero (sū'gä·rō) *m* cork

sugna (sū'nyâ) *f* grease; lard

sugo (sū'gō) *m* juice; gravy; *(fig)* main point; pièce de résistance

suicida (swē·chē'dâ) *m&f* suicide *(person)*; —**rsi** (swē·chē·dâr'sē) *vr* to commit suicide

suicidio (swē·chē'dyō) *m* suicide *(act)*

suino (swē'nō) *m* swine; — *a* swinish

sunto (sūn'tō) *m* summary, résumé

suo (sū'ō) *a&pron* his, hers, its, your

suocera (swō'chä·râ) *f* mother-in-law

suocero (swō'chä·rō) *m* father-in-law

suola (swō'lâ) *f* sole *(shoe)*

suolo (swō'lō) *m* soil, earth; ground

suonare (swō·nâ'rā) *vt (mus)* to play; to ring

suonatore (swō·nâ·tō'rā) *m* player, musician

suono (swō'nō) *m* sound; chime, ringing *(bell)*

suora (swō'râ) *f* nun

superare (sū·pä·râ'rā) *vt* to exceed; to do better than

superbia (sū·per'byâ) *f* pride, conceit

superbo (sū·pär'bō) *a* conceited; splendid; haughty

superficiale (sū·pär·fē·châ'lä) *a* superficial

superficie (sū·pär·fē'chä) *f* surface; area

superiore (sū·pä·ryō'rä) *a* superior; higher, upper

superfluo (sū·per'flūō) *a* superflous; — *m* surplus

supermercato (sū·pär·mär·kâ'tō) *m* supermarket

superstite (sū·per'stē·tä) *m* survivor; — *a* surviving

superstizione (sū·pär·stē·tsyō'nä) *f* superstition

superstizioso (sū·pär·stē·tsyō'zō) *a* superstitious

superuomo (sū·pä·rūō'mō) *m* superman

supino (sū·pē'nō) *a* on one's back; supine

supplementare (sūp·plä·mān·tâ'rā) *a* auxiliary, supplementary

supplemento (sūp·plä·mān'tō) *m* supplement; extra fare; additional fee

supplente (sūp·plän'tä) *m* substitute, alternate

â ârm, **ā** bāby, **e** bet, **ē** bē, **ō** gō, **ô** gône, **ū** blūe, **b** bad, **ch** child, **d** dad, **f** fat, **g** gay, **j** jet

supplenza (sŭp·plăn′tsâ) *f* temporary position; position of an alternate

supplica (sŭp′plē·kâ) *f* request; entreaty; **–re** (sŭp·plē·kâ′rā) *vt* to implore

supplizio (sŭp·plē′tsyō) *m* torment; torture; intense suffering

supporre * (sŭp·pōr′rā) *vt&i* to suppose; to conjecture

supposizione (sŭp·pō·zē·tsyō′nā) *f* supposition

supposta (sŭp·pō′stâ) *f* suppository

suppurare (sŭp·pū·râ′rā) *vi* to discharge pus, suppurate

suppurazione (sŭp·pū·râ·tsyō′nā) *f* discharge of pus, suppuration

supremo (sū·prā′mō) *a* ultimate, last; supreme, absolute

surrealista (sūr·rā·â·lē′stâ) *a&m* surrealist

surrogato (sūr·rō·gâ′tō) *m* substitute, replacement

susina (sū·zē′nâ) *f* plum

sussidiare (sūs·sē·dyâ′rā) *vt* to subsidize, bolster

sussidiario (sūs·sē·dyâ′ryō) *a* additional, subsidiary

sussidio (sūs·sē′dyō) *m* subsidy; contribution

sussiego (sūs·syâ′gō) *m* primness, stiffness

sussultare (sūs·sūl·tâ′rā) *vi* to quake; to start, be startled; to throb

sussulto (sūs·sūl′tō) *m* tremble, jump, jerk

sussurrare (sūs·sūr·râ′rā) *vt&i* to sigh, sough *(wind)*; to whisper

sussurro (sūs·sūr′rō) *m* whisper; soughing

svagarsi (zvâ·gâr′sē) *vr* to distract one's mind; to amuse oneself

svago (zvâ′gō) *m* entertainment, recreation

svaligiare (zvâ·lē·jâ′rā) *vt* to burglarize, rob; to strip bare, plunder

svaligiatore (zvâ·lē·jâ·tō′rā) *m* burglar, robber

svalutare (zvâ·lū·tâ′rā) *vt* to depreciate; to devaluate

svalutazione (zvâ·lū·tâ·tsyō′nā) *f* depreciation; devaluating

svanire (zvâ·nē′rā) *vi* to vanish; to evaporate; to fade out; to weaken, lose its force

svantaggiosamente (zvân·tâj·jō·zâ·mân′tā) *adv* unfavorably; prejudicially

svantaggio (zvân·tâj′jō) *m* disadvantage

svariato (zvâ·ryâ′tō) *a* assorted, sundry, divers; not a few

svedese (zvā·dā′zā) *a* Swedish; — *m* Swede

svegliare (zvā·lyâ′rā) *vt* to awake, wake up, awaken; *(fig)* to stimulate

svegliarsi (zvā·lyâr′sē) *vr* to wake up; to be awakened; to be aroused

svelare (zvā·lâ′rā) *vt* to reveal

svelarsi (zvā·lâr′sē) *vr* to show one's true colors; to disclose one's real motives

sveltezza (zvāl·tā′tsâ) *f* slenderness; promptness, rapidity; alertness

svelto (zvāl′tō) *a* alert; slender; quick

svendere (zven′dā·rā) *vt* to sell below cost

svenimento (zvā·nē·mān′tō) *m* faint

svenire * (zvā·nē′rā) *vi* to faint

sventato (zvān·tâ′tō) *a* heedless, careless; — *m* scatterbrain

sventura (zvān·tū′râ) *f* misfortune, mischance

svenuto (zvā·nū′tō) *a* fainted; unconscious

svergognare (zvār·gō·nyâ′rā) *vt* to put to shame; to discountenance

svergognato (zvār·gō·nyâ′tō) *a* shameless, brazen

svestirsi (zvā·stēr′sē) *vr* to undress

Svezia (zve′tsyâ) *f* Sweden

svezzare (zvā·tsâ′rā) *vt* to wean

sviare (zvyâ′rā) *vt* to mislead; to deviate; *(rail)* to switch

sviarsi (zvyâr′sē) *vr* to become lost; to go astray

svignarsela (zvē·nyâr′sā·lâ) *vr* to decamp, abscond; to slip away

sviluppare (zvē·lūp·pâ′rā) *vt* to develop

svilupparsi (zvē·lūp·pâr′sē) *vr* to enlarge; to develop; to grow

sviluppo (zvē·lūp′pō) *m* development; **età dello —** puberty

svincolare (zvēn·kō·lâ′rā) *vt* to redeem; to clear through customs

svincolarsi (zvēn·kō·lâr′sē) *vr* to disengage oneself; to free oneself; to escape

svista (zvē′stâ) *f* oversight

svitare (zvē·tâ′rā) *vt* to unscrew

Svizzera (zvē′tsā·râ) *f* Switzerland

svizzero (zvē′tsā·rō) *a&m* Swiss

svogliatamente (zvō·lyâ·tâ·mân′tā) *adv* unwillingly; grudgingly

svogliato (zvō·lyâ′tō) *a* inattentive; averse, grudging; lackadaisical

svolgere * (zvōl′jā·rā) *vt* to unroll; to display; to carry out; to elaborate on, develop

svolgersi * (zvōl′jâr·sē) *vr* to take place; to unfold; to develop

svolgimento (zvōl·jē·mân′tō) *m* handling; solution *(problem)*; development, event

svolta (zvōl′tâ) *f* turn; bend; curve; **–re** (zvōl·tâ′rā) *vt&i* to turn

svotare (zvō·tâ′rā) *vt* to discharge, empty

k kid, **l** let, **m** met, **n** not, **p** pat, **r** very, **s** sat, **sh** shop, **t** tell, **v** vat, **w** we, **y** yet, **z** zero

T

tabaccaio (tâ·bâk·kâ′yō) *m* tobacco dealer, tobacconist
tabaccheria (tâ·bâk·kä·rē′â) *f* cigar store, tobacco shop
tabacco (tâ·bâk′kō) *m* tobacco
tabella (tâ·bāl′lâ) *f* table, chart; bulletin board
tabellone (tâ·bāl·lō′nä) *m* poster
tabernacolo (tâ·bär·nâ′kō·lō) *m* tabernacle
taccagno (tâk·kâ′nyō) *a* stingy, tight-fisted
taccheggiatore (tâk·kāj·jâ·tō′rä) *m* shoplifter
tacchino (tâk·kē′nō) *m* turkey
tacciare (tâ·châ′rä) *vt* to accuse; to blame for
tacco (tâk′kō) *m* heel
taccuino (tâk·kwē′nō) *m* notebook
tacere * (tâ·châ′rä) *vi* to keep quiet; — *vt* to omit; not to mention
taciturno (tâ·chē·tūr′nō) *a* taciturn, uncommunicative; sullen
tachimetro (tâ·kē′mä·trō) *m* speedometer
tafferuglio (tâf·fä·rū′lyō) *m* scuffle
taffetà (tâf·fä·tâ′) *m* adhesive tape; taffeta
taglia (tâ′lyâ) *f* reward; size; —carte (tâ·lyâ·kâr′tä) *m* paper knife; —legna (tâ·lyâ·lā′nyâ) *m* lumberjack; —ndo (tâ·lyân′dō) *m* coupon; —re (tâ·lyâ′rä) *vt* to cut; —rsi (tâ·lyâr′sē) *vr* to cut oneself; —telle (tâ·lyâ·tāl′lä) *fpl* noodles; —tore (tâ·lyâ·tō′rä) *m* cutter; tailor
tagliente (tâ·lyān′tä) *a* sharp; *(fig)* sarcastic, trenchant
tagliere (tâ·lyä′rä) *m* platter
taglierina (tâ·lyä·rē′nâ) *f* paper cutter
taglio (tâ′lyō) *m* cut; edge, cut side; blade, cutting edge; denomination *(money)*
tagliuola (tâ·lywō′lâ) *f* trap
talco (tâl′kō) *m* talcum powder
tale (tâ′lä) *a* such, so; like, similar; certain, particular
talento (tâ·lān′tō) *m* talent, skill, great ability
talloncino (tâl·lōn·chē′nō) *m* coupon; check stub; voucher
tallone (tâl·lō′nä) *m* heel; *(com)* stub
talmente (tâl·mān′tä) *adv* so very; so much; in that way; so, in such a way
talpa (tâl′pâ) *f* mole
taluno (tâ·lū′nō) *pron* someone, somebody
talvolta (tâl·vōl′tâ) *adv* on occasion, sometimes
tamburello (tâm·bū·rāl′lō) *m* tambourine

tamburino (tâm·bū·rē′nō) *m* drummer
tamburo (tâm·bū′rō) *m* drum
tamponare (tâm·pō·nâ′rä) *vt* to stop up, plug up
tampone (tâm·pō′nä) *m* stamp pad; stopper
tana (tâ′nâ) *f* lair, cave
tanaglie (tâ·nâ′lyä) *fpl* pincers; tongs
tanè (tâ·nä′) *a* chestnut color
tanfo (tân′fō) *m* stench; bad odor
tangente (tân·jän′tä) *f&a* tangent
tanghero (tân′gä·rō) *m* boor, yokel
tanti (tân′tē) *a* so many, a great many
tantino (tân·tē′nō) *m* little bit
tanto (tân′tō) *a&adv* so much; so; — quanto as much as
tappa (tâp′pâ) *f* stop; lap *(race)*; —re (tâp·pâ′rä) *vt* to plug up, plug
tappeto (tâp·pā′tō) *m* rug, carpet
tappezzare (tâp·pä·tsâ′rä) *vt* to upholster; to wallpaper
tappezzeria (tâp·pä·tsä·rē′â) *f* upholstery; wallpaper; **fare —** to be a wallflower *(coll)*
tappezziere (tâp·pä·tsyä′rä) *m* upholsterer; decorator
tappo (tâp′pō) *m* plug, cork; cap, cover
tarantola (tâ·rân′tō·lâ) *f* tarantula
tarchiato (târ·kyâ′tō) *a* stocky
tardare (târ·dâ′rä) *vi* to be late; to be long
tardi (târ′dē) *adv* late
targa (târ′gâ) *f* license plate; — stradale street sign
tariffa (tâ·rēf′fâ) *f* scale, rate; price list; tariff, duty
tarlato (târ·lâ′tō) *a* moth-eaten; worm-eaten
tarlo (târ′lō)´*m* woodworm, clothes moth
tarma (târ′mâ) *f* moth
tartagliare (târ·tâ·lyâ′rä) *vi* to stammer
tartaruga (târ·tâ·rū′gâ) *f* tortoise, turtle
tartassare (târ·tâs·sâ′rä) *vt* to manhandle, mistreat
tartina (târ·tē′nâ) *f* sandwich
tartufo (târ·tū′fō) *m* truffle
tasca (tâs′kâ) *f* pocket; —bile (tâ·skâ′bē·lä) *a* pocket; portable; —pane (tâ·skâ·pâ′nä) *m* haversack, shoulder sack
taschino (tâ·skē′nō) *m* vest pocket
tassa (tâs′sâ) *f* tax; duty; —metro (tâs·sâ′mä·trō) *m* taximeter; —re (tâs·sâ′rä) *vt* to tax; —tivamente (tâs·sâ·tē·vâ·mân′tä) *adv* exactly; explicitly; positively; —tivo (tâs·sâ·tē′vō) *a* exact; compulsory
tassello (tâs·sāl′lō) *m* dowel

â ârm, ā bāby, e bet, ē bē, ō gō, ô gône, ū blūe, b bad, ch child, d dad, f fat, g gay, j jet

tassì (tâs·sē′) *m* taxi, cab

tassista (tâs·sē′stâ) *m* taxi driver, cab driver

tasso (tâs′sō) *m* rate of interest

tasso (tâs′sō) *m* badger

tastare (tâ·stâ′rā) *vt* to feel, finger; *(med)* to palpate

tastiera (tâ·styā′râ) *f* keyboard

tasto (tâ′stō) *m* *(mus, mech)* key; subject

tastoni (tâ·stō′nē) *adv* by groping, gropingly

tattica (tât′tē·kâ) *f* tactics

tatto (tât′tō) *m* sense of touch; tact

tatuaggio (tâ·twâj′jō) *m* tattoo

tatuare (tâ·twâ′rā) *vt* to tattoo

taumaturgo (tâū·mâ·tūr′gō) *m* miracle worker

taurino (tâū·rē′nō) *a* bullish; bull, bull-like

tauromachia (tâū·rō·mâ·kē′â) *f* bull-fighting

taverna (tâ·vār′nâ) *f* tavern

taverniere (tâ·vār·nyā′râ) *m* tavern owner

tavola (tâ′vō·lâ) *f* board; table; plank

tavoletta (tâ·vō·lāt′tâ) *f* tablet

tavolino (tâ·vō·lē′nō) *m* worktable; small table

tavolozza (tâ·vō·lō′tsâ) *f* palette

tazza (tâ′tsâ) *f* cup

te (tā) *pron* you; to you

tè (tā) *m* tea

teatro (tā·â′trō) *m* theater; — **lirico** opera; — **di prosa** legitimate theater; drama

teca (tā′kâ) *f* reliquary; jewel case

tecnica (tek′nē·kâ) *f* technique

tecnicamente (tāk·nē·kâ·mān′tâ) *adv* technically

tecnico (tek′nē·kō) *a* technical; — *m* technician; expert

tedesco (tā·dâ′skō) *a&m* German

tedio (te′dyō) *m* boredom, ennui; –**so** (tā·dyō′zō) *a* boring

tegame (tā·gâ′mā) *m* pan

teglia (te′lyâ) *f* casserole, baking dish

tegola (te′gō·lâ) *f* roofing tile

teiera (tā·yā′râ) *f* teapot

tela (tā′lâ) *f* cloth; linen; canvas; painting; *(theat)* curtain; — **incerata** oil cloth; — **di ragno** cobweb; –**io** (tâ·lâ′yō) *m* *(auto)* chassis; framework; loom

telearma (tā·lā·âr′mâ) *f* guided missile

telecamera (tā·lā·kâ′mā·râ) *f* television camera

telecomandato (tā·lā·kō·mân·dâ′tō) *a* remote-controlled

telecomando (tā·lā·kō·mân′dō) *m* remote control

teleferica (tā·lā·fe′rē·kâ) *f* overhead cable railway, funicular

telefonare (tā·lā·fō·nâ′rā) *vt* to telephone

telefonico (tā·lā·fô′nē·kō) *a* telephone; **elenco** — telephone directory

telefonista (tā·lā·fō·nē′stâ) *m&f* telephone operator

telefono (tā·le′fō·nō) *m* telephone

telefoto (tā·lā·fō′tō) *f* telephotograph

telegenico (tā·lā·je′nē·kō) *a* telegenic

telegiornale (tā·lā·jōr·nâ′lâ) *m* television news

telegrafare (tā·lā·grâ·fâ′rā) *vt* to wire, cable

telegrafista (tā·lā·grâ·fē′stâ) *m&f* telegraph operator

telegrafo (tā·le′grâ·fō) *m* telegraph

telegramma (tā·lā·grâm′mâ) *m* telegram

telemetro (tā·le′mā·trō) *m* range finder

teleobiettivo (tā·lā·ō·byât·tē′vō) *m* telephoto lens

telepatia (tā·lā·pâ·tē′â) *f* telepathy

teleromanzo (tā·lā·rō·mân′dzō) *m* play for television

teleschermo (tā·lā·skâr′mō) *m* television screen

telescopio (tā·lā·skō′pyō) *m* telescope

telescrivente (tā·lā·skrē·vân′tâ) *f* teletypewriter, teleprinter

telespettatore (tā·lā·spât·tâ·tō′râ) *m* televiewer

telespresso (tā·lā·sprās′sō) *m* telephone message; telegraph message

teletrasmettere (tā·lā·trâ·zmet′tā·rā) *vt* to telecast

teletrasmissione (tā·lā·trâ·zmēs·syō′nâ) *f* telecast

televisionare (tā·lā·vē·zyō·nâ′rā) *vt* to telecast, televise

televisione (tā·lā·vē·zyō′nâ) *f* television

televisivo (tā·lā·vē·zē′vō) *a* television

televisore (tā·lā·vē·zō′râ) *m* television set

telone (tā·lō′nâ) *m* *(theat)* curtain

tema (tā′mâ) *m* subject, theme; problem

temerario (tā·mā·râ′ryō) *a* foolhardy

temere (tā·mā′rā) *vi* to be afraid; — *vt* to fear, be afraid of

temibile (tā·mē′bē·lâ) *a* formidable, frightful

temperalapis (tām·pā·râ·lâ′pēs) *m* pencil sharpener

temperamento (tām·pā·râ·mân′tō) *m* temperament

temperanza (tām·pā·rân′tsâ) *f* temperance

temperare (tām·pā·râ′rā) *vt* to temper, lessen; to sharpen; to moderate

temperato (tām·pā·râ′tō) *a* temperate; restrained, reserved

temperatura (tām·pā·râ·tū′râ) *f* tempera-

ture
temperino (tām·pä·rē'nō) *m* penknife
tempesta (tām·pä'stä) *f* storm
tempestivamente (tām·pä·stē·vâ·mān'tā)
adv promptly; at the right time
tempestoso (tām·pä·stō'zō) *a* stormy
tempia (tem'pyâ) *f* (*anat*) temple
tempio (tem'pyō) *m* temple (*building*)
tempo (tām'pō) *m* time; weather; (*gram*)
tense; **–rale** (tām·pō·râ'lä) *m* storm;
–rale *a* temporal; **–raneo** (tām·pō·râ'-
nā·ō) *a* temporary, transitory; **–reggia-
mento** (tām·pō·rāj·jâ·mān'tō) *m* procrastination; **–reggiare** (tām·pō·rāj·jâ'-
rā) *vi* to procrastinate; **–reggiatore** (tām·
pō·rāj·jâ·tō'rā) *m* procrastinator
tempra (tām'prâ) *f* vigor; moral tone,
character; attitude; **–re** (tām·prâ'rā) *vt*
to harden; to temper
tenace (tā·nâ'chä) *a* tenacious, constant
tenacità (tā·nâ·chē·tâ') *f* stick-to-itiveness
(*coll*); tenacity
tenaglia (tā·nâ'lyâ) *f* pincers
tenda (tān'dâ) *f* curtain; tent; awning
tendenza (tān·dān'tsâ) *f* bent, propensity
tendenzioso (tān·dān·tsyō'zō) *a* biased,
prejudiced
tendere * (ten'dā·rā) *vt* to stretch out; to
hand over; — *vi* to tend, lean
tendina (tān·dē'nâ) *f* window curtain;
blind
tenebre (te'nā·brä) *fpl* darkness; gloominess
tenebroso (tā·nā·brō'zō) *a* dark; somber
tenente (tā·nān'tā) *m* lieutenant
tenere * (tā·nā'rā) *vt&i* to hold, hold onto;
to maintain, keep; to care for, have an
interest in; — **la destra** to keep to the
right; — **a mente** to bear in mind; —
conto di to consider, take into consideration; **non c'è motivo che tenga** there is
no reason for it; **non ci tiene affatto** he
doesn't care at all; — **al proprio nome**
to care about one's reputation
tenerezza (tā·nā·rā'tsâ) *f* tenderness;
fondness
tenersi * (tā·nār'sē) *vr* to keep from; to
hold oneself; — **per intelligente** to deem
oneself clever; — **al corrent dei fatti** to
keep abreast of the news; — **in piedi** to
remain standing
tenero (te'nā·rō) *a* tender; affectionate;
— *m* soft part; weakness, foible
tenia (te'nyâ) *f* tapeworm
tennista (tān·nē'stâ) *m* tennis player
tenore (tā·nō'rā) *m* tenor; text; (*mus*)
tenor; tendency; meaning; — **di vita**
standard of living

tensione (tān·syō'nā) *f* tension
tentacolo (tān·tâ'kō·lō) *m* tentacle
tentare (tān·tâ'rā) *vt* to try, attempt; to
tempt; to touch
tentativo (tān·tâ·tē'vō) *m* attempt
tentatore (tān·tâ·tō'rā) *m* tempter
tentatrice (tān·tâ·trē'chä) *f* temptress
tentazione (tān·tâ·tsyō'nā) *f* temptation
tentennare (tān·tān·nâ'rā) *vi* to waver; to
be indecisive; — *vt* to shake
tenue (te'nwā) *a* thin, slight
tenuta (tā·nū'tâ) *f* uniform; estate; landed
holdings
teologo (tā·ô'lō·gō) *m* theologian
teoria (tā·ō·rē'â) *f* theory
teorico (tā·ô'rē·kō) *a* theoretical
teorizzare (tā·ō·rē·dzâ'rā) *vi* to theorize
tepido (te'pē·dō) *a* lukewarm, tepid
tepore (tā·pō'rā) *m* warmth
teppa (tāp'pâ) *f* underworld, gangland
teppista (tāp·pē'stâ) *m* gangster
terapia (tā·râ·pē'â) *f* therapy; therapeutics
tergere * (ter'jā·rā) *vt* to wipe, polish
tergicristallo (tār·jē·krē·stâl'lō) *m* windshield wiper
tergiversare (tār·jē·vār·sâ'rā) *vi* to be
evasive; to quibble
tergo (tār'gō) *m* back
termale (tār·mâ'lä) *a* thermal; **stazione —**
spa, health resort
terme (tār'mä) *fpl* hot springs
terminatamente (tār·mē·nâ·tâ·mān'tā)
adv exactly; definitively; once and for
all
terminare (tār·mē·nâ'rā) *vt&i* to finish,
conclude
termine (ter'mē·nä) *m* end; termination;
term; stipulation; **a rigor di —** strictly
speaking; **in altri termini** in other words
terminologia (tār·mē·nō·lō·jē'â) *f* terminology
termodinamica (tār·mō·dē·nâ'mē·kâ) *f*
thermodynamics
termoelettrico (tār·mō·ā·let'trē·kō) *a*
thermoelectric
termogeno (tār·mô'jä·nō) *a* thermogenic,
heat-producing
termomagnetico (tār·mō·mâ·nye'tē·kō) *a*
thermomagnetic
termometro (tār·mô'mä·trō) *m* thermometer
termosifone (tār·mō·sē·fō'nā) *m* radiator
termostato (tār·mō·stâ'tō) *m* thermostat
terra (tār'râ) *f* soil, ground; earth; (*naut*)
land; (*elec*) ground; **scendere a —** to
land, go ashore; **via —** by land
terraglia (tār·râ'lyâ) *f* earthenware
terrazza (tār·râ'tsâ) *f*, **terrazzo** (tār·râ'-

â ârm, ā bāby, e bet, ē bē, ō gō, ô gône, ū blūe, b bad, ch child, d dad, f fat, g gay, j jet

tsō) *m* terrace; balcony
terremoto (tär·rä·mō'tō) *m* earthquake
terreno (tär·rä'nō) *m* soil; plot of land;
— *a* worldly, temporal
terrestre (tär·rä'strä) *a* terrestrial
terribile (tär·rē'bē·lä) *a* awful, terrible
terrificante (tär·rē·fē·kän'tä) *a* appalling,
frightening, horrifying
terrificare (tär·rē·fē·kå'rä) *vt* to appall;
to terrify, horrify
terrifico (tär·rē'fē·kō) *a* dreadful, horrible
territoriale (tär·rē·tō·ryâ'lä) *a* territorial
territorio (tär·rē·tō'ryō) *m* territory, region
terrore (tär·rō'rä) *m* terror, fear
terrorizzare (tär·rō·rē·dzä'rä) *vt* to terrorize
terzetto (tär·tsät'tō) *m* trio; group of three
terzino (tär·tsē'nō) *m* fullback (*football*)
terzo (tär'tsō) *a* third
tesa (tä'zâ) *f* hat brim
teschio (te'skyō) *m* skull
tesi (tä'zē) *f* thesis
teso (tä'zō) *a* taut, tightly stretched;
strained
tesoreria (tä·zō·rä·rē'â) *f* treasury
tesoriere (tä·zō·ryä'rä) *m* treasurer
tesoro (tä·zō'rō) *m* treasure; sweetheart
tessera (tes'sä·râ) *f* card; identification
card
tessere (tes'sä·rä) *vt* to weave
tessile (tes'sē·lä) *a* textile
tessilsacco (täs·sēl·säk'kō) *m* garment bag
tessuto (täs·sū'tō) *m* fabric, material;
(*anat*) tissue
testa (tä'stâ) *f* head; top; **dolor di** — headache; **in testa alla pagina** at the top
of the page
testamento (tä·stä·män'tō) *m* will
testardaggine (tä·stär·dâj'jē·nä) *f* stub-
bornness
testardo (tä·stär'dō) *a* stubborn
testata (tä·stä'tâ) *f* headline; heading;
(*mil*) warhead
testicolo (tä·stē'kō·lō) *m* testicle
testimone (tä·stē·mō'nä) *m* witness
testimonianza (tä·stē·mō·nyân'tsä) *f* testimony, evidence
testimoniare (tä·stē·mō·nyä'rä) *vt* to testify to, give evidence to, attest to
testo (tä'stō) *m* text; copy
testuale (tä·stwä'lä) *a* verbatim; word-for-
word
testualmente (tä·stwâl·män'tä) *adv* verbatim
tetano (te'tâ·nō) *m* tetanus, lockjaw
tetraedro (tä·trä·ä'drō) *m* tetrahedron
tetragono (tä·trâ'gō·nō) *m* tetragon; —

a (*fig*) steadfast, constant, stable
tetro (tä'trō) *a* gloomy, dark
tetto (tät'tō) *m* roof; **–ia** (tät·tô'yâ) *f*
shed; marquee
ti (tē) *pron* you; to you
tiara (tyâ'râ) *f* tiara
tibia (tē'byâ) *f* shinbone, tibia
ticchio (tēk'kyō) *m* caprice, whim; (*med*)
tic
tiepido (tye'pē·dō) *a* lukewarm
tifo (tē'fō) *m* typhus; **–ide** (tē·fô'ē·dä) *f*
typhoid fever; **–so** (tē·fō'zō) *m* typhus
patient; (*fig*) sports enthusiast, fan
tifone (tē·fō'nä) *m* hurricane; typhoon
tiglio (tē'lyō) *m* linden tree
tigna (tē'nyâ) *f* ringworm
tignola (tē·nyō'lâ) *f* moth
tigre (tē'grä) *f* tiger
tigrotto (tē·grōt'tō) *m* tiger cub
timballo (tēm·bâl'lō) *m* (*cooking*) timbale;
kettle drum
timbrare (tēm·brâ'rä) *vt* to postmark; to
affix a stamp to, stamp
timbro (tēm'brō) *m* stamp; timbre
timidamente (tē·mē·dâ·män'tä) *adv* with
shyness, timidly
timidezza (tē·mē·dä'tsâ) *f* shyness; ti-
midity
timido (tē'mē·dō) *a* shy; diffident
timone (tē·mō'nä) *m* helm; rudder
timoniere (tē·mō·nyä'rä) *m* helmsman
timore (tē·mō'rä) *m* fear
timoroso (tē·mō·rō'zō) *a* timid, afraid
timpano (tēm'pâ·nō) *m* eardrum; kettle-
drum
tina (tē'nâ) *f* tub
tinello (tē·nâl'lō) *m* dinette, small dining
room
tingere * (tēn'jä·rä) *vt* to dye
tingersi * (tēn'jär·sē) *vr* to dye; — **le**
labbra to put on lipstick
tino (tē'nō) *m* tub, vat; **–zza** (tē·nō'tsâ) *f*
tub; bathtub
tinta (tēn'tâ) *f* shade; color; **–rella** (tēn·
tâ·rälʹlâ) *f* (*coll*) suntan
tintinnare (tēn·tēn·nâ'rä) *vi* to clink; to
jingle; to tinkle
tintinnio (tēn·tēn·nē'ō) *m* clinking; jin-
gling; tinkling
tintore (tēn·tō'rä) *m* dry cleaner; dyer
tintoria (tēn·tō·rē'â) *f* dry cleaning shop
tintura (tēn·tū'râ) *f* tincture
tipicamente (tē·pē·kâ·män'tä) *adv* typi-
cally
tipico (tē'pē·kō) *a* typical
tipo (tē'pō) *m* type; pattern, standard; **bel**
— **originale** oddball (*coll*); **–grafia** (tē·
pō·grä·fē'â) *f* printing office; **–grafo**

k kid, **l** let, **m** met, **n** not, **p** pat, **r** very, **s** sat, **sh** shop, **t** tell, **v** vat, **w** we, **y** yet, **z** zero

(tē·pô'grâ·fō) *m* printer
tiraggio (tē·râj'jō) *m* draft (*drawing*)
tiralinee (tē·râ·lē'nâ·ā) *m* ruling pen
tiranneggiare (tē·rân·nâj·jâ'rā) *vt* to
tyrannize, oppress; to lord it over
tirannia (tē·rân·nē'â) *f* tyranny
tiranno (tē·rân'nō) *m* tyrant
tirapiedi (tē·râ·pyâ'dē) *m* henchman, collaborator
tirapranzi (tē·râ·prân'dzē) *m* dumbwaiter
tirare (tē·râ'rā) *vt* to pull; to throw; to
shoot at; to print, run off an impression
of; — *vi* to tend; to blow (*wind*); — **la
somma** to find the sum; — **sul prezzo**
to bargain; — **le conclusioni** to draw the
conclusion; — **avanti** to get ahead; —
diritto to go straight ahead
tirarsi (tē·râr'sē) *vr* to draw to oneself,
pull in; — **indietro** to draw back; (*fig*)
to retract one's statement; — **su** to stand
up; (*fig*) to pull oneself together; — **dai
pasticci** to get out of trouble
tirato (tē·râ'tō) *a* taut, pulled tight; stingy
tiratore (tē·râ·tō'rā) *m* marksman; —
scelto sharpshooter; **franco** — sniper;
— **d'arco** archer: — **di scherma** fencer
tiratura (tē·râ·tū'râ) *f* run (*printing*);
circulation; printing; extension
tirchio (tēr'kyō) *a* stingy
tiretto (tē·rât'tō) *m* drawer
tiritera (tē·rē·tā'râ) *f* rigmarole; nonsense tale; wordy speech
tiro (tē'rō) *m* pull; extent; throw; shot;
stroke (*billiards*); — **a segno** shooting
gallery; **venire a** — (*coll*) to get one's
hands on; —**cinio** (tē·rō·chē'nyō) *m*
apprenticeship, training period
tiroide (tē·rô'ē·dā) *f* (*anat*) thyroid
tisana (tē·zâ'nâ) *f* tisane
tisi (tē'zē) *f* tuberculosis; —**co** (tē'zē·kō) *a*
tuberculous, tubercular
titolare (tē·tō·lâ'rā) *m* owner of a firm;
company president; — *a* titular
titolo (tē'tō·lō) *m* title; right; headline,
heading; qualification, requisite; — **di
studio** degree; **a** — **di** by way of; in
one's capacity as
titubante (tē·tū·bân'tā) *a* hesitant, reluctant
tizio (tē'tsyō) *m* a certain individual, some
person, so-and-so
tizzone (tē·tsō'nā) *m* firebrand
toccare (tōk·kâ'rā) *vt&i* to touch; to
affect; to be one's turn; — **sul vivo** to
hurt deeply, cut to the quick; — **con
mano** to make sure of
toccarsi (tōk·kâr'sē) *vr* to meet, reach
toccasana (tōk·kâ·sâ'nâ) *m* panacea, cure-
all
tocco (tōk'kō) *m* touch; (*med*) stroke;
hint, indication; — *a* touched; crackbrained; **al** — at one o'clock
toga (tō'gà) *f* official garb; toga
togliere * (tô'lyā·rā) *vt* to take away; to
lift off
togliersi * (tô'lyār·sē) *vr* to get away; to
extricate oneself; to deprive oneself;
— **la vita** to commit suicide; — **di
mezzo** to get out of the way; — **le scarpe** to take off one's shoes
tolda (tōl'dâ) *f* (*naut*) deck
toletta (tō·lāt'tâ) *f* dressing table, vanity;
toilette, grooming
tollerante (tōl·lā·rân'tā) *a* tolerant, liberal; understanding
tolleranza (tōl·lā·rân'tsâ) *f* leeway, tolerance; understanding; **casa di** —
brothel
tollerare (tōl·lā·râ'rā) *vt* to tolerate, bear;
to allow, sanction
tomaia (tō·mâ'yâ) *f* vamp; upper (*shoe*)
tomba (tōm'bâ) *f* tomb; grave
tombino (tōm·bē'nō) *m* manhole
tombola (tôm'bō·lâ) *f* lotto; bingo
tomo (tō'mō) *m* volume, tome
tondo (tōn'dō) *a* round; obvious, patent
tonfo (tōn'fō) *m* splash; thud; flop
tonnellaggio (tōn·nāl·lâj'jō) *m* tonnage
tonnellata (tōn·nāl·lâ'tâ) *f* ton
tonno (tōn'nō) *m* tuna, tuna fish
tono (tō'nō) *m* tone; tune; pitch; style,
fashion
tonsilla (tōn·sēl'lâ) *f* tonsil
topazio (tō·pâ'tsyō) *m* topaz
topica (tô'pē·kâ) *f* blunder; **fare una** —
to put one's foot in it
topo (tō'pō) *m* mouse; — **d'auto** automobile thief; — **di biblioteca** bookworm
(*fig*)
topografia (tō·pō·grâ·fē'â) *f* topography
toppa (tōp'pâ) *f* patch; lock
torace (tō·râ'châ) *m* thorax
torbido (tôr'bē·dō) *a* muddy, roiled
torcere * (tôr'châ·rā) *vt* to twist; to
wrench
torcersi * (tôr'châr·sē) *vr* to squirm,
wriggle
torchio (tôr'kyō) *m* press
torcia (tôr'châ) *f* candle, torch
torcicollo (tôr·chē·kōl'lō) *m* stiff neck;
torticollis
torinese (tō·rē·nâ'zā) *a&m* Turinese
Torino (tō·rē'nō) *f* Turin
torlo (tôr'lō) *m* yolk
tormenta (tôr·mān'tâ) *f* blizzard; —**re** (tôr·
mān·tâ'rā) *vt* to torment, plague; —**rsi**

(tŏr·mān·târ'sē) *vr* to worry oneself, be uneasy; to hound oneself

tormento (tŏr·mān'tō) *m* torture; anguish, suffering

tornaconto (tŏr·nâ·kōn'tō) *m* advantage, account

tornare (tŏr·nâ'rā) *vi* to return; to recur

torneo (tŏr·nā'ō) *m* competition; jousting

tornio (tôr'nyō) *m* lathe

tornitore (tŏr·nē·tō'rā) *m* turner

toro (tō'rō) *m* bull

torpedine (tŏr·pe'dē·nā) *f* torpedo

torpediniera (tŏr·pā·dē·nyā'râ) *f* torpedo boat

torpedone (tŏr·pā·dō'nā) *m* sightseeing bus; motor coach

torpore (tŏr·pō'rā) *m* lethargy, drowsiness

torre (tŏr'rā) *f* tower

torrente (tŏr·rān'tā) *m* torrent, rapids

torrone (tŏr·rō'nā) *m* nougat

torsione (tŏr·syō'nā) *f* twist, torsion

torso (tŏr'sō) *m* (*anat*) trunk, torso

torsolo (tŏr'sō·lō) *m* core, pit, stone (*fruit*)

torta (tŏr'tâ) *f* cake; pie

torto (tŏr'tō) *m* wrong; condemnation; injustice; — *a* twisted, out of shape; **aver** — to be wrong, be in error

tortora (tôr'tō·râ) *f* turtledove

tortuosamente (tŏr·twō·zâ·mān'tā) *adv* tortuously; laboriously

tortuoso (tŏr·twō'zō) *a* winding; crooked; laborious

tortura (tŏr·tū'rā) *f* torture; **–re** (tŏr·tū·râ'rā) *vt* to torture; **–rsi** (tŏr·tū·râr'sē) *vr* to plague oneself, torture oneself; to hound oneself; — **il cervello** to cudgel one's brains

torvo (tŏr'vō) *a* surly, grim

tosare (tō·zâ'rā) *vt* to clip, cut; to shear

Toscana (tō·skâ'nä) *f* Tuscany

toscano (tō·skâ'nō) *m&a* Tuscan

tosse (tōs'sä) *f* cough

tossico (tôs'sē·kō) *m* poison; — *a* toxic; **–mane** (tōs·sē·kō'mâ·nä) *m* drug addict

tostapane (tō·stâ·pâ'nä) *m* toaster

tostare (tō·stâ'rā) *vt* to roast; to toast

tosto (tō'stō) *adv* immediately; soon; — **che** just as soon as, when

tosto (tō'stō) *a* brazen, impudent; toasted

totale (tō·tâ'lä) *m&a* total

totalizzatore (tō·tâ·lē·dzâ·tō'rā) *m* totalizator; pari-mutuel

totocalcio (tō·tō·kâl'chō) *m* football pool

tovaglia (tō·vâ'lyâ) *f* tablecloth

tovagliolo (tō·vâ·lyō'lō) *m* napkin

tozzo (tō'tsō) *a* stocky; chunky; — *m* piece, chunk

tra (trâ) *prep* among; between

traballare (trâ·bâl·lâ'rā) *vi* to totter; to reel

trabeazione (trâ·bā·â·tsyō'nä) *f* entablature

traboccare (trâ·bōk·kâ'rā) *vi* to overflow

trabocchetto (trâ·bōk·kāt'tō) *m* trap, pitfall

traccia (trâ'châ) *f* trace; **–re** (trâ·châ'rā) *vt* to sketch; to trail; to lay out; **–to** (trâ·châ'tō) *m* tracing; layout

tracolla (trâ·kōl'lâ) *f* shoulder belt; **a** — across the shoulders

tracollo (trâ·kōl'lō) *m* downfall, collapse; (*mech*) breakdown, failure; (*com*) decline, recession

tradimento (trâ·dē·mān'tō) *m* betrayal; deception

tradire (trâ·dē'rā) *vt* to betray; to cheat

tradirsi (trâ·dēr'sē) *vr* to give away one's motives; to defeat one's own purpose

traditore (trâ·dē·tō'rā) *m* traitor; deceiver

tradizione (trâ·dē·tsyō'nä) *f* tradition, custom

tradotta (trâ·dōt'tâ) *f* troop train

tradurre * (trâ·dūr'rā) *vt* to translate

traduttore (trâ·dūt·tō'rā) *m* translator

traduzione (trâ·dū·tsyō'nä) *f* translation

trafelato (trâ·fā·lâ'tō) *a* breathless, out of breath, breathing hard

traffichino (trâf·fē·kē'nō) *m* schemer, meddler

traffico (trâf'fē·kō) *m* traffic; business, trade

trafiletto (trâ·fē·lāt'tō) *m* brief article

traforare (trâ·fō·râ'rā) *vt* to drill through; to pierce

traforo (trâ·fō'rō) *m* tunnel; openwork embroidery

tragedia (trâ·je'dyâ) *f* tragedy

traghetto (trâ·gāt'tō) *m* ferryboat

tragico (trâ'jē·kō) *a* tragic

tragitto (trâ·jēt'tō) *m* run, trip; route

traguardo (trâ·gwâr'dō) *m* (*sport*) finish line; aim, purpose

tralasciare (trâ·lâ·shâ'rā) *vt* to interrupt; to omit; to give up

tram (trâm) *m* streetcar

trama (trâ'mâ) *f* plot; intrigue

trambusto (trâm·bū'stō) *m* confusion; hustle and bustle

tramezza (trâ·mā'dzâ) *f* partition; division

tramezzino (trâ·mā·dzē'nō) *m* sandwich man

tramite (trâ'mē·tā) *m* procedure, course, channel; **per** — **di** by means of, by way of

tramontana (trâ·mōn·tâ'nâ) *f* north wind

---

k kid, **l** let, **m** met, **n** not, **p** pat, **r** very, **s** sat, **sh** shop, **t** tell, **v** vat, **w** we, **y** yet, **z** zero

tramontare (trâ·mōn·tâ′rā) *vi* to go down, set *(sun)*

tramonto (trâ·mōn′tō) *m* sunset; setting

trampolino (trâm·pō·lē′nō) *m* springboard; trampoline

tranello (trâ·nāl′lō) *m* trap

tranne (trân′nä) *prep* except, with the exception of

tranquillità (trân·kwēl·lē·tâ′) *f* tranquillity, peace

tranquillizzare (trân·kwēl·lē·dzâ′rā) *vt* to calm; to pacify

tranquillizzarsi (trân·kwēl·lē·dzâr′sē) *vr* to become quiet, calm down

tranquillo (trân·kwēl′lō) *a* calm, peaceful; restful

transatlantico (trân·zât·lân′tē·kō) *m* ocean liner; — *a* transatlantic

transazione (trân·zâ·tsyō′nä) *f* compromise, agreement to terms; dealing, transaction

transigere * (trân·zē′jä·rā) *vi* to compromise; to agree on terms; to transact business

transito (trân′sē·tō) *m* transit; **vietato il** — no entrance, no admittance; **–rio** (trân·sē·tô′ryō) *a* fleeting, transitory

tranvia (trân·vē′â) *f* streetcar

tranviere (trân·vyä′rā) *m* streetcar conductor

trapano (trâ′pâ·nō) *m* drill

trapelare (trâ·pä·lâ′rā) *vi* to ooze out; to leak through

trapezio (trâ·pe′tsyō) *m* trapeze; *(math)* trapezoid

trapianto (trâ·pyân′tō) *m* transplant, graft; transfer

trappola (trâp′pō·lâ) *f* trap

trapunta (trâ·pūn′tâ) *f* quilt; **–re** (trâ·pūn·tâ′rā) *vt* to quilt

trarre * (trâr′rā) *vt* to draw in, take in, haul in; — **in inganno** to deceive; — **un sospiro** to heave a sigh

trarsi * (trâr′sē) *vr* to extricate oneself, free oneself; — **d'impaccio** to get out of a difficult situation

trasalire (trâ·sâ·lē′rā) *vi* to jump, start; to be startled, taken unaware

trasandato (trâ·zân·dâ′tō) *a* careless, slovenly; abandoned, neglected

trascendere * (trâ·shen′dā·rā) *vt* to transcend; to overstep; to exaggerate; to lose one's composure

trascinare (trâ·shē·nâ′rā) *vt* to drag along; to shuffle *(feet)*; to pull along

trascinarsi (trâ·shē·nâr′sē) *vr* to pull oneself along with effort

trascorrere * (trâ·scôr′râ·rā) *vt* to spend

(time); — *vi* to elapse, go by

trascorso (trâ·skôr′sō) *m* lapse *(time)*; slight error; — *a* travelled, traversed

trascurare (trâ·skū·râ′rā) *vt* to neglect; to be careless about

trascurato (trâ·skū·râ′tō) *a* careless, neglectful

trasferire (trâ·sfâ·rē′rā) *vt* to transfer; to make over

trasferirsi (trâ·sfâ·rēr′sē) *vr* to move to a new address

trasferta (trâ·sfâr′tâ) *f* travel allowance

trasfigurazione (trâ·sfē·gū·râ·tsyō′nä) *f* transfiguration

trasformare (trâ·sfōr·mâ′rā) *vt* to transform

trasformatore (trâ·sfōr·mâ·tō′rā) *m* transformer, converter; changer

trasformazione (trâ·sfōr·mâ·tsyō′nä) *f* transformation; changeover

trasfusione (trâ·sfū·zyō′nä) *f* transfusion

trasgredire (trâ·zgrâ·dē′rā) *vt&i* to infringe upon; to violate; to sin against

trasgressione (trâ·zgrās·syō′nä) *f* violation; encroachment

traslocare (trâ·zlō·kâ′rā) *vt&i* to move; to change one's address; to relocate

trasloco (trâ·zlō′kō) *m* moving, change of residence; relocation

trasmettere * (trâ·zmet′tā·rā) *vt (rad)* to broadcast; to forward, transmit

trasmigrazione (trâ·zmē·grâ·tsyō′nä) *f* transmigration

trasmissione (trâ·zmēs·syō′nä) *f* broadcast; transmission

trasmissore (trâ·zmēs·sō′rā) *m* transmitter, forwarder

trasmittente (trân·zmēt·tän′tä) *m* sending set, transmitter; — *a* transmitting

trasognato (trâ·sō·nyâ′tō) *a* visionary, impractical; dreamy, woolgathering

trasparente (trâ·spâ·rân′tä) *a* transparent; obvious; *(fig)* sincere, straightforward

trasparenza (trâ·spâ·rân′tsâ) *f* transparency; obviousness; *(fig)* sincerity

trasportare (trâ·spōr·tâ′rā) *vt* to transport; to transpose; to draw; to inspire

trasporto (trâ·spōr′tō) *m* transportation; ecstasy, inspiration

trasvolare (trâ·zvō·lâ′rā) *vt* to fly over, fly above

tratta (trât′tâ) *f* bank draft; run, stretch, section; — **delle bianche** white slavery; **–mento** (trât·tâ·mān′tō) *m* treatment, use; **–re** (trât·tâ′rā) *vt* to treat; to make use of; **–rsi** (trât·târ′sē) *vr* to be a matter of; to concern; to fare, live, do; **–rsi di vita o di morte** to be a question of life or death; **si tratta di ciò** that's the question, that's just the point; **–tiva** (trât·tâ·tē′vâ) *f* negotiation; **–to** (trât· tâ′tō) *m* treaty

trattenere * (trât·tā·nā′rā) *vt* to withhold; to check; to hold in, restrain

trattenersi * (trât·tā·nār′sē) *vr* to stay, prolong one's stay; to control oneself, keep one's emotions under control

trattenimento (trât·tā·nē·mān′tō) *m* party; entertainment

trattenuta (trât·tā·nū′tâ) *f* (*com*) deduction

tratto (trât′tō) *m* stroke; jerk; distance; way, manner; time period; **— d'unione** hyphen; **tutto ad un —** without warning, suddenly; **di — in —** occasionally, periodically

trattoria (trât·tō·rē′â) *m* restaurant

trattore (trât·tō′rā) *m* restaurateur; (*mech*) tractor

trattrice (trât·trē′chā) *f* tractor

trave (trâ′vā) *f* rafter, beam

traversare (trâ·vār·sâ′rā) *vt* to cross, go across

traversata (trâ·vār·sâ′tâ) *f* crossing, trip across, trip over

travestito (trâ·vā·stē′tō) *a* disguised; misrepresented

traviare (trâ·vyâ′rā) *vt* to lead astray; to corrupt

travolgente (trâ·vōl·jān′tā) *a* overwhelming, decisive

travolgere * (trâ·vōl′jā·rā) *vt* to overcome; to sweep away; to upset

trazione (trâ·tsyō′nā) *f* drayage, cartage; traction

tre (trā) *a* three

trebbiare (trāb·byâ′rā) *vt&i* to thresh

trebbiatrice (trāb·byâ·trē′chā) *f* threshing machine

treccia (trē′châ) *f* braid

trecento (trā·chān′tō) *a* three hundred; **il T–** the fourteenth century

tredicenne (trā·dē·chān′nā) *a* thirteen years old

tredicesimo (trā·dē·che′zē·mō) *a* thirteenth

tredici (tre′dē·chē) *a* thirteen; **–mila** (trâ·dē·chē·mē′lâ) *a* thirteen thousand

tregua (tre′gwâ) *f* truce; rest, peace (*fig*)

tremare (trā·mâ′rā) *vi* to shake, tremble

tremendo (trā·mān′dō) *a* dire; tremendous; dreadful

trementina (trā·mān·tē′nâ) *f* turpentine

tremila (trā·mē′lâ) *a* three thousand

treno (trā′nō) *m* train; **— letto** sleeping car

trenta (trān′tâ) *a* thirty; **–mila** (trān·tâ· mē′lâ) *a* thirty thousand

trentesimo (trān·te′zē·mō) *a&m* thirtieth

tresca (trā′skâ) *f* love affair

triangolare (tryân·gō·lâ′rā) *a* triangular

triangolo (tryân′gō·lō) *m* triangle

tribolazione (trē·bō·lâ·tsyō′nā) *f* tribulation, ordeal

tribù (trē·bū′) *f* tribe

tribuna (trē·bū′nâ) *f* stand; gallery; **–le** (trē·bū·nâ′lā) *m* court, tribunal

triciclo (trē·chē′klō) *m* tricycle

triennale (tryân·nâ′lā) *a* triennial

trienne (tryân′nā) *a* three years old

Trieste (tryâ′stā) *f* Trieste

triestino (tryâ·stē′nō) *a* Triestine

trifase (trē·fâ′zā) *a* (*elec*) three-phase

trifoglio (trē·fō′lyō) *m* clover

trimestre (trē·mâ′strā) *m* quarter (*year*); period of three months

trimotore (trē·mō·tō′rā) *m* (*avi*) trimotor

trincea (trēn·chā′â) *f* trench

trinciare (trēn·châ′rā) *vt* to carve; to slice, cut

trionfo (tryōn′fō) *m* triumph

triplo (trē′plō) *a&m* triple

trippa (trēp′pâ) *f* tripe

triste (trē′stā) *a* unhappy; sad; **–zza** (trē· stâ′tsâ) *f* sorrow, sadness

tristo (trē′stō) *a* evil, wicked

tritacarne (trē·tâ·kâr′nā) *vt* meat grinder

tritare (trē·tâ′rā) *vt* to grind; to chop fine, mince

tritolo (trē·tō′lō) *m* trinitrotoluene, TNT

trivellare (trē·vāl·lâ′rā) *vt* to drill, perforate

triviale (trē·vyâ′lā) *a* uncultured, vulgar, common

trofeo (trō·fā′ō) *m* trophy

troia (trō′yâ) *f* sow

Troia (trō′yâ) *f* Troy

troiano (trō·yâ′nō) *m&a* Trojan

tromba (trōm′bâ) *f* horn

trombaio (trōm·bâ′yō) *m* plumber

trombato (trōm·bâ′tō) *a* rejected; defeated at the polls

trombettiere (trōm·bāt·tyâ′rā) *m* bugler; trumpeter

trombone (trōm·bō′nā) *m* trombone

troncare (trōn·kâ′rā) *vt* to cut off; to reduce sharply

tronco (trōn′kō) *m* trunk, log; (*rail*) siding; **— a** cut off; curtailed; truncated

trono (trō′nō) *m* throne

tropico (trō′pē·kō) *m* tropic

troppi (trōp′pē) *a* too many

troppo (trōp′pō) *adv* too; too much; **—** *a&pron* too much

---

k kid, **l** let, **m** met, **n** not, **p** pat, **r** very, **s** sat, **sh** shop, **t** tell, **v** vat, **w** we, **y** yet, **z** zero

trota (trō'tâ) *f* trout
trotto (trōt'tō) *m* trot
trottola (trôt'tō·lâ) *f* top (*toy*)
trovare (trō·vâ'rā) *vt* to find; to believe, be of the opinion
trovarsi (trō·vâr'sē) *vr* to meet; to feel, be; to be by chance
trovata (trō·vâ'tâ) *f* makeshift; invention
truccare (trūk·kâ'rā) *vt* to trick, deceive
truccarsi (trūk·kâr'sē) *vr* to make up, put on one's makeup
truccatore (trūk·kâ·tō'rā) *m* (*theat*) make-up man
trucco (trūk'kō) *m* trick; cosmetics
truce (trū'chā) *a* savage; merciless, grim; horrifying
truciolo (trū'chō·lō) *m* wood shaving; chip of wood
truffa (trūf'fâ) *f* fraud; — **all'americana** confidence game; **–re** (trūf·fâ'rā) *vt* to swindle; to dupe; **–tore** (trūf·fâ·tō'rā) *m* swindler; confidence man; crook
truppa (trūp'pâ) *f* troop
tu (tū) *pron* you (*fam*)
tubatura (tū·bâ·tū'râ) *f* plumbing system, plumbing
tubercolosario (tū·bâr·kō·lō·zâ'ryō) *m* tuberculosis sanatorium
tubercolosi (tū·bâr·kō·lō'zē) *f* tuberculosis, consumption
tubercoloso (tū·bâr·kō·lō'zō) *a* tubercular; — *m&a* consumptive
tubo (tū'bō) *m* pipe, tube
tuffare (tūf·fâ'râ) *vt* to plunge
tuffarsi (tūf·fâr'sē) *vr* to plunge, dive
tuffo (tūf'fō) *m* dive
tumulto (tū·mūl'tō) *m* din, uproar
tumultuoso (tū·mūl·twō'zō) *a* tumultuous
tuo (tū'ō) *a* your, yours; — *pron* yours
tuono (twō'nō) *m* thundering, thunder
tuorlo (twōr'lō) *m* yolk
turacciolo (tū·râ'chō·lō) *m* stopper, cork

turare (tū·râ'rā) *vt* to cork, plug up; to obstruct, block
turarsi (tū·râr'sē) *vr* to be stopped up
turba (tūr'bâ) *f* disorderly crowd; mob; **–mento** (tūr·bâ·mān'tō) *m* excitement; disturbance; anxiety
turbante (tūr·bân'tā) *m* turban
turbare (tūr·bâ'rā) *vt* to disturb, bother
turbarsi (tūr·bâr'sē) *vr* to become upset; to become perturbed; to grow overcast (*sky*)
turbina (tūr·bē'nâ) *f* turbine
turbine (tūr'bē·nā) *m* whirlwind
turbinosamente (tūr·bē·nō·zâ·mān'tā) *adv* stormily
turbogeneratore (tūr·bō·jā·nā·râ·tō'rā) *m* turbogenerator
turbogetto (tūr·bō·jāt'tō) *m* turbojet
turboreattore (tūr·bō·rā·ât·tō'rā) *m* turbojet
turchese (tūr·kā'zā) *f* turquoise
turchino (tūr·kē'nō) *a* deep blue
turco (tūr'kō) *m* Turk; — *a* Turkish
turista (tū·rē'stâ) *m&f* tourist
turlupinare (tūr·lū·pē·nâ'râ) *vt* to swindle; to hoodwink; to defraud
turlupinatura (tūr·lū·pē·nâ·tū'râ) *f* fraud; trickery; deceit
turno (tūr'nō) *m* shift; turn
turpiloquio (tūr·pē·lô'kwēō) *m* obscene speech, foul language
tuta (tū'tâ) *f* overalls
tutela (tū·tā'lâ) *f* protection; sponsorship, safeguard
tutore (tū·tō'rā) *m* guardian; protector; sponsor
tuttavia (tūt·tâ·vē'â) *adv* notwithstanding, nonetheless; — *conj* in spite of, notwithstanding
tutto (tūt'tō) *a* all; — *m* everything; overall effect; **–ra** (tūt·tō'râ) *adv* still; as yet

U

ubbidiente (ūb·bē·dyān'tâ) *a* obedient; meek
ubbidienza (ūb·bē·dyān'tsâ) *f* obedience; meekness
ubbidire (ūb·bē·dē'râ) *vt* to obey; to comply with, fulfill
ubicazione (ū·bē·kâ·tsyō'nâ) *f* whereabouts; site, situation
ubriacarsi (ū·bryâ·kâr'sē) *vr* to become drunk; to drink to excess
ubriachezza (ū·bryâ·kā'tsâ) *f* inebriation, drunkenness

ubriaco (ū·bryâ'kō) *a&m* drunk; **–ne** (ū·bryâ'kō·nā) *m* drunk, drunkard
uccello (ū·chāl'lō) *m* bird
uccidere * (ū·chē'dā·râ) *vt* to kill, do away with
uccidersi * (ū·chē'dār·sē) *vr* to kill oneself, do away with oneself
uccisione (ū·chē·zyō'nâ) *f* killing
udienza (ū·dyān'tsâ) *f* (*law*) hearing; audience; consideration
udire * (ū·dē'râ) *vt* to hear
udito (ū·dē'tō) *m* sense of hearing; **–rio**

â ârm, *ā* bāby, *e* bet, *ē* bē, *ō* gō, *ô* gône, *ū* blūe, **b** bad, **ch** child, **d** dad, **f** fat, **g** gay, **j** jet

(ū·dē·tô′ryō) *m* audience, spectators

ufficiale (ūf·fē·châ′lā) *m* officer; — *a* official; — **pagatore** paymaster

ufficialmente (ūf·fē·chäl·män′tā) *adv* officially; through official channels

ufficio (ūf·fē′chō) *m* office; –**so** (ūf·fē·chō′zō) *a* informal; semiofficial

uggioso (ūj·jō′zō) *a* boring; uninteresting; distasteful

uguaglianza (ū·gwâ·lyân′tsâ) *f* likeness; equality

uguale (ū·gwâ′lā) *a* equal; — *m* peer, equal

ugualmente (ū·gwâl·män′tā) *adv* just the same; equally

ultimare (ūl·tē·mâ′rā) *vt* to complete, terminate

ultimo (ūl′tē·mō) *a* last, final; recent.

umanità (ū·mâ·nē·tâ′) *f* humanity

umanitario (ū·mâ·nē·tâ′ryō) *a&m* humanitarian

umano (ū·mâ′nō) *a* human

umbro (ūm′brō) *m&a* Umbrian

umidità (ū·mē·dē·tâ′) *f* humidity

umido (ū′mē·dō) *a* humid, damp; — *m* dampness; stew

umile (ū′mē·lā) *a* humble; lacking in pretention

umiliante (ū·mē·lyân′tā) *a* degrading, humiliating

umiliare (ū·mē·lyâ′rā) *vt* to mortify, humiliate; to degrade

umiliarsi (ū·mē·lyâr′sē) *vr* to humble oneself, degrade oneself

umiliazione (ū·mē·lyâ·tsyô′nā) *f* degradation, humiliation

umiltà (ū·mēl·tâ′) *f* humility; unpretentiousness, modesty

umore (ū·mō′rā) *m* mood, humor; **di cattivo** — in a bad mood, out of sorts

umorista (ū·mō·rē′stâ) *m* humorist; wit

umoristico (ū·mō·rē′stē·kō) *a* witty; funny

un (ūn) *art m* the

una (ū′nâ) *art f* the

uncinetto (ūn·chē·nāt′tō) *m* crocheting needle

uncino (ūn·chē′nō) *m* hook

undicesimo (ūn·dē·che′zē·mō) *a&m* eleventh

undici (ūn′dē·chē) *a* eleven

ungere * (ūn′jä·rā) *vt* to grease; to smear grease on

ungherese (ūn·gā·rā′zā) *a&m* Hungarian

Ungheria (ūn·gā·rē′â) *f* Hungary

unghia (ūn′gyâ) *f* fingernail; toenail; claw

unguento (ūn·gwän′tō) *m* salve, ointment

unicamente (ū·nē·kâ·män′tā) *adv* only,

specifically

unificare (ū·nē·fē·kâ′rā) *vt* to unify, join, bring together

unificarsi (ū·nē·fē·kâr′sē) *vr* to be unified, be joined, unite

unificazione (ū·nē·fē·kâ·tsyō′nā) *f* unification, joining

unico (ū′nē·kō) *a* unique; only; specific

uniforme (ū·nē·fōr′mā) *f* uniform; — *a* even, standard, uniform

unione (ū·nyō′nā) *f* union; fusion, blending

unire (ū·nē′rā) *vt* to unite; to attach

unirsi (ū·nēr′sē) *vr* to fuse together; to join, become united

universale (ū·nē·vär·sâ′lā) *a* general; universal; blanket, all-inclusive; **Giudizio** — Last Judgment; **Diluvio** — Deluge, Flood (*eccl*)

università (ū·nē·vär·sē·tâ′) *f* university

universitario (ū·nē·vär·sē·tâ′ryō) *a* university; — *m* university student

universo (ū·nē·vär′sō) *m* universe

uno (ū′nō) *art m* the; — *a* one, a, an, any; — *pron* one, a certain one

unto (ūn′tō) *m* fat; grease; — *a* greasy; (*fig*) unclean, dirty

untuoso (ūn·twō′zō) *a* greasy, oily

unzione (ūn·tsyō′nā) *f* ointment; **estrema** — (*eccl*) extreme unction

uomini (wô′mē·nē) *mpl* men

uomo (wô′mō) *m* man; fellow, individual; **come un sol** — with one accord

uova (wō′vâ) *fpl* eggs; — **sode** hard boiled eggs; — **strapazzate** scrambled eggs; — **sbattute** beaten eggs; **caminare sulle** — (*fig*) to walk with mincing steps

uovo (wō′vō) *m* egg; — **fresco** fresh egg; **tuorlo d'** — egg yolk; **cercare il pelo nell'** — to make trivial distinctions; to be petty

uragano (ū·râ·gâ′nō) *m* hurricane

uranio (ū·râ′nyō) *m* uranium

urbanesimo (ūr·bâ·ne′zē·mō) *m* urbanism

urbanistica (ūr·bâ·nē′stē·kâ) *f* city planning

urbanità (ūr·bâ·nē·tâ′) *f* politeness, gentility; savoir faire

urbano (ūr·bâ′nō) *a* urban; genteel; — *m* local telephone call

urgente (ūr·jän′tā) *a* urgent; –**mente** (ūr·jän·tâ·män′tā) *adv* urgently

urgenza (ūr·jän′tsâ) *f* urgency, emergency

urina (ū·rē′nâ) *f* urine

urlare (ūr·lâ′rā) *vi* to scream, yell; to holler; to cry out

urlo (ūr′lō) *m* scream, shout; outcry

urna (ūr′nâ) *f* urn; (*pol*) ballot box

---

k kid, **l** let, **m** met, **n** not, **p** pat, **r** very, **s** sat, **sh** shop, **t** tell, **v** vat, **w** we, **y** yet, **z** zero

urtante (ūr·tân′tä) *a* (*fig*) annoying, exasperating

urtare (ūr·tâ′rä) *vt* to bump into; to shove; to run into, collide with

urtarsi (ūr·târ′sē) *vr* to shove one another; to collide; (*fig*) to become annoyed; to dispute

urto (ūr′tō) *m* shove, push; impact; **essere in — con** (*fig*) to be angry with; not to be on speaking terms with; **mettersi in — con** to quarrel with, have a misunderstanding with

usanza (ū·zân′tsä) *f* custom; usage

usare (ū·zâ′rä) *vt* to use; — *vi* to be accustomed to, have the habit of

usarsi (ū·zâr′sē) *vr* to be the fashion; to be in use

usato (ū·zâ′tō) *a* used; usual; second-hand; **più dell'** — unusual, more than usual

usciere (ū·shā′rä) *m* usher; process server

uscio (ū′shō) *m* door; exit

uscire * (ū·shē′rä) *vi* to go out; to exit

uscita (ū·shē′tä) *f* exit; (*fig*) witty remark; (*com*) expenditure; **entrata e —** (*com*) assets and liabilities

usignuolo (ū·zē·nywō′lō) *m* nightingale

uso (ū′zō) *m* custom; usage; — *a* used, accustomed; **essere in —** to be customary, be in use, be considered fashion-

able; **secondo l'—** in keeping with tradition; **fuori d'—** obsolete; out of working order

usuale (ū·zwâ′lä) *a* customary; traditional

usualmente (ū·zwâl·mān′tä) *adv* ordinarily, usually; traditionally

usufruire (ū·zū·frūē′rä) *vi* to benefit by, derive advantage from

usura (ū·zū′rä) *f* wear and tear, use; usury; **–io** (ū·zū·râ′yō) *m* usurer, loan shark; (*coll*) money lender

usurpare (ū·zūr·pâ′rä) *vt* to usurp, take over

utensile (ū·tän·sē′lä) *m* utensil; **macchina — machine tool**

utente (ū·tän′tä) *m* user; subscriber

utenza (ū·tän′tsä) *f* consumers

utero (ū′tä·rō) *m* uterus

utile (ū′tē·lä) *a* useful; — *m* profit; (*com*) dividend

utilità (ū·tē·lē·tâ′) *f* utility, service

utilitaria (ū·tē·lē·tâ′ryâ) *f* compact car

utilizzare (ū·tē·lē·dzâ′rä) *vt* to utilize, make use of; to derive profit from

utilizzazione (ū·tē·lē·dzâ·tsyō′nä) *f* utilization, utilizing

utilmente (ū·tēl·mān′tä) *adv* usefully

uva (ū′vâ) *f* grape; **— passa** raisin

uzzolo (ū′dzō·lō) *m* caprice, whim; secret desire

V

vacante (vâ·kân′tä) *a* empty; not in use

vacanza (vâ·kân′tsä) *f* vacation

vacca (vâk′kâ) *f* cow

vacchetta (vâk·kāt′tâ) *f* cowhide

vaccinare (vâ·chē·nâ′rä) *vt* to vaccinate

vaccino (vâ·chē′nō) *m* vaccine

vacillare (vâ·chēl·lâ′rä) *vt* to waver, be undecided

vacillazione (vâ·chēl·lâ·tsyō′nä) *f* vacillation, indecision; flickering

vacuo (vâ′kwō) *a* empty, meaningless

vagabondo (vâ·gâ·bōn′dō) *m* idler; vagabond

vagamente (vâ·gâ·mān′tä) *adv* vaguely; in a charming way

vaglia (vâ′lyâ) *m* money order; — *f* capability; mettle; worth; **–re** (vâ·lyâ′rä) *vt* to test the merit of, evaluate; to pick out

vago (vâ′gō) *a* vague; lovely, desirable

vagone (vâ·gō′nä) *m* railroad car; **— da letto** sleeping car; **— ristorante** dining car

vaiolo (vâ·yō′lō) *m* smallpox

valanga (vâ·lân′gâ) *f* avalanche

valente (vâ·lān′tä) *a* able; skillful; apt

valere * (vâ·lā′rä) *vi* to be worth; to be valid; to be worthwhile; to be of use, worth the effort; **quanto vale ciò?** what is the price of this? **non —** (*sport*) not to count; **farsi —** to make oneself a name; **vale a dire** in other words, that is to say

valersi * (vâ·lār′sē) *vr* to utilize, make use of; **— di ogni mezzo per raggiungere la meta** to use any means to gain an end

valevole (vâ·le′vō·lä) *a* valid; of help, of use

valico (vâ′lē·kō) *m* pass, gap; break in a mountain range

validità (vâ·lē·dē·tâ′) *f* effect, validness; effectiveness

valido (vâ′lē·dō) *a* valid, good; worthwhile

valigia (vâ·lē′jâ) *f* suitcase

valle (vâl′lä) *f* valley

valore (vâ·lō′rä) *m* value; valor

valoroso (vâ·lō·rō′zō) *a* brave, stout-hearted

valuta (vâ·lū′tâ) *f* currency; worth, value;

–re (vâ·lū·tâ'rā) *vt* to value; to evaluate; **–zione** (vâ·lū·tâ·tsyō'nā) *f* estimate; evaluation

valvola (vâl'vō·lâ) *f* valve; radio tube

vaneggiare (vâ·nāj·jâ'rā) *vi* to rant wildly, rave; to talk deliriously

vanga (vân'gâ) *f* spade

vangelo (vân·jâ'lō) *m* Gospel; (*fig*) absolute truth

vaniglia (vâ·nē'lyâ) *f* vanilla

vanità (vâ·nē·tâ') *f* conceitedness, vainness; shallowness

vanitoso (vâ·nē·tō'zō) *a* vain, conceited; shallow

vano (vâ'nō) *m* room; open space; — *a* vain, empty; conceited

vantaggio (vân·tâj'jō) *m* advantage; **–so** (vân·tâj·jō'zō) *a* advantageous

vantare (vân·tâ'rā) *vt&i* to boast of; to pride oneself on

vantarsi (vân·târ'sē) *vr* to boast, show off

vanto (vân'tō) *m* boast; pride

vanvera (vân'vā·râ) *f* heedlessness; **a —** thoughtlessly, carelessly

vapore (vâ·pō'rā) *m* steam; steamship; **–tto** (vâ·pō·rāt'tō) *m* steamboat

vaporizzatore (vâ·pō·rē·dzâ·tō'rā) *m* atomizer

vaporoso (vâ·pō·rō'zō) *a* diaphanous, filmy; vaporous

varare (vâ·râ'rā) *vt* to launch; — **un affare** (*com*) to set up a business; — **una legge** (*pol*) to pass a bill

varcare (vâr·kâ'rā) *vt* to cross; to overcome; to go beyond

varechina (vâ·rā·kē'nâ) *f* bleach

variazione (vâ·ryâ·tsyō'nā) *f* diversity, variety; modifying

varicella (vâ·rē·châl'lâ) *f* chicken pox

varietà (vâ·ryā·tâ') *f* variety; vaudeville; **spettacolo di —** variety show; **teatro di —** music hall

vario (vâ'ryō) *a* different; changing; various, several

varo (vâ'rō) *m* launching; introduction, debut

vasca (vâ'skâ) *f* tub

vasellame (vâ·zāl·lâ'mā) *m* pottery; set of dishes

vaso (vâ'zō) *m* vase; pot

vassoio (vâs·sô'yō) *m* tray

vastità (vâ·stē·tâ') *f* expanse, width, vastness, extension

vasto (vâ'stō) *a* vast, broad; immense

Vaticano (vâ·tē·kâ'nō) *m* Vatican

vaticinio (vâ·tē·chē'nyō) *m* prophecy

ve (vā) *pron* to you, you; — *adv* there

ve'! (vā) *interj* Look! See!

vecchia (vek'kyâ) *f* old woman

vecchiaia (vāk·kyâ'yâ) *f* old age

vecchio (vek'kyō) *a* old; — *m* old man

vece (vā'chā) *f* place, stead; **fare la — di** to substitute for, replace; **in — di** instead of

vedere * (vā·dā'rā) *vt* to see; to understand; to make note of; — **la luce** to be born; **non — l'ora di** to long for; to look forward to

vedersi * (vā·dār'sē) *vr* to get together, meet

vedova (ve'dō·vâ) *f* widow

vedovo (ve'dō·vō) *m* widower

veduta (vā·dū'tâ) *f* scene, view

vegetale (vā·jā·tâ'lā) *a* vegetable

vegetariano (vā·jā·tâ·ryâ'nō) *a&m* vegetarian

vegetazione (vā·jā·tâ·tsyō'nā) *f* vegetation

vegeto (ve'jā·tō) *a* hardy, thriving

veglia (ve'lyâ) *f* vigil, wake, watch; **–re** (vā·lyâ'rā) *vt* to watch over; to guard

veglione (vā·lyō'nā) *m* costume party, masked ball

veicolo (vā·ē'kō·lō) *m* vehicle

vela (vā'lâ) *f* sail; **–re** (vā·lâ'rā) *vt* to cover up, disguise; **–rsi** (vā·lâr'sē) *vr* to become thick (*voice*); to wear a veil; **–to** (vā·lâ'tō) *a* veiled

veleno (vā·lā'nō) *m* poison; **–so** (vā·lā·nō'zō) *a* poisonous

veliero (vā·lyā'rō) *m* sailing ship

velivolo (vā·lē'vō·lō) *m (avi)* glider

vellicare (vāl·lē·kâ'rā) *vt* to tickle; to give a pleasant feeling; to please

vello (vāl'lō) *m* fleece; **–so** (vāl·lō'zō) *a* shaggy

velluto (vāl·lū'tō) *m* velvet, velours

velo (vā'lō) *m* gauze; veil

veloce (vā·lō'chā) *a* fast, speedy; **–mente** (vā·lō·chā·mān'tā) *adv* rapidly, quickly

velocipede (vā·lō·chē'pā·dā) *m* tricycle

velocista (vā·lō·chē'stâ) *m* sprinter

velocità (vā·lō·chē·tâ') *f* speed; **eccesso di —** speeding, exceeding the speed limit

velodromo (vā·lô'drō·mō) *m* bicycle track

vena (vā'nâ) *f* vein; lode (*mining*); **essere in buona —** to be in the mood

venale (vā·nâ'lā) *a* corruptible; marketable; **prezzo —** sales price

venalità (vā·nâ·lē·tâ') *f* venality, susceptibility to bribes

vendemmia (vān·dem'myâ) *f* grape harvest; vintage season

vendere (ven'dā·rā) *vt* to sell; — **fumo** (*fig*) to bluff; to dupe; **aver ragione da — ** (*coll*) to be completely justified; to be absolutely right

vendetta (vān·dāt′tâ) *f* revenge

vendicare (vān·dē·kâ′rā) *vt* to avenge

vendicarsi (vān·dē·kâr′sē) *vr* to take revenge; to wreak vengeance

vendicativo (vān·dē·kâ·tē′vō) *a* vengeful, vindictive

vendita (ven′dē·tâ) *f* sale

venditore (vān·dē·tō′rā) *m* salesman; dealer

venduto (vān·dū′tō) *a* sold; *(fig)* corrupted, bribed

venerazione (vā·nā·râ·tsyō′nā) *f* deep respect, veneration; worship

venerdì (vā·nār·dē′) *m* Friday

venereo (vā·ne′rā·ō) *a* venereal

Venezia (vā·ne′tsyâ) *f* Venice

veneziano (vā·nā·tsyâ′nō) *a&m* Venetian

venire * (vā·nē′rā) *vi* to come; to occur, take place; — **in mente** to get into one's head; to come to one; to come back to one; — **a galla** to float; to come to the surface; *(fig)* to be revealed, show up

ventaglio (vān·tâ′lyō) *m* fan

ventennio (vān·ten′nyō) *m* twenty-year period

ventesimo (vān·te′zē·mō) *a* twentieth

venti (vān′tē) *a* twenty

ventilatore (vān·tē·lâ·tō′rā) *m* electric fan; ventilator, vent

ventilazione (vān·tē·lâ·tsyō′nā) *f* ventilation

ventina (vān·tē′nâ) *f* score; roughly twenty

vento (vān′tō) *m* wind

ventre (vān′trā) *m* womb; stomach, belly

ventriera (vān·tryâ′râ) *f* belt; bellyband

ventriloquo (vān·trē′lō·kwō) *m* ventriloquist

ventura (vān·tū′râ) *f* destiny, fortune

venturo (vān·tū′rō) *a* future; next *(in order)*; coming; **l'anno —** next year

venuta (vā·nū′tâ) *f* arrival; advent

venuto (vā·nū′tō) *a* arrived; **ben —** welcome

veramente (vā·râ·mān′tā) *adv* actually, in fact; really

veranda (vā·rân′dâ) *f* veranda

verbale (vār·bâ′lā) *a* verbal; — *m* minutes of a meeting; declaration

verbo (vār′bō) *m* verb

verdastro (vār·dâ′strō) *a* greenish

verde (vār′dā) *a* green; **ridere —** to laugh out of the wrong side of one's mouth; **essere al —** *(fig)* to be penniless; **età —** tender years, young age

verderame (vār·dā·râ′mā) *m* verdigris

verdetto (vār·dāt′tō) *m* verdict

verdura (vār·dū′râ) *f* vegetables

verecondo (vā·rā·kōn′dō) *a* modest, unassuming

verga (vār′gâ) *f* rod, stick

vergine (ver′jē·nā) *f&a* virgin

vergogna (vār·gō′nyâ) *f* shame, disgrace; modestness

vergognarsi (vār·gō·nyâr′sē) *vr* to feel ashamed, be covered with shame

vergognosamente (vār·gō·nyō·zâ·mān′tā) *adv* shamefully; shamelessly

vergognoso (vār·gō·nyō′zō) *a* bashful, shy; shameful; shameless

verifica (vā·rē′fē·kâ) *f* control; verification; **–re** (vā·rē·fē·kâ′rā) *vt* to check, confirm; **–rsi** (vā·rē·fē·kâr′sē) *vr* to come true, actually happen

verità (vā·rē·tâ′) *f* veracity, truth

veritiero (vā·rē·tyâ′rō) *a* truthful, honest

verme (vār′mā) *m* worm

vermiglio (vār·mē′lyō) *m* vermilion

vermut (vār′mūt) *m* vermouth

vernice (vār·nē′châ) *f* paint; varnish; preview; patent leather; — **fresca** fresh paint

verniciare (vār·nē·châ′rā) *vt* to paint; to varnish

vero (vā′rō) *a* true; absolute, complete; — *m* truth; **dal —** from life; from nature *(arts)*; **–simiglianza** (vā·rō·sē·mē·lyân′tsâ) *f* likelihood; **–simile** (vā·rō·sē′mē·lā) *a* likely

versamento (vār·sâ·mān′tō) *m* payment; pouring in; investment

versare (vār·sâ′rā) *vt* to pour; to pay in; to invest *(money)*

versione (vār·syō′nā) *f* translation; version

verso (vār′sō) *m* verse; — *prep* towards; about

vertenza (vār·tān′tsâ) *f* quarrel, dispute

verticale (vār·tē·kâ′lā) *a* vertical

vertice (ver′tē·châ) *m* top, summit; *(math)* vertex

vertigine (vār·tē′jē·nā) *f* dizziness

vertiginoso (vār·tē·jē·nō′zō) *a* dizzy

verza (vār′dzâ) *f* cabbage

vescica (vā·shē′kâ) *f* blister; bladder

vescovo (ve′skō·vō) *m* bishop

vespa (vā′spâ) *f* wasp

vestaglia (vā·stâ′lyâ) *f* lady's robe; negligee

veste (vā′stā) *m* dress; — **da camera** dressing gown

vestiario (vā·styâ′ryō) *m* clothes

vestire (vā·stē′rā) *vt* to dress

vestirsi (vā·stēr′sē) *vr* to get dressed

vestito (vā·stē′tō) *m* suit; dress; — *a*

â ârm, ā bāby, e bet, ē bē, ō gō, ô gône, ū blūe, b bad, ch child, d dad, f fat, g gay, j jet

dressed; clad

veterinario (vä·tä·rē·nâ'ryō) *m&a* veterinary

vetrata (vä·trâ'tâ) *f* glass partition; glass door

vetrina (vä·trē'nâ) *f* showcase; display window; store window

vetrinista (vä·trē·nē'stâ) *m* window trimmer

vetrino (vä·trē'nō) *m* microscopic slide

vetro (vä'trō) *m* glass; sheet of glass

vetta (vāt'tâ) *f* peak; summit; top

vettura (vät·tū'râ) *f* car, vehicle

vezzeggiare (vā·tsāj·jâ'râ) *vt* to fondle

vezzeggiativo (vā·tsāj·jâ·tē'vō) *m* pet name, term of endearment; *(gram)* diminutive

vi (vē) *pron* you, to you; — *adv* there

via (vē'â) *f* way; street; — *adv* away; —! *interj* Go away!

viaggiare (vyâj·jâ'râ) *vi* to travel

viaggiatore (vyâj·jâ·tō'râ) *m* passenger; traveler; wayfarer

viaggio (vyâj'jō) *m* trip; voyage; **Buon** —! Have a nice trip!

viale (vyâ'lā) *m* boulevard, avenue

vibrazione (vē·brâ·tsyō'nâ) *f* vibration

vicenda (vē·chän'dâ) *f* alteration, change; event, development

vicendevole (vē·chän·de'vō·lā) *a* reciprocal; in common

vicendevolmente (vē·chän·dā·vōl·mān'tā) *adv* mutually

viceré (vē·chā·râ') *m* viceroy

viceversa (vē·chā·vär'sâ) *adv* conversely; vice versa

vicinanza (vē·chē·nân'tsâ) *f* neighborhood, area

vicinato (vē·chē·nâ'tō) *m* neighborhood; collective neighbors

vicino (vē·chē'nō) *m* neighbor; — *a&adv* near, close

vicolo (vē'kō·lō) *m* alley

vidimare (vē·dē·mâ'râ) *vt* to visa

vidimazione (vē·dē·mâ·tsyō'nâ) *f* visé; validation

vietare (vyâ·tâ'râ) *vt* to forbid

vietato (vyâ·tâ'tō) *a* forbidden; — **fumare** no smoking

vigilare (vē·jē·lâ'râ) *vt* to keep watch over; to keep an eye on

vigile (vē'jē·lā) *m* policeman; — **del fuoco** fireman; — *a* watchful, mindful

vigilia (vē·jē'lyâ) *f* eve; vigil

vigliacco (vē·lyâk'kō) *a* cowardly; yellow *(coll)*; — *m* coward

vigna (vē'nyâ) *f* vineyard

vignetta (vē·nyät'tâ) *f* sketch, vignette

vigogna (vē·gō'nyâ) *f* vicuna

vigore (vē·gō'râ) *m* energy; vigor; effect, influence; **entrare in** — *(law)* to take effect, go into effect.

vigorosamente (vē·gō·rō·zâ·mān'tâ) *adv* energetically, with vigor

vigoroso (vē·gō·rō'zō) *a* strong; vigorous

vile (vē'lā) *a* dastardly; contemptible, mean; — *m* coward; low character

villa (vēl'lâ) *f* villa; country home; **–ggio** (vēl·lâj'jō) *m* village

villano (vēl·lâ'nō) *m* peasant; — *a* rude; coarse; — **rifatto** upstart

villeggiare (vēl·lāj·jâ'râ) *vi* to vacation in the country

villeggiatura (vēl·lāj·jâ·tū'râ) *f* summer vacation in the country

villino (vēl·lē'nō) *m* cottage

viltà (vēl·tâ') *f* cowardliness, cowardice; vile nature

vincere * (vēn'chā·râ) *vt&i* to win; to vanquish

vincersi * (vēn'chär·sē) *vr* to control one's emotions, hold in one's feelings

vincita (vēn'chē·tâ) *f* victory; winning

vincitore (vēn·chē·tō'râ) *m* winner

vincolare (vēn·kō·lâ'râ) *vt* to tie together, bind

vincolo (vēn'kō·lō) *m* lien, attachment; bond, fetter, restraint

vino (vē'nō) *m* wine

viola (vyō'lâ) *f* violet; viola

violare (vyō·lâ'râ) *vt* to violate; to break *(law)*; to desecrate; to rape, ravish

violazione (vyō·lâ·tsyō'nâ) *f* rape; violation; — **di domicilio** housebreaking

violentare (vyō·lān·tâ'râ) *vt* to do violence to; to rape

violento (vyō·lān'tō) *a* violent; bestial

violenza (vyō·lān'tsâ) *f* violence

violino (vyō·lē'nō) *m* violin

violoncello (vyō·lōn·chāl'lō) *m* cello

viottolo (vyōt'tō·lō) *m* path, trail

vipera (vē'pā·râ) *f* viper

virare (vē·râ'râ) *vi* *(naut)* to tack; *(avi)* to bank

virgola (vēr'gō·lâ) *f* comma

virgolette (vēr·gō·lāt'tâ) *fpl* quotation marks; **fra** — in quotation marks

virile (vē·rē'lā) *a* manful, courageous, virile

virilità (vē·rē·lē·tâ') *f* courage; power; virility; manhood

virtù (vēr·tū') *f* virtue; ability; strength

virtuoso (vēr·twō'zō) *a* honorable, virtuous

viscere (vē'shā·râ) *fpl* viscera

vischio (vē'skyō) *m* mistletoe

---

k kid, **l** let, **m** met, **n** not, **p** pat, **r** very, **s** sat, **sh** shop, **t** tell, **v** vat, **w** we, **y** yet, **z** zero

visibilio (vē·zē·bē′lyō) *m* abundance; **andare in —** to go into raptures; to be entranced
visibilità (vē·zē·bē·lē·tâ′) *f* visibility
visiera (vē·zyā′râ) *f* peak; visor
visione (vē·zyō′nä) *f* apparition; mental image; vision
visita (vē′zē·tâ) *f* visit; examination; **— doganale** customs inspection; **— medica** medical examination; **–re** (vē·zē·tâ′rä) *vt* to visit, call on
viso (vē′zō) *m* face
visone (vē·zō′nä) *m* mink
vissuto (vēs·sū′tō) *a* lived; worldly-wise, blasé
vista (vē′stâ) *f* view; outlook; sight; **–re** (vē·stâ′rä) *vt* to visa
visto (vē′stō) *a* seen; **—** *m* visa; **–so** (vē·stō′zō) *a* tawdry, cheap; extensive
vita (vē′tâ) *f* life; waist
vitalità (vē·tâ·lē·tâ′) *f* vivacity, animation, vitality
vitalizio (vē·tâ·lē′tsyō) *a* for life; **—** *m (com)* life annuity
vite (vē′tä) *f* screw; vine; *(avi)* tailspin
vitello (vē·tāl′lō) *m* veal; calf; **–ne** (vē·tāl·lō′nä) *m (coll)* playboy, idler
vittima (vēt′tē·mâ) *f* victim
vitto (vēt′tō) *m* food; **— e alloggio** room and board
vittoria (vēt·tô′ryâ) *f* victory
vittorioso (vēt·tō·ryō′zō) *a* victorious
vituperare (vē·tū·pä·râ′rä) *vt* to abuse; to cast aspersions on
vituperio (vē·tū·pe′ryō) *m* vituperation; defamation; outrage; aspersion
vivace (vē·vâ′chä) *a* vivacious, lively
vivacità (vē·vâ·chē·tâ′) *f* exhilaration; vivacity; activeness
vivaio (vē·vâ′yō) *m* nursery, greenhouse; hatchery
vivente (vē·vān′tä) *a* living
vivere * (vē′vä·rä) *vt&i* to live
viveri (vē′vä·rē) *mpl* provisions
vivisezione (vē·vē·sä·tsyō′nä) *f* vivisection
vivo (vē′vō) *a* alive; living
viziare (vē·tsyâ′rä) *vt* to ruin, spoil; to corrupt
viziarsi (vē·tsyâr′sē) *vr* to be spoiled; to be corrupted
vizio (vē′tsyō) *m* vice; bad habit; malfunction, defect; **–so** (vē·tsyō′zō) *a* dissolute; corrupt, vicious
vocabolario (vō·kâ·bō·lâ′ryō) *m* vocabulary
vocabolo (vō·kâ′bō·lō) *m* word; term
vocale (vō·kâ′lä) *a* vocal; **—** *f* vowel

voce (vō′chä) *f* voice; rumor; word; **— pubblica** public opinion
vogare (vō·gâ′rä) *vi* to row
voglia (vô′lyä) *f* wish; desire; birthmark
voi (vō′ē) *pron* you; **–altri** (vōē·âl′trē) *pron* you, you others
volante (vō·lân′tä) *m* steering wheel; **—** *a* flying
volantino (vō·lân·tē′nō) *m* handbill
volare (vō·lâ′rä) *vi* to fly
volatile (vō·lâ′tē·lä) *m* bird; **—** *a* winged; volatile
volenteroso (vō·lān·tä·rō′zō) *a* willing, pleased; zealous
volentieri (vō·lân·tyä′rē) *adv* willingly
volere * (vō·lā′ra) *vt&i* to wish, want; to feel like; **— bene** to love, be fond of **— dire** to mean; to signify
volgare (vōl·gâ′rä) *a* vulgar; **—** *m* dialect, vernacular
volgere * (vôl′jä·rä) *vt&i* to turn
volgersi * (vôl′jär·sē) *vr* to turn around, turn about
volgo (vōl′gō) *m* rabble, mob; masses
volitivo (vō·lē·tē′vō) *a* strong-willed; impetuous
volo (vō′lō) *m* flight
volontà (vō·lōn·tâ′) *f* will
volontario (vō·lōn·tâ′ryō) *a* voluntary; **—** *m* volunteer
volpe (vōl′pä) *f* fox; **— argentata** silver fox
volta (vōl′tä) *f* turn; time; **di — in —** once in a while; **altre volte** in the past, previously
volta (vōl′tâ) *m (elec)* volt
voltaggio (vōl·tâj′jō) *m (elec)* voltage
voltare (vōl·tâ′rä) *vt&i* to turn
voltarsi (vōl·târ′sē) *vr* to turn around
volto (vōl′tō) *m* face
volubile (vō·lū′bē·lä) *a* inconstant; garrulous
volume (vō·lū′mä) *m* mass, volume; book, tome
voluminoso (vō·lū·mē·nō′zō) *a* roomy; voluminous
voluttà (vō·lūt·tâ′) *f* lasciviousness, lust
vomitare (vō·mē·tâ′rä) *vt&i* to vomit; to spew forth
vongola (vôn′gō·lâ) *f* clam, mussel
vorace (vō·râ′chä) *a* voracious
voracità (vō·râ·chē·tâ′) *f* greed; voracity, hunger
voragine (vō·râ′jē·nä) *f* gulf; abyss
vortice (vôr′tē·chä) *m* whirlwind; whirlpool
vostro (vō′strō) *a* your; **— pron** yours
votare (vō·tâ′rä) *vt&i* to vote
votazione (vō·tâ·tsyō′nä) *f* voting

â ârm, ā bāby, e bet, ē bē, ō gō, ô gône, ū blūe, b bad, ch child, d dad, f fat, g gay, j jet

voto (vō′tō) *m* vote; vow; prayer; desire
vulcanizzare (vŭl·kâ·nē·dzâ′rā) *vt* to vulcanize
vulcano (vŭl·kâ′nō) *m* volcano
vuotare (vwō·tâ′rā) *vt* to empty; — **il sacco** to speak one's piece; to get something off one's chest
vuotarsi (vwō·târ′sē) *vr* to empty out, become empty
vuoto (vwō′tō) *a* empty; — *m* void; *(phys)* vacuum; emptiness; **a** — to no avail, without result

X

xenofobia (ksā·nō·fō·bē′â) *f* fear of foreigners, xenophobia
Xeres (ksā′rās) *m* Sherry wine
xilofonista (ksē·lō·fō·nē′stâ) *m* xylophone player
xilofono (ksē·lô′fō·nō) *m* xylophone
xilografia (ksē·lō·grâ·fē′â) *m* wood carving; printing with woodcuts
xilografo (ksē·lô′grâ·fō) *m* wood-carver, xylographer

Z

zabaione (dzâ·bâ·yō′nā) *m* eggnog
zafferano (dzâf·fâ·râ′nō) *m* saffron
zaffiro (dzâf′fē·rō) *m* sapphire
zaino (dzâ′ē·nō) *m* knapsack
zampa (dzâm′pâ) *f* claw; paw
zampillare (dzâm·pēl·lâ′rā) *vi* to gush forth, pour out
zampillo (dzâm·pēl′lō) *m* squirt, stream; jet, gush
zampino (dzâm·pē′nō) *m* little paw; **mettere lo — dappertutto** *(fig)* to have a finger in every pie; to have many irons in the fire
zampogna (dzâm·pō′nyâ) *f* bagpipe; **–ro** (dzâm·pō·nyâ′rō) *m* bagpipe player
zanna (dzân′nâ) *f* fang; tusk
zanzara (dzân·dzâ′râ) *f* mosquito
zanzariera (dzân·zâ·ryā′râ) *f* mosquito netting
zappa (dzâp′pâ) *f* hoe; **–re** (dzâp·pâ′rā) *vt* to dig in, work *(soil)*
zar (dzâr) *m* czar, **–ina** (dzâ·rē′nā) *f* czarina
zattera (dzât′tā·râ) *f* raft
zavorra (dzâ·vōr′râ) *f* weight, ballast
zebra (dzā′brâ) *f* zebra
zecca (dzāk′kâ) *f* mint; **nuovo di —** brand-new
zelante (dzā·lân′tā) *a* zealous; ambitious
zeppo (dzâp′pō) *a* chock-full, stuffed
zerbino (zār·bē′nō) *m* doormat
zerbinotto (dzār·bē·nōt′tō) *m* dandy; ladies' man
zero (dzā′rō) *m* zero
zia (dzē′â) *f* aunt
zibellino (dzē·bâl·lē′nō) *m* sable
zigomo (dzē′gō·mō) *m* cheekbone
zimbello (dzēm·bâl′lō) *m* laughingstock, butt of humor
zinco (dzēn′kō) *m* zinc
zingaro (dzēn′gâ·rō) *m* gypsy
zio (dzē′ō) *m* uncle
zitella (dzē·tāl′lâ) *f* spinster
zitto (dzēt′tō) *a* silent
zizzania (dzē·dzâ′nyâ) *f* disagreement, discord
zoccolo (dzôk′kō·lō) *m* wooden shoe; wainscotting
zolfanello (dzōl·fâ·nāl′lō) *m* kitchen match
zolfo (dzōl′fō) *m* sulphur
zolla (dzōl′lâ) *f* lump of sod; clod of earth
zolletta (dzōl·lāt′tâ) *f* lump of sugar
zona (dzō′nâ) *f* zone
zoologia (dzō·ō·lō·jē′â) *f* zoology
zoologico (dzō·ō·lô′jē·kō) *a* zoological
zoppicare (dzōp·pē·kâ′rā) *vi* to limp; to be lopsided
zoppo (dzōp′pō) *a* lame; lopsided, uneven
zotico (dzō′tē·kō) *a* rustic, boorish
zucca (dzŭk′kâ) *f* squash; pumpkin; *(coll)* ignoramus, dunce
zuccheriera (dzŭk·kā·ryā′râ) *f* sugar bowl
zuccherino (dzŭk·kā·rē′nō) *m* candy
zucchero (dzŭk′kâ·rō) *m* sugar
zucchino (dzŭk·kē′nō) *m* zucchini
zuffa (dzŭf′fâ) *f* scuffle, tussle; quarrel, argument
zuppa (dzŭp′pâ) *f* soup
zuppiera (dzŭp·pyā′râ) *f* tureen

ITALIAN-ENGLISH FIRST NAMES

A

Abramo (â·brâ′mō) Abraham
Ada (â′dâ) Ada
Adamo (â·dâ′mō) Adam
Adelina (â·dā·lē′nâ) Adeline
Adriano (â·dryâ′nō) Adrian
Agata (â′gâ·tâ) Agatha
Agnese (â·nyā′zā) Agnes
Agnesina (â·nyā·zē′nâ) Aggie
Agostino (â·gō·stē′nō) Austin
Alberto (âl·bār′tō) Albert
Alessandrino (â·lās·sân·drē′nō) Alex, Alec
Alessandro (â·lās·sân′drō) Alexander
Alessio (â·les′syō) Alexis
Alfonso (âl·fōn′sō) Alphonse
Alfredo (âl·frā′dō) Alfred
Alice (â·lē′chā) Alice
Aloisio (â·lō·ē′zyō) Aloysius
Ambrogio (âm·brô′jō) Ambrose
Andrea (ân·drā′â) Andrew
Andreuccio (ân·drā·ū′chō) Andy
Angela (ân′jā·lâ) Angela
Angelica (ân·je′lē·kâ) Angelica
Angelina (ân·jā·lē′nâ) Angeline
Angelo (ân′jā·lō) Angelus
Anna (ân′nâ) Ann
Annetta (ân·nāt′tâ) Annette, Nancy, Annie
Annina (ân·nē′nâ) Nancy, Annie
Anselmo (ân·sāl′mō) Anselm

Antonia (ân·tô′nyâ) Antonia
Antonietta (ân·tō·nyāt′tâ) Antoinette
Antonio (ân·tô′nyō) Anthony, Antoine
Apollodoro (â·pōl·lō·dō′rō) Apollodorus
Arianna (â·ryân′nâ) Ariadne
Arnaldo (âr·nâl′dō) Arnold
Aroldo (â·rōl′dō) Harold
Aronne (â·rōn′nâ) Aaron
Arrigo (âr·rē′gō) Henry
Arturo (âr·tū′rō) Arthur
Augusto (âū·gū′stō) August
Aurelia (âū·re′lyâ) Aurelia

B

Baldassarre (bâl·dâs·sâr′rā) Balthazar
Baldovino (bâl·dō·vē′nō) Baldwin
Barbara (bâr′bâ·râ) Barbara
Barnaba (bâr′nâ·bâ) Barnaby
Bartolomeo (bâr·tō·lō·mā′ō) Bartholomew
Basilio (bâ·zē′lyō) Basil
Beatrice (bā·â·trē′chā) Beatrice
Benedetto (bā·nā·dāt′tō) Benedict
Beniamino (bā·nyâ·mē′nō) Benjamin
Berenice (bā·rā·nē′chā) Bernice

Bernardina (bär·när·dē′nä) Bernadine

Bernardino (bär·när·dē′nō) Barney

Bernardo (bär·när′dō) Bernard

Berta (bär′tä) Bertha

Bertrando (bär·trän′dō) Bertram, Bertrand

Bianca (byän′kä) Blanche

Brigida (brē′jē·dä) Bridget

C

Calvino (käl·vē′nō) Calvin

Camilla (kä·mēl′lä) Camille

Carletto (kär·lät′tō) Charlie

Carlo (kär′lō) Charles

Carlotta (kär·lōt′tä) Charlotte

Carolina (kä·rō·lē′nä) Caroline

Caterina (kä·tä·rē′nä) Catherine, Katherine, Kathie

Cecilia (chä·chē′lyä) Cecilia, Cecily

Cecilio (chä·chē′lyō) Cecil

Cesare (che′zä·rä) Caesar

Chiara (kyä′rä) Clare, Clara

Clarice (klä′rē·chä) Clarissa

Clarissa (klä·rēs′sä) Clarissa

Claudia (klä′ū·dyä) Claudia

Claudiano (kläü·dyä′nō) Claudian

Claudio (klä′ū·dyō) Claude

Clemente (klä·mān′tä) Clement

Clemenza (klä·mān′tsä) Clemence

Clio (klē′ō) Clio

Cloe (klō′ä) Chloe

Cordelia (kōr·de′lyä) Cordelia

Corinna (kō·rēn′nä) Corinne

Cornelia (kōr·ne′lyä) Cornelia

Cornelio (kōr·ne′lyō) Cornelius

Corradino (kōr·rä·dē′nō) Conrad

Corrado (kōr·rä′dō) Conrad

Costanza (kō·stän′tsä) Constance

Cristiano (krē·styä′nō) Christian

Cristina (krē·stē′nä) Christine

Cristoforo (krē·stô′fō·rō) Christopher

D

Dafne (däf′nä) Daphne

Damiano (dä·myâ′nō) Damian

Damone (dä·mō′nä) Damon

Daniele (dä·nyä′lä) Daniel

Dante (dän′tä) Dante

Dario (dâ′ryō) Darien

Davide (dâ′vē·dä) David

Davidino (dâ·vē·dē′nō) Davy

Delia (de′lyä) Delia

Demetrio (dä·me′tryō) Demetrius

Diana (dyâ′nä) Diane, Diana

Dionigi (dyō·nē′jē) Dennis

Domenico (dō·me′nē·kō) Dominic

Donato (dō·nâ′tō) Donatus

Dora (dō′rä) Dora

Doride (dô′rē·dä) Doris

Dorotea (dō·rō·tä′â) Dorothy

Durante (dū·rän′tä) Durand

E

Edgardo (ād·gâr′dō) Edgar
Editta (ā·dēt′tâ) Edith
Edmondo (ād·mōn′dō) Edmund
Edoardo (ā·dō·âr′dō) Edward
Egidio (ā·jē′dyō) Giles
Elena (e′lā·nâ) Helen, Ellen, Helena
Eleonora (ā·lā·ō·nō′râ) Eleanor
Elia (ā·lē′â) Elias
Elisa (ā·lē′zâ) Eliza
Elisabetta (ā·lē·zâ·bāt′tâ) Elizabeth
Eloisa (ā·lō·ē′zâ) Eloise
Elvira (āl·vē′râ) Elvira
Emilia (ā·mē′lyâ) Emily, Emilia
Emilio (ā·mē′lyō) Emile
Emma (ām′mâ) Emma
Enrichetta (ān·rē·kāt′tâ) Harriet, Hatty, Hetty
Enrico (ān·rē′kō) Henry
Erberto (ār·bār′tō) Herbert
Erico (ā·rē′kō) Eric
Ermione (ār·myō′nā) Hermione
Ernestina (ār·nā·stē′nâ) Ernestine
Ernesto (ār·nā′stō) Ernest
Esmondo (ā·zmōn′dō) Esmund
Ester (ā′stār) Esther
Ettore (et′tō·rā) Hector
Eugenia (āū·je′nyâ) Eugenia
Eugenio (āū·je′nyō) Eugene
Eva (ā′vâ) Eve
Evelina (ā·vā·lē′nâ) Evelyn
Ezechiele (ā·dzā·kyā′lā) Ezekiel

F

Fabiano (fâ·byâ′nō) Fabian
Fabrizio (fâ·brē′tsyō) Fabricius
Federica (fā·dā·rē′kâ) Frederica
Federico (fā·dā·rē′kō) Frederick, Fred
Felice (fā·lē′chā) Felix
Felicia (fā·lē′châ) Felicia
Feliciano (fā·lē·châ′nō) Felician
Felicita (fā·lē′chē·tâ) Felicity
Ferdinando (fār·dē·nân′dō) Ferdinand
Fernando (fār·nân′dō) Ferdinand
Filemone (fē·le′mō·nā) Philemon
Filippo (fē·lēp′pō) Philip
Fiorenza (fyō·rān′tsâ) Florence
Flaviano (flâ·vyâ′nō) Flavian
Flavio (flâ′vyō) Flavius
Fortunata (fōr·tū·nâ′tâ) Fortune
Fortunato (fōr·tū·nâ′tō) Fortunatus
Francesca (frân·chā′skâ) Frances
Francesco (frân·chā′skō) Francis, Frank
Fulvia (fūl′vyâ) Fulvia
Fulvio (fūl′vyō) Fulvius

G

Gabriele (gâ·bryā′lā) Gabriel
Gabriella (gâ·bryāl′lâ) Gabriella
Galileo (gâ·lē·lā′ō) Galileo
Geltrude (jāl·trū′dā) Gertrude
Genoveffa (jā·nō·vāf′fâ) Genevieve

272

Geraldina (jā·râl·dē′nâ) Geraldine

Geraldo (jā·râl′dō) Gerald

Gerardo (jā·râr′dō) Gerard

Geronimo (jā·rô′nē·mō) Jerome

Gervasio (jār·vâ′zyō) Gervase

Giacinta (jâ·chēn′tâ) Hyacinth

Giacobbe (jâ·kōb′bâ) Jacob

Giacomina (jâ·kō·mē′nâ) Jenny

Giacomo (jâ′kō·mō) James, Jacques

Giampietro (jâm·pyā′trō) John Peter

Gian Andrea (jân ân·drā′â) John Andrew

Gian Carlo (jân kâr′lō) John Charles

Gian Lorenzo (jân lō·rān′dzō) John Lawrence

Gianmaria (jân·mâ·rē′â) John Marion

Giannetta (jân·nāt′tâ) Jeanette, Jenny

Giannetto (jân·nāt′tō) Jack

Giano (jâ′nō) Ian

Giasone (jâ·zō′nâ) Jason

Gilberto (jēl·bār′tō) Gilbert

Gina (jē′nâ) Jean

Gino (jē′nō) Gene

Gioconda (jō·kōn′dâ) Jocunda

Gionata (jô′nâ·tâ) Jonathan

Giordano (jōr·dâ′nō) Jordan

Giorgetto (jōr·jāt′tō) Georgie

Giorgiana (jōr·jâ′nâ) Georgiane

Giorgio (jôr′jō) George

Giovanna (jō·vân′nâ) Jane, Joan, Johanna

Giovanni (jō·vân′nē) John

Giovannina (jō·vân·nē′nâ) Jean

Giuditta (jū·dēt′tâ) Judith

Giulia (jū′lyâ) Julia, Julie

Giuliana (jū·lyâ′nâ) Juliana

Giuliano (jū·lyâ′nō) Julian

Giulietta (jū·lyāt′tâ) Juliet

Giulio (jū′lyō) Julius, Jules

Giuseppe (jū·zāp′pâ) Joseph

Giuseppina (jū·zāp·pē′nâ) Josephine

Giustina (jū·stē′nâ) Justina

Giustiniano (jū·stē·nyâ′nō) Justinian

Giustino (jū·stē′nō) Justin

Giusto (jū′stō) Justus

Goffredo (gōf·frā′dō) Godfrey

Gregorio (grā·gô′ryō) Gregory

Gualtiero (gwâl·tyā′rō) Walter

Guglielmino (gū·lyāl·mē′nō) Bill

Guglielmo (gū·lyāl′mō) William

Guido (gwē′dō) Guy

Guntero (gūn·tā′rō) Gunther

Gustavo (gū·stâ′vō) Gustav

I

Ida (ē′dâ) Ida

Ilario (ē·lâ′ryō) Hilary

Irene (ē·rā′nā) Irene

Isabella (ē·zâ·bāl′lâ) Isabel

Isacco (ē·zâk′kō) Isaac

Ivonne (ē·vōn′nâ) Yves

L

Lamberto (lâm·bār'tō) Lambert
Laura (lâ'ū·râ) Laura
Lavinia (lâ·vē'nyâ) Lavinia
Leandro (lā·ân'drō) Leander
Leonardo (lā·ō·nâr'dō) Leonard
Leone (lā·ō'nā) Leo
Leonia (lā·ô'nyâ) Leonia
Leonora (lā·ō·nō'râ) Leonore
Leopoldo (lā·ō·pōl'dō) Leopold
Lea (lā'â) Leah
Lidia (lē'dyâ) Lydia
Lionello (lyō·nāl'lō) Lionel
Lisa (lē'zâ) Betty
Lisetta (lē·zāt'tâ) Betsy
Livia (lē'vyâ) Livia
Lodovico (lō·dō·vē'kō) Lewis
Lorena (lō·rā'nâ) Lorraine
Lorenzo (lō·rān'dzō) Lawrence
Luca (lū'kâ) Luke, Lucas
Lucano (lū·kâ'nō) Lucan
Lucia (lū·chē'â) Lucy, Lucia
Luciano (lū·châ'nō) Lucian
Lucio (lū'chō) Lucius
Lucrezio (lū·krē'tsyō) Lucretius
Luigi (lwē'jē) Louis
Luisa (lwē'zâ) Louisa

M

Maddalena (mâd·dâ·lā'nâ) Madeleine, Madeline
Magda (mâg'dâ) Maud
Manfredo (mân·frā'dō) Manfred

Manlio (mân'lyō) Manlius
Manuele (mâ·nwā'lā) Manuel
Marcantonio (mâr·kân·tô'nyō) Mark Anthony
Marcellina (mâr·chāl·lē'nâ) Marcelline
Marcellino (mâr·chāl·lē'nō) Marcellinus
Marcello (mâr·chāl'lō) Marcel
Marco (mâr'kō) Mark
Margherita (mâr·gā·rē'tâ) Margaret, Margery, Margot, Madge
Maria (mâ·rē'â) Mary, Marie
Marianna (mâ·ryân'nâ) Marianne
Marietta (mâ·ryāt'tâ) Peggy, Marion, May
Mario (mâ'ryō) Marius
Marta (mâr'tâ) Martha
Martino (mâr·tē'nō) Martin
Massimiliano (mâs·sē·mē·lyâ'nō) Maximilian
Matilde (mâ·tēl'dâ) Mathilda
Matteo (mât·tā'ō) Matthew
Maurizio (mâū·rē'tsyō) Maurice
Melissa (mā·lēs'sâ) Melissa
Mercede (mâr·châ'dâ) Mercedes
Michelangelo (mē·kā·lân'jâ·lō) Michaelangelo
Michele (mē·kā'lā) Michael
Michelino (mē·kā·lē'nō) Mike
Minerva (mē·nār'vâ) Minerva
Miranda (mē·rân'dâ) Miranda
Modesto (mō·dā'stō) Modestus
Monica (mô'nē·ka) Monica, Monique

N

Nannetta (nân·nāt'tâ) Nannette
Natale (nâ·tâ'lā) Noel
Natalia (nâ·tâ·lē'â) Natalie
Nataniele (nâ·tâ·nyā'lā) Nathaniel
Nicola (nē·kō'lâ) Nicholas
Nicoletta (nē·kō·lāt'tâ) Nicolette
Nicolò (nē·kō·lō') Nicholas
Nicoluccio (nē·kō·lū'chō) Nick
Nina (nē'nâ) Nina, Nan
Nino (nē'nō) Nino

O

Ofelia (ō·fe'lyâ) Ophelia
Olivia (ō·lē'vyâ) Olive, Olivia
Oliviero (ō·lē·vyā'rō) Oliver
Omero (ō·mā'rō) Homer
Onofredo (ō·nō·frā'dō) Humphrey
Onorato (ō·nō·râ'tō) Honore
Orazio (ō·râ'tsyō) Horace, Horatio
Orlando (ōr·lân'dō) Orlando
Orsola (ôr'sō·lâ) Ursula
Ortensia (ōr·ten'syâ) Hortense, Hortensia
Oscar (ō'skâr) Oscar
Osvaldo (ō·zvâl'dō) Oswald
Ottavia (ōt·tâ'vyâ) Octavia
Ottaviano (ōt·tâ·vyā'nō) Octavian
Ottavio (ōt·tâ'vyō) Octavius
Ovidio (ō·vē'dyō) Ovid

P

Panfilo (pân'fē·lō) Pamphilus
Paola (pâ'ō·lâ) Paula
Paolina (pâ·ō·lē'nâ) Paulina
Paolino (pâ·ō·lē'nō) Paulinus
Paolo (pâ'ō·lō) Paul
Pasquale (pâ·skwâ'lā) Pascal
Patrizia (pâ·trē'tsyâ) Patricia
Patrizio (pā·trē'tsyō) Patrick
Penelope (pā·ne'lō·pā) Penelope
Petronilla (pā·trō·nēl'lâ) Petronella
Petronio (pā·trô'nyō) Petronius
Piero (pyā'rō) Peter
Pietro (pyā'trō) Peter
Pietruccio (pyā·trū'chō) Pete
Pindaro (pēn'dâ·rō) Pindar
Placidia (plâ·chē'dyâ) Placidia
Platone (plâ·tō'nā) Plato
Plauto (plâ'ū·tō) Plautus
Plinio (plē'nyō) Pliny
Pompeo (pōm·pā'ō) Pompey
Porfirio (pōr·fē'ryō) Porphyry
Porzia (pôr'tsyâ) Portia
Priscilla (prē·shēl'lâ) Priscilla
Prospero (prô'spā·rō) Prosper
Proteo (prô'tā·ō) Proteus
Prudenza (prū·dān'tsâ) Prudence

Q

Quintiliano (kwēn·tē·lyâ'nō) Quintilian
Quintino (kwēn·tē'nō) Quentin

R

Rachele (râ·kā'lā) Rachel
Raffaele (râf·fâ·ā'lā) Raphael
Raimondo (râē·mōn'dō) Raymond
Randolfo (rân·dōl'fō) Randolph
Raniero (râ·nyā'rō)
Raulo (râ'ū·lō) Ralph
Rea (rā'â) Rhea
Rebecca (rā·bāk'kâ) Rebecca
Reginaldo (rā·jē·nâl'dō) Reginald
Reinardo (rāē·nâr'dō) Reinhard
Renato (rā·nâ'tō) Renatus
Riccardino (rēk·kâr·dē'nō) Dick
Riccardo (rēk·kâr'dō) Richard
Rinaldo (rē·nâl'dō) Reynold, Reggie, Ronald
Roberto (rō·bār'tō) Robert
Rodolfo (rō·dōl'fō) Rudolph, Ralph
Rodrigo (rō·drē'gō) Roderick
Rolando (rō·lân'dō) Roland
Romolo (rô'mō·lō) Romulus
Rosa (rō'zâ) Rose
Rosalia (rō·zâ·lē'â) Rosalie
Rosalinda (rō·zâ·lēn'dâ) Rosalind
Rosamonda (rō·zâ·mōn'dâ) Rosamund
Rosetta (rō·zāt'tâ) Rosette
Rosina (rō·zē'nâ) Rosalie
Rossana (rōs·sâ'nâ) Roxanne
Rufo (rū'fō) Rufus
Ruggero (rūj·jā'rō) Roger
Ruth (rūt) Ruth

S

Salomone (sâ·lō·mō'nā) Solomon
Samuele (sâ·mwā'lā) Samuel
Sandro (sân'drō) Andrew
Sansone (sân·sō'nā) Samson
Sara (sâ'râ) Sarah, Sally
Saul (sâ'ūl) Saul
Saverio (sâ·ve'ryō) Xavier
Sebastiana (sā·bâ·styâ'nâ) Sebastiana
Sebastiano (sā·bâ·styâ'nō) Sebastian
Sempronia (sām·prô'nyâ) Sempronia
Sempronio (sām·prô'nyō) Sempronius
Severo (sā·vā'rō) Severus
Sibilla (sē·bēl'lâ) Sibyl
Sigfrido (sēg·frē'dō) Siegfried
Sigismondo (sē·jē·zmōn'dō) Sigmund
Silvestro (sēl·vā'strō) Silvester
Silvia (sēl'vyâ) Sylvia
Silvio (sēl'vyō) Sylvius
Simeone (sē·mā·ō'nā) Simeon
Simone (sē·mō'nā) Simon
Sofia (sō·fē'â) Sophie
Stefania (stā·fâ'nyâ) Stephanie
Stefano (ste'fâ·nō) Stephen
Stella (stāl'lâ) Estelle, Stella
Stentore (stān·tō'rā) Stentor
Susanna (sū·zân'nâ) Susan, Sue, Susannah
Susetta (sū·zāt'tâ) Susie

T

Tacito (tâ′chē·tō) Tacitus
Taddeo (tâd·dā′ō) Thaddeus
Teobaldo (tā·ō·bâl′dō) Theobald
Teodato (tā·ō·dâ′tō) Theodatus
Teodora (tā·ō·dō′râ) Theodora
Teodorico (tā·ō·dō·rē′kō) Theodoric
Teodoro (tā·ō·dō′rō) Theodore
Teodosia (tā·ō·dô′zyâ) Theodosia
Teodosio (tā·ō·dô′zyō) Theodosius
Terenzio (tā·ren′tsyō) Terence
Teresa (tā·rā′zā) Therese, Teresa
Tibaldo (tē·bâl′dō) Tybald
Timeo (tē·mā′ō) Timaeus
Timoteo (tē·mô′tā·ō) Timothy
Tirone (tē·rō′nā) Tyrone
Tito (tē′tō) Titus
Tommasina (tōm·mâ·zē′nâ) Thomasina
Tommasino (tōm·mâ·zē′nō) Tom
Tommaso (tōm·mâ′zō) Thomas
Tonio (tô′nyō) Tony

U

Ubaldo (ū·bâl′dō) Hubaldus
Uberto (ū·bār′tō) Hubert
Ugo (ū′gō) Hugh
Ulisse (ū·lēs′sā) Ulysses
Ulrico (ūl·rē′kō) Ulric
Umberto (ūm·bār′tō) Humbert
Urania (ū·râ′nyâ) Urania
Urbano (ūr·bâ′nō) Urban

V

Valentina (vâ·lān·tē′nâ) Valentina
Valentino (vâ·lān·tē′nō) Valentine
Valeria (vâ·le′ryâ) Valerie
Valeriano (vâ·lā·ryâ′nō) Valerian
Venere (ve′nā·rā) Venus
Veronica (vā·rô′nē·kâ) Veronica
Vincenza (vēn·chān′dzâ) Vincentia
Vincenzina (vēn·chān·dzē′nâ) Vinny
Vincenzo (vēn·chān′dzō) Vincent
Vilfrido (vēl·frē′dō) Wilfred
Vinfrido (vēn·frē′dō) Winfred
Viola (vyō′lâ) Violet
Virgilio (vēr·jē′lyō) Virgil
Virginia (vēr·jē′nyâ) Virginia
Vitale (vē·tâ′lā) Vitellius
Vito (vē′tō) Vitus
Vittore (vēt·tō′rā) Victor
Vittoria (vēt·tô′ryâ) Victoria
Vittoriano (vēt·tō·ryâ′nō) Victorian
Vittorio (vēt·tô′ryō) Victor
Viviana (vē·vyâ′nâ) Vivian

Z

Zaccaria (dzâk·kâ·rē′â) Zachary
Zaccheo (dzâk·kā′ō) Zaccheus
Zenobia (dzā·nô′byâ) Zenobia
Zenone (dzā·nō′nā) Zeno

ABBREVIATIONS

a	adjective	*interj*	interjection
adv	adverb	*lit*	literature
aesp	aerospace	*m*	masculine
agr	agriculture	*math*	mathematics
anat	anatomy	*mech*	mechanics
arch	architecture	*med*	medicine
art	article	*mil*	military
ast	astronomy	*min*	mineralogy
auto	automobile	*mus*	music
avi	aviation	*n*	noun
biol	biology	*naut*	nautical
bot	botany	*phot*	photography
chem	chemistry	*phys*	physics
coll	colloquial	*pl*	plural
com	commerce	*pol*	politics
comp	compound	*prep*	preposition
conj	conjunction	*print*	printing
dent	dentistry	*pron*	pronoun
eccl	ecclesiastic	*rad*	radio
elec	electricity	*rail*	railway
f	feminine	*sl*	slang
fam	familiar	*theat*	theatre
fig	figuratively	*TV*	television
for	formal	*vi*	verb intransitive
geog	geography	*vt*	verb transitive
geol	geology	*vt&i*	verb transitive and intransitive
gram	grammar	*zool*	zoology

English-Italian

A

a *art* un, uno, una, un'
aback *adv* indietro; **be taken —** rimanere di sasso
abacus *n* abbaco
abandon *vt* abbandonare; **–ment** *n* abbandono
abase *vt* umiliare; **–ment** *n* degradazione, umiliazione
abash *vt* intimidare, svergognare, umiliare
abate *vi* diminuire; **–ment** *n* diminuzione, indebolimento, sconto
abbey *n* abbazia
abbot *n* abate *m*
abbreviate *vt* abbreviare
abbreviation *n* abbreviazione
abdicate *vt&i* abdicare, rinunciare
abdication *n* abdicazione
abdomen *n* addome *m,* ventre *m*
abdominal *a* addominale
abduct *vt* rapire; **–ion** *n* ratto; **–or** *n* rapitore *m*
abed *adv* a letto, infermo
aberration *n* aberrazione
abet *vt* favoreggiare
abeyance *n* giacenza; **in — giacente,
•** pendente, sospeso
abhor *vt* aborrire; **–rence** *n* aborrimento; **–rent** *a* aborrevole, odioso
abide *vt* sopportare; resistere; **— *vi*** dimorare, continuare; **— by** sostenere, mantenere
abiding *a* dimorante, costante
ability *n* capacità, facoltà
abject *a* abietto, basso, vile
abjure *vt* abiurare
ablative *a* ablativo
ablaze *adv* in fiamme; splendente
able *a* abile, capace; **be — to** potere, essere in grado di, sapere
able-bodied *a* robusto, vigoroso
ablution *n* abluzione
ably *adv* abilmente
abnegate *vt* rinunziare
abnegation *n* rinunzia
abnormal *a* anormale; **–ity** *n* anormalità
aboard *adv&prep* a bordo; **all —! in carrozza!: go — imbarcarsi
abode *n* dimora
abolish *vt* abolire
abolition *n* abolizione
A-bomb *n* bomba atomica
abominable *a* abominevole, infame
abominate *vt* detestare
abomination *n* abominazione, infamia
aboriginal *a* aborigeno, primitivo
abort *n (aesp)* fallimento
abortion *n* aborto
abortive *a* abortivo; senza esito
abound *vi* abbondare; **–ing** *a* abbondante
about *prep* intorno, intorno a; *(time)* verso, circa; **be — to** essere sul punto di, stare per
above *adv&prep* sopra, su; **— all** soprattutto
above-mentioned *a* sopraccitato
aboveboard *a* sincero; **— *adv*** lealmente
abrasion *n* abrasione, logoramento
abrasive *a* abrasivo; **— *n*** abrasivo
abreast *adv* in linea; **— of the times** conforme ai tempi
abridge *vt* accorciare
abroad *adv* all'estero
abrogate *vt* abrogare; *(abolish)* abolire; *(annul)* annullare
abrupt *a* brusco, improvviso
abscess *n* ascesso

abscond *vi* scappare, sparire; nascondersi
absence *n* assenza; **leave of** — licenza, congedo
absent *a* assente; **–ee** *n* assenteista *m*
absent-minded *a* distratto
absolute *a* assoluto; **–ly** *adv* assolutamente
absolution *n* assoluzione
absolve *vt* assolvere
absorb *vt* assorbire
absorbent *a* assorbente; — **cotton** cotone idrofilo
absorption *n* assorbimento
abstain *v* astenersi
abstemious *a* astemio
abstinence *n* astinenza
abstract *vt* sottrarre; — *n&a* astratto, estratto; — *n (com)* riassunto; **in the** — in astratto; **–ly** *adv* astrattamente
abstracted *a* distratto; **–ly** *adv* distrattamente
abstraction *n* astrazione
abstruse *a* astruso
absurd *a* assurdo; **–ity** *n* assurdità
abundance *n* abbondanza
abundant *a* abbondante
abuse *vt* maltrattare; — *vi* abusare; — *n* abuso, insulto
abusive *a* abusivo
abut *vi* sfociare, confinare
abyss *n* abisso, profondità
Abyssinia *n* Abissinia
Abyssinian *n&a* abissino
academic *a* accademico, classico
academy *n* accademia, scuola
accede *vi* accedere, consentire, assentire
accelerate *vt* accelerare; — *vi* affrettarsi
acceleration *n* accelerazione
accelerator *n* acceleratore *m*
accent *n* accento, tono; — *vt* accentare, accentuare; **–uate** *vt* accentuare
accept *vt* accettare, accogliere; *(approve)* approvare; **–able** *a* accettabile, ammissibile; **–ance** *n* accettazione; approvazione; *(com)* cambiale *f*
access *n* accesso, entrata
accessory *a* accessorio; — *n* accessorio; *(partner)* complice *m*
accident *n* incidente *m;* **–al** *a* accidentale, fortuito; **–ally** *adv* accidentalmente, per caso
acclaim *vt* acclamare; — *n* acclamazione
acclamation *n* acclamazione
acclimate *vt* acclimatare
accomodate *vt* accomodare, favorire; *(house)* alloggiare; — *vi* accomodarsi, prestarsi, conformarsi; — **oneself** adattarsi
accommodating *a* cortese, accomodante

accommodation *n* accomodamento; **–s** *npl* *(hotel)* alloggiamento
accompaniment *n* accompagnamento
accompanist *n* accompagnatore *m*, accompagnatrice *f*
accompany *vt* accompagnare
accomplice *n* complice *m*
accomplish *vt* realizzare; **–ed** *a* adempiuto, compiuto; **–ment** *n* complimento, effettuazione
accord *vt* accordare; *(grant)* concedere; — *vi* accordarsi; — *n* accordo, concordia; **of one's own** — spontaneamente; **with one** — simultaneamente, di comune accordo; **–ance** *n* conformità
according *a* concedente; — *adv* secondo, conforme a; **–ly** *adv* così, pertanto
accordion *n* fisarmonica; — **player** fisarmonicista *m&f*
accost *vt* accostare, abbordare
account *n (com)* conto; *(report)* resoconto; *(story)* racconto, versione; **of no** — di nessuna importanza; **on** — *(com)* per conto; **on** — **of** per causa di; **on my** — per conto mio, a causa mia; **on no** — in nessun modo
account *vt (com)* contare; — **for** render conto di
accountant *n* ragioniere *m*, contabile *m*
accounting *n* contabilità
accredit *vt* accreditare; **–ed** *a* accreditato
accrual *a* crescente, montante
accrue *vi* accumularsi; **–d** *a* accumulato
accumulate *vt* accumulare, ammucchiare; — *vi* accumularsi
accumulation *n* accumulazione
accuracy *n* precisione, esattezza
accurate *a* esatto, giusto, preciso
accursed *a* maledetto
accusation *n* accusa
accusative *a&n* accusativo
accuse *vt* accusare; **–d** *a* accusato
accuser *n* accusatore *m*
accustom *vt* abituare; **become –ed** abituarsi
ace *n* asso
acetate *n* acetato
acetic *a* acetico
acetone *n* acetone *m*
acetylene *n* acetilene *m*
ache *n* dolore *m;* — *vi* sentir male, dolere; far male
achieve *vt* raggiungere, conseguire, pervenire; **–ment** *n* raggiungimento; *(goal)* meta; *(result)* esito
acid *n&a* acido; — **test** analisi finale
acid-forming *a* acidico
acidity *n* acidità
acidosis *n* acidosi *f*

acknowledge *vt* riconoscere; — **receipt** accusare ricevuta
acknowledgment *n* riconoscimento, confessione
acme *n* acme *m*, crisi *f*, apogeo
acorn *n* ghianda
acoustic *a* acustico; **–s** *npl* acustica
acquaint *vt* informare; **be –ed** conoscere; **be –ed with** essere edotto di; — **oneself with** fare la conoscenza di
acquaintance *n* conoscenza
acquiesce *vi* consentire a
acquiescence *n* acquiescenza
acquiescent *a* acquiescente, accomodante
acquire *vt* acquistare
acquisition *n* acquisizione, acquisto
acquit *vt* assolvere; — **oneself well** fare buona figura
acquittal *n* assoluzione
acre *n* acro; **–age** *n* superficie *f*
acrid *a* agro
acrobat *n* acrobata *m&f*; **–ics** *npl* acrobazie *fpl*; **–ic** *a* acrobatico
across *adv* dirimpetto; **come** — imbattersi in; — *prep* attraverso
act *n* atto, azione; *(law)* legge *f*; *(of a play)* atto; *(theat)* recitazione, rappresentazione; — *vt* fare; *(behavior)* agire; rappresentare; funzionare; — **as** fungere da
acting *n* azione, recitazione
action *n* azione, fatto; **legal** — azione legale; **–s** condotta
activate *v* attivare
active *a* attivo; **–ly** *adv* attivamente
activity *n* attività
actor *n* attore, interprete *m*
actress *n* attrice, interprete *f*
actual *a* effettivo, reale; **–ly** *adv* effettivamente
actuality *n* attualità
acumen *n* acume *m*
acute *a* acuto; **–ly** *adv* acutamente
adage *n* adagio, proverbio
adamant *a* inflessibile
adapt *v* adattare; **–able** *a* adattabile; **–ability** *n* adattabilità; **–ation** *n* adattamento; **–er** *n (theat)* adattatore *m*
add *vt* aggiungere; *(math)* addizionare, sommare
addendum *n* aggiunta; addendo
addict *vt* assuefare; **drug —** tossicomane *m*
addiction *n* inclinazione; propensione
adding machine *n* addizionatrice *f*
addition *n* aggiunta; *(math)* addizione; **in — to** oltre a; **–al** *a* supplementare, addizionale
addle *vt* confondere; — *vi* confondersi
addle-brained *a* stupido
address *n* indirizzo; — *vt* indirizzare;

— *vi* indirizzarsi; **–ee** *n* destinatario
address *n* discorso; — *vt* rivolgere la parola a; — *vi* rivolgersi
adduce *vt* addurre, aggiungere
adenoids *npl* adenoidi *fpl*
adept *n&a* esperto, adepto
adequate *a* sufficiente, adeguato; **–ly** *adv* sufficientemente; **–ness** *n* adeguamento
adhere *vi* aderire
adherent *a&n* aderente *m&f*; **–ly** *adv* aderentemente
adhesion *n* adesione *f*
adhesive *a* adesivo; — **tape** nastro adesivo; — *n* cerotto; **–ness** *n* vischiosità
adipose *a* adiposo, grasso
adit *n* entrata
adjacent *a* contiguo, adiacente
adjective *n* aggettivo
adjoin *vt* aggiungere; — *vi* confinare, essere contiguo; **–ing** *a* contiguo
adjourn *vt* rinviare; — *vi* fare rinvio; *(discussion)* aggiornare; *(meeting)* sciogliere l'adunanza; **–ment** *n* rinvio
adjudication *n* aggiudicazione; condanna, sentenza
adjunct *n* aggiunto
adjust *vt* aggiustare; — **oneself** adattarsi; **–able** *a* aggiustabile; **–ment** *n* accomodamento
adjutant *n* aiutante *m*
ad-lib *vt* improvvisare
administer *vt* amministrare; — *vi* contribuire, somministrare
administrator *n* amministratore *m*
administration *n* amministrazione, governo
admirable *a* ammirevole
admirably *adv* mirabilmente
admiral *n* ammiraglio
admiration *n* ammirazione
admire *vt* ammirare; **–r** *n* ammiratore *m*, ammiratrice *f*
admissible *a* ammissibile
admission *n (acknowledgment)* ammissione, *(entrance)* ingresso, entrata
admit *vt* ammettere; *(acknowledge)* confessare, riconoscere
admittance *n* entrata, ingresso; **no —** vietato l'ingresso
admittedly *adv* ammissibilmente
admix *vt* mischiare; — *vi* mescolarsi con; **–ture** *n* miscela
admonish *vt* ammonire, riprendere
admonition *n* ammonizione
ado *n* rumore *m*, confusione
adobe *n&a* mattone crudo
adolescence *n* adolescenza
adolescent *a* adolescente

adopt *vt* adottare; **–ed** *a* adottato, addottivo
adoption *n* adozione
adorable *a* adorabile
adoration *a* adorazione
adore *vt* adorare; — *vi* fare atto di adorazione
adorn *vt* adornare, fregiare; — **one's self** adornarsi, abbellirsi
adrenal *a* adrenale; **–in** *n* adrenalina
adrift *a&adv* alla deriva
adroit *a* destro, abile
adsorb *vt* raccogliere, riunire, assorbire
adulation *n* adulazione
adult *a&n* adulto
adulterant *n&a* adulterante
adulterer *n* adultero; adultera
adulterate *vt* adulterare, falsificare
adultery *n* adulterio
advance *vt* avanzare; *(money)* prestare; **pay in** — anticipare; — *vi* andare avanti; **–d** *a* avanzato; — *n* anticipo; *(price, wage)* aumento; — **allowance** anticipo di trasferta; **in** — in anticipo; anticipatamente; **–ment** *n* promozione; anticipo; **make –s** fare approcci, tentar di amicarsi
advantage *n* vantaggio; **take** — **of** approfittarsi di; **–ous** *a* vantaggioso, conveniente
advent *n* avvenimento
Advent *n* Avvento
adventure *n* avventura; **–some** *a* ardito, corraggioso; **–r** *n* avventuriero; — *vt* avventurare; — *vi* avventurarsi
adventurous *a* avventuroso, corraggioso
adverb *n* avverbio; **–ial** *a* avverbiale
adversary *n* avversario
adverse *a* avverso, contrario
adversity *n* avversità
advertise *vt&i* annunziare; inserire un annunzio; *(publicize)* fare pubblicità; **–ment** *n* pubblicitario
advertiser *n* inserzionista *m*
advertising *n* pubblicità
advice *n* consiglio
advisability *n* prudenza, sagacità
advisable *a* consigliabile; *(suitable)* conveniente; *(wise)* prudente
advise *vt* consigliare; — **with** consultare
advisor *n* consigliere *m*
advisory *a* consultivo
advocate *n* *(law)* avvocato; *(of cause)* sostenitore *m*, difensore *m*; *(promoter)* propugnatore *m;* — *vt* avvocare, difendere
aerate *vt* aerare, arieggiare
aerial *a* aereo; — *n* *(rad&TV)* antenna; **–ist** *n* ginnasta *m*, funambulo
aerodynamics *npl* aerodinamica

aeroembolism *n* aeroembolismo
aeromedicine *n* aeromedicina
aeronautics *n* aeronautica
aerosol *n* particola dell'aria; — **bomb** spruzzatore
aerospace *a* aerospazio
aerostat *n* aerostato; **–ic** *a* aerostatico
aerothermodynamics *npl* aerotermodinamica
aesthetic *a* estetico; **–s** *n* estetica
afar *adv* lontano; **from** — da lontano
affability *n* affabilità
affable *a* affabile
affair *n* affare *m*; *(love)* relazione amorosa; *(party)* festa
affect *vt* affettare; *(emotions)* commuovere; **–ed** *a* *(emotions)* commoso; *(manners)* affettato; **–edly** *adv* affettosamente; **–ing** *a* influente
affection *n* affezione; **–ate** *a* affettuoso; **–ately** *adv* affezionatamente
affidavit *n* affidavit *m*; dichiarazione giurata, certificato legale
affiliate *vt* affiliare, associarsi
affiliation *n* affiliazione, associazione
affirm *vt* affermare; **–ation** *n* affermazione, ratifica
affirmative *n* affermativa; — *a* affermativo
affix *vt* affiggere
afflict *vt* affliggere
affliction *n* afflizione
affluence *n* affluenza
affluent *a* affluente
afflux *n* afflusso
afford *vt* fornire
affray *n* rissa
affront *n* affronto; — *vt* affrontare
afield *adv* lontano; in campo
afire *a* in fiamme
afloat *a* a galla, galleggiante
afoot *a&adv* a piedi, camminando
aforesaid *a* sopraddetto
afoul *a&adv* in collisione
afraid *a* pauroso; **be** — aver paura, temere
African *a&n* africano
aft *adv* *(naut)* a poppa; posteriore
after *prep&adv* dopo; **day** — **tomorrow** dopodomani; — *conj* dopo che; **–ward** *adv* dopo, più tardi
afterburner *n* *(avi)* tubo di scappamento di aviogetto
aftereffect *n* conseguenza, risultato
aftermath *n* postumo; conseguenza
afternoon *n* pomeriggio
afterthought *n* cambiamento di idea
again *adv* ancora, di nuovo, nuovamente, un'altra volta; — **and** — ripetutamente
against *prep* contro

agape *a&adv* spalancato; con la bocca aperta

age *n* età, era; **–less** *a* sempre giovane; **of** — maggiorenne; — *vt&i* invecchiare; **–d** *a* vecchio, invecchiato

agency *n* agenzia; **government** — ente governativo

agent *n* agente, rappresentante *m&f;* sostanza

agglomerate *vt* agglomerare

agglomeration *n* agglomerazione

agglutinin *n* anticorpo agglutinante

aggrandize *vt* ingrandire; **–ment** *n* ingrandimento

aggravate *vt* aggravare, irritare

aggravation *n* aggravazione, provocazione

aggregate *a* totale; — *n* aggregato, totale; — *vt* aggregare

aggregation *n* aggregato, riunione

aggression *n* aggressione

aggressive *a* aggressivo, invadente

aggressor *n* aggressore *m*

aghast *a* terrorizzato

agile *a* agile

agility *n* agilità

agitate *vt* agitare

agitation *n* agitazione

agitator *n* agitatore *m*

aglow *a* infuocato, ardente

agnostic *n&a* agnostico

ago *adv* passato, fa; **long** — molto tempo fa

agog *a* eccitato, agitato; — *adv* agitatamente; **be all** — essere emozionato

agonize *vi* agonizzare

agonizing *a* agonizzante

agony *n* agonia

agrarian *a* agrario

agree *vi* acconsentire; andare d'accordo, essere d'accordo, mettersi d'accordo; **–able** *a* piacevole

agreement *n* accordo, patto; *(gram)* concordanza; — **with** accordo con; **general** — unanimità; **reach an** — pervenire ad un accordo

agricultural *a* agricolo

agriculture *n* agricoltura

agronomy *n* agronomia

aground *a&adv* incagliato, arenato; **run** — arenare

ahead *adv* avanti, d'avanti; **get** — oltrepassare; **go** — avanzare, andare avanti; — **of time** in anticipo

aid *vt* aiutare; — *n* aiuto, assistenza; **first** — pronto soccorso

aide *n* aiutante *m*

ail *vt* addolorare; — *vi* soffrire; **What —s you?** Che cosa ti fa soffrire?; **–ment** *n* indisposizione; **–ing** *a* sofferente

aileron *n* alerone *m*

aim *vt* aspirare; *(gun)* mirare; — *n* mira; *(purpose)* scopo; **–less** *a* senza scopo

air *n* atmosfera, aria; *(manner)* aspetto, maniera; — **brush** aerografo; — **chamber** camera d'aria; — **gun** fucile ad aria compressa; — **lift** ponte aereo; — **mail** posta aerea; — **pocket** *(avi)* vuoto d'aria; — **pump** pompa pneumatica; — **shaft** *(mine)* pozzo d'aerazione; **up in the** — in aria

air *n* *(avi)* aria; — **base** base aerea; **by** — per via aerea; — **freight** trasporto aereo; — **line** aviolinea; — **terminal** aerostazione; **–way** rotta aerea

air– *(in comp)* **—borne** *a* aerotrasportato; — **condition** *vt* applicare l'aria condizionata; **—mail** *a* per via aerea

air *vt* *(opinion)* esprimere; *(ventilation)* aerare, ventilare

airily *a* leggermente, delicatamente

airless *a* senz'aria

airing *n* passeggiata; *(things)* esposizione all'aria

airplane *n* aeroplano; — **carrier** nave portaerei

airport *n* aeroporto

airtight *a* ermetico

airy *a* arioso

aisle *n* corridoio; *(church)* navata

ajar *a* socchiuso

akin *a* imparentato

alacrity *n* alacrità

a la mode alla moda, di moda

alarm *n* allarme *m*; *(fright)* spavento; — **clock** sveglia; — **signal** segnale d'allarme; — *vt* allarmare

alarming *a* allarmante

alas *interj* ahimè

albeit *adv* benchè

album *n* album *m*

albumen *n* albume *m*, albumina

alcohol *n* alcool *m*, spirito

alcoholic *n* alcolizzato; — *a* alcoolico

alcove *n* alcova, nicchia

alderman *n* consigliere municipale

ale *n* birra forte

alert *n* allarme *m*; — *a* sveglio, svelto, vigilante

alertness *n* vigilanza

algae *npl* alghe *fpl*

algebra *n* algebra

alias *adv* alias, altrimenti detto

alibi *n* alibi *m*; *(excuse)* scusa

alien *a&n* straniero, forestiero

alienate *vt* alienare

alight *vi (get off)* scendere, uscire

align *vt* allineare

alignment *n* allineamento

alike *a* simile

alimentary *a* alimentare
alimony *n* alimenti *mpl*
alive *a* vivo, vivente
alkali *n* alcali *m*
alkaline *a* alcalino
all *a&adv* tutto; — **around** tutt'intorno; — **at once** improvvisamente; *(immediately)* subito; — **right** bene, molto bene; — **the better** tanto meglio; **be** — **in** *(coll)* essere esausto; **by** — **means** in assoluto; **not at** — nient'affatto; **with** — **my heart** di tutto cuore
all— *(in comp)* —**out** *a (coll)* massimo; totale; —**over** *a* dalla testa ai piedi *(fig)*; *(coll)* completo; —**round** *a* perfetto
allay *vt* calmare, mitigare
allegation *n* allegazione
allege *vt* dichiarare, pretendere, allegare; —**d** *a* presunto
allegiance *n* lealtà, fedeltà
allegorical *a* allegorico
allegory *n* allegoria
allegro *a* allegro
allergic *a* allergico
allergy *n* allergia
alleviate *vt* alleviare, lenire
alley *n* vicolo; **blind** — vicolo cieco
alliance *n* alleanza
allied *a* alleato
alligator *n* alligatore *m*
alliteration *n* allitterazione
allocate *vt* assegnare, ripartire
allocation *n* collocamento, distribuzione
allot *vt* ripartire; *(assign)* assegnare; *(award)* accordare; —**ment** *n* divisione, porzione
allow *vt* permettere, ammettere, lasciare; — **for** prevedere; —**able** *a* permissibile; —**ance** *n* assegno
alloy *n* lega; — *vt* fondere
allspice *n* pepe di Giamaica
allude *vt* alludere
allure *vt* lusingare, sedurre
allurement *n* simpatia, attrazione
alluring *a* seducente
allusion *n* allusione
alluvial *a* alluviale, alluvionale
ally *n* alleato; — *vt* alleare, collegare
almanac *n* almanacco
almighty *a* onnipotente
Almighty (The) *n* Dio , l'Onnipotente
almond *n* mandorla; — **tree** mandorlo
almost *adv* quasi
alms *npl* limosina, elemosina
aloft *adv* in alto
alone *a* solo; — *adv* solamente, solo, soltanto; **let** — lasciare in pace, lasciare tranquillo
along *adv* avanti; — *prep* per, lungo; —

with assieme a; **go** — **with** andare con; **get** — **with** *(sl, agree)* andare d'accordo con
alongside *adv* lungo il bordo
aloof *adv* in disparte; — *a* riservato
aloud *adv* ad alta voce
alphabet *n* alfabeto; —**ical** *a* alfabetico; —**ize** *vt* disporre in ordine alfabetico
Alps *npl* Alpi *fpl*
already *adv* già
also *adv* anche, pure
altar *n* altare *m;* **high** — altare maggiore
alter *vt* modificare, cambiare; —**ation** *n* modificazione
altercation *n* alterco
alternate *vt* alternare; — *n* supplente *m&f*, sostituto
alternating *a* alternante; — **current** corrente alternata
alternative *n* alternativa
although *conj* benchè, quantunque, sebbene
altimeter *n* altimetro
altitude *n* altitudine *f*, altezza
alto *n* contralto; — *a (mus)* alto
altogether *adv* tutto, completamente; nell'insieme
altruism *n* altruismo
alum *n* allume *m*
aluminum *n* alluminio
always *adv* sempre
A.M., ante meridiem antimeridiano, del mattino
amalgamate *vi* amalgamare, fondere; — *vi* amalgamarsi, fondersi
amass *vt* ammassare
amateur *n&a* dilettante *m&f;* —**ish** *a* dilettante, dilettantesco, da dilettante
amaze *vt* stupire, meravigliare; —**ment** *n* stupore *m*, meraviglia
amazing *a* meraviglioso, stupefacente
amazon *n* amazzone *f*
Amazon River Rio delle Amazzoni
ambassador *n* ambasciatore *m;* — **at large** Ministro senza portafoglio
amber *n* ambra
ambidextrous *a* ambidestro; versatile *(fig)*
ambiguity *n* ambiguità
ambiguous *a* ambiguo
ambition *n* ambizione
ambitious *a* ambizioso
amble *vi* incedere tranquillamente; *(horse)* ambiare; — *n* ambio; andatura tranquilla
ambulance *n* ambulanza
ambulatory *n&a* ambulatorio, ambulante
ambuscade *n* imboscata

ambush *n* imboscata; — *vt* imboscare
ameliorate *vt* migliorare
amen *interj* così sia; amen
amenable *a* sottomesso, arrendevole
amelioration *n* miglioramento
amend *vt* emendare, riformare; **–ed** *a* in compenso; **–ment** *n* emendamento; **–s** *npl* ammenda; **make –s** dar in compenso
amenity *n* amenità
American *n&a* americano; americana
amiable *a* affabile
amiableness *n* amabilità, cordialità
amicable *a* amichevole
amid *prep* fra, nel mezzo di
amiss *adv* male; di traverso, in senso contrario; **take** — prendere in mala parte
amity *n* amicizia, intesa
ammeter *n* amperometro
ammonia *n* ammoniaca
ammunition *n* munizioni *fpl*
amnesia *n* amnesia
amnesty *n* amnistia
amoeba *n* ameba
among *prep* fra, in mezzo di; in mezzo a
amoral *a* amorale
amorous *a* amoroso
amorphous *a* amorfo
amortization *n* amortizzamento
amortize *vt* ammortizzare
amount *n* quantità, somma; *(large)* somma considerevole; *(small)* piccola somma; — *vi* ammontare; — **to something** arrivare a qualcosa *(fig)*
ampere *n* ampere *m*
amperage *n* amperaggio
amphibian *n* anfibio
amphitheater *n* anfiteatro
ample *a* ampio, vasto
amplification *n* ampliazione, amplificazione
amplifier *n* amplificatore *m*
amplify *vt* amplificare, ampliare, *(enlarge)* ingrandire
amplitude *n* ampiezza
amplitude modulation, (AM) *(rad)* ampia modulazione
amply *adv* ampiamente
amputate *vt* amputare
amputation *n* amputazione
amputee *n* amputato, invalido
amulet *n* amuleto
amuse *vt* divertire
amusement *n* divertimento; — **park** parco di divertimenti
amusing *a* divertente; *(funny)* buffo
an *art* un, uno, una, un'
anachronism *n* anacronismo
anagram *n* anagramma *m*
analgesic *n* analgesico; — *a* analgesico

analogous *a* analogo
analogy *n* analogia
analysis *n* analisi *f*
analytical *a* analitico
analyze *vt* analizzare
anarchy *n* anarchia
anathema *n* anatema *m*
anatomical *a* anatomico
anatomy *n* anatomia
ancestor *n* antenato; **–s** *npl* antenati *mpl*
ancestral *a* atavico
ancestry *n* discendenza, origine *f*
anchor *n* ancora; **lie (ride) at** — stare all'ancora; **–age** *n* ancoraggio; — *vt* ancorare; — *vi* ancorarsi
anchorite *n* anacoreta *m*
anchovy *n* acciuga
ancient *a* antico; **very** — antichissimo
and *conj* e, ed; — **so on** e così via
andiron *n* alare *m*
anecdote *n* aneddoto
anemia *n* anemia
anemic *a* anemico
anemometer *n* anemometro
anesthesia *n* anestesia
anesthetic *n&a* anestetico
anew *adv* di nuovo, da capo
angel *n* angelo; *(sl)* finanziatore *m*;
angelic *a* angelico
anger *n* collera, rabbia, stizza
angle *n* angolo; *(corner)* canto; *(opinion)* punto di vista; — *vi* pescare
angler *n* pescatore
Anglo-Saxon *n&a* anglo-sassone *m&f*
angry *a* arrabbiato; **get** — andare in collera; *(med)* infiammato
anguish *n* angoscia
angular *a* angolare
animal *n&a* animale *m*
animate *vt* animare; — *a* animato; **–d** *a* animato, vivace
animation *n* animazione
animosity *n* animosità
anise *n* anice *m*
ankle *n* caviglia
anklets *npl* calzini *mpl*
annals *npl* annali *mpl*
annex *vt* annettere; — *n* *(building)* annesso; *(com)* succursale; **–ation** *n* annessione
annihilate *vt* annichilire, annichilare, annientare
annihilation *n* annientamento, annichilazione
anniversary *n&a* anniversario
annotate *vt* annotare
annotation *n* annotazione
announce *vt* annunziare, far noto, proclamare; **–ment** *n* annunzio, proclama *m*,

partecipazione
announcer *n (rad)* annunciatore *m*
annoy *vt* annoiare, seccare, incomodare;
–**ance** *n* noia, molestia, disturbo;
–**ing** *a* noioso, fastidioso, seccante
annual *a* annuo; — *n* annuale *m*
annuity *n* annualità, pensione annuale;
life — rendita vitalizia
annul *vt* annullare
annulment *n* annullamento
annunciation *n* annunciazione
anode *n* anodo
anoint *vt* ungere, consacrare
anomaly *n* anomalia
anon *adv* subito
anonym *n* anonimo
anonymous *a* anonimo, sconosciuto
another *a* un altro, un'altra
answer *n* risposta; –**able** *a* corrispondente; — *vi* rispondere; — **back** *(coll)*
ribattere *(fig)*; — **for** essere responsabile; — **the description** corrispondere alla descrizione; — **the purpose**
servire allo scopo
ant *n* formica
antacid *a&n* antiacido
antagonism *n* antagonismo
antagonist *n* antagonista *m*; –**ic** *a* anta-
gonistico
antagonize *vt* affrontare, mettersi contro
antarctic *a&n* antartico
ante *n* piatto *(coll)*
antecedent *a&n* antecedente, anteriore *m*
antedate *vt* antidatare, prevenire
antelope *n* antilope *m*
antenna *n* antenna
anterior *a* anteriore
anteroom *n* anticamera
anthem *n* inno
anthology *n* antologia
anthracite *n* antracite *f*
anthropoid *a&n* antropoide *m*
anthropology *n* antropologia
antiaircraft *n&a* antiaereo
antibiotic *n&a* antibiotico
antibody *n* anticorpo
antics *npl* buffoni *mpl*; farse *fpl*
anticipate *vt* prevedere, precedere,
prevenire
anticipation *n* anticipo, anticipazio-
ne; *(qualm)* presentimento
antidote *n* antidoto
antifreeze *n* anticongelante *m*
antihistamine *n* antistamina
antimycin *n* antimicina
antipathy *n* antipatia
antipodes *npl* antipodi *mpl*
antiquated *a* antiquato
antique *a* antico; — *n* oggetto antico

antiquity *n* antichità
antiseptic *a&n* antisettico
antisocial *a* antisociale
antithesis *n* antitesi *f*
antitoxin *n* antitossina
antitrust *a* contro i monopoli
antler *n* corno del cervo
antonym *n* antinomia
anvil *n* incudine *f*
anxiety *n* ansia; *(eagerness)* premura
anxious *a* desideroso; *(worry)* preoccupato; impaziente
any *a&pron* alcuno; — **at all** qualsiasi;
qualunque; — **mail** della posta; — **money** del danaro; — **more** di più; — **old
thing** *(sl)* qualunque cosa; **not** —
nessuno; **not on** — **account** per niente
al mondo
anybody, anyone *pron* uno; — **at all**
chiunque, chichessia; — **who** chi;
not — nessuno
anyhow *adv* in qualsiasi modo, in ogni
caso, comunque
anyone *pron* chi, chiunque
anything *pron* qualsiasi cosa
anyway *adv* insomma, in ogni caso, comunque
anywhere *adv* dovunque, in qualsiasi
parte
apart *adv* separatamente, in disparte
apartment *n* appartamento; — **house**
casa d'appartamenti
apathetic *a* apatico
apathy *n* apatia
ape *n* scimmia; — *vt* imitare
aperture *n* apertura
apex *n* apice *m*, cima, apogeo
aphorism *a* aforisma *m*
apiary *n* apiario, luogo delle api
apiece *adv* ciascuno, ognuno, l'uno
apocryphal *a* apocrifo
apogee *n* apogeo
apologetic *a* apologetico
apologize *vi* scusarsi, chiedere perdono;
fare le scuse
apology *n* scusa, apologia
apoplexy *n* apoplessia
apostle *n* apostolo
apostolic *a* apostolico
apostrophe *n* apostrofo
appall *vi* impallidire; –**ing** *a* spaventevole
apparatus *n* apparecchio
apparel *n* vestiario, indumenti *mpl*, abbigliamento
apparent *a* apparente, chiaro; –**ly** *adv*
apparentemente
apparition *n* apparizione
appeal *vi* fare appello, ricorrere in appello; *(attract)* attrarre, fare sim-

patia; — *vt* sottomettere a; — *n* attrazione, atrattiva; *(law)* appello; –ing *a* supplichevole

appear *vi* apparire; *(seem)* parere, sembrare; *(show oneself)* esibirsi; presentarsi; –ance *n* apparenza; apparizione; *(aspect)* aspetto, aria

appease *vt* calmare, ammansire; –ment *n* pacificazione

append *vt* appendere; –age *n* appendice *f*

appendectomy *n* appenditomia

appendicitis *n* appendicite *f*

appendix *n* appendice *f*; *(book)* aggiunta

appertain *vi* appartenere

appetite *n* appetito

appetizer *n* *(drink)* aperitivo; *(food)* antipasto

appetizing *a* aperitivo, stimolante d'appetito

applaud *vt* applaudire; — *vi* felicitarsi

applause *n* applauso

apple *n* mela, pomo; — **of one's eye** pupilla dell'occhio; — **orchard** pometo; — **polisher** *(sl)* cortigiano *(fig)*; leccapiedi *m* *(sl)*; — **tree** melo

apple-pie order *(coll)* ordine perfetto

applesauce *n* salsa di mela; *(sl)* storie *fpl* *(fig)*; un sacco di sciocchezze *(fig)*

appliance *n* apparecchio, attrezzo; *(elec)* elettrodomestico

applicable *a* applicabile

applicant *n* candidato

application *n* domanda, applicazione

applied *a* applicato

apply *vt* applicare; — *vi* applicarsi; — **for** sollecitare, chiedere; — **to** rivolgersi a

appoint *vt* nominare; –ment *n* appuntamento; nomina

apportion *vt* distribuire; –ment *n* distribuzione

apposition *n* apposizione

appraisal *n* stima, valutazione

appraise *vt* valutare

appreciable *a* apprezzabile

appreciate *vt* apprezzare, stimare, gradire; *(realize)* rendersi conto di; — *vi* aumentare di prezzo

appreciation *n* apprezzamento

appreciative *a* apprezzativo

apprehend *vt* comprendere; *(dread)* temere; — *vi* comprendere, supporre

apprehension *n* apprensione, timore *m*

apprehensive *a* apprensivo, timoroso

apprentice *n* apprendista *m&f*

approach *vt* accostarsi, avvicinarsi; — *vi* avvicinarsi, appressarsi; — *n* accesso, approccio

approbation *n* approvazione

appropriate *a* acconcio, adatto, appro-

priato; — *vt* stanziare; *(sl)* appropriarsi di

appropriation *n* appropriazione; *(money)* stanziamento

approval *n* approvazione, conferma

approve *vt* approvare, confermare

approving *a* favorevole

approximate *a* approssimativo; –ly *adv* approssimativamente, presso a poco, verso; — *vt* approssimare

approximation *n* approssimazione

apricot *n* albicocca; — **tree** albicocco

April *n* aprile *m;* — **Fools' Day** Primo d'aprile

apron *n* grembiule *m*

apropos *adv* a proposito

apt *a* *(proper)* adatto, atto; *(inclined)* disposto, inclinato; –ness *n* attitudine *f*

aptitude *n* abilità, attitudine *f*, disposizione

aqualung *n* serbatoio dell'aria

aquaplane *n* acquaplano

aquarium *n* acquario

aquatic *a* acquatico

aqueduct *n* acquedotto

aquiline *a* aquilino

Arabia Arabia

Arab, Arabian *n&a* arabo

arable *a* arabile

arbiter *n* arbitro

arbitrary *a* arbitrario

arbitrate *vt* arbitrare — *vi* arbitrarsi, fare da arbitro

arbitrator *n* arbitro

arbor *n* pergola; –eal *a* arboreo; –etum *n* arboreto

arc *n* arco; — **lamp** lampada ad arco voltaico; — **light** luce d'arco voltaico; — **welding** arco voltaico

arcade *n* arcata

arch *n* arco, volta; –way *n* arcale *m*; passaggio a volta; — *a* principale; *(crafty)* furbo; –ed *a* arcato; –ly *adv* accortamente; — *vt* arcuare; — *vi* formare arco

archaic *a* arcaico

archbishop *n* arcivescovo

archdiocese *n* arcidiocesi *f*

archeology *n* archeologia

archer *n* arciere *m*; –y *n* tiro all'arco

architect *n* architetto; –ural *a* architettonico; –ure *n* architettura

archives *npl* archivio

arctic *n&a* artico

ardent *a* ardente

ardor *n* ardore *m*

arduous *a* arduo

area *n* zona, regione *f*; *(surface)* superficie *f*

arena *n* anfiteatro, arena, stadio

argot *n* gergo
argue *vt* discutere, disputare, litigare; — *vi* argomentare, fare discussione
argument *n* discussione, diverbio
arid *a* arido; sterile
arise *vi* alzarzi, levarsi
aristrocracy *n* aristocrazia
aristrocrat *n* aristrocratico; **-ic** *a* aristocratico
arithmetic *n* aritmetica
arm *n* braccio; *(mil)* arma; — **in** — a braccetto; **at** **-s length** a distanza; **-chair** *n* poltrona; **-ful** *n* bracciata; **-hole** *n* giro; **-pit** *n* ascella; — *vt* armare; — *vi* armarsi
armament *n* armamento
armistice *n* armistizio
armor *n* corazza, blinda; **-y** *n* armeria
armored *a* corazzato, blindato; — **car** autoblinda
army *n* esercito
aroma *n* profumo, fragranza; **-tic** *a* aromatico
around *prep* attorno; — *adv* intorno; all'intorno; *(turning)* in giro
arouse *vt (wake)* svegliare; *(foment)* suscitare; — *vi* svegliarsi
arraign *vt* tradurre; **-ment** *n* traduzione
arrange *vt* ordinare, disporre; **-ment** *n (order)* disposizione, ordine *m; (agreement)* accordo
arrant *a* insigne
array *n* schiera; *(dress)* abbigliamento; — *vt* parare, disporre
arrears *n* arretrati; **be in** — essere in arretrati
arrest *n* arresto; — *vt* arrestare; fermare; — **attention** chiamare l'attenzione
arresting *a* che arresta
arrival *n* arrivo
arrive *vi* arrivare, giungere
arrogance *n* arroganza
arrogant *a* arrogante, prepotente
arrow *n* freccia; **-head** *n* punta di freccia
arsenal *n* arsenale *m*
arsenic *n* arsenico
arson *n* incendio doloso
art *n* arte *f;* **-less** *a* semplice, senz'arte; **the fine -s** le belle arti
artery *n* arteria
artful *a* artificiale; **-ness** *n* artificialità; **-ly** *adv* artificialmente
arthritis *n* artrite *f*
artichoke *n* carciofo
article *n* articolo, oggetto
articulate *vt* articolare, pronunziare; — *vi* pronunziarsi
articulation *n* articolazione
artifact *n* artefatto
artifice *n* artefice *m*

artificial *a* artificiale; — **insemination** fecondazione artificiale
artillery *n* artiglieria
artisan *n* artigiano
artist *n* artista *m&f;* **-ic** *a* artistico
as *conj&adv* come; — **far** — fino a; — **for** quanto a; — **if** come se; — **it were** generalmente parlando *(coll);* — **large** — grande come; — **much** — tanto quanto; — **soon** — **possible** il più presto possibile; — **to** quanto a; — **well** *(also)* anche, pure; **just** — così; **the same** — come, lo stesso che
asbestos *n* amianto
ascend *vi* montare, salire; — *vt* ascendere, salire; **-ancy** *n* ascendente *m*
ascendant *n* ascendente *m;* — *a* ascendente
ascension *n* ascesa, ascensione
Ascension *n* Ascensione
ascent *n* ascesa, salita, erta
ascertain *vt* accertarsi, constatare, appurare
ascetic *n* asceta *m;* — *a* ascetico
ascribe *vt* ascrivere, attribuire
ash *n* cenere *f; (bot)* frassino; **-can** *n* pattumiera; **-tray** *n* portacenere *m;* **A- Wednesday** Giorno delle Ceneri
ashamed *a* vergognoso; **be** — vergognarsi
ashen *a* di frassino
ashore *adv* a terra; **go** — sbarcare, scendere a terra
Asian, Asiatic *n&a* asiatico
aside *adv* a parte; — **from** eccetto, a parte
asinine *a* asinino
ask *vt* domandare, chiedere; *(invite)* invitare; — *vi* informarsi di; — **about** domandare circa
askance *adv.* lateralmente, di traverso
askew *adv* obliquamente; — *a* obliquo
asleep *a* addormentato; **be** — dormire; **fall** — addormentarsi
asparagus *n* asparago
aspect *n* aspetto
asperity *n* asprezza, rudezza
aspersion *n* aspersione, denigrazione
asphalt *n* asfalto; — *vt* asfaltare
asphyxiate *vt* asfissiare; — *vi* asfissiarsi
asphyxiation *n* asfissia
aspirant *n* aspirante *m;* — *a* aspirante
aspiration *n* aspirazione
aspire *vi* aspirare, bramare
aspirin *n* aspirina
ass *n* asino
assail *vt* assalire, attaccare; **-ant** *n* assalitore *m,* assalitrice *f*
assassin *n* assassino; **-ate** *vt* assassinare, ammazzare
assassination *n* assassinio
assault *n* assalto; — *vt* assalire, attac-

care
assay vt saggiare; — n assaggio, saggio
assemblage n raccolta; assemblea
assemble vt riunire; — vi riunirsi, adunarsi
assembly n (people) assemblea, riunione; (mech) montaggio; — **line** linea di montaggio; — **line production** produzione in serie
assent vi assentire; — n consenso
assert vt asserire, affermare
assertion n asserzione
assess vt tassare; –ment n tassazione, imposta; –or n assessore m; agente delle tasse
asset n assetto; –s npl (com) attività
assiduous a assiduo; –ly adv assiduamente
assign vt assegnare, attribuire; –ment n (school) compito; (task) incarico; missione
assimilate vt assimilare; — vi assimilarsi
assimilation n assimilazione
assist vt aiutare, assistere; — vi aiutare, contribuire a; –ance n assistenza, aiuto, soccorso, sussidio; –ant n assistente m, aiutante m; aggiunto
associate vt associare, unire; — vi associarsi con; — **with** frequentare; –d a associato, relazionato
associate n compagno di lavoro, collega; — a associato
association n associazione, società
assort vt assortire; — vi essere d'accordo; –ed a assortito; –ment n scelta; assortimento
assuage vt calmare; — vi calmarsi
assume vt assumere, supporre, usurpare; — vi arrogarsi; –d a assunto; preso; pervenuto a
assuming a presuntuoso, altero; — **that** supponendo che
assumption n supposizione; arroganza
Assumption n Assunzione
assurance n certezza, sicurezza, conferma
assure vt assicurare, rassicurare; — vi assicurarsi di
assured a assicurato, sicuro; –ly adv certamente, sicuramente
aster n astero
asterisk n asterisco
astern adv a poppa
asthma n asma; –tic a asmatico
astigmatism n astigmatismo
astir a&adv in movimento
astonish vt stupire, meravigliare; –ing a stupefacente, stupendo, straordinario; –ment n stupore m, maraviglia
astound vt sbalordire, stupefare

astray a sviato; (lost) smarrito; — adv fuori strada; go — fuorviarsi, perdersi; **lead** — sviare, traviare, fuorviare
astride a a cavalcioni
astringent a&n astringente m
astrobiology n (aesp) astrobiologia
astronaut n astronauta m
astronavigation n astronavigazione
astronomy n astronomia
astrophysics n astrofisica
astute a astuto, furbo
asunder adv separatamente; **put** — collocare separatamente; **tear** – stracciare; —a separato
asylum n asilo; **insane** — manicomio
at prep a, in, da; — **all events** in ogni modo; — **large** in libertà; — **last** finalmente; — **once** subito
atheism n ateismo
atheist n ateo; –ic a ateistico
Athens Atene f
athlete n atleta m&f; —'s **foot** (med) piede d'atleta
athletic a atletico; — **field** campo sportivo; –s npl atletica
Atlantic n&a atlantico
atlas n atlante m
atmosphere n atmosfera; (surroundings) ambiente m
atmospheric a atmosferico
atom n atomo; — **bomb** bomba atomica
atomic a atomico; — **blast** esplosione atomica; — **energy** energia atomica; — **pile** pila atomica, reattore m
atomize vt atomizzare, polverizzare; –r n polverizzatore m
atone vt riparare, fare ammenda, espiare; — vi riparare a; –ment n espiazione
atrocious a atroce
atrocity n atrocità
atrophy n atrofia; — vt atrofizzare; — vi atrofizzarsi
attach vt attaccare, unire; (importance) attribuire; (law) sequestrare, requisire; –ment n attaccamento; (fondness) affetto; (law) sequestro
attack vt attaccare; — n attacco, aggressione, assalto
attain vt raggiungere; –able a attaccabile; –ment n attaccamento
attempt vt tentare; –ed a tentato; — n tentativo; (crime) attentato; (effort) sforzo
attend vt (to) attendere; (be present) assistere; (escort) scortare; — vi essere presente, presenziare; — **to** incaricarsi di; –ance n presenza; (care) servizio; (audience) pubblico; frequenza; –ant n attendente, inserviente m&f
attention n attenzione; at — (mil) sul-

l'attenti; **attract** — attirare l'attenzione; **call** — richiamare l'attenzione; **give** — **to** prestare attenzione a; **pay** — stare attento, fare attenzione; **to the** — **of** attenzione personale

attentive *a* attento; **–ly** *adv* attentamente

attenuate *vt* attenuare, far dimagrire

attest *vt* attestare, legalizzare; — *vi (law)* testimoniare

attic *n* soffitta; — *a* attico, dell'Attica

attire *n* vestito; — *vt* vestire, abbigliare

attitude *n* attitudine *f*, posizione; *(behavior)* contegno, atteggiamento

attorney *n* avvocato, procuratore *m*

attract *vt* attrarre, attirare; — *vi* esercitare attrazione; **–ive** *a* attraente, bello, gradevole, simpatico

attraction *n* attrazione, simpatia, attrattiva

attribute *vt* attribuire

attribute *n* attributo, qualità; *(trait)* tratto

attributive *a* attributivo

attrition *n* attrito

attune *vt* accordare, mettere a tono

auburn *a* castagno rossiccio

auction *n* asta pubblica; **–eer** *n* imbonitore *m*

audacious *a* audace, ardito

audacity *n* audacia

audible *a* udibile, percettibile

audience *n* pubblico; *(interview)* udienza

audiophile *n* audiofilo, audio-amatore *m*

audio-visual *a* audio-visuale

audit *n* controllo; **–or** *n (com)* revisore dei conti; — *vt* controllare, verificare; **–ing** *n* verifica

audition *n* audizione

auditorium *n* auditorio, sala

auditory *a* uditivo

auger *n* succhiello, trivella

augment *vt&i* aumentare

augur *vt&i* augurare

August *n* agosto

august *a* augusto

aunt *n* zia

aura *n* aura, esalazione

aureomycin *n* aureomicina

auricle *n* auricola

aurora *n* aurora

auspices *npl* auspici *mpl*; **under the** — **of** sotto l'egida di

auspicious *a* auspice, propizio; **–ly** *adv* propiziamente

austere *a* austero

austerity *n* austerità

Australia Australia

Australian *n&a* australiano

Austrian *n&a* austriaco

authentic *a* autentico; **–ity** *n* autenticità

author *a* autore *m*

authoritative *a* autoritario

authority *n* autenticità

authorization *n* autorizzazione

authorize *vt* autorizzare

autobiography *n* autobiografia

autocade *n* treno (*or* fila) di automezzi

autocracy *n* autocrazia

autocrat *n* autocrate *m*; **–ic** *a* autocratico

autogiro *n* autogiro

autograph *n* autografo; — *vt* autografare

automatic *a* automatico; — *n (mech)* distributore automatico

automation *n* automazione

automaton *n* automa *m*

automobile, auto *n* automobile *f*; — **show** autosalone *m*

automotive *a* automobilistico

autonomous *a* autonomo

autonomy *n* autonomia

autopilot *n* autopilota *m*, pilota automatico

autopsy *n* autopsia

autumn *n* autunno; **–al** *a* autunnale

auxiliary *a* ausiliario; — *n* ausiliare *m*

avail *vt&i* valere, servire, giovare; — **oneself of** servirsi di; — *n* vantaggio, effetto; **of no** — vano, inutile; **–able** *a* disponibile, trovabile; **–ability** *n* disponibilità

avalanche *n* valanga

avarice *n* avarizia

avaricious *a* avaro; **–ly** *adv* avidamente

avenge *vt* vendicare; vendicarsi di

avenger *n* vendicatore *m*

avenue *n* corso, viale *m*

aver *vt* affermare, certificare

average *n* media; — *a* medio; — *vt* fare una media; — *vi* mostrare la media

averse *a* avverso, contrario

aversion *n* antipatia, avversione; **pet** — antipatia cordiale

avert *vt* allontanare, distogliere

aviary *n* uccelliera

aviation *n* aviazione

aviator *n* aviatore *m*, aviatrice *f*

avid *a* avido; **–ity** *n* avidità

avocation *n* passatempo

avoid *vt* evitare, schivare, scansare, fuggire; **–able** *a* evitabile; **–ance** *n* l'evitare; *(law)* annullamento

avow *vt* confessare; **–al** *n* confessione

await *vt* attendere, aspettare; — *vi* aspettarsi

awake *vt* svegliare; — *vi* svegliarsi;

— *a* desto, sveglio
awaken *vt* destare
awakening *n* risveglio; — *a* eccitante
award *n* premio; — *vt* aggiudicare, conferire
aware *a* informato, consapevole; **become** — accorgersi
away *a* assente; — *adv* via; **be** — distare; **go** — andarsene; **keep** — **(from)** tener lontano
awe *n* soggezione
awe-inspiring *a* imponente
awe-struck *a* atterrito, impaurito
awful *a* terribile, spaventoso

awhile *adv* un poco, un momento
awkward *a* goffo, maldestro; **–ly** *adv* goffamente, maldestramente
awl *n* lesina
awning *n* tenda
awry *a&adv* di traverso, di sghembo
ax (axe) *n* scure *f*
axiom *n* assioma *m*
axis *n* asse *m*
axle *n* assale *m*
azalea *n* azalea
azon bomb *n* proiettile radiocomandato, bomba radiocomandata
azure *a* azzurro, blu

B

B.A., Bachelor of Arts diplomato in lettere
babble *n* balbettio; — *vt* balbettare; — *vi* dire e ridire, ripetersi
babbling *a* balbettante
babel *n* confusione, parapiglia *m*
baboon *n* babbuino
baby *n* bambino, bambina; *(in affection)* bimbo, bimba; — *a* bambinesco; — **carriage** carrozzino; — **grand piano** pianoforte a mezzacoda
baby *vt* vezzeggiare
baby– *(in comp)* **–sit** *vi* fare da bambinaia; **–sitter** *n* bambinaia
babyhood *n* prima fanciullezza, infanzia
babyish *a* infantile
bachelor *n* scapolo
back *n* dorso; *(chair)* schienale *m; (human)* schiena; *(shoulders)* spalle *fpl*; **turn one's** — **on** dare la schiena; — *a* di dietro; — **seat** posto di dietro; — **stairs** scala di servizio; — *adv* addietro, dietro; **call** — richiamare; **come** — ritornare; — *vt&i* appoggiare, indietreggiare; *(com)* finanziare; munire di indietro; *(auto)* far marcia indietro; — **down, out** ritirarsi; — **up** indietreggiare
backbite *vt&i* diffamare
backbone *n* spina dorsale; *(fig)* energia *(fig)*
backer *n* protettore *m; (sport)* secondo
backfielder *n (sport)* giocatore di retrolinea
backfire *n* contraccolpo; *(auto)* ritorno di fiamma
background *n* sfondo; *(environment)* ambiente *m; (past)* precedenti *mpl*
backing *n* appoggio, *(com)* sostegno
backlog *n* ceppo
backnumber *n (fig)* parruccone *m; (print)* numero arretrato

backstage *n* dietro le quinte
backstitch *n* punto indietro; — *vt&i* cucire a punto indietro
backstop *n (sport)* ostacolo per la palla
backward *a* tardivo; — *adv* di dietro, indietro
backwash *n* risacca
bacon *n* pancetta affumicata
bacteria *npl* batteri *mpl*
bacterial *a* batterico
bacteriology *n* batteriologia
bad *a* cattivo; *(evil)* malo; *(spoiled)* guasto; — **blood** cattivo sangue; — **humor** malumore *m;* — **look** cattivo aspetto; **–ly** *adv* male, malamente; gravemente
badge *n* distintivo, placca
badger *n* tasso; — *vt* seccare, tormentare, stuzzicare
badinage *n* scherzo
baffle *vt* lasciare perplesso, confondere
baffling *a* frustrante, sconcertante
bag *n* sacco; *(luggage)* valigia; *(paper)* sacchetto; *(purse)* borsa; — *vt* insaccare; — *vi* gonfiarsi
baggage *n* bagaglio; — **car** carro-bagagli; — **check** scontrino del bagaglio; — **master** bagagliere *m;* — **room** deposito bagagli
baggy *a* come un sacco; *(hanging)* pendente; *(swollen)* gonfio
bail *n* cauzione; **on** — sotto cauzione; — *vt* rilasciare sotto cauzione; — **out** *(avi)* lanciarsi col paracadute
bailiff *n* ufficiale giudiziario
bailiwick *n* giurisdizione
bait *vt* adescare; — *n* esca
bake *vt* cuocere al forno; — *vi* essere cotto, dissecarsi; **–d** *a* al forno; infornato

baker *n* fornaio; **—y** *n (bread)* panificio, panetteria; *(sweet goods)* pasticceria

baking *n* infornata; **— powder** lievito; **— soda** bicarbonato di soda

balance *n (com)* saldo; *(remainder)* resto; *(scales)* bilancia, bilancio; equilibrio; **— of power** equilibrio politico; **— of trade** bilancia del commercio; **— sheet** bilancio; **lose one's —** perdere l'equilibrio

balance *vt (com)* saldare; *(equalize)* pareggiare, equilibrare; **—** *vi* equilibrarsi, pareggiarsi; **— an account** chiudere un conto, accertare il saldo

balcony *n* loggia; *(theat)* galleria; *(window)* balcone *m*

bald *a* calvo; **—ness** *n* calvizie *f*

bale *n* balla; **—ful** *a* calamitoso, maligno

balk *vt (hinder)* intralciare; **—** *vi* impuntarsi, arrestarsi; **—** *n (coll)* puntiglio; *(obstacle)* ostacolo; **—y** *a* puntiglioso

ball *n* palla, pallone *m*; *(dance)* ballo; **— bearing** cuscinetto a sfere

ballpoint pen *n* penna a sfera

ballad *n* canzone popolare

ballast *n* zavorra

ballet *n* balletto; **— dancer** ballerino, ballerina

ballistic missile *n* missile balistico

ballistics *n* balistica

balloon *n* pallone *m*, palloncino; **— tire** gomma ballon

ballot *n* voto; scheda di votazione; **— box** urna; **— count** scrutinio; **—** *vt&i* votare a scrutinio segreto

ballplayer *n* giocatore di baseball

ballyhoo *n (sl)* baccano, montatura, propaganda sensazionale

balm *n* unguento; **—y** *a* imbalsamato

balsam *n* balsamo

balustrade *n* balaustrata

bamboo *n* bambù *m*; **— curtain** tendina di bambù

bamboozle *vt (coll)* turlupinare; **—** *vi* turlupinarsi

ban *n* bando; **—** *vt* interdire, proibire, vietare

banal *a* banale; **—ity** *n* banalità

banana *n* banana

band *n* banda; *(cloth)* striscia, nastro, fascia; *(group)* gruppo; *(mus)* orchestra; **—** *vt* unire, unirsi; **—** *vi* associarsi; legarsi con

bandage *n* benda, fascia; **—** *vt* fasciare, bendare

bandanna *n* fazzoletto

bandit *n* bandito

bandstand *n* piattaforma per orchestra

bane *n* flagello

bang *n* colpo; *(explosion)* detonazione;

—s *npl (hair)* frangetta; **—** *vt* colpire, sbattere; **—** *vi* rumoreggiare, saltare

bangle *n* braccialetto

banish *vt* esiliare, bandire; **—ment** *n* bando, proscrizione, esilio

banister *n* ringhiera

banjo *n* banjo *m*

bank *n (com)* banca, banco; *(river)* riva; *(savings)* cassa di risparmio; **—book** *n* libretto di banca; **—** *vt* arginare; coprire; depositare in banca; **—** *vi (embank)* fare banchi; fare il banchiere; *(avi)* virare

banker *n* banchiere *m*

banking *n* servizio bancario

bankrupt *a* fallito; **—cy** *n* bancarotta, fallimento; **—** *vt* fallire

banner *n* stendardo, bandiera; *(standard)* gonfalone *m*, vessillo

banns *npl* bandi *mpl*, pubblicazione

banquet *n* banchetto

bantamweight *n* peso bantam *(fig)*

banter *n* burla, scherno; **—** *vt* burlare, schernire; **—** *vi* burlarsi di

baptism *n* battesimo; **—al** *a* battesimale

baptize *vt* battezzare; *(eccl)* amministrare il battesimo

bar *n (barricade)* sbarra; *(candy)* tavoletta; *(inn)* bar *m*, taverna; *(law)* avvocatura; *(line)* verga; *(mus)* battuta; *(obstacle)* ostacolo; **—keeper, —maid** *n* barista *m&f*; **—** *prep* eccettuato; **—** *vt* sbarrare; *(exclude)* escludere

barb *n* punta, spina; **—ed** *a* spinato

barbarian *n&a* barbaro

barbarism *n* barbarie *f*; *(language)* barbarismo

barbarity *n* barbarie *f*, crudeltà

barbarous *a* barbaro

barbecue *n* carne arrostita; **—** *vt* arrostire

barber *n* barbiere, parrucchiere *m*; **—shop** *n* bottega di barbiere

barbiturate *n* barbiturico

bare *a* nudo; **—faced** *a* sfacciato; col viso scoperto; **—foot** *a* scalzo; **—headed** *a* a testa scoperta; **lay —** svelare; **—** *vt* scoprire; **—ly** *adv* appena, nudamente

bareness *n* nudità, nudezza

bargain *n* occasione; **—** *vt* decidere, regolare; **—** *vi* mercanteggiare

barge *n* chiatta, zattera; **—** *vt* trasportare con chiatta; **—** *vi* muoversi lentamente

baritone *n* baritono

bark *n (dog)* abbaiamento; *(tree)* scorza; **—** *vt* scorticare; **—** *vi* abbaiare, latrare

barley *n* orzo

barn n stalla; granaio; **–yard** n aia
barometer n barometro
baron n barone m; **–ess** n baronessa
baronet n baronetto
barracks npl caserma
barrage n sbarramento
barrel n barile m, botte f; — vt imbarilare
barren a sterile, arido
barrette n fermaglio per i capelli
barricade n barricata; — vt barricare
barrier n barriera
barring prep eccettuato, salvo
barrister n avvocato
barroom n bar m; taverna
bartender n barista m
barter vt barattare; — vi fare baratto; — n baratto, permuta
basal a fondamentale, basico; — **metabolism** metabolismo basale
base n base f; fondamento; — a basso; vile; **–less** a infondato, senza base; **–ness** n bassezza; — vt basare
baseball n palla a basi, baseball m
baseboard n zoccolo
basement n cantina, sottosuolo
bashful a timido; **–ness** n timidezza
basic a basilare, fondamentale
basil n basilico
basin n (hand) catinella, lavabo; (river) bacino di un fiume
basis n base f
bask vt scaldare; — vi scaldarsi
basket n paniere m, sporta, cesta; (waste) cestino; **–ball** n pallacanestro; **–ry** n mestiere del panieraio
bass n (fish) pesce persico; (mus) basso; — **horn** corno di bassetto; — **viol** violoncello
bassinet n culla
bassoon n fagotto
bastard n&a bastardo; **–ly** a bastardamente
baste vt (abuse) bastonare, frustare; (cooking) umettare; (sewing) imbastire
bastion n bastione m
bat n (animal) pipistrello; (club) mazza, bastone m; **go on a —** (sl) bighellonare; — vt battere; — **an eye** batter ciglio
batch n (bread) infornata; (lot) partita
batch n infornata; partita
bated a turbato; **with — breath** con voce turbata
bath n bagno; **–ometer** n batometro; **–robe** n accappatoio; **–room** n stanza da bagno; **–tub** n vasca da bagno
bathe vt lavare, bagnare; farsi il bagno; — vi fare il bagno
bathing n bagno; — **cap** cuffia da bagno; — **suit** costume da bagno

bathyscaphe n batiscafo
bathysphere n batisfera
baton n bacchetta; bastone di comando
battalion n battaglione m
batter n (baseball) battitore m; (cookery) pastetta; — vt battere; (wreck) guastare
battery n batteria; — **charge** carica della batteria
battle n battaglia; **–field** n campo di battaglia; — **royal** battaglia strenua; **pitched —** battaglia campale; **sham —** battaglia finta; **–ship** n nave da guerra; — vt combattere qualcuno; — vi battagliare; battersi
bauble n bagatella
Bavaria Baviera
Bavarian n&a bavarese m&f
bawl vt sgridare; — **out** (coll) dare una lavata di testa (coll); — n sgridata, lavata di testa
bay n (arch) alcova; (bot) lauro, alloro; (color) baio; (geog) baia; — a baio; — **leaf** foglia d'alloro; — **window** finestra sporgente; **hold at —** tenere in iscacco; **keep at —** tenere a bada; **stand at —** essere in iscacco; essere appressato
bay vt (arch) arginare; — vi (animal) abbaiare
baying n (animal) abbaiamento
bayonet n baionetta
bayou n canaletta
bazaar n bazar m, emporio; **charity —** pesca di beneficenza
B.C., Before Christ adv avanti Cristo
be vi essere, esistere, stare; — **ill** star male; — **in a hurry** avere fretta; — **right** aver ragione; — **that as it may** comunque; — **well** star bene
beach n spiaggia; **–comber** n vagabondo di spiaggia; **–head** n (mil) spiaggia di sbarco
beach vt tirare in secco
bead n grano, chicco; (pearl) perla; **tell one's –s** sgranare il rosario
beading n inserto per nastrino
beaded a perliforme
beady a rotondo come perla; (eyes) lucente
beak n becco
beaker n bicchierone m, provino
beam n (arch) trave f; sorriso; (light) raggio; (scale) asta; **fly on the —** seguire la rotta del radar; — vt raggiare, irradiare; — vi sorridere
bean n fagiolo; (broad) fava; (coffee) chicco di caffè; (navy) fagiolo; (string) fagiolino; **spill the –s** (fig) divulgare un segreto
beanpole n sostegno per piante; **thin as a —** (sl) stecchito

bear *n* orso; **–ish** *a* d'orso, rozzo

bear *vt (carry)* portare; *(endure)* sopportare; **— in mind** ricordarsi; **— out** *(prove)* convalidare; **— up** sostenersi, mantenersi

bearable *a* tollerabile, sopportabile

bearer *n* portatore *m*

bearing *n (manner)* comportamento, contegno; *(mech)* cuscinetto; *(naut)* rilevamento; *(reference to)* riferimento; **— on** *prep* relativo; **get one's –s** orientarsi

beard *n* barba; **–ed** *a* barbuto; **–less** *a* imberbe, senza barba

beard *vt (dare)* sfidare; *(defy)* bravare

beast *n* bestia, animale *m*, bruto; **— of burden** bestia da soma; **–ly** *a* bestiale

beat *n* battito; **—** *vt* battere, picchiare; *(coll)* vincere; *(whip up)* frullare; **—** *vi* battere, bussare

beaten *a* abbattuto, vinto *(fig)*; battuto; *(defeated)* sconfitto

beater *n* battitore; *(egg)* frullino

beating *n* battito; *(defeat)* sconfitta

beatitude *n* beatitudine *f*

beatific *a* beatifico

beatnik *n (sl)* anticonformista, bohemian

beau *n* fidanzato, innamorato

beautician *n* imbellitore *m*; addetto all'imbellimento

beautiful *a* bello

beautify *vi* abbellire

beauty *n* bellezza; **— contest** concorso di bellezza; **— parlor** salone di bellezza, istituto di bellezza

beaver *n* castoro

becalm *vt* calmare

because *conj* perchè; **— of** per, a causa di, per motivo di

beck *n* **at the — and call of** agli ordini di

beckon *vi* far cenno; **—** *vt* far cenno a

become *vi* diventare, divenire; *(befit)* convenire; **—** *vt* addirsi a; **— worthy** essere degno di

becoming *a* conveniente, grazioso

bed *n* letto; *(garden)* aiuola; *(river)* greto; **–clothes, –ding** *npl* biancheria da letto; **–fellow** *n* compagno di letto; **–ridden** *a* degente; **–room** *n* camera da letto; **–sheet** *n* lenzuolo; **–spread** *n* coperta; **–spring** *n* elastico; **–stead** *n* telaio del letto; letto; **–time** *n* ora di andare a letto

bedbug *n* cimice *f*

bedevil *vt* violentare, tormentare

bedlam *n* caos *m*, pandemonio

bedraggle *vt* infangare

bedrock *n* fondamento solido

bedside *n* bordo del letto; **—** *a* da letto; di capezzale

bee *n* ape *f*; **have a — in one's bonnet** avere un'idea fissa, aver qualcosa nella manica; **make a –line** *(fig)* andare in linea retta

beech *n* faggio

beef *n* manzo; *(meat)* carne bovina; *(ox)* bue *m*; **–steak** *n* bistecca; **–y** *a* grasso, grosso

beehive *n* alveare *m*

beer *n* birra; **— garden** birreria, barristorante *m*; **draft —** birra alla pompa

beeswax *n* cera d'api

beet *n* barbabietola; **— sugar** zucchero di barbabietola

beetle *n* scarafaggio

befall *vi* accadere, capitare, succedere

befit *vt* convenire a; *(adapt)* adattarsi a

befitting *a* conveniente

before *adv* prima; **— prep** prima di; davanti a; **— conj** prima che

beforehand *adv* in anticipo

befriend *vt* aiutare; trattare da amico

befuddle *vt* confondere con sofisma

beg *vt* mendicare; pregare, implorare, chiedere; **—** *vi* domandare, chiedere l'elemosina; **— the question** dare per ammesso

beggar *n* mendicante *m*; **–ly** *a* povero

beget *vt* causare, generare

begin *vt&i* cominciare, principiare; **to — with** prima di tutto

beginner *n* principiante *m*

beginning *n* principio; **in the —** al principio

begrudge *vt* invidiare

beguile *vt (cheat)* ingannare; *(distract)* distrarre; *(entice)* sedurre

behalf *n* beneficio, difesa; **in — of a** favore di; **on — of** a nome di

behave, — oneself *vi* comportarsi

behavior *n* comportamento; **–ism** *n* comportismo

behead *vt* decapitare

behest *n* ingiunzione, mandato

behind *prep* dietro, dietro di; **— adv** dietro, indietro; in ritardo

behold *vt* vedere, contemplare, scorgere; **—!** *interj* ecco! guarda!

behoove *vt* convenire, essere utile *(or* conveniente); **—** *vi* essere conveniente

being *n* essere *m*, esistenza; creatura; *(human)* essere umano

belabor *vt* lavorare, colpire

belated *a* ritardato

belch *vt&i* eruttare

belfry *n* torre *f*, campanile *m*

Belgian *a&n* belga

Belgium Belgio

belie *vt* diffamare, travisare

belief *n* fede *f;* opinione *f*
believable *a* credibile
believe *vt* credere, pensare; — *vi* credere in
believer *n* credente *m&f*
bell *n* campana; *(door)* campanello; **ring the** — suonare; **–boy** *n* ragazzo, groom d'albergo
belle *n* bella donna
bellicose *a* bellicoso
belligerency *n* aggressività, belligeranza
belligerent *n&a* belligerante *m*
bellow *vt&i* muggire, mugghiare; **–s** *n* mantice *m*
belly *n* pancia, ventre *m*
belong *vi (membership)* far parte; *(ownership)* spettare, appartenere; **–ings** *npl* proprietà, beni *mpl*
beloved *a* benamato, caro, amato, diletto, adorato
below *adv* sotto, giù; — *prep* sotto, al disotto di
belt *n* cintura; *(geog)* zona; *(girdle)* cinghia; — **conveyor** trasportatore a nastro; **hit below the** — fare un tiro mancino; **tighten one's** — stringere la cinghia di un buco; — *vt* cingere; *(coll)* battere
bemoan *vt* deplorare, lamentare, piangere
bench *n* banco; *(garden)* panchina; *(law)* tribunale *m;* — **warrant** mandato di cattura; — *vt* esibire
bend *n* piega, curva; — *vt* piegare; — *vi* piegarsi
beneath *adv* sotto, giù; — *prep* sotto, al disotto di
benediction *n* benedizione
benefactor *n* benefattore *m*
beneficence *n* beneficenza
beneficent *a* caritatevole
beneficial *a* buono, benefico, utile, salutare, vantaggioso
beneficiary *n* beneficiario
benefit *n* beneficio, vantaggio; *(subsidy)* sussidio; **for the** — **of** a beneficio di; — *vt* beneficare
benevolence *n* benevolenza
benevolent *a* buono, benevolo; *(charitable)* caritatevole
benighted *a* ignorante, oscurato
benign *a* benigno
bent *n* attitudine *f;* disposizione; *(tendency)* tendenza; — *a (crooked)* curvo; *(twisted)* torto
benumb *vt* intorpidire, intirizzire
benzine *n* benzolo
bequeath *vt* fare testamento, testare
bequest *n* lascito
berate *vt* rimproverare

bereave *vt* privare; **–ment** *n* perdita; lutto
bereft *a* privato, spogliato
beret *n* berretto, basco
berkelium *n (chem)* berchelio
berry *n* bacca
berserk *a* vandalico, distruttivo
berth *n* cuccetta, letto; **give a wide** — **to** evitare
beseech *vt* supplicare, pregare
beset *vt* circondare, assediare
besetting *a* circondante
beside *prep* accanto a; — **oneself** fuori di sè; — *adv* d'altronde, inoltre
besides *adv* inoltre, per giunta; — *prep* inoltre a
besiege *vt* assediare
bespeak *vt* ordinare, prenotare, sollecitare
best *a* migliore; ottimo; — **man** testimone *m;* — *adv* meglio; **do one's** — fare il possibile; **for the** — per il meglio; **get the** — **of** aver il meglio di; **make the** — **of** trar vantaggio di
bestial *a* bestiale; **–ity** *n* bestialità
bestir *vt* eccitare
bestow *vt* elargire, conferire
bet *n* scommessa; **You** —! *interj (coll)* Per certo!; — *vt* scommettere; — *vi* fare una scommessa
beta ray raggio beta
betake *vt* — **oneself** andarsene per conto proprio
betatron *n* betatrone *m*
betide *vt&i* accadere
betray *vt* tradire; — **oneself** tradirsi; **–al** *n* tradimento
betroth *vt* fidanzare; **–al** *n* fidanzamento; **–ed** *n&a* fidanzato
better *n* meglio, vantaggio; **for the** — per il meglio; **so much the** — tanto meglio; — *adv* meglio; — **and** — di bene in meglio; — *a* meglio, migliore; **think** — **of** pensarci meglio; — *vt* migliorare; — **oneself** migliorarsi; **get** — migliorare
between *prep* fra, tra; **betwixt and** — nè l'uno nè l'altro, fra i due; — *adv* nel mezzo, fra i due
bevel *n* angolo; — *vt&i* smussare
bevelled *a* smussato
beverage *n* bevanda, bibita
bevatron *n* bevatrone *m*
bevy *n* gruppo; *(swarm)* sciame *m*
bewail *vt* lamentare; *(regret)* rimpiangere; — *vi* lamentarsi
beware *vt&i* guardarsi da, stare in guardia
bewilder *vt* sgomentare, confondere, turbare; **–ing** *a* sgomentevole; **–ment** *n*

sgomento; estasi *f*
bewitch *vt* ammaliare, stregare, incantare; **–ing** *a* affascinante
beyond *prep* al di là di; — *adv&n* al di là; **go** — andare più lontano di
biannual *a* biennale
bias *n* inclinazione; *(prejudice)* pregiudizio; **on the** — di sbieco; **–ed** *a* prevenuto; — *vt* influenzare
bib *n* bavaglino
Bible *n* Bibbia
biblical *a* biblico
bibliography *n* bibliografia
bicarbonate *n* bicarbonato
bicentennial *a* bicentennale
biceps *npl* bicipiti *mpl*
bicker *vi* far questione, litigare, bisticciare
bicycle *n* bicicletta; **ride a** — andare in bicicletta
bid *vt (command)* ordinare; *(offer)* offrire; — *vi* offrire un prezzo; — **adieu** dire addio; — **fair** promettere di; — *n* offerta, licitazione
bidder *n* offerente *m*
bidding *n* invito, offerta, ordine *m*
bide *vt* attendere, aspettare, sopportare; — **one's time** attendere l'occasione
biennial *a&n* biennale
bier *n* bara
bifocal *a* bifocale
big *a* grosso, grande; importante; — **shot** *(sl)* pezzo grosso; **look** — darsi delle arie; **talk** — darsi importanza; **B–Dipper** Orsa Maggiore
bigamist *n* bigamo
bigamous *a* bigamo
bigamy *n* bigamia
big-hearted *a* di buon cuore, generoso
bigot *n* bigotto; **–ry** *n* bigottismo, fanatismo
bigotted *a* bigotto, fanatico
bigwig *n (coll)* pezzo grosso
bilateral *a* bilaterale
bile *n* bile *f*
bilingual *a* bilingue
bilious *a* bilioso
bill *n* conto; *(bird)* becco; *(com)* fattura; — **of fare** lista delle vivande; — **of health** certificato di salute; — **of lading** polizza di carico; **dollar** — biglietto da un dollaro; **–fold** *n* portafogli *m*, portafoglio; **–ing** *n* carezze *fpl*; — *vt* affigere; *(com)* fatturare; — **and coo** coccolare
billboard *n* albo di avvisi
billet *n (lodging)* accantonamento, alloggio: *(note)* lettera; — *vt* assengnare, collocare

billiards *npl* biliardo
billion *n* miliardo
billionnaire *n* miliardario
billow *n* maroso; — *vi* mareggiare, beccheggiare, rollare; **–y** *a* ondoso, agitato
bimonthly *a&n* bimestrale *m*; *(fortnight)* quindicinale *m*; — *adv* bimestralmente; quindicinalmente
bin *n* madia
bind *vt* legare; *(again)* rilegare; — **oneself** impegnarsi; **–er** *n* legatore *m*
binding *n* legatura; — *a* obbligatorio
bingo *n* tombola
biochemistry *n* biochimica
binoculars *npl* binoccolo
biographer *n* biografo
biographical *a* biografico
biography *n* biografia
biological *a* biologico; — **warfare** *n* guerra biologica
biologist *n* biologo
biology *n* biologia
bionics *npl* bionica
biophysics *n* biofisica
biopsy *n* biopsia
biotin *n (growth factor)* biotina
bipartisan *a* che fa doppio gioco
biped *n* bipede *m&f*
birch *n* betulla
bird *n* uccello; **–'s-eye** *a* a vista d'uccello
birdseed *n* becchime *m*
biretta *n* berretta
birth *n* nascita; **–day** *n* compleanno; **–mark** *n* voglia; **–place** *n* luogo di nascita; **–right** *n* diritto di nascita, primogenitura; **give** — **to** partorire; dare alla luce
biscuit *n* panino
bisect *vt* bisecare; — *vi* tagliare in due
bishop *n* vescovo; **–ric** *n* vescovato
bit *n (amount)* pezzetto; *(horse)* morso; *(restraint)* freno; *(tool)* punta da trapano; **two –s** *(sl)* un quarto di dollaro
bitch *n* cagna; — *vi (sl)* lagnarsi
bite *vt&i* mordere; *(sting)* pungere; — *vi (fish)* abboccare; — *n* morso; *(mouthful)* boccone *m*
biting *a* mordente, aspro, sarcastico
bitter *a* amaro; **fight to the** — **end** lottare fino alla fine; **–ly** *adv* amaramente
bitterness *n* amarezza
bituminous *a* bituminoso
bivouac *n* bivacco; — *vi* bivaccare
biweekly *a&adv* ogni due settimane; bisettimanale; due volte la settimana; — *n* bisettimanale *m*
bizarre *a* bizzarro

blab *vi* chiacchierare; — *vt* raccontare

black *a* nero, scuro; — **eye** occhio pesto; — **list** lista nera; — **market** mercato nero, borsa nera; — **sheep** pecora nera; **–smith** *n* fabbro

blackball *vt* votare contro, bocciare, rigettare

blackberry *n* mora selvatica; *(bush)* moro

blackbird *n* merlo

blackboard *n* lavagna

blacken *vt* annerire, infamare; — *vi* annerirsi

blackguard *n* briccone *m*, mascalzone *m*

blackhead *n* punto nero

blackmail *n* ricatto; — *vt* ricattare; **–er** *n* ricattatore *m*

blackout *n* oscuramento; *(med)* amnesia; — *vt* oscurare, obliare

bladder *n* vescica

blade *n* lama; *(grass)* filo; **propeller —** pala d'elica

blame *n* colpa; **–less** *a* innocente; — *vt* dare la colpa

blameworthy *a* biasimevole

blanche *vt* imbiancare; evitare; — *vi* impallidire; tergiversare

bland *a* blando, soave; **–ness** *n* affabilità; **–ly** *adv* blandamente

blandishment *n* blandizia

blank *n&a* bianco; *(void)* vuoto; — **cartridge** cartuccia; — **check** assegno a vuoto; — **verse** verso libero; **–ly** *adv* vagamente

blanket *n (cover)* coperta; — **instructions** ordini generali *mpl;* **–ing** *(rad)* interferenza; — *a* generale; — *vt* coprire con coperta

blare *vi* risuonare, muggire; — *vt* proclamare a suon di tromba; — *n* suono, muggito

blarney *n* adulazione

blasé *a* scettico, blasé, abulico, indifferente

blaspheme *vi* bestemmiare

blasphemous *a* blasfematorio, sacrilego

blasphemy *n* bestemmia

blast *n* colpo di vento; esplosione; *(loud noise)* squillo; **–off** *n (aesp)* lancio; — *vt* far saltare; fare appassire; — **off** *(coll)* esplodere da impazienza; **–ed** *a* appassito, rovinato; **–ing** *n* distruzione, rovina

blatant *a* risuonante; **–ly** *adv* risuonatamente, sonoramente

blaze *n* incendio, fiamma; — *vi* divampare; *(glitter)* brillare; — *vt* far brillare; — **a trail** marchiare una pista

blazing *a* sfolgorante

bleach *vt&i* imbiancare; — *n* varecchina

bleachers *npl (stadium)* scalinate *fpl*

bleak *a* pallido

blear *vt* offuscare; *(vision)* velare; **–ed** offuscato

bleary *a* offuscato; *(of eyes)* infiammato; *(teary)* lagrimoso

bleat *n* belato; — *vi* belare

bleed *vi* sanguinare; — *vt* salassare; **–er** *n (med)* emofiliaco

bleeding *n* emorragia; — *a* sanguinante

blemish *vt* macchiare; — *n* macchia

blend *vt (mingle)* mischiare; *(mix)* mescolare; — *n* miscela; **–er** *n* frullatore *m*

bless *vt* benedire, consacrare; **–ed** *a* felice; **–ing** *n* benedizione

blight *n* ruggine *f; (bot)* golpe *f;* — *vt* danneggiare, riardere; *(fig)* guastare

blind *a* cieco; — **alley** vicolo cieco; — **flying** volo cieco; — *vt* accecare; — *n* sotterfugio, pretesto; persiana; *(fig)* finta; **Venetian –s** tende alla veneziana, persiane avvolgibili *fpl*

blinder *n (horse)* paraocchi *m*

blindfold *vt* bendare gli occhi, — *n* benda

blindly *adv* alla cieca

blink *vi (eyes)* sbattere gli occhi; **–er** *n (auto)* segnale di svolta

bliss *n* felicità; **–ful** *a* felice; **–fully** *adv* felicemente

blister *n* vescica, bollicina; — *vi* produrre vesciche

blithe *a* gaio, giocondo

blitz *n* attacco a sorpresa

blizzard *n* tormenta; bufera

bloat *vt* gonfiare; — *vi* gonfiarsi; **–ed** *a* gonfio, gonfiato

blob *n* goccia, macchia

bloc *n (pol)* blocco, gruppo

block *n* blocco; *(of houses)* isolato di case; — **and tackle** paranco; **stumbling —** intoppo; — *vt* bloccare

blockade *n* blocco; *(war)* assedio; **run a —** rompere il blocco; — *vt* bloccare; assediare

blockhead *n* testardo

blonde *a&n* biondo

blood *n* sangue *m; —* **plasma** plasma sanguigno

bloodcurdling *a* atterrito

bloodhound *n* segugio

bloodless *a* esangue

bloodshed *n* spargimento di sangue

bloodshot *a* congestionato

bloodstain *n* macchia di sangue

bloodthirsty *a* assetato di sangue

bloody *a* sanguinario

bloom *n* fiore *m; —* *vi* fiorire; **–ing** *a* in fiore, fiorente

blossom *n* fiore *m; —* *vi* fiorire, sbocciare

blot *vt* disonorare; *(hide)* oscurare; *(spot)*

macchiare; — **out** cancellare; — *vi* macchiarsi; — *n* macchia
blotch *n* pustola, grossa macchia
blotter *n* carta sugante, brogliaccio
blotting paper carta asciugante
blouse *n* camicetta; blusa
blow *n* colpo; **–gun**, **–pipe** *n* cerbottana; **–torch** *n* cannello ossidrico; **come to –s** azzuffarsi; — *vi* soffiare, sbuffare; *(wind)* tirare; — **away** dissipare; — **out** *(fuse)* fulminare; *(light)* spegnere; — **over** soffiar via, rovesciare; — **up** gonfiare; *(photo)* ingrandire
blowout *n (tire)* scoppio
blubber *n* pianto; — *vi* piangere a dirotto; **–ing** *n* singhiozzo
bludgeon *n* randello, mazza; — *vt* colpire con mazza
blue *n* blu; *(azure)* azzurro; *(dark)* turchino; *(light)* celeste; *(sky)* azzurrocielo; **be —** essere depresso; **–berry** *n* mirtillo blu; **–bird** *n* beccafico; **–jay** *n* ghiandaia blu; **–print** *n* cianotipia; **once in a — moon** ad ogni morte di papa; **turn the air —** bestemmiare
blueing *n* indaco
blues *n pl* melanconia; **have the —** essere giù di spirito; *(mus)* musica nostalgica
bluff *n (geog)* scogliera; *(sham)* bluff *m*, smargiassata; — *vt* ingannare, bluffare; — *vi* vantarsi di
bluffer *n* vanaglorioso
bluish *a* bluastro
blunder *n* topica; sbaglio grossolano; — *vi* fare una topica, commettere un errore, equivocarsi
blunt *a* smussato; *(abrupt)* brusco; *(dull)* ottuso; — *vt* ottundere, rintuzzare
bluntly *adv* rudemente
blur *n* disonore *m*; *(mark)* macchia, segno indistinto; — *vt* offuscare, rendere indistinto; — *vi* confondersi
blurb *n* encomio
blurry *a* macchiato
blurt *vt* soffiare, singhiozzare
blush *n* rossore *m*; — *vi* arrossire
bluster *n* fanfaronata; — *vi* fare chiasso; *(weather)* infuriare
blustering *a* rumoroso
blustery *a* tempestoso
boar *n* verro; **wild —** cinghiale
board *n (com)* consiglio; *(food)* tavola; *(wood)* asse *m*; **— of directors** consiglio di amministrazione; **— of health** ufficio d'igiene; **— of trade** camera di commercio; **on —** a bordo
board *vt* impalcare; prendere a pensione; — *vi (boat)* imbarcarsi; stare a pensione; *(train)* salire in treno
boarder *n* pensionato; *(school)* convittore

m
boardinghouse *n* pensione
boarding school pensionato, collegio, convitto
boardwalk *n* passeggio, lungomare *m*
boast *n* vanto; — *vt* vantare; — *vi* vantarsi, gloriarsi; **–er** *n* spaccone *m*
boastful *a* millantatore; **–ness** *n* millantaria
boat *n* barca, battello; *(steam)* piroscafo; **in the same —** *(coll)* nella stessa situazione
boating *n* canottaggio
boatman *n* battelliere *m*
boatswain *n* nostromo
bob *n (hair)* orecchino
bob *vt* battere, scuotere; — *vi* dondolare; — **up** *(appear)* apparire improvvisamente
bobby pin molletta per i capelli
bobby socks *(coll)* braccialetti *mpl*
bobby soxer *(coll)* ragazzina, adolescente *f*
bobcat *n* gatto selvatico
bobsled *n* slitta
bode *vt&i* presagire; — **well, (ill)** promettere bene, (male)
bodice *n* busto
bodiless *a* incorporeo
bodily *a* corporeo; — *adv* di peso
body *n* corpo; *(airplane)* fusoliera; *(auto)* carrozzeria; *(corpse)* cadavere *m*; — **politic** corpo governativo; **in a —** tutti insieme
bodyguard *n* guardia del corpo *(or* personale*)*
bog *n* pantano; — *vt&i* impantanare; — **down** affondare nel pantano
boil *n* bollitura; *(med)* foruncolo; — *vi* bollire; — *vt* lessare, fare bollire; **–ed** *a* bollito
boiler *n* bollitore *m*, caldaia
boiling *a* bollente; — **point** punto d'ebollizione
boisterous *a* turbolento, chiassoso
bold *a* temerario; **–ly** *adv* temerariamente
boldness *n* ardimento, coraggio
boldface *n (type)* grassetto
bold-faced *a* sfrontato, sfacciato
bolero *n* bolero
boll *n* capsula; **— weevil** acaro del cotone
bolster *n* cuscino, cuscinetto; — *vt* accomodare con cuscini; *(fig)* rafforzare
bolt *n* bullone *m*; *(thunder)* fulmine *m*; — **upright** tutto dritto
bolt *vt* scattare; *(food)* tranguigiare
bomb *n* bomba; — **bay** *(avi)* forma di sgancio; — **shelter** rifugio aereo; **–proof** *a* a prova di bomba; **–shell** *n* bossolo;

–**sight** n strumento di sgancio

bombard vt bombardare; –**ment** n bombardamento

bombast n ampollosità; –**ic** a ampolloso

bomber n bombardiere m

bonanza n prosperità, fortuna; (mine) miniera ricca

bonbon n bombone m

bond n legame m, vincolo; (com) obbligazione, titolo; — vt depositare, immagazzinare; –**ed** a depositato; –**holder** n portatore m

bondage n servitù f

bondsman n avallo, garante m; schiavo

bone n osso; (fish) lisca; **feel in one's** –**s**; intuire; **have a — to pick** avere un punto da chiarire; **make no** –**s about** non avere scrupoli per; — vt disossare; — **up on** riassumere; –**less** a disossato, senz' osso

bone-dry a secco come un osso

boner n (sl) sproposito

bonehead n (sl) testa dura, stupido

bonfire n falò

bonnet n cuffia

bonus n gratifica

bony a ossuto

boo interj bu! — vt burlare, fischiare

booby n stupido; — **prize** premio per l'ultimo arrivato; — **trap** tranello, trappola esplosiva

book n libro; — **end** appoggialibri m; — **jacket** coprilibro; **memorandum** — libretto d'appunti; –**binder** n rilegatore m; –**case** n libreria, scaffale m; –**let** n libretto; –**mark** n segnalibro; –**plate** n etichetta di un libro; –**seller** n libraio; –**shelf** n scaffale m; –**store** n libreria, negozio di libri

book vt registrare; (reserve) prenotare, riservare; (theat) scritturare; — vi (travel) prendere il biglietto; –**ing** n registrazione

bookkeeper n contabile m&f

bookkeeping n contabilità

bookmaker n (sport) allibratore m

bookworm n tarlo, tignola; (fig) topo di biblioteca

boom n rimbombo; (com) prosperità improvvisa; (naut) boma, asta; — vi progredire, prosperare; — vt promuovere

boomerang n boomerang; — vi ritorcersi contro l'autore

boon n favore m, beneficio; — a gaio; buono

boondoggle n (sl) lavoro di poco profitto; — vi (sl) lavorare per poco

boor n zotico; –**ish** a rozzo, grossolano, volgare

boost n (help) aiuto; (rise) rialzo; — vt (praise) esaltare; (increase) aumentare

booster n connessione elettrica a combinazione; — **rocket** (aesp) razzo comandato

boot n stivale m; **to** — in più, in aggiunta; –**less** a inutile

bootblack n lustrascarpe m

booth n baracca

bootleg a contrabbandato; — vt&i contrabbandare

bootlegger n contrabbandiere m

booty n bottino

borax n borace m

border n (edge) orlo; (geog) frontiera; — vt orlare, confinare; — vi essere limitrofo; — **on** confinare con

borderland n paese limitrofo

borderline n confine m; — a incerto, dubbioso; — **case** caso incerto

bore n buco; (gun) calibro; (mech) alesaggio; (person) noia, seccatore m, seccatrice f; impiastro (fig); — vt (pierce) bucare, forare; (weary) annoiare, seccare

boredom n noia

boring a noioso, seccante

born a nato; **be** — (birth) nascere

borrow vt prendere a prestito; — vi fare un prestito; –**er** n mutuatario; colui che chiede prestito

bosh n (coll) assurdità, stupidaggine f

bosom n seno; — **friend** amico amato

boss n (coll) principale, padrone m

botanical a botanico

botany n botanica

botch vt rammendare; — n rappezzo, rattoppo

both a&pron ambedue, tutt'e due; — conj così come, tanto quanto; — **hands** ambe le mani

bother n fastidio; — vt molestare, dar fastidio, seccare; — vi infastidirsi di

bothersome a fastidioso, noioso

bottle n bottiglia; (flask) fiasco; (vial) fiala

bottle vt imbottigliare; — **up one's feeling** nascondere l'emozione

bottleneck n intoppo, congestione di traffico

bottom n fondo; **at the** — in fondo; — a del fondo, inferiore; infimo, ultimo; –**less** a senza fondo

bottom vt fondare; (naut) sondare

botulism n botulismo

boudoir n spogliatoio, salottino da signora

bough n ramo

bouillon n brodo

boulder n ciottolo, sasso

boulevard n corso, viale m

bounce *vi* rimbalzare; — *vt* battere, far saltare; — *n* balzo, rimbalzo
bouncing *a* robusto; pieno di salute
bound *n* rimbalzo; **out of –s** fuori limite; — *a* obbligato, impegnato, rilegato; — **for** diretto a; — **to happen** inevitabile; **–less** *a* illimitato
bound *vi (jump)* balzare; — *vt (limit)* limitare
boundary *n* confine *m*
bountiful *a* generoso, benifico
bounty *n* generosità, bontà
bouquet *n* mazzolino; *(smell)* profumo; *(wine)* aroma *m*
bout *n* partita, turno
bow *n* inchino; *(naut)* prora; — *vi* inchinarsi; *(yield)* cedere; — *vt* inclinare; *(head)* abbassare la testa
bow *n* arco; *(mus)* archetto; *(ribbon)* nodo; *(tie)* cravatta; **draw a long —** esagerare; — *vt* piegare, curvare
bowels *npl* intestini *mpl*, budella *fpl*
bower *n* capanna
bowl *n* scodella, boccia; — *vi* giuocare ai birilli; giocare alle bocce; — **over** stravolgere
bowlegged *a* gambistorto
bowling *n* le bocce; — **alley** pista *(or* salone) di bocce; — **ball** boccia; — **pin** birillo
box *n* scatola; *(case)* cassa; *(slap)* ceffone *m; (theat)* palco; — **office** botteghino
box *vt* incassare; *(ears)* schiaffeggiare; *(sport)* fare del pugilato
boxcar *n* furgone, vagone *m*
boxer *n (packer)* imballatore *m; (sport)* pugile *m*
boxing *n* pugilato; — **glove** guanto da pugilato; — **match** partita di pugilato
boy *n* ragazzo; — **scout** Giovane Esploratore
boycott *n* boicottaggio; — *vt* boicottare
boyhood *n* puerizia, adolescenza
boyish *a* fanciullesco
brace *n* sopporto, sostegno; — *vt (bind)* legare; *(support)* sostenere; — **up** rianimarsi
bracelet *n* braccialetto
bracing *a* corroborante, tonico
bracket *n* mensola; *(print)* parentesi quadra
brad *n* chiodino
brag *n* vanteria; — *vi* vantarsi; — *vt* vantarsi di
braggart *n* millantatore *m*
braid *n* cordoncino, spighetta; *(hair)* treccia; — *vt* intrecciare
braille *n* Braille *m*, sistema braille
brain *n* cervello; — **fever** meningite ce-

rebro-spinale; — **storm** *(coll)* confusione mentale; **electronic —** cervello elettronico; **beat one's –s out** *(sl)* spremere il cervello; **rack one's –s** scervellarsi; **–less** *a* poco intelligente, stupido; **–y** *a (coll)* intelligente; — *vt* far saltare le cervella
brainwash *n* psico-inquisizione, lavaggio mentale
braise *vt* brasare; **–d** *a* brasato
brake *n* freno; — **band** freno a nastro; — **lining** tessuto per freni; **apply the —** usare il freno; **release the —** rilasciare il freno; — *vt* frenare
brakeman *n* frenatore *m*
bramble *n* pruno, rovo
bran *n* crusca
branch *n (com)* succursale *f; (rail)* biforcazione; *(tree)* ramo; — *vt* suddividere, ramificare; — *vi* ramificarsi; — **off** diramarsi, biforcarsi; — **out** espandersi
brand *n* marca; — *vt* bollare, marchiare
brandish *vt* brandire
brand-new *a* fiammante
brandy *n* acquavite *f*
brash *a* arrogante
brass *n* ottone *m;* — **band** fanfara; **bold as —** *(coll)* spudorato
brassiere *n* reggiseno, reggipetto
brat *n* moccioso
bravado *n* spacconata
brave *a* coraggioso; — *vt* sfidare; — *n (American Indian)* bravo
bravery *n* coraggio, eroismo
brawl *n* zuffa, rissa; — *vi* sbraitare, gridare
brawn *n* polpa di carne; **–y** *a* muscoloso, forte
bray *n* raglio; — *vi* ragliare
brazen *a* sfrontato, impudente, sfacciato; — *vt* trattare con disprezzo
brazier *n* ottonaio
Brazil Brasile *m*
Brazilian *a&n* brasiliano
breach *n* breccia, rottura, violazione; — **of promise** violazione di promessa; — **of trust, faith** abuso di fiducia; — *vt* aprire una breccia, infrangere
bread *n* pane *m; (graham, wholewheat)* pane integrale; *(rye)* pane di segala; **earn one's —** guadagnarsi il pane; **fresh —** pane fresco; **know which side one's — is buttered on** sapere barcarmenarsi; **–board** *n* tagliere per pane; **–line** *n* fila di persone per ricevere alimento gratis; **–winner** *n* lavoratore *m*
bread *vt* impanare; **–ed** *a* impanato
breadth *n* larghezza, estensione

break vt rompere, spezzare; (news) comunicare; — vi rompersi; — **away** farla finita; — **down** (health) ammalarsi; (mech) avere una panna; — **in on** irrompere su, interrompere; — **into** invadere; — **one's word** mancare alla promessa; — **off** cessare di, smettere; — **out** scoppiare; (flare) divampare; (rise up) sorgere; — **up** distruggere, abbattere; cessare
break n rottura; (bone) frattura; (pause) interruzione; (weather) cambiamento; — **of day** alba; **bad** — sfortuna, scalogna; **give a** — concedere una occasione
breakable a fragile
breakage n rottura
breakdown n (auto) panna; (damage) guasto; (med) crollo; (separation) classificazione
breakfast n prima colazione
breakneck a sfrenato; (foolhardy) azzardato; — adv a rompicollo
breakwater n frangiflutti m
breast n (anat) petto, seno; (woman's) mammella; — **stroke** nuoto a rana; **make a clean** — **of it** confessare tutto
breast vt affrontare
breath n fiato, respiro; **be out of** — essere senza fiato; **gasp for** — ansare; **take one's** — **away** sconcertare
breathless a senza fiato
breathe vi respirare, fiatare; — vt infondere
breathing n respiro; — **space** tempo di tirare il fiato (fig)
breath-taking a emozionante, sfiatante
breech n posteriore m; (gun) culatta
breed vt generare; allevare; — vi moltiplicare; — n razza, stirpe f; –**er** n allevatore m
breeding n educazione, modi garbati, allevamento
breeze n brezza
breezy a arieggiato, brioso, vivace
breve n breve m
breviary n breviario
brevity n brevità, concisione
brew n miscela, fermentazione; — vt (beer) fare la birra; (ferment) fermentare; (infuse) fare un infuso di; (mix) miscelare; (plot) tramare; **something** –**ing** gatta ci cova (fig)
brewery n fabbrica di birra
briar n rovo
bribe n subornazione, corruzione, seduzione; — vt corrompere, subornare
bribery n subornazione, corruzione
brick n mattone m; –**layer** n muratore m; –**yard** n fabbrica di mattoni
bridal a nuziale; — **gown** abito da sposa

bride n sposa, sposina; — **and groom** gli sposi
bridegroom m sposo
bridesmaid n damigella d'onore
bridge n ponte m; (dent) ponte dentale; (game) bridge m; (suspension) ponte sospeso; –**head** n testa di ponte; — vt costruire un ponte su, fare ponte su
bridle n briglia; — **path** galoppatoio; — vt frenare; — vi raddrizzarsi
brief a breve; **in** — in breve; — n memoriale m, riassunto; (law) esposto, citazione; **hold no** — **for** non essere d'accordo con; –**ly** adv in modo conciso; — vt dare istruzioni precise; –**ing** (avi) n istruzione di volo
brig n (naut) brigantino
brigade n brigata
bright a vivace, brillante, chiaro, intelligente; –**ness** n splendore m; (light) chiarore m; (mirth) allegria
brighten vt rischiarare; — vi rischiararsi
brilliance, brilliancy n splendore m
brilliant a brillante; — n brillante m, diamante m
brim n orlo; — **over** traboccare
brimful a ricolmo
brine n salamoia
bring vt (carry) portare; (lead) condurre; — **about** effettuare, causare; — **around** convincere; — **forth** produrre; — **oneself to** persuadersi; — **out** emettere; — **to** (revive) ravvivare; — **to one's mind** chiamare l'attenzione; — **up** (child) educare, allevare; (subject) tirare su
brink n orlo
brisk a attivo, vivace
bristle n setola; — vi arricciare, rizzare; — vt rizzarsi, arricciarsi
bristly a setoloso
British a britannico
brittle a fragile, friabile
broach vt introdurre, intavolare, abbordarsi
broad a largo; –**jump** (sport) salto in lungo; –**side** n (naut) bordo; bordato
broadcast n radiotrasmissione; — vt divulgare; (rad&TV) radiotrasmettere
broadcasting n radiodiffusione; — a trasmittente, radiotrasmittente; –**station** stazione radiotrasmettente
broaden vi allargare; — vt allargarsi
broad-minded a tollerante, liberale, di larghe vedute
brocade n broccato
broccoli n broccolo
brochure n opuscolo
broil vt arrostire in graticola; –**ed** a ai

ferri; **–er** n arrostitrice f

broke a (sl) al verde, senza quattrini

broken a rotto; — **English** cattivo inglese

broken– (in comp) **–down** a scoraggiato; **–hearted** a disperato

broker n (com) sensale m, mediatore m; agente m

brokerage n mediazione

bromide n bromuro

bronchial a bronchiale; — **tube** bronco

bronchitis n bronchite f

bronchoscope n bronchiscopio

bronze n bronzo; — a bronzeo; di bronzo

brooch n spilla, fermaglio

brood n nidiata, covata; vt&i covare, meditare; — **over** angosciarsi

brook n ruscello; — vt supportare; — **no interference** non tollerare intrusione

broom n scopa; (bot) ginestra; **–stick** n manico di scopa

broth n brodo

brothel n postribolo

brother n fratello; frate m; **–hood** n fratellanza; **–ly** a fraterno

brother-in-law n cognato

brow n fronte f; **knit one's –s** accigliarsi

browbeat vt imporre, intimidire

brown a bruno; (hair) castagno; (skin) abbronzato; — **paper** carta straccia; — **sugar** zucchero greggio; — vt abbrunire; (cooking) dorare, rosolare

browse vt pascolare, brucare; — vi (in books) scartabellare

bruise vt ammaccare; — n livido, contusione

bruiser n pugile m

brunch n (coll) combinazione di colazione e pranzo

brunette a&n brunetta, bruna

brunt n attacco, urto

brush n pennello; (carbon) elettrodi di carbonio; (shoe) spazzola per le scarpe; (tooth) spazzolino da denti; — vt spazzolare; — **past** sfiorare

brush-off n (sl) scoraggiamento

brushwood n macchia

brusque a brusco, rude

Brussels Brusselle; — **sprouts** npl cavoli di Brusselle

brutal a brutale; **–ity** n brutalità

brute n bruto, bestia; — a bruto

B.S., Bachelor of Science diploma in scienze; diplomato in scienze

bubble n bolla, bollicina; — vt far bollire; — vi bollire; — **over** traboccare

buccaneer n bucaniere, pirata m

buck n daino; (sl) dollaro; **pass the —** (sl) scaricare la responsabilità; — vi sgroppare; (auto) andare a strappi (fig);

(horse) imbizzarrirsi; — vt opporsi a (coll); — **up** (coll) rallegrare

bucket n secchia, secchio; — **seat** (auto) strapuntino

buckle n fibbia; — vt affibbiare; — vi piegarsi; torcersi

buckshot n pallini da caccia

buckwheat n grano saraceno

bucolic a bucolico

bud n bottone m; gemma; **nip in the —** prevenire; — vi germogliare; — vt innestare

buddy n (coll) compare m, amicone m; camerata m

budge vi muoversi, indietreggiare; — vt spostare

budget n bilancio; — vt fare il bilancio

buff n colpo; — a marrone chiaro, fulvo; — vt lisciare, lucidare

buffalo n buffalo

buffer n paraurti m; (rail) respingente m

buffet n (furniture) credenza; (meal) tavola calda; (service) servizio di buffet

buffet vt colpire, schiaffeggiare; — vi fare a pugni

buffoon n buffone m

bug n insetto; (coll) microbo

bugbear n spauracchio

buggy n calesse m; **baby —** carrozzina

bugle n tromba

bugler n trombettiere m

build n (stature) struttura fisica; **–up** n opinione precostruita, propaganda; **–er** n costruttore m; **–ing** n edifizio, fabbricato; — vt&i costruire

bulb n bulbo, globo; (elec) lampadina elettrica; **–ous** a bulboso

Bulgarian n&a bulgaro

bulge vt&i gonfiarsi; — n protuberanza

bulk n massa, volume m; **in —** sciolto; **–head** n paratia; **–y** a voluminoso

bull n toro; — **market** mercato in aumento; **papal —** bolla papale

bulldog n mastino

bulldoze vt (coll) intimidire

bulldozer n apripista m; livellatrice f

bullet n pallottola; **–proof** a a prova di pallottole

bulletin n bollettino; — **board** albo, tabella per gli avvisi pubblici

bullfight n tauromachia, toreo, corrida

bullfighter n toreador m, torero

bullfrog n rana toro

bullion n lingotto d'oro (or d'argento)

bully n prepotente m, gradasso; — vi fare il prepotente; — vt maltrattare, tiranneggiare

bulwark n baluardo; — vt fortificare

bum n (coll) lazzarone, straccione m

bumblebee n calabrone m

bump n colpo, urto, collisione; *(head)* bernoccolo; **-y** a pieno di bozze; — vt urtare; — vi sbattere contro

bumper n *(auto)* paraurti m, respingente m; — **crop** raccolta eccezionale

bumpkin n rusticone, cafone m

bumptious a presuntuoso

bun n panino, focaccia; *(hair)* boccolo

bunch n mazzetto; *(grapes)* grappolo; **in -es** a grappoli; — vt riunire in fascio; raccogliere; — vi gonfiarsi, raccogliersi in

bundle n involto, pacco, collo, fascio; *(sticks)* fagotto; — vt impaccare, avvolgere; — **off, out** svignarsela

bungalow n villino, casetta

bungle vi lavorare alla carlona; — vt storpiare

bungler n incapace m

bunion n grosso callo al piede

bunk n cuccetta; *(sl)* stupidaggine f

bunt vt&i spingere, cozzare; — n *(baseball)* spintone m

bunting n bandiere fpl

buoy n boa; — vt sostenere a galla; — vi galleggiare

buoyancy n leggerezza, elasticità, vivacità

buoyant a leggero, galleggiante; *(gay)* allegro

burden n fardello, carico; **-some** a pesante, opprimente; — vt gravare, caricare

bureau n *(furniture)* comò, cassettone m; *(office)* ufficio, ente governativo; **travel** — agenzia di viaggio

bureaucracy n burocrazia

burglar n svaligiatore, scassinatore m; **-y** n furto con scasso

burial n sepoltura, interramento; — **ground** cimitero

burlap n tela da sacco

burlesque a burlesco; — n burletta; — vt&i parodiare, imitare mettendo in ridicolo

burly a corpulento

Burma Birmania

burn n scottatura, ustione f; **-er** n bruciatore m; — vt bruciare

burning n incendio; — a ardente

burnish vt brunire

burnt a bruciato

burr n *(accent)* pronuncia forte dell'erre; *(bot)* involucro della castagna; *(mech)* limatura, bava, scoria; *(sound)* suono confuso; *(tool)* trapano; — vt&i parlare in erre

burrow n tana; — vt&i rintanarsi, fare un buco

bursitis n borsite f

burst vi scoppiare; — **into tears** scoppiare in pianto; — vt far esplodere; — n scoppio, esplosione; accesso; — **of applause** ovazione; esplosione di applausi

bury vt seppellire, sotterrare

bus n autobus m, pullman m

busboy n garzone, fattorino

bush n cespuglio, macchia; **beat around the** — menar il can per l'aia

bushel n staio

bushing n *(mech)* boccola

bushy a folto

busily adv attivamente

business n azienda, commercio, affare m; *(kind of work)* faccenda, occupazione; — **cycle** giro d'affari; — **house** casa di commercio; — **office** amministrazione; **make it one's** — prendere per proprio conto; **-man** n uomo d'affari

businesslike a commerciale, pratico

bust n busto; — vi *(sl)* andare in rovina

bustle n trambusto, chiasso; **hustle and** — andirivieni m; — vi affaccendarsi

busy a occupato, affaccendato, impegnato; — **oneself** occuparsi

busybody n ficcanaso, intrigante m

but prep, conj&adv ma, però, salvo, eccetto; — **for** senza; **no one** — nessuno eccetto; **all** — quasi

butane n butano

butcher n macellaio, — **shop** macelleria; — vt massacrare

butchery n massacro

butler n maggiordomo

butt n *(humor)* zimbello; *(cigar)* mozzicone m, cicca *(coll)*; *(gun)* calcio; *(target)* bersaglio; — vt&i cozzare; — **in** *(coll)* intromettersi

butter n burro; — **dish** burriera; — **knife** coltello del burro; — vt imburrare; — **up** *(coll)* lusingare; **-ed** a imburrato

butterfly n farfalla

buttermilk n siero del latte

butterscotch n caramella al burro

buttocks npl natiche fpl

button n bottone m; — vt abbottonare; abbottonarsi

buttonhole n occhiello; — vt attaccare un bottone *(fig)*

buttress n pilastro

buxom a procace, grassoccio

buy n compra; **a good** — un buon acquisto

buyer n compratore m, compratrice f

buy vt comprare, acquistare; — **off** corrompere; — **up** accaparrare; — vi fare compere

buzz n ronzio; — vi ronzare; — vt sussurrare; *(avi)* ronzare

buzzard *n* bozzagro
buzzer *n* cicalino
by *prep (according to)* secondo; *(near)* presso, vicino a; *(per)* da, per; *(time)* non più tardi di, entro; — *adv* vicino, accanto, in disparte; — **air** per via aerea; — **all means** a tutti i costi; — **and** — prossimamente, fra poco, — **and large** comunque; — **your leave** a tuo beneplacito; — **the way** a proposito;

— **train** col treno
bygone *a* passato; — *n* cosa passata
bylaw *n* statuto, regolamento
bypass *n* circonvallazione, strada di deviazione; — *vt* deviare
by-product *n* sottoprodotto
bystander *n* astante, spettatore *m*
byway *n* disvio
byword *n* proverbio; *(ridicule)* oggetto di derisione

C

cab *n* tassì *m;* **–stand** *n* stazione di vetture
cabal *n* cabala; — *vi* intrigare, complottare
cabaret *n* ritrovo notturno, tabarin *m*
cabbage *n* cavolo
cabin *n* cabina; — **steward** cameriere di bordo
cabinet *n (cupboard)* armadio; *(curio)* stipo; *(pol)* consiglio dei ministri; **–maker** *n* ebanista *m;* **–work** *n* ebanisteria
cable *n* cablogramma *m; (elec)* filo elettrico, cavo; *(rope)* corda; *(wire)* cavo metallico; — **railway** funivia, funicolare; — *vt* telegrafare; *(rope)* legare con corda; — *vi* mandare un cablogramma
cabman *n* vetturino, fiaccheraio
caboose *n (naut)* cucina, cambusa
cackle *n* chiacchierio; *(hen)* chioccolio; — *vt&i* chiacchierare, chioccolare, chiocciare
cacophony *n* cacofonia
cactus *n* agave *f,* cacto
cad *n* mascalzone *m*
cadaver *n* cadavere *m;* **–ous** *a* cadaverico
caddy *n (golf)* portabastoni *m; (tea)* scatola da tè
cadence *n* cadenza
cadenza *n* cadenza
cadet *n* cadetto
café *n* caffè, bar *m;* — **keeper** barista *m*
cafeteria *n* tavola calda, caffè, pasticceria
cage *n* gabbia; — *vt* mettere in gabbia
cagey *a (sl)* astuto
caisson *n (arch)* cassone *m*
cajole *vt* accarezzare, adulare; — *vi* fare carezze, fare adulazioni
cake *n* dolce *m; (little)* pasticcino; *(manylayered)* torta; *(soap)* saponetta; — *vt (coagulate)* far quagliare; *(harden)* fare indurire; — *vi* quagliarsi; indurirsi
calamity *n* calamità
calcification *n* calcificazione
calcify *vt* calcificare; — *vi* calcificarsi

calcimine *n* tinta a calce
calcium *n* calcio
calculable *a* calcolabile
calculate *vt* calcolare; — *vi* fare calcoli; *(rely on)* contare su
calculating *a* calcolatore; — **machine** macchina calcolatrice
calculation *n* calcolo, previsione
calculus *n* calcolo
calendar *n* calendario
calf *n* vitello; *(leg)* polpaccio
caliber *n* calibro
calibrate *vt* calibrare
calibration *n* calibrazione
californium *n (chem)* californio
calipers *npl* compassi *mpl*
call *n (appeal)* appello; *(request)* invito; *(social)* visita; *(sound)* voce; *(summons)* chiamata; **make a** — **on** visitare; **with-in** — a portata di voce; **–er** *n* visitatore *m,* visitatrice *f;* chiamatore *m,* chiamatrice *f;* **–ing** *n* chiamata, appello; *(work)* professione, vocazione
call *vt&i* chiamare; — **away** attirare; — **back** richiamare; — **down** *(sl)* rimarcare; — **for** esigere; — **forth** designare; — **names** vituperare; — **off** distrarre; — **to mind** ricordarsi; — **to order** richiamare all'ordine; — **the roll** fare l'appello; — **together** riunire; — **up** evocare; *(phone)* telefonare
callous *a* duro, calloso, insensibile; — *vt* incallire; — *vi* incallirsi
callow *a* implume
callus, callous *n* callo
calm *n* calma, tranquillità; — *a* calmo; — *vi* calmarsi; — **down** ammansire, tranquillizzarsi; **become** — calmarsi
calorie *n* caloria
calumny *n* calunnia
calypso *a* calipso
calyx *n* calice *m*
cam *n (mech)* camma
camel *n* cammello; **—'s hair** *(cloth)* pelo di cammello
cameo *n* cammeo

camera *n* macchina fotografica; *(movie)* macchina cinematografica da presa
camerman *n* cineoperatore *m*
camouflage *n* mimetizzazione; — *vt* mascherare, camuffare
camp *n* campo, accampamento; **break** — levare il campo; **–ground** area per campeggio; — *vi* campeggiare, far campeggio; **accamparsi**
campaign *n* campagna; — *vi* fare una campagna
camphor *n* canfora
campus *n* area scolastica
can *n* latta; *(tiny)* barattolo; — **opener** apriscatole *m;* — *vt* inscatolare, inlattare, mettere in conserva; *(com)* mettere in latta; *(dismiss, sl)* dimettere; — *vi* *(able)* potere, sapere
Canadian *a&n* canadese
canal *n* canale *m*
canary *n* canarino
cancel *vt* annullare, cancellare; **–ed** *a* cancellato, annullato
cancellation *n* annullamento, cancellazione
cancer *n* cancro; **–ous** *a* canceroso, cancrenoso
candid *a* sincero, franco; **–ly** *adv* candidamente
candidate *n* candidato, aspirante *m*
candied *a* candito
candle *n* candela; *(church)* cero; **–light** *n* luce di candela; **–stick** *n* candeliere *m;* **–wick** *n* lucignolo per candele
candor *n* candore, ingenuità
candy *n* dolci, dolciumi, zuccherini *mpl;* — **store** negozio di dolci, pasticceria; — *vt* candire
cane *n* canna; bastone *m;* — *(or* **caned) furniture** mobili di vimini *(or* di canna*);* **sugar** — canna da zucchero
canine *a* canino
canister *n* scatola di latta
canker *n* cancro
canned *a* inscatolato, inlattato; *(mus)* inciso in dischi; *(sl)* dimesso
cannery *n* fabbrica di conserve
cannibal *n* cannibale *m;* **–ism** *n* cannibalismo
cannon *n* cannone *m*
canny *a* abile, prudente
canoe *n* canoa, canotto, sandalino; — *vi* remare in canoa
canon *n* canone *m; (mus)* fuga; — **law** diritto canonico
canonize *vt* canonizzare
canopy *n* baldacchino, tenda
cant *n* ipocrisia, affettazione
cantaloupe *n* melone *m*
cantankerous *a* sgradevole, litigioso

cantata *n* cantata
canteen *n* *(container)* borraccia; *(mil)* casa del soldato, spaccio
canter *n* piccolo galoppo; — *vt&i* andare al piccolo galoppo
cantor *n* cantore *m*
canvas *n* canovaccio; *(cloth)* tela
canvass *vt* sollecitare; *(examine)* vagliare; — *vi* sollecitare voti; **–er** *n* propagandista; *(com)* piazzista; *(solicitation)* sollecitatore *m; (pol)* agente elettorale
canyon *n* vallone profondo, burrone *m*
cap *n* berretto; *(lid)* coperchio; *(mech)* tappo; — *vt* *(cover)* coprire, *(finish)* completare; **to** — **it all** per rendere la cosa completa
capability *n* capacità
capable *a* capace, abile; in gamba *(coll)*
capacity *n* abilità, capacità, qualità; **seating** — capacità di luogo
cape *n* mantellina, mantella; *(geog)* capo
caper *n* capriola, salto; *(bot)* cappero; — *vi* far capriole
capillary *n* vaso capillare; — *a* capillare; — **action** forza capillare
capital *a* capitale, importante, principale, maiuscolo; — **punishment** pena di morte, pena capitale; — *n (arch)* capitello; *(com)* capitale *m; (geog)* capitale *f; (print)* maiuscola; **provincial** — capoluogo di provincia
capitalist *n* capitalista *m&f*
capitalization *n* capitalizzazione
capitalize *vt* capitalizzare
capitol *n* Capitolio
capitulate *vi* capitolare
capitulation *n* capitolazione
capon *n* cappone *m*
caprice *n* capriccio
capricious *a* capriccioso
capsize *vt* capovolgere; — *vi* capovolgersi
capsule *n* capsula; *(aesp)* capsula, calotta
captain *n* capitano
caption *n* sottotitolo, didascalia
captivate *vt* *(charm)* sedurre; *(win)* conquistare, cattivare
captivating *a* seducente
captive *n&a* prigioniero, schiavo
captivity *n* cattività, schiavitù *f,* prigionia
capture *n* cattura, arresto; — *vt* catturare, impadronirsi di
car *n* automobile *f,* macchina *(coll); (*veicolo; *(rail)* vagone ferroviario; — **pool** intercambio di guida; **armored** — autoblinda; **baggage** — vagone bagagli; **dining** — vagone ristorante; **freight** —

vagone merci; **sleeping** — vagone letto; **smoking** — scompartimento fumatori; **side–** n motocarrozzino, sidecar m
carafe n caraffa
caramel n caramella; **–ize** vt&i candire, caramellare
carat n carato
caravan n carovana
caraway n carvi m, comino
carbolic acid n acido fenico
carbon n carbone m; — **paper** carta carbone
carbuncle n carbonchio; (med) foruncolo
carburetor n carburatore m
carcass n carcassa, carcame m
card n cartolina, carta; (catalog, index) schedario; (greeting) cartolina di auguri; — **game** giuoco di carte
cardboard n cartone m
cardiac a&n cardiaco
cardinal a cardinale, principale; (color) rosso vivo; — n cardinale m
cardiogram n cardiogramma
cardiograph n cardiografia
cardsharp n baro
care n attenzione; (nursing) cura; (worry) preoccupazione; **take** — **of** occuparsi di; (med) curare; — vi curarsi di, badare; — **about** interessarsi di; — **for** (like, love) voler bene a; **I don't** — Non m'importa; **What do I** —? Che m'importa?
careen vt carenare
career n carriera
carefree a spensierato
careful a accurato, attento; **Be** —! Attenzione!
careless a imprudente, negligente; **–ness** n negligenza, noncuranza
caress n carezza; — vt accarezzare
caret n segno di richiamo
caretaker n custode m, portinaio
careworn a preoccupato
carfare n prezzo della corsa
cargo n carico
caricature n caricatura; — vt mettere in caricatura, caricaturare
caries npl carie f
carillon n cariglione m, carillon m
carload n carico, limite di carico; — **lot** (com) lotto di carico, unità di carico
carnage n strage f, carneficina
carnal a carnale
carnation n garofano
carnival n carnevale m, fiera
carnivorous a carnivoro
carol n canto, canzone f
carouse vi gozzovigliare
carousel n carosello

carp n (fish) carpio; — vi (blame) censurare; (quibble) cavillare
carpenter n falegname m, carpentiere m
carpentry n falegnameria
carpet n tappeto; — **sweeper** scopa automatica, macchina spazzatrice; **on the** — (sl) sul tappeto; **–ing** n materiale per tappeti; — vt tappetare, coprire con tappeto
carport n cappotta
carriage n carrozza, carrozzella; (behavior) portamento
carrier n portatore, vettore m; (aircraft) nave portaerei; (luggage) portabagaglio; (pigeon) piccione viaggiatore
carrion n carogna
carrot n carota
carry vi portare, trasportare; — **away** portar via; — **forward** riportare; — **off** portar via, asportare; — **on** continuare; spingere; — **out** (accomplish) realizzare; (complete) portare a termine; (execute) eseguire; (move) portare fuori; — **over** trasportare
cart n carretto; **–load** n carrettata; — vt trasportare
cartage n carreggio, trasporto
cartel n cartello
cartilage n cartilagine f
cartographer n cartografo
cartography n cartografia
carton n scatola di cartone; — **of cigarettes** stecca di sigarette
cartoon n caricatura; vignetta; **–ist** n caricaturista; **animated** — cartone animato
cartridge n cartuccia; — **belt** cartucciera; (mil) giberna; — **clip** bossolo di cartuccia
cartwheel n salto obliquo
carve vt scolpire, intagliare; (food) trinciare; decorare con figure intagliate
carver n intagliatore m, (food) trinciante m
carving n intaglio, scultura; — **knife** trinciante m
casaba n melone d'inverno
cascade n cascata; — vi cadere in cascata
case n cassetta; (chance) caso; (container) astuccio; (gram) caso; **just in** — nel caso che; **–ment** n finestra a battenti
cash n contante m; — **on delivery, C.O.D.** pagamento alla consegna; — **register** registratore di cassa; **hard** — contanti; **pay** — pagare in contanti; — vt pagare; incassare
cashbook n libro di cassa
cashbox n scrigno
cashew (nut) n anacardo

cashier n cassiere m; — vt destituire

cashmere n casimiro

casing n (cover) copertura; (frame) telaio; (packing) incassamento

cask n botte f, fusto, barile m

casket n bara; cofanetto, scrigno

casserole n casseruola

cassock n tonaca, sottana

cast vt (metal) fondere; (show) dare le parti; (throw) gettare; — **about for** considerare; cercare; — **off** (discard) scartare, rigettare; (naut) mollare gli ormeggi; — **a ballot** votare; — n (eye) leggero strabismo; (plaster) calco; (theat) complesso

castanets npl nacchere fpl

castaway n naufrago

caste n casta

caster n gettatore m; (foundry) fonditore m; (furniture) rotella

castigate vt castigare, punire, correggere

casting n (sport) lancio

cast iron ghisa

castle n castello, palazzo; fortezza

castoff n (discard) scarto; (jettison) gettito

castor oil olio di ricino

castrate vt castrare

casual a accidentale, casuale, fortuito; (nonchalant) indifferente, disinvolto; — **clothes** vestito da casa; **-ty** n (mishap) accidente; (victim) vittima

cat n gatto; — **nap** pisolino; **let the** — **out of the bag** (fig) svelare un segreto; **be a —'s paw** fare la testa di ferro (fig)

catabolism n catabolismo

cataclysm n cataclisma; **-ic** a disastroso

catafalque n catafalco

catalog n catalogo; — vt catalogare

catalyst n catalizzatore m

catapult n catapulta; — vt catapultare

cataract n cascata; (med) cataratta

catarrh n catarro

catastrophe n catastrofe f

catastrophic a catastrofico

catcall n miagolio

catch vt (grab) afferrare, prendere; (nab) acchiappare; — vi afferrarsi; — **a glimpse of** intravedere; — **cold** prendere un raffreddore; — **fire** incendiarsi; — **the train** prendere il treno

catch n (arrest) cattura; (door) anelli di porta; (fish) pesca; (jewelry) fermaglio; (window) gancio; — **basin** marginatore m; **-word** n grido popolare, slogan m

catching a contagioso

catchy a (attractive) attraente; (deceitful) ingannevole; (mus) orecchiabile

catechism n catechismo

categorical a categorico

category n categoria

cater vt provvedere; **-er** n provveditore, fornitore m

caterpillar n bruco; (mech) trattore a cingoli

caterwaul vi miagolare; — n miagolio

catfish n pesce gatto

catgut n minugia

cathartic a&n catartico

cathedral n cattedrale f

catheter n catetere m

cathode n catodo; **-ray tube** lampada a raggi catodici

catholic a cattolico

Catholicism n Cattolicismo, Cattolicesimo

catnip n erba dei gatti

catsup n salsa di pomodori

cattiness n felinità

cattle n bestiame m; — **ranch** fattoria di allevamento bovino; **-man** n allevatore di bovini

catty a dispettoso

Caucasian n&a caucasico

caucus n comitato elettorale

caudal a caudale

cauliflower n cavolfiore m

causative a causativo

cause n causa, motivo; **make common —** **with** far causa comune con; — vt causare

causeway n marciapiedi m

caustic a caustico; — n (chem) caustico

cauterize vt cauterizzare

caution n prudenza; cautela; — vt prevenire

cautious a cauto, prudente

cavalcade n cavalcata

cavalier n cavaliere m

cavalry n cavalleria

cave n grotta, caverna; — **man** uomo delle caverne, troglodita m; — vt scavare; — vi (fail) fallire; (sag) afflosciarsi; — **in** scassare; (coll) cedere

cavern n caverna

caviar n caviale m

cavil n cavillo; — vi cavillare

cavity n buco; (tooth) carie f

caw n gracchiamento; — vi gracchiare

cayenne n pepe di Caienna

cease vt&i cessare; (give up) smettere; (interrupt) interrompere; **-less** a incessante

cease-fire n tregua

cedar n cedro

cede vt cedere

cedilla n cediglia

ceiling n soffitto; (avi) massima alti-

tudine
celebrant *n (eccl)* celebrante *m*
celebrate *vt&i* festeggiare, celebrare, commemorare
celebrated *a* celebre, famoso
celebration *n* celebrazione, festa
celebrity *n* celebrità, persona celebre
celery *n* sedano
celestial *a* celeste, divino
celestial mechanics meccanica celeste
celibacy *n* celibato
celibate *n&a* celibe *m*
cell *n* cella; *(anat)* cellula; *(elec)* pila; *(prison)* cella; **-ular** *a* cellulare
cellar *n* cantina
cellist *n* violoncellista *m&f*
cello *n* violoncello
cellophane *n* cellofane *f*
celluloid *n* celluloide *f*
cellulose *n* cellulosa
cement *n* cemento, mastice *m*; *(adhesive)* adesivo; *(dent)* resina indiana; — cementare, collegare con cemento; attacare; *(dent)* otturare; *(stick)* incollare; — *vi* cementarsi
cemetery *n* cimitero, camposanto
censer *n* incensiere *m*, turibolo
censor *n* censore *m*; — *vt* censurare; **-ship** *n* censura
censure *n* censura; *(reproof)* rimprovero; — *vt* censurare
census *n* censimento
cent *n* centesimo, cento
centenary *n&a* centenario
centennial *a* secolare; — *n* centenario
center *n* centro; — **of attraction** centro d'attrazione; — *vt* centrare; — *vi* essere in centro
centigrade *a* centigrado
centigram *n* centigrammo
centimeter *n* centimetro
centipede *n* millepiedi *m*
central *a* centrale; **-ize** *vt* centralizzare
Central America America Centrale
centralization *n* centralizazzione
centrifugal *a* centrifugo
centripetal *a* centripeto
century *n* secolo
ceramic *a* ceramico; **-s** *npl* ceramica
cereal *n* cereale *m*
cerebellum *n* cervelletto
cerebral *a* cerebrale; — **palsy** paralisi cerebrale
cerebrum *n* cervello, cerebro
ceremonial *a&n* rituale, cerimoniale *m*
ceremonious *a* cerimonioso; **-ly** *adv* cerimoniosamente
ceremony *n* rito, cerimonia, solennità; **without** — senza complimenti

cerise *n* color ciliegia; — *a* di color ciliegia
certain *a* certo, sicuro; — **man** un tale; **for** — di sicuro, in forma certa
certainly *adv* sicuro, certo, certamente; senz'altro, senza dubbio
certainty *n* certezza, sicurezza; **with** — con sicurezza
certificate *n* certificato; *(com)* titolo
certified *a* certificato; — **check** assegno garantito dalla banca; — **milk** latte certificato; — **public accountant, C.P.A.** ragioniere abilitato
certify *vt* certificare, legalizzare; — **to** garantire
certitude *n* certezza
cervical *a* cervicale
cessation *n* cessazione
cesspool *n* pozzo nero
chafe *vt* irritare; scaldare *(fig)*
chaff *n (husk)* loglio; *(ridicule)* beffa; — *vt&i* beffare
chafing dish scaldavivande *m*
chagrin *n* cruccio, mortificazione
chain *n* catena; — **reaction** reazione a catena; — **store** succursale *f*; — **of events** serie d'eventi
chair *n* sedia; *(deck)* sedia a sdraio; *(folding)* sedia pieghevole; *(professorial)* cattedra; *(wheel)* sedia con rotelle; **take the** — insediarsi; assumere la presidenza
chairman *n* presidente *m*; **-ship** *n* presidenza
chalice *n* calice *m*
chalk *n* gesso; — *vt* scrivere col gesso; — **up** sommare a conto di qualcuno; **-y** *a* calcareo, gessoso
challenge *n* sfida; *(mil)* chi va là; *(law)* ricusazione; — *vt* sfidare, provocare; — **attention** chiamare l'attenzione
challenger *n* sfidante *m*, provocatore *m*, aggressore *m*
chamber *n* camera; *(hall)* aula; *(room)* stanza, sala; **air** — camera d'aria; — **music** musica da camera
chambermaid *n (hotel)* cameriera
Chamber of Comerce Camera di Commercio
chamois *n* camoscio
champ *vt* mordere, masticare; — *n (sl)* campione *m*
champagne *n* spumante *m*, sciampagna *m*
champion *n* campione *m*; **-ship** *n* campionato
chance *n* combinazione, imprevisto; ventura; caso; **by** — per caso, per combinazione; — *a* fortuito, accidentale; — *vi* accadere per caso; — *vt (coll)* tentare, avventurare; — **on** imbattersi con
chancellor *n* cancelliere *m*

chancery n cancelleria
chandelier n lampadario
change vt cambiare, scambiare; cambiarsi; — **hands** cambiare di proprietario; — **one's mind** cambiare idea
change n cambio; (money) piccolo cambio; — **of heart** conversione; — **of life** cambio di vita; — **of venue** cambio di giurisdizione; **make a** — cambiare, fare un cambiamento
changeable a cambiabile, variabile, mutabile
changeless a immutabile, costante
changeover n cambio
channel n canale m, stretto; (rad, TV) stazione; (river) canale m; **The English C-La Manica**; — vt scannellare, scavare un canale
chant n canto; — vt&i cantare; **-er** n cantore m
chaos n caos m
chaotic a caotico
chap vt&i crepare; — n uomo, giovanotto
chapel n cappella
chaperon n istitutrice f, aia; — vt accompagnare
chaplain n cappellano
chapter n capitolo
char vt carbonizzare; — vi carbonizzarsi
character n carattere m, temperamento; (print) carattere m; (theat) personaggio
characteristic a caratteristico; — n caratteristica
characterization n caratterizzazione
characterize vt caratterizzare
charcoal n carbone di legna, carbonella; — **burner** carbonaio
charge n carica; (care) custodia; (cost) prezzo, costo; (law) accusa; — **account** conto; **be in** — essere in carico di; **free of** — gratis; **in** — **of** in custodia di; — vt caricare, accusare; — vi (mil) caricare, andare alla carica; — **to account** mettere in conto
chargeable a accusabile, imponibile, imputabile
charger n (horse) destriero da carica; (elec) carica-batterie
chariot n carro; **-eer** n carrista m, cocchiere m
charitable a caritatevole
charity n carità, bontà; **out of** — a beneficienza
charlatan n ciarlatano
charm n fascino; (luck) portafortuna m, amuleto; — vt incantare, affascinare; **-ing** a affascinante, grazioso, delizioso
chart n carta; (med) storia clinica; —

vt fare un piano, tracciare
charter n carta, brevetto; — **member** socio fondatore; — vt (com) concedere una licenza; (hire) noleggiare
chase vt cacciare, dare la caccia; — n caccia, inseguimento; **give** — dare la caccia a
chasm n baratro, abisso, voragine f
chassis n telaio
chaste a casto, puro
chasten vt castigare, punire
chastise vt castigare, punire
chastisement n castigo
chastity n castità
chasuble n pianeta
chat vi chiacchierare, far due chiacchiere; — n chiacchiera
chattel n mobile m; — **mortgage** ipoteca mobiliare
chatter n chiacchiera; **-box** n chiacchierone m; — vi chiacchierare, ciarlare
chattering n ciarla, chiacchiera; — a ciarliero
chatty a ciarliero, loquace
cheap a economico; a buon mercato
cheapen vt deprezzare, svilire; (price) diminuire di prezzo
cheapness n buon mercato
cheat vt ingannare; frodare; **-er** n imbroglione, truffatore m; **-ing** n inganno, imbroglio
check vt verificare, controllare; (stop) fermare, arrestare; (store) lasciare in deposito; — vi provare di aver ragione, — **in** (register) registrarsi; — **out** dimettersi
check n (baggage) scontrino bagagli; (bank) assegno; (blank) assegno in bianco; (cashier's) assegno di cassa; (mark) segno; (obstacle) ostacolo; (traveler's) assegno per viaggiatore; — **list** lista di verifica; **-book** n libretto d'assegni; **-er** n controllore m; **-up** n esame generale, controllo, verifica; **-ed** a a quadretti
checkered a quadrettato; — **career** vita avventurosa
checkerboard n scacchiera
checkers npl (game) scacchi mpl
checkmate n scacco matto; — vt dare scacco matto
checkroom n vestiario, guardaroba; (rail) deposito bagagli
cheek n guancia; **-y** a (coll) sfacciato
cheekbone n zigomo
cheep n pigolio; — vi pigolare
cheer n allegria, gioia; (hurrah) grido di gioia; **-less** a triste, malinconico; **-y** a gioioso, contento; — vt rallegrare, consolare, incoraggiare; — **up** gioi-

re, animarsi
cheerful *a* allegro; **–ly** *adv* graziosamente, gaiamente; **–ness** *n* vivacità
cheese *n* cacio, formaggio
chef *n* capo cuoco
chemical *a* chimico; — **engineering** ingegneria chimica; — *n* prodotto chimico
chemist *n* chimico; **–ry** *n* chimica
cherish *vt* accarezzare, nutrire
cherry *n&a* ciliegia; — **tree** ciliegio
cherub *n* cherubino, cherubo; **–ic** *a* cherubico
chess *n* scacchi; **–board** *n* scacchiera; **–men** *npl* pedine degli scacchi
chest *n* (*anat*) petto, torace *m*; (*container*) cassa, cassone *m*; (*furniture*) comò, cassetone *m*
chestnut *n* marrone *m*, castagna; — **tree** castagno; — *a* (*color*) castano, marrone, castagno
chevalier *n* cavaliere *m*
chevron *n* (*mil*) gallone *m*
chew *vt* masticare
chewing gum gomma da masticare, cicla
chiaroscuro *n* (*arts*) chiaroscuro
chic *a* scic
chicanery *n* intrigo; (*cavil*) sofisticheria
chicken *n* pollo; **–pox** *n* varicella, morbiglione *m*
chicken-hearted *a* timido, pauroso
chicory *n* cicoria
chide *vi* sgridare, rimproverare
chief *n* capo; — *a* principale; — **justice** giudice supremo; — **of staff** capo reparto; **–ly** *adv* sopratutto
chieftain *n* capo, capobanda; condottiero
chiffon *n* sciffon *m*
chilblains *npl* geloni *mpl*
child *n* bambino, bambina, fanciulla, fanciullo; bimbo, bimba; creatura; **with** — incinta; **–birth** *n* parto; **–hood** *n* fanciullezza; (*infancy*) infanzia; **–ish** *a* puerile, infantile; **–less** *a* senza figli; **–like** *a* bambinesco
children *npl* bambini, fanciulli, figli *mpl*
Chile Cile; **–an** *n&a* cileno
chili *n* peperone, peperosso; — **sauce** salsa pepata
chill *n* brivido, raffreddore *m*; — *a* freddo, glaciale; **–y** *a* freddo; (*people*) freddoloso
chill *vt* raffreddare; — *vi* raffreddarsi
chime *n* (*bell*) cariglione *m*; (*harmony*) concerto; (*mus*) accordo; — *vt* far risuonare; — *vi* scampanare; risuonare; — **in with** prender parte al concerto; accordarsi con
chimerical *a* chimerico
chimney *n* camino, fumaiolo

chiming *a* scampanante; — *n* scampanio
chimpanzee *n* scimpanzè
chin *n* mento
china *n* porcellana; **–ware** *n* porcellana
chinchilla *n* cinciglia
Chinese *n&a* cinese *m&f*
chink *n* screziatura, fessura
chip *n* frammento, scheggia; — *vt* scheggiare, tagliuzzare; — *vi* scheggiarsi, — **in** (*coll*) pagare la propria quota; **have a — on one's shoulder** (*coll*) essere aggressivo
chipmunk *n* scoiattolo striato
chipper *a* (*coll*) vivace
chiropractor *n* ortopedico
chirp *vi* cinguettare, trillare; — *n* cinguettio
chisel *n* scalpello, cesello; — *vt* cesellare; (*coll*) turlupinare; **–ed** *a* cesellato
chivalrous *a* cavalleresco, cortese
chivalry *n* cavalleria
chives *npl* cipollina verde
chloremia *n* clorimia
chloride *n* cloruro
chlorinate *vt* clorurare
chlorination *n* clorurazione
chlorine *n* cloro
chloroform *n* cloroformio
chlorophyll *n* clorofilla
chock-full *a* colmo, completamente pieno
chocolate *n* cioccolata, cioccolatino; — *a* di cioccolata
choice *n* scelta; — *a* scelto, raro, squisito
choir *n* coro
choke *vt* strangolare, soffocare; — *vi* (*block*) ingombrarsi, ostruirsi; — **back** ricacciar dentro; — **down** ringoiare; — **off** soffocare; — **up** ingorgare; — *n* (*auto*) diffusore *m*, valvola dell'aria; (*mech*) regolatore *m*
choler *n* collera; **–ic** *a* collerico
cholera *n* colera
cholesterol *n* colesterina
choose *vt* (*desire*) preferire, decidere; (*select*) scegliere; — *vi* preferirsi, volere, decidersi a
choosy *a* (*coll*) sofistico (*coll*)
chop *vt* tritare, tagliuzzare; (*meat*) sminuzzare; — *n* taglio; (*meat*) costoletta, cotoletta; **–s** *npl* (*jaws*) mascelle *fpl*; **lick one's –s** leccarsi le labbra
chopped *a* tagliato, tritato
choppy *a* screpolato, increspato
choral *a* corale
chord *n* corda; (*mus*) accordo
chore *n* lavoro, faccenda
choreography *n* coreografia
chorister *n* corista *m&f*
chortle *n* sogghigno; — *vt&i* ridacchiare

chorus *n (people)* coro; *(song)* ritornello; — **girl** ballerina; — *vt* far coro a
chosen *a* scelto, preferito
Christ *n* Cristo
christen *vt* battezzare; *(coll)* usare per la prima volta; **–ing** *n* battesimo
Christian *n&a* cristiano; — **name** nome di battesimo
Christianity *n* cristianità
Christmas *n* Natale *m*; **Merry** — Buon Natale
chrome *n* cromo
chrome-plated *a* cromato
chromium *n* cromio
chromogen *n* cromogeno
chromosome *n* cromosomo
chromosphere *n* (ast) cromosfera
chronic *a* cronico
chronicle *n* cronaca
chronological *a* cronologico
chronology *n* cronologia
chrysalis *n* crisalide *f*
chrysanthemum *n* crisantemo
chubby *a* paffuto, grassoccio
chuck *vt (throw)* buttare, gettare; — **under the chin** dare un colpetto sotto il mento; — **out** buttare fuori; — *n (mech)* mandrino
chuckle *vi* ridacchiare; ridere sotto i baffi; — *n* sogghigno, riso represso
chug *n (motor)* rumore d'esplosione; — *vi* fare rumore di esplosione; — **along** guidare provocando esplosioni
chum *n (coll)* amico intimo, compagno; — *vi (coll)* amicarsi
chump *n (coll)* scemo
chunk *n* ceppo; **–y** *a* tozzo
church *n* chiesa, tempio; — **music** musica sacra; — **service** ufficio divino
churlish *a* grossolano
churn *n* zangola; — *vt&i* zangolare; *(froth)* spumeggiare
ᵇute *n* canale di scolo
cider *n* sidro
cigar *n* sigaro; — **store** rivendita di tabacchi; tabaccheria; — **holder** bocchino
cigarette *n* sigaretta; — **butt** cicca, mozzicone; — **case** portasigarette *m*; — **holder** bocchino; — **lighter** accendisigari *m*; **filter** — sigaretta con filtro
cilia *npl* ciglia *fpl*
cinch *n* sottopancia, cigna; *(coll)* certezza; — *vt* assicurare con cigna
cincture *n* cintura
cinder *n* cenere, carbon fossile
cinemascope *n* cinemascopio
cinnamon *n* cannella
cipher *n* cifra *m*, zero
circle *n* circolo; *(astr)* orbita; **dress**

— **prima galleria**; — *vt* circondare, accerchiare; — *vi* formare circolo
circuit *n* circuito; **short** — corto circuito
circuitous *a* tortuoso, indiretto
circular *a&n* circolare *m*
circulate *vt* mettere in circolazione
circulating *a* circolante; — **library** biblioteca circolante
circulation *n* circolazione; *(newspaper)* tiratura
circumcise *vt* circoncidere
circumference *n* circonferenza
circumflex *a* circonflesso
circumlocution *n* circonlocuzione
circumnavigate *vt* circumnavigare
circumscribe *vt* circoscrivere
circumspect *a* circospetto; **–ive** *a* circospettivo
circumspection *n* circospezione
circumstance *n* circostanza, condizione; stato, incidente *m*
circumstances *npl* circostanze *fpl*; **under no** — sotto nessun concetto; in nessun caso; **under the** — nelle circostanze
circumstantial *a* circostanziale; — **evidence** evidenza circostanziale
circumstantiate *vt* dettagliare
circumvent *vt* circonvenire, circuire
circus *n* circo equestre
cirrhosis *n* cirrosi *f*
cirrus *a (ast)* cirro; — **cloud** cirro
cistern *n* cisterna
citadel *n* cittadella
citation *n* citazione
cite *vt* citare; allegare testimonianze
citified *a* cittadinizzato
citizen *n* cittadino; **–ship** *n* cittadinanza
citric acid acido citrico
citron *n* cedro
citrus *a* citro; — **fruit** agrume *m*; — **grove** agrumeto
city *n* città; **–hall** municipio; — **planning** piano regolatore; — **editor** redattore del notiziario locale
civic *a* civico, **–s** *npl* diritto civile
civil *a* civile; *(manner)* cortese, urbano; — **engineer** ingegnere civile; — **ser vice** amministrazione civile
civilian *n* borghese *m*
civilization *n* civiltà, civilizzazione
civility *n* cortesia, gentilezza
civilize *vt* civilizzare
civilized *a* civile
clabber *n* quaglio; — *vi* quagliare
clack *vi* scoppiettare, scoccare; — *n* scoppiettamento
clad *a* vestito; *(covered)* coperto
claim *vt* pretendere, reclamare; — *n* pretesa, reclamo

claimant *n* reclamante *m*, pretendente *m*

clairvoyance *n* chiaroveggenza

clairvoyant *a&n* chiaroveggente *m*

clam *n* pettine *m*, vongola; *(person, coll)* chiuso in sè *(fig);* — **up** *(coll)* rinchiudersi in sè

clamber *vi* arrampicarsi

clammy *a* viscido, colloso, *(humid)* umidiccio

clamor *n* clamore *m;* –**ous** *a* chiassoso

clamp *n* rampone *m*, grappa; *(vise)* morsa; — *vt* stringere con la morsa; — **down** *(coll)* irrigidirsi

clan *n* clan *m*; tribù *f;* *(faction)* fazione

clandestine *a* clandestino

clang, clank *vt&i* risuonare; — *n* clangore *m*

clannish *a* tradizionalista; strettamente unito alla famiglia

clap *vi* applaudire, battere le mani; — *vt* battere; *(fling)* gettare, lanciare; — *n (blow)* colpo; *(hands)* battimano; *(thunder)* scoppio

clapboard *n* assicella per rivestimento; — *a* di assicella per rivestimento

clapping *n* applauso, battimano

claptrap *n* sciocchezza, — *a* sciocco

claque *n* clac *f;* gente pagata per applaudire

claret *n* vino di Borgogna; chiaretto

clarify *vt&i* chiarire, chiarificare

clarinet *n* clarinetto

clarity *n* splendore *m*, chiarezza

clash *vi (collide)* urtarsi, cozzare; *(oppose)* opporsi, contrastare; — *vt* far produrre rumore

clash *n* urto, scontro, contrasto

clasp *n* fermaglio; — *vt* affibbiare, stringere, allacciare

class *n* classe *f;* lezione *f;* –**mate** *n* compagno di scuola; –**room** *n* aula; — **consciousness** coscienza di classe; — *vt* classificare

classic, –al *n&a* classico

classification *n* classificazione

classified *a* classificato; *(confidential)* riservato, segreto

classify *vt* classificare

clatter *n* rumore *m;* fracasso; — *vi* far rumore; — *vt* far fare rumore

clause *n* articolo; *(gram)* clausola; *(law)* proposizione

claustrophobia *n* claustrofobia

clavicle *n* clavicola

claw *n* artiglio; *(hammer)* taglio; *(shellfish)* pinza; — *vt* graffiare, lacerare

clay *n* creta, argilla; — **pigeon** piattello per tiro

clean *a* pulito, –**liness** *n* pulizia, nitidezza; –**ly** *adv* pulitamente

clean *vt* pulire, nettare; — **up** far pulizia; –**ing** *n* pulizia, pulitura

clean-cut *a* delineato, ben delineato

cleaner *n* nettatore, pulitore *m*

cleanse *vt* nettare, pulire

cleanser *n* nettatore, pulitore *m*

clean-shaven *a* rapato a zero

clear *a* chiaro, netto; — **complexion** bella carnagione; **be in the** — essere in regola; **keep** — **of** tenersi lontano da; –**ly** *adv* chiaramente; –**ness** *n* chiarezza

clear *vt* chiarire, chiarificare; — *vi* rischiararsi, schiarirsi; *(weather)* rasserenarsi, rimettersi; — **away** dissipare, svanire; — **the table** sgombrare; — **up** rischiararsi

clear– *(in comp)* —**cut** *a* tagliato nettamente, positivo; —**headed** *a* dalla mente chiara; —**sighted** *a* chiaroveggente

clearance *n (sale)* liquidazione; *(space)* spazio libero

clearing *n* chiarimento; *(debt)* regolamento dei conti; *(explanation)* schiarimento; *(land)* sgombero, dissodamento; *(woods)* radura; — **house** *(com)* stanza di compensazione

clearness *n* chiarezza

cleat *n* gattello

cleavage *n* taglio, fessura

cleave *vi* aderire a, attaccarsi a; — *vt* fendere, spaccare

cleaver *n* scure *f*

clef *n* chiave *f*

cleft *n* fessura; — **palate** labbro leporino

clemency *n* clemenza, mitezza

clement *a* clemente

clench *vt* impugnare; *(teeth, fist)* stringere

clergy *n* clero; –**man** *n* ecclesiastico, pastore *m*; *(priest)* sacerdote *m*, prete *m*

cleric *n* chierico; –**al** *a* clericale –**al work** lavoro d'ufficio

clerk *n* impiegato d'ufficio, commesso di negozio; — *vi* fare l'impiegato d'ufficio

clever *a* abile, capace, scaltro; ingegnoso; –**ly** *adv* abilmente

cleverness *n* abilità, intelligenza, merito

click *n* tintinnio; — *vi* tintinnare; *(sl)* accordarsi

client *n* cliente *m*; –**ele** *n* clientela

cliff *n* scogliera

climactic *a* climatico

climate *n* clima *m*

climax *n* culmine *m*, punto culminante; — *vi* ascendere, culminare

climb *vt&i* montare; *(clamber)* arrampicarsi; *(scale)* scalare; — *n* ascensione; scalata; — **indicator** *(avi)* ascensimetro; **–er** n ascensionista m

clinch n stretta; (boxing) abbraccio; — vt impugnare, (boxing) stringere in pugno; — **a bargain** concludere un affare

clincher n rampone m, gancio

cling vi aderire, aggrapparsi; **–ing** a agganciato

clingy a tenace

clinic n clinica; — a clinico; **–al** a clinico

clink vt&i tintinnare; — **glasses** toccare; (toast) fare un brindisi a; — n tintinnio; (sl) carcere f

clinker n (coal) scoria

clip vt tagliare; (cut out) ritagliare; (cut short) tagliar corto; (shear) tosare; (words) storpiare le parole; — n gancio; (coll) colpo; (hair) tosatura, taglio di capelli; (paper) fermaglio; **go at a good** — camminare speditamente

clipper n macchinetta per tosure; (naut) veliero rapido

clippers npl (hair) tosatrice f

clipping n ritaglio di giornale

clique n cricca

cloak n cappotto; (mask) maschera; (pretext) pretesto; — vt (hide) celare; coprire con mantello

cloakroom n guardaroba

clobber vt (sl) bastonare

clock n pendola, orologio; (alarm) sveglia; (sock) ricamo; **–maker** n orologiaio; **–wise** a destrorso, da sinistra

clockwork n orologeria; **go like** — andare come un orologio

clod n massa; (sod) gleba

clodhopper n tanghero; **–s** npl scarponi mpl

clog n intoppo; (shoe) zoccolo; — vt impacciare, ostruire; — vi incagliarsi

cloister n chiostro; **–ed** a solitario; ritirato dal mondo

close vt chiudere; (end) finire; — **quarters** corpo a corpo; — **the ranks** serrare le file; — vi chiudersi; — a (airless) senz'aria; (compact) stretto, serrato; (nearby) vicino; (reserved) riservato; — **call** (coll) stretta scappatoia; — **friendship** amicizia stretta; — **shave** scampato liscio; — adv vicino; strettamente; — **by** vicino a

close- (in comp) **–mouthed** a reticente, incomunicativo; **–up** n fotografia di primo piano

closed a chiuso; — **circuit** circuito chiuso

closefisted a misero, avaro

closer a più vicino

closet n ripostiglio, armadio a muro; — vt chiudere nell'armadio

closing n chiusura, conclusione; — **of accounts** (com) chiusura dei conti

clot n coagulo; — vi coagularsi; — vt coagulare

cloth n stoffa, tessuto; — **binding** rilegatura in tela

clothe vt vestire, rivestire

clothes npl abiti mpl; **suit of** — abito completo; — **closet** guardaroba; armadio, guardaroba a muro; **–line** n corda per biancheria; **–pin** n moletta per la biancheria

clothier n (maker) fabbricante di tessuti; (seller) commerciante in tessuti

clothing n abiti mpl, vestiario

cloud n nuvola; **–burst** n acquazzone m; **be in the –s** essere fra le nuvole (coll); **–less** a sereno; **–y** a nuvoloso

cloud vt annuvolare; — vi rannuvolarsi

clove n chiodo di garofano

clover n trifoglio; **in** — nella bambagia (coll); **be in** — vivere agiatamente

cloverleaf n quadrifoglio

clown n pagliaccio, buffone m; (harlequin) arlecchino; — vi fare il pagliaccio

cloy vt saziare; — vi saziarsi

club n circolo; (card) fiore m; (weapon) mazza; — **car** vagone bar; — **sandwich** panino imbottito; — **steak** lombo di manzo

club vt bastonare; — vi riunirsi

clubfoot n piede storto

clubhouse circolo

cluck vi chiocciare

clue n gomitolo, filo

clump n blocco, massa; — vi camminare pesantemente; — vt ammassare

clumsiness n grossolanità; (weight) pesantezza

clumsy a goffo, maldestro

cluster n grappolo; mazzetto; — vt riunire, aggrappolare; — vi riunirsi, aggrappolarsi

clutch n presa; (auto) frizione; (mech) innesto; — **pedal** pedale di frizione; — vt stringere, afferrare; **throw in the** — (mech) ingranare

clutches npl grinfie fpl; **in the** — nelle grinfie

clutter n disordine m, confusione; — vt ingombrare

coach n (pupil's) ripetitore m; (sport) allenatore m; (teacher) istruttore m; (vehicle) vettura, carrozza; — vt addestrare, preparare, dar lezione di ripetizione; — vi scarrozzare; andare in carrozza

coachman n cocchiere m

coagulant n coagulante m

coagulate vt coagulare; — vi coagularsi

coagulation n coagulazione

coal n carbone m; — **mine** miniera di carbone; — **oil** petrolio, kerosina; — **pit** pozzo di carbone; — **tar** catrame di carbone; **bituminous** — carbone bituminoso; **hard** — carbone duro; **soft** — carbone dolce; **rake over the –s** rimproverare, ridicolizzare

coalesce *vi* unirsi, fondersi, coalizzarsi

coalition *n* coalizione

coarse *a* grossolano, volgare, ruvido; **–ly** *adv* grossolanamente; **–ness** *n* grossolanità

coarsen *vt* rendere grossolano; — *vi* arrozzire, diventare grossolano

coast *n* costa, litorale *m;* — **line** litorale; — **guard** guardacosta; **have a clear** — essere fuori pericolo; **–al** *a* costiero; — *vi* costeggiare

coaster *n (glass)* sottobicchiere *m; (naut)* nave costiera; — **brake** freno contro pedale

coat *n* soprabito, pastrano; *(jacket)* giacca; *(paint, varnish)* strato; **–ing** *n (cloth)* stoffa; *(film)* strato; *(paint)* mano *f;* — **of arms** cotta d'arme; scudo nobiliare; **–ed** *a* vestito, coperto; — *vt* rivestire

coatroom *n* guardaroba

coax *vt* pregare con lusinghe; persuadere con moine; — *vi* usare persuasione

coaxing *n* adulazione; **–ingly** *adv* carezzevolmente, adulatamente

coaxial *a* coassiale; — **cable** cavo coassiale

cob *n (corn)* pannocchia; *(swan)* cigno

cobalt *n* cobalto

cobble *vt* rammendare; *(shoes)* rattoppare

cobbler *n* ciabattino

cobra *n* cobra

cobweb *n* ragnatela

cocaine *n* cocaina

cock *n* gallo; *(gun)* cane *m; (mech)* ago; — **and bull story** fandonia; **–ade** *n* coccarda; **–roach** *n* scarafaggio; **–sure** *a* sicurissimo; **–y** *a (coll)* vanitoso; arrogante; — *vt* drizzare; — *vi* drizzarsi

cocked *a* drizzato; — **hat** cappello a due punte; **knock into a** — **hat** sconfiggere completamente

cockeyed *a* strabico; *(sl)* a sghembo; alla ventitrè *(coll)*

cockpit *n (avi)* carlinga, abitacolo

cocksure *a* sicurissimo

cocktail *n* cocktail *m;* — **shaker** shaker *m*, bottiglia da cocktail

cocoa *n* cacao; — **butter** burro di cacao

coconut *n* noce di cocco

cocoon *n* bozzolo

C.O.D. contro assegno, pagamento alla consegna

cod, –fish *n* merluzzo; **dried** — baccalà *m*

coda *n* codetta

coddle *vt* vezzeggiare; *(cooking)* cuocere lentamente

code *n* codice *m;* **secret** — cifrario; — *vt* cifrare

codex *n* manoscritto antico

codicil *n* codicillo

cod-liver oil olio di fegato di merluzzo

coeducation *n* coeducazione

coeducational *a* coeducazionale; — **school** scuola mista

coefficient *n* coefficiente *m*

coequal *a* eguale, coeguale

coerce *vt* forzare, costringere, obbligare

coexist *vi* coesistere; **–ence** *n* coesistenza

coffee *n* caffè *m;* — **bean** chicco di caffè; — **mill** macinino da caffè; — **plantation** piantagione di caffè; — **pot** caffettiera; — **shop** caffè, ristorante *m*

coffer *n* cofano, scrigno

coffin *n* bara, cassa da morto

cog *n* dente di ruota; — **railway** ferrovia a cremagliera; **–wheel** *n* ruota dentata, ingranaggio

cogent *a* evidente; urgente; *(strong)* forte, potente

cogitate *vi* cogitare, meditare

cognac *n* cognac *m*

cognate *a* parente, consanguineo

cognizance *n* cognizione

cognizant *a* competente, istruito

cognomen *n* cognome *m*

cohabit *vi* coabitare; **–ation** *n* coabitazione

cohere *vi* aderire a; *(agree)* concordare

coherence *n* coerenza

coherent *a* coerente

cohesion *n* aderenza, coesione

cohesive *a* coesivo

cohort *n* coorte *f*

coiffure *n* pettinatura

coil *vt* avvolgere, arrotolare; — *vi* piegarsi, avvolgersi; — *n* rotolo; *(elec)* bobina

coin *n* moneta; **–age** *n* conio; invenzione; — *vt* coniare, battere moneta; — **a word** inventare una parola

coincide *vi* coincidere

coincidence *n* combinazione, coincidenza, concordanza

coincident *a* coincidente; **–al** *a* coincidentale

coke *n (fuel)* coke *m*

colander *n* colatoio, colabrodo

cold *n* freddo, *(med)* raffreddore *m;* **take** — pigliare un raffreddore, raffreddarsi; — *a* freddo; **be** — *(person)* aver freddo; — **cream** *(cosmetic)* crema di bellezza; — **storage** conservazione a freddo; — **weather** tempo freddo; **–ness** n freddezza, freddo; **–ly** adv freddamente

cold– (in comp) **–blooded** a di sangue freddo, insensibile; **–wave** n (weather) ondata di freddo

colic n colica

coliseum n colosseo

colitis n colite f

collaborate vt&i collaborare

collaboration n collaborazione

collaborator n collaboratore m

collapse vi crollare, avere un collasso; — vt provocare collasso; — n crollo; sfacelo; (med) collasso, prostrazione; **nervous** — esaurimento nervoso

collapsible a pieghevole, ribaltabile

collar vt prendere per il collo; (fig) catturare

collar n collare m; (coat) bavero; (shirt) colletto; **–bone** n clavicola

collate vt collazionare

collateral n&a collaterale m

colleague n collega m&f

collect vi raccogliere, collezionare, riscuotere; (money) incassare; **–or** n collezionista m; (com) controllore m; (tax) esattore m

collective a collettivo; — **bargaining** contratto collettivo

collection n raccolta, collezione

collectivism n collettivismo

college n collegio; scuola superiore; università; facoltà di università; **electoral** — collegio elettorale

collegiate a collegiato

collide vi scontrarsi, urtarsi

collie n cane da pastore scozzese

collision n collisione, scontro, investimento, urto

collocate vt collocare

collocation n collocamento, collocazione

colloid n&a colloide m

colloquial a familiare; della lingua parlata; **–ism** n parola familiare; espressione familiare

colloquy n colloquio

collusion n collusione, connivenza, complicità

cologne n colonia (coll); **C–** Colonia

colon n (anat) colon m; (gram) due punti

colonel n colonnello

colonial a coloniale

colonist n colono

colonize vt colonizzare; — vi formare una colonia

colony n colonia

color n colore m, colorito; **change** — cambiar colore; **–less** a incolore, insulso; — vt colorare

coloration n colorazione

colorblindness n daltonismo

colored a colorato; — **people** npl gente di colore

coloring n colore m; colorito; (skin) carnagione f

colossal a colossale

colt n puledro

columbine n aquilegia

column n colonna; (newspaper) rubrica, colonna di giornale

coma n coma m

comatose a comatoso

comb n pettine m; (cock) cresta; (hair) pettine per capelli; (honey) favo; — vt pettinare; — **out** (fig) eliminare; — vi pettinarsi

combat n combattimento; — **fatigue** psicopatia di guerra

combat vt combattere; — vi contendere con; **–ive** a combattivo, litigioso

combatant n&a combattente m

combination n combinazione; — **lock** serratura a combinazione

combine vt combinare; — vi combinarsi, allearsi; — n (coll) consorzio, combriccola; (com) società; (mech) macchina trebbiatrice

combined a combinato; — **efforts** sforzi combinati

combustible a&n combustibile m

combustion n combustione; — **chamber** camera di scoppio

come vi venire; — **about** accadere; — **after** (follow) seguire; (get) venire a prendere; — **again** ritornare; — **apart** separarsi, — **away** venire via; — **back** tornare; — **between** intervenire; — **by** (get) ottenare, acquistare; (pass) passare; — **down** scendere; — **for** venire per; — **forward** avanzarsi; — **home** tornare a casa; — **in** entrare; **C– in!** Avanti!; **May I (we) — in?** Si può?; — **near** avvicinarsi; — **of age** diventare maggiorenne; **off** staccarsi; **C– on!** Andiamo!; — **out** uscire; (stain) scomparire; — **through** riuscire; — **to** (amount to) ammontare; (revive) riaversi; — **to terms** mettersi d'accordo; — **undone** sfarsi; — **up** venire su; venire a galla (fig); — **what may** qualunque cosa avvenga (fig); — **up with** raggiungere

comeback n ritorno

comedian n comico, buffone m; (theat) commediante m

comedown n (coll) caduta

comedy n commedia; **musical** — burletta, opera comica, operetta

comeliness n bellezza, avvenenza

comely a avvenente, grazioso, bello

comet *n* cometa
comfort *n* consolazione, conforto; *(body)* comodità; **–er** *n* confortatore *m*; *(bedding)* imbottita, coltrone *m*; **–able** *a* confortevole; comodo; **–ably** *adv* comodamente; — *vt* confortare, consolare; **–ing** *a* confortante
comic *n* comico; — **book** giornalino per i piccoli; — **opera** opera buffa; — **strip** fumetto; vignetta
comical *a* comico
coming *n* venuta, arrivo; — *a* prossimo
comma *n* virgola
command *vt* comandare, ordinare; — *vi* essere al comando; — *n* comando, ordine *m*, padronanza; **–er** *n* comandante *m*, capo; **–ment** *n* comandamento
commanding *a* autoritario
commando *n* reparto di truppe d'assalto
commandeer *vt* requisire
commemorate *vt* commemorare
commemoration *n* commemorazione
commemorative *a* commemorativo
commence *vt&i* cominciare, incominciare, iniziare, mettersi a
commencement *n (beginning)* inizio; *(graduation)* cerimonia della consegna del diploma
commend *vt (praise)* lodare, elogiare; *(recommend)* raccomandare; **–able** *a* raccomandabile; **–ation** *n* raccomandazione; **–atory** *a* raccomandatorio
commensurate *a* commisurato
comment *n* commento, osservazione; — *vt* commentare, criticare; — *vi* fare commento
commentary *n* commento, annotazioni *fpl*
commentator *n* commentatore *m*
commerce *n* commercio
commercial *a* commerciale; — **art** arte commerciale; — **college** scuola commerciale; — *n (rad, TV)* annunzio pubblicitario; **–ize** *vt* commercializzare
commiserate *vt* commiserare
commiseration *n* commiserazione
commissar *n* commissario; **–iat** *n* commissariato
commissary *n* commissario
commission *n* commissione; provvigione *f*; — **house** ditta per commissioni; — **merchant** commissionario; **out of** — fuori uso; — *vt* commissionare; incaricare con una missione
commissioned *a* inviato in missione, commissionato
commit *vt* fare, affidare, commettere; — **to memory** imparare a memoria
commitment *n* consegna
committee *n* comitato, commissione
commodious *a* comodo

commodity *n* prodotto, derrata
commodore *n* commodoro
common *a* comune; *(usual)* ordinario; *(vulgar)* triviale; — **carrier** vettore *m*; — **sense** buon senso; — **stock** *(com)* titolo in comune; **in** — in comune
commonplace *n* banalità; — *a* banale; volgare
commonwealth *n* stato; repubblica
commotion *n* agitazione, tumulto, chiasso
communal *a* comunale
commune *vi* conferire, discorrere; — **with oneself** meditare
commune *n* comune *m*
communicable *a* comunicabile
communicant *n* comunicando
communicate *vt* comunicare, trasmettere; — *vi* comunicarsi, fare la comunione
communication *n* comunicazione
communicative *a* comunicativo
communion *n* comunione; **take** — comunicarsi
communiqué *n* comunicato ufficiale
communism *n* comunismo
communist *n* comunista *m&f*; **–ic** *a* comunista, comunistico
community *n* comunità, collettività; *(locality)* vicinato; *(village)* paese *m*; — **chest** fondo di comunità; — **center** luogo di riunione di una comunità
communize *vt* socializzare, accomunare
commutation *n* commutazione; — **ticket** abbonamento combinato
commutator *n* commutatore *m*
commute *vt* commutare; sostituire; — *vi* fare sostituzione di; viaggiare giornalmente con abbonamento combinato
commuter *n* colui che viaggia al lavoro
compact *a* compatto; **–ly** *adv* concisamente
compact *n (agreement)* patto, contratto; *(auto)* piccola automobile; *(powder)* portacipria *m*
companion *n* compagno, compagna; **–ship** *n* compagnia, cameratismo, amicizia
companionable *a* socievole
companionway *n* scaletta
company *n* compagnia, società; **part** — separarsi
comparable *a* paragonabile
comparative *a* comparativo, relativo; **–ly** *adv* comparativamente, relativamente
compare *vt* paragonare, confrontare; — **notes** fare uno scambio di idee
comparison *n* paragone *m*, confronto; **beyond** — senza confronto, senza paragone; **in** — **with** in confronto a
compartment *n* compartimento, scompartimento
compass *n (naut)* bussola; *(range)* limite

m, portata; — *vt* circondare, andare attorno; *(achieve)* compiere
compassion *n* compassione, pietà; **-ate** *a* compassivo, compassionevole
compatible *a* compatibile
compatriot *n* compatriota *m&f*
compel *vt* costringere, obbligare, forzare
compellation *n* appello
compensate *vt* compensare, risarcire; — *vi* compensarsi
compensation *n* compenso, ricompensa, indennità
compensator *n* compensatore *m*, compensatrice *f*
compensatory *a* compensativo
compete *vi* concorrere, gareggiare
competence *n* competenza
competent *a* competente, capace, abile
competition *n* competizione, gara, concorso
competitive *a* competitivo
competitor *n* competitore, concorrente *m*
compilation *n* compilazione, raccolta
compile *vt* compilare
compiler *n* compilatore *m*
complain *vi* lamentarsi
complainant *n* accusatore, querelante *m*
complaint *n* lamento; *(protest)* protesta, reclamo, accusa; *(law)* querela; *(med)* malattia, disturbo; **lodge a** — dar querela
complaisance *n* compiacenza
complaisant *a* compiacente
complement *n* complemento; — *vt* completare, riempiere; **-ary** *a* complementare
complete *a* finito, completo; — *vt* completare, terminare, finire; **-ly** *adv* completamente
completion *n* complemento, fine *f*, termine *m*
complex *a&n* complesso; **inferiority** — *n* complesso di inferiorità
complexion *n* carnagione *f*, colorito
complexity *n* complessità; complicazione
compliance *n* obbedienza, acquiescenza; **in** — **with** in conformità con
compliant *a* condiscendente
complicate *vt* complicare; **-d** *a* complicato
complication *n* complicazione
complicity *n* complicità
compliment *n* complimento; *(eulogy)* elogio; *(homage)* omaggio; — *vt* felicitare, lodare
complimentary *a* laudativo, complimentoso; *(gratis)* gratuito, in omaggio, di favore; — **ticket** biglietto-omaggio
component *a&n* componente
compose *vt* comporre; — *vi* fare composizioni, creare; **-d** *a* disinvolto, calmo,

tranquillo; **be -d of** consistere di
composer *n* compositore *m*
composite *a* composto
composition *n* composizione, natura, componimento
compositor *n* compositore *m*
compost *n* composto
composure *n* disinvoltura, calma; sangue freddo
compote *n* composta, conserva
compound *vt* comporre, combinare; — *vi* venire a una transazione; — **a felony** comporre *(or* sospendere) un'accusa di delitto; — *n* composto; — *a* composto, composito
comprehend *vt* comprendere, concepire, capire, includere
comprehensible *a* comprensibile
comprehension *n* comprensione
comprehensive *a* comprensivo, spazioso, vasto
compress *n* compressa
compress *vt* comprimere, condensare; **-ed** *a* compresso
compressor *n (mech)* compressore *m*
compression *n* compressione
comprise *vt* comprendere, includere; **-d** *a* compreso, incluso
compromise *n* compromesso, transazione; — *vt* compromettere, transigere; — *vi* compromettersi
comptometer *n* comptometro
comptroller *n* controllore *m;* **-ship** *n* controlleria
compulsion *n* compulsione, costrizione
compulsive *a* obbligatorio, forzato; **-ly** *adv* forzosamente
compulsory *a* obbligatorio
compunction *n* compunzione
computation *n* computo
compute *vt* calcolare
computer *n* computatore *m*, computatrice *f*
comrade *n* camerata *m*, compagno; **-ship** *n* cameratismo
concave *a* concavo
conceal *vt* celare, nascondere; **-ed** *a* celato, nascosto
concealment *n (deception)* dissimulazione; *(hiding)* celamento
concede *vt* concedere, ammettere
conceit *n* vanità, amor proprio, presunzione, boria; **-ed** *a* presuntuoso, vanitoso, vanesio; **-edly** *adv* vanamente; infatuatamente
conceivable *a* concepibile
conceive *vt&i* concepire, immaginare
concentrate *vt* concentrare; — *vi* concentrarsi, raccogliersi; — **on** convergere; **-d** *a* concentrato

concentrate *n* concentrato, essenza
concentration *n* concentrazione
concentric *a* concentrico
concept *n* concetto, idea
conception *n* concezione; *(idea)* concetto
concern *vt* riguardare, concernere, interessare; — oneself interessarsi, occuparsi
concern *n* *(com)* ditta, azienda; *(interest)* cura, interesse *m*, faccenda, affare *m*; *(worry)* preoccupazione
concerned *a* preoccupato; interessato; as far as . . . is — per ciò che riguarda
concerning *prep* di; quanto a, relativo a, riguardante a
concert *n* concerto; –ed *a* concertato
concert *vt* concertare; — *vi* concertarsi
concession *n* concessione
conciliate *vt* conciliare
conciliation *n* conciliazione
conciliatory *a* conciliatorio
concise *a* conciso
conclave *n* conclave *m*
conclude *vt&i* concludere, terminare, finire; *(deduce)* dedurre
conclusion *n* conclusione
conclusive *a* conclusivo; –ly *adv* conclusivamente
concoct *vt* *(develop)* elaborare; *(plot)* complottare; *(prepare)* preparare
concoction *n* elaborazione; complottazione; *(mixture)* miscela
concomitant *a* concomitante, accessorio; — *n* compagno, accessorio
concord *n* concordia, armonia; — grape uva concordia; — *vi* concordare
concourse *n* concorso, affluenza
concrete *n* cemento, *(arch)* calcestruzzo; — mixer betoniera; — *a* concreto; di calcestruzzo
concubine *n* concubina
concupescence *n* concupiscenza
concur *vi* convenire con, concordare con, accordarsi
concurrence *n* concorrenza
concurrent *a* concorrente, simultaneo; –ly *adv* simultaneamente
concussion *n* scossa, concussione; *(brain)* trauma, commozione cerebrale
condemn *vt* condannare, biasimare
condemnation *n* condanna
condensation *n* condensazione
condense *vt* condensare, abbreviare
condenser *n* condensatore *m*
condescend *vi* accondiscendere; *(deign)* degnarsi; –ing *a* condiscendente
condescension *n* condiscendenza
condiment *n* condimento
condition *n* condizione; –al *a* condizionale; — *vt* imporre condizioni; — *vi* stipulare

condole *vi* fare le condoglianze, condolersi
condolence *n* condoglianza
condone *vt* condonare, perdonare, scusare
conduce *vi* contribuire, tendere
conducive *a* tendente, favorevole
conduct *n* condotta, contegno, procedimento
conduct *vt* guidare, dirigere; condurre a; — oneself *(behave)* comportarsi; — *vi* *(phy)* condurre
conductivity *n* *(elec)* conduttività
conduction *n* conduzione
conductor *n* capotreno; *(streetcar)* conduttore *m*; *(elec)* conduttore *m*; *(mus)* direttore *m*, direttrice *f*
conduit *n* condotto, condotta
cone *n* cono; *(bot)* pigna, pina; *(ice cream)* cono gelato; *(paper)* cartoccio
confection *n* confetto, conserva
confectionery *n* confetturerìa; — store confetteria
confederacy *n* confederazione; lega
confederate *a&n* confederato; — *vt* federare, confederare; — *vi* federarsi, confederarsi
confederation *n* confederazione
confer *vt&i* conferire; — with conferire con; avere una conferenza con
conference *n* conferenza, colloquio; *(meeting)* riunione *f*
confess *vt* confessare; — *vi* confessarsi; — to ammettere di
confession *n* confessione; –al *n* confessionale *m*
confessor *n* confessore *m*
confetti *npl* coriandoli *mpl*
confidant *n* confidente *m*
confide *vt&i* confidare; aver fiducia
confidence *n* fiducia; in strict — in stretta confidenza; — game abuso di fiducia; — man abusatore di fiducia
confident *a* confidente; –ly *adv* fiduciosamente
confidential *a* confidenziale
confiding *a* confidente, fiducioso
configuration *n* configurazione
confine *vt* confinare; — oneself limitarsi; –d to bed obbligato a letto
confinement *n* confino, ritiro; *(law)* reclusione; solitary — segregazione cellulare
confirm *vt* confermare; *(eccl)* cresimare; –ation *n* conferma; cresima; –atory *a* confermatorio; –ative *a* confermativo; –ed *a* inveterato; –ing *a* confermante
confiscate *vt* confiscare
confiscation *n* confisca

conflagration n conflagrazione, accensione
conflict n conflitto, contrasto
conflict vi contrastare, essere in conflitto; **–ing** a in conflitto, contrastante
conform vt conformare, adattare; — vi adattarsi, conformarsi; **–able** a conforme a; sottomesso a; **–ation** n conformazione; **–ist** n conformista m; **–ity** n conformità
confound vt confondere; **–ed** a confuso
confront vt confrontare, affrontare
confuse vt confondere, turbare, sconcertare; **–ed** a confuso, disordinato
confusedly adv confusamente
confusion n confusione; **be covered with** — essere imbarazzato
confute vt confutare
congeal vt congelare, gelare; coagulare; — vi congelarsi; coagularsi; **–ed** a congelato
congenial a simpatico, gradevole
congenital a congenito
congest vt&i riunire, ammassare, congestionare
congested a riunito, congestionato; — **district** settore superpopolato
congestion n congestione f
conglomerate a conglomerato
conglomeration n conglomerazione, conglomerato
congratulate vt felicitare
congratulation n congratulazione; **–s** npl congratulazioni, complimenti
congregate vt radunare, riunire; — vi adunarsi, riunirsi
congregation n congregazione; **–al** a congregazionale
congress n congresso; **–man** n congressista m
congressional a congressionale, del congresso
congruent a congruente
congruity n congruismo, congruità
congruous a congruo
conical a conico
conifer n conifera
conjecture n congettura, supposizione; — vt&i congetturare
conjugal a coniugale
conjugate vt coniugare
conjugation n coniugazione
conjunction n congiunzione
conjunctive a congiuntivo
conjunctivitis n congiuntivite f
conjure vt&i scongiurare
conjurer n prestigiatore m
connect vt connettere, unire; — vi far coincidenza, connettersi, unirsi; **–ing** a d'unione, di comunicazione; **–ed** a con-

nesso, unito, imparentato
connection n rapporto, relazione; (elec) connessione, contatto
connivance n connivenza
connive vi avere connivenza con
conniving a connivente
connoisseur n intenditore m, intenditrice f; buongustaio
connotation n senso, significato
connote vt implicare; significare indirettamente
connubial a coniugale, connubiale
conquer vt&i vincere, conquistare; **–or** n vincitore m
conquest n conquista
consanguinity n consanguinità
conscience n coscienza; **in all** — in tutta coscienza
conscience-stricken a con peso di coscienza (fig)
conscientious a coscienzioso; **–ly** adv coscienziosamente
conscious a conscio, consapevole; **–ly** adv consciamente; **–ness** n conoscenza, coscienza
conscript vt coscrivere, reclutare
conscription n coscrizione, reclutamento
consecrate vt consacrare, benedire; **–d** a consacrato
consecration n consacrazione
consecutive a consecutivo
consensus n consenso
consent vi acconsentire; approvare, accettare; — n consenso, accordo
consequence n conseguenza; **take the –s** pagare le conseguenze
consequent a conseguente; **–ly** adv in conseguenza, conseguentemente
consequential a conseguenziale, logico
conservation n conservazione
conservative a conservativo; — n conservatore m, conservatrice f
conservatory n conservatorio musicale; (hothouse) serra; — a conservativo
conserve vt conservare; (in syrup) mettere in conserva
conserve n conserva
consider vt&i considerare, riflettere sopra; **–ed** a considerato; **–able** a considerabile; **–ate** a considerato, di considerazione
consideration n considerazione; **in — of** in considerazione di; **under no —** sotto nessuna circostanza; **take into —** prendere in considerazione; **under —** in esame, allo studio
considering that in considerazione di; considerando che
consign vt&i consegnare; **—ee** n consegnatario; **–or** n depositante m; (sender)

mittente *m*

consignment *n* consegna; deposito; **on —** in deposito

consist *vi* ·consistere; **–ency** *n* consistenza; **–ent** *a* consistente

consistory *n* concistoro

consolation *n* consolazione

console *vt* consolare

console *n* mensola

consolidate *vt* consolidare; **—** *vi* consolidarsi

consolidation *n* consolidamento

consommé *n* brodo ristretto

consonant *a&n* consonante *f*

consort *n* consorte *m*

consort *vt* associare, unire; **—** *vi* associarsi, unirsi; **— with** associarsi con

conspicuous *a* cospicuo; **–ly** *adv* cospicuamente

conspiracy *n* congiura, complotto, cospirazione

conspirator *n* cospiratore *m*, cospiratrice *f*

conspire *vt&i* complottare, congiurare

constabulary *npl* corpo di polizia

constancy *n* costanza

constant *a* costante, ininterrotto; **—** *n* (*math*) costante *f*; **–ly** *adv* costantemente

constellation *n* costellazione

consternate *vt* costernare; **–d** *a* costernato

consternation *n* costernazione, sgomento

constipate *vt* costipare; **–d** *a* costipato

constipation *n* costipazione

constituency *n* circoscrizione elettorale

constituent *a* costituente

constitute *vt* costituire

constitution *n* costituzione

constitutional *a* costituzionale; **—** *n* passeggiata igienica

constitutionality *n* costituzionalità

constrain *vt* costringere; **–ed** *a* costretto

constraint *n* costrizione

constrict *vt* costringere

constriction *n* costrizione

constrictor *n* costrittore *m*; **boa —** *n* serpente boa

construct *vt* costruire; **–or** *n* costruttore *m*

construction *n* costruzione; **give a wrong —** mal interpretare; **–al** *a* strutturale; di costruzione

constructive *a* costruttivo

construe *vt* interpretare

consubstantiate *vt* consustanziare

consul *n* console *m*; **–ar** *a* consolare

consulate *n* consolato

consult *vt* consultare; **—** *vi* consultarsi con; **–ing** *a* consultante; **–ation** *n*

consulto; **–ant** *n* consultante *m*

consume *vt* consumare; **—** *vi* consumarsi; **–d** *a* consumato

consumer *n* consumatore *m*

consummate *a* consumato

consummate *vt* consumare, finire

consummation *n* consumazione

consumption *n* consumazione; (*med*) consunzione

contact *n* contatto; **— lenses** *npl* lenti di contatto

contact *vt&i* fare contatto, mettersi a contatto

contagion *n* contagio

contagious *a* contagioso

contain *vt* contenere; **— oneself** contenersi

contaminate *vt* contaminare

contamination *n* contaminazione

contemplate *vt&i* contemplare, meditare

contemplation *n* contemplazione, meditazione

contemporaneous *a* contemporaneo; **–ly** *adv* contemporaneamente

contemporary *n&a* contemporaneo

contempt *n* disprezzo; **–ible** *a* spregevole

contemptuous *a* sprezzante

contend *vt* contendere, contestare; **—** *vi* pretendere

content *n* contentezza; **to one's heart's —** a volontà; **—** *a* contento; **–ed** *a* contento, contentato; **—** *vt* accontentare

contention *n* controversia; **bone of —** seme di discordia

contentment *n* contentamento

contents *npl* contenuto; **table of —** indice *m*

contest *vt* contestare; **—** *vi* lottare, concorrere; **–ant** *n* contestante *m*

contest *n* contestazione, concorso; **beauty —** concorso di bellezza

context *n* contesto, senso

contextual *a* contestuale

contiguity *n* contiguità

contiguous *a* contiguo

continence *n* continenza

continent *n* continente *m*; **–al** *a* continentale

contingency *n* contingenza

contingent *a* contingente; **—** *n* contingente *m*

continual *a* continuo; **–ly** *adv* continuamente

continuance *n* continuazione, continuità

continuation *n* continuazione

continue *vt&i* continuare; **–d** *a* continuo

continuity *n* continuità; (*movies*) copione cinematografico; (*radio*) copione per radio

continuous *a* continuo

contort *vt* contorcere, attorcigliare
contortion *n* contorsione; **–ist** *n* contorsionista *m&f*
contour *n* contorno; **— plowing** rilievo topografico
contraband *n* contrabbando
contraception *n* contracconcezione, antifecondazione
contract *n* contratto; **party to a —** contraente *m;* **–ing** *a* contrattante; **–or** *n* contraente *m*, imprenditore *m;* **—** *vt (com)* contrarre
contract *vt (med)* contrarre; **–ed** *a* contrattato; **–ible** *a* contrattile; **–ibility** *n* contrattilità
contraction *n* contrazione
contradict *vt&i* contraddire; **–ory** *a* contraddittorio
contradiction *n* contraddizione
contrail *n (avi)* fumeggio, scia
contralto *n* contralto
contrariness *n* contrarietà
contrary *a&n* contrario; **on the —** al contrario
contrast *vi* contrastare; **—** *vt* mettere in contrasto; **—** *n* contrasto; **–ing** *a* contrastante
contravene *vt* contravvenire
contribute *vt&i* contribuire
contribution *n* contributo
contributor *n* contributore *m*, contributrice *f*
contributory *a* contributivo
contrite *a* contrito
contrition *n* contrizione
contrivance *n* escogitazione, invenzione
contrive *vt* escogitare; **—** *vi* ingegnarsi
control *vt* controllare; **— oneself** controllarsi; **—** *n* controllo; **— stick** *(avi)* cloche *f*, leva di comando; **— tower** *(avi)* torre di controllo
controller *n* controllore *m*
controversial *a* di controversia, controverso
controversy *n* controversia
contusion *n* contusione
conundrum *n* indovinello
convalesce *vi* essere convalescente
convalescence *n* convalescenza
convalescent *a&n* convalescente *m&f;* **— home** convalescenziario
convection *n* convezione
convene *vt* convenire; **—** *vi* adunarsi
convenience *n* convenienza, **at one's —** con comodità; **a bell'agio**
convenient *a* conveniente; **–ly** *adv* convenientemente
convent *n* convento
convention *n* convenzione; **–al** *a* convenzionale

converge *vt&i* convergere
convergence *n* convergenza
convergent *a* convergente
converging *a* convergente
conversant *a* versato in
conversation *n* conversazione, **— piece** *(arts)* gruppo; **–al** *a* di conversazione; **–alist** *n* parlatore *m*, parlatrice *f*
converse *vi* conversare
converse *a* reciproco; **–ly** *adv* reciprocamente, per converso
conversion *n* conversione
convert *vt* convertire; **—** *vi* convertirsi; **–er** *(elec)* convertitore *m*
convert *n* convertito
convertibility *n* convertibilità
convertible *a* convertibile; **—** *n (auto)* convertibile, decapottabile *m*
convex *a* convesso
convey *vt* portare, trasmettere, trasferire; **— thanks** inviare ringraziamenti
conveyance *n* trasporto
conveyor *n* trasportatore *m*, trasportatrice *f*
convict *vt* condannare
convict *n* condannato, detenuto, forzato
conviction *n* convinzione
convince *vt* convincere
convincible *a* convincibile
convincing *a* convincente; **–ly** *adv* in modo convincente
convivial *a* conviviale; **–ity** *n* convivialità
convocation *n* convocazione; **–al** *a* convocazionale
convolution *n* convoluzione
convoy *n* convoglio, scorta; **—** *vt* convogliare, scortare
convulse *vt* agitare, mettere in convulsione; **–d** *a* convulso
convulsion *n* convulsione
convulsive *a* convulsivo
coo *vi* tubare, gemere; **–ing** *n* il tubare
cook *n* cuoco; **—** *vt&i* cuocere; **— one's goose** *(fig)* dare il colpo di grazia; **— up** *(coll)* arrangiare; **–ed** *a* cotto; *(coll)* falsificato; **–ing** *n* cucina
cookie *n* pasticcino
cool *a* fresco; **—** *vt&i* raffreddare, rinfrescare; **— down** calmarsi; **–ly** *adv* indifferentemente; **–ing** *a* rinfrescante
cooler *n* rinfrescatoio
cooling-off period periodo di assestamento
coolness *n* fresco; *(manner)* indifferenza
coop *n* stia; **—** *vt* rinchiudere
co-operate *vi* cooperare
co-operation *n* cooperazione
co-operative *a* cooperativo; **—** *n* cooperativa
co-ordinate *vt* coordinare; **—** *vi* coordi-

narsi
co-ordination *n* coordinazione
co-ordinator *n* coordinatore *m*
coot *n* folaga
cop *n* (*sl*) poliziotto; — *vt* (*sl*) acchiappare, afferrare
copartner *n* socio
cope *n* cappa; — *vt* coprire; — **with** lottare contro
coping *n* comignolo
copious *a* copioso
copper *n* rame *m*; **-y** *a* di rame
copra *n* copra *m*
copse *n* bosco ceduo
copy *n* copia; — *vt&i* copiare, imitare; **-book** *n* quaderno; **-cat** *n* scimmia (*fig*)
copyright *n* diritto d'autore; — *vt* patentare; assicurare (*or* comprare) la esclusiva artistica
coquette *n* civetta (*fig*)
coquettish *a* civettuolo, vezzoso
coral *n* corallo; — *a* corallino; di corallo; — **reef** banco di corallo
cord *n* corda, cordone *m*; (*elec*) filo; cavo elettrico; **spinal** — spina dorsale; — *vt* legare con corda; (*wood*) misurare
cordage *n* cordame *m*
corded *a* fatto a corda, di corda
cordial *a* cordiale; — *n* cordiale *m*; **-ly** *adv* cordialmente; **-ity** *n* cordialità
cording *n* legamento; (*wood*) misura
cordon *n* cordone *m*
corduroy *n* corderoy *m*, fustagno; — *a* di corderoy
core *n* cuore *m*; nocciolo; — *vt* vuotare, estrarre il torsolo
co-respondent *n* coimputato
cork *n* sughero, turacciolo; — *a* di sughero; — *vt* turare, tappare; **-screw** *n* cavaturaccioli *m*
corn *vt* salare
corn *n* grano, cereale *m*, granturco; (*foot*) callo; — **borer** *n* parassita del granturco
corncob *n* pannocchia
corner *vt* rincantucciare; — *vi* essere in angolo; trovarsi all'angolo; — *n* angolo; **turn the** — girare l'angolo; **cut -s** (*fig*) accorciare; **-ed** *a* ad angolo, angoloso
cornerstone *n* pietra angolare
cornet *n* (*mus*) cornetta; (*paper*) cartoccio
cornice *n* cornice *f*
cornstarch *n* amido di grano, fecola di grano
corollary *n* corollario
corona *n* corona
coronary *a* coronario; — **thrombosis** *n*

trombosi coronaria
coronation *n* incoronazione
coroner *n* giudice istruttore
coronet *n* corona, diadema
corporal *n* (*mil*) caporale *m*; (*eccl*) corporale *m*; — *a* corporeo; corporale; — **punishment** punizione corporale
corporate *a* corporativo
corporation *n* corporazione
corporeal *a* corporeo
corps *n* corpo; (*avi*) aviazione, corpo areonautico
corpse *n* corpo, cadavere *m*
corpulence *n* corpulenza
corpulent *a* corpulento
corpuscle *n* corpuscolo
corral *n* recinto; — *vt* raccogliere
correct *vt* correggere; — *a* corretto; **-ive** *a* correttivo, di correzione; **-ness** *n* correttezza; **-ional** *a* correzionale; **-ly** *adv* correttamente
correction *n* correzione
correlate *a* correlazionato, correlativo; — *vt* correlazionare; — *vi* essere in relazione
correlation *n* correlazione
correlative *a&n* correlativo
correspond *vi* corrispondere; **-ent** *n* corrispondente *m*; **-ing** *a* corrispondente
correspondence *n* corrispondenza, — **school** scuola per corrispondenza
corridor *n* corridore *m*
corrigible *a* correggibile
corroborate *vt* corroborare
corroboration *n* corroboramento, corroborazione
corroborator *n* corroboratore; **-y** *a* corroborante
corrode *vt* corrodere, rodere; — *vi* corrodersi, rodersi
corrosion *n* corrosione
corrosive *a* corrosivo
corrugate *vt* corrugare, ondulare; — *vi* corrugarsi, ondularsi, **-d** *a* corrugato, ondulato
corrupt *vt* corrompere; — *vi* corrompersi; **-ibility** *n* corruttibilità; **-ible** *a* corruttibile; **-ive** *a* corruttivo
corruption *n* corruzione
corsage *n* mazzolino
corset *n* corsetto
cortege *n* corteo
cortex *n* (*anat*) cortice *m*; (*bot*) corteccia
cortisone *n* cortisona
coseismal *a* cosismico
cosine *n* coseno
cosmetic *a&n* cosmetico; **-ian** *n* cosmetico
cosmic *a* cosmico, — **dust** particella cosmica, pulviscolo cosmico; — **rays**

raggi cosmici
cosmonaut *n (aesp)* cosmonauta *m&f*
cosmopolitan *a&n* cosmopolita *m*
cosmotron *n* cosmotrone *m*
Cossack *n* Cosacco
cost *n* costo; — **of living** costo della vita; — **price** prezzo di costo; **whatever the** — a qualunque costo; **at all** —**s** ad ogni costo; —**liness** *n* costosità; —**ly** *a* costoso, caro; — *vt* stimare; — *vi* costare
costume *n* costume *m;* — *vt* vestire in costume
costumer *n* costumista *m&f*, costumiere *m*
cot *n* lettino; culla
cote *n* stabbio; *(dove)* piccionaia; colombaia
coterie *n* combriccola
cottage *n* capanna, villetta
cotton *n* cotone *m;* — *a* di cotone, cotoniero; **absorbent** — cotone idrofilo; — **gin** macchina cardatrice del cotone; —**seed oil** olio di cotone; —**y** *a* cotonato
couch *n* divano, sofà; — *vt* coricare; — *vi* coricarsi, stendersi
cough *n* tosse *f;* — **drop** pastiglia per la tosse; — **syrup** sciroppo per la tosse; **whooping** — tosse asinina; — *vt* espettorare; — *vi* tossire
coughing *n* tosse *f*
council *n* consiglio, concilio; **city** — consiglio comunale; —**or** *n* membro del consiglio, consigliere *m*
counsel *n* consiglio, opinione; **keep one's own** — tenere per sè le proprie opinioni; **take** — consultare; — *vt* consigliare
counselor *n* consigliere *m*
count *vt* contare; *(mus)* solfeggiare; — **me in** conta con me; — **on** contare su; fare affidamento; — *n* conto, calcolo; *(title)* conte *m*; —**down** *n (aesp)* conteggio
countenance *n* viso, sembiante *m;* — *vt&i* appoggiare, favorire, secondare, sostenere; **put out of** — fare confusione; sconcertare
counter *n (calculator)* calcolatore *m*, calcolatrice *f; (game)* gettone *m; (person)* contante *m&f*; contatore *m*, contatrice *f; (store)* banco; **Geiger** — contatore Geiger; — *a* oppositore, controcorrente *(fig);* — *adv* contro, contrariamente; — *vt* opporre; — *vi* rispondere; *(sport)* controbattere
counteract *vt* contrariare
counterattack *n* contrattacco; — *vt&i* contrattaccare
counterbalance *vt* contrappesare; — *n* contrappeso
counterclaim *n* controreclamo; — *vi* con-

troreclamare
counterclockwise *a* opposto all'orologio
counterfeit *a* contraffatto; — *n* contraffazione; — *vt* contraffare; — *vi* fingere; —**er** *n* contraffattore *m*, contraffatrice *f*
counterirritant *n* contrirritante
countermand *vt* contromandare, annullare
countermarch *n* contromarcia
countermove *n* contromossa; — *vt&i* contromuovere
counteroffensive *n* controffensiva
counterpane *n* contrappunta, coltre *f*
counterpart *n* controparte *f*
counterpoint *n* contrappunto
counterpoise *n* contrappeso; — *vt* controbilanciare
counterrevolution *n* controrivoluzione
countersign *vt* contrassegnare
countersink *vt* fresare, accecare, incassare
counterweight *n* contrappeso
countess *n* contessa
countless *a* innumerevole
countrified *a* rustico
country *n* paese *m*, regione *f*, patria; campagna; *(native)* paese natio; — **club** circolo campestre; *(golf)* campo di golf; —**man** *n* compatriotta *m&f*, contadino, paesano; —**side** *n* campagna, paese; —**wide** *a* in tutto il paese *(fig);* — *a* rurale, di campagna
county *n* contea; — **poor farm** campo di ritiro per i poveri; — **seat** *(privincial)* capoluogo
coup *n* colpo
coupé *n* cupè *m*
couple *n* coppia, paio; — *vt* accoppiare, appaiare; — *vi* accoppiarsi, appaiarsi
coupling *n (mech)* accoppiamento, attacco
coupon *n* cupone *m*, cedola; *(com)* cupone
courage *n* coraggio; — **of one's convictions** coraggio delle proprie opinioni; —**ous** *a* coraggioso
courier *n* corriere *m*
course *n* corso, corsa, carriera; *(meal)* portata; *(river)* corso; *(study)* corso di studi; **a matter of** — cosa naturale; **in due** — regolarmente; **in the** — **of** durante, **of** — naturalmente; **run its** — seguire il suo corso; — *vt&i* correre
court *n* corte *f*, assemblea; **out of** — extra legale; —**house** *n* tribunale *m*, corte *f*, palazzo di giustizia; — *a* di corte, della corte; —**room** *n* sala di corte
court *vt* corteggiare, fare la corte; —**ship** *n* corte *f*, assiduità
courteous *a* cortese
courtesan *n* cortigiana

courtesy n cortesia
courtliness n cortesia
courtly a cortese
court-martial n corte marziale
court plaster n taffettà inglese
cousin n cugino, cugina; **first —** cugino germano
covalence n (phys) covalenza
cove n (arch) arco; (geog) seno
covenant n covenzione
cover vt coprire; celare, nascondere; **— oneself** coprirsi; **— up** dissimulare, ricoprire interamante; **—** n copertura, coperta; **— charge** prezzo di coperto; **book —** copertina; **take —** proteggersi; **under separate —** separatamente; **–ed** a coperto, ricoperto
coverall n spolverina
covering n copertura
coverlet n copriletto
covert a coperto, nascosto
covet vt&i desiderare; **—** vt bramare, agognare; avere un cattivo desiderio; **–ous** a avido, cupido
covey n covata, branco
cow n vacca; **–boy** n vaccaro; **–catcher** n (engine) paraurti; **–hand** n vaccaro; **–hide** n pelle di vacca; **—** vt intimidire; scoraggiare
coward n codardo, vile m; **–ice** n codardia, viltà; **–ly** a codardo, vigliacco
cower vi accoccolarsi, accovacciarsi
cowl n cappuccio
cowlick n ciuffo
co-worker n compagno di lavore, collaboratore m
coy a modesto, timido
coyote n sciacallo americano
cozily adv gradevolmente, comodamente
coziness n comodità
cozy a accogliente
C.P.A., certified public accountant n ragioniere abilitato
crab n granchio; **— apple** mela selvatica; **–grass** n gramigna; **—** vt&i (coll) avvilire
crack vt spaccare, fendere; **—** vi spaccarsi, fendersi; **— a joke** fare scherzi; **— down** (coll) costringere con severità; **— up** (coll) crollare; (praise) vantare
crack n fessura, crepa; **— of dawn** n prime ore del mattino; **–brained** a matto, pazzo; **—** a spaccato; (coll) balzano
cracker n biscotto; (fireworks) galletta
crackle vt&i screpolare; (sound) crepitare
cracking n scoppiettio, crepito
crack-up n collisione; (med) collasso
cradle n culla; **—** vt mettere nella culla
craft n arte f; (naut) battello; (slyness) astuzia; (trade) mestiere m; **–ily** adv

abilmente; (slyly) con inganno; **–iness** n astuzia **–y** a (able) astuto, capace; (sly) furbo
craftsman n artigiano; **–ship** n artefice m
crag n rupe f, picco
craggy a roccioso, scosceso
cram vt riempire; **—** vi riempirsi; (coll) rimpinzare
cramp n crampo; **—** vt dare crampi; **–ed** a indolenzito, con i crampi
cranberry n mortella; **— sauce** salsa di mortella
crane n gru f; **—** vt&i sollevare con la gru; **— one's neck** allungare il collo
cranial a cranico
crank n gomito; (coll) eccentrico; **–case** n (auto) carter m; **–shaft** n albero a gomito; **–y** a debole, capriccioso
cranny n fessura, incrinatura; **in nook and —** in ogni dove (coll)
crash vt fracassare; **—** vi far rumore; **—** n fracasso; (com) fallimento; **— landing** (avi) atterraggio irregolare
crash-dive vt (avi) picchiare
crass a crasso, grossolano
crate n gabbia per imballaggio; **—** vt ingabbiare
crater n cratere m
cravat n cravatta
crave vt&i supplicare, chiedere insistentemente
craven a codardo
craving n aspirazione, desiderio
craw n (bird) gozzo; **stick in one's —** (coll) stare nello stomaco (coll)
crawfish n gameto; **—** vi (coll) indietreggiare
crawl vi strisciare; **— with** formicolare; **—** n strisciamento, (swimming) stile libero, crawl m
crayon n matita, lapis m
craze vt squilibrare, fare impazzire; **–d** a folle; ammatassato (fig); **—** n mania
crazy a matto, pazzo; illogico; **— bone** gomito
cream n crema, panna; (best) il meglio; **— cheese** formaggio grasso; **— pitcher** vaso per la crema; **— puff** bignola; **— sauce** salsa bianca; **whipped —** panna montana; **–y** a cremoso; **–ery** n cri- meria; **—** vt (sauce) aggiungere la salsa bianca; (whip) frullare
crease n piega; **—** vt&i piegare, fare pieghe, sgualcire
crease-resistant a antipiega
create vt creare
creation n creazione
creative a creativo
creator n creatore m
creature n creatura; **— comforts** prov-

viste *fpl*
credence *n* credito; *(eccl)* credenza
credential *n* credenziale *f*; **-s** *npl* credenziali *fpl*
credenza *n* credenza
credibility *n* credibilità
credible *a* credibile
credit *n* credito; *(school)* attestato scolastico; **—** **card** lettera di credito; **— rating** credito commerciale; **— union** cooperativa di credito; **–able** *a* degno di credito; **–or** *n* creditore *m;* **—** *vt* credere a, fare *(or* dare) credito
credulity *n* credulità
credulous *a* credulo; **-ly** *adv* credulamente
creed *n* credo, fede *f*, simbolo
creek *n* seno, caletta
creel *n* paniere da pesca, nassa
creep *vt&i* strisciare; *(bot)* arrampicarsi; **—** *n (sl)* rettile *m (fig);* **-er** *n* rettile *m; (bot)* rampicante *m;* **-ing** *a* strisciante; *(bot)* rampicante; **-s** *npl* brividi *mpl;* **-y** *a* strisciante
cremate *vt* cremare, incenerire
cremation *n* cremazione
crematory *n* crematorio
creosote *n* creosoto
crêpe *n* crespo; **— paper** carta increspata
crepitation *n* crepitio, crepitazione
crescendo *n&adv* crescendo
crescent *n* crescente *m;* **—** *adj* crescente; **— moon** luna crescente
crest *n* cresta; *(bird)* cresta, ciuffo; *(wave)* cresta dell'onda; **-ed** *a* crestato, con la cresta
crestfallen *a* depresso
Crete Creta
cretinism *n* cretinismo
cretonne *n* creton *m*, cotonina
crevice *n* fessura, incrinatura; **-d** *a* fesso, incrinato
crew *n* ciurma, equipaggio; **— cut** capelli a spazzola
crib *n (bed)* culla; *(eccl)* presepe *m; (food)* mangiatoia; **—** *vt* copiare, sottrarre, plagiare
cribbing *n (coll)* plagio
crick *n* crampo, spasimo; **—** *vt* dare crampi
cricket *n* grillo
crier *n* banditore *m*
crime *n* delitto, crimine *m;* **— wave** onda di delitti
criminal *n&a* criminale
criminologist *n* criminalista *m*, criminologo
criminology *n* criminologia
crimp *vt* arricciare, arruolare; **—** *n* arruolatore *m;* **put a — in** *(coll)* mettere il bastone fra le ruote *(coll);* **-y** *a*

riccio, ricciuto; arricciato
crimson *n* cremisi *m;* **—** *a* cremisino, cremisi; **—** *vt&i* arrossire
cringe *vt* contrarre; **—** *vi* inchinarsi, fare riverenza
cringing *a* servile; **—** *n* servilità
crinkle *n* crespa, grinza; ondulazione; **—** *vt* aggrinzare; **—** *vi* increspare, incresparsi
cripple *n&a* storpio, zoppo; **—** *vt* storpiare
crisis *n* crisi *f*
crisp *a* crespo, riccio; *(air)* crespo; *(manner)* insinuante; *(repartee)* vivace; **—** *vt* ondulare, arricciare, increspare; **—** *vi* ondularsi, arricciarsi, incresparsi; **-ly** *adv* acutamente; **-ness** *n* l'esser crespo; **-y** *a* crespo
crisscross *a* crociato, incrociato; **—** *adv* a croce; **—** *vt&i* incrociare; *(sign)* firmare con la croce; **—** *n (signature)* segno di croce
criterion *n* criterio
critic *n* critico; **-al** *a* critico; **-ism** *n* critica; **-ize** *vt&i* criticare
croak *vt&i* gracchiare; **—** n gracchiamento; **-y** *a* rauco
crochet *n* uncinetto; **—** *vt&i* lavorare all'uncinetto; **— hook** uncinetto
crock *n* pignatta; **-ery** *n* maiolica
crocodile *n* coccodrillo; **— tears** *(fig)* lagrime di coccodrillo
crocus *n* croco, zafferano
crony *n* compagno, amico
crook *n* curvatura; *(coll)* truffatore, **-ed** *a* curvo, piegato; *(person)* perverso; **-edness** *n* curvatura, perversità; **—** *vt* curvare, piegare; **—** *vi* curvarsi, piegarsi
croon *vt&i* gemere, canticchiare; **-er** *n* canticchiatore *m*
crop *n* raccolto; *(zool)* gozzo; **—** *vt (grass)* pascolare; *(hair)* tosare; *(reap)* cogliere; **— off** tagliare; **— up** affiorare, sopravvenire
cropper *n* collasso; *(coll)* caduta; **come a —** stramazzare; fare un capitombolo
cross *n* croce *f;* **— reference** rimando, richiamo; **—** *a* incrociato, traversale; *(humor)* di malumore; **as a bear** di pessimo umore; **-bow** *n* balestra; **-walk** *n* passaggio pedonale; **—** *vt* incrociare, attraversare; **—** *vi* incrociarsi, attraversarsi; **— out** cancellare
crossbreed *n* incrocio, ibrido; **—** *vt&i* incrociare razze
cross- *(in comp)* **—country** *a&adv* attraverso i campi; **— examine** *vt* fare contro interrogatorio; **—eyed** *a* strabico; **—grained** *a* a fibre irregolari; *(peevish)* bisbetico; **—hatch** *vt (print)* tratteggia-

re; —legged a&adv a gambe incrociate; —patch n bisbetico; —piece n traversa; —road n crocevia; —section n sezione trasversale; —town a transurbano

crosscut saw n sega a due mani

crossing n incrocio; (rail) intersezione; level — passaggio a livello

cross-purpose n equivoco, contradizione, malinteso; work at —s contrastare

crosswise adv&a di traverso

crossword puzzle n cruciverba m

crotch n forca; (anat, pants) inforcatura

crouch vi accovacciarsi; essere servile

croup n groppa; (med) crup m; —y a (med) crupale

crouton n crostino

crow n corvo, cornacchia; as the — flies a volo d'uccello; eat — umiliarsi; — vi (cock) cantare; (fig) cantar vittoria

crowbar n leva

crowd n folla, ressa; — vt affollare, ingombrare; — vi affollarsi, affluire; —ed a affollato, sovraccaricato

crown n corona, cima; (head) sommità; — vt incoronare; — prince principe ereditario; —ing a finale, supremo, ultimo

crow's feet npl rughe fpl, zampe di gallina (coll)

crow's-nest n (naut) coffa

crucial a cruciale, decisivo

crucible n crogiuolo

crucifix n crocifisso

crucify vt crocifiggere

crude a crudo; — oil olio grezzo; —ly adv crudamente; —ness n crudezza

cruel a crudele; —ty n crudeltà

cruet n ampolla

cruise vi incrociare, andare in crociera; — n crociera

cruiser n incrociatore m

crumb n mollica, briciola; — vt sbriciolare, impanare; —ed a sbriciolato, grattugiato; —y a pieno di briciole; (sl) schifoso

crumble vt grattugiare, sbriciolare; — vi sbriciolarsi

crumbling n sbriciolamento; crollo

crumbly a midolloso, friabile

crumple vt raggrinzare; — vi raggrinzarsi

crunch vt&i scricchiolare, sgranocchiare, sgretolare; — n scricchiolio; —ing a scricchiolante

crusade n crociata; — vi fare una crociata

crusader n crociato

crush vt schiacciare; — vi schiacciarsi; — n (coll) infatuazione; (crowd) affollamento; —ing a schiacciante

crust n crosta; (sediment) deposito; —

vt incrostare; — vi incrostarsi; —y a incrostato

crustacean n&a crostaceo

crutch n gruccia, stampella

crux n difficoltà; (puzzle) indovinello, rebus m; — of the matter punto cruciale

cry vt&i piangere; (yell) gridare; —baby n piagnucolone (coll); — n pianto; grido; —ing n pianti mpl; grida fpl

cryogenics npl criogenica

crypt n cripta; —ic a segreto, nascosto

cryptography n criptografia, crittografia

crystal n cristallo; — a cristallino; di cristallo

crystalline a cristallino

crystallize vt&i cristallizzare

cub n cucciolo; bear — orsacchiotto; — reporter (coll) giornalista inesperto

cubbyhole n sgabuzzino

cube n cubo; — vt cubare; — root n radice cubica

cubic a cubico; — measure volume m

cubicle n cubicolo

cuckoo n cuculo; — clock orologio a cuculo, pendola

cucumber n cetriolo

cud n bolo alimentare; chew the — ruminare

cuddle vt serrare, stringere; — vi serrarsi, stringersi, rannicchiarsi; —some a vezzoso, coccolone

cudgel n bastone m, randello; take up the —s for difendere; — vt bastonare

cue n (billiard) stecca; (hair) codino; (line) coda, fila, linea; (theat) parola, suggerimento; give a — dare lo spunto

cuff n (blow) schiaffo, ceffone m; (shirt) polsino; (trouser) risvolto dei pantaloni; — button bottone da polsino; — links npl gemelli mpl; off the — (sl) ufficioso; on the — (sl) sulla parola; — vt schiaffeggiare; prendere a pugni

cuirass n corazza

cuisine n cucina

culinary a culinario

cull vt cogliere, scegliere

culminate vi culminare

culmination n culminazione

culpability n colpevolezza, colpabilità

culpable a colpabile

culprit n colpevole m; (law) imputato

cult n culto

cultivate vt coltivare

cultivation n coltivazione

cultivator n aratro; (mech) coltivatore m

cultural a culturale

culture n cultura; — vt coltivare

culvert n sottopassaggio

cumber vt ingombrare, oberare; —some a

ingombrante
cumulative *a* cumulativo
cumulous *a* cumuloso *m*
cumulus (cloud) *n* cumulo
cunning *a* abile; — *n* abilità
cup *n* tazza; — *vt* applicare la ventosa;
–ful *n* tazza piena; contenuto della tazza
cupboard *n* armadio, credenza
Cupid *n* Cupido
cupidity *n* cupidigia
cupola *n* cupola
cur *n* degenerato; *(dog)* cane bastardo
curable *a* curabile, guaribile
curate *n* curato
curative *a* curativo
curator *n* curatore *m*
curb *n (check)* giogo, freno, barbazzale *m*;
(street) ciglio di strada; **–ing** *n (fig)*
freno; — *vt* frenare, reprimere, mettere
il freno
curd *n* latte quagliato
curdle *vt* coagulare, quagliare; — *vi* coagularsi; — **one's blood** agghiacciare il
sangue
cure *n* cura; — *vt* curare, guarire; *(by
salting)* salare; *(by smoking)* affumicare; *(pelt)* conciare
cure-all *n* toccasana, curatutto, panacea
curfew *n* coprifuoco
curia *n (eccl)* curia
curio *n* anticaglia
curiosity *n* curiosità
curious *a* curioso
curl *vt* arricciare, inanellare; — *vi* arricciarsi, inanellarsi; — **up** aggrovigliarsi; — *n* ricciolo, boccolo; **–y** *a*
ricciuto
curlicue *n* ghirigoro
currant *n* ribes *m*
currency *n* circolazione; **foreign** — valuta
straniera
current *a* corrente; **–ly** *adv* correntemente; — **events** attualità *fpl*; — **expenses**
spese correnti
current *n* corrente *f*; — **density** densità di
corrente; **alternating** — corrente alternata; **direct** — corrente diretta
curricular *a* curriculare
curriculum *n* curricolo
curry *vt* condire; — **favor** entrare in grazia
curse *n* maledizione, afflizione; — *vt* maledire; — *vi* bestemmiare; **be –d with**
essere afflitto da; **–d** *a* maledetto, afflitto
cursing *n* maledizione
cursive *a* corsivo
cursory *a* rapido, affrettato
curt *a* corto, breve
curtail *vt* accorciare, abbreviare; **–ment**
n abbreviazione
curtain *n* cortina, tenda; — **call** pre-

sentazione agli applausi; — **lecture**
rimprovero coniugale; — **raiser** avan-
spettacolo; **iron** — cortina di ferro;
— *vt* applicare le cortine; *(hide)* velare
curtsy *n* cortesia, inchino; — *vi* fare cortesia
curvature *n* curvatura
curve *n* curva; — *vt* curvare; — *vi* curvarsi; **–d** *a* curvo
cushion *n* cuscino; — *vt* collocare sopra
cuscini; *(pad)* imbottire
cusp *n* cuspide *f*; **–id** *n* dente canino; — *a*
cuspidato, acuto
cuspidor *n* sputacchiera
custard *n* crostata
custodial *a* di custodia
custodian *n* custode *m*
custody *n* custodia; **in** — in custodia,
arrestato; **take into** — prendere in
custodia, arrestare; **have** — **of** avere
custodia di
custom *n* costume *m*, usanza; **–ary** *a* con-
suetudinario; **–arily** *adv* consuetudina-
riamente; **–er** *n* cliente *m*; **–house** *n* dogana
custom-built, –made *a* fatto a richiesta
customs *npl* dogana; — **declaration**
dichiarazione doganale; — **inspection**
ispezione doganale; — **inspector** ispettore doganale
cut *n* taglio; *(blow)* colpo; *(wound)* incisione; *(fig)* affronto; — **and dried**
preelaborato, preparato; — **glass** cristallo intagliato
cut *vt&i* tagliare; *(cards)* alzare; *(class)*
(sl) marinare la scuola; *(omit)* omettere;
(a person, sl) far finta di non vedere;
(prices) ribassare; *(teeth)* mettere i
denti; — **and run** *(sl)* svignarsela; tagliare la corda *(coll)*; — **down to size** *(sl)*
mettere a posto *(coll)*; — **off** ritagliare,
(detach) staccare; *(interrupt)* interrompere; — **short** tagliar corto *(coll)*;
C– it out! Smettila!; — *n (print)* cliché
m
cutaneous *a* cutaneo
cutback *n* riduzione
cute *a (coll)* grazioso
cut-glass *a* di vetro intagliato
cuticle *n* cuticola, pellicola
cutlery *n* coltelleria
cutlet *n* cotoletta, braciola
cutoff *n* scorciatoia
cutout *n* interruttore *m*; *(auto)* valvola;
(picture) disegno *(or* figura) da ritagliare
cut-rate *a&adv* a buon mercato
cutthroat *n* assassino, sicario; — *a* omicida
cutting *n* taglio; — *a* tagliente

cyanide *n* cianuro
cyclamen *n* ciclamino
cycle *n* ciclo
cyclic, cyclical *a* ciclico
cyclist *n* ciclista *m&f*
cyclone *n* ciclone *m*
cyclotron *n* ciclotrone *m*
cylinder *n* cilindro; — **head** camera di combustione
cylindrical *a* cilindrico

cymbal *n* cembalo; —**ist** *n* suonatore di piatti
cynic *n* cinico; —**ism** *n* cinismo
cynical *a* cinico
cynosure *n* cinosura, *(ast)* Orsa Minore
cypress *n* cipresso
Cyprus Cipro
cyst *n* ciste *f*
Czech *n&a* czeco, ceco
Czechoslovakia Cecoslovacchia

D

dab *vt&i* comprimere; *(pat)* battere leggermente; — **at** macchiare; *(food)* piluccare; — *n* colpetto; *(mud)* zacchera; *(paint)* schizzo; *(small bit)* pizzicotto
dabber *n* tampone *m*
dabble *vt* immergere, bagnare; — *vi* guazzare, immischiarsi
dactyl *n* dattilo
dad, daddy *n* papà *m*, babbo
dadaism *n* dadaismo
dado *n* *(arch)* dado
daffodil *n* narciso prataiolo
dagger *n* daga, pugnale *m*
dahlia *n* dalia
daily *a* quotidiano, giornaliero; — **newspaper** giornale quotidiano; — *adv* quotidianamente, giornalmente
daintily *adv* delicatamente, gustosamente
daintiness *n* delicatezza, leccornia
dainty *a* delicato, ghiotto
dairy *n* latteria; — **farm** vaccheria; — **products** latticini *mpl*
dais *n* palco
daisy *n* margherita
dale *n* valle *f*
dalliance *n* indugio, ritardo
dally *vi* indugiare, ritardare, dimorarsi
dam *n* diga; *(animal)* madre; **give a tinker's** — non dare nessun valore; — *vt* fornire di diga, frenare, arginare
damage *n* danno; — *vt* danneggiare, nuocere; — *vi* subire danno; —**able** *a* danneggiabile; —**d** *a* danneggiato
damaging *a* danneggiante, dannoso
damask *n* damasco
dame *n* dama, signora
damn *vt* maledire, dannare; — *a* dannato; —**able** *a* maledetto, odioso; —**ation** *n* dannazione; —**ed** *a* dannato
damp *n* umidità, *(mine)* vapore *m*; — *a* umido, umidiccio; —**er** *n* *(fig)* guastafeste *m*; *(flue)* regolatore *m*; *(mus)* sordina; —**ness** *n* umidità
dampen *vt* inumidire, abbattere; — *vi* inumidirsi; abbattersi
dance *vi* danzare, ballare; **make — an-**

other tune far cambiare di tono *(coll)*; — **attendance on** servire con attenzione; — *n* ballo, danza
dancer *n* ballerino, danzatore *m*
dandelion *n* radicchiella
dander *n* *(coll)* collera; **get one's — up** montare in collera
dandle *vt* dondolare, cullare, accarezzare
dandruff *n* forfora
dandy *n* damerino; — *a* *(sl)* elegante, ricercato
Dane, Danish *n&a* danese
danger *n* pericolo
dangerous *a* pericoloso; —**ously** *adv* pericolosamente
dangle *vt* far penzolare; — *vi* penzolare, penzolarsi
dank *a* umido, madido
dapper *a* gentile, grazioso
dapple *a* screziato; — *vt* macchiettare, screziare; — *vi* screziarsi, macchiettarsi; —**d** *a* macchiettato, screziato
dare *vt* sfidare; — **say** osare di dire; —**devil** *n* audace *m&f*, temerario
daring *a* ardito, audace; — *n* ardimento, audacia
dark *a* oscuro, nero; — **horse** *(pol)* candidato insignificante; — **secret** segreto profondo; **in the** — all'oscuro; **keep** — lasciare all'oscuro; — *n* oscurità; —**ness** *n* oscurità; —**room** *n* camera oscura
darken *vt* oscurare; — *vi* oscurarsi, imbrunire
darling *n* favorito, diletto; — *a* caro, prediletto
darn *vt* rammendare; — *n* rammendo; —**ed** *a* rammendato; —**ing needle** ago da rammendo
dart *n* dardo; — *vt* dardeggiare; — *vi* slanciarsi, balzare
dash *vt* colpire, rompere; — *vi* rompersi; — **hopes** togliere la speranza; — **off** *(do)* fare frettolosamente; *(go)* precipitarsi *(coll)*
dash *n* impeto, slancio; *(print)* lineeta; *(small amount)* goccia; pizzico

dashing *a* vivace, impetuoso
dashboard *n* cruscotto; *(mudguard)* parafango
dastard *n* vile *m*, codardo; — *a* codardo; **–liness** *n* codardia; **–ly** *adv* codardamente
data *npl* dati *mpl*; — **processing** progressione di date *(or* datista)
date *n* data; *(bot)* dattero; *(coll)* appuntamento; **out of** — passato, fuori moda; **until now, this** — fino ad oggi, alla data; **up to** — moderno; di moda; — *vt* datare; — *vi* datare da
daub *vt&i (blob)* sgorbiare; *(plaster)* intonacare; *(stain)* imbrattare; — *n* imbratto, sgorbio; *(plaster)* intonaco; **–er** imbrattatore *m*
daughter *n* figlia
daughter-in-law *n* nuora
daunt *vt* intimidire; **–less** *a* intrepido
dauphin *n* delfino
davenport *n* sofà *m*
davit *n (naut)* gru *f*
dawdle *vi* bighellonare
dawdler *n* perdigiorno
dawdling *a* bighellone, fannullone; — *n* bighellonamento
dawn *n* alba, aurora; — *vi* albeggiare; — **on** balenare *(fig)*
day *n* giorno; — **after** — ogni giorno; — **after tomorrow** dopodomani; — **before yesterday** avantieri; — **by** — giorno per giorno; — **in,** — **out** un giorno dopo l'altro; **by the** — alla giornata; **call it a** — averne abbastanza; **every other** — ogni due giorni; **from** — **to** — da un giorno all'altro
daybreak *n* alba
daydream *n* sogno ad occhi aperti; — *vi* sognare ad occhi aperti
day-laborer *n* giornaliere *m*
daylight *n* giorno; **by** — di giorno; — **saving time** ora estiva
day nursery asilo infantile
daytime *n* il giorno; — *a* di giorno
day school scuola diurna
daze *vt* stupefare, sbalordire; — *n* stupore *m*
dazedly *adv* sbalorditamente
dazzle *vt* abbagliare; — *vi* brillare; — *n* abbagliamento
dazzling *a* abbagliante
deacon *n* diacono; **–ess** *n* diaconessa
deactivate *vt* annullare, neutralizzare
dead *a* morto; *(color)* smorto; *(elec)* senza corrente; *(exhaustion, fire)* spento; *(sound)* sordo; — **center** punto morto; **—drunk** ubriaco fradicio; — **end** vicolo cieco; **in a** — **heat** alla stessa distanza del traguardo; — **letter** giacente *f*; — **loss**

perdita totale; — **sleep** sonno profondo; — **sure** sicurissimo; — **weight** peso morto; **the** — i morti
deadliness *n* letalità, natura mortale
deadlock *n* paralisi *f*, ostruzione; — *vt* paralizzare, ostruire
deadly *a* mortale, letale; — *adv* mortalmente, a morte
deaf *a* sordo; **–ness** *n* sordità
deafen *vt* assordare; **–ing** *a* assordante
deaf-mute *n* sordomuto
deal *vt* distribuire; — *vi* agire, comportarsi; *(com)* commerciare, trattare
deal *n (amount)* quantità, parte *f; (cards)* mano *f; (com)* affare *m; (pol)* arrangiamento politico; — **in** *(com)* commerciare in; — **with** aver a che fare, *(concern)* concernere; **a good** — un buon affare; molto; **a great** — moltissimo; **give a square** — trattare giustamente; **make a** — fare un affare; — *a (wood)* di legno di pino
dealer *n (card)* chi distribuisce le carte; *(com)* esercente, distributore *m*
dealing *n* azione, condotta; *(manner of)* modo d'agire; **–s** *npl* pratiche *fpl*
dean *n* decano
dear *n* diletto, caro; — *a* caro, prezioso; *(costly)* costoso; **–ly** *adv* caramente, teneramente; *(amount)* molto; **–ness** *n* carezza; alto prezzo; — **friend** caro amico, cara amica
dearth *n* carestia, scarsità
death *n* morte *f;* — **rate** mortalità; — **rattle** rantolo mortale; — **warrant** ordine d'esecuzione; **–bed** *n* letto di morte; **–less** *a* immortale; **–ly** *a* mortale
debacle *n* sfacelo, disfatta
debar *vt* escludere; *(law)* prescrivere
debark *vt* sbarcare; **–ation** *n* sbarco
debase *vt* avvilire; **–ment** *n* avvilimento; **–basing** *a* degradante
debatable *a* discutibile
debate *vt* dibattere, discutere; — *n* dibattito, discussione
debater *n* dibattente *m*, oratore *m*, parlamentare *m*
debauch *vt* pervertire; — *vi* pervertirsi; **–edly** *adv* perversamente; **–ery** *n* pervertimento
debenture *n* obbligazione
debilitate *vt* debilitare
debilitation *n* debilitazione
debility *n* debolezza
debit *n* debito; — *vt* addebitare
debonaire *a* bonario
debris *n* frammenti *mpl*
debt *n* debito, obbligo; **get into** — andare in deficit; **–or** *n* debitore *m*
debunk *vt (coll)* sgonfiare

debut *n* debutto, esordio; **–ante** *n* debuttante, esordiente *m&f*
decade *n* decade *f*
decadence *n* decadenza
decadent *a* decadente
decalcify *vt* decalcificare
decamp *vi (escape)* svignarsela, scappare; levare il campo *(or* le tende)
decant *vt* decantare; **–er** *n* caraffa
decapitate *vt* decapitare
decapitation *n* decapitazione
decay *vi* decadere, deperire; — *n* decadenza, decadimento; *(putrifaction)* marciume *m; (tooth)* carie *f*
decease *vi* decedere; **–d** *a* deceduto
decedent *n* defunto
deceit *n* inganno, frode *f;* **–ful** *a* falso, ingannevole
deceive *vt* ingannare; **–r** *n* ingannatore *m*
December *n* dicembre *m*
decency *n* decenza, modestia
decent *a* decente, modesto
decentralize *vt* decentrare
deception *n* decezione; frode *f;* delusione; inganno
deceptive *a* ingannevole
decibel *n (elec)* decibel *m*
decide *vt* decidere; — *vi* decidersi
decidedly *adv* decisamente
decimal *a&n* decimale *m*
decimate *vt* decimare
decipher *vt* decifrare; **–able** *a* decifrabile
decision *n* decisione; **come to a** — giungere a una decisione
decisive *a* decisivo, deciso
deck *n* ponte *m,* tolda; *(sl)* terra; *(cards)* mazzo di carte; **— chair** sedia a sdraio; **–hand** *n* marinaio di ponte
declaim *vt&i* declamare
declamation *n* declamazione
declamatory *a* declamatorio
declaration *n* dichiarazione
declare *vt* dichiarare; **— oneself** dichiararsi, rivelarsi
declension *n* declino; *(gram)* declinazione
decline *vt&i* declinare; **— *n*** declino; consunzione
decoction *n* decotto, decozione
decode *vt* decifrare
decompose *vt* decomporre, scomporre; — *vi* decomporsi, scomporsi
decomposition *n* decomposizione
decontaminate *vt* decontaminare
decontrol *vt* liberare dal controllo; — *n* cessazione di controllo
décor *n* decorazione
decorate *vt* decorare
decoration *n* decorazione
decorative *a* decorativo, ornamentale
decorator *n* decoratore *m*

decorous *a* decoroso
decorum *n* decoro
decoy *n (bait)* esca; *(snare)* trappola; **— *vt*** allettare
decrease *vt&i* diminuire, decrescere
decreasing *a* descrescente; **–ly** *adv* in diminuzione
decree *n* decreto, sentenza; **— *vt*** decretare
decrepit *a* decrepito
decry *vt* screditare; *(censure)* biasimare; *(disparage)* deprezzare
dedicate *vt* dedicare; *(coll)* inaugurare
dedication *n* dedica
deduce *vt* dedurre, derivare, desumere
deduct *vt* dedurre; **–ible** *a* deducibile
deduction *n* deduzione *f*
deed *n* atto, fatto; **in —** in realtà
deem *vt&i* giudicare, pensare, credere
deep *a* profondo, grave; **–freeze** *vt* congelare; **— seated** profondo; intimo; **go off the — end** *(coll)* passare i limiti; **in — water** *(fig)* in difficoltà, in cattive acque *(coll);* **–ly** *adv* profondamente
deepness *n* profondità
deepen *vt* approfondire; **— *vi*** approfondirsi
deep-rooted *a* inveterato
deer *n* cervo
deface *vt* sfigurare; *(discredit)* screditare
defalcation *n* diffalco
defamation *n* diffamazione
defamatory *a* diffamatorio
defame *vt* diffamare
default *n* difetto; *(lack)* mancanza; — *vt* condannare in contumacia; — *vi* essere contumace; **–er** *n* imputato, contumace *m;* **in — of** in mancanza di
defeat *vt* sconfiggere; **— *n*** sconfitta, disfatta; **–ist** *n* disfattista *m*
defect *n* difetto; **–ive** *a* difettoso
defection *n* defezione *f*
defend *vt* difendere; **–ant** *n (law)* accusato; **–er** *n* difensore *m*
defense *n* difesa; **–less** *a* indifeso
defensive *a* difensivo; **— *n*** difensiva
defer *vt* differire; **— *vi*** deferire; **–ence** *n* deferenza
deferential *a* deferente
deferment *n* differimento
deferred *a* differito, deferito
defiance *n* sfida, disfida; **in — of** a dispetto di
defiant *a* provocante
deficiency *n* deficienza, difetto
deficient *a* deficiente
deficit *n (com)* deficit *m,* ammanco
defile *vt* disonorare; *(sully)* macchiare; **— *vi*** sfilare; **–ment** *n* profanazione,

macchia
definable *a* definibile
define *vt* definire
definite *a* definito; — **article** articolo determinativo; **–ly** *adv* definitamente; certamente; **–ness** *n* determinatezza
definition *n* definizione
deflate *vt* sgonfiare
deflation *n* sgonfiamento; *(economics)* deflazione
deflect *vt&i* deflettere
deflection *n* deviazione
deform *vt* deformare; — *vi* deformarsi; **–ation** *n* deformazione; **–ed** *a* deforme
deformity *n* deformità
defraud *vt* defraudare
defray *vt* pagare
defrock *vt* svestire; *(eccl)* spretare
defrost *vt* sgelare; rimuovere il ghiaccio; **–er** *n* disgelatore *m; (windshield)* visiera termica; **–ing** *n* disgelo
deft *a* destro, abile
defunct *a&n* defunto
defy *vt* sfidare, scartare, resistere a
degeneracy *n* degenerazione
degenerate *a&n* degenerato; — *vi* degenerare
degeneration *n* degenerazione
deglutinate *vt* deglutinare
degradation *n* degradazione
degrade *vt* degradare; **–d** *a* degradato
degrading *a* digradante
degree *n* grado; diploma; **in some** — fino a un certo punto; **to a** — all'estremo; **by –s** gradatamente; a poco a poco
degression *n* degressione, regressione, diminuzione
dehumidify *vt* deumidificare; diminuire l'umidità
dehydrate *vt* disidratare
dehydration *n* disidratazione
deice *vt* prevenire la formazione di ghiaccio; **–r** *n* scioglighiaccio
deification *n* deificazione
deify *vt* deificare
deign *vt* concedere; — *vi* degnarsi
deity *n* deità
deject *vt* abbattere; **–ed** *a* abbattuto
dejection *n* abbattimento; *(med)* deiezione
delay *vt* differire, ritardare; — *vi* indugiare; — *n* indugio; *(deferment)* rinvio
delaying *a* ritardante
delectable *a* dilettevole
delegate *n* delegato; — *vt* delegare
delegation *n* delegazione
delete *vt* cancellare
deletion *n* cancellazione
deliberate *vt&i* deliberare
deliberate *a* deliberato; *(cautious)* cauto

deliberation *n* deliberazione, riflessione
delicacy *n* delicatezza
delicate *a* delicato
delicatessen *n* negozio di cibi prelibati
delicious *a* delizioso, squisito
delight *vt* dilettare; — *vi* dilettarsi; — *n* diletto; **–ed** *a* deliziato
delightful *a* dilettevole
delineate *vt* delineare
delineation *n* delineazione
delineator *n* disegnatore *m,* delineatore *m*
delinquency *n* delinquenza
delinquent *a&n* delinquente *m&f;* **juvenile** — delinquente giovanile
delirious *a* delirante
delirium *n* delirio
deliver *vt* liberare; *(blow)* lanciare; *(goods)* consegnare; *(med)* far sgravare; *(save)* salvare; *(speech)* enunciare; **be –ed of** partorire; **–ance** *n* rilascio, liberazione
delivery *n* liberazione; *(goods)* consegna; *(mail)* distribuzione; *(med)* parto; *(speech)* dizione; *(sport)* lancio; **general** — fermo in posta; **special** — lettera espresso
delude *vt* deludere
deluge *n* diluvio; — *vt* inondare
delusion *n* delusione, illusione
delve *vt* vangare, sondare
demagogue *n* demagogo; **–ry** *n* pratica demagogica
demand *vt* domandare; *(require)* esigere; — *n* domanda; *(complaint)* reclamo; **in** — ricercato; **on** — *(com)* su domanda
demanding *a* esigente
demarcation *n* demarcazione
demean *vt* degradare, abbassare; — **one's self** avvilirsi
demeanor *n* condotta
demented *a* demente
demerit *n* demerito
demigod *n* semidio
demijohn *n* damigiana
demilitarize *vt* smilitarizzare; sostituire la legge civile a quella marziale
demise *n* morte *m,* decesso; *(law)* cessione, trapasso
demitasse *n* tazzina
demobilization *n* smobilitazione
demobilize *vt* smobilitare
democracy *n* democrazia
democrat *n* democrata *m&f;* **–ic** *a* democratico; **–ically** *adv* democraticamente
demolish *vt* demolire
demolition *n* demolizione
demon *n* demone *m,* demonio; **–iacal** *a* demoniaco, diabolico

demonstrable *a* dimostrabile
demonstrate *vt* dimostrare; — *vi* fare (*or* participare a) dimostrazione
demonstration *n* dimostrazione
demonstrative *a* dimostrativo
demonstrator *n* dimostratore *m*; dimostratrice *f;* dimostrante *m&f*
demoralization *n* demoralizzazione
demoralize *vt* demoralizzare
demote *vt* retrocedere
demotion *n* retrocessione
demount *vt* smontare
demur *vi* esitare, temporeggiare; — *n* esitazione, temporeggiamento
demure *a* sobrio; *(modest)* pudico
demurrage *n* sosta, controstallie *fpl; (charges)* magazzinaggio
den *n* covo, tana; *(private room)* studio intimo
denatured *a* denaturato
deniable *a* negabile
deniably *adv* negabilmente
denial *n* diniego, rinnegazione
denizen *n* abitante *m; (citizen)* cittadino
Denmark Danimarca
denomination *n* denominazione; *(coin)* taglio, conio; **–al** *a* particolare, settario
denominator *n* denominatore *m*
denote *vt* denotare
denounce *vt* denunciare; **–ment** *n* denuncia
dense *a* denso; *(stupid)* sciocco
density *n* densità
dent *n* incavo, intaccatura; — *vt* incavare, intaccare, dentellare; **–ed** *a* dentellato, intaccato
dental *a* dentale; — **floss** filo per pulire i denti
dentate *a* dentato, dentellato
dentation *n (bot)* dentellatura; *(med)* dentizione
dentifrice *n* dentifricio
dentist *n* dentista *m;* **–ry** *n* odontoiatria
denture *n* dentiera, dentatura
denude *vt* denudare
denunciation *n* denuncia
deny *vt* negare, rifiutare; — **oneself** negarsi, privarsi
deodorant *a&n* disodorante, deodorante *m*
deodorize *vt* deodorare
deodorizer *n* deodorante *m&f*
deontology *n* deontologia
depart *(deviate from)* deviare, derogare; *(go)* partire; **–ed** *a* morto, passato; **–ure** *n* partenza, dipartita; morte *f*
department *n* dipartimento; — **store** grande magazzino, bazar *m,* emporio; **–al** *a* dipartimentale
depend *vi* dipendere; — **on** dipendere da; **–ability** *n* affidamento; **–able** *a* fidato; **–ably** *adv* fidatamente; **–ence** *n* di-

pendenza, fiducia; **–ency** *n* dipendenza; **–ent** *a* dipendente
depict *vt* dipingere
depilatory *n&a* depilatorio
deplete *vt (empty)* vuotare; *(exhaust)* esaurire
depletion *n* deplezione, diminuzione, esaurimento
deplorable *a* deplorabile
deplore *vt* deplorare
deploy *vt* dispiegare
depopulate *vt* spopolare; — *vi* spopolarsi
deport *vt* deportare; **–ation** *n* deportazione; **–ment** *n* condotta, comportamento
depose *vt* deporre
deposit *vt* depositare; — *n* deposito; **–or** *n* depositante *m&f;* **–ory** *n* deposito, depositario
deposition *n* deposizione; *(law)* testimonianza, deposizione
depot *n* deposito; *(rail)* stazione
deprave *vt* depravare; **–d** *a* depravato
depravity *n* depravazione
deprecate *vt* deprecare
deprecating *a* screditante
depreciate *vt* deprezzare; — *vi* deprezzarsi
depreciation *n* deprezzamento
depredation *n* depredamento
depress *vt* deprimere; **–ed** *a* depresso; **–ant** *n&a (med)* deprimente *m;* **–ing** *a* deprimente, depressivo
depression *n* depressione
deprivation *n* privazione; *(dismissal from office)* deposizione
deprive *vt* privare; *(dismiss)* deporre
depth *n* profondità, abisso *(fig)*; colmo *(fig)*; **beyond one's** — senza fondo *(coll)*
deputation *n* deputazione
deputize *vt* delegare
deputy *n* deputato, delegato
derail *vt* far deragliare; — *vi* deragliare; **–ment** *n* deragliamento
derange *vt* disordinare; **–d** *a* disordinato; *(insane)* pazzo; **–ment** *n* disordine *m;* pazzia
derby *n (hat)* bombetta; *(race)* derby *m*
derelict *a* derelitto; — *n* relitto
dereliction *n* abbandono; *(law)* delinquenza
deride *vt* deridere
derision *n* derisione
derisive *a* derisivo
derivation *n* derivazione
derivative *a* derivato, derivativo; — *n* derivato
derive *vt&i* derivare
dermatitis *n* dermatite *f*

dermatologist n dermatologo
derogate vi derogare
derogation n calunnia
derogatory a derogatorio
derrick n gru meccanica
dervish n dervis m, dervigio
descant n (mus) melodia
descend vt&i discendere; **be –ed from** discendere da
descendant n discendente m&f; **–s** npl discendenti mpl
descent n discesa
describe vt descrivere
description n descrizione; **of all –s** di tutti i generi
descriptive a descrittivo
desecrate vt profanare, sconsacrare
desecration n profanazione
desegregate vt integrare, contro-discriminare
desegregation n integrazione, antidiscriminazione
desensitize vt insensibilizzare
desert vt&i disertare; **–er** n disertore m
desert n (geog) deserto
desertion n diserzione
deserts npl (just reward) ricompensa secondo il merito
deserve vt&i meritare; **–d** a meritato
deserving a meritevole, degno
desiccate vt essicare; **—** vi essicarsi, seccare
design vt disegnare; (plan) progettare; **—** n disegno; **–s** npl piani mpl
designer n disegnatore m; modellista f
designing a astuto, intrigante
designate vt designare
desirability n desiderabilità
desirable a desiderabile
desire vt desiderare; **—** n desiderio
desirous a desideroso
desist vi desistere
desk n scrivania
desolate a desolato
desolation n desolazione
despair vi disperare, disperarsi; **—** n disperazione; **–ing** a disperante, disperato
desperate a disperato
desperation n disperazione
despicable a vile, spregevole
despise vt disprezzare
despite prep nonostante
despoil vt spogliare (fig)
despondency n scoraggiamento
despondent a scoraggiato
despot n despota m; **–ic** a dispotico; **–ism** n dispotismo
dessert n dolci e frutta
destination n destinazione
destine vt destinare; **–d** a destinato

destiny n destino
destitute a destituito, bisognoso
destitution n destituzione, bisogno
destroy vt distruggere; **–er** n (naut) cacciatorpediniere m
destructible a distruttibile
destruction n distruzione
destructive a distruttivo; **–ness** n distruttività
desultory a saltuario
detach vt staccare; **–able** a staccabile; **–ed** a staccato; **–ment** n distacco; (mil) distaccamento
detail n dettaglio; (mil) distaccamento; **go into —** entrare in particolari; **in —** in dettaglio; **–ed** a particolareggiato; **—** vt dettagliare
detain vt detenere
detect vt svelare
detective a&n rivelatore m, investigatore m
detection n scoperta, rivelazione
detector n scopritore, rivelatore m; (elec) coesore m; (rad) detettore m
detention n detenzione, arresto; (delay) ritardo
deter vt scoraggiare, dissuadere; (detain) trattenere; **–rent** a&n preventivo, dissuadente m
detergent a&n detergente, detersivo
deteriorate vt deteriorare; **—** vi deteriorarsi
deterioration n deterioramento
determinable a determinabile
determinate a definito, determinato
determination n determinazione, risoluzione
determinative a determinativo, definitivo
determine vt determinare, decidere; **—** vi determinarsi, decidersi; **–d** a risoluto, determinato, deciso
detest vt detestare; **–able** a detestabile; **–ation** n detestazione
dethrone vt detronizzare; **–ment** n detronizzazione
detonate vi detonare; **—** vt far detonare
detonation n detonazione
detonator n detonatore m
detour n deviazione, giravolta; **—** vt&i deviare
detract vt&i detrarre, denigrare; **— from** sparlare di; **–or** n detrattore, denigratore m
detraction n detrazione, diffamazione
detriment n detrimento; **–al** a dannoso
deuce n (cards, dice) due; (tennis) 40 pari
devaluate vt svalutare
devaluation n svalutazione
devalue vt svalutare
devastate vt devastare; **–d** a devastato
devastating a devastante, devastatore

devastation *n* devastazione
develop *vt* sviluppare; — *vi* svilupparsi; **–ment** *n* sviluppo
developer *n (photo)* sviluppatore *m*
deviate *vi* deviare
deviation *n* deviazione
device *n* disegno; *(plan)* progetto, stratagemma *m*; **leave to one's own –s** lasciare in balia della propria volontà
devil *n* diavolo; **between the — and the deep blue sea** fra l'incudine e il martello *(coll)*; **give the — his due** render giustizia all'avversario; **play the — with** *(coll)* mandare in rovina completa; **–ish** *a* diabolico; **–ment** *n* diavoleria; **–try** *n* diavoleria, azione diabolica
devil-may-care *a (careless)* trascurato; *(dissolute)* scapestrato
devious *a* indiretto, deviato
devise *vt* escogitare; *(law)* legare per testamento
devitalize *vt* privare della vitalità; indebolire
devoid *a* destituito; privo di
devolve *vt* devolvere, passare a, trasferire
devote *vt* dedicare; — **oneself to** dedicarsi a; **–d** *a* devoto
devotee *n* devoto, fanatico; persona dedita
devotion *n* devozione; **–al** *a* devozionale; religioso; **–s** *npl* devozioni *fpl,* preghiere *fpl*
devour *vt* divorare
devout *a* devoto, pio; **–ness** *n* devozione, religiosità
dew *n* rugiada; — **claw** sprone *m*
dewy *a* rugiadoso
dexterity *n* destrezza
dexterous *a* abile, destro
dextrin *n* destrina
dextrose *n* destrosio
diabetes *n* diabete *m*
diabetic *a* diabetico
diabolic, –al *a* diabolico
diacritical *a* diacritico; — **mark** segno diacritico
diadem *n* diadema *m*
diaeresis *n* dieresi *f*
diagnose *vt* diagnosticare
diagnosis *n* diagnosi *f*
diagonal *a&n* diagonale; **–ly** *adv* diagonalmente
diagram *n* diagramma *m;* **–matic** *a* diagrammatico
dial *n* quadrante *m*; *(sun)* meridiana; *(telephone)* disco; — *vt* misurare, indicare sul quadrante; — *vi (telephone)* discare; fare il numero
dialect *n* dialetto; **–ic, –ical** *a* dialettale, dialettico; **–ics** *npl* dialettica

dialogue *n* dialogo
diameter *n* diametro
diametric, diametrical *a* diametrale
diametrically *adv* diametralmente; — **opposed** diametralmente opposto
diamond *n* rombo; *(baseball)* campo di giuoco; *(cards)* quadri *mpl;* *(gem)* diamante *m*; — **in the rough** *(fig)* diamante grezzo
diapason *n* diapason *m*
diaper *n (baby's)* pannolino
diaphanous *a* diafano
diaphragm *n* diaframma *m*
diarrhea *n* diarrea
diary *n* diario
diastase *n* diastasi *f*
diathermy *n* diatermia
diatonic *a* diatonico
diatribe *n* diatriba
dice *npl* dadi *mpl;* — *vi* giuocare ai dadi, — *vt (food)* tagliare in dadi
dicker *vi (sl)* contrattare; — *vt* barattare; — *n* buon affare
dictaphone *n* dittafono
dictate *vt&i* dettare; — *n* dettame *m*
dictation *n* dettatura; *(order)* comando
dictator *n* dittatore *m;* **–ship** *n* dittatura
dicatatorial *a* dittatorio, dittatoriale
diction *n* dizione
dictionary *n* dizionario
dictograph *n* dittografo
dictum *n* detto, massima
didactic *a* didattico; **–s** *npl* didattica
die *vi* morire; — **away** morire lentamente, languire; — **off** estinguersi; *(wither)* appassire, svanire; — **out** perire; estinguersi; **–hard** *n* intransigente *m*
die *n (coin)* conio; *(dice)* dado; *(mech)* stampo, marchio; — **casting** pressa, fusione; **the — is cast** il dado è tratto; **–maker** *n* tecnico formista
diesel engine motore Diesel
diet *n (pol)* dieta, assemblea
diet *n* dieta, regime *m*; **be on a** — essere a dieta; **put on a** — mettere a dieta
dietetic *a* dietetico; **–s** *n* dietetica
dietitian *n* dietista *m&f; (med)* medico dietista
differ *vi* differire; *(disagree)* dissentire
difference *n* differenza; **split the** — dividere la differenza
different *a* differente, diverso
differential *n&a* differenziale *m*
differentiate *vt* differenziare; — *vi* differenziarsi
differentiation *n* differenziazione
difficult *a* difficile; **–y** *n* difficoltà
difficulties *npl* difficoltà *fpl;* **be in** — essere in difficoltà
diffidence *n* diffidenza, timidezza

diffident *a* diffidente, timido
diffract *vt* diffrangere
diffraction *n* diffrazione
diffuse *a* diffuso; **–r** *n* diffusore *m*
diffusion *n* diffusione
dig *vt&i* scavare; *(hoe)* zappare; — **in** rintanarsi; *(coll)* indagare; — **up** dissotterrare; *(find out)* scoprire; — *n* *(coll)* sarcasmo; *(push)* spinta; *(sl)* sgobbone *m*
digest *n* digesto, compendio
digest *vt* considerare; *(summarize)* riassumere; — *vt&i* *(food)* digerire
digestible *a* digeribile
digestive *a* digestivo
digger *n* *(mech)* scavatrice *f*
diggings *npl* *(coll)* alloggio
digit *n* dito; *(number)* cifra; **–al** *a* digitale
dignified *a* austero, nobile, dignitoso
dignify *vt* dignificare, nobilitare
dignitary *n* dignitario
dignity *n* dignità
digraph *n* digramma *m*
digress *vi* digredire
digression *n* digressione
dike *n* diga
dilapidate *vt* dilapidare; — *vi* dilapidarsi; **–d** *a* dilapidato
dilapidation *n* dilapidazione
dilate *vt* dilatare; — *vi* dilatarsi, espandersi
dilation *n* dilazione, dilatazione
dilatory *a* dilatorio
dilemma *n* dilemma *m*; **the horns of a —** i corni di un dilemma
diligence *n* perserveranza
diligent *a* diligente
dill *n* aneto
dillydally *vi* tentennare, nicchiare
dilute *vt* diluire
diluted *a* diluito; **be —** diluirsi
dilution *n* diluzione
dim *a* oscuro, confuso; — *vt* oscurare, offuscare; **–ly** *adv* oscuramente, confusamente
dime *n* moneta da 10 cents
dimension *n* dimensione; **–al** *a* dimensionale; di dimensione
diminish *vt&i* diminuire
diminutive *a&n* diminutivo
dimmer *n* reostato
dimness *n* oscurità
dimout *n* oscuramento
dimple *n* fossetta, affossamento; — *vi* formare fossette; **–d** *a* increspato
din *n* fracasso; — *vt* stordire
dine *vi* pranzare, desinare; — **out** pranzare fuori
diner *n* chi pranza; *(rail)* vagone ristorante
dinghy *n* *(naut)* dingo

dinginess *n* oscurità; sporcizia
dingy *a* *(dark)* oscuro; *(dirty)* sporco
dining *n* pranzo; — **room** sala da pranzo
dinner *n* pranzo, desinare *m*; — **jacket** abito da sera; smoking *m*
dinosaur *n* dinosauro
dint *n* forza; **by — of** a forza di
diocese *n* diocesi *f*
diorama *n* diorama *m*
dioxide *n* biossido
dip *vt* immergere; *(plunge into)* tuffare; — *vi* immergersi; tuffarsi; — **into** attingere a; — **the flag** abbassare la bandiera; — *n* immersione, tuffo
diphtheria *n* difterite *f*
diphthong *n* dittongo
diploma *n* diploma *m*
diplomacy *n* diplomazia
diplomat *n* diplomatico; **–ic** *a* diplomatico
dipper *n* *(person)* immersionista; *(spoon)* cucchiaione *m*; **Big D–** Orsa Maggiore; **Little D–** Orsa Minore
direct *a* diretto, diritto; — **current** corrente continua; — **object** *(gram)* accusativo; **–ly** *adv* *(direction)* direttamente; *(time)* immediatamente; **–ive** *n* direttiva
direction *n* direzione; *(address)* indirizzo; — **finder** *(rad)* ondascopio
directions *npl* direzioni *fpl*; *(instructions)* istruzioni, indicazioni *fpl*
director *n* direttore *m*; *(actors)* regista *m*; *(mus)* direttore d'orchestra; **board of –s** consiglio di amministrazione
directory *n* direttorio, guida; *(phone)* guida telefonica
dirge *n* canto funebre
dirt *n* sudiciume *m*
dirtiness *n* sporcizia; *(baseness)* bassezza
dirty *a* sporco, sudicio; — *vt* sporcare, imbrattare
disability *n* incapacità, invalidità; — **insurance** assicurazione per l'invalidità
disable *vt* inabilitare; **–d** *a* invalido
disablement *n* incapacità
disabuse *vt* disingannare
disadvantage *n* svantaggio, perdita, inconveniente *m*
disagree *vi* dissentire, non essere d'accordo
disagreeable *a* antipatico, spiacevole, sgradevole
disagreement *n* disaccordo, divergenza
disallow *vt* disapprovare
disappear *vi* sparire; **–ance** *n* scomparsa
disappoint *vt* ingannare, deludere
disappointment *n* delusione, disappunto
disapproval *n* disapprovazione
disapprove *vt* disapprovare; — *vi* avere cattiva opinione
disarm *vt&i* disarmare

disarming *a* ingenuo

disarmament *n* disarmo; — **conference** conferenza del disarmo

disarrange *vt* scompigliare

disarray *n* confusione

disaster *n* disastro, sciagura

disastrous *a* disastroso, catastrofico

disavow *vt* negare

disband *vt* sbandare, congedare; — *vi* sbandarsi; essere licenziato

disbar *vt* (*law*) cancellare dall'albo degli avvocati

disbelieve *vt* diffidare, discredere

disburse *vt* sborsare; –**ment** *n* sborso, spese *fpl*

discard *n* rifiuto; (*card*) scarto

discard *vt&i* scartare

discern *vt* discernere, distinguere; — *vi* discriminare; –**ible** *a* percettibile; –**ing** *a* perspicace, giudizioso; –**ment** *n* discernimento

discharge *n* (*elec*) scarico; (*med*) spurgo; (*mil*) congedo, rilascio

discharge *vt&i* (*dismiss*) licenziare; (*a duty*) compiere; (*elec*) scaricare; (*gun*) sparare; (*mil*) congedare; (*release*) rilasciare; (*unload*) scaricare; — **an obligation** adempiere un dovere

disciple *n* discepolo

disciplinarian *a* disciplinare

discipline *n* disciplina; — *vt* punire; castigare

disclaim *vt* rinunciare

disclose *vt* svelare, manifestare

disclosure *n* rivelazione

discolor *vt* scolorare, scolorire, cambiar colore; –**ation** *n* scoloramento

discomfort *n* disagio, incomodo

disconcert *vt* sconcertare

disconnect *vt* staccare, tagliare; (*part*) separare; (*elec*) interrompere

discontent *n* malcontento, scontento

discontinue *vt* sospendere, prosciogliere; — *vi* desistere

discontinued *a* sospeso, soppresso, esaurito

discord *n* discordia; –**ant** *a* discordante

discount *n* sconto, ribasso; — **rate** tasso di sconto; — *vt* scontare

discountenance *vt* turbare, sconcertare

discourage *vt* scoraggiare; (*deter*) dissuadere; —**ment** *n* scoraggiamento, scoramento

discouraging *a* scoraggiante

discourse *n* discorso, trattato

discourtesy *n* scortesia

discourteous *a* scortese, sgarbato

discover *vt* scoprire, trovare; –**er** *n* scopritore *m*; –**y** *n* scoperta

discredit *vt* screditare

discreet *a* discreto, prudente

discrepancy *n* discrepanza, divergenza, contraddizione

discretion *n* discrezione, prudenza

discriminate *vt&i* discriminare, distinguere; far distinzione; — **against** far distinzioni nocive contro

discriminating *a* discretivo, da intenditore

discrimination *n* discriminazione, distinzione

discus *n* (*sport*) disco

discuss *vt* dibattere, parlare di, discutere, ragionare di

discussion *n* discussione

disdain *n* disdegno, disprezzo; — *vt* disdegnare; –**ful** *a* sdegnoso

disease *n* malattia; –*d a* malato

disembark *vt* sbarcare; –**ation** *n* sbarco

disenchant *vt* disincantare; –**ment** *n* disincanto, disillusione

disencumber *vt* sgombrare

disengage *vt* liberare; (*mech*) sganciare; — *vi* separarsi da

disfavor *n* disgrazia, sfavore *m*

disfigure *vt* sfigurare, sfregiare

disfranchise *vt* privare della franchigia

disgorge *vt* vomitare, recere

disgrace *n* vergogna, disonore *m*; — *vt* disonorare; –**ful** *a* vergognoso, disonorevole

disgruntled *a* malcontento, di malumore, imbronciato

disguise *vt* travestire, mascherare; — *n* travestimento, finzione, maschera; **in** — camuffato

disgust *n* schifo, disgusto; — *vt* disgustare; –**ing** *a* disgustoso, schifoso

dish *n* piatto, pietanza; — *vt* servire, scodellare; –**water** *n* lavatura di piatti; –**cloth** *n* strofinaccio da piatti; –**pan** *n* recipiente per lavare i piatti; –**towel** *n* strofinaccio per asciugare i piatti

dishearten *vt* scoraggiare

dishevel *vt* scapigliare, scarmigliare; –**ed** *a* scapigliato

dishonest *a* disonesto

dishonor *n* disonore *m*, infamia; — *vt* disonorare, svergognare; –**able** *a* disonorevole; –**ably** *adv* disonorevolmente

dishwarmer *n* scaldavivande *m*

dishwasher *n* lavapiatti *m*; (*person*) sguattero

disillusion *n* disillusione; –**ment** *n* liberazione d'una illusione; — *vt* disilludere

disinclined *a* contrario

disinfect *vt* disinfettare; –**ant** *n&a* disinfettante *m*; –**ion** *n* disinfezione

disinherit *vt* diseredare

disintegrate *vt* disintegrare

disintegration *n* disintegrazione

disinter *vt* disseppellire; **–ment** *n* dissotterramento
disinterested *a* disinteressato
disjoin *vt* disgiungere; — *vi* disgiungersi
disjoint *vt* slogare, disgiungere; **–ed** *a* slogato
disk *n* disco; — **jockey** presentatore di dischi
dislike *n* antipatia, avversione; — *vt* avere in antipatia
dislocate *vt* slogare
dislocation *n (med)* slogatura
dislodge *vt&i* sloggiare, scacciare
disloyal *a* sleale; **–ty** *n* infedeltà, slealtà
dismal *a* triste, misero, funesto
dismantle *vt* smantellare
dismay *vt* costernare; — *n* costernazione
dismember *vt* smembrare
dismiss *vt* licenziare, destituire, congedare; **—a meeting** togliere una seduta; *(oust)* scacciare; **–al** *n* licenziamento, destituzione, congedo
dismount *vi* smontare, scavalcare
disobedience *n* disobbedienza
disobedient *a* disobbediente
disobey *vt* disobbedire a
disobliging *a* senza gentilezza
disorder *n* disordine *m;* **–ed mind** psicopatico; **–ly** *a* disordinato
disorganization *n* disorganizzazione
disorganize *vt* disorganizzare
disown *vt* negare, non confessare, rinunciare
disparage *vt* menomare
disparaging *a* offensivo
dispassionate *a* spassionato; **–ly** *adv* spassionatamente
dispatch *n* prontezza, urgenza, fretta; *(com)* dispaccio, spedizione; — *vt* inviare, spacciare, spedire; *(kill)* uccidere
dispel *vt* dissipare; — *vi* dissiparsi
dispensable *a* non indispensabile
dispensary *n* dispensario
dispensation *n* distribuzione; *(excuse from)* dispensa
dispense *vt* distribuire; *(administer)* amministrare; *(exempt)* dispensare, esentare
dispersal *n* dispersione
disperse *vt* disperdere, spargere; — *vi* disperdersi
dispirit *vt* scoraggiare; **–ed** *a* abbattuto; scoraggiato; *(dismayed)* sgomento
displaced *a* spostato — **person** profugo
displacement *n* spostamento; *(naut)* stazzo; **cylinder** — cilindrata
display *n* mostra, esibizione; — *vt* esporre, mostrare
displease *vt* offendere, dispiacere a
displeasure *n* dispiacere *m,* disapprovazione

disposable *a* disponibile
disposal *n* disposizione
dispose *vt* disporre; — **of** disporre di; *(sell)* vendere
disposed *a* disposto; **ill** — maldisposto, malintenzionato; **be** — **to** avere dispozione per; essere incline per
disposition *n* inclinazione, carattere *m;* *(disposal of)* disposizione; *(temper)* indole *f*
dispossess *vt* espropriare; **–ed** *a* espropriato
disproportionate *a* sproporzionato
disprove *vt* confutare, invalidare
disputable *a* disputabile
dispute *n* disputa, dibattito
disqualification *n* inabilitazione; squalifica
disqualify *vt* squalificare
disquiet *n* inquietudine *f;* travaglio; — *vt* inquietare, tribolare; **–ing** *a* inquietante
disregard *vt* non dare importanza a, trascurare; — *n* negligenza, indifferenza
disreputable *a* vergognoso; screditato, malfamato
disrepute *n* disonore *m,* discredito
disrespect *n* insolenza; mancanza di rispetto; **–ful** *a* irriverente, incivile; **–fully** *adv* irrispettosamente
disrobe *vt* svestire, spogliare; — *vi* spogliarsi
disrupt *vt* rompere
dissatisfaction *n* malcontento
dissatisfied *a* malcontento
dissatisfy *vt* scontentare, dispiacere
dissect *vt* notomizzare, sezionare; **–ion** *n* dissezione
dissemble *vt&i* simulare
dissemblingly *adv* dissimulatamente
disseminate *vt* disseminare, diffondere
dissemination *n* disseminazione
dissension *n* discordia
dissent *vi* dissentire; — *n* dissenso
dissertation *n* dissertazione; *(school)* tesi di laurea
disservice *n* disservizio
dissimilar *a* dissimile; **–ity** *n* dissimilitudine *f*
dissimulate *vt* dissimulare
dissimulation *n* dissimulazione
dissipate *vt* dissipare; — *vi* dissiparsi
dissipation *n* dispersione, dissipazione
dissolute *a* dissoluto, licenzioso; **–ly** *adv* dissolutamente
dissolution *n* dissoluzione, licenza
dissolve *vt* sciogliere, dissolvere; — *vi* disciogliersi
dissonance *n* dissonanza
dissonant *a* dissonante, differente

dissuade *vt* dissuadere
dissuasion *n* dissuasione
distaff *n* rocca, conocchia
distance *n* distanza; **at a — of** alla distanza di
distant *a* distante, lontano; *(reticent)* riservato
distantly *adv (far)* lontanamente; *(coldly)* con distanza
distaste *n* disgusto, dispiacere *m*; *(dislike)* avversione, idiosincrasia
distasteful *a* fastidioso, sgradevole, antipatico
distemper *n* indisposizione; *(med)* malattia; **—** *vt (disturb)* turbare; fare male, fare ammalare
distend *vt* stendere, allargare; **—** *vi* distendersi, allargarsi
distill *vt* distillare; **–ed** *a* distillato; **–ation** *n* distillazione
distillery *n* distilleria
distinct *a* distinto; **–ive** *a* distintivo
distinction *n* distinzione
distinguish *vt* distinguere; **–ed** *a* distinto
distinguishing *a* distintivo
distort *vt* contorcere, distorcere; *(alter)* travisare *(fig)*
distortion *n* distorsione
distract *vt* distrarre, svagare; turbare
distracted *a* distratto; divertito; *(upset)* sconvolto; **–ly** *adv* distrattamente
distraction *n* distrazione
distress *n* sfortuna, guaio, miseria, pena, angoscia; **— signal** segnalazione di soccorso; **–ed** *a* spiacente; **—** *vt* inquietare, affliggere
distribute *vt* distribuire
distribution *n* distribuzione
distributor *n* distributore *m*
district *n* distretto; **— attorney** procuratore di stato
distrust *vt* sospettare; diffidare di; non aver fiducia in; **—** *n* diffidenza, sfiducia; **–ful** *a* sospettoso
disturb *vt* disturbare; **–ance** *n* disturbo
disuse *n* disuso
ditch *n* fosso, fossato; **fight to the last —** resistere ad oltranza
ditto *n* idem *m*, lo stesso
diuretic *a* diuretico
divan *n* divano, sofà
dive *vi* tuffarsi; *(naut)* immergersi; **—** *n* immersione, tuffo; *(coll)* bettola; *(avi)* scesa in picchiata
dive– *(in comp)* **—bomber** *n* aereo da picchiata; **— bombing** *n* bombardamento in picchiata
diver *n* tuffatore *m*; *(deep-sea)* palombaro; *(skin)* sommozzatore *m*
diverge *vi* divergere, deviare, differire

divergence *n* divergenza
diverging *a* divergente
divers *a* assortito
diverse *a* diverso, differente, vario
diversion *n* diversione, divertimento, passatempo; *(turning from)* deviazione; **–ary** *a* ricreativo
diversity *n* diversità
divert *vt* divertire; *(amuse)* svagare; **–ing** *a* divertente
divest *vt* svestire, spogliare; **— oneself** svestirsi, spogliarsi
divide *vt* dividere; **—** *vi* dividersi, scindersi; **–d** *a* diviso; **—** *n (geog)* spartiacque *m*
dividend *n* dividendo
divider *n* divisore *m*; **–s** *npl (compass)* compasso a molla
divination *n* divinazione
divine *a* divino; **—** *vi* profetizzare, fare profezia
diving *n* immersione, tuffo; **— bell** campana da palombaro; **— suit** scafandro
divinity *n* divinità
division *n* divisione; **–al** *a* divisorio, divisionale
divisor *n* divisore *m*
divorce *n* divorzio; **—** *vt* divorziare, divorziarsi; **— court** tribunale dei divorzi; **sue for a —** chiedere un divorzio
divorcé *n* divorziato, **–e** *n* divorziata
divot *n (golf)* zolla erbosa strappata dal bastone
divulge *vt* rivelare, divulgare
dizziness *n* vertigini *fpl*, stordimento
dizzy *a* vertiginoso; *(coll)* stordito; **feel —** avere le vertigini; **make one —** stordire, dare le vertigini a
D.N.A., deoxyribonucleic acid *n* D.N.A., acido diossigenucleico
do *vt&i* fare; **— away with** sopprimere; distruggere; **— dishes** lavare i piatti; **— in** *(coll)* rovinare; *(kill)* uccidere; **— one's best** fare del proprio meglio; **— out of** frodare; **— up** rifare, riparare, involgere, abbottonare; **— without** fare senza; **have to — with** aver che fare con; **make —** aggiustarsi con; **this will —** ciò basta
docile *a* docile
dock *n* molo, imbarcadero; **dry —** bacino di carenaggio; **—** *vt* abbreviare; *(ship)* far entrare in bacino; *(tail)* tagliare la coda; *(wages)* far dedurre dalla paga
docket *n* registro; *(law)* attergato
dockyard *n* cantiere navale
doctor *n* dottore *m*; **–ate** *n* dottorato; **—** *vt* adulterare; **— oneself** curarsi da sè; **be under a –'s care** essere assistito dal

dottore
doctrine *n* dottrina
document *n* documento; **–ary** *a* documentario
documentation *n* documentazione
dodder *vi* tremare; **–ing** *a* tremante
dodge *n* balzo; *(coll)* trucco *(fig);* — *vt* evitare, schivare, eludere; — *vi* cambiare di posto; sfuggire con sotterfugi
doe *n* daina
doff *vt* cavarsi, togliersi; sbarazzarsi di
dog *n* cane *m;* — **days** canicola; — **one's footsteps** pedinare qualcuno; **let sleeping –s lie** lasciare dormire il cane che dorme; — *vt (follow)* pedinare; *(spy on)* spiare, seguire le orme
dog– *(in comp)* **—eared** *a* sfogliato, spiegazzato; **—eared page** pagina con gli angoli sfogliati; **—tired** *a* stanco morto
dogged *a* ostinato, accanito; **–ly** *adv* risolutamente; *(firmly)* tenacemente; *(stubbornly)* ostinatamente
doghouse *n* canile *m;* **be in the** — *(sl)* essere nei pasticci *(coll)*
dogma *n* dogma *m;* **–tic** *a* dogmatico
doily *n* tovagliolino, sottocoppa *m; (coaster)* sottobicchiere *m*
doing *n* fatto, evento; **be worth** — valere la pena; **–s** *npl* faccende *fpl,* fatti *mpl*
doldrums *npl (naut)* calme equatoriali *fpl;* **be in the** — essere malinconico
dole *n* elemosina, piccola quantità; **–ful** *a* doloroso, lamentevole; — *vt* fare la carità; — **out** distribuire
doll *n* bambola
dollar *n* dollaro
dolly *n (toy)* bambolina; *(truck)* carrello
dolor *n* dolore *m*
dolorous *a* doloroso
dolt *n* balordo, stupido
domain *n* dominio, proprietà
dome *n* cupola
domestic *a* domestico, di famiglia; nazionale; locale; — *n (servant)* domestico
domesticate *vt* addomesticare
domicile *n* domicilio
dominance *n* dominio
dominant *a* dominante
dominate *vt* dominare, predominare
domination *n* dominazione
domineer *vt&i* tiranneggiare, signoreggiare; **–ing** *a* tirannico, prepotente
Dominican Republic *n* Republica domenicana
dominion *n* dominio; colonia autonoma
domino *n* domino
don *vt* indossare; — *n* signore *m*
donate *vt* donare, dare
donation *n* offerta, dono
donkey *n* asino; **make a** — **of** far passa-

re per stupido *(coll)*
donor *n* donatore *m,* donatrice *f*
doodle *n* allocco, ingenuo; — *vt&i* disegnare *(or* scrivere) distrattamente
doom *n* condanna; **voice of** — la voce della Giustizia Divina; — *vt* condannare; **–ed** *a* predestinato; *(condemned)* condannato
doomsday *n* la fine del mondo
door *n* porta, uscio; **–bell** *n* campanello; **–knob** *n* maniglia della porta; **–man** *n* portiere *m;* **–mat** *n* nettapiedi *m;* **–step** *n* soglia; **–way** *n* vano della porta; **back** — porta di servizio
dope *n* stupefacente *m; (sl)* narcotico; *(low-down, sl)* informazione *(fig);* — *vt (sl)* affettare con stupefacenti
dormant *a* dormiente
dormer window abbaino
dormitory *n* dormitorio
dose *n* dose *f;* — *vt* dosare, somministrare dosi
dossier *n* incartamento
dot *n* punto; **on the** — a punto
dotage *n* rimbambimento
dote *vi* rimbambire; — **on** amare pazzamente
double *n&a* duplicato, doppio; — **feature** due film d'un programma; **one's** — l'altro sè stesso; — *vt* doppiare, raddoppiare; — **back** *(fold)* piegare indietro; *(retrace)* ritornare sui propri passi; — *vi* ripiegare; tornare indietro, girarsi
double– *(in comp)* **—breasted** *a* a due petti; **—cross** *n (sl)* tradimento; doppio giuoco; — *vt* tradire; fare il doppio giuoco; **—edged** *a* a due tagli; — **faced** *a (cloth)* a doppia faccia; *(person)* ipocrita, falso; di faccia doppia *(coll)*
doubt *n* dubbio; **no** — senza dubbio; **put in** — mettere in dubbio; **–ful** *a* dubbioso; **–less** *adv* certamente; senza dubbio; — *vt* dubitare
douche *n* doccia
dough *n* pasta; *(sl)* denaro, soldi *mpl*
doughnut *n* frittella
dove *n* colomba
dovetail *n* coda di rondine; — *vt* unire a coda di rondine
dowager *n (coll)* matrona di prestigio
dowdy *a* malvestito, trasandato
down *n (feather)* piuma; *(hair)* lanugine *f;* — *adv* giù abasso; in basso; — **to** fino a; — **the street** *(be)* giù per la strada; *(go)* per la strada; **go** — scendere; **pay** — pagare la prima quota
down *vt (debase)* umiliare; (lower) abbassare; *(pull)* abbattere; *(swallow)* buttar giù
downcast *a* abbattuto

downfall n rovina, caduta

downgrade n discesa; — vt degradare

downhearted a abbattuto, scoraggiato

downhill a scendente; — adv in discesa

downpour n acquazzone m; pioggia a catinelle

downright a diretto, assoluto, completo; — adv assolutamente

downstairs adv giù, abbasso, di sotto, in basso, al piano di sotto; — n pianterreno

downtown n centro della città; — adv in città

downwards adv abbasso

dowry n dote f

doze vi sonnecchiare

dozen n dozzina

drab a grigiobruno, monotono; (color) nocciuola

draft n tiro; (air) corrente d'aria; (com) tratta; (drink) sorsata; (mil) leva, coscrizione; (plan) disegno; (sketch) schizzo; — **beer** birra spillata; **rough** — minuta, brutta copia

draft vt disegnare; (compose) redigere; (sketch) tracciare

draftsman n disegnatore m

drag n draga; (sl) influenza, favore m; — vt trascinare; — vi trascinarsi

drag chute (avi) paracaduta che frena l'atterraggio

dragnet n rete f; (police) retata

dragon n drago

drain vt scolare, prosciugare; (empty) vuotare; –**pipe** n tubo di scarico, tubo di drenaggio

drain n canale m; (med) drenaggio; –**age** n drenaggio

drama n dramma m

dramatic a drammatico

dramatist n drammaturgo; autore drammatico

dramatize vt drammatizzare

drape n drappo; — vt drappeggiare; — vi pendere flosciamente

drapery n drappeggio, tendaggio, drapperia

drastic a drastico

draw vt disegnare; (attract) attrarre; (pull) tirare; (sword) sguainare; (water) attingere; — **a sigh** sospirare; — **away** sorpassare; — **back** indietreggiare; — **lots** sorteggiare; — **near** avvicinarsi; — **oneself up** mettersi ritto; — **out** tirar fuori

draw n attrazione; (score) parte indecisa

drawback n svantaggio, inconveniente m

drawbridge n ponte levatoio

drawer n cassetto

drawers npl (clothing) mutande f

drawing n disegno; (lottery) lotteria; (pulling) tiraggio; (raffle) sorteggio; — **card** specchio per le allodole (fig); — **pen** tiralinee m; — **room** sala da ricevimento, salone m

drawl n voce affettata; — vi strascicare le parole

drawn a indeciso; (face) emaciato; (sword) sguainato

dread n paura, terrore m; — vt avere orrore di

dreadful a terribile, spaventevole

dream n sogno; — vt avere una visione di; — vi sognare; — **up** inventare; –**er** n sognatore m

dreamy a sognante; (fantastic) chimerico

dreary a lugubre, cupo, desolato, monotono

dregs npl feccia, sedimento

drench vt inzuppare, bagnare

dress n abbigliamento; vestito da donna; — vt vestire; (med) medicare; (wrap) fasciare; — vi vestirsi; –**y** a (coll) elegante, vistoso

dresser n (furniture) comò, cassettone m; (theat) guardarobiere m; **a good** — persona ben vestita

dressing n (meat, fowl) ripieno; (med) medicazione; (salad) condimento per l'insalata; — **table** toletta

dressmaker n sarta; sarto

dribble vi gocciolare; — vt far gocciolare

dried a secco

drift n (avi) deriva; deviazione a causa del vento; (meaning) significato; (naut) deriva, direzione; (snow) cumulo di neve; **get the** — (sl) comprendere; — vi andare alla deriva; — vt accumulare

drill n (mech) trapano, perforatrice f; (mil) esercitazione; (training) addestramento; — vt forare, perforare, (train) addestrare

drink n bibita, bevanda; –**able** a potabile; — vt bere; — **a toast** fare un brindisi; — **in** assimilare

drip vi sgocciolare; — vt far sgocciolare; — n sgocciolamento

drive n energia, sforzo; (mech) trasmissione; (pressure) pressione; (ride) passeggiata in carrozza; — vt guidare; — **away** allontanare; — **back** respingere; — **mad** far ammattire; — vi guidare; essere sospinto; andare in veicolo; (rush) precipitarsi; — **a bargain** condurre un affare; — **at** tendere a

drive-in n (restaurant) autoristorante m, autoristoratore m; (theat) autocinema m, cineparco

driver n (auto) automobilista, autista m; (bus) conduttore m; (coachman) coc-

chiere *m*
driver's license patente *f*
driveway *n* vialetto d'entrata; passo carreggiabile
driving *a* movente; di guida; — **power** forza di propulsione
drizzle *vt&i* piovigginare; — *n* pioggerella
droll *a* bizzarro, scherzoso, burlone
drone *n* fuco, pecchione *m*; *(avi)* aereo a controllo remoto; — *vt* dire come ronzando; — *vi* ronzare
drool *vi* sbavare, far bava
droop *vi* curvarsi; *(hang)* pendere; — *vt* abbassare
drop *n* goccia; *(descent)* caduta; *(ear)* pendente *m*; *(globule)* globulo
drop *vi* gocciolare; *(prices)* ribassare; — *vt* lasciar cadere; abbandonare, negligere; — **behind** rimanere indietro; — **in** capitare per caso; — **out** mettersi fuori
drop- *(in comp)* —**kick** *(football)* *n* calcio di rimbalzo; — *vt&i* dare un calcio di rimbalzo; —**leaf** *n* asse accessoria per allungare un tavolo
dropper *n (med)* contagocce *m*
dropsy *n* idropisia, edema *m*
drought *n* siccità
drove *n* gregge *m*, mandra; *(crowd)* folla
drown *vt&i* annegare
drowse *vt* assopire; — *vi* assopirsi
drowsiness *n* sonnolenza, assopimento
drowsy *a* sonnacchioso, sonnolento
drudge *n* sgobbone *m;* uomo di fatica; — *vi* sfacchinare
drudgery *n* facchinata, lavoraccio
drug *n* droga, stupefacente *m*; *(med)* medicinale *m;* — **addict** tossicomane *m;* **be a — on the market** *(com)* essere in troppa concorrenza; — *vt* narcotizzare
druggist *n* farmacista *m*
drugstore *n* farmacia
drum *n (ear)* timpano; *(mus)* tamburo; — *vi (fingers)* tamburellare; *(mus)* tamburreggiare; — **into** *(fig)* inculcare; — *vt* tamburellare; — **up** *(get)* sollecitare, ottenere ostentando
drummer *n (com)* commesso viaggiatore; *(mus)* tamburino
drumstick *n (fowl)* coscia; *(mus)* bacchetta di tamburo
drunk *n&a* ubriaco, ebbro; bevuto *(coll)*; —**ard** *n* ubriacone, beone *m;* —**en** *a* ubriaco, ebbro; —**enly** *adv* ebbramente, ubriacamente; da ubriaco
drunkenness *n* ubriachezza
dry *a* secco; — **cell** cellula elettrica secca; — **cleaner** tintore *m;* — **cleaning** pulitura a secco; — **dock** bacino di carenaggio; — **goods** mercerie *fpl;* — *vt*

seccare; — **up** seccarsi
dryness *n* aridità
dual *a* doppio, duplice, — **control** doppio controllo
dub *vt* investire; armare cavaliere; *(name)* soprannominare; — **in** *(movies)* doppiare
dubious *a* dubbio, incerto, equivoco
duchess *n* duchessa
duchy *n* ducato
duck *n* anitra; — *vt (avoid)* schivare; *(dip)* immergere; *(plunge)* tuffare; — **the head** chinare la testa; — *vi* immergersi; tuffarsi; schivarsi
duct *n* condotto, tubo
ductless *a* senza condotti; — **gland** ghiandola endocrina
dud *n (failure)* cosa che fa cilecca; *(rag)* cencio; — *a* inutile
dude *n* bellimbusto, zerbinotto
duds *npl (sl, clothes)* abiti *mpl; (things)* roba
due *n&a* debito, dovuto; — **bill** *(com)* cambiale *f,* tratta; **fall** —, **be** — scadere; **in** — **time** a tempo debito; — *adv* direttamente
dues *npl* quota, diritti *mpl,* ammontare dovuto
duet *n* duetto
duel *n* duello
duke *n* duca *m*
dull *a* ottuso, noioso; *(color)* oscuro; *(edge)* smussato; — **pain** dolore sordo; —**ness** *n* povertà di spirito; *(surface)* opacità
duly *adv* regolarmente, debitamente
dumb *a* muto; *(coll)* stupido, cretino
dumbly *a* mutamente
dumbbell *n* manubrio
dumbwaiter *n* calapranzi *m*
dumbfound *vt* confondere; far tacere
dummy *n* prestanome *m*; *(cards)* morto; *(manikin)* manichino; *(print)* menabò; *(sl)* stupido; *(straw)* uomo di paglia; — *a* falso, finto
dump *n* mondezzaio; *(sl)* luogo malandato; — *vt* scaricare; svendere in quantità; — *vi* cadere improvvisamente; scaricarsi; —**y** *a* tozzo; *(thickset)* tarchiato
dumps *npl (sl)* malinconia; **be in the** — essere malinconico
dumping ground posto dei rifiuti
dumpling *n* gnocco
dun *vt&i* importunare; *(for money)* insistere nella riscossione
dunce *n* stupido, ignorante *m*, balordo, asino
dune *n* duna
dungeon *n* carcere sotterraneo
dupe *n* gonzo; — *vt* gabbare, truffare,

imbrogliare
duplex *n* a doppio, duplice
duplicate *n* copia; — *n&a* duplicato; — *vt* riprodurre, duplicare
duplicity *n* doppiezza, duplicità
durable *a* durevole
durability *n* durabilità
duration *n* durata
duress *n* coercizione; **under** — per forza, dietro minaccia
during *prep* durante
dusk *n* crepuscolo, imbrunire *m*
dusky *a* scuro, nerastro, bruno
dust *n* polvere *f*; — **storm** tormenta di sabbia; **throw** — **in the eyes** *(fig)* gettare polvere negli occhi *(fig)*; **-y** *a* polveroso
dust *vt* spolverare, spazzolare; — *vi* impolverarsi; levare la polvere dai mobili
duster *n* strofinaccio
Dutch *n&a* olandese *m&f*; — **treat** pagamento alla romana *(coll)*; **go** — *(coll)* fare alla romana
duties *npl* funzioni *fpl*; doveri *mpl*; *(tax)*

diritti di dogana
dutiful *a* obbediente
duty *n* dovere *m*; *(mil)* servizio; **on** — di servizio
duty-free *a* franco di dazio; in franchigia
dwarf *n&a* nano; — *vt* rimpicciolire
dwell *vi* abitare, risiedere; — **on** *(a subject)* insistere su
dwelling *n* dimora
dwindle *vt* ridurre; — *vi* diminuire, deperire, ridursi
dye *vt* tingere, colorire; — *vi* tingersi, colorarsi; — *n* tinta, tintura, colore *m*
dyed-in-the-wool *a* tinto prima della confezione
dyer *n* tintore *m*
dying *a* moribondo, morente
dynamic *a* dinamico; **-s** *n* dinamica
dynamite *n* dinamite *f*
dynamo *n* dinamo *f*
dynasty *n* dinastia
dysentery *n* dissenteria
dyspepsia *n* dispepsia
dyspeptic *a* dispeptico

E

each *a* ciascuno, ogni; — *pron* ognuno, ciascheduno; — **other** l'un l'altro
eager *a* desideroso, avido, volenteroso, impaziente; **-ness** *n* ardore *m*, impazienza
eagle *n* aquila
eagle-eyed *a* dalla vista d'aquila
ear *n* orecchio; *(corn)* pannocchia; **in one** — **and out the other** entrato in un orecchio e uscito dall'altro *(coll)*; **-ache** *n* dolore all'orecchio; mal d'orecchi; **-drum** *n* timpano
earl *n* conte *m*
early *a* mattutino, mattiniero; — **bird** la prima rondine *(fig)*; l'uccello mattiniero; — *adv* di buon'ora, in anticipo
earmark *vt* destinare, serbare, designare
earmuffs *npl* copriorecchi *mpl*
earn *vt&i* guadagnare; *(deserve)* meritare
earnest *a* serio, sincero; — **money** caparra
earnings *npl* salario, guadagni *mpl*
earphone *n* cuffia telefonica
earring *n* orecchino
earth *n* terra; **-ly** *a* terrestre
earthen *a* terreo, di terra; **-ware** *n* terraglie *fpl*
earthquake *n* terremoto
earthworm *n* verme di terra, verme anellide
earwax *n* cerume *m*
ease *n* agio, facilità, disinvoltura; **at** — **a** proprio agio; **ill at** — in imbaraz-

zo; — *vt* calmare, sollevare
easel *n* cavalletto
easily *adv* facilmente, senza difficoltà
east *n* est, oriente *m*; **the E**– Oriente; **the Far E**– l'estrem'Oriente
Easter *n* Pasqua; — **Sunday** Pasqua; — *a* pasquale
easterly *a&adv* orientale, dell'est
eastern *a* orientale, dell'oriente
easy *a* facile, disinvolto, comodo; — **money** *(coll)* danaro guadagnato facilmente; — **chair** poltrona; **-going** *a* tranquillo, sereno, bonario
eat *vt* mangiare; *(breakfast)* far colazione; *(dinner)* pranzare; — **one's words** ricredersi; **-en** *a* mangiato
eatable *n* commestibile *m*, alimento; —, **edible** *a* commestibile, mangiabile; **-s** *npl* commestibili *mpl*
eavesdrop *vi* origliare
ebb *n* riflusso; — **tide** bassa marea; — *vi* rifluire, abbassarsi; *(decline)* decadere
ebony *n* ebano; — *a* d'ebano
ebullition *n* ebollizione, bollore *m*; *(fig)* agitazione
eccentric *a&n* eccentrico; **-ity** *n* eccentricità
ecclesiastic, -al *n&a* ecclesiastico
echelon *n* scaglione *m*
echo *n* eco *m&f*; — *vt* far eco a; — *vi* echeggiare

eclair n pasta di crema
éclat n successo, applauso, effetto
eclipse n eclisse m&f; — vt eclissare, superare; — vi ecclissarsi
ecliptic a (ast) eclittico
economics n scienza economica
economist n economista m
economize vt&i economizzare
economy n economia
ecru a color seta crudo
ecstasy n estasi f
ecstatic a estatico
ecumenical a ecumenico
eddy n turbine m, vortice m; — vt&i turbinare
edema n edema, gonfiore m
edge n bordo, margine m; (knife) filo; **have the** — **on** (coll) aver vantaggio; **on** — sul filo; sull'orlo; (nervous) irritabile; -**wise** adv di taglio; di profilo; — vi avanzare gradatamente; camminare di traverso (fig); (border) orlare; — vt bordare, orlare; (whet) affilare
edging n bordo, orlo
edible a commestibile, mangereccio
edict n editto
edifice n edificio
edify vt edificare
edit vt curare, redigere, rivedere
edition n edizione
editor n (book, magazine) redattore, curatore m; (newspaper) direttore m
editorial n editoriale m; articolo di fondo
educate vt istruire; (rear) allevare; -**d** a istruito, colto
education n istruzione, insegnamento; **physical** — educazione fisica
educational a educativo, pedagogico, scolastico
educator n educatore m, insegnante m, maestro
educe vt estrarre; (infer) dedurre
eel n anguilla
eerie a lugubre, tetro, irreale, magico
effable a esprimibile, pronunciabile
efface vt cancellare
effect n effetto; — vt effettuare, produrre; -**ual** a efficace
effective a efficace, effettivo
effervescent a spumante
efficacious a efficace
efficiency n efficienza, efficacia
efficient a efficiente, capace
effort n sforzo
effusive a espansivo, esuberante
egg n uovo; (fried) uovo fritto; (hardboiled) uovo sodo; (poached) uovo affogato; (scrambled) uovo strapazzato; (soft-boiled) uovo da bere, uovo appena bollito; (sunny side up) uovo ad occhio di bue; — **white** chiara d'uovo, albume m; — **yolk** tuorlo d'uovo; — vt lanciare uova contro; — **on** incitare
eggnog n zabaione m
eggplant n melanzana
ego n ego
egocentric a egocentrico
egoism, egotism n egoismo, egotismo
egotist n egotista m
egress n egresso
egret n ciuffetto
Egypt Egitto; -**ian** n&a egiziano
eider down peluria, lanugine f
eight a otto; -**ieth** a ottantesimo; -**y** a ottanta
eighteen a diciotto; -**th** a diciottesimo; -**th century** il Settecento
eighth a ottavo
either pron&a ambi; l'uno e l'altro; uno dei due; **in** — **case** i ambo i casi; **not** — nemmeno; —... **or** o ... o
ejaculation n eiaculazione, emissione
eject vt espellere, scacciare
ejection n espulsione; — (law) sfratto
eke vt allungare, prolungare; — **out** complementare
elaborate vt elaborare; — a elaborato, accurato
elan n slancio
elapse vi decorrere, passare, trascorrere
elastic n&a elastico
elated a allegro, esultante
elbow n gomito; **out at the** -**s** malconcio; -**room** n libertà d'azione; — vt dare gomitata a; — vi fare gomito; avanzare a gomitate
elder a maggiore, anziano
elderly a d'una certa età
eldest a il maggiore, il più anziano, il più vecchio
elect a eletto, nominato; — vt eleggere; **the** — gli eletti
election n elezione
electioneer vt sollecitare voti
electoral a elettorale
electric, -al a elettrico
electrician n elettricista m, elettrotecnico
electricity n elettricità
electrify vt elettrizzare
electrocardiogram n elettrocardiogramma m
electrocute vt folgorare, fulminare
electrocution n elettrocuzione
electrode n elettrodo
electrodynamics n elettrodinamica
electromagnet n elettromagnete m
electron n elettrone m
electronic a elettronico; — **brain** cervello elettronico; -**s** n elettronica
electroplate vt placcare con galvanopla-

stica
elegance *n* eleganza, buon gusto
elegant *a* elegante, di buon gusto
element *n* elemento; **–al** *a* elementare
elements *npl* rudimenti *mpl*
elementary *a* elementare; — **school** scuola elementare
elephant *n* elefante *m*
elevate *vt* elevare, innalzare
elevated *a* elevato; — **railway** ferrovia soprelevata
elevation *n* elevazione
elevator *n* ascensore *m*; **freight** — montacarichi *m*; — **boy** ragazzo
eleven *a* undici
eleventh *a* undicesimo; — **hour** l'undicesima ora, l'ultima ora per fare qualcosa
elf *n* folletto, fata; **–in** *a* di folletto, incantato
elicit *vt* incitare, educere
elide *vt* elidere
eliminate *vt* eliminare
elimination *n* eliminazione
elision *n* elisione
elite *a* seletto, alto; — *n* il meglio, elite *m*
elk *n* alce *f*
ell *n (building)* ala
eligible *a* eleggibile, desiderabile
ellipse *n* ellisse *f*
ellipsis *n* ellissi *f*
elm *n* olmo
elongate *vt* allungare, estendere; — *vi* aumentare la lunghezza
elope *vi* fuggire per sposarsi
elopement *n* fuga con l'amante
eloquence *n* eloquenza
eloquent *a* eloquente
else *a* altro; **anybody** — chiunque altro; **anything** —? qualche cosa d'altro? **anywhere** — ogni altro luogo; **everything** — tutto il resto; **nobody** — nessun altro; **nothing** — nient'altro; **nowhere** — nessun altro luogo
elsewhere *adv* altrove, in altro luogo
elucidate *vt* chiarire, delucidare
elusive *a* evasivo, elusivo
em *n (print)* unità di spazio
emaciate *vt* emaciare; — *vi* emaciarsi
emaciated *a* magro, smunto, scarno
emancipate *vt* emancipare
emasculation *n* evirazione, sterilizzazione
embalm *vt* imbalsamare
embankment *n* argine *m*, diga; terrapieno
embargo *n* embargo
embark *vt* imbarcare; — *vi* imbarcarsi
embarkation *n* imbarco
embarrass *vt* imbarazzare, mettere in imbarazzo; **–ing** *a* imbarazzante; **–ment** *n*

imbarazzo
embassy *n* ambasciata
embellish *vt* abbellire
ember *n* tizzone *m*, brace *f*; **E– Day** Quattro Tempora
embezzle *vt* appropriarsi fraudolentemente
embezzler *n* prevaricatore *m*
emblem *n* emblema *m*
embolism *n* embolia
emboss *vt* lavorare d'incavo, damaschinare
embossed *a* in rilievo
embrace *vt* stringere, abbracciare; — *vi* abbracciarsi; — *n* stretta, abbraccio
embroider *vt* ricamare; **–y** *n* ricamo
embroil *vt* imbrogliare
embryo *n* embrione *m*; **–nic** *a* embrionale
emcee, M.C. *n* cerimoniere *m*; — *vt&i* fare il maestro di cerimonie
emerald *n* smeraldo
emerge *vi* emergere
emergency *n* emergenza; — **exist** uscita di sicurezza; — **landing** atterraggio di fortuna
emery *n* smeriglio
emetic *n&a* emetico
emigrant *n* emigrante *m&f*
emigrate *vi* emigrare
emigration *n* emigrazione
eminence *n* eminenza
eminent *a* eminente
emissary *n* emissario
emit *vt* emettere
emollient *a&n* emolliente *m*
emolument *n* emolumento
emotion *n* emozione; **–al** *a* emotivo
empanel *vt* formare la lista dei giurati
emperor *n* imperatore *m*
emphasis *n* enfasi *f*
emphasize *vt* mettere in rilievo; *(insist on)* insistere su; *(underline)* sottolineare
emphatic *a* enfatico, energico, deciso
emphatically *adv* decisamente
empire *n* impero
employ *vt* impiegare, usare; — *n* impiego
employee *n* impiegato
employer *n* principale *m*; datore di lavoro
employment *n* impiego, occupazione
empower *vt* autorizzare; conferire potere
empress *n* imperatrice *f*
emptiness *n* vuoto, vanità; *(frivolity)* frivolità
empty *a* vuoto; — *vt* vuotare; *(remove)* sgombrare
empty– *(in comp)* **–handed** *a* a mani vuote; **–headed** *a* senza cervello
empyema *n* empiema *m*
emulate *vt* emulare
emulsify *vt* emulsionare

en *n (print)* mezza unità di spazio

enable *vt* consentire; abilitare

enact *vt* decretare, promulgare; **–ment** *n* decreto, promulgazione

enamel *n* smalto; — *vt* smaltare

enamor *vt* innamorare

encamp *vt* accampare; — *vi* accamparsi; **–ment** *n* accampamento

encase, incase *vt* incassare, incassonare; *(cover)* coprire

enchant *vt* incantare; **–ing** *a* incantevole

enchantment *n* incanto, incantesimo

encircle *vt* accerchiare, cingere, circondare

enclose *vt* allegare; *(include)* accludere; *(shut in)* racchiudere

enclosure *n* allegato; *(pen)* recinto

encompass *vt* circondare, abbracciare, racchiudere

encore *n* bis *m*; ripetizione; — *vt (ask for)* chiedere il bis; *(give)* ripetere, bissare

encounter *n* incontro, scontro; *(battle)* combattimento; — *vt* affrontare; *(meet)* incontrare; — *vi* ingaggiare battaglia; incontrarsi

encourage *vt* incoraggiare

encouragement *n* incoraggiamento

encouraging *a* incoraggiante

encroach *vt&i* usurpare, invadere; abusarsi di

encumber *vt* ingombrare, imbarazzare; *(burden)* opprimere

encyclopedia *n* enciclopedia

end *n* fine *m&f*, estremità: *(purpose)* scopo; **by the** — **of** prima della fine di; **make both –s meet** sbarcare il lunario; **odds and –s** cianfrusaglie *fpl;* **on** — ritto; **put an** — **to** mettere fine a

end *vt* terminare, finire; — *vi* finire, cessare

endanger *vt* mettere in pericolo

endear *vt* rendere caro a; fare amare da

endearment *n* amabilità; *(tenderness)* tenerezza

endeavor *vt&i* cercare, tentare; *(strive)* sforzarsi; — *n* tentativo; sforzo

ending *n* fine *f*, conclusione; *(gram)* desinenza

endive *n* indivia

endless *a* interminabile

endocarditis *n* endocardite *f*

endocrine *n&a* endocrina; **–ology** *n* endocrinologia

endorse *vt* approvare *(fig); (check)* indorsare, girare; *(guaranty)* garantire, avallare; *(law)* girare

endorsement *n* avallo, girata, approvazione *(fig)*

endow *vt* dotare; **–ment** *n* dotazione,

dono

endurable *a* tollerabile, sopportabile

endurance *n* resistenza, pazienza; **beyond** — intolerabile

endure *vt&i* soffrire, sopportare, *(last)* durare, continuare

enema *n* clistere *m*, enteroclisma *m*, lavativo

enemy *n* nemico

energetic *a* energico, dinamico

energy *n* energia; **atomic** — energia atomica

enervate *vt* scoraggiare

enforce *vt* imporre; *(law)* far rispettare la legge; **–ment** *n* esecuzione; *(law)* applicazione della legge

enfranchise *vt* affrancare

engage *vt* riservare; *(hire)* impegnare; *(reserve)* prenotare; — **in conversation** entrare in conversazione

engaged *a* fidanzato; *(busy)* occupato; *(employed)* impegnato

engagement *n (marital)* fidanzamento; *(mil)* scontro; *(promise)* impegno; **keep an** — andare a un appuntamento

engaging *a* attraente

engender *vt* ingenerare, produrre; *(cause)* causare, far nascere

engine *n* motore *m; (rail)* locomotiva

engineer *n* ingegnere *m; (avi)* motorista *m; (mil)* geniere *m; (rail)* macchinista *m;* — *vt* combinare; *(scheme)* macchinare

engineering *n* ingegneria

England Inghilterra

English *n&a* inglese *m&f;* **in plain** — per essere chiaro; in parole povere

Englishman, –woman *n* inglese *m&f*

engrave *vt* incidere, scolpire

engraver *n* incisore *m*

engraving *n* incisione

engross *vt* occupare, assorbire; **be –ed** essere assorto; **–ing** *a* interessante; avvincente

engulf *vt* inghiottire; gettare nel gorgo *(fig)*

enhance *vt* intensificare, aumentare, elevare

enhancement *n* aumento

enigma *n* enigma *m* **–tic** *a* enigmatico

enjoy *vt* godere, gustare; aver piacere di; **–able** *a* piacevole, divertente

enjoyment *n* godimento, piacere *m*

enlarge *vt* ingrandire; — *vi* ingrandirsi

enlargement *n* ingrandimento

enlighten *vt* illuminare, dare schiarimenti; **–ment** *n* schiarimento

enlist *vt* arruolare; — *vi* arruolarsi

enlistment *n* arruolamento

enliven *vt* animare, ravvivare

enmity *n* inimicizia
enormous *a* enorme
enough *a&adv* abbastanza; **be — bastare**; essere sufficiente; **That's —! Basta!**
enrage *vt* irritare, arrabbiare
enrapture *vt* mandare in estasi, estasiare
enrich *vt* arricchire
enrichment *n* arricchimento
enroll *vt* iscrivere; **— vi iscriversi**
ensconce *vt* accomodare; *(hide)* nascondere; *(protect)* proteggere
ensemble *n* insieme *m*; complesso
ensign *n* *(banner)* bandiera; *(insignia)* insegna; *(officer)* guardiamarina *m*
enslave *vt* schiavizzare, cautivare
ensnare *vt* sedurre, allettare; prendere in trappola *(fig)*
ensue *vi* seguire, risultare, derivare
ensuing *a* seguente, successivo, prossimo
entail *vt* importare, occasionare; *(law)* assegnare
entangle *vt* imbrogliare, arruffare, coinvolgere
entente *n* intesa, patto
enter *vt* entrare, penetrare; *(accounting)* portare; *(law)* intentare; *(record)* iscrivere
enterprise *n* impresa
enterprising *a* intraprendente
entertain *vt* divertire; dare un ricevimento; **—ing a divertente**
entertainment *n* divertimento, spettacolo
enthrall *vt* incantare, cattivare; *(enslave)* soggiogare
enthrone *vt* incoronare; *(eccl)* investire, intronizzare
enthusiasm *n* entusiasmo
enthusiast *n* entusiasta *m*; **—ic a entusiastico**
entice *vt* incitare, adescare, sedurre
enticement *n* fascino, seduzione
enticing *a* seducente, tentatore
entire *a* intero; **—ly adv interamente**
entirety *n* tutto, intero, totalità; **in its —** nella sua pienezza; nella sua totalità
entitle *vt* intitolare, nominare; dare un diritto
entity *n* entità
entomologist *n* entomologo
entrails *npl* interiora *fpl*, intestini *mpl*, viscere *fpl*
entrance *n* ingresso, entrata
entrance *vt* estasiare
entrant *n* inscritto, participante *m*; *(beginner)* novizio
entreat *vt* implorare, supplicare
entreaty *n* supplica, sollecitazione, insistenza
entrench *vt* trincerare; **— vi trasgredire**
entrust *vt* affidare a

entry *n* entrata; *(com)* iscrizione, registrazione; **— blank domanda; double —** *(bookkeeping)* partita doppia
enumerate *vt* enumerare
enumeration *n* enumerazione
enunciate *vt* pronunziare, enunciare
enunciation *n* enunciazione
envelop *vt* avviluppare, involgere
envelope busta; **window — busta con** finestrina
enviable *a* invidiabile
envious *a* invidioso
environment *n* ambiente *m*
environs *npl* dintorni *mpl*
envoy *n* messo; inviato diplomatico
envy *n* invidia; **be green with — essere** verde d'invidia; **— vt invidiare**
enzyme *n* enzimo
eon *n* era, età
ephedrine *n* efedrina
ephemeral *a* effimero
epic *a* epico; **— n epopea; — poem epico**
epicure *n* epicureo; **–an a epicureo**
epidemic *n* epidemia; **— a epidemico**
epidermis *n* epidermide *f*
epiglottis *n* epiglotide *f*
epigram *n* epigramma *m*
epigrammatic *a* epigrammatico
epigraph *n* epigrafe *f*
epilepsy *n* epilessia
epileptic *a* epilettico
epilogue *n* epilogo
Epiphany *n* Epifania
episode *n* episodio
epitaph *n* epitaffio
epitome *n* epitome *f*, compendio
epithet *n* epiteto
epoch *n* epoca
Epsom salts sale inglese, solfato di magnesia
equidistant *a* equidistante
equal *n&a* eguale; **— vt eguagliare; –ly** *adv* egualmente
equalization *n* equalizzazione
equality *n* eguaglianza
equalize *vt* egualizzare
equanimity *n* equanimità
equation *n* equazione
equator *n* equatore *m*
equatorial *a* equatoriale
equilibrium *n* equilibrio
equinox *n* equinozio
equip *vt* dotare, attrezzare, equipaggiare
equipment *n* macchinario, dotazione, attrezzatura
equitable *a* equo, giusto
equity *n* equità
equivalent *a&n* equivalente *m*
equivocation *n* equivoco
era *n* era, epoca

eradicate vt estirpare, sradicare
erase vt cancellare
eraser n gomma da cancellare
erasure n cancellatura
erect vt erigere; — a eretto, diritto
erg n ergon m
ergo adv ergo, dunque
ergot n granosprone m, malattia di cereali
ermine n ermellino
erode vt rodere, consumare
erosion n erosione
erotic a erotico
err vi sbagliarsi; –ing a errante
errand n commissione; — boy commesso, fattorino
erratic a irregolare, eccentrico
erroneous a erroneo
error n errore m, sbaglio; **typographical** — errore di stampa
erudite a erudito
erupt vi eruttare
eruption n eruzione
erysipelas n risipola
escalator n scala mobile
escapade n scappata, follia
escape vt fuggire, evadere; (evade) evitare, scansare; — vi scappare
escape n evasione, fuga; — valve (mech) valvola di scappamento; fire — uscita d'incendio, uscita d'emergenza; have a narrow — scampare per miracolo; make one's — evadere
escort n scorta, compagno; — vt scortare, accompagnare
escrow n contratto in deposito presso un terzo; deposito di caparra
Eskimo n&a esquimese
esophagus n esofago
esoteric a esoterico
especially adv particolarmente, specialmente
espionage n spionaggio
essay n saggio; — vt provare
essence n essenza, profumo
essential a essenziale; –ly adv essenzialmente
establish vt stabilire, fondare
establishment n stabilimento, organizzazione; complesso; (company) ditta
estate n proprietà; real — beni immobili mpl
esteem vt stimare, rispettare; — n stima, considerazione
ester n estere m
esthete n esteta m&f
esthetic a estetico
estimate vt stimare, valutare; (calculate) calcolare; — n valutazione, perizia, preventivo; (com) stima
estimation n giudizio, opinone f, stima

Estonia Estonia
et cetera (etc.) n eccetera m (ecc.)
etch vt disegnare (fig); incidere all'acquaforte
etching n incisione, acquaforte f
eternal a eterno
eternity n eternità
ether n etere m
ethical a etico
ethics npl etica
ethnology n etnologia
ethyl n etile m
etiquette n etichetta, cerimoniale m, convenienza
etude n (arts) studio
etymology n etimologia
Eucharist n Eucaristia
eugenics npl eugenetica
eulogy n elogio
eunuch n eunuco
euphonious a eufonico, armonioso
European n&a europeo
eurythmics npl euritmica, euritmia
euthanasia n eutanasia
evacuate vt evacuare; (people) sfollare
evacuee n sfollato
evade vt scansare, eludere, schivare
evaluate vt valutare
evangelist n evangelista m&f
evaporate vt far evaporare; — vi evaporare, svaporare
evaporated a evaporato
evaporation n evaporazione
evasion n evasione, pretesto, sotterfugio
evasive a evasivo
eve n vigilia
even a pari, eguale; — number numero pari; — temper carattere pacifico; be — with essere alla pari; get — with sdebitarsi con; — adv persino, anche; — as nel momento in cui; — if anche se; — so anche così; — then anche allora, di già, a quel tempo; — though benchè; not — neppure; — vt rendere equale, eguagliare; (com, scale) bilanciare
evening n sera, serata; during the — di sera, durante la sera; every — ogni sera; in the — alla sera; the — before la sera precedente; — a di sera, serale; — clothes abiti da sera
evenly adv uniformemente
event n evento, avvenimento, caso; (contest) gara; in the — that in caso che
eventful a movimentato, avventuroso; importante
eventual a eventuale, finale; –ly adv finalmente, alla fine, eventualmente
eventuality n eventualità
ever adv sempre, mai; — since dopo, a

decorrere da; **for — and —** per sempre; **more than —** più che mai; **scarcely —** quasi mai

evergreen *n* sempreverde *m*

everlasting *a* eterno; *(ceaseless)* incessante; **—** *n* eternità

every *a* ogni, ciascuno; **— now and then** di tanto in tanto; **— other** uno sì uno no; **— time** ogni volta; **— day** giornalmente; ogni giorno; **–one, –body** *pron* ognuno, ciascuno; *(all)* tutti

everyday *a* quotidiano, comune, per ogni giorno

everything *n* tutto, ogni cosa

everywhere *adv* dovunque

evict *vt* sfrattare; *(dispossess)* espellere, spossessare

eviction *n* sfratto, espulsione

evidence *n* prova, testimonianza; **give —** testimoniare

evident *a* evidente, ovvio

evil *a* cattivo; **—** *n* male *m*, danno

evildoer *n* malfattore *m*, malfattrice *f*

evil-minded *a* malevolo, perverso, malintenzionato

eviscerate *vt* sviscerare, sventrare

evocation *n* evocazione

evoke *vt* evocare

evolution *n* evoluzione

evolve *vt* evolvere; **—** *vi* evolversi

ewe *n* pecora

ewer *n* brocca, boccale *m*

exact *a* esatto, preciso; **–ing** *a* esigente; **–ly** *adv* esattamente, precisamente; **–ness** *n* esattezza; **—** *vt* esigere, pretendere

exaggerate *vt* esagerare

exaggeration *n* esagerazione

exalt *vt* esaltare; **–ed** *a* esaltato, sommo, altolocato; **–ation** *n* esaltazione

examination *n* esame *m*; *(med)* visita; **competitive —** esame di concorso

examine *vt* esaminare

examiner *n* esaminatore *m*, esaminatrice *f*

example *n* esempio

exasperate *vt* esasperare

exasperation *n* esasperazione

excavate *vt* scavare

excavation *n* scavo

exceed *vt* superare, eccedere

exceedingly *adv* eccessivamente

excel *vt* eccellere, superare

excellence, excellency *n* eccellenza

Excellency *n* *(eccl)* Eccellenza

excellent *a* eccellente, ottimo

excelsior *n* l'eccelso, il migliore

except *vt* escludere, eccettuare; **—** *prep* fuori di, salvo, eccetto, tranne

exception *n* obiezione, eccezione; **take —** *(object)* obiettare; *(offense)* risentirsi di

exceptional *a* eccezionale

excerpt *vt* estrarre; **—** *n* estratto, brano, passo

excess *n* eccesso, soverchio; *(exaggeration)* esagerazione; **— baggage** bagaglio in eccedenza; **–ive** *a* troppo, eccessivo

exchange *vt* scambiare; **— greetings** scambiare auguri

exchange *n* cambio; *(com)* borsa; **rate of —** prezzo di cambio

excise *n* dazio, imposta; tributi indiretti *mpl*; **—** *vt* tassare, daziare; *(cut out)* tagliare

excitable *a* eccitabile, emotivo

excite *vt* eccitare, provocare, suscitare

excited *a* eccitato; **get —** eccitarsi, esaltarsi

excitement *n* agitazione, emozione; *(confusion)* trambusto

exciting *a* emozionante, vivificativo

exclaim *vt* esclamare

exclamation *n* esclamazione; **— point** punto esclamativo

exclude *vt* escludere

exclusion *n* esclusione

exclusive *a* esclusivo, scelto, aristocratico; di classe; **— of** a prescindere da

excommunicate *vt* scomunicare

excommunication *n* scomunica

excresence *n* escrescenza

excrete *vt* escretare

excretion *n* escrezione

excruciating *a* atroce, terribile

excursion *n* escursione, gita

excuse *n* scusa, pretesto; **—** *vt* scusare; **— oneself** scusarsi

execration *n* esecrazione

execute *vt* eseguire; *(penal)* giustiziare

execution *n* adempimento; esecuzione

executive *a* esecutivo; **—** *n* dirigente *m*

exemplary *a* esemplare

exemplify *vt* servire d'esempio

exempt *a* esente; **—** *vt* esentare, dispensare

exemption *n* esenzione

exercise *n* esercizio; **—** *vt* esercitare, far esercizi, addestrare; **—** *vi* esercitarsi, addestrarsi

exert *vt* esercitare, compiere; **— oneself** sforzarsi

exertion *n* sforzo

exhale *vt* esalare

exhaust *n* scappamento; *(auto)* tubo di scappamento; **—** *vt* esaurire

exhausted *a* esaurito, sfinito

exhausting *a* spossante

exhaustion *n* esaurimento

exhaustive *a* esauriente

exhibit *vt* esporre, mostrare; **—** *n* mostra; *(object)* oggetto esposto; **–or** *n* espositore *m*, esibitore *m*

exhibition *n* mostra, esposizione

exhibitionism *n* esibizionismo

exhilarate *vt* rallegrare, esilarare

exhilarating *a* esilarante

exhilaration *n* ilarità, allegrezza

exhort *vt* esortare; **–ation** *n* esortazione

exhume *vt* esumare

exigencies *npl* esigenze, necessità *fpl*; bisogni *mpl*

exigent *a* urgente, esigente

exile *n* esilio, bando; *(person)* esule *m;* **–** *vt* esiliare, proscrivere

exist *vi* vivere, esistere; **–ence** *n* esistenza, vita; **–ing** *a* esistente, attuale

existent *a* esistente

existential *a* esistenziale

existentialism *n* esistenzialismo

existentialist *n* esistenzialista *m&f*

exit *n* uscita

exodontist *n* chirurgo odontoiatra

exodus *n* esodo

exonerate *vt* discolpare, prosciogliere

exoneration *n* esonero

exorbitant *a* esorbitante

exorcize *vt* esorcizzare

exotic *a* esotico

expand *vt* espandere, stendere; **—** *vi* espandersi, dilatarsi

expanse *n* espansione, distesa

expansion *n* espansione

expansive *a* espansivo

expatriate *vt* espatriare

expect *vt (anticipate)* prevedere; *(await)* attendere; *(require)* pretendere; **–ancy** *n* attesa, aspettativa

expectant *a* aspettante

expectation *n* aspettativa, speranza

expedient *a* utile, pratico, vantaggioso; **—** *n* espediente *m*, mezzo, ripiego

expedite *vt* affrettare, sbrigare

expedition *n* spedizione; *(speed)* prontezza

expel *vt* scacciare, espellere

expend *vt* spendere, consumare; **–able** *a* spendibile, consumabile

expenditure *n* spesa

expense *n* spesa, costo

expensive *a* caro, costoso; **be —** essere dispendioso; essere caro

experience *n* pratica, esperienza; **—** *vt* provare

experienced *a* pratico, esperto

experiment *n* esperimento, prova, esperienza; **–al** *a* sperimentale

expert *a* pratico, esperto; **—** *n* intenditore *m*, specialista *m*; perito

expertly *adv* destramente

expertness *n* abilità, capacità, destrezza

expiration *n* scadenza, termine *m*

expire *vt (die)* spirare; *(end)* scadere

explain *vt* spiegare

explainable *a* spiegabile

explanation *n* spiegazione

explanatory *a* spiegativo, esplicativo, espositivo

explicate *vt* spiegare

explicit *a* esplicito

explode *vi* scoppiare, esplodere; **—** *vt* far scoppiare; *(theory)* demolire

exploit *n* prodezza, impresa; **—** *vt* utilizzare, sfruttare

exploration *n* esplorazione

explore *vt* esplorare; *(investigate)* indagare

explorer *n* esploratore *m*

explosion *n* scoppio, esplosione

explosive *a* esplosivo

exponent *n* esponente *m*, rappresentante *m*

export *n* esportazione; **— house** casa d'esportazione

export *vt* esportare; **–er** *n* esportatore *m*

expose *vt* esporre; *(uncover)* smascherare; **–d** *a* esposto, scoperto

exposé *n* esposto, esposizione

exposition *n* mostra, esposizione

expository *a* espositivo

expostulate *vi* lagnarsi, fare rimostranze

expostulation *n* disputa, protesta

exposure *n* esposto, esposizione; *(frostbite)* assideramento; *(photo)* posa; **— meter** *(photo)* esposimetro

express *vt (speech)* esprimere, espressare; *(transport)* spedire per espresso; **—** *a (exact)* formale, esplicito; *(speed)* espresso; **–ed** *a* espresso; **—** *n* espresso

expression *n* espressione

expressive *a* espressivo

expressway *n* autostrada

expropriation *n* espropriazione

expurgate *vt* espurgare

exquisite *a* squisito

extant *a* esistente

extemporaneous *a* estemporaneo, improvviso

extend *vt* estendere, prolungare, allargare; *(put out)* porgere; **—** *vi* stendersi, prolungarsi, estendersi

extended *a* esteso, prolungato; *(taut)* teso

extension *n* estensione; prolungamento; **— of time** proroga

extensive *a* diffuso, vasto, esteso

extensively *adv* estesamente, considerevolmente

extent *n* grado, punto, limite *m;* **to a certain —** fino ad un certo punto

extenuating *a* estenuante; *(law)* attenuante; **— circumstances** circostanze attenuanti

exterior *n&a* esterno
exterminate *vt* estirpare, sterminare
extermination *n* sterminio
exterminator *n* sterminatore *m*, distruttore *m*
external *a* esterno
extinct *a* estinto; **–ion** *n* estinzione
extinguish *vt* spegnere
extinguisher *n* estintore *m*; spegnitoio; **fire —** estintore d'incendio
extirpate *vt* estirpare, sradicare
extol *vt* estollere, esaltare, vantare
extort *vt* estorcere
extortion *n* estorsione; **–ist** *n* estorsionista *m&f*, strozzino
extra *a* supplementare; **— charges** spese supplementari *fpl*; **— edition** edizione straordinaria; **— pay** supplemento di paga; **—** *adv* in più
extra *n* supplemento; *(theat)* comparsa *m&f*
extract *vt* estrarre; **—** *n* estratto
extraction *n* estrazione; *(lineage)* discendenza, origine *f*
extracurricular *a* fuori dell'ordinario, extracurricolare
extradite *vt* estradare
extradition *n* estradizione
extraneous *a* estraneo
extraordinary *a* straordinario; *(wonderful)* stupendo
extrasensory *a* estrasensoriale; **— perception** percezione estrasensoriale

extravagance *n* prodigalità, spreco
extravagant *a* esagerato; *(price)* esorbitante; *(wasteful)* prodigo
extreme *a&n* estremo; **—** *a* ultimo
extremity *n* estremità
extricate *vt* districare
extrovert *n* estroverso
extrude *vt* espellere; **—** *vi* uscire
exuberance *n* esuberanza
exuberant *a* esuberante
exude *vt* traspirare, trasudare; *(display)* manifestare
exult *vt* esultare; **–ant** *a* esultante
exultation *n* esultazione; *(joy)* giubilo; *(triumph)* trionfo
exultingly *adv* esultando
eye *n* occhio; **— to —** in accordo assoluto; **in the twinkling of an —** in un batter d'occhi; **keep an — on** tenere d'occhio; **cry one's –s out** disfarsi in pianto; **–ball** *n* globo dell'occhio; **–cup** *n* bacinella per gli occhi; **–lid** *n* palpebra; **–sight** *n* vista; **–strain** *n* fatica degli occhi; **–wash** *n* lozione per gli occhi; **—** *vt* sbirciare
eyebrow *n* sopracciglio; **— pencil** matita per le sopracciglia
eyeful *n* occhiata
eyeglasses *npl* occhiali *mpl*, lenti *fpl*
eyelash *n* ciglio; **–es** *npl* ciglia *fpl*
eyelet *n* occhiello
eyetooth *n* dente canino
eyewitness *n* testimone oculare *m&f*

F

fable *n* favola
fabric *n* tessuto, stoffa
fabricate *vt (construct)* costruire; *(create)* creare; *(lie)* inventare, mentire
fabrication *n* fabbricazione; *(invention)* invenzione; *(untruth)* bugia
face *n* faccia, viso; **— card** figura; **— down** a faccia in giù; al rovescio; **— to —** faccia a faccia; **— powder** cipria; **— value** valore nominale; valore apparente; **about —** fare volta faccia; **fall on one's —** cadere con la faccia in giù; **lose —** far cattiva figura; perdere prestigio; **make a —** far boccacce; **on the — of it** sulla faccia; secondo l'apparenza; **save —** salvare la faccia *(fig)*; **—** *vt* confrontare; fronteggiare; **— the issue** confrontare la situazione
facet *n* faccetta; **—** *vt* sfaccettare
facial *a* facciale
facilitate *vt* facilitare
facilities *npl* agevolazioni, facilità, installazioni *fpl*; *(services)* servizi *mpl*; **toilet**

— bagno di decenza
facility *n* facilità
facing *n* risvolta; *(building)* rivestimento; *(cloth)* guarnizione
facsimile *n* facsimile *m*
fact *n* fatto; **as a matter of —** in linea di fatto; **in —** effettivamente, infatti; **matter of —** effettivo, positivo; **the — is** il fatto è
faction *n* fazione; *(discord)* discordia *(fig)*; dissenso *(fig)*
factor *n* fattore *m*; *(math)* coefficiente *m*
factory *n* fabbrica
factual *a* effettivo, fattivo
faculty *n (ability)* facoltà, talento; *(school)* corpo degli insegnanti; il personale insegnante
fad *n* capriccio del gusto; moda del momento
fade *vt* far appassire; far sbiadire; **—** *vi (color)* sbiadire; *(wither)* appassire; **— away** appassire; **— out** svanire gradualmente

fade-out n sparizione; *(movies, TV, rad)* sparizione graduale

fag vt stancare, affaticare; — vi affaticarsi, sfinirsi di lavoro

fagged out sfinito

fail vt mancare, abbandonare; — **to pass** *(examination)* essere bocciato; — **to do** mancare di fare; — vi venir meno; non riuscire; *(decline)* deperire; **without** — senza fallo, senz'altro

failing n difetto, fallo; — *prep* in mancanza di, in difetto di; — **for** debolezza per

failure n insuccesso, fallimento, fiasco; *(person)* fallito, caduto

faint n svenimento, deliquio; — a debole, lieve; *(pale)* pallido; — vi svenire; — **away** svenire

fainthearted a timido; *(cowardly)* pusillanime

fainting n svenimento

faintly adv debolmente

faintness n languore m

fair a leale, equo giusto; *(beautiful)* bello; *(hair)* biondo; *(skin)* bianco; — **chance** buona occasione; — **deal** lealtà; — **name** buona reputazione; — **play** lealtà, giustizia; — **possibility** alta probabilità; — **sex** sesso debole; — **weather** buon tempo

fair n fiera, esposizione; **–ground** n campo della fiera

fair-minded a imparziale, senza pregiudizi

fairness n giustizia; **in all** — per essere giusto

fairy n fata; — **tale** racconto delle fate, fiaba

faith n fede f, fiducia; **breach of** — slealtà; mancanza di parola

faithful a fedele, leale; **–ness** n fedeltà, costanza

faithfully adv fedelmente; con fedeltà

faithless a infedele, miscredente, sleale

fake a *(coll)* falso; — vt *(coll)* far finta di, simulare; — n *(coll)* contraffazione

faker n *(coll)* imbroglione m

fakir n fachiro

fall n caduta, cascata; *(season)* autunno

fall vt cascare, cadere; — **asleep** addormentarsi; — **back** indietreggiare, rinculare; — **behind** rimanere indietro; — — **by the wayside** perdere la giusta via *(fig)*; — **due** scadere; — **for** *(coll)* accettare *(fig)*; essere attratto; — **headlong** cadere a testa giù; — **in love** innamorarsi; — **into a trap** cadere in trappola *(fig)*; — **off** cadere, staccarsi, diminuire; — **on deaf ears** essere ignorato; — **out** rompere, litigare; —

through fallire; fare fiasco

fallacy n fallacia, errore m

fallible a fallibile

falling n caduta; — a cadente

fall-out n polvere radioattiva

false a falso, fallace; *(unfaithful)* infedele; — **alarm** falso allarme; — **bottom** doppio fondo; — **face** maschera; — **teeth** denti finti; **make a** — **step** mettere un passo in falso *(fig)*; fare un passo falso *(fig)*

falsehood n menzogna, bugia

falsely adv falsamente, fintamente

falsetto n falsetto

falsify vt falsificare

falsity n falsità

falter vt&i *(move)* esitare; *(stammer)* balbettare

fame n fama, celebrità

famed a rinomato, celebre, conosciuto, famoso

familiar a familiare, conosciuto, intimo; **be** — **with** essere familiare con; essere in confidenza con

familiarity n familiarità; confidenza; *(knowledge)* conoscenza

family n famiglia; — **name** cognome m; — **tree** albero genealogico; **be in the** — essere familiare; **be in the** — **way** essere incinta; — a di famiglia

famine n carestia

famish vt affamare; — vi soffrire la fame; aver fame

famished a affamato

famous a famoso, celebre

fan n ventaglio; *(elec)* ventilatore m; *(coll)* tifoso, entusiasta di uno sport; — vt ventilare; far vento; stimolare *(fig)*; — vi *(spread out)* aprirsi a ventaglio

fanatic a&n fanatico

fanatical a fanatico

fanaticism n fanatismo

fanciful a fantastico, fantasioso

fancy a di fantasia; — n fantasia, capriccio; **take a** — **to** simpatizzare per; — vt immaginare; — **oneself to be** presumere di sè stesso

fancy– *(in comp)* **—dress party** festa in costume; ballo in maschera; **—free** a col cuore libero

fang n zanna

fantastic a fantastico, bizzarro

fantasy n fantasia

far a&adv lontano, distante; — **and away** oltremodo; — **and wide** da tutti i lati; — **be it from me** lungi da mè; — **better** molto meglio; — **between** a lunghi intervalli; — **from it** tutt'al contrario; **as** — **as** *(distance)* lontano quanto;

by — oltremodo; **go** — andar lontano; **just so** — fino a; **so** — finora, talmente

far– *(in comp)* **—fetched** *a* improbabile; forzato; remotamente connesso; **—off** *a* lontano; **—reaching** *a* esteso, di lunga portata

farad *n (elec)* farad *m*

faraway *a* lontano; *(absent)* assente

farce *n* farsa

farcical *a* burlesco

fare *n (food)* cibo; *(transportation)* prezzo di un biglietto; passeggero; **half** — metà prezzo; **full** — prezzo intero

fare *vi* barcamenarsi; — **well** prosperare

farewell *n* addio, commiato; — *a* d'addio

farinaceous *a* farinaceo

farm *n* podere *m*, fattoria; — **hand** bracciante agricolo; **–house** *n* cascina; casa colonica **–yard** *n* aia; — *vt&i* coltivare; *(rent)* affittare

farmer *n* agricoltore *m*

farming *n* agricoltura; — *a* agricolo

farseeing *a* sagace, lungimirante

farsighted *a* previdente; *(sight)* presbite

farther *a* più lontano; — **back** più indietro; — *adv* più lontano, al di là; ancora di più

farthest *a* il più lontano; — *adv* più lontano

fascinate *vt* affascinare, ammaliare, incantare

fascination *n* fascino

fascinating *a* affascinante

Fascism *n* fascismo

fashion *n* moda; *(way)* maniera; — **show** sfilata di moda; **after a** — in certo modo; **in** — di moda

fashion *vi* adattare, foggiare, formare

fashionable *a* elegante, di moda, alla moda

fast *vt* digiunare; — *n* digiuno; — **day** giorno di digiuno; — *a* rapido, veloce; *(color)* solido; *(dissolute)* dissoluto; *(faithful)* fedele; *(secure)* fermo, stabile; **make** — *(secure)* fissare, assicurare; **sleep** — *(soundly)* dormire profondamente

fasten *vt* attaccare

fastener, fastening *n* fermaglio, legame *m*; *(bolt, latch)* chiavistello

fastidious *a* delicato, schizzinoso; *(exacting)* esigente

fat *n&a* grasso; **get** — diventar grasso, ingrassare

fatal *a* mortale, fatale; decisivo, importante; **–ity** *n* fatalità

fate *n* fato, destino, fatalità; sorte *f*

father *n* padre *m*; **–land** patria; **–ly** *a* paterno; **–less** *a* orfano di padre

father-in-law *n* suocero

fathom *n (measure)* braccio; — *vt* sondare scandagliare; *(understand)* profondizzare, capir bene

fatten *vt* ingrassare

fatuous *a* fatuo, vano

faucet *n* rubinetto

fault *n* colpa, mancanza; **at** — in difetto; **find** — criticare, trovare a ridire; **to a** — fino alla meticolosità; **–less** *a* perfetto, irreprensibile; **–y** *a* difettoso

faultfinder *n* critico, censore *m*

faultfinding *n* biasimo, rimprovero

favor *n* favore *m*; **be in** — **of** essere in favore di; **do a** — fare un favore; **find** — **with** essere ben accetto; **show** — mostrare preferenza *(fig)*; — *vt* favorire

favorable *a* favorevole

favorite *a&n* prediletto, favorito

fawn *n* daino, cerbiatto; — *a (color)* fulvo; — *vi* adulare

fawning *a* servile

fear *n* timore *m*, paura; **–ful** *a* terribile; timoroso; **–less** *a* intrepido, senza paura

feasibility *n* possibilità, praticabilità

feasible *a* praticabile, fattibile, probabile

feast *n* banchetto, festa, festino; — *vt* banchettare, far festa a

feat *n* impresa, prodezza

feather *n* piuma, penna; — **in one's cap** distinzione, vanto; **birds of a** — persone di una sola risma; — *vt* piumare; **–ed** *a* piumato, pennuto

featherbedding *n* obbligazione sindacale di pagare i lavoranti per lavoro non eseguito

featherweight *n* peso piuma

feature *n* tratto, caratteristica; **double** — due film principali; — **story** articolo di fondo; — *vt* ritrarre, rappresentare

features *npl* fattezze *fpl*, fisionomia; *(face)* viso

February *n* febbraio

fecundity *n* fecondità

federal *a* federale

federation *n* federazione

fee *n* onorario; *(law)* diritti *mpl*; *(tax)* tassa; **admission** — *(school)* quota d'iscrizione; *(theat)* prezzo d'entrata

feeble *a* debole, fiacco; **–ness** *n* debolezza

feebly *adv* debolmente

feed *n* foraggio, mangime *m*; — *vt* alimentare, dar da mangiare; — *vi* mangiare; — **on** nutrirsi di

feedback *a (elec)* controcircuitico, controgenerante; — *n* sistema controgenerante

feeding *n* alimentazione, mangiata, pascolo; *(animal)* alimento, foraggio; *(meal)* pasto

feel *n (sense)* tatto; **–ing** *n* senso, sensazione

feel *vt&i* sentire, sentirsi; *(believe)* credere, ritenere; *(touch)* toccare, tastare; **— better** sentirsi meglio; **— like** aver voglia di; sentirsi come; **— one's way** procedere con prudenza; **— strongly about** avere una opinione positiva

feeler *n* antenna; *(insect)* tentacolo

feeling *n* sensazione, sentimento

feelings *npl (emotions)* sensibilità

feet *npl* piedi *mpl*

feign *vt* simulare, fingere; **—** *vi* fingersi

felicitation *n* felicitazione

felicitous *a* felice, appropriato

feline *a* felino

fell *vt* atterrare, abbattere, ribattere

fellow *n* compagno, collega *m*; *(coll)* persona; **—** *a* dello stesso gruppo; **–ship** *n* cameratismo; *(scholarship)* borsa di studi

felon *n* malfattore *m*, traditore *m*; *(med)* patereccio

felony *n* fellonia, reato grave

felt *n* feltro

female *n* femmina; **—** *a* femminile

feminine *a* femminile

femur *n* femore *m*

fence *n* steccato, recinto; *(stolen goods)* ricettatore *m*; **be on the —** essere indeciso; **—** *vt* cingere; **—** *vi (sport)* tirare di scherma

fencing *n (sport)* scherma

fend *vt* parare; **— for oneself** difendersi, arrangiarsi; **— off** parare, sviare

fender *n* parafanghi *m*; *(fireplace)* parafuoco

ferment *n* fermento; agitazione; **—** *vi* fermentare

fermentation *n* fermentazione; *(yeast)* lievito

fern *n* felce *f*

ferocious *a* feroce

ferret *n* furetto; **—** *vt&i* cacciare col furetto; **— out** snidare

ferric *a* ferrico

ferry *n* traghetto; **—** *vt&i* traghettare

fertile *a* fertile

fertility *a* fertilità

fertilize *vt* fertilizzare

fertilizer *n* fertilizzante *m*; *(manure)* concime *m*

fervency *n* calore, fervore, ardore *m*

fervent *a* fervente; **–ly** *adv* con fervore; fervorosamente

fervid *a* fervido, ardente, caloroso

fester *vi* suppurare; **–ing** *a* ulcerante, suppurante, infezioso

festival *n* festivale *m*, festa

festive *a* festivo, gaio

festivity *n* festività

festoon *n* festone *m*; **—** *vt* festonare; ornare con festoni

fetching *a* seducente, attraente

fete *n* festa; **—** *vt* far festa a

fetish *n* feticcio

fetters *npl* ceppi *mpl*, catene *fpl*; schiavitù *f (fig)*

fettle *n* stato, ordine *m*, condizione; **in fine —** in ottimo stato

fetlock *n* garretto

fetus *n* feto

feud *n* vendetta, ostilità; inimicizia di famiglie, fra due famiglie; **—al** *a* feudale

fever *n* febbre *f*; **get into a —** eccitarsi

feverish *a* febbricitante, febbrile

few *a&pron* pochi, poche; **a —** alcuni, alcune; **–er** *a* meno; di meno

fiancé *n* fidanzato

fiancée *n* fidanzata

fiasco *n* fiasco

fiat *n* decreto, comando, ordine *m*

fib *n* menzognetta, frottola; **—** *vt* dire una piccola bugia

fibber *n* bugiardo

fiber *n* fibra

fibrous *a* fibroso

fickle *a* volubile, inconstante, capriccioso

fiction *n* invenzione; *(lit)* romanzo, narrativa

fictitious *a* fittizio, immaginario

fidelity *n* fedeltà; **high —** alta fedeltà

fiddle *n* violino ordinario; **play second —** essere di second'ordine; **—** *vi (coll)* suonare il violino; **— around** *(coll)* gironzolare

fidget *vi* agitarsi, essere irrequieto

fiduciary *n&a* fiduciario

field *n* campo; *(subject)* settore *m*, soggetto; **— day** giornata campale; **— glasses** binocolo da campo; **— mouse** arvicola; **—** *a* campale; di campo; **–er** *n (baseball)* ribattitore *m*

fiend *n* diavolo, demonio; **–ish** *a* cattivo, diabolico, perfido

fierce *a* feroce, accanito; **–ness** *n* ferocia, fierezza

fiery *a* focoso, ardente, infocato

fifteen *a* quindici

fifteenth *a* quindicesimo, decimoquinto

fifth *a* quinto; *(mus)* quinta

fiftieth *a* cinquantesimo

fifty *a* cinquanta

fifty-fifty *a&adv* mezzo e mezzo; *(so-so)* così così, nè bene nè male

fig *n* fico; **— tree** fico; **not be worth a —** non valere niente

fight *vt* combattere, lottare; **— a way through** aprirsi un cammino; **— it out**

combattere ad oltranza

fight n lotta, combattimento, disputa, rissa; **pick a — with** provocare

fighter n lottatore m, combattente m

fighting n combattimento, battaglia; — a combattente, battagliero

figment n finzione, invenzione; — **of the imagination** opera della immaginazione

figurative a traslato, figurato, allegorico, metaforico

figure n taglia, statura; (math) cifra; (mus) figura; — **of speech** modo di dire; **cut a poor —** fare brutta figura; **–head** n (naut) polena; figura di prua; (fig) prestanome m; — vt calcolare; esprimere in figure; (coll) supporre; — **out** (coll) comprendere, calcolare; — vi calcolare; lavorare con figure numeriche; — **on** (coll) contare su

figurine n statuetta, figurina

filament n filamento

filbert n nocciuola, avellana

filch vt rubacchiare

file n (folder) cartella; (tool) lima; — **card** cartellino di agendario; — **clerk** impiegato; **in single —** in fila indiana; — vt limare; archiviare; classificare; — **by** sfilare

filial a filiale

filibuster n filibustiere m; — vi fare il filibustiere

filigree n filigrana

filing n limatura; collezione; — **cabinet** schedario

fill vt riempire; — vi riempirsi; — **in** inserire; riempire; — **out** riempire; — n sufficienza; **–er** n riempitore m

fillet n benda; (meat) filetto

filling n ripieno; — **station** stazione di servizio; **tooth —** otturazione, impiombatura; — a sazievole

filly n cavallina

film n film m, pellicola; — **library** cineteca; **–y** a trasparente

filmstrip n film a proiezione fissa

filter n filtro; (photo) filtro luce; — **tipped** con filtro; — vt filtrare

filth n sudiciume m, sporcizia; **–y** a sporco, sudicio; (obscene) osceno

filtrate n liquido filtrato; — vt&i filtrare

filtration n filtrazione

fin n pinna; natatoia

final a finale; **–s** npl esami finali

finally adv finalmente

finality a finalità

finance n finanza, **–s** npl finanze fpl; — vt sovvenzionare, finanziare

financier n finanziere m

financial a finanziario

financing n finanziamento

find vi trovare; (law) dichiarare; — **out** indovinare, scoprire; — **fault** trovare a ridire; — **for oneself** trovare per proprio conto; — n trovata, scoperta

findings npl utensili mpl, arnesi mpl

fine a fino; (beauty) bello; — n multa, ammenda; — **arts** belle arti fpl; — vt multare; fare una contravvenzione; **F–!** interj Bene!, Molto bene!

Finland Finlandia

finesse n finezza, delicatezza

finger n dito; — **bowl** lavadita m; — **mark** ditata; **ring —** anulare m; **–nail** n unghia; **–print** n impronta digitale; — vt tastare, maneggiare

fingering n tocco, il tastare; (mus) diteggio, tocco

finicky a meticoloso; di gusti difficili

finish vt terminare, finire; — n fine f

Finnish a finlandese

fir tree n abete m

fire n fuoco, incendio; — **department** servizio di pompieri; — **engine** pompa d'incendio; — **escape** uscita di sicurezza; — **extinguisher** estintore m; — **screen** parafuoco; — **station** stazione dei pompieri; **–man** n vigile del fuoco; **–plug** n idrante m, bocca d'incendio

fire vt incendiare; (ceramics) cuocere; (coll) licenziare, congedare; (weapon) sparare; — **with enthusiasm** infiammare d'entusiasmo

firearms npl armi da fuoco fpl

firebrand n tizzone m, testa calda (fig)

firecracker n castagnuola, petardo

fireplace n focolare m, camino

fireproof a incombustibile, resistente al fuoco

firewood n legna da ardere

fireworks npl fuochi d'artificio

firing n (furnace) alimentazione del fuoco; — **line** linea di tiro; — **pin** percussore m; — **squad** plotone d'esecuzione

firm a solido, fermo; — n (com) ditta, azienda, società

firmament n cielo, firmamento

first a primo; — **aid** pronto soccorso; — **base** (sport) prima base; — **night** (theat) première m; notte di debutto; — adv prima, dapprima; in primo luogo; — **and last time** per prima ed ultima volta; **get to — base** (sl) giungere all'oggettivo (fig); raggiungere il proposito

first– (in comp) — **born** n primogenito; primo nato; **–class** a di prima classe; di prima qualità; **–rate** a di primo ordine

firsthand a&adv di prima mano

fiscal a fiscale

fish n pesce m; — **bone** lisca; **a queer —** (coll) un eccentrico; –**hook** n amo; –**line** lenza; — vt&i pescare; — **for information** sondare, indagare, cercare informazioni

fishing n pesca; — **rod** canna da pesca; — **tackle** aggeggi da pesca

fisherman n pescatore m

fishy a pescoso; di pesce; (coll) ambiguo, equivoco

fission n scissione, fissione; **nuclear —** scissione dell'atomo

fissure n fessura, crepatura

fist n pugno; **shake a — at** mostrare i pugni a (fig); –**ful** n pugnata

fit n (clothes) taglio; (med) attacco, accesso; **by –s and starts** saltuariamente; — a adatto, conveniente, idoneo; (health) sano; — **to be tied** (coll) furioso; — **to drink** buono da bere; see — **to** considerare appropriato; — vt adattarsi; star bene; — **in with** accordarsi con

fitful a saltuario, irregolare; –**ly** adv a salti

fitness n convenienza, attitudine f

fix n difficoltà; **in a bad —** nei pasticci; — vt fissare, stabilire; (adjust, repair) aggiustare, riparare

fixation n fissazione

fixative n fissativo

fixed a fisso, stabilito, convenuto; — **charge** spesa di manutenzione

fixings npl (coll) accessori mpl

fixture n infisso; (elec) impianto elettrico

fizz n spuma; sciampagna (coll); — vi spumare, spumeggiare; –**y** a gassoso

fizzle n (coll) fiasco, fallimento; — vi (froth) spumeggiare; (hiss) fischiare

flabbiness n flaccidità, languidezza

flabby a fiacco

flag n bandiera; –**pole** n asta di bandiera; –**ship** n nave ammiraglia

flag vt (signal) segnalare con bandiera; — vi languire; (droop) pendere

flagging a diminuente

flagrant a flagrante, palese

flair n fiuto, attitudine f, acume m

flake n fiocco, falda; —, — **off** vt sfaldare; — vi sfioccarsi, sfaldarsi

flaky a a falde, scaglioso

flamboyant a fiammeggiante, sfavillante

flame n fiamma; — vi fiammeggiare

flaming a fiammeggiante; (emotion) ardente

flange n fiangia

flank n lato, fianco; — vt fiancheggiare

flannel n flanella

flap n lembo, tesa; (noise) battuta; (avi) ipersostentatore m, deflettore m; — vt

sbattere, agitare

flare n fuoco, fiamma; (flash) bagliore m; (gift) talento; (rocket) razzo; — vi divampare; — **up** sfuriare, perdere le staffe (fig)

flare-up n sfuriata

flaring a sfolgorante, fiammante

flash n flash m, lampo, splendore; **in a —** in un lampo; **lightning —** lampo

flash vi sfolgorare, lampeggiare; (lightning) balenare; — **by** passare come una freccia

flashing n lampo, bagliore m; — a scintillante, lampeggiante

flashlight n lampadina tascabile

flashy a sgargiante, vistoso

flask n fiasco; (hip) fiaschetta

flat n apartamento; (mus) bemolle m

flat a piano, piatto; — **broke** (sl) in bolletta, al verde; — **denial** deciso rifiuto; — **rate** cifra esatta; — **refusal** rifiuto categorico; **fall —** far fiasco

flat vt (mus) fare un bemolle

flat– (in comp) —**bottomed** a a fondo piatto; —**footed** a dai piedi piatti

flatiron n ferro da stiro

flatten vt livellare, appiattire

flatter vt lusingare, adulare

flattery n lusinga, adulazione

flatware n coperti mpl, argenteria

flatulent a flatulento; vuoto

flaunt vt ostentare; — vi pavoneggiarsi

flavor n gusto, sapore m, aroma m

flavoring n condimento; ciò che dà sapore

flaw n difetto, pecca; –**less** a perfetto, senza difetti

flax n lino; –**en** a di lino; (hair) biondo

flea n pulce f

fleck n macchia

fledgling n novellino; (bird) uccelletto

flee vi scappare, fuggire

fleecy a lanoso

fleet n flotta, marina; (trucks) equipaggiamento di veicoli; **merchant —** flotta mercantile; — a veloce

fleet-footed a veloce, svelto

fleeting a fugace, effimero

flesh n carne f; — **color** color carne; — **wound** ferita superficiale

fleshy a pingue, carnoso

flex vt flettere, piegare

flexible a flessibile

flexibility n flessibilità

flick n buffetto, colpettino; (whip) frustatina; — vt dare un colpetto a

flicker vt tremolare, guizzare, vacillare; — n guizzo, tremolio; — **of an eyelash** batter d'occhio

flier n aviatore m; (advertisement) volantino

flight *n* volo; *(escape)* fuga; *(stairs)* rampa di scale; — **pattern** *(avi)* formazione; **put to** — mettere in fuga; **–iness** *n* leggerezza, volubilità; **–y** *a* leggero, volubile, frivolo

flimsiness *n* leggerezza, inconsistenza, frivolità

flimsy *a* sottile, fragile

flinch *vi* ritirarsi, esitare, titubare, indietreggiare

fling *vt* scagliare, lanciare; — *vi* precipitarsi, scagliarsi

fling *n* getto, colpo, lancio; *(attempt)* tentativo

flint *n* pietra focaia

flip *n* ditata, buffetto; — *a* impertinente

flippant *a* impertinente, frivolo

flipper *n* natatoia, pinna

flirt *vi* flirtare; — *n* civetta, fraschetta

flirtation *n* flirt *m*; amoreggiamento

flit *vi* svolazzare

float *vi* galleggiare, fluttuare; — *n* carro allegorico; **–er** *n* spostato

floating *a* galleggiante; — **dock** bacino galleggiante

flock *n* gregge *m*; — *vi* affollarsi, adunarsi

floe *n* banco di ghiaccio

flog *vt* sferzare, staffilare

flood *n* inondazione; — **tide** alta marea; **–gate** *n* chiusa; **–light** *n* proiettore *m*; — *vt* inondare

floor *n* pavimento, suolo; *(building story)* piano; — **polish** lucido per pavimento; **ground** — pianterreno; **tiled** — pavimento a mattonelle; **have the** — avere turno per parlare; — *vt* pavimentare; *(coll)* ridurre in silenzio

flooring *n* pavimentazione

floorwalker *n* capo reparto

flop *n* caduta; *(coll)* insuccesso; — *vt&i* cadere; *(fish)* dibattersi; *(coll)* far fiasco

floral *a* floreale

Florence Firenze *f*

Florentine *a&n* fiorentino

florid *a* florido

florist *n* fioraio, fiorista *m&f*

floss *n* piumino, cascame di seta; **–y** *a* lanuginoso

flounce *n* balza; — *vt* ornare di gale; — **about** dimenarsi; — **out** precipitarsi fuori

flounder *vi* dibattersi; *(speech)* impappinarsi

flour *n* farina; — *vt* infarinare; **–y** *a* farinoso, infarinato

flourish *vt&i* prosperare, fiorire; *(brandish)* brandire; — *n* svolazzo; *(mus)* fioritura, fanfara; *(sword)* mulinello

flourishing *a* fiorente, prosperoso

flout *vt&i* schernire, beffarsi

flow *vi* scorrere; — **into** affluire, influire; **ebb and** — flusso e riflusso; — *n* corso, flusso, corrente *f*; **–ing** *a* fluente, scorrevole; *(tide)* montante

flower *n* fiore *m*; — **shop** negozio di fioraio; — **stand** portafiori *m*, giardiniera; — *vt&i* fiorire; **–ed** *a* fiorito, a fiori

flowering *a* fiorito; — *n* fioritura

flowery *a* infiorato; in fiore; *(language)* fiorito

flu *n* *(med)* influenza

fluctuate *vi* oscillare, fluttuare

flue *n* tubo, condotto, gola

fluency *n* scorrevolezza, facilità

fluent *a* fluente, scorrevole; **–ly** *adv* correntemente, speditamente

fluff *n* borra; *(hair)* lanugine *f*, peluria; — *vt* rendere soffice; *(bird)* scuotere le penne; — *vi (fig)* scuotersi le penne; **–y** *a* lanuginoso

fluid *a&n* fluido; — **drive** *(auto)* giunto idraulico

fluke *n* colpo di fortuna; caso inaspettato; — *vi (coll)* avere un colpo di fortuna

flunk *vt (coll)* bocciare; — *vi* essere bocciato agli esami; far fiasco

fluorescent *a* fluorescente

fluoridation *n* fluoridazione, fluorazione

fluoride *n* fluorite *f*

fluoroscope *n* fluoroscopio

flurry *n* trambusto, agitazione; *(snow)* mulinello di neve

flush *n* rossore *m*, accesso *(fig)*; *(cards)* flusso; — *vt* snidare *(fig)*; *(level)* livellare; *(rinse)* sciacquare; — *vi* arrossire; — *a* ripieno; *(coll)* a livello; *(print)* allineato

fluster *vt* agitare; — *vi* agitarsi, turbarsi; — *n* agitazione, trambusto

flustered *a* sconcertato

flute *n* flauto

fluting *n* scanalatura

flutter *vt* svolazzare, agitare; — *vi* agitarsi

fly *vi* volare; *(flee)* fuggire; — *vt* sventolare, far volare; *(avi)* pilotare; — **away** scappare; volar via; — **into a rage** perdere il freno *(fig)*; — **off the handle** uscire dai gangheri *(fig)*; — **on the beam** *(avi)* volare radio-guidato; — **over** sorvolare; volare sopra

fly *n* mosca; **–leaf** *n* foglio di guardia; **–paper** *n* carta moschicida; **–weight** *n* *(sport)* peso mosca; **–wheel** *n (mech)* volante *m*; **on the** — al volo

flying *n* volo, aviazione; — **saucer** disco volante; **blind** — volo cieco; — *a* volante

F.M., frequency modulation modulazione

di frequenza

foal *n* puledro, asinello

foam *n* schiuma; — **rubber** gomma piuma

F.O.B., free on board F.O.B., consegna a bordo

focus *n* fuoco, centro; — *vt* mettere a fuoco; **in** — a fuoco; **out of** — sfocato

fodder *n* foraggio

foe *n* avversario, nemico

fog *n* nebbia; **–horn** *n* sirena

foggy *a* nebbioso; **It's** — C'è nebbia

fogy *n* persona antiquata; **–ish** *a* antiquato

foible *n* debole *m*

foil *vt* sventare; *(block)* impedire, — *n* lamina metallica; *(person)* contrasto

foist *vt* imporre, affibbiare

fold *vt* piegare; — *n* piega, piegatura; *(sheep)* ovile *m*; **–er** *n (file)* cartella; **–ing** *a* pieghevole

foliage *n* fogliame *m*

folio *n* folio; — *vt* numerare le pagine

folk *n* gente *f*, popolo; — *a* popolare; del popolo; **–lore** *n* folclore *m*; — **song** canto popolare

follicle *n* follicolo

follow *vt* seguire; — *vi* risultare

following *n* seguito; — *a* seguente

folly *n* follia, assurdità

foment *vt* fomentare

fond *a* affezionato, affettuoso, tenero; amante di; **be** — **of** voler bene a

fondle *vt* carezzare

fondly *adv* teneramente

fondness *n* affetto, amore *m*

food *n* cibo

fool *n* cretino; **make a** — **of oneself** mostrarsi sciocco; **–hardy** *a* pericoloso; — *vt* ingannare; — **away** sperperare

foolish *a* sciocco, stupido

foolishness *n* scemenza

foolproof *a* semplicissimo, sicurissimo

foolscap *n (paper)* carta protocollo *f*

foot *n* piede *m*; *(animal)* zampa; *(measure)* piede; *(stand)* base *f*; — **brake** freno a pedale; **have one** — **in the grave** avere un piede nella fossa *(fig)*; **on** — in piedi; **put one's** — **down** puntare i piedi; **put one's** — **in it** mettere lo zampino; **–bridge** *n* passerella; **–hill** *n* collinetta, rialzo di terreno; **–lights** *npl* luci della ribalta; **–print** *n* pedata, traccia, orma; **–sore** *a* con mal di piedi; **–step** *n* passo; **–stool** *n* sgabello; **–wear** *n* calzatura

foot *vt (math)* fare la somma; — *vi* camminare; andare a piedi; — **the bill** pagare il conto

football *n* pallone *m*, palla; *(game)* giuoco del calcio

footing *n* piede *m*, sostegno, base *f*; **lose**

one's — perdere l'equilibrio

fop *n* bellimbusto, zerbinotto

for *prep* per; — *conj* perchè; **What** —? A che scopo?

forage *vi* foraggiare

foray *n* scorreria

forbear *vt&i* evitare, pazientare; astenersi da, fare a meno di

forbearance *n* indulgenza, pazienza

forbid *vt* proibire

forbidden *a* proibito, vietato

force *n* forza; **air** — aereonautica; **in** — in vigore; **–s** *npl* forze *fpl*; — *vt* costringere, sforzare, obbligare; — **back** respingere; — **one's way in** aprirsi il cammino con la forza; **–d** *a* costretto, forzato

forceful *a* potente, vigoroso

forceps *npl* forcipi *mpl*

forcibly *adv* energicamente; con forza

ford *n* guado; — *vt* guadare

forearm *n* avambraccio; — *vt* premunire

forebear *n* avo, antenato

foreboding *n* presagio, presentimento

forecast *n* previsione; *(weather)* previsione del tempo, bollettino meteorologico; — *vt* prevedere

foreclose *vt* precludere

foreclosure *n* preclusione

forefather *n* avo, antenato

forefinger *n* dito indice

forefront *n* la parte anteriore, l'anteriore *m*, il davanti *m*

forego *vt&i* precedere

foregoing *a* precedente, summenzionato

foregone *a* predeterminato, preconcetto; — **conclusion** deduzione ovvia

foreground *n* primo piano

forehead *n* fronte *f*

foreign *a* estero, forestiero; — **affairs** affari esteri; — **legion** legione straniera; — **trade** commercio estero

foreigner *n* straniero, straniera

Foreign Office *n* Ministero degli Affari Esteri

foreman *n* caposquadra, capotecnico, capomastro, capo operaio; *(jury)* capo della giuria

foremost *a* primo, principale; il migliore; il più grande

forenoon *n* mattino

forerunner *n* precursore *m*

foresee *vt* prevedere

foreshadow *vt* adombrare, prefigurare; far presentire

foresight *n* previdenza

forest *n* foresta, bosco; — **ranger** guardia forestale, guardaboschi *m*

forestall *vt* prevenire, anticipare, accaparrare

foretell *vt* predire
forethought *n* previdenza, previsione, premeditazione
forever *adv* sempre
forewarn *vt* preavvisare
foreword *n* proemio, prefazione
forfeit *n* multa, ammenda; — *vt* demeritare; perdere il diritto di
forge *n* fucina, forgia; — *vt* fucinare, forgiare, fabbricare; contraffare, falsificare
forgery *n* falsificazione, contraffazione
forget *vt* dimenticare; non ricordarsi
forgetful *a* dimentico, smemorato, negligente; **–ness** *n* dimenticanza; negligenza, smemoratezza
forget-me-not *n* nontiscordardimè *m*
forgive *vt* perdonare; **–ness** *n* perdono
forgiving *a* clemente, indulgente
forgotten *a* dimenticato, rimesso; fatto grazia
fork *n (road)* biforcazione; *(table)* forchetta; *(tool)* forca; *(tree)* forcella; *(trousers)* inforcatura; **tuning** — diapason *m*; — *vt* rimuovere con forca; — *vi* biforcarsi
forlorn *a* infelice, sconsolato, abbandonato
form *n* forma, modulo; — **letter** lettera circolare; **matter of** — questione di forma; **proper** — forma appropriata; **–ation** *n* formazione; **–less** *a* informe, amorfo; — *vt* formare, foggiare; — *vi* formarsi
formal *a* formale, d'etichetta, ufficiale; — **dress** abito da cerimonia
formality *n* cerimonia, formalità
former *a* precedente, passato; **the** — qello, questo; il primo; **–ly** *adv* altre volte, anteriormente, già, precedentemente; tempo fa
formidable *a* formidabile, minaccioso
formula *n* formula
formulate *vt* formulare
fornicate *vi* fornicare
forsake *vt* lasciare, abbandonare; *(renounce)* rinunziare
forsaken *a* abbandonato
fort *n* forte *m*, fortezza
forte *n&adv* forte *m*
forth *adv* avanti; *(outward)* fuori; **and so** — e così via; **–coming** *a* prossimo, futuro, imminente; **–right** *a* franco, esplicito, sincero; **–with** *adv* subito, immediatamente
fortieth *a* quarantesimo
fortification *n* fortificazione
fortify *vt* fortificare
fortitude *n* fortezza, fermezza, coraggio
fortnight *n* due settimane; quindici gior-

ni; una quindicina; **–ly** *a* quindicinale, bisettimanale
fortuitous *a* accidentale, fortuito; **–ly** *adv* fortuitamente, accidentalmente
fortunate *a* fortunato; **–ly** *adv* per fortuna
fortune *n* fortuna; *(fate)* sorte *f*; — **hunter** cacciatore di dote
fortuneteller *n* indovino, indovina
forty *a* quaranta
forum *n* foro, tribunale *m*; dibattito pubblico
forward *a (ahead)* avanzato, inoltrato; *(brash)* audace, impertinente, sfacciato; *(daring)* spinto; — *adv* avanti; — *vt* inoltrare; far seguire
forwardness *n* progresso; *(manner)* impertinenza; precocità
forwards *adv* avanti
fossil *n* fossile *m*; **–ize** *vt* fossilizzare; **–ize** *vi* fossilizzarsi
foster *vt (encourage)* incoraggiare, secondare; *(shelter)* allevare, incrementare
foster child figlio adottato, affiliato
foster father padre adottivo
foster mother balia, nutrice, madre adottiva
foster parents genitori adottivi
foul *a* sporco; *(improper)* scorretto; — **ball** palla fuori campo; — **play** giuoco scorretto; condotta disonesta
foul-mouthed *a* osceno, sboccato
found *vt* fondare
foundation *n* fondazione; fondamento, base *f*; *(arch)* fondamenta *fpl*; — **garment** reggicalze *m*
founder *n* fondatore *m*; — *vt* affondare; — *vi* sprofondare
foundling *n* trovatello
foundry *n* fonderia
fountain *n* fontana; — **pen** penna stilografica
four *a* quattro
four-footed *a* a quattro piedi, a quattro gambe
foursome *n* gruppo di quattro persone; *(golf, cards)* partita a quattro
fourteen *a* quattordici; **–th** *a* quattordicesimo
fourth *a* quarto
fowl *n* pollame *m*
fox *n* volpe *f*; **–hole** *n* trincea; **–y** *a* astuto, furbo
fracas *n* chiasso, fracasso
fraction *n* frazione
fracture *n* frattura; — *vt* rompere, fratturare
fragile *a* fragile
fragility *n* fragilità
fragment *n* frammento; **–ary** *a* frammenta-

rio

fragrance n odore m, fragranza, profumo

fragrant a fragrante, profumato, odoroso

frail a fragile, delicato; **–ty** n fragilità, debolezza

frame n forma, struttura; (mech) telaio; (picture) cornice f; — **house** casa con struttura di legno; — **of mind** stato d'animo; **–work** n struttura, armatura

frame vt formare, incorniciare; (coll) incriminare con intrigo

framed a composto, escogitato, forgiato, incorniciato

France Francia

franchise n franchigia; (com) esclusiva, privativa

frank a sincero, franco

frankly adv francamente

frankfurter n salsicciotto

frantic a frenetico, furioso

frantically adv pazzamente, freneticamente

fraternal a fraterno

fraternity n fratellanza, confraternità

fraternize vt fraternizzare

fraud n frode f; **–ulent** a fraudolento

fray n lotta, cambattimento; (scuffle) zuffa; — vt consumare; (ravel) sfilacciare; (wear) logorare; — vi consumarsi, logorarsi, sfilacciarsi; **–ed** a consumato, logoro, sfilacciato

freak n ghiribizzo; (monster) mostro; (whim) capriccio; **–ish** a capriccioso; (abnormal) strano, anormale

freckle n lentiggine f; — vi divenire lentigginoso; **–d** a lentigginoso

free a libero, gratuito; — **and easy** senza complimenti; — **enterprise** impresa privata; — **hand** mano libera; — **of charge** gratis; — **speech** libertà di parola; — **will** libero arbitrio; **make — with** stralimitarsi; **of one's own — will** di spontanea volontà

free vt svincolare; (exempt) esimere; (liberate) liberare

freedom n libertà

free-for-all n (coll) giuoco (or concorso) aperto a chiunque

free fall n (aesp) mozione nello spazio

freehand a a mano libera

freemason n framassone m

freeway n autostrada

freeze vt gelare, congelare; — n gelo, congelamento

freezer n congelatore m; **deep —** frigorifero a temperatura bassa

freezing a gelido, glaciale; — **cold** freddo glaciale

freight n carico mercantile; — **train** treno merci

freightage n nolo

French a&n francese m; — **dressing** condimento francese; — **door** porta a due battenti; — **horn** corno inglese; — **leave** uscita alla chetichella; — **seam** orlo francese; — **window** finestra a due battenti

Frenchman, –woman n francese m&f

frenzied a frenetico

frenzy n pazzia, frenesia

frequency n frequenza; — **modulation** modulazione di frequenza

frequent a frequente; **–ly** adv frequentemente

fresh a fresco; (sl) presuntuoso, impertinente; **–ness** n freschezza; (strength) vigore m; **–ly** adv di fresco; di recente; **–en** vt&i rinfrescare

freshman n matricolino, matricola

fresh-water a d'acqua dolce

fret n agitazione; (stringed instrument) tasto; — vi agitarsi, irritarsi

fretful a irritato, impaziente, inquieto; (peevish) stizzoso, scontroso

fretfulness n irritabilità

friable a friabile

friar n frate m

friction n frizione

Friday n venerdì; **Good —** Venerdì Santo

fried a fritto

friend n amico, amica; **make a —** farsi un amico; **–less** a senza amici; **–ly** a amichevole; **–ship** n amicizia

frieze n (arch) fregio

fright n spavento; **–en** vt spaventare; **–ened** a spaventato, impaurito, intimidito; **–ful** a spaventoso, spaventevole

frigid a freddo, frigido, glaciale

frigidity n freddezza, frigidezza, frigidità

frill a trina, gala, fronzolo; — vt guarnire, orlare; ornare di trine

fringe n frangia; — **benefit** introito extrasalariale; — vt orlare, ornare con frangia

frisk vi sgambettare, saltellare, folleggiare; — vt (coll) perquisire addosso; **–y** a vispo, vivace

fritter n frittella; — vt gingillare; — **away** disperdere; (time) sprecare il tempo

frivolity n frivolità, frivolezza

frivolous a frivolo

frizzle vt arrostire alla griglia; — vi far rumore di friggere

frizzy a arricciato

fro adv indietro; **to and —** avanti e indietro

frock n veste f; costume m; vestito; (eccl) tonaca; sottana

frog n rana, ranocchio; (rail) incrocio, raccordo; (trimming) alamaro; — **in the**

throat raucedine *f*

frolic *n* trastullo; — *vi* trastullarsi; **–some** *a* allegro, giocoso, festevole

from *prep* da; da parte di; — **now on** da ora in poi; **take** — *(accept)* accettare; *(deprive of)* privare di

front *n* davanti *m*, facciata; — *a* di avanti; del davanti; **in** — **of** in faccia, dirimpetto; — *vt&i* affrontare

frontier *n* frontiera, confine *m*

frontispiece *n* frontespizio

frost *n* gelo; **hoar** — brina; **–bite** *n* congelamento; **–bitten** *a* congelato, gelato

frosted *a (food)* candito; *(hoary)* brinato; — **glass** vetro smerigliato

frosting *n* ghiacciata; *(cake)* crosta di zucchero

froth *n* schiuma; — *vt* far spumare; — *vi* spumeggiare, schiumare, spumare

frown *n* cipiglio; sguardo corrucciato; — *vi* accigliarsi; — **on** disapprovare

frowning *a* corrucciato

frowsy *a* sporco, scalcinato

frozen *a* gelato, congelato

frugal *a* parco, frugale

fruit *n* frutto, frutta; — **dealer** fruttivendolo; — **stand** banco di fruttivendolo

fruitful *a* fruttifero; *(profitable)* proficuo

fruition *n* soddisfazione, adempimento

fruitless *a* improduttivo; *(useless)* vano

frustrate *vt* deludere, frustrare

frustration *n* insuccesso, delusione

fry *vt* friggere; — *vi* friggersi

frying pan padella

fuel *n* combustibile *m;* — **oil** petrolio da ardere; — **tank** cisterna per carburanti; — *vt* alimentare con combustibile; — *vi* rifornirsi di carburante

fugitive *a* fuggiasco, evaso; — *n* disertore *m*

fugue *n* fuga

fulcrum *n* fulcro

fulfil *vt* compiere, eseguire, esaudire

fulfilment *n* realizzazione

full *a* pieno; **at** — **blast** al massimo; — **dress** abito da cerimonie; — **house** *(poker)* un tris e una coppia; *(theat)* teatro esaurito; — **moon** luna piena; — **stop** fermata completa; **at** — **speed** a tutta velocità; **in** — per esteso; **in** pieno; **–back** *n (football)* terzino

full– *(in comp)* **–blooded** *a* pieno di vitalità; *(breeding)* puro sangue, di razza; **–blown** *a* in piena fioritura; **–bodied** *a* grasso, pingue; **–faced** *a* dalla faccia piena; **–fledged** *a* completo; — **grown** *a* adulto, maturo; **–length** *a* dalla testa ai piedi; **–term** *a* di periodo completo

fullness *n* pienezza

fully *adv* tutto, interamente, perfettamente

fume *n* emanazione, esalazione; — *vt* affumicare, offuscare; — *vi (anger)* arrabbiarsi, smaniare

fumigate *vt* disinfettare, soffumicare

fumigation *n* fumigazione

fuming *a* collerico, adirato

fun *n* divertimento; **full of** — molto divertente; **have** — divertirsi; **in** — per scherzo; **make** — **of** burlarsi di

function *n* funzione; — *vi* funzionare

fund *n* capitale liquido, fondo monetario; **sinking** — fondo di ammortamento

fundamental *a* fondamentale

funeral *n* funerale *m;* — **director** assistente funebre; — **home** ditta di pompe funebri

funereal *a* funebre, lugubre

fungicide *n* funghicida *m*

fungus *n* fungo

funnel *n* imbuto

funny *a* buffo, comico, divertente; *(odd)* strano, curioso; — **bone** nervo del gomito

fur *n* pelliccia; — **store** pellicceria

furbish *vt* forbire, lucidare

furious *a* furioso; **–ly** *adv* furiosamente

furlough *n* licenza, congedo

furnace *n* fornace *f*

furnish *vt* ammobiliare; *(supply)* fornire

furnished *a* ammobiliato; — **room** camera ammobiliata

furnishings *npl* arredamenti *mpl*

furniture *n* mobili *mpl*, mobilia

furor *n* furore *m*

furrier *n* pellicciaio

furrow *n* solco

furry *a* peloso; *(tongue)* patinoso

further *a* ulteriore; — *adv* oltre, più in là, oltre a ciò; — *vt* assecondare, agevolare; **without** — **ado** senza ulteriori difficoltà

furtherance *a* promozione, avanzamento

furthermore *adv* inoltre, d'altronde

furthest *a* il più lontano; — *adv* alla massima distanza

furtive *a* furtivo, occulto; **–ly** *adv* furtivamente

fury *n* furore *m*

fuse *n* valvola, fusibile *m*

fuselage *n (avi)* fusoliera

fuss *n* chiasso, trambusto; — **over nothing** trambusto per un nonnulla; — *vi* inquietarsi, affannarsi

fussy *a* meticoloso, schifiltoso

futile *a* inutile, futile, frivolo, vano

futility *n* futilità

future *a* futuro; — *n* futuro, avvenire *m;*

in the — nel futuro
futurist *n* futurista *m&f*

futurity *n* avvenire *m*, futuro
fuzz *n* materia volatile (*or* impalpabile)

G

G– (*in comp*) **—force** *n* forza di gravità; **—man** *n* agente federale; **—suit** *n* (*avi*) scafandro spaziale
gab *n* loquacità, cicaleccio; **gift of —** lingua sciolta; — *vi* cicalare
gabardine *n* gabardina
gabby *a* loquace
gable *n* frontone *m*; **— roof** tetto spiovente
gad *vi* gironzare, girellare; **— about** vagare, andare qua e là
gadabout *n* giramondo
gadget *n* aggeggio, congegno; (*mech*) meccanismo
gaff *n* rampone *m*, uncino; (*naut*) picco di randa
gag *n* bavaglio; (*coll*) scherzo, battuta, trovata; — *vt* imbavagliare; — *vi* (*theat*) improvvisare
gaiety *n* allegria, gaiezza
gaily *a* gaiamente
gain *n* guadagno; — *vt&i* guadagnare; — **on** diminuire la distanza; — **weight** ingrossare
gainful *a* vantaggioso, lucrativo
gainsay *vt* contraddire; dire di no
gait *n* andatura, portamento, passo
gala *a* di gala
galaxy *n* galassia; (*ast*) Via Lattea
gale *n* tormenta, bufera; — **of laughter** scroscio di risa
gall *n* bile *f*; (*coll*) impudenza, sfacciataggine *f*; — *vt* irritare
gallant *a* galante; (*brave*) coraggioso; (*gay*) gaio; (*imposing*) imponente
gallantry *n* galanteria, coraggio
gallbladder *n* cistifellea
gallery *n* galleria; (*theat*) loggione *m*
galley *n* cucina di bordo; (*naut*) galera; (*print*) bozza di stampa
gallivant *vi* bighellonare, andare a zonzo
gallon *n* gallone *m*
gallop *n* galoppo; — *vi* galoppare
gallows *npl* forca, patibolo
gallstone *n* calcolo biliare, mal della pietra
galore *adv* a iosa, in abbondanza
galoshes *npl* galosce *fpl*
galvanize *vt* galvanizzare
galvanometer *n* galvanometro
gamble *n* giuoco d'azzardo; — *n* (*coll*) rischio, azzardo; — *vi* giuocare d'azzardo; — *vt* fare scommessa
gambler *n* giocatore *m*
gambling *n* giuoco d'azzardo; — **house** bisca
game *n* giuoco; (*food*) cacciagione *f*; (*coll*) sotterfugio; (*sport*) partita; **make a — of** giocarsi di; **play the — right** essere onesto; — *a* coraggioso; (*lame*) zoppo; **die —** resistere fino in fondo
gamekeeper *n* guardacaccia *m*
gamma *n* gamma; — **globulin** emoglobina; — **ray** raggio gamma
gander *n* maschio dell'oca
gang *n* banda, combriccola; (*work*) squadra; **–plank** *n* passerella; plancia di sbarco
ganglion *n* ganglio
gangrene *n* cancrena
gangrenous *a* cancrenoso
gangster *n* gangster *m*, bandito, delinquente *m*
gangway *n* passaggio, corridoio; (*naut*) pontile *m*; (*mine*) tunnel di miniera
gantlet *n* (*fig*) sfida; **run the —** superare gli ostacoli
gantry tower *n* (*aesp*) torre di lancio
gap *n* (*blank*) lacuna; (*breach*) breccia; (*mountain*) gola, valico
gape *vi* (*open*) spalancarsi; (*yawn*) sbadigliare; restare a bocca aperta; — **at** guardare attonito
gaping *a* sbadigliante; (*agape*) stordito
garage *n* autorimessa, garage *m*
garb *n* abbigliamento
garbage *n* immondizie *fpl*
garble *vt* mutilare; (*falsify*) falsificare
garden *n* giardino
gardener *n* giardiniere *m*
gardenia *n* gardenia
gargle *vt* gargarizzare; — *n* gargarismo
gargoyle *n* garguglia
garish *a* vistoso, sfarzoso, abbagliante
garland *n* ghirlanda
garlic *n* aglio; — **clove** capo d'aglio
garment *n* indumento; — **industry** industria dell'abbigliamento
garnish *n* guarnizione; (*food*) contorno; — *vt* abbellire, guarnire
garnishee *vt* imporre trattenute sul salario
garrison *n* guarnigione *f*
garret *n* soffitta
garrote *n* cappio; — *vt* strangolare
garter *n* giarrettiera; — **belt** reggicalze *m*; — **snake** biscia
gas *n* gas *m*; (*coll*) benzina; — **heater** stufa a gas; — **meter** contatore del gas; —

stove cucina a gas; — **tank** *(auto)* serbatoio; **–light** *n* luce di gas
gaseous *a* gassoso
gash *n* taglio, sfregio; — *vt* sguarciare
gasoline *n* benzina
gasp *vi* ansare, boccheggiare; — *n* sospiro, anelito; **last** — ultimo respiro
gasping *n* ansito, affanno; — *a* ansimante, affannoso
gastrectomy *n* rettogastrotomia, gastrorettotomia
gate *n* cancello; porta del cancello
gateway *n* portone *m*
gather *vt* raccogliere; *(infer)* dedurre; *(sewing)* increspare, pieghettare; — *vi* *(meet)* adunarsi
gathering *n* adunata, riunione *f; (harvest)* raccolta; *(med)* ascesso, suppurazione; *(people)* adunanza
gaudy *a* sgargiante, vistoso
gauge *n* misura; *(mech)* indicatore *m;* — *vt* misurare; stimare
gaunt *a* sparuto
gauntlet *n* guanto da moschettiere; **take up the** — accettare la sfida; **throw down the** — tirare il guanto di sfida *(fig)*
gauze *n* garza
gavel *n* tributo, gabella
gawk *vi* guardare attorno stupidamente; **–y** *a* balordo, sguaiato
gay *a* allegro, gaio
gaze *vi* guardare; — **at** fissare; — *n* sguardo fisso
gazeteer *n* gazzettiere *m; dizionario geografico*
gear *n* arnesi *mpl,* arredo; *(auto)* meccanismo, ingranaggio; *(equipment)* corredo; *(mech)* congegno; *(tools)* arnesi *mpl;* — **shift** cambio di velocità; **in** — funzionante; **throw out of** — arrestare; *(disable)* mettere fuori posto; — *vt* abbigliare; *(mech)* ingranare
gearing *n* ingranaggio
geiger counter contatore Geiger
gelatin *n* gelatina
gem *n* gemma, gioiello
gender *n* genere *m*
gene *n* tipo genetico
genealogy *n* genealogia
general *a&n* generale *m;* — **delivery** fermo in posta; **in** — in generale
generality *n* generalità
generalization *n* generalizzazione
generally *adv* generalmente; — **speaking** generalmente parlando
generate *vt* generare, produrre
generation *n* generazione
generator *n* generatore *m*
generic *a* generico

generosity *n* generosità
generous *a* generoso
genesis *n* genesi *f,* origine *f*
genetics *n* genetica
Geneva Ginevra
genial *a* cordiale, cortese
geniality *n* genialità
genitals *npl* genitali *mpl*
genitive *a* genitivo
genius *n* genio
Genoa Genova
Genoese *a&n* genovese *m&f*
genteel *a* ammanierato, affettato, ricercato
gentility *n* gentilezza; *(breeding)* nascita aristocratica
gentle *a (mild)* dolce, moderato; *(genteel)* raffinato, cortese
gentleman *n* signore *m;* gentiluomo
gentlemen *ipl* gentiluomini *mpl;* signori *mpl*
gentleness *n* dolcezza, tenerezza
gently *adv* dolcemente
gentry *n* gente per bene; benestanti di campagna
genuflection *n* genuflessione
genuine *a* autentico, genuino
genus *n* genere *m*
geochemistry *n* geochimica
geographic, –al *a* geografico
geography *n* geografia
geologist *n* geologo
geology *n* geologia
geometric, –al *a* geometrico
geometry *n* geometria; **solid** — geometria solida; **plane** — geometria piana
geophysics *n* geofisica
geopolitics *n* geopolitica
geranium *n* geranio
geriatrics *n* gériatria
germ *n* germe *m,* microbo
German *a&n* tedesco, tedesca; — **measles** rosolia
germane *a* relativo, pertinente; *(akin)* germano
Germany Germania
germicide *n* germicida
germinate *vi* germinare
gerund *n* gerundio
gestation *n* gestazione
gesticulate *vi* gesticolare
gesture *n* atto, gesto; — *vi* gestire, gesticolare
get *vt* avere, ottenere; *(fetch)* portare; *(receive)* ricevere; — *vi (become)* diventare, farsi; *(come)* arrivare; — **about** andare attorno; — **along** avanzare, andare avanti; *(agree with)* andare d'accordo con; — **around** *(avoid)* girare; — **at** raggiungere il segno *(fig);* —

away allontanarsi; — **down** scendere; — **even with** vendicarsi, far da pagare; — **into** entrare, mettersi in; — **rid of** sbarazzarsi di; — **up** alzarsi; — **wind of** avere sentore di

get– *(in comp)* —**together** *n* adunata; —**up** *n (arrangement)* formata; *(coll, dress)* costume *m*; —**up-and-go** *n* energia

getaway *n* fuga

geyser *n* geyser, soffione *m*; *(mech)* stufa a gas

ghastliness *n* orrore, squallore *m*; *(paleness)* pallidezza

ghastly *a* orribile, macabro, cadaverico

ghost *n* spettro, fantasma *m;* — **town** città abbandonata; — **writer** chi scrive in nome altrui; **give up the** — perdersi d'animo; **Holy G**– Spirito Santo

G.I. *(mil)* soldato americano

giant *n* gigante *m*

gibberish *n* ciancia

gibe, (jibe) *n* scherno, beffa; — *vt&i* schernire, beffarsi di

giblets *npl* frattaglie, rigaglie *fpl*

giddiness *n* vertigine *f*, capogiro; *(frivolity)* frivolità

giddy *a* vertiginoso; spensierato *(fig)*; *(scatterbrained)* scervellato; **feel** — avere le vertigini

gift *n* regalo, dono; –**ed** *a* valente, d'ingegno

gigantic *a* enorme, gigantesco

giggle *vi* fare risatine sciocche; — *n* riso sciocco

giggling *a* che ride scioccamente

gild *vt&i* dorare

gills *npl* branchie *fpl*

gilt *n* indoratura, doratura; — *a* dorato

gilt-edged *a* di prim'ordine; dorato sul taglio; — **securities** azioni solide

gimlet *n* succhiello

gimmick *n (sl)* trucco, espediente *m*

gin *n* gin *m*

ginger *n* zenzero; — **ale** gassosa allo zenzero

gingerly *adv* cautamente, delicatamente; — *a* cauto

gingham *n* rigatino

gingivitis *n* gengivite *f*

gird *vt* cingere; *(invest with)* investire; — *vi* schernire

girder *n* trave *f*; **steel** — putrella

girdle *n (belt)* cintura; *(garment)* ventriera elastica; — *vt* cingere; *(circle)* circondare

girl *n* ragazza, fanciulla; *(miss)* signorina; *(coll)* innamorata; **hired** — donna di servizio; –**ish** *a* fanciullesco, femminile; –**hood** *n* fanciullezza

girth *n* circonferenza

gist *n* essenza, sostanza, sunto, punto principale

give *vt* dare; — **account** rendere conto; — **away** presentare; dar via; — **back** restituire; — **birth to** dare alla luce; — **evidence** offrire evidenza; *(show)* dare indicazione; — **off** emettere; — **out** *(emit)* emettere; *(fail)* esaurirsi; — **rise to** dare origine a; — **up** *(renounce)* rinunciare; *(yield)* cedere; — **way** cedere, ritirarsi

given *a* dato, stabilito; disposto; — **name** nome di battesimo; — **time** tempo dato

give-and-take *n* compromesso

giver *n* donatore *m*

gizzard *n* ventriglio

glacial *a* glaciale

glacier *n* ghiacciaio

glad *a* contento, lieto, felice; –**ly** *adv* con piacere, volentieri; –**ness** *n* contentezza, gioia, piacere *m*

gladden *vt* rallegrare, allietare

gladiolus *n* gladiolo

glamour *n* fascino; –**ous** *a* affascinante

glance *n* occhiata, sguardo; **at first** — a prima vista; — *vi* dare un'occhiata; dare uno sguardo

gland *n* glandola; –**ular** *a* glandolare, ghiandolare

glare *n* bagliore *m*, sfolgorio; *(eye)* occhiataccia; — *vi* sfolgorare; gettare sguardi sfologoranti

glaring *a* abbagliante, evidente, lampante

glass *n* vetro, cristallo; — **blower** soffiatore di vetro; — **making** fabbricazione del vetro; **cut** — cristallo tagliato; **drinking** — bicchiere *m*; **magnifying** — lente d'ingrandimento; **stained** — vetrata colorata; –**ful** *n* bicchiere pieno; –**ware** *n* cristalleria; vetrame *m*

glasses *npl (drinking)* bicchieri *mpl*; *(eye)* occhiali *mpl*, lenti *fpl*

glassy *a* vitreo, trasparente, cristallino

glaucoma *n* glaucoma *m*

glaze *n* smalto; — *vt* smaltare

glazier *n* vetraio

gleam *n* raggio; — *vi* luccicare, raggiare

gleaming *a* lucente

glee *n (hilarity)* ilarità; *(joy)* gioia; — **club** circolo di coristi

glib *a* loquace, scorrevole

glide *vi* scivolare; — *n* scivolata

glider *n (avi)* aliante *m*

glimmer *n* barlume *m*

glimpse *n* occhiata, sguardo di sfuggita; — *vt&i* intravedere

glint *n* scintillio, sprazzo di luce; — *vi* scintillare, brillare

glisten *vi* brillare, luccicare

glitter *vi* scintillare; — *n* scintillio

gloat *vi* gongolare; divorare con gli occhi *(fig)*

global *a* globale

globe *n* sfera, globo

globular *a* sferico, globulare

gloom *n (darkness)* tenebre *fpl*, oscurità; *(sorrow)* tristezza; **-y** *a (dark)* tetro, oscuro; *(sad)* melanconico, cupo

glorify *vt* glorificare, magnificare, esaltare

glorious *a* glorioso, splendido

glory *n* gloria, onore *m*; — *vi* gloriarsi

gloss *n* lucidezza; **give a** — lustrare; — *vt* lustrare; lucidare;. — **over** adonestare; **-y** *a* lucido

glove *n* guanto, — **shop** guanteria, guantificio; negozio di guanti

glow *vi (flush)* arrossire; *(shine)* brillare; — *n (warmth)* calore *m*; ardore *m*; *(reflection)* riflesso

glower *vi* guardare torvamente

glowing *a* brillante, animato; *(hot)* acceso

glucose *n* glucosio

glue *n* colla; — *vt* incollare

gluey *a* attaccaticcio

glum *a* cupo, arcigno

glut *vt* saziare; *(obstruct)* ingombrare

glutten *n* glutine *m*

glutton *n* ghiottone *m*

gluttonous *a* ghiotto

gluttony *n* ghiottoneria, gola

gnarl *n* nodo

gnarled *a* nodoso

gnarly *a* nodoso

gnat *n* moscerino

gnaw *vt* rosicchiare, rodere

gnawing *n* rodimento; corrosione; — *a* rosicante

go *vi* andare; — **against** andar contro; — **astray** perdersi; — **away** partire; — **back** tornare indietro; — **back on** *(fig)* rinnegare; — **backward** camminare all'indietro; — **beyond** oltrepassare; — **for** *(coll)* andare in cerca di; — **forward** avanzare; — **out** uscire; — **out of one's way** *(detour)* deviarsi; sviarsi; *(favor)* disturbarsi per qualcuno; — **over** *(pass over)* dare una scorsa; *(repeat)* ripetere; *(to)* andare da; — **to sleep** addormentarsi; — **through with** condurre a termine; — **to it** *(coll)* sbrigarsi; — **under** affondare; *(fail)* soccombere; — **with** *(agree)* andare d'accordo; stare con; — **without** fare a meno; **let** — **of** lasciare

go *n (coll)* energia *(fig)*; **all the** — di moda; **have a** — **at it** trattare di fare; **It's a** —! Accettato!; **make a** — **of it** aver esito; **on the** — in movimento; *(busy)*

attivo; **no** — *(sl)* impossibile; di nessun profitto

goad *n* pungolo; — *vt* stimolare

goal *n* meta, mira, scopo

goat *n* capro, capra

goatee *n* barbetta, pizzo

gobble *vt* trangugiare

gobbler *n* ghiottone *m*; **turkey** — tacchino

go-between *n* mediatore *m*, intermediario

goblet *n* coppa

God *n* Dio; — **willing** se piace a Dio; **-speed** *n* buon viaggio

god *n* dio; **-child** *n* figlioccio; **-father** *n* padrino; **-mother** *n* madrina; **-send** *n* bazza *(coll)*; fortuna inaspettata; **-less** *a* ateo, empio; **-like** *a* divino; **-liness** *n* santità

goddess *n* dea

goggle-eyed *a* con gli occhi stralunati

goggles *npl* occhialoni *mpl*

goiter *n* gozzo

gold *n* oro

golden *a* dorato, aureo

gold-filled *a* aurifero

golf *n* golf *m*; — **clubs** bastoni *mpl*; — **course** campo di golf; **-bag** *n* borsa dei bastoni; — *vi* giocare al golf

gonad *n* gonade *f*; tessuto generativo

gondola *n* gondola

gone *a* andato, partito; *(finished)* finito; *(used up)* esaurito

gonorrhea *n* gonorrea

good *n* bene *m*; *(usefulness)* utilità; — **breeding** buona educazione; **G— for you!** *interj* Molto bene!; **do** — far bene; **make** — riuscir bene; — *a* buono; — **afternoon, day** buon giorno; — **evening** buona sera; — **nature** indole buona, buona qualità; — **night** buona notte; — **sense** buon senso; — **turn** buon'azione, favore *m*; — *adv* bene; **be** — essere buono; **for** — **and all** per sempre

good- *(in comp)* **-by** *n* addio, arrivederci, arriverderla; **-for-nothing** *n&a* buonanulla *m&f*; **-hearted** *a* di buon cuore; **-humored** *a* di buon umore; **-looking** *a* attraente; **-natured** *a* di buona indole; **-night** *a* di buonanotte; **-sized** *a* grande

Good Friday Venerdì Santo

goodness *n* bontà; **thank** — *interj* grazie a Dio!

goods *npl* merci *fpl*, beni *mpl*; **catch with the** — *(coll)* prendere in flagrante; **deliver the** — *(coll)* consegnare la merce; **household** — masserizie *fpl*; *(utensils)* utensileria

goose *n* oca; — **flesh,** — **pimples** pelle d'oca *(fig)* **wild** — **chase** la luna nel pozzo *(fig)*

gooseberry *n* ribes *m*, uva spina

gore *n (blood)* grumo di sangue; *(sewing)* taglio di stoffa che compone la gonna; — *vt* incornare

gorge *n* burrone *m*; — *vt&i* gozzovigliare

gorgeous *a* splendido, brillante; *(sumptuous)* fastoso; **-ly** *adv* sontuosamente; con gran fastosità

gorilla *n* gorilla *m*

gory *a* insanguinato

gosling *n* papero

gospel *n* vangelo; — **truth** verità sacrosanta; verità di Vangelo

gossamer *n (gauze)* garza; *(web)* ragnatela; **-y** *a* sottilissimo, tenue

gossip *n* pettegolezzo; — *vi* spettegolare

Gothic *a* gotico

gouge *n* sgorbio; — *vt* sgorbiare

gourd *n* zucca

gourmand *n* ghiottone *m*

gourmet *n* buongustaio

gout *n* gotta

govern *vt* governare

governess *n* governante, istitutrice *f*

government *n* governo, controllo; **-al** *a* governativo

governor *n* governatore *m*

gown *n (coverall)* camice *m*; *(dress)* vestito; **dressing** — veste da camera

grab *vt* afferrare, agguantare; — *n* presa, stretta; — **bag** *(coll)* sacco di regali-sopresa

grace *n* grazia; *(pardon)* perdono; — **note** *(mus)* fioritura; **say** — recitare il benedicite; — *vt* adornare

graceful *a* leggiadro, grazioso

gradation *n* gradazione

grade *n* grado, punto; *(school)* voto; — **crossing** *(rail)* passaggio a livello; — **school** scuola elementare; — *vt* classificare; *(score)* dare i punti; *(surface)* livellare

gradual *a* graduale; **-ly** *adv* man mano, via via

graduate *vt* graduare; conferire un diploma; — *vi* diplomarsi, laurearsi; — *a* diplomato; graduato; — *n* laureato; *(measure)* bicchiere graduato

graduation *n* graduazione

graft *n (bot)* innesto; *(med)* trapianto; *(pol, coll)* corruzione; — *vt (bot)* innestare; *(med)* trapiantare

grain *n (cereal)* grano; *(seed)* chicco; *(texture)* filo; *(weight)* grano; *(wood)* filo, venatura; — **alcohol** alcool di grano; **against the** — di malavoglia; controvoglia

gram *n* grammo

grammar *n* grammatica; — **school** scuola elementare

grammarian *n* grammatico

grammatical *a* grammaticale

grand *a* grande, grandioso, magnifico; — **opera** opera; — **piano** pianoforte a coda; **-stand** *n* tribuna

grandchild *n* nipotino, nipotina

granddaughter, grandson *n* nipote *m&f*

grandfather *n* nonno

grandmother *n* nonna

grandparent *n* nonno, nonna

grandeur *n* grandezza, fasto, grandiosità, magnificenza

grandiloquent *a* magniloquente

grandiose *a* grandioso

granite *n* granito

grant *n* dono, concessione; *(school)* borsa di studio; — *vt* accordare; *(acknowledge)* ammettere, riconoscere; **-ing that** dato che; **take for -ed** accettare come vero

granulate *vt* granulare; — *vi* granularsi

granulated *a* granulato; — **sugar** zucchero cristallizzato

grape *n* uva; — **seed** acino; **bunch of -s** grappolo d'uva

grapefruit *n* pompelmo

grapevine *n* vigna coltivata; *(coll)* confidenza di notizie non ufficiali

graph *n* grafico, diagramma *m*; **-ic** *a* grafico

graphite *n* grafite *f*

grapple *n* rampone *m*; — *vt (wrestling)* aggrappare; — *vi* afferrarsi; — **with** *(fig)* lottare contro; *(problems)* trattare

grasp *vt* afferrare; *(understand)* capire; — *n* stretta; *(scope)* portata

grasping *a* avaro, tirchio, spilorcio

grass *n* erba; **blade of** — filo d'erba; **-hopper** *n* cavalletta; **-land** *n* prateria; **-y** *a* erboso

grate *n (framework)* inferriata; *(grid)* griglia; *(grill)* graticola; — *vt* grattuggiare; *(sound)* raspare; — *vi* stridere

grateful *a* riconoscente, grato; *(pleasing)* gradito; **-ness** *n* gradevolezza, gratitudine *f*

gratification *n (granting of)* appagamento, raggiungimento della meta; *(pleasure)* soddisfazione

gratified *a* gratificato, soddisfatto

gratify *vt* soddisfare; *(please)* accontentare; **-ing** *a* gradevole

grating *n* griglia, inferriata; *(sound)* stridore *m*

gratis *a* gratuito; — *adv* gratis, gratuitamente

gratitude *n* riconoscenza

gratuity *n* mancia

grave *n* tomba, fossa; **-digger** *n* becchino;

–yard *n* cimitero; — *a* grave, austero

gravel *n* ghiaia

gravitate *vi* propendere, gravitare

gravity *n* gravità

gravy *n* sugo di carne; **–boat** *n* salsiera

gray *a&n* grigio

gray-haired *a* dai capelli grigi

grayness *n* grigiore *m*

graze *vt* rasentare, sfiorare; — *vi* pascolare

grease *n* unto, grasso; — **paint** cerone *m*; **remove** — sgrassare; *(spots)* smacchiare

greasing *n* *(auto)* ingrassaggio

greasy *a* untuoso, oleoso

great *a* grande, illustre; **a** — **deal** molto; **a** — **many** molti, gran numero; **to a** — **extent** estesamente

great-grandchild *n* pronipote *m&f*

great-grandparents *npl* bisnonni *mpl*

greatly *adv* molto

greatness *n* grandezza

Grecian, Greek *a&n* greco

Greece Grecia

greed, greediness *n* avidità

greedy *a* avido, ingordo

green *a&n* verde *m*; — *n* *(grassy field)* prato; — **light** *(coll)* luce verde *(fig)*; **–ish** *a* verdastro; **–ness** *n* verdezza, freschezza; *(untrained)* inesperienza

green-eyed *a* dagli occhi verdi; *(fig)* geloso

greenhouse *n* serra

greens *npl* verdura, ortaggio; *(herbs)* erbe *fpl*

greet *vt* salutare

greeting *n* saluto

gregarious *a* socievole, gregario

grenadier *n* granatiere *m*

grenadine *n* *(pomegranite juice)* granatina

grid *n* grata; *(elec)* sistema di elettrificazione; *(rad, TV)* griglia di valvola

griddle *n* tegamino; plancia per cuocere dolci

gridiron *n* griglia; *(football)* campo di calcio demarcato

grief *n* dolore *m*, pena; **come to** — finire male

grief-stricken *a* afflitto, angosciato

grievance *n* rancore *m*; *(complaint)* gravame *m*, reclamo; *(grudge)* ruggine *f* *(fig)*; *(wrong)* torto

grieve *vt* addolorare, affliggere, rattristare; — *vi* affliggersi, crucciarsi, addolorarsi

grievious *a* penoso

grill *vt* cuocere sulla graticola; — *n* graticola

grim *a* sinistro; *(cruel)* implacabile; *(stern)* austero

grimace *n* boccaccia, smorfia

grime *n* sudiciume *m*

grimy *a* sudicio

grin *vi* sogghignare; — *n* gran sorriso, smorfia

grind *vt* *(glass)* smerigliare; *(mill)* macinare; *(teeth)* digrignare; — *n* sgobbamento; *(coll)* fatica; **daily** — *(sl)* fatica quotidiana

grinder *n* macinatore *m*; **knife** — arrotino; **meat** — tritacarne *m*; **organ** — suonatore d'organetto

grinding *n* macinatura; *(sharpening)* affilatura; — *a* *(sound)* stridente

grindstone *n* mola

grip *vt* stringere, afferrare; — *n* presa, stretta; *(luggage)* valigetta; **come to –s with** essere nel punto critico di una decisione; venire alle mani

gripe *n* crampo, colica; *(sl)* lamentela; — *vt* afferrare, dare crampi di ventre; — *vi* *(sl)* lamentarsi

gripping *a* impressionante, eccitante

gristle *n* cartilagine *f*

grit *n* sabbia, arenaria; *(coll)* fermezza, coraggio; — *vt* *(teeth)* digrignare

gritty *a* sabbioso; *(brave)* coraggioso

groan *vi* gemere; — *n* lamento, gemito

grocer *n* rivenditore di generi alimentari

groceries *npl* alimenti *mpl*

grocery *n* negozio di generi alimentari

groggy *a* *(drunk)* ubbriaco; *(unsteady)* malfermo

groin *n* inguine *m*

groom *n* stalliere *m*; mozzo di stalla; *(wedding)* sposo; — *vt* *(horse)* strigliare; addestrare; — *vi* addestrarsi

groove *n* incastro, scanalatura; — *vt* scanalare

grope *vi* andare a tastoni; brancolare; — **for** cercare a tastoni

groping *a* brancolante; **–ly** *adv* a tastoni, brancolando

gross *n* grossa; — *a* grosso, volgare, grossolano; *(com)* lordo; — **ignorance** ignoranza crassa

grotesque *a* grottesco

grouch *n* malinconico, tetro; **have a** — essere di malumore; — *vi* lamentarsi, essere di malumore

grouchy *a* *(coll)* burbero, di cattivo umore

ground *n* suolo, terra; *(basis)* fondamento, fondo; — **floor** pianterreno; **break** — dare inizio a, cominciare; **forbidden** — terreno proibito; **give** — *(retreat)* retrocedere; **hold one's** — star saldo; **–less** *a* infondato, senza base

ground *vt* fondare; *(avi)* proibire il volo; *(elec)* mettere a terra; **–ed** *a* fondato, basato; *(naut)* arenato

ground-control *n* *(avi)* controllo da terra

grounds *npl (basis)* fondamento; *(coffee)* fondo di caffè, feccia di caffè; *(land)* parco, giardini *mpl;* — **for divorce** movente per il divorzio

groundwork *n* fondamenta, basi *fpl*

group *n* gruppo; — *vt* raggruppare, adunare; — *vi* raggrupparsi

grove *n* boschetto; *(plantation)* piantagione *f*

grovel *vi (flatter)* strisciare; *(stoop)* abbassarsi, umiliarsi

grow *vt* coltivare; — *vi* ingrandire, crescere; *(progress)* progredire; — **better** *(improve)* migliorare; — **dark** oscurare; — **from** provenire; — **into** *(become)* diventare; — **old** invecchiare; — **soft** diventare indulgente; — **up** *(age)* crescere, ingrandire; — **worse** peggiorare

growl *v* ringhiare; — *n* ringhio, brontolio

grown *a* adulto, cresciuto, fatto

grown-up *a&n* adulto, adulta

growth *n* vegetazione; *(increase)* crescita; *(med)* escrescenza

grub *n* verme *m*, bruco; *(coll)* cibo; — *vt* sradicare, estirpare; — *vi* zappare; *(coll)* mangiare

grubby *a* sudicio, sporco, bacato

grudge *n* rancore *m;* **bear a** — aver rancore contro; **have a** — **against** aver malanimo contro

grudgingly *adv* malvolentieri

gruel *n* farina d'avena cotta in acqua

grueling *a* estenuante, faticoso

gruesome *a* orrendo, macabro, raccapricciante

gruff *a* brusco; **−ness** *n* asprezza, rozzezza

grumble *vt* borbottare; — *vi* lamentarsi

grumpy *a* irritabile, bisbetico; di cattivo umore

grunt *vi* grugnire; — *n* grugnito

guarantee *vt* garantire; — *n* garanzia, garante *m*

guarantor *n* garante *m*, mallevadore *m*

guaranty *n* garanzia

guard *n* protettore *m;* *(person)* guardia *m;* *(rail)* capotreno; **under** — sotto vigilanza; **−rail** *n* controrotaia; — *vt* sorvegliare, proteggere; — **against** premunirsi contro

guardian *n* tutore *m*, tutrice *f;* *(custodian)* custode *m*

guerilla *n* partigiano, guerrigliero; — **warfare** guerriglia

guess *vt&i* indovinare; *(surmise)* credere, supporre; — *n* supposizione, congettura; **rough** — occhio e croce; **−work** *n* congettura

guest *n* invitato

guffaw *n* risata; scoppio di risa

Guiana Guiana

guidance *n* guida, norma; — **beam** luceguida

guide *n* guida; — **rope** *(avi)* stabilizzatore *m;* **−book** *n* guida; **−post** *n* cartello indicatore; — *vt* guidare

guided missile missile guidato

guiding *a* dirigente

guild *n* associazione, corporazione

guile *n* astuzia, frode *f;* **−less** *a* ingenuo

guillotine *n* ghigliottina; — *vt* ghigliottinare

guilt *n* colpa; **−less** *a* innocente; **−y** *a* colpevole

guinea pig porcellino d'India

guise *n* forma, guisa, sembianza

guitar *n* chitarra; **−ist** *n* chitarrista *m*

gulch *n* burrone profondo, baratro

gulf *n* golfo

gull *n* gabbiano; **sea** — gabbiano di mare

gullible *a* credulone

gully *n* burrone *m*, condotto, cunicolo

gulp *n* sorsata, boccone *m;* — *vt* ingoiare

gum *n* gomma; *(anat)* gengiva; *(bot)* resina; — **tree** albero da gomma
bubble — cicla bomba; **chewing** — gomma da masticare

gumdrop *n* pasticca di gomma

gummed *a* gommato, ingommato; — **tape** nastro adesivo

gummy *a (adherent)* aderente; *(rubber)* gommoso; *(sticky)* attaccaticcio

gumption *n (coll)* spirito d'iniziativa

gun *n* cannone, fucile *m*, pistola; — **barrel** canna di fucile; — **butt** calcio di fucile; — **permit** porto d'armi; **−fire** *n* sparo di cannone; **−man** *n* assassino; **−powder** *n* polvere da sparo; **−shot** *n* tiro di arma da fuoco; **−smith** *n* armaiolo

gunner *n* artigliere *m;* **−y** *n* artiglieria, balistica

gun-shy *a* pauroso delle armi da fuoco

gurgle *vi* gorgogliare; — *n* gorgoglio

gush *vi* zampillare; sgorgare; *(coll)* entusiasmarsi eccessivamente; — *n* zampillo; **−er** *n (oil)* getto di petrolio; **−ing** *a* sgorgante; *(person)* espansivo; **−y** *a* meloso, affettatamente sentimentale

gust *n* raffica; *(rush)* impeto

gusto *n* trasporto, entusiasmo

gusty *a* burrascoso, tempestoso, ventoso

gut *n* budello; — *vt* sventare

guts *npl* intestini *mpl;* budella *fpl;* *(sl)* coraggio, fegato *(fig);* **have** — *(sl)* aver coraggio

gutter *n (curb)* cunetta; *(roof)* gronda

guttersnipe *n* monello

guttural *a* gutturale

guy *n (sl)* tipo, individuo
gymnasium *n* palestra
gymnastics *npl* ginnastica
gypsy *n* zingaro

gypsum *n* gesso
gyrate *vi* girare
gyration *n* rotazione
gyroscope *n* giroscopio

H

haberdashery *n* merceria
habit *n* abitudine *f*
habitable *a* abitabile
habitation *n* dimora, abitazione
hack *vt* mutilare; tagliare all'azzardo; — *vi* tossicchiare; — *n* lacerazione, taglio; *(cab)* carrozza; — **writer** scrittorello *(fig)*
hackneyed *a* trito, banale
haddock *n* merluzzo; **dried** — baccalà *m*
hag *n* vecchia strega
haggard *a* sparuto, allampanato; *(wild)* selvatico
haggle *vi* mercanteggiare
Hague, The L'Aia
hail *n* grandine *f*; *(greeting)* saluto; **-stone** *n* chicco di grandine; **-storm** *n* grandinata; — *vi* grandinare; — *vt* salutare, acclamare
hair *n (animal)* peli *mpl*; *(human)* capelli *mpl*; **split -s** cercare il pelo nell'uovo *(fig)*; **-brush** *n* spazzola; **-cut** *n* taglio di capelli; **-dresser** *n* parrucchiere *m*, pettinatrice *f*; **-pin** *n* forcina; **-spring** *n (mech)* molla del bilanciere
hair- *(in comp)* **-do** *n* pettinatura; **-raising** *a (coll)* raccapricciante
hairy *a* capelluto, peloso
hale *a* sano, vigoroso
half *n* metà; — **a dozen** mezza dozzina; — **as much** la metà di; — *a* mezzo; — **brother** fratellastro; fratello uterino; — **sister** sorellastra; sorella uterina; — *adv* a metà; in mezzo
half- *(in comp)* **-and-half** *a* mezzo e mezzo; sì e no; così; **-baked** *a (food)* cotto a metà; *(person)* inesperto; **-breed, -caste** *n* meticcio, mezzosangue *m*; **-holiday** *n* mezza festa; **-hour** *n* mezz'ora; **-life** *n* semisviluppo di una reazione nucleare; **-light** *n* mezza luce; **-slip** *n* sottogonna, sottoveste a vita; **-truth** *n* verità detta a metà; **-turn** *n* mezza volta; **-wit** *n* mezzo stupido
halfhearted *a* indifferente, apatico; senza entusiasmo
half sole mezza suola
halfway *a* equidistante, mezzo; — *adv* a metà, a metà strada
halibut *n* rombo
halitosis *n* alito pesante

hall *n* sala, aula, **-way** *n* corridoio
hallmark *n* marchio ufficiale per garantire il grado di purezza
hallow *vt* consacrare
hallucination *n* allucinazione
halo *n* alone *m*
halt *vi* fermarsi; — *n* fermata, pausa
halter *n* cavezza
halve *vt* dimezzare
halves *npl* **by** — a metà; **go** — dividere la spesa
ham *n* prosciutto; *(coll, rad)* radioamatore *m*, *(coll, theat)* cattivo attore; — **and eggs** uova e prosciutto
hamburger *n* carne macinata *f*; — **on a bun** panino ripieno di polpetta
hammer *n* martello; — *vt* martellare
hamper *n* canestro; — *vt* ostacolare
hamstring *vt* sgarrettare, tagliare i garretti
hand *n* mano *f*; *(measure)* spanna; *(watch)* lancetta; — **and glove** strettamente confidenziale; come pane e cacio; — **in** — strettamente confidenziale *(fig)*; con la mano in mano; — **over** — una mano dopo l'altra; — **to** — di mano in mano; **at** — a portata di mano; **by** — a mano; **by the** — per mano; **out of** — fuori controllo; **have the upper** — aver controllo; **lend a** — dare una mano *(fig)*; **old** — esperto; **on** — fra le mani, alla mano; **on the other** — dall'altro lato, d'altra parte; **show one's** — rivelare le proprie intenzioni; **upper** — sopravvento
hand *vt* porgere; — **down** trasmettere per successione; — **over** *(com)* consegnare
hand- *(in comp)* **-made** *a* fatto a mano; **live -to-mouth** vivere alla giornata
handbag *n* borsa; *(luggage)* valigetta
handbill *n* annunzio, avviso
handbook *n* manuale *m*
handcuff *n* manetta; — *vt* ammanettare
handful *n* pugno, manata; — **of** mano piena di
handicap *n* ostacolo; *(disadvantage)* svantaggio; — *vt* ostacolare
handicraft *n* artigianato
handkerchief *n* fazzoletto
handle *n* manico; — *vt* maneggiare, toccare
handling *n* manipolazione, maneggio, trat-

tamento
handout n (sl) elemosina
hands npl mani fpl; **— down** adv facilmente; **— off** interj giù le mani; **— up** interj mani in alto; **change —** cambiar mani; **wash one's — of** lavarsi le mani (fig)
handshake n stretta di mano
handsome a bello, simpatico, generoso
handspring n salto acrobatico
handwork n lavoro manuale
handwriting n scrittura
handwritten a manoscritto; scritto a mano
handy a comodo, abile; a portata di mano
handyman n fasservizi m
hang vi pendere, penzolare; (execute) impiccare; **— around** indugiare; **— back** esitare; **— in the balance** stare in bilico; **— on** tenersi attaccato a; **— one's head** chinare la testa; **— together** accordarsi; essere attaccato l'un l'altro (fig); **— up** appendere, sospendere
hangar n hangar m, aviorimessa
hangdog a abbattuto
hanger n gancio; **coat —** attaccapanni m
hanger-on n parassita, scroccone m, seguace m
hanging n sospensione; **—** a pensile, pendente; **-s** npl tappezzerie fpl, tendine fpl
hangman n boia, carnefice m
hangnail n pipita
hangover n mal di testa dopo una bevuta
hank n matassa
hanker vi bramare
hankering n desiderio ardente
haphazard a fortuito, accidentale
happen vi accadere, avvenire, capitare; **— on** capitare, imbattersi
happening n avvenimento
happily adv felicemente
happiness n felicità, contentezza
happy a felice, contento, lieto
happy-go-lucky a spensierato
harangue n arringa; **—** vt&i arringare
harass vt molestare, tormentare
harbor n porto; **—** vt&i albergare
hard a duro; difficile, severo; **— and fast** saldo; **— cash** contanti mpl; **— coal** antracite f; **— luck** scalogna, iella; **— of hearing** duro d'orecchio; **— put** (coll) ostacolato; **— to please** difficile d'accontentare; **— up** (coll) al verde, nei guai
hard adv fortemente; **try —** sforzarsi arduamente
hard- (in comp) **—boiled** a duro; (coll) molto sofisticato; **—earned** a guadagnato con fatica; **—working** a laborioso,

lavoratore
harden vt indurare; (steel) temprare; **–ed** a indurito
hardhearted a inumano, duro
hardihood n resistenza
hardiness n vigore m, robustezza
hardly adv appena, difficilmente, quasi, duramente
hardness n durezza, difficoltà
hardship n avversità, pena
hardware n ferramenta fpl, utensileria; **— store** negozio di ferramenta
hardwood n legno duro
hardy a robusto, vigoroso; (daring) audace
harebrained a temerario, imprudente
harlot n prostituta
harm n male m, danno; **–ful** a nocivo, dannoso; **–less** a innocuo; **—** vt nuocere, fare del male
harmonica n armonica
harmonious a armonioso, armonico
harmonize vt&i armonizzare; (agree) concordare; **— with** andar bene con
harmony n armonia
harness n bardatura, finimenti mpl; armatura; (fig) restrizione; **—** vt bardare; (connect) attaccare
harp n arpa; **—** vi suonare l'arpa; **— on** (fig) insistere, ripetere
harpoon n rampone m, fiocina
harridan n vecchiaccia
harrow n erpice m; **—** vt straziare; (agri) erpicare; **–ing** a straziante, atroce
harry vt devastare, saccheggiare
harsh a rude, brusco
harshness n asprezza; (sound) discordanza
harum-scarum a scervellato, sventato
harvest n raccolto, messe f; **— moon** luna della mietitura; **—** vt mietere, fare il raccolto; **-er** n mietitore m; (mech) mietitrice f
has-been n (coll) decaduto
hash n carne macinata; carne tritata con patate
hasp n serramento, fermaglio
hassock n cuscino
haste n furia, fretta; **— makes waste** chi va piano va sano
hasten vt affrettare, accelerare; **—** vi affrettarsi
hastily adv in fretta, affrettatamente, presto
hasty a frettoloso
hat n cappello; **— rack** poggia-cappello; **pass the —** fare una colletta; **top —** cappello a cilindro; **-band** n nastro del cappello; **-box** n cappelliera; **-less** a scappellato; senza cappello
hatch n covata; (naut) boccaporto; **—** vt

(eggs) covare; *(idea)* tramare; *(print)* trattegiare; — *vi* uscire dall'uovo

hatchet *n* accetta; **bury the** — riconciliarsi

hate *n* odio; **–ful** *a* odioso; — *vt* detestare, odiare, abominare

hatred *n* odio

haughtily *adv* arrogantemente

haughtiness *n* superbia, alterigia

haughty *a* altezzoso

haul *vt* trasportare, rimorchiare, tirare

haunch *n* anca; *(meat)* coscia

haunt *vt* frequentare; *(follow)* perseguitare; — *n* ricovero, covo, ritiro; **–s** *npl* locali preferiti

haunted *a* visitato dagli spiriti

have *vt* possedere, avere; — **a look at** dare una guardata a; — **on** *(wear)* indossare; — **something done** far fare qualche cosa

haven *n* rifugio, porto

havoc *n* strage *f*, rovina; **play** — **with** devastare

hawk *n* falcone *m*; — *vi* fare il venditore ambulante

hawser *n* gomena

hawthorn *n* biancospino

hay *n* fieno; — **fever** febbre del fieno; **–loft** *n* fienile *m*; **–maker** *n* fienatore *m*; *(boxing)* pugno decisivo; **–rack** *n* covone di fieno; **–stack** *n* mucchio di fieno

hazard *m* rischio, azzardo; — *vt&i* arrischiare; **–ous** *a* azzardato

haze *n* bruma, caligine *f*; — *vt* annebbiare

hazel *n* nocciuolo; — **nut** nocciuola; — *a* di nocciuola

hazy *a* confuso, indistinto; *(misty)* caliginoso

he *pron* egli, lui; — **who** colui che

head *n* testa, capo; *(river)* sorgente *f*; — **of hair** capigliatura; — **over heels** *a* gambe levate, capovolto; **–s or tails** testa o croce; **at the** — in capo a; **alla testa di**; **come to a** — raggiungere il colmo; *(med)* suppurare; **from** — **to foot** da capo a piedi; **go to one's** — montare alla testa; **keep one's** — tenere la testa a posto; **lose one's** — perdere la testa; **out of one's** — fuori di mente

head *vt* capeggiare, dirigere; — **off** stornare, deviare

headache *n* dolor di testa; mal di capo

headdress *n* pettinatura

headfirst *adv* a capofitto

headgear *n* copricapo; *(cap)* cuffia; *(hat)* cappello

heading *n* titolo

headland *n* promontorio, capo

headlight *n* faro, fanale *m*

headline *n* titolo, intestazione *f*

headlong *adv* a capofitto, precipitatamente; — *a* violento, impetuoso

head-on *a&adv* testa-testa

headphone *n* cuffia telefonica

headquarters *npl* sede *f*; quartier generale; ufficio centrale

headrest *n* poggiatesta

headstone *n* lapide *f*

headstrong *a* testardo

headway *n* progresso, cammino; **make** — progredire, far strada

heady *a* che da alla testa

heal *vt* guarire, sanare

healing *n* guarigione *f*; — *a* curativo

health *n* salute *f*, sanità; — **officer** ufficiale sanitario; — **resort** stazione climatica; **bill of** — certificato di salute; **–y** *a* sano; in buona salute

healthful *a* sano; **–ness** *n* salute, salubrità

heap *n* mucchio, cumulo; — *vt* ammassare, ammucchiare

hear *vt* sentire, udire; — **about** sentire riguardo a; — **from** aver notizie di; — **of** essere informato circa

hearing *n* *(audience)* udienza; *(sense)* udito; — **aid** apparecchio acustico; **hard of** — duro d'orecchio

hearsay *n* diceria, voce *f*

hearse *n* carro funebre

heart *n* cuore *m;* **to one's –'s content** a piacimento, con gioia di cuore; — **trouble** disturbo cardiaco; **by** — **a** memoria; **with all my** — con tutto il mio cuore; — *a* cardiaco

heartbreaking *a* straziante

heartbroken *a* angosciato, straziato, affranto

heartburn *n* bruciore di stomaco

heartfelt *a* sincero, caldo, profondo, intenso

hearten *vt* incoraggiare

heartiness *n* cordialità

hearth *n* focolare *m*

heartless *a* spietato, senza cuore

heart-rending *a* straziante

heartsick *a* afflitto, abbattuto; **con la morte nel cuore** *(fig)*

heart-to-heart *a* cuore a cuore

hearty *a* cordiale, vigoroso; *(abundant)* abbondante

heat *n* calore *m*, caldo; *(sport)* eliminatoria, preliminare *m*; **dead** — *(sport)* corsa alla pari; **prickly** — eruzione della pelle per il caldo; **–stroke** *n* insolazione; colpo di caldo; — **wave** ondata di caldo; — *vt* scaldare, riscaldare, infiammare; — *vi* scaldarsi, infiammarsi

heated *a* riscaldato; *(excited)* agitato;

(inflammed) infiammato

heater *n* riscaldatore *m*; **electric —** stufettina elettrica; **water —** scaldabagno

heathen *n&a* pagano

heating *n* riscaldamento; **— pad** cuscino termico

heat-resistant *a* refrattario al calore; resistente al calore

heave *vt* gettare, sollevare; **—** *vi* (bulge) gonfiarsi; *(emit)* vomitare; *(lift)* sollevarsi; **— a sigh** emettere un sospiro; **— in sight** apparire; **—** *n* sollevamento, sussulto

heaven *n* paradiso; *(sky)* cielo; **-ly** *a* celeste, divino

heavily *adv* pesantemente; *(much)* molto, assai; *(seriously)* gravemente

heaviness *n* pesantezza

heavy *a* pesante; **-weight** *n* *(sport)* peso massimo

heavy-handed *a* severo, oppressivo

Hebrew *n&a* ebreo, ebrea

heckle *vt* cardare, pettinare; interrompere importunamente; **-r** *n* interruttore importuno

hectic *a* agitato, movimentato; *(feverish)* febbrile

hectogram *n* ettogrammo, etto *(coll)*

hedge *n* siepe *f*; barriera; *(defense)* protezione; **—** *vt* assiepare, circondare di siepe; **— in** *(restrict)* restringere; **—** *vi* fare siepi; evadere una domanda

hedgehop *vi* *(avi)* volare a bassa quota; **—** *n* volo a bassa quota

hedonist *n* edonista *m&f*

heed *vt* badare; dar retta; **—** *n* attenzione

heel *n* *(foot)* tallone *m*; *(shoe)* tacco; *(coll)* carogna *(fig)* **—** *vt* rattacconare; **—** *vi* *(naut)* sbandarsi

heels *npl* tacchi *mpl*; **fall head over —** cadere a gambe levate; **take to one's —** svignarsela; battere i tacchi

hefty *a* vigoroso, robusto, gagliardo

heifer *n* giovenca

height *n* *(altitude)* elevatezza; *(avi)* quota; *(loftiness)* altezza, *(people)* statura; **-en** *vt* aumentare, intensificare

heir *n* erede *m&f*; **— apparant** erede diretto; **— presumptive** erede presunto

heiress *n* ereditiera

heirloom *n* ereditato; mobile di famiglia

hegemony *n* egemonia

helicopter *n* elicottero

heliotherapy *n* elioterapia

heliport *n* eliporto

hell *n* inferno; **-ish** *a* infernale

hellcat *n* megera

hello *interj* salve, ciao; *(phone)* pronto

helm *n* timone *m*; *(control)* comando

helmet *n* casco, elmo

help *vt* aiutare; **— down** aiutare a scendere; **— oneself** aiutarsi; **— out** aiutare; **H— yourself!** Si serva!; **I can't —** it Non è colpa mia

help *n* aiuto, soccorso; *(assistant)* aiutante *m*; *(remedy)* rimedio; **no — for it** è fatale; **-ful** *a* utile; **-less** *a* impotente, debole, indifeso

helping *n* porzione *f*; **—** *a* utile, soccorrevole

helpmate *n* consorte *m&f*, marito, moglie *f*

helter-skelter *adv* alla rinfusa

hem *n* orlo; **—** *vt* orlare; **— in** cingere, circondare

hemisphere *n* emisfero

hemoglobin *n* emoglobina

hemolysin *n* *(immunology)* emolisina, anticorpo del sangue

hemophilia *n* emofilia

hemophyliac *n* emofiliaco

hemorrhage *n* emorragia

hemorrhoids *npl* emorroidi *fpl*

hemp *n* canapa

hemstitch *n* orlo a giorno; **—** *vt* orlare a giorno

hen *n* gallina; *(birds)* femmina; **— tracks** *(writing)* zampa di gallina *(fig)*; **-coop** *n* gallinaio; piccolo pollaio

hence *adv* di qui, da ora; *(therefore)* perciò

henceforth *adv* da ora in poi

henna *n* ennè *f*

hepatic *a* epatico

her *pron* la; lei; **—** *a* il suo, la sua; **-self** *pron* sè; lei stessa, sè stessa

herald *n* araldo; **—** *vt* annunziare, proclamare; **-ry** *n* araldica

herb *n* erba; **-ivorous** *a* erbivoro

herd *n* gregge *m*, folla; **the common —** gente ordinaria; **—** *vi* far gregge

here *adv* qui; qua; **— is, — are** ecco; **that's neither — nor there** è di poca importanza; **-abouts** *adv* da queste parti; qui vicino; **-by** *adv* per questo mezzo; per mezzo della presente; **-in** *adv* qui, in questo; qui accluso; **-with** *adv* unitamente

hereafter *adv* da ora in poi; in avvenire; **—** *n* l'altro mondo

hereditary *a* ereditario

heredity *n* eredità

heresy *n* eresia

heretic *n* eretico

heretofore *adv* fin qui

heritage *n* retaggio

hermaphrodite *n* ermafrodite *m&f*

hermetic *a* ermetico; **-ally** *a* ermeticamente

hermit *n* eremita *m*

hernia *n* ernia

hero *n* eroe *m*; *(theat)* protagonista *m*; **-ic** *a* eroico; **-ics** *npl* eroica; linguaggio letterario; **-ism** *n* eroismo

heroin *n* eroina

heroine *n* eroina, protagonista

herring *n* aringa

hers *pron* il suo, la sua

hesitancy *n* esitazione

hesitate *vi* esitare

hesitation *n* esitazione *f*

heterodox *a* eterodosso

hew *vt* fendere; — **down** abbattere; — **to the line** rimanere negli stretti limiti

hexameter *n* esametro

hiatus *n* iato; lacuna *(fig)*

hibernate *vi* svernare; svernare in letargo

hibernation *n* ibernazione

hiccough *n* singhiozzo; — *vi* avere il singhiozzo

hidden *a* celato, nascosto; segreto, occulto

hide *vt* nascondere, celare; — *vi* nascondersi; — *n* pelle *f*

hide– *(in comp)* **–and-seek** *n* rimpiattino; **–out** *n* nascondiglio

hidebound *a* testardo; di corte vedute *(fig)*

hideous *a* bruttissimo, orribile

hiding *a* che nasconde, che si nasconde

hierarchy *n* gerarchia

hieroglyphics *npl* geroglifici *mpl*

hi-fi *n (rad, coll)* alta fedeltà

high *a* alto, elevato; *(drunk, sl)* brillo, ubbriaco; — **and low** ovunque; — **and mighty** arrogante; — **jump** salto in alto; — **noon** pieno mezzogiorno; — **seas** alto mare; — **school** scuola media; — **spirits** coraggio, animo; — **tide** punto culminante; — **time** ultimo momento

high– *(in comp)* **–class** *a* d'alta classe; di qualità superiore; **–grade** *a* di qualità superiore; d'alto grado; **–handed** *a* arbitrario; **–minded** *a* magnanimo; **–necked** *a* dal colletto alto; **–pitched** *a* stridulo, acuto; **–priced** *a* caro, costoso; **–sounding** *a* sonoro, altisonante; **–spirited** *a* audace, vivo, pieno di coraggio *(or* d'energia*)*; **–strung** *a* nervoso, emotivo; **–tension** ad alta tensione; **–test** *a* d'alta prova, con basso grado d'ebollizione

highball *n* whisky con soda e ghiaccio

highbrow *n* sapientone, intellettuale

higher *a* più elevato, superiore

highest *a* il più alto, massimo

highhanded *a* arrogante, prepotente

High Mass *n* Messa Alta

highness *n* elevatezza, altezza; **Your H–** Sua Altezza

highway *n* camionale *f*; strada maestra;

–man *n* grassatore *m*, bandito, ladrone di strada

hijack *vt (coll)* contrabbandare; rubare; **–ing** *n* contrabbando; furto

hike *n* marcia; gita a piedi; — *vi* vagabondare

hiking *n* escursione, marcia; — *a* d'escursione, di marcia

hilarious *a* ilare, molto allegro

hilarity *n* ilarità

hill *n* collina, colle *m*; **–side** *n* fianco di collina

hilly *a* collinoso, montuoso

hilt *n* elsa, impugnatura

him *pron* lo, lui; **–self** *pron* sè, egli stesso; lui stesso, sè stesso

hind *n (zool)* cerva, daina; — *a* posteriore, dietro, di dietro; — **legs** gambe posteriori; **–quarters** *n* quarti di dietro; **–sight** *n* retrospezione

hinder *vt* impedire, ostacolare

hindrance *n* ostacolo, inciampo

hinge *n* cardine *m*; — *vt* incardinare; — **on** dipendere da

hint *n* cenno, traccia; **drop a** — fare una insinuazione; **take a** — capire a volo *(fig)*; — *vt&i* insinuare; — **at** alludere

hip *n* anca, fianco

hippodrome *n* ippodromo

hire *vt* noleggiare, prendere in affitto; — *n* noleggio, salario; **for** — da nolo

hireling *n* prezzolato, mercenario

hirsute *a* ispido, irsuto

his *pron* il suo, la sua

hiss *vt&i* fischiare; — *n* sibilo

histamine *n* istamina

historian *n* storico

historic, historical *a* storico

history *n* storia

histrionics *npl* drammaturgia

hit *vt* colpire, battere; — **the ceiling** *(coll)* perdere le staffe *(fig)*; — **the jackpot** *(coll)* avere una fortuna sfacciata; — **the mark** dare nel segno; — **the spot** dare giusto nel punto; — *n* colpo, successo; *(coll)* battuta; — **or miss** trascuratamente, a casaccio

hitch *n* impedimento; *(naut)* nodo; — *vt&i* attaccare; **–hike** viaggiare con l'autostop

hitherto *adv* finora; fin qui

hit-or-miss *a* negligente

hive *n* alveare *m*; **–s** *n (med)* orticaria

hoard *n* cumulo, mucchio; — *vt* accumulare, ammassare

hoarse *a* rauco

hoary *a* canuto, bianco; *(old)* vecchio

hoax *n* beffa, inganno; *(joke)* scherzo; —

vt fare uno scherzo; corbellare

hobble *n* imbarazzo, pastoia; *(limp)* zoppicamento; — *vi* zoppicare; — *vt (horse)* impastoiare

hobby *n* passatempo, distrazione; — **horse** cavallino a dondolo

hobnob *vi* bere insieme, dare del tu, prendersi confidenza

hobo *n* vagabondo

hock *n* garretto; **in** — *(coll)* in pegno; al Monte di Pietà *(coll)*; — *vt* sgarrettare

hocus-pocus *n* giuoco di prestigio

hodgepodge *n* guazzabuglio

hoe *n* zappa; — *vt&i* zappare

hog *n* maiale *m*, porco; **–gish** *a* porcino, suino; *(fig)* bestiale, sporco; **–wash** *n* beverone del porco

hoist *vt* alzare, innalzare; *(naut)* issare; — *n* montacarichi *m*

hold *n* presa; sostegno, appoggio; *(naut)* stiva; — *vt* occupare; *(keep)* tenere; *(sustain)* sopportare; — **back** frenare, impedire; — **forth** offrire, promettere; — **on** star fermo; — **one's tongue** tener la lingua a freno; — **out** resistere a; — **over** aggiornare, posporre, detenere; — **up** sostenere; **get** — **of** impugnare; aver in pugno; **have a** — **on** far presa su; **take** — **of** afferrare; dar di piglio a

holdup *n* furto a mano armata; *(delay)* ritardo

hole *n* foro, buco; **in the** — *(coll)* in debito; **put in a** — *(coll)* imbarazzare

holiday *n* festa

holiness *n* santità

Holland Olanda

hollow *n* vuoto; — *a* cavo, concavo; *(empty)* vuoto; *(deep)* cupo; *(fig)* falso, vano; *(sound)* sordo; — *vt* scavare

hollow– *(in comp)* **–cheeked** *a* dalle guance infossate; **–eyed** *a* dagli occhi infossati

holly *n* agrifoglio

hollyhock *n* malvarosa, alcea

holster *n* fondina

holy *a* santo; — **water;** acqua santa; **H–ｗeek** settimana santa

homage *n* omaggio, rispetto

home *n* casa, focolare *m*; — **stretch** *(race)* retta finale; — **town** paese natio; **–land** *n* patria; **–less** *a* senza tetto; **–like** *a* comodo, intimo; **–made** *a* casalingo; fatto in casa; **–maker** *n* massaia; padrona di casa; — *a* casalingo, nostrano; di casa

home-coming *n* ritorno a casa

homely *a* brutto, sgraziato

homesick *a* nostalgico; **–ness** *n* nostal-gia

homeward *adv&a* verso casa

homicidal *a* omicida

homicide *n* omicidio

homogenized *a* omogeneizzato

homogenous *a* omogeneo

homonym *n* omonimo

homosexual *n* omosessuale

hone *vt* affilare con cote; — *n* cote *f*

honest *a* onesto; *(frank)* veritiero, sincero, leale; **–y** *n* onestà, probità, *(morals)* correttezza

honey *n* miele *m*; *(fig)* tesoro *(fig)*, carino; **–comb** *n* favo; **–dew melon** melone melato

honeymoon *n* luna di miele

honor *n* onore *m*; *(glory)* onorificenza; **on my** — sul mio onore; **point of** — punto d'onore; **word of** — parola d'onore; — *vt* onorare; — **a draft** accettare una cambiale; **–ed** *a* onorato, rispettato; **–s** *npl* onori *mpl*

honorable *a* onorevole

honorary *a* onorario, onorifico

hood *n* cappuccio; *(auto)* cofano; *(sl)* mascalzone *m*; camorrista *m (coll)*; **–ed** *a* incappucciato

hoodlum *n (coll* malvivente *m*, teppista *m*

hoodoo *(coll)* iettatore *m*

hoodwink *vt* ingannare

hoof *n* zoccolo, unghia

hook *n* uncino; — **and eye** gancio ad occhio; **by** — **or crook** con le buone o con le cattive *(coll)*; **on one's own** — indipendente; **–up** *n (rad, TV)* connessione; **–worm** *n* verme intestinale; — *vt* agganciare, uncinare

hooky *n* play — marinare la scuola

hoop *n* cerchione *m*, cerchio, anello

hop *vi* saltellare; — *n* salto, salto su piede; **–s** *npl (bot)* luppoli *mpl*

hope *n* speranza; — *vt&i* sperare, aver fiducia, confidare; **–ful** *a* promettente; pieno di speranza; **–less** *a* disperato

hopper *n* tramoggia

hopscotch *n* giuoco fanciullesco dove si saltella

horde *n* orda

horizon *n* orizzonte *m*

hormone *n* ormone *m*

horn *n* tromba; *(animal)* corno; *(auto)* clacson *m*; — **in** *(sl, intrude)* intromettersi; **blow one's own** — lodarsi; **blow the** — strombettare; **–ed** *a* cornuto, cornifero; **–y** *a* corneo, calloso

horns *npl* corna *fpl*; **pull in one's** — mordere il freno *(fig)*

hornet *n* calabrone *m*; **—'s nest** vespaio

horoscope *n* oroscopo

horrible *a* orribile

horrid *a* orrendo, brutto
horrify *vt* atterrire
horror *n* orrore *m*
hors d'œuvres *npl* antipasto
horse *n* cavallo; — **sense** buon senso; — **trainer** cavallerizzo; allenatore di cavalli; **race** — cavallo da corsa; **get on one's high** — *(fig)* darsi delle arie *(coll)*; **work like a** — lavorare come un cavallo; **–man** *n* cavaliere *m*; **–play** *n* giuochi di mano *(fig)*; **–power** *n* cavalli vapore; **–shoe** *n* ferro di cavallo
horseback *n* groppa; — *adv* in groppa
horseradish *n* rafano
horticulture *n* orticultura
hose *n* manichetta, tubo flessibile; — *npl* calze *fpl*
hosiery *n* calze *fpl*; — **store** negozio di calze
hospitable *a* ospitale
hospital *n* ospedale *m*; clinica; — **insurance** assicurazione ospitaliera; **maternity** — casa di maternità
hospitality *n* ospitalità
hospitalize *vt* ricoverare in ospedale, ospitalizzare
host *n* ospite *m*, padrone di casa *(coll)*; *(inn)* oste *m*; *(crowd)* moltitudine *f*
Host *n (eccl)* Ostia, Particola
hostage *n* ostaggio
hostel *n* locanda; **youth** — albergo per la gioventù
hostess *n* ospite *f*; padrona di casa *(coll)*; *(inn)* ostessa; *(avi)* hostess *f*
hostile *a* ostile
hostility *n* ostilità
hot *a* caldo; *(food)* piccante; **be in** — **water** *(coll)* essere nei guai; **make it** — **for** *(coll)* dare filo da torcere; **–bed** *n* concimaia; **–foot** *adv* in fretta e furia; **–house** *n* serra; **–water bag** borsa dell'acqua calda
hot– *(in comp)* **—blooded** *a* ardente, impetuoso; **—headed** *a* impetuoso; **—rod** *(sl)* vecchia automobile con motore sovralimentato; **—tempered** *a* collerico
hotel *n* albergo, hotel *m*
hotly *adv* caldamente; *(passionately)* vementemente
hound *n* bracco; — *vt (fig)* perseguitare
hour *n* ora; **half an** — mezz'ora; — **hand** lancetta delle ore; **per** — per ora; **work by the** — lavorare a ore
hourly *adv* ogni ora, tutte le ore; — *a* frequente, che accade ogni ora
house *n* casa; *(com)* ditta; *(legislative)* camera; **full** — *(theat)* sala al completo; **–fly** *n* mosca domestica; **–keeper** *n* governante *f*; **–wife** *n* massaia; **–work** *n* lavoro di casa, faccenda di casa; — *vt* alloggiare

housedog *n* cane da guardia
household *n* famiglia, focolare domestico *(fig)*; — **management** gestione della casa
house physician medico residente
housing *n* alloggio; *(mech)* carter *m*
hovel *n* bicocca, capanna, tugurio
hover *vi* gravitare, esitare, attardarsi; — **over** librarsi su
how *adv* come; — **many** quanti *mpl*, quante *fpl*; — **much** quanto; — **often** quante volte
however *conj* però; per quanto; — *adv* ciononostante, comunque
howl *vi* urlare; — *n* urlo, lamento
hub *n* centro; *(auto)* mozzo; **–cap** *n* piatto della ruota
hubbub *n* tumulto
huckster *n* merciaiolo, trafficante *m*
huddle *n* calca, folla, confusione; — *vt* mettere insieme; — *vi* accalcarsi, affollarsi
hue *n* tinta; — **and cry** clamore di grida
huff *n* sfuriata; **–y** *a* stizzito
hug *vt* stringere, abbracciare; — *n* abbraccio
huge *a* enorme; **–ly** *adv* enormemente; **–ness** *n* enormità
hulk *n (naut)* carcassa di nave; **–ing** *a* grosso, goffo, pesante
hull *n* guscio, baccello; *(bot)* guscio, mallo; — *vt* sgusciare
hullabaloo *n* baccano
hum *vt&i (buzz)* ronzare; *(murmur)* mormorare; *(tune)* canticchiare; — *vi (tune)* cantarellare; — *n* mormorio
human *a* umano; — *n* esser umano; **–ly** *adv* umanamente
humane *a* umano, compassionevole
humanitarian *a* umanitario
humanity *n* umanità
humankind *n* umanità; genere umano
humble *a* umile; — *vt* umiliare; — **oneself** umiliarsi
humbly *a* umilmente
humbug *n* inganno, imbroglio; *(quack)* ciarlatano, impostore *m*; — *vt* ingannare, imbrogliare
humdrum *a* banale, monotono
humid *a* umido; **–ity** *n* umidità
humiliate *vt* umiliare
humiliation *n* umiliazione
humility *n* umiltà
humor *n* umore *m*, spirito; **bad** — malumore; **good** — buonumore; — *vt* compiacere; lasciar fare; **–ous** *a* comico, spiritoso, bizzarro, fantastico; *(whimsical)* capriccioso

humorist *n* umorista *m*
hump *n* gobba
hunch *n* gobba; *(coll)* presentimento, intuizione *f*; **–back** *n* gobbo
hundred *a&n* cento; **about a —** un centinaio; **–th** *a* centesimo
Hungarian *a&n* ungherese *m&f*
Hungary Ungheria
hunger *n* fame *f*; **—** *vi* aver fame, affamarsi, patir fame; **—** *vt* affamare; **— for** bramare
hungrily *adv* famelicamente
hungry *a* affamato; **be —** aver fame
hunk *n* massa
hunt *n* caccia, inseguimento; **—** *vt* inseguire, perseguitare, cacciare; **— down** perseguire; **—** *vi* andare a caccia; **— for** cercare; **–er** *n* cacciatore *m*; **–ing** *n* caccia
hurdle *n* ostacolo; **—** *vt* superare
hurdy-gurdy *n* organetto di Barberia
hurl *vt* scagliare, lanciare; **— back** rilanciare; *(reply)* ribattere *(fig)*
Hurrah! *interj* Bravo!; Evviva!
hurricane *n* uragano
hurried *a* affrettato; **–ly** *adv* affrettatamente
hurry *n* fretta; **be in a —** aver fretta; **in a —** in fretta; **—** *vt* affrettare, sollecitare; **—** *vi* affrettarsi, far presto; **— away** svignarsela, andarsene in fretta, **— back** tornare in fretta; **— on** affrettare, affrettarsi; **— over** fare in fretta, affrettare; **— up** affrettarsi, spicciarsi
hurt *vt* far male a; *(feelings)* offendere; **—** *vi* dolere; **—** *n* ferita, male *m*, danno; **—** *a* danneggiato; ferito; offeso
hurtle *vi (dash)* precipitarsi; **—** *vt* lanciare
husband *n* marito
husbandry *n* agricoltura
hush *n* silenzio; **—** *vt&i* azzittire, far tacere, tacere; **H–!** *interj* Stai zitto!
husk *n* guscio, baccello; **—** *vt* sgusciare; **–iness** *n* raucedine *f*; **–y** *a* robusto; rauco
hussy *n* donna impertinente, sfacciata
hustle *n (coll)* energia; **—** *vt&i (hurry)*

sbrigarsi; *(push)* spingere, dare spintoni; **— and bustle** andirivieni *m*
hustler *n (coll)* persona energica
hut *n* capanna
hutch *n* capanna; **rabbit—** conigliera
hyacinth *n* giacinto
hybrid *n* ibrido
hydrant *n* idrante *m*
hydraulic *a* idraulico; **–s** *npl* idraulica
hydrocarbon *n* idrocarburo
hydrocephalus *n* idrocefalo
hydrochloric *a* idroclorico
hydrofoil *n* aliscafo
hydrogen *n* idrogeno; **— bomb** bomba all'idrogeno; **— peroxide** *n* perossido d'idrogeno, *(chem)* acqua ossigenata
hydrolysis *n* idrolisi *f*
hydrophobia *n* idrofobia
hydroplane *n* idroplano
hydroponics *npl* idrocultura, idroponia
hydrostatics *npl* idrostatica
hydrotherapy *n* idroterapia
hyena *n* iena
hygiene *n* igiene *f*
hygienic *a* igienico
hymn *n* inno
hyperacidity *n* iperacidità
hyperbole *n* iperbole *f*
hypersonic *a* ipersonico, supersonico
hypertension *n* ipertensione
hypertrophy *n* ipertrofia
hyphen *n* trattino, lineetta
hypnotic *a* ipnotico
hypnotism *n* ipnotismo
hypnotize *vt* ipnotizzare
hypochondriac *n&a* ipocondriaco, ipocondriaca
hypocrisy *n* ipocrisia
hypocrite *n* ipocrita *m*
hypocritical *a* ipocrito
hypodermic *a* ipodermico
hypothesis *n* ipotesi *f*
hypothetical *a* ipotetico
hysterectomy *n* isterettomia
hysteria *n* isteria, isterismo
hysterical *a* isterico
hysterics *npl* accesso d'isterismo

I

I *pron* io
ice *n* ghiaccio; **— age** era glaciale; **— bag** *(med)* borsa da ghiaccio; **— cream** gelato; **— pack** lastrone di ghiaccio; **— skates** pattini da ghiaccio; **— water** acqua ghiacciata; **–berg** *n* borgognone *m*; iceberg *m*; **–box** *n* ghiacciaia; **–d** *a* ghiacciato, gelato; *(frosted)* candito; **— a cake** candire un dolce

ice-cream cone cono di gelato
ice-skate *vi* pattinare sul ghiaccio
icicle *n* ghiacciuolo
icily *adv* frigidamente, glacialmente
iciness *n* gelidità; freddo glaciale
icing *n* ghiacciata; *(cake)* canditura
iconoclast *n* iconoclasta *m*
iconoscope *n (TV)* iconoscopio
icy *a* glaciale; gelido

idea n idea
ideal n&a ideale m; **–ist** n idealista m&f;
 –ly adv idealmente; **–ism** n idealismo;
 –istic a idealista
identical a identico
identification n identità, identificazione;
 — card carta d'identità
identify vt (recognize) riconoscere; **—
 oneself** farsi riconoscere
identity n identità
ideological a ideologico
ideology n ideologia
idiocy n idiozia
idiom n (language) idioma m; (phrase)
 idiotismo; **–atic** a idiomatico
idiosyncracy n peculiarità
idiot n idiota m; **–ic** a stupido
idle a ozioso; **— capital** capitale congelato; **—** vt&i oziare, impigrire; (motor)
 funzionare al minimo; (time) perder
 tempo; **— away** sprecare; **–ness** n ozio
idler n fannullone m; perditempo
idol n idolo; **–ize** vt indolatrare
idolater n idolatra m&f
idyllic a idillico
i.e., that is ciò è
if conj se; **— ever** se mai; **— not** senò;
 — so se è così
ignite vt accendere
ignition n accensione; **— switch** chiave
 d'accensione
ignoble a ignobile
ignominious a infamante, ignominioso
ignominy n ignominia
ignoramous n ignorante m, asino (fig);
 (boor) zotico
ignorance n ignoranza
ignorant a ignorante
ignore vt ignorare; (inattention) non dare importanza
ill a ammalato; **— adv** male; **— will**
 malvolere m; malanimo; mala voglia;
 — at ease inquieto, incomodo; **–ness**
 n malattia, male m
ill– (in comp) **–advised** a malaccorto;
 –bred a maleducato; **–disposed** a maldisposto; **–humored** a di cattivo umore;
 –mannered a maleducato, scortese,
 sgarbato; **–natured** a malvagio, cattivo, bisbetico; **–tempered** a collerico,
 irritabile; **–timed** a inopportuno, intempestivo
ill-gotten a mal acquisto; **— gains**
 guadagni illeciti
illegal a illegale; **–ly** adv illegalmente
illegible a illeggibile
illegitimate a illegittimo
illicit a illecito
illiteracy n analfabetismo
illiterate a&n analfabeta m&f

illogical a illogico
illuminate vt illuminare
illumination n illuminazione
illusion n illusione
illusive a fallace, illusorio
illustrate vt illustrare
illustration n (example) esempio; (picture) illustrazione, figura
illustrious a illustre
illustrative a illustrativo
image n immagine f
imaginary a immaginario
imagination n immaginazione
imaginative a immaginativo, fantastico
imagine vt&i immaginare, fantasticare;
 supporre
imbecile a&n imbecille m
imbecility n imbecillaggine f, imbecill-
 ità; (foolishness) sciocchezza; (stupidity) ebetismo
imbibe vt imbevere, assimilare, assorbire
imbroglio n imbroglio
imbue vt inculcare, infondere; (fig) imbevere
imitate vt imitare
imitation n imitazione; **— a** falso, artificiale
imitator n imitatore m
immaculate a immacolato
immanent a immanente
immaterial a indifferente; incorporeo
immature a immaturo
immaturity n immaturità
immeasurable a immisurabile, smisurato
immediate a immediato; **–ly** adv subito
immemorial a immemorabile
immense a immenso
immensity n immensità
immerse vt tuffare, immergere
immersion n immersione
immigrant n&a immigrante m
immigrate vi immigrare
immigration n immigrazione
imminent a imminente
immobile a immobile, fermo
immobility n immobilità
immobilize vt immobilizzare
immoderate a smodato, immoderato, eccessivo
immodest a immodesto, sfacciato, presuntuoso
immoral a immorale
immorality n immoralità
immortal a immortale
immortality n immortalità
immovable a fermo, irremovibile; (law)
 inamovibile
immune a esente, immune
immunology n immunologia
immunity n immunità; (exemption) esen-

zione
immunization *n* immunizzazione
immunize *vt* immunizzare
imp *n* diavoletto; *(child)* birichino; *(goblin)* folletto; **–ish** *a* birichino, sbarazzino; **–ishly** *adv (malice)* maliziosamente; *(mischief)* birichinamente
impact *n* urto; — *vt* ficcare
impair *vt* danneggiare, pregiudicare; nuocere a
impalpable *a* impalpabile
impart *vt* impartire, comunicare, riferire
impartial *a* imparziale; **–ity** *n* imparzialità
impass *n* difficoltà insormontabile; vicolo cieco *(fig)*; **–able, –ive** *a* impassibile
impatience *n* impazienza
impatient *a* impaziente; **get** — impazientirsi
impeach *vt* incriminare; **–able** *a* incriminabile; **–ment** *n* incriminazione, accusa
impeccable *a* impeccabile
impedance *n (elec)* reattanza; *(phy)* trasmittività relativa acustica
impede *vt* ritardare, impedire, ostacolare
impediment *n* ostacolo
impel *vt* costringere, spingere
impend *vi* incombere, soprastare; *(threaten)* minacciare; essere imminente; **–ing** *a* imminente; minaccioso
impenetrable *a* impenetrabile
imperative *a* imperativo, indispensabile
imperfect *a&n* imperfetto
imperfection *n* imperfezione
imperial *a* imperiale, supremo; **–istic** *a* imperialistico; **–ism** *n* imperialismo
imperil *vt* arrischiare, mettere in pericolo
imperishable *a* indistruttibile, imperituro
impermeable *a* impermeabile
impersonal *a* impersonale
impersonate *vt* impersonare, personificare, imitare
impersonation *n* personificazione; *(law)* supposizione di persona
impertinence *n* impertinenza
impertinent *a* impertinente, insolente
imperturbable *a* imperturbabile
impervious *a* impervio
impetuous *a* impetuoso
impetus *n* impulso, impeto, slancio
impiety *n* empietà
impinge *vi* sbattere; — **on** sbattere contro
impious *a* empio
implant *vt* piantare; *(fig)* imprimere, inculcare
implement *n* utensile *m*; implemento; — *vt* effettuare
implicate *vt* implicare

implication *n* implicazione
implicit *a* implicito, assoluto; *(implied)* sottinteso
implied *a* implicito
implore *vt* implorare
imploring *a* supplichevole, implorante; — *n* supplica
imply *vt* implicare, insinuare, suggerire
impolite *a* sgarbato; **–ness** *n* scortesia, villania; maleducazione
imponderable *a* imponderabile
import *vt* importare; — *n* importanza; *(meaning)* senso, significato; **–ation** *n* importazione; — **duties** *npl* diritti doganali; **–er** *n* importatore *m*
importance *n* importanza
important *a* importante; **–ly** *adv* con importanza
impose *vt* imporre; — **on** praticare inganno
imposing *a* imponente
imposition *n* imposizione; *(outrage)* sopruso; *(swindle)* frode *f*
impossibility *n* impossibiltà
impossible *a* impossibile
impost *n* tassa, imposta
impostor *n* impostore *m*
imposture *n* frode *f*, impostura, inganno
impotence *n* impotenza
impotent *a* impotente
impound *vt* sequestrare, confiscare; *(animals)* rinchiudere
impoverish *vt* impoverire
impracticability *n* impraticabilità
impractical *a* non pratico, impraticabile
imprecate *vt* imprecare
imprecation *n* imprecazione
impregnable *a* imprendibile, inespugnabile
impregnate *vt* fecondare, impregnare, imbevere
impress *vt* imprimere; impressionare
impression *n* impressione, idea
impressive *a* imponente, impressionante
imprint *vt* stampare, imprimere; *(fix)* fissare; — *n* stampa
imprison *vt* imprigionare; **–ment** *n* imprigionamento
improbability *n* improbabilità
improbable *a* improbabile
impromptu *a* improvvisato
improper *a* scorretto, indecente
impropriety *n* sconvenienza; *(gram)* improprietà; *(wrong)* erroneità
improve *vt* migliorare; — *vi* migliorarsi; far progressi; **–ment** *n* miglioramento, perfezionamento
improvident *a* imprudente, imprevidente
improvise *vt* improvvisare
imprudence *n* imprudenza
imprudent *a* imprudente

impudence *n* impudenza
impudent *a* impudente
impugn *vt* impugnare, accusare; contraddire
impunity *n* impunità
impulse *n* impeto, impulso, slancio; **act on** — agire d'impulso
impulsive *a* impulsivo; **–ly** *adv* impulsivamente
impure *a* impuro; *(filthy)* immondo; *(immodest)* impudico
impurity *n* impudicizia, impurità
imputation *n* accusa, imputazione, addebito
impute *vt* imputare
in *prep* in, a, entro; — **spite of** nonostante; — **writing** per iscritto; **be all** — essere sfinito; **have it** — **for** aver rancore per; **know the –s and outs** sapere dell'a alla zeta; **take** — *(absorb)* assorbire; *(attend)* assistere a; *(deceive)* ingannare; — *adv* dentro; **be** — *(at home)* essere a casa
inability *n* incapacità
inaccessible *a* inaccessibile
inaccuracy *n* inesattezza
inaccurate *a* inesatto
inaction *n* inerzia, inazione
inactive *a* inattivo
inactivity *n* inoperosità, inattività
inadvertent *a* incauto, disattento; *(unplanned)* impremeditato; **–ly** *adv* inavvertitamente
inadequacy *n* inettitudine *f*; insufficienza
inadequate *a* inadeguato; *(inexperienced)* inesperto; *(worthless)* inetto
inalienable *a* inalienabile
inane *a* inane, vano, vuoto
inanimate *a* inanimato
inappropriate *a* disadatto; improprio
inaptitude *n* incapacità, inettitudine *f*
inarticulate *a* inarticolato
inasmuch as *conj* poichè, dacchè; in quanto che
inattention *n* disattenzione; *(carelessness)* trascuratezza
inattentive *a* distratto, disattento, trascurato
inaudible *a* inaudibile
inaugurate *vt* inaugurare
inauguration *n* inaugurazione
inauspicious *a* *(ominous)* infausto; *(unfortunate)* infelice; malaugurato
inborn *a* innato
inbound *a* entrante
incalculable *a* incalcolabile
incapability *n* inettitudine *f*, incapacità
incapable *a* incapace
incapacitate *vt* inabilitare, incapacitare
incapacity *n* inabilità, incapacità

incarcerate *vt* incarcerare
incarnation *n* incarnazione
incase *vt* incassare; chiudere; *(cover)* coprire
incendiary *n&a* incendiario
incense *n* incenso; — *vt* incensare; *(anger)* fare arrabbiare
incentive *n* stimolo, incentivo
incessant *a* incessante
incest *n* incesto
inch *n* dito, pollice *m*; — **by** — gradualmente; **every** — del tutto, completamente; **within an** — **of** per un pelo; — *vt* far avanzare gradualmente; — *vi* avanzare gradualmente
incident *n* incidente *m*; **–al** *a* incidentale; **–ally** *adv* a proposito
incinerate *vt* incenerire
incinerator *n* inceneritore *m*
incipient *a* iniziale, incipiente
incision *n* incisione
incite *vt* incitare
incivility *n* scortesia, villania
inclement *a* duro, inclemente
inclination *n* inclinazione, voglia
incline *n* pendio, pendenza; — *vt&i* inclinare; essere disposto a
inclose, enclose *vt* accludere; *(encircle)* circondare
include *vt* includere, comprendere
including *a* compreso
inclusion *n* inclusione
inclusive *a* inclusivo, incluso
incognito *a* incognito; — *adv* in incognito
incoherence *n* incoerenza
incoherent *a* sconnesso, incoerente
incombustible *a* incombustibile
income *n* stipendio; — **tax** tassa sul reddito
incoming *a* prossimo; *(arriving)* in arrivo
incommode *vt* scomodare, incomodare
incommunicado *a* incommunicato
incommutable *a* incommutabile
incomparable *a* impareggiabile, incomparabile
incompatibility *n* incompatibilità
incompatible *a* incompatibile
incompetence *n* incompetenza
incompetent *a* incompetente
incomplete *a* incompleto, imperfetto
incomprehensible *a* incomprensibile
inconceivable *a* inconcepibile
inconclusive *a* inconclusivo, inconcludente
incongruity *n* assurdità, incongruenza
incongruous *a* assurdo, incongruente
inconsequential *a* illogico, inconseguente
inconsiderable *a* trascurabile, inconsiderabile
inconsiderate *a* sconsiderato, senza

riguardi

inconsistency *n* inconsistenza, incongruenza

inconsistent *a* inconsistente, incongruente, incompatibile

incontinent *a* incontinente

incontestable *a* incontrastabile, incontestibile

inconvenience *n* incomodo, disturbo; — *vt* incomodare

inconvenient *a* scomodo

incorporate *vi* fondersi, unirsi; — *vt* incorporare; *(com)* costituire in società anonima; **–d** *a* incorporato, associato

incorporation *n* incorporazione

incorrect *a* sbagliato, scorretto; *(etiquette)* sconveniente

incorrigible *a* incorregibile

incorruptible *a* incorruttibile

increase *vt&i* crescere; aumentare; — *n* aumento

increasing *a* crescente; **–ly** *adv* in aumento

incredible *a* incredibile

incredulity *n* incredulità

incredulous *a* incredulo

increment *n* incremento

incriminate *vt* incriminare, incolpare, imputare

incubate *vt&i* incubare, covare

incubation *n* incubazione

incumbent *n* incaricato, responsabile *m*; — *a* incombente

incur *vt* contrarre; incorrere

incurable *a* inguaribile

indebted *a* obbligato, tenuto, indebitato; **–ness** *n* debito, obbligazione

indecency *n* indecenza; *(immodesty)* scorrettezza

indecent *a* scorretto, indecente

indecision *n* indecisione, perplessità, forse *m*

indecisive *a* non decisivo

indeed *adv* veramente, infatti, davvero

indefatigable *a* instancabile, infaticabile

indefensible *a* indifendibile, insostenibile

indefinable *a* indefinibile

indefinite *a* indeterminato, indefinito

indelicate *a* indelicato, sconveniente

indemnity *n* indennità

indent *vt* frastagliare, intaccare; *(print)* spaziare; **—ation** *n* incavo, intacco

independence *n* indipendenza

independent *a* indipendente

indescribable *a* indescrivibile

indestructible *a* indistruttibile

indeterminate *a* vago, indeterminato

index *n* indice *m*; — **finger** indice; — *vt* fornire di un indice

India India; — **ink** inchiostro di Cina

Indian *a&n* indiano; *(American)* pelliros-

sa *m*; — **summer** estate di San Martino

indicate *vt* indicare

indication *n* indicazione; *(sign)* segno

Indies Indie *fpl*; **East** — Indie orientali; **West** — Indie occidentali

indicative *n&a* indicativo

indicator *n* indicatore *m*

indict *vt* accusare; *(law)* processare; **–ment** *n* atto di accusa

indifference *n* indifferenza

indifferent *a* indifferente

indigenous *a* indigeno

indigent *a* indigente

indigestible *a* indigesto, indigeribile

indigestion *n* indigestione

indignant *a* adirato, sdegnato; **–ly** *adv* indignatamente

indignity *n* indegnità

indirect *a* indiretto

indiscernible *a* impercettibile, indiscernibile

indiscreet *a* indiscreto

indiscretion *n* indiscrezione

indiscriminate *a* indiscriminato, confuso

indispensable *a* indispensabile

indisposed *a* ammalato, indisposto

indisposition *n* indisposizione

indisputable *a* incontestabile, indiscutibile

indistinct *a* indistinto

indistinguishable *a* indiscernibile, indistinguibile

individual *n* individuo; — *a* individuale; **–ism** *n* individualismo; **–ist** *n* individualista *m&f*

indivisible *a* indivisibile

indoctrinate *vt* addottrinare

indolence *n* indolenza

indolent *a* indolente

indomitable *a* indomabile

Indonesia Indonesia

indoor *a* interno; **–s** *adv* dentro, in casa

induce *vt* persuadere, indurre

inducement *n* allettamento, persuasione; *(flattery)* lusinga; *(stimulus)* stimolo

induct *vt* insediare

induction *n* induzione; *(mil)* arruolamento; *(to office)* insediamento; — **coil** rocchetto d'induzione

indulge *vt* contentare, soddisfare, accarezzare *(fig)*; — *vi* indulgere in; abbandonarsi a; — **in** permettersi il lusso di

indulgence *n* indulgenza, privilegio; *(kindness)* favore *m*

indulgent *a* indulgente

industrial *a* industriale; **–ist** *n* industrialista *m&f*; **–ize** *vt* industrializzare; **–ization** *n* industrializzazione

industrious *a* laborioso, industrioso

industry *n* industria, lavoro; *(activity)* attività
inebriate *n* ubbriaco; — *vt* inebriare, ubbriacare; **-d** *a* ubbriacato, inebriato
inedible *a* immangiabile
ineffable *a* ineffabile
ineffective, ineffectual *a* ineffettivo, inefficace, inutile; **-ness** *n* inefficacia, inutilità
inefficacy *n* inefficacia
inefficiency *n* incapacità, inefficienza
inefficient *a* incapace, inefficiente
ineligible *a* ineleggibile
inept *a* incapace, inetto
inert *a* inerte
inertia *n* inerzia
inequality *n* disuguaglianza, ineguaglianza
inequitable *a* ingiusto
ineradicable *a* inestirpabile
inescapable *a* inevitabile
inestimable *a* incalcolabile; *(invaluable)* preziosissimo
inevitable *a* inevitabile
inexcusable *a* imperdonabile, ingiustificabile
inexhaustible *a* inesauribile
inexpedient *a* inefficace
inexpensive *a* economico; poco costoso
inexperience *n* inesperienza
inexperienced *a* inesperto
inexplicable *a* incomprensibile
inexpressible *a* inesprimibile
inexpressive *a* inespressivo
inextricable *a* inestricabile
infallible *a* infallibile
infallibility *n* infallibilità
infamous *a* infame
infancy *n* infanzia; *(law)* minorità
infant *n* infante *m*
infantile *a* bambinesco, puerile; — **paralysis** poliomielite *f*
infantry *n* fanteria
infatuate *vt* infatuare; **become -d** infatuarsi
infatuation *n* infatuazione; *(craze)* pazzia
infect *vt* infettare
infection *n* infezione
infectious *a* infettivo
infer *vt* dedurre, inferire
inference *n* illazione, inferenza
inferior *a* inferiore
inferiority *n* inferiorità; — **complex** complesso d'inferiorità
infernal *a* infernale
inferno *n* inferno
infest *vt* infestare; molestare *(fig)*; **-ation** *n* infestazione, infestamento
infidel *n&a* miscredente *m*
infidelity *n* infedeltà

infiltrate *vt&i* infiltrare, infiltrarsi
infinite *n&a* infinito; **-ly** *adv* infinitamente
infinitive *n* infinito
infinity *n* infinità
infirm *a* debole, infermo, malfermo; **-ity** *n* infermità
infirmary *n* infermeria
inflame *vt* infiammare, irritare; *(fig)* infervorare
inflammable *a* infiammabile
inflammation *n* infiammazione
inflate *vt* dilatare, gonfiare
inflation *n* *(com)* inflazione; *(gas)* gonfiamento; *(of an idea)* esagerazione
inflection *n* inflessione; *(gram)* flessione
inflexible *a* inflessibile
inflict *vt* infliggere
influence *n* influsso; ascendente *m*; — *vt* influenzare, influire
influential *a* influente
influenza *n* influenza
influx *n* affluenza
inform *vt* informare, avvisare; far sapere; — **against** denunciare, accusare **-ant** *n* informatore *m*, informatrice *f*; **-er** *n* delatore *m*, delatrice *f*; **-ed** *a* informato
informal *a* senza cerimonie, intimo; alla mano *(fig)*; **-ity** *n* semplicità; mancanza di cerimonie
information *n* informazione; *(notice)* notizia, avviso; — **bureau** ufficio informazioni
infraction *n* infrazione, contravvenzione, violazione
infrared *a* infrarosso
infrequent *a* infrequente, raro
infringe *vt* contravvenire, trasgredire, violare, infrangere; **-ment** *n* infrazione, contravvenzione, violazione
infuriate *vt* infuriare; **-d** *a* infuriato, furioso, furibondo, furente
infuse *vt* infondere; *(inspire)* ispirare
infusion *n* infusione; ispirazione
ingenious *a* ingegnoso
ingenuity *n* ingegnosità
ingenuous *a* ingenuo, sincero, semplice
inglorious *a* inglorioso; oscuro *(fig)*
ingrained *a* inerente, inveterato, radicato
ingratiate *vt* ingraziare; — **oneself** ingraziarsi; entrare nelle grazie di
ingratitude *n* ingratitudine *f*
inhabit *vt* abitare; **-able** *a* abitabile **-ant** *n* abitante *m*
inhalant *n* inalatore *m*
inhale *vt* aspirare
inharmonious *a* inarmonioso
inherent *a* inerente
inherit *vt* ereditare; **-ance** *n* eredità
inhibit *vt* proibire, inibire

inhibition *n* inibizione, repressione
inhospitable *a* inospitale
inhuman *a* crudele, inumano; **–ity** *n* crudeltà, inumanità
inimical *a* contrario, ostile, avverso, nemico
inimitable *a* inimitabile
iniquitous *a* iniquo
iniquity *n* iniquità
initial *n&a* iniziale *f*; **–ly** *adv* da principio, inizialmente
initiate *vt* iniziare, cominciare; **—** *n* iniziato
initiation *n* iniziazione
initiative *n* iniziativa
initiator *n* iniziatore *m*
inject *vt* iniettare; **–or** *n (mech)* iniettore *m*
injection *n* iniezione; **— pump** pompa ad iniezione
injudicious *a* sventato, insensato; poco giudizioso
injunction *n* ingiunzione
injure *vt* danneggiare, nuocere; *(wound)* ferire; far male a
injurious *a* dannoso, nocivo
injury *n* ferita, danno; *(wrong)* torto
injustice *n* ingiustizia
ink *n* inchiostro; **— pad** cuscinetto per timbri; **–y** *a (dirty with)* sporco d'inchiostro; color inchiostro; **—** *vt* inchiostrare
inkling *n* sospetto, sentore *m*, indizio
inkstand, inkwell *n* calamaio
inlaid *a* intarsiato
inland *n&a* interno, entroterra; **—** *adv* all'interno
in-laws *npl* parenti acquisiti
inlay *n* intarsio; **—** *vt* intarsiare
inlet *n (geog)* baia, insenatura; braccio di mare; *(mech)* immissione
inmate *n* ricoverato
inn *n* locanda, taverna, osteria
innate *a* ingenito, innato
inner *a* interiore; **— tube** camera d'aria; **–most** *a* il più segreto; il più intimo
inning *n* volta, turno
innocence *n* innocenza
innocent *n&a* innocente *m*
innocuous *a* innocuo
innovate *vi* innovare
innovation *n* innovazione
innuendo *n* malignazione, insinuazione
innumerable *a* innumerevole
inoculate *vt* inoculare
inoculation *n* inoculazione
inoffensive *a* innocuo
inopportune *a* intempestivo, inopportuno
inordinate *a* smoderato, disordinato
inorganic *a* inorganico
inquest *n* inchiesta giudiziaria

inquire *vt&i* chiedere, domandare, investigare; **— after** informarsi di
inquiry *n* domanda, inchiesta
inquisitive *a* curioso
inroad *n* irruzione, incursione, invasione; **make –s on** *(supply)* togliere dalla riserva
insane *a* pazzo, demente; **— asylum** manicomio
insanity *n* pazzia
insatiable *a* ingordo, insaziabile
inscribe *vt* inscrivere, iscrivere
inscription *n* iscrizione
insect *n* insetto; **–icide** *n* insetticida *m*
insecure *a* malfermo, insicuro
insecurity *n* precarietà, instabilità, incertezza
inseminate *vt* inseminare, seminare
insensible *a* insensibile, insensato
insensitive *a* insensitivo
inseparable *a* inseparabile
insert *n* allegato, inserto; **—** *vt* inserire
insertion *n* inserzione
inset *n* inserto, inserzione, riquadro
inside *a&n* interno; **— of** dentro di; *(time, coll)* entro; **— out** a rovescio; **–s** *npl (anat, coll)* intestini *mpl*
insidious *a* insidioso
insight *n* discernimento, perspicacia
insignia *npl* insegne *fpl*
insignificance *n* insignificanza, futilità
insignificant *a* insignificante
insincere *a* insincero, ipocrita
insincerity *n* ipocrisia
insinuate *vt* insinuare; dare ad intendere
insinuation *n* insinuazione
insipid *a* insipido, scipito, sciocco, uggioso
insist *vi* insistere
insistence *n* insistenza
insistent *a* insistente
insolation *n* insolazione
insole *n* soletta
insolence *n* insolenza
insolent *a* insolente
insoluble *a* insolubile
insolvent *a* insolvente
insomnia *n* insonnia
insomuch (as) *conj* a tal punto, talmente che
inspect *vt* visitare, ispezionare
inspection *n* ispezione, visita
inspector *n* ispettore *m*
inspiration *n* ispirazione; **–al** *a* ispirato
inspire *vt* ispirare
inspiring *a* ispirante, suggestivo
install *vt* collocare, installare; **–ation** *n* impianto, installazione; *(to office)* insediamento
installment *n* rata; *(serial)* puntata; **monthly —** rata mensile

instance *n* caso; *(example)* esempio; **for —** per esempio; **in the first —** in primo luogo
instant *n* attimo; **this —** subito; **—** *a* urgente; **—ly** *adv* immediatamente
instantaneous *a* istantaneo
instead *adv* invece; **— of** in luogo di
instep *n* collo del piede
instigate *vt* incitare, istigare; promuovere
instigation *n* istigazione
instigator *n* incitatore *m*, istigatore *m*
instill *vt* istillare, inculcare
instinct *n* istinto; **—ive** *a* istintivo
institute *n* istituto, **—** *vt* istituire
institution *n* istituzione
instruct *vt* istruire; **—or** *n* insegnante *m*
instruction *n* istruzione
instrument *n* strumento; **— flying** volo strumentale
instrumental *a* strumentale, utile; **— in** che contribuisce a; **—ist** *n* strumentista *m*
insubordination *n* insubordinazione
insubstantial *a* inconsistente
insufferable *a* insopportabile, insoffribile
insufficiency *n* insufficienza
insufficient *a* insufficiente; **—ly** *adv* insufficientemente
insulate *vt* isolare, separare
insulating *a* isolante
insulation *n* isolamento
insulin *n* insulina
insult *n* insulto, offesa, ingiuria; **—** *vt* insultare
insuperable *a* insuperabile
insupportable *a* insopportabile
insurable *a* assicurabile
insurance *n* assicurazione; **— broker** agente di assicurazione; **life —** assicurazione sulla vita
insure *vt* assicurare
insurgent *n&a* insorgente *m&f*, insorto, ribelle *m&f*
insurrection *n* sommossa, insurrezione
insurmountable *a* insormontabile
intact *a* intatto; *(safe)* illeso
intake *n* immissione, presa; *(mech)* energia assorbita
intangible *a* intangibile
integral *n* totalità; **—** *a* integrale
integrate *vt* integrare
integration *n* integrazione
integrity *n* integrità
intellect *n* intelletto
intellectual *a&n* intellettuale *m&f*
intelligence *n* sagacia
intelligent *a* intelligente
intelligible *a* intelligibile
intemperance *n* alcoolismo, intemperanza
intemperate *a* immoderato, intemperato

intend *vt* intendere, *(plan)* progettare
intense *a* intenso, forte
intensify *vt* intensificare, rafforzare
intent *n* intenzione; **—** *a* intento, attento
intention *n* intenzione; **—al** *a* premeditato
interact *vi* reagire reciprocamente
interaction *n* azione reciproca
intercede *vi* intercedere
intercellular *a* intercellulare
intercept *vt* arrestare, intercettare
interception *n* intercettazione
interceptor *n* intercettatore *m*, intercettatrice *f*
intercession *n* intercessione
interchange *n* intercambio, scambio, contraccambio; **—** *vt* contraccambiare, scambiare, alternare; **—able** *a* intercambiabile
intercollegiate *a* intercollegiato
intercolonial *a* intercoloniale
intercommunication *n* intercomunicazione
intercostal *a* intercostale
intercourse *n* comunicazioni *fpl*, relazioni *fpl*; *(com)* commercio, traffico; *(sex)* coito
interdenominational *a* interdenominazionale
interdepartmental *a* interdipartimentale
interdependence *n* interdipendenza
interest *n* interesse *m*; **— rate** saggio d'interesse; **—ed** *a* interessato; **—ing** *a* interessante
interfere *vi* interferire; *(meddle)* immischiarsi
interference *n* ingerenza, intervento
interim *n* intervallo; *(meantime)* frattempo; *(tenure)* interinato; **—** *a* temporaneo; interinale; *(temporary)* provvisorio
interior *a* interno
interject *vt* intercalare, interporre
interjection *n* interiezione
interlace *vt* allacciare, intrecciare
interline *vt* interlineare
interlining *n* ultrafodera
interlock *vt* collegare; **— vi** collegarsi
interloper *n* intruso; *(stranger)* estraneo
interlude *n* intermezzo
intermarriage *n* matrimonio fra parenti; matrimonio fra diverse razze
intermarry *vi* sposarsi fra parenti; sposarsi fra diverse razze
intermediate *a* frapposto, intermedio
intermediary *a&n* intermediario
interminable *a* interminabile
interminably *adv* interminabilmente
intermingle *vt* mescolare, intramezzare; **— vi** mescolarsi, intramezzarsi
intermission *n* intervallo, pausa
intermittent *a* intermittente

intern *vi* internare; — *vt* confinare; — *n (med)* interno; **-al** *a* interno; **-ment** *n* confino, internamento; **-ist** *n* specialista delle malattie interne; **-ship** *n* internato

international *a* internazionale; — **law** diritto internazionale

interplanetary *a* interplanetario

interpolate *vt* inserire, interpolare, intercalare

interpolation *n* interpolazione

interpret *vt* interpretare; **-er** *n* interprete *m&f*; **-ation** *n* interpretazione

interpretative *a* interpretativo

interracial *a* interrazziale

interrelationship *n* correlazione

interrogate *vt* interrogare

interrogation *n* interrogazione; — **mark** punto interrogativo

interrupt *vt* interrompere; **-er** *n (elec)* interruttore *m*

interruption *n* interruzione

intersect *vt* incrociare, intersecare

intersection *n* intersezione; *(street)* incrocio stradale

intersperse *vt* seminare, cospargere, alternare

interstate *a* interstatale

interurban *a* interurbano

interval *n* intervallo

intervene *vi* intervenire

intervention *n* intervento, interposizione

interview *n* colloquio, intervista; — *vt* intervistare

interweave *vt* intrecciare, intessere

interwoven *a* intrecciato, intessuto

intestate *a* intestato

intestinal *a* intestinale

intestines *npl* intestini *mpl*

intimacy *n* intimità

intimate *a* intimo

intimate *vt* accennare, notificare

intimation *n* intimazione, notifica

intimidate *vt* intimidire

intimidation *n* minaccia

into *prep* in

intolerable *a* intollerabile

intolerance *n* intolleranza

intolerant *a* intollerante

intone *vt* intonare

intoxicated *a* ebbro, ubriaco

intoxicating *a* inebriante

intoxication *n* intossicazione; *(alcohol)* ubriachezza

intractable *a* intrattabile

intransitive *a* intransitivo

intravenous *a* endovenoso

intrepid *a* intrepido

intricate *a* complicato, difficile

intrigue *n* intrigo; — *vt* stuzzicare; — *vi* intrigare

intriguing *a* intrigante

intrinsic *a* intrinseco

introduce *vt* introdurre; *(people)* presentare

introduction *n* introduzione; *(people)* presentazione

introductory *a* introduttivo, preliminare

introspection *n* introspezione

introspective *a* introspettivo

introvert *n* introverso

intrude *vt* intrudere; — *vi* ingerirsi, immischiarsi; — **on** disturbare, importunare

intrusion *n* intrusione

intuition *n* intuizione

intuitive *a* intuitivo

inundate *vt* inondare

inundation *n* inondazione

inure *vt* abituare

invade *vt* invadere, violare, assalire; **-r** *n* invasore *m*

invalid *n&a* ammalato, infermo

invalid *a* invalido, non valido

invaluable *a* incalcolabile, inestimabile

invariable *a* invariabile

invariably *adv* sempre, invariabilmente

invasion *n* invasione

inveigle *vt* allettare, sedurre; *(allure)* persuadere; *(deceive)* ingannare

invent *vt* inventare; **-ive** *a* inventivo; **-or** *n* inventore *m*, inventrice *f*

inventory *n* inventario; — *vt* inventariare

inverse *a* inverso

inversion *n* inversione

invert *vt* invertire

invest *vt* impiegare; *(com)* investire; **-or** *n* azionista *m&f*, inversionista *m&f*; **-ment** *n* investimento, impiego

investigate *vt* investigare, esaminare, indagare

investigation *n* inchiesta, investigazione, indagine *f*

investigator *n* investigatore *m*

inveterate *a* inveterato

invigorate *vt* rinvigorire, rinforzare

invigorating *a* corroborante, fortificante

invincible *a* invincibile

inviolable *a* inviolabile

invisibility *n* invisibilità

invisible *a* invisibile

invitation *n* invito

invite *vt* invitare

inviting *a* invitante, attraente, seducente

invocation *n* invocazione

invoice *n* fattura; — *vt* fatturare

invoke *vt* implorare, invocare

involuntary *a* involontario

involve *vt* coinvolgere, implicare; comprendere

involved *a* coinvolto, implicato; **become — essere coinvolto**
invulnerable *a* invulnerabile
inward *a* interno; **— self** fra sè; **–ly** *adv* dentro
iodine *n* iodio
ion *n* ione *m*, iono
iota *n* iota *m*
I.O.U, I owe you cambiale *f*
Iran Iran *m*
Iraq Irac, Irak *m*
irascible *a* irascibile
irate *a* incollerito, irato
IRBM, intermediate range ballistic missile MBMP; missile balistico di media portata
ire *n* collera, ira, rabbia
Ireland Irlanda
iridescent *a* iridescente
iris *n* iris *m*, iride *f*
Irish *a* irlandese
irk *vt* turbare, affligere, annoiare
irksome *a* noioso, seccante
iron *n* ferro; **— curtain** cortina di ferro; **— lung** polmone d'acciaio; **cast —** ghisa; **sheet —** lamiera; **wrought —** ferro battuto; **–clad** *a* irrevocabile, **— vt** stirare; **–ing** *n* stiratura
ironic, –al *a* ironico
irony *n* ironia
irradiate *vt* illuminare, irradiare; *(med)* trattare con radioterapia
irrational *a* irrazionale, illogico
irreconcilable *a* inconciliabile, irreconciliabile
irredeemable *a* irredimibile
irreducible *a* irreducibile
irrefutable *a* irrefutabile
irregular *a* irregolare; **–ity** *n* irregolarità
irrelevance *n* irrilevanza
irrelevant *a* irrilevante
irreligious *a* irreligioso
irremovable *a* irremovibile
irreparable *a* irreparabile
irreproachable *a* irreprensibile, impeccabile
irresolute *a* irresoluto
irresistible *a* irresistibile

irrespective *a* indipendente; **— adv** indipendentemente; **— of** a prescindere da
irresponsibility *n* irresponsabilità
irresponsible *a* irresponsabile
irreverence *n* irriverenza
irreverent *a* irriverente
irreversible *a* irreversibile, irrevocabile
irrigate *vt* irrigare
irrigation *n* irrigazione
irritability *n* irritabilità
irritable *a* irritabile
irritant *n&a* irritante *m*
irritate *vt* irritare
irritating *a* irritante
irritation *n* provocazione, irritazione
Islamism *n* islamismo
island *n* isola; **–er** *n* isolano
isobar *n* isobara
isolate *vt* isolare
isolation *n* isolazione, isolamento **–ism** *n* isolazionismo; **–ist** *n* isolazionista *m&f*
isomer *n* isomero
isothermal *a* isotermico
isotope *n* isotopo
Israel Israele *m*; **–ite** *n* israelita *m&f*
Israeli *a&n* israeliano
issue *n* *(periodical)* fascicolo; *(problem)* soggetto; *(progeny)* prole *f*; *(result)* esito; **take — with** non essere d'accordo
isthmus *n* istmo
it *pron* esso, essa; lo, la
Italian *a&n* italiano, italiana
italics *npl* corsivi *mpl*
Italy Italia
itch *n* prurito, scabbia; **— vi** prudere, pizzicare; **–ing** *n* prurito, pizzicore *m*; **–y** *a* rognoso
item *n* articolo; **–ize** *vt* specificare; fare la distinta
iterate *vt* ripetere, iterare
itinerant *a* girovago, ambulante
intinerary *n* itinerario
its *pron&a* il suo; la sua
itself *pron* si; sè; esso stesso, sè stesso, essa stessa, sè stessa; **by —** da solo
ivory *n* avorio; **— a** d'avorio
ivy *n* edera

J

jab *n* punzecchiatura; *(stab)* pugnalata; **— vt** punzecchiare, pugnalare
jabber *vi* ciarlare; *(grumble)* borbottare
jabbering *n* chiacchierio, cicaleccio; **— a** ciarlante
jack *vt* levare; **— n** *(cards)* fante *m*; *(mech)* martinetto, cricco; **— rabbit** lepre *m*

jack– (in comp) —in-the-box *n* saltamartino; **—of-all-trades** *n* factotum *m*; tuttofare *m&f*
jackass *n* asino
jacket *n* giacchetta, giacca; *(book)* sopraccopertina, coprilibro
jackknife *n* coltello a serramanico
jackpot *n* *(cards)* monte *m*; *(coll)* suc-

cesso; *(poker)* piatto; **hit the** — *(sl)* aver fortuna

jade *n (horse)* ronzino; *(min)* giada; *(woman)* donnaccia; — *vt* affaticare, spossare; **–d** *a* spossato

jag *n* tacca, intaccatura; dente di sega; — *vt* frastagliare, dentellare

jagged *a* dentellato, intaccato

jail *n* prigione *f*; carcere *m*; — *vt* incarcerare

jalopy *n (coll)* carcassa

jam *n (cooking)* conserva, marmellata

jam *n* inceppamento, blocco; *(traffic)* ingorgo stradale; **in a** — *(coll)* nelle difficoltà; — *vt* bloccare, intasare; *(mech)* grippare; *(rad)* disturbare; — **on the brakes** frenare di colpo; — **the fingers** schiacciarsi le dita

jangle *vt* far tintinnare; *(bells)* scampanellare; — *vi* stonare, altercare

jangling *a* stonato; — *n (fig)* contesa, alterco

janitor *n* portinaio, custode *m*

January *n* gennaio

Japan Giappone *m*

Japanese *a&n* giapponese *m&f*

jar *vt&i (clash)* urtarsi; *(shake)* vibrare, scuotere; — **one's nerves** dare ai nervi *(fig)*; — *n* scossa, vibrazione; *(clash)* urto, dissonanza; *(container)* giara, boccale *m*

jargon *n* gergo

jaundice *n* itterizia; **–d** *a* geloso

jaunt *n* escursione, gita; **–y** *a* gaio; *(wearing apparel)* azzimato; — *vi* andare a spasso

jaw *n* mascella; **–bone** *n* mandibola; — *vi (sl)* ciarlare; rimbrottare

jealous *a* invidioso, geloso

jealousy *n* gelosia, invidia

jeans *npl* tuta di lavoro

jeep *n* camionetta, gip *m*

jeer *n* scherno; — *vt&i* burlare, schernire; — **at** beffarsi di

jeering *n* scherno; — *a* derisorio, beffardo

jellied *a* gelatinato, gelatinoso

jelly *n* gelatina

jeopardize *vt* compromettere, mettere a repentaglio

jeopardy *n* pericolo, rischio, repentaglio

jerk *n* strappo, stratta, scatto; *(sl)* puzzone *m (sl)*; — *vt* strappare; — *vi* scattare; **–y** *a* a sbalzi, spasmodico

jersey *n* maglia

jest *n* scherzo, facezia; **–er** *n* burlone *m*, buffone *m*; — *vi* scherzare

Jesus Christ *n* Gesù Cristo

jet *n (avi)* aerogetto; *(flame)* getto; vampa; *(gas)* becco a gas; *(min)* giavazzo, ambra nera; — **plane** aeroplano a reazione,

aviogetto; — **propulsion** spinta a getto; — *vt* emettere, buttar fuori; — *vi* sgorgare

jet-black *a* nero lucente

jettison *vt* gettare fuori bordo

Jew *n* israelita *m&f*

jewel *n* gioiello; **watch** — rubino; **–er** *n* gioielliere *m*; **–ry** *n* gioielleria

Jewish *a* ebreo

jib *n (naut)* fiocco, vela di bompresso

jibe *vi* accordarsi

jiffy *n (coll)* momento

jig *n (dance)* giga; — *vi* ballare la giga; — *vt* balzellare; **the** — **is up** *(sl)* è finita la cuccagna *(fig)*; **–saw** *n* sega verticale

jigger *n (measure)* un'oncia e mezzo

jiggle *vt&i* scuotere, agitarsi

jilt *vt* abbandonare; piantare *(coll)*

jingle *n (metal)* tintinnio; *(rhyme)* filastrocca; — *vt* far tintinnare; — *vi* tintinnare

jitters *npl (sl)* nervosità eccessiva; **have the** — essere sulle spine

job *n* lavoro, faccenda; — **lot** *(com)* merce di liquidazione; **–less** *a* disoccupato; — *vi* lavorare a cottimo

jobber *n (com)* cottimista *m*; *(middleman)* grossista *m*, distributore *m*

jockey *n* fantino; — *vt&i (deceive)* ingannare; *(defraud)* imbrogliare; *(racing)* fare il fantino; — **for position** brigare, intrigare

jocular *a* allegro, piacevole, vivace

jog *n* scossa leggera; *(nudge)* spinta; *(road, line)* rientranza; — **trot** trotto regolare; — *vt* scuotere, spingere; — *vi (along)* trotterellare

joggle *vt* scuotere; — *vi* scuotersi

join *vt* congiungere; — *vi* unirsi a; associarsi con; — **in** partecipare

joint *n (anat)* articolazione; *(bot)* nodo; *(geol)* fessura; *(junction)* giuntura; **out of** — *(med)* slogato; in disordine; — **account** conto corrente in comune; — **heir** coerede *m*

joist *n* trave *f*

joke *n* scherzo, barzelletta; **practical** — un tiro birbone; — *vi* scherzare, celiare

joker *n* burlone *m*; *(card)* matta

joking *a* scherzoso, faceto; **–ly** *adv* scherzosamente

jolly *a* gioviale, allegro, divertente

jolt *n* scossa; — *vt&i* scuotere

jostle *vt* pigiare, spingere; — *vi* spingersi, urtarsi, pigiarsi

jot *n* quisquilia; — *vt (down)* prender nota

jounce *vt* scuotere; far sobbalzare; — *vi* scuotersi, sobbalzare

journal *n* *(bookkeeping)* giornale *m*; *(diary)* diario; *(magazine)* rivista; *(newspaper)* giornale *m*
journalism *n* giornalismo
journalist *n* giornalista *m*
journey *n* viaggio; — *vi* viaggiare
jovial *a* gioviale
joy *n* gioia
joyful *a* allegro, gioioso, festivo; –**ly** *adv* allegramente
joyous *a* gioioso
jubilant *a* giubilante
jubilation *n* giubilo
jubilee *n* giubileo
judge *n* giudice *m*, arbitro; — *vt&i* giudicare; *(think)* credere, intendere, reputare
judgment *n* giudizio; **pass** — **on** giudicare in materia
judicial *a* giudiziario
judicious *a* giudizioso, assennato
jug *n* boccale *m*, brocca
juggle *vi* giocolare
juggler *n* giocoliere *m*
jugular *a* giugulare
juice *n* succo, sugo
juiciness *n* sugosità
juicy *a* succoso
jukebox *n* fonografo automatico a gettone
July *n* luglio
jumble *n* guazzabuglio; — *vt* confondere, gettare alla rinfusa
jumbo *a* colossale, gigantesco, enorme; — *n* colosso, gigante *m*; *(mammoth)* mastodonte *m* *(fig)*
jump *vt&i* saltare; — **around** darsi d'attorno; — **to conclusions** arrivare a giudizi precipitati; — *n* salto; **be on the** — essere in agitazione; –**y** *a* agitato
jumping *n* salto; — *a* saltatore, saltante; — **jack** saltamartino
junction *n* incrocio, bivio; *(forking)* biforcazione
June *n* giugno
jungle *n* giungla
junior *a* iuniore, cadetto; — *n* giovane *m&f*; figlio minore; *(student)* studente di terzo anno
junk *n* rottami *mpl*; *(rags)* stracci *mpl*; –**man** *n* rigattiere *m*
junta *n* giunta
jurisdiction *n* giurisdizione
jurisprudence *n* giurisprudenza
jurist *n* giurista *m*
juror *n* giurato
jury *n* giuria; — **box** banco della giuria; **grand** — gran giurì
just *a* giusto; — *adv* appena, soltanto; — **as** nello stesso momente che; — **gone** appena uscito; — **now** or ora; –**ly** *adv* giustamente; a buon diritto
justice *n* giustizia; *(judge)* giudice *m*
justifiable *a* giustificabile, lecito
justification *n* scusa, giustificazione
justify *vt* giustificare
jut *vi* protendersi, sporgere
jute *n* iuta
juvenile *a* giovanile; — *n* giovane *m&f*; — **delinquency** delinquenza minorile; — **delinquent** delinquente giovanile, giovane delinquente
juxtaposition *n* giustapposizione

K

kale *n* cavolo riccio
kaleidoscope *n* caleidoscopio
kaleidoscopic *a* caleidoscopico
kangaroo *n* canguro
kaolin *n* caolino
kapok *n* capoc, kapok *m*
keel *n* *(naut)* chiglia; — *vi* rollare; capovolgersi; — *vt* *(naut)* capovolgere; — **over** *(naut)* capovolgersi; *(person)* svenire
keen *a* acuto, affilato, perspicace; *(desirous)* desideroso, –**ly** *adv* acutamente; –**ness** *n* acutezza, vivacità
keep *n* mantenimento; — *vt* tenere, mantenere; — *vi* tenersi; mantenersi; — **aloof** tenersi in disparte; — **an eye on** tener d'occhio; — **back** *(conceal)* nascondere *(fig)*; *(restrain)* trattenere; — **books** tenere la contabilità; — **from** astenersi; — **house** mantenere casa; — **mum** tacere; — **on** continuare
keeping *n* cura, mantenimento; *(care)* custodia; **in** — **with** d'accordo con, in armonia con
keepsake *n* ricordo
ken *n* conoscenza, comprensione
kennel *n* covo, canile *m*
kernel *n* essenza; *(center)* nucleo; *(grain)* chicco; *(nut)* nocciolo
kerosene *n* petrolio; — **lamp** lampada a petrolio
kettle *n* pentola, bollitore *m*; –**drum** *n* timpano
key *n* *(door, mus)* chiave *f*; *(elec)* chiavetta; *(piano)* tasto; **master** — chiave generale; –**board** *n* tastiera; –**hole** *n* buco della serratura; –**note** *n* tonica, nota dominante; –**stone** *n* *(arch)* chiave di

volta; — *a* principale; — *vt* chiudere a chiave; *(mus)* intonare, accordare

kick *vt&i* prendere a calci; dare un calcio; *(coll)* lamentarsi; — *n* calcio, pedata; *(coll)* lamento; **–off** *n (sport)* calcio d'inizio

kid *n* capretto; *(coll)* bimbo; **handle with — gloves** trattare con guanti di velluto; **–skin** *n* pelle di capretto; — *a* di capretto; — *vt (coll)* burlare

kidnap *vt* rapire

kidney *n* rene *m*; — **bean** fagiuolo

kill *vt* ammazzare, uccidere; — *n* uccisione; **–er** *n* assassino

killing *n* assassinio, uccisione; **make a — *(coll)*** fare man bassa *(fig)*; — *a (coll)* schiacciante; *(funny)* esilarante; *(weather)* micidiale

kill-joy *n* guastafeste *m*

kiln *n* fornace *m*, forno

kilo *n* chilo; **–cycle** *n* chilociclo; **–gram** *n* chilogramma *m*, chilo; **–meter** *n* chilometro; **–watt** *n* chilowatt *m*

kin *n* famiglia, parentela; **next of —** il parente più prossimo; **–ship** *n* parentela

kind *a* gentile, buono; — *n* maniera, genere *m*, specie *f*; **nothing of the —** niente del genere; **–hearted** *a* buono, benevolo; **–ly** *adv* gentilmente; **–ness** *n* gentilezza, bontà

kindergarten *n* giardino d'infanzia

kindle *vt* provocare, accendere; dar fuoco a; *(excite)* eccitare; — *vi* accendersi; prender fuoco

kindliness *n* amabilità

kindling wood legna minuta per accendere

kindred *n* parentela, parenti *mpl*; — *a* affine; imparentato

kinetic *a* cinetico; **–s** *npl* cinetica

king *n* re *m*

kingdom *n* regno

kingpin *n (bowling)* birillo centrale; *(coll)* principale *m*, pezzo grosso

king-size *a* di formato gigante

kink *n (knot)* arricciatura; *(muscle)* crampo; **–y** *a* ricciuto

kiss *n* bacio; — *vt* baciare

kit *n* armamentario, corredo; cassetta di arnesi

kitchen *n* cucina; — **stove** fornello, cucina

kite *n (com)* cambiale di favore; *(toy)* aquilone *m*; *(zool)* nibbio; — *vi (com)* aver denaro con cambiale di favore; *(hurry)* volare *(fig)*

kitten *n* gattino; **–ish** *a* come un gattino

kitty *n (cat)* gattino, micino; *(money pool)* piatto, monte *m*

kleptomaniac *n* cleptomane *m&f*

knack *n* abilità

knave *n* briccone *m*, mariuolo; *(cards)* fante *m*

knead *vt* impastare

knee *n* ginocchio; **on one's –s** ginocchioni, in ginocchio; **–cap** *n* rotula

knee– *(in comp)* **–deep** *a* fino alle ginocchia; **–high** *a* all'altezza del ginocchio

kneel *vi* inginocchiarsi

knell *n* rintocco a morto, suono a morto

knickknack *n* ninnolo, gingillo, bagatella

knife *n* coltello; — **grinder** arrotino; — *vt* pugnalare, accoltellare

knight *n* cavaliere *m*; *(chess)* cavallo; **–hood** *n* cavalleria; **–ly** *a* cavalleresco; — *vt* fare cavaliere, creare cavaliere

knight-errant *n* cavaliere errante

knit *vt&i* unire; lavorare a maglia; *(bone)* saldarsi; — **one's brows** aggrottare le ciglia

knitting *n* lavoro a maglia; — **needle** ferro da calza

knob *n* bozza, protuberanza, pomo; **–by** *a* nodoso

knock *vt&i* bussare, picchiare; *(against)* urtare, — **around** *(coll)* sballottare; — **down** atterrare; — **off** *(price)* ribassare; *(work)* smettere il lavoro; — **out** vincere, sopraffare; *(boxing)* mettere fuori combattimento

knocker *n (door)* battente *m*

knocking *n* colpi *mpl*

knock-kneed *a* con le gambe storte

knockout *n* successone; *(boxing)* fuori combattimento

knot *n* nodo; **–hole** *n* foro rimasto nel legno allo staccarsi di un nodo; **–ted** *a* annodato, nodoso; **–ty** *a* nodoso; difficile

knottiness *n (fig)* difficoltà; complicazione; complessità

know *n* conoscenza; **be in the —** saperla lunga

know *vt* sapere; *(acquaint)* conoscere

knowingly *adv* accortamente

known *a* noto, conosciuto

know– *(in comp)* **–how** *n (coll)* conoscenza pratica; il saper fare; **–nothing** *n* ignorante

knowledge *n* sapere *m*; conoscenza, erudizione *f*; *(science)* scienza

knuckle *n (anat)* articolazione; *(finger)* nocca; *(meat)* ossobuco; *(mech)* giunto; — **under** sottomettersi, cedere; **rap over the –s** battere sulle nocche

kowtow *vi (bow)* salutare, toccando il suolo con la fronte, *(submit)* mostrare devozione

L

label *n* etichetta; — *vt* classificare; *(mark)* marcare
labial *a* labiale
labor *n* lavoro; — **market** offerta e domanda di lavoro; — **union** sindicato operaio; **hard** — lavori forzati; **-er** *n* bracciante, lavoratore *m*; — *vt&i* lavorare; *(distress)* angosciare, soffrire; **be in** — *(birth)* avere le doglie; **-ed** *a* stentato, elaborato
labor-saving *a* che evita fatica
laboratory *n* laboratorio
labyrinth *n* labirinto
lace *n* merletto, trina; *(shoe)* laccio, stringa; — *vt (beat)* battere; *(berate)* strigliare *(fig)*; *(connect)* allacciare; *(trim)* gallonare
laceration *n* strappo, lacerazione
lachrymose *a* lagrimoso
lacing *n* allacciamento; *(beating)* battuta; *(diatribe)* strigliata *(fig)*
lack *n* mancanza, difetto; **for** — **of** — mancanza di; — *vt&i* mancare, scarseggiare
lackadaisical *a* lezioso, languido, svenevole
lacking *a* mancante, difettante; — **in** privo di
lackluster *a* opaco
laconic *a* laconico
lacquer *n* lacca
lacrimose *a* lagrimoso
lactation *n* allattamento
lactic *a* lattico; — **acid** acido lattico
lactose *n* lattosio
lacy *a* traforato, calato; di pizzo
lad *n* ragazzo
ladder *n* scala a piuoli
lade *vt* imbarcare, caricare
lading *n* carico, caricamento; **bill of** — polizza di carico
ladle *n* mestolo; — *vt* scodellare; — **out** distribuire
lady *n* signora; *(nobility)* nobildonna; **-like** *a* distinto, fine, signorile; **-love** innamorata
lag *vi* attardarsi; restare indietro; — *n* ritardo
laggard *n* infingardo
lagoon *n* laguna
laid up *(sick)* ammalato; *(stored)* accumulato
lair *n* tana, covo, nascondiglio
laity *n* laicato; laici *mpl*
lake *n* lago
lamb *n* agnello; **-skin** *n* pelle d'agnello
lame *a* storpio, zoppo; — **excuse** scusa magra; **-ness** *n* difetto; *(med)* zoppi-

camento; — *vt* storpiare; **-ly** *adv* zoppicando, imperfettamente
lament *vt&i* lamentare, lamentarsi; — *n* lamento; **-ation** *n* lamentela, lamentazione; **-able** *a* lamentabile
laminate *vt* laminare; **-d plastic** laminati plastici
lamp *n* lampada; **-black** *n* nerofumo; **-post** *n* lampione *m*; **-shade** *n* paralume *m*
lampoon *n* libello, satira; — *vt* satireggiare
lance *n* lancia; *(med)* lancetta; — *vt (med)* incidere con la lancetta
land *n* terra; *(country)* paese *m*; *(soil)* terreno; — *vi (naut)* sbarcare, approdare; *(avi)* atterrare, arrivare; — *vt* tirare a terra; — **on one's feet** cadere in piedi
landholder *n* proprietario terriero
landing *n (avi)* atterraggio; *(naut)* approdo, sbarco; *(arch)* pianerottolo; **blind** — atterraggio cieco *or* radiocomandato; — **place** sbarcatoio; — **gear** carrello; — **strip** pista di atterraggio
landlady *n* affittacamere *f*; padrona di casa
landlord *n* locatore *m*
landmark *n* segno di confine; punto di riferimento
land office catasto
landowner *n* proprietario terriero
landscape *n* paesaggio; — **painter** paesista *m*
landslide *n* frana; *(pol)* elezione per maggioranza schiacciante
lane *n (auto)* corsia stradale; *(path)* sentiero; *(street)* vicolo
language *n* lingua, linguaggio; **bad** — turpiloquio
languid *a* languido
languish *vi* languire; **-ing** *a* languido, languente
languor *n* languore *m*; **-ous** *a* languido
lanky *a* allampanato
lanolin *n* lanolina
lantern *n* lanterna
lantern-jawed *a* macilento
Laos Laos
lap *n (anat)* grembo; *(cloth)* falda; *(sport)* giro; — *vt* piegare; *(animal)* lappare; *(water)* lambire
lapel *n* risvolto
lapping *a* lambente
lapse *n* dimenticanza; intervallo; *(gap)* lacuna; *(expiration)* decadenza; — *vi* trascorrere; decadere, ricadere
larceny *n* furto

lard *n* strutto, sugna; — *vt* lardellare

larder *n* dispensa

large *a* grosso, ampio; — **as life** in bella vista; **at** — in libertà; **al largo** *(coll)*; in generale; nell'insieme; **–ly** *adv* ampiamente

large-scale *a* in larga scala

largess *n* liberalità, regalo, dono

lariat *n* laccio

lark *n* allodola; *(fun)* divertimento; **go on a** — divertirsi

laryngitis *n* laringite *f*

larynx *n* laringe *f*

laser *n* amplificazione di luce per mezzo d'emissione stimolata di radiazione

lash *n* *(scourge)* sferza, frusta, flagello; *(eye)* ciglio; — *vt* frustare, sferzare; *(tie)* legare **–ing** *n* battitura; *(punishment)* castigo, flagellazione; *(cable)* gomena

lassitude *n* sfinimento, lassitudine

last *n* fine *f*; *(shoe)* forma da scarpe; — *a* ultimo; — **night** la notte scorsa; — **time** ultima volta; — **week** la settimana scorsa; **at** — finalmente; **next to** — penultimo; **–ly** *adv* finalmente, ultimamente, infine; — *vi* durare; **–ing** *a* duraturo, durevole, durabile

latch *n* *(door)* serratura, chiavistello; *(gate)* spranga; **–key** *n* chiave di casa; — *vt* chiudere con chiavistello

late *adv* tardi, in ritardo; **of** — recentemente; — *a* tardivo, recente; *(deceased)* fu, defunto, buonanima; **–ly** *adv* recentemente; — **in the night** a notte tarda; — **in the week** verso la fine della settimana

latent *a* latente

later *a* posteriore; *(following)* seguente; — *adv* più tardi

lateral *a* laterale

latest *a* ultimo, più recente; **at the** — al più tardi

lath *n* listello; — *vt* coprire di assicelle; **–ing** *n* listellatura

lathe *n* tornio

lather *n* schiuma, saponata; — *vt* insaponare, schiumare; *(coll)* bastonare; — *vi* spumeggiare

Latin *a&n* latino; — **America** America latina

latitude *n* latitudine *f*; *(of action)* ampiezza; libertà d'azione; carta bianca *(fig)*

latter *a* ultimo; **the** — quest'ultimo, questi

lattice *n* traliccio, graticcio, grata; **–work** *n* graticolato, graticcio, traliccio

laud *vt* esaltare; **–able** *a* lodevole

laugh *vi* ridere; — **at** farsi beffe di; — *n* riso; **–ter** *n* risata, ilarità; — **up one's sleeve** ridere sotto i baffi; **–able** *a* risibile, ridicolo

laughing *a* allegro, ridente; **no** — **matter** niente da ridere; **–stock** *n* zimbello; **–ly** *adv* ridendo

launch *vt* lanciare, varare; — *vi* imbarcarsi *(fig)*; — *n* varo; *(boat)* lancia

launching *n* lancio, varo; — **pad** *(aesp)* piattaforma di lancio

launder *vi* fare il bucato; — *vt* lavare

laundress *n* lavandaia, stiratrice *f*

laundry *n* bucato; *(place)* lavanderia

lavatory *n* lavabo; *(restroom)* gabinetto di decenza

lavender *n* lavanda; — *a* color lavanda

lavish *a* abbondante, prodigo; — *vt* prodigare, largire; **–ness** *n* prodigalità, profusione, sciupio *(coll)*

law *n* legge *f*, diritto; **according to** — secondo la legge; **lay down the** — dettar legge; **civil** — diritto civile; **–breaker** *n* violatore delle legge; **–maker** *n* legislatore *m*; **–suit** *n* causa, querela

law-abiding *a* rispettoso della legge

lawful *a* legale, legittimo; **–ly** *adv* legittimamente

lawless *a* sfrenato; senza legge; **–ness** *n* licenza, sfrenatezza

lawn *n* praticello, tappeto erboso

lawnmower *n* falciatrice meccanica

lawyer *n* avvocato

lax *a* negligente, trascurato; *(morally)* immorale; **–ity** *n* negligenza; immoralità

laxative *n* lassativo, purgante *m*; — *a* purgativo

lay *vt* collocare, mettere, posare; *(paint)* coprire di pittura; *(spread)* stendere; — **aside** mettere da parte; — **a bet** fare una scommessa; — **bare** scoprire; — **a hand on** mettere le mani su; — **low** abbattere; *(hide)* appiattarsi; — **open** esporre; — **out** preparare, esporre, *(money)* spendere; — **up** conservare; mettere da parte; — *vi (bet)* scommettere; far scommessa; *(egg)* deporre uova

lay *n* *(position)* situazione, posizione; — **of the land** sistemazione del terreno; **–off** *n* sospensione di lavoro

lay *a* laico, secolare; **–man** *n* laico, secolare *m*

layer *n* strato

layette *n* corredo di neonato

layout *n* progetto, disegno; *(print)* menabò

laze *vi* oziare; esser pigro; vivere nell'inerzia

laziness *n* indolenza, pigrizia

lazy *a* pigro, indolente; **–bones** *n* *(coll)* indolente *m*

lead *vt (guide)* condurre, guidare; *(head)* capeggiare; *(cause)* indurre; **— away, off** condurre via; **— the way** mostrare il cammino; andare avanti; **—** *n* direzione, comando; *(elec)* cavo maestro; *(theat)* primo attore; **take the —** prendere il comando

lead *n (min)* piombo; **—** *a* plumbeo, di piombo; **–en** *a* pesante, plumbeo, di piombo; **— poisoning** saturnismo, colica saturnina; **—** *vt* impiombare

leader *n* capo, guida, persona autorevole; **–ship** *n* direzione, direttiva

leading *a* principale, primario, primo; **— question** domanda capziosa *or* suggestiva

leaf *n (book)* pagina, foglio; *(bot)* foglia; *(table)* aggiunta; **–let** *n (print)* foglietto, fasciolo; **–less** *a* senza foglie; **–y** *a* frondoso, carico di foglie; **—** *vi (bot)* frondeggiare; *(book)* sfogliare le pagine di

league *n (measure)* lega; *(organization)* lega, associazione; **in — with** in lega con

leak *n* fuga, perdita; *(gas)* fuga di gas; **spring a —** *(gas)* fare fuga; *(liquid)* fare acqua; **–age** *n* falla, scolo, filtrazione; **—** *vt&i* perdere, colare; **— out** *(secret)* trapelare

leaky *a* fesso; che ha una falla

lean *n&a* magro; **–ness** *n* magrezza; **—** *vt&i* inclinare, appoggiare; **— back one's head** piegare la testa indietro; **— on** appoggiarsi a; **— out** sporgersi

leaning *n* inclinazione, tendenza, pendenza; **—** *a* tendente, inclinato, pendente

lean-to *n* tettoia, baracchino

leap *vt&i* saltare; **—** *n* salto; **— year** anno bisestile

leapfrog *n* saltamontone *m*, cavallina

learn *vt* imparare, apprendere; **–er** *n* allievo, scolaro; **–ing** *n* sapere *m*, conoscenza, scienza

learned *a* dotto, erudito, sapiente

lease *n* contratto d'affitto; **—** *vt* dare *(or* prendere) in affitto

leash *n* laccio, guinzaglio; **—** *vt* tenere al guinzaglio

least *n&a* minimo; **—** *adv* minimamente; meno possibile; **at —** almeno; **not in the —** in nessun modo, per nulla

leather *n* pelle *f*, cuoio

leathery *a* coriaceo

leave *n* licenza, congedo; permesso; **take — of** accomiatarsi da; **—** *vt&i* lasciare; *(depart)* partire, andarsene; **— alone** lasciare in pace; **— behind** lasciare indietro; **on —** in licenza; **— out** omettere, tralasciare; **sick —** licenza di convalescenza

leaven *n* lievito; **—** *vt* lievitare

leavening *n* lievitazione, fermentazione, lievito; **—** *a* in fermentazione

leavings *npl* avanzi, resti *mpl*

Lebanon Libano

lecher *n* libertino

lecherous *a* lascivo, osceno

lechery *n* libertinaggio, lascivia

lecture *n* conferenza, discorso; *(scolding)* ramanzina; **— vi** far conferenze; **—** *vt* rimproverare, ammonire

lecturer *n* conferenziere *m*

ledge *n* sporgenza, bordo; *(geol)* strato; *(mountain)* cornice *f*; *(window)* davanzale *m*

ledger *n* libro mastro

leech *n* sanguisuga; **stick like a —** attaccarsi come una sanguisuga

leek *n* porro

leer *n* sbirciata; **—** *vi* sbirciare; **— at** sogguardare

lees *npl* sedimento

leeward *a&n* sottovento

leeway *n* deriva

left *a&n* sinistra; *(neglected)* trascurato; **— behind** sorpassato, lasciato indietro; **on the —** a sinistra; **–over** *n* rimasuglio; **–ward** *adv* verso sinistra; **left–** *(in comp)* **–hand** *a* sinistro; **–handed** *a* mancino; ambiguo; **–wing** *a (pol)* di sinistra; **–winger** *n (pol)* appartenente alla sinistra

leftist *n* persona di sinistra

leg *n* gamba; *(animal)* zampa; *(fowl)* coscia; *(trip)* tappa; **pull someone's —** fare un tiro scherzoso a qualcuno, prendere in giro qualcuno; **shake a —** *(sl)* sbrigarsi; **stand on one's own two legs** essere indipendente; **without a —** **to stand on** senza nessuna ragione; **on one's last –s** essere alle ultime risorse

legacy *n* eredità

legal *a* giuridico, legale; **–ity** *n* legalità; **–ize** *vt* legalizzare

legate *n* nunzio, legato

legation *n* legazione *f*

legend *n* leggenda; **–ary** *a* leggendario

legerdemain *n* gioco di prestigio

leggings *npl* uose *fpl*

legible *a* leggibile

legion *n* legione *f*

legislate *vi* legiferare

legislation *n* legislazione

legislator *n* legislatore *m*

legislature *n* legislatura

legitimacy *n* legittimità

legitimate *a* legittimo

legume *n* legume *m*

leisure *n* comodo, agio; **at —** a proprio

agio; **–ly** *a* deliberato, calmo; **–ly** *adv* comodamente, con comodo; **in a –ly way** senza fretta

lemon *n* limone *m*; **—** **squeezer** spremilimoni *m*; **—** **tree** limone *m*; **–ade** *n* limonata

lend *vt* dare in prestito, prestare, imprestare; fornire; **–er** *n* prestatore *m*, prestante *m*; **—** **a hand** prestar man forte

lending *a* di prestito; **—** *n* prestito; **—** **library** biblioteca circolante

lend-lease *n* prestito di guerra

length *n* lunghezza; *(time)* durata; **at —** finalmente; per esteso, diffusamente; **–wise** *a* per il lungo; **–y** *a* lungo; **–en** *vt* allungare

leniency *n* benevolenza, indulgenza

lenient *a* indulgente

lens *n* lente *f*; *(eye)* cristallino; *(magnifying)* lente d'ingrandimento; **—** **shutter** *(photo)* otturatore *m*

Lent *n* quaresima; **–en** *a* quaresimale, magro

lentil *n* lenticchia, lente *f*

leopard *n* leopardo

leper *n* lebbroso

leprosy *n* lebbra

leprous *a* lebbroso

lesion *n* lesione

less *a* meno, minore, inferiore; **—** *adv &* *prep* meno; **–er** *a* minore; più piccolo; **–en** *vt&i* diminuire; **for —than** per meno di; **in — than no time** in men che non si dica; **— and —** sempre meno; **none the —** nondimeno

lessee *n* locatario, affittuario

lesson *n* lezione

lessor *n* locatore *m*

lest *conj* per tema che, affinchè non

let *vt* lasciare, permettere; **—** **alone** lasciare in pace; **—** **down** deludere; **—** **go** **(of)** lasciare andare *(coll)*; **—** **in** lasciar entrare; **—** **know** far sapere; **—** **off** perdonare; lasciar passare *(fig)*; **—** **out** far uscire; *(dress)* allargare; *(secret)* divulgare; **—** **up** *(coll)* diventar meno rigido; *(slacken)* mollare; **–down** *n* *(coll)* disappunto; **–up** *n* rallentamento

lethargy *n* letargo

letter *n* *(alphabet, mail)* lettera; **—** **box** *n* cassetta postale; **—** **carrier** postino; **–head** intestazione; **—** **of attorney** mandato di procura; **—** **of credit** lettera di credito; **—** **opener** aprilettere *m*; **capital —** maiuscola; **dead —** lettera morta; **form —** lettera circolare; **lower-case —** *(print)* minuscola; **registered —** lettera raccomandata; **small —** minuscola; **—** *vt* scrivere con caratteri alfabetici

lettering *n* caratteri alfabetici; iscrizione

lettuce *n* lattuga

leucocyte *n* leucocite *m*

leukemia *n* leucemia

levee *n* argine *m*; diga

level *a* piano; **—** **with** a livello con; **do one's —** **best** fare del proprio meglio; **—** *n* livello; piano; **be on the —** avere intenzioni oneste; **—** *vt* livellare; *(aim)* puntare; *(avi)* volare raso terra; **—** **to the ground** radere al suolo

level-headed *a* equilibrato, di buon senso

lever *n* leva; **control —** *(avi)* asta di comando; **–age** *n* punto d'appoggio, fulcro; influenza, vantaggio

levity *n* leggerezza, frivolità

levulose *n* levulosio

levy *n* imposizione, esazione; **—** *vt* requisire, esigere; **—** **a tax** imporre un tributo

lewd *a* libidinoso, dissoluto

lewdness *n* oscenità, libidine *f*

lexicographer *n* lessicografo

lexicon *n* lessico

liabilities *npl* *(com)* passività; *(debts)* impegni *mpl*

liability *n* responsabilità; svantaggio

liable *a* responsabile; *(likely)* suscettibile di

liar *n* bugiardo

libel *n* diffamazione *f*; **—** *vt* diffamare

liberal *a* generoso, liberale; **–ism** *n* liberalismo; **–ity** *n* liberalità; **–ly** *adv* liberalmente; **–ize** *vt* rendere liberale

liberate *vt* liberare

liberation *n* liberazione

liberator *n* liberatore *m*

libertine *n* libertino; **—** *a* licenzioso

liberty *n* libertà; **take the —** prendersi la libertà

libidinous *a* libidinoso

libido *n* libidine *f*

librarian *n* bibliotecario

library *n* biblioteca

librettist *n* librettista *m&f*

libretto *n* libretto

Libya Libia

license *n* licenza, permesso; **—** **plate** targa di circolazione; **driver's —** patente di guida; **hunting —** porto d'armi; **—** *vt* autorizzare

licentious *a* licenzioso, libertino

licentiousness *n* licenziosità

licit *a* lecito

lick *vt* leccare; *(coll)* battere, sconfiggere; **—** **one's chops** *(fig)* leccarsi i baffi *(fig)*; **—** **someone's boots** leccare i piedi a qualcuno; **—** *n* leccata; **give a — and a promise** *(fig)* fare qualche cosa superficialmente

licorice n liquirizia
lid n coperchio; (eye) palpebra
lie n menzogna, bugia; — vi mentire
lie vi trovarsi, stare; giacere; — **down** sdraiarsi, stendersi, coricarsi; — **still** star fermo
lien n diritto di rivalsa
lieu n luogo; **in — of** in vece di, in luogo di
lieutenant n tenente m; **second —** sottotenente m
life n vita; — **annuity** vitalizio; — **belt** salvagente m; — **buoy** gavitello di salvataggio; — **expectancy** probabilità di vivere; — **insurance** assicurazione sulla vita; — **preserver** apparecchio di salvataggio, sfollagente m; **come to —** ritornare in vita; **for — a** vita; **high — alta** società; **matter of — and death** questione di vita o morte; –**blood** n anima (fig); –**boat** n battello di salvataggio; –**guard** n bagnino; –**long** a perpetuo; –**saver** n salvavita; –**time** a a vita, per la vita; –**work** n lavoro di una vita; **still —** natura morta
lifeless a inanimato
likelike a verosimile, dal vero
life-size a al vero, al naturale
lift vt sollevare, alzare; — vi disiparsi; alzarsi; — n sollevamento; (air) ponte aereo; (auto) passaggio
ligament n legamento
ligature n legatura
light n luce f; — **beam** raggio di luce; — **bulb** lampadina; — **meter** (phot) fotometro; — **wave** onda luminosa; **bring to —** mettere in luce; **come to —** venire in luce, manifestarsi; **throw — on** gettar luce su (fig); –**hearted** a allegro, gaio; –**house** n faro; –**weight** n (sport) peso leggero
light a chiaro; (weight) leggero
light vt accendere; illuminare; — vi accendersi; illuminarsi; — **on** (encounter) imbattersi in
lighten vt illuminare; (weight) alleggerire; — vi illuminarsi; balenare; alleggerirsi
light– (in comp) –**fingered** a lesto di mano; –**footed** a agile, veloce; –**headed** a svenato, leggero; –**year** n (ast) anno luce
lighting n illuminazione
lightning n baleno; — **rod** parafulmine m; **flash of —** un lampo; **fork —** saetta; **sheet —** lampeggio
ligneous a ligneo
likable a simpatico, piacevole
like a simile, somigliante; — prep simile a, come; — vt piacere a; voler bene a, aver simpatia per; — adv come, da,

nella maniera di; –**ly** a probabile; –**ness** n rassomiglianza; –**wise** adv così, ugualmente; –**lihood** n probabilità, verosimiglianza; **feel —** aver voglia di; **look —** somigliare a
liken vt confrontare, paragonare
liking n (affection) affetto, simpatia; (desire) inclinazione; (taste) gusto; **take a — to** prendere in simpatia
lilac n lilla
lily n giglio
limb n membro; (tree) ramo
limber a flessibile, agile; — vt rendere flessibile
lime n calce f; (fruit) limetta; –**stone** n calcare m; pietra calcarea
limelight n evidenza (fig); **be in the —** essere prominente
limit n limite m; — vt limitare; –**ed** a ristretto, limitato; –**less** a illimitato
limitation n limitazione, limite m, riserva
limp n zoppicamento; — vi zoppicare; –**ing** a zoppicante
limp a floscio, fiacco, molle; –**ly** adv flosciamente
limpid a chiaro, limpido, terso
line n linea, riga; (com) linea d'affari; (poet) verso; **draw the —** (fig) segnare il limite; — vt rigare, segnare; (articles) rivestire, ricoprire, foderare; (rule) allineare; — **up** allinearsi
lineage n lignaggio, stirpe f, razza
lined a (inside) rivestito, ricoperto, foderato; (ruled) lineato
lineal a lineale
linear n lineare
lineman n (rail) guardalinea m
linen n tela di lino; **bed —** biancheria; — a di lino
liner n (boat) transatlantico
linesman n (sport) arbitro
line-up n sfilata
linger vi attardarsi; –**ing** a ritardato, lungo, lento; (lasting) persistente
lingual a linguale
linguist n linguista m&f; –**ics** npl linguistica; –**ic** a linguistico
liniment n linimento
lining n fodera, rivestimento
link n vincolo; anello di congiunzione; — vt concatenare, unire
linoleum n linoleum m
linotype n macchina linotipo
linseed n seme di lino; — **oil** olio di lino
lint n peluria, cascame m
lion n leone m
lion-hearted a dal cuor di leone
lip n labbro; — **reading** il capire dal moto delle labbra; — **service** fedeltà a parole

lipstick *n* rossetto per le labbra
liquefaction *n* liquefazione
liquefy *vt* liquefare; — *vi* liquefarsi
liqueur *n* liquore *m*
liquid *a&n* liquido
liquidate *vt* liquidare
liquidation *n* liquidazione
liquor *n* liquore *m*; — **store** negozio di liquori; **hard** — bevanda di alto grado alcoolico
Lisbon Lisbona
lisp *vt&i* parlare bleso; — *n* pronunzia blesa
list *n* elenco, lista; *(naut)* sbandamento; — **price** prezzo marcato; — *vt* elencare; — *vi (naut)* sbandare
listen *vi* ascoltare; **-er** *n* ascoltatore *m*; **-ing** *a* ascoltante
listless *a* indifferente; svogliato; **-ness** svogliatezza
litany *n* litania
liter *n* litro
literacy *n* il saper leggere e scrivere
literal *a* letterale; **-ly** *adv* letteralmente
literary *a* letterario
literate *a* letterato; che sa leggere e scrivere; — *n* letterato, erudito in lettere
literature *n* letteratura
lithe *a* snello, pieghevole
lithograph *n* litografia; **-er** *n* litografo
lithography *n* litografia
litigant *n* litigante *m&f*; parte in causa
litigate *vt (law)* discutere; — *vi* avere una causa in corso; litigare
litigation *n* lite legale
litmus *n* tornasole *m*; — **paper** carta di tornasole
litter *n (animal)* figliata; *(mess)* disordine, sossopra *m*; — *vt* disordinare; — *vi (animal)* partorire; **-ed** *a* disordinato, sossopra
little *a* piccolo; — *n&adv* poco; — **by** — a poco a poco; **a** — **while** un po' di tempo; **L- Bear** Orsa Minore
liturgy *n* liturgia
live *vt&i* vivere; *(reside)* abitare; — **down** *(past)* far dimenticare; — **from hand to mouth** vivere alla giornata; — *a* vivo, vivente; ardente; — **show** *(TV)* scena dal vero; — **steam** vapore compresso; **-liness** *n* vivacità
livelihood *n* sussistenza, mantenimento
lively *a* vivo, vivace
liven *vt* animare; — *vi* ravvivarsi
liver *n* fegato
livery *n* livrea; — **stable** stalla dove si noleggiano cavalli
livestock *n* bestiame *m*

livid *a* livido
living *n* esistenza, vita, pane quotidiano; — **room** salotto; — **wage** salario livellato alle esigenze vitali; **earn a** — guadagnarsi il pane; **standard of** — tenore di vita; — *a* vivente
lizard *n* lucertola; — *a* di lucertola
llama *n* lama
load *vt* caricare; — *n* carico, peso; **-s of** *(coll)* mucchi di
loaded *a* caricato; — **dice** dadi truccati
loaf *n* pane *m*, forma di pane; — *vi* bighellonare; **-er** *n* bighellone *m*, ozioso; **-ing** *n* ozio
loan *n* prestito; — **shark** strozzino; — *vt* prestare
loathe *vt* detestare; avere a schifo
loathing *n* ripugnanza
loathsome *a* schifoso, disgustoso
lobby *n* vestibolo, atrio; — *vi (pol)* sollecitare voti con manovre influenzabili
lobe *n* lobo
lobster *n* aragosta
local *a* locale; **-ity** *n* località; **-ize** *vt* localizzare; **-ly** *a* localmente
locale *n* scena
locate *vt* collocare; individuare, reperire; **be -d** essere situato
location *n* posto, posizione
lock *n (canal)* chiusa; *(gun)* percussore *m*; *(hair)* ricciolo, ciocca, bioccolo; *(latch)* serratura, toppa; **air** — camera di pressione intermedia; **pick a** — aprire con grimaldello; **under** — **and key** sotto chiave; **-smith** *n* magnano, chiavaio; **-out** *n (labor)* serrata; **-ed** *a* chiuso a chiave
lock *vt* chiudere a chiave; — *vi* chiudersi; — **in** rinserrare; — **out** chiuder fuori; — **up** rinchiudere
locker *n* ripostiglio; armadietto; baule *m*; tiretto; — **room** spogliatoio
locket *n* ciondolo reliquiario
lockjaw *n* tetano
lockup *n* prigione *f*
locomotion *n* locomozione
locomotive *n* locomotiva; — *a* locomotivo, mobile
locomotor ataxia atassia locomotrice
locus *n (geom)* luogo
locust *n* locusta; — **tree** carrubo
lode *n (geol)* filone metallifero
lodge *n* villetta; locale notturno; — *vt&i* alloggiare; — **a complaint** sporgere querela
lodger *n* inquilino
lodging *n* alloggio
loft *n (attic)* solaio, soffitta; *(dove)* piccionaia; — *vt* mettere in soffitta

lofty *a* elevato, alto; *(noble)* nobile
log *n* ceppo, tronco; *(naut)* libro di bordo; — **cabin** capanna di tronchi d'albero; . — *vt&i* tagliare in ceppi
logarithm *n* logaritmo
logger *n* boscaiolo
loggerhead *n* stupido; **be at** —s essere alle prese
logic *n* logica; **-al** *a* logico
logistics *npl* logistica
loin *n* lombo; *(meat)* lombata; —s *npl* lombi *mpl*, reni *fpl*
loiter *vi* indugiarsi; gironzolare; **-er** *n* bighellone *m*, ozioso, sfaccendato; **-ing** *n* l'andare a zonzo
loll *vi* penzolare; afflosciarsi — *vt* lasciar penzolare
lollipop *n* caramella
London Londra
lone *a* solo, solitario; **-liness** *n* solitudine *f*; **-ly** *a* solitario, isolato, desolato; **-some** *a* solitario, solo
long *a* lungo; — *adv* per molto tempo, a lungo; **in the** — **run** nell'insieme; **a** — **time** molto tempo; **as** — **as** fin tanto che; **before** — fra poco; — **for** desiderare vivamente, agognare; **-ing** *n* desiderio, brama
long— *(in comp)* —**distance** *a* di lunga distanza; *(phone)* interurbano; —**faced** *a* malinconico, triste; —**legged** *a* dalle gambe lunghe; —**lived** *a* longevo, dalla vita lunga; —**lost** *a* perduto da lungo tempo; —**playing record, LP** disco microsolco; —**standing** *a* esistente da lungo tempo; —**suffering** *a* paziente; —**winded** *a* che ha grande resistenza per correre; *(fig)* tedioso, parolaio
longevity *n* longevità
longhand *n* scrittura ordinaria
longitude *n* longitudine *f*
longshoreman *n* scaricatore del porto
look *vt&i* guardare; *(appear)* sembrare; — **after** aver cura di; — **as if** sembrare che; — **at** guardare, esaminare; *(consider)* considerare; — **away** girar gli occhi; — **back (on)** ricordarsi (di); — **bad** aver cattivo aspetto; — **down on** *(fig)* disprezzare; — **for** cercare; *(expect)* aspettare; — **into** esaminare; — **like** somigliare; — **on** *(face)* dare su; **L**— **out!** Bada!, Guarda!, Attento! Attenzione!; — **over** esaminare, sorvegliare; — **up** *(word)* cercare; *(glance)* alzare lo sguardo; — **up to** *(admire)* ammirare, rispettare; **as it** —**s to me** come mi sembra, secondo me; **by the** —**s of it** secondo le apparenze
look *n* aria, sguardo, cera
looking glass specchio

lookout *n* guardia; **be on the** — stare all'erta *(or* in guardia); **That's my** — Ciò spetta a me, È affar mio
loom *n* telaio; — *vi* apparire, profilarsi
loop *n* cappio; asola; *(avi)* volta, gran volta; —**hole** *n* scappatoia
loose *a* sciolto, libero; sfrenato, dissoluto; **at** — **ends** trascurato, disordinato; indeciso; — **change** spiccioli *mpl*; **-ly** *a* scioltamente; vagamente; **-n** *vt* sciogliere, slegare; — *vi* sciogliersi, allentarsi
loose— *(in comp)* —**jointed** *a* dinoccolato; —**leaf** *a* dai fogli sciolti
looseness *n* scioltezza; *(moral)* immoralità
loot *n* bottino; — *vt* predare
lop *vt* potare; recidere; mozzare; **-sided** *a* mal equilibrato; pendente; asimetrico; — **off** mozzare
lope *vi* correre a lunghi passi; — *n* *(gait)* passo lungo
lop-eared *a* con gli orecchi penzoloni
loquacious *a* loquace; **-ness** *n* loquacità
Lord *n* Signore *m*, Dio
lord *n* signore, padrone *m*
Lord's Prayer Paternostro
lore *n* sapienza, erudizione
lose *vt&i* perdere; — **one's temper** andare in collera; — **one's way** smarrirsi; — **sight of** perdere di vista; **-r** *n* perditore *m*, perdente *m&f*
losing *a* in perdita, perdente
loss *n* perdita; **be at a** — non sapere cosa fare, essere confuso; **sell at a** — vendere in perdita
lost *a* perduto, perso; *(ruin)* rovinato
lot *n* sorte *f*, destino; *(land)* lotto; *(goods)* partita; **draw** —s tirare a sorte
lotion *n* lozione *f*
lots *npl* *(coll)* grande quantità, un mucchio
lottery *n* lotteria
loud *a* forte; sgargiante; **-ness** *n* forza, rumorosità; *(of dress)* vistosità
loudspeaker *n* altoparlante *m*
loudmouthed *a* volgare, grossolano
lounge *n* atrio, vestibolo; divano, sofà *m*; — *vi* andare a zonzo, oziare
louse *n* pidocchio
lousy *a* pidocchioso; *(sl)* schifoso
lout *n* villanzone *m*
lovable *a* caro, amabile
love *n* amore *m*, affetto; — **affair** amoruccio, passioncella; **be in** — essere innamorato; **fall in** — **with** innamorarsi di; **make** — corteggiare; **-less** *a* senza amore; **-liness** *a* bellezza, grazia, incanto; **-lorn** *a* infelice in amore; **-ly** *a* bello, grazioso, piacevole; **-r** *n* amante *m&f*; innamorato; **-sick** *a* innamorato
love *vt* amare, voler bene a

love-making n corte, flirteo
loving a amoroso; affettuoso; devoto
low a basso; vile; depresso; — adv basso;
   — vi muggire; — n (cow) muggito; **-ly** a
   umile
low- (in comp) **—cut** a scollato, decoltè;
   —down a (coll) vile, meschino;
   —pitched a (tone) di tono basso; (roof)
   di bassa inclinazione; **—pressure** a di
   bassa pressione; **—spirited** a triste,
   scoraggiato, abbattuto
lowdown n (sl) il nocciolo della questione
   (fig)
lower a più basso; **— berth** cuccetta bassa; **— vt** abbassare; (shame) avvilire;
   — vi abbassarsi; avvilirsi; (sink) af-
   fondarsi
lower-case a minuscolo
lowland n pianura, bassopiano; **-s** pianura del sudest scozzese
lowliness n umiltà
lox n (chem) ossigeno liquido; salmone affumicato
loyal a fedele; **-ist** n monarchico; **-ty** n
   fedeltà
lozenge n pasticca, pastiglia; (geom) lo-
   sanga
lube n olio lubrificante
lubricant n lubrificante m
lubricate vt lubrificare
lubricating lubrificante; **— oil** olio
   lubrificante
lubrication n lubrificazione
lucid a lucido; brillante; **-ity** n lucidità
luck n fortuna; **bad —** disdetta; **good —**
   buona fortuna; **-ily** adv fortunatamente
lucky a felice, fortunato; **— charm**
   amuleto
lucrative a lucrativo
ludicrous a ridicolo, comico; assurdo,
   ludicro
lug n (pull) strappone m; (mech) aletta,
   aggetto; (projection) sporgenza; — vt
   spingere; trascinare
luggage n bagaglio
lugubrious a lugubre
lukewarm a tiepido; (fig) indifferente
lull n sosta, bonaccia, intervallo di calma; **— vt** cullare, calmare; **— vi**
   calmarsi
lullaby n ninnananna
lumber n legname m; **— dealer** commer-

ciante di legname; **-jack** n boscaiolo;
   -man n taglialegna m; commerciante in
   legname; **-yard** n deposito di legname;
   — vi tagliar legna; **-ing** a pesante,
   ingombrante, goffo
lumen n lumen m
luminary n luminare m
lump n pezzo; bernoccolo; **— in the
   throat** nodo alla gola; **— sum** somma
   globale; **— vt** ammucchiare; prendere
   all'ingrosso, ammassare; **— vi** muoversi
   pesantemente; fare mucchio
lunacy n demenza, follia, alienazione
   mentale
lunar a lunare
lunatic a&n pazzo, matto
lunch, luncheon n colazione f; **— vi** far
   colazione
lung n polmone m; **iron —** (med) polmone
   d'acciaio
lunge n slancio; (fencing) a fondo; **— vi**
   slanciarsi; (fencing) fare un a fondo
lurch n scarto; (naut) bordata; (auto)
   sbandata; **leave in the —** lasciare nei
   guai; **— vi** rollare, sbandare, traballare
lure n (fishing) esca; (fig) lusinga, allettamento; **— away** sviare; **— vt** adescare, allettare
lurid a lurido; scandaloso
lurk vi nascondersi; stare in agguato
luscious a succolento
lush a lussureggiante
lust n concupiscenza, lussuria; inconti-
   nenza; **— vi** agognare, bramare; **-y** a
   vigoroso, forte
luster n splendore m, lustro
lustiness n vigore m
lustrous a lucido, brillante, splendente,
   lustro
lute n liuto
luxuriant a rigoglioso, lussureggiante
luxurious a lussuoso, suntuoso
luxury n lusso
lye n liscivia; soda caustica
lying n mendacia, falsità; **— a** giacente;
   (false) mendace
lying-in hospital casa di maternità
lymph n linfa; **— gland** n glandola lin-
   fatica; **-atic** a linfatico
Lyons Lione
lyric n lirica; **— a** lirico
lyrical a lirico

M

M. A., Master of Arts n diplomato in
   lettere
macabre a macabro
macadam n macadam m, massicciata; **— a**

   macadamizzato, massicciato
macaroni n maccheroni mpl
macaroon n amaretto
mace n (spice) macis m; (club) mazza

macerate *vt* macerare

machination *n* macchinazione, complotto

machine *n* macchina; — **gun** mitragliatrice *f*; — **shop** officina meccanica; — **tool** macchina utensile

machine-gun *vt* mitragliare

machine-made *a* fatto a macchina

machinery *n* macchine *fpl*; meccanismo; congegno

machinist *n* macchinista *m*, meccanico

mackerel *n* sgombro; — **sky** cielo a pecorelle

macrocosm *n* macrocosmo

macron *n* (*gram*) lunga

mad *a* pazzo; (*coll*) arrabbiato; **stark** — matto del tutto; **drive** — far impazzire; **get** — (*coll*) adirarsi; **go** — impazzire; **-cap** *n* scervellato, impulsivo; **-man** *n* pazzo, matto, folle *m*

madam *n* madama, signora

madden *vt* far diventar matto, far ammattire; **-ing** *a* da far impazzire

made *a* fatto

Madeira Madera

made-to-order *a* fatto su misura

made-up *a* artificiale, falso; (*cosmetics*) truccato

madly *adv* pazzamente

madness *n* pazzia, follia

Madonna *n* Madonna

madrigal *n* madrigale *m*

magazine *n* rivista; (*mil*) arsenale *m*; **powder** — polveriera

magenta *n&a* cremisi

maggot *n* verme *m*, baco; (*fig*) capriccio, ubbia

magic *n* magia; — *a* magico; **-al** *a* magico; **-ian** *n* mago; illusionista *m*

magistrate *n* magistrato

magnanimity *n* magnanimità

magnanimous *a* magnanimo

magnate *n* magnate *m*; (*coll*) pezzo grosso (*coll*)

magnesia *n* magnesia

magnesium *n* magnesio; — **light** luce al magnesio

magnet *n* calamita; **-ic** *a* magnetico; **-ic recorder** magnetofono; **-ism** *n* magnetismo; **-ize** calamitare, magnetizzare

magneto *n* magnete *m*

magnetohydrodynamics *npl* (*phy*) magnetoidrodinamica

magnetron *n* tubo catodico regolato con campo magnetico

magnification *n* amplificazione, ingrandimento

magnificence *n* magnificenza

magnificent *a* magnifico

magnify *vt* ingrandire, esagerare

magnifying *a* ingranditore; — *n* ingran-

dimento; — **glass** lente d'ingrandimento

magnitude *n* grandezza; **of the first** — di somma importanza

magpie *n* gazza

mahogany *n* mogano

maid *n* cameriera, donna di servizio; — **of honor** damigella d'onore; **old** — vecchia zitella

maiden *n* zitella; ragazza; vergine *f*; — **voyage** viaggio inaugurale; — *a* verginale, nubile; — **name** nome da signorina

mail *n* (*armor*) maglia di ferro

mail *n* posta, corriere *m*; **by return** — a giro di posta; — **delivery** distribuzione della posta; **registered** — posta raccomandata; **-box** *n* cassetta delle lettere; **-man** *n* portalettere *m*; — *vt* imbucare, impostare

mail-order house casa di commercio per corrispondenza

maim *vt* mutilare

main *n* (*utility*) conduttura principale; — *a* principale; — **office** ufficio principale, sede centrale; — **thing** l'essenziale, il principale; **-land** *n* continente *m*, terraferma; **-ly** *adv* principalmente; **-spring** *n* molla principale di meccanismo; (*fig*) causa basica; **-stay** (*naut*) straglio di maestra; (*fig*) appoggio principale

maintain *vt* sostenere; mantenere

maintenance *n* mantenimento, manutenzione

maize *n* granturco

majestic *a* maestoso; **-ally** *adv* maestosamente

majesty *n* maestà

majolica *n* maiolica

major *a* maggiore; — **general** (*mil*) maggiore generale; — *n* (*mil*) maggiore *m*; (*law*) maggiorenne *m*; **-domo** *n* maggiordomo; — *vi* (*study*) specializzarsi

majority *n* maggioranza

make *vt* fare; fabbricare; obbligare; costringere; — **a fool of** prendere per stupido; — **a living** guadagnarsi la vita; — **headway** progredire; — **a point** raggiungere lo scopo; — **believe** far finta di; dar ad intendere; — **no difference** non avere importanza; — **out** (*list, check*) compilare; (*document*) stendere; (*succeed*) riuscire; — **over** (*remake*) rifare; (*transfer*) trasmettere; — **ready** preparare, approntare; — **room** far posto; — **up** (*compose*) comporre; (*complete*) completare; (*reconcile*) fare la pace; — *n* fattura, fabbricazione; marca

make-believe *n* finzione, sembianza; — *a* finto

maker n fattore m
Maker n Creatore m
makeshift n espediente m; — a improvvisato
make-up n (print) impaginazione f; (cosmetics) truccatura; (composition) composizione, costituzione, struttura; (theat) trucco
making n fattura, creazione; struttura; **have the –s of** avere la stoffa di
maladjusted a inadatto
maladjustment n cattivo accomodamento, aggiustatura malfatta
maladroit a malaccorto
malady n malattia
malar a zigomatico; — n zigomo
malaria n malaria
malcontent n&a malcontento
male a maschile; — n maschio
malefactor n malfattore m
malevolent a malevolo
malfeasance n cattiva condotta, misfatto
malformation n malformazione, deformazione
malformed a deforme
malfunction n cattivo funzionamento; — vi funzionare male
malice n malizia, cattiveria; **with —aforethought** con premeditazione
malicious a malevolo, maligno; **–ness** n maliziosità
malign vt diffamare, calunniare
malignancy n malignità
malignant a maligno, nocivo
malinger vi fingersi ammalato
malleability n malleabilità
malleable a malleabile
mallet n mazzuola; martello di legno
malnutrition n denutrizione
malodorous a puzzolente
malpractice n negligenza professionale
malt n malto; **–ed** a di malto
Malta Malta
maltreat vt maltrattare; **–ment** n maltrattamento
mamma n mamma, madre f
mammal n mammifero
mammary a mammario
mammoth n mammut m; — a (coll) grande, enorme
man n uomo; **old —** vecchio; **young —** giovane m, giovanotto; **–hole** n chiusino; **–hood** n virilità, umanità; **–kind** n genere umano; umanità; **–liness** n virilità, mascolinità; fermezza virile; — vt equipaggiare; **–ly** a virile, mascolino, **–ly** adv virilmente
manacle n manetta; — vt ammanettare
manage vt dirigere, amministrare, manipolare; — vi arrangiarsi, cavarsela

(coll); **–able** a maneggevole, trattabile; **–ment** n direzione f; gestione f
manager n direttore m; **–ial** a direttivo
managing a gerente, amministratore
mandate n mandato
mandatory a impositorio, obbligatorio
mandible n mandibola
mandolin n mandolino
mane n criniera
man-eating a antropofago
maneuver n manovra; — vt manovrare
manganese n manganese m
mange n rogna, scabbia
manger n greppia; (eccl) presepio
mangle n mangano; — vt (iron) manganare; lacerare, sfigurare
mangy a scabbioso
manhandle vt malmenare
mania n mania, pazzia
maniac n&a maniaco
manicure n manicura; — vt far la manicura
manicurist n manicure f
manifest n manifesto; — a evidente; — vt manifestare; — vi manifestarsi; **–ation** n manifestazione
manifesto n proclama, manifesto
manifold a molteplice; multiforme; — n (mech) tubo collettore
manikin n manichino
manipulate vt manipolare
manipulation n manipolazione
manipulator n manipolatore m
manna n manna
manner n maniera; modo; aria; **in a —of speaking** per modo di dire; **in this —** in questo modo; **–ly** a cortese, educato; **–ism** n manierismo; **–s** npl modo di comportarsi; educazione
man-of-war n nave da guerra
manor n maniero; feudo, castello
mansion n casa signorile
manslaughter n omicidio preterintenzionale
mantel n mensola di camino
mantilla n mantiglia
mantle n (cape) mantello; manto; (fireplace) cappa
manual a&n manuale m; **— training** pratica apprendista
manufacture n fabbrica, manifattura; — vt manifatturare, fabbricare; **–r** n manifatturiere, fabbricante m
manufacturing n fabbricazione; — a manifatturante
manumit vt emancipare
manure n letame, concime m
manuscript n manoscritto
many n&a molti, tanti; **how —, so —** quanti; **as — as** tanti quanti; **too —**

troppi
many-sided *a* con molti lati (*or* aspetti)
map *n* carta geografica; — **maker** *n* cartografo; — *vt* fare una carta di; — **out** tracciare; progettare in dettaglio
maple *n* acero
mar *vt* (*ruin*) guastare; (*spoil*) avariare; (*disfigure*) sfigurare; — *n* guasto, rovina, danno
maraschino *n* maraschino
marathon *n* maratona
marauder *n* predone, predatore *m*
marble *n* marmo; — *a* di marmo; **-d** *a* marmoreo, marmorizzato; — *vt* marmorare, marmorizzare
March *n* marzo
march *n* marcia; — *vi* marciare; — *vt* far marciare; — **by** sfilare
mare *n* giumenta
margarine *n* margarina
margin *n* margine *m*, orlo; — (*com*) deposito di garanzia marginale; **-al** *a* marginale
marginate *vt* marginare
marigold *n* fiorrancio
marimba *n* silofono
marinate *vt* marinare
marine *n* marinaio; **M– Corps** marina; — *a* marino, marittimo
mariner *n* marinaio
marionette *n* marionetta
marital *a* maritale
maritime *a* marittimo
marjoram *n* maggiorana
mark *n* segno; (*school*) voto, punto; (*target*) bersaglio; — **of distinction** segno di distinzione; **question** — punto interrogativo; — *vt* marcare; — **down** (*com*) diminuire il prezzo; — **time** segnare il passo; marcare il tempo; — **up** aumentare il prezzo; **-ed** *a* marcato, distinto, noto; **-er** *n* segnatore *m*; marcatore *m*; **-ing** *n* marchio; segno; **trade–** *n* marca di fabbrica
marked– (*as comp*) **—down** *a* a prezzo ribassato; **—up** *a* a prezzo aumentato
market *n* mercato; — **place** piazza del mercato; — **price** (*com*) prezzo di mercato; **-able** *a* mercantile, commerciabile; **on the** — sul mercato; — *vt* vendere
marketing *n* commercio; — **research** indagine di mercato
marksman *n* tiratore esperto
markup *n* (*com*) margine di rivendita
marmalade *n* marmellata
maroon *n&a* (*color*) marrone; — *vt* abbandonare su un'isola
marquee *n* pensilina
marquis *n* marchese *m*

marriage *n* matrimonio; **–able** *a* maritabile, in età da marito; — **license** dispensa di matrimonio
married *a* sposato; (*conjugal*) matrimoniale, coniugale; (*man*) ammogliato; (*woman*) maritata; **get** — sposarsi; — **couple** coniugi *mpl*
marrow *n* midollo
marry *vt* sposare; — *vi* sposarsi
Mars *n* Marte *m*
Marseilles Marsiglia
marsh *n* palude *f*; **–y** *a* paludoso
marshal *n* maresciallo; — **law** legge marziale; — *vt* ordinare; mettere in ordine; — **one's forces** riunire le forze
marshmallow *n* (*bot*) altea
marsupial *n&a* marsupiale *m*
mart *n* mercato, centro commerciale
marten *n* martora
martial *a* marziale
Martian *a&n* marziano
martinet *n* rigorista *m*
martyr *n* martire *m&f*; **–dom** *n* martirio; — *vt* martirizzare
marvel *n* meraviglia; — *vt* meravigliare; — *vi* meravigliarsi; **–ous** *a* meraviglioso; **–ously** *adv* meravigliosamente
marzipan *n* marzapane *m*
mascara *n* rimmel *m*
mascot *n* mascotte *f*; (*charm*) talismano, portafortuna *m*
masculine *a* maschile
masculinity *n* maschilità, mascolinità
mash *vt* ridurre in polpa, pestare; **–ed** *a* ridotto in poltiglia, schiacciato; passato
mask *n* maschera; — *vt* mascherare
masochism *n* masochismo
mason *n* muratore *m*
masquerade *n* mascherata; (*dance*) ballo in maschera; — *vi* mascherarsi
mass *n* massa, mucchio; — **meeting** comizio; — **production** produzione in massa; **–es** *npl* (*people*) masse popolari; — *vt* ammassare; — *vi* ammassarsi
Mass *n* Santa Messa
massacre *n* massacro; — *vt* massacrare
massage *n* massaggio; — *vt* massaggiare
masseur *n* massaggiatore *m*
massive *a* massivo
mast *n* (*naut*) albero
master *n* padrone; maestro *m*; — **hand** mano maestra; — **key** chiave maestra; — **of ceremonies** maestro di cerimonie; — **stroke** colpo maestro; **–ly** *a* magistrale; abile; **–ful** prepotente; **–piece** *n* capolavoro; **–y** *n* possesso; padronanza; maestria; — *vt* dominare
mastermind *n* genio, mente superiore; — *vt* organizzare, dirigere
masticate *vt* masticare

mastication *n* masticazione
mastiff *n* mastino
mastoid *n* mastoide *f*; — *a* mastoideo
mat *n* stuoia; **door** — zerbino; **table** — sottopiatto; **-ted** *a* arruffato; intrecciato
mat *a* opaco
match *n* simile *m*; *(matrimonial)* partito; *(sport)* partita, gara; — *vt (marry)* maritare; *(couple)* accoppiare; *(agree)* accordare; — *vi* maritarsi; **-less** *a* incomparabile
match *n (flame)* fiammifero; **book -es** fiammiferi Minerva *(coll)*
matchbox *n* scatola di fiammiferi
matchmaker *n* combinatore di matrimoni
mate *n* sposo; compagno; *(naut)* secondo di bordo; — *vt&i* accoppiare; accoppiarsi, unirsi
material *a* materiale; — *n* materia, stoffa; materiali *mpl*; **raw —s** materie prime *fpl*; **-ism** materialismo; **-ist** materialista *m*; **-ize** *vi* realizzarsi; **-ly** *adv* materialmente
maternal *a* materno
maternity *n* maternità
mathematical *a* matematico
mathematician *n* matematico
mathematics *npl* matematica
matinee *n* mattinata; rappresentazione diurna
matriarch *n* materfamilias *f*
matriculate *vt* immatricolare; — *vi* immatricolarsi
matriculation *n* immatricolazione
matrimonial *a* matrimoniale
matrimony *n* matrimonio
matrix *n* matrice *f*
matron *n* matrona; *(caretaker)* sorvegliante *f*
matter *n* materia; soggetto; *(med)* pus *m*; **it does not** — non importa; **What is the** —? Cosa c'è?, Che succede?; **as a — of fact** in verità, in realtà; **no** — **what** non importa che; — *vi* importare; *(med)* produrre pus
matter-of-fact *a* prosaico; effettivo
matting *n (floor covering)* stuoia
mattress *n* materasso; **innerspring** — materasso a molle
mature *a* maturo; — *vt&i* maturare; *(com)* scadere
maturity *n* maturità; *(com)* scadenza
maudlin *a* piagnucoloso, sentimentalone
maul *n* mazza; — *vt* malmenare, stracciare
mausoleum *n* mausoleo
maverick *n* vitello *(or puledro)* non marcato; *(fig)* individuo indipendente
mawkish *a* sdolcinato
maxim *n* massima, principio
maximum *a&n* massimo

May *n* maggio
may *vi* potere, esser possibile; **it** — **be** può darsi; forse; può essere
maybe *adv* forse
mayhem *n* sfregio
mayonnaise *n* maionese *f*
mayor *n* sindaco
maze *n* labirinto
M.C., Master of Ceremonies presentatore *m*; maestro di cerimonie
M.D., Doctor of Medicine dottore in medicina
me *pron* me, mi
meadow *n* prato
meager *a* scarso
meal *n* pasto; *(grain)* farina; **-time** *n* ora del pasto; **-y** *a* farinoso
mean *a* cattivo, vile; meschino; avaro; *(average)* mediocre, medio; — *n* medio, mezzo; *(math)* media; — *vt&i* significare, voler dire; **-ness** *n* inferiorità; spregevolezza; avarizia
meander *vi* vagare; serpeggiare; — *n* meandro
meaning *n* significato; **-ful** *a* pieno di significato; **-fulness** *n* significanza; **-less** *a* senza significato
means *npl* mezzi; **by all** — senz'altro, certamente; **by** — **of** per mezzo di; **by no** — niente affatto
meantime *n* frattempo; — *adv* nel frattempo, frattanto
meanwhile *adv* intanto
measles *npl* morbillo
measly *a (coll)* insignificante
measurable *a* misurabile
measurably *adv* misurabilmente
measure *n* misura; **in some** — in parte; **-ment** *n* misura, dimensione; — *vt* misurare
meat *n* carne *f*; *(fig)* il punto più importante; **-ball** *n* polpetta; **-less** *a* senza carne; **-man** *n* macellaio; **-market** *n* macelleria; **-y** *a* carnoso
mechanic *n* meccanico, macchinista *m*; **-s** *npl* meccanica
mechanical *a* meccanico; — **engineer** ingegnere meccanico; — **engineering** ingegneria meccanica
mechanism *n* meccanismo
mechanize *vt* meccanizzare
medal *n* medaglia
medallion *n* medaglione *m*
meddle *vi* ingerirsi, immischiarsi; ficcare il naso *(fig)*
meddlesome *a* intrigante; intromettente; — **person** ficcanaso
media *npl* mezzi *mpl*; **advertising** — veicoli pubblicitari
median *a&n* medio; mediano

mediate *vt* intercedere; arbitrare; far da moderatore
mediation *n* mediazione
mediator *n* mediatore *m*, intermediario
medical *a* medico; — **examination** visita medica; — **school** facoltà di medicina
medicate *vt* medicare
medication *n* medicatura
medicinal *a* medicinale
medicine *n* medicina; — **chest** cassetta di medicinali; — **dropper** contagocce *m*; — **man** stregone *m*
medieval *a* medioevale
mediocre *a* mediocre
mediocrity *n* mediocrità
meditate *vt&i* contemplare, meditare; *(plan)* tramare
meditation *n* meditazione
meditative *a* meditativo
Mediterranean *a* mediterraneo; — **Sea** mare mediterraneo
medium *n* mezzo; *(spiritualist)* medium *m*; — *a* medio, mediano
medium-sized *a* di media dimensione *or* grandezza
medley *n* mescolanza, miscuglio; farragine *f*
medulla *n (anat)* midollo
meek *a* mite, docile; —**ness** *n* mansuetudine, mitezza
meerschaum *n* schiuma di mare
meet *n* raduno; — *a* appropriato; convenevole; — *vt* incontrare; *(acquaintance)* far la conoscenza di; soddisfare; — *vi* riunirsi; incontrarsi; — **with** incontrarsi con; **go to** — andare incontro a; **make both ends** — *(fig)* sbarcare il lunario
meeting *n (reunion)* riunione *f*; assemblea; *(encounter)* incontro; — **place** ritrovo
megaphone *n* megafono
megaton *n* megatonnellata
melancholy *a* melanconico; — *n* melanconia
meld *n (card)* dichiarazione; — *vt* unire; — *vi* fondersi; *(cards)* dichiararsi
mellow *a* tenero; succoso; maturo; — *vt* maturare; *(soften)* ammorbidire; — *vi* maturarsi; ammorbidirsi
mellowing *n* maturazione; — *a* maturante
mellowness *n* maturità
melodious *a* melodioso
melodrama *n* melodramma *m*
melodramatic *a* melodrammatico
melody *n* melodia
melon *n* melone, popone *m*
melt *vt* fondere, sciogliere; — *vi* fondersi, sciogliersi
melting *n* fusione; liquefazione; *(fig)* intenerimento; — *a* fondente; — **point**

punto di fusione; — **pot** crogiuolo
member *n* membro; socio; —**ship** *n* insieme di soci
membrane *n* membrana
memento *n* memento, ricordo, nota
memorable *a* memorabile
memorandum, memo *n* memorandum *m*, appunto
memorial *n* monumento; commemorazione; — *a* commemorativo
memorize *vt* imparare a memoria
memory *n* memoria, ricordo; **commit to** — imparare a memoria
menace *n* minaccia; — *vt* minacciare
menacing *a* minacciante; —**ly** minacciosamente
menagerie *n* serraglio
mend *vt* riparare; raccomodare; — *vi* migliorare
mendable *a* riparabile
mendicant *n&a* mendicante *m*
mending *n* accomodamento, rammendo, riparazione
menial *a* servile, basso
meningitis *n* meningite *f*
meniscus *n* menisco
menopause *n* menopausa
menstruate *vi* aver mestrui
menstruation *n* mestruazione
mental *a* mentale; — **hospital** *n* manicomio
mentality *n* mentalità
mention *n* menzione; — *vt* menzionare; **don't** — **it** prego; si figuri; niente
mentor *n* mentore *m*
menu *n* carta, lista delle vivande
mercantile *a* mercantile
mercantilism *n* mercantilismo
mercenary *n&a* mercenario
mercerize *vt* mercerizzare
merchandise *n* mercanzia; — *vt&i* commerciare
merchant *n* commerciante *m*; —**man** *n* nave mercantile; — **marine** marina mercantile
merciful *a* pio; misericordioso
merciless *a* spietato
mercurial *a* mercuriale
mercury *n* mercurio
mercy *n* misericordia; clemenza; **at the** — **of** alla mercè di; **have** — **on** aver pietà di; aver misericordia di; — **killing** eutanasia
mere *a* solo; semplice; —**ly** *adv* puramente; solamente
merge *vt&i* unire, fondere, fondersi, unirsi; —**r** *n* assorbimento; incorporamento
meridian *n&a* meridiano
meringue *n* meringa
merit *n* merito; — *vt* meritare; —**orious**

a meritorio; *(person)* meritevole
mermaid *n* sirena
merman *n* tritone *m*
merrily *adv* allegramente
merriment *n* allegria, festevolezza
merry *a* gaio, allegro; **–making** *n* festa; divertimento
merry-go-round *n* carosello, giostra
mesa *n* altipiano
mesh *n* maglia; — *vt&i* ingranare; **in —** in ingranaggio
mesmerize *vt* ipnotizzare
mess *n (mil, naut)* mensa, rancio; **— hall** mensa; **— kit** gavetta e stoviglie da campo
mess *n (dirt)* sporcizia; *(muss)* impiccio; guazzabuglio; *(trouble)* imbroglio; pasticcio *(fig)*; — *vt* sporcare; imbrogliare; **–y** *a* confuso, in disordine
message *n* messaggio
messenger *n* messaggero, fattorino
Messiah *n* Messia *m*
metabolic *a* metabolico
metabolism *n* metabolismo
metal *n* metallo; **—, –lic** *a* metallico
metallurgist *n* metallurgico
metallurgy *n* metallurgia
metamorphose *vt* metamorfosare; — *vi* metamorfosarsi
metamorphosis *a* metamorfosi *f*
metaphor *n* metafora
metaphysical *a* metafisico
metaphysics *npl* metafisica
metatarsal *a* metatarsico
mete *vt* distribuire
meteor *n* meteora; **–ic** *a* meteorico; **–ite** meteorite *f*; **–ological** *a* meteorologico; **–ologist** *n* meteorologo; **–ology** *n* meteorologia
meter *n (distance)* metro; *(device)* contatore, misuratore *m*
method *n* metodo; **–ical** *a* metodico
methyl *n (chem)* metile *m*
meticulous *a* meticoloso
metric *a* metrico; **— system** sistema decimale
metronome *n* metronomo
metropolis *n* metropoli *f*
metropolitan *a* metropolitano
mettle *n* ardore *m*, coraggio, foga
mew *n* miagolio; — *vi* miagolare
Mexican *a&n* messicano
Mexico Messico
mezzanine *n* mezzanino
microbe *n* microbo
microbiology *n* microbiologia
microcosm *n* microcosmo
microfilm *n* microfilm *m*; — *vt* microfilmare
microgroove *n* microsolco

micrometer *n* micrometro
microorganism *n* microrganismo
microphone *n* microfono
microscope *n* microscopio
microscopic, –al *a* microscopico
microwave *n* micro-onda
mid *a* di mezzo, medio; **–day** *n* mezzodì *m*; **–night** *n* mezzanotte *f*
middle *n* mezzo; **— class** borghesia; **–man** *n* intermediario; **–weight** *n (sport)* peso medio
middle-aged *a* di mezz'età
Middle Ages *npl* medioevo
middle-class *a* borghese
middling *a* mediocre; benino
midget *n&a* nano
midriff *n* diaframma *m*
midshipman *n* guardiamarina *m*
midst *n* mezzo; **in the — of** nel mezzo di
midsummer *n* mezza estate
midway *a* a metà strada; intermedio; — *adv* a mezza strada
midwife *n* levatrice *f*
midwinter *n* cuore dell'inverno
mien *n* aria, aspetto, cera
might *n* potere *m*; **— and main** tutte le forze; **–y** *a* potente
migraine *n* emicrania
migrant *n* emigrante, migratore *m*; — *a* migratore
migrate *vi* migrare, emigrare
migration *n* migrazione, emigrazione
migratory *a* migratorio
Milan Milano
milch *a* lattifero
mild *a* mite; **–ly** *adv* mitemente; **–ness** *n* mitezza, dolcezza
mildew *n* muffa; — *vt* macchiare; far ammuffire; — *vi* ammuffirsi
mile *n* miglio; **–stone** *n* pietra miliare
mileage *n* chilometraggio; distanza in miglia
militant *a* militante
militarism *n* militarismo
military *a* militare
militate *vi* militare; combattere
militia *n* milizia
milk *n* latte *m*; **— sugar** lattosio; **–man** *n* lattaio; **— vt** mungere
milky *a* latteo; **the M– Way** la Via Lattea
milksop *n* uomo effeminato
mill *n* mulino; **–stone** *n* mola, macina; — *vt* macinare; *(money)* zigrinare; *(wood)* modellare
millennium *n* millennio
millepede *n* millepiedi *m*
miller *n* mugnaio
milligram *n* milligrammo
millimeter *n* millimetro

milliner *n* modista; **-y** *n* modisteria
million *n* milione *m*; **-aire** *n* milionario; **-th** *a* milionesimo
mime *n* mima; *(person)* mimo; — *vt* mimare
mimeograph *n* mimeografo; ciclostile *m*; — *vt* mimeografare
mimic *n* mimo; — *a* mimico; — *vt* imitare, fare la mimica di; **-ry** *n* mimica
minaret *n* minareto
mince *vt* tritare, tagliuzzare; *(weaken)* indebolire; — *vi* camminare affettatamente — **words** mangiarsi le parole; **-d meat** carne tritata
mind *n* mente *f*; spirito; intenzione; — **reader**- che legge il pensiero altrui; **bear in** — tener presente; **be of one** — essere d'accordo; **change one's** — cambiar di parere *or* d'opinione; **have in** — aver in mente, ricordarsi; **make up one's** — decidersi; **peace of** — tranquillità d'animo; **state of** — stato d'animo; **of no** — di nessuna importanza; **-ful** *a* attento; memore; — *vt (heed)* badare a; *(dislike)* dispiacersi; *(look after)* curare
mine *pron* il mio, la mia, i miei, le mie
mine *n* miniera; — **field** campo minato; — **sweeper** dragamine *m*; **-r** *n* minatore *m*; — *vt* minare; *(minerals)* scavare
mineral *a&n* minerale *m*; **-ogist** *n* minerologo; **-ogy** *n* mineralogia
mingle *vt&i* mischiare; mischiarsi
miniature *n* miniatura; — *a* in miniatura, in piccolo
minimize *vt* sottovalutare, diminuire; dar poca importanza a
minimum *a&n* minimo
mining *n* industria mineraria; — *a* minerario
minion *n* favorito
minister *n* ministro; pastore evangelico; — *vi* soddisfare le necessità
ministry *n (eccl)* sacerdozio; *(pol)* ministero
mink *n* visone *m*
minor *a&n* minorenne *m&f*
minority *n* minoranza
minstrel *n* menestrello
mint *n (bot)* menta; *(fig)* tesoro; *(money)* zecca; — *vt* coniare
minuet *n* minuetto
minus *prep* meno; *(coll)* senza; *n (quantity)* quantità negativa; *(sign)* segno di sottrazione
minute *n* minuto; istante *m*; **any** — da un momento all'altro; — **hand** lancetta dei minuti; **this** — immediatamente
minute *a* minuto, piccolo
minx *n* birichina, sbarazzina

miracle *n* miracolo; — **worker** taumaturgo
miraculous *a* miracoloso
mirage *n* miraggio
mire *n* fango, pantano; — *vt* infangare; — *vi* impantanarsi
mirror *n* specchio; **rear-view** — specchio retrovisivo; — *vt* riflettere; rispecchiare
mirth *n* allegria; ilarità; **-ful** *a* gaio
misadventure *n* disavventura
misalliance *n* cattiva alleanza; matrimonio mal riuscito
misanthrope *n* misantropo
misanthropic *a* misantropico
misapplied *a* mal applicato
misapplication *n* cattiva applicazione
misapprenhension *n* malinteso; equivoco
misappropriate *vt* usare abusivamente
misappropriation *n* appropriazione indebita
misbehave *vi* comportarsi male
misbehavior *n* cattiva condotta
miscalculate *vt* calcolare male; — *vi* sbagliarsi nel calcolo
miscalculation *n* errore di calcolo
miscarriage *n* errore *m*; fiasco; *(med)* aborto; — **of justice** errore giudiziario
miscarry *vi* fallire; *(med)* abortire
miscellaneous *a* miscellaneo
mischance *n* sfortuna
mischief *n* danno; cattiveria; male *m*; *(person)* birichino; *(prank)* birichinata
mischievous *a* dannoso, nocivo; birichino
misconception *n* malinteso; idea sbagliata
misconduct *n* cattiva condotta *or* gestione
misconstruction *n* errata interpretazione
misconstrue *vt* mal interpretare, fraintendere
miscount *n* conto sbagliato
miscreant *n&a* scellerato
misdeal *n* cattiva distribuzione; — *vt&i* distribuire male
misdeed *n* misfatto
misdemeanor *n* reato non grave
misdirect *vt* indirizzare *(or* dirigere) male
miser *n* avaro
miserly *a* avaro
miserable *a* infelice; pietoso; sciagurato
misery *n* angoscia; miseria
misfire *vi* far cilecca
misfit *n* fuori-luogo *m*; pesce fuor d'acqua *(fig)*
misfortune *n* sfortuna; disgrazia
misgiving *n* presentimento, timore *m*, sospetto
misguide *vt* fuorviare, sviare; dirigere male; **-d** *a* maldiretto
mishap *n* incidente *m*
misinform *vt* informare male

misinterpret vt interpretare male
misinterpretation n malinteso
misjudge vt mal giudicare
mislay vt mal collocare; (lose) smarrire
mislead vt fuorviare; –ing a ingannevole
mismanage vt amministrar male
mismanagement n cattiva gestione or amministrazione
mismatch vt assortire male
misnomer n uso errato di un titolo or nome
misogamist n misogamo
misprint n errore di stampa; — vt stampare erroneamente
mispronounce vt pronunziare male
misquote vt citare erroneamente
misrepresent vt mal rappresentare; –ation alterazione
misrule n malgoverno; — vt governare male
Miss n signorina
miss n colpo mancato; — vt mancare; (person) rimpiangere; (train) perdere
misshapen a mal fatto
missile n missile m, razzo; **guided** — missile telecomandato; — **base** n base per missili
missing a mancante, disperso
mission n missione; –ary n missionario
missive n missiva
misspell vt&i compitar male; fare errori d'ortografia
misstate vt travisare, esporre erroneamente
misstatement n affermazione sbagliata
misstep n passo falso
mist n bruma; nebbia; –y a nebbioso; (fig) oscuro
mistake n errore m; sbaglio; — vt sbagliare, confondere; **make a** — commetter uno sbaglio
mistaken a erroneo; sbagliato
mistimed a intempestivo
mistranslate vt tradurre male
mistranslation n traduzione errata
mistreat vt maltrattare; –ment n maltrattamento
mistress n direttrice f; (paramour) amante f
mistrust n diffidenza; — vt diffidare di; –ful a diffidente
misunderstand vt fraintendere, capir male; –ing n malinteso
misunderstood a malinteso, frainteso
misuse n cattivo uso; abuso
misuse vt abusare; usar male
mite n pochettino; cosa piccolissima
miter n (eccl) mitra; (joint) ugnatura; — **square** squadra zoppa; — vt commettere ad angolo retto
mitigate vt mitigare

mitigating a mitigante
mitigation n mitigamento, mitigazione
mitten n mezzo guanto
mix n miscela; — vt mischiare, confondere; — vi mischiarsi; –ed a mischiato, mescolato; misto
mixed-up a confuso
mixture n mescolanza, miscuglio
mix-up n confusione, guazzabuglio
mizzenmast n albero di mezzana
moan n lamento; — vi lamentarsi, gemere; — vt piangere, lamentare
moat n fossato
mob n folla, canaglia; — vt assalire in tumulto; — vi tumultuare
mobile a mobile
mobility n mobilità
mobilization n mobilitazione
moccasin n mocassino
mock a falso, finto; — vt canzonare, deridere; –ery n canzonatura, beffa; –ing a canzonatorio
modal a modale
mode n modo, maniera; (fashion) moda
model n modello, campione m; (artist) modella; (mannequin) indossatrice f; — vt modellare, plasmare; — vi posare, fare la modella; — a esemplare
moderate a moderato
moderate vt moderare; — vi moderarsi
moderation n moderazione
modern n moderno; –ize vt modernizzare; –istic a modernista, modernistico
modest a modesto; –y n modestia
modicum n quantità modica
modification n modifica, modificazione
modify vt modificare
modulate vt modulare
modulation n modulazione
Mohammedan n&a maomettano; –ism n islamismo
moist a umido; –ness n umidità; –ure n umidità; –en vt umettare
molar a&n molare m
molasses n melassa
mold n stampo; modello; (bot) muffa; — vt modellare; — vi ammuffire; –y a ammuffito, muffoso; –iness n muffa
molding n formatura, getto, modellazione; (trim) modanatura
mole n neo; (zool) talpa
molecular a molecolare; — **biology** biologia molecolare
molecule n molecola
molehill n tana di talpa; **make a mountain out of a** — fare di una paglia un trave (fig)
moleskin n pelle di talpa
molest vt molestare
mollify vt ammollire

mollusk *n* mollusco
molt *vi* mudare, rimpiumarsi; **–en** *a* fuso
mollycoddle *n* vezzeggiato
moment *n* momento; **–ary** *a* momentaneo; **–arily** *adv* momentaneamente; **–ous** *a* critico, decisivo
momentum *n* impulso
monarch *n* monarca *m*; **–y** *n* monarchia
monastery *n* monastero, convento
monastic *a* monastico
Monday *n* lunedì *m*
monetary *a* monetario
money *n* danaro, moneta; *(paper)* banconota; *(counterfeit)* moneta falsa; **—box** salvadanaio; **— order** vaglia; **ready —** danaro contante; **–ed** *a* ricco
money-making *a* redditizio
mongrel *n* meticcio; **—** *a* meticcio, ibrido
monitor *n* *(class)* capoclasse *m*; *(rad)* monitore *m*
monk *n* monaco, frate *m*
monkey *n* scimmia; **— wrench** chiave inglese; **—** *vi* *(coll)* gingillarsi; **— with** toccare, manomettere
monochromatic *a* monocromatico
monocle *n* monocolo
monogamist *n* monogamo
monogamous *a* monogamo
monogamy *n* monogamia
monogram *n* monogramma *m*
monograph *n* monografia
monologue *n* monologo
monomania *n* monomania
monoplane *n* monoplano
monopolistic *a* monopolista
monopolize *vt* monopolizzare
monopoly *n* monopolio
monorail *n* monovia
monosyllabic *a* monosillabico
monosyllable *n* monosillabo
monotonous *a* monotono
monotony *n* monotonia
monotype *n* *(print)* monotipo *f*
monoxide *n* monossido; **carbon —** ossido carbonico
monsoon *n* monsone *m*
monster *n* mostro; **—** *a* enorme
monstrance *n* *(eccl)* ostensorio
monstrosity *n* mostruosità
monstrous *a* mostruoso
montage *n* fotomontaggio
month *n* mese *m*; **—'s allowance** quota mensile; **once a —** una volta al mese; **–ly** *a* mensile; **–ly** *adv* mensilmente
monument *n* monumento; **–al** *a* monumentale
moo *vi* muggire
mood *n* umore *m*; disposizione, stato d'animo; *(gram)* modo; **–y** *a* scontroso, mutevole, di cattivo umore; **be in the — to**
essere in vena di
moodiness *n* scontrosità, mutevolezza
moon *n* luna; **—** *vi* bighellonare; **–light** *n* chiaro di luna
moonbeam *n* raggio di luna
moonstruck *a* lunatico
moor *n* moro; **–ish** *a* moresco
moor *n* brughiera, landa; **—** *vt* *(naut)* ormeggiare, amarrare; **—** *vi* ormeggiarsi; **–ing** *n* ormeggio
moose *n* alce *m*
moot *a* discutibile
mop *n* radazza; *(hair)* zazzera; **—** *vt* radazzare
mope *vi* essere malinconico, avere la luna *(fig)*
moral *a&n* morale *f*; **–s** costumi *mpl*; **–ist** *n* moralista *m*; **–ly** *adv* moralmente **–ize** *vt&i* moralizzare; **–ity** *n* moralità
morale *n* morale *m*, stato d'anima
morass *n* palude *f*
moratorium *n* moratoria
morbid *a* malsano; morboso
more *a* più, maggiore; **—** *adv* più, ancora; **all the —** al massimo; **not any —** non più; **once —** ancora una volta; **— and — più** e più; **— or less** più o meno **–over** *adv* inoltre, per giunta, di più
mores *npl* usanze *fpl*
morgue *n* camera mortuaria
moribund *a* moribondo
Mormon *n&a* mormone *m*
morning *n* mattina, mattino; **—** *a* del mattino
moron *n* idiota *m&f*; **–ic** *a* idiota
morose *a* burbero; orso *(fig)*; **–ness** *n* scontrosità
morphine *n* morfina
morsel *n* pezzetto
mortal *a&n* mortale *m*; **–ly** *adv* mortalmente, a morte; **–ity** *n* mortalità
mortar *n* mortaio; *(arch)* malta
mortgage *n* ipoteca; **—** *vt* ipotecare
mortician *n* impresario di pompe funebri
mortification *n* mortificazione; *(med)* cancrena
mortify *vt* mortificare
mortuary *n* camera mortuaria; **—** *a* mortuario
mosaic *n&a* mosaico
Moscow Mosca
Moslem *n&a* mussulmano, maomettano
mosque *n* moschea
mosquito *n* zanzara; **— netting** zanzariera
moss *n* musco; **–y** *a* muschioso
most *a* il più, la maggior parte di; **—** *adv* molto, il più; **at the —** tutt'al più; **for the — part** nella maggior parte; **— likely** probabilmente; **— of all**

sopratutto; **–ly** *adv* principalmente
motel *n* autostello
moth *n* falena; *(clothes)* tarma; **— ball** naftalina in palline
mother *n* madre *f;* **–hood** *n* maternità; **–less** *a* orfano di madre; **–ly** *a* materno; **— tongue** lingua materna; **—** *vt* dar vita a; fare da madre a
mother-in-law *n* suocera
mother-of-pearl *n* madreperla
motif *n* motivo
motion *n* moto, movimento; *(parliamentary)* mozione; **— picture** pellicola cinematografica, film *m;* **—** *vt* fare segno; far cenno a; **–less** *a* immobile
motivate *vt* motivare, cagionare
motive *n* motivo
motley *a* multicolore; screziato, eterogeneo
motor *n* motore *m;* **–boat** *n* motoscafo; **–bus** *n* autobus *m;* **–cade** *n* sfilata di automezzi; **–car** *n* automobile *f;* **–cycle** *n* motocicletta; **–ist** *n* automobilista *m;* **–man** *n* manovratore *m;* **–scooter** *n* motoretta
motorize *vt* motorizzare
mottle *vt* screziare; macchiare; **–d** *a* screziato; chiazzato
motto *n* divisa, motto
mound *n (pile)* tumulo; *(small hill)* poggio, collinetta
mount *n* monte *m; (horse)* cavalcatura; **—** *vt* ascendere, salire; *(horse)* montare; *(gem)* incastonare; **—** *vi* salire, innalzarsi; **–ed** *a* montato
mountain *n* montagna; monte *m;* **— climber** alpinista *m;* **— climbing** alpinismo; **— range** catena di montagne; **–eer** *n* montanaro; **–ous** *a* montuoso
mountebank *n* saltimbanco
mounting *n* montaggio; ascensione; *(gem)* incastonatura; **—** *a* montante; ascendente
mourn *vt&i* piangere, rimpiangere; **–ful** *a* lugubre, triste; **–er** *n* dolente *m&f;* infelice *m&f*
mourning *n* lutto; **—** *a* dolente, afflitto; **go into —** prendere il lutto
mouse *n* topo; **–trap** *n* trappola per topi; **–y** *a* come un topo
moustache *n* baffi *mpl*
mouth *n (anat)* bocca; *(river)* foce *f;* **by word of —** a viva voce; **make the — water** far venire l'acquolina in bocca; **— organ** armonica; **–piece** *n* imboccatura; **—** *vt* declamare; mettere in bocca; **—** *vi* parlare gonfio; **–ful** *n* boccone *m*
movable *a* mobile
move *n* movimento; *(household)* trasloco; *(game)* mossa; **–r** *n* motore *m; (household)* traslocatore *m;* **–ment** *n* movi-

mento; **—** *vt* muovere, far muovere; *(emotions)* commuovere; **—** *vi* muoversi; progredire; traslocare; **— away** allontanare; **— off** togliere, rimuovere; **— out** portar fuori
movie *n (coll)* pellicola cinematografica; **–s** *npl (coll)* cinema *m*
moving *n* movimento; trasloco; **— van** carro-trasporti *(or* traslochi) *m;* **—** *a* mobile; *(emotional)* commovente
mow *vt* falciare; **— the grass** tagliare l'erba
Mr., Mister *n* signor, signore *m*
Mrs., Missis *n* signora
much *a&adv* molto; **as — as** tanto quanto; **how —** quanto; **so —** tanto; **too —** troppo; **very —** moltissimo; **make — of** dare molta importanza a
mucilage *n* mucillagine *f*
muck *n* letame *m,* fango
mucous *n* mucoso
mucus *n* muco
mud *n* fango
muddle *vt* confondere, far pasticci; **—** *n* imbroglio, confusione
muddy *a* fangoso; **—** *vt* intorbidare, infangare
mudguard *n* parafango
muff *n* manicotto; **—** *vt* impasticciare
muffin *n* panino
muffle *vt* avviluppare, coprire; *(sound)* soffocare
muffler *n* sciarpa da collo; *(auto)* silenziatore *m*
mug *n* boccale *m*
muggy *a* umido
mule *n* mulo
muleteer *n* mulattiere *m*
mulish *a* di mulo; testardo
mull *n* mussola; **—** *vt (wine)* aromatizzare; **— &i** *(coll)* meditare, ruminare *(fig)*
multicolored *a* multicolore
multigraph *n* ciclostile *m*
multiple *a&n* multiplo
multiplex *a* molteplice, multiplo
multiplication *n* moltiplicazione; **— table** tavola pitagorica
multiplicity *n* molteplicità
multiply *vt* moltiplicare; **—** *vi* moltiplicarsi
multistage rocket *(aesp)* razzo plurifasico
multitude *n* moltitudine *f*
mumble *vt&i* borbottare
mummify *vt* mummificare
mummy *n* mummia
mumps *npl* orecchioni *mpl*
munch *vt&i* masticare
mundane *a* mondano
municipal *a* municipale
municipality *n* comune *m,* municipio

munificence n munificenza
munificent a munificente
munitions npl munizioni fpl
mural n pittura murale; — a murale
murder n omicidio premeditato; — vt assassinare; **–er** n assassino; **–ess** n assassina; **–ous** a micidiale
murky a nero, oscuro, tenebroso
murmur n mormorio; — vt&i mormorare
muscatel n moscato
muscle n muscolo
muscle-bound a dai muscoli induriti
muscular a muscolare; — **dystrophy** distrofia muscolare
muscularity n muscolosità
musculature n muscolatura
muse n musa; — vt&i riflettere, meditare
museum n museo
mush n polenta, poltiglia; **–y** a (coll) sentimentale; — vi viaggiare con slitta tirata da cani
mushroom n fungo
music n musica; — **hall** sala-concerti f; **–al** a musicale; **–ally** adv musicalmente
musicale n programma musicale in una riunione
musing n meditazione; fantasticheria
musk n muschio
musket n moschetto; **–eer** n moschettiere m
muskrat n ondatra
muss n (coll) disordine m; — vt (coll) mettere in disordine; **–y** a (coll) in disordine; sciatto
mussel n dattero di mare
must n (wine) mosto; (bot) muffa; **–iness** n muffa; **–y** a ammuffitto; — vi ammuffire, ammuffirsi; (obligation) dovere

mustard n mostarda, senape f; — **plaster** senapismo
muster n appello; — vt (mil) adunare; **to** — **courage** farsi coraggio
mutability n mutabilità
mutable a mutabile, mutevole
mutation n cambiamento, mutazione
mute n muto; (mus) sordina; — a muto; — vt mettere la sordina; **–d** a silenziato; (mus) in sordina
mutilate vt mutilare
mutilation n mutilazione
mutinous a ammutinato, sedizioso
mutiny n ammutinamento; — vi ammutinarsi
mutter vt&i mormorare
mutton n montone m, castrato
mutual a mutuo
muzzle n (animal nose) muso; (device) museruola; (gun) bocca; — vt imbavagliare; far tacere
my a il mio, la mia, i miei, le mie
myopia n miopia
myopic a miope
myosin n miosina
myriad n miriade f; — a innumerabile
myrrh n mirra
myrtle n mirto
myself pron me, mi, me stesso
mysterious a misterioso
mystery n mistero
mystic n&a mistico; **–al** a mistico; **–ism** n misticismo
mystification n mistificazione
mystified a mistificato
mystify vt mistificare
myth n mito; **–ical** a mitico; **–ological** a mitologico; **–ology** n mitologia

N

nab vt (coll) acchiappare
nacelle n (avi) navicella
nag n ronzino; — vt rimbrottare
nagging n rimbrotto; — a rimbrottante
nail n chiodo; (finger) unghia; — **file** lima per le unghie; — **polish** smalto per le unghie; **hit the** — **on the head** (fig) colpire giusto; mettere un dito sulla piaga (fig); — vt inchiodare
naive a ingenuo
naked a nudo; **–ness** n nudità
namby-pamby a insulso
name n nome m, rappresentazione; **–sake** n omonimo; **–plate** n placca per il nome; **–less** a senza nome; **–ly** adv cioè, ossia; — vt menzionare; nominare
nap n sonnellino; (cloth) pelo
naphtha n nafta

napkin n tovagliuolo
Naples Napoli
narcissus n narciso
narcosis n narcosi f
narcotic a&n narcotico
narcotize vt narcotizzare
narrate vt narrare
narration n narrazione
narrative n narrativa
narrator n narratore m
narrow a&n stretto; — **escape** scappatoia miracolosa (coll); — vt restringere; — vi restringersi
narrow– (in comp) **—gauge** a a scartamento ridotto; **—minded** a gretto
narrowly adv (almost) pressoché; strettamente
narrowness n grettezza; strettezza

nasal *a* nasale; **–ize** *vt* nasalizzare
nascent *a* nascente
nastiness *n* malvagità; sporcizia
nasty *a* sporco; schifoso, brutto
natal *a* natale
nation *n* nazione
national *a* nazionale; **–ism** *n* nazionalismo; **–ist** *n&a* nazionalista *m&f*; **–ization** *n* nazionalizzazione; **–ize** *vt* nazionalizzare
nationality *n* nazionalità
nationwide *a* attraverso l'intero paese
native *a&n* indigeno, nativo; **— land** paese natio
native-born *a* nato in un luogo indicato
nativity *n* natività
natty *a* ordinato, netto, elegante
natural *a* naturale; **—** *n (mus)* bequadro; **— history** storia naturale; **–ism** *n* naturalismo; **–ist** *n* naturalista *m&f*; **–ization** *n* naturalizzazione; **–ize** *vt* naturalizzare; **–ly** *adv* naturalmente; **–ness** *n* naturalezza; **— resources** ricchezze naturali
nature *n* natura; **by —** per natura; **from —** dal naturale; **good —** bontà
naught *n* niente *m*, zero
naughtiness *n* cattiveria
naughty *a* cattivello
nausea *n* nausea
nauseate *vt* nauseare; **—** *vi* sentir nausea
nauseating *a* nauseante
nauseous *a* nauseabondo
nautical *a* nautico; **— mile** miglio marino *or* nautico
nautilus *n* nautilo
naval *a* navale; **— academy** accademia navale; **— officer** ufficiale di marina
nave *n* navata; *(wheel)* mozzo di ruota
navel *n* ombelico
navigable *a* navigabile
navigate *vt&i* navigare
navigation *n* navigazione
navigator *n* navigatore *m*
navy *n* marina; **— bean** fagiuolo bianco; **— blue** blu marino; **— yard** arsenale *m*
nay *n* voto negativo
Nazi *n* nazista *m&f*
neap *a* basso; **— tide** bassa marea
Neapolitan *n&a* napoletano
near *prep* vicino a, presso di; **—** *a&adv* vicino; **–by** *a&adv* vicino; **–ly** *adv* quasi, pressappoco; **–sighted** *a* miope; **—** *vt&i* avvicinarsi
neat *a* pulito, lindo; **–ly** *adv* nettamente, pulitamente; **–ness** *n* lindezza, nettezza
nebula *n (ast)* nebulosa
nebulous *a* nebuloso, nuvoloso
necessarily *adv* necessariamente
necessary *a* necessario; **be —** occorrere, bisognare, essere necessario

necessitate *vt* costringere, rendere necessario
necesity *n* necessità
neck *n* collo; *(bottle)* collo; *(dress)* colletto; *(geog)* lingua di terra; **–lace** *n* collana; **–tie** *n* cravatta; **–wear** *n* cravatte e colletti
necromancer *n* negromante *m&f*
necromancy *n* negromanzia
nectar *n* nettare *m*; **–ine** *n* pesca-noce *f*
née *a* nata
need *n* bisogno; **—** *vt&i* aver bisogno di; **–iness** *n* indigenza; **–less** *a* superfluo; **–lessly** *adv* inutilmente, innecessariamente; **–y** *a* bisognoso
needle *n* ago; **—** *vt* cucire con l'ago; **—** *vi* lavorare all'ago; **–work** *n* lavoro all'ago
ne'er-do-well *n* fannullone *m*, buono a nulla
nefarious *a* nefario, ribaldo
negate *vt* negare
negation *n* negazione
negative *n* negazione; *(photo)* negativa; **—** *a* negativo
neglect *vt* trascurare; **—** *n* negligenza; **–ful** *a* trascurato
negligee *n* vestaglia
negligence *n* negligenza
negligent *a* negligente
negligible *a* trascurabile
negotiable *a* negoziabile
negotiate *vt&i* negoziare; *(coll)* superare
negotiation *n* negoziato
negotiator *n* negoziatore *m*
Negro *n&a* negro
neigh *n* nitrito; **—** *vi* nitrire
neighbor *n* vicino; **–hood** *n* vicinato; quartiere *m*; **–ing** *a* vicino; *(country)* limitrofo; **–ly** *a* amichevole
neither *conj* nè; neppure, neanche; **— . . . nor** nè . . . nè; **— of the two** nessuno dei due
nemesis *n* nemesi *f*
neon *n* neon *m*; **— sign** insegna al neon
neophyte *n* neofito
nephew *n* nipote *m*
nepotism *n* nepotismo
nerve *n* nervo; coraggio; *(coll)* audacia
nerve-racking *a* snervante
nervous *a* nervoso; **— system** sistema nervoso; **–ness** *n* nervosità
nervy *a* coraggioso; *(coll)* audace
nest *n* nido; **—** *vi* annidarsi; **— egg** gruzzolo
nestle *vi* coccolarsi
net *n* rete *f*; *(police)* retata; **—** *vt* irretire
net *(com)* *n* guadagno netto; **—** *a* netto; **— profit** utile netto; **—** *vt* ricavare,

guadagnarsi
nether a basso
Netherlands Paesi Bassi, Olanda
netting n reticolato
nettle n ortica; — vt irritare; pungere
network n rete f; (rad) rete radiofonica
neuralgia n nevralgia
neurasthenia n nevrastenia
neuritis n nevrite f
neurologist n neurologo
neurology n neurologia
neurosis n neurosi f
neurotic a nevrotico
neuter n&n neutro, neutrale
neutral a&n neutrale; neutro; **–ity** n neutralità; **–ize** vt neutralizzare
neutron n neutrone m
never adv mai; — **ending** infinito; — **mind** non importa, pazienza
nevermore adv mai più
nevertheless adv però, pure; tuttavia
new a nuovo; **–born** a neonato, nato da poco; rigenerato; **–comer** n nuovo venuto; **–ly** adv recentemente; **–ness** n novità
newfangled a di nuova invenzione
newlywed n sposino
New Orleans Nuova Orlean
news npl notizia; notizie fpl; novità; **–boy** n strillone m, giornalaio; **–cast** n giornale radio; **–man** n giornalista m; **–paper** n giornale m; **–print** n carta per la stampa di giornale; **–reel** n notiziario cinematografico, **–stand** n edicola di giornali
New Year anno nuovo; **—'s Day** primo dell'anno, capodanno
New World Nuovo Mondo
New York Nuova York
next a prossimo, contiguo; — **day** il giorno successivo, il giorno dopo; — adv dopo, poi; — **of kin** il parente più prossimo — **to** accanto a
niacin n acido nicotinico
nib n punta, pennino
nibble n rosicchiamento; bocconcino; — vt&i rosicchiare; beccare
nice a bello, grazioso, gentile, simpatico; **–ly** adv scrupolosamente, esattamente; **–ty** n finezza
niche n nicchia
nick n tacca, incisione f; **in the — of time** nel momento più propizio; — vt incidere tacche
nickel n (min) nichelio, nichel m; — vt nichelare
nickel-plated a nichelato
nicknack n gingillo
nickname n nomignolo
nicotine n nicotina

niece n nipote f
niggardliness n avarizia
niggardly a avaro, taccagno
night n notte f; — **blindness** emeralopia; — **club** ritrovo notturno; — **letter** lettera notturna; — **owl** (coll) nottambulo; **at —** di notte; **by —** di notte; **–cap** n berretto da notte; **–dress**, **–gown** n indumento da notte; **–fall** n il cader della notte; **–mare** n incubo; **–shirt** n camicia da notte
nightingale n usignolo
nightlong a di tutta la notte; — adv nottetempo; durante tutta la notte
nightly adv di notte, nottetempo; — a notturno, di ogni notte
nihilism n nichilismo
nihilist n nichilista m&f
nil n niente, nulla m; — a nullo
Nile Nilo
nimble a agile
nimbus n nimbo; (cloud) nembo
nincompoop n semplicione m
nine a nove; **–teen** a diciannove; **–teenth** a diciannovesimo; **–ty** a novanta
ninny n imbecille m
ninth a nono
nip n (pinch) pizzicotto; (bite) morsicotto; — vt pizzicare; mordere; (squeeze) spremere; — **in the bud** tagliare il male alla radice (fig)
nippers npl pinze
nipple n capezzolo
nippy a piccante; (cold) pungente
nit n lendine m
nitric a nitrico
niter n nitrato di potassio or di sodio
nitrate n nitrato
nitrogen n azoto; **–ous** a di nitrogeno, d'azoto; azotato
nitroglycerin n nitroglicerina
nitrous a nitroso
nitwit n persona poco intelligente
no adv no; — a nessuno; **by — means** in nessun modo; **in — way** di nessun modo; — **doubt** senza dubbio; — **end** infine m; — **less** nientemeno; — **longer** non più; basta; — **such thing** impossible; — **smoking** proibito fumare; — n no, voto negativo
nobility n nobiltà
noble a nobile; **–man** n nobiluomo; **–ness** n nobiltà
nobly adv nobilmente
nobody pron nessuno; — **else** nessun altro
nocturnal a notturno
nocturne n notturno
nod n cenno della testa; — vt accennare col capo; — vi (doze) sonnecchiare
node n nodo; (bot) nocchio

nodule *n* nodulo
noise *n* rumore *m*, chiasso; **make —** far rumore; **—** *vt* divulgare; **—** *vi* far rumore
noiseless *a* silenzioso; **–ly** *adv* silenziosamente
noisily *adv* rumorosamente
noisome *a* nocivo
noisiness *n* rumorosità
noisy *a* chiassoso
nomad *n* nomade *m&f*; **–ic** *a* nomade
nomenclature *n* nomenclatura
nominal *a* nominale; **–ly** *adv* nominalmente
nominate *vt* nominare, designare come candidato
nomination *n* nomina, designazione
nominative *a&n* nominativo
nominee *n* designato, candidato
nonacceptance *n* rifiuto di accettazione
nonaggression *n* mancata aggressione
nonaggressive *a* inaggressivo
nonallergic *a* inallergico, non-allergico
nonattendance *n* assenza
nonchalance *n* disinvoltura
nonchalant *a* disinvolto
noncombattant *n* non-combattente
noncombattive *a* non-combattivo
noncommissioned *a* (*mil*) senza brevetto; **— officer** sottufficiale *m*
noncommittal *a* evasivo, che non vuole impegnarsi
noncompliance *n* inadempienza; opposizione
nonconductor *n* cattivo conduttore, nonconduttore
nonconformist *n* anticonformista, dissidente *m&f*
nondescript *a* indefinibile, inclassificabile
none *pron* nessuno, niente, nulla *m*; **—** *adv* non; **I have —** non ne ho; **— the less** nondimeno
nonentity *n* nullità, inesistenza
nonessential *n* inessenzialità; **—** *a* inessenziale
nonexistent *a* inesistente
nonintervention *n* non-intervento, neutralità
nonpareil *a* ineguagliato
nonpayment *n* mancato pagamento
nonplussed *a* imbarazzato
nonprofit *a* senza profitto
nonresistance *n* ubbidienza passiva
nonresident *a&n* non-residente *m*
nonresistant *a* irresistente, passivo
nonrestrictive *a* non-restrittivo
nonsectarian *a* non-settario
nonsense *n* assurdità; **N–!** (*interj*) Macchè!
nonsensical *a* assurdo
nonskid *a* antisdrucciolevole

nonstop *a&adv* (*avi*) senza scalo; senza fermate
nonsupport *n* (*law*) mancato sostentamento
nonunion *a* indipendente dai sindacati
noodles *npl* tagliatelle *fpl*
nook *n* angolo
noon *n* mezzogiorno; **—** *a* meridiano
noose *n* nodo scorsoio; (*fig*) trappola
nor *conj* nè; neppure, neanche; **neither ...** **—** nè ... nè
Nordic *n&a* nordico
norm *n* modello, norma, tipo
normal *a&n* normale *m*; **–cy** *n* normalità; **–ly** *adv* normalmente
Norman *n&a* normanno
north *n* nord *m*; **—** *a* settentrionale; **–east** *n* nord-est *m*; **–erly, –ern** *a* settentrionale; **–ward** *adv* verso il nord; **–west** *n* nord-ovest *m*; **N– America** America del Nord; **N– Pole** Polo Nord; **N– Star** stella polare
Norway Norvegia
Norwegian *a&n* norvegese *m&f*
nose *n* naso; (*animal*) muso; (*scent*) fiuto; **— dive** (*avi*) picchiata; **blow one's —** soffiarsi il naso; **lead by the —** menar per il naso; **— bag** (*horse*) sacchetto mangiatoia; **–bleed** *n* sangue del naso, epistassi *f*; **–y** *a* (*coll*) inquisitivo, ficcanaso; **—** *vt&i* (*sniff*) fiutare, annusare; (*pry*) curiosare
nose-dive *vi* (*avi*) calarsi in picchiata
nostalgia *n* nostalgia
nostril *n* narice *f*; (*horse*) frogia
nostrum *n* toccasana *m*, panacea, sanatoria
not *adv* non; **— even** neppure; **— at all** niente affatto
notability *n* notabilità
notable *a* notabile, notevole; **—** *n* notabile *m*
notably *adv* notabilmente
notary *n* notaio
notation *n* notazione
notch *n* incisione, intaglio; **—** *vt* incidere, intagliare
note *n* (*memo*) nota; (*letter*) biglietto; distinzione; (*mus*) nota musicale; **bank —** banconota; **make — of**, **take — of** prendere nota di; **sour —** stonatura; **take –s** prendere appunti; **—** *vt* annotare
notebook *n* taccuino; **loose-leaf —** quaderno d'appunti a fogli staccabili; **— filler** fogli di ricambio
noted *a* noto, famoso
noteworthy *a* degno di nota
nothing *n* niente, nulla *m*; **— but** nient'altro che; **— else** nient'altro; **good for —** buono a nulla
nothingness *n* nulla *m*, oblio

notice *n* avviso; **at short —** con breve dilazione; **give —** licenziare; **take — of** rilevare, osservare; **until further —** fino a nuovo avviso; **—** *vt* notare, osservare; **–able** *a* apparente
notification *n* notificazione
notify *vt* notificare
notion *n* nozione, idea, opinione *f*
notions *npl* idee *fpl*; *(articles)* piccolezze *fpl*
notoriety *n* notorietà, cattiva fama
notorious *a* famigerato
notwithstanding *prep* malgrado; **—** *conj* nonostante, malgrado, quantunque, tuttavia
nougat *n* torrone *m*
nought *n* nulla *m*
noun *n* sostantivo
nourish *vt* nutrire; **–ment** *n* nutrimento; **–ing** *a* nutriente
novel *n* romanzo; **—** *a* nuovo
novelette *n* novella
novelist *n* romanziere *m&f*
novelty *n* novità
November *n* novembre
novena *n* novena
novice *n* novizio
novitiate *n* tirocinio, noviziato
now *adv* ora, adesso; **N–!** *interj* Via! Dunque!; **— and again** di tempo in tempo; **—** qua e là; **— and then** di quando in quando; **till —** finora
nowadays *adv* oggigiorno
nowhere *adv* in nessun luogo
nowise *adv* in nessun modo
noxious *a* nocivo
nozzle *n* ugello, beccuccio
nuance *n* sfumatura
nubile *a* nubile
nuclear *a* nucleare; **— physics** fisica nucleare
nucleus *n* nucleo
nude *n&a* nudo
nudge *n* leggera gomitata; **—** *vt* attirare l'attenzione con leggera gomitata
nudism *n* nudismo

nudist *n* nudista *m&f*
nudity *n* nudità
nugget *n* pepita
nuisance *n* seccatura
null *a* nullo; **— and void** annullato
nullification *n* annullamento
nullify *vt* annullare
numb *a* intorpidito; **—** *vt* intorpidire; **–ness** *n* torpore *m*
number *n* numero; **—** *vt* numerare; **–ed** *a* numerato
numbering *n* numerazione; **—** *a* numerante; **— machine** numeratrice *f*
numeral *n* numero; **—** *a* numerale
numerator *n (math)* numeratore *m*
numerical *a* numerico
numerous *a* numeroso
numerousness *n* numerosità
numismatics *npl* numismatica
numismatist *n* numismatico
numskull *n* babbeo, semplicione *m*
nun *n* monaca, suora
nuncio *n (eccl)* nunzio
nunnery *n* convento
nuptial *a* nuziale; **–s** *npl* nozze *fpl*
nurse *n* infermiera; **wet —** balia; **—** *vt* curare; allattare; **–maid** *n* bambinaia
nursery *n* stanza dei bambini; **— school** asilo infantile
nursing *n* allattamento; **—** *a* allattante; **— home** casa di salute
nurture *vt* nutrire, alimentare; allevare; **—** *n* nutrimento
nut *n* noce *f*; *(mech)* dado; **–cracker** *n* schiaccianoci *m*; *(zool)* nocciolaia; **–ty** *a* di nocciola; *(sl)* pazzoide
nutmeg *n* noce moscata
nutrient *n* nutritivo, nutriente *m*
nutriment *n* alimento, nutrimento
nutrition *n* nutrimento
nutritious *a* nutritivo
nutshell *n* guscio di noce; **in a —** in breve
nuzzle *vt&i* fregare col muso, accarezzare col muso
nylon *n* nailon *m*
nymph *n* ninfa

O

oaf *n* semplicione *m*, zotico
oak *n* quercia; **–en** *a* di quercia
oakum *n* stoppa
oar *n* remo
oarlock *n* scalmiera
oarsman *n* rematore *m*
oasis *n* oasi *f*
oath *n* giuramento; bestemmia
oatmeal *n* farinata d'avena
oats *npl* avena; **sow wild —** far vita

dissipata
obduracy *n* ostinazione, durezza
obdurate *a* ostinato, duro
obedience *n* ubbidienza
obedient *a* ubbidiente
obeisance *n* deferenza; *(bow)* riverenza
obelisk *n* obelisco
obese *a* obeso
obesity *n* obesità
obey *vt&i* ubbidire

obfuscate *vt* offuscare
obituary *n* necrologia
object *n* oggetto; *(gram)* complemento oggetto; — **lesson** esempio pratico
object *vt&i* fare obiezione, opporsi
objection *n* obiezione; **raise an** — sollevare un'obiezione; **–able** *a* biasimevole
objective *n&a* obbiettivo; **–ly** *adv* obbiettivamente; oggettivamente
objectivity *n* obbiettività
objector *n* oppositore *m*; **consciencious** — obiettore di coscienza
oblation *n* oblazione
obligate *vt* obbligare
obligation *n* obbligo; impegno
obligatory *a* obbligatorio
oblige *vt (require)* obbligare; *(please)* fare un piacere a
obliged *a* riconoscente, obbligato; **be** — *(indebted)* essere obbligato a qualcuno; *(required)* esser costretto a fare qualcosa
obliging *a* compiacente
oblique *a* obliquo
obliterate *vt* cancellare
obliteration *n* obliterazione, cancellazione
oblivion *n* oblio
oblivious *a* immemore, dimentico
oblong *a* oblungo; — *n* rettangolo
obnoxious *a* offensivo, odioso
oboe *n (mus)* oboe *m*
oboist *n* oboista *m&f*
obscene *a* osceno
obscenity *n* oscenità
obscure *a* oscuro; — *vt* offuscare
obscurity *n* oscurità
obsequies *npl* esequie *fpl*
obsequious *a* ossequioso; **–ness** *n* ossequiosità
observable *a* notevole
observance *n* osservanza
observant *a* osservante
observation *n* osservazione; — **car** vagone belvedere
observatory *n* osservatorio
observe *vt&i* osservare; **–r** *n* osservatore *m*
observing *a* osservante
obsess *vt* ossessionare
obsession *n* ossessione
obsessive *a* ossessionante
obsidian *n* ossidiana
obsolescence *n* disuso
obsolete *a* antiquato, fuori uso; **become** — cadere in disuso
obstacle *n* ostacolo
obstetrician *n* ostetrico
obstetrics *npl* ostetricia

obstinacy *n* ostinazione
obstinate *a* ostinato
obstreperous *a* clamoroso
obstruct *vt* ostruire; impedire; **–ive** *a* ostruttivo
obstruction *n* ostruzione, ostacolo; **–ist** *n* ostruzionista *m&f*
obtain *vt* ottenere; — *vi* prevalere; essere in voga; **–able** *a* ottenibile
obtrusive *a* importuno
obtuse *a* ottuso
obverse *a* obverso; — *n* diritto
obviate *vt* ovviare
obvious *a* evidente, ovvio; **–ly** *adv* ovviamente
occasion *n* occasione; **–al** *a* occasionale, casuale; **–ally** *adv* sporadicamente; **a** — *vt* causare
occident *n* occidente *m*; **–al** *a&n* occidentale
occiput *n* occipite *m*
occult *a* occulto; **–ism** *n* occultismo
occupancy *n* occupazione
occupant *n* occupante *m&f*; *(tenant)* locatario, inquilino
occupation *n* occupazione, impiego
occupy *vt* occupare
occur *vi* accadere, succedere; venire in mente, **–ing** *a* occorrente
occurrence *n* occorrenza, contingenza, incidente *m*, avvenimento
ocean *n* oceano; **–ic** *a* oceanico; **–ography** *n* oceanografia
ocher *n* ocra
o'clock *adv* **one** — l'una; **two** — le due
octad *n* gruppo di otto
octagon *n* ottagono; **–al** *a* ottagonale
octane *n (chem)* ottano
octave *n* ottavo
octet *n (mus)* ottetto
October *n* ottobre *m*
octopus *n* polpo
ocular *a* oculare
oculist *n* oculista *m*
odd *a (uneven)* dispari, ineguale; *(queer)* originale; **–ity, –ness** *n* bizzarria; **–ly** *adv* bizzarramente
odds *npl* probabilità, vantaggio; — **and ends** ritagli *mpl*, cianfrusaglie *fpl*; **be at** — **with** essere in lotta con
ode *n* ode *f*
odious *a* odioso
odium *n* odio
odor *n* odore *m*; **–ous** *a* odoroso, fragrante; **–less** *a* inodoro
of *prep* di
off *adv* lontano, distante; — *prep* da, fuori di; — **and on** di quando in quando; — **the record** ufficioso; — **limits** extralimite; **come** — *(loosen)* stac-

carsi; **far** — remoto; **put** — rinviare
right — *(coll)* subito; **set** — mettere
in rilievo; partire; **take** — *(avi)* decollare; *(remove)* togliere, staccare; **turn** —
(lights, motor) spegnere; *(road)* cambiare di direzione; **Hands** —! Non toccare!

offal *n* avanzi, rifiuti *mpl*

offbeat *a* originale, strano

off-color *a* difettoso di colore; improprio

offend *vt* offendere; **–er** *n* offensore *m*;
–ing *a* offensivo

offense *n* offesa; delitto; attacco

offensive *n* offensiva; — *a* offensivo,
ingiurioso; **–ly** *adv* offensivamente

offer *vt* offrire; — *n* offerta; proposta;
–ing *n* offerta; sacrificio

offertory *n (eccl)* offertorio

offhand *a* estemporaneo, impensato, sul
momento, impreparato

office *n (business)* ufficio; *(position)*
carica; — **boy** fattorino; **–holder** *n*
impiegato statale; — **hours** orario
d'ufficio

officer *n* ufficiale *m*; poliziotto

official *a* ufficiale; — *n* funzionario; **–ly** *a*
ufficialmente

officiate *vi* esercitare le funzioni; *(eccl)*
officiare

officious *a* inframmettente

offing *n (naut)* largo; **in the** — in vista

offset *vt* compensare; — *n (print)* roto-
calcografia

offshoot *n* germoglio

offshore *a&adv* vicino alla costa

offside *a* fuori giuoco

offspring *n* prole *f*

often *adv* spesso, frequentemente; **how**
—? quante volte?

ogle *vt* adocchiare, sbirciare, occhieggiare

ogre *n* orco

ohm *n* ohm *m*

oil *n* olio; **crude** — petrolio grezzo;
mineral — olio minerale; — **field**
campo petrolifero; — **painting** pittura
ad olio; — **paints** pitture ad olio;
— **well** pozzo petrolifero; — *vt* lubrificare; **–y** *a* untuoso, oleoso

oilcloth *n* tela cerata

ointment *n* unguento

OK, okay *a* buono; — *adv* molto bene;
— *n* approvazione; — *vt (coll)* approvare

okra *n* ambretta commestibile

old *a* vecchio; — **age** vecchiaia; —
maid zitellona; **–ish** *a* vecchiotto;
–ness *n* vecchiaia, antichità

old– *(in comp)* **–fashioned** *a* antiquato,
fuori moda; **–time** *a* antico; **–timer** *n*
(coll) persona all'antica; **–world** *a*

del Vecchio Mondo

Old World Vecchio Mondo

oleomargarine *n* oleomargarina

olfactory *a* olfattivo

oligarchy *n* oligarchia

olive *n* oliva; — **branch** ramo d'olivo;
— **oil** olio d'oliva; — **tree** olivo; — *a*
verde oliva

Olympic Games giuochi olimpici

omelet *n* frittata

omen *n* presagio, augurio

ominous *a* infausto, di malaugurio

omission *n* omissione

omit *vt* omettere

omnibus *n* omnibus, autobus *m*

omnipotence *n* onnipotenza

omnipotent *a* onnipotente

omnipresence *n* onnipresenza

omnipresent *a* onnipresente

omniscience *n* onniscienza

omniscient *a* onnisciente

omniverous *a* onnivoro

on *prep* su, sopra; — *adv* avanti; **and so** —
e così via

once *adv* una volta; **all at** — ad un tratto; **at** — subito; immediatamente; —
for all una volta per tutte; — **more**
ancora una volta

oncoming *n* l'approssimarsi; — *a* prossimo, che si avvicina

one *n&a* uno, una; — **by** — uno a uno; **at**
— **stroke** d'un colpo; **–ness** *n* unicità,
unità; — *pron* l'uno, l'una; qualcuno,
qualcuna; — **another** l'un l'altro

one– *(in comp)* — **armed** *a* monco; — **eyed**
a guercio, che manca d'un occhio; —
horse *a* con un solo cavallo; *(fig)* povero;
insignificante; **–legged** *a* mutilato
d'una gamba; **–sided** *a* unilaterale,
parziale; **–time** *a* d'una volta; **–track** *a*
(coll) limitato

onerous *a* oneroso

oneself *pron* sè, se stesso, si

one-way *a* a senso unico; — **ticket** biglietto
di sola andata

onion *n* cipolla

onlooker *n* spettatore *m*; spettatrice *f*

only *a* unico, solo; — *adv* solamente, soltanto

onomatopoeia *n* onomatopeia

onrush *n* irruzione

onset *n* assalto, carica, attacco

onslaught *n* assalto, aggressione

onto *prep* sulla cima di, sopra

onus *n* onere, gravame *m*

onward *adv* in avanti

ooze *vi* filtrare; trapelare; — *n* fango;
essudazione

oozing *n* gocciolamento; filtrazione; — *a*
gocciolante; filtrante

opal *n* opale *f*; **–escent** *a* opalescente
opaque *a* opaco
open *a* aperto; franco; **–handed** *a* generoso; **–hearted** *a* franco, sincero; **—house** ricevimento informale; **— letter** lettera aperta; **–ly** *adv* apertamente; **–ness** *n* franchezza; **— question** questione indecisa; **— secret** segreto di Pulcinella *(coll)*; **— shop** officina indipendente dai sindacati; **—** *vt* aprire
open— *(in comp)* **—air** *a* all' aperto; **—eyed** *a* attento, sveglio; **—faced** *a* a viso aperto *(fig)*; **—minded** *a* spregiudicato; **—mouthed** *a* a bocca aperta
opener *n* apritore *m*, apritrice *f*; **eye —** rivelazione; **can —** apriscatole *m*
opening *n* apertura
opera *n* opera; **comic —** opera comica; **light —** operetta; **— glasses** binocolo da teatro; **— hat** gibus *m*; **–tic** *a* lirico; operistico
operate *vt&i* operare, agire, gestire, funzionare
operation *n* operazione; **–al** *a* operazionale *(mil)*
operator *n* operatore, monovratore *m*; *(com)* speculatore *m*; **telegraph —** telegrafista *m&f*; **telephone —** centralinista
opiate *n* narcotico
opine *vt&i* opinare
opinion *n* opinione *f*, parere *m*; **–ated** *a* ostinato, dogmatico; **in my —** a mio parere, secondo il mio avviso
opium *n* oppio
opossum *n* opossum *m*
opponent *n* avversario
opportune *a* opportuno; **–ness** *n* convenienza; **–ly** *adv* a proposito
opportunism *n* opportunismo
opportunist *n* opportunista *m&f*
opportunity *n* occasione
oppose *vt* opporre, avversare
opposing *a* avverso, opposto
opposite *a* opposto; **—** *prep* in faccia a; **—** *n* contrario
opposition *n* opposizione
oppress *vt* opprimere; **–ion** *n* oppressione; **–ive** *a* oppressivo; **–or** *n* oppressore *m*
opprobrious *a* obbrobrioso
opprobrium *n* obbrobrio
optic, –al *a* ottico
optician *n* ottico
optics *npl* ottica
optimism *n* ottimismo
optimist *n* ottimista *m&f*; **–ic** *a* ottimistico
optimum *n&a* ottimo
option *n* opzione; **–al** *a* facoltativo
optometry *n* optometria
opulence *n* opulenza

opulent *a* opulento
or *conj* o, ovvero, ossia; **either . . . —** o . . . o, sia . . . sia; **— else** altrimenti, oppure
oracle *n* oracolo
oral *a* orale; **–ly** *adv* oralmente
orange *n* arancia; **— tree** arancio; **—** *a (color)* arancione; **–ade** *n* aranciata
orangutan *n* orango
orate *vt&i* arringare, declamare
oration *n* orazione
orator *n* oratore *m*; **–y** *n* oratorio; **–ical** *a* oratorio
orb *n* orbe *m*
orbit *n* orbita; **—** *vt* mettere in orbita
orchard *n* frutteto
orchestra *n* orchestra; **–l** *a* orchestrale; **— seat** poltrona
orchestrate *vt* orchestrare
orchestration *n* orchestrazione
orchid *n* orchidea
ordain *vt* ordinare, decretare
ordeal *n* cimento, prova
order *n* ordine *m*; *(com)* ordinazione; **call to —** richiamare all'ordine; **in — that** affinchè, acciocchè; **in — to** allo scopo di; **make to —** fare su ordinazione; **on —** su ordinazione; **out of —** guasto; **—** *vt* ordinare
orderly *n (mil)* ordinanza, attendente *m*; *(hospital)* inserviente *m*; **—** *a* ordinato; **—** *adv* ordinatamente
ordinal *a* ordinale
ordinance *n* ordinanza
ordinary *a* ordinario; **out of the —** straordinario
ordination *n* ordinazione
ordnance *n* artiglieria
ore *n* minerale *m*
organ *n* organo; **–ic** *a* organico; **–ism** *n* organismo; **–ist** *n* organista *m&f*; **— grinder** suonatore d'organetto; **— stop** registro d'organo
organdy *n* organdis *m*
organization *n* organizzazione, complesso
organize *vt* organizzare
organizer *n* organizzatore *m*
orgy *n* orgia
orient *vt* orientare; **—** *vi* orientarsi
Orient *n* oriente *m*; **–al** *n&a* orientale *m&f*
orientation *n* orientamento
orifice *n* orifizio
origin *n* origine *f*
original *a* originale; **–ity** *n* originalità; **–ly** *adv* originalmente, originariamente
originate *vt&i* creare; derivare, originare
originator *n* originatore *m*
ornament *n* ornamento; **–al** ornamentale; **–ation** ornamentazione; **—** *vt* ornare, adornare

ornate *a* adorno, ornato
ornithologist *n* ornitologo
ornithology *n* ornitologia
orphan *n* orfano; **–age** *n* orfanotrofio
orthodontia *n* ortodontoiatria
orthodox *a* ortodosso
orthography *n* ortografia
orthopedics *npl* ortopedia
orthopedist *n* ortopedico, ortopedista *m&f*
oscillate *vi* oscillare
oscillation *n* oscillazione
osmosis *n* osmosi *f*
ossification *n* ossificazione
ossify *vt* ossificare; — *vi* ossificarsi
ostensible *a* ostensibile, apparente
ostensibly *adv* apparentemente
ostentation *n* ostentazione
ostentatious *a* ostentativo
osteomyelitis *n* osteomelite *f*
ostracism *n* ostracismo
ostracize *vt* ostracizzare
ostrich *n* struzzo
other *adv* altrimenti; — *a&pron* altro;
  each — l'un l'altro; **every** — **day** un
  giorno sì e uno no; **the** —**s** gli altri
  mpl, le altre *fpl*; **the** — **world** l'altro
  mondo
otherworldliness *n* spiritualità
otherworldly *a* spirituale
otherwise *adv* altrimenti
ottoman *n* divano
ought *n* nulla, niente *m*
ought *vi* dovere
ounce *n* oncia
our *a* nostro, nostra; *(pl)* nostri, nostre
ours *pron* il nostro, la nostra; *(pl)* i
  nostri, le nostre
ourselves *pron* ci, noi stessi
oust *vt* espellere, scacciare
out *adv* fuori; — *a* di fuori; — *n (sport)*
  fuori *m*, fallo; — **of** fuori di, fuori
  da; da, di; *(lacking)* senza; **in and** —
  a zig zag; **way** — uscita
out– *(in comp)* —**and-out** *a* da cima a fondo; —**of-date** *a* sorpassato, fuori moda;
  —**of-doors** *a&adv* all'aperto, fuori casa;
  —**of-the-way** *a* remoto, appartato;
  insolito
outbalance *vt* sbilanciare
outboard *a&adv* fuoribordo; — **motor**
  motore fuoribordo
outbid *vt (price)* superare l'offerta di
outbound *a* partente
outbreak *n* scoppio; sommossa
outbuilding *n* dipendenza, annesso
outburst *n (anger)* trasporto; esplosione
outcast *n* proscritto
outclass *vt* superare in qualità
outcome *n* risultato, esito
outcry *n* grido

outdated *a* fuori moda, sorpassato
outdistance *vt* lasciar indietro
outdo *vt* sorpassare, superare
outdoor *a* all'aperto; — **exercise** esercizi
  all'aria libera *or* all'aperto
outdoors *adv* all'aria aperta
outer *a* esterno
outfit *n* equipaggiamento; corredo; gruppo; — *vt* equipaggiare, corredare
outflank *vt* aggirare
outgoing *a* uscente; *(rail)* in partenza
outgrow *vt* superare le misure; **–th** *n*
  escrescenza; prodotto
outing *n* escursione, gita
outlandish *a* bizzarro, strano
outlast *vt* durare più di, durare oltre
outlaw *n* fuorilegge *m*, bandito; — *vt*
  proscrivere, bandire
outlay *n (com)* uscita, sborso
outlet *n* sbocco; *(com)* smercio; *(elec)*
  presa
outline *n* schizzo, abbozzo, — *vt* abbozzare; disegnare
outlive *vt* sopravvivere a
outlook *n* prospettiva
outlying *a* remoto, lontano; *(external)*
  esterno
outmaneuver *vt* sventare
outmoded *a* messo fuori moda *or* stile
outnumber *vt* sorpassare in numero
outpatient *n (not hospitalized)* malato
  esterno
outpost *n* avamposto
outpouring *n* spargimento
output *n* produzione
outrage *n* scandalo, oltraggio; — *vt*
  oltraggiare; **–ous** *a* vergognoso, intollerabile, infame
outrank *vt* superare in rango *or* grado
outright *adv* subito; completamente; — *a*
  matricolato, completo
outrun *vt* superare in corsa
outs *npl* politici non più in carica; **ins**
  and — il pro e il contro; **on the** —
  in discordia
outset *n* principio
outside *a&n* esterno; — *adv* fuori, di
  fuori; **–r** *n* estraneo
outshine *vi* scintillare, brillare; — *vt*
  ecclissare
outskirts *npl* dintorni *mpl*
outspoken *a* franco
outspread *a* steso, spiegato; cosparso
outstanding *a* eminente; in sospeso; *(debt)*
  insoluto, non pagato
outstay *vt* trattenersi più a lungo di;
  — **one's welcome** restare più del necessario
outstretched *a* steso; allungato
outward *a* esterno; **–ly** *adv* esternamente;

all'esterno

outwear *vt* consumare; *(last longer)* durare di più

outweigh *vt* superare in importanza; superare in peso

outwit *vt* superare in intelligenza

outworn *a* consumato; *(obsolete)* superato; *(trite)* banale

oval *a&n* ovale

ovary *n* ovaia

ovate *a* ovato

ovation *n* ovazione

oven *n* forno; **Dutch** — forno olandese

over *prep* sopra; — una volta ancora; — **and** — ripetutamente

overabundance *n* sovrabbondanza

overabundant *a* sovrabbondante

overact *vt&i* esagerare, eccedere; **–ive** *a* eccessivamente attivo

overage *a* troppo vecchio

over-all *a* complessivo

overalls *npl* tuta

overawe *vt* intimidire; **–d** *a* intimidito

overbearing *a* altezzoso

overboard *adv* in mare

overburden *vt* sovraccaricare

overcast *a* offuscato, oscuro; — *vt (sewing)* cucire a punto rasato; *(sky)* offuscare, oscurare; **–ing** *n (sewing)* ricucitura; *(weather)* offuscamento

overcharge *n* sovraccarico; — *vt* sovraccaricare

overcoat *n* soprabito

overcome *vt&i* sormontare, vincere, superare

overconfidence *n* eccesso di fiducia

overconfident *a* troppo fiducioso

overcooked *a* stracotto

overcrowd *vt* affollare in eccesso; **–ing** *n* ingombro

overdeveloped *a* eccessivamente sviluppato

overdo *vt* fare troppo; esagerare; — *vi* strafare

overdone *a* esagerato; *(food)* stracotto

overdose *n* dose eccessiva

overdraft *n (com)* assegno eccedente il deposito; *(mech)* corrente d'aria sul fuoco

overdraw *vt* eccedere

overdrawn *a* esagerato; troppo teso

overdrive *n (auto)* marcia sovramoltiplicata

overdue *a* scaduto, moroso

overeat *vt* mangiare troppo

overestimate *vt* sovrastimare, sopravalutare

overexcite *vt* sovreccitare; **–ment** *n* sovreccitazione

overexertion *n* sforzo eccessivo

overexpose *vt* esporre troppo

overexposure *n* sovresposizione

overfatigue *n* fatica eccessiva

overfeed *vt* rimpinzare; — *vi* rimpinzarsi

overfill *vt* sovraccaricare; — *vi* sovraccaricarsi

overflow *n* inondazione, eccedenza; — *vi* traboccare; — *vt* inondare; **–ing** *a* inondante

overgrown *a* cresciuto eccessivamente; coperto completamente

overgrowth *n* cresciuta eccessiva

overhang *vt* soprastare a; — *vi* soprastare; pendere; **–ing** *a* soprasospeso; *(menacing)* minacciante

overhaul *vt* ispezionare, esaminare

overhead *a* di sopra; — *adv* in alto; — *n (com)* spese generali

overhear *vt* sorprendere, udire involontariamente

overheat *vt* surriscaldare

overindulgence *n* intemperanza

overindulgent *a* intemperante; troppo indulgente

overjoyed *a* pieno d'allegria, colmo di gioia

overland *a* terrestre; — *a&adv* per terra, via terra

overlap *vt* sovrappore; — *vi* sovrapporsi; **–ing** *a* sovrapponente

overload *n* sovraccarico; — *vt* sovraccaricare

overlook *vt* passar sopra a, non far caso di; *(position)* dare su

overnight *adv* durante la notte; dall'oggi al domani; — *a* notturno, di una notte

overpass *n* soprappassaggio

overpay *vt* pagare troppo; **–ment** *n* pagamento eccessivo

overpopulated *a* sovrapopolato

overpower *vt* sopraffare; **–ing** *a* prepotente, soggiogante

overproduction *n* sovraproduzione

overrate *vt* sopravvalutare

overreach *vt* oltrepassare; — *vi* andar troppo oltre; — **oneself** strafare

overripe *a* troppo maturo

overrule *vt&i* dominare; *(prevail)* prevalere

overruling *n* prevalenza, dominazione; — *a* prevalente, dominante

overrun *vt* infestare, invadere

overseas *adv* oltremare; — *a* d'oltremare

oversee *vt* sopraintendere; **–r** *n* sopraintendente *m*

overshadow *vt* ombreggiare; *(eclipse)* eclissare

overshoes *npl* soprascarpe, galosce *fpl*

overshoot *vt* oltrepassare

oversight *n* svista, errore *m*

oversleep vi dormire fino a tardi
overstatement n esagerazione
overstep vt oltrepassare
oversupply n sovrabbondanza
overt a visibile, pubblico, manifesto
overtake vt raggiungere
overtax vt soprattassare
overthrow n disfatta; — vt rovesciare
overtime n ore straordinarie
overtire vt sopraffaticare, strapazzare
overtone n superfrequenza sonica
overture n proposta; (mus) preludio
overturn vt capovolgere; — vi capovolgersi
overvalue vt sopravvalutare
overweight n eccesso di peso; — a troppo
  ● pesante
overwhelm vt sopraffare, opprimere; **-ing**
  a schiacciante
overwork vt far lavorare troppo; — vi

lavorare troppo; — n eccesso di lavoro
overwrought a sovreccitato
overzealous a troppo zelante
oviparous a oviparo
ovum n uovo
owe vt dovere; — vi essere in debito
owing a dovuto; — **to** a causa di
own a proprio; — vt possedere; — **up to**
  confessare
owner n proprietario; **-ship** n possidenza
ox n bue m; **-en** npl buoi mpl
oxalic a ossalico
oxidation n ossidazione
oxide n ossido
oxidize vt ossidare; — vi ossidarsi
oxiacetylene a ossiacetilenico
oxygen n ossigeno; — **tent** campana
  d'ossigeno
oyster n ostrica
ozone n ozono

P

pace n passo; — vt misurare a passi;
  percorrere; — vi camminare; **keep —
  with** mantenersi al passo con
pachyderm n pachiderma m
pacific a pacifico
pacifier n pacificatore m
pacifism n pacifismo
pacifist n pacifista m&f
pacify vt placare, calmare
pacifying n pacificazione; — a pacificatore
pack n pacchetto; pacco; (cards) mazzo di
  carte; — **animal** animale da soma; —
  horse cavallo da basto or da soma;
  -er n imballatore m, imballatrice f
pack vt impaccare; — **one's bags** far le
  valigie; — **off** scacciare, licenziare;
  — **up** impaccare, imballare; far fagotto
  (fig)
package n involto, pacco; — vt impacchettare; mettere in cassa (or involucro)
packing n imballaggio; (mech) guarnizione
packsaddle n basto
pact n patto
pad n cuscinetto; tampone m; (paper)
  blocco; — vt imbottire; — vi viaggiare
  a piedi
padding n imbottitura; materiale per
  imbottire
paddle vi pagaiare; — vt (coll) sculacciare; — n pagaia; — **steamer** nave a ruote; — **wheel** ruota a pale
paddock n passeggiatoio
padlock n lucchetto; — vt allucchettare
pagan n&a pagano; **-ism** n paganismo
page n (book) pagina; (lefthand) verso;

(righthand) recto; (boy) paggio; (messenger) fattorino (coll); — vt (print)
numerare le pagine, impaginare; (call)
chiamare a voce alta
pageant n corteo storico, spettacolo; **-ry**
  n corteo, parata, spettacolo fastoso
pagination n impaginazione
pail n secchio, secchia
pain n dolore m; pena; **be in —** soffrire;
  take —s affannarsi, darsi da fare; — vt
  far male a, affliggere, far soffrire;
  -ful a penoso, doloroso
painstaking a accurato, diligente
paint n pittura; colore m; vernice f;
  — vt dipingere; **-er** n pittore m;
  (house) verniciatore m; imbianchino;
  -ing n pittura, quadro
paintbrush n pennello
pair n paio, coppia; — vt accoppiare;
  — **off** accoppiarsi, mettersi per due
pajamas npl pigiama m
pal n (coll) compagno, amicone m
palace n palazzo
paladin n paladino
palatable a saporito
palate n palato
palatial a grandioso
palatinate n palatinato
palatine n&a palatino
pale a pallido; — vt far impallidire; — vi
  impallidire; — n palo; confine m; **beyond the —** impossibile; smoderato;
  -ness n pallore m
paleography n paleografia
paleolithic a paleolitico
paleontologist n paleontologo

paleontology n paleontologia
Palestine Palestina
palette n tavolozza; — **knife** spatoletta di pittore
palisade n palizzata
pall n drappo funebre; coltre f; — vi diventare insipido; — vt rendere insipido; (fig) deprimere; **–bearer** n chi regge i cordoni in un funerale
pallet n giaciglio
palliate vt palliare
palliative n&a palliativo
pallid a pallido
pallor n pallore m
palm n (anat) palmo; (bot) palma; **–ist** n chiromante m&f; — **off** imporre con la frode
Palm Sunday Domenica delle Palme
palpitate vi palpitare
palpitation n palpitazione
palsied a paralizzato
palsy n paralisi f; — vt paralizzare
paltry a piccolo; vile, meschino
pamper vt viziare, vezzeggiare
pamphlet n opuscolo; **–eer** n scrittore di opuscoli
pan n padella; — **out** aver successo; — **someone** (coll) criticare qualcuno
panacea n panacea
Pan-American a panamericano
pancake n frittella
pancreas n pancreas m
pancreatic a pancreatico
pandemonium n pandemonio
pander n mezzano, ruffiano; — vi fare il mezzano
pane n vetro; pannello
panegyric n panegirico
panel n pannello; (law) giuria; **jury —** lista dei giurati; — vt decorare con pannelli; **–ing** n lavoro a pannelli; pannelli mpl
pang n trafitta; dolore m
panic n panico; — vt procurare panico; — vi essere preso da panico; **–ky** a timido, pauroso, atterrito
panoply n panoplia
panorama n panorama
panoramic a panoramico
pansy n viola del pensiero
pant vi ansare, palpitare; — n anelito, palpito
panties npl mutandine fpl
pantheism n panteismo
pantheist n panteista m
pantheistic a panteistico
Pantheon n Panteon m
panther n pantera
pantograph n pantografo
pantomime n pantomima

pantomimist n pantomimo
pantry n dispensa
pants npl calzoni mpl
papacy n papato
papal a papale
paper n carta; documento; **blotting —** carta assorbente; **carbon —** carta carbone; — **clip** fermacarte m; — **hanger** tappezziere in carta; — **knife** tagliacarte m; **–weight** fermacarte m; — a cartaceo; — vt (walls) tappezzare con carta
paperboy n strillone m
papier-mâché n cartapesta
papist n papista m&f
paprika n paprica
papyrus n papiro
par n pari f; **at —** alla pari
parable n parabola
parabola n (math) parabola
parabolic a parabolico
parachute n paracadute m; — vt paracadutare; — vi lanciarsi con il paracadute
parachutist n paracadutista m&f
parade n sfilata; (mil) parata; — vt ostentare; — vi sfilare in parata
paradise n paradiso
paradox n paradosso
paradoxical a paradossale
paraffin n paraffina
paragon n esempio, modello
paragraph n paragrafo; — vt paragrafare
parallel a&n parallelo; — vt parallelizzare; **be — with** essere in parallelo con
parallelogram n parallelogramma m
paralogism n paralogismo
paralysis n paralisi f
paralytic a&n paralitico
paralyze vt paralizzare
paramount a supremo
paramour n amante m&f
paranoia n paranoia
paranoiac n paranoico
parapet n parapetto
paraphernalia npl accessori mpl
paraphrase n parafrasi f; — vt parafrasare; — vi fare una parafrasi
paraplegia n (med) paraplegia
parasite n parassita m
parasitic a parassitico
parasol n parasole m
parataxis n paratassi f
paratrooper n (mil) paracadutista m
paratroops npl corpo di paracadutisti
parboil vt far bollire a mezzo
parcel n pacchetto; — **post** pacco postale; — vt dividere in parti, spartire; impacchettare

parch *vt* arrostire; *(dry)* inaridire; — *vi* arrostirsi; inaridirsi
parchment *n* pergamena
pardon *n* perdono; — *vt* perdonare; **-able** *a* perdonabile
pare *vt* pelare; sbucciare
paregoric *n&a (med)* paregorico
parent *n* genitore *m*, genitrice *f*; — *a* madre; natale; nativo; **-age** *n* discendenza, origine *f*, generazione; **-hood** *n* paternità, maternità; genitura; **-s** *npl* genitori *mpl*
parental *a* dei genitori
parenthesis *n* parentesi *f*
parenthetical *a* fra parentisi, parentetico
pariah *n* paria *m&f*
paring *n (peeling)* buccia; sbucciatura; — **knife** trincetto, spacchino
Paris Parigi
parish *n* parrocchia; — *a* parrocchiale; **-ioner** *n* parrocchiano
parity *n* parità
park *n* giardino pubblico, parco; — *vt* parcheggiare
parking *n* parcheggio, posteggio; — **meter** parchimetro; **no** — vietata la sosta *(or* il parcheggio)
parlance *n* linguaggio; il parlare; **in common** — nel linguaggio corrente
parley *n* trattattiva parlamentare; — *vi* parlamentare
parliament *n* parlamento; **-arian** *n* parlamentare *m*
parliamentary *a* parlamentare
parlor *n* salotto; **beauty** — salone di bellezza
Parnassian *a&n* parnassiano
parochial *a* parrocchiale
parody *n* parodia; — *vt* parodiare, imitare
parole *n (law)* condizionale *f*, libertà provvisoria; — *vt* concedere la libertà provvisoria
paroxysm *n* parossismo
parquet *n* parchetto, parchè *m*; — *vt* pavimentare a parchè
parrot *n* pappagallo
parry *vt* evitare, parare
parse *vt (gram)* analizzare
parsley *n* prezzemolo
parsnip *n* pastinaca
parson *n* parroco; **-age** *n* canonica
part *n* parte *f*; *(hair)* riga, scriminatura; *(spare)* pezzo di ricambio; *(speech)* parte del discorso; *(theat)* parte *f*; — *a* parziale; — *adv* in parte; **for my** — per parte mia; **for the most** — per la maggior parte; **from all -s** da ogni lato; **in** — in parte, **take** — in participare a; **take someone's** — prender la parte di qualcuno; **-s** *npl* parti *fpl*; regione; abilità

part *vt* separare; — *vi* separarsi; — **from, with** separarsi da
partake *vi* partecipare, condividere
partial *a* parziale; **-ity** *n* parzialità
participant *n* partecipante *m&f*
participate *vt&i* partecipare
participation *n* partecipazione
participator *n* partecipante *m&f*
participial *a (gram)* participiale
participle *n (gram)* participio
particle *n* particella; granello
particular *n&a* particolare *m*; **-ity** *n* particolarità; **-ization** *n* particolarizzazione; **-ize** *vt* particolareggiare; **-ly** *adv* particolarmente
parting *n* separazione
partisan *n&a* partigiano
partition *n* partizione; tramezzo; divisorio; — *vt* dividere in parti
partitive *a (gram)* partitivo
partly *adv* in parte
partner *n* socio; **-ship** *n* società
party *n* festa; partito; **be a** — **to** essere complice in; — **line** *(pol)* partito di linea; *(telephone)* ramificazione telefonica
parvenu *n* nuovo ricco, villano rifatto
pass *vi* passare; — *vt* sorpassare; — **away** morire; — **by** passar presso; *(omit)* omettere; — **on** passar oltre; — **out** *(exit)* uscire; *(distribute)* distribuire; *(faint sl)* perdere i sensi; — **over** omettere, tralasciare
pass *n* passo, valico; *(mountain)* gola; *(permit)* permesso; **-able** *a* passabile; attraversabile; **-ive** *a* passivo
passage, -way *n* passaggio
passbook *n* libretto di banca
passenger *n* passeggero
passer-by *n* passante *m*
passing *a* passeggero; — *n (death)* decesso; **in** — fra parentesi
passion *n* passione; **-ate** *a* ardente
passkey *n* chiave comune
Passover *n* Pasqua ebrea
passport *n* passaporto
password *n* parola d'ordine
past *n&a* passato; — **master** maestro, esperto; — **participle** *(gram)* participio passato; — **perfect** *(gram)* passato anteriore; — *prep* dopo, oltre
paste *n* colla; *(food)* pasta; — *vt* incollare
pasteboard *n* cartone *m*
pasteurization *n* pastorizzazione
pasteurize *vt* pastorizzare
pastime *n* passatempo
pastor *n* pastore *m*; **-al** *n&a* pastorale

pastry *n* pasticceria; — **cook** pasticciere *m*; — **shop** pasticceria
pasture *n* pascolo; — *vt&i* pascolare
pasty *a* pastoso
pat *n* colpetto; *(butter)* pezzo; — *a* apposito; opportuno; — *vt* dare un colpetto; accarezzare; **stand** — impuntarsi *(fig)*
patch *n* toppa, pezza; — *vt* rattoppare
patchwork *n* raffazzonatura, rappezzatura
pate *n* testa
patella *n (zool)* patella; rotula
paten *n* disco; *(eccl)* patena
patent *n* brevetto; — **leather** coppale *m*; — *vt* brevettare
patent *a* patente, evidente, ovvio
paternal *a* paterno; **-ism** *n* paternalismo; **-istic** *a* paternalistico
paternity *n* paternità
path *n* sentiero; *(track)* corso, traiettoria
pathetic *a* patetico
pathfinder *n* esploratore *m*
pathological *a* patologico
pathology *n* patologia
pathos *n* patos *m*
pathway *n* sentiero, via
patience *n* pazienza; **loose** — impazientirsi
patient *n&a* paziente *m&f*
patina *n* patina
patriarch *n* patriarca *m*
patrician *n&a* patrizio
patricide *n* parricida *m&f*; *(crime)* parricidio
patrimony *n* patrimonio
patriot *n* patriotta *m*; **-ic** *a* patriottico
patriotism *n* patriottismo
patrol *n* pattuglia; ronda; — *vt* perlustrare
patron *n* patrono, mecenate *m*; *(customer)* cliente *m*
patronize *vt* frequentare; patrocinare; trattare con fare condiscendente
patter *n* picchiettio; — *vt (rain)* picchiettare
pattern *n* disegno; modello; — *vt* modellare
paunch *n* pancia; **-y** *a* panciuto
pauper *n* indigente *m&f*
pause *n* pausa; — *vi* far pausa
pave *vt* pavimentare; — **the way** *(fig)* preparare il cammino *(fig)*
pavement *n* lastricato
pavilion *n* padiglione *m*
paving *n* pavimento; pavimentazione
paw *n* zampa; — *vt* colpire, raspare con le zampe, maneggiare
pawl *n (mech)* dente d'arresto
pawn *n* pegno; *(chess)* pedina; **-broker** *n* prestatore su pegno; **-shop** *n* Monte di Pietà, casa di pegno; — **ticket** polizza di pegno; — *vt* impegnare, dare in pegno
pay *n* paga, salario; **-able** *a* pagabile; **-day** *n* giorno di paga; **-ee** *n* beneficiario; **-er** *n* pagatore *m*, pagatrice *f*; **-ment** *n* pagamento; — **roll** foglio-paga; — *vt* pagare; — **back** restituire; rimborsare; — **no attention** non prestare attenzione; — **off** ammortizzare; liquidare; — **up** pagare completamente, saldare
pay-off *n (coll)* resa dei conti; cosa inaspettata
pea *n* pisello; **-shooter** *n* cerbottana; — **soup** passata di piselli
peace pace *f*; — **offering** sacrifizio propiziatorio; **make** — **with** rappacificarsi con; **-ably** *adv* pacificamente; **-ful** *a* pacifico, calmo; **-maker** *n* pacificatore *m*
peach *n* pesca; *(tree)* pesco
peacock *n* pavone *m*
peak *n* picco, cima, vetta; *(zenith)* apogeo; **-ed** *a* a punta, appuntito; *(drawn)* scarno
peal *n* scampanio; *(laughter)* risata squillante; *(thunder)* scoppio; — *vi* sonare; scampanare; — *vt* far risonare
peanut *n* arachide *f*
pear *n* pera; *(tree)* pero
pearl *n* perla; — **diver** pescatore di perle; — **oyster** ostrica perlifera
peasant *n* contadino
peasantry *n* contadini *mpl*
peat *n* torba
pebble *n* ciottolo
pebbly *a* ciottoloso
peccadillo *n* peccatuccio
pecan *n* noce americana; *(tree)* noce americano
peck *n* beccata; *(measure)* quantità di due galloni; — *vt&i* beccare; *(food)* sbocconcellare; — **at** *(criticize)* biasimare; mangiare delicatamente
pectoral *a* pettorale
peculiar *a* strano; **-ity** *n* peculiarità; caratteristica
pedagogical *a* pedagogico
pedagogue *n* pedagogo
pedagogy *n* pedagogia
pedal *n* pedale *m*; — *vt* pedalare
pedant *n* pedante *m*
pedantic *a* pedante
pedantry *n* pedanteria
peddle *vt* vendere in piccole quantità; — *vi* fare il venditore ambulante; **-r** *n* venditore ambulante
pedestal *n* piedestallo
pedestrian *n* pedone *m*
pediatrician *n* pediatra *m*
pedicure *n* callista *m&f*

pedigree *n* genealogia
pediment *n* frontone *m*
pedometer *n* pedometro; passimetro
peek *n* sguardo fugace; — *vi* far capolino
peel *vt* pelare, sbucciare; — *n* buccia
peep *vi (sound)* pigolare; *(look at)* sbirciare, spiare; — *n (sound)* pigolio; occhiata; **-hole** *n* buco; *(opening)* spiraglio; *(slit)* fessura
peer *n* pari *m*; — *vi* spuntare; scuriosare; **-age** *n (pol)* Pari *mpl*; aristocrazia; almanacco nobiliare; **-less** *a* incomparabile
peevish *a* irritabile; stizzoso; **-ness** *n* irritabilità
peg *n* caviglia; — *vt (fasten)* incavicchiare, incavigliare; *(com)* stabilizzare
pell-mell *adv* alla rinfusa; — *a* disordinato
pelt *n* colpo; velocità; *(animal)* pelliccia; *(rain)* scroscio; — *vt* lanciare, scagliare
pelting *n (of objects)* assalto; — *a (rain)* furioso
pelvic *a* pelvico
pelvis *n* pelvi *f*
pen *n* recinto; *(writing)* penna; — **name** pseudonimo d'arte; **ballpoint** — penna a sfera; **-holder** *n* portapenna *m*; — *vt* scrivere a penna; *(enclose)* rinchiudere
penal *a* penale; **-ty** *n* penalità; pena, punizione; **-ize** *vt* penalizzare
penance *n* penitenza
pencil *n* matita, lapis *m*
pendant *n&a* pendente *m*
pending *a* pendente; — *prep* durante; in attesa di
pendulum *n* pendolo
penetrate *vt* penetrare
penetrating *a* penetrante
penetration *n* penetrazione; intuizione
penicillin *n* penicillina
peninsula *n* penisola
peninsular *a* peninsulare
penis *n* pene *m*
penitence *n* penitenza
penitent *a&n* penitente *m*
penitentiary *n* penitenziario
penknife *n* temperino
penmanship *n* calligrafia
pennant *n* fiamma, stendardo, gagliardetto
penniless *a* senza un soldo
penny *n* centesimo di dollaro; soldo
pension *n* pensione *f*; — *vt* pensionare
pensioner *n* pensionato
pensive *a* pensoso
pentagon *n* pentagono; **-al** *a* pentagonale
pentameter *n* pentametro
penthouse *n* tettoia
pent-up *a* confinato

penumbra *n* penombra
penurious *a* povero, bisognoso; avaro
penury *n* penuria
people *n* popolo; gente *f*; — *vt* popolare
pep *n (sl)* energia, vigore *m*
pepper *n* pepe *m*; peperone *m*; — *vt* pepare; **-corn** *n* granello di pepe; **-mint** *n* menta peperina; **-y** *a* pepato
pepsin *n* pepsina
peptic *a* peptico
per *prep* per; — **capita** a testa
perambulate *vi* passeggiare, vagare
perambulatory *a* vagante, perambulatorio
perceivable *a* percettibile
perceive *vt* osservare, accorgersi, percepire
percent *n* per cento; **-age** *n* percentuale *f*
perceptibility *n* percettibilità
perception *n* percezione
perceptive *a* percettivo
perch *n* posatoio; *(fish)* pesce persico; — *vi* posarsi
perchance *adv* per caso
percolate *vt&i* filtrare
percolator *n* filtro, colino
percussion *n* percussione; — **cap** capsula di percussione
perdition *n* perdizione
peremptory *a* perentorio
perennial *a* perenne; — *n* pianta perenne
perfect *a* perfetto
perfect *vt* perfezionare
perfectibility *n* perfezionabilità
perfectible *a* perfettibile
perfection *n* perfezione
perfidious *a* perfido
perfidy *n* perfidia
perforate *vt* perforare
perforation *n* perforazione
perforce *adv* per forza
perform *vt* fare, eseguire; *(theat)* rappresentare, recitare
performance *n* esecuzione; rappresentazione
performer *n* artista *m&f*; esecutore *m*; *(theat)* attore *m*, attrice *f*
perfume *n* profumo; — *vt* profumare
perfumery *n* profumeria
perfunctory *a* negligente, superficiale, formale
perhaps *adv* forse
pericardium *n* pericardio
perigee *n* perigeo
peril *n* pericolo; **-ous** *a* rischioso, pericoloso; — *vt* esporre a pericolo; **be in** — pericolare
perimeter *n* perimetro
period *n* periodo; epoca; *(gram)* punto
periodic *a* periodico
periodical *n* periodico

peripatetic *n&a* peripatetico
peripheral *a* periferico
periphery *n* periferia
periphrasis *n* perifrasi *f*
periscope *n* periscopio
perish *vi* perire; **–able** *a* deperibile
peristalsis *n* peristalsi *f*
peristaltic *a* peristaltico
peritoneum *n* peritoneo
peritonitis *n* peritonite *f*
perjure *vt* spergiurare
perjurer *n* spergiuratore *m*
perjury *n* giuramento falso
perky *a* vivace
permanence *n* permanenza
permanent *a* permanente; **— wave** ondulazione permanente, permanente *f*; **–ly** *adv* permanentemente
permanganate *n* permanganato
permeability *n* permeabilità
permeable *a* permeabile
permeate *vt* permeare
permeation *n* permeazione
permissible *a* permissibile
permission *n* permesso
permissive *a* permissivo, indulgente
permit *n* permesso
permit *vt&i* permettere; lasciare
permutation *n* permuta
pernicious *a* pernicioso
peroration *n* perorazione
peroxide *n* acqua ossigenata
perpendicular *n&a* perpendicolare *f*
perpetrate *vt* perpetrare
perpetration *n* perpetrazione
perpetrator *n* perpetratore *m*
perpetual *a* perpetuo
perpetuate *vt* perpetuare
perpetuation *n* perpetuazione
perplex *vt* imbarazzare, rendere perplesso; **–ing** *a* imbarazzante; **–ity** *n* perplessità
perquisite *n* incerto, mancia; *(right)* requisito
persecute *vt* perseguitare
persecution *n* persecuzione
persecutor *n* persecutore *m*
perseverance *n* perseveranza
persevere *vi* perseverare
persevering *a* perseverante
Persian *a&n* persiano
persiflage *n* frivolezza
persist *vi* persistere; **–ence** *n* persistenza; **–ent** *a* persistente
person *n* persona; **–able** *a* ben fatto, bello; **–age** *n* personaggio; **–al** *a* personale; **–ality** *n* personalità; **–ification** *n* personificazione; **–ify** *vt* personificare
personnel *n* personale *m*
perspective *n* prospettiva

perspicacity *n* perspicacia
perspiration *n* sudore *m*
perspire *vi* traspirare, sudare
persuade *vt* persuadere
persuasion *n* persuasione
persuasive *a* persuasivo
pert *a* impertinente
pertain *vi* riguardare, appartenere; riferirsi a
pertinacious *a* pertinace
pertinacity *n* pertinacia
pertinence *n* pertinenza
pertinent *a* pertinente
perturb *vt* turbare, perturbare; **–ation** *n* perturbazione, perturbamento
Peru Perù
perusal *n* lettura accurata
peruse *vt* leggere attentamente
pervade *vt* pervadere, penetrare
pervasion *n* penetrazione
pervasive *a* penetrante
perverse *a* perverso
perversion *n* perversione
perversity *n* perversità
pervert *vt* depravare, pervertire; **— n** pervertito; **–er** *n* pervertitore *m*
pervious *a* permeabile
pessimism *n* pessimismo
pessimist *n* pessimista *m&f*; **–ic** *a* pessimistico
pest *n* parassita *m*; *(nuisance)* seccatura; **–er** *vt* infastidire
pestilence *n* pestilenza
pestilent *a* pestilente; noioso
pestle *n* pestello
pet *n* favorito, beniamino; **— vt** vezzeggiare; **— name** vezzeggiativo
petal *n* petalo
petition *n* petizione, preghiera; **— vt** rivolgere un'istanza; **–er** *n* richiedente *m*
petrel *n* procellaria
petrify *vt* pietrificare; **— vi** pietrificarsi
petroleum *n* petrolio; **— a** a petrolio, di petrolio
petticoat *n* sottana
pettifog *vi* fare l'azzeccagarbugli; **–ger** *n* azzeccagarbugli *m*; **–ging** *n* cavilli *mpl*
pettiness *n* piccolezza
petty *a* meschino; **— cash** piccola cassa; **— larceny** furterello, piccolo furto; **— officer** sottufficiale di marina
petulance *n* petulanza
petulant *a* petulante
pew *n* panca di chiesa
pewter *a* di peltro; **— n** peltro
phagocyte *n* fagocito
phalanx *n* falange *f*
phallic *a* fallico
phallus *n* fallo
phantom *n* fantasma *m*

Pharaoh n Faraone m
pharisaic a farisaico
Pharisee n Fariseo m
pharmaceutical a farmaceutico
pharmaceutics npl farmaceutica
pharmacist n farmacista m
pharmacologist n farmacologo
pharmacology n farmacologia
pharmacopoeia n farmacopea
pharmacy n farmacia
pharynx n faringe f
phase n aspetto, fase f
pheasant n fagiano
phenol n fenolo
phenomenal a fenomenale
phenomenon n fenomeno
Philadelphia Filadelfia
philander vi amoreggiare; **-er** n donnaiuolo
philanthropic a filantropico
philanthropist n filantropo
philanthropy n filantropia
philatelic a filatelico
philatelist n filatelico
philately n filatelia
philharmonic a filarmonico
Philippines Filippine
philological a filologico
philologist n filologo
philology n filologia
philosopher n filosofo
philosophize vi filosofare
philosophy n filosofia
phlegm n flemma; muco
phlegmatic a flemmatico
phobia n fobia
phoenix n fenice f
phone n (coll) telefono; — vt&i telefonare
phonetic a fonetico; **-s** npl fonetica
phonic a fonico
phonograph n grammofono, fonografo
phosphate n fosfato
phosphite n fosfito
phosphorescence n fosforescenza
phosphorescent a fosforescente
phosphoric a fosforico
phosphorous a fosforoso
phosphorus n fosforo
photodynamics npl fotodinamica
photoelectric a fotoelettrico; — **cell** cellula
  fotoelettrica
photoengrave vt fotoincidere
photoengraving n fotoincisione
photogenic a fotogenico
photograph n fotografia; **-er** n fotografo;
  -ic a fotografico; **-y** n fotografia; — vt
  fotografare
photogravure n fotoincisione
photometer n fotometro
photomicrograph n microfoto f
photostat n fotostato; macchina fotosta-

tica; — vt fare una copia fotostatica di
photosynthesis n fotosintesi f
phrase n frase f; — vt formulare; (mus)
  fraseggiare
phraseology n fraseologia
phrenetic a frenetico
phrenology n frenologia
physic n purgante m
physical a fisico
physician n medico
physicist n fisico
physics npl fisica; **solid state** — elettrofisica degli stati solidi
physiognomy n fisonomia
physiological a fisiologico
physiologist n fisiologo
physiology n fisiologia
physiotherapy n fisioterapia
physique n fisico
pianist n pianista m&f
piano n pianoforte m; **baby grand** —
  pianino; **grand** — pianoforte a coda;
  upright — pianoforte verticale; —
  a&adv piano
pica n (print) pica
picayune a meschino
piccolo n ottavino
pick n piccone m; scelta; — vt scegliere; cogliere; — **out** scegliere; — **up**
  (tidy) raccogliere, rassetare
pickax n piccone m
picket n (stake) stacca, picchetto; —
  fence palizzata; — vt picchettare
pickle n sottaceto; (coll) imbarazzo; **in**
  a — nei pasticci; — vt mettere sotto
  aceto
picklock n grimaldello
pickpocket n borsaiuolo
pickup n (auto) furgoncino; (speed) accelerazione; (phonograph) pickup, diaframma m; (coll) conoscenza casuale
picnic n merenda in campagna
pictorial a pittorico, illustrato; — n
  giornale illustrato
picture n quadro; ritratto; — vt dipingere;
  descrivere
picturesque a pittoresco
piddling a insignificante
pie n torta
piebald a pezzato; (fig) misto, eterogeneo
piece n pezzo; — **of one's mind** rimprovero; — **rate** (com) compenso a cottimo;
  — vt congiungere; rappezzare
piecemeal a separato; a pezzi; — adv
  gradatamente; separatamente; pezzo a
  pezzo
piecework n lavoro a cottimo
pied a pezzato; variopinto
Piedmont Piemonte; **-ese** a&n piemontese m&f

pier n molo

pierce vt&i perforare

piercing a pungente, penetrante

piety n pietà, devozione

pig n porco, maiale m; — **iron** ghisa; **-headed** a (fig) ostinato

pigeon n piccione m, colombo; **clay** — piccione artificiale; **homing** — piccione viaggiatore

pigeon- (in comp) **-breasted** a di petto a sterno convesso; dal petto di gallina (fig); **-toed** a con gli alluci in dentro

pigeonhole n nicchia; casella; — vt depositare in casellario; (delay) posporre

piggish a porcino; ghiottone; sporco

piggyback adv addosso; a spalle

pigment n pigmento; **-ation** n pigmentazione

pigpen n porcile m

pigtail n codino; **-s** npl (hair) trecce fpl

pike n picca; (fish) luccio; **-r** n giocatore timido

pilaster n (arch) pilastro

pile n mucchio; (elec) pila; (cloth) pelo; — vt ammucchiare

piles npl (med) emorroidi mpl

pilfer vt&i rubacchiare; **-er** n ladruncolo; **-ing** n rubacchiamento

pilgrim n pellegrino; **-age** n pellegrinaggio

pill n pillola; **-box** scatoletta per le pillole; (mil) fortino di cemento

pillar n pilastro, colonna

pillory n gogna; — vt mettere alla gogna

pillow n cuscino; **-case** n federa; — vt adagiare su cuscini

pilot n pilota m; — **light** fiammella d'alimentazione; lampada pilota; — vt pilotare, guidare

pimiento n pimento di Giamaica

pimple n pustoletta

pimply a foruncoloso, pustoloso

pin n spilla, spillo; — **money** denaro dato alla moglie per le spese personali; **on -s and needles** sulle spine, impacciato; — vt fissare, attaccare con uno spillo

pinafore n grembiulino

pincers npl pinze fpl, tenaglie fpl

pinch vt pizzicare; — n (nip) pizzicotto; (quantity) presa; (need) bisogno

pinch-hit vi (baseball) sostituire un giuocatore; — **for** sostituire in emergenza

pinch-hitter n sostituto; (baseball) giuocatore sostituto

pincushion n portaspilli m

pine n pino; — vi languire; **to — for** spasimare per

pineapple n ananasso m; — a d'ananasso

ping-pong n tennis da tavola

pink a color rosa; — **of condition** con-

dizione ideale

pinnacle n pinnacolo; apogeo

pinion, vt immobilizzare, inceppare

pinpoint vt precisare; localizzare; — n punta di spillo

pinprick n puntata di spillo

pint n pinta

pinwheel n girandola

pioneer n pioniere m; — vt preparare, aprire; — vi fare il pioniere

pious a devoto, pio

pipe n pipa; tubo; (mus) flauto; **-line** n tubatura; **-r** n flautista m

piping n tubazione; suono di zampogna (or cornamusa); (food) decorazione; (clothing) orlo ricamato; — **hot** (liquid) bollente, caldo caldo

piquancy n piccante m

piquant a piccante

pique n picca; — vt piccare; — **oneself on** piccarsi di

piracy n pirateria; (lit) plagio

pirate n pirata m; — vi pirateggiare, corseggiare; — vt plagiare, saccheggiare

pirouette n piroetta; — vi piroettare

pistachio n pistacchio

pistol n pistola

piston n pistone m; — **rod** stelo di stantuffo

pit n buca, fossa; cava; (nut) nocciolo; — vt (into ground) interrare; (mark) marcare; (competition) mettere in gara

pitch n punto, grado; (mus) tono; (min) pece f; — **pipe** diapason da fiato; — vt buttare, gettare; — vi (naut) beccheggiare; **to — in** lavorare alacremente

pitch- (in comp) **-black** a nerissimo; **-dark** a oscuro, nero come la pece

pitchblende n pechblenda

pitcher n brocca; **baseball** — lanciatore m

pitchfork n forca; forcone m

piteous a pietoso; commovente

pitfall n trappola; inganno

pith n forza; essenza; (anat, bot) midollo; **-y** a (marrow) midolloso; (essence) essenziale, vigoroso

pitiable a compassionevole; pietoso; degno di pietà

pitiful a pietoso

pitiless a spietato, crudele; incompassionevole

pittance n (portion) porzioncina; (charity) elemosina

pitted a butterato

pitter-patter n scalpiccio, picchiettio; — vi scalpicciare, picchiettare

pituitary a pituitario

pity n pietà, compassione; — vt compiangere

pivot n perno; — vt imperniare; — vi

imperniarsi
pixie *n* fata
placard *n* cartellone *m*
placate *vt* placare
place *n* posto, luogo; **in —** **of** in luogo di; al posto di; invece; **out of —** inopportuno; fuori luogo; fuori posto; **—** *vi (racing)* piazzare; **—** *vt* collocare; **take —** succedere; aver luogo; **–ment** *n* collocamento
placenta *n* placenta
plagiarism *n* plagio
plagiarist *n* plagiario
plagiarize *vt* plagiare
plague *n* peste *f*; **—** *vt* tormentare; appestare
plaid *n* mantello scozzese; **—** *a (design)* scozzese
plain *n* pianura; **—** *a* semplice; ovvio; evidente; **–ly** *adv* semplicemente; **–ness** *n* evidenza; semplicità; assenza di bellezza
plainsman *n* abitante della pianura
plain-spoken *a* schietto, franco
plaintiff *n* attore *m*, parte civile
plaintive *a* lamentoso, triste
plan *n* piano; progetto; **—** *vt* progettare; pianificare
plane *n* pialla; *(avi)* aeroplano; *(level)* piano; **—** *vt* piallare; spianare
planet *n* pianeta *m*; **–ary** *a* planetario, di pianeta; **–arium** *n* planetario
plank *n* tavola; *(pol)* caposaldo; **—** *vt* intavolare; *(coll)* pagare; **–ing** *n* impalcatura, intavolatura
plant *n* pianta; *(com)* stabilimento; **—** *vt* piantare, impiantare; fissare; **–er** *n* piantatore *m*
plantation *n* piantagione *f*
plaque *n* placca
plasma *n* plasma *m*; **—** **physics** *(phys)* fisica dei plasmi
plaster *n* intonaco; gesso; **adhesive —** sparadrappo; **corn —** cerotto callicida; **— cast** riproduzione in gesso; **— of Paris** gesso da scultore, stucco; **–er** *n* gessaio; intonachista *m&f*; **–ing** *n* ingessatura; intonaco
plasterboard *n* tavola di gesso compensato
plastic *a* plastico; **—** *n* materia plastica
plasticity *n* plasticità
plat *n* pezzo di terra; **—** *vt (map or chart)* progettare
plate *n* piatto; placca; *(metal)* lamiera, *(dental)* dentiera, protesi dentale; *(print)* incisione; **— glass** lastra di cristallo *(or* vetro); **–ful** *n* piatto pieno; contenuto di un piatto; **—** *vt* placcare, laminare
platen *n* rullo dattilografico; *(print)* pir-

rone *m*
plateau *n* altipiano
platform *n* piattaforma; *(pol)* programma *m*
plating *n* placcatura
platinum *n* platino; **—** *a* di platino
platitude *n* banalità; insulsaggine *f*
platitudinous *a* banale
platonic *a* platonico
platter *n* piatto
plaudit *n* applauso
plausibility *n* plausibilità
plausible *a* plausibile
play *n* giuoco; *(theat)* spettacolo; **— on words** giuoco di parole; **—** *vt&i* giuocare; *(instrument)* suonare; **–ful** *a* scherzevole; **–ground** *n* luogo di ricreazione; campo di giuoco; **–mate** *n* compagno di giuoco; **–off** *n (sports)* partita decisiva; **–thing** *n* trastullo, balocco
playback *n* collaudo di dischi *(or* nastri)
player *n (game)* giocatore; *(mus)* suonatore *m*; *(theat)* attore *m*
playhouse *n* teatro
playing *n* giuoco; **— cards** carte da giuoco; **— field** campo sportivo
playwright *n* drammaturgo
plea *n* supplica
plead *vi* sollecitare; **—** *vt* perorare
pleasant *a* ameno, gradevole; **–ness** *n* amenità
please *vt&i* accontentare; **—!** *interj* per favore!; **as you —** come ti piace
pleased *a* soddisfatto, contento; **— to meet you** *(coll)* lieto di conoscerti
pleasing *a* piacevole
pleasurable *a* piacevole
pleasure *n* piacere *m*
pleat *vt* pieghettare; intrecciare; **—** *n* piega
plebeian *a* plebeo, volgare; **—** *n* plebeo
plebiscite *n* plebiscito
plectrum *n* plettro
pledge *n* pegno; brindisi; **—** *vt* impegnare; brindare a
plenary *a* plenario
plenipotentiary *n&a* plenipotenziario
plentiful *a* copioso, abbondante
plenty *n* abbondanza
plethora *n* pletora
pleurisy *n* pleurite *f*
plexus *n* plesso
pliability *n* pieghevolezza, arrendevolezza
pliable *a* cedevole, arrendevole
pliant *a* pieghevole, flessibile, arrendevole
pliers *npl* pinze *fpl*
plight *n* situazione critica
plod *vi* andare a stento; sgobbare
plodder *n* sgobbone *m*; chi va avanti a stento

plodding *n* stento, sgobbo; — *a* laborioso, sgobbone

plop *n* tonfo; — *vi* fare un tonfo

plot *n* trama; *(intrigue)* complotto; — *vt* complottare, tramare

plotting *n* complotto

plow *n* aratro; **gang** — aratro multiplo; **rotary** — aratro rotativo; — *vt* arare; — **through** profondizzare, sprofondarsi *(fig)*

plowshare *n* vomere *m*

pluck *n* coraggio, fegato *(fig)*; — *vt* cogliere, togliere; *(pull up)* strappare; —**y** *a* corraggioso

plug *n* tappo; *(elec)* spina; *(advertising, sl)* intromissione reclamistica; **spark** — candela; — *vt* tappare; — **in** inserire la spina; — *vi (coll)* sgobbare

plum *n* susina

plumb *n* piombo; — **line** filo a piombo; — *a* verticale, a piombo; — *adv* a piombo, verticalmente; — *vt* sondare, scandagliare; —**er** *n* idraulico; —**ing** *n* piombatura; lavoro d'idraulico

plume *n* piuma, penna

plummet *n* piombino; *(naut)* scandaglio; — *vi* cadere a piombo

plump *a* paffuto, grassoccio; — *vt* gettare giù; — *vi* piombare; —**ness** *n* grassezza

plunder *n* bottino; — *vt* saccheggiare; rubare

plunge *vt* tuffare; immergere; — *vi* tuffarsi; immergersi; — *n* tuffo, immersione

pluperfect *n (gram)* passato anteriore

plural *a&n* plurale *m*; —**ity** *n* pluralità; *(pol)* maggioranza relativa

plus *prep* più

plush *n* felpa

plutocracy *n* plutocrazia

plutocrat *n* plutocrate *m&f*; —**ic** *a* plutocratico

plutonium *n* plutonio

ply *n (fold)* piega; *(thickness)* spessore *m*; — *vi (work)* applicarsi; viaggiare rutinariamente; — *vt (trade)* esercitare; adoperare; — **with questions** investire con domande

plywood *n* legno compensato

P.M. post meridiem dopo mezzogiorno, del pomeriggio, pomeridiano

pneumatic *a* pneumatico

pneumonia *n* polmonite *f*

poach *vi* sconfinare; — *vt (cooking)* bollire uova in camicia; —**er** *n* bracconiere *m*

pock *n* pustola; —**mark** *n* buttero

pocket *n* tasca; — **book** libro tascabile; **line one's** —**s** riempirsi le tasche *(fig)*; —**book** *n* portafogli *m*; borsetta da donna; —**knife** *n* temperino; — *a* tascabile; — *vt* intascare; *(feelings)* contenere

pock-marked *a* butterato

pod *n* baccello; *(flock)* branco

poem *n* poesia; poema *m*

poet *n* poeta *m*; —**ic**, —**ical** *a* poetico; —**ry** *n* poesia

poetics *npl* poetica

poignancy *n* acutezza

poignant *a* piccante

point *n* punto; punta; grado; mira; — **of view** punto di vista; **get to the** — andare al fatto; **make a** — **of** farsi un dovere di; **on the** — **of** sul punto di; **stretch a** — fare un'eccezione; — *vt* indicare; *(sharpen)* appuntare; **to** — **out** segnalare, notare; **to the** — in proposito

point-blank *a* a bruciapelo

pointer *n (dog)* cane da punta; bacchetta

pointless *a* inutile

poise *n* equilibrio; portamento; dignità; — *vt* equilibrare; — *vi* equilibrarsi; esser sospeso

poised *a* disinvolto, imperturbabile

poison *n* veleno; — *vt* avvelenare; —**ing** *n* avvelenamento; —**ous** *a* velenoso

poke *n* colpo, spinta; — *vi* dar colpi; — *vt* cacciare, spingere; — **along** poltrire; — **fun at** scherzare; **buy a pig in a** — comprare alla cieca *(fig)*

poker *n* attizzatoio; *(game)* poker *m*

Poland Polonia

polar *a* polare; — **bear** orso bianco

polarity *n* polarità

polarize *vt* polarizzare

Pole *n* polacco

pole *n* palo; *(geog)* polo; — **vault** salto all'asta

polecat *n* puzzola

police *n* polizia; — **station** commissariato, questura; — *vt* mantenere l'ordine con la polizia; —**man** *n* guardia, poliziotto, vigile urbano

policy *n* politica; — **holder** assicurato; **insurance** — polizza d'assicurazione

poliomyelitis *n* poliomelite *f*

Polish *a* polacco

polish *vt* pulire, levigare; — *n* lucido, vernice *f*; —**ed** *a* raffinato

polite *a* cortese, garbato; —**ness** *n* cortesia

politic, —al *a* politico

politics *npl* politica

politician *n* politico, politicante *m*

polka *n* polka, polca

poll *n (pol)* votazione; *(opinion)* referendum *m*; — **tax** testatico; —**s** *npl* urne *fpl*; — *vt* tosare, potare, cimare; ottenere

pollen *n* polline *m*

pollinate vt coprire di polline
polling n votazione; — **booth** cabina elettorale
pollute vt contaminare; violare; **-d** a impuro, sudicio; corrotto
pollution n polluzione; profanazione
polo n (sport) polo
polychrome a policromo
polyclinic n policlinico
polygamist n poligamo
polygamous a poligamo
polygamy n poligamia
polyglot n poliglotta m&f
polygon n poligono; **-al** a poligonale
polymer n polimero; — **chemistry** polimerologia, chimica dei polimeri
polymerization n polimerizzazione
polymorphism n polimorfismo
polymorphous a polimorfo
Polynesia Polinesia
polyp n polipo
polyphonic a polifonico
polyphony n polifonia
polysyllabic a polisillabo
polysyllable n polisillabo
polytechnic a politecnico
polytheism n politeismo
polytheist n politeista m&f
polytheistic a politeistico
pomade n pomata
pomegranate n melagrana
pommel n pomo; — vt battere
pomp n pompa, fasto; **-ous** a pomposo; **-ousness** n pomposità
ponder vt&i ponderare; riflettere; meditare; **-ous** a ponderoso
poniard n pugnale m; — vt pugnalare
pontiff n pontefice m
pontifical a pontificale
pontificate n pontificato
pontoon n pontone m
pony n cavallino
poodle n cane barbone
pool n stagno; (betting) piatto di scommesse; (money) fondo comune; (swimming) piscina; — vt mettere in comune
poop n (naut) poppa
poor a povero, cattivo, scadente; — npl i poveri mpl; **-house** n ricovero di mendicità; **-ly** adv malamente, male, scarsamente
pop n sparo; (beverage) gasosa; **-corn** n granturco arrostito; **-gun** n pistola ad aria compressa; — vt&i esplodere, sparare
Pope n Papa m
poplar n pioppo
poplin n poplina
poppy n papavero
populace n plebaglia, popolino

popular a popolare; **-ity** n popolarità; **-ize** vt popolarizzare
populate vt popolare
population n popolazione
populous a popoloso
porcelain n porcellana
porch n veranda; portico
porcupine n porcospino
pore n poro
pore (over) vi ponderare; studiare attentamente
pork n carne di porco; — **chop** costoletta di porco
pornographic a pornografico
pornography n pornografia
porosity n porosità
porous a poroso
porphyry n porfido
porpoise n focena
port n porto; (naut) babordo; (wine) vino d'Oporto; **-folio** n cartella; (pol) portafoglio; **-hole** n portello; oblò; **-able** a portabile, portatile
portend vt presagire
portent n portento; presagio
portentous a portentoso, prodigioso
porter n facchino, portatore m
portion n porzione; — vt ripartire; dotare
portly a corpulento
portrait n ritratto; — **painter** ritrattista m&f
portray vt ritrarre; descrivere; **-al** n pittura, descrizione
Portugal Portogallo
Portuguese a&n portoghese m
pose n posa, atteggiamento; — vt far posare; — vi posare; atteggiarsi; — **as** atteggiarsi; — **questions** porre domande
position n posizione; posto; (job) impiego; **be in a — to** essere in grado di; — vt collocare
positive a positivo, assoluto; **-ly** adv positivamente
positivism n positivismo
positron n positrone m; elletrone positivo
posse n pattuglia
possess vt possedere; **-ed** a posseduto; invasato; **-ive** a possessivo; **-or** n possessore m
possibility n possibilità
possible a possibile
possibly adv possibilmente; forse
post n posto; palo; — vt affiggere; impostare; — **no bills** proibita l'affissione; — **office** ufficio postale
postage n affrancatura; — **stamp** francobollo
postal a postale
postcard n cartolina postale
postdate vt posdatare

poster n cartellone m
posterior a&n posteriore m
posterity n i posteri mpl
postgraduate n&a universitario
posthaste adv subito, immediatamente
posthumous a postumo
postman n portalettere m
postmark n timbro postale
postmaster n direttore postale
postpaid a porto pagato
postpone vt rimandare; **–ment** n rinvio
postscript n poscritto
posture n atteggiamento; *(manner)* attitudine f
postwar a del dopoguerra
pot n pentola; vaso; — **roast** arrosto in tegame; — **shot** sparo a caso; — vt invasare; — vi *(coll)* sparare; **–hook** n gancio del focolare
potable a potabile
potash n potassa
potassium n potassio
potato n patata; **sweet —** patata americana
potbellied a panciuto
potency n potenza, potere m
potent a potente
potentate n potentato
potential n potenzialità; — a potenziale; **–ity** n potenzialità
potion n pozione
potluck n pasto quotidiano; — a alla buona; **take —** desinare alla buona
potter n vasaio; **–'s field** cimitero dei poveri; **–'s wheel** ruota del vasaio
pottery n ceramica; terraglie, stoviglie fpl
pouch n borsa
poultice n cataplasma
poultry n pollame m
pounce *(on)* vi balzare su, gettarsi sopra
pound n libbra; — vt battere, colpire; camminare pesantemente; pulsare
pound n *(animal)* rinchiuso
pour vt versare; — vi diluviare, piovere a dirotto; — **off** colare, drenare; **–ing** a torrenziale
pout vi fare il broncio; — n broncio
poverty n povertà, miseria
poverty-stricken a caduto in miseria, impoverito
powder n polvere f; cipria; — **magazine** polveriera; — **puff** piumino; — **room** toletta per signore; — vt impolverare; incipriare; — vi incipriarsi; impolverarsi; **–y** a polveroso
powdered a in polvere; incipriato, impolverato; — **sugar** zucchero al velo
power n forza; energia; facoltà; autorità; **–ful** a potente; **–less** a impotente; **–lessness** n impotenza; — **plant** apparato motore; **central** elettrica

practicability n praticabilità
practicable a praticabile
practical a pratico; — **joke** beffa, burla; **–ly** adv praticamente; quasi
practice n pratica; *(exercise)* esercizio, uso; *(professional)* clientela; — vt praticare, esercitare
practiced a abile, esperto
practitioner n professionista m&f
pragmatic a pragmatico
pragmatism n pragmatismo
pragmatist n pragmatista m
prairie n prateria
praise n lode f, elogio; — vt lodare; **–worthy** a lodevole
prance vi impennarsi; pavoneggiarsi
prancing n impennata; — a rampante
prank n burla, tiro birbone
prate vi ciarlare, cicalare
prattle n ciarla; — vi chiacchierare, ciarlare
pray vt&i pregare; **–er** n preghiera
prayerful a devoto, pio
preach vt&i predicare; **–er** n predicatore m; *(minister)* pastore m; **–ing** n sermone m, predica
preamble n preambolo
prearrange vt predisporre; **–ment** n preordinamento
prebend n *(eccl)* prebenda
precarious a precario; **–ly** adv precariamente; **–ness** n precarietà
precaution n precauzione; **–ary** a precauzionale
precede vt&i precedere
precedence n precedenza
precedent n precedente m
precedent a precedente
preceding a precedente
precept n precetto; **–or** n precettore m
precinct n distretto; **–s** npl dintorni mpl
precious a prezioso, caro
precipice n precipizio
precipitant n&a precipitante m
precipitate n *(chem)* precipitato; — vt&i precipitare
precipitation n precipitazione
precipitous a precipitoso
précis n sunto
precise a preciso; **–ly** adv precisamente; **–ness** n precisione
precision n precisione
preclude vt precludere
preclusion n preclusione
preclusive a preclusivo
precocious a precoce; **–ness** n precocità
precocity n precocità
preconceive vt preconcepire; **–d** a preconcepito
preconception n preconcetto

precursor *n* precursore *m*; **-y** *a* introduttivo
predate *vt* antidatare; predatare; **-d** *a* predatato
predatory *a* rapace; predatorio
predecessor *n* predecessore *m*
predestinate *vt* predestinare; — *a* predestinato
predestination *n* predestinazione
predestine *vt* predestinare
predetermine *vt* predeterminare; **-d** *a* predeterminato
predicament *n* imbarazzo, situazione difficile
predicate *vt* affermare; — *n* predicato
predication *n* predicazione
predict *vt* predire; **-ion** *n* predizione, presagio
predilection *n* predilezione
predispose *vt* predisporre; **-d** *a* predisposto
predisposition *n* predisposizione
predominance *n* predominanza
predominant *a* predominante
predominate *vt&i* predominare, prevalere
preeminence *n* preminenza
preeminent *a* preminente
preempt *vt* acquistare in precedenza
preen *vt&i* lisciarsi le penne; leccarsi *(fig)*
preestablish *vt* prestabilire; **-d** *a* prestabilito
preexist *vt&i* preesistere; **-ence** *n* preesistenza; **-ent** *a* preesistente
prefabricate *vt* prefabbricare; **-d** *a* prefabbricato
preface *n* prefazione; — *vt (book)* fare una prefazione a
prefatory *a* preliminare
prefer *vt* preferire; **-able** *a* preferibile; **-ence** *n* preferenza; **-ential** *a* preferenziale
preferred *a* preferito; *(stock)* privilegiato
prefix *n* prefisso; — *vt* prefiggere, premettere
pregnable *a* prendibile
pregnancy *n* gravidanza, gestazione
pregnant *a* incinta; gravido
preheat *vt* prescaldare; **-ed** *a* prescaldato
prehensile *a* prensile
prehistoric *a* preistorico
prehistory *n* preistoria
prejudge *vt* pregiudicare
prejudgment *n* giudizio prematuro
prejudice *n* pregiudizio; — *vt* pregiudicare; danneggiare
prejudicial *a* pregiudiziale
prelate *n* prelato
preliminary *a&n* preliminare
prelude *n* preludio
premature *a* prematuro; **-ly** *adv* prematu-

ramente; **-ness** *n* prematurità
premeditate *vt* premeditare; **-d** *a* premeditato
premeditation *n* premeditazione
premier *n (pol)* primo ministro
première *n (theat)* prima
premise *n* premessa; **-s** *npl* locali *mpl*; *(logic)* premesse *fpl*; — *vt* premettere
premium *n* premio
premonition *n* presentimento
prenatal *a* prenatale
preoccupation *n* preoccupazione
preoccupy *vt* preoccupare
preordain *vt* preordinare; **-ed** *a* preordinato
prepaid *a* franco di porto
preparation *n* preparazione, preparativo
preparatory *a* preparatorio; — **school** scuola preparatoria
prepare *vt* preparare; — *vi* prepararsi
prepay *vt* pagare in anticipo; **-ment** *n* pagamento anticipato
preponderance *n* preponderanza
preponderant *a* preponderante
preposition *n (gram)* preposizione
prepossessing *a* attraente
prepossession *n* pregiudizio; preoccupazione; prevenzione
preposterous *a* assurdo
prerequisite *a* indispensabile; — *n* requisito
prerogative *n* prerogativa
presage *vt* presagire
prescience *n* prescienza
prescient *a* presciente
prescribe *vt&i* prescrivere
prescription *n* ricetta; prescrizione *f*
presence *n* presenza; — **of mind** prontezza d'animo; **in the — of** alla presenza di
present *n (gift)* regalo, dono; *(time)* presente *m*; — *a* attuale, presente; **at — ora, adesso**
present *vt* presentare, offrire; — **oneself** presentarsi, comparire; **-ation** *n* offerta, presentazione; *(theat)* rappresentazione
presentable *a* presentabile
presentably *adv* presentabilmente
presentiment *n* presentimento
preservation *n* preservazione
preservative *n* preservativo, preservatore *m*
preserve *vt* preservare, conservare
preserve *n* marmellata, conserva
preside *vi* presiedere
presidency *n* presidenza
president *n* presidente *m*
press *vt&i* premere; stringere; stirare; — *n* pressa; torchio; *(print)* stampa,

stamperia; *(mech)* pressa; **the — *(news)*** la stampa

pressing *a* urgente, pressante, insistente; **—** *n* urgenza; pressione; stiratura

pressure *n* pressione; **— cooker** pentola a pressione; **blood —** pressione sanguigna

pressurize *vt (avi&naut)* mantenere la pressione di, pressurizzare

pressurized *a* a pressione; pressurizzato

prestige *n* prestigio

presumable *a* presumibile

presumably *adv* presumibilmente

presume *vt&i* presumere, supporre

presuming *a* presuntuoso

presumption *n* presunzione

presumptive *a* presunto

presumptuous *a* presuntuoso

presuppose *vt* presupporre

presupposition *n* presupposizione

pretend *vt&i* fingere, far finta di

pretender *n* pretendente *m&f*

pretense *n* finzione, pretesto; pretesa

pretention *n* pretesa

pretentious *a* pretenzioso; **–ness** *n* pretenziosità

preterit *n (gram)* preterito

pretext *n* pretesto; **on the — of** col pretesto di

prettiness *n* grazia, leggiadria; eleganza

prettily *adv* graziosamente

pretty *a* carino, grazioso, bello; **—** *adv* discretamente

prevail *vi* prevalere; **–ing** *a* prevalente; comune

prevalence *n* prevalenza

prevalent *a* generale, comune; prevalente

prevaricate *vi* prevaricare; tergiversare

prevarication *n* tergiversazione; prevaricazione

prevaricator *n* prevaricatore *m*

prevent *vt* impedire, prevenire, evitare; **–able** *a* prevenibile; **–ion** *n* prevenzione; **–ative** *n* preventivo

preventive *n* misura preventiva; **—** *a* preventivo

preview *n* anteprima

previous *a* precedente; **–ly** *adv* prima, anteriormente

prewar *a* d'anteguerra

prey *n* preda; **—** *vi* predare

price *n* prezzo; **at any —** ad ogni costo; **— cutting** ribasso; **–less** *a* senza prezzo, inestimabile; **—** *vt* valutare; *(coll)* chiedere il prezzo di

prick *n* puntura; **–ly** *a* spinoso; **—** *vt* pungere

pride *n* orgoglio, fierezza; **take — in** essere fiero *(or* orgoglioso) di; **— oneself on** vantarsi di; gloriarsi di

priest *n* prete, sacerdote *m*; **–hood** *n* sacerdozio; **–ly** *a* sacerdotale

prig *n* meticoloso, sofistico, presuntuoso

prim *a* meticoloso, cerimonioso; affettato; **–ness** *n* formalità

primacy *n* supremazia

primarily *adv* principalmente; prima di tutto

primary *a* primario

prime *a* primo, principale; **—** *n* colmo, perfezione; fiore *m*; **in its —** nel suo fiore; **—** *vt (person)* preparare, istruire; *(gun)* caricare; *(mech)* adescare

primer *n* primo libro

primeval *a* primitivo; **— forests** foreste vergini

priming *n* innesco

primitive *a* primitivo; **–ness** *n* primitività

primogeniture *n* primogenitura

primordial *a* primordiale

primp *vi* prepararsi meticolosamente

primrose *n* primula

prince *n* principe *m*; **–ly** *a* principesco

princess *n* principessa

principal *a* principale; **—** *n (com)* capitale *m*

principle *n* principio

print *vt&i* stampare; *(letter)* scrivere a stampatello; **out of —** esaurito; **—** *n* stampa, impressione; *(photo)* positiva; *(type)* caratteri *mpl*; **–er** *n* tipografo

printed *a* stampato; **— matter** stampe *fpl*

printing *n* stampa, tiratura; **—** *a* tipografico, da stampa; **— press** torchio tipografico

prior *a* precedente, antecedente; **— to** prima di; **–ity** *n* priorità

prior *(eccl)* priore *m*

prism *n* prisma; **–atic** *a* prismatico

prison *n* prigione *f*; **–er** *n* prigioniero

pristine *a* pristino

privacy *n* intimità; segreto

private *a* privato; **—** *n (mil)* soldato semplice; **–ly** *adv* privatamente, in privato; personalmente

privation *n* privazione

privilege *n* privilegio; **—** *vt* privilegiare

prize *n* premio; **—** *a* pregiato

prizefight *n* partita di pugilato; **–er** *n* pugile *m*

pro *n (coll)* professionista *m&f*; **—** *a* favorevole; **the –s and cons** il pro ed il contro; **—** *adv* pro, in favore

probability *n* probabilità

probable *a* probabile

probate *vt* provare l'autenticità di

probation *n* periodo di prova; libertà condizionale

probe *n* sonda; investigazione; **—** *vt* sondare

probity *n* integrità

problem *n* problema *m*; **–atical** *a* problematico

proboscis *n* proboscide *f*

procedure *n* procedimento, procedura

proceed *vi* procedere, continuare; derivare

proceedings *npl* procedimenti *mpl*; *(law)* procedura

proceeds *npl* ricavo; incasso

process *n* corso; procedimento; processo

procession *n* processione; **funeral —** corteo funebre; **–al** *a&n* processionale *m*

proclivity *n* proclività, inclinazione

procrastinate *vt&i* procrastinare, posporre

procrastination *n* procrastinazione

procreate *vt&i* procreare

procreative *a* procreatore, generativo

procreator *n* procreatore *m*

procurable *a* procurabile

procure *vt* procurare, ottenere; **–ment** *n* ottenimento

prod *n* pungolo; **—** *vt* pungere; *(push)* spingere

prodigal *a* prodigo

prodigious *a* prodigioso; **–ness** *n* prodigiosità

prodigy *n* prodigio

produce *n* frutto; profitto; prodotto

produce *vt* produrre, fabbricare; **–r** *n* produttore *m*

producible *a* producibile

product *n* prodotto

production *n* produzione

productive *a* produttivo; **–ness** produttività

profane *a* profano; **—** *vt* violare, profanare

profaner *n* profanatore *m*

profanity *n* profanità

profess *vt* professare; pretendere, dichiarare

professed *a* dichiarato; **–ly** *adv* dichiaratamente

profession *n* professione

professional *a* professionale; **—** *n* professionista *m&f*

professor *n* professore *m*; **–ial** *a* professorale; **–ship** *n* cattedra

proffer *vt* proferire

proficiency *n* abilità

proficient *a* abile, provetto, esperto; **–ly** *adv* espertamente

profile *n* profilo; **—** *vt* profilare

profit *n* profitto; guadagno; **—** *vi* profittare, trarre vantaggio; **–able** *a* utile, vantaggioso; **–less** *a* senza profitto, inutile; **— by** trarre profitto da

profiteer *n* profittatore *m*; **–ing** *n* sfruttamento

profligate *a* dissoluto

profound *a* profondo; **–ly** *adv* profondamente; **–ness** *n* profondità

profundity *n* profondità

profuse *a* profuso; prodigo; **–ly** *adv* profusamente; prodigalmente; **–ness** *n* profusione

profusion *n* profusione

progenitor *n* progenitore *m*

progeny *n* progenie *f*

prognosis *n* prognosi *f*

prognosticate *vt* pronosticare

prognostication *n* pronosticazione

program *n* programma *m*; **—** *vt* progettare, fare programma per

programming *n* *(for computers)* programmazione

progress *n* progresso

progress *vi* progredire, far progressi; **–ive** *a* progressivo

progression *n* progressione

prohibit *vt* proibire

prohibition *n* proibizione

prohibitive *a* proibitivo

project *n* progetto; **–ile** *n* proiettile *m*; **–ion** *(action)* proiezione; sporgenza; **–or** *n* proiettore *m*

project *vt* progettare; **—** *vi* sporgersi

proletarian *a* proletario

proletariat *n* proletariato

prolific *a* prolifico

prologue *n* prologo

prolong *vt* prolungare; **–ation** *n* prolungazione

promenade *n* passeggiata; **—** *vi* passeggiare

prominence *n* eminenza, importanza; risalto

prominent *a* eminente; saliente; **–ly** *adv* prominentemente

promiscuous *a* promiscuo

promise *n* promessa; **—** *vt&i* promettere

promising *a* promettente

promissory *a* promettente; **— note** cambiale *f*

promontory *n* promontorio

promote *vt* promuovere

promoter *n* fautore *m*

promotion *n* avanzamento, promozione

prompt *a* pronto, immediato; puntuale; **–ly** *adv* subito, prontamente; **–ness** *n* prontezza; **–er** *n* suggeritore *m*; **—** *vt* incitare; *(theat)* suggerire

promulgate *vt* promulgare

promulgation *n* promulgazione

prone *a* prono; **— to** inclinato a *(fig)*

prong *n* rebbio; **–ed** *a* con rebbi

pronominal *a* pronominale

pronoun *n* pronome *m*

pronounce *vt&i* pronunziare; **–able** *a* pronunziabile; **–d** *a* pronunziato; **–ment** *n* dichiarazione

pronunciation *n* pronunzia

proof *n* prova; *(print)* bozza di stampa; **galley —** bozza di composizione; **–reader** *n* corretore di bozze; **–reading** *n* correzione di bozze; **—** *vt* tirare una bozza

prop *n* puntello; *(theat)* attrezzatura; **—** *vt* puntellare

propaganda *n* propaganda

propagandist *n* propagandista *m&f*

propagandize *vt* propagandare; **—** *vi* fare propaganda

propagate *vt* propagare; **—** *vi* propagarsi

propagation *n* propagazione

propel *vt* spingere avanti

propellant *n* propulsore *m*

propellent *a* motore, propulsore

propeller *n* elica

propensity *n* propensione

proper *a* proprio, corretto; **–ly** *adv* propriamente, appropriatamente; **–ness** *n* convenienza

property *n* proprietà; beni *mpl*

prophecy *n* profezia

prophesy *vt&i* profetizzare

prophet *n* profeta *m*

prophylactic *a* profilattico

prophylaxis *n* profilassi *f*

propinquity *n* propinquità

propitiate *vt* propiziare

propitiation *n* propiziazione

propitious *a* propizio

proponent *n* proponente *m*

proportion *n* proporzione; **–al** *a* proporzionale; **–ate** *a* proporzionato; **—** *vt* proporzionare

proposal *n* proposta

propose *vt* proporre; **—** *vi* fare una proposta di matrimonio

proposition *n* proposta, proposizione

propound *vt* proporre

proprietary *a* di proprietà

proprietor *n* proprietario

propriety *n* proprietà

propulsion *n* propulsione; **jet —** propulsione a reazione

prorate *vt* ripartire proporzionalmente; dividere proporzionalmente

prosaic *a* prosaico

proscenium *n* proscenio

proscribe *vt* proscrivere

proscription *n* proscrizione

prose *n* prosa

prosecute *vt (law)* processare

prosecution *n (law)* processo, querela

prosecutor *n* accusatore *m*; pubblico ministero; *(plaintiff)* parte civile

proselyte *n* proselito

proselytize *vt* convertire

prospect *n* prospetto; *(view)* vista; **–ive** *a* previsto, futuro; **—** *vt&i* esplorare; cercare

prospector *n* prospettore *m*

prospectus *n* prospetto

prosper *vi* prosperare; **—** *vt* far prosperare; **–ous** *a* prospero

prosperity *n* prosperità

prostate *n* prostata

prostitute *n* prostituta; **—** *vt* prostituire

prostitution *n* prostituzione

prostrate *a* abbattuto; prosternato; **—** *vt* prostrare

prostration *n* prostrazione

protagonist *n* protagonista *m&f*

protect *vt* proteggere; **–ion** *n* protezione; **–ive** *a* protettivo; **–or** *n* protettore *m*; **–orate** *m* protettorato

protein *n* proteina

protest *n* protesta

protest *vt&i* protestare

Protestant *a&n* protestante *m&f*; **–ism** *n* protestantesimo

protestation *n* protestazione

protocol *n* protocollo

proton *n* protone *m*

protoplasm *n* protoplasma *m*; **–ic** *a* di protoplasma

prototype *n* prototipo

Protozoa *npl* protozoi *mpl*

protozoan *n* protozoo

protract *vt* protrarre; **–or** *n* protrattore *m*; *(anat)* muscolo estensore; *(geometry)* goniometro

protrude *vt* spingere avanti; far uscire; **—** *vi* sporgersi; proiettarsi

protruding *a* sporgente; spingente avanti

protrusion *n* sporgenza, prominenza

protuberance *n* protuberanza

protuberant *a* protuberante

proud *a* fiero, orgoglioso

provable *a* provabile

prove *vt* provare; **—** *vi* provarsi

proverb *n* proverbio; **–ial** *a* proverbiale

provide *vt&i* fornire; **–r** *n* provveditore *m*

provided *conj* purchè; **— that** *a* condizione che

providence *n* provvidenza

provident *a* provvido, previdente; **–ial** *a* provvidenziale

province *n* provincia

provincial *a* provinciale

provision *n* stipulazione *f*; **–al** *a* provvisorio, **–s** *npl* viveri *mpl*; provviste *fpl*

proviso *n* condizione; clausola

provisory *a* provvisorio

provocation *n* provocazione

provocative *a* provocativo

provoke *vt* provocare

provoking *a* provocante

prow *n* prua, prora; **–ess** *n* valore *m*, prodezza

prowl *vi* vagare, gironzolare; **–er** *n* vagabondo
proximity *n* prossimità
proxy *n* procura; **by —** per procura
prudence *n* prudenza
prude *n* schizzinoso; **–ry** *n* schifiltà
prudent *a* prudente; **–ly** *adv* prudentemente
prudish *a* schifiltoso
prune *n* prugna secca; **—** *vt* potare
pruning *n* potatura
prurience *n* sensualità
prurient *a* lascivo
pry *vi* spiare; ficcare il naso; **—** *vt* sollevare con una leva; **—** *n (tool)* leva, palanca
prying *n* curiosità; **—** *a* curioso, ficcanaso
psalm *n* salmo; **–ist** *n* salmista *m*
psalter *n* salterio
pseudonym *n* pseudonimo
psyche *n* psiche *f*
psychiatric *a* psichiatrico
psychiatrist *n* psichiatra *m&f*
psychiatry *n* psichiatria
psychic *a* psichico
psychoanalist *n* psicoanalista *m&f*
psychoanalysis *n* psicoanalisi *f*
psychological *a* psicologico
psychologist *n* psicologo
psychology *n* psicologia
psychopath *n* psicopatico
psychopathic *a* psicopatico
psychopathology *n* psicopatologia
psychopathy *n* psicopatia
psychosis *n* psicosi *f*
psychosomatic *a* psicosomatico
psychotherapy *n* psicoterapia
puberty *n* pubertà
public *n&a* pubblico; **— works** lavori pubblici *mpl*; **make —** pubblicare
public-spirited *a* con senso civico
publication *n* pubblicazione
publicity *n* pubblicità
publicize *vt* pubblicare
publish *vt* pubblicare; **–er** *n* editore *m*
publishing *n* pubblicazione; **—** *a* editoriale; **— house** *n* casa editrice
pucker *n* grinza; piega; **—** *vt* increspare; **—** *vi* raggrinzarsi
pudding *n* budino
puddle *n* pozzanghera
pudgy *a* tozzo
puerile *a* puerile
Puerto Rico Portorico
puff *n* soffio; **— pastry** pasta sfoglia
puff *vi* soffiare; gonfiarsi; **—** *vt* gonfiare
puffiness *n* gonfiore *m*; gonfiatura
puffy *a* gonfio
pug *n* cane bolognese; **— nose** naso camuso

pugilism *n* pugilato
pugilist *n* pugilista *m*
pugilistic *a* pugilistico
pugnacious *a* pugnace
pugnacity *n* pugnacità
pug-nosed *a* dal naso camuso
pull *vt* tirare; **— apart** staccare; **— off** cavare, tirar via; **— out** estrarre, strappare; **— oneself together** ricomporsi; **— through** *(recover)* guarire, rimettersi
pull *n* strappo, tiro; *(sl)* influenza, vantaggio
pullet *n* pollastrella
pulley *n* puleggia
pullover *n* pullover *m*
pulmonary *a* polmonare
pulp *n* polpa
pulpit *n* pulpito
pulpy *a* polposo
pulsate *vi* pulsare
pulsation *n* pulsazione
pulse *n* polso
pulverization *n* polverizzazione
pulverize *vt* polverizzare; **—** *vi* polverizzarsi
pumice *n* pomice *f*
pump *n* pompa; *(shoe)* scarpetta; **—** *vt&i* pompare; *(inflate)* gonfiare
pumpkin *n* zucca
pun *n* giuoco di parole
punch *n* cazzotto, pugno; *(mech)* punzone *m*; *(drink)* ponce *m*; **—** *vt* punzonare; perforare; dare un pugno a
punctilious *a* scrupoloso, puntiglioso, meticoloso
punctual *a* puntuale; **–ity** *n* puntualità
punctuate *vt* punteggiare
punctuation *n* punteggiatura
puncture *n* puntura; *(tire)* foratura; **—** *vt* pungere, bucare, forare
punctureproof *a* antiperforante
pungency *n* agrezza, natura piccante
pungent *a* pungente
puniness *n* debolezza
punish *vt* castigare, punire; **–able** *a* punibile
punishment *n* punizione; **capital —** pena capitale
punitive *a* punitivo
puny *a* floscio, debole
pup, puppy *n* cucciolo; cagnolino
pupa *n* crisalide *f*
pupil *n (eye)* pupilla; *(school)* allievo; alunno, alunna; scolaro, scolara
puppet *n* burattino; **— show** recita di marionette
purchase *n* acquisto, compera; **—** *vt* acquistare, comperare
purchaser *n* acquirente *m&f*
pure *a* puro; **–ly** *adv* puramente

purgative *n&a* purgante *m*; purgativo
purgatory *n* purgatorio
purge *n* purga, purgante *m*; — *vt* purgare; — *vi* purgarsi
purification *n* purificazione
purifier *n* purificatore *m*
purify *vt* purificare
purism *n* purismo
purist *n* purista *m*
puritan *n* puritano; –**ical** *a* puritanico
purity *n* purezza
purl *vt (knitting)* smerlare; –**ing** *n* smerlo
purloin *vt&i* rubare
purple *n&a (color)* viola; **born to the —** *(fig)* di origine regale — *vt* imporporare; — *vi* imporporarsi
purport *n* significato; tenore *m*
purport *vt* significare; presumere, pretendere
purpose *n* scopo; **for the — of** allo scopo di; **on —** intenzionalmente; apposta; **to no —** invano; inutilmente; –**ful** *a* intenzionale; *(resolute)* risoluto; –**ly** *adv* intenzionalmente
purr *n* fusa *fpl*; — *vi* far le fusa; –**ing** *n* fusa *fpl*
purse *n* borsa; *(prize)* denaro; — *vt* increspare; — **the lips** contrarre le labbra; –**r** *n (naut)* commissario di bordo
pursuance *n* esecuzione, effettuazione
pursuant *a* inseguente
pursue *vt* perseguire
persuer *n* inseguitore *m*
pursuit *n* inseguimento; **in — of** alla ricerca di
purvey *vt* fornire

purveyor *n* fornitore *m*
pus *n* pus *m*, marcia; –**tule** *n* pustola
push *vt&i* spingere; — **ahead** progressare; — **back** respingere; — **one's way** farsi largo; — *n* spinta; — **button** pulsante *m*
pushover *n (sl)* cosa facile
puss *n* micino
put *vt* mettere; collocare; — **down** deporre, metter giù; — **off** posporre; — **on** indossare, mettersi; — **on airs** darsi arie; — **oneself out** disturbarsi *(coll)*; — **out** insoddisfatto; scontento; — **up** *(house)* soggiornare; *(can)* conservare; — **up with** tollerare, soffrire, sopportare
put-up *a* macchinato; — **job** intrigo, truffa
putrefaction *n* putrefazione
putrefy *vt* putrefare; — *vi* putrefarsi
putrid *a* putrido
putty *n* stucco; — **knife** spatola da stucco; — *vt* stuccare
puzzle *n* enigma *m*, rompicapo; **crossword —** cruciverba *m*; — *vt* rendere perplesso; — *vi* scervellarsi; –**ment** *n* sbalordimento, perplessità; –**r** *n* enigma *m*; *(person)* sfinge *f (fig)*
puzzling *a* problematico
pygmy, pigmy *n&a* pigmeo
pylon *n* pilone *m*
pyorrhea *n* piorrea
pyramid *n* piramide *f*
pyre *n* pira
pyromaniac *n* piromane *m&f*
pyrometer *n* pirometro
pyrotechnics *npl* pirotecnica
python *n* pitone *m*

Q

quack *n* ciarlatano, impostore *m*; *(duck)* gracidio; — *vi* schiamazzare, gracidare
quackery *n* ciarlataneria
quad *n (print)* quadratino
quadrangle *n* quadrangolo
quadrangular *a* quadrangolare
quadrant *n* quadrante *m*
quadratic *n&a* quadratico; — **equation** equazione quadratica
quadrilateral *a* quadrilatero
quadruped *n&a* quadrupede *m*
quadruple *n (math)* quadruplo; — *vt* quadruplicare
quadruplets *npl* quartetto di gemelli
quaff *vt&i* tracannare
quagmire *n* acquitrino
quail *n* quaglia; — *vi* scoraggiarsi
quaint *a* strano, pittoresco, originale; –**ness** *n* il pittoresco, originalità

quake *vi* tremare; — *n* tremore *m*, scossa; terremoto
quaking *n* tremolio; — *a* tremolante
qualification *n* qualifica; capacità; limitazione
qualified *a* idoneo; limitato
qualifier *n* qualificatore *m*; *(gram)* qualificativo
qualify *vt* abilitare, qualificare; limitare; — *vi* rendersi idoneo; qualificarsi
qualifying *a* qualificativo; — **heat** *(sport)* eliminatoria
qualitative *a* qualitativo
quality *n* qualità
qualm *n* apprensione; nausea; — **of conscience** scrupolo
quandary *n* dilemma *m*, imbarazzo
quantitative *a* quantitativo

quantity n quantità
quantum n quanto
quarantine n quarantena; — vt mettere in quarantena
quarrel n lite f, disputa; — vi litigare; bisticciare; **–some** a litigioso
quarry n (mine) cava; (prey) preda; (hunting) selvaggina
quart n quarto di gallone
quarter n (math) quarta parte, quarto; (money) un quarto di dollaro; **–back** n (football) terzino; centro attacco; **–master** n (naut) secondo capo timoniere; **–s** (living) quartiere m; alloggio; — vt (mil) alloggiare; squartare
quarter n (time) un quarto d'ora; **a — past** e un quarto; **a — to** meno un quarto
quarter– (as comp) **—deck** n (naut) cassero di poppa; **—hour** n quarto d'ora
quarterly n pubblicazione trimestrale; — a trimestrale; — adv trimestralmente
quartet n quartetto
quartz n quarzo
quash vt schiacciare
quasi a&adv quasi
quatrain n quartina
quaver n tremolo; (mus) croma; — vi vibrare; trillare
quay n molo
queasy a nauseato
queen n regina; — vt (chess) fare regina; — vi fare la regina; **–ly** a regale
queer a strano, bizzarro; — vt (sl) rovinare; **–ness** n stranezza, bizzarria
quell vt reprimere
quench vt (thirst) dissetare; spegnere; — **a fire** estinguere un incendio
querulous a querulo
query n domanda; — vt domandare
quest n ricerca; richiesta; **in — of** in cerca di
question n domanda; questione f; **— mark** punto interrogativo; **ask a —** fare una domanda; **in —** in questione; **out of the —** impossibile; **without —** senza dubbio; **a — of** una questione di; **–able** a discutibile; — vt interrogare; (doubt) discutere, mettere in dubbio
questioner n interrogatore m
questioning n inchiesta; — a interrogante, (dubious) dubbioso; **–ly** adv interrogativamente
questionnaire n questionario
queue n (hair) codino; (line) coda, fila
quibble vi sofisticare, cavillare
quibbler n cavillatore m
quibbling n sofisma m, cavillo
quick n vivo; **the — and the dead** i vivi e i morti; — a lesto, pronto, rapido;

–ness n rapidità, vivacità; **–ly** adv presto, rapidamente; **–en** vt animare; stimolare; — vi animarsi; affrettarsi
quickening n accelerazione; — a eccitante; accelerato
quicklime n calce viva
quicksand n sabbia mobile
quicksilver n mercurio
quick-tempered a irascibile
quick-witted a di pronto ingegno
quiescence n quiescenza
quiescent a quiescente; silente
quiet a quieto, tranquillo; modesto; calmo; **Keep —!** interj Sta zitto!; **be —** stare tranquillo (or in silenzio); — n calma, quiete f; **–ness** n quiete f; silenzio; **–ly** adv silenziosamente; quietamente; — vt calmare; quietare; — vi calmarsi, quietarsi
quill n penna
quilt n trapunta; — vt trapuntare; **–ed** a imbottito
quince n cotogna
quinine n chinino
quinsy n squinanzia
quintal n quintale m
quintessence n quintessenza
quintet n quintetto
quintuple n&a quintuplo; — vt quintuplicare
quip n bottata; frizzo
quire n quinterno, quaderno
quirk n sotterfugio; (peculiarity) singolarità; **— of fate** capriccio del destino
quisling n disfattista m&f; quintacolonnista m&f
quit vt abbandonare, lasciare
quitclaim n (law) remissione, rinunzia
quits a pari; **be —** essere pari; **call it —** dichiarare la fine
quitter n (coward) codardo; rinunciatario
quite adv completamente; realmente; (coll) abbastanza
quiver vi tremolare; — n (archery) faretra; tremito
quivering n fremito, tremito
quixotic a donchisciottesco
quiz vt interrogare, esaminare; — n esame superficiale
quizzical a interrogante; (bantering) beffardo
quondam a già, antico
quorum n numero legale
quota n quota, porzione
quotable a citabile
quotation n citazione; (com) quotazione di borsa; **— marks** virgolette fpl
quote vt citare; (com) quotare
quotient n quoziente m

R

rabbi *n* rabbino
rabbit *n* coniglio
rabble *n* plebaglia; ressa
rabid *a* rabbioso; *(rabies)* idrofobo
rabies *npl* rabbia, idrofobia
raccoon *n* procione *m*
race *n (people)* razza, stirpe *f*
race *n* corsa; **arms** — corsa agli armamenti; **boat** — regata; **foot** — corsa a piedi; **horse** — corsa di cavalli; — **horse** cavallo da corsa; — **track** pista; — *vi* correre; *(compete)* gareggiare; — *vt* far correre; *(motor)* imballare; **-r** *n* corridore *m*
racial *a* razziale
raciness *n* brio
racing *n* corsa, corse *fpl*; — *a* di corsa; dedicato alle corse
racism *n* razzismo
rack *n (clouds)* nembo; rastrelliera; *(coat)* attaccapanni *m*; *(luggage)* reticella; — *vt* torturare; — **one's brains** *(fig)* torturarsi il cervello; — **up** *(score)* accumulare
racket *n* gazzarra; *(sl)* traffico delittuoso; **tennis** — racchetta; **-eer** *n (sl)* camorrista *m (sl)*
racking *a* terribile, atroce
racy *a* caratteristico; piccante
radar *n* radar *m*
radial *a* radiale
radiance *n* splendore *m*
radiant *a* radiante
radiate *vi* raggiare, irradiarsi; — *vt* irradiare
radiation *n* radiazione
radiator *n* radiatore *m*
radical *a&n* radicale *m*; — **sign** segno di radice; **-ism** *n* radicalismo
radicle *n* radice *f*
radio *n* radio *f*; — **beacon** radiofaro; — **frequency** radiofrequenza; — **set** apparecchio; — **station** stazione radio; — *vt* trasmettere per radio
radioactive *a* radioattivo
radioactivity *n* radioattività
radiobroadcast *n* radiotrasmissione
radiocarbon *n* carbonio radioattivo; — **dating** determinazione dell'età di sostanze organiche per mezzo del contenuto di carbonio radioattivo
radiogram *n* radiogramma *m*
radiograph *n* radiografo
radiography *n* radiografia
radiolocation *n* radiolocalizzazione
radiologist *n* radiologo
radiology *n* radiologia

radiometer *n* radiometro
radioscopy *n* radioscopia
radiosensitive *a* radiosensibile
radiotelegraphy *n* radiotelegrafia
radiotherapy *n* radioterapia
radish *n* ravanello
radium *n* radio
radius *n* raggio; **within a** — **of** entro un raggio di
raffle *n* riffa, tombola; — *vt&i* sorteggiare
raft *n* zattera; *(coll)* quantità di
rafter *n* trave *f*
rag *n* straccio, cencio; **-man** *n* cenciaiolo
ragamuffin *n* straccione *m*
rage *n* furore *m*; **fly into a** — montare in furia; — *vi* arrabbiarsi; infuriare
ragged *a* cencioso
raging *a* furioso, violento
ragout *n* ragù *m*
rags *npl* stracci *mpl*; **be in** — *(fig)* essere in cenci *(or* stracciato)
raid *n* incursione; — *vt* invadere; predare
rail *n* sbarra; ringhiera; **by** — per ferrovia, con il treno; — *vi* rimbrottare; — **at, against** ingiuriare; proferire ingiurie; **-ing** *n* ringhiera; cancellata
raillery *n* derisione
railroad *n* ferrovia; — **station** stazione ferroviaria; — **tracks** rotaie *fpl*, binari *mpl*; — **train** treno; **narrow-gauge** — ferrovia a scartamento ridotto; — *vt (coll)* affrettare
rain *n* pioggia; — **water** acqua piovana; **in the** — alla pioggia; **-bow** *n* arcobaleno; — **check** biglietto per spettacolo all'aperto riusabile in caso di pioggia; **-coat** *n* impermeabile *m*; **-fall** *n* pioggia, precipitazione atmosferica; **-proof** *a* impermeabile; **-storm** *n* uragano di pioggia; **-y** *a* piovoso
raise *vt* alzare, sollevare; *(child)* allevare; *(money)* procurare; — *n* rialzo; aumento
raisin *n* uva passa
rake *n (tool)* rastrello; *(person)* libertino, scapestrato; *(naut)* inclinazione; — *vt* rastrellare, riunire; — **through** frugare; — *vi (naut)* inclinarsi
rakish *a* elegante
rally *n* riunione *f*; *(tennis)* ripresa; — *vt* adunare; *(banter)* beffare; — *vi* adunarsi; riprendersi
ram *n (mech)* stantuffo; *(naut)* sperone *m*; *(animal)* montone *m*; — *vt (beat)* battere; *(cram)* riempire; imbottire; *(naut)* speronare; **-rod** *n* bacchetta di fucile
ramble *vi* vagare; divagare; — *n (stroll)*

passeggiata
rambling *a* errante, divagante; — *n* divagazione
ramification *n* ramificazione
ramp *n* rampa
rampage *n* furia, violenza; — *vi* esser violento, sfuriare
rampant *a* violento, aggressivo; *(unchecked)* sfrenato; *(heraldry)* rampante; **be —** imperversare
rampart *n* bastione *m*
ramshackle *a* pericolante, cadente
ranch *n* fattoria per bestiame; **-er** *n* fattore *m*, allevatore di bestiame
rancid *a* rancido; **-ity** *n* rancidezza
rancor *n* rancore *m*
random *a* fortuito; **at —** a casaccio
range *n* catena di montagne; distesa; portata; **— finder** telemetro; **kitchen —** fornello; **in —** a tiro; **out of —** fuori di portata; **-r** *n (forest)* guardia forestale; — *vt* attraversare; — *vi* vagare; variare
rank *n* grado, rango; — *a* rancido, forte; grossolano; *(growth)* esuberante; — *vt* classificare; — *vi* essere classificato; **— with** essere alla pari di
ranking *a* eminente
rankle *vi* infiammarsi
ransack *vt* perquisire; saccheggiare; frugare
ransom *vt* riscattare; — *n* riscatto
rant *vi* smaniare; — *vt* declamare
rap *n* colpetto; *(coll)* condanna, fio; — *vt* battere; — *vi* bussare
rapacious *a* rapace; **-ly** *adv* rapacemente; **-nous** *a* rapacità
rape *n* violenza carnale, stupro; — *vt* violare, fare violenza carnale, stuprare; rapire
rapid *a* veloce, rapido; **-ity** *n* rapidità; **-s** *npl* rapida
rapid-fire *a* a tiro rapido
rapier *n* spada
rapport *n* armonia
rapt *a* rapito, estatico
rapture *n* trasporto; estasi *f*
rapturous *a* estatico
rare *a* raro; *(meat)* poco cotto; **-ly** *adv* di rado, raramente
rarefaction *n* rarefazione
rarefied *a* rarefatto
rarefy *vt* rarefare; — *vi* rarefarsi
rarity *n* rarità
rascal *n* briccone *m*
rash *n (med)* eruzione; — *a* temerario; **-ness** *n* imprudenza, avventatezza; **-ly** *adv* imprudentemente; irriflessivamente
rasp *n* raspa; — *vt* raspare; *(fig)* irritare; — *vi (sound)* raschiare

rasping *n* raschiamento; — *a* rauco
raspberry *n* lampone *m*
rat *n* topo, sorcio; **-trap** trappola per topi; **smell a —** subodorare, mangiare la foglia *(fig)*
ratchet *n* rocchetto
rate *n* proporzione; tariffa; velocità; **at the — of** al tasso di; **at any —** (fig) comunque, in ogni modo; **exchange —** quotazione di cambio; **interest —** saggio d'interesse; — *vt* stimare; valutare; — *vi* classificarsi
rather *adv* piuttosto, abbastanza
ratification *n* ratifica
ratify *vt* ratificare
rating *n* classificazione
ratio *n* ragione *f*
ration *n* razione; — *vt* razionare; **-ing** *n* razionamento
rational *a* razionale; **-ize** *vt* razionalizzare
rattle *vi* risonare; sbatacchiare; — *vt* far rumoreggiare; **become -d** *(coll)* confondersi; turbarsi; — *n* rumore *m*; chiacchierio; *(death)* rantolo; *(toy)* sonaglio
rattlebrain *n* chiacchierone *m*
rattlesnake *n* serpente a sonagli
raucous *a* rauco
ravage *vt* devastare; — *n* devastazione
ravaging *a* rovinoso
rave *vi* delirare, vaneggiare; *(coll)* entusiasmarsi
ravel *vt* avviluppare; imbrogliare
ravelling *n* filaccio
raven *n* corvo
ravenous *a* vorace; affamato
ravine *n* burrone *m*, voragine *f*
raving *a* delirante; *(coll)* straordinario; **-s** *npl* deliri *mpl (fig)*
ravish *vt* violare; *(delight)* incantare; **-ing** *a* incantevole
raw *a* crudo; inesperto; **— materials** materie prime; **-ness** *n* crudezza; rozzezza; escoriazione; inesperienza
rawboned *a* scarno
rawhide *n* cuoio greggio
ray *n* raggio; *(zool)* razza; — *vi* raggiare; — *vt* irradiare
rayon *n* raion *m*
raze *vt* radere; *(destroy)* distruggere
razor *n* rasoio; **— blade** lametta da barba; **safety —** rasoio di sicurezza
re *n* **in —** in merito a
reach *vt* raggiungere; arrivare; stendere; — *vi* estendersi; — *n* distesa, portata; **within —** possibile; a portata di mano
react *vi* reagire
reaction *n* reazione; **-ary** *a&n* reazionario
reactor *n* reattore *m*

read *vt* leggere; **–able** *a* leggibile; **–ing** *n* lettura; **–er** *n* lettore *m*; libro di lettura
readily *adv* volentieri; prontamente; facilmente
readiness *n* prontezza; facilità; **in —** pronto, alla mano
readjust *vt* raggiustare; riordinare; **–ment** *n* raggiustamento, riordinamento
readmission *n* riammissione
readmit *vt* riammettere
ready *a* pronto; **— money** contanti *mpl*; **—** *vt* preparare, predisporre
ready-made *a* confezionato
reaffirm *vt* riaffermare; **–ation** *n* riaffermazione
reagent *n* reagente *m*
real *a* reale; **— estate** beni immobili; **–ism** *n* realismo; **–ist** *n* realista *m&f*; **–istic** *a* realistico; **–istically** *adv* realisticamente; **–ity** *n* realtà
realization *n* realizzazione
realize *vt* accorgersi di; *(com)* realizzare
really *adv* veramente, davvero, effettivamente
realm *n* regno, reame *m*
realtor *n* agente immobiliare
realty *n* beni immobili
ream *vt* alesare; **–er** *n (machine)* alesatrice *f*; *(person)* alesatore *m*
reanimate *vt* rianimare
reanimation *n* rianimazione
reap *vt* mietere; falciare
reaper *n (mech)* mietitrice *f*; *(person)* mietitore *m*, mietitrice *f*
reappear *vi* riapparire; **–ance** *n* riapparizione, ricomparsa
reappoint *vt* rinominare; **–ment** *n* rinomina
reapproach *vt* ravvicinare
rear *n* di dietro, tergo; *(mil)* retroguardia; **—** *a* posteriore; **— admiral** contrammiraglio; **— guard** retroguardia; **—** *vt (lift)* erigere; *(young)* allevare; **—** *vi (horse)* impennarsi
rearm *vt* riarmare; **–ament** *n* riarmo, riarmamento
rearrange *vt* riordinare; **–ment** *n* riordinamento
reascend *vt&i* riascendere
reason *n* motivo, ragione *f*; **by — of** per causa di; **for this —** per questa ragione; **have — to** aver motivo di; **listen to —** ascoltar la ragione; **stand to —** essere innegabile; **–ing** *n* ragionamento; **—** *vi* ragionare; **—** *vt* razionalizzare; analizzare
reasonable *a* ragionevole; *(price)* conveniente
reasonably *adv* abbastanza; ragionevolmente

reassemble *vt* riunire ancora; **—** *vi* riunirsi ancora
reassurance *n* rassicurazione
reassure *vt* rassicurare
reawaken *vt* risvegliare; **—** *vi* risvegliarsi; **–ing** *n* risveglio
rebate *n* bonifica, sconto, diminuzione; **—** *vt* dedurre, diminuire
rebel *a&n* ribelle *m*
rebel *vi* ribellarsi
rebellion *n* rivolta
rebellious *a* ribelle
rebind *vt* rilegare, ricostruire
rebirth *n* rinascita
reborn *a* rinato
rebound *n* rimbalzo
rebound *vi* rimbalzare
rebroadcast *n* ritrasmissione; **—** *vt* ritrasmettere
rebuff *n (refusal)* rifiuto; *(repulse)* rigetto
rebuild *vt* ricostruire
rebuke *vt* rimproverare; **—** *n* rimprovero
recalcitrance *n* ricalcitramento
recalcitrant *a* ricalcitrante
recall *vt* richiamare; *(remember)* rammentare, ricordare; revocare
recall *n* richiamo; revoca
recant *vt* ritrattare; ripudiare; **—** *vi* ritrattarsi
recap *vt (auto)* ricostruire il battistrada
recapitulate *vt&i* ricapitolare
recapitulation *n* ricapitolazione
recapture *n* ripresa, ricupero; **—** *vt* ricatturare
recede *vi* recedere, indietreggiare
receding *a* recedente, indietreggiante
receipt *n* quietanza, ricevuta; **—** *vt* quietanzare
receivable *a* ricevibile; **accounts —** *(com)* conti esigibili
receive *vt* ricevere; **–r** *n* ricevitore *m*, destinatario; *(law)* curatore *m*
receiving *n* ricevimento; *(stolen goods)* ricettazione
recent *a* recente; fresco; **–ly** *adv* recentemente, poco fa
receptacle *n* ricettacolo
reception *n* accoglienza; ricevimento; *(radio)* ricezione
receptionist *n* accoglitrice *f*
receptive *a* ricettivo; **–ness** *n* recettività
recess *n* recesso; nicchia; **school —** ricreazione
recess *vi* aggiornarsi; **—** *vt* formare rientranza
recession *n* regresso; *(com)* crisi economica; **–al** *a* recessionale
recidivist *n* recidivo
recipe *n* ricetta

recipient n recipiente, ricevente m
reciprocal a reciproco
reciprocate vt contraccambiare, reciprocare
reciprocity n reciprocità
recital n recita; *(telling)* rappresentazione
recitation n recitazione
recite vt recitare; declamare
reckless a temerario
reckon vi calcolare; *(coll)* supporre, credere
reckoning n computo; **day of** — giorno del giudizio; giorno di retribuzione
reclaim vt redimere; *(land)* bonificare
reclamation n redenzione; correzione; riforma; *(land)* bonifica
recline vi sdraiarsi; adagiarsi; — vt reclinare, adagiare
reclining a adagiato
recluse n eremita m
recognition n riconoscimento
recognizable a riconoscibile
recognizance n malleveria
recognize vt riconoscere
recoil vi ritirarsi, indietreggiare; rimbalzare; *(gun)* rinculare; — n indietreggiamento; rimbalzo; *(gun)* rinculo
recollect vt ricordare; **–ion** n ricordo; memoria
recommence vt&i ricominciare
recommend vt raccomandare; **–ation** n raccomandazione
recompense n ricompensa; — vt ricompensare
reconcilable a riconciliabile
reconcile vt riconciliare
reconciliation n riconciliazione
reconciliatory a riconciliatorio
recondite a recondito
recondition vt riaccondizionare; **–ing** n riaccondizionamento
reconnaisance n ricognizione
reconnoiter vt perlustrare; — vi fare una ricognizione
reconquer vt riconquistare
reconsider vt riconsiderare; **–ation** n riconsiderazione
reconstitute vt ricostituire
reconstruct vt ricostruire; **–ion** n ricostruzione
record vt registrare; *(phonograph)* incidere
record n registro; *(phonograph)* disco; *(sport)* primato; — **player** giradischi m; **off the** — non ufficiale; **–ing** n incisione; registrazione; **–s** npl *(law)* precedenti mpl
recorder n registratore m; archivista m; **tape** — fonografo *(or incisore)* a nastro
record-breaking a primatista
recount n ricomputo; riconto; — vt ricomputare, ricontare; *(narrate)* raccontare
recountal n racconto
recoup vt ricuperare, compensare; **–ment** n ricupero
recourse n rifugio, ricorso; **have** — **to** ricorrere a
recover vi guarire, rimettersi; — vt ricuperare; **–y** n guarigione f, ricupero
re-cover vt ricoprire
recreant a codardo
recreate vt svagare, ristorare; — vi ristorarsi, divertirsi
re-create vt ricreare
recreation n ricreazione, divertimento, svago; **–al** a ricreativo
recriminate vi recriminare
recrimination n recriminazione
recruit vt reclutare; — n recluta; **–ing** n reclutamento
rectal a rettale
rectangle n rettangolo
rectangular a rettangolare
rectifiable a correggibile
rectification n rettificazione
rectifier n *(elec)* raddrizzatore di corrente
rectify vt rettificare; *(elec)* raddrizzare
rectilinear a rettilineo
rectitude n rettitudine f
rector n *(eccl)* parroco, pastore m; **–y** n casa parrocchiale
rectum n retto
recumbent a giacente
recuperate vi guarire, rimettersi; — vt ricuperare
recuperation n ricuperazione, ricupero
recur vi ricorrere; **–rence** n ricorrenza; ritorno; **–rent** a periodico, ricorrente
red n&a rosso; — **light** pericolo; — **pepper** pepe di Caienna; — **tape** *(fig)* burocrazia; **be in the** — *(com)* essere in deficit *(or passivo)*; **–cap** n facchino; **–head** n chi ha i capelli rossi; **–ness** n rossore m; **–skin** n *(Indian)* pellerossa m
red– *(in comp)* **–blooded** a energico; — **eyed** cogli occhi infiammati; **–haired** a dai capelli rossi; **–handed** a con le mani nel sacco; **–hot** a rovente; **–letter day** giorno festivo
redden vi arrossire; — vt colorare di rosso
reddish a rossiccio
redecorate vt ridecorare
redeem vt redimere, riscattare; **–able** a redimibile; **–er** n chi riscatta
Redeemer n Redentore m
redemption n redenzione, riscatto
rediscover vt scoprire di nuovo
redistribute vt ridistribuire
redistribution n ridistribuzione
redolence n fragranza, profumo

redolent *a* fragrante, profumato

redouble *vt* raddoppiare; — *vi* raddoppiarsi

redoubtable *a* formidabile

redound *vi* ridondare

redraft *vt* redigere di nuovo

redress *n* rettifica, riparazione

redress *vt* rettificare

reduce *vt&i* ridurre; *(weight)* dimagrare, dimagrire

reducible *a* riducibile

reduction *n* riduzione

redundancy *n* ridondanza

redundant *a* ridondante

reduplicate *vt* raddoppiare

reduplication *n* raddoppiamento

reecho *vi&t* riecheggiare

reed *n* canna; *(musical instrument)* ancia; — *a* di canna

reeducate *vt* rieducare

reeducation *n* rieducazione

reef *n* scoglio; *(naut)* terzaruolo; — *vt* terzaruolare

reek *vt&i* fumare; esalare; *(stink)* puzzare

reel *n* aspo, bobina; *(spinning)* vacillamento; — **off** snocciolare; **news** — notiziario cinematografico; — *vt* avvolgere; — *vi* girare, vacillare

reeling *n* vacillamento; — *a* vacillante

reelect *vt* rieleggere; **-ion** *n* rielezione

reembark *vi* rimbarcarsi

reembody *vt* rincorporare

reenact *vt* eseguire di nuovo; *(law)* rimettere in vigore

reenlist *vi* riarruolarsi

reenter *vt* rientrare

reentry *n* rientrata

reequip *vt* riequipaggiare

reestablish *vt* ristabilire; **-ment** *n* ristabilimento, restaurazione

reexamination *n* riesame *m*

reexamine *vt* riesaminare

reexport *vt* riesportare; **-ation** *n* riesporto

reface *vt* rifare la facciata di

refashion *vt* rimodernare

refasten *vt* rilegare, riassicurare

refectory *n* refettorio

refer *vi* alludere; — *vt* riferire

referable *a* referibile

reference *n* allusione; referenza; richiamo; **letter of** — lettera di raccomandazione; — **book** libro di consultazione; — **library** biblioteca di consultazione; **with** — **to** rispetto a

referee *n* arbitro; — *vt* arbitrare

referendum *n* referendum *m*

referral *n* riferimento

refill *vt* riempire; — *n* rifornimento, ricambio

refine *vt* raffinare; **-d** *a* colto, raffinato; **-ment** *n* raffinatezza

refinery *n* raffineria

refit *vt* riparare

reflect *vt&i* riflettere, reflettersi, meditare; **-or** *n* riflettore *m*

reflection *n* riflessione; riflesso; critica

reflex *n* riflesso; **-ive** *a* riflessivo

reforest *vt* rimboscare; **-ation** *n* rimboscamento

reform *vt* riformare; — *vi* riformarsi; — *n* riforma; **-atory** *n* riformatorio; **-er** *n* riformatore *m*

reformation *n* *(moral)* emendamento; riforma

refract *vt* rifrangere; **-ion** *n* rifrazione; **-ive** *a* rifrattivo; **-or** *n* rifrattore *m*; **-ory** *a* rifrangente

refrain *vi* astenersi; — *n* ritornello; aria

refresh *vt* rinfrescare; **-ment** *n* rinfresco; **-ing** *a* rinfrescante

refrigerate *vt* refrigerare

refrigeration *n* refrigerazione

refrigerator *n* frigorifero

refuel *vt&i* rifornire di carburante

refuge *n* ricovero; rifugio; **take** — rifugiarsi

refugee *n* profugo

refulgence *n* splendore *m*

refulgent *a* rifulgente

refund *vt* rimborsare

refund, -ing *n* rimborso

refundable *a* rimborsabile

refurnish *vt* riprovvedere, riammobiliare

refusal *n* rifiuto

refuse *n* rifiuto; immondizie *fpl*

refuse *vt&i* rifiutare

refutation *n* confutazione

refute *vt* refutare

regain *vt* ricuperare, riguadagnare; — **consciousness** riprendersi

regal *a* regale; **-ia** *n* insegne regali

regale *vt* *(delight)* deliziare; *(fete)* festeggiare

regard *n* riguardo, stima; **have no** — **for** non aver riguardo per; **in** — **to** riguardo a; **in this** — sotto questo rispetto; — *vt* riguardare; stimare

regarding *prep* riguardo a

regardless *a* noncurante; — *adv* in ogni modo; — **of** nonostante

regards *npl* saluti *mpl*; **give** — presentare gli omaggi

regatta *n* regata

regency *n* reggenza

regenerate *vt* rigenerare; — *vi* rigenerarsi

regenerate *a* rigenerato

regeneration *n* rigenerazione

regent *n* reggente *m&f*

regime *n* regime *m*

regiment *n* reggimento; — *vt* irreggimentare; **–al** *a* reggimentale; **–ation** *n* reggimentazione
region *n* regione *f*; **–al** *a* regionale
register *n* registro; **cash** — registratore di cassa; — *vt* registrare; *(mail)* raccomandare; — *vi* iscriversi
registrar *n* archivista *m*; segretario
registration *n* registrazione; *(mail)* raccomandazione
registry *n* segretariato
regnant *a* regnante
regress *vi* regredire
regression *n* regressione
regressive *a* regressivo
regret *n* rammarico; **–ful** *a* rincresciuto; **–fully** *adv* con dispiacere; — *vt* rimpiangere; dispiacere di
regrettable *a* increscioso
regroup *vt* raggruppare di nuovo
regular *a* regolare; **–ity** *n* regolarità; **–ly** *adv* regolarmente; **–ize** *vt* regolarizzare
regulate *vt* regolare
regulation *n* regolamento; regola; — *a* regolamentare
regulator *n* regolatore *m*
regurgitate *vt&i* rigurgitare
regurgitation *n* rigurgito
rehabilitate *vt* riabilitare
rehabilitation *n* riabilitazione
rehearsal *n* prova
rehearse *vt* provare, ripetere
reheat *vt* riscaldare
reign *n* regno; — *vi* regnare; **–ing** *a* regnante
reimbursable *a* rimborsabile
reimburse *vt* rimborsare; **–ment** *n* rimborso
rein *n* redine *f*; — *vt* imbrigliare, frenare, controllare
reincarnation *n* reincarnazione
reincorporate *vt* reincorporare
reindeer *n* renna
reinforce *vt* rinforzare; **–d** *a* rinforzato; **–ment** *n* rinforzo
reinsert *vt* inserire di nuovo
reinstate *vt (position)* reintegrare; *(re-establish)* ristabilire; *(replace)* ricollocare; **–ment** *n* ristabilimento; ripristino
reinsurance *n* riassicurazione
reinsure *vt* riassicurare
reinvest *vt* rinvestire; **–ment** *n* rinvestimento
reissue *vt* riemettere; ripubblicare; — *n* riemissione; ripubblicazione
reiterate *vt* reiterare
reiteration *n* reiterazione
reject *n* respinto, rifiuto
reject *vt* scartare

rejection *n* rigetto; reiezione
rejoice *vi* rallegrarsi, gioire; — *vt* rallegrare
rejoicing *n* allegria; gioia
rejoin *vt* riunire di nuovo; *(meet)* raggiungere; *(reply)* replicare; — *vi* riunirsi di nuovo
rejoinder *n* replica
rejuvenate *vt* ringiovanire
rejuvenation *n* ringiovanimento
rekindle *vt* riaccendere; — *vi* riaccendersi
relapse *vi* ricadere; — *n* ricaduta
relate *vt (narrate)* raccontare; mettere in relazione; — *vi* riguardare; **–d** *a* imparentato; *(similar)* affine
relating *a* relativo
relation *n* rapporto, relazione; **in — to** in riferimento a; inerente a; **–ship** *n* rapporto, relazione, parentela
relative *n* parente *m&f*; — *a* relativo
relativity *n* relatività
relax *vt* rilassare; — *vi* rilassarsi, distrarsi; **–ation** *n* distensione, svago; **–ing** *a* calmante
relay *n* cambio, muta; *(elec)* raddrizzatore di corrente; *(rad)* trasmissione; — *vt (mail)* distribuire; *(rebroadcast)* ritrasmettere
release *vt* liberare, rilasciare; — *n* liberazione, rilascio; esonero; *(mech)* scarico
relegate *vt* relegare
relegation *n* relegazione
relent *vi* cedere, attenuarsi; **–less** *a* inflessibile; **–lessness** *n* implacabilità, inflessibilità
relevance *n* applicabilità, rapporto; pertinenza
relevant *a* pertinente, a proposito
reliability *n* fidatezza
reliable *a* degno di fiducia
reliably *adv* fidatamente
reliant *a* fiducioso
reliance *n* fiducia
relic *n* reliquia
relief *n* sollievo; *(help)* sussidio, aiuto; *(replace)* rilievo
relieve *vt* alleviare; esonerare; dare il cambio a
relight *vt* riaccendere
religion *n* religione *f*
religiosity *n* religiosità
religious *a* religioso
reline *vt* rifoderare; *(brakes)* rifasciare
relinquish *vt* abbandonare, rinunciare; **–ment** *n* rinuncia, abbandono
reliquary *n* reliquario
relish *n* gusto; condimento; — *vt (enjoy)* godere; *(taste)* gustare; — *vi* aver sapore di

relive *vt* rivivere
reload *vt* ricaricare
relocate *vt* ricollocare
relocation *n* ricollocazione
reluctance *n* riluttanza
reluctant *a* restio, poco disposto; –ly *adv* a malincuore
rely *vi* contare su
remain *vi* restare, rimanere; –s *npl* spoglie *fpl*, resti *mpl*
remainder *n* resto
remaining *a* rimanente
remake *vt* rifare
remark *n* osservazione, commento; — *vt* commentare; *(notice)* osservare, notare; –able *a* straordinario, notevole
re-mark *vt* marcare di nuovo
remarkably *adv* notevolmente
remarry *vi* risposarsi; — *vt* risposare
remediable *a* rimediabile
remedial *a* curativo, riparatore
remedy *n* rimedio; — *vt* rimediare
remember *vt&i* ricordare, ricordarsi
remembrance *n* memoria, ricordo, rimembranza
remind *vt&i* ricordare; –er *n* ricordo, memorandum *m*
reminiscence *n* reminiscenza, ricordo
reminiscent *a* reminiscente, memore
remiss *a* negligente; *(slow)* lento
remissible *a* remissibile
remission *n* remissione, perdono, condono
remit *vt* rimettere; *(decrease)* scemare; –tal *n* remissione; –tance *n* rimessa; –ter *n* mittente *m&f*
remnant *n* resto; scampolo
remodel *vt* ricostruire; rimodellare
remonstrance *n* rimostranza
remonstrate *vt* esprimere protestando; — *vi* rimostrare, protestare
remorse *n* rimorso; –less *a* spietato, senza rimorsi; –ful *a* pieno di rimorsi, contrito
remote *a* lontano, remoto; — control *n* radiotelecomando; –ly *adv* remotamente; –ness *n* lontananza
remold *vt* rimodellare
remount *vt* rimontare
removable *a* rimovibile
removal *n* trasloco, cambio
remove *vt* togliere, portar via; destituire; –d *a* lontano
remunerate *vt* rimunerare
remuneration *n* rimunerazione
remunerative *a* rimunerativo
renaissance *n* rinascimento
renal *a* renale
rename *vt* rinominare
renascence *n* rinascita
renascent *a* rinascente

rend *vt* stracciare, fendere; — *vi* lacerarsi, stracciarsi
render *vt* rendere; *(fat)* sciogliere; *(mus)* eseguire
rendezvous *n* appuntamento; — *vt* radunare; — *vi* riunirsi
rendition *n* *(mus)* esecuzione
renegade *n* rinnegato; apostata *m*
renege *vi* *(coll)* rinnegare la parola *(fig)*
renew *vt* rinnovare; ricominciare; — *vi* rinnovarsi; –al *n* rinnovo; –able *a* rinnovabile
renounce *vt* rinunciare; ripudiare; –ment *n* rinuncia
renovate *vt* rinnovare
renovation *n* rinnovazione
renown *n* rinomanza; celebrità, fama; distinzione; –ed *a* rinomato
rent *n* *(cloth)* strappo, spacco; *(income)* reddito; *(property)* affitto; –al *n* affitto; *(income)* rendita locativa
rent *vt* affittare, noleggiare; — *vi* venir affittato
renunciation *n* rinuncia
reoccupation *n* rioccupazione
reoccupy *vt* rioccupare
reopen *vt* riaprire; — *vi* riaprirsi; –ing *n* riapertura
reorder *vt* riordinare
reorganization *n* riorganizzazione
reorganize *vt&i* riorganizzare
repack *vi* rifare le valige
repaint *vt* ridipingere
repair *vt* riparare, accomodare; — *vi* recarsi; *(withdraw)* ritirarsi; —, –ing *n* riparazione; –able *a* riparabile; –man *n* riparatore *m*
reparable *a* rimediabile, riparabile
reparation *n* riparazione
repartee *n* frizzo, risposta pronta
repast *n* pasto
repatriate *vt&i* rimpatriare
repatriation *n* rimpatrio
repave *vt* rilastricare, ripavimentare
repay *vt* rimborsare, ripagare; valere la pena di, ricompensare; –able *a* ricompensabile, rimborsabile; –ment *n* restituzione; ricompensa
repeal *n* revoca, abrogazione; — *vt* revocare, abrogare
repeat *vt* ripetere; — *vi* ripetersi; — *n* ripetizione; risuono; –er *n* ripetitore *m*; *(law)* recidivo; –ed *a* ripetuto; –edly *adv* ripetutamente
repeating *a* periodico, ricorrente; — decimal decimale periodico
repel *vt* respingere
repellent *a* repellente
repelling *a* repulsivo
repent *vt&i* pentirsi di; –ance *n* penti-

mento; **–ant** *a* penitente; pentito
repercussion *n* ripercussione
repertoire *n* repertorio
repertory *n* deposito; *(theat)* repertorio
repetend *n (math)* decimale periodico
repetition *n* ripetizione
replace *vt* rimettere; sostituire; **–able** *a* rimpiazzabile, sostituibile; **–ment** *n* sostituzione
replant *vt* ripiantare
replate *vt* riplaccare
replay *vt (game)* giocare di nuovo; *(mus)* suonare di nuovo
replenish *vt* empire di nuovo; **–ment** *n* riempimento
replete *a* pieno, sazio
replica *n* copia, replica
reply *vt&i* replicare, rispondere; — *n* replica, risposta
repopulate *vt* ripopolare
repopulation *n* ripopolamento
report *vt* riferire; — *vi* presentarsi, consegnarsi; — *n* rapporto; rendiconto; *(gun)* detonazione; **–ing** *n* cronaca; **–er** *n* cronista *m*; *(newspaper)* giornalista *m&f*
repose *n* riposo; — *vi* riposare; riposarsi
repository *n* deposito, magazzino; *(cemetery)* cripta
repossess *vt* ripossedere, riavere
repossession *n* ripossessione
reprehend *vt* biasimare
reprehensible *a* riprensibile
reprehensibly *adv* reprensibilmente
reprehension *n* riprensione
represent *vt* rappresentare
representation *n* rappresentanza
representative *n* rappresentante *m*; deputato; — *a* rappresentativo; tipico
repress *vt* reprimere; **–ed** *a* represso
repression *n* repressione
repressive *a* repressivo
reprieve *n* sospensione, grazia; — *vt* graziare; *(penal)* rinviare l'esecuzione
reprimand *n* rimprovero; — *vt* rimproverare
reprint *n* ristampa; estratto di stampa; — *vt* ristampare; **–ing** *n* ristampa
reprisal *n* rappresaglia
reproach *n* biasimo, rimprovero; — *vt* rimproverare, sgridare; **–able** *a* riprovevole; **–ful** *a* accusante, criticante; **–less** *a* irreprensibile
reprobate *n&a* reprobo, immorale *m&f*; — *vt* riprovare
reprobation *n* riprovazione
reproduce *vt* riprodurre; — *vi* riprodursi
reproducible *a* riproducibile
reproduction *n* riproduzione
reproductive *a* riproduttivo

reproof *n* rimprovero, biasimo
reprove *vt* rimproverare, riprovare, censurare
reptile *n* rettile *m*
republic *n* repubblica; **–an** *n&a* repubblicano
republish *vt* ripubblicare
repudiate *vt* ripudiare, rigettare
repudiation *n* ripudio, ripulsa; *(law)* interdizione
repugnance *n* ripulsione, ripugnanza
repugnant *a* ripugnante
repulse *vt* respingere, repellere; ricusare; — *n* ripulsa, rifiuto
repulsion *n* repulsione, ripulsa
repulsive *a* schifoso, nauseante, ripulsivo
repurchase *n* ricompera; — *vt* ricomperare
reputable *a* stimabile, rispettabile
reputation *n* riputazione
repute *n* riputazione, stima; **–d** *a* reputato; — *vt* ritenere, reputare
request *n* richiesta; — *vt* chiedere, richiedere; **on** — in base a richiesta
require *vt* esigere; **–ment** *n* requisito, bisogno, necessità
requisite *n* requisito; — *a* richiesto, necessario
requisition *vt* requisire; — *n* requisizione
requital *n* contraccambio; *(retaliation)* rappresaglia
requite *vt* contraccambiare, ricompensare, ripagare
reroute *vt* desviare
resaddle *vt* risellare
resale *n* rivendita
rescind *vt* rescindere, abrogare
rescue *n* liberazione, riscatto; — *vt* liberare, salvare; **–r** *n* liberatore *m*
research *n* ricerca, investigazione; — *vt* investigare; — *vi* fare ricerca
resell *vt* rivendere
resemblance *n* rassomiglianza
resemble *vt* rassomigliare a
resent *vt* risentirsi di; **–ful** *a* rancoroso; **–ment** *n* risentimento
reservation *n* prenotazione; riserva
reserve *n* riserva; — *vt* riservare; *(engage)* prenotare
reserved *a* circospetto, riservato; **–ly** *adv* con riserbo
reservist *n* riservista *m*
reservoir *n* serbatoio, cisterna
reset *vt* rimettere; ricollocare; *(gem)* rincastonare; *(print)* ricomporre
resettle *vt* ristabilire; — *vi* ristabilirsi
reside *vi* risiedere
residence *n* domicilio, residenza
resident *n&a* abitante, residente *m*; **–ial** *a* residenziale
residual *a* residuale

residue n residuo
resign vt dare le dimissioni; rinunciare; — oneself rassegnarsi; -ed a rassegnato; -edly con rassegnazione
resignation n rassegnazione; dimissioni fpl
resilience n elasticità
resilient a elastico
resin n resina; -ous a di resina, resinoso
resist vt&i resistere; -ance n resistenza; -ant a resistente; -ible a resistibile; -or n (elec) resistenza
resole vt risuolare
resolute a risoluto
resolution n risoluzione; proponimento
resolve vt risolvere, decidere; — vi risolversi, decidersi
resonance n risonanza
resonant a risonante
resonator n risonatore m
resort n ricorso; (summer) luogo di villeggiatura; — vi ricorrere
resound vi risonare; -ing a risonante
resource n risorsa; -ful a abile, intraprendente, ingegnoso; pieno di risorse; -fulness n intraprendenza
resources npl (financial) mezzi economici; (natural) risorse naturali
respect n rispetto; in this — sotto questo riguardo; with — to riguardo a; con rispetto a; -able a rispettabile; -ability n rispettabilità; -ful a rispettoso; -fully adv con rispetto; — vt rispettare
respecting prep riguardo a, circa
respective a rispettivo; -ly adv rispettivamente
respiration n respirazione
respirator n respiratore m
respiratory a respiratorio
respire vt&i respirare
respite n tregua, respiro
resplendent a risplendente
respond vt&i rispondere
respondent n (law) imputato; — a rispondente
response n responso, risposta; (med) riflesso
responsibility n responsabilità
responsible a responsabile
responsive a accondiscendente, corresponsivo
rest n resto; riposo; (mus) pausa; (support) appoggio, sostegno; take a — riposarsi, prendere un riposo; -ful a calmo; riposante; -fully adv riposatamente; — vt&i riposare; riposarsi
restate vt riesporre, ridire
restaurant n ristorante m
restive a restio; ostinato; -ness n ostinatezza; restio

restless a inquieto, irrequieto; -ness n inquietudine f
restock vt rifornire
restorable a restaurabile
restoration n restaurazione, restauro
restorative n&a ristorativo
restore vt restaurare; restituire
restrain vt trattenere
restraint n restrizione; detenzione; (manner) riservatezza
restrict vt restringere; -ive a restrittivo
restriction n restrizione
rest room gabinetto di decenza
result n risultato; — vi risultare; as a — of in seguito a
resultant a risultante
résumé n riassunto
resume vt&i riprendere
resumption n ripresa
resurge vi risorgere
resurgence n risorgimento
resurgent a risorgente
resurrect vt risuscitare
resurrection n risurrezione
resuscitate vt&i risuscitare
resuscitation n ristabilimento, ravvivamento
ret vt macerare
retail n (com) dettaglio; vendita al minuto; — a al minuto; — vt vendere al minuto; dettagliare; -er n venditore al minuto; dettagliante m
retain vt ritenere; -er n servitore m; (law) onorario
retaining a che ritiene; — wall muro di sostegno
retake vt riprendere
retaliate vi render pan per focaccia (fig), rivalersi; — vt ritorcere, rendere
retaliation n rappresaglia; contraccambio; ritorsione
retaliatory a di rappresaglia
retard vt ritardare, rallentare; -ed a deficiente, mentalmente ritardato
retch vi recere; -ing n conato di vomito
retell vt riraccontare, ridire
retention n conservazione; ritenzione
retentive a ritentivo; -ness n ritenitiva, ritentiva
reticence n reticenza
reticent a reticente
retina n retina
retinue n corteo, seguito
retire vt ritirare; — vi ritirarsi; (to bed) andare a letto; (from work) andare in pensione; -d a in pensione; a riposo; -ment n riposo, ritiro
retiring a riservato, ritirato
retort n ritorsione; (chem) storta; —

vt&i ribattere, rimbeccare, ritorcere
retouch *vt* ritoccare
retrace *vt* riandare, ricalcare
retract *vt* ritirare; ritrattare; — *vi* ritirarsi; ritrattarsi
retractable *a* ritrattabile
retractile *a* retrattile
retraction *n* ritrattazione
retractor *n (anat)* muscolo retrattore
retread *vt (auto)* rifare il battistrada
retreat *n* ritirata; ritiro; — *vi* ritirarsi; recedere; **-ing** *a* ritirante; *(mil)* in ritirata
retrench *vt* ridurre; — *vi* risparmiare; **-ment** *n* risparmio
retribution *n* castigo; ricompensa, retribuzione
retrieve *vt* ricuperare
retroact *vi* retroagire
retroaction *n* retroazione
retroactive *a* retroattivo
retrogradation *n* retrogradazione
retrograde *vi* ritirarsi, retrogradare; — *a* retrogrado
retrogress *vi* retrogredire; **-ion** *n* retrogressione; **-ive** *a* retrogressivo
retrospect, retrospection *n* retrospetto, retrospezione
retroversion *n* retroversione
return *vt* restituire; *(send back)* rinviare; *(reciprocate)* contraccambiare; — *vi* ritornare; — *n* ritorno; — *a* di ritorno; — **match** *(sport)* partita di ritorno; — **ticket** biglietto di andata e ritorno; **in** — per contro; a cambio; **in** — **for** in cambio di
returnable *a* restituibile
reunion *n* riunione *f*
reunite *vt* riunire; — *vi* riunirsi
revalue *vt* rivalutare
revamp *vt* riorganizzare, rifare
reveal *vt* rivelare
reveille *n (mil)* diana
revel *n* baldoria, festa; — *vi* far baldoria *(or festa)*; **-ler** *n* crapulone *m*; **-ry** *n* baldoria
revelation *n* rivelazione *f*
revenge *n* vendetta; **-ful** *a* vendicativo; — *vt* vendicare; **take** — **on** vendicarsi con
revenue *n* reddito, entrata; fisco
reverberate *vt&i* riverberare, ripercuotere, riflettere
reverberation *n* riverbero
revere *vt* riverire
reverence *n* riverenza; venerazione
reverend *a* reverendo
reverent *a* riverente
reverie *n* fantasticheria; meditazione
reversal *n* inversione; revoca

reverse *n* rovescio; opposto, contrario; — *(auto)* retromarcia; — **side** parte opposta; — *a* opposto; — *vt* invertire
reversion *n* riversione, ritorno
revert *vi* rivolgersi, ritornare
review *n* rivista; *(book)* recensione *f*; — *vt* rivedere; recensire; **-er** *n* recensore *m*, critico
revile *vt* insultare
revise *vt* correggere, rivedere
reviser *n* revisore *m*
revision *n* revisione
revisit *vt* rivisitare
revival *n* risorgimento; risveglio; ravvivamento; *(arts)* riesumazione; *(eccl)* risveglio religioso; **-ist** *n* promotore di risvegli religiosi
revive *vt* ravvivare; — *vi* rianimarsi, rivivere
reviver *n* ravvivatore *m*
revocable *a* revocabile
revocation *n* revoca
revoke *vt* revocare
revolt *vi* ribellarsi; — *vt* nauseare; — *n* rivolta; **-ing** *a* nauseante
revolution *n* rivoluzione; *(mech)* giro; **-ary** *a* rivoluzionario; **-ize** *vt* rivoluzionare
revolve *vt&i* girare
revolver *n* revolver *m*, rivoltella
revolving *a* girevole, giratorio
revue *n (theat)* rivista
revulsion *n* repulsione
revulsive *n&a* revulsivo
reward *n* ricompensa; — *vt* rimunerare, premiare; **-ing** *a* ricompensatore, di ricompensa
rewin *vt* rivincere
rewind *vt* avvolgere di nuovo
reword *vt* ripetere; mettere in altre parole
rewrite *vt* riscrivere; — *n* riscritto
rhapsodical *a* rapsodico
rhapsody *n* rapsodia
Rhenish *a* del Reno
rheometer *n* reometro
rheoscope *n* reoscopo
rheostat *n* reostato
rhetoric *n* rettorica; **-al** *a* rettorico; **-ian** *n* retore *m*
rheumatic *a* reumatico; — **fever** febbre reumatica
rheumatism *n* reumatismo
Rh factor fattore Rh
Rhine Reno; — **wine** vino del Reno
rhinestone *n* strasso
rhinoceros *n* rinoceronte *m*
rhizome *n (bot)* rizoma
rhombus *n (math)* rombo
rhubarb *n* rabarbaro
rhyme *n* rima; — *vt&i* rimare; **no** — **or**

reason senza capo nè coda *(fig)*
rhymester *n* rimatore *m*
rhythm *n* ritmo; **–ic** *a* ritmico
rib *n* costola; — *vt* centinare; *(coll)* beffare, deridere
ribald *a* licenzioso, scurrile; **–ry** *n* scurrilità
ribbing *n* costole *fpl*; centinatura; *(coll)* beffa, presa in giro
ribbon *n* nastro; **tear to —s** fare a brandelli
rice *n* riso; — **field** risaia; — **paper** carta riso *(or* cinese); — **pudding** riso al latte
rich *a* ricco; **–es** *npl* ricchezza; **–ness** *n* ricchezza; **grow —** arricchirsi; **the —** i ricchi
rickets *npl (med)* rachitismo
rickety *a* rachitico
ricochet *vi* rimbalzare; — *n* rimbalzo
rid *vt* sbarazzare, liberare; **get — of** sbarazzarsi di
riddance *n* liberazione
riddle *n* indovinello, enigma *m*; — *vt* risolvere; spiegare; — *vi* parlare per enigmi
riddle *vt (perforate)* crivellare
ride *vt&i* cavalcare; andare in *(or* a); — *n* corsa; cavalcata; passeggiata
rider *n (horseback)* cavaliere *m*; *(jockey)* fantino; *(law)* codicillo, aggiunta
ridge *n* cresta; *(roof)* colmo, comignolo
ridicule *n* ridicolo; — *vt* deridere, mettere in ridicolo
ridiculous *a* ridicolo
riding *n* equitazione; — **boots** stivali per equitazione; — **breeches** calzoni per equitazione; — **habit** abito da amazzone; — **master** maestro d'equitazione; — **school** scuola d'equitazione
rife *a* prevalente, comune; abbondante; — **with** abbondante di
riffraff *n* rifiuti *mpl*; canaglia, marmaglia
rifle *n* fucile *m*; — **range** campo di tiro; **within — shot** a portata di fucile; — *vt* predare, derubare
rifleman *n* fuciliere *m*
rift *n* crepa, fessura
rig *n* arnese *m*; — *vt (naut)* attrezzare; equipaggiare; *(tamper)* manipolare fraudolentemente
rigging *n (naut)* attrezzatura
right *n* ragione, diritto; — **and wrong** il giusto e l'ingiusto; — **of way** *(law)* diritto di passaggio; — **side** destra; *(material)* dritto; — **side up** a faccia in sù *(fig)*; **have the —** aver il diritto
right *a* giusto, diritto, corretto; — **angle** angolo retto; **all —** benissimo; **be —** aver ragione
right *adv (directly)* dirittamente; *(justly)* giustamente; *(well)* bene; — **and left** destra e sinistra; — **away** subito; **do —** far bene
right *vt* raddrizzare, correggere; — *vi* raddrizzarsi
righteous *a* retto; giusto; virtuoso; **–ly** *adv* rettamente; **–ness** *n* rettitudine *f*
rightful *a* legittimo; giusto; equo; **–ly** *adv* legittimamente; equamente; giustamente
right-handed *a* destro
rightly *adv* rettamente, esattamente
rights *npl* diritti *mpl*; **by —** a rigore, per diritto; **within one's —** nei propri diritti
rigid *a* rigido, severo; **–ity** *n* rigidità, severità; rigidezza; **–ly** *adv* rigidamente
rigmarole *n* tiritera
rigor *n* rigidità, severità; *(med)* brivido; **–ous** *a* rigoroso; **–ousness** *n* rigorosità; — **mortis** rigidità cadaverica
rile *vt (coll)* irritare
rill *n* ruscello
rim *n (wheel)* cerchione *m*; orlo; *(eyeglass)* montatura; — *vt* orlare, bordare; **–less** *a* senza montatura
rime *vt* brinare; — *n* brina
rind *n* buccia, scorza
rinderpest *n* peste bovina
ring *n* anello; cerchio; — **finger** anulare *m*; **boxing —** ring *m*, quadrato; **wedding —** anello nuziale, fede *f*, vera; — *vt&i* suonare; *(surround)* circondare; **–leader** *n* agitatore, capobanda *m*; **–worm** *n* tigna
ringing *n* suono, scampanio; — *a* risuonante, sonoro
rink *n* pista di pattinaggio
rinse *vt* sciacquare; — *n* risciacquata
riot *n* sommossa; **–er** *n* rivoltoso, sedizioso; **–ing** *n* sedizia; libertinaggio; **–ous** *a* sedizioso; libertino
rip *vt* lacerare, scucire; — *vi* lacerarsi; — **open** aprire; — *n* scucitura; strappo; *(coll)* furfante *m*; **–cord** *n* cordella per aprire il paracadute *(or* la valvola del pallone aerostatico)
ripe *a* maturo; **–ness** *n* maturità
ripen *vt&i* maturare; **–ing** *n* maturazione
ripple *n* increspatura; mormorio; — *vt* increspare; — *vi* incresparsi
rippling *n* increspamento; mormorio; — *a* increspato
rise *vi* alzarsi; sorgere; *(increase)* aumentare; — *n* alzata; ascesa; *(ground)* salita, elevazione; **–r** *n* chi si alza; *(stair)* alzata di gradino
risibility *n* risibilità
risible *a* risibile
rising *n* rivolta; levata; *(tide)* flusso; — *a*

sorgente, crescente
risk *n* rischio; — *vt* rischiare; **-y** *a* rischioso; **run a** — correre un rischio
riskiness *n* rischiosità
risqué *a* salace
rite *n* rito, cerimonia
ritual *n&a* rituale, cerimoniale *m*; **-ism** *n* ritualismo; **-ist** *n* ritualista *m&f*; **-istic** *a* ritualistico
rival *n&a* rivale; **-ry** *n* rivalità; — *vt* emulare
rive *vt* fendere; — *vi* fendersi
river *n* fiume *m*; **down-** *adv* a valle; **-head** *n* sorgente *f*; **-side** *n* sponda di fiume; **up-** *adv* a monte
rivet *n* bullone *m*, ribattino; — *vt* ribadire, fissare; **-er** ribaditore *m*, ribaditrice *f*
Riviera Riviera
rivulet *n* ruscelletto
roach *n (fish)* lasca; scarafaggio
road *n* strada; — **map** mappa stradale; **main** — strada maestra; **on the** — in cammino; **-bed** *n* fondo stradale; **-block** *n* barricata stradale; **-house** *n* ostello, locanda, albergo; **-side** *n* bordo stradale; **-stead** *n (naut)* rada, ancoraggio; **-way** *n* carreggiata
roadster *n* automobile da sport
roam *vt&i* vagare, percorrere; **-er** *n* vagabondo
roan *a&n* roano
roar *vi* ruggire; — *vt* urlare; — *n* ruggito; *(laughter)* scroscio; **-ing** *a* ruggente; — **with laughter** scoppiare dalle risa
roast *vt* arrostire, torrefare; *(coll)* criticare; — *n* arrosto; — *a* arrostito
roaster *n (coffee)* tostino; *(person)* rosticciere *m*
rob *vt* derubare, rubare
robber *n* ladro; **-y** *n* furto, rapina
robe *n* veste *f*; *(law)* toga; — *vt* vestire; — *vi* vestirsi
robin *n* pettirosso
robot *n* automa *m*
robust *a* vigoroso, robusto; **-ness** *n* robustezza
rock *n* roccia, pietra; — **bottom** il punto più basso; — **crystal** quarzo; — **garden** giardino alpino; — **salt** salgemma *m*; — **wool** *(min)* fibra minerale; — *vt* cullare; — *vi* cullarsi; *(totter)* barcollare; — *vt&i* dondolare; **-y** *a* roccioso
rock-bottom *a* il più basso
rocker *n* dondolo
rocket *n* razzo; — **propulsion** propulsione a razzo
rocking *n* oscillazione; — *a* oscillante; *a* dondolo; — **chair** sedia a dondolo; —

horse cavallo a dondolo
rococo *n* rococò
rod *n* verga, pertica; *(curtain)* bacchetta da tenda; *(fishing)* canna; *(measure)* 5 metri circa
rodent *n&a* roditore *m*
roe *n (deer)* capriolo
Roentgen rays raggi Roentgen
rogue *n* furfante *m*
roguish *a* furfante; malizioso; **-ness** *n* furfanteria
roil *vt (turbid)* intorbidire; irritare
roisterer *n* millantatore *m*; schiamazzatore *m*
role *n* parte *f*
roll *n* rotolo; *(bread)* panino; *(film)* bobina di pellicola; *(list)* lista; — **call** appello; — *vt* arrotolare, rotolare; — **over** rovesciarsi; — **up** *(sleeves)* rimboccare; — *vi* rotolarsi; arrotolarsi; rullare; oscillare
roller *n (mech)* cilindro; rullo; — **bearing** cuscinetto a sfere; — **skates** pattini a rotelle
rolling *n* rotolamento; rullio; — **in wealth** ricchissimo; — **mill** laminatoio; — **pin** matterello
roly-poly *a* tozzo
Roman *a&n* romano
Romania Rumania; **-n** *a&n* rumeno
romance *n&a* romanzo; *(mus)* romanza; — *vi* favoleggiare
Romance *a* neolatino, romanzo; — **languages** lingue romanze
Romanesque *n&a* romanico
romantic *a* romantico; **-ism** *n* romanticismo
romp *vi* ruzzare; **-ers** *npl* tuta da bambino
rood *n* crocifisso
roof *n (house)* tetto; *(mouth)* palato; **-ing** *n* tetto; — *vt* ricoprire con tetto; mettere il tetto
rook *n (chess)* torre *f*; *(zool)* cornacchia; — *vt* truffare
room *n* stanza; *(space)* posto, spazio; **make** — **for** far posto per; — **and board** pensione completa; **-er** *n* inquilino; **-ette** *n* *(rail)* cabina; **-y** *a* spazioso, ampio; — *vt&i* alloggiare
roost *n* pollaio; — *vi* appollaiarsi
rooster *n* gallo
root *n* radice *f*; **square** — radice quadrata; — *vi* radicarsi; — *vt (establish)* radicare; *(plant)* piantare; — **out** sradicare; **-ed** *a* radicato
rope *n* corda; — *vt* allacciare; — **in** *(sl)* coinvolgere
ropy *a* viscido, viscoso
rosary *n* rosario, corona
rose *a&n* rosa; **-bud** *n* bocciuolo di rosa;

–bush n rosaio; — **water** acqua di rose; — **window** rosone m

rose-colored a di color rosa; ottimista; **look through** — **glasses** veder tutto rosa (fig)

rosemary n rosmarino

rosin n resina

roster n lista, ruolo

rostrum n rostro, tribuna

rosy a roseo

rot vt&i imputridire; — n putrefazione, carie f; (sl) assurdità

rotary a rotatorio; — **press** rotativa

rotate vt&i girare, ruotare

rotation n rotazione

rote n rutina; **by** — a memoria

rotten a bacato, putrido, marcio; **–ness** n putrefazione

rotund a rotondo; **–ity** n rotondità

rotunda n rotonda

rouge n rossetto, belletto; — vt imbellettare

rough a ruvido; rozzo; (coll) difficile; — **draft** abbozzo; **–neck** n (sl) grossolano; **–ly** adv ruvidamente; aspramente; rozzamente; **–ness** n ruvidità

rough vt irruvidire; abbozzare

roughen vt irruvidire; arrozzire; — vi arrozzarsi; irruvidirsi

roughshod a ferrato grossolanamente; **ride** — **over** trattare duramente

round a rotondo; — **number** cifra tonda; — **trip** viaggio di andata e ritorno; **–up** n (cattle) raduno, retata (fig); — n cerchio; (gun) scarica; (patrol) ronda; (series) serie f; (sport) ripresa; giro, ciclo; — adv intorno; attorno; in giro; — prep intorno a; — vt arrotondare; completare; circondare; — vi arrotondarsi, girarsi; — **up** (coll) riunire

roundabout a evasivo, indiretto

roundness n rotondità

round-shouldered a dalle spalle rotonde (or curve)

round-the-clock a&adv giorno e notte

rouse vt svegliare; suscitare; — vi svegliarsi

rousing a animatore, eccitante

rout vt sbaragliare; — n sconfitta

route n rotta, via

routine n rutina, abito; — a rutinario, abitudinario; abituale

rove vi vagare, errare; **–r** n girovago

roving a vagabondo

row n baruffa, litigio; lite f, rissa; — vi litigare; bisticciare

row n riga, fila; **–boat** n barca a remi; — vi remare; — vt muovere a remi

royal a regale, reale, regio; **–ist** n mo-

narchico; **–ly** adv regalmente

royalty n regalità, maestà, monarchia; reali mpl; (book) diritto d'autore; (patent) percentuale sugli utili

rub n fregata; ostacolo; frizione; **–down** n massaggio; — vt&i strofinare, fregare; — **the wrong way** offendere; — **out** cancellare; (kill, sl) fare fuori (sl)

rubber n gomma; (cards) partita; — **band** elastico; — **stamp** stampino di gomma; **–ize** vt gommare

rubberneck n (sl) ficcanaso; — vi (sl) ficcare il naso

rubbers npl soprascarpe, galosce fpl

rubbish n immondizie fpl; corbellerie fpl

rubble n pietrisco, breccia

rubric n rubrica

ruby n rubino

rudder n timone m

ruddy a rubizzo

rude a maleducato; rozzo; **–ly** adv grossolanamente, rozzamente; **–ness** n rozzezza; grossolanità

rudiment n rudimento; **–ary** a rudimentale

rue n (bot) ruta; — vt deplorare; pentirsi di; — vi pentirsi; addolorarsi; **–ful** a malinconico, doloroso

ruff n gorgiera

ruffian n malfattore m, ruffiano

ruffle vt arruffare; increspare; turbare; — vi arruffarsi; incresparsi; turbarsi; — n increspatura; (drum) rullio

rug n tappeto

rugged a ruvido; austero; robusto; **–ness** n ruvidezza, inflessibilità

rugose a rugoso

rugosity n rugosità

ruin n rovina; — vt rovinare; **–ation** n rovina; — vt rovinare; **–ed** a rovinato; **–ous** a rovinoso; in rovina

rule n regola; riga; governo; — **of thumb** regola per esperienza; **as a** — di regola; **slide** — regolo calcolatore; — vi regnare; — vt regolare; governare; (draw lines) rigare; **–d** a rigato; governato; **–d paper** carta rigata

ruler n (measure) regolo; governante m

ruling n rigatura; governo; (law) verdetto; — a dominante

rum n rum m

rumble n rimbombo, rintruono; — vi rombare, rintronare

rumbling a rimbombo, brontolio, rintruono; — a rimbombante

ruminant n (zool) ruminante m

ruminate vt&i ruminare; meditare

rumination n ruminazione

rummage vt&i frugare, rovistare

rumor n diceria; — vt divulgare; **it is –ed that** corre voce che

rump *n* posteriore *m*, deretano, culo; *(horse)* groppa

rumple *vt* sgualcire, scompigliare

rumpus *n (coll)* strepito, chiasso

run *n* corsa; *(cattle)* recinto; *(cycle)* serie; *(itinerary)* percorso; *(stocking)* smagliatura; **first —** *(movies)* prima visione; **in the long —** a lungo andare; **on the —** in fuga

run *vt&i* correre; *(extend)* stendersi, spandersi; *(machine)* funzionare; *(manage)* dirigere; *(com)* gestire; *(wound)* suppurare; **— away** fuggire; **— across** imbattersi in; **— down** investire; **— for it** darsela a gambe *(fig)*; **— into** cadere in, raggiungere; **— off** fuggire; stampare; versare; **— over** scorrere; *(auto)* investire; ripetere; **— up** accumulare; **— up against** discordare con

runaway *n&a* fuggitivo

rundown *n* ripasso rapido

run-down *a (clock)* scaricato; *(person)* esaurito, debilitato

rung *n* piuolo

run-in *n (coll)* disaccordo

run-of-the-mill *a* comune, ordinario

runner *n (sport)* corridore *m*; *(stocking)* smagliatura

runner-up *n (sport)* secondo arrivato

running *a* corrente; da corsa; *(med)* purulento; **— n** corsa; marcia; funzionamento; **— board** montatoio

runt *n* nano, pigmeo

runway *n* pista

rupture *n* rottura; *(med)* ernia; **— vt** rompere; erniare; **— vi** rompersi; erniarsi

rural *a* rurale

ruse *n* stratagemma *m*

rush *n* furia; **— vi** affrettarsi, sbrigarsi; **— vt** affrettare, sbrigare; **— hour** ora di punta *(coll)*

rush *n (bot)* giunco

rushing *a* precipitoso

russet *n&a* rossetto

Russia Russia

Russian *a&n* russo

rust *n* ruggine *f*; **— vt** arrugginire; **— vi** arrugginirsi; **-y** *a* rugginoso

rustic *a* rustico

rustiness *n* rugginosità

rustle *n* fruscio, mormorio; **— vi** frusciare, stormire

rustler *n* ladro di bestiame

rut *n* solco; trantran *m (coll)*

ruthless *a* spietato; **-ly** *adv* spietatamente

rye *n* segala; *(bread)* pane di segala

S

Sabbath *n (Christian)* domenica; *(Jewish)* sabato

saber *n* sciabola; **— vt** sciabolare

sable *n* zibellino; **— a** di zibellino

sabotage *n* sabotaggio; **— vt** sabotare

saccharin *n* saccarina

sack *n* sacco; **— cloth** *n* tela da sacco; **— vt** insaccare; *(discharge)* licenziare

sack *n (pillage)* saccheggio; **— vt** saccheggiare

sacrament *n* sacramento; **-al** *a* sacramentale

sacred *a* sacro; inviolabile; **-ness** *n* santità

sacrifice *n* sacrifizio; **— vt** sacrificare; *(com)* vendere con perdita

sacrificial *a* sacrificatorio, di sacrifizio

sacrilege *n* sacrilegio

sacrilegious *a* sacrilego

sacristan *n* sagrestano

sacristy *n* sagrestia

sacrosanct *a* sacrosanto

sacrum *n (anat)* osso sacro

sad *a* triste; **-ly** *adv* tristemente; gravemente; dolorosamente; **-ness** *n* tristezza

sadden *vt* rattristare; **— vi** rattristarsi

saddle *n* sella; **-bag** *n* bisaccia; **— horse** cavallo da sella; **— vt** sellare; accollare; gravare; **be -d with** accollarsi di

safe *a* salvo, sicuro; **— n** cassaforte *f*; **— and sound** sano e salvo; **-guard** *n* salvaguardia; **-keeping** *n* custodia; **-ly** *adv* con sicurezza; **-ness** *n* sicurezza

safe-conduct *n* salvacondotto

safety *n* salvezza, sicurezza; impunità; **— belt** cintura di salvataggio; **— glass** vetro compensato, vetro infrangibile; **— match** fiammifero svedese; **— pin** spilla di sicurezza; **— razor** macchinetta da barba; **— valve** valvola di sicurezza

saffron *n* zafferano

sag *vi* cedere; abbassarsi; **— n** cedimento, depressione

sagacious *a* sagace

sagacity *n* sagacità, sagacia

sage *n* savio; *(bot)* salvia; **— a** prudente, saggio

sagging *a* cascante, cedente; spiegazzato; **— n** cedimento

said *a* suddetto, detto, sopradetto

sail *n* vela; **— vt&i** veleggiare; salpare, partire, navigare; **-boat** *n* barca a vela

sailing *n* navigazione; **— ship** nave a vela

sailor *n* marinaio

saint *n* santo; **-ed** *a* sacro, santo, santificato; **-ly** *a* santo, devoto, pio; **— vt**

canonizzare

sake *n* amore *m*; ragione *f*; **for the —
of** per amor di

salaam *n* salamelecco; **—** *vt* fare salame-
lecchi a

salable *a* vendibile

salacious *a* salace

salacity *n* salacità

salad *n* insalata; **fruit —** macedonia di
frutta; **— bowl** insalatiera; **— dressing**
condimento per insalata

salamander *n* salamandra

salaried *a* salariato

salary *n* stipendio; salario

sale *n* vendita; **auction —** vendita al-
l'asta; **clearance —** liquidazione; **for
—** da vendere

sales *npl* vendite *fpl*; **— tax** tassa sulle
vendite; **–clerk** *n* venditore in negozio,
commesso; **–room** *n* sala di vendita

salesman *n* venditore *m*, commesso; **–ship**
n arte del vendere; **traveling —** commesso viaggiatore, piazzista *m*

salient *n&a* saliente *m*

saline *a* salino, salso; **—** *n* salina

saliva *n* saliva

salivary *a* salivare

salivate *vi* salivare

sallow *a* giallastro pallido

sally *n (mil)* sortita; uscita; escursione;
— *vi* fare una sortita

salmon *n* salmone *m*

saloon *n* taverna; bar *m*

salt *n* sale *m*; **— water** acqua salata (or
di mare); **rock —** salgemma; **table —**
sale da tavola; **–cellar** *n* saliera; **–peter**
n salnitro; **–shaker** *n* saliera; **—** *vt*
salare; **–ed** *a* salato; **–y** *a* salato

saltiness *n* salsezza

saltworks *n* salina

salubrious *a* salubre

salutary *a* salutare

salutation *n* saluto

salute *vt* salutare; **—** *n* saluto; *(cannon)*
salva

salvage *n* salvataggio; **—** *vt* ricuperare,
salvare

salvation *n* salvezza, salute *f*

salve *n* unguento, emolliente *m*; **—** *vt* calmare, lenire

salver *n* vassoio

salvo *n* salva

Samaritan *n* samaritano

same *a* stesso; **all the —** ciò nonostante;
lo stesso, tutt'uno; **at the — time**
con tutto ciò, ciò nonostante, pure;
–ness *n* uniformità; monotonia

sample *n* campione *m*, esempio; **—** *vt* saggiare, provare

sampling *n* campionatura

sanatorium *n* casa di cura; stazione climatica

sanctify *vt* santificare

sanctimonious *a* bigotto

sanction *n* sanzione; **—** *vt* approvare

sanctity *n* santità

sanctuary *n* santuario

sanctum *n* santuario, sacrario; studio riservato; **inner —** sancta sanctorum *(fig)*

sand *n* sabbia, rena; **–s** *npl* spiaggia; **–bag**
n sacco a terra; **— bar** banco di sabbia;
–box *n* sabbiera; **–stone** *n* arenaria;
–storm *n* tempesta di sabbia; **—** *vt*
sabbiare, smerigliare

sandal *n* sandalo; **–wood** *n* legno di sandalo

sandblast *n (mech)* sabbiatrice *f*; **—** *vt*
smerigliare, sabbiare

sandpaper *n* carta vetrata; **—** *vt* levigare
con carta vetrata

sandwich *n* panino ripieno; **—** *vt* inserire

sandy *a* sabbioso; *(hair)* biondastro

sane *a* equilibrato, savio

sanguinary *a* sanguinario

sanguine *a* sanguigno; ottimista

sanitary *a* igienico; **— napkin** pannolino
igienico

sanitarium *n* sanatorio

sanitation igiene *f*

sanity *n* sanità di mente

Sanskrit *n &a* sanscrito

Santa Claus *n* Befana; Babbo Natale, Papà
Natale

sap *n* linfa; *(sl)* grullo; **—** *vt* sottominare,
indebolire

sapling *n* arboscello

sarcasm *n* sarcasmo

sarcastic *a* sarcastico

sarcophagus *n* sarcofago

sardine *n* sardina

Sardinia *n* Sardegna; **–n** *a&n* sardo

sardonic *a* sardonico

sash *n* sciarpa; *(window)* telaio

Satan *n* Satana *m*

satanic *a* satanico

satchel *n* borsa, cartella

satellite *n* satellite *m*

satiate *vt* saziare

satiety *n* sazietà

satin *n* raso, satin *m*; **–y** *a* di raso, sa-
tinato

satire *n* satira

satirical *a* satirico

satirist *n* satirico

satirize *vt* satireggiare

satisfaction *n* soddisfazione *f*

satisfactory *a* soddisfacente

satisfy *vt&i* soddisfare, contentare

saturate *vt* saturare

saturation *n* saturazione

Saturday *n* sabato
saturnism *n* saturnismo
satyr *n* satiro
sauce *n* salsa; **–box** *n* (coll) sfacciato, insolente *m*; **–pan** *n* casseruola; — *vt* condire
saucer *n* piattino
sauciness *n* sfacciataggine *f*
saucy *a* insolente, sfacciato
Saudi Arabia Arabia Saudita
sauerkraut *n* crauti *mpl*
saunter *vi* bighellonare
sausage *n* salciccia; carne insaccata
savage *a&n* selvaggio; **–ry** *n* barbarie *f*; ferocia
savannah *n* savana
savant *n* dotto
save *vt* salvare; (keep) conservare, — *vt&i* risparmiare; — *prep* salvo, tranne, eccetto; **–r** *n* liberatore *m*; (money) risparmiatore *m*
saving *a* economico, frugale; — *n* economia
savings *npl* risparmi *mpl*; — **bank** cassa di risparmio; — **account** conto di risparmio
Saviour *n* Salvatore, Redentore *m*
savor *n* sapore *m*, gusto; aroma; — *vt* assaporare; dar sapore; — *vi* aver sapore di, sapere di
savory *a* saporito
saw *n* (tool) sega; (adage) proverbio; **–dust** *n* segatura; **–horse** *n* cavalletto per segare; **–mill** *n* segheria
saw-toothed *a* dentato, dentellato
Saxon *n&a* sassone *m&f*
saxaphone *n* sassofono
say *vt&i* dire; **have one's** — dire la sua; **that is to** — vale a dire, cioè
saying *n* detto, massima; **it goes without** — non è neppure il caso di dirlo
scab *n* crosta; (labor) crumiro; — *vi* cicatrizzarsi; formar crosta; fare il crumiro
scabbard *n* fodero, guaina
scabby *a* coperto di croste
scabrous *a* osceno; scabroso
scaffold *n* patibolo; impalcatura; **–ing** *n* impalcatura, intelaiatura
scalawag *n* scapestrato, furfante *m*
scald *vt* scottare; — *n* scottata; **–ing** *a* scottante; **–ing** *n* scottatura
scale *n* (fish) squama; (measurement) scala; (weight) bilancia; — *vt* scalare, assendere; graduare; (fish) squamare
scalene *a* (math) scaleno
scales *npl* bilancia; **platform** — basculla
scaling *n* scalata; desquamazione
scallion *n* scalogno
scallop *n* (sewing) smerlo, orlatura;

(zool) mollusco; — *vt* (cooking) cuocere al gratin; (sewing) festonare, orlare
scalp *n* cuoio capelluto; — *vt* scotennare; **–er** *n* (ticket seller) bagarino, incettatore *m*
scalpel *n* bisturi *m*
scaly *a* squamoso, scaglioso; (sl) meschino, ladro
scamp *n* furfante *m*
scamper *n* scampo, fuga precipitosa; — *vi* scampare, fuggire precipitosamente
scan *vt* (mus) scandire; esaminare; (TV) esplorare
scandal *n* scandalo; **–ize** *vt* scandalizzare; **–monger** *n* maldicente *m&f*; **–ous** *a* scandaloso
Scandinavia Scandinavia
Scandinavian *a&n* scandinavo
scant, scanty *a* scarso
scantily *adv* scarsamente
scantiness *n* scarsezza
scapegoat *n* capro espiatorio
scapegrace *n* scapestrato
scapula *n* scapola
scapular *n* (eccl) scapolare *m*
scar *n* cicatrice *f*; sfregio; — *vi* cicatrizzarsi; — *vt* cicatrizzare, sfregiare
scarab *n* scarabeo
scarce *a* scarso; **–ly** *adv* appena, quasi
scarcity *n* scarsità
scare *n* spavento; — *vt* impaurire, spaventare
scarecrow *n* spauracchio, spaventapasseri *m*
scarf *n* sciarpa, scialle *m*
scarlet *a&n* scarlatto; — **fever** scarlattina
scathing *a* caustico, severo, pungente
scatter *vt* sparpagliare; — *vi* disperdersi; **–ed** *a* sparso; disseminato
scatterbrain *n* scervellato
scattering *n* sparpagliamento
scavenger *n* spazzino
scenario *n* canovaccio
scene *n* scena; **–ry** *n* paesaggio; (view) veduta; (theat) scenario
scenic *a* scenico
scenography *n* scenografia
scent *n* odore *m*; fiuto; — *vt* odorare; profumare
scepter *n* scettro
schedule *n* programma *m*; tabella; orario; — *vt* programmare
schema *n* schema *m*
schematic *a* schematico
scheme *n* complotto; progetto; — *vi* macchinare; progettare; — *vi* far progetti; intrigare; **color** — armonizzazione di colori
schemer *n* intrigante *m&f*

scheming n macchinazione; progetti mpl; — a scaltro, intrigante; progettante
scherzo n (mus) scherzo
schism n scisma m; **-atic** n&a scismatico
schist n (geol) schisto
schizophrenia n schizofrenia
schizophrenic n&a schizofrenico
scholar n alunno, studente m, scolaro; (erudite) studioso, erudito; **-ly** a erudito, dotto; **-ship** n erudizione; borsa di studio
scholastic a scolastico; **-ism** n scolasticismo
school n scuola; **high** — scuola media; **-book** n libro scolastico; **-boy** n scolaro; **-girl** n scolara; **-house** n scuola, edificio scolastico; **-room** n aula scolastica; **-teacher** n maestro, maestra; insegnante m&f; — vt disciplinare; istruire
schooling n istruzione; (cost) costo di studi
schooner n (boat) goletta; (glass) bicchierone da birra
sciatica n (med) sciatica
science n scienza; — **fiction** fantascienza
scientific a scientifico
scientist n scienziato
scimitar n scimitarra
scintillate vi scintillare
scintillating a scintillante
scion n discendente m
scissors npl forbici fpl
sclerosis n (med) sclerosi f
scoff vt&i schernire, deridere; **-er** n derisore, schernitore m
scoffing n scherno, derisione; — a derisorio
scold vt&i sgridare, rimproverare; — n megera, bisbetica
scolding n rimprovero, sgridata; **-ly** adv sgridando, con rimprovero
scone n focaccina
scoop n ramaiolo, cucchiaione m; (news) colpo giornalistico; — vt vuotare, scavare
scoot vi (coll) darsela a gambe, scappare; **-er** n monopattino; **motor -er** motonetta
scope n portata
scorbutic a scorbutico
scorch vt bruciare, arrostire; — vi bruciacchiarsi, arrostirsi; **-ed** a bruciato; **-er** n giorno scottante
scorching a bruciante; (remark) sarcastico; — n bruciatura, ustione f
score n (game) punteggio; (mus) spartito, partitura; (number) venti m, ventina; — vt segnare; — vi far punti
scoring n (mus) orchestrazione

scorn n disprezzo; **-ful** a sprezzante, sdegnoso; **-fully** adv sdegnosamente; — vt sdegnare, disprezzare
scorpion n scorpione m
Scot n scozzese m
Scotch n whisky scozzese; — a scozzese
scotch vt sopprimere
scot-free a impune, impunito; (gratis) gratuito
Scotland Scozia
Scotsman n scozzese m
Scottish n&a scozzese m
scoundrel n mascalzone m
scour vt (scout) perlustrare, percorrere; (clean) ripulire; — **the country** battere la campagna (fig); **-ing** n smacchiatura, pulitura
scourge n sferza; — vt sferzare
scout n esploratore m; **-master** n capo esploratore m; **boy** — giovane esploratore; **girl** — giovane esploratrice; — vt&i esplorare
scow n chiatta
scowl n sguardo torvo, cipiglio; — vi accigliarsi
scragginess n magrezza
scraggy a scarno, magro
scramble n mischia, tafferuglio; (climb) scalata; — vt agitare, mischiare, strapazzare; — vi (climb) inerpicarsi; agitarsi; (struggle) azzuffarsi; **-d** a agitato, strapazzato; **-d eggs** uova strapazzate
scrap n pezzo; briciola; **-book** n album m; — **heap** mucchio di rifiuti; — vt rigettare, scartare
scrap n (sl) baruffa, zuffa; — vi (sl) altercare, bisticciare
scrape n imbroglio; (skin) spellatura; (sound) stridore m; — vt raschiare; **together** raggranellare; **-r** n raschietto
scratch n graffio; (sport) linea di partenza; — **pad** blocco di carta per minuta; — **paper** carta per minuta; **from** — dal niente; — vt grattare; graffiare; (sport) eliminare; **-y** a graffiante, aspro; (writing) scarabocchiato
scrawl n scarabocchio; — vt&i scarabocchiare
scrawny a magro
scream n grido, strillo; **-ing** n strilli mpl, urla fpl; — vt&i gridare, urlare
screech n grido, urlo; — **owl** barbagianni m; — vt&i strillare
screen n schermo; paravento; — vt nascondere; vagliare
screw n vite f; — **propellor** propulsore a elica; — **thread** impanatura; — vt avvitare; (distort) torcere; — vi avvitarsi; — **up one's courage** farsi coraggio

screwdriver *n* cacciavite *m*

scribble *n* scarabocchio; mala scrittura; — *vt* scribacchiare

scribe *n* scrivano

scrimmage *n* schermaglia

scrimp *vi* economizzare; restringere; **–iness** esiguità; **–y** *a* esiguo

scrip *n* certificato provvisorio

script *n* scrittura, manoscritto; *(print)* corsivo; *(theat)* copione *m*

scriptural *a* scritturale, conforme alla Sacra Scrittura

Scripture *n* Sacra Scrittura

scriptwriter *n* sceneggiatore *m*

scrofula *n (med)* scrofola

scroll *n* rotolo, papiro; *(design)* spirale *m*, voluta; — **saw** sega da traforo; **–work** *n* traforo, arabesco, intarsio

scrotum *(anat)* scroto

scrounge *vt (sl)* scroccare

scrub *vt* strofinare, pulire; — *n* boscaglia, macchia

scrubby *a* stentato

scruff *n* nuca

scruple *n* scrupolo

scrupulous *a* scrupoloso

scrutinize *vt* scrutare

scrutiny *n* indagine *f,* esame *m*

scuba *n* apparato di respirazione per la pesca subacquea

scuff *n (slipper)* ciabatta, pianella; *(shuffle)* scalpiccio; logorio; — *vt&i* logorare; scalpicciare

scuffle *n* rissa, parapiglia; *(shuffling)* scalpiccio; — *vi* azzuffarsi; scalpicciare

sculptor *n* scultore *m,* scultrice *f*

sculpture *n* scultura; — *vt* scolpire

scum *n* schiuma; scoria

scurrilous *a* scurrile; **–ness** *n* scurrilità

scurry *n* sgambetto, fretta; — *vi* sgam-bettare, affrettarsi

scurvy *n (med)* scorbuto; — *a* meschino, vile

scuttle *n* secchio; *(naut)* boccaporto; — *vi* affrettarsi; — *vt* affondare; — **away** scappare

scythe *n* falce *f*

sea *n* mare *m;* **–board** *n* litorale *m,* spiag-gia; **–going** *a* atto al mare; — **breeze** brezza marina; — **gull** gabbiano; — **horse** ippocampo; — **legs** equilibrio da marinaio; — **level** livello del mare; — **lion** otaria; — **of** *(fig)* mare di; — **power** potenza marittima; — **shell** conchiglia marina; — **urchin** echino; — **wall** diga; **at** — in mare; *(confused)* perplesso; **heavy** — mare agitato; **rough** — mare grosso

seacoast *n* costa

seafarer *n* marinaio

seafaring *a* di mare, marino

seal *n* sigillo; *(zool)* foca; — *vt* sigil-lare; chiudere; **–skin** *n* pelle di foca

sealing *n* sigillazione; — **wax** ceralacca

seam *n* cucitura; **–less** *a* senza cucitura

seaman *n* marinaio; **–like** *a* marinaresco; **–ship** *n* arte marinaresca

seamstress *n* cucitrice *f*

seaplane *n* idrovolante *m*

seaport *n* porto marittimo

sear *vt* cauterizzare; bruciare; insecchire

search *vt&i* cercare, perquisire; far ri-cerche; — *n* ricerca, perquisizione

searching *n* ricerca, indagine *f;* — *a* pe-netrante, scrutatore

searchlight *n* riflettore *m*

seashore *n* spiaggia, lido

seasickness *n* mal di mare

seaside *n* marina

season *n* stagione; — **ticket** biglietto d'abbonamento; **out of** — fuori stagio-ne; **–al** *a* stagionale; **–able** *a* di stagione; opportuno

season *vt* condire; *(mature)* stagionare; **–ed** *a (food)* condito; *(aged)* stagionato; **seasoning** *n* (wood) stagionatura; *(food)* condimento

seat *n* posto; sedia; sedile *m;* — *vt* far sedere; insediare; provvedere di posti a sedere; **–ed** *a* seduto

seaweed *n* alga marina

seaworthy *a* a tenuta di mare, atto ad af-frontare il mare

secede *vi* staccarsi

secession *n* secessione

seclude *vt* secludere, isolare, ritirare; **–d** *a* ritirato, appartato

seclusion *n* ritiro, solitudine *f*

second *a&n* secondo; — **hand** *(watch)* lan-cetta dei secondi; — **floor** secondo pia-no; — **nature** seconda natura; — **sight** prescienza; sesto senso, intuizione; **on** — **thought** tutto ben considerato; — *vt* assecondare

secondhand *a* di seconda mano; d'occa-sione; per sentito dire

second-rate *a* di seconda qualità

secrecy *n* segretezza

secret *n&a* segreto; **keep a** — mantenere il segreto; **–ive** *a* segreto; secretivo; **–ly** *adv* segretamente

secretary *n* segretario; *(desk)* scrittoio

secrete *vt* nascondere; *(exude)* secernere

secretion *n* secrezione

sect *n* setta; **–arian** *a* settario; **–ar-ianism** *n* spirito settario

section *n* sezione; *(city)* quartiere *m;* **–al** *a* sezionale, parziale; — *vt* sezionare

sector *n* settore *m*

secular *a* secolare; *(laic)* laico; *(worldly)*

mondano; **–ism** n secolarismo; **–ize** vt secolarizzare

secure a sicuro, al sicuro; — vt ottenere, assicurare

security n sicurezza; garanzia

securities npl (com) titoli mpl

sedate a posato, calmo, tranquillo; **–ness** n posatezza, calma, tranquillità

sedative n&n sedativo

sedentary a sedentario

sedge n giunco

sediment n deposito, sedimento; **–ary** a sedimentario; **–ation** n sedimentazione

sedition n sedizione

seditious a sedizioso

seduce vt sedurre

seducer n seduttore m

seduction n seduzione

seductive a seducente, seduttore

sedulity n diligenza

sedulous a diligente

see vt&i vedere; — **about** vedere di; — **through** (understand) percepire, intuire; — **to** occuparsi di; **as far as I can** — per quanto io possa vedere; **The Holy S–** La Santa Sede

seed n seme m, chicco; **–ling** n pianticella, piantina; **–y** a granoso; pieno di semi; (fig) logoro; — vt (deseed) sgranare; (sow) seminare; — vi sgranarsi

seeing n vista, visione; — a vidente; — **that** visto che

seek vt&i ricercare, cercare; — **to** tentare di

seeker n cercatore m

seem vi sembrare, parere; **–ing** a apparente; **–ingly** adv apparentemente; **–ly** a decente, conveniente

seemliness n decenza

seep vi filtrare; **–age** n gocciolamento; trasudamento

seer n profeta m, veggente m&f

seer n (viewer) spettatore m

seesaw n altalena; — vi fare l'altalena; dondolare

seethe vi agitarsi, fermentare; bollire

segment n segmento

segregate vt segregare

segregation n segregazione

seiche n fluttuazione lacustre

seine n sciabica

Seine Senna

seismic a sismico

seismograph n sismografo

seize vt afferrare; (law) confiscare

seizure n cattura; (law) confisca; (med) attacco, accesso

seldom adv raramente

select vt scegliere; — a scelto; **–ion** n scelta, selezione; **–ive** a selettivo; **–ivity**

selettività

selenite n selenite f

selenium n selenio

self n personalità; sè stesso, ego

self- (in comp) —**acting** a automatico; —**addressed** a indirizzato a sè stesso; —**assurance** n sicurezza di sè; —**assured** a sicuro di sè; —**centered** a egocentrico; —**confidence** n fiducia in sè stesso; —**confident** a sicuro di sè; —**conscious** a imbarazzato; —**contained** riservato; —**control** n padronanza di sè; —**defense** n legittima difesa; —**denial** n astinenza, abnegazione; —**determined** a con autodecisione; —**discipline** n autodisciplina; —**educated** a autodidatta; —**esteem** n amor proprio; —**evident** a evidente; —**explanatory** a ovvio; —**expression** n espressione dell'individuo; —**governed** a autonomo; —**government** n autogoverno, autonomia, indipendenza; —**help** n autosufficienza; azione senza l'aiuto altrui; —**importance** n boria; —**important** a borioso; —**indulgence** n indulgenza per sè stesso; —**interest** n interesse personale; —**made** a fatto da sè; —**possessed** a calmo; —**possession** n padronanza di sè stesso; —**preservation** n istinto di conservazione; —**propelled** a automotore; —**regard** n rispetto di sè stesso; —**regulating** a a regolazione automatica; —**reliance** n fiducia in sè; — **reliant** a fiducioso di sè stesso; —**respect** n dignità; —**restraint** n controllo di sè stesso; riservatezza; —**sacrifice** n abnegazione; sacrificio di sè stesso; —**satisfied** a vanitoso; —**service** n autoservizio; —**starter** n (auto) avviamento; —**styled** a sedicente; —**sufficient** a autosufficiente; —**supporting** a indipendente; —**taught** a autodidatta; —**willed** a ostinato

selfish a egoistico; egoista; **–ness** n egoismo

selfless a altruista

selfsame a identico; esattamente lo stesso

sell vt&i vendere; (coll) ingannare; — **out** vender tutto; (betray) vendere; **–out** n vendita totale, liquidazione; **–er** n venditore m; negoziante m; **–ing** n vendita

seltzer n acqua di Seltz

selvage n cimosa

semantic a semantico

semantics npl semantica

semaphore n semaforo

semblance n apparenza, sembianza

semen n sperma

semester n semestre m

semiannual a semestrale; **–ly** adv semestralmente

semicircle *n* semicerchio
semicolon *n* punto e virgola
semiconscious *a* semicosciente
semifinal *n* semifinale *m*
semimonthly *a* bimensile; quindicinale
seminar *n* seminario
seminary *n* seminario
semination *n* semina
semiofficial *a* semiufficiale
semiprecious *a* semiprezioso
Semitic *a* semitico
semitransparent *a* semitrasparente
semitropical *a* semitropicale
semiweekly *a* bisettimanale
senate *n* senato
senator *n* senatore *m*
send *vt* inviare, mandare, spedire; —
away mandar via, congedare; — **for**
mandar a chiamare; **–er** *n* mittente *m&f*
senile *a* senile
senility *n* senilità
senior *n* anziano, decano; — *a* maggiore;
seniore; **–ity** *n* anzianità
sensation *n* sensazione; **–al** *a* sensazionale
sense *n* senso; **common** — buon senso;
make — aver significato, essere logico;
talk — parlare con senno; **–less** *a*
insensibile; *(silly)* insensato; *(absurd)*
assurdo; **–s** *npl* sensi *mpl*; — *vt&i*
intuire
sensibility *n* sensibilità
sensible *a* assennato, giudizioso
sensitive *a* sensibile, suscettibile
sensitivity *n* sensibilità
sensitize *vt* sensibilizzare
sensory *a* sensorio
sensual *a* sensuale; **–ism** *n* sensualismo;
–ist *n* sensualista *m&f*; **–ity** *n* sensualità
sensuous *a* sensuale, sensitivo
sentence *n* sentenza; condanna; *(gram)*
frase *f*, periodo; — *vt* condannare
sententious *a* sentenzioso
sentiment *n* sentimento; **–al** *a* sentimentale;
–alism *n* sentimentalismo; **–alist** *n*
sentimentale *m&f*; **–ality** *n* sentimenta-
lità
sentinel *n* sentinella
sentry *n* guardia; — **box** garitta
sepal *n* sepalo
separable *a* separabile
separate *vt* separare; — *vi* separarsi; —
a diviso, separato; **–ly** *adv* a parte,
separatamente
separation *n* separazione
separatism *n* separatismo
sepia *n (color)* seppia
September *n* settembre *m*
septic *a* settico
septicemia *n (med)* setticemia
sepulcher *n* sepolcro

sepulchral *a* sepolcrale
sequel *n* sequela, conseguenza
sequence *n* sequenza, serie *f*, successione
sequester *vt* sequestrare; separare; **–ed** *a*
ritirato; sequestrato
sequin *n* lustrino
seraph *n* serafino
seraphic *a* serafico
serenade *n* serenata; — *vt* fare una serenata a
serene *a* sereno; **–ly** *a* serenamente
serenity *n* serenità
serf *n* schiavo, servo; **–dom** *n* servaggio
sergeant *n* sergente *m*
sergeant-at-arms *n* usciere *m*
serial *n* romanzo a puntate; — *a* di serie;
periodico; — **number** numero di serie
series *n* serie *f*
serious *a* grave, serio; **–ly** *adv* seriamente,
sul serio; **–ness** *n* serietà; **take –ly**
prendere sul serio
sermon *n* predica, sermone *m*; **–ize** *vt* sermoneggiare
serous *a* sieroso
serpent *n* serpente *m*; **–ine** *a* serpentino;
(twisting) tortuoso
serrate *a* dentellato
serried *a* serrato
serum *n* siero
servant *n* domestico; servo; **civil** —
impiegato statale
serve *vt&i* servire; — **as** servire da;
— **time** *(mil)* prestare servizio; *(law)*
scontare una sentenza
service *n* servizio, prestazione; — **station**
stazione di servizio; **at your** — ai vostri
ordini; **be of** — essere utile; **–s** *npl*
prestazioni *fpl*, servizi *mpl*; — *vt*
mettere in uso
serviceable *a* durevole; pratico
serviceman *n* militare *m*
servile *a* servile
servility *n* servilità
servitude *n* servitù
sesame *n* sesamo
session *n* sessione, seduta
set *n* servizio, serie *f*, collezione; *(group)*
gruppo; *(hair)* messa in piega; *(rad)* apparecchio; *(sport)* partita; *(theat)*
scenario
set *vt* mettere, porre, regolare; *(gem)* incastonare; *(table)* apparecchiare; *(type)*
comporre; — *vi* mettersi; *(sun)* tramontare; *(congeal)* coagularsi; *(hen)* covare;
— **aside** metter da parte; *(law)* annullare; — **forth** mostrare; — **out** *(place)*
mettere, posare; *(start)* partire; *(begin)*
incominciare; *(plant)* piantare
set *a (firm)* fisso; *(established)* stabilito;
(stubborn) testardo

setback *n* arresto; *(retreat)* indietreggiamento

settee *n* canapè *m*

setting *n* *(gem)* incastonatura; *(table)* apparecchiatura, coperto; *(birds)* covata; *(surroundings)* dintorni *mpl*

settle *vt* *(establish)* stabilire; comporre, aggiustare; *(pay)* saldare; — *vi* stabilirsi; **–ment** *n* accomodamento; pagamento; colonia

settler *n* colono

set-to *n* *(coll)* abboccamento; *(argument)* discussione

setup *n* organizzazione; *(mech)* montaggio

seven *a* sette; **–teen** *a* diciasette; **–th** *a* settimo; **–ty** *a* settanta

seventeenth *a* diciassettesimo; — **century** secolo diciasettesimo, il seicento

sever *vt* dividere, recidere; — *vi* dividersi; **–ance** *n* separazione, distacco

several *a* parecchi

severe *a* severo; grave

severity *n* severità

sew *vt&i* cucire

sewage *n* acque di scolo

sewer *n* conduttura, fogna, cloaca

sewing *n* cucito; — **machine** macchina da cucire

sex *n* sesso; — **appeal** fascino

sextant *n* sestante *m*

sextet *n* sestetto

sexton *n* sagrestano

sexual *a* sessuale; **–ity** *n* sessualità; **–ly** *adv* sessualmente

shabbiness *n* stato logoro

shabby *a* logoro; mal vestito; — **trick** meschinità

shack *n* baracca

shackle *n* ceppo; — *vt* inceppare

shad *n* alosa; — **roe** uova di alosa

shade *n* *(color)* tinta; *(shadow)* ombra; *(window)* scuretto; *(lamp)* paralume *m*; **–d** *a* ombreggiato; protetto; all'ombra; — *vt* ombreggiare

shadiness *n* ombrosità

shading *n* sfumatura

shadow *n* ombra; — *vt* oscurare; ombreggiare; *(follow)* pedinare; **–y** *a* ombroso; oscuro; *(ghostly)* spettrale

shady *a* ombroso; sospetto

shaft *n* *(light)* raggio; *(lightning)* fulmine *m*; *(mech)* albero, asse *m*; *(mine)* pozzo; **crank–** *n* albero a gomito

shaggy *a* irsuto, ispido, scabroso

shah *n* scià *m*

shake *vt* scuotere; — *vi* tremare; — **hands** stringere la mano; **–down** *n* giaciglio improvvisato; *(sl)* estorsione; — **off** disfarsi di

shake-up *n* riorganizzazione energica

shaking *n* scossa, scuotimento; — *a* agitato; debole; *(voice)* tremante

shale *n* schisto

shallop *n* scialuppa

shallow *a* poco profondo; **–ness** *n* poca profondità, superficialità

sham *a* finto, falso; — *n* finzione, finta, impostura; — *vt* simulare, fingere

shambles *npl* macello; strage *f*, carneficina

shame *n* vergogna; pudore *m*; **what a —!** che peccato!; — *vt* disonorare, svergognare; **–faced** *a* timido, vergognoso; **–ful** *a* vergognoso; **–less** *a* svergognato, spudorato

shammy *n* pelle di camoscio

shampoo *n* saponatura; — *vt* lavare

shamrock *n* trifoglio

shank *n* stinco, tibia; gamba

shanty *n* capanna

shape *vt* formare, foggiare; — *vi* *(coll)* prender forma; — *n* forma; **–less** *a* informe; **–liness** *n* bellezza; simmetria; **–ly** *a* bello; simmetrico

shard *n* coccio

share *n* parte *f*; *(com)* azione *f*; — *vt* dividere, spartire, condividere; — *vi* partecipare; **–cropper** *n* mezzadro; **–holder** *n* azionista *m&f*

sharing *n* spartizione

shark *n* pescecane *m*, squalo; **loan —** strozzino

sharp *a* acuto, tagliente, affilato; *(clever)* astuto, furbo; — **curve** curva stretta; — *n* *(mus)* diesis *m*; — *adv* preciso; in punto; **two o'clock —** alle due in punto; **–ly** *adv* acutamente; astutamente; **–ness** *n* acume *m*; astuzia; asprezza; **–shooter** *n* tiratore scelto

sharpen *vt* affilare, appuntare; acuire

sharpener *n* *(mech)* affilatrice *f*; *(grindstone)* arrotino; *(pencil)* temperalapis *m*

sharp-edged *a* affilato

sharp-witted *a* intelligente, acuto

shatter *vt* fracassare; — *vi* fracassarsi

shatterproof *a* infrangibile

shave *vt* fare la barba a; — *vi* radersi, farsi la barba; — *n* sbarbata; **have a close —** *(fig)* cavarsela a malapena; **–r** *n* *(coll)* imberbe *m*

shaving *n* ritaglio, truciolo; *(beard)* sbarbata; *(hair)* tosatura; — **brush** pennello da barba; — **cream** sapone *(or* crema) da barba

shawl *n* scialle *m*

she *pron* lei, ella, essa

sheaf *n* fascio, covone *m*; — *vt* legare in covoni

shear *n* cesoia; cesoiata; **–ing** *n* tosatura; — *vt* tranciare; *(hair)* tosare; **–s** *npl* cesoie *fpl*

shearer *n* tosatore *m*

sheath *n* fodero, guaina

sheathe *vt* ringuainare

shed *vt (tears)* versare, spargere; *(skin)* spogliarsi di; — **light on** far luce su; — *n* tettoia, capannone *m*

sheen *n* splendore *m*

sheep *n* pecora; **-ish** *a* timido, impacciato; **black** — pecora nera *(fig)*; — **dog** cane da pastore

sheepskin *n (parchment)* pergamena; pelle di pecora

sheer *a* trasparente; *(mere)* mero, semplice, pretto; *(steep)* profondo

sheer *vi (naut)* virare

sheet *n (bed)* lenzuolo; *(glass)* lastra; *(ice)* distesa, lastra; *(metal)* lamiera, lamina; *(paper)* foglio; — *vt* rivestire, foderare; *(laminate)* laminare; **-ing** *n (material)* tela da lenzuola; *(lining)* fodera

sheik *n* sceicco

shelf *n* mensola, scaffale *m*; **put on the —** mettere in disparte

shell *n* conchiglia; guscio; *(mil)* proiettile *m*; — *vt* sbucciare; bombardare; sgranare

shellac *n* gomma-lacca; — *vt* lucidare a spirito

shellfire *n* tiro d'artiglieria

shellfish *n* crostaceo

shellshock *n* psicosi di guerra

shelter *n* rifugio; — *vt* ricoverare, proteggere; nascondere; — *vi* ricoverarsi, mettersi al coperto

shelve *vt* disporre in scaffale; mettere da parte; licenziare; **-s** *npl* scaffali *mpl*

shelving *n* scaffalatura; pendenza

shepherd *n* pastore *m*; **-ess** *n* pastorella; — *vt* guidare, scortare

sherbet *n* sorbetto

sheriff *n* sceriffo

sherry *n* vino di Xeres

shibboleth *n* parola d'ordine

shield *n* scudo, protezione *f*; *(mech)* schermo; — *vt* proteggere, difendere, coprire

shift *vt* cambiare, spostare; — *vi* spostarsi; — **for oneself** indipendenzarsi, cavarsela; — *n (auto)* cambiamento; *(squad)* squadra; *(labor)* turno; *(typewriter)* tasto per maiuscole; **-less** *a* pigro, inetto; **-y** *a* scaltro; *(eyes)* sfuggente

shiftiness *n* scaltrezza

shilling *n* scellino

shilly-shally *vi* esitare

shimmer *n* barlume, luccichio; **-y** *a* luccicante; — *vt* luccicare, brillare

shin *n* stinco, tibia; — **up** arrampicarsi

shine *vi* brillare; — *vt* lucidare, lustrare; — *n* splendore *m*; **take a — to** *(coll)* sentir simpatia per

shiner *n (coll)* occhio pesto

shingle *n (roof)* assicella, tegola di legno; *(gravel)* ghiaia; *(hair)* sfumatura di capelli; **hang out one's —** *(coll)* debuttare nella professione; **-s** *(med)* zona, erpete *m*; — *vt (hair)* tagliare corti; *(roof)* coprire di tegole

shining, shiny *a* lucente

ship *n* nave *f*; — *vt* spedire; — *vi* imbarcarsi; **-builder** *n* costruttore navale; **-owner** *n* armatore *m*; **-per** *n* speditore, caricatore *m*; **-shape** *a* ordinato; in ordine; **-wright** *n* impiegato di cantiere navale; **-yard** *n* cantiere navale, arsenale *m*; **on -board** a bordo

shipping *n* imbarco, spedizione; — **room** cantiere di spedizioni; — **clerk** impiegato spedizioniere

shipment *n* spedizione *f*, carico

shipwreck *n* naufragio; — *vt* far naufragare

shire *n* contea

shirk *vt* schivare, scansare

shirker *n* scansafatiche *m*

shirt *n* camicia; **-front** *n* sparato; **-maker** *n* camiciaio, **-waist** *n* blusa; **in — sleeves** in maniche di camicia

shiver *vi* rabbrividire; — *n* brivido, fremito

shoal *n* bassofondo

shock *n* scossa; *(emotion)* emozione; — **absorber** ammortizzatore *m*; — **treatment** *(med)* elettroterapia; — **wave** ripercussione; — *vt* scuotere, *(scandel)* scandalizzare; *(stun)* stordire. colpire; **-ing** *a* ripugnante, scandaloso

shoddy *a* falso; scadente

shoe *n* scarpa; — **polish** lucido da scarpe; — **brush** spazzola da scarpe; **-horn** *n* calzatoio; **-lace** *n* stringa, laccio; **-less** *a* scalzo; **-maker** *n* calzolaio; — **store** calzoleria; — **tree** forma da scarpe; — *vt* calzare; *(horse)* ferrare

shoestring *n* stringa, laccio; piccolo capitale *m*

shoo *vt* spaventare; cacciare via

shoot *vt&i* sparare; scattare; *(kill)* fucilare; *(bot)* germogliare; — **up** balzare, saltare; — *n (bot)* germoglio

shooting *n* tiro; — **gallery** tiro al bersaglio; — **star** stella filante

shop *n* bottega; — *vi* fare delle compere; **-girl** *n* commessa; **-keeper** *n* negoziante *m*; **-lifter** *n* taccheggiatore *m*; **-per** *n* chi va a far spese; **-window** *n* vetrina; **-worn** *a* sciupato

shopping *n* compere *fpl*; — **bag** borsa da spesa; **go —** andare a far spese

shore *n* costa, lido, riva; *(prop)* puntello; — *vt* puntellare

short *a* corto; *(height)* basso; — **circuit** corto circuito; — **cut** scorciatoia; — **story** novella; — **wave** onda corta; **for** — per brevità; **in** — in breve; **make** — **work of** sbarazzarsi in breve di; —**age** *n* mancanza, deficienza; —**ly** *adv* presto, in breve, tra poco; — *vt (elec)* provocare un corto circuito

short— *(in comp)* —**circuit** *vt (elec)* provocare un corto circuito; —**handed** *a* con personale insufficiente; —**lived** *a* di breve durata, caduco; —**spoken** *a* di poche parole; —**tempered** *a* collerico, irascibile; —**term** *a* a breve scadenza; —**winded** *a* affannoso; *(animals)* bolso

shortcake *n* pasta frolla

shortchange *vt (coll)* imbrogliare nel dare il resto

shortcoming *n* manchevolezza, deficienza

shorten *vt* accorciare, abbreviare, ridurre; — *vi* accorciarsi, ridursi

shortening *n* accorciamento, riduzione, diminuzione; *(cooking)* grasso

shorthand *n* stenografia

shortness *n* piccolezza; scarsità; — **of temper** irascibilità

shorts *npl* mutande *fpl*, calzoni corti, calzoncini *mpl*

shortsighted *a* miope; *(fig)* imprevidente; —**ness** *n* miopia, imprevidenza

shot *n* sparo; *(buckshot)* pallottola, pallini *mpl*; *(drink)* cicchetto *(coll)*; *(person)* tiratore *m*; *(med)* iniezione; *(photo)* scatto; **good** — tiratore scelto

shotgun *n* fucile da caccia; — **shell** cartuccia, bossolo

shoulder *n* spalla; — **blade** scapola — **strap** spallina; — *vt* caricarsi sulle spalle; spingere a spalla; assumere

shout *vt&i* gridare, urlare; — *n* grido; schiamazzo

shove *n* spinta, spintone *m*; — *vt* spingere con forza

shovel *n* pala; — *vt (coal)* scavare; spalare; *(food)* mangiare avidamente, divorare

show *n* spettacolo; *(arts)* mostra, esposizione; — **card** cartello; — **window** vetrata; —**case** *n* vetrina; —**down** *n (coll)* carte in tavola *(fig)*; —**man** *n* espositore *m*; —**manship** *n* abile esposizione; —**room** *n* sala d'esposizione; —**y** *a* vistoso

show *vt* mostrare; — *vi* farsi vedere; — **off** ostentare; — **up** smascherare; smascherarsi

shower *n* acquazzone *m*; doccia; — *vi* fare la doccia; piovere a rovesci; — *vt* riversare, inondare

showiness *n* vistosità

show-off *n* ostentazione; *(person)* millantatore *m*, presuntuoso

shrapnel *n (mil)* granata

shred *n* brandello; — *vt* fare a brandelli, sbrindellare

shrew *n* bisbetica, megera; *(zool)* toporagno; —**ish** *a* bisbetico; —**ishness** *n* temperamento bisbetico

shrewd *a* scaltro, fino; —**ly** *adv* sagacemente; scaltramente; —**ness** *n* sagacia; scaltrezza

shriek *n* grido, urlo; — *vt&i* strillare, gridare

shrill *a* acuto, stridulo; —**ness** *n* acutezza, stridore *m*

shrimp *n* gamberetto di mare

shrine *n* sacrario; reliquario

shrink *vi* restringersi, contrarsi; — *vt* restringere, contrarre; —**age** *n* restringimento, contrazione; — **back** indietreggiare

shrinking *n* diminuzione, contrazione; — *a* restringente

shrivel *vi* contrarsi, raggrinzarsi; — *vt* contrarre, raggrinzare

shroud *n* sudario, velo; *(naut)* sartia; — *vt* avvolgere in sudario, coprire, nascondere

Shrove Tuesday Martedì Grasso

shrub *n* arbusto; —**bery** *n* arbusti *mpl*

shrug *n* scrollata di spalle; — *vi* scrollare le spalle

shrunken *a* accorciato

shuck *vt* sbucciare, sgranare

shudder *vi* rabbrividire; — *n* fremito, brivido

shuffle *n* strascichio; *(deceit)* sotterfugio; *(dance)* passo doppio; *(mus)* scompiglio; — *vt (scuffle)* strascicare; *(confuse)* scompigliare; *(mix)* mischiare; — *vi* strascicarsi; vacillare; *(quibble)* tergiversare; — **off** sbarazzarsi di

shuffleboard *n* giuoco delle piastrelle

shuffling *a* strascicante, evasivo; — *n* *(feet)* strascichio; *(mixing)* rimescolamento

shun *vt* evitare

shunt *vt&i* derivare; *(discard)* scartare; *(rail)* smistare

shut *vt&i* chiudere, chiudersi; — **down** cessare il lavoro; — **in** rinchiudere; — **off** chiudere; — **out** chiuder fuori; — **up** *(coll)* tacere; far tacere — *a* chiuso; —**down** *n* cessazione del lavoro; —**off** *n* chiusura

shut-in *n* rinchiuso, recluso

shutter *n* scuro, imposta, persiana; *(phot)* otturatore *m*

shuttle *n* spoletta, navetta; — *vi* fare la

spola
shuttlecock *n* volano
shy *a* timido; sospettoso; *(lacking)* corto di, mancante di; — *vi* adombrarsi; indietreggiare; **–ly** *adv* timidamente; *(suspiciously)* sospettosamente; **–ness** *n* timidezza, diffidenza
shyster *n* imbroglione, azzeccagarbugli *m*
Siamese *a* siamese; — **twins** fratelli siamesi
sibilant *a* sibilante
sibyl *n* sibilla
Sicilian *a&n* siciliano
Sicily Sicilia
sick *a* ammalato; **–ly** *a* malaticcio; **–bed** letto di dolore; — **leave** licenza di convalescenza
sicken *vt* dar nausea; infastidire; — *vi* ammalarsi; nausearsi; **–ing** *a* nauseante, repulsivo
sickle *n* falce *f*
sickness *n* malattia
side *n* lato; — **by** — fianco a fianco; **–car** *n* motocarrozzella; — **dish** portata secondaria; — **issue** questione secondaria; — **light** fanale laterale; — **line** attività secondaria; supplemento di lavoro; **–long** *a* di lato, obliquo; — **show** baraccone *m*; mostra secondaria; — **street** traversa; **–walk** *n* marciapiede *m*; **–ways** *adv* di lato, a sghembo; **on all** **–s** da ogni parte; **on one** — da una parte, — *vt* chiudere con pareti; *(coll)* mettere a parte; **–track** *vt&i* sviare; — **with** prendere le parti di; appoggiare; — *a* di fianco, laterale, obliquo
sideboard *n* credenza
side-step *vt* evitare
siding *n* *(rail)* binario laterale
sidle *vi* camminare di fianco
siege *n* assedio; **lay** — **to** assediare
siesta *n* siesta
sieve *n* staccio, crivello; — *vt* stacciare
sift *vt* stacciare, vagliare; **–er** *n* staccio
sigh *vt&i* sospirare; — *n* sospiro; **–ing** *n* sospiri *mpl*
sight *n* vista; *(gun)* mirino; — **draft** tratta a vista; **at first** — a prima vista; **in** — in vista; **lose** — **of** perdere di vista; **on** — a vista; **out of** — fuori di vista; — *vt* avvistare; prendere di mira; — *vi* mirare; **–less** *a* cieco; invisibile; **–seer** *n* osservatore *m*
sight-see *vi* fare una passeggiata turistica; **–ing** *n* veduta, osservazione, ispezione
sign *n* segno, insegna; — **language** linguaggio a gesti, linguaggio mimico; — **painter** pittore d'insegne; **–post** *n* palo indicatore — *vt&i (signature)* firmare; segnare; — **away** cedere; — **off**

(rad&TV) finire la trasmissione; — **on** ingaggiarsi; — **up** sottoscriversi
signal *n* segnale *m*; — **light** fanale *m*; — *vt&i* segnalare; far segnali; — *a* notevole; esemplare; **S– Corps** *(mil)* corpo segnalatori
signature *n* firma
signboard *n* insegna
signer *n* firmatario
signet *n* sigillo; — **ring** anello con sigillo
significance *n* significato
significant *a* significante, significativo; importante
signify *vt* significare
silence *n* silenzio; — *vt* far tacere, calmare; *(rebellion)* soffocare *(fig)*
silencer *n* smorzatore *m*
silent *a* silenzioso; — **partner** socio non attivo
silhouette *n* sagoma, profilo; — *vt* delineare, siluettare
silica *n* silice *f*
silicon *n* silicio
silk *n* seta; — *a* di seta; **–en** *a* di seta; serico; dolce; — **screen** stampino di seta; **–iness** *n* setosità; **–worm** *n* baco da seta; **–y** *a* setaceo; di seta, serico; *(fig)* dolce
sill *n* *(door)* soglia; *(window)* davanzale *m*
silliness *n* sciocchezza, stupidaggine *f*
silly *a* sciocco, scemo
silo *n* silo
silver *n* argento; — *a* d'argento; — **plate** posate e vasellame argentati; **–smith** *n* argentiere *m*; **–ware** *n* argenteria; **–y** *a* inargentato
silver-plate *vt* argentare
silver-tongued *a* eloquente
similar *a* somigliante, simile; **–ity** *n* analogia; similitudine *f*; somiglianza; **–ly** *adv* similmente
simile *n* paragone *m*; similitudine *f*
similitude *n* somiglianza
simmer *vt&i* bollire; **–ing** *n* bollore *m*, ebollizione
simony *n* simonia
simper *n* smorfia; sorriso affettato; **–ing** *n* affettazione; smorfie *fpl*; — *vi* sorridere con affettazione
simple *a* semplice
simple-minded *a* semplicione, candido; *(med)* deficiente
simpleton *n* semplicione *m*
simplicity *n* semplicità
simplification *n* semplificazione
simplify *vt* semplificare
simply *adv* semplicemente
simulate *vt* simulare
simulation *n* simulazione
simultaneous *a* simultaneo; **–ly** *adv* simul-

taneamente

sin *n* peccato; — *vi* peccare; **–ful** *a* peccaminoso; **–fulness** *n* colpevolezza; **–ner** *n* peccatore *m*

since *prep* dopo, da; — *conj* dacchè, poichè, giacchè; dopo che; — *adv* dopo, di poi, dopo d'allora

sincere *a* sincero; **–ly** *adv* sinceramente

sincerity *n* sincerità

sine *n* (*math*) sino

sinecure *n* sinecura

sinew *n* tendine *m*; nervo

sinewy *a* nerboruto, nervoso

sing *vt&i* cantare; **–able** *a* cantabile

singe *vt* bruciacchiare; — *n* bruciacchiata

single *a* singolo; (*man*) celibe; (*woman*) nubile; — **file** fila indiana; **–ness** *n* sincerità; — **out** scegliere, separare, distinguere

single– (*in comp*) **–breasted** *a* a un petto; **–handed** *a* da sè; senza aiuto altrui; **–minded** *a* schietto, sincero

singly *a* uno ad uno, individualmente

singsong *n* cantilena; — *a* monotono

singular *a* singolare; — *n* singolarità; **–ize** *vt* singolarizzare; **–ly** *adv* singolarmente

sinister *a* sinistro

sink *vt&i* affondare; (*money*) investire; (*well*) scavare; — *n* acquaio; **–er** *n* (*fish line*) piombo; **–age** *n* calo, diminuzione; affondamento

sinking *a* affondante; — **fund** *n* fondo d'ammortamento

sinuosity *n* sinuosità

sinuous *a* sinuoso

sinus *n* (*anat*) seno nasale, seno frontale

sinusitis *n* sinusite *f*

sip *n* sorso; — *vt&i* sorseggiare

siphon *vt* sifonare; — *n* sifone *m*

sir *n* signore *m*

sire *n* sire, signore *m*; padre; — *vt* procreare, generare

siren *n* sirena

sirloin *n* lombo

sissy *n* (*coll*) maschio effeminato

sister *n* sorella; (*nun*) suora, monaca, religiosa

sister-in-law *n* cognata

sit *vi* sedere; sedersi; — *vt* far sedere; **–down strike** sciopero bianco; — **up** (*wait up*) vegliare; tenersi dritto

site *n* sito, posizione

sitter *n* modello; (*baby*) bambinaia; (*hen*) chioccia

sitting *n* seduta; riunione; (*arts*) posa; — *a* seduto; posante; — **room** salotto

situate *vt* collocare; **–d** *a* posto, situato; **be –d** trovarsi

situation *n* situazione; impiego

six *a* sei; **–teen** *a* sedici; **–teenth** *a* sedicesimo; **–th** *a* sesto; **–tieth** *a* sessantesimo; **–ty** *a* sessanta

sizable *a* abbastanza grande

size *n* misura, formato, grandezza; — *vt* graduare secondo misura; — **up** giudicare, pesare

sizing *n* (*fabric*) imbozzimatura

sizzle *vi* sfrigolare; friggere; — *n* sfrigolio

sizzling *a* caldo fumante

skate *n* pattino; **ice** — pattino da ghiaccio; **roller** — pattino a rotelle; — *vi* pattinare; **–r** *n* pattinatore *m*, pattinatrice *f*

skating *n* pattinaggio; — **rink** pista di pattinaggio; **figure** — pattinaggio artistico

skein *n* matassa; gomitolo

skeleton *n* scheletro; — **key** chiave maestra

skeptic *n* scettico *m*; **–al** *a* scettico; **–ism** *n* scetticismo

sketch *vt&i* abbozzare, schizzare; — *n* abozzo, schizzo; **–book** *n* album di schizzi; **–ily** *adv* senza dettagli; **–y** *a* non dettagliato

skew *a* a sghembo, obliquo

skewer *n* spiedo

ski *n* sci *m*; **–er** *n* sciatore *m*, sciatrice *f*; — **lift** sciovia; **–ing** *n* sport dello sci; — *vi* sciare

skid *n* (*avi*) pattino di coda; (*mech*) freno a scarpa; (*slip*) slittamento, slittata; — *vi* slittare

skiff *n* schifo

skill *n* abilità, destrezza; **–ful** *a* abile, destro, **–fully** *adv* abilmente, accortamente

skilled *a* abile, addestrato; esperto; — **labor** mano d'opera specializzata; — **worker** specialista *m*

skillet *n* padella

skim *vt&i* scremare; scorrere; — **milk** latte scremato

skimp *vt&i* (*coll*) esser tirchio; economizzare; **–y** *a* (*coll*) meschino; scarso; tirchio

skin *n* pelle *f*; — **diver** pescatore subacqueo; **–flint** *n* spilorcio; avaro; — *vt* pelare, scorticare; sbucciare

skin-deep *a* superficiale

skinny *a* scarno, magro

skin-tight *a* indossante come un guanto

skip *vi* saltellare; — *vt* omettere; — *n* salto

skipper *n* capitano di mare

skirmish *n* schermaglia; (*mil*) scaramuccia; — *vi* scaramucciare

skirt *n* gonna; — *vt&i* rasentare, orlare, costeggiare

skit *n* parodia, scherzo, farsa
skittish *a* volubile; *(horse)* bizzarro, ombroso
skoal *interj* salute!
skulk *vi* strisciare, accovacciarsi
skull *n* cranio; **–cap** *n* papalina
skunk *n* moffetta; *(coll)* farabutto
sky *n* cielo; **–light** *n* lucernario, abbaino; **–line** *n* orizzonte *m*; **–scraper** *n* grattacielo; **–writing** *n* scrittura con fumi di aeroplano
sky-high *a&adv* fino alle nuvole *(fig)*
skylark *n* allodola
skyrocket *n* razzo; — *vi (coll)* salire con grande velocità
slab *n* lastra
slack *a* lento; fiacco; debole; negligente; — *n (rope)* imbando; — **time** stagione morta; **–er** *n* poltrone *m*; **–ness** *n* incuranza; allentamento; — **off** allentare; allentarsi
slacken *vt* allentare; moderare; — *vi* allentarsi; moderarsi; diminuire
slacks *npl* calzoni *mpl*
slag *n* scoria
slain *n* ucciso; morto
slake *vt* spegnere, placare; *(thirst)* dissetare; — *vi* spegnersi, placarsi
slalom *n (skiing)* slalom *m*
slam *n (door)* sbattuta di porta; *(sl)* critica severa; **grand —** *(cards)* cappotto; — *vt* sbattere; chiudere rumorosamente; *(sl)* criticare severamente; — *vi* sbattersi
slander *n* calunnia; — *vt* calunniare; **–er** calunniatore *m*
slanderous *a* calunnioso
slang *n* gergo populare
slant *n* pendio, declivio; *(viewpoint)* punto di vista; **–ing** *a* inclinato, obliquo; — *vt* far pendere, inclinare; — *vi* pendere, inclinarsi
slap *n* ceffone *m*; *(face)* schiaffo; — *vt* schiaffeggiare
slapstick *n* scena grottesca, farsa; — *a* grottesco
slash *n* taglio; — *vt (cut)* tagliare; *(gash)* squarciare; *(whip)* sferzare; *(reduce)* ridurre
slat *n* striscia; stecca, assicella
slate *n* ardesia; lavagna; tegola d'ardesia; *(pol)* lista dei candidati; — *vt* mettere sulla lista dei candidati; *(coll)* stroncare; coprire d'ardesia
slattern *n* sciattona
slaughter *n* strage *f*, carneficina; macellazione; **–house** *n* mattatoio; macello; — *vt* massacrare; *(animals)* macellare
slave *n* schiavo; — **driver** negriero; *(fig)* aguzzino; — *vi* lavorare come schiavo;

logorarsi; **–ry** *n* schiavitù *f*
slavish *a* servile; abietto; **–ly** *adv* da schiavo; servilmente; bassamente
slaw *n* insalata di cavoli
slay *vt* uccidere; **–er** *n* assassino; **–ing** *n* uccisione
sleaziness *n* mancanza di consistenza
sleazy *a* senza consistenza
sled *n* slitta
sledge *n* traino; **–hammer** mazza
sleek *a* liscio, levigato; lucido
sleep *vi* dormire; **go to —** addormentarsi
sleep *n* sonno; *(fig)* quiete *f*; **–less** *a* insonne; **–less night** notte bianca; **–ily** *adv* sonnolentemente; **–iness** *n* sonnolenza; **–y** *a* assonnato, sonnacchioso; **be –y** aver sonno
sleeping *n* sonno, riposo; — **car** vagone letto; — **pill** sonnifero; — **sickness** malattia del sonno
sleepwalker *n* sonnambulo
sleepwalking *n* sonnambulismo
sleepyhead *n* dormiglione *m*
sleet *n* nevischio; **–y** *a* nevischioso; — *vi* nevicare e piovere insieme
sleeve *n* manica; **–less** *a* senza maniche; **laugh up one's —** ridere sotto i baffi
sleigh *n* slitta
sleight *n* destrezza; — **of hand** giuoco di prestigio, prestigiazione
slender *a* esile, smilzo, snello; **–ness** *n* snellezza
sleuth *n* segugio
slice *n* fetta; — *vt* affettare
slick *a* destro, abile; scivoloso; — *vt* lisciare, appianare; **–er** *n (coll, person)* imbroglione *m*; *(raincoat)* impermeabile *m*
slide *vi* scivolare; scorrere; — *vt* far scorrere; — *n* scivolata; slitta; *(microscope)* vetrino per microscopio; *(photo)* diapositiva; *(rock)* frana; — **rule** regolo calcolatore; — **valve** valvola a cassetto
slight *a* leggero, minimo; smilzo; — *n* affronto; — *vt* trascurare; disprezzare, denigrare; **–ly** *adv* lievemente, superficialmente; **–ness** *n* snellezza
slim *a* smilzo; **–ness** *n* esiguità, esilità, sottigliezza; — *vi* dimagrire
slime *n* limo, fanghiglia
sliminess *n* viscosità
slimy *a* viscido, viscoso
sling *n* fionda; benda per sostenere un braccio al collo; **–shot** *n* fionda, tirelastico; — *vt* sospendere; *(throw)* lanciare
slink *vi* strisciare; sgusciare; **–y** *a* strisciante
slip *n (error)* sbaglio, svista; *(slide)* scivolata; *(underwear)* sottoveste *f*,

combinazione; **–cover** n fodera di mobile; **–knot** n nodo scorsoio; — vt&i sdrucciolare; sgusciare, sfuggire; scorrere, infilare; sbagliarsi

slipper n pantofola

slipperiness n sdrucciolosità

slippery a sdrucciolevole

slipshod a trascurato

slipup n sbaglio, errore m

slipway n (naut) scalo

slit vt fendere; — n fessura

sliver n scheggia

slobber vi sbavare; — n bava; **–y** a bavoso

sloe n prugnola; — **gin** liquore di prugnola

slog vi avanzare a stento

slogan n slogan m

sloop n scialuppa

slop n risciacquatura di piatti, pozzanghera; — vt versare, spandere; — vi traboccare

slope n pendio; — vt&i inclinare

sloppy a fangoso; (coll) sciatto, trascurato; viscido

slosh vi sguazzare; — vt agitare ; — n fanghiglia

slot n fessura; — **machine** distributore automatico

sloth n indolenza; (zool) bradipo; **–ful** a pigro; **–fulness** n pigrizia

slouch n scompostura; (person) persona goffa, persona curva; negligente m; — **hat** cappello a tesa in giù; **–y** a scomposto; — vi stare (or camminare) scompostamente

slough n (swamp) palude f

slough n spoglia; (med) crosta; — vt&i spogliarsi di; cambiare la pelle

slovenliness n trascuratezza

slovenly a trascurato, sudicio

slow n lento; ottuso; (clock) in ritardo; **–down** n rallentamento; **–ly** adv adagio, piano, lentamente; **–ness** n lentezza; — vt ritardare; — vi rallentare; — **down** rallentare

slow-motion a al rallentatore

sludge n melma, fanghiglia

slug n (metal) lingotto; (bullet) pallottola; (zool) lumaca; (token) gettone m; — vt (coll) percuotere

sluggard n pigrone m

sluggish a lento; pigro; **–ness** n indolenza; pigrizia

sluice n chiusa; canale m; cateratta; — vt&i inondare, defluire, affluire

slumber n sonno; — vi dormire; sonnecchiare

slump n abbassamento improvviso, tracollo, caduta brusca; — vi precipitare; avere un tracollo; affondare

slums npl quartieri poveri

slur n macchia; diffamazione; (mus) legatura; — vt pronunciare male; diffamare; (mus) legare

slush n fanghiglia di neve

slut n donnaccia

sly a furbo, truffaldino; **on the** — alla chetichella; **–ly** a astutamente; furtivamente

smack n gusto; aroma; sapore m; schiocco; schiaffo; bacione m; — vt far schioccare, schiaffeggiare; baciare sonoramente; — vi sapere di, aver sapore

small a piccolo, minuto; — **of the back** n le reni fpl; — **change** (money) spiccioli mpl; — **letter** minuscola; — **talk** chiacchiera, banalità

small-minded a gretto

smallpox n vaiolo

small-town a provinciale

smart n bruciore, dolore m; — a intelligente; scaltro; elegante; — **aleck** (coll) presuntuoso e antipatico; **–ing** n bruciore m; **–ing** a bruciante; **–ly** adv vivacemente; elegantemente; acutamente; dolorosamente; **–ness** n acutezza, prontezza di spirito; eleganza

smarten vt adornare; abbellire

smash n collisione; sconquasso; rovina; — vt fracassare; rovinare; — vi fallire; fracassarsi; spezzarsi

smashup n catastrofe f; rovina; crollo; collisione

smattering n conoscimento superficiale, infarinatura

smear n spalmata; calunnia; — vt&i spalmare; calunniare

smell vt&i odorare; fiutare; **–y** a puzzolente; — n odore m; (sense of) odorato, fiuto, olfatto; **–ing salts** sali mpl

smelt n (fish) eperlano; — vt fondere; **–er** n fonditore m; **–ing** n fusione; **–ing furnace** alto forno

smile n sorriso; — vi sorridere

smiling a sorridente

smirch vt insudiciare

smirk n sorriso affettato; — vi sorridere affettatamente

smite vt percuotere, colpire; (kill) uccidere

smith n fabbro; **–y** fucina

smithereens npl (coll) schegge fpl; pezzi mpl; frantumi mpl; frammenti mpl; **break to** — andare in frantumi; mandare in frantumi

smock n blusa; camice m; camiciotto

smoke n fumo; — **screen** cortina di fuma; **–stack** n fumaiolo; **–less** a senza fumo; — vt&i fumare; affumicare; **–d** a affumicato; **–r** n fumatore m, fumatrice f

smokiness n fumosità

smoking n fumo, il fumare; — **jacket**

giacca da fumo; **no** — proibito fumare
smoky *a* fumoso, fumante
smolder *vt&i* bruciare senza fiamma; covare nelle ceneri; **–ing** *a* covante, che cova
smooth *a* liscio; — *vt* lisciare; piallare; appianare, calmare; **–ly** *adv* agevolmente; **–ness** *n* levigatezza; calma; agevolezza
smooth-shaved *a* imberbe
smooth-tongued *a* adulatore, mellifluo
smother *vt&i* soffocare; nascondere
smudge *n* sgorbio, macchia; — *vt&i* macchiare, sporcare
smudgy *a* macchiato
smug *a* vanitoso, affettato; **–ness** *n* vanità, affettazione
smuggle *vt&i* contrabbandare; **–r** *n* contrabbandiere *m*
smuggling *n* frodo, contrabbando
smut *n* fuliggine *f*; oscenità
smuttiness *n* oscenità
smutty *a* fuligginoso, nero, osceno
snack *n* spuntino; pasto frugale; — *vi* fare uno spuntino
snag *n* nodo; troncone *m*; intoppo; ramo sommerso; — *vt* ostacolare
snail *n* lumaca, chiocciola; **at a —'s pace** a passo di lumaca *(coll)*
snake *n* serpente *m*; — *vi* serpeggiare
snaky *a* tortuoso, serpentino; *(fig)* scaltro
snap *vt&i* spezzare; mordere, azzannare, cercare di mordere; scattare, schioccare; spezzarsi; — *n* scatto, schiocco; morso; *(sl)* cosa facile da farsi; *(coll)* vivacità; **cold** — periodo di freddo; **–shot** *n (photo)* istantanea
snapdragon *n (bot)* bocca di leone
snappish *a* irascibile, bisbetico
snappy *a (coll)* vivo, pungente; elegante; **make it** — *(sl)* fa presto
snare *n* trappola; — *vt* prendere al laccio
snarl *n (animal)* ringhio; *(tangle)* groviglio; — *vi* ringhiare; aggrovigliarsi; — *vt* aggrovigliare
snatch *vt* strappare, ghermire; — *n* presa; strappone *m*
sneak *n* spia; vile *m*; — **thief** ladruncolo; **–y** *a* servile, basso; ficcanaso; — *vt (coll)* rubare, sottrarre; — *vi* strisciare; spiare; — **in** intrufolarsi; — **out** uscire alla chetichella
sneakers *npl* scarpe da ginnastica
sneaking *a* meschino, basso; sospettoso; **–ly** *adv* bassamente; sospettosamente
sneer *n* sogghigno; — *vi* sogghignare; **–ing** *a* derisorio
sneeze *vi* starnutire; — *n* starnuto
snicker *n* risatina celata; — *vi* ridacchiare
sniff *n* fiutata; — *vi* succhiare col naso; frignare

sniffle *n* succhiata di naso; — *vi* succhiare col naso; frignare
snip *n* ritaglio; taglio; brandello; pezzettino; — *vt&i* tagliuzzare
snipe *n (zool)* beccaccino; **–r** *n* cecchino; — *vi* sparare in appostamento
snippy *a* presuntuoso, arioso
snivel *vi* moccicare, piagnucolare, frignare
snob *n* snob *m*
snobbish *a* snobistico; affettato; **–ness** *n* snobismo; affettazione
snoop *vi (coll)* curiosare, ficcare il naso; **–er** *n* ficcanaso
snoot *n (coll)* naso; faccia, smorfia; **–y** *a* arrogante
snooze *n* pisolino; — *vi* sonnecchiare
snore *vi&n* russare *m*
snorer *n* russatore *m*
snoring *n* il russare
snorkel *n* presa d'aria
snort *n* sbuffo; — *vi* sbuffare; **–ing** *n* sbuffamento; **–ing** *a* sbuffante
snout *n* muso; *(pig)* grugno; *(mech)* beccuccio
snow *n* neve *f*; **–bound** *a* bloccato dalla neve; **–drift** *n* ammasso di neve; **–fall** *n* nevicata; **–flake** *n* fiocco di neve; — **line** limite delle nevi perpetue; **–plow** *n* spazzaneve *m*; **–slide** *n* valanga; **–storm** *n* tempesta di neve; **–suit** *n* vestito da neve; — *vi* nevicare; **it is –ing** nevica
snow– *(in comp)* **–blind** *a* accecato dalla neve; **–capped** *a* coronato di neve
snowball *n* palla di neve; — *vt* lanciare palle di neve; — *vi (enlarge)* crescere rapidamente
snowy *a* nevoso
snub *n* rimprovero, affronto; — *vt* trattare freddamente, offendere; — **nose** naso camuso
snuff *n* moccolo; tabacco da fiuto; presa di tabacco; fiutata; — *vt* smoccolare; fiutare
snuffbox *n* tabacchiera
snuffle *vi* fiutare rumorosamente
snug *a* comodo, agevole; ritirato, nascosto, riparato; **–ly** *adv* comodamente, agevolmente; **–ness** *n* comodità
snuggle *vt* vezzeggiare, abbracciare; — *vi* accomodarsi, rannicchiarsi
so *adv&conj* così, tanto, talmente; quindi; di modo che; **and** — **forth** e così via; eccetera; — **as to** in modo da; — **long!** ciao!, arrivederci!; — **much** tanto; — **then** bene, allora; — **to speak** per così dire
soak *vt* inzuppare; — *vi* inzupparsi, assorbirsi; filtrare
soaking *a* gocciolante, — *n* bagno, immer-

sione
so-and-so *n (coll)* Tal dei Tali
soap *n* sapone *m*; — **bubble** bolla di sapone; —**dish** portasapone *m*; –**stone** *n* steatite *f*; –**suds** *npl* saponata, soluzione saponosa; **bar** — sapone in barre; **toilet** — saponetta; –**y** *a* saponoso; insaponato; — *vt* insaponare
soar *vi* volare; librarsi, acquistare quota; prendere lo slancio
sob *n* singhiozzo; — *vi* singhiozzare
sober *a* sobrio; –**ness** *n* sobrietà; moderazione; — *vt&i* smaltire la sbornia; rinsavire, calmarsi; ritornare in sè
sober-minded *a* serio, sobrio
sobersides *n* musoduro
sobriety *n* sobrietà
sobriquet *n* soprannome *m*
so-called *a* cosiddetto
sociability *n* sociabilità
sociable *a* socievole, affabile
sociably *adv* socievolmente
social *n* trattenimento sociale; — **security** assicurazione sociale; — *a* sociale; socievole, affabile; –**ism** *n* socialismo; –**ist** *n* socialista *m&f*; –**istic** *a* socialista, socialistico; –**ite** *n* persona dell'alta società; –**ize** *vt* socializzare
society *n* società
sociological *a* sociologico
sociologist *n* sociologo
sociology *n* sociologia
sock *n* calzetta, calzino; *(sl)* pugno; — *vt (sl)* colpire, dare un pugno
socket *n (elec)* incavo, portalampada *m*; *(eye)* orbita; *(joint)* manicotto, giunto; *(anat)* articolazione; (tooth) alveolo
sod *n* zolla erbosa
soda *n* soda; **baking** — bicarbonato di soda; — **water** selz *m*, acqua gassosa
sodium *n* sodio; — **chloride** clorato di sodio
sodomy *n* sodomia
sofa *n* sofà, canapè *m*; — **bed** sofà a letto, divano-letto
soft *a* molle; dolce; — **coal** carbone bituminoso; — **drink** bevanda analcoolica; –**ness** *n* morbidezza; tenerezza; debolezza; — **pedal** sordina
soft– *(in comp)* –**boiled** bassotto; — **pedal** *vt (coll)* abbassare il tono; diminuire; —**soap** *vt (coll)* adulare; —**spoken** *a* mellifluo; affabile
soften *vt* ammollire, addolcire, mitigare; — *vi* rammollirsi; addolcirsi; mitigarsi
softhead *n* imbecille *m*
softhearted *a* di buon cuore
soggy *a* inzuppato
soil *n* suolo; terra; sporcizia, macchia; letame; — *vi* sporcarsi

sojourn *n* soggiorno; — *vi* soggiornare
sol *n (mus)* sol *m*
solace *n* consolazione, conforto, — *vt* consolare
solar *a* solare; — **plexus** plesso solare; — **system** sistema solare
sold *a* venduto
solder *vt* saldare; — *vi* saldarsi; — *n* saldatura
soldering *n* saldatura; — **iron** saldatore *m*
soldier *n* soldato; — *vi* fare il soldato
sole *n (fish)* sogliola; *(foot)* pianta del piede; *(shoe)* suola; — *a* solo, unico; — *vt* risolare, solare
solecism *n* solecismo
solemn *a* solenne; grave; –**ity** *n* solennità; –**ization** *n* solennizzamento; –**ize** *vt* solennizzare
solicit *vt&i* sollecitare; fare colletta; pregare; –**ation** *n* sollecitazione, richiesta; –**or** *n* piazzista, propagandista *m*; –**ous** *a* sollecito; –**ude** *n* sollecitudine *f*
solid *a&n* solido; –**arity** solidarietà; — **color** tinta unita; –**ity** *n* solidezza, solidità; –**ify** *vt* solidificare; –**ify** *vi* solidificarsi
solid state physics elettrofisica degli stati solidi
soliloquy *n* soliloquio
solitaire *n* solitario
solitariness *n* solitudine *f*
solitary *a* solitario; — **confinement** segregazione cellulare
solitude *n* solitudine *f*
solo *n&a (mus)* assolo
soloist *n* solista *m&f*
solstice *n* solstizio
solubility *n* solubilità
soluble *a* solubile
solution *n* soluzione
solve *vt* risolvere
solvency *n* solvibilità
solvent *a&n* solvente
somber *a* oscuro, ombroso, fosco; –**ness** *n* foscaggine *f*
some *a* qualche, un po'di; qualcuno; del, della, dei, delle; — *pron* alcuni *mpl*; alcune *fpl*; certi *mpl*; certe *fpl*; ne; — *adv* circa
some *(in comb)* –**body** *pron* qualcuno; –**day** *adv* qualche giorno; –**how** *adv* in qualche modo; –**one** *pron* qualcuno; –**one else** un altro; –**thing** *n* qualcosa; qualche cosa; –**time** *adv* qualche volta, uno di questi giorni; –**times** *adv* qualche volta, talvolta; –**what** *adv* alquanto, un poco; –**where** *adv* in qualche luogo; –**where else** altrove
somersault *n* capitombolo, capriola; — *vi*

far salti mortali (or capriole)
somnambulism *n* sonnambulismo
somnambulist *n* sonnambulo
somnolence sonnolenza
somnolent *a* sonnolente
son *n* figlio
sonata *n* sonata
song *n* canzone *f*; **–ster** *n* cantante *m*;
 –stress *n* cantante *f*
sonic *a* di suono, sonico; **— boom** *(avi)*
 strepito di aviogetto
son-in-law *n* genero
sonnet *n* sonetto
sonneteer *n* sonettista *m&f*
sonority *n* sonorità
sonorous *a* sonoro
soon *adv* presto, subito; **as — as** appena
 che; **How —?** Quando?; **–er** *adv* più
 presto; piuttosto; prima
soot *n* fuliggine *f*; **–y** *a* fuligginoso, nero
soothe *vt* calmare, lenire
soothing *a* calmante, mite; adulante
soothsayer *n* indovino
soothsaying *n* divinazione
sop *n* zuppa, pappa; **—, — up** *vt* inzuppare, assorbire; **— vi** inzupparsi;
 –ing *a* bagnato, inzuppato
sophist *n* sofista *m&f*
sophisticated *a* sofisticato; ricercato;
 raffinato
sophistication *n* sofisticazione; adulte-
 razione
sophistry *n* sofisticheria
sophomore *n* studente di secondo anno;
 fagiolo *(student sl)*
sophomoric *a* inesperto, poco giudizioso
soporific *n&a* soporifero
soprano *n* soprano
sorcerer *n* mago, stregone *m*
sorceress *n* maga, strega
sorcery *n* magia, stregoneria
sordid *a* sordido; **–ly** *adv* sordidamente;
 –ness sordidezza
sore *n* piaga; **— a** doloroso; *(coll)* arrabbiato; **–ness** *n* dolore *m*
sorghum *n* sorgo
sorority *n* associazione fra donne
sorrel *n (bot)* acetosa; **— a&n** sauro
sorrow *n* dolore *m*, pena; **–ful** *a* triste;
 addolorato; doloroso; **— vi** addolorarsi,
 affliggersi
sorry *a* spiacente, afflitto, dolente; meschino; **be —** essere spiacente
sort *n* sorta, genere *m*; specie *f*; **— vt**
 assortire
sortie *n (mil)* sortita
so-so *a&adv* così così
sot *n* ubriacone *m*
sough *vi* stormire, sussurrare
sought *a* cercato, ricercato

soul *n* anima; **–ful** *a* spirituale; **–less** *a*
 senz'anima
sound *n* suono; rumore *m*; *(geog)* stretto;
 — barrier barriera del suono; **— track**
 (movies) colonna sonora; **— wave** onda
 sonora; **— a** sano; solido; *(com)* solvente; **–ly** *adv* bene; profondamente; **–ness**
 n sanità; validità; **–less** *a* muto, senza
 suono
sound *vt* suonare, far suonare; sondare;
 — vi suonare, risuonare; sembrare
sounding *n (naut)* sondaggio; scandaglio;
 — a sonante, risonante, sonoro; **—
 board** tavola armonica; **— line** *(naut)*
 sonda, scandaglio
soundproof *a* refrattario al suono, anti-
 acustico
soup *n* minestra; zuppa; **— plate** scodella;
 –spoon *n* cucchiaione *m*; **— tureen**
 zuppiera; **–y** *a* come zuppa
soupçon *n* pizzico
sour *a* agro; aspro; **–ness** *n* acidità;
 asprezza; **— vt&i** rendere agro, inacidire;
 –ly *adv* aspramente
source *n* fonte *f*
souse *vt* mettere in salamoia; immergere,
 inzuppare, tuffare; **— vi** immergersi,
 inzupparsi, tuffarsi
south *n* sud *m*; **S– America** America del
 Sud; **S– American** sudamericano
southeast *n* sud-est *m*
southern *a* meridionale
southerner *n* meridionale *m&f*
southpaw *n&a (coll)* mancino
southwest *n* sud-ovest *m*
souvenir *n* ricordo
sovereign *a&n* sovrano
sovereignty *n* sovranità
soviet *n* soviet *m*; **— a** sovietico
sow *n* troia, scrofa
sow *vt&i* seminare; **–er** *n* seminatore *m*;
 –ing *n* semina
soy, soybean *n* soia
spa *n* stazione termale
space *n* spazio; **— capsule** capsula spaziale; **— platform** piattaforma interplane-
 tare; **— suit** tuta spaziale; **— travel**
 viaggio spaziale; **–man** *n* astronauta
 m; **–ship** *n* astronave *f*; **— station**
 stazione spaziale; **— vt** spaziare; inter-
 vallare
spacing *n* spaziatura
spacious *a* ampio; **–ness** *n* ampiezza
spade *n (cards)* picca; *(tool)* vanga; **call
 a — a —** dire pane al pane; **— vt** vangare
Spain Spagna
span *n* durata, portata; *(measure)* spanna;
 — vt attraversare, stendersi attraverso;
 abbracciare; *(measure)* misurare a

spanne
spangle *n* paglietta, lustrino; — *vt* adornare con lustrini; — *vi* luccicare
Spaniard *n* spagnolo
spaniel *n* bracco spagnolo
Spanish *n&a* spagnolo
spank *vt* sculacciare; **–ing** *n* sculacciamento
spar *n* antenna; *(avi)* alerone *m*; *(geol)* spato; *(naut)* albero; — *vi* fare un incontro di pugilato, combattere; discutere
spare *vt&i* risparmiare; tralasciare; — *a* di ricambio; smilzo; — **parts** pezzi di ricambio; — **time** tempo libero; — **tire** gomma di ricambio
spareness *n* scarnezza
sparerib *n* costoletta di maiale
sparing *a* frugale; parco, economo
spark *n* scintilla; — **plug** candela
sparkle *vi* scintillare; essere effervescente
sparkling *a* scintillante; effervescente
sparrow *n* passero
sparse *a* rado; **–ly** *adv* radamente; **–ness** *n* radezza
Spartan *n&a* spartano
spasm *n* spasmo, spasimo; **–odic** *a* spasmodico; **–odically** *adv* spasmodicamente
spastic *n&a* spastico
spat *n* battibecco; **–s** *npl (footwear)* ghette *fpl*; — *vi* bisticciare
spatial, spacial *a* spaziale
spatter *vt&i* spruzzare; **–ing** *n* spruzzata
spatula *n* spatola
spawn *n* progenie *f*; *(fish)* uova *fpl*; — *vt&i* generare; deporre uova
spay *vt* sterilizzare
speak *vt&i* parlare; — **out** parlar chiaro; — **up** parlare forte
speaker *n* parlatore, conferenziere, oratore *m*; *(mech)* altoparlante *m*
spear *n (grass)* stelo; fiocina; spiedo; lancia; **–fishing** pesca subacquea; — **gun** fucile subacqueo; **–head** *n* punta di lancia; **–mint** *n* menta; — *vt* trafiggere, fiocinare
special *a* speciale; — **delivery** per espresso; **–ist** *n* specialista *m*; **–ization** *n* specializzazione; **–ize** *vi* specializzarsi; **–ize** *vt* specializzare; **–ty** *n* specialità
specie *n* moneta metallica
species *n* specie *f*
specific *a* specifico; — **gravity** peso specifico; **–ally** *adv* specificamente
specification *n* specificazione
specious *a* specioso
specify *vt* specificare
specimen *n* campione *m*
speck *n (amount)* tantino; macchiolina

speckle *vt* variegare; marcare a puntini; — *n* puntino, macchiolina; **–d** *a* variegato, macchiettato
spectacle *n* spettacolo
spectacles *npl (glasses)* occhiali *mpl*
spectacular *a* spettacoloso, spettacolare, sensazionale
spectator *n* spettatore *m*; spettatrice *f*
specter *n* spettro
spectral *a* spettrale
spectroscope *n* spettroscopio
spectrum *n* spettro
speculate *vi* speculare
speculation *n* speculazione
speculator *n* speculatore *m*
speculative *a* speculativo
speech *n* discorso; linguaggio; **–less** *a* muto; **figure of** — figura rettorica
speed *n* velocità; **–boat** *n* motoscafo; **–ily** *adv* velocemente; **–iness** *n* rapidità; — **limit** velocità massima; **–ometer** *n* contachilometri *m*; **–way** *n* autopista; **–y** *a* rapido; — *vt* affrettare, far accelerare; — *vi* affrettarsi, accelerare, aumentare la velocità
speed-up *n* accelerazione, acceleramento
spell *n* malia; **–bound** *a* affascinato, incantato; **–binder** *n (coll)* oratore che conquista l'auditorio
spell *vt* compitare, sillabare; **–er** *n (book)* sillabario; *(person)* chi compita
spelling *n* ortografia; — **bee** emulazione *(or* gara) in ortografia
spend *vt* spendere; *(time)* trascorrere; esaurire; **–er** *n* consumatore *m*
spendthrift *n* scialacquatore *m*
spent *a* speso; esaurito
sperm *n* sperma *m*; — **whale** capidoglio
spermatozoa *npl* spermatozoi *mpl*
spew *vt&i* vomitare
sphere *n* sfera
spherical *a* sferico
spheroid *n&a* sferoide *m*
sphincter *n (anat)* sfintere *m*
sphinx *n* sfinge *f*
spice *n* spezie *f*; — *vt* condire con spezie
spiciness *n* gusto piccante
spick-and-span *a* pulito alla perfezione
spicy *a* drogato, pepato, piccante
spider *n* ragno; **–y** *a* come un ragno; — **web** ragnatela
spigot *n* turacciolo; zipolo; rubinetto
spike *n* punta; chiodo; *(bot)* aculeo; *(corn)* spiga; — *vt* inchiodare; infilzare
spill *n* caduta; zipolo, legnetto; — *vt* spargere, versare; confessare; — *vi* versarsi, rovesciarsi
spin *vt* filare; girare; — *n* giro; rotazione; *(avi)* vite *f*; avvitamento; corsa
spinach *n* spinaci *mpl*

spinal *a* vertebrale; — **cord** midollo spinale; — **column** colonna vertebrale
spindle *n* fuso, asse *m*
spine *n* *(anat)* spina dorsale; *(book)* dorso del libro; *(bot)* spina; **–less** *a* invertebrato; slombato
spinet *n* *(mus)* spinetta
spinning *n* filatura; — **jenny** filatoio; — **mill** filanda; — **wheel** ruota per filare; filatoio; — *a* girante, rollante
spinster *n* zitella
spiny *a* spinoso; difficile
spiral *a&n* spirale *f*
spire *n* cuspide *f*, guglia; *(bot)* stelo
spirit *n* spirito; — **level** livello ad aria; **–less** *a* abbattuto, avvilito; **–ed** *a* vivace, coraggioso; — *vt* animare, ravvivare; — **away** trafugare
spirits *npl* bevande alcooliche; liquori *mpl*; **in high** — di buon umore
spiritual *a* spirituale; **–ism** *n* *(philosophy)* spiritualismo; spiritismo; **–ist** *n* spiritista *m&f*
spit *n* sputo; *(cooking)* spiedo; *(land)* lingua di terra; — *vt&i* sputare
spite *n* dispetto, rancore *m*, **in** — **of** malgrado; **–ful** *a* dispettoso; — *vt* vessare; far dispetto a
spitfire *n* stizzoso, irascibile *m*; *(avi)* spitfire *m*
spittle *n* saliva, sputo
spittoon *n* sputacchiera
splash *n* schizzo; — *vt&i* schizzare
spleen *n* *(organ)* milza; malinconia, malumore *m*; **–ful** *a* bisbetico, imbronciato
splendid *a* splendido, magnifico; **–ly** *adv* splendidamente
splendor *n* splendore *m*
splice *n* calettatura, unione *f*, impiombatura; — *vt* calettare, unire, impiombare
splint *n* stecca
splinter *n* scheggia; — *vt* scheggiare; — *vi* scheggiarsi
split *vt&i* fendere, scindere; spaccarsi; dividere; — *n* fessura, scissione; *(dance)* spaccata
splitting *a* fendente, spaccante; — *n* *(atom)* scissione; — **headache** mal di testa lancinante
splotch *vt* macchiare, chiazzare; — *n* macchia, chiazza; **–ed** *a* macchiato, chiazzato; **–y** *a* macchiato
splurge *n* *(coll)* sfoggio, ostentazione; — *vt* *(coll)* sfoggiare, ostentare
splutter *vi* barbugliare
spoil *vt* guastare, viziare, rovinare; — *vi* guastarsi; infradiciarsi; **–age** *n* deterioramento
spoils *npl* bottino
spoilsport *n* guastafeste *m*

spoke *n* raggio
spokesman *n* portavoce *m&f*
sponge *n* spugna; — *vt&i* usare la spugna; *(coll)* scroccare
sponger *n* *(coll)* scroccone *m*
sponginess *n* spugnosità
spongy *a* spugnoso
sponsor *n* garante *m*; padrino, madrina; *(rad, TV)* patrocinatore *m*; — *vt* garantire; **–ship** *n* garanzia
spontaneity *n* spontaneità
spontaneous *a* spontaneo; **–ly** *adv* spontaneamente
spool *n* bobina
spoon *n* cucchiaio; **–ful** *n* cucchiaiata
spoor *n* traccia, pista, orma
sporadic *a* sporadico
spore *n* spora
sport *n* sport *m*; *(biol)* anomalia; **–ing** *a* sportivo; **–ive** *a* scherzevole; — *vi* divertirsi; giuocare; — *vt* *(coll)* ostentare
sportsman *n* sportivo
spot *n* macchia, punto; *(place)* luogo; **be on the** — *(sl)* essere nei guai; **–light** *n* fascio di luce; proiettore *m*; **–less** *a* immacolato; — *vt* *(place)* collocare; *(blemish)* macchiare; punteggiare
spotted *a* macchiato
spotty *a* macchiato; picchiettato
spouse *n* sposo, sposa
spout *vt* spruzzare; — *vi* sgorgare — *n* sgorgo; becco, tubo
sprain *n* storta; — *vt* storcere
sprawl *vi* sdraiarsi, distendersi; **–ing** *a* sdraiato, disteso
spray *vt* spruzzare, vaporizzare; — *n* *(flowers)* ramoscello; spruzzo, getto; raffica; *(device)* spruzzatore *m*
spread *n* distesa; *(bed)* coperta da letto; *(bread)* companatico da spalmare; *(coll)* festa, banchetto
spread *vt&i* spargere; *(news)* divulgare, diffondere; stendere, spalmare
spree *n* baldoria
sprig *n* ramoscello; rampollo
sprightliness *n* vivacità
sprightly *a* vivace
spring *n* *(elasticity)* elasticità; *(leap)* salto, balzo; *(metal)* molla; *(movement)* scatto; *(season)* primavera; *(water)* sorgente *f*; **–board** *n* trampolino; **–lock** *n* serratura a scatto; — **fever** *(fig)* indolenza primaverile; **–y** *a* elastico; — *vt&i* molleggiare; *(water)* scaturire; *(jump)* saltare; *(leak)* aprire; — **from** originare da, provenire da; — **up** balzare su; *(rise)* nascere, sorgere
springlike *a* primaverile
sprinkle *n* aspersione; spruzzata; — *vt* spruzzare; cospargere; — *vi* pioviggi-

nare; **–r** *n* spruzzatore *m*
sprinkling *n* spruzzata; spruzzo
sprint *n* *(sport)* volata; — *vi* fare una volata, correre in volata; **–er** *n* velocista *m*
sprite *n* folletto
sprocket *n* dente di ruota
sprout *n* germoglio; rampollo; — *vi* germogliare
spruce *a* lindo; — *n* *(bot)* abete *m*; — *vt* allindare; — *vi* allindarsi
spry *a* agile, lesto; **–ness** agilità
spume *n* schiuma, spuma
spumy *a* spumoso
spun *a* filato
spunk *n* *(coll)* coraggio
spunky *a* *(coll)* coraggioso
spur *n* sperone *m*; stimolo; **on the — of the moment** lì per lì, senza riflettere; — *vt* incitare, spronare
spurious *a* spurio
spurn *vt* sdegnare, respingere; **–ing** *n* respingimento
spurt *n* getto, zampillo; *(sport)* scatto, volata; — *vt&i* spruzzare, zampillare, scaturire
sputter *n* spruzzo; balbettio; — *vi* spruzzare; schizzare; balbettare; **–ing** *a* balbettante
sputum *n* sputo
spy *n* spia; — *vt&i* spiare; far la spia
spyglass *n* cannocchiale *m*
squab *n* piccioncino
squabble *n* lite *f*; — *vi* litigare
squad *n* squadra
squadron *n* squadrone *m*; *(avi)* squadriglia
squalid *a* squallido
squall *n* *(storm)* turbine *m*; strillo; — *vi* strillare, sbraitare; turbinare
squalor *n* squallore *m*
squander *vt* sperperare
square *n* quadrato; piazza; — *a* quadrato; *(com)* saldato; giusto; — *vt* quadrare; **— measure** misura di superficie; **— root** radice quadrata
square-rigged *a* *(naut)* a vele quadre
squash *n* zucca; schiacciamento; — *vt* schiacciare
squat *vi* accosciarsi; **–ty** *a* tozzo
squawk *n* strido, gracidio; — *vi* gracidare
squeak *vi* squittire; — *n* strido
squeal *n* strillo; *(coll)* delazione; — *vt&i* strillare; *(coll)* delatare
squeamish *a* schifiltoso; **–ness** *n* schizzinosità
squeeze *n* stretta; estorsione; — *vt* spremere; stringere; — *vi* insinuarsi, intromettersi; **— out** spremere; **lemon –r** spremilimone *m*
squelch *n* risposta mordace; — *vt* schiac-

ciare; tacitare, soffocare
squib *n* satira
squid *n* calamaro
squint *n* sguardo strabico; *(med)* strabismo; *(coll)* occhiata di sbieco; — *vi* guardare con gli occhi socchiusi; *(med)* essere strabico
squint-eyed *a* strabico
squinting *n* strabismo; — *a* con gli occhi socchiusi; *(med)* strabico
squire *n* gentiluomo di campagna; scudiere *m*; — *vt* scortare
squirm *vi* contorcersi; **–ing** *n* contorcimento
squirrel *n* scoiattolo
squirt *n* *(syringe)* siringa; spruzzo; *(coll)* persona meschina, omiciattolo; — *vt&i* spruzzare, zampillare
stab *n* pugnalata, stoccata; — *vt* accoltellare, pugnalare; **— in the back** pugnalare alle spalle; **make a — at** fare un tentativo
stability *n* stabilità
stabilization *n* stabilizzazione
stabilize *vt* stabilizzare; **–r** *n* stabilizzatore *m*
stable *a* fermo, stabile — *n* scuderia, stalla — *vt* mettere nella stalla
staccato *a* staccato
stack *n* mucchio, ammasso; — *vt* ammucchiare; *(cards)* preparare per barare
stadium *n* stadio
staff *n* bastone *m*; *(editorial)* corpo redazionale; *(mus)* pentagramma *m*; *(office)* personale *m*; *(teaching)* corpo degli insegnanti; **— of life** mezzo di prima necessità; il pane quotidiano *(fig)*
stag *n* cervo; **— party** serata per uomini soli
stage *n* scena, palcoscenico, teatro; tappa; **— fright** panico dell'attore; **— manager** direttore di scena; **–coach** *n* diligenza; **–craft** *n* arte scenica; **–hand** *n* macchinista scenico; — *vt* mettere in scena
stagger *vi* vacillare; esitare; — *vt* sconcertare; far barcollare; scuotere; **–ed** *a* a intervalli, d'intervallo, alternato; **–ing** *a* barcollante; titubante
staging *n* messa in scena
stagnancy *n* ristagno
stagnant *a* stagnante
stagnate *vi* ristagnare
stagy *a* teatrale
staid *a* posato, severo, serio; **–ness** *n* gravità, posatezza
stain *n* macchia; — *vt* tingere, macchiare, sporcare; — *vi* sporcarsi, macchiarsi; **–ed** *a* macchiato; sfregiato; **–ed glass**

vetro colorato

stainless *a* senza macchia, immacolato; — **steel** acciaio inossidabile

stair *n* gradino, scalino; **–case, –way** *n* scala; **–s** *npl* scale *fpl*; scalinata

stake *n (wager)* posta, scommessa; *(wooden)* palo, stecco; — *vt* scommettere; puntellare; sostenere; — **a claim** dichiararsi proprietario

stalactite *n* stalattite *f*

stalagmite *n* stalagmite *f*

stale *a* rafferno, stantio; — *vt&i* invecchiare; *(baked products)* seccare; **–ness** *n* vecchiezza

stalk *n* stelo; picciuolo; torsolo; — *vi* camminare impettito; — *vt* seguire la pista di

stallion *n* stallone *m*

stalwart *a* robusto; coraggioso

stamen *n* stame *m*

stamina *n* resistenza fisica, vigore *m*

stammer *vt&i* balbettare; **–er** *n* balbuziente *m*; **–ing** *n* balbuzie *f*

stamp *n* impressione; stampa; *(postage)* francobollo; *(revenue)* marca da bollo; *(rubber)* timbro di gomma; — **pad** cuscinetto per timbri; — *vt* battere, pestare, imprimere; *(mail)* affrancare; — *vi* scalpicciare, battere i piedi; — **out** estirpare, sradicare

stampede *n* fuga precipitosa; — *vi* fuggire precipitosamente; — *vt* mettere in fuga precipitosa

stance *n* atteggiamento

stand *n* edicola; fermata; posizione; pausa, sosta; tribuna; **–point** *n* punto di vista; **–still** *n* arresto, fermata; — *vi* stare; fermarsi; star diritto; essere; rimanere; alzarsi; — *vt* mettere; tollerare; — **aside** tenersi da parte; — **back** rispondere per, garantire per; *(behind)* stare dietro di; — **by** assistere, difendere, sostenere; — **for** tollerare; significare; prendere la parte di; sostituire; — **off** tenersi da parte; **it –s to reason** è ovvio; — **up** tenersi ritto; — **up against** opporsi a; essere contro; — **up for** sostenere, difendere

standard *n* stendardo; criterio, norma; — **of living** tenore di vita; — *a* normale, usuale; standardizzato; **–ization** *n* standardizzazione; **–ize** *vt* standardizzare

standard-bearer *n* portabandiera *m*

stand- *(in comp)* **—by** *n* appoggio; **–in** *n* controfigura

standing *a* permanente, fisso; — *n (duration)* durata; posizione, rango; — **army;** esercito permanente; — **order** ordine permanente; — **room** posto in piedi

standoffish *a* superbo, altero, riservato

stanza *n* strofa

staple *n* prodotto principale; *(metal)* chiodo ad U; — *a* stabilito, principale; **–r** *n (paper)* cucitrice a grappe

star *n* stella, astro; *(print)* asterisco; **evening** — espero; **shooting** — stella filante; **–board** *n* tribordo; **–board** *a* di tribordo; **–gazer** *n* astronomo; — **less** *a* senza stelle; **–light** *n* luce stellare; **–lit** *a* stellato, illuminato di stelle; **–ry** *a* stellato; — *vi* essere un astro cinematografico *(or* teatrale); primeggiare; — *vt* cospargere di stelle; *(mark)* indicare con asterisco

starch *n* amido; — *vt* inamidare; **–iness** *n* inamidatezza; **–y** *a* amidoso

stare *vt&i* guardare fisso; — *n* sguardo fisso

starfish *n* stella di mare

stark *a* inflessibile, rigido; proprio; completo; desolato; — *adv* completamente

starling *n* stornello

starry-eyed *a* dagli occhi scintillanti, dagli occhi sognanti

star-spangled *a* stellato, punteggiato di stelle

start *n* principio; sussulto; vantaggio; partenza; avviamento; — *vt&i* cominciare; trasalire; partire; mettere in moto, fondare; — **again** ricominciare; **starter** *n (auto)* avviamento; iniziatore *m*; partente *m*

starting *n* partenza; sussulto; *(beginning)* inizio, principio; *(business)* lancio; — **gate, post** palo di partenza; — **point** punto di partenza

startle *vt* far trasalire, sorprendere, spaventare

startling *a* sorprendente; emozionante; allarmante

starvation *n* inedia; fame *f*

starve *vi* morire di fame; — *vt* affamare, far morire di fame

starving *a* famelico

state *n* stato; condizione; **–craft** *n* arte di governo; **–ly** *a* maestoso; **–liness** *n* imponenza, maestà; **–room** *n* cabina; — *a* statale; — *vt* dichiarare

statement *n* dichiarazione, affermazione; *(com)* rendiconto; distinta

statesman *n* uomo di stato; **–ship** *n* arte di governo, politica

static *n* disturbi atmosferici; — *a* statico

station *n* stazione; posto; *(social)* posizione sociale; — **agent, –master** capostazione *m*; — **break** *(rad)* intervallo; — **wagon** giardinetta; — *vt* mettere a posto; collocare

stationary *a* stazionario

stationer *n* cartolaio

stationery *n* articoli di cancelleria; — **store** cartoleria

Stations of the Cross Stazioni della Via Crucis

statistic, -al *a* statistico

statistics *npl* statistica

statistician *n* statistico, esperto in statistica

statuary *n* scultura; statue *fpl*

statue *n* statua; **-sque** *a* scultoreo; statuario

statuette *n* figurina, statuetta

stature *n* statura

status *n* stato, condizione, rango

statute *n* statuto; — **law** legge statutaria

statutory *a* statutario

staunch *a* fermo; leale, fido; — *vt* stagnare

stave *n* doga; *(ladder)* piuola; *(lit)* strofa; — *vt* dogare; — **in** sfondare; — **off** stornare

stay *n* soggiorno; sostegno; *(delay)* proroga; — *vi (remain)* soggiornare, rimanere; *(bear up)* sostenersi; — *vt* prorogare; *(prop)* puntellare; *(stop)* fermare; — **up** *(in place)* stare; *(awake)* vegliare; **-ing power** resistenza

stay-at-home *n* casalingo, persona che ama la propria casa

stead *n* posto; vece *f*; **-fast** *a* risoluto, costante; **-iness** *n* stabilità; **-y** *a* stabile; fisso, fermo

steak *n* bistecca

steal *n (coll)* guadagno senza scrupoli, vantaggio disonesto; — *vt&i* rubare; — **away** allontanarsi furtivamente

stealth *n* segreto; **-ily** *adv* furtivamente; **-y** *a* furtivo, segreto

steam *n* vapore *m*; **-ing** *a* fumante; — **roller** rullo compressore; **-ship** *n* piroscafo; bastimento

steel *n* acciaio; **stainless** — acciaio inossidabile; **tempered** — acciaio temperato; — **engraving** incisione su acciaio; — **mill** acciaieria; — *a* d'acciaio; **-y** *a* acciaioso; duro; — *vt* fortificare, indurire; temprare; — **oneself** indurirsi

steelyard *n* stadera

steep *a* ripido; *(coll)* caro; **-ly** *adv* ripidamente; **-ness** *n* ripidità; — *vt* imbevere, impregnare

steeple *n* campanile *m*, guglia

steeplechase *n* corsa ad ostacoli

steer *n* manzo

steer *vt* guidare; *(naut)* pilotare; — *vi* sterzare; — **clear of** evitare, girar al largo da

steerage *n* pilotaggio, viraggio, guida; terza classe

steering *n* direzione; *(naut)* governo; *(auto)* guida; — **gear** comando; sterzo;

— **wheel** volante *m*

steersman *n* timoniere *m*

stein *n* boccale da birra

stellar *a* stellare

stellate *a* stellato

stem *n* gambo; *(bot)* stelo; *(gram)* radice *f*: *(mus)* gamba; *(naut)* prua; *(watch)* caricatore *m*; — *vt* resistere a, arginare; — **from** aver origine da

stench *n* puzza

stencil *n* stampino; — *vt* stampinare

stenographer *n* stenografo, stenografa

stenographic *a* stenagrafico

stenography *n* stenografia

stenotype *n* macchina da stenodattilografia

stentorian *a* stentoreo

step *n* passo; *(stairs)* gradino; *(door)* soglia; — *vi* fare un passo, camminare; — **in** entrare; — **off** misurare a passi; — **on** calpestare; — **out** uscire; **take -s** fare passi *(fig)*

stepbrother *n* fratellastro

stepchild *n* figliastro, figliastra

stepdaughter *n* figliastra

stepfather *n* patrigno

stepladder *n* scala a piuoli

stepmother *n* matrigna

steppe *n* steppa

steppingstone *n* pietra a guado; *(fig)* trampolino *(fig)*

stepsister *n* sorellastra

stepson *n* figliastro

stereographic *a* stereografico

stereophonic *a* stereofonico

stereoscope *n* stereoscopio

stereotype *n* stereotipo; — *vt* stereotipare

sterile *a* sterile

sterility *n* sterilità

sterilization *n* sterilizzazione

sterilize *vt* sterilizzare

sterling *a* genuino, vero; — **silver** argento puro

stern *a* austero, severo; — *n (naut)* poppa; **-ly** *adv* severamente; **-ness** *n* severità, austerità

sternum *n* sterno

stethoscope *n* stetoscopio

stevedore *n* stivatore *m*

stew *n* stufatino, ragù *m*; **be in a —** *(coll)* essere in imbarazzo; — *vt* cuocere lentamente; — *vi* cuocersi lentamente

steward *n* economo; *(ship)* cameriere di bordo; **-ess** *(avi)* hostess *f*; **chief —** capo commissario

stick *n* bastone *m*; **-er** *n (label)* etichetta; **-ler** *n* pedante *m&f*; rigido; — *vt* attaccare, fissare, conficcare, appiccicare; *(pierce)* trafiggere; pungere; — *vi* aderire, appiccicarsi; persistere, ostinarsi, preseverare; — **out** sporgersi; —

up alzarsi; *(rob)* rapinare; — up for parlare in difesa di; -y *a* appiccicoso
stiff *a* rigido; -ly *adv* con difficoltà; rigidamente; — **neck** torcicollo; -ness *n* severità, rigidezza; consistenza
stiffen *vt* irrigidire; rassodare; — *vi* irrigidirsi; rassodarsi
stiffening *n* irrigidimento; *(cloth)* rinforzo, imbozzimatura
stifle *vt&i* soffocare
stifling *a* soffocante
stigma *n* stigma
stigmata *npl* stimmate *fpl*
stiletto *n* stiletto
still *vt* calmare; silenziare; — *a* silenzioso; calmo; fermo; — *n* quiete *f*; silenzio; — *adv* ancora, tuttora; -born *a* nato morto; — life natura morta; -ness *n* silenzio, quiete *f*; immobilità
stilted *a* affettato, pomposo
stilts *npl* trampoli *mpl*
stimulant *a&n* stimolante *m*
stimulate *vt* stimolare
stimulation *n* stimolo, incitamento
stimulus *n* stimolo
sting *vt&i* pungere, bruciare, dolere; — *n* puntura d'insetto; bruciore *m*; *(object)* pungiglione *m*; pungolo; -ing *a* pungente, mordace
stinginess *n* grettezza
stingy *a* spilorcio; meschino
stink *vi* puzzare; — *n* puzza; -er *n (sl)* puzzone *(sl) m*
stint *n* limite *m*; restrizione; compito; — *vt* limitare; — *vi* economizzare
stipend *n* stipendio
stipple *vt* punteggiare
stippling *n* punteggiatura
stipulate *vt&i* stipulare
stipulation *n* stipulazione
stir *vt* rimescolare; agitare, scuotere; attizzare; — *vi* agitarsi, scuotersi; stormire; — *n* eccitamento; moto; tumulto
stirring *a* emozionante
stirrup *n* staffa
stitch *vt* cucire; — *n* punto; *(knitting)* maglia
stock *n* assortimento; scorta, *(cattle)* bestiame *m*; *(com)* valore *m*, titolo; *(cooking)* brodo; *(gun)* fusto; *(handle)* manico: *(material)* materiale *m*; *(lineage)* schiatta; -broker *n* operatore di borsa; — **company** *(theat)* repertorio; compagnia stabile; — **exchange** borsa valori, -holder *n* azionista *m*; — in trade mercanzia; **take** — of inventariare — *a* disponibile; — *vt* provvedere, fornire; popolare, immettere
stockade *n* stecconata

stocking *n* calza; in — feet senza scarpe
stockpile *n* riserva; — *vt* accumulare; *(reserve)* immagazzinare
stock-still *a* immobile
stocky *a* tozzo
stockyards *npl* chiusa per il bestiame
stodgy *a* pesante; ingombrante; noioso
stoic *n&a* stoico; -al *a* stoico; -ism *n* stoicismo
stoke *vt* attizzare; -er *n (mech)* fochista
stole *n* stola
stolid *a* stolido; impassibile; -ity *n* impassibilità, stolidità
stomach *n* stomaco; -ache *n* dolore di stomaco; — *vt* digerire, mangiare; tollerare; **turn one's** — nauseare, stomacare
stone *n* pietra; sasso; *(fruit)* nocciolo; *(med)* calcolo; -cutter *n* tagliapietra *m*; -hearted *a* dal cuore di pietra; -less *a* senza pietre *(or* nocciuolo); -mason *n* muratore *m*; -work *n* muratura; -y *a* sassoso; — *a* di pietra; — *vt* lapidare; *(fruit)* togliere il nocciolo a; *(pave)* acciottolare
stone- *(in comp)* —blind *a* completamente cieco; —broke *a (sl)* in bolletta *(coll)*; —dead *a* morto stecchito; —deaf *a* sordo come una campana
stoning *n* lapidazione
stooge *n (coll)* tirapiedi *m*
stool *n* sgabello; escremento, feci *mpl*
stoop *vi* chinarsi, abbassarsi; — *vt* inchinare, abbassare; — *n (porch)* portico; curvatura
stop *n* fermata; sosta; interruzione; *(mus)* registro; -gap *n* stoppabuchi, turabuchi *m*; sostituto; -light *n* semaforo; -over *n* sosta, fermata; — **sign** segnale di fermata; — **watch** cronometro; — *vt* fermare; sospendere, cessare; impedire; — *vi* fermarsi; smettere; — in visitare; — off, over sostare, fermarsi; — up otturare
stoppage *n* cessazione
stopper *n* fermante *m*; tappo; chiusura; — *vt* turare, tappare
stopping *n* arresto, fermata; otturazione; — *a* fermante; tappante
storage *n* magazzinaggio; — battery accumulatore
store *n* negozio; scorta; magazzino; in — in riserva, in deposito; set — by dare importanza a; -house *n* magazzino; -keeper *n* magazziniere; negoziante *m*; -room *n* magazzino; — *vt* conservare; immagazzinare; fornire
storied *a* istoriato
stork *n* cicogna

storm *n* tempesta; — **cellar** rifugio per tempesta; — **door** porta antintemperie; — **window** finestra da tempesta; **–bound** *a* bloccato da tempesta; **–proof** *a* a prova di tempesta; **–y** *a* tempestoso; — *vt* assalire; — *vi* imperversare

story *n* favola, racconto; *(building)* piano; **–teller** *n* novelliere *m*; raccontatore *m*; *(liar)* bugiardo

storybook *n* libro di racconti

stout *a* robusto; tarchiato; **–ness** *n* corpulenza; risolutezza

stouthearted *a* intrepido

stove *n (cooking)* fornello; cucina; *(heating)* stufa; **–pipe** *n* tubo della stufa; **–pipe hat** *(coll)* cappello a cilindro

stow *vt* stivare; smettere; — **away** *(naut)* imbarcarsi clandestinamente; **–away** *n* viaggiatore clandestino

straddle *vi* divaricare le gambe; — *vt* sedere a cavalcioni; *(coll)* essere equivoco

straggle *vi* sbandarsi; sperdersi; **–r** *n* disperso; sbandato

straight *a* diritto; retto, onesto; *(drink)* liscio; **–forward** *a* franco, schietto; **–ness** *n* dirittura; rettitudine *f*; **–way** *adv* immediatamente, subito; — *adv* direttamente

straighten *vt* raddrizzare; rassettare; — *vi* raddrizzarsi

strain *n* sforzo, strappo; razza; *(mus)* ritmo, motivo; tono; — *vt* colare, filtrare; sforzare; storcere; — *vi* sforzarsi; storcersi; colarsi

strainer *n* colatoio, colabrodo

strait *n (geog)* stretto; — **jacket** camicia di forza; **–s** *npl* difficoltà *fpl*

straiten *vt* restringere

strait-laced *a* scrupoloso, rigoroso

strand *n* spiaggia, riva, lido; *(thread)* filo; — *vt* far arenare; far incagliare; — *vi* arenarsi; incagliarsi; **be –ed** essere abbandonato

strange *a* strano, singolare; **–ness** *n* singolarità, stranezza; **–ly** *adv* curiosamente, stranamente; **–r** *n* straniero

strangle *vt* strangolare; — *vi* strangolarsi; **–hold** *n* stretta mortale

strangling *n* strangolatura

strangulate *vt* strangolare, strozzare

strangulation *n* strozzatura, strangolatura

strap *n* correggia, cinghia; — *vt* legare, con cinghia; *(punish)* staffilare

strapping *a* robusto

stratagem *n* stratagemma *m*

strategic *a* strategico

strategist *n* stratega *m*

strategy *n* strategia

stratification *n* stratificazione

stratify *vt* stratificare

stratosphere *n* stratosfera

stratum *n* strato

straw *n* paglia; — **vote** votazione preliminare; **last** — *(fig)* colmo

strawberry *n* fragola

stray *vi* fuorviarsi, smarrirsi; — *a* smarrito; sperso; randagio; *(fig)* fortuito; — *n* animale randagio

streak *vt* striare; — *n* striscia; **–y** *a* striato

stream *n* fiume, corso d'aqua, corrente *f*; — *vi* scorrere; fluire; **–er** *n* pennone *m*, banderuola

streamline *vt* sveltire, modernizzare; rendere aerodinamico; **–d** *a* aerodinamico

street *n* strada, via; **–car** *n* tram *m*; **–light** *m* fanale, lampione *m*; — **sweeper** spazzino; *(mech)* spazzatrice meccanica; **–walker** *n* prostituta, donna di marciapiede *(coll)*

strength *n* potenza, forza, energia; resistenza; **at full** — in pieno, al completo

strengthen *vt* rinforzare; consolidare; — *vi* rafforzarsi; consolidarsi

strenuous *a* energico, vigoroso; **–ness** *n* strenuità

streptococcus *n* streptococco

streptomycin *n* streptomicina

stress *n* risalto; sforzo; *(gram)* accento tonico; *(med)* tensione *f*; *(mech)* pressione; — *vt* accentuare, accentare, far risaltare

stretch *n* tensione; stiramento; sforzo; distesa; periodo; **at a** — d'un tratto; — *vt* tendere; stirare; esagerare; sforzare; — *vi* stendersi; stirarsi; allungarsi

stretcher *n (frame)* telaio; *(med)* barella; **–bearer** *n* portabarelle *m*

strew *vt* sparpagliare

striated *a* striato

stricken *a* colpito

strict *a* severo, stretto; **–ly** *adv* strettamente; esattamente; **–ness** *n* esatezza; rigore *m*; **–ure** *n* censura, critica; *(med)* restringimento

stride *n* passo lungo; — *vi* camminare a gran passi

strident *a* stridente

strife *n* conflitto

strike *n* colpo; *(baseball)* battuta; *(labor)* sciopero; *(mine)* scoperta; **be on** — essere in isciopero; **go on** — scioperare; **–breaker** *n* crumiro; **–r** *n (labor)* scioperante *m*; — *vt* colpire; *(mine)* scoprire; *(hour)* scoccare; *(match)* accendere; — **a bargain** concludere un affare; — **out** *(delete)* cancellare; partire; — *vi* scioperare

striking *a* impressionante, notevole, sensazionale; **–ingly** *adv* sensazionalmente

string *n* filo, spago, laccio; *(mus)* corda; — **beans** fagiolini *mpl*; **-y** *a* fibroso
string *vt* legare; — **up** *(hang)* impiccare; — **out** prolungare; — **along** *(coll)* ingannare; **-ed instrument** strumento a corde
stringency *n* severità; limitazione; penuria
stringent *a* stringente; urgente, rigido
strings *npl (mus)* corde; fili; *(coll)* limitazioni *fpl*; **no** — **attached** senz'obbligazione
strip *n* striscia; — *vt* privare; *(undress)* spogliare; — *vi* spogliarsi; — **tease** spogliarello *(coll)*; **comic** — fumetti *mpl*
stripe *n* striscia, riga; *(mil)* gallone *m*; sferzata; — *vt* rigare
striped *a* rigato
stripling *n* giovanotto
strive *vi* sforzarsi
striving *n* sforzo; — *a* sforzato, forzoso
stroke *n* colpo; tratto; accesso; *(swimming)* bracciata; *(med)* colpo apoplettico; — **of luck** colpo di fortuna; **on the** — **of** allo scoccare di; — *vt* accarezzare, lisciare
stroll *n* passeggiatina; — *vi* vagare, fare una passeggiata; **-ing** *a* vagabondo, ambulante; **-er** *n (person)* vagabondo, girovago; *(baby's)* carrozzina per neonati, portinfante *m*
strong *a* forte; duro, robusto; **-box** *n* cassaforte *f*; **-hold** *n* fortezza; caposaldo; **-ly** *adv* fortemente
strong-minded *a* ardito, risoluto
strong-willed *a* risoluto
strontium *n* stronzio
strop *n* coramella; — *vt* affilare sulla coramella
strophe *n* strofa
structural *a* strutturale; — **steel** ferro trafilato per strutture
structure *n* struttura, edifizio, costruzione
struggle *n* lotta; — *vi* lottare
strum *vt&i* strimpellare
strumpet *n* prostituta
strut *n* tronfiezza, modo impettito di camminare; *(prop)* puntello; *(avi)* montante *m*; — *vi* pavoneggiarsi
strychnine *n* stricnina
stub *n* ceppo; mozzicone *m*; *(ticket)* matrice *f*; — *vt* estirpare; *(hit)* sbattere; **-by** *a* tozzo; pieno di ceppi
stubble *n* stoppia
stubbly *a* stopposo; *(hair)* ispido
stubborn *a* ostinato, testardo; **-ness** *n* ostinazione
stucco *n* stucco
stuck *a* attaccato; traffitto; incollato
stud *n* borchia; *(stable)* scuderia; *(prop)*

pilastrino; **-horse** *n* cavallo da razza; — *vt* guarnire con borchie
student *n* studente *m*, studentessa
studied *a* studiato, affettato
studio *n* studio; — **couch** letto alla turca
studious *a* studioso; **-ness** studiosità
study *n* studio; cura, diligenza; — *vt&i* studiare
stuff *vt (cram)* riempire, imbottire, rimpinzare; *(crowd)* pigiare; *(cooking)* infarcire; imbottire; — *n (things)* stoffa, roba, materia; — **and nonsense** insensatezza; **-ed** *a* imbottito, rimpinzato; **-ing** *n (pillow)* imbottitura; *(food)* ripieno; **-y** *a* soffocante, chiuso; *(coll)* rigido, inflessibile
stultify *vt* rendere ridicolo *(or* insignificante); svalorare
stumble *vi* inciampare; barcollare; — *n (in speech)* papera; inciampata
stumbling *a* inciampante; — *n* inciampamento; *(in speech)* balbettio; — **block** ostacolo; scoglio *(fig)*
stump *n* ceppo, tronco, mozzicone *m*; *(art)* sfumino; — *vt* disorientare, confondere; — *vi* camminare pesantemente; *(pol)* fare tournée di comizi politici
stun *vt* stordire
stunning *a* stupendo, sbalorditivo, meraviglioso; che stordisce
stunt *n (coll)* esibizione, montatura; — **flying** acrobazia aviatoria; — *vt* ostacolare; arrestare lo sviluppo di; — *vi* esibirsi
stupefaction *n* stupefazione
stupefy *vt* istupidire, stupefare; **-ing** *a* stupefacente
stupendous *a* stupendo
stupid *a* stupido, sciocco; **-ity** *n* stupidaggine *f*
stupor *n* stupore, torpore *m*
sturdily *adv* vigorosamente
sturdiness *n* vigore *m*, robustezza
sturdy *a* forte, resistente
stutter *vt&i* tartagliare; — *n* balbuzie *f*; **-er** *n* balbuziente *m&f*; **-ing** *n* balbettamento; **-ing** *a* balbettante
sty *n (med)* orzaiuolo; *(pig)* porcile *m*
style *n* stile *m*, moda; maniera; — *vt* disegnare, stilizzare; chiamare, nominare
stylish *a* elegante
stylist *n* stilista *m&f*
stylistic *a* stilistico
stylize *vt* stilizzare
stylus *n* stilo; puntina di fonografo
stymie *vt* ostacolare
styptic *n&a* astringente; — **pencil** matita emostatica
suable *a* processabile
suave *a* soave, dolce, blando; **-ly** *adv* dol-

cemente; soavemente; **–ness** n soavità
suavity n soavità
subagent n subagente m
subaltern n&a subalterno
subcommittee n sottocomitato
subconscious n&a subcosciente m
subconsciousness n subcoscienza
subcontract n subcontratto, subappalto;
— vt subappaltare; **–er** n subcontratti-
sta, subappaltatore m
subcutaneous a subcutaneo, sottocutaneo
subdivide vt suddividere
subdivision n suddivisione
subdue vt domare, reprimere; *(light)* attenuare
subheading n sottotitolo
subject n&a soggetto; suddito; — vt sottomettere; **–ive** a soggettivo; **–ively**
adv soggettivamente; **–ivity** n sogget-
tività
subjugate vt soggiogare
subjugation n soggiogamento, soggiogo
subjunctive a&n soggiuntivo, congiuntivo
sublease vt subaffittare; — n subaffitto
sublet vt subaffittare
sublimate vt sublimare; — n&a sublimato
sublimation n sublimazione
sublime n&a sublime
sublimity n sublimità
submarine n&a sottomarino
submerge vt sommergere; — vi sommergersi
submergible a sommergibile
submersion n sommersione
submission n sottomissione
submissive a sottomesso; **–ness** n sottomissione
submit vt presentare; — vi sottomettersi
subnormal a subnormale
subordinate a&n subordinato; — vt subor-
dinare
subordination n subordinazione
suborn vt subornare
subpoena n citazione legale di comparizione; — vt fare una citazione legale di
comparizione
subscribe vi abbonarsi; sottoscriversi,
aderire; — vt sottoscrivere, abbonare
subscriber n abbonato; sottoscrittore m
subscription n abbonamento
subsequent a susseguente; **–ly** adv sus-
seguentemente
subservience n subordinazione, servilismo
subservient a subordinato, servile
subside vi cedere, sprofondare; diminuire,
cessare
subsidiary n&a sussidiario
subsidize vt sovvenzionare
subsidy n sussidio
subsist vi sussistere, mantenersi

subsistence n sussistenza
subsoil n sottosuolo
subspecies n sottospecie f
substance n sostanza, essenza
substantial a sostanziale; **–ity** n sostan-
zialità; **–ly** adv sostanzialmente
substantive n&a sostantivo
substation n stazione sussidiaria
substitute vt sostituire; — vi sostituirsi;
— n sostituto; surrogato; — a sostituto,
supplente
substitution n sostituzione
substratum n sostrato
substructure n sostruzione
subterfuge n sotterfugio
subterranean a sotterraneo
subtitle n sottotitolo; didascalia
subtle a fino, delicato; subdolo, sottile;
–ty n sottigliezza
subtly adv sottilmente
subtract vt sottrarre
subtrahend n sottraendo
subtraction n sottrazione
subtropical a quasi tropicale
suburb n sobborgo
suburban a periferico, suburbano; **–ite** n
abitante dei sobborghi
subvention n sovvenzione
subversive a sovversivo
subversion n sovversione
subvert vt sovvertire
subway n ferrovia sotterranea, metropolitana; sottopassaggio
succeed vi riuscire, succedere; — vt succedere a
succeeding a succedente
success n successo, riuscita; **–ful** a di
successo, vittorioso, riuscito; **–ive** a
successivo
succession n successione
successor n successore m
succinct a succinto; **–ly** adv succintamen-
te; **–ness** n brevità
succor n soccorso; — vt soccorrere
succumb vi soccombere
succulence n succolenza
succulent a succolento
such a tale, simile; — pron tale; — **as**
come quale
suck vt succhiare, poppare; assorbire; —
n succhiata, poppata; *(coll)* sorsetto;
–er n *(candy)* caramella; *(mech)* stantuffo; *(zool)* succhiatoio; *(bot)* suc-
chione m; *(sl)* gonzo
suckle vt allattare
suckling n lattante m&f; — **pig** porcellino
di latte
sucrose n saccarosio; zucchero di canna
suction n aspirazione; — **pump** pompa
aspirante

sudden *a* improvviso, inaspettato; **all of a** — tutt'a un tratto; **—ly** *adv* improvvisamente; **—ness** *n* istantaneità, subitaneità
suds *npl* schiuma di sapone; acqua saponata
sue *vt&i* querelare, citare
suede *n* pelle scamosciata
suet *n* sugna
suffer *vi&i* soffrire subire; permettere; **—ing** *a* sofferente; **—ing** *n* sofferenza
suffice *vt&i* bastare
sufficiency *n* sufficienza
sufficient *a* sufficiente; **—ly** *adv* sufficientemente
suffix *n* suffisso
suffocate *vt&i* soffocare
suffocating *a* soffocante
suffocation *n* soffocazione, asfissia
sufferage *n* suffragio
suffuse *vt* aspergere; bagnare; spandere sopra
suffusion *n* suffusione
sugar *n* zucchero; **beet** — zucchero di barbabietola; **brown** — zucchero greggio; **granulated** — zucchero granulato; **lump** — zucchero in zollette; **bowl** zuccheriera; — **cane** canna da zucchero; — *vt* inzuccherare; addolcire; **—y** *a* zuccherino
sugar-coated *a* candito, coperto di zucchero; inzuccherato *(fig, manner)* meloso
suggest *vt* proporre, suggerire, suggestionare; **—ive** *a* suggestivo
suggestion *n* consiglio, proposta, suggerimento
suicide *n* suicida *m&f*; *(act)* suicidio; **commit** — suicidarsi, uccidersi
suit *n* *(clothing)* abito completo; *(law)* azione; *(courtship)* corte *f*; *(cards)* seme *m*; *(request)* petizione; — *vt&i* convenire; piacere a; **follow** — seguire l'esempio; **—able** *a* conveniente; **—ability** *n* accordo, convenienza; adattabilità, opportunità; **—case** *n* valigia; **—ing** *n* stoffa
suite *n* seguito; serie *f*; appartamento; *(furniture)* mobilia
suitor *n* richiedente *m*; pretendente *m*; *(law)* querelante *m*
sulfate *n* solfato
sulfide *n* solfuro
sulfur *n* zolfo
sulk *vi* accigliarsi, essere di malumore; **—iness** *n* malumore *m*; **—y** *a* scontroso
sullen *a* taciturno; imbronciato
sully *vt* sporcare, macchiare
sultan *n* sultano
sultry *a* soffocante, afoso
sum *n* somma, totale *m*; — *vt* sommare; — **up** riassumere

sumac *n* *(bot)* sommacco
summarize *vt* riassumere
summarily *adv* sommariamente
summary *n* sommario
summer *n* estate *f*; **—house** *n* padiglione di giardino; — **resort** stazione estiva; **—time** estate *f*, stagione estiva; — **vacation** vacanze estive; **—y** *a* estivo; — *vi* *(vacation)* villeggiare, passare l'estate
summit *n* vetta, cima; — **conference** conferenza al vertice
summon *vt* convocare; *(law)* citare; **—s** *n* *(law)* citazione
sumptuous *a* suntuoso; **—ly** *adv* suntuosamente; **—ness** *n* suntuosità
sun *n* sole *m*; **—bath** *n* bagno di sole; **—beam** *n* raggio di sole; **—dial** *n* meridiana; **—down** *n* tramonto; **—glasses** *npl* occhiali da sole; **—lamp** *n* lampada per raggi ultravioletti; **—light**, **—shine** *n* luce del sole; **—rise** *n* alba, aurora; **—set** *n* tramonto; **—spot** *n* macchia solare; **—stroke** *n* insolazione, colpo di sole; **—lit** *a* soleggiato; **—ny** *a* solatio; allegro
sun *vt* esporre al sole
sunburn *n* abbronzatura, tintarella *(coll)*; scottatura di sole; — *vt* abbronzare; bruciare al sole; — *vi* abbonzarsi; **—ed** *a* abbronzato; bruciato dal sole
Sunday *n* domenica; — **school** scuola domenicale
sundries *npl* generi diversi
sundry *a* diversi, parecchi
sunken *a* infossato
suntan *n* abbronzatura
sun-tanned *a* abbronzato
sup *vt* sorseggiare; — *vi* cenare
superable *a* sormontabile
superabundance *n* sovrabbondanza
superabundant *a* sovrabbondante
superb *a* superbo
supercilious *a* sdegnoso, arrogante; **—ness** *n* arroganza
superficial *a* superficiale; **—ity** *n* superficialità
superfine *a* sopraffino
superfluity *n* superfluità
superfluous *a* superfluo
superhighway *n* autostrada
superhuman *a* sovrumano
superimpose *vt* sovrimporre
superintend *vt* sovrintendere; **—ence** *n* soprintendenza; **—end** *n* sovrintendente, soprintendente *m*
superior *a&n* superiore *m*; **—ity** *n* superiorità
superlative *a&n* superlativo
superman *n* superuomo
supermarket *n* supermercato
supernatural *a* sovrannaturale

supernumerary *a* in soprannumero; — *n* soprannumerario; *(theat)* comparsa
supersaturated *a* soprasaturato
supersede *vt* rimpiazzare, soppiantare
supersensitive *a* ipersensibile
supersonic *a* supersonico, ultrasonoro
superstition *n* superstizione
superstitious *a* superstizioso
superstructure *n* soprastruttura
supervene *vi* sopravvenire
supervise *vt* sorvegliare, sovraintendere
supervision *n* sorveglianza
supervisor *n* sovrintendente, controllore *m*
supine *a* supino
supper *n* cena; **The Last S–** L'Ultima Cena; **–time** *n* ora di cena
supplant *vt* soppiantare
supple *a* flessibile, cedevole, docile, arrendevole; servile; **–ness** *n* flessibilità; arrendevolezza; docilità, servilità
supplement *n* supplemento; — *vt* completare; **–ary** *a* supplementare
supplicate *vt&i* supplicare
supplicant *n* supplicante *m&f*
supplication *n* supplica
supplier *n* fornitore *m*
supply *vt* fornire; colmare, soddisfare; — *n* rifornimento, provvista; — **and demand** offerta e domanda
support *vt* mantenere; confermare; appoggiare; — *n* mantenimento, sostegno; **–er** *n (person)* fautore, sostenitore *m*; *(hosiery)* giarrettiera; *(med)* sospensorio
supposable *a* supponibile
suppose *vt* supporre, credere; **–d** *a* supposto, putativo
supposing *conj* supposto che
supposition *n* supposizione, congettura
suppository *n (med)* supposta
suppress *vt* sopprimere; nascondere
suppression *n* soppressione
suppurate *vi* suppurare
suppuration *n* suppurazione
supremacy *n* supremazia
supreme *a* supremo
surcharge *n* sovraccarico; — *vt* sovraccaricare
sure *a* sicuro, certo; **–ly** *adv* certamente, senz'altro; **make — (that)** accertarsi che; — *adv (coll)* certo, sicuro; **–ly** *adv* certamente; **–ness** *n* sicurezza
sure-footed *a* a piè fermo
surety *n* garanzia; garante *m&f*
surf *n* risacca; **–board** *n* idroscì
surface *n* superficie *f*; **on the —** superficiale; **in superficie**; — *vt* dare una superficie; lisciare; — *vi* venire alla superficie; — *a* superficiale
surfeit *vt* saziare; — *vi* rimpinzarsi; saziarsi; — *n* sazietà, eccesso
surge *n* ondata; — *vi* sollevarsi
surgeon *n* chirurgo
surgery *n* chirurgia
surgical *a* chirurgico
surging *a* agitato; ondeggiante; — *n* agitazione
surliness *n* arcignezza
surly *a* arcigno
surmise *vt&i* congetturare, supporre; — *n* supposizione; sospetto
surmount *vt* sorpassare, sormontare; **–able** *a* sormontabile
surname *n* cognome *m*
surpass *vt* sorpassare
surplice *n (eccl)* cotta
surplus *n* eccedenza; — *a* in eccedenza
surprise *vt* sorprendere; — *n* sorpresa
surprising *a* sorprendente; **–ly** *adv* sorprendentemente
surrealism *n* surrealismo
surrealist *n* surrealista *m&f*
surrender *n* resa; abbandono; — *vi* arrendersi; — *vt* cedere; rinunziare a
surrepetitious *a* surrettizio; clandestino
surrogate *n* sostituto; surrogato; — *vt* surrogare
surround *vt* circondare; **–ing** *a* circostante
surroundings *npl* dintorni *mpl*; ambiente *m*
surtax *n* sopratassa
surveillance *n* sorveglianza
survey *vt* osservare, stimare; far perizia di, misurare
survey *n* veduta, agrimensura, esame *m*; inchiesta; rilevamento topografico; **–or** *n* agrimensore *m*; geometra *m*
survival *n* sopravvivenza
survive *vi* sopravvivere
surviving *a* sopravvivente
survivor *n* superstite *m&f*
susceptibility *n* suscettibilità
susceptible *a* suscettibile
susceptive *a* suscettivo
suspect *vt&i* sospettare; supporre; — *n* sospetto
suspend *vt* sospendere; **–ers** *npl* bretelle *fpl*
suspense *n* incertezza, ansia, dubbio, **keep in —** tenere con l'animo sospeso
suspension *n* sospensione; — **bridge** ponte sospeso
suspicion *n* sospetto, traccia
suspicious *a* sospettoso, sospetto; **–ness** *n* sospettosità
sustain *vt* sostenere; subire; prolungare; **–ed** *a* sostenuto
sustenance *n* vitto, mantenimento
suture *n* sutura; — *vt* suturare
swab *n* strofinaccio; radazza; tampone *m*;

— *vt* lavare, radazzare; tamponare
swaddle *vt* fasciare, involgere
swaddling clothes fasce *fpl*; pannolini per bambini
swagger *n* spacconata; — *vi* darsi arie; camminare pavoneggiandosi; **-er** *n* fanfarone, spaccone *m*
swallow *n* boccone *m*; sorsata; sorso; *(bird)* rondine *f*; — *vt* inghiottire; — **up** assorbire, inghiottire; divorare
swamp *n* palude *f*; — *vt&i* inondare, sommergere; impantanare; rovinare; **-y** *a* paludoso
swan *n* cigno; **-sdown** *n* piuma di cigno
swap *vt (coll)* barattare, scambiare
sward *n* erba
swarm *n* sciame *m*; — *vi* sciamare, brulicare
swarthy *a* bruno, olivastro
swashbuckler *n* rodomonte *m*
swatch *n* campione di stoffa
swath *n* falciata; solco falciato
swathe *n* fascia; — *vt* fasciare
sway *n* oscillazione; dominio; — *vt&i* oscillare; vacillare, dondolare; influenzare; deviare; **-ing** *n* oscillazione
sway-backed *a* insellato; con la schiena curva
swear *vt&i* bestemmiare; giurare; — **by** giurare su; — **in** far fare giuramento; — **to** giurare di; **-ing** *n* giuramento; bestemmia
swearword *n* bestemmia
sweat *n* sudore *m*; fatica; — *vt* sudare; far sudare; *(exploit)* sfruttare; — *vi* trasudare; traspirare
sweater *n* golf *m*, maglia
Swede svedese *m&f*
Sweden Svezia
Swedish *a* svedese
sweep *n* colpo, spazzata, distesa; portata; strascicamento; **chimney** — spazzacamino; **in one** — di un colpo; **make a clean** — far piazza pulita; — **away, off** portar via; — **up, out** spazzare via; **-er** *n* spazzino; *(machine)* spazzatrice *f*; **-ing** *a* rapido, violento; completo, totale; **-ing** *n* spazzatura; lo spazzare; — *vt* spazzare; scopare; sfiorare; percorrere; — *vi* scopare; incedere; stendersi
sweepstakes *npl* lotteria sportiva
sweet *a* dolce; amabile; — *n* dolce *m*; dolcezza; fragranza; — **tooth** *(coll)* goloso; bocca dolce *(fig)*
sweeten *vt* inzuccherare; addolcire; **-ing** *n* inzuccheramento; addolcimento
sweetly *adv* dolcemente
sweetness *n* dolcezza
swell *vt&i* gonfiare; — *n (coll)* elegantone *m (coll)*; elevazione; ondulazione;

— *a (coll)* elegante; *(sl)* magnifico
swelling *n* gonfiore *m*
swelter *vi* soffocare dal caldo; — *n* afa
swerve *vi* deviare, sviarsi; — *n* deviazione; — *vt* sviare, deviare
swift *a* rapido; — *n (bird)* rondone *m*; **-ly** *adv* rapidamente, celermente; **-ness** *n* rapidità, velocità
swill *n* rifiuti *mpl*, risciaquatura
swim *vi* nuotare, bagnarsi; *(head)* girare; — *vt* attraversare a nuoto; — *n* nuotata; **be in the** — essere al corrente; **go for a** — fare il bagno; **-suit** *n* costume da bagno
swimmer *n* nuotatore *m*
swimming *n* nuoto; *(head)* vertigine *f*; — **pool** piscina
swindle *vt* turlupinare, imbrogliare; — *n* truffa
swine *n* maiale *m*; **-herd** *n* porcaio
swing *vi* dondolare; oscillare, rotare; bilanciarsi; — *vt* far girare; far oscillare; — *n* altalena; oscillazione; slancio, dondolio; **in full** — in piena attività
swinging *a* oscillante; ritmico; — **door** porta battente
swipe *n (coll)* colpo; pugno; — *vt (coll)* battere forte; prendere a pugni; *(sl)* rubare
swirl *n* turbine *m*; — *vi* turbinare, vorticare; — *vt* far turbinare
swish *n* sibilo, sferzata; *(water)* sciabordio; *(silk)* fruscio; — *vi* frusciare, sibilare; — *vt* sferzare; far sibilare; **-ing** *a* sferzante, frusciante; **-ing** *n* fruscio
Swiss *a&n* svizzero
switch *n* cambiamento; *(elec)* interruttore *m*; *(rail)* scambio; verga; sferzata; **-board** *n* centralino telefonico; — *vt* sferzare; dimenare; intercambiare; *(rail)* deviare; — *vi* deviarsi; — **off** *(light)* spegnere; chiudere; — **on** *(light)* accendere; aprire
Switzerland Svizzera
swivel *n* perno; mulinello; — **chair** sedia girevole; — *vi* girarsi; imperniarsi; — *vt* rotare
swollen *a* gonfiato
swoon *vi* svenire; — *n* svenimento
swoop *n* colpo, avventata; attacco; — *vi* slanciarsi, avventarsi, piombare su, calarsi su; — *vt* ghermire
sword *n* spada; **-fish** *n* pesce spada; **-sman** *n* spadaccino
sworn *a* giurato
sycophant *n* sicofante *m&f*
syllabic *a* sillabico
syllable *n* sillaba

syllabus *n* compendio; *(eccl)* sillabo
syllogism *n* sillogismo
sylph *n* silfide *f*
sylvan *a* silvestre
symbiosis *n* simbiosi *f*
symbol *n* simbolo; **-ic** *a* simbolico; **-ism** *n* simbolismo; **-ize** *vt* simbolizzare
symmetrical *a* simmetrico
symmetry *n* simmetria
sympathetic *a* simpatizzante; comprensivo
sympathize *vi* condividere i sentimenti; simpatizzare
sympathy *n* compassione; condoglianza; simpatia
symphonic *a* sinfonico
symphony *n* sinfonia
symposium *n* simposio
symptom *n* sintomo; **-atic** *a* sintomatico
synagogue *n* sinagoga
synchronize *vt&i* sincronizzare
synchronization *n* sincronizzazione

syncopate *vt* sincopare
syncopation *n* sincopatura *f*; musica sincopata
syndicate *n* *(com)* sindacato, consorzio; associazione
synonym *n* sinonimo
synonymous *a* sinonimo
synopsis *n* sinossi *f*
syntax *n* sintassi *f*
synthesis *n* sintesi *f*
synthesize *vt* sintetizzare
synthetic *a* sintetico
syphilis *n* sifilide *f*
syphilitic *a* sifilitico
Syria Siria; **-c** *a* siriaco; **-n** *n&a* siriano
syringe *n* siringa; — *vt* iniettare, siringare
syrup *n* sciroppo; **-y** *a* sciropposo
system *n* sistema *m*, metodo; *(rail)* rete *f*; **-atic** *a* sistematico; **-atize** *vt* sistematizzare, sistemare

T

tab *n* linguetta; *(label)* etichetta; **keep — on** *(coll)* sorvegliare; *(expenses)* mantenere controllo di; — *vt* fornire di linguetta
tabernacle *n* tabernacolo
table *n* tavola; tabella, indice *m*; **-cloth** *n* tovaglia; **-land** *n* altipiano, acrocoro; **-spoon** *n* cucchiaio da minestra; **turn the —s** capovolgere la situazione; — *vt* posporre
tablet *n* tavoletta; pastiglia; lapide *f*; *(paper)* taccuino
tableware *n* servizio da tavola
taboo *n* tabù *m*; — *a* proibito; — *vt* interdire, proibire
tabular *a* tabellare, tavolare, tabulare
tabulate *vt* catalogare, classificare, disporre in tabelle
tachometer *n* tachimetro
tacit *a* tacito
taciturn *a* taciturno
tack *n* bulletta, chiodino; *(sewing)* imbastitura; *(naut)* virata, bordeggio; — *vt* inchiodare; imbastire; *(naut)* virare
tackle *n* *(naut)* paranco; carrucola; *(gear)* attrezzatura; *(football)* attacco; — *vt* attaccare; afferrarsi a; intraprendere; *(horse)* bardare
tacky *a* vischioso, attaccaticcio
tact *n* tatto, diplomazia; **-ful** *a* diplomatico; accorto; **-less** *a* senza tatto; **-fully** *adv* con tatto; diplomaticamente
tactical *a* tattico
tactics *npl* tattica
tadpole *n* girino

taffeta *n* taffetà *m*
tag *n* etichetta; — *vt* aggiungere; *(coll)* seguire; mettere l'etichetta a; — **along** *(coll)* accompagnare
tail *n* coda; *(hair)* treccia; — **end** estremità; — **spin** *n* avvitamento; — **wind** vento in poppa; **turn** — darsela a gambe; **-s** *npl* *(coll)* marsina, frac *m*; — *vt* *(sl)* pedinare; — *vi* accodarsi
taillight *n* fanale di coda
tailor *n* sarto; — *vi* fare il sarto; — *vt* confezionare; **-ing** *n* sartoria
tailor-made *a* fatto dal sarto, tailleur
taint *n* magagna, infezione; — *vt* contaminare, corrompere, guastare; — *vi* corrompersi, guastarsi
take *n* presa; *(earnings)* guadagno, profitto
take *vt* prendere; portare; accettare, ricevere; — *vi* riuscire; — **after** *(resemble)* rassomigliarsi a; — **away** togliere, levare; — **back** riprendere; — **care of** prendersi cura di; attendere a; — **down** *(lower)* abbassare; *(write)* scrivere, prender nota; — **in** *(comprise)* includere; *(deceive)* ingannare, raggirare; — **off** *(disrobe)* levarsi; *(remove)* levare; *(avi)* decollare; — **on** *(add)* assumere; *(coll)* prendersela; — **on oneself** attribuirsi; — **one's time** non affrettarsi innecessariamente, fare con calma; — **out** togliere, levare, asportare; — **over for** succedere, rilevare; — **place** aver luogo; — **to** *(like)* affezionarsi a; — **up** *(consider)* considerare, trattare
take-off *n* *(coll)* caricatura; *(avi)* decollo

taking *a* attraente; *(med)* contagioso

talcum *n* talco

tale *n* racconto; *(lie)* fiaba; **–bearer** *n* maldicente *m*

talent *n* talento; **–ed** *a* intelligente, abile, ingegnoso

talk *n* discorso; conversazione, ciarla; *(gossip)* pettegolezzo; — *vi* parlare, conversare; — *vt* dire; esprimere; — **over** discutere su; **–ative** *a* loquace, chiacchierone, ciarliero

talker *n* parlatore *m*; chiacchierone *m*

talking *n* conversazione; chiacchiere *fpl*; — *a* parlante

talking-to *n (coll)* lavata di testa *(fig)*

tall *a* alto, grande; *(coll)* stravagante, straordinario; **–ness** *n* altezza; — **story** panzana

tallow *n* sego

tally *n* targa; tacca; duplicato; conto, verifica; — *vt* registrare; calcolare; far coincidere; — *vi* coincidere

talon *n* artiglio

tambourine *n* tamburino

tame *a* addomesticato; mansueto, docile; **–ness** *n* mansuetudine *f*; **–r** *n* domatore *m*, domatrice *f*; — *vt* addomesticare, domare

tamp *vt (cover)* tamponare; *(beat down)* pestare

tamper *vi* immischiarsi; metterci le mani

tampon *n* tampone *m*

tan *vt (leather)* conciare; abbronzare; *(coll)* percuotere, malmenare; — *a* abbronzato; — *n* abbronzatura; concia

tang *n* aroma forte, sapore *m*

tangent *n&a* tangente *f*; **go (fly) off on a —** filare per la tangente

tangerine *n* mandarino

tangible *a* tangibile

Tangier Tangeri

tangle *vt* ingarbugliare; — *n* groviglio

tank *n* serbatoio; cisterna; *(mil)* carro armato; **gas —** gazometro; **–age** *n* capacità di serbatoio

tankard *n* boccale *m*

tanner *n* conciatore *m*; **–y** conceria

tannic *a* tannico

tannin *n* tannino

tantalize *vt* tormentare; tentare

tantalizing *a* seducente; tormentante, tormentoso; — *n* supplizio di Tantalo, tormento

tantalum *n* tantalio

tantamount *a* equivalente

tantrum *n* escandescenza

tap *vt* colpire leggermente, bussare; *(cask)* spillare; — *n* colpetto; *(water)* rubinetto; *(elec)* presa, spina; — **dance** tip-tap *m*

tape *n* nastro; *(adhesive)* sparadrappo, nastro adesivo; *(recording)* nastro fonografico; **red —** pedanteria burocratica; — **measure** metro a nastro; — **recorder** magnetofono; registratore a nastro; — *vt (tie)* legare con nastro; incidere su nastro

taper *n* cero, candela; assottigliamento; — *vi* affusolarsi, assottigliarsi; diminuirsi; — *vt* affusolare, assottigliare; diminuire; **–ing** *a* conico, affusolato

tapestry *n* arazzo

tapeworm *n* tenia

taproot *n* fittone *m*

taps *npl (mil)* silenzio

tar *n* pece *f*, catrame *m*; **–ry** *a* incatramato; — *vt* incatramare

tarantula *n* tarantola

tardiness *n* ritardo

tardy *a* in ritardo

target *n* bersaglio

tariff *n* tariffa

tarnish *n* appannamento; — *vt* macchiare, appannare; — *vi* macchiarsi, appannarsi

tarpaulin *n* tela incatramata; copertone *m*

tarry *vi* fermarsi, arrestarsi, sostare, indugiare, attardarsi, trattenersi

tart *n* crostata; *(woman)* donnaccia; — *a* acido, acerbo; *(fig)* aspro; **–ly** *adv* acidamente, mordacemente; **–ness** *n* acidità, mordacità

tartar *n* tartaro; *(person, fig)* scontroso; **cream of —** cremor di tartaro

task *n* compito; **–master** *n* padrone *m*; **take to —** rimproverare; — *vt* esaurire, affaticare

tassel *n* nappa, fiocco

taste *n* gusto, sapore *m*; — *vt* assaggiare; — *vi* sapere di; **–fully** *adv* elegantemente; **–less** *a* insipido, senza gusto

tastiness *n* squisitezza

tasty *a* saporito

tatter *n* straccio, brandello; — *vt* stracciare; **–ed** *a* cencioso

tatterdemalion *n* straccione *m*

tattle *vi* chiacchierare, pettegolare; **–tale** *n* gazzettino

tatto *n* tatuaggio; *(mil)* ritirata; **beat a —** battere una ritirata; — *vt* tatuare

taunt *vt* punzecchiare, beffare; — *n* punzecchiatura

taupe *a&n* color talpa

taut *a* teso, rigido; **–ness** *n* tensione, rigidezza

tautology *n* tautologia

tavern *n* osteria; bettola, taverna; **–keeper** *n* oste *m*

tawdriness *n* vistosità

tawdry *a* sfarzoso, chiamativo, vistoso

tawny *a* fulvo, abbronzato

tax *n* imposta, tassa, gravame *m*; — *vt* tassare, gravare; accusare; — **collector** esattore delle imposte; **–payer** *n* contribuente *m&f*; **income** — imposta sul reddito; **–able** *a* tassabile, imponibile; **–ation** *n* tassazione, tasse *fpl*

taxi *n* tassì *m*; — **driver** tassista *m*; — *vi* andare in tassì; *(avi)* rullare

taxidermist *n* impagliatore *m*, tassidermista *m&f*

taxidermy *n* tassidermia

taximeter *n* tassametro

tea *n* tè *m*; **–cup** *n* tazza da tè; **–kettle** *n* bollitore *m*; **–pot** *n* teiera; **–room** *n* sala da tè; **–spoon** *n* cucchiaino

teach *vt* insegnare; **–er** *n* insegnante *m&f*; maestro, maestra; **–ing** *n* insegnamento

team *n* squadra; gruppo; **–mate** *n* compagno di squadra; **–work** *n* sforzo combinato; — *vt* accoppiare, aggruppare

teamster *n* guidatore, carrettiere *m*

tear *n* lagrima; — **gas** gas lacrimogeno; **–ful** *a* lagrimoso, pieno di lagrime; **–fully** *adv* lagrimosamente, piangendo; **–y** *a* lagrimoso; **burst into –s** scoppiare in lagrime; **shed –s** versare lagrime

tear *vt* lacerare, stracciare; — *vi* strapparsi; — **down** precipitarsi, scendere precipitosamente; *(dismantle)* smontare; — **oneself away** andarsene a malincuore; — **up** salire precipitosamente; — *n* strappo; lacerazione; **wear and —** logorìo

tease *vt* stuzzicare; importunare; — *n* seccatore *m*

teasing *n* seccatura; — *a* seccante

teat *n* capezzolo, mammella

technical *a* tecnico; **–ity** *n* tecnicismo

technician *n* tecnico

technique *n* tecnica, metodo

technological *a* tecnologico

technology *n* tecnologia

tedious *a* tedioso; **–ly** *adv* tediosamente

tedium *n* tedio, noia

teem *vi* formicolare; abbondare; **–ing** *a* formicolante, abbondante di; fecondo

teen-age *a* adolescente

teen-ager *n* adolescente *m&f*

teeter *vt* dondolare, — *vi* dondolarsi

teeter-totter *n* altalena

teeth *npl* denti *mpl*; **–ing** *n* dentizione

teethe *vi* mettere i denti

teetotaler *n* astemio

telecast *n* teletrasmissione; — *vt&i* teletrasmettere

telegram *n* telegramma *m*

telegraph *n* telegrafo; **–ic** *a* telegrafico; — *vt&i* telegrafare

telegraphy *n* telegrafia

telelens *n* telelente *f*

telemeter *n* telemetro

teleological *a* teleologico

teleology *n* teleologia

telepathic *a* telepatico

telepathy *n* telepatia

telephone *n* telefono; — **book** guida telefonica; — **booth** cabina telefonica; — **dial** disco del telefono; — **exchange** centralino telefonico; — **operator** centralinista, telefonista *m&f*; — *vt&i* telefonare

telephonic *a* telefonico

telephony *n* telefonia

telephoto *a* telefotografico; — **lens** telelente *f*

telephotograph *vt* telefotografare; — *n* telefotografia

telephotography *n* telefotografia

teleprinter *n* telescrivente *m*

telescope *n* telescopio; — *vt* incastrare, introdurre uno dentro l'altro; — *vi* incastrarsi, mettersi uno dentro l'altro

telescopic *a* telescopico

teletypewriter *n* telescrivente *m*, teletipo

televise *vt* trasmettere per televisione

television *n* televisione; — **set** televisore *m*

tell *vt&i* dire, raccontare; — **apart** distinguere; **–er** *n* narratore *m*; **bank –er** *n* cassiere *m*; **–tale** *a* chiacchierone, indiscreto; informatore

telling *n* racconto; — *a* efficace, energico

tellurium *n* *(chem)* tellurio

temerity *n* temerità

temper *n* umore *m*, indole *f*; collera; tempera; **lose one's —** adirarsi, perdere la calma; — *vt* mitigare, temperare; — *vi* mitigarsi, temperarsi

tempera *n* tempera

temperament *n* temperamento; **–al** *a* temperamentale, impetuoso

temperance *n* temperanza

temperate *a* temperato

temperature *n* temperatura

tempest *n* tempesta

tempestuous *a* tempestoso

temple *n* tempio; *(anat)* tempia

temporal *a* temporale

temporarily *adv* provvisoriamente

temporary *a* temporaneo

temporize *vi* temporeggiare

tempt *vt* tentare, allettare, attrarre; **–ation** *n* tentazione; **–er** *n* tentatore *m*; **–ing** *a* tentatore, seducente; **–ress** *n* tentatrice *f*

ten *a* dieci; **–th** *a* decimo

tenable *a* sostenibile

tenacious *a* adesivo; tenace

tenacity *n* tenacia

tenancy *n* locazione

tenant *n* locatario, inquilino

tend *vt* curare, custodire; — *vi* tendere, piegare
tendency *n* tendenza
tendentious *a* tendenzioso
tender *a* tenero, affettuoso; delicato; **–ness** *n* tenerezza; **–ly** *adv* teneramente
tender *n* offerta; *(money)* valuta; — *vt* porgere, offrire
tenderhearted *a* sensibile, di cuore tenero
tenderloin *n* filetto
tendon *n* tendine *m*
tendril *n* viticcio
tenement *n* casa popolare
tenet *n* dogma *m*; principio; opinione *f*; canone *m*
tennis *n* tennis *m*; — **court** campo da tennis
tenor *n* *(meaning)* tenore *m*; corso; *(mus)* tenore *m*
tense *a* teso, tenso, rigido; — *n* tempo; — *vt* tendere, rendere teso; — *vi* tendersi; **–ness** *n* tensione
tensile *a* tensile
tension *n* tensione
tent *n* tenda; *(med)* cappa per ossigeno; *(med)* sonda, drenaggio; — *vi* attendarsi
tentacle *n* tentacolo
tentative *a* sperimentale
tenuous *a* tenue
tenure *n* tenuta, possesso, occupazione; gestione *f*
tepid *a* tiepido
term *n* sessione; termine *m*; durata; *(name)* nome; *(office)* periodo uffiale; *(school)* periodo scolastico; — *vt* definire, nominare
terminal *n* terminale *m*; *(elec)* serrafilo; — *a* terminale
terminate *vt&i* finire, concludere, terminare
termination *n* fine *f*; *(gram)* desinenza
terminology *n* terminologia
terminus *n* termine, limite *m*
termite *n* termite *f*
terms *npl* condizioni *fpl*; *(com)* rapporti *mpl*; relazioni *fpl*; patti *mpl*; termini *mpl*; **come to** — venire a condizioni; **on good** — in buoni rapporti
tern *n* *(zool)* sterna
terrace *n* terrazza; — *vt* terrazzare
terrain *n* terreno
terrestrial *a* terrestre
terrible *a* terribile
terrier *m* *(zool)* terrier *m*
terrific *a* terrificante; *(coll)* fantastico, fenomenale; **–ally** *adv* spaventevolmente
terrify *vt* spaventare
territorial *a* territoriale
territory *n* territorio

terror *n* terrore *m*; **–ism** *n* terrorismo; **–ist** *n* terrorista *m*
terrorize *vt* terrorizzare
terror-stricken *a* atterrito
terse *a* terso; conciso
tertiary *a* terziario
test *n* esame *m*, prova, collaudo; — **pilot** pilota collaudatore; — **tube** provino; — *vt* provare, analizzare, collaudare; **–er** *n* sperimentatore, collaudatore *m*
testament *n* testamento; **–ary** *a* testamentario
testate *a* testante
testator *n* testatore *m*
testicle *n* testicolo
testify *vt&i* attestare; testimoniare
testimonial *n* attestato
testimony *n* testimonianza
testiness *n* irascibilità
testy *a* permaloso, irascibile
tetanus *n* tetano
tether *n* fune *f*, catena, cavezza; *(abilities)* risorse *fpl*; — *vt* legare, impastoiare
tetrad *n* quaterna; quattro
tetragon *n* tetragono
tetragonal *a* tetragonale, tetragono
tetrahedron *n* tetraedro
tetrameter *n* tetrametro
tetrarch *n* tetrarca *n*
tetrode *n* tetrodo
text *n* testo; **–book** *n* libro di testo; *(manual)* manuale scolastico; **–ual** *a* testuale
textile *a* tessile; — *n* tessuto
texture *n* tessitura; struttura
Thames Tamigi
than *conj* che, che non; di
thank *vt* ringraziare; — **you** grazie
thankful *a* riconoscente; **–fulness** *n* riconoscenza, gratitudine *f*
thankless *a* ingrato
thanks *npl* ringraziamenti *mpl*; grazie *fpl*; **–giving** *n* ringraziamento
that *a&pron* quello, quella; cotesto, cotesta; — *pron* che, ciò, il quale, la quale; — *conj* che; — *adv* tanto, così
thatch *n* paglia; tetto di paglia; stoppia; — *vt* coprire di paglia; **–ed** *a* coperto di paglia; di paglia
thaw *vt&i* disgelare; — *n* disgelo
the *art*, il, lo, la; i, gli *mpl*; le *fpl*
theater *n* teatro
theatrical *a* teatrale
theft *n* furto
their, **–s** *a&pron* il loro, la loro; i loro *mpl*; le loro *fpl*
theism *n* teismo
theist *n* teista *m&f*
theistic *a* teistico
them *pron* li, loro, essi *mpl*; le, loro, esse *fpl*

theme n tema m, soggetto
themselves pron pl si, sè, sè stessi mpl; sè stesse fpl
then adv allora, in seguito, poi; dunque; anche; **now and —** di tanto in tanto
thence adv dunque, quindi
thenceforth adv d'allora in poi
theocracy n teocrazia
theocratic, -al a teocratico
theologian n teologo
theological a teologico
theology n teologia
theorem n teorema m
theoretical a teoretico; **-ly** adv teoreticamente
theorist n teorico
theorize vi teorizzare
theory n teoria
theosophy n teosofia
therapeutic a terapeutico
therapy n terapia, terapeutica
there adv lì, colà, là; ci, vi; **here and —** qua e là; **— is** c'è, v'è; ecco; **— are** ci sono, vi sono; ecco
thereabouts adv nei dintorni; all'incirca
thereafter adv d'allora in poi
thereby adv con ciò; così
therefore adv quindi, perciò
therein adv vi, in ciò, in esso
thereon adv su ciò, a questo proposito
thereupon adv in seguito a ciò, in conseguenza
therewith adv con ciò, in seguito a ciò
therm n caloria, unità termica; **-ic** termico
thermal a termale; **— barrier** (aesp) barriera termica
thermodynamics npl termodinamica
thermoelectricity n termoelettricità
thermometer n termometro
thermonuclear a termonucleare
thermostat n termostato
thermotherapy n termoterapia
these pron & a pl questi mpl; queste fpl
thesis n tesi f
they pron pl essi mpl, esse fpl; loro m&fpl; **— say** si dice
thick a spesso, folto; (coll) intimo; **-ness** n spessore m; consistenza; densità
thick- (in comp) —skinned a insensibile, dalla pelle dura; **—witted** a melenso, stupido
thicken vt rendere spesso; **— vi** ispessirsi; **-ing** n ispessimento; condensazione
thicket n boschetto, macchia
thickheaded a babbeo, stupido
thickset a denso, folto; robusto, tarchiato
thief n ladro
thievery n ladrocinio, furto
thievish ladresco
thigh n coscia; **-bone** n femore m

thimble n ditale m
thin a magro; (hair) rado; (line) sottile; (voice) acuto; **-ness** n sottigliezza, finezza; (growth) radezza; magrezza; **-ly** adv sottilmente; **— vt** assottigliare; diradare; **— vi** assottigliarsi; diradarsi
thing n cosa; oggetto; affare m; **latest —** ultima creazione, ultima moda
think vt&i pensare, credere; figurarsi; stimare; **— over** pensarci su; riflettere su; **— so** pensare così; credere di sì; **-able** a concepibile, pensabile; **-er** n pensatore m
thinking n pensiero; opinione f; **— a** pensante, intelligente, ragionante
thinner n solvente m
thin-skinned a sensibile; dalla pelle delicata
third terzo; **-ly** adv in terzo luogo
third-rate a di terza categoria, scadente
thirst n sete f; **-y** a assetato; avido; **— vi** aver sete; **be -y** aver sete
thirteen a tredici; **-th** a tredicesimo
thirtieth a trentesimo
thirty a trenta
this a&pron questo, questa; **— pron** ciò; **like —** così
thistle n cardo
thong n cinghia, correggia
thorax n torace m
thorium n torio
thorn n spina; **— in the flesh** (fig) una spada nel fianco (fig), grattacapo; **-y** a spinoso
thorough a completo, intero, perfetto; meticoloso; **-ness** n completezza; perfezione; meticolosità; **-ly** adv completamente
thoroughbred n (horse) puro-sangue; (person) nobile m&f
thoroughgoing a meticoloso
thoroughfare n via pubblica, strada frequentata
those pron pl quelli, cotesti mpl; quelle, coteste fpl; **— a pl** quei, quegli, quelle, cotesti, coteste
though conj quantunque, benchè; **— adv** ciononostante; **as —** come se; **even —** anche se
thought n pensiero; idea; **-ful** a previdente; riguardoso; pensieroso; **-fulness** n premura, sollecitudine f; previdenza; **-less** a sbadato; irriflessivo, spensierato; **-lessness** n spensieratezza, sbadataggine f
thousand a mille; **-th** a millesimo
thrash vt bastonare; trebbiare; **-ing** n battitura, bastonatura
thread n filo; (screw) filetto, impanatura; **— vt** infilare; **— vi** serpeggiare; **—**

one's way passare attraverso, infilarsi; **–bare** *a* logoro; trito
threat *n* minaccia
threaten *vt&i* minacciare; **–ing** *a* minaccioso
three *a* tre; **–fold** *a* triplo, triplice
three– *(in comp)* **–cornered** *a* triangolare; **–dimensional** *a* tridimensionale; **–legged** *a* a tre gambe; a tre piedi; **–ply** *a* di tre fili; **–quarter** *a* di tre quarti; **–speed gear** *(mech)* cambio a tre velocità; **–wheeled** *a* a tre ruote
thresh *vt* trebbiare, battere
thresher *n (mech)* trebbiatrice *f*; *(person)* trebbiatore *m*
threshing *n* trebbiatura; **— machine** trebbiatrice *f*
threshold *n* soglia
thrice *adv* tre volte
thrift *n* economia, risparmio; **–y** *a* frugale, economico
thriftiness *n* frugalità, economia
thrill *vt* commuovere; **—** *vi* emozionarsi; **—** *n* emozione
thrilling *a* eccitante, emozionante
thrive *vi* prosperare; aver successo
thriving *a* prospero; vigoroso
throat *n* gola; **sore —** mal di gola; **–y** *a* di gola; gutturale; **clear one's —** schiarirsi la voce
throb *n* pulsazione; battito; **—** *vi* palpitare
throbbing *n* pulsazione, palpitazione; battito; **—** *a* pulsante; palpitante
throes *npl* dolori *mpl*; angoscie *fpl*; pene *fpl*; *(childbirth)* doglie *fpl*
thrombosis *n* trombosi *f*
throne *n* trono
throng *n* folla; **—** *vi* accalcarsi; affollarsi; **—** *vt* affollare; accalcare
throttle *n* valvola, farfalla; **—** *vt* strozzare, strangolare; *(mech)* regolare con valvola
through *prep* attraverso; per; durante; a causa di; per mezzo di; **—** *adv* dal principio alla fine; completamente; **—** *a* diretto; finito; **–out** *prep* in tutto; da un capo all'altro di; **–out** *adv* dappertutto
throw *n* getto, lancio; **–back** *n* riversione; **—** *vt* buttare, gettare; **— away** buttar via; *(waste)* scialacquare; **— off** liberarsi di; eludere; **— up** *(hands)* gettare in aria; *(vomit)* rigettare
thrust *n* spinta; *(fencing)* stoccata; *(mech)* propulsione, pressione; **—** *vt* spingere; imporre; trafiggere, ficcare; **—** *vi* cacciarsi
thud *n* tonfo, rumore sordo; **—** *vi* fare un tonfo *(or* un rumore sordo)

thug *n* assassino, strangolatore *m*, sicario
thumb *n* pollice *m*; **–tack** *n* puntina da disegno; **—** *vt* sporcare con il pollice; **— through** dare uno sguardo a, scartabellare
thump *n* colpo, percossa; tonfo; **—** *vt* dar pugni a; percuotere; **—** *vi* fare un tonfo; palpitare
thunder *n* tuono; **–bolt** *n* fulmine *m*; **–cloud, –head** *n* nuvolone *m*; nembo temporalesco; **–storm** *n* temporale *m*; **–struck** *a* stupefatto; **—** *vi* tuonare
thundering *n* tuono; **—** *a* tuonante; assordante
Thursday *n* giovedì *m*
thus *adv* così; **— far** fin qui, a questo punto
thwart *vt* impedire
thyme *r:* timo
thyroid *n&a* tiroide *f*
tiara *n* tiara
Tiber Tevere
tic *n (med)* ticchio
tick *n (zool)* zecca; *(watch)* tic-tac *m*, battito; **—** *vi* ticchettare, battere
ticket *n* biglietto; *(label)* etichetta; *(pol)* lista elettorale; *(fine)* contravvenzione, multa; **complimentary —** biglietto di favore; **season —** abbonamento; **— collector** controllore *m*; **— window** sportello
ticking *n* ticchettio; *(cloth)* traliccio; **—** *a* ticchettante
tickle *n* solletico; **—** *vt* solleticare; divertire; **—** *vi* provare solletico
ticklish *a* suscettibile; solleticoso; difficile
tidal *a* di marea; **— wave** maremoto
tidbit *n* bocconcino prelibato
tide *n* marea
tidiness *n* pulizia, nettezza; ordinatezza
tidings *npl* informazioni *fpl*
tidy *a* ordinato, lindo; *(coll)* considerevole; **—** *n* coprisedia
tie *vt* legare; annodare; pareggiare; **—** *vi* pareggiarsi; legarsi; **—** *n* legame *m*; *(neck)* cravatta; *(rail)* traversina; *(sport)* pareggio; *(mus)* legatura
tiepin *n* spillo per la cravatta
tier *n* fila
tie-up *n* interruzione temporanea
tiff *n* bisticcio, stizza
tiger *n* tigre *f*
tight *a* stretto; teso; ermetico; fermo; *(coll)* spilorcio; *(sl)* ubriaco; **–ness** *n* strettezza; **–rope, –rope walker** funambolo; **–ly** *adv* strettamente; **–en** *vt* stringere; **–en** *vi* stringersi
tightfisted *a* avaro
tight-fitting *a* attillato

tight-lipped *a* impassibile; silenzioso
tights *npl* maglia
tile *n* tegola; mattonella, piastrella; — *vt* coprire con tegole; **–d** *a* coperto di tegole
tiling *n* tegolato
till *prep* fino a; — *conj* finchè; — *n* tiretto di cassa, cassa
till *vt* arare; **–able** *a* coltivabile; **–ing** *n* coltivazione; **–er** *n* coltivatore *m*
tiller *n (naut)* barra del timone
tilt *n* inclinazione; torneo; **full** — a gran velocità; — *vt* inclinare; — *vi* inclinarsi; giostrare; **–ed** *a* inclinato
timber *n* legname *m*; boschi *mpl*
timbre *n* timbro
time *n* tempo; ora; *(era)* epoca; momento; volta; — **after** — tante volte; — **and (—) again** ripetutamente; **at the same** — nello stesso tempo; **from** — **to** — di quando in quando; **in, on** — in tempo; **keep** — tenere il tempo; **short** — poco tempo, breve tempo; **a short** — **after** poco dopo; **–less** *a* interminabile; eterno; **–worn** *a* logoro; — *vt* regolare; calcolare il tempo; *(sport)* cronometrare; sincronizzare; cogliere il momento per
time-honored *a* venerabile
timekeeper *n (sport)* cronometrista *m*
timeliness *n* tempestività
timely *a* tempestivo, opportuno, a tempo
timepiece *n* orologio
timetable *n* orario
timid *a* timido
timing *n* sincronizzazione, tempo
tin *n* stagno; latta; — **can** scatola; — **foil** stagnola; — **plate** latta stagnata; **–smith** *n* lattoniere *m*; **–ware** *n* articoli di latta; — *vt* stagnare
tincture *n* tintura
tinder *n* esca
tine *n* rebbio, punta
tinge *n* tintura; pizzico; — *vt* tingere
tingle *n* formicolio, puntura, prurito; — *vi* formicolare
tingling *n* prurito, formicolio
tinker *vi* affaccendarsi
tinkle *vi* tintinnare; — *vt* far tintinnare; — *n* tintinnio
tin-plate *vt* stagnare
tinsel *n* orpello; finzione
tint *n* tinta; — *vt* colorire
tiny *a* minuscolo, piccino
tip *n* punta; *(advice)* consiglio; *(fee)* mancia; *(information)* informazione segreta; — *vt* appuntare; dar la mancia a; inclinare; rivelare una informazione utile; toccare leggermente; — *vi* inclinarsi; — **over** rovesciare; rovesciarsi

tipple *vi* sbevazzare
tippler *n* sbevazzatore *m*
tipsiness *n* ubriachezza
tipsy *a* brillo
tiptoe *vi* camminare in punta di piedi; — *adv* in punta di piedi
tiptop *n (coll)* massimo; colmo; — *a (coll)* eccellente, sommo
tirade *n* sfuriata
tire *n* pneumatico, gomma; — *vt* stancare; annoiare; — *vi* annoiarsi, stancarsi; **–d** *a* stanco; **–dness** *n* stanchezza; **–less** *a* instancabile; **–some** *a* faticoso; noioso, fastidioso
tissue *n* tessuto; — **paper** *n* carta velina
tit *n* — **for tat** colpo per colpo; contraccambio; **give** — **for tat** rendere pan per focaccia
titanic *a* titanico
titanium *n* titanio
tithe *n* decima
title *n* titolo; diritto; — **page** frontespizio; — *vt* intitolare
titlist *n* campione *m*
titrate *vt (chem)* titolare
titration *n (chem)* analisi volumetrica
titter *n* risolino, ridacchiamento; — *vi* ridacchiare
titular *a&n* titolare *m*
to *prep* a; verso; per; in; di; **come** — rinvenire; **up** — fino a
toad *n* rospo
toadstool *n* fungo velenoso
toady *n* parassita *m&f*; adulatore *m*; — *vt* adulare
toast *vt* abbrustolire; — *vi* brindare; — *n* pane abbrustolito; brindisi *m*
toaster *n* tostapane *m*
toastmaster *n* direttore dei brindisi
tobacco *n* tabacco
toboggan *n* toboga; — *vi* andare in toboga
today *n&adv* oggi *m*; **a week from** — fra una settimana; **a week ago** — una settimana fa
toddle *vi* camminare a passi incerti; **–r** *n* bambino
to-do *n (coll)* daffare *m*
toe *n* dito del piede; *(shoe)* punta; — **the mark (line)** essere ligio al dovere; — *vt* toccare con la punta del piede; fornire di punta
toe-dance *vi* ballare sulle punte dei piedi
toenail *n* unghia del piede
toffee *n* caramella
together *adv* insieme
toggle *n (naut)* coccinello; — **switch** *(elec)* interruttore a coltello
togs *npl (coll)* indumenti *mpl*
toil *vi* faticare; — *n* fatica, lavoro; **–er** *n* sgobbone *m*; lavoratore *m*; **–some**

a faticoso, penoso; **–worn** *a* sfinito dalla fatica

toilet *n* toletta; gabinetto; ritirata; — **paper** carta igienica; — **water** acqua di Colonia

token *n* segno; ricordo; prova; *(coin)* gettone; — **payment** pagamento simbolico; **by the same** — per ciò, a conferma di quanto detto; **in** — **of** in pegno di *(coll)*

tolerable *a* tollerabile

tolerably *adv* tollerabilmente

tolerance *n* tolleranza

tolerant *a* tollerante

tolerate *vt* tollerare

toleration *n* tolleranza

toll *n* pedaggio dazio; *(bells)* rintocco; — **bridge** ponte di pedaggio; — **call** telefonata interurbana; **–house** *n* ufficio daziario; **pay a** — pagare il dazio; — *vi* rintoccare; — *vt* suonare a rintocchi

tomato *n* pomodoro

tomb *n* tomba; **–stone** *n* lapide *f*, pietra sepolcrale

tomboy *n* maschietta

tomcat *n* gatto

tome *n* tomo, volume *m*

tomfoolery *n* sciocchezza

tomorrow *adv&n* domani *m*; **the day after** — dopodomani; — **morning** domattina; **a week from** — domani a otto

tom-tom *n* tam-tam *m*

ton *n* tonnellata; **–nage** *n* tonnellaggio; *(naut)* stazza

tonal *a* tonale

tonality *n* tonalità

tone *n* tono, intonazione; sfumatura; — **down** attenuare; **–less** senza tono; — *vt* intonare

tongs *npl* molle *fpl*, tenaglie *fpl*

tongue *n* lingua; *(shoe)* linguetta; *(bell)* battaglio; *(buckle)* puntale *m*; **on the tip of the** — sulla punta della lingua; **with** — **in cheek** con ironia, con arguzia

tongue-tied *a* bleso

tonic *a&n* tonico; — *n (mus)* tonica

tonight *adv&n* stanotte *f*, stasera

tonsil *n* tonsilla; **–lectomy** *n* tonsillotomia; **–litis** *n* tonsillite *f*

tonsure *vt* tonsurare; — *n* tonsura

too *adv* troppo; anche, pure; — **much** troppo

tool *n* utensile *m*; *(person)* agente *m*

toot *n* suono di corno; — *vt&i* suonare, fischiettare

tooth *n* dente *m*; — *vt* dentellare

toothache *n* mal di denti

toothbrush *n* spazzolino da denti

toothpaste *n* dentifricio

toothpick *n* stuzzicadenti *m*, stecchino

top *n* sommo; colmo; testa; *(bus)* imperiale *m*; *(mountain)* vetta; *(toy)* trottola; **–coat** *n* soprabito; **–flight** *a (coll)* di primissimo ordine; — **hat** cappello a cilindro; — *a* massimo, primo; — *vt* coronare; raggiungere la vetta; sorpassare; svettare

toper *n* ubriacone *m*

topic *n* tema *m*; argomento; **–al** *a* attuale; topico

topmost *a* più elevato, più in alto

top-notch *a (coll)* eccellente

topographer *n* topografo

topographic *a* topografico

topography *n* topografia

topping *n* cima

topple *vi* capitombolare; — *vt* ribaltare

top-secret *a* estremamente segreto

topsy-turvy *a* capovolto

torch *n* fiaccola

torchlight *n* luce di fiaccola; — **parade** fiaccolata

torero *n* torero, toreadore *m*

torment *n* tormento; — *vt* tormentare; **–ing** *a* tormentoso; **–or** *n* tormentatore *m*

torn *a* stracciato

tornado *n* tromba d'aria, ciclone *m*, uragano

torpedo *n* siluro; — **boat** torpediniera; — **tube** tubo lanciasiluri; — *vt* silurare

torpid *a* tardo; intorpidito

torpor *n* torpore *m*

torrent *n* torrente *m*; **in –s** a torrenti; **–ial** *a* torrenziale

torrid *a* torrido

torsion *n* torsione

torso *n* torso

tort *n (law)* torto

tortoise *n* tartaruga

tortuosity *n* tortuosità

tortuous *a* tortuoso

torture *n* tortura; **–r** *n* torturatore *m*; — *vt* torturare, tormentare

toss *n* scossa, colpo; *(naut)* beccheggio; — **off** tracannare; sbrigare; **–up** *n* testa o croce; **–ing** *n* agitazione, scossa; sballottamento; — *vi* agitarsi; — *vt* gettare, lanciare, sballottare; alzare di colpo

tot *n* bambino, bimbo

total *n* totale *m*, somma; — *a* totale; — *vt* addizionare, sommare; ammontare a; **–ization** *n* totalizzazione; **–ity** *n* totalità

totalitarian *n&a* totalitario; **–ism** *n* totalitarismo

totter *vi* vacillare, **–ing** *a* barcollante

toucan *n* tucano

touch *n* tatto, contatto; *(sl)* stoccata

(*fig*); pizzico; tocco; leggero attacco; **-ing** *a* commovente; **-iness** *n* suscettibilità; **-y** *a* suscettibile; — *vt* toccare; commuovere; concernere, trattare; — *vi* toccarsi; *(naut)* fare scalo

touch-and-go *a* arrischiato; incerto

touchstone *n* pietra di paragone

tough *a* duro; difficile; resistente; violento; ostinato; — *n* tipaccio; **-ly** *adv* difficilmente; ostinatamente; duramente; **-ness** *n* ostinazione; durezza; difficoltà

toughen *vt* indurire; — *vi* indurirsi

tour *n* viaggio, giro; visita; **conducted** — gita in comitiva; — *vi* viaggiare; girare; — *vt* viaggiare attraverso; **-ism** *n* turismo; **-ist** *n* turista *m&f*

tournament *n* torneo; concorso, gara

tousle *vt* scompigliare, disordinare

tow *n* rimorchio; stoppa; **-headed** dai capelli di stoppa *(fig)*; **-line** *n* cavo di rimorchio; — *vt* rimorchiare

toward **-s** *prep* verso

towel *n* asciugamano; **-ing** *n* stoffa d'asciugamani; — *vt* asciugare

tower *n* torre *f*; *(church)* campanile *m*; — *vi* torreggiare; **-ing** *a* torreggiante

town *n* paese *m*, borgo, città; — **hall** municipio; **-ship** *n* comune *m*

townsman *n* borghese *m*, cittadino

townspeople *npl* cittadinanza

toxic *a* tossico, velenoso

toxicology *n* tossicologia

toxin *n* tossina

toy *n* giocattolo, balocco; — *vi* giocare

trace *n* vestigio, traccia; *(horse)* tirella; — *vt* rintracciare; ricalcare; attribuire; **-able** *a* decalcabile; tracciabile; **-r** *n* ricalcatore, tracciatore *m*; **-ry** *n* intaglio

trachea *n (anat)* trachea

tracheotomy *n* tracheotomia

tracing *n* tracciato, ricalco; — **paper** carta per ricalcare

track *n* orma; sentiero; *(rail)* binario; *(sports)* pista, corsa su pista; — **down** scovare, snidare, catturare; **keep** — **of** seguire il corso di; — *vt* pedinare, seguire la pista di; lasciare le tracce

trackless *a* deserto, senza sentieri

tract *n* tratto, spazio; opuscolo; **-able** *a* trattabile

tractability *n* trattabilità

traction *n* trazione *f*

tractor *n* trattrice *f*

trade *n* commercio; mestiere *m*; — **name** nome commerciale; — **union** sindacato operaio; **-mark** marca di fabbrica; **-r** *n* commerciante, negoziante *m&f*; — *vi* commerciare; — *vt* barattare

tradesman *n* commerciante *m*

tradespeople *npl* gente di commercio, commercianti *mpl*

trading *n* commercio, traffico commerciale; baratto; — *a* commerciale; — **stamps** buoni-regalo

tradition *n* tradizione *f*

traditional *a* tradizionale

traditionalism *n* tradizionalismo

traffic *n* traffico, circolazione *f*; commercio; — **jam** congestione di traffico; — **light** semaforo; — **manager** capo traffico; — **policeman** vigile *m*; — **sign** segnale di traffico; — *vi* commerciare, trafficare

tragedian *n* tragico, attore tragico; *(author)* tragedo *m*, dramaturgo

tragedy *n* tragedia

tragic *a* tragico

tragicomedy *n* tragicommedia

trail *n* pista; orme *fpl*; sentiero; strascico; — *vt* trascinare, strascicare; pedinare; seguire a stento; — *vi* trascinarsi

trailer *n* rimorchio; *(movie)* cortometraggio pubblicitario

trailing *a* strisciante

train *n* treno; seguito; *(dress)* strascico; — *vt* addestrare, allenare; *(an animal)* ammaestrare; *(sports)* allenare; istruire; *(gun)* puntare; — *vi* allenarsi; **-ed** *a* ammaestrato, allenato

trainee *n* recluta *m*; novizio

trainer *n* allenatore *m*

training *n* allenamento, addestramento; — *a* allenante; esercitante

trait *n* tratto, caratteristica

traitor *n* traditore *m*; **-ous** *a* traditore

trajectory *n* traiettoria

trammel *vt* impedire, impastoiare; irretire; — *n* pastoia

tramp *n* rumore di passi; camminata; vagabondo; — *vi* camminare pesantemente; vagabondare; — *vt* calpestare; percorrere camminando

trample *vt* calpestare

trance *n* trance *m*

tranquil *a* tranquillo; **-ity** *n* tranquillità; **-ize** *vt* tranquillizzare; **-izer** *n* tranquillante *m*

transact *vt* trattare, negoziare

transaction *n* affare *m*, operazione, transazione

transatlantic *a* transatlantico

transcend *vt* trascendere; **-ency** *n* trascendenza; **-ent** *a* trascendente; **-ental** *a* trascendentale; **-entalism** *n* trascendentalismo

transcontinental *a* transcontinentale

transcribe *vt* trascrivere

transcription *n* trascrizione, copia; *(rad)* registrazione di radiotrasmissione

translation *n* traduzione
translator *n* traduttore *m*
transliterate *vt* trascrivere
translucent *a* translucido
transmigrate *vi* trasmigrare
transmigration *n* trasmigrazione
transmit *vt* trasmettere
transmitter *n* trasmettitore *m*
transmutation *n* trasformazione, trasmutazione
transmute *vt* trasmutare
transoceanic *a* transoceanico
transom *n* lunetta; traversa
transparency *n* trasparenza; *(phot)* diapositiva
transparent *a* trasparente
transpiration *n* traspirazione
transpire *vt&i* traspirare, esalare; *(happen)* accadere
transplant *vt* trapiantare; **-ation** *n* trapianto
transport *vt* trasportare; — *n* trasporto; **-ation** *n* trasporto; mezzo di trasporto; biglietto di viaggio
transpose *vt* trasportare, invertire, trasporre
transposition *n* trasposizione
transship *vt* trasbordare; **-ment** *n* trasbordo
transverse *a* trasversale
trap *n* trappola; inganno; — **door** *n* botola; **set a** — tendere una trappola; — *vt* prendere in trappola; — *vi*
transfer *vt* riportare; cedere; trasferire; — *vi* fare coincidenza; trasferirsi; — **able** *a* trasferibile; — *n* trasferimento; cessione; *(ticket)* biglietto cumulativo
transfiguration *n* trasfigurazione
transfigure *vt* trasfigurare
transfix *vt* trafiggere
transform *vt* trasformare; — *vi* trasformarsi; **-ation** *n* trasformazione
transformer *n* *(elec)* trasformatore *m*
transfusion *n* trasfusione
transgress *vt* trasgredire; — *vi* peccare, errare
transgression *n* trasgressione
transgressor *n* trasgressore *m*
transience *n* temporaneità
transient *a* transitorio, temporaneo; — *n* transeunte *m&f*
transit *n* transito, trasporto; **in** — **di** passaggio, di transito, in transito
transition *n* transizione
transitional *a* di transizione
transitive *a* transitivo
transitoriness *n* transitorietà
transitory *a* transitorio
translatable *a* traducibile
translate *vt* tradurre; — *vi* tradursi

stendere trappole
trapeze *n* trapezio
trapezoid *n* trapezoide *m*
trapper *n* cacciatore con trappole
trappings *npl* ornamenti *mpl*
trash *n* immondizie *fpl*; robaccia, **-y** *a* di scarto
trauma *n* *(med)* trauma *m*; **-tic** *a* traumatico
travail *n* travaglio, doglia; doglia del parto
travel *vi* viaggiare; — *vt* percorrere; — *n* viaggio; *(mech)* corsa, percorso; **-ogue** *n* conferenza su viaggi
traveler *n* viaggiatore *m*, viaggiatrice *f*; **-'s check** *n* assegno per viaggiatori
traveling *a* viaggiante; — *n* il viaggiare; — **salesman** commesso viaggiatore
traversal *n* attraversamento
traverse *vt* attraversare; — *n* traversa; — *a* trasversale
travesty *n* parodia; travisazione; — *vt* travestire
trawl *vt&i* pescare a rete
trawler *n* imbarcazione peschereccia
tray *n* vassoio
treacherous *a* perfido
treachery *n* perfidia
tread *vt* calpestare; percorrere; *(auto)* mettere il battistrada; — *vi* camminare; porre piede; — **water** nuotare diritto; — *n* passo; *(stair)* gradino; *(auto)* battistrada *m*
treadle *n* pedale *m*
treason *n* tradimento; **-able** *a* proditorio; **-ous** *a* sedizioso
treasure *n* tesoro; — *vt* apprezzare, tesaurizzare
treasurer *n* tesoriere *m*
treasury *n* tesoreria
treat *vt&i* trattare; curare; — *vi* negoziare; — *vt* offrire, invitare; — *n* regalo; festa; piacere *m*
treatise *n* trattato
treatment *n* trattamento; cura
treaty *n* trattato
treble *n* *(math)* triplo: *(mus)* soprano; suono acuto; — *a* triplice; acuto; — *vt* triplicare; — *vi* triplicarsi; — **clef** chiave di sol
tree *n* albero; **-top** *n* cima d'albero; **family** — albero genealogico
trellis *n* graticciata
tremble *n* tremito; — *vi* tremare
trembling *n* tremolio; — *a* tremante
tremendous *a* tremendo; *(coll)* enorme, meraviglioso
tremolo *n* tremolo
tremor *n* tremore *m*, tremito
tremulous *a* tremolante
trench *n* trincea; — **coat** impermeabile *m*

trenchant *a* penetrante, tagliente
trencherman *n* forte mangiatore, buona forchetta
trend *n* tendenza, direzione; — *vi* tendere, dirigersi
trepan *vt (med)* trapanare; — *n* trapano
trepidation *n* trepidazione
trespass *vi* oltrepassare, sconfinare; trasgredire; peccare; **-er** *n* trasgressore *m*
tress *n* treccia
trestle *n* trespolo; cavalletto
trey *n (cards)* tre *m*
triad *n* triade *f*
trial *n* prova; saggio, collaudo; dolore *m*; *(law)* processo
triangle *n* triangolo
triangular *a* triangolare
triangulate *vt* triangolare
triangulation *n* triangolazione
tribal *a* di tribù
tribe *n* tribù *f*
tribesman *n* membro di tribù
tribulation *n* tribolazione
tribunal *n* tribunale *m*
tribune *n* tribuno; *(dais)* tribuna
tributary *n&a* tributario
tribute *n* tributo
triceps *n* tricipite *m*
trick *n* tiro; inganno; destrezza; giuoco di prestigio; **-ery** *n* astuzia, fraudolenza; **-y** *a* scaltro, malizioso, ingannevole; **-iness** *n* furberia, malizia; — *vt* ingannare; **do the** — eliminare il problema
trickle *n* gocciolio; — *vi* gocciolare, stillare
trickling *n* gocciolio
tricolor *n&a* tricolore *m*
tricycle *n* triciclo
tried *a* provato, fido
triennial *a* triennale
trifle *n* inezia, nonnulla *m*; — *vi* gingillarsi; — *vt* sprecare
trifling *a* frivolo; insignificante
trigger *n* grilletto
trigonometry *n* trigonometria
trill *n* trillo; — *vi* trillare; — *vt* far trillare
trillion *n* trilione *m*
trilogy *n* trilogia
trim *a* lindo, attillato; — *vt* decorare, ornare; aggiustare; ordinare; piallare; *(hair)* spuntare; *(sewing)* guarnire; *(trees)* potare; — *n* assetto, ordine *m*; decorazione; **in** — in ordine; **-ness** *n* nettezza; eleganza
trimming *n* ornamento, guarnizione, decorazione
Trinidad La Trinità
trinity *n* trinità
Trinity *n (eccl)* Trinità
trinket *n* gingillo

trio *n* trio
trip *n* viaggio; **take a** — fare un viaggio; **-hammer** *n* maglio a leva, maglio meccanico
trip *vi (stumble)* incespicare; fare uno sbaglio; saltellare; — *vt* far inciampare; cogliere in fallo; *(mech)* sganciare
tripe *n* trippa
triple *a* triplo; **-t** *n* terzina; *(mus)* tripletta; **-ts** *npl* trigemini *mpl*; *vi* triplicare
triplicate *a* triplice; in tre copie; — *n* triplo
tripod *n* tripode *m*
triptych *n* trittico
trite *a* banale; trito
triumph *n* trionfo; vittoria; — *vi* trionfare; **-ant** *a* trionfante
triumvirate *n* triumvirato
triune *a* trino ed uno
trivet *n* treppiede *m*
trivial *a* banale; da nulla
triviality *n* banalità
trochaic *a* trocaico
Trojan *n&a* troiano
troll *vt&i* pescare con esca girante
trolley *n* puleggia; *(bus)* carrello; **-bus** *n* filobus *m*
trollop *n* prostituta, sgualdrina
trombone *n* trombone *m*
troop *n* truppa; **-er** *n* soldato di cavalleria; — *vi* schierarsi, adunarsi; sfilare; affluire; — *vt* raggruppare, radunare
troopship *n* trasporto
trophy *n* trofeo
tropic *n* tropico
tropical *a* tropicale
tropics *npl* i tropici *mpl*
trot *n* trotto; — *vi* trottare; — *vt* far trottare
troubadour *n* trovatore *m*
trouble *n* guaio; disturbo; male *m*; imbarazzo; **-maker** *n* disturbatore, provocatore *m*; **be in** — trovarsi nei pasticci; **take the** — **to** prendersi la pena di; **be worth the** — valer la pena; — *vt* disturbare; turbare; — *vi* disturbarsi; turbarsi; infastidirsi; **-d** *a* turbato, afflitto
troublesome *a* molesto; fastidioso; noioso
trough *n (kneading)* madia; abbeveratoio
trounce *vt* malmenare, battere; *(coll)* sconfiggere
troupe *n* compagnia
trousers *npl* calzoni *mpl*; **short** — *npl* calzoncini *mpl*
trousseau *n* corredo da sposa
trout *n* trota
trowel *n* cazzuola; vanghetta per trapiantare
Troy Troia

truant *a* chi marina la scuola
truce *n* tregua
truck *n* camione *m*; autocarro; — **driver** camionista *m*; — **farm** orto; — **farming** ortofrutticoltura; — **farmer** trafficante d'ortaggi; **have no** — **with** evitare di trattare con; — *vi* scambiare, barattare; carreggiare
truculence *n* trucolenza
truculent *a* trucolento
trudge *vi* camminare faticosamente
true *a* vero; esatto; leale; — *adv* veramente; lealmente; **come** — realizzarsi, avverarsi; — *vt* rettificare, regolare, conformizzare
true-blue *a* costante, fido
truffle *n* tartufo
truism *n* luogo comune, verità banale
truly *adv* veramente
trump *n* (*card*) briscola; (*coll*) brav'uomo; — *vt* prendere con la briscola; — **up** inventare
trumpery *n* frottole *fpl*
trumpet *n* tromba; — *vi* strombazzare; strombettare; (*elephant*) barrire; **-er** *n* trombettiere *m*
truncate *vt* troncare
truncheon *n* bastone *m*
trundle *vt* far ruzzolare, far rotolare; — *vi* ruzzolare, rotolare
trunk *n* baule *m*; (*auto*) portabagagli *m*; (*body*) torso; (*elephant*) proboscide *f*; (*tree*) tronco
trunks *npl* calzoncini *mpl*, slip *m*, mutandine *fpl*
truss *n* cinto erniario; travata; — *vt* legare; (*prop*) puntellare
trust *n* fiducia, credito; (*com*) trust *m*, consorzio; **-worthy** *a* fidato; **in** — in deposito; — *vt* dar credito a, fidarsi di; — *vi* fidarsi; **-ing** *a* fiducioso; **-ed** *a* fidato
trustee *n* amministratore *m*; **-ship** *n* amministrazione, curatela
truth *n* verità; **to tell the** — a dire il vero; **-ful** *a* sincero, verace
truthfulness *n* veracità
try *vt* provare, tentare; (*law*) giudicare; (*tire*) stancare; — **out** collaudare; mettere a prova; — **on** provare; — *n* tentativo, prova
trying *a* difficile, penoso, seccante
tryout *n* prova, saggio
tryst *n* appuntamento
T-shirt *n* maglietta estiva, canottiera
tub *n* tino; — **bath** bagno in vasca; **-by** *a* obeso, grasso, paffuto
tuba *n* tuba
tube *n* tubo, canale *m*; (*rad*) valvola; **inner** — camera d'aria

tuber *n* tubero
tubercle *n* tubercolo
tubercular *a* tubercolare
tuberculosis *n* tubercolosi *f*
tuberous *a* tuberoso
tubing *n* tubatura
tubular *a* tubolare
tuck *n* piegatura; — *vt* ripiegare, rimboccare
Tuesday *n* martedì; **Shrove** — Martedì Grasso
tuft *n* ciuffo; (*wool*) fiocco; (*bird*) cresta; **-ed** *a* crestato; fiocchettato; con ciuffi; — *vt* trapuntare
tug *vt* tirare con forza; rimorchiare; — *n* strappo, tirone *m*; rimorchiatore *m*; — **of war** tiro della fune
tugboat *n* rimorchiatore *m*
tuition *n* tassa scolastica
tulip *n* tulipano
tumble *vi* cadere; agitarsi; capitombolare; — *vt* rovesciare, scompigliare — *n* caduta; capitombolo
tumbler *n* (*acrobat*) acrobata *m&f*, saltimbanco; (*glass*) bicchiere *m*; (*lock*) nasello
tumble-down *a* caduco, crollante
tumefaction *n* tumefazione
tumor *n* tumore *m*
tumult *n* tumulto; **-ous** *a* tumultuoso
tun *n* barile *m*
tuna, tuna fish *n* tonno
tunable *a* accordabile
tundra *n* tundra
tune *n* melodia, aria; **in** — d'accordo, a tono, intonato; **out of** — fuori tono, in disaccordo, stonato; **-ful** *a* intonato, melodioso; **-r** *n* accordatore *m*; **-vt** accordare; (*motor*) regolare
tune-up *n* regolazione
tungsten *n* tungsteno
tunic *n* tunica
tuning *n* accordatura; — **fork** diapason *m*
Tunisia Tunisia; **-n** *n&a* tunisino
tunnel *n* galleria, traforo; — *vt* traforare
turban *n* turbante *m*
turbid *a* torbido
turbine *n* turbina
turbojet *n* turboreattore *m*, turbogetto
turboprop *n* turbopropulsore *m*, turboelica
turbulence *n* turbolenza
turbulent *a* turbolento
tureen *n* zuppiera
turf *n* zolla erbosa; torba; ippodromo, pista
turgid *a* turgido; **-ity** *n* turgidezza
Turin Torino
Turk *n* turco
Turkey Turchia
turkey *n* tacchino

Turkish *n&a* turco; — **bath** bagno turco
turmoil *n* agitazione
turn *vt* voltare; girare; *(blunt)* smussare; cambiare; — *vi* voltarsi; diventare; girare; — **about, around** voltarsi indietro; — **back** tornare indietro; — **off** chiudere; — **on** aprire; dipendere da; — **out** uscire; riuscire; far uscire; *(light)* spegnere; — **over** voltarsi; — **up** presentarsi; scoprire; accadere
turn *n* svolta; turno; giro; cambio; **done to a** — fatto a perfezione; **good** — buona azione; **sharp** — curva stretta; **–coat** *n* opportunista *m*; **–down** *a* rovesciato; **–out** *n (com)* produzione; *(audience)* uditorio; **–over** *n (com)* giro d'affare; rovesciamento; *(pastry)* focaccia; **–stile** *n* molinello; **–table** *n (rail)* piattaforma girevole; *(rad)* piatto giradischi
turpentine *n* trementina
turpitude *n* turpitudine *f*
turquoise *n* turchese *f*
turret *n* torricella
turtle *n* tartaruga; **–dove** tortora; **turn** — capovolgersi
Tuscan *a&n* toscano
Tuscany Toscana
tusk *n* zanna
tussle *n* rissa, zuffa; — *vi* azzuffarsi
tutelage *n* tutela
tutelary *a* tutelare
tutor *n* istitutore *m*; — *vt* istruire, insegnare
tuxedo *n* smoking *m*
twaddle *n* ciancia; — *vi* cianciare
twang *n* tono vibratorio; accento nasale; **speak with a** — parlare col naso
tweak *vt* pizzicare, ritorcere
tweet *vi* cinguettare
tweezers *npl* pinzette *fpl*; *(hair)* mollette *fpl*
twelfth *a* dodicesimo
twelve *a* dodici
twentieth *a* ventesimo
twenty *a* venti
twice *adv* due volte
twiddle *vt* far girare
twig *n* ramoscello
twilight *n* crepuscolo
twin *a&n* gemello
twine *n* spago, corda; — *vt* intrecciare;

attorcigliare; legare; — *vi* attorcigliarsi; serpeggiare
twin-engine *a* bimotore
twinge *n* dolore *m*; spasimo; — *vt* pungere — *vi* dolere
twinkle *vi* scintillare; ammiccare; — *n* scintillio; strizzatina d'occhio, occhiolino
twinkling *n* scintillio, balenio, sfavillio; istante *m*; **in the** — **of an eye** in un batter d'occhio
twirl *vt&i* rigirare
twist *n* attorcigliamento; torsione; tendenza; treccia; **–er** *n (storm)* turbine *m*, tromba d'aria; — *vt* torcere, contorcere; intrecciare; — *vi* torcersi, contorcersi; **–ed** *a* storto; **–ing** *n* contorcimento
twit *vt* rimproverare, rinfacciare
twitch *n* spasimo; strappo; — *vi* contrarsi, contorcersi; — *vt* strappare
twitter *n* pigolio, cinguettio; agitazione; **all of a** — agitato, nervoso; — *vi* pigolare, cinguettare
two *a* due; **–fold** *a* doppio
two- *(in comp)* **–edged** *a* a doppio taglio; **–faced** *a* a due facce; ipocrito; **–fisted** virile, vigoroso; **–handed** *a* a due mani; **–legged** *a* a due gambe, bipede; **–piece** *a* a due pezzi; **–step** *n* passo doppio; **–way** *a* a doppio senso
tycoon *n* magnate *m*
tympanum *n* timpano
type *n* tipo; *(print)* carattere *m*; — *vt* scrivere a macchina; classificare
typesetter *n* compositore *m*
typewriter *n* macchina da scrivere
typhoid (fever) *n* tifoide *f*
typhoon *n* tifone *m*
typhus *n* tifo
typical *a* tipico; **–ly** *adv* tipicamente
typify *vt* rappresentare, figurare, tipificare
typing *n* dattilografia
typist *n* dattilografo, dattilografa
typographer *n* tipografo
typographical *a* tipografico
typography *n* tipografia
tyrannical *a* tirannico
tyrannize *vt&i* tiranneggiare
tyranny *n* tirannia
tyrant *n* tiranno
Tyrol Tirolo

U

ubiquitous *a* onnipresente
udder *n* poppa
ugliness *n* bruttezza
ugly *a* brutto

ulcer *n* ulcera; **–ate** *vt* ulcerare; **–ate** *vi* ulcerarsi; **–ation** *n* ulcerazione; **–ous** *a* ulceroso
ulterior *a* ulteriore; — **motive** secondo

fine
ultimate *a* finale, ultimo
ultimatum *n* ultimatum *m*
ultra *a&n* ultra; **–modern** *a* ultramoderno; **–sonic** *a* ultrasonico; **–violet** *a* ultravioletto
umbilical *a* ombelicale; — **cord** cordone ombelicale
umbilicus *n* ombelico
umbrage *n* ombra, offesa; fogliame *m*; **take** — adombrarsi
umbrella *n* ombrello, parapioggia, paracqua
umpire *n* arbitro; — *vt&i* arbitrare
umpiring *n* arbitraggio
UN, United Nations O.N.U., Organizzazione delle Nazioni Unite
unabashed *a* imperturbato; svergognato
unabated *a* inesausto, non esausto
unabating *a* infaticabile, senza diminuzione di energia
unable *a* incapace; **be** — **to** non potere, essere incapacitato per
unabridged *a* completo, intero
unaccented *a* non accentato, inaccentuato; atono
unacceptable *a* inaccettabile
unaccomodating *a* inadattabile, incondiscendente
unaccompanied *a* solo, non accompagnato; *(mus)* senza accompagnamento
unaccomplished *a* incompiuto
unaccountable *a* inesplicabile; irresponsabile
unaccounted (for) *a* inspiegato; *(missing)* mancante
unaccredited *a* non accreditato
unaccustomed *a* non abituato
unacknowledged *a* non riconosciuto; *(letter)* senza risposta, senza riscontro
unacquainted *a* non informato; — **with** senza familiarità circa
unacquired *a* naturale
unadapted *a* inadatto
unaddressed *a* senza indirizzo
unadorned *a* disadorno
unadulterated *a* genuino, non adulterato, inalterato
unadvisable *a* non consigliabile
unaffected *a* non affettato; *(naive)* semplice
unaffectedness *n* semplicità
unafraid *a* intrepido, senza paura, temerario
unagreeable *a* sgradevole
unaggressive *a* non aggressivo
unaided *a* senz'aiuto
unallowed *a* non permesso
unalloyed *a* puro, senza lega
unalterable *a* inalterabile
unaltered *a* inalterato

unambitious *a* senz'ambizione
unanimity *n* unanimità
unanimous *a* unanime
unannounced *a* non annunziato, inaspettato
unanswerable *a* irrefutabile
unanswered *a* senza risposta
unanticipated *a* non anticipato
unappeased *a* implacato, insoddisfatto
unappetizing *a* poco appetitoso
unappreciated *a* non apprezzato
unappreciative *a* non apprezzativo
unapproachable *a* inaccessibile
unarmed *a* indifeso, inerme
unashamed *a* spudorato, svergognato
unasked *a* non richiesto
unassailable *a* inattaccabile
unassimilated *a* non assimilato
unassisted *a* non assistito
unassuming *a* modesto, senza pretese
unattached *a* libero; non fidanzato; separato
unattainable *a* irraggiungibile
unattended *a* non accompagnato, solo
unattractive *a* poco attraente
unauthentic *a* non autentico
unavailable *a* non disponibile
unavailing *a* inutile, inefficace
unavenged *a* non vendicato
unavoidable *a* inevitabile
unavowed *a* non riconosciuto; inconfessato
unaware *a* inconsapevole; **be** — **of** ignorare
unawares *adv* all'insaputa; di sorpresa
unbalanced *a* squilibrato
unbandage *vt* sbendare
unbaptized *a* non battezzato
unbar *vt* aprire
unbearable *a* insopportabile
unbearably *adv* insopportabilmente
unbeatable *a* imbattibile
unbeaten *a* imbattuto
unbecoming *a* indecoroso
unbefitting *a* sconvenevole
unbeknown *a* sconosciuto; — **to** all'insaputa di
unbelief *n* incredulità
unbelievable *a* incredibile
unbeliever *n* miscredente *m&f*
unbelieving *a* incredulo
unbend *vt* raddrizzare; allentare; — *vi* *(relax)* rilassarsi; raddrizzarsi; **–ing** *a* inflessibile
unbiased *a* imparziale
unbidden *a* spontaneo; senza invito
unbind *vt* sciogliere
unblamable *a* innocente, irreprensibile
unbleached *a* non candeggiato
unblemished *a* senza macchia, puro

unblock *vt* sbloccare; **-ed** *a* sbloccato
unblushing *a* svergognato
unbolt *vt* aprire, levare il catenaccio; **-ed** *a* aperto, senza catenaccio
unborn *a* non nato, inesistente
unbosom *vt* rivelare, confidare; **— one-self** sfogarsi
unbound *a* sciolto, libero; *(book)* senza rilegare; **-ed** *a* illimitato
unbowed *a* indomito
unbreakable *a* irrompibile, infrangibile
unbred *a* maleducato, grossolano
unbridled *a* sbrigliato, sfrenato
unbroken *a* intatto, non rotto; ininterrotto
unbuckle *vt* sciogliere, sfibbiare
unburden *vt* scaricare
unburied *a* insepolto
unbusinesslike *a* poco commerciale, poco pratico
unbutton *vt* sbottonare; **-ed** *a* sbottonato
uncalled *a* non chiamato
uncalled-for *a* innecessario; impertinente
uncanny *a* irreale, soprannaturale
uncared-for *a* trascurato, negletto
unceasing *a* incessante; **-ly** *adv* continuamente, incessantemente
uncensored *a* incensurato
unceremonious *a* senza cerimonie
uncertain *a* incerto; **-ty** *n* incertezza
uncertified *a* non certificato, non legalizzato
unchain *vt* liberare, sciogliere dalle catene, scatenare
unchallenged *a* non sfidato, senza obbiezione
unchangeable *a* invariabile, immutabile
unchanged *a* inalterato, immutato, invariato
unchanging *a* costante, invariabile
uncharitable *a* non caritatevole, senza carità
uncharted *a* non indicato in una carta marittima
unchaste *a* non casto
unchecked *a* incontrollato, sfrenato
unchivalrous *a* non cavalleresco
unchristian *a* indegno d'un cristiano, poco cristiano
unchristened *a* non battezzato
uncircumspect *a* imprudente
uncircumcised *a* incirconciso
uncivil *a* sgarbato; **-ized** *a* incivile, barbaro
unclaimed *a* non reclamato, non domandato
unclasp *vt* slacciare; **-ed** *a* slacciato, aperto
uncle *n* zio
unclean *a* sporco, sudicio; poco pulito;

-liness *n* sporcizia; impurità
unclench *vt* aprire
unclothed *a* svestito
unclouded *a* senza nuvole
uncock *vt* disarmare
uncoil *vt* svolgere, srotolare
uncollected *a* non raccolto, non riunito
uncolored *a* non colorato, incoloro
uncombed *a* spettinato
uncomfortable *a* scomodo, a disagio
uncomfortably *adv* scomodamente
uncommitted *a* non commesso; non impegnato, non compromesso
uncommon *a* non comune, raro
uncommunicative *a* riservato, incommunicativo
uncomplaining *a* rassegnato
uncomplete *a* incompleto, incompiuto
uncomplicated *a* semplice
uncomplimentary *a* poco lusinghiero, offensivo
uncompromising *a* intransigente, inflessibile
unconcealed *a* non nascosto, manifesto
unconcern *n* indifferenza; **-ed** *a* indifferente, noncurante
unconditional *a* incondizionale
unconfirmed *a* non confermato
uncongenial *a* incompatibile, antipatico
unconnected *a* sconnesso; staccato, separato; estraneo
unconquerable *a* inconquistabile, invincibile
unconquered *a* invitto, indomito
unconscious *a* inconscio, inconsapevole, privo di sensi; **be — of** ignorare; **-ly** *adv* inconsciamente; **-ness** *n* incoscienza
unconscionable *a* senza scrupoli
unconsecrated *a* non consacrato
unconsidered *a* sconsiderato, inconsiderato
unconstitutional *a* incostituzionale
unconstrained *a* senza costrizione, disinvolto
unconsumed *a* non consumato
uncontaminated *a* incontaminato
uncontested *a* incontestato
uncontradicted *a* non contraddetto
uncontrollable *a* incontrollabile
uncontrolled *a* sfrenato, senza controllo
unconventional *a* non convenzionale
unconverted *a* non convertito
unconvinced *a* non convinto
unconvincing *a* non convincente
uncooked *a* non cotto, non cucinato, crudo
uncork *vt* stappare, sturare, **-ed** *a* sturato, stappato
uncorrected *a* non corretto
uncorroborated *a* non corroborato

uncorrupted *a* incorrotto
uncouple *vt* spaiare, sconnettere
uncouth *a* goffo, grossolano; **–ness** *n* grossolanità, goffaggine *f*
uncover *vt* scoprire; — *vi* scoprirsi
uncrowned *a* senza corona
unction *n* unzione; unguento; **extreme** — *(eccl)* estrema unzione
unctuous *a* untuoso
uncultivated *a* incolto
uncultured *a* incolto
uncurbed *a* indomito
uncured *a* non guarito
uncurtailed *a* non diminuito
uncustomary *a* inusato
uncut *a* intonso, non tagliato
undamaged *a* non danneggiato, indenne
undamped *a* non scoraggiato
undated *a* non datato, senza data
undaunted *a* intrepido
undeceive *vt* disingannare
undecided *a* incerto, indeciso
undecipherable *a* indecifrabile
undefeated *a* invitto, non vinto
undefended *a* indifeso
undefinable *a* indefinibile
undefined *a* indefinito
undelivered *a* non recapitato
undemonstrative *a* non aperto, chiuso, riservato
undeniable *a* innegabile
undeniably *adv* innegabilmente
under *prep* sotto, meno di; — **the circumstances** in tali circostanze, nelle circostanze; — *a* di sotto; inferiore; — *adv* al di sotto, sotto
underage *a* minorenne
underage *n* deficit *m*
underbid *vt* offrire un prezzo inferiòre a, fare offerta più bassa di
underbrush *n* cespugli *mpl*, macchie *fpl*
undercarriage *n* carrello d'atterraggio; *(auto)* telaio
undercharge *vt* riscuotere al di sotto del prezzo guisto; caricare insufficientemente
underclothing *n* biancheria personale
undercover *a* segreto, occulto, clandestino
undercurrent *n* corrente subacquea; influenza segreta
undercut *n* *(tennis)* tiro di taglio; — *vt* vendere (*or* lavorare) a prezzo inferiore a
underdeveloped *a* insufficientemente sviluppato
underdog *n* persona sottomessa
underdone *a* poco cotto; *(meat)* al sangue
underestimate *vt* sottostimare, svalutare
underexpose *vt* dare esposizione insufficiente a

underexposure *n* *(photo)* esposizione insufficiente
underfed *a* malnutrito
underfoot *adv* sotto i piedi
undergarment *n* sottoveste *f*, indumento personale
undergo *vt* subire
undergraduate studente d'università
underground *a* sotterraneo; — *n* *(pol)* resistenza clandestina, cospiratori *mpl*; — *adv* sottoterra
undergrowth *n* cespuglio, macchia
underhanded *a* subdolo, furbo; corto di personale; **–ly** *adv* clandestinamente, sottomano, segretamente
underhung *a* sporgente
underlie *vt* costituire la base (*or* fondamenta) di; essere sottoposto a
underline *vt* sottolineare
underling *n* subalterno
underlying *a* fondamentale
undermine *vt* sottominare
undermost *a* infimo
underneath *adv* al di sotto; — *prep* sotto; al di sotto di
undernourished *a* denutrito
undernourishment *n* denutrizione
underpaid *a* mal pagato
underpay *vt* pagare insufficientemente
underpass *n* sottopassaggio
underpinning *n* sottomuro
underprivileged *a* privo del benestare; povero
underproduction *n* produzione insufficiente
underrate *vt* sottovalutare; **–d** *a* sottovalutato
underscore *vt* sottolineare
undersea *a* subacqueo, sottomarino
undersecretary *n* sottosegretario
undersell *vt* svendere, vendere in concorrenza
undershirt *n* maglietta
underside *n* parte inferiore
undersign *vt* sottoscrivere; **–ed** *n&a* sottoscritto
undersized *a* di dimensione al di sotto del normale
underskirt *n* sottogonna
understand *vt&i* capire, comprendere; **–able** *a* comprensibile
understanding *n* comprensione, intesa; intelletto, intelligenza, giudizio; **have an** — **with** accordarsi con, aver un'intesa con; **on the** — **that** a condizione che; — *a* intelligente, comprensivo
understate *vt* attenuare; **–ment** *n* affermazione incompleta
understood *a* inteso, sottinteso, capito

understudy *n (theat)* sostituto; — *vt* studiare la parte di
undertake *vt* intraprendere, **-r** *n* imprenditore *m*, imprenditrice *f*; impresario di pompe funebri
undertaking *n* impresa
undertone *n* tono basso (*or* fievole); sfumatura; **in an** — sottovoce
undervalue *vt* sottovalutare, svalutare
underwear *n* biancheria intima
underweight *a* troppo magro
underworld *n* oltretomba; inferno; bassifondi *mpl*; — *a* d'oltretomba; dei bassifondi
underwrite *vt* sottoscrivere, garantire, assicurare; **-r** *n* assicuratore *m*; garante *m*
undeserved *a* immeritato, ingiusto; **-ly** *adv* immeritatamente, ingiustamente
undeserving *a* immeritevole
undesirable *a* sgradito, indesiderabile
undetected *a* nascosto, segreto, non scoperto
undetermined *a* indeterminato, indeciso
undeterred *a* non scoraggiato, non distolto
undeveloped *a* non sviluppato
undeviating *a* diritto, costante, non deviante
undigested *a* indigesto, non digerito
undignified *a* senza dignità
undiluted *a* non diluito
undiminished *a* non diminuito, intero
undiplomatic *a* poco diplomatico
undirected *a* senza direzione
undiscerned *a* inosservato
undiscernible *a* indiscernibile
undiscerning *a* senza discernimento
undisciplined *a* indisciplinato
undiscovered *a* non scoperto
undisclosed *a* nascosto, segreto
undiscriminating *a* senza discernimento, di cattivo gusto
undisguised *a* aperto, non mascherato; **-ly** *adv* apertamente, francamente
undismayed *a* non scoraggiato, senza paura, fermo
undisputed *a* indisputato, indiscusso, incontrastato; fuori discussione
undissolved *a* non disciolto
undistinguishable *a* indistinguibile
undistinguished *a* non distinto; non famoso; volgare, comune
undistorted *a* non distorto
undisturbed *a* indisturbato
undivided *a* indiviso
undo *vt* disfare, sciogliere
undoing *n* rovina; annullamento
undone *a* sciolto, disfatto; rovinato; **come** — sciogliersi

undoubtedly *adv* indubbiamente, senza dubbio
undress *vt* spogliare; — *vi* spogliarsi, svestirsi; **-ed** *a* svestito; non preparato, grezzo
undrinkable *a* imbevibile
undue *a* eccessivo, inconveniente
undulate *vi* ondeggiare; fluttuare; — *vt* far ondeggiare, ondulare
unduly *adv* eccessivamente
undying *a* imperituro, immortale
unearned *a* immeritato, non guadagnato
unearth *vt* dissotterrare scavare; scoprire; **-ed** *a* dissotterrato; scoperto; **-ly** *a* soprannaturale
uneasiness *n* disagio, inquietudine *f*, turbamento
uneasy *a* inquieto, turbato
uneaten *a* non mangiato
unedible *a* immangiabile
uneducated *a* incolto, ignorante
unemotional *a* impassibile, non emotivo
unemployed *a&n* disoccupato
unemployment *n* disoccupazione; — **insurance** assicurazione contro la disoccupazione
unencumbered *a* sgombro; libero di gravami, non ipotecato
unending *a* interminabile
unendurable *a* insopportabile, intollerabile
unenlightened *a* ignorante
unenterprising *a* poco intraprendente
unenviable *a* non invidiabile
unequal *a* ineguale, disuguale; inadatto; **-ed** *a* ineguagliato; **-ly** *adv* inegualmente
unequivocal *a* franco, chiaro; inequivocabile
unerring *a* infallibile
unessential *a* non essenziale, superfluo
uneven *a* ineguale; non piano; dispari; **-ness** *n* ineguaglianza, disuguaglianza; disparità
uneventful *a* senza novità, calmo, monotono
unexampled *a* senza precedenti, inaudito
unexcelled *a* non sorpassato, insuperato
unexceptionable *a* irreprensibile
unexciting *a* non eccitante
unexpected *a* inatteso, inaspettato; **-ly** all'improvviso
unexpired *a* non spirato, non scaduto
unexplained *a* non spiegato, inesplicato
unexplored *a* inesplorato
unexposed *a* non esposto, protetto; nascosto, segreto
unexpressed *a* inespresso
unexpurgated *a* integro, inespurgato
unfaded *a* non appassito, non scolorito

unfailing *a* infallibile
unfair *a* ingiusto; parziale; **–ly** *adv* disonestamente, ingiustamente; **–ness** *n* ingiustizia; parzialità
unfaithful *a* infedele; **–ness** *n* infedeltà
unfaltering *a* deciso, fermo
unfamiliar *a* poco pratico; sconosciuto; **–ity** *n* mancanza di familiarità
unfashionable *a* fuori moda
unfasten *vt* slegare, aprire, sciogliere; — *vi* slegarsi
unfathomable *a* insondabile
unfavorable *a* sfavorevole
unfeasible *a* impraticabile, non fattibile
unfeeling *a* insensibile
unfeigned *a* genuino, non finto
unfertile *a* non fertile, sterile
unfettered *a* senza catene, senza ceppi; libero, illimitato
unfilled *a* vuoto; vacante
unfinished *a* incompleto
unfit *a* incapace; inadatto; **–ness** *n* incapacità; **–ting** *a* sconveniente
unflagging *a* infaticabile
unflattering *a* poco lusinghiero
unflinching *a* risoluto, imperterrito
unfold *vt* spiegare, rivelare; — *vt* spiegarsi
unforced *a* spontaneo
unforeseen *a* inatteso, imprevisto
unforgettable *a* indimenticabile
unforgivable *a* imperdonabile
unforgiven *a* senza perdono, non perdonato
unforgiving *a* implacabile
unforgotten *a* non dimenticato
unformulated *a* non formulato
unfortified *a* debole, non fortificato, indifeso
unfortunate *a* disgraziato, sfortunato, infelice; **–ly** *adv* sfortunatamente, per sfortuna
unfounded *a* infondato
unfrequented *a* infrequentato
unfriendliness *n* inimicizia
unfriendly *a* mal disposto, poco amichevole, sfavorevole; ostile
unfrock *vt (eccl)* spretare
unfruitful *a* infruttuoso; sterile
unfulfilled *a* incompiuto, inadempiuto
unfurl *vt* spiegare, aprire; — *vi* distendersi
unfurnished *a* non ammobiliato
ungainliness *n* goffaggine *f*
ungainly *a* maldestro, goffo; — *adv* maldestramente, goffamente
ungenerous *a* meschino, ingeneroso
ungentlemanly *a* grossolano, rozzo, volgare
ungird *vt* scingere

unglazed *a* senza vetri; non lucidato
ungodliness *a* empietà
ungodly *a* empio; *(coll)* orrendo
ungovernable *a* ingovernabile
ungraceful *a* sgraziato, senza grazia
ungracious *a* scortese; antipatico; **–ly** *adv* scortesemente; **–ness** *n* scortesia, grossolanità
ungrammatical *a* scorretto, non grammaticale
ungrateful *a* ingrato, non riconoscente; **–ness** ingratitudine *f*
ungratified *a* insoddisfatto, non appagato
ungrounded *a* infondato
ungrudging *a* liberale, generoso, dí buon cuore; **–ly** *adv* generosamente, di buon cuore, volentieri
unguarded *a* incostudito
unguent *n* unguento
ungulate *n&a* ungulato
unhallowed *a* profano, non consacrato
unhampered *a* non impedito, disimbarazzato
unhand *vt* lasciar andare, lasciare
unhandy *a* maldestro
unhappily *adv* sfortunatamente
unhappiness *n* infelicità, sfortuna
unhappy *a* infelice, scontento, sfortunato
unharmed, unhurt *a* illeso, sano e salvo
unhealthful *a* insalubre
unhealthiness *n* insalubrità
unhealthy *a* malsano, malaticcio
unheard *a* non udito
unheard-of *a* inaudito
unheated *a* non riscaldato
unheeding *a* negligente, disattento
unhesitating *a* risoluto, non esitante; **–ly** *adv* senza esitazione, risolutamente
unhindered *a* disimpacciato, non ostacolato
unhinge *vt* sgangherare; *(mind)* disordinare
unhitch *vt* staccare
unholy *a* empio; *(coll)* terribile
unhoped-for *a* insperato
unhorse *vt* scavalcare
unhook *vt* sganciare
unhurried *a* calmo; **–ly** *adv* senza fretta
unicorn *n* unicorno
unidentified *a* non identificato
unification *n* unificazione
uniform *a&n* uniforme *f*; **–ly** *a* uniformemente
uniformity *n* uniformità
unify *vt* unificare
unilateral *a* unilaterale
unimaginable *a* inimmaginabile
unimaginative *a* senza immaginazione
unimpaired *a* integro, non indebolito
unimpeachable *a* inattaccabile, inconte-

stabile

unimpeded *a* senza ostacoli, non impedito

unimportant *a* poco importante, insignificante

unimposed *a* volontario

unimposing *a* poco imponente

unimpressed *a* non impressionato

unimpressionable *a* non impressionabile

unimpressive *a* poco impressionante

unimproved *a* non migliorato

uninflammable *a* non infiammabile

uninfluenced *a* non influenzato

uninfluential *a* senza influenza

uninformed *a* ignaro, non informato, ignorante

uninhabitable *a* inabitabile

uninhabited *a* disabitato, inabitato

uninitiated *a* non iniziato

uninjured *a* incolume, illeso

uninspired *a* senza ispirazione, non ispirato

unintelligent *a* stupido, poco intelligente

unintelligible *a* incomprensibile

unintentional *a* involontario

uninterested *a* disinteressato

uninteresting *a* poco interessante

uninterrupted *a* ininterrotto

uninvited *a* non invitato

uninviting *a* poco attraente

union *n* unione *f*; **labor —** sindacato; **–ist** *n* unionista *m&f*

unique *a* solo, unico

unison *n* unisono; **in —** all'unisono

unit *n* unità; *(mil)* reparto

Unitarian *n&a* unitario

unite *vt* unire; **—** *vi* unirsi

united *a* unito

United Arab Republic Repubbliche Arabe Unite

United Kingdom Regno Unito

United Nations Nazioni Unite

United States of America Stati Uniti d'America

unity *n* unità

univalent *a* univalente, monovalente

universal *a* universale; **–ity** *n* universalità; **–ly** *adv* universalmente

universe *n* universo

university *n* università; **—** *a* universitario

unjust *a* ingiusto; **–ly** *adv* ingiustamente

unjustifiable *a* ingiustificabile

unjustified *a* ingiustificato

unkempt *a* trasandato, spettinato, scarmigliato

unkind *a* sgarbato, poco gentile; **–ness** scortesia

unknot *vt* slegare, snodare

unknowable *a* inconoscibile

unknowingly *adv* inconsapevolmente

unknown *n* sconosciuto; *(math)* incognita;

— *a* sconosciuto, ignoto

unlace *vt* slacciare; **–d** *a* slacciato

unladylike *a* non degno d'una signora

unlatch *vt* disserrare

unlawful *a* illegale, illegittimo, illecito; **–ly** *adv* illecitamente; **–ness** *n* illegalità

unlearn *vt* disimparare; **–ed** non imparato; *(person)* ignorante

unleash *vt* sguinzagliare

unleavened *a* senza lievito, non fermentato; **— bread** pane azzimo

unless *conj* a meno che, salvo che, se non

unlettered *a* ignorante, illetterato, analfabeta

unlicensed *a* senza licenza *(or permesso)*

unlifelike *a* inverosimile

unlike *a* dissimile; **—** *prep* diverso di; **–lihood** *n* improbabilità, inverosimiglianza

unlikely *a* improbabile

unlimited illimitato

unlined *a (paper)* senza righe; *(clothing)* non foderato

unload *vt* scaricare; disfarsi di; **–ing** *n* scarico; **–ed** *a* scaricato, scarico

unlock *vt* disserrare, aprire; **–ed** aperto, dischiuso

unlooked-for inaspettato, inatteso

unloosen *vt* sciogliere, allentare

unlovable *a* antipatico, detestabile

unloving *a* insensibile, non sentimentale, impassivo

unluckiness *n* sfortuna

unlucky *a* sfortunato, disgraziato, sventurato

unman *vt* snervare

unmanageable *a* ribelle, intrattabile

unmanly *a* effeminato, vile, pusillanime

unmannerly *adv* grossolanamente, rozzamente; **—** *a* scortese, sgarbato

unmarked *a* non marcato, non contrassegnato

unmarketable *a* invendibile

unmarried *a* non sposato

unmask *vt* smascherare; **—** *vi* smascherasi

unmatched *a* scompagnato, spaiato; incomparato

unmeant *a* involontario

unmeasurable *a* immisurabile

unmelodious *a* stonato, discordante

unmentionable *a* innominabile

unmerciful *a* spietato, senza misericordia

unmerited *a* immeritato

unmindful *a* negligente, smemorato, sventato

unmistakable *a* indubbio, evidente

unmistakably *adv* evidentemente, senza errore, senza dubbio, inequivocabilmente

unmitigated non mitigato; *(complete)*

assoluto
unmixed *a* puro, non mischiato, non misto
unmodified *a* non modificato
unmolested *a* indisturbato
unmounted *a (jewel)* non incastonato
unmoor *vt* disormeggiare
unmourned *a* illagrimato
unmoved *a* immobile; impassibile, inesorabile
unmurmering *a* rassegnato
unnamed anonimo, innominato
unnatural *a* innaturale, non naturale; snaturato, contro natura
unnavigable *a* innavigabile
unnecessary *a* superfluo
unneeded *a* innecessario
unnegotiable *a (com)* non negoziabile
unnerve *vt* snervare
unnoticeable *a* inosservabile
unnoticed, unobserved *a* inosservato
unnumbered *a* innumerabile
unobjectionable *a* ineccepibile
unobliging *a* scompiacente
unobservant *a* inosservante
unobstructed *a* inostruito, non impedito
unobtainable *a* inottenibile
unobtrusive *a* modesto, discreto, riservato; **–ly** *adv* modestamente, discretamente
unoccupied *a* disoccupato; libero, vacante, non occupato
unofficial *a* non ufficiale, ufficioso
unopened *a* chiuso, non aperto
unopposed *a* incontrastato, senza opposizione
unoriginal *a* non originale
unorthodox *a* eterodosso
unostentatious *a* semplice, senza fasto
unpack *vt* disfare, spacchettare, sballare; **—** *vi* disfare i bagagli
unpaid *a* non pagato; *(com)* in sospeso; non saldato
unpalatable *a* sgradevole
unparalleled *a* ineguagliabile, incomparato, senza paralleli *(coll)*
unpardonable *a* imperdonabile
unpatriotic *a* non patriottico, poco patriottico
unpaved *a* non pavimentato, senza selciato
unperceivable *a* inosservabile
unperceived *a* inosservato
unperturbed *a* imperturbato
unpin *vt* levare gli spilli da; staccare
unpitying *a* spietato
unpleasant *a* spiacevole; **–ness** *n* spiacevolezza; disaccordo
unpleasing *a* spiacevole
unpolished *a (person)* grossolano, rozzo; *(surface)* grezzo, non lucidato

unpolluted *a* incontaminato
unpopular *a* non popolare, impopolare, non gradito; **–ity** *n* impopolarità
unpracticed *a* inesperto
unprecedented *a* senza precedenti, inaudito
unprejudiced *a* spregiudicato, senza pregiudizi, imparziale
unpremeditated *a* impremeditato
unprepared *a* impreparato
unprepossessing *a* poco attraente
unpresentable *a* impresentabile
unpresuming *a* senza presunzione
unpretentious *a* senza pretese
unpreventable inevitabile
unprincipled *a* immorale, senza principi
unprintable *a* inatto alla stampa, non pubblicabile
unproductive *a* improduttivo
unprofitable *a* inutile, senza profitto, non vantaggioso
unprogressive *a* conservatore, antiprogressivo
unpromising *a* non promettente
unprompted *a* spontaneo, senza suggerimento
unpronounceable *a* impronunziabile
unpropitious *a* impropizio, sfavorevole
unprotected *a* senza protezione, improtetto
unprovable *a* indimostrabile, improvabile
unproved *a* indimostrato, improvato
unprovided *a* sprovvisto
unprovoked *a* non provocato, senza provocazione
unpublished *a* inedito
unpunished *a* impunito
unqualified *a* incompetente; senza riserva; *(law)* senza titoli; *(official)* non autorizzato
unquenchable *a* inestinguibile, insaziabile, indomabile
unquestionable *a* indiscutibile
unquestioned *a* incontestato; non interrogato
unquestioning *a* indiscusso, assoluto
unravel *vt* sbrogliare, dipanare, sfilacciare
unraveled *a* sciolto, dipanato
unread *a (not)* non letto; *(uneducated)* ignorante, incolto; **–able** *a* illeggibile
unreal *a* irreale
unreasonable *a* irragionevole
unreasoning *a* irragionevole
unreciprocated *a* non contraccambiato
unrecognizable *a* irriconoscibile
unrecognized *a* sconosciuto, misconosciuto
unreconcilable *a* inconciliabile
unreconciled *a* inconciliato
unrecorded *a* dimenticato; non registrato

unrectified *a* non rettificato
unredeemed *a* irredento, non riscattato; non ammortizzato; non rimborsato
unredressed *a* non riparato
unreel *vt* svolgere, sgomitolare; — *vi* svolgersi, sgomitolarsi
unreformed *a* non corretto, non riformato
unrefined *a* crudo, grezzo, non raffinato; rozzo
unrefuted *a* irrefutato
unrehearsed *a* improvvisato
unrelated *a* senza rapporti, non imparentato
unrelenting *a* inesorabile, inflessibile
unreliability *n* inattendibilità
unreliable *a* inattendibile; instabile
unremitting *a* assiduo, incessante, senza tregua
unremunerative *a* infruttifero, non rimunerativo
unrepealed *a* non revocato
unrepentant *a* impenitente, incorreggibile
unrepresentative *a* non rappresentativo
unrequited *a* non ricambiato, non corrisposto
unreserved *a* schietto, non riservato; illimitato
unresponsible irresponsabile
unresponsive *a* insensibile, impassibile
unrest *n* inquietudine *f*; sedizione
unrestrained *a* sfrenato, irrepresso
unrestricted *a* illimitato, senza restrizione
unrevenged *a* invendicato
unrewarded *a* irretribuito, senza ricompensa
unrighteous *a* malvagio, iniquo
unripe *a* acerbo, immaturo
unrivaled *a* impareggiabile, senza rivale
unroll *vt* svolgere; — *vi* svolgersi
unromantic *a* non romantico
unruffled *a* calmo, liscio; non increspato
unruled *a* senza righe
unruliness *n* indisciplina
unruly *a* indisciplinato
unsaddle *vt* dissellare, disarcionare
unsafe *a* malsicuro, pericoloso
unsaid *a* non detto
unsalable *a* invendibile
unsalted *a* non salato
unsanctioned *a* non sanzionato
unsanitary *a* insalubre, antigienico
unsatiable *a* insaziabile
unsatisfactory *a* non soddisfacente
unsatisfied *a* insoddisfatto
unsatisfying *a* insoddisfacente
unscathed *a* illeso, incolume
unschooled *a* inesperto, non istruito
unscientific *a* non scientifico
unscrew *vt* svitare
unscrupulous *a* senza scrupoli

unseal *vt* togliere i sigilli da; aprire, dissigillare; **–ed** *a* aperto, non sigillato
unseasonable *a* inopportuno, intempestivo; fuori stagione
unseasoned *a* non stagionato; *(food)* non condito; *(unaccustomed)* non abituato
unseat *vt* deporre; *(horse)* disarcionare; *(pol)* silurare *(fig)*
unseeing *a* non veggente, cieco
unseemliness *a* sconvenienza, indecenza
unseemly *a* sconveniente
unseen *a* invisibile; non visto
unselfish *a* altruista, non egoista; **–ly** *adv* disinteressatamente; **–ness** *n* altruismo, disinteresse *m*
unserviceable *a* inservibile, fuori uso
unsettle *vt* sconvolgere, turbare, disorganizzare
unsettled *a* incerto, disordinato; squilibrato; inabitato; — **accounts** conti pendenti, conti non saldati
unshakeable *a* fermo, irremovibile
unshaken *a* fermo, saldo; imperturbato, imperterrito
unshapely *a* informe, deforme, sgraziato
unshaven *a* non sbarbato
unsheathe *vt* sfoderare, sguainare
unsheltered *a* improtetto, non riparato
unshoe *vt (horse)* togliere i ferri a
unshrinkable *a* irrestringibile
unsightly *a* brutto, sgradevole, deforme
unsigned *a* non firmato, senza firma
unsinkable *a* inaffondabile, non sommergibile
unskillful *a* imperito, inesperto, malaccorto
unskilled *a* inesperto; non specializzato
unsociable *a* insocievole
unsoiled *a* puro, non sporcato, pulito
unsold *a* invenduto
unsolicited *a* non sollecitato, non richiesto
unsolicitous *a* non preoccupato, incurante
unsolved *a* insoluto
unsophisticated *a* semplice
unsought *a* non richiesto
unsound *a* difettoso; errato; malsicuro, debole; **–ness** *n* instabilità; insalubrità; **–ly** *adv* instabilmente, male; non sanamente
unsounded *a* non sondato
unsparing *a* prodigo; inesorabile
unspeakable *a* indicibile; orribile
unspecified *a* non specificato
unspoiled *a* non rovinato, non guasto; *(child)* ben allevato
unspoken *a* non detto, taciuto
unsportsmanlike *a* antisportivo
unstable *a* instabile
unstained *a (character)* immacolato, senza macchia; non dipinto

unstamped *a* non affrancato
unstarched *a* non inamidato
unstated *a* non dichiarato
unsteadiness *n* instabilità
unsteady *a* instabile
unstinted *a* copioso, abbondante
unstrap *vt* sfasciare, slegare
unstressed *a* atono, senza accento
unstring *vt* slegare, sfilare; *(nerves)* snervare
unstrung *a (mus)* senza corde; snervato
unstudied *a* naturale, non sforzato
unsubdued *a* indomato, non sottomesso, indomito
unsubstantial *a* poco sostanziale, poco solido
unsubstantiated *a* non confermato
unsuccessful *a* infruttuoso, senza successo, vano; **–ly** *adv* infruttuosamente, senza successo
unsuitable *a* inadatto, non appropriato, intempestivo
unsuited *a* inadatto, inadeguato
unsullied *a* immacolato, senza macchia, non sporcato
unsung *a* non celebrato
unsupported *a* non sostenuto, non confermato
unsure *a* malsicuro, incerto, pericolante
unsurmountable *a* insormontabile
unsurpassable *a* insorpassabile
unsurpassed *a* insuperato
unsusceptible *a* non suscettibile
unsuspected *a* insospettato
unsuspecting *a* senza sospetto
unsuspicious *a* non sospettoso
unswayed *a* non influenzato
unsweetened *a* non addolcito
unswerving *a* non deviante, fermo, irremovibile
unsymmetrical *a* asimmetrico
unsympathetic *a* non simpatico; ostico; incompassionevole; **–ally** *adv* ostilmente; senza simpatia
unsystematic *a* senza metodo, non sistematico
untainted *a* incorrotto, non guasto
untalented *a* senza talento
untamable *a* indomabile
untamed *a* indomito, non addomesticato
untangle *vt* dipanare, sbrogliare
untapped *a* non utilizzato
untarnished *a* non macchiato, puro; *(moral)* senza macchia
untenable *a* insostenibile
untenanted *a* sfitto, senza inquilini
untended *a* incustodito
untested *a* non collaudato
unthinkable *a* impensabile
unthinking *a* sventato, spensierato

unthought-of impensato
untidiness *n* disordine *m*
untidy *a* disordinato
untie *vt* sciogliere, slegare
until *prep* fino a; — *conj* finchè, finchè non; fino a quando
untillable *a* non coltivabile
untilled *a* non coltivato
untimeliness *n* intempestività
untimely *a* prematuro; inopportuno
untiring *a* indefesso, instancabile
untold *a* non detto; incalcolabile, inesprimibile
untouchable *a* intoccabile, impalpabile
untouched *a* intatto, intoccato
untrained *a* inesperto, non esercitato, non allenato
untrammeled *a* senza impacci, non inceppato
untranslatable *a* intraducibile
untraveled *a (person)* che non ha viaggiato molto; *(road)* non percorso, infrequentato
untried *a* non provato, intentato; non processato
untrimmed *a* disadorno, non guarnito; intonso
untrodden *a* non frequentato
untroubled *a* imperturbato, sereno
untrue *a* mendace, falso; *(faithless)* infedele
untrustworthy *a* mendace, indegno di fede
untruth *n* bugia, menzogna, falsità; **–ful** *a* bugiardo; **–fully** *adv* falsamente; **–fulness** *n* falsità
unfurned *a* non girato, non voltato
untutored *a* ignorante, senza istruzione
unusable *a* inusabile, fuori uso
unused *a* non abituato
unusual *a* insolito; **–ness** *n* stranezza, straordinarietà; **–ly** *adv* straordinariamente, insolitamente
unvanquished *a* invitto
unvaried *a* invariato
unvarnished *a* non verniciato; *(fig)* naturale, schietto
unvarying *a* invariabile
unveil *vt* svelare; rivelare; **–ing** *n* scoprimento, inaugurazione
unverifiable *a* non verificabile
unverified *a* non verificato
unversed *a* inabile, inesperto
unvoiced *a* inespresso, non pronunciato; *(gram)* muto
unwanted *a* non richiesto, indesiderato
unwarranted *a* ingiustificato; *(com)* senza garanzia, gratuito
unwary *a* sventato, imprudente
unwavering *a* irremovibile, incrollabile
unweakened *a* non indebolito

unwearing *a* instancabile
unwelcome *a* sgradito
unwell *a* indisposto
unwholesome *a* malsano, nocivo
unwieldy *a* ingombrante, poco maneggevole; *(clumsy)* goffo
unwilling *a* restio, maldisposto, riluttante; **–ly** *adv* malvolentieri
unwind *vt* svolgere, srotolare; — *vi* srotolarsi, svolgersi
unwise *a* imprudente
unwitnessed *n* senza testimoni
unwitting *a* inconsapevole, inconscio; **–ly** *adv* inconsapevolmente
unwonted *a* non abituato
unworkable *a* non lavorabile, inattuabile
unworked *a* non lavorato, incoltivato
unworldly *a* non mondano, spirituale
unworthiness *n* indegnità
unworthy *a* indegno
unwounded *a* illeso
unwrap *vt* aprire, districare, togliere da un involucro
unwrapped *a* sfasciato, non involto
unwrinkled *a* liscio, spianato, senza grinze
unwritten *a* tradizionale, non scritto
unyielding *a* inflessibile, rigido
unyoke *vt* togliere il giogo a
up *n* aumento; **–s and downs** alti e bassi; — *a* in su; montante, salente; scaduto; in piedi; *(sport)* in vantaggio; — *prep* su; su per, verso l'alto di; — to fino a
up *vt* mettere su, alzare; — *vi* alzarsi; **be — to** *(coll)* essere capace di, essere in grado di; **bring — *(child)*** educare, allevare; **make —** inventare; *(peace)* rapacificarsi; *(cosmetics)* truccarsi; **speak —** *(openly)* parlare chiaro; *(loudly)* parlare ad alta voce; **walk — and down** camminare su e giù
upbraid *vt* rimproverare
upbringing *n* allevamento, educazione
upheaval *n* sollevamento, tumulto, confusione
uphill *adv* in salita, in su; — *a* montante, difficile
uphold *vt* sostenere, sollevare; **–er** *n* sostenitore *m*
upholster *vt* tappezzare, imbottire; **–y** *n* tappezzeria; **–er** *n* tappezziere *m*
upkeep *n* mantenimento
upland *n* altipiano
uplift *n* edificazione; sollevazione; **–ed** *a* sollevato, elevato, edificato; — *vt* elevare, edificare
uplifting *a* edificante
upon *prep&adv* su, sopra
upper *a* superiore, più in alto; **— case** maiuscole *fpl*; **–cut** *n (boxing)* colpo all'insù; **— hand** superiorità, vantaggio

upper-case *a* maiuscolo
upper-class *a* di classe alta
uppermost *a* superiore, il più alto; — *adv* su, sopra, in alto, al disopra di tutti
upright *a* diritto; onesto
uprising *n* insurrezione
uproar *n* tumulto; **–ious** *a* tumultuoso
uproot *vt* sradicare, estirpare
upset *vt* sconvolgere, rovesciare, agitare; — *vi* capovolgersi; turbarsi; — *a* rovesciato; — *n* sconvolgimento
upshot *n* esito, conclusione
upside-down *a* disordinato
upstairs *adv* sopra, su; — *a* disopra; — *n* piano superiore
upstanding *a* diritto, eretto, onorabile
upstart *n* villano rifatto, nuovo ricco
upstream *adv* a monte
up-to-date *a* aggiornato
upturn *vt* volgere in su; **–ed** *a* volto in su
upward *a&adv* in su, in alto
uranium *n* uranio
urban *a* urbano; **–ity** urbanità
urbane *a* cortese
urchin *n* monello
urea *n* urea
uremia *n* uremia
uremic *a* uremico
ureter *n* uretere *m*
urge *vt* esortare, pregare; — *n* impulso, impeto
urgency *n* urgenza; bisogno
urgent *a* urgente
urging *n* sollecitazione
uric *a* urico
urinal *n* orinale *m*, orinatoio; **–ysis** *n* analisi delle urine
urinate *vi* orinare
urine *n* orina
urn *n* urna; **coffee —** caffettiera
us *pron* noi; ci
usable *a* servibile
usage *n* usanza, uso
use *n* uso, impiego; **–fulness** *n* utilità; **be of —** essere utile; **make — of** far uso di; **What's the —?** A che serve? **–r** *n* utente *m*, chi usa; **–ful** *a* utile; **–less** *a* inutile
use *vt* usare, adoperare, utilizzare; trattare
used *a* usato; abituato; **be — to** essere abituato a; **get — to** abituarsi a; **— up** esaurito, esausto, consumato
usher *n* usciere, portiere *m*; *(theat)* accompagnatore *m*; — *vt* scortare; **— in** annunciare
USSR, Union of Soviet Socialist Republics Unione Repubbliche Sovietiche Socialiste
usual *a* solito, comune; **as —** come al solito; **–ly** *adv* ordinariamente, di solito
usurp *vt* usurpare; **–er** *n* usurpatore *m*,

usurpatrice *f*
usurpation *n* usurpazione
usury *n* usura
utensil *n* utensile *m*
uterus *n* utero
utilitarian *a* utilitario
utility *n* utilità; **public —** servizio di pubblica utilità

utilization *n* utilizzazione
utilize *vt* utilizzare
utmost *a* sommo, estremo; **—** *n* massimo
utter *a* estremo, totale; **—** *vt* dire, proferire
utterance *n* espressione
utterly *adv* assolutamente, completamente
uvula *n* ugola

V

vacancy *n* posto libero, vacanza, spazio libero; stanza (*or* appartamento) da affittare
vacant *a* vuoto, libero; (*person*) distratto
vacate *vt* sgombrare, lasciar libero
vacation *n* vacanze, ferie *fpl*
vaccinate *vt* vaccinare
vaccination *n* vaccinazione
vaccine *n* vaccino
vacillate *vi* vacillare
vacillation *n* vacillazione
vacuum *n* vuoto; **— cleaner** aspirapolvere *m*; **— tube** (*elec*) valvola termoionica; **—** *vt* pulire con l'aspirapolvere
vagabond *a&n* vagabondo
vagary *n* capriccio
vagina *n* (*anat*) vagina
vagrancy *n* vagabondaggio
vagrant *n&a* vagabondo
vague *a* vago, incerto; **–ly** *adv* vagamente; **–ness** *n* vaghezza
vain *a* vano; vanitoso; **in —** invano; **–ness — *n* vanità; inutilità
vainglorious *a* vanitoso, vanaglorioso
vainglory *n* vanagloria
valedictorian *n* (*school*) oratore che pronuncia il commiato
valedictory *n* discorso di commiato **—** *a* di commiato
valence *n* (*chem*) valenza
valet *n* valletto
valiant *a* prode, valoroso; **–ly** *adv* valorosamente
valid *a* valido; **–ation** *n* convalidazione
validate *vt* convalidare
validity *n* validità
valise *n* valigia
valley *n* valle *f*, vallata
valor *n* valore *m*; **–ous** *a* valoroso; **–ously** *adv* valorosamente
valuable *a* costoso, prezioso, valutabile; **–s** *npl* preziosi *mpl*
valuation *n* stima, valutazione
value *n* valore *m*; **of no —** senza valore; **face —** valore nominale; **–d** *a* stimato, valutato; **–less** *a* senza valore; **—** *vt* valutare, stimare
valve *n* valvola; **exhaust —** valvola di

scappamento; **safety —** valvola di sicurezza
valvular *a* valvolare
vamp *n* (*shoe*) tomaia; (*flirt*) donna fatale, civetta; (*mus*) improvvisazione; **—** *vt* mettere la tomaia; (*patch*) rappezzare; (*beguile*) adescare
vampire *n* vampiro
van *n* furgone *m*, carro; **–guard** avanguardia
vanadium *n* vanadio
Van Allen radiation belt zona radioattiva Van Allen
vandal *n* vandalo; **–ism** *n* vandalismo
Vandyke *n* pizzo a punta
vane *n* banderuola
vanilla *n* vaniglia; **— bean** chicco di vaniglia
vanish *vi* svanire, sparire; **–ed** *a* svanito, sparito, scomparso
vanishing *n* sparizione, scomparsa; **—** *a* che sparisce, evanescente; **— cream** crema evanescente (*or* volatile); **— point** punto all'infinito
vanity *n* vanità; (*furniture*) pettiniera; **— case** portacipria
vanquish *vt* vincere, sopraffare; **–ed** *a* vinto, conquistato; **–er** *n* vincitore *m*
vantage *n* vantaggio; **— point** punto di vantaggio
vapid *a* insipido; **–ity** *n* insipidità; **–ness** *n* insipidezza
vapor *n* vapore *m*; **–ous** *a* vaporoso
vaporization *n* vaporizzazione
vaporize *vt* vaporizzare; **—** *vi* evaporizzare; **–r** *n* vaporizzatore *m*
variability *n* variabilità
variable *a* variabile
variably *adv* variabilmente
variance *n* disaccordo; divergenza; **at — with** in disaccordo con
variant *n* variante *f*; **—** *a* vario, variante, variabile
variation *n* variazione; modifica
varicose *a* varicoso; **— vein** vena varicosa
varied *a* vario, assortito, variato
variegate *vt* variare
variety *n* varietà

various *a* vario, diverso
varnish *n* vernice *f*; — *vt* verniciare; **–ing** *n* verniciatura
vary *vt&i* variare; **–ing** *a* variante
vascular *a* vascolare
vase *n* vaso
vaseline *n* vaselina
vasomotor *a (anat)* vasomotore
vassal *n* vassallo
vast *a* immenso, vasto; **–ness** *n* vastità, immensità; **–ly** *adv* vastamente
vat *n* tino
Vatican *n* Vaticano; — **City** Città del Vaticano
vaudeville *n* operetta
vault *n* salto; *(arch)* volta; *(bank)* camera blindata; *(burial)* tomba; *(cellar)* sotterraneo, cantina; **–ing** *n* volteggio; — *vi (jump)* volteggiare; — *vt (arch)* costruire a volta
vaunt *vt* vantare; — *n* vanto; **–ing** *n* millanteria
veal *n* vitello; — **cutlet** cotoletta di vitello
vedette *n (mil)* vedetta
veer *n* virata; — *vi* virare, cambiare direzione; — *vt* voltare
vegetable *n* legume *m*, verdura; — *a* vegetale
vegetarian *a&n* vegetariano; **–ism** *n* vegetarianismo
vegetate *vi* vegetare
vegetation *n* vegetazione
vehemence *n* veemenza
vehement *a* veemente; **–ly** *adv* veementemente
vehicle *n* veicolo
vehicular *a* di veicolo
veil *n* velo; **–ed** *a* velato; — *vt* velare; nascondere
vein *n* vena; umore *m*; **–ing** *n* venatura; **–ed** *a* venato
veiny *a* venoso
vellum *n* pergamena, cartapecora
velocipede *n* velocipede *m*
velocity *n* velocità
velum *n (anat)* velo
velvet *n* velluto; — *a* di velluto, vellutato
velveteen *n* velluto di cotone
venal *a* venale; **–ity** *n* venalità, **–ly** *adv* venalmente
vend *vt* vendere
vending machine distributore automatico, distributrice a gettone
vendor *n* venditore *m*, venditrice *f*
veneer *n (furniture)* impiallacciatura; — *vt* impiallacciare
venerability *n* venerabilità
venerable *a* venerabile
venerably *adv* venerabilmente
venerate *vt* venerare

veneration *n* venerazione
venereal *a* venereo; — **disease** malattia venerea
Venetian *n&a* veneziano; — **blinds** persiane, gelosie *fpl*
vengeance *n* vendetta; **to wreak** — vendicarsi
vengeful *a* vendicativo; **–ly** *adv* vendicativamente
venial *a* veniale; — **sin** peccato veniale; **–ity** *n* venialità
Venice Venezia
venison *n* carne di cervo
venom *n* veleno; **–ous** *a* velenoso; *(person)* maldicente, malevolo
vent *n* apertura, sfogo; **to give** — **to** dar sfogo a; — *vt* sfogare
ventilate *vt* ventilare
ventilation *n* ventilazione
ventilator *n* ventilatore *m*
ventral *a* ventrale
ventricle *n* ventricolo
ventriloquism *n* ventriloquio
ventriloquist *n* ventriloquo
venture *n* impresa; **–some** *a* avventuroso; — *vt&i* tentare, azzardare, avventurarsi, rischiare
venue *n (law)* sede *f*
veracious *a* verace
veracity *n* veracità
verb *n* verbo
verbal *a* verbale; — **ly** *adv* oralmente
verbatim *a* testuale; — *adv* testualmente
verbose *a* verboso
verbosity *n* verbosità
verdant *a* verdeggiante
verdict *n* verdetto
verdigris *n* verderame *m*
verdure *n* verzura
verge *n* orlo; limite *m*; **on the** — **of** sull'orlo di; — *vi* propendere, tendere; — **on** essere vicino a
verger *n* sagrestano
verifiable *a* verificabile
verification *n* verifica
verify *vt* verificare
verisimilitude *n* verosimiglianza
veritable *a* vero
verity *n* verità
vermiform *a* vermiforme; — **appendix** appendice vermiforme
vermilion *n&a* vermiglione *m*
vermin *npl* insetti e animali nocivi; **–ous** *a* verminoso
vermouth *n* vermut *m*
vernacular *a&n* volgare *m*
vernal *a* primaverile; — **equinox** equinozio di primavera
versatile *a* versatile
versatility *n* versatilità

verse *n* verso, strofa; poesia; **–d** *a* versato
versifier *n* versificatore *m*
versify *vt* versificare
version *n* versione
versus *prep* contro
vertebra *n (anat)* vertebra
vertebral *a* vertebrale
vertebrate *n&a* vertebrato
vertex *n* vertice *m*
vertical *a* verticale
vertiginous *a* vertiginoso
vertigo *n (med)* vertigine *f*
verve *n* entusiasmo, vigore *m*, brio
very *adv* molto; — *a* stesso, vero; **at the**
— **last** proprio all'ultimo
vesicle *n* vescichetta, pustola
vespers *npl* vespri *mpl*
vessel *n* nave *f*, vascello; *(anat)* vaso; *(container)* recipiente *m*
vest *n* gilè *m*, panciotto
vest *vt* investire, conferire
vestibule *n* vestibolo
vestige *n* traccia
vestigial *a* rudimentale
vest-pocket *a* tascabile
vestment *n (eccl)* paramento sacerdotale
vestry *n (eccl)* sagrestia
Vesuvius *n* Vesuvio
veteran *n&a* veterano
veterinary *n&a* veterinario
veto *n* veto; — *vt* porre il veto a
vex *vt* irritare; **–ation** *n* vessazione dispiacere *m*; **–atious** *a* fastidioso, irritante; **–ed** *a* vessato, irritato; seccato; contrariato; **–ing** *a* vessante, irritante, contrariante
via *prep* via, per, attraverso
viability *n* viabilità
viable *a* viabile
viaduct *a* viadotto
vial *n* fiala
viand *n* vivanda, cibo
vibrant *a* vibrante
vibrate *vi* vibrare, oscillare; — *vt* far vibrare
vibration *n* vibrazione
vibrator *n* vibratore *m*
vicar *n* vicario; **–age** *n* vicariato, canonica
vicarious *a* indiretto; **–ly** *adv* indirettamente
vice *n* vizio, difetto; depravazione
viceroy *n* viceré *m*
vice-admiral *n* viceammiraglio
vice-consul *n* viceconsole *m*
vice-president *n* vicepresidente *m*
vicinity *n* vicinanza; **in the** — **of** nei dintorni di
vicious *a* violento; cattivo, maligno, vizioso; **–ness** viziosità; — **circle** circolo vizioso

vicissitude *n* vicenda, vicissitudine *f*
victim *n* vittima; **–ize** *vt* far vittima di
victor *n* vincitore *m*; **–y** *n* vittoria; **–ious** *a* vittorioso
victuals *npl* vettovaglie *fpl*
vicuña *n* vigogna
video *n* televisione; — *a* televisivo
vie *vi* rivaleggiare, gareggiare
Vienna Vienna
Viennese *a&n* Viennese
view *n* veduta, panorama, vista; opinione *f*; **–er** *n* spettatore *m*, spettatrice *f*; **–finder** *n* mirino; **–point** *n* punto di vista; **bird's-eye** — veduta a volo d'uccello; **in** — **of** in vista di; **point of** — punto di vista; — *vt* guardare; considerare
vigil *n* vigilia, veglia; **keep a** — vegliare
vigilance *n* vigilanza; *(med)* insonnia
vigilant *a* vigilante; **–ly** *adv* vigilmente, vigilatamente
vignette *n* vignetta
vigor *n* vigore *m*
vigorous *a* vigoroso; **–ly** *adv* vigorosamente; **–ness** *n* vigorosità
viking *n* vichingo, normanno
vile *a* vile, basso, disgustoso, abbietto; **–ness** *n* bassezza, viltà
vilification *n* vilipendio
vilifier *n* diffamatore *m*
vilify *vt* calunniare, diffamare
villa *n* villa
village *n* villaggio
villager *n* villico
villain *n* farabutto, mascalzone *m*; **–y** *n* infamia, malvagità; **–ous** *a* malvagio, vile, infame
vim *n* vigore *m*, forza
vincible *a* vincibile
vindicable *a* rivendicabile
vindicate *vt* giustificare, rivendicare
vindication *n* rivendicazione
vindicator *n* rivendicatore *m*
vindictive *a* vendicativo; **–ly** *adv* vendicativamente; **–ness** *n* carattere vendicativo
vine *n* pianta rampicante; *(grape)* vite *f*
vinegar *n* aceto
vineyard *n* vigneto, vigna
vintage *n* vendemmia; anno di raccolto di vino; vini *mpl*
vintery *n* vinaio
vinyl *n* vinile *m*; — *a* vinilico
viola *n* viola
violable *a* violabile
violate *vt* violare, violentare, rapire
violation *n* violazione, infrazione
violator *n* violatore, trasgressore *m*
violence *n* violenza
violent *a* violento; **–ly** *adv* violentemente

violet *n* viola mammola, violetta; — *a* violetto

violin *n* violino

violinist *n* violinista *m&f*

viper *n* vipera; **-ous** *a* viperino

virago *n* virago *f*

virgin *a&n* vergine *f*; **-al** *a* verginale; **-ity** *n* verginità

virile *a* maschio, virile

virility *n* virilità

virology *n* virologia

virtual *a* virtuale; **-ly** *adv* virtualmente

virtue *n* virtù *f*; castità; rettitudine *f*; **by — of** in virtù di

virtuosity *n* virtuosità

virtuoso *n* virtuoso

virtuous *a* virtuoso

virulence *n* virulenza

virulent *a* virulento

virus *n* virus *m*

visa *n* visto; — *vt* vidimare

visage *n* viso, aspetto

vis-a-vis *adv* a faccia a faccia; — *prep* dirimpetto

viscera *npl (anat)* visceri *mpl*

visceral *a* viscerale

viscid *a* viscido

viscosity *n* viscosità

viscount *n* visconte *m*

viscountess *n* viscontessa

viscous *a* viscoso, vischioso

vise *n* morsetto, morsa

visé *n* visto

visibility *n* visibilità

visible *a* visibile

visibly *adv* visibilmente

vision *n* apparizione, visione; *(sense)* vista; **-ary** *a&n* visionario

visit *vt* visitare; *(inflict)* affliggere, infliggere; — *n* visita; **-ation** *n* visita ufficiale; *(eccl)* visitazione; castigo divino; **-ing** *a* da visita

visitor *n* visitatore *m*, visitatrice *f*

visor *n* visiera

vista *n* vista, prospettiva; visuale *f*

visual *a* visivo

visualize *vt* figurarsi, immaginare

vital *a* vitale, — **statistics** statistiche anagrafiche; **-ly** *adv* vitalmente

vitalism *n* vitalismo

vitality *n* vitalità

vitals *npl* organi vitali

vitamin *n* vitamina

vitiate *vt* corrompere, viziare

vitreous *a* vitreo

vitrify *vt* vetrificare; — *vi* vetrificarsi

vitriol *n* vetriolo; **-ic** *a* vetriolico

vituperation *n* vituperio, vituperazione, insulto

vituperative *a* vituperativo

vivacious *a* vivace, brioso

vivacity *n* vivacità, brio

vivid *a* vivido, vivo; **-ly** *adv* vividamente; **-ness** *n* vividezza

vivify *vt* vivificare

viviparous *a* viviparo

vivisect *vt* vivisezionare; **-ion** *n* vivisezione

vixen *n* volpe femmina; *(woman)* megera; **-ish** *a* bisbetico

viz *adv* cioè, ossia, vale a dire

vocabulary *n* vocabolario

vocal *a* vocale; loquace; **-ist** *n* cantante, vocalista *m&f*; — **cords** corde vocali

vocalization *n* vocalizzazione

vocalize *vt&i* vocalizzare

vocation *n* vocazione, professione; **-al** professionale, di mestiere; **-al school** scuola d'arti e mestieri

vociferous *a* clamoroso, rumoroso; **-ly** *adv* clamorosamente, rumorosamente

vodka *n* vodka

vogue *n* moda, voga; **in —** di moda, in voga

voice *n* voce; **-less** *a* muto, senza voce; — *vt* esprimere; **-d** *a* espresso, nominato; sonoro

void *n&a* vuoto; — *vt* annullare; — **of** privo di

voidance *n* annullamento

volatile *a* incostante, volatile

volatility *n* volatilità

volatilize *vt* volatilizzare

volcanic *a* vulcanico

volcano *n* vulcano

volition *n* volere *m*, volontà

volley *n* scarica, raffica; **-ball** *n* pallarete, palla a volo; — *vt* lanciare; *(sport)* colpire al volo; *(mil)* sparare a salve

volt *n* volta; **-age** *n* voltaggio; **-ameter** *m* voltametro

volubility *n* volubilità

voluble *a* loquace, volubile

volume *n* volume *m*; massa

volumetric *a* volumetrico

voluminous *a* voluminoso; **-ly** *adv* voluminosamente; **-ness** *n* voluminosità

voluntarily *a* spontaneamente

voluntary *a* volontario

volunteer *n* volontario; — *vt* offrire; — *vi* arruolarsi; offrirsi

voluptuous *a* voluttuoso; **-ness** *n* sensualità

vomit *vt&i* vomitare; **-ing** *n* vomito

voracious *a* vorace; **-ly** *adv* voracemente; **-ness** *n* voracità

voracity *n* voracità

vortex *n* turbine, vortice *m*, gorgo

votary *n* devoto, fedele *m&f*

vote *n* voto; **put to a —** mettere a voto; **-r** *n* elettore *m*, votante *m&f*; — *vt&i* vo-

tare
voting *n* votazione, scrutinio; — *a* votante
votive *a* votivo
vouch (for) *vi* rispondere di, garantire per
voucher *n* pezza giustificativa, scontrino
vow *n* voto; — *vt* giurare, far voto di
vowel *n* vocale *f*
voyage *n* viaggio di mare; **-r** *n* viaggiatore *m*; — *vi* navigare
vulcanite *n* vulcanite *f*

vulcanization *n* vulcanizzazione
vulcanize *vt* vulcanizzare
vulgar *a* volgare, triviale, **-ism** *n* volgarità, volgarismo; espressione volgare; **-ity** *n* volgarità; **-ization** *n* volgarizzazione; **-ize** *vt* volgarizzare; **-ly** *adv* volgarmente
Vulgate *n* Vulgata
vulnerability *n* vulnerabilità
vulnerable *a* vulnerabile
vulture *n* avvoltoio
vying *a* in concorrenza

W

wadding *n* ovatta, bambagia
waddle *vi* camminare dondolando, barcollare; — *n* dondolio
wade *vt&i* guadare; — **across** passare a guado
wading *n* guado
wafer cialda; *(eccl)* ostia
waffle *n* cialda; — **iron** *n* ferro per cialde
waft *vt* sollevare, trasportare per aria; spargere; — *vi* levarsi, sollevarsi; fluttuare
wag *n (tail)* scodinzolio; scuotimento; *(person)* buontempone *m*; — *vt* scuotere; — *vi* dimenarsi; — **the tail** scodinzolare
wage *n* paga, salario; — **earner** salariato; — *vt* intraprendere; — **war** fare la guerra
wager *n* scommessa; — *vt* scommettere
waggish *a* scherzevole
wagon *n* carro, furgone *m*
waif *n* trovatello
wail *vi* lamentarsi; — *n* lamento, gemito
wainscoting *n* zoccolo di parete
waist *n* cintura; *(blouse)* camicetta; **-line** *n* vita
wait *vt&i* aspettare, attendere; — *n* attesa; **lie in** — stare in agguato, appostarsi
waiter *n* cameriere *m*; **head-** *n* capocameriere *m*
waiting *n* attesa; — **game** temporeggiamento; — **list** prenotazione; — *a* d'aspetto; — **room** anticamera, camera d'aspetto; *(rail)* sala d'aspetto
waitress *n* cameriera
waive *vt* rinunciare a, abbandonare
waiver *n* rinuncia
wake *n (death)* veglia funebre; *(naut)* scia; **in the — of** a conseguenza di; — *vi* svegliarsi; — *vt* svegliare
wakeful *a* sveglio; vigile; insonne; **-ness** *n* vigilanza; insonnia
waken *vi* svegliarsi; — *vt* svegliare
Wales Galles

walk *n* passeggiata, camminata; *(path)* sentiero; *(gait)* andatura; **-away** *n* facile vittoria; **-out** *n (coll)* sciopero; — *vi* camminare, passeggiare; — *vt* percorrere; **-ing** *a* passeggiante, camminante
walker *n (child's)* andarino; camminatore *m*, pedone *m&f*
walkie-talkie *n* trasmittente-ricevente portatile
walk-up *n (coll)* casa senza ascensore
wall *n* muro, parete *f*; *(arch)* paratia, tramezza; **-eyed** *a* strabico; **-paper** *n* carta da parati; — **plug** presa di corrente; **drive to the** — mettere con le spalle al muro *(fig)*; **go to the** — andare contro il muro *(fig)*; — *vt* cingere di mura
wallet *n* portafogli *m*
wallop *vt (coll)* colpire violentemente
walloping *a (coll)* madornale
wallow *vi* avvoltolarsi
walnut *n* noce *f*
walrus *n (zool)* tricheco
waltz *n* valzer *m*; — *vi* ballare il valzer, valzare
wan *a* pallido, smunto
wand *n* verga, bacchetta
wander *vi* errare, vagare; **-er** *n* nomade *m*
wandering *n* vagabondaggio; — *a* errante, nomade
wanderlust *n* istinto nomade
wane *n* declino; — *vi* decrescere, declinare, decadere, calare
waning *a* decadente, declinante; *(moon)* calante
want *vt* volere, desiderare; mancare, aver bisogno di; — *n* desiderio; mancanza, bisogno; **-ing** *a* deficiente, mancante
wanted *a* ricercato
wanton *a* lascivo, immorale; ingiustificato; sfrenato, sconsiderato; **-ness** *n* licenza
war *n* guerra; **cold** — guerra fredda; **-fare** *n* guerra; **-like** *a* bellicoso; **-monger** *n* guerrafondaio; **-path** *n* spedizione mili-

tare; **–ship** *n* nave da guerra; **–time** *n* tempo di guerra; — *vi* fare la guerra, guerreggiare

warble *vt&i* gorgheggiare

ward *n* pupillo; *(care)* tutela; *(city)* rione, quartiere *m*; *(hospital)* corsia; — **off** respingere, schivare

warden *n* custode *m*; direttore di prigione

wardrobe *n* guardaroba; *(to wear)* vestiario; — **mistress** *(theat)* vestiarista; — **trunk** baule armadio

wardroom *n* *(naut)* quadrato degli ufficiali

warehouse *n* magazzino; **–man** *n* magazziniere *m*

wares *npl* mercanzia, merci *fpl*

warhead *n* spoletta esplosiva

warily *a* cautamente

wariness *n* cautela, precauzione

warm *a* caldo; caloroso; **be** — *(person)* aver caldo; *(weather)* fare caldo; **–hearted** *a* di buon cuore, affettuoso; **–ly** calorosamente; — *vt* riscaldare; — *vi* riscaldarsi

warm-blooded *a* dal sangue caldo

warming *n* riscaldamento; — **pan** scaldaletto

warmth *n* calore *m*

warn *vt* ammonire, avvertire

warning *n* avvertimento, preavviso; — *a* avvertente

warp *n* *(cloth)* ordito, trama; *(wood)* curvatura, inarcamento; *(fig)* deformazione; — *vi* curvarsi; deviarsi; — *vt* ordire; far curvare; *(fig)* stornare, pervertire, influenzare; **–ed** *a* ordito; incurvato; *(fig)* pervertito; influenzato

warrant *vt* giustificare; autorizzare; garantire; — *n* ordine *m*; autorizzazione, giustificazione; *(law)* mandato di cattura; — **officer** sottufficiale; **–ed** *a* certificato, garantito; giustificato

warranty *n* garanzia

warren *n* garenna

warring *a* in conflitto, avverso, ostile

warrior *n* guerriero

Warsaw Varsavia

wart *n* porro, verruca

wary *a* circospetto, cauto; **be** — **of** diffidare di, non fidarsi di

wash *n* lavatura; bucato; *(ship)* sciaquio, risucchio; **–bowl**, **–stand** *n* lavabo, lavandino; **–room** *n* stanza per lavarsi; gabinetto; **–tub** mastello, tinozza

wash *vt* lavare; — *vi* lavarsi; — **one's hands** lavarsi le mani

washable *a* lavabile

washed-out *a* *(tired)* sfinito, esausto; *(color)* sbiadito

washer *n* *(mech)* rosetta, rondella

washerwoman *n* lavandaia

washing *n* lavatura; *(laundry)* lavaggio, bucato; — **machine** macchina lavapanni, lavatrice *f*

washout *n* alluvione *f*, erosione; *(sl)* fiasco; *(school)* bocciato

washy *a* acquoso, bagnato; debole, fiacco

wasp *n* vespa; **–ish** irascibile, stizzoso; **–s' nest** vespaio

wastage *n* sciupio; consumo

waste *n* spreco, perdita; rifiuti *mpl*; sciupio, devastazione; regione incolta; — *a* di scarto, scartato; *(land)* incolto; — *vt* sprecare; sciupare; devastare; dissipare; — *vi* deperire, consumarsi; logorarsi; — **away** sciuparsi; — **of time** perdita di tempo; **–paper** *n* carta straccia; — **pipe** tubo di scarico; **–ed** *a* sciupato, perduto, mancato, sprecato

wastebasket *n* cestino dei rifiuti

wasteful *a* spendereccio, prodigo; **–ness** *n* prodigalità

wasting *n* dissipazione, sperpero

wastrel *n* sprecone *m*

watch *n* veglia; *(naut)* guardia; *(observance)* osservazione; *(care)* sorveglianza; *(timepiece)* orologio da polso; **–er** *n* sorvegliante *m&f*; — *vt&i* *(care for)* vigilare, sorvegliare; *(observe)* osservare; *(sit up)* vegliare; **–ful** *a* guardingo, cauto, circospetto; **–fulness** *n* vigilanza

watchdog *n* cane da guardia

watchmaker *n* orologiaio

watchman *n* guardiano

watchtower *n* torre d'osservazione

watchword *n* parola d'ordine

water *n* acqua; *(med)* urina; — **bug** insetto acquatico; — **color** acquerello; **–fall** *n* cascata; — **front** settore portuale; **–line** *n* linea d'acqua *(or* d'immersione; **–mark** *n* filigrana di carta; **–melon** *n* cocomero; — **power** energia idraulica; **–proof** *a* impermeabile; **–shed** *n* spartiacque *m*; **–spout** *n* tromba d'acqua; **–tight** *a* impermeabile; **–way** *n* canale navigabile; **–works** *npl* impianto idraulico

water *vt* annacquare; inumidire; *(com)* aumentare il capitale nominale; *(stock)* provvedere d'acqua; *(land)* innaffiare, irrigare; — *vi* rifornirsi d'acqua; *(eyes)* piangere; abbeverarsi; **–ed** *a* annacquato; abbeverato

water– *(in comp)* **–cooled** *a* raffreddato ad acqua; **–logged** *a* inzuppato d'acqua; **–repellent** *a* antiassorbente; **–soaked** *a* inzuppato d'acqua; **–waved** *a* ondulato all'acqua

watering *n* *(land)* irrigazione; *(stock)* abbeveraggio; rifornimento d'acqua; *(of eyes)* lagrimazione; — **can** innaffiatoio

watery *a* acquoso; annacquato

watt *n* watt *m*

wave *n* onda; *(hair)* ondulazione; *(gesture)* cenno, segno; — **length** *(rad, TV)* lunghezza d'onda; — *vt* ondulare; agitare, brandire; — *vi* ondeggiare; far cenno; **-d** *a* ondulato

waver *vi* vacillare, esitare; ondeggiare; **-ing** *a* vacillante, esitante, indeciso, irresoluto; **-ing** *n* vacillazione

wavy *a* ondulato, ondeggiante, ondoso; *(line)* serpeggiante

wax *n* cera; *(ear)* cerume *m*; — **paper** carta cerata; **sealing** — ceralacca; — *vt* incerare; — *vi* divenire, crescere; **-y** *a* cereo

way *n* via, strada; mezzo; maniera, usanza; **all the** — lungo tutto il cammino; in tutti i modi, completamente; **be in the** — ingombrare, impedire; **by the** — a proposito; **by** — **of** via; a titolo di; **give** — cedere, accondiscendere; **give** — **to** lasciare il passo a; **have one's own** — fare a proprio modo; **lose one's** — smarrirsi; **make one's** — farsi largo *(coll);* **make** — aprire il cammino *(coll);* **on the** — per istrada, lungo il cammino; **out of the** — fuori strada, fuori mano; **right** — la via giusta; **under** — in marcia, in lavorazione; — **in** entrata; — **out** uscita

wayfarer *n* viaggiatore *m*

wayfaring *a* viaggiante

waylay *vt* appostare; tendere un agguato

wayside *n* bordo della strada; **leave by the** — lasciare per strada, lasciare indietro, abbandonare

wayward *a* ostinato; capriccioso; **-ness** *n* ostinatezza

we *pron* noi

weak *a* debole; leggero; fievole, infermo; **-ly** *adv* debolmente; **-ling** *n* debole *m&f;* **-ness** *n* debolezza, fievolezza, delicatezza

weaken *vt* indebolire; diluire; attenuare; affievolire; — *vi* indebolirsi; **-ing** *n* indebolimento

weak– *(in comp)* **—kneed** *a* cedevole, timido; debole di ginocchia; **—minded** *a* poco intelligente; **—sighted** *a* debole di vista

weakhearted *a* poco coraggioso

wealth *n* ricchezza; abbondanza; **-y** *a* ricco

wean *vt* slattare, svezzare, disabituare; — *vi* slattarsi; svezzarsi, disabituarsi

weapon *n* arma

wear *vt* portare; stancare; — *vi* logorarsi; *(last)* durare; **-able** *a* portabile, indossabile; — **away** consumare; — **out**

consumare, logorare; — *n* uso; logorio; — **and tear** logorio

weariless *a* instancabile

wearily *adv* con fatica

weariness *n* stanchezza

wearing *a* da indossare; faticoso, esauriente; — **apparel** *n* indumenti *mpl,* vestiario

wearisome *a* faticoso, noioso, fastidioso

weary *a* stanco, esausto; noioso, pesante; — *vt* stancare, esaurire; — *vi* stancarsi

weasel *n* *(zool)* donnola

weather *n* tempo; — **bureau** centro meteorologico; **-man** *n* meteorologo; **-proof** *a* antintemperie; — **report** previsioni meteorologiche; — **vane** banderola; **-worn** *a* logorato dalle intemperie, — *vi* deteriorarsi alle intemperie; — *vt* esporre alle intemperie; resistere; — **the storm** sormontare gli ostacoli

weather-beaten *a* battuto dalle intemperie

weave *vt* tessere; ordire; intrecciare; — *n* tessitura

weaver *n* tessitore *m*

weaving *n* tessitura

web *n* tela, tessuto; rete *f;* *(spider)* ragnatela

webbed *a* palmato

webbing *n* trama, tessuto, ordito

web-footed *a* palmipede

wed *vt* sposare; — *vi* sposarsi

wedded *a* coniugale; sposato

wedding *n* matrimonio; nozze *fpl;* — **cake** torta nuziale; — **ring** anello nuziale

wedge *n* cuneo; — *vt* incuneare

wedlock *n* matrimonio, nozze *fpl*

Wednesday *n* mercoledì *m*

wee *a* minuscolo

weed *n* erbaccia; **-y** *a* pieno d'erbacce; — *vt&i* sarchiare; **—ing** *n* sarchiatura; **—er** *n* sarchiatore *m;* *(mech)* sarchiatrice *f*

weeds *npl* *(mourning)* gramaglie *fpl*

week *n* settimana; **-day** *n* giorno feriale; **-end** *n* fine di settimana; **a** — **from today** oggi a otto

weekly *n&a* settimanale *m;* — *adv* ogni settimana

weep *vt&i* piangere; **-y** *a* lagrimoso

weeping *vt&i* pianto; — *a* piangente; — **willow** salice piangente

weevil *n* *(zool)* punteruolo

weft *n* trama

weigh *vt* pesare; considerare, valutare; *(naut)* levare; — *vi* pesare, avere il peso di; aver importanza; — **down** opprimere; — **in** pesarsi; — **one's words** pesare le parole *(fig)*

weigh-in *n* *(sport)* pesaggio

weight *n* peso; influenza, importanza;

-iness *n* importanza; **-lessness** *n (aesp)* agravitazione; **-y** *a* pesante, grave; potente; — *vt* caricare con peso; **gain** — ingrassare; **lose** — dimagrire

weir *n* chiusa, cateratta

weird *a* misterioso, strano, bizzarro, fantastico

welcome *n* accoglienza; — *a* benvenuto, gradito; — *interj* ben venuto!; **You're** — Non c'è di che, Prego; — *vt* dare il benvenuto a, fare buon'accoglienza a; gradire

weld *vt* saldare; **-er** *n* saldatore *m*; **-ing** *n* saldatura

welfare *n* benessere *m*; — **state** *(pol)* stato socialista; — **work** lavoro assistenziale

well *n* pozzo; *(stairs)* tromba di scale; — *a* buono, bene; sano; fortunato; — *adv* bene; **-born** *a* ben nato, di origine altolocata; **be** — star bene

well *vi* sgorgare

well- *(in comp)* **—advised** *a* prudente, saggio; **—balanced** *a* equilibrato; **—behaved** *a* cortese; **—being** *n* benessere *m*; **—bred** *a* costumato, beneducato; **—done** *a* benfatto; *(food)* ben cotto; **—earned** *a* ben meritato; **—educated** *a* colto; **—founded** *a* ben fondato; **—informed** *a* ben informato, istruito; **—kept** *a* ben tenuto; **—known** *a* ben noto; **—mannered** *a* di buone maniere; **—meaning** *a* ben intenzionato; **—off** *a* agiato, benestante; **—read** *a* erudito; **—spent** *a* ben impiegato; **—suited** *a* adatto; **—timed** *a* opportuno; **—to-do** agiato, ricco

Welsh *n&a* gallese *m*

Welshman *n* gallese *m*

welt *n* bordo, orlo

welter *vi* avvoltolarsi; — *n* confusione

welterweight *n (sport)* peso medio-leggero

wen *n* cisti sebacea

wench *n* popolana

west *n* ovest, occidente *m*; — *a* d'ovest; **-ern** *a* occidentale; **W- Indies** Indie occidentali

wet *a* bagnato, umido; *(paint)* fresco; — **blanket** guastafeste *m (fig)*; **-ness** umidità; — **nurse** balia; — *vt* bagnare

whack *vi (coll)* colpire; — *n (coll)* colpo; legnata, bastonata

whale *n* balena

whaling *n* pesca della balena; — **ship** baleniera

wharf *n* molo, scalo

what *pron* che, cosa, che cosa, ciò; quel che; — *a* che; — *adv* come, che; — *interj* che!? cosa!? **W- did you say?** Come? Che cosa hai detto? **W- is it?** Cos'è? Cosa c'è?

whatever *a* qualsiasi, qualunque; — *pron* qualsiasi cosa, qualunque cosa

whatsoever *pron* checchessia, qualunque cosa; — *a* qualunque, qualsiasi

wheat *n* frumento

wheedle *vt* adulare, vezzeggiare, ottenere con blandizie

wheedling *n* moine *fpl*

wheel *n* ruota; *(naut)* barra; *(auto)* volante *m*; — **chair** sedia a rotelle; — *vi* girare, voltarsi; — *vt* far rotare; trasportare su ruote

wheelbarrow *n* carriola

wheeling *n* rotazione, roteamento; **free-** *n* ruota libera

wheelwright *n* carraio

wheeze *n* respiro ansimante; — *vi* ansimare

wheezing *n* respirazione ansimante; — *a* ansimante, asmatico

wheezy *a* asmatico, ansimante

whelp *m* cucciolo; — *vi* partorire, sgravare

when *conj&adv* quando, qualora; **since** — da quando

whenever *conj* quando, ogni qualvolta che, qualora

where *adv&conj&pron* dove

whereabouts *n* ubicazione; — *adv* dove, in che posto

whereas *conj* stante che, siccome, poichè, mentre

whereat *conj* al che

whereby *adv* per cui, per mezzo del quale

wherefore *adv* perciò, onde, per la qual cosa

wherein *adv* dove

whereupon *conj* al che, dopo di che

wherever *conj* dovunque

wherewithal *n* soldi *mpl*; mezzi *mpl*

whet *vt (knife)* affilare; *(appetite)* stimolare

whether *conj* se, sia, sia che

whetstone *n* cote *f*

whey *n* siero di latte

which *pron* il quale, la quale, che, i quali *mpl*, le quali *fpl*; — *a* quale; — **way** per dove, dove

whichever *a* qualunque, qualsiasi; — *pron* chechessia

whiff *n* sbuffo, soffio

while *n* tempo; momento; — *conj* mentre, intanto che; — **away** trascorrere, passare; **a short** — **ago** poco fa; **be worth** — valere la pena; **in a little** — tra poco; **once in a** — una volta tanto

whim *n* capriccio

whimper *n* piagnucolio, piagnisteo, lagna; **-er** *n* piagnone, piagnucolone *m*; **-ing** *n* piagnucolio, pianisteo; **-ing** *a* pia-

gnucolante; — *vi* piagnucolare, lagnarsi
whimsical *a* bizzarro, capriccioso
whimsy *n* ubbia, capriccio
whine *vi* piagnucolare; — *n* piagnisteo
whining *n* piagnucolio, piagnisteo, lagna; — *a* piagnucolante, lagnante
whinny *n* nitrito; — *vi* nitrire
whip *n* frusta; sferzata; *(pol)* organizzatore politico; — **hand** vantaggio; — *vt* frustare; frullare; stimolare; *(coll)* sopraffare; — *vi* agitarsi; slanciarsi
whipped *a* frullato; — **cream** panna montata
whipping *n* frustata, battitura
whir *n* fruscio; — *vi* frusciare
whirl — *vi* girare rapidamente; — *vi* far turbinare; — *n* giro rapido, vortice *m*; confusione
whirligig *n* carosello; *(toy)* trottola
whirlpool *n* vortice *m*
whirlwind *n* turbine *m*
whisk *n* spazzata, spazzolata; **–broom** scopetta, scopino; — *vt* spazzare, spazzolare, asportare rapidamente; — *vi* muoversi con leggerezza
whisker *n* pelo di barba
whiskers *npl* barba; *(animal)* baffi *mpl*
whisky *n* whisky *m*
whisper *vt&i* sussurrare; — *n* susurro, bisbiglio; *(rumor)* diceria
whistle *vt&i* fischiare; — *n* fischio; *(instrument)* fischietto
whistler *n* fischiatore *m*
whistling *n* fischiamento
whit *n* iota *m*, inezia
white *a* bianco; pallido; **show the —** **feather** dar prova di viltà; — **elephant** cosa ingombrante; — **heat** incandescenza; — **lie** bugia innocente; — *n* bianco; *(egg)* albume *m*; **–ness** *n* bianchezza, pallore *m*; purezza, candore *m*
whitecap *n* cresta d'onda
white-faced *a* pallido
whitefish *n* pesce bianco, lavareto
white-hot *a* incandescente
white-livered *a* vigliacco, codardo
whiten *vt* imbiancare; — *vi* impallidire; imbiancarsi
whitewash *n* calce da imbiancare; — *vi* imbiancare con calce; dare una mano di bianco
whither *adv* dove
whiting *n* *(fish)* merlano
whitish *a* biancastro
whittle *vt* tagliuzzare, assottigliare
whiz *n* sibilo; *(sl)* esperto, perito; — *vi* fischiare, sibilare; *(hurry)* sfrecciare
who *pron* che; chi; il quale, la quale, i quali, le quali
whoa *interj* ferma!

whole *a* intero, completo; tutto insieme; — **number** numero intero; — **note** semibreve *f*; — **wheat** grano integrale; — **wheat bread** pane integrale; — *n* intero, totale *m*; **in the —** in fin dei conti, in totale
wholeness *n* interezza, totalità
wholesale *n* vendita all'ingrosso; — *a* *&adv* all'ingrosso; — *a* generale; — *vt* *&i* vendere all'ingrosso
wholesaler *n* grossista *m*
wholesome *a* salubre, sano; **–ness** salubrità
wholly *adv* del tutto, interamente
whom *pron* chi, che, cui; il quale, la quale, i quali, le quali; **–ever** *pron* chiunque
whoop *n* urlo, grido; **–ing cough** pertosse *f*, tosse canina; — *vi* gridare, urlare
whore *n* prostituta, sgualdrina
whorl *n* spirale *m*, spira
whose *pron* di chi; di cui; il cui, la cui, i cui, le cui
why *adv* perchè
wick *n* lucignolo
wicked *a* cattivo, scellerato; **–ness** *n* malvagità
wicker *n* vimine *m*
wide *a* largo; esteso; lontano; **–spread** *a* diffuso largamente; **far and —** in lungo e in largo; **–ly** *adv* largamente
wide– *(in comp)* **–awake** *a* sveglio; vigile; **–eyed** *a* con gli occhi sbarrati; **–open** *a* spalancato
widen *vt* allargare, ampliare; — *vi* allargarsi, ampliarsi, estendersi
widow *n* vedova; — *vt* vedovare; **–hood** *n* vedovanza
widower *n* vedovo
width *n* larghezza; *(cloth)* altezza
wield *vt* maneggiare; esercitare
wieldy *a* maneggiabile
wife *n* moglie *f*; **–ly** *a* di moglie, coniugale
wig *n* parrucca
wiggle *vt* dimenare; — *vi* dimenarsi; — *n* dimenamento, agitazione; **–r** *n* dimenante *m&f*
wigwag *n* segnalazione con bandierine; — *vi* fare segnalazioni con bandierine
wild *a* selvaggio, selvatico, silvestre, impetuoso; **–s** luoghi inesplorati; **–cat** *n* gatto selvatico; **–cat strike** sciopero non autorizzato; **–ness** *n* selvatichezza; sfrenatezza; **–ly** *adv* selvaticamente, selvaggiamente; sfrenatamente
wilderness *n* luogo selvaggio
wildfire *n* fuoco greco
wild-goose chase tentativo inutile, impresa vana
wile *n* astuzia, raggiro

wiliness n malizia, astuzia

will n volontà; desiderio; testamento; **free** — libero arbitrio, — vt&i ordinare, volere; — vt disporre per testamento

willful a premeditato, intenzionale; osti-nato; **-ness** n premeditazione; osti-nazione; **-ly** adv premeditatamente; osti-natamente

willing a pronto, volenteroso; **be** — volere; **-ness** n buona volontà; accon-discendenza; **-ly** adv volentieri

will-o'-the-wisp n fuoco fatuo

willow n salice m; **-y** a pieno di salici; svelto, grazioso

willy-nilly adv volente o nolente

wilt vi appassire; — vt far appassire

wily a astuto, malizioso

wimple n soggolo

win vt&i vincere, guadagnare; — **over** persuadere; — n vittoria, vincita

wince vi trasalire, indietreggiare

winch n argano, manubrio, manovella

wind n vento; (breath) fiato; **-bag** n (coll) chiacchierone m, ciarlatano; **-breaker** n giacca a vento; **-fall** n fortuna ina-spettata; **-mill** n mulino a vento; **-pipe** n trachea; **-storm** n bufera da vento; — **tunnel** (avi) tunnel per vento arti-ficiale; **get** — **of** aver sentore di; **-less** a senza vento; **-y** a ventoso; ver-boso, — vt far perdere il fiato; **-ed** a ansimante, sfiatato

wind vt avvolgere; (clock) caricare; — vi serpeggiare, avvolgersi; — n curva

wind- (in comp) **-blown** a portato dal vento; scompigliato; **-borne** a tra-sportato dal vento; **-swept** a esposto al vento

winding n svolta, sinuosità; giro; — a serpeggiante, sinuoso; — **sheet** lenzuo-lo mortuario, sudario

windjammer n veliere m

windlass n argano

window n finestra; (auto, rail) finestrino; (store) vetrina; (box office) sportello; — **dresser** n vetrinista m&f; **-pane** n vetro di finestra; **-sill** n davanzale m; **display** — n vetrina

window-shop vi guardare vetrine; **-er** n chi guarda le vetrine

windshield n parabrezza m; — **wiper** tergicristallo

windup n (end) conclusione

wine n vino; — **cellar** n cantina; **-glass** n bicchiere da vino; **-grower** n viticultore m; — **growing** viticultura; **-ry** n vineria; — **shop** spaccio di vino; — vt provvedere di vino

wing n ala; **-spread** n apertura d'ali; **-less** a senz'ali; **-s** npl (theat) quinte

fpl; **take** — prendere il volo; **under the** — **of** sotto la protezione di; — vt sorvolare; — vi volare

wink vi strizzare l'occhio; — n ammicco, strizzata d'occhi, occhiolino; istante m

winner n vincitore m, vincitrice f

winning a vincente, vincitore; seducente; **-s** npl guadagni mpl, vincita

winnow vt vagliare

winsome a seducente, affascinante; **-ness** n fascino, attrattività

winter n inverno; — vi svernare; **-ize** vt equipaggiare per l'inverno; **-time** n stagione invernale

wintriness n qualità invernale; freddezza

wintry a invernale; freddo; (fig) triste, brullo

wipe vt asciugare, pulire; — **one's nose** asciugarsi il naso; — **out** cancellare, distruggere

wire n filo metallico; (coll) telegramma m; **barbed** — filo spinato; **-photo** n radio-foto f; — **tapping** uso di apparecchio speciale per captare conversazioni tele-foniche altrui; **-puller** n potenza occulta (fig); **-pulling** n manovra dei fili (fig); eminenza grigia (fig); — vt installare i fili; (coll) telegrafare; legare con filo

wire-haired a dal pelo rigido; setoloso

wireless a senza fili, radiotelegrafico; — n radiotelegrafia

wiriness n nerbo, nervo; (hair) rigidezza

wiring n instalazione elettrica

wiry a di filo metallico; (person) nervoso, nerboruto; (hair) rigido

wisdom n saggezza; — **tooth** dente del giudizio

wise a saggio; — n guisa, maniera, modo; **-ly** adv saggiamente

wiseacre n sapientone m, presuntuoso

wish n desiderio, voglia, augurio; **-bone** n forcella; — vt&i desiderare, volere, augurare

wishful a desideroso; — **thinking** illusioni fpl

wishy-washy a insipido

wisp n ciuffo, strofinaccio

wisteria n glicine m

wistful a pensoso; nostalgico, sognante; **-ness** n nostalgia

wit n spirito, arguzia; **to** — cioè, vale a dire; **-less** a povero di spirito, senza intelligenza; **-ty** a arguto, spiritoso

witch n strega; **-craft** n stregoneria; — **doctor** stregone m; **-ing** a incantevole; magico

with prep con; **-in** prep dentro di; entro; **-in** adv dentro; **-out** prep senza; fuori di; **-out** adv fuori

withdraw vt ritirare; — vi ritirarsi

withdrawal *n* ritirata, ritiro

wither *vi* appassire; — *vt* far appassire; **-ing** *a* languente; sprezzante

withers *npl* garrese *m*

withhold *vt* trattenere; rifiutare; — *vi* astenersi; **-ing** *n* astensione; rifiuto; detenzione

withstand *vt&i* resistere a, opporsi a

witness *n* testimone *m&f*; testimonianza; **bear** — fare testimonianza; — *vt* testimoniare, presenziare, attestare

witticism *n* frizzo spiritoso, arguzia

wittily *adv* spiritosamente

wittingly *adv* intenzionalmente, apposta

wizard *n* mago, stregone *m*; **-ry** *n* stregoneria, magia

wizen *vt* raggrinzire; — *vi* raggrinzarsi; **-ed** *a* magro, secco, raggrinzito

wobble *vi* vacillare, tremare

wobbling *a* vacillante; — *n* barcollamento

wobbly *a* malfermo, debole

woe *n* guaio, sventura; **-begone** *a* sconsolato; **-ful** *a* triste, doloroso; **-fully** *adv* dolorosamente

wolf *n* lupo; **-ish** *a* lupesco, di lupo, rapace; — *vt* mangiare con voracità

woman *n* donna; **-hood** *n* femminilità; **-ish** *a* effeminato; **-ly** *a* femminino, femminile, muliebre

woman-hater *n* misogino

womb *n* utero; grembo

wonder *n* meraviglia, stupore *m;* **-ful** *a* meraviglioso; **-fully** *adv* mirabilmente, meravigliosamente; **-land** *n* terra delle meraviglie; **-ment** *n* stupore *m*, meraviglia; — *vt&i* meravigliarsi, domandarsi

wondrous *a* meraviglioso, mirabile

wont *n* abitudine *f*

woo *vt* fare la corte a; **-ing** *n* corteggiamento

wood *n* legno; — **alcohol** alcool metilico; **-craft** *n* lavorazione del legno; **-carving** scultura in legno; **-cut** *n* intaglio su legno; **-cutter** *n* boscaiolo, taglialegna; intagliatore in legno; **-land** *n* terreno boscoso; **-pecker** picchio; **-work** *n* lavoro in legno; infissi di legno; intavolato; **-ed** *a* boscoso; **-en** *a* di legno; duro, goffo; inespressivo

wood-carver *n* scultore in legno

woods *npl* bosco, foresta; **-man** *n* boscaiolo; **-y** *a* boscoso, boschivo

woof *n* trama

woofer *n* altoparlante di bassa frequenza

wool *n* lana; **cotton** — ovatta; **steel** — lana d'acciaio; **pull the** — **over one's eyes** gettar polvere agli occhi *(fig)*; **-en** *a* di lana; **-ly** *a* lanoso, lanuto; *(hair)* crespo

word *n* parola; notizia; **by** — **of mouth** *adv* oralmente, a voce; **in a** — in una parola; **leave** — lasciar detto; **-less** *a* senza parola, muto; non espresso; **give one's** — dare la propria parola, dare la parola d'onore; **have -s with** aver parole con, litigare; **in other -s** in altre parole; — *vt* esprimere, formulare

wordiness *n* verbosità

wording *n* dicitura; espressione; modo di dire

wordy *a* parolaio, verboso

work *vt* lavorare; far funzionare; far lavorare; causare; — *vi* funzionare; lavorare; fare effetto; — **out** *(succeed)* riuscire, aver esito; — **up** elaborare; *(excite)* eccitare; *(mix)* mischiare; **-able** *a* lavorabile; sfruttabile; **-er** *n* operaio; lavoratore *m*, lavoratrice *f*

work *n* lavoro; opera; **-aday** *a* ordinario; **-bag** *n* borsa degli attrezzi; **-book** *n* manuale *m*; libro di esercizi; diario di lavoro; **-man** *n* artigiano, operaio; **-manship** *n* mano d'opera, esecuzione; abilità artigiana, finitezza; **-out** *n* *(sport)* allenamento; **at** — all'opera; **-s** *npl* opere *fpl*; *(mech)* meccanismo; fabbrica

working *n* funzionamento, operazione; — **capital** capitale d'esercizio; — **class** classe lavoratrice; — **day** giorno di lavoro; — **hours** orario di lavoro

world *n* mondo; — **without end** fino alla fine dei secoli *(fig)*; **for all the** — per tutto l'oro del mondo *(coll)*; **-liness** *n* mondanità; **-ly** *a* mondano, umano, materialista

world-wide *a* mondiale

worm *n* verme *m*; *(screw)* impanatura; — *vt* liberare dai vermi; fare subdolamente; *(secret)* strappare; — *vi* agire subdolamente; serpeggiare; **-s** *npl (med)* parassiti *mpl*; — **one's way into** insinuarsi in

worm-eaten *a* tarlato, bacato; *(out-of-date)* antiquato

wormwood *n* *(fig)* tribulazione; *(bot)* assenzio

worn *a* consumato, logoro

worn-out *a* esausto; logoro

worried *a* preoccupato, ansioso

worry *n* ansia, preoccupazione; angoscia; — *vi* preoccuparsi, affliggersi; — *vt* preoccupare, annoiare, disturbare

worse *a* peggiore; — *adv* peggio; **be** — **off** star peggio; **so much the** — tanto peggio

worsen *vt&i* peggiorare

worship *n* adorazione, culto; — *vt&i* adorare, venerare; partecipare a una funzione religiosa

worst *a* il peggiore, il più cattivo; — *adv* alla peggio; — *n* il peggio; — *vt* sopraffare

worsted *n* tessuto di lana pettinata

worth *n* valore *m*, merito; — *a* degno di, del valore di; **be** — valere; **–less** *a* di nessun valore; **–y** *a* degno

worthily *adv* degnamente

worthiness *n* merito

worthwhile *a* che vale la pena

would-be *a* sedicente, preteso; mancato

wound *n* piaga, ferita; — *vt* ferire; offendere

woven *a* tessuto

wraith *n* spettro, fantasma

wrangle *n* bisticcio, alterco, rissa; — *vi* bisticciarsi; altercare

wrap *vt* avvolgere, impaccare, incartare; **–vi** avvolgersi; — *n* mantello

wrapper *n* fascia, involucro

wrapping *n* imballaggio

wrath *n* ira, rabbia

wreak *vt* sfogare; — **vengeance** vendicarsi

wreath *n* corona, ghirlanda; **–e** *vt* inghirlandare, festonare; **–ed** *a* festonato, inghirlandato

wreck *n* naufragio; relitto; rovina; avanzi *mpl*; — *vt* distruggere, rovinare, demolire; **–age** *n* relitto; **–ed** *a* mancato; rovinato; naufragato; **–ing** *a (naut)* di salvataggio

wren *n (zool)* scriciolo

wrench *vt* storcere; — *n* torsione violenta; *(med)* slogatura, distorsione, lussazione; *(mech)* chiave fissa; **monkey** — chiave inglese

wrest *vt* strappare, torcere; — *n* strappo

wrestle *vi* lottare; — *n* lotta; — **with** lottare contro; **–r** *n* lottatore *m*

wrestling *n* lotta; **catch-as-catch-can** — lotta libera

wretch *n* sciagurato, miserabile *m*; **–ed** *a* infelice, meschino, pessimo; **–edness** *n* miseria; meschinità

wrick *n* storta; — *vt* storcersi

wriggle *n* contorsione; dimenamento; — *vi* torcersi, dimenarsi; — *vt* torcere; — **out of** levarsi da

wriggling *n* contorsione

wring *vt* torcere, stringere, spremere; estorcere; — *vi* torcersi; **–er** *n* cilindro da bucato

wringing *n* torsione

wringing-wet *a* inzuppato, gocciolante, bagnato

wrinkle *n* ruga, grinza; **latest** — *(coll)* ultimo grido, ultima moda; — *vt* corrugare; sgualcire; — *vi* raggrinzirsi; **–d** *a* grinzoso, rugoso

wrinkling *n* grinza

wrist *n* polso; **–band** *n* polsino; **–let** *n* braccialetto; — **watch** orologio da polso

writ *n (law)* mandato; **Holy W–** la Sacra Scrittura

write *vt&i* scrivere; — **down** mettere per iscritto; — **off** cancellare; scrivere con facilità

writer *n* scrittore *m*, scrittrice *f*; scrivente *m&f*

write-up *n* resoconto, rapporto

writhe *vi* contorcersi

writhing *n* contorsione

writing *n* scrittura, grafia, scritto; opera; — **desk** scrivania; — **pad** cartella per scrivere; — **paper** carta da scrivere; **in** — per iscritto

written *a* per iscritto, scritto

wrong *n* male *m*; torto; danno; ingiustizia; **–doer** *n* malfattore *m*, malfattrice *f*; peccatore *m*, peccatrice *f*; **–doing** *n* malazione; **be** — aver torto; **do** — far male; peccare; **go** — sbagliar strada *(fig)*; **in the** — dalla parte del torto; in torto; **What's** —? Che c'è di male?

wrong *vt* far male a, danneggiare; offendere; accusare a torto; — *adv* erroneamente, malamente, a torto; **–ly** *adv* male; ingiustamente

wrongful *a* ingiusto; **–ly** *adv* ingiustamente

wroth *a* arrabbiato, stizzito

wrought *a* lavorato; — **iron** ferro battuto

wry *a* storto, torto; **make a** — **face** fare una smorfia

wryneck *n* torcicollo

X

xenon *n (chem)* xeno

Xmas, Christmas *n* Natale *m*

X ray raggio X

X-ray *vt* fare una radiografia di; — **pic-** **ture** radiografia

xylography *n* silografia

xylophone *n* silofono

xylophonist *n* silofonista *m*

Y

yacht *n* panfilo

yank *n* strappo; — *vt* strappare; — *vi* dare uno strappone

Yankee *n&a* americano, statunitense *m&f*

yap *n* abbaiamento, latrato, guaito; — *vi* abbaiare; guaire

yard *n* recinto, cortile *m; (naut)* antenna; norma; *(measure)* iarda; *(rail)* stazione di smistamento; **–man** *n (rail) n* manovratore *m;* **–stick** stecca d'una iarda

yarn *n* filato; *(coll)* racconto immaginario

yaw *vi (naut)* cambiar rotta, orzare

yawl *n (naut)* iole *f*

yawn *n* sbadiglio; — *vi* sbadigliare; spalancarsi; **–ing** *a* spalancato; sonnolento, sbadigliante; **–ing** *n* sbadiglio

yea *adv* già; sì; — *n* voto affermativo

year *n* anno; **leap** — anno bisestile; **last** — l'anno scorso, l'anno passato; **school** — anno scolastico; **–book** *n* annuario; **–ling** *n* animale d'un anno

yearly *a* annuale; — *adv* ogni anno

yearn *vi* desiderare ardentemente; bramare, agognare; struggersi per

yearning *n* vivo desiderio; — *a* bramoso

yeast *n* lievito

yell *n* strillo, urlo; — *vt&i* urlare, gridare

yellow *a* giallo; *(coll)* vigliacco; — **fever** febbre gialla; — **journalism** giornalismo sensazionale; **–ish** *a* giallastro; **–ness** *n* giallore *m;* — *vt&i* ingiallire

yelp *n* guaito; — *vi* guaire, latrare

yelping *n* guaiti *mpl;* — *a* che guaisce

yen *n (coll)* desiderio vivo; — *vi* agognare, bramare

yes *adv* sì, già

yesterday *adv* ieri; **day before** — ieri l'altro, avant'ieri

yet *conj* però, tuttavia, nondimento; — *adv* ancora, finora; **as** — finora; **not** — non ancora

yew *n (bot)* tasso

yield *vt&i* produrre, rendere, cedere — *n* raccolto, rendita

yodel *n* canto tirolese; — *vi* cantare alla tirolese

yogurt *n* yogurt *m*

yoke *n* giogo; paio; — *vt* accoppiare; aggiogare

yokel *n* zoticone *m*, villano

yolk *n* tuorlo

yonder *adv* laggiù, là

yore *n; of* — di un tempo, anticamente

you *pron* tu; Lei, la, Loro; voi

young *a* giovane; — *npl* i nati; *(animal)* cuccioli *mpl, (chicks)* pulcini *mpl; (people)* i giovani *mpl;* **–ster** *n* fanciullo; — **lady** signorina; — **man** giovanotto

your *a* tuo, vostro; Suo, Loro, tua, vostra, Sua

yours *pron* il tuo, il vostro, il Suo, la tua, la vostra, la Sua, il Loro, la Loro

yourself *pron* tu stesso, voi stesso, Lei stesso, Lei stessa, voi stessa, ti, si, vi

yourselves *pron pl* voi stessi, voi stesse, Loro stessi, Loro stesse, si, vi

youth *n* gioventù *f*, giovinezza; giovane *m;* **–ful** *a* giovanile; **–fulness** *n* giovinezza

yowl *vi* ululare; — *n* ululato

yule *n* Natale *m;* **–tide** *n* feste natalizie

Z

zany *a* comico, buffo; — *n* buffone *m*, semplicione *m*

zeal *n* zelo

zealot *n* zelante *m&f*, zelatore *m*, zelatrice *f;* fanatico

zealous *a* fervente, zelante

zenith *n* zenit, apogeo *m*

zephyr *n* zeffiro

zero *n* zero, nulla *m;* — **hour** ora zero

zest *n* gusto, sapore *m; interesse, ardore m;* **–ful** *a* saporito, aromatico; piacevole, gustoso

zigzag *n* zigzag *m;* — *a&adv* a zigzag; — *vi* andare a zigzag, serpeggiare

zinc *n* zinco

zip *n (coll)* energia; sibilo; — *vi* muoversi fulmineamente, scattare, frecciare; sibilare

zipper *n* chiusura lampo

zodiac *n* zodiaco

zone *n* zona; — *vi* dividere in zone; **–d** *a* a zone

zoo *n* giardino zoologico

zoological *a* zoologico

zoologist *n* zoologo

zoology *n* zoologia

zoom *n (avi)* ascesa verticale; rimbombo; — *vi* rimbombare; *(avi)* salire verticalmente

zoonosis *n* zoonosi *f*

ENGLISH-ITALIAN FIRST NAMES

A

Aaron Aronne
Abel Abele
Abraham Abramo
Ada Ada
Adam Adamo
Adelaide Adelaide
Adele Adele
Adeline Adelina
Adolph Adolfo
Adrian Adriano
Agatha Agata
Aggie Agnesina
Agnes Agnese
Albert Alberto
Alec, Alex Alessandrino
Alexander Alessandro
Alexandra Alessandra
Alfred Alfredo
Alice Alice
Althea Altea
Ambrose Ambrogio
Amelia Amelia
Amy Amata
Andrew Andrea, Sandro
Andy Andreuccio
Angela Angela
Ann Anna
Annie Annina, Annetta
Anthony Antonio
Antoine Antonio
Antoinette Antonietta

Antony Antonio
Archibald Arcibaldo
Arnold Arnaldo
Arthur Arturo
August Augusto
Augusta Augusta
Augustine Agostino
Austin Agostino

B

Baldwin Baldovino
Barbara Barbara
Barnaby Barnaba
Barnard Bernardo
Barney Bernardino
Bartholomew Bartolomeo
Basil Basilio
Beatrice Beatrice
Benedict Benedetto
Benjamin Beniamino
Bernadine Bernardina
Bernard Bernardo
Bernice Berenice
Bertha Berta
Bertram Bertrando
Bertrand Bertrando
Betsy Lisetta
Betty Lisa
Bill Guglielmino
Blanche Bianca
Bob Robertuccio
Bridget Brigida

C

Camille Camilla
Caroline Carolina
Catherine Caterina
Cecil Cecilio
Cecilia, Cecily Cecilia
Charles Carlo
Charlie Carletto
Charlotte Carlotta
Chloe Cloe
Christian Cristiano
Christine Cristina
Christopher Cristoforo
Clara, Clare Chiara
Clarissa Clarissa, Clarice
Claude Claudio
Claudia Claudia
Clement Clemente
Clementine Clementina
Clio Clio
Conrad Corrado, Corradino
Constance Costanza
Cordelia Cordelia
Corinne Corinna
Cornelia Cornelia
Cornelius Cornelio
Cyrus Ciro

D

Daniel Daniele
Daphne Dafne
David Davide
Davy Davidino

Delia Delia
Delilah Dalila
Dennis Diogini
Diana, Diane Diana
Dick Riccardino
Dolores Dolores
Donald Donaldo
Dora Dora
Doris Doride
Dorothy Dorotea

E

Edgar Edgardo
Edith Editta
Edmund Edmondo
Edward Edoardo
Eleanor Eleonora
Elias Elia
Eliza Elisa
Elizabeth Elisabetta
Ellen Elena
Eloise Eloisa
Elvira Elvira
Emanuel Emanuele
Emilia Emilia
Emily Emilia
Emma Emma
Emmie Emmina
Eric Erico
Ernest Ernesto
Ernestine Ernestina
Esmund Esmondo
Estelle Stella
Esther Ester

Eugene Eugenio
Eugenia Eugenia
Eunice Eunice
Evangeline Evangelina
Eve Eva
Evelyn Evelina

F

Fabian Fabiano
Felicia Felicia
Felix Felice
Ferdinand Ferdinando
Flora Flora
Florence Fiorenza
Frances Francesca
Francis Francesco
Frank Francesco
Fred Federico
Frederica Federica
Frederick Federico

G

Gabriel Gabriele
Gabriella Gabriella
Gaylord Gagliardo
Gene Gino
Genevieve Genoveffa
Geoffrey Goffredo
George Giorgio
Georgette Giorgetta
Georgia Giorgia
Georgiane Giorgiana
Georgie Giorgetto

Gerald Geraldo
Geraldine Geraldina
Gerard Gerardo
Gertrude Geltrude
Gilbert Gilberto
Giles Egidio
Godfrey Goffredo
Gregory Gregorio
Gustav Gustavo
Guy Guido

H

Hal Enrico
Hannah Anna
Harold Aroldo
Harriet Enrichetta
Harry Arrigo
Hatty Enrichetta
Hector Ettore
Helen, Helena Elena
Henrietta Enrichetta
Henry Enrico, Arrigo
Herbert Erberto
Hermione Ermione
Hilary Hilario
Homer Omero
Horace Orazio
Horatio Orazio
Hortense Ortensia
Hubert Uberto
Hugh Ugo
Hughie Ugolino
Humbert Umberto
Humphrey Onofredo

I

Ian Giano
Ida Ida
Immanuel Emanuele
Inez Ines
Irene Irene
Iris Iris
Isaac Isacco
Isabel Isabella
Ivan Ivano

J

Jack Giannetto
Jacob Giacobbe
James Giacomo
Jane Giovanna
Jean Giovannina, Gina
Jenny Giannetta, Giacomina
Jeremiah Geremia
Jeremy Geremia
Jerome Geronimo
Jessica Gessica
Jimmy Giacomino
Joan, Joanna Giovanna
Joe Giuseppino
Joey Peppino
Johanna Giovanna
John Giovanni
Johnny Giannino, Giovannino
Jonah Giona
Jonathan Gionata
Jordan Giordano
Joseph Giuseppe

Josephine Giuseppina
Joshua Giosuè
Judith Giuditta
Jules Giulio
Julia Giulia
Julian Giuliano
Juliana Giuliana
Julie Giulia
Juliet Giulietta
Julius Giulio
Justin Giustino
Justina Giustina

K

Katherine Caterina
Kathie Caterina
Kitty Caterina

L

Lambert Lamberto
Larry Lorenzino
Laura Laura
Lavinia Lavinia
Lawrence Lorenzo
Leah Lea
Leda Leda
Lelia Lelia
Leo Leone
Leonard Leonardo
Leonore Leonora
Leopold Leopoldo
Letitia Letizia
Lewie Luigino

Lewis Luigi
Lionel Lionello
Lisa Lisa
Lorraine Lorena
Lou Luigino
Louie Gigi
Louis Luigi
Louisa Luisa
Louise Luigia
Lucas Luca
Lucia Lucia
Lucian Luciano
Lucinda Lucinda
Lucius Lucio
Lucretia Lucrezia
Lucy Lucia
Ludwig Ludovico
Luke Luca
Luther Lutero
Lydia Lidia

Martha Marta
Martin Martino
Mary Maria
Mathilda Matilde
Matthew Matteo
Maude Magda
Maurice Maurizio
Maximilian Massimiliano
May Marietta
Melissa Melissa
Mercedes Mercede
Mercia Mercia
Michael Michele
Mike Michelino
Minerva Minerva
Miranda Miranda
Miriam Miriam
Monica Monica
Monique Monica
Morris Maurizio
Moses Mosè

M

Madeleine Maddalena
Madeline Maddalena
Malcolm Malcomo
Manfred Manfredo
Manuel Manuele
Margery Margherita
Margot Margherita
Marianne Marianna
Marie Maria
Marion Marietta
Marius Mario
Mark Marco

N

Nan Nina
Nancy Annetta, Annina
Nannette Nannetta
Naomi Noemi
Natalie Natalia
Nathaniel Nataniele
Nicholas Nicola, Nicolò
Nick Nicoluccio
Nicolette Nicoletta
Nina Nina
Noah Noè

Noel Natale
Nora Nora

O

Olive Olivia
Oliver Oliviero
Olivia Olivia
Ophelia Ofelia
Orlando Orlando
Oscar Oscar
Oswald Osvaldo
Otto Ottone

P

Patrick Patrizio
Paul Paolo
Paula Paola
Peggy Marietta
Penelope Penelope
Pete Pietruccio
Peter Pietro
Phil Filippuccio
Philip Filippo
Phoebe Feba
Polly Mariuccia
Priscilla Priscilla
Prudence Prudenza

R

Rachel Rachele
Ralph Rodolfo, Raulo
Randall Randolfo

Randolph Randolfo
Raymond Raimondo
Rebecca Rebecca
Reggie Rinaldo
Reginald Reginaldo
Reynold Rinaldo
Richard Riccardo
Robert Roberto
Robin Robertuccio
Roderick Rodrigo
Roger Ruggero
Roland Rolando
Ronald Rinaldo
Rosalie Rosalia, Rosina
Rosalind Rosalinda
Rose Rosa
Rosette Rosetta
Rowland Rolando
Roxanne Rossana
Rudolph Rodolfo
Rufus Rufo
Rupert Ruperto
Ruth Rut

S

Sally Sara
Samson Sansone
Samuel Samuele
Sarah Sara
Saul Saul
Sebastian Sebastiano
Sibyl Sibilla
Siegfried Sigfrido
Sigmund Sigismondo

Silvester Silvestro
Simon Simone
Solomon Salomone
Sophie Sofia
Stanislas Stanislao
Stella Stella
Stephanie Stefania
Stephen Stefano
Sue Susanna
Susan Susanna
Susannah Susanna
Susie Susetta
Sylvia Silvia

T

Terence Terenzio
Teresa Teresa
Thaddeus Taddeo
Theodora Teodora
Theodore Teodoro
Therese Teresa
Thomas Tommaso
Timothy Timoteo
Titus Tito
Tobias Tobia
Toby Tobia
Tom Tommasino
Tony Tonio
Tyrone Tirone

U

Ulric Ulrico
Ursula Orsola

V

Valentine Valentino
Valerie Veleria
Veronica Veronica
Vic Vittorino
Vicky Vittorina
Victor Vittorio
Victoria Vittoria
Virgil Virgilio
Vincent Vincenzo
Vinny Vincenzina
Violet Viola
Virginia Virginia
Vitus Vito
Vivian Viviana
Vladimir Vladimiro

W

Walter Gualtiero
Wilfred Vilfrido
Wilhelm Guglielmo
Wilhelmina Guglielmina
William Guglielmo
Winfred Vinfrido

Y

Yves Ivonne
Yvette Ivetta

Z

Zachary Zaccaria

TRAVELER'S CONVERSATION GUIDE

ARRIVAL

Where is customs, please?

My baggage? I think the ones over there are mine.

I have nothing to declare.

There are only personal belongings in that trunk.

Excuse me, where can I find a porter?

Take everything to a taxi, please.

How much do I owe you?
How much is it?

TAXI

Will you get a cab for me, please?

Take me to Hotel _____.

Is it very far?
Go more slowly, please!

Slower!
Stop here a moment, please.

Go ahead.
Faster, please.

Turn to the left.
Turn to the right.
Keep going straight.

How much is it?
Can you change ten thousand lire?

L'ARRIVO

La dogana, dov'è, per favore? (lâ dō·gâ'nâ dō·vā' pär fâ·vō'rā)

I miei bagagli? Credo che siano quelli là. (ē myā'ē bâ·gâ'lyē krā'dō kā sē'â·nō kwāl'lē lâ)

Non ho niente da dichiarare. (nōn ō nyān'tä dâ dē·kyâ·râ'rā)

In quel baule ci sono solo effetti personali. (ēn kwāl bâ·ū'lā chē sō'nō sō'lō äf·fāt'tē pär·sō·nâ'lē)

Scusi, dove posso trovare un facchino? (skū'zē dō'vā pōs'sō trō·vâ'rā ūn fâk·kē'nō)

Porti tutto in un tassì, per piacere. (pōr'tē tūt'tō ē·nūn' tâs·sē' pär pyâ·chā'rā)

Quanto Le devo? (kwân'tō lā dā'vō)
Quant'è? (kwân·tā')

IL TASSÌ

Mi vuol trovare un tassì, per favore. (mē vwōl trō·vâ'rā ūn tâs·sē' pär fâ·vō'rā)

Mi porti all'Albergo _____. (mē pōr'tē âl·lâl·bär'gō)

È molto distante? (ā mōl'tō dē·stân'tā)
Vada più piano, La prego! (vâ'dâ pyū pyâ'nō lâ prā'gō)

Più adagio! (pyū â·dâ'jō)
Si fermi un momento, per favore. (sē fär'mē ūn mō·mân'tō pär fâ·vō'rā)

Avanti. (â·vân'tē)
Acceleri, per favore. (â·che'lä·rē pär fâ·vō'rā)

Volti a sinistra. (vōl'tē â sē·nē'strâ)
Giri a destra. (jē'rē â dā'strâ)
Vada sempre diritto. (vâ'dâ sām'prā dē·rēt'tō)

Quant'è? (kwân·tā')
Può cambiarmi un biglietto da dieci mila? (pwō kâm·byâr'mē ūn bē·lyāt'tō dâ dyā'chē mē'lâ)

HOTEL | L'ALBERGO

Where is the desk?

Dov'è la direzione? (dō·vā' lâ dē·rā·tsyō'nä)

Have you reserved a room for me? My name is _____.

È stata prenotata una camera per me? Mi chiamo _____. (ā stä'tâ prä·nō·tâ'tâ ū'nâ kâ'mä·râ pār mā mē kyâ'mō)

Can I pay by the week?

Posso pagare la camera per settimana? (pōs'sō pâ·gâ'rā lâ kâ'mä·râ pār sat·tē·mâ'nâ)

Are meals included?

I pasti sono compresi? (ē pâ'stē sō'nō cōm·prä'zē)

What are your meal times?

A che ore si servono i pasti? (â kā ō'rā sē ser'vō·nō ē pâ'stē)

I'd like a room with two beds, a bath, and air conditioning.

Vorrei una camera a due letti con bagno ed aria condizionata. (vōr·rä'ē ū'nâ kâ'mä·râ â dü'ä lät'tē kōn bâ'nyō ā·dâ'ryâ kōn·dē·tsyō·nâ'tâ)

I am going to stay a week (two weeks).

Resterò una settimana (due settimane). (rā·stä·rō' ū'nâ sät·tē·mâ'nâ [dü'ä sät·tē·mâ'nā])

I want a single room overlooking the square.

Desidero una stanza a un letto che guardi sulla piazza. (dā·zē'dā·rō ū'nâ stân'tsâ â ün lät'tō kā gwâr'dē sūl'lâ pyâ'tsâ)

A room on the lake (on the sea) for two nights.

Una camera sul lago (sul mare) per due notti. (ū'nâ kâ'mä·râ sūl lâ'gō [sūl mâ'rä] pār dü'ä nōt'tē)

Will you carry my bag for me?

Mi vuol portare la valigia? (mē vwōl pōr·tâ'rä lâ vâ·lē'jä)

This room is too expensive. Don't you have something a little cheaper?

Questa camera è troppo cara. Non ha una più a buon mercato? (kwä'stâ kâ'mä·râ ā trōp'pō kâ'râ nōn â ū'nâ pyū â bwōn mār·kâ'tō)

Please bring me some ice.

Mi porti del ghiaccio, per favore. (mē pōr'tē dāl gyâ'chō pār fâ·vō'râ)

Bring me another blanket and another towel, if you please.

Mi dia un'altra coperta e un altro asciugamano, se non Le dispiace. (mē dē'â ū·nâl'trâ kō·pār'tâ ā ū·nâl'trō â·shū·gâ·mâ'nō sā nōn lā dē·spyâ'chä)

Do you have laundry service? I should like to have some things washed.

Avete il servizio per il bucato? Vorrei far lavare della biancheria. (â·vä'tâ ēl sār·vē'tsyō pā·rēl' bū·kâ'tō vōr·rä'ē fâr lâ·vâ'rä dāl'lâ byân·kā·rē'â)

Please wake me at eight o'clock.

Mi faccia il piacere di svegliarmi alle otto. (mē fâ'châ ēl pyâ·chā'rä dē zvā·lyâr'mē âl'lā ōt'tō)

Conversation

I want this suit pressed.

Vorrei far stirare quest'abito. (vōr·rā'ē fâr stē·râ'rā qwā·stâ'bē·tō)

I have a suit to be dry cleaned, a shirt to be ironed, and shoes to be polished.

Ho un vestito da pulire, una camicia da stirare e le scarpe da lucidare. (ō ūn vā·stē'tō dâ pū·lē'rā ū'nâ kâ·mē'châ dâ stē·râ'rā ā lā skâr'pā dâ lū·chē·dâ'rā)

When will they be ready?

Quando saranno pronti? (kwân'do sâ·rân'nō prōn'tē)

Do you have a map of the city?

Ha una pianta della città? (â ū'nâ pyân'tâ dāl'lâ chēt·tâ')

Do you have stamps?

Ha francobolli? (â frân·kō·bōl'lē)

You can buy stamps at the tobacco shop.

I francobolli si comprano dal tabaccaio. (ē frân·kō·bōl'lē sē kōm'prâ·nō dâl tâ·bâk·kâ'yō)

Are there any letters for me?

Ci sono lettere per me? (chē sō'nō let'tā·rā pār mā)

Please give me my bill.

Mi dia il conto per favore. (mē dē'â ēl kōn'tō pār fâ·vō'rā)

Are taxes and service included?

Il servizio e le tasse sono compresi? (ēl sār·vē'tsyō ā lā tâs'sā sō'nō kōm·prā'zē)

Will you take a traveler's check?

Mi può cambiare un assegno per viaggiatori? (mē pwō kâm·byâ'rā ū·nâs·sā'nyō pār vyâj·jâ·tō'rē)

Have my luggage taken down.

Mi faccia portar giù le valigie. (mē fâ'châ pōr·târ' jū lā vâ·lē'jā)

AT THE RESTAURANT

Waiter, bring me the menu please.

Cameriere, il menù, per favore. (kâ·mā·ryā'rā ēl mā·nū' pār fâ·vō'rā)

I'd like an American breakfast.

Voglio fare colazione all'inglese. (vō'lyō fâ'rā kō·lâ·tsyō'nā âl·lēn·glā'zā)

Bring me two eggs with bacon (with ham), toast, and coffee.

Mi dia due uova con pancetta (con prosciutto), crostini e caffè. (mē dē'â dū'ā wō'vâ kōn pân·chāt'tâ [kōn prō·shūt'tō] krō·stē'nē ā kâf·fā')

I'd like the Italian breakfast.

Vorrei la colazione italiana. (vōr·rā'ē lâ kō·lâ·tsyō'nā ē·tâ·lyâ'nâ)

Café au lait with rolls, butter, and marmelade.

Caffelatte con brioche, burro e marmellata. (kâf·fā·lât'tā kōn brē·ōsh' būr'rō ā mâr·māl·lâ'tâ)

To begin with, a cocktail.

Per cominciare, un aperitivo. (pār kō·mēn·châ'rā ū·nâ·pā·rē·tē'vō)

I'll have the table d'hôte.

Desidero il pasto a prezzo fisso. (dā·zē'dā·rō ēl pâ'stō â prā'tsō fēs'sō)

522

Chicken broth, breaded veal cutlet with peas, wine, and fruit.	*Brodo di pollo, cotolette alla milanese con piselli, vino e frutta.* (brō'dō dē pōl'lō kō·tō·lāt'tā âl'lâ mē·lâ·nä'zä kōn pē·zāl'lē vē'nō ā frūt'tâ)
Bring some hors d'oeuvres, tagliatelle Bologna style, roast veal with fried potatoes, and a pint of white wine.	*Porti dell'antipasto, tagliatelle alla bolognese, vitello arrosto con patate fritte e un quartino di bianco.* (pōr'tē dāl·lân·tē·pâ'stō tâ·lyâ·tāl'lā âl'lâ bō·lō·nyä'zä vē·tāl'lō âr·rō'stō kōn pâ·tâ'tā frēt'tā ā ūn kwâr·tē'nō dē byân'kō)
Do you have fresh beer?	*Ha della birra fresca?* (â dāl'lâ bēr'râ frä'skâ)
Strong (weak, spiked) coffee and coffee with cream.	*Un caffè ristretto (lungo, macchiato) e un cappuccino.* (ūn kâf·fā' rē·strät'tō [lūn'gō mâk·kyâ'tō] ā ūn kâp·pū·chē'nō)
Where is the washroom, please?	*Mi dica dov'è la toletta, per favore?* (mē dē'kâ dō·vä' lâ tō·lāt'tâ pār fâ·vō'rā)
Waiter, a fork (spoon, glass, napkin, knife), please.	*Cameriere, una forchetta (un cucchiaio, un bicchiere, un tovagliolo, un coltello) per favore.* (kâ·mā·ryä'rā ū'nâ fōr·kāt'tâ [ūn kūk·kyâ'yō ūn bēk·kyä'rā ūn tō·vâ·lyō'lō ūn kōl·tāl'lō] pār fâ·vō'rā)
Please bring me some butter.	*Mi dia un po' di burro, La prego.* (mē dē'â ūn pō dē būr'rō lâ prä'gō)
Waiter, some more bread, please.	*Cameriere, del pane, per piacere.* (kâ·mā·ryä'rā dāl pâ'nä pār pyâ·chä'rā)
May I please have a glass of milk?	*Mi può dare un bicchiere di latte?* (mē pwō dâ'rā ūn bēk·kyä'rā dē lât'tā)
Cheese	*Formaggio* (fōr·mäj'jō)
Grilled steak	*Bistecca ai ferri* (bē·stäk'kâ â'ē fär'rē)
Macaroni and cheese	*Pasta asciutta* (pâ'stâ â·shūt'tâ)
Mashed potatoes	*Purè di patate* (pū·rä' dē pâ·tâ'tā)
Mineral water	*Acqua minerale* (âk'kwâ mē·nä·râ'lā)
Steak Florentine style	*Bistecca alla fiorentina* (bē·stäk'kâ âl'lâ fyō·rän·tē'nâ)
Stuffed macaroni in broth	*Tagliatelle in brodo* (tâ·lyâ·tāl'lā ēn brō'dō)
Tomato salad	*Insalata di pomodori* (ēn·sâ·lâ'tâ dē pō·mō·dō'rē)
Veal roll in spiced sauce	*Saltimbocca alla romana* (sâl·tēm·bōk'kâ âl'lâ rō·mâ'nâ)
Whipped cream	*Panna montata* (pân'nâ mōn·tâ'tâ)

Conversation

MONEY

Can I cash a check here or do I have to go to the bank?

Is there a bank near here?

Where can I cash a check?

What is the rate of exchange?

Here is my passport.

Please give me two 10,000-lire notes and one 5,000.

AT THE POST OFFICE

Where is the post office?
Is it far from here?
Is that the telegraph window?

I'd like to send a wire to Chicago.

Give me two 100-lire stamps.

I'd like this letter sent registered and this package insured.

Please send it airmail.

Please give me a post card.

Is this the window for general delivery?

Are there any letters for me?

IL DENARO

Posso cambiare qui un assegno o devo andare alla banca? (pōs′sō kâm·byâ′rā kwē ū·nâs·sā′nyō ō dā′vō ân·dâ′rā âl′lâ bân′kâ)

C'è una banca qui vicino? (châ ū′nâ bân′kâ kwē vē·chē′nō)

Dove posso riscuotere un assegno? (dō′vā pōs′sō rē·skwô′tā·rā ū·nâs·sā′nyō)

Quant'è il cambio? (kwân·tā′ ēl kâm′byō)

Ecco il mio passaporto. (āk′kō ēl mē′ō pâs·sâ·pōr′tō)

Mi dia due biglietti da dieci mila lire ed uno da cinque mila, per piacere. (mē dē′â dū′ā bē·lyāt′tē dâ dyā′chē mē′lâ lē′rā ā·dū′nō dâ chēn′kwā mē′lâ pār pyâ·chā′rā)

ALLA POSTA

Dov'è la posta? (dō·vā′ lâ pō′stâ)
È lontano? (ā lōn·tâ′nō)
È quello lo sportello dei telegrammi? (ā kwāl′lō lō spōr·tāl′lō dā′ē tā·lā·grâm′mē)

Vorrei mandare un telegramma a Chicago. (vōr·rā′ē mân·dâ′rā ūn tā·lā·grâm′mâ â chē·kâ′gō)

Mi dia due francobolli da cento lire. (mē dē′â dū′ā frân·kō·bōl′lē dâ chān′tō lē′rā)

Questa lettera me la fa raccomandata e questo pacchetto assicurato. (kwā′stâ let′tā·râ mā lâ fâ râk·kō·mân·dâ′tâ ā kwā′stō pâk·kāt′tō âs·sē·kū·râ′tō)

Me la spedisca per via aerea, per piacere. (mā lâ spā·dē′skâ pār vē′â â·e′rā·â pār pyâ·chā′rā)

Mi dia una cartolina postale. (mē dē′â ū′nâ kâr·tō·lē′nâ pō·stâ′lā)

È qui lo sportello di fermo posta? (ā kwē lō spōr·tāl′lō dē fār′mō pō′stâ)

Ci sono lettere per me? (chē sō′nō let′tā·rā pār mā)

STORES	**I NEGOZI**
Bakery	*Fornaio, Panetteria* (fōr·nâ'yō pâ·nāt·tā·rē'â)
Barber shop	*Barbiere* (bâr·byā'rā)
Beauty shop	*Salone di bellezza* (sâ·lō'nā dē bāl·lā'tsâ)
Book store	*Libreria* (lē·brā·rē'â)
Dairy store	*Latteria* (lât·tā·rē'â)
Drug store	*Farmacia* (fâr·mâ·chē'â)
Florist	*Fiorista* (fyō·rē'stâ)
Food shop	*Alimentari* (â·lē·mān·tâ'rē)
Butcher shop	*Macelleria* (mâ·chāl·lā·rē'â)
Grocery store	*Salumeria* (sâ·lū·mā·rē'â)
Delicatessen	*Drogheria* (drō·gā·rē'â)
Jewelry shop	*Gioielleria* (jō·yāl·lā·rē'â)
Watchmaker	*Orologeria* (ō·rō·lō·jā·rē'â)
Dress shop	*Casa di mode* (kâ'zâ dē mō'dā)
Dressmaker	*Modisteria* (mō·dē·stā·rē'â)
Tailor shop	*Sartoria* (sâr·tō·rē'â)
Tobacco shop	*Tabacchaio, Tabaccheria, Sali e tabacchi* (tâ·bâk·kâ'yō tâ·bâk·kā·rē'â sâ'lē ā tâ·bâk'kē)
Shoe repair shop	*Ciabattino* (châ·bât·tē'nō)
Shoe store	*Calzoleria* (kâl·tsō·lā·rē'â)
Department store	*Bazar* (bâ·dzâr')
Bar	*Osteria* (ō·stā·rē'â)
Restaurant	*Trattoria* (trât·tō·rē'â)
Liquor store	*Fiaschetteria* (fyâ·skāt·tā·rē'â)
Dry goods store	*Merceria* (mār·chā·rē'â)
Stationery shop	*Cartoleria* (kâr·tō·lā·rē'â)
Perfume shop	*Profumeria* (prō·fū·mā·rē'â)

SHOPPING	**GLI ACQUISTI**
I am going shopping.	*Vado a fare delle compere.* (vâ'dō â fâ'rā dāl'lā kōm'pā·rā)
I'm going shopping for groceries.	*Vado a far la spesa.* (vâ'dō â fâr lâ spā'zâ)
Is there a grocery store near here?	*C'è un mercato qui vicino?* (chā ūn mār·kâ'tō kwē vē·chē'nō)
Are there any dress shops?	*Ci sono negozi di mode?* (chē sō'nō nā·gō'tsē dē mō'dā)
How much is this hat?	*Quant'è questo cappello?* (kwân·tā' kwā'stō kâp·pāl'lō)

Conversation

What's the price of a dozen handkerchiefs?

Quanto costa una dozzina di fazzoletti? (kwân'tō kō'stâ ū'nâ dō·dzē'nâ dē fâ·tsō·lāt'tē)

Could you show me some blouses?

Può mostrarmi delle bluse? (pwō mō·strâr'mē dāl'lā blū'zā)

May I see some stockings (shirts, ties)?

Mi vuol far vedere delle calze (camicie, cravatte)? (mē vwōl fâr vā·dā'rā dāl'lā kâl'tsā [kâ·mē'chā krâ·vât'tā])

Show me some leather gloves.

Mi faccia vedere dei guanti di pelle. (mē fâ'châ vā·dā'rā dā'ē gwân'tē dē pāl'lā)

What color?

Di che colore? (dē kā kō·lō'rā)

What size?

Di che misura? (dē kā mē·zū'râ)

May I see something better?

Mi vuol far vedere una qualità migliore? (mē vwōl fâr vā·dā'rā ū'nâ kwâ·lē·tâ' mē·lyō'rā)

These shoes go well with the dress.

Queste scarpe combinano con il vestito. (kwā'stā skâr'pā kōm·bē'nâ·nō kō·nēl' vā·stē'tō)

I prefer solid colors.

Preferisco le tinte unite. (prā·fā·rē'skō lā tēn'tā ū·nē'tā)

Do you have it in white?

Ce l'ha bianco? (chā lâ byân'kō)

Do you deliver?

Fanno servizio a domicilio? (fân'nō sār·vē'tsyō â dō·mē·chē'lyō)

You can send everything to the hotel.

Mi può mandare tutto all'albergo. (mē pwō mân·dâ'rā tūt'tō âl·lâl·bār'gō)

Can you give me a discount?

Mi può fare uno sconto? (mē pwō fâ'rā ū'nō skōn'tō)

I'm very sorry, but our prices are fixed.

Mi dispiace, ma qui si vende a prezzo fisso. (mē dē·spyâ'chā mâ kwē sē vān'dā â prā'tsō fēs'sō)

We'll give you a ten-percent reduction.

Le faremo un ribasso del dieci per cento. (lē fâ·rā'mō ūn rē·bâs'sō dāl dyā'chē pār chān'tō)

Thank you very much! Please take one of these complimentary gifts.

Molte grazie! La prego, si serva di uno di questi omaggi. (mōl'tā grā'tsyā lâ prā'gō sē sār'vâ dē ū'nō dē kwā'stē ō·mâj'jē)

I'll take this figurine; it will make a nice souvenir of the Alps.

Scelgo questa statuetta. È un bel ricordo delle Alpi. (shāl'gō kwā'stâ stâ·twāt'tâ ā ūn bāl rē·kōr'dō dāl'lā âl'pē)

We'll send everything out before noon.

Le manderemo tutto prima di mezzogiorno. (lē mân·dā·rā'mō tūt'tō prē'mâ dē mā·dzō·jōr'nō)

PHOTOGRAPHY

May I take pictures?

May I take my camera into the museum?

How much is the fee for taking pictures?

I need some color film.

Where can I buy camera supplies?

Can you have this roll of films developed?

Does the price include development?

I want three prints of each negative.

Do you have movie film?

Will you put in the film?

EVERYDAY EXPRESSIONS

Good morning!
Good evening!
Good night!
My name is _____.
I understand Italian pretty well, but I don't speak it.

Do you speak English?
Where are you going?
Come here, please.

I want to show you something.

Speak slowly, please.

LA FOTOGRAFIA

È permesso fare fotografie? (ā pär·mäs'sō fâ'rā fō·tō·grâ·fē'ä)

Posso entrare con la macchina fotografica nel museo? (pōs'sō ān·trä'rā kōn lâ mâk'kē·nâ fō·tō·grâ'fē·kâ näl mū·zā'ō)

Quanto si paga per fare delle fotografie? (kwän'tō sē pâ'gâ pär fâ'rā dāl'lā fō·tō·grâ·fē'ä)

Vorrei delle pellicole per fotografia a colori. (vōr·rā'ē dāl'lä pāl·lē'kō·lā pär fō·tō·grä·fē'â â kō·lō'rē)

Dove posso comprare articoli fotografici? (dō'vä pōs'sō kōm·prâ'rā âr·tē'kō·lē fō·tō·grâ'fē·chē)

Può sviluppare questo rullo? (pwō zvē·lūp·pâ'rā kwä'stō rūl'lō)

Il costo include anche lo sviluppo? (ēl kō'stō ēn·klū'dā ân'kä lō zvē·lūp'·pō)

Desidero tre copie di ciascun negativo. (dā·zē'dä·rō trā kô'pyä dē châ·skūn' nä·gâ·tē'vō)

Ha pellicole per macchine da presa? (â pāl·lē'kō·lä pär mâk'kē·nä dâ prā'zâ)

Vuol caricare la macchina? (vwōl kâ·rē·kâ'rā lâ mâk'kē·nâ)

CONVERSAZIONE GENERALE

Buon giorno! (bwōn jōr'nō)
Buona sera! (bwō'nâ sā'râ)
Buona notte! (bwō'nâ nōt'tä)
Mi chiamo _____. (mē kyâ'mō)
Capisco l'italiano abbastanza bene, ma non lo parlo. (kâ·pē'skō lē·tâ·lyâ'·nō âb·bâ·stän'tsâ bā'nä mâ nōn lō pâr'lō)

Parla inglese? (pâr'lâ ēn·glā'zä)
Dove va? (dō'vä vâ)
Venga qua, per piacere. (vān'gâ kwâ pär pyâ·chā'râ)
Le vorrei far vedere una cosa. (lā vōr·rä'ē fâr vâ·dā'rā ū'nä kō'zâ)
Parli adagio, per favore. (pâr'lē â·dâ'·jō pär fâ·vō'rä)

Conversation

I have no time today.	*Oggi non ho tempo.* (ōj'jē nō·nō' tām'pō)
What can I do for you?	*Desidera?* (dā·zē'dā·râ)
Will you tell me the time?	*Mi vuol dire l'ora?* (mē vwōl dē'rā lō'râ)
Is there a doctor near here?	*C'è un dottore qui vicino?* (chā ūn dōt·tō'rā kwē vē·chē'nō)
How do you say _____ in Italian?	*Come si dice in italiano _____?* (kō'mā sē dē'chā ē·nē·tâ·lyâ'nō)
What does _____ mean?	*Cosa vuol dire _____?* (kō'zâ vwōl dē'rā)
What is that for?	*A che serve?* (â kā sār'vā)
You know what I mean?	*M'intende?* (mēn·tān'dā)
Do you understand me?	*Mi capisce?* (mē kâ·pē'shā)
I'm sorry, but I don't understand you.	*Mi rincresce, ma non La capisco.* (mē rēn·krā'shā mâ nōn lâ kâ·pē'skō)
I understand you when you speak slowly.	*La capisco quando parla adagio.* (lâ kâ·pē'skō kwân'dō pâr'lâ â·dâ'jō)
Where is the Catholic church?	*Dov'è la chiesa cattolica?* (dō·vā' lâ kyā'zâ kât·tô'lē·kâ)
What time is Mass?	*A che ora c'è messa?* (â kā ō'râ chā mās'sâ)
Thank you very much.	*Mille grazie.* (mēl'lā grâ'tsyā)
You are welcome.	*Prego.* (prā'gō)
How are you?	*Come sta?* (kō'mā stâ)
Fine, thank you, and you?	*Bene, grazie, e Lei?* (bā'nā grâ'tsyâ ā lā'ē)
Please repeat.	*Ripeta, per favore.* (rē·pā'tâ pār fâ·vō'rā)
Excuse me.	*Mi scusi.* (mē skū'zē)
Keep the change.	*Si tenga il resto.* (sē tān'gâ ēl rā'stō)
Think nothing of it!	*S'immagini!* (sēm·mâ'jē·nē)
Of course!	*Senz'altro!* (sān·dzâl'trō)
Please send for a doctor.	*Vorrei un medico, per favore.* (vōr·rā'ē ūn me'dē·kō pār fâ·vō'rā)
Where is the lost-and-found office?	*Da che parte si trova l'ufficio oggetti smarriti?* (dâ kā pâr'tā sē trō'vâ lūf·fē'chō ōj·jāt'tē zmâr·rē'tē)
I'm very happy to hear that.	*Ne sono proprio contento.* (nā sō'nō prô'pryō kōn·tān'tō)
Very glad to meet you!	*Fortunatissimo!* (fōr·tū·nâ·tēs'sē·mō)
It's a real pleasure to make your acquaintance.	*È un vero piacere di fare la Sua conoscenza.* (ā ūn vā'rō pyâ·chā'rā dē fâ'rā lā sū'â kō·nō·shān'tsâ)

528

Allow me to introduce you to _____.	*Permetta che Le presenti* _____. (pär·mät'tâ kā lā prā·zän'tē)
Good-bye!	*Addio.* (âd·dē'ō)
So long.	*Ciao.* (châ'ō)
Have a pleasant trip!	*Buon viaggio!* (bwōn vyâj'jō)
See you later!	*Arrivederci!* (âr·rē·vā·dār'chē)
Is there someone here who speaks English?	*C'è qui qualcuno che parli inglese?* (chā kwē kwâl·kū'nō kā pâr'lē ēn·glā'zā)
I need an English-speaking guide.	*Ho bisogno d'un cicerone che parli inglese.* (ō bē·zō'nyō dūn chē·chā·rō'nā kā pâr'lē ēn·glā'zā)

WEATHER	IL TEMPO
What's the weather like?	*Che tempo fa?* (kā tām'pō fâ)
The weather is nice.	*Fa bel tempo.* (fâ bāl tām'pō)
The weather is bad.	*Fa cattivo tempo.* (fâ kât·tē'vō tām'pō)
It's cold out.	*Fa freddo.* (fâ frād'dō)
It's hot out.	*Fa caldo.* (fâ kâl'dó)
It's cool.	*Fa fresco.* (fâ frā'skō)
It's sunny.	*Fa sole.* (fâ sō'lā)
It's foggy.	*C'è nebbia.* (chā neb'byâ)
It's windy.	*Tira vento.* (tē'râ vān'tō)
It's cloudy.	*È coperto.* (ā kō·pār'tō)
It's snowing.	*Nevica.* (ne'vē·kâ)
It's raining.	*Piove.* (pyō'vā)
It's a beautiful, sunny day.	*C'è un bel sole.* (chā ūn bāl sō'lā)
It's thundering.	*Tuona.* (twō'nâ)
It's lightning.	*Lampeggia.* (lâm·pej'jâ)

TIME	L'ORA
What time is it?	*Che ora è?* (kā ō'râ ā)
It is one o'clock.	*È l'una.* (ā lū'nâ)
It is two o'clock.	*Sono le due.* (sō'nō lā dū'ā)
It is eight o'clock.	*Sono le otto.* (sō'nō lā ōt'tō)
It is noon.	*È mezzogiorno.* (ā mā·dzō·jōr'nō)
It is 10:15.	*Sono le dieci e un quarto.* (sō'nō lā dyā'chē ā ūn kwâr'tō)
It is midnight.	*È mezzanotte.* (ā mā·dzâ·nōt'tā)

Conversation

It is quarter to eleven.	*Sono le undici meno un quarto.* (sō'nō lā ūn'dē·chē mā'nō ūn kwâr'tō)
It is twenty minutes to seven.	*Sono le sette meno venti.* (sō'nō lā sāt'tā mā'nō vān'tē)
The train leaves at 2 P.M.	*Il treno parte alle quattordici.* (ēl trā'nō pâr'tā âl·lā kwât·tôr'dē·chē)
The concert begins at 9 P.M.	*Il concerto comincia alle ventuno.* (ēl kōn·chār'tō kō·mēn'châ âl'lā vān·tū'nō)

(Note that in the last two sentences above the twenty-four hour system of telling time is used, which counts the hours from midnight to midnight. In Italy, the twenty-four hour system is used for all official functions and for train and airline schedules.)

DAYS / I GIORNI

Sunday	*domenica* (dō·me'nē·kâ)
Monday	*lunedì* (lū·nā·dē')
Tuesday	*martedì* (mâr·tā·dē')
Wednesday	*mercoledì* (mār·kō·lā·dē')
Thursday	*giovedì* (jō·vā·dē')
Friday	*venerdì* (vā·nār·dē')
Saturday	*sabato* (sâ'bâ·tō)

MONTHS / I MESI

January	*gennaio* (jān·nâ'yō)
February	*febbraio* (fāb·brâ'yō)
March	*marzo* (mâr'tsō)
April	*aprile* (â·prē'lā)
May	*maggio* (mâj'jō)
June	*giugno* (jū'nyō)
July	*luglio* (lū'lyō)
August	*agosto* (â·gō'stō)
September	*settembre* (sāt·tām'brā)
October	*ottobre* (ōt·tō'brā)
November	*novembre* (nō·vām'brā)
December	*dicembre* (dē·chām'brā)

THE SEASONS / LE STAGIONI

Spring	*la primavera* (lâ prē·mâ·vā'râ)
Summer	*l'estate* (lā·stâ'tā)
Fall	*l'autunno* (lâū·tūn'nō)
Winter	*l'inverno* (lēn·vār'nō)

AT THE AIRPORT

What is the flying time to Milan?

Will there be many stops?

Please give me a one-way ticket only.

How many pounds of luggage are permitted each passenger?

What is the rate for excess weight?

What time do we leave?

What time do we arrive?

I'd like to reserve a seat, please.

Is that the waiting room?

I'll leave my suitcases here.

I'll take this overnight case and my purse with me.

The gate to your plane is number three.

At what altitude are we flying?

We're already a half-hour late.

RAILROAD

Where is the ticket window?

I want two first class tickets for _____.

One way, please.

ALL'AEROPORTO

Quante ore di volo ci vorranno per arrivare a Milano? (kwân'tā ō'rā dē vō'lō chē vōr·rân'nō pā·râr·rē·vâ'-rā â mē·lâ'nō)

Farà molti scali? (fâ·râ' mōl'tē skâ'lē)

Mi dia solo il biglietto d'andata, per piacere. (mē dē'â sō'lō ēl bē·lyāt'tō dân·dâ'tâ pār pyâ·chā'rā)

Quanti chili di bagaglio sono permessi ad ogni passeggero? (kwân'tē kē'lē dē bâ·gâ'lyō sō'nō pār·mās'sē â·dō'nyē pâs·sâj·jā'rō)

Qual'è la tariffa per il peso in eccedenza? (kwâ·lā' lâ tâ·rēf'fâ pā·rēl' pā'zō ē·nâ·chā·dān'tsâ)

A che ora si parte? (â kā ō'râ sē pâr'tā)

A que ora si arriva? (â kā ō'râ sē âr·rē'vâ)

Vorrei prenotare un posto, per favore. (vōr·rā'ē prā·nō·tâ'rā ūn pō'stō pār fâ·vō'râ)

È quella la sala d'aspetto? (ā kwāl'lâ lâ sâ'lâ dâ·spāt'tō)

Le valigie le lascio qui. (lā vâ·lē'jâ lā lâ'shō kwē)

Questa valigetta e la borsa le porto con me. (kwā'stâ vâ·lē·jāt'tâ ā lâ bōr'sâ lā pōr'tō kōn mā)

Il passaggio numero tre è quello del Suo aeroplano. (ēl pâs·sâj'jō nū'mā·rō trā ā kwāl'lō dāl sū'ō â·ā·rō·plâ'-nō)

A che altitudine stiamo volando? (â kā âl·tē·tū'dē·nā styâ'mō vō·lân'dō)

Già siamo in ritardo di mezz'ora. (jâ syâ'mō ēn rē·târ'dō dē mâ·dzō'râ)

LA FERROVIA

Dov'è la biglietteria? (dō·vā' lâ bē·lyāt·tā·rē'â)

Desidero due biglietti di prima classe per _____. (dā·zē'dā·rō dū'ā bē·lyāt'tē dē prē'mâ klâs'sâ pār)

Di sola andata, per favore. (dē sō'lâ ân·dâ'tâ pār fâ·vō'râ)

Conversation

Round trip.	*Di andata e ritorno.* (dē ân·dâ'tâ ā rē·tōr'nō)
Is the train air-conditioned?	*C'è l'aria condizionata sul treno?* (chā l'â'ryâ kōn·dē·tsyō·nâ'tâ sūl trā'nō)
Is this the train to _____?	*Questo è il treno per _____?* (kwā'stō ā ēl trā'nō pär)
Where is the train to Ravenna?	*Dove si prende il treno per Ravenna?* (dō'vä sē prān'dä ēl trā'nō pär râ·vän'nâ)
I want an upper (lower) berth.	*Vorrei una cuccetta superiore (inferiore).* (vōr·rā'ē ū'nâ kū·chāt'tâ sū·pā·ryō'rā [ēn·fā·ryō'rā])
I want a private compartment.	*Vorrei una cabina ad un letto.* (vōr·rā'ē ū'nâ kâ·bē'nâ â·dūn' lāt'tō)
On what track is the train?	*Su che binario è il treno?* (sū kā bē·nâ'ryō ā ēl trā'nō)
When do we reach _____?	*A che ora arriveremo a _____?* (â kā ō'râ âr·rē·vā·rā'mō â)
Are we on time?	*Siamo in orario?* (syâ'mō ē·nō·râ'ryō)
How late are we?	*Quanto siamo in ritardo?* (kwân'tō syâ'mō ēn rē·târ'dō)
Is there a dining car?	*C'è un vagone ristorante?* (chā ūn vâ·gō'nä rē·stō·rân'tä)
How late do you serve breakfast?	*Fino a che ora si serve la prima colazione?* (fē'nō â kā ō'râ sē sār'vā lâ prē'mâ kō·lâ·tsyō'nä)
When do you start serving lunch?	*A che ora si serve la colazione?* (â kā ō'râ sē sār'vā lâ kō·lâ·tsyō'nä)
Where is the smoking car?	*Da che parte è lo scompartimento per fumatori?* (dâ kā pâr'tā ā lō skōm·pâr·tē·mān'tō pär fū·mā·tō'rē)
Is the berth made up?	*È fatto il letto?* (ā fât'tō ēl lāt'tō)
Please take down the suitcase.	*Porti giù quella valigia, per favore.* (pōr'tē jū kwāl'lâ vâ·lē'jâ pär fâ·vō'rā)
Is this seat vacant?	*È libero questo posto?* (ā lē'bā·rō kwā'stō pō'stō)
May I open the door?	*Le disturba se apro la porta?* (lā dē·stūr'bâ sā â'prō lâ pōr'tâ)
Do you think we could turn off the fan?	*Non sarebbe bene spegnere il ventilatore?* (nōn sâ·rāb'bā bā'nä spe'nyā·rā ēl vän·tē·lâ·tō'rā)
Have you seen the conductor?	*Ha visto il controllore?* (â vē'stō ēl kōn·trōl·lō'rā)
Can I check this suitcase?	*Posso depositare questa valigia?* (pōs'sō dā·pō·zē·tâ'rā kwā'stâ vâ·lē'jâ)

AUTOMOBILE	L'AUTOMOBILE
Forty liters of gas, please.	*Quaranta litri di benzina, per favore.* (kwâ·rân'tâ lē'trē dē bān·dzē'nâ pār fâ·vō'rā)
Check the oil.	*Verifichi l'olio.* (vā·rē'fē·kē lô'lyō)
Fill her up.	*Faccia il pieno.* (fâ'châ ēl pyā'nō)
I have a flat tire.	*Ho una gomma a terra.* (ō ū'nâ gōm'mâ â tār'rā)
Can you fix this puncture?	*Può accomodare la foratura?* (pwō âk·kō·mō·dâ'rā lâ fō·râ·tū'râ)
Where is the next gasoline station?	*Dove si trova il distributore più vicino?* (dō'vā sē trō'vâ ēl dē·strē·bū·tō'rā pyū vē·chē'nō)
My car has developed engine trouble.	*La mia macchina ha un guasto.* (lâ mē'â mâk'kē·nâ â ūn gwā'stō)
Can you tow the car to town?	*Si può rimorchiare la macchina fino in città?* (sē pwō rē·mōr·kyâ'rā lâ mâk'kē·nâ fē'nō ēn chēt'tâ)
Wash it, change the oil, and check the tires.	*La lavi, cambi l'olio, e verifichi le gomme.* (lâ lâ'vē kâm'bē lô'lyō ā vā·rē'fē·kē lā gōm'mā)
What do you charge for a grease job?	*Quanto costa l'ingrassaggio?* (kwân'tō kō'stâ lēn·grâs·sâj'jō)
Is the road in good condition?	*È buona la strada?* (ā bwō'nâ lâ strâ'dâ)

CONVERTING TEMPERATURES

Fahrenheit to Centigrade	Centigrade to Fahrenheit
Subtract 32° and multiply by 5/9.	Multiply by 9/5 and add 32°.
50°F = 10°C −4°F = −20°C	40°C = 104°F 20°C = 68°F

CONVERTING MEASUREMENTS

American to Italian	Italian to American
1 gallon = 3.8 liters	1 liter = .26 gallons
1 pound = .45 kilos	1 kilo = 2.2 pounds
1 inch = 2.5 centimeters	1 centimeter = .4 inches
1 yard = .9 meters	1 meter = 1.1 yards
1 mile = 1.6 kilometers	1 kilometer = .6 miles
1 acre = .4 hectares	1 hectare = 2.5 acres

The figures given above are approximate equivalents.

To convert American measurements into their Italian equivalents, or vice versa, multiply as indicated in the examples below.

Examples: To determine the approximate number of liters in ten gallons, multiply 3.8 (liters per gallon) x 10 = 38.1 liters.

To determine the approximate number of miles in 14 kilometers, multiply .6 (miles per kilometer) x 14 = 8.4 miles.

Numbers

CARDINAL NUMBERS	I NUMERI CARDINALI
1	*uno, una* (ū'nō ū'nâ)
2	*due* (dū'ā)
3	*tre* (trā)
4	*quattro* (kwât'trō)
5	*cinque* (chēn'kwā)
6	*sei* (sā'ē)
7	*sette* (sāt'tā)
8	*otto* (ōt'tō)
9	*nove* (nō'vā)
10	*dieci* (dyā'chē)
11	*undici* (ūn'dē·chē)
12	*dodici* (dô'dē·chē)
13	*tredici* (tre'dē·chē)
14	*quattordici* (kwât·tôr'dē·chē)
15	*quindici* (kwēn'dē·chē)
16	*sedici* (se'dē·chē)
17	*diciassette* (dē·châs·sāt'tā)
18	*diciotto* (dē·chōt'tō)
19	*diciannove* (dē·chân·nō'vā)
20	*venti* (vān'tē)
21	*ventuno* (vān·tū'nō)
22	*ventidue* (vān·tē·dū'ā)
30	*trenta* (trān'tâ)
31	*trentuno* (trān·tū'nō)
40	*quaranta* (kwâ·rân'tâ)
50	*cinquanta* (chēn·kwân'tâ)
60	*sessanta* (sās·sân'tâ)
70	*settanta* (sāt·tân'tâ)
80	*ottanta* (ōt·tân'tâ)
90	*novanta* (nō·vân'tâ)
100	*cento* (chān'tō)
101	*centuno* (chān'tū'nō)
200	*duecento* (dwā·chān'tō)
201	*duecento uno* (dwā·chān'tō ū'nō)
300	*trecento* (trā·chān'tō)
400	*quattrocento* (kwât·trō·chān'tō)
500	*cinquecento* (chēn·kwā·chān'tō)
600	*seicento* (sāē·chān'tō)
700	*settecento* (sāt·tā·chān'tō)

800	*ottocento* (ōt·tō·chän'tō)
900	*novecento* (nō·vä·chän'tō)
1,000	*mille* (mēl'lā)
1,001	*mille e uno* (mēl'lā ā ū'nō)
2,000	*due mila* (dū'ā mē'lâ)
3,000	*tre mila* (trā mē'lâ)
1 million	*un milione* (ūn mē·lyō'nā)
1 billion	*un miliardo* (ūn mē·lyâr'dō)

ORDINAL NUMBERS — I NUMERI ORDINALI

First	*primo* (prē'mō)
Second	*secondo* (sā·kōn'dō)
Third	*terzo* (tär'tsō)
Fourth	*quarto* (kwâr'tō)
Fifth	*quinto* (kwēn'tō)
Sixth	*sesto* (sā'stō)
Seventh	*settimo* (set'tē·mō)
Eighth	*ottavo* (ōt·tâ'vō)
Ninth	*nono* (nō'nō)
Tenth	*decimo* (de'chē·mō)
Eleventh	*undicesimo* (ūn·dē·che'zē·mō)
Twelfth	*dodicesimo* (dō·dē·che'zē·mō)
Thirteenth	*tredicesimo* (trā·dē·che'zē·mō)
Fourteenth	*quattordicesimo* (kwât·tōr·dē·che'zē·mō)
Fifteenth	*quindicesimo* (kwēn·dē·che'zē·mō)
Sixteenth	*sedicesimo* (sā·dē·che'zē·mō)
Seventeenth	*diciassettesimo* (dē·châs·sät·te'zē·mō)
Eighteenth	*diciottesimo* (dē·chōt·te'zē·mō)
Nineteenth	*diciannovesimo* (dē·chân·nō·ve'zē·mō)
Twentieth	*ventesimo* (vān·te'zē·mō)
Twenty-first	*ventesimo primo* (vān·te'zē·mō prē'mō)
Hundredth	*centesimo* (chān·te'zē·mō)
Hundred-and-first	*centesimo primo* (chān·te'zē·mō prē'mō)
Thousandth	*millesimo* (mēl·le'zē·mō)
Millionth	*milionesimo* (mē·lyō·ne'zē·mō)

Road Signs

ITALIAN ROAD SIGNS

Italian road signs, like those in the United States, have typical shapes depending on their function. Many bear worded instructions, but others have only symbols that relay information to the motorist at a glance. The three distinct shapes and their functions are as follows:

 a triangular sign indicates danger.

 a circular sign gives definite instructions.

 a rectangular sign contains special information.

As in the United States, traffic in Italy proceeds on the right-hand side of the street or highway.

SEGNALAZIONI STRADALI	ROAD SIGNS
Curva (kūr′vâ)	*Curve*
Curva pericolosa (kūr′vâ pā·rē·kō·lō′zâ)	*Dangerous curve*
Curva e controcurva (kūr′vâ ā kōn·trō·kūr′vâ)	*S-curve*
Svolta (zvōl′tâ)	*Turn*
Discesa pericolosa (dē·shā′zâ pā·rē·kō·lō′zâ)	*Dangerous descent*
Cunetta (kū·nāt′tâ)	*Dip*
Svolta stretta (zvōl′tâ strāt′tâ)	*Sharp turn*
Dosso (dōs′sō)	*Bump*
Strettoia (strāt·tô′yâ)	*Road narrows*
Incrocio (ēn·krô′chō)	*Intersection*
Arresto all'incrocio (âr·rā′stō âl·lēn·krô′chō)	*Stop at intersection*
Divieto di svolta (dē·vyā′tō dē zvōl′tâ)	*No turns*
Divieto di svolta a destra (dē·vyā′tō dē zvōl′tâ â dā′strâ)	*No right turn*
Divieto di svolta a sinistra (dē·vyā′tō dē zvōl′tâ â sē·nē′strâ)	*No left turn*
Divieto di inversione ad U (dē·vyā′tō dē ēn·vār·syō′nā â·dū′)	*No U-turns*
Direzioni consentite (dē·rā·tsyō′nē kōn·sān·tē′tâ)	*Right or left turn permitted*
Direzione obbligatoria a destra (dē·rā·tsyō′nā ōb·blē·gâ·tô′ryâ â dā′strâ)	*Right turn only*
Direzione obbligatoria a sinistra (dē·rā·tsyō′nā ōb·blē·gâ·tô′ryâ â sē·nē′strâ)	*Left turn only*

Senso obbligatorio (sän'sō ōb·blē·gâ·tô'ryō) — *One-way traffic (indicated by arrow)*

Senso proibito (sän'sō prōē·bē'tō) — *No entry, one-way traffic*

Senso unico (sän'sō ū'nē·kō) — *One-way traffic (indicated by arrow)*

Tenere la destra (tā·nä'rä lâ dä'strâ) — *Keep to the right*

Divieto di accesso (dē·vyä'tō dē â·chäs'sō) — *Do not enter*

Confluenza a destra (kōn·flūän'tsâ â dä'strâ) — *Road entering right*

Preavviso di dare precedenza (prä·âv·vē'zō dē dâ'rä prä·chä·dän'tsâ) — *Priority road ahead*

Dare precedenza (dâ'rä prä·chä·dän'tsâ) — *Yield right-of-way*

Doppio senso di circolazione (dôp'pyō sän'sō dē chēr·kō·lâ·tsyō'nä) — *Two-way traffic*

Fine del doppio senso di circolazione (fē'nä dāl dôp'pyō sän'sō dē chēr·kō·lâ·tsyō'nä) — *End of two-way traffic*

Corsia riservata ai veicoli lenti (kōr·sē'â rē·zär·vâ'tâ â'ē vä·ē'kō·lē län'tē) — *Lane for slow vehicles*

Semaforo a 150 m. (sä·mâ'fō·rō â chän'tō chēn·kwân'tâ mä'trē) — *Traffic signal, 150 meters*

Semafori sincronizzati 40 km. (sä·mâ'fō·rē sēn·krō·nē·dzâ'tē kwâ·rân'tâ kē·lô'mä·trē) — *Signals set for 40 kilometers per hour*

Rotaia (rō·tâ'yâ) — *Traffic circle*

Divieto di transito ai pedoni (dē·vyä'tō dē trân'sē·tō â'ē pä·dō'nē) — *No pedestrians*

Passaggio per pedoni (pâs·sâj'jō pär pä·dō'nē) — *Pedestrian crosswalk*

Sottopassaggio (sōt·tō·pâs·sâj'jō) — *Underpass*

Parcheggio avanti (pâr·kej'jō â·vân'tē) — *Parking ahead*

Sosta vietata (sō'stâ vyä·tâ'tâ) — *No parking*

Sosta regolamentata (sō'stâ rā·gō·lâ·mân·tâ'tâ) — *Limited parking*

Sosta di emergenza (sō'stâ dē ā·mär·jän'tsâ) — *Emergency parking*

Vicolo cieco (vē'kō·lō chä'kō) — *Dead end*

Rallentare (râl·län·tâ'rä) — *Slow down*

Strada sdrucciolevole (strâ'dâ zdrū·chō·le'vō·lä) — *Slippery when wet*

Lavori (lâ·vō'rē) — *Men working*

Ponte mobile (pōn'tä mô'bē·lä) — *Drawbridge*

Prudenza (prū·dän'tsâ) — *Caution*

Road Signs

Bambini (bâm·bē′nē)
Watch for children

Divieto di sorpasso (dē·vyā′tō dē sōr·pâs′sō)
No passing

Fine del divieto di sorpasso (fē′nä däl dē·vyā′tō dē sōr·pâs′sō)
End no passing

Divieto di sorpasso tra autotreni (dē·vyā′tō dē sōr·pâs′sō trâ āū·tō·trā′nē)
No passing for trailer trucks

Fine del divieto di sorpasso tra autotreni (fē′nä däl dē·vyā′tō dē sōr·pâs′sō trâ āū·tō·trā′nē)
End no passing for trailer trucks

Riservato alle autovetture (rē·zär·vâ′tō âl′lä âū·tō·vät·tū′rä)
Automobile traffic only

Divieto di transito alle biciclette (dē·vyā′tō dē trân′sē·tō âl′lä bē·chē·klāt′tä)
No bicycles

Pista ciclabile (pē′stâ chē·klâ′bē·lä)
Bicycle path

Divieto di transito ai motocicli (dē·vyā′tō dē trân′sē·tō â′ē mō·tō·chē′·klē)
No motorcycles

Fermata di autobus (fär·mâ′tâ dē â′ū·tō·būs)
Bus stop

Via in costruzione (vē′â ēn kō·strū·tsyō′nä)
Road under construction

Passaggio a livello con barriere (pâs·sâj′jō â lē·väl′lō kōn bâr·ryā′rä)
Guarded railroad crossing

Passaggio a livello senza barriere (pâs·sâj′jō â lē·väl′lō sän′tsâ bâr·ryā′rä)
Unguarded railroad crossing

Limite massimo di velocità 75 km. (lē′mē·tä mâs′sē·mō dē vä·lō·chē·tâ′ sä·tân·tâ·chēn′kwä kē·lō′mä·trē)
Speed limit 75 kilometers per hour

Limite minimo di velocità 45 km. (lē′mē·tä mē′nē·mō dē vä·lō·chē·tâ′ kwâ·rân·tâ·chēn′kwä kē·lō′mä·trē)
Minimum speed 45 kilometers per hour

Limitazione di velocità (lē·mē·tâ·tsyō′nä dē vä·lō·chē·tâ′)
Speed zone ahead

Fine della limitazione di velocità (fē′nä däl′lâ lē·mē·tâ·tsyō′nä dē vä·lō·chē·tâ′)
End speed zone

Deviazione (dä·vyâ·tsyō′nä)
Detour

Autostrada (âū·tō·strâ′dâ)
Expressway, throughway

Preavviso di bivio Firenze (prā·âv·vē′·zō dē bē·vē′ō fē·rän′tsä)
Approaching exit for Florence

Preavviso di canalizzazione (prā·âv·vē′zō dē kâ·nâ·lē·dzâ·tsyō′nä)
Enter proper lanes ahead

Uscita operai (ū·shē′tâ ō·pä·râ′ē)
Employee exit

Alt! Dogana (âlt dō·gâ′nä)
Stop! Customs

Assistenza meccanica (âs·sē·stän'tsâ mäk·kâ'nē·kâ) — *Garage*

Rifornimento benzina (rē·fōr·nē·män'tō bān·dzē'nâ) — *Filling station*

Transito con catene (trân'sē·tō kōn kâ·tā'nā) — *Proceed with chains*

Divieto di segnalazioni acustiche (dē·vyā'tō dē sā·nyâ·lâ·tsyō'nē â·kū'stē·kā) — *No horns*

Ospedale (ō·spā·dâ'lā) — *Hospital*

Pronto soccorso (prōn'tō sōk·kōr'sō) — *First aid*

Telefono (tā·le'fō·nō) — *Telephone*

Campeggio (kâm·pej'jō) — *Camp site*

Terreno per rimorchi (tär·rā'nō pär rē·mōr'kē) — *Trailer park*

Campeggio e rimorchi (kâm·pej'jō ā rē·mōr'kē) — *Camp site with trailer facilities*

Ostello della gioventù (ō·stāl'lō dāl'lâ jō·vān·tū') — *Youth hostel*

Banchine non transitabili (bân·kē'nā nōn trân·sē·tâ'bē·lē) — *Keep off shoulders*

Caduta di masse (kâ·dū'tâ dē mâs'sā) — *Rock slide*

Frana (frâ'nâ) — *Road washed out*

Strada dissestata (strâ'dâ dēs·sâ·stâ'tâ) — *Road in bad repair*

Spegnere i fari (spe'nyā·rā ē fâ'rē) — *Turn off headlights*

ROAD SYMBOLS

All the following symbols are in use throughout Western Europe except those marked (*ITAL*), which are to be found only in Italy.

1 Danger

Uneven Road

Dangerous Curve

Right Curve

S-curve

Intersection

Traffic Circle

Railroad Crossing, Guarded

Railroad Crossing, Unguarded

Railroad Crossing, Unguarded

Dangerous Hill

Road Symbols

 Road Narrows

 Drawbridge

 Men Working

 Slippery When Wet

 Pedestrian Crosswalk

 Watch Out For Children

 Cattle Crossing

 Side Road

 Low-flying Aircraft

 Beware of Animals

 Caution

 Priority Road Ahead

 Two-way Traffic

 Traffic Signals Ahead

2 Instructions

 Road Closed

 No Entry

 Motor Vehicles Only (*ITAL*)

 Motorcycles Only (*ITAL*)

 Pedestrians Only (*ITAL*)

 No Motorcycles

 No Motor Vehicles

 No Bicycles

 No Horns

 No Left Turn

 No Passing

 Maximum Width

 Maximum Height

 Maximum Weight

 Speed Limit

Stop at
Intersection

Stop
Customs

No
Parking

No Parking
I Uneven Days
II Even Days

Yield Right-
of-way

End Speed
Limit

End No
Passing

Direction of
Traffic

One-way
Street (*ITAL*)

Minimum
Speed

3 Information

Priority
Road

End of
Priority Road

Parking

You Have
Right-of-way

Hospital

First Aid

First Aid

Garage

Telephone

Filling
Station

Camp Site

Trailer Park

Camp Site
with Trailer
Facilities

Distance to
Camp Site

Expressway
(Undivided)

End
Expressway
(Undivided)

Expressway
(Divided)

END
Expressway
(Divided)

COUNTRIES OF EUROPE

Country	Capital	Area in Sq. Miles	Population
Albania	Tirane	11,096	1,865,000
Andorra	Andorra	174	14,000
Austria	Vienna	32,374	7,290,000
Belgium	Brussels	11.779	9,499,000
Bulgaria	Sofia	42,729	8,258,000
Czechoslovakia	Prague	49,370	14,274,000
Denmark	Copenhagen	16,619	4,768,000
Finland	Helsinki	130,120	4,651,000
France	Paris	212,822	49,570,000
Germany—Democratic Rep. (East Germany)	East Berlin	41,646	16,000,000
Federal Rep. (West Germany)	Bonn	95,928	57,485,000
Gr. Britain, see Un. Kingdom			
Greece	Athens	50,548	8,612,000
Hungary	Budapest	35,919	10,198,000
Iceland	Reykjavik	39,758	192,000
Ireland, Rep. of	Dublin	27,135	2,881,000
Italy	Rome	116,303	51,945,000
Liechtenstein	Vaduz	61	19,000
Luxembourg	Luxembourg	998	330,000
Malta	Valletta	122	319,000
Monaco	Monaco-Ville	0.77	23,000
Netherlands	Amsterdam & the Hague	12,978	12,523,000
Norway	Oslo	125,065	3,753,000
Poland	Warsaw	120,359	31,811,000
Portugal	Lisbon	35,340	9,228,000
Rumania	Bucharest	91,699	19,027,000
San Marino	......	23	18,000
Spain	Madrid	194,884	32,005,000
Sweden	Stockholm	173,666	7,844,000
Switzerland	Berne	15,941	5,945,000
Turkey	Ankara	301,380	
in Asia	......	292,291	28,720,000
in Europe	......	9,089	2,664,000
Union of Soviet Socialist Republics (Soviet Union)	Moscow	8,649,512	233,200,000
in Asia	......	6,619,000	54,015,000
in Europe	......	2,030,512	173,672,000
United Kingdom of Great Britain and North. Ireland		94,198	54,744,000
England and Wales	London	58,348	48,075,000
Scotland	Edinburgh	30,411	5,204,000
Northern Ireland	Belfast	5,439	1,478,000

Vatican City	. . . . . .	0.17	1,000
Yugoslavia	Belgrade	98,766	19,845,000

SOURCES: *UN Statistical Yearbook, 1963; UN Population and Vital Statistics Report, 1 April, 1967*

UNITED STATES OF AMERICA

Area	3,615,150 square miles	(from *Statistical Abstract of the U.S., 1966*)
Population	latest official estimate	197,807,000

(Census Bureau and *UN Population and Vital Statistics Report*, 1 April, 1967)

EUROPEAN CITIES OVER 1,000,000

(UN Demographic Yearbook, 1965)

Name and Country	Population	Name and Country	Population
Moscow, USSR	6,366,000	Milan, Italy	1,661,970*
Leningrad, USSR	3,329,000	Vienna, Austria	1,638,584
Berlin, Germany	3,273,297	Kiev, USSR	1,332,000
East	1,071,462	Bucharest, Rumania	1,239,458
West	2,201,835	Warsaw, Poland	1,232,000
London, England	3,184,600	Naples, Italy	1,212,790*
Paris, France	2,790,091	Munich, Fed. Rep. of Ger.	1,182,411
Madrid, Spain	2,558,583*	Turin, Italy	1,115,466*
Rome, Italy	2,417,140*	Birmingham, England	1,106,040
Budapest, Hungary	1,928,000	Gorki, USSR	1,085,000
Hamburg, Fed. Rep.		Kharkov, USSR	1,070,000
of Germany	1,856,530	Glasgow, Scotland	1,018,582
Barcelona, Spain	1,696,008	Prague, Czechoslovakia	1,017,156

* Denotes metropolitan population, including both city and suburban areas

ITALIAN CITIES OVER 250,000

(UN Demographic Yearbook, 1965)

English Name	Italian Name	Population
Rome	Roma (rō'mâ)	2,417,140
Milan	Milano (mē·lâ'nō)	1,661,970
Naples	Napoli (nâ'pō·lē)	1,212,790
Turin	Torino (tō·rē'nō)	1,115,466
Genoa	Genova (je'nō·vâ)	834,103
Palermo	Palermo (pâ·lär'mō)	618,327
Bologna	Bologna (bō·lō'nyâ)	479,051
Florence	Firenze (fē·rän'tsā)	455,314
Catania	Catania (kâ·tâ'nyâ)	383,739
Venice	Venezia (vā·nā'tsyâ)	357,951
Bari	Bari (bâ'rē)	326,446
Trieste	Trieste (tryä'stā)	278,996
Messina	Messina (mäs·sē'nâ)	260,802

*Census data for Italy reports metropolitan population only.

U.S. CITIES OVER 250,000
(1960 Official Census)

City and State	Population	City and State	Population
New York, N.Y.	7,781,984	Indianapolis, Ind.	476,258
Chicago, Ill.	3,550,404	Kansas City, Mo.	475,539
Los Angeles, Calif.	2,479,015	Columbus, Ohio	471,316
Philadelphia, Pa.	2,002,512	Phoenix, Ariz.	439,170
Detroit, Mich.	1,670,144	Newark, N.J.	405,220
Baltimore, Md.	939,024	Louisville, Ky.	390,639
Houston, Texas	938,219	Portland, Oreg.	372,676
Cleveland, Ohio	876,050	Oakland, Calif.	367,548
Washington, D.C.	763,956	Fort Worth, Texas	356,268
St. Louis, Mo.	750,026	Long Beach, Calif.	344,168
Milwaukee, Wisc.	741,324	Birmingham, Ala.	340,887
San Francisco, Calif.	740,316	Oklahoma City, Okla.	324,253
Boston, Mass.	697,197	Rochester, N.Y.	318,611
Dallas, Texas	679,684	Toledo, Ohio	318,003
New Orleans, La.	627,525	St. Paul, Minn.	313,411
Pittsburgh, Pa.	604,332	Norfolk, Va.	304,869
San Antonio, Texas	587,718	Omaha, Nebr.	301,598
San Diego, Calif.	573,224	Honolulu, Hawaii	294,194
Seattle, Wash.	557,087	Miami, Fla.	291,688
Buffalo, N.Y.	532,759	Akron, Ohio	290,351
Cincinnati, Ohio	502,550	El Paso, Texas	276,687
Memphis, Tenn.	497,524	Jersey City, N.J.	276,101
Denver, Colo.	493,887	Tampa, Fla.	274,970
Atlanta, Ga.	487,455	Dayton, Ohio	262,332
Minneapolis, Minn.	482,872	Tulsa, Okla.	261,685
Wichita, Kans.	254,698		